British Literature 1640–1789

BLACKWELL ANTHOLOGIES
Editorial Advisers

Blackwell Anthologies are a series of extensive and comprehensive volumes designed to address the numerous issues raised by recent debates regarding the literary canon, value, text, context, gender, genre, and period. While providing the reader with key canonical writings in their entirety, the series is also ambitious in its coverage of hitherto marginalised texts, and flexible in the overall variety of its approaches to periods and movements. Each volume has been thoroughly researched to meet the current needs of teachers and students.

Romanticism: An Anthology
edited by Duncan Wu

Victorian Women Poets: An Anthology
edited by Angela Leighton and Margaret Reynolds

Nineteenth-century American Women Writers: An Anthology
edited by Karen L. Kilcup

Forthcoming

Old and Middle English: An Anthology
edited by Elaine Treharne

Chaucer to Spenser: An Anthology
edited by Derek Pearsall

Renaissance Literature: An Anthology
edited by Michael Payne

Romantic Women Poets: An Anthology
edited by Duncan Wu

The Victorians: An Anthology
edited by Valentine Cunningham

Modernism: An Anthology
edited by Lawrence Rainey

Early African-American Literature: An Anthology
edited by Phillip M. Richards

Nineteenth-century American Literature: An Anthology
edited by Kenny J. Williams

Nineteenth-century American Women Poets: An Anthology
edited by Paula Bennett

Native American Women Writers c. 1800–1925: An Anthology
edited by Karen L. Kilcup

BRITISH LITERATURE
1640-1789
AN ANTHOLOGY

EDITED BY

ROBERT DEMARIA JR

BLACKWELL
Publishers

Copyright © Blackwell Publishers Ltd, 1996
Introduction, selection, arrangement and apparatus
© Robert DeMaria Jr, 1996

First published 1996
2 4 6 8 10 9 7 5 3 1

Blackwell Publishers Ltd
108 Cowley Road
Oxford OX4 1JF
UK

Blackwell Publishers Inc.
238 Main Street
Cambridge, Massachusetts 02142, USA

Library of Congress Cataloging-in-Publication Data
British literature, 1640–1789: an anthology/edited by Robert DeMaria, Jr.
p.   cm. – (Blackwell anthologies)
Includes index.
ISBN 0-631-19527-0 (hbk.: alk. paper). – ISBN 0-631-19528-9
(pbk.: alk. paper)
1. English literature – 18th century.   2. English literature – Early modern, 1500–1700.
3. Great Britain – Literary collections.   I. DeMaria, Robert.   II. Series.
PR1134.B74   1996   96-6257
820.8'005 – dc20   CIP

British Library Cataloguing in Publication Data

A CIP catalogue record for this book is available from the British Library.

Commissioning Editor: Andrew McNeillie
Desk Editor: Alison Truefitt
Production Controller: Lisa Eaton
Text Designer: Lisa Eaton

Typeset in 9.5 on 11 pt Garamond 3 by Best-set Typesetter Ltd, Hong Kong
Printed in Great Britain by T.J. Press (Padstow), Cornwall

This book is printed on acid-free paper

Contents

List of Authors

Introduction

Unlike books, real life histories (including literary histories) do not have neat beginnings and ends. Like any other time period one might choose, the years from 1640 to 1789 do not comprise a perfectly coherent or discrete field of social or literary history. However, this is a period bounded by two crucially important events: the British Civil War and the French Revolution. Both events influenced literature, as well as every other aspect of culture. Very roughly speaking, the Civil War divided the country into Puritans, or Roundheads, and Royalists, and each group had literary as well as political and religious (and even tonsorial) habits that distinguished them. Of course, the lines along which the country split were infinitely more complex. A host of radical groups emerged, such as the Diggers, the Levellers, and the Muggletonians, who argued with each other as well as with well-established Puritans and Presbyterians, even though all agreed about the evils of the high-church Royalists whose supposedly satanic overlord was the Roman Catholic Church. The most radical groups did not flourish for long: Oliver Cromwell's militant Puritan Commonwealth did not support them, and by the time the Stuart monarchy was restored in 1660 they were at least twice removed from political influence. However, aspects of their prophetic religious, political, and literary modes persisted as part of a complex culture of dissent that maintained itself throughout the eighteenth century and produced some of its best and most popular literature.

The prophetic strain of the radicals is visible in the writings of John Bunyan, including his immensely popular *Pilgrim's Progress*; Daniel Defoe was a dissenter who landed in the stocks for ridiculing the suppression of dissent; and William Blake's visions arose from his Muggletonian background. It is tempting to suggest that the French Revolution parallels the Civil War and represents another outbreak of democratic idealism, and that between two such outbreaks lies the dominant culture of the eighteenth century, holding them both in abeyance. But there were always crosscurrents of thought and feeling. Even Samuel Johnson, who certainly belonged to the dominant, high-church culture of the eighteenth century, was deeply influenced by dissenting religion and loved Bunyan and Defoe. Moreover, the democratic reforms urged by radicals in the 1640s drew gradually closer to enactment throughout the period, though many had to wait for Emancipation in 1807, the Reform Bills of 1832 and 1867, and for even later legislation. When the Representation of the People Act in 1918 gave

British women the right to vote in Parliamentary elections, it fulfilled another of the many desiderata of radical groups formed in the 1640s.

Of course, the French Revolution did not have as great or as direct an effect on Britain as its own Civil War. Nevertheless, especially in view of the violent anti-government Gordon Riots of 1780 and the recently concluded American Revolutionary War (1775–83), the French Revolution was regarded with millennial hopes and fears in Britain. The Gordon Riots led to the establishment of a fulltime police force in London, and the French Revolution, followed as it was by the Terror and then the Napoleonic Wars, led to further state anxiety. Those who founded hopes of reform on the events of 1789, such as Mary Wollstonecraft and William Godwin, soon found it prudent to express more moderate views or none at all. William Wordsworth and Samuel T. Coleridge turned their discussion from politics to philosophy, but still found themselves suspected because a wary citizen heard them discussing Spinoza and thought they were planning acts of espionage (Spy-nosy). Blake, a genuine grandchild of the radicals of the Civil War, was one of the few who openly celebrated the Revolution through it all. However, whether it was openly expressed or not, the French Revolution revitalized radical sentiment in Britain, and it galvanized the opposition. Another divide occurred in the culture, one which was dramatically expressed by Edmund Burke's *Reflections on the Revolution in France* and the angry replies it drew from Mary Wollstonecraft, Thomas Paine, and other proponents of equal rights.

For Burke, the French Revolution, and British sympathy for it, signaled the end of chivalry, decency, good manners, and civil respect. But these were not his only fears and objections. What repelled him most, he said, was the commitment in the Revolution to ideas and theories, and the willingness of the revolutionaries to put their abstract ideals ahead of consideration for real people. Burke felt that the real state of things, the real situation of human beings, who are and always will be mutually dependent on each other, was forgotten in the blaze of theories, slogans, and enthusiasm. That an abstraction like "The Rights of Man" could take the place of consideration for individual men and women was what Burke said horrified him the most. Paine and Wollstonecraft saw Burke's rhetoric merely as a defense of the status quo, with all its cruelties of class distinction, its lack of regard for the poor, its disrespect for the intellectual potential of women, and its idolatry of the rich and high-born. They also made an appeal to real experience and pointed to the real sufferings in the many millions of lives sacrificed to the romantic fictions of chivalry that Burke took for real life. In a way, the opponents in this fight were arguing over the high ground of eighteenth-century culture: the appeal to experience and the real state of things as they are. Throughout the period, such appeals usually won out over ideals, theories, visions, and other products of the imagination.

The eighteenth century did not lack imagination or ideals, and it was not antagonistic to imaginative writing or to the democratic impulses expressed in the British Civil War and the French Revolution. However, many of the writers of the period were, like Burke, skeptical about the efficacy and the value of mere ideas. John Locke's empiricism was the dominant philosophy of the period for most thinkers, no matter what their political preferences, whereas Berkeley's idealist notions were generally regarded as odd. In social thought, the dominant view favored gradual change, based on precedent and received views; rational forms of Christianity were in the ascendant and most platonic or ideal forms (despite the likes of John Norris and Henry More) in decline; in literary criticism, as in science, the most influential writers endorsed empirical procedures; and in literature, they tended to reject utopian solutions and epic inclusiveness. Samuel Johnson was fond of remarking the way in which theory is perpetually giving way to experience in all intellectual fields, and in saying so, he was expressing a very important strand of thought in his century.

Many of the writers of the eighteenth century are better known for their critiques of existing ideas than for presenting new systems of their own. In fact, novelty was one of the ideas about which the period was most skeptical. The great targets of attack throughout this contentious age were innovators of various kinds, and they were invariably seen as people who confuse ideas and reality. Jonathan Swift's satires on scientific and social inventors (or "projectors") are perhaps the most famous attacks of this kind, but Samuel Johnson was equally hard on the "aeronautical projector" and the many unrealistic philosophers who offer solutions to the great questions of life in *Rasselas*. The radical thinkers who favored the regicide of 1649 and those who applauded the *beau jour* of the French Revolution, were particularly open to attack as promulgators of unrealistic ideas. Most members of society throughout the period believed that the voice of experience, rather than that of innovation, held the greatest share of the truth.

Although John Milton rebelled against the established government of Charles I, helped frame the Commonwealth's idea of government, and conceived justifications for the regicide in 1649, Milton's villains in *Paradise Lost* (1667) are, nevertheless, innovators with strange ideas. The fact is that Milton did not see himself or describe himself as a rebel. Milton's God and His government are images of the world seen from the point of view of the Puritans' brief period of empowerment (*c.* 1640–60). Milton's rebel angels are the Royalists and highchurchmen of the Stuart monarchy, whom he saw as departing from the true, God-given, Puritan path. For many readers, this is counter-intuitive: Milton's connection with Cromwell makes him so unmistakably a rebel, that they see his rebel angels as the true heroes of *Paradise Lost*. But, however we feel about Milton's God or his Satan, the poem undeniably delivers us into a world of experience and bars the way to the ideal, pastoral world of Eden. Moreover, Milton tells us that this new world of experience is ultimately better than Eden, even though living in it is hard work. In the real world men and women must work out the details of marriage and family life; men and women must labor; and everyone has to work out his or her own salvation. Speech, too, is more complicated in the world of experience and can enjoy no Edenic perfection; it is, for example, riddled with irony, which is perhaps the most characteristic linguistic mode of the literature written in the wake of *Paradise Lost*. The two perfect people of Eden become the much more numerous but much more imperfect people of history. It is an oversimplification, of course, but in a way *Paradise Lost* is the epic of experience, and it ushers in an age devoted to working out the ramifications of an outlook that gave precedence to experience in all things.

Most literary constructions of the Commonwealth rule did not achieve the prominence of *Paradise Lost*; Andrew Marvell's excellent "Horatian Ode upon Cromwell's Return from Ireland," for example, was expunged from the books and not circulated in print until after the next revolution, the less traumatic Glorious Revolution of 1688–9. *Paradise Lost*, however, was immediately felt to be great literature, so great that it transcended political commitments and quickly became the most frequently cited poem in English for writers of almost all political persuasions. Partly out of helplessness before its grandeur, partly in reaction to its splendor, and partly in obedience to its message, poets began writing more about history, more about experience, and more than ever before about the ironies inherent in the difference between the old ideals and the new real world in which they lived. The best of epic poetry was ironic; the historical mode was as high as poets dared to soar, and even then they rarely did so without irony; and there was a renewed awareness that the best of art had been discovered by giants before the flood: ancients, especially Homer, Virgil, Horace, and Juvenal, and giant Englishmen, Shakespeare, Ben Jonson, and Milton.

But if the modern writers lacked greatness, they enjoyed numerical superiority. In addition to releasing a flood of new ideas, the British Civil War engendered new races of authors: pamphlets, newsbooks, and other ephemera increased so much that they can almost be said to have been born at this time. A hunger for news expanded the reading public, especially among the middle class and, later, among the working classes. The social range of those doing the writing also increased vastly, and print was resoundingly confirmed as the supreme medium for the dissemination of literature. Earlier in the seventeenth century manuscript circulation of poetry was still very highly respected, and publication was regarded as somewhat vulgar. Ben Jonson carefully shepherded his works through the press, but he was unusual for his time. Such famous writers as John Donne and George Herbert favored manuscript circulation, and this preference lived on well into the seventeenth century. John Wilmot, Earl of Rochester, authorized the publication of only a few of his poems, for example, and many, many poets claimed that they submitted to publication only because they learned that manuscripts of their work had been obtained by piratical booksellers about to make a profit on their efforts. The percentage of such claims that were disingenuous steadily increased, however, and by the eighteenth century proper more writers were willing to be frank about their wish to appear in print. Still, it was not common for writers to put their names on the title pages of their works, and part of the reason for this was fidelity to the older idea of authorship in which the writer was separate from the vulgar world of publication. Even Samuel Johnson, who was frank about the fact that he published for a living, did not put his name on a published work until 1749, when he was forty years old.

By mid-century the author's passion for publication had survived so many lampoons that it was almost universally accepted. The medium of print sought broader avenues of circulation than the coteries which exchanged manuscripts among themselves, and new parts of society made their mark in the new medium: women published in much greater numbers in the eighteenth century than ever before, and some inroads were made by working people. Subscription publication, which began in the mid-seventeenth century, had something to do with this: the capital for the publication of these projects was supplied by the public, who bought books before the first printing and enjoyed the privilege of seeing their names on the list of subscribers in the preliminary matter of the book. Such lists replaced, or at least competed with, dedications to wealthy individuals who supported publication in the old regime of literary production. Like readers and writers, the patrons of literature grew numerically and became more widely distributed across the social spectrum.

The democratization of literature did not occur without resistance, however. A great deal of the most famous literature in the early eighteenth century satirizes writers, new modes of writing, and print itself. Highly successful writers like John Dryden and Alexander Pope were constantly at war with the lesser writers who, in their view, tended to reduce the prestige of the guild or bring down the dignity of the new print-world class of authors. (Of course, there were counter-attacks, and Dryden in particular had to defend himself both against new-world hacks and old-world, aristocratic writers.) Many authors made anxious attempts to link themselves with classical and earlier English writers and to distinguish themselves from the "common herd" of their contemporaries. Pope's grandest and most laborious work, the *Dunciad*, is designed largely to distance himself from what he describes as the countless and culturally unwashed mass of writers emerging in his time. For Pope, as for Dryden, there had to be an aristocracy of writers based on skill rather than class. Swift carried his version of elitism even further than Pope and found that all modern writing, most writing of any age, and nearly all of what passes for thought is a stupendous waste of time. Swift's *Tale of a Tub* should have done more than any book in history to discourage publication, but Swift was wise, or cynical, enough to know that not even his *Tub* could long distract the Leviathan of society from its follies.

Though they may never have kept a single author from publishing, writers like Pope and Swift seem to have had an immense influence on the critics and scholars who specialize in the eighteenth century. Perhaps this is – ironically – because they are particularly critical of scholars and critics and make even more fun of them than of other poets and prose writers. Whatever the reason, and nineteenth-century attitudes may have more to do with it than Pope and Swift, the canon of eighteenth-century works was for a long time intensively focused on a few writers selected as supreme. Arguably, students of the eighteenth century imbibed the period's high standards for elegance and other forms of esthetic excellence in writing, and they could be satisfied with nothing much less than the best. This is another pleasant fiction, and there may be some truth in it, but it is also true that elements of class awareness, snobbery, and politics played into the construction of these esthetic standards. Moreover, whatever the validity of the esthetic standards, the feeling that they had to be upheld through the exclusion and derision of many writers was as much an expression of anxiety as of taste or judgement.

In the past two decades the focus on the central figures of the eighteenth century has diminished a bit, and attention has shifted to the so-called margins. For quite some time now there has been a desire, as well as a demand, to hear other voices than those that have traditionally spoken for the century and a half represented in this anthology. The strongest, most welcome, and most productive desire has been to hear the voices of women: the reappearance of women writers on the scene has made for the greatest change in eighteenth-century studies over the last twenty-five years. Shortly before that, in 1969, a fine new anthology of the literature of the "long" eighteenth century (1660–1798) appeared, edited by three excellent scholars. But of the three thousand columns in this large book, with a wide, double-column page format, a total of three were occupied by the writings of women. What's more, as far as I know, few people objected or were even surprised. That book is a monument to a certain kind of fine taste and mature judgement, with very large selections from Dryden, Pope, Swift, and Johnson, but also with selections from numerous lesser figures. There are over ninety in the supporting cast, but their inferior position is carefully marked. The majority of writers, including the three women, do not get introductions and so are clearly relegated to a more distant circle of the esthetic society. In the present anthology about a quarter of the writers present are women; they contribute about twenty percent of the writing, and they are all introduced. The difference by no means represents an innovation of my own; it merely reflects significant changes in the study and teaching of this period that have occurred over the last twenty-five years.

The rediscovery of the women writers of the period is the most important development in eighteenth-century studies, but it is not the only one. The literature of the British Civil War has undergone long overdue reconsideration. At the other end of the chronology, the roots of Romanticism have been very widely explored and found to lie deep in the eighteenth century, as early as James Thomson, who was born in 1700, the year Dryden died, and even in the writings of Richard Savage, who was born in the seventeenth century. Along with a recognition of Romantic elements in eighteenth-century writing has come a richer understanding of related movements, such as the interest in sensibility, which grew throughout the eighteenth century proper. But the eighteenth century has not been seen merely as the seedbed of Romanticism. The most active and productive branches of literary criticism in recent years have flourished partly through looking anew at the eighteenth century: feminist literary criticism, the renewed interest in the historical contexts of literature, and the revitalized study of bibliography, which has blossomed into the sociology of literary texts, and its attendant interest in the history of print. The study of the eighteenth century has provided interesting material for all of these approaches, and it is essential to their full development.

With all of these changes, few things have remained exactly as they were. Milton is still the most important poet in the seventeenth century (and perhaps any century), but he is re-situated in the period in which he wrote his most important work (rather than located among the Elizabethans, as he was in the old days). This has meant a demotion for Dryden. When Dryden was seen as the major poet in the first part of the "long" eighteenth century, he was naturally given greater prominence than he is now. If that is a loss, there are undeniably great advantages to having Milton among us. *Paradise Lost* makes almost everything that comes after it in this *Anthology* more intelligible. It was a great pleasure to be able to refer students to passages in *Paradise Lost* throughout my footnotes on later works in the book. Another major competitor for space once reserved for Dryden is certainly Aphra Behn, represented here by *Oroonoko* and a selection of her poetry. She competed with Dryden for the Royalist theater audiences of their time, but was successfully lampooned into disrepute by the following generation. It is a pleasure to restore her to her place in the historical scene with Dryden and her other competitors for fame.

As Milton is of his, Pope is still the most prominent poet of his century, and the *Anthology* reflects this, but his proportions are diminished in order to admit other voices. Poetry in general has given way on some fronts to prose. There is no question that much of the poetry of Pope excluded from this anthology is, line for line, linguistically richer than the prose stories for the sake of which, in part, it was sacrificed. But verbal beauty is only one of the attractions of literature, and it seemed more important to include something by Eliza Haywood, a popular and interesting writer whom Pope lampooned in the *Dunciad*, than to have more Pope. A number of the longest works included in full here are works of prose: *Oroonoko*, *A Tale of a Tub*, and *Rasselas*. This partly reflects the increased interest in prose over the last twenty-five years, but it also serves the very practical purpose of providing teachers with some complete texts between two covers, so they can reduce the number of books they require students to buy. The *Anthology* aims to provide a complete syllabus for a variety of courses on the period. Perhaps everyone will want one other text, but it is hoped that not much more than that will be needed. The one other text for many teachers is likely to be a play; drama is a glaring omission in this collection, but I despaired of selecting the play or two, at best, that most teachers would prefer. Here too, the interest in prose works, which take up more space than poetry, had an effect.

Among the prose works included throughout the *Anthology*, and sometimes nudging out well-known works of poetry, are a few pieces that a generation ago would often have been considered part of the background of literature rather than literature itself. Some of the journal entries and letters, as well as some of the fragments of historical and philosophical works used to seem somewhat infra-literary to the most influential critics. But this was very much not the case in the eighteenth century itself because the word "literature" still meant almost everything that appeared in letters, all examples of written learning. The century had a great deal to do with creating the specialized nineteenth-century meaning of the term "literature," but it resisted it even as it created the word "literary" and glided towards a more restricted sense of the phrase "literary history."

In restoring some of the old meaning of "literature," recent trends have been true to the outlook of the period itself. This is also so when it comes to the re-introduction of women onto the scene. There were plenty of places in the eighteenth century world where women were not seen – the polling places, for example, the universities, and the ecclesiastical benefices. They may not have been prominent in the literary scene, but they were more present than we used to think. Several of Samuel Johnson's closest associates were women writers: Hester Thrale, his best friend; Elizabeth Carter who was already working for *The Gentleman's Magazine* when Johnson arrived in London; Charlotte Lennox; and Frances Burney, to name a few. He much preferred the novels of Sarah Fielding to those of her brother Henry. Three of the four *Ramblers* which he did not write himself he assigned to women writers; he subscribed to the publication of several volumes of poetry by women, and he participated in the mixed company of Samuel Richardson's literary circle. Women worked under numerous disadvantages as writers in the eighteenth century, and they did not produce as much as men, but they were present in publications of the period, and they deserve to be restored to something like the prominence they once struggled to enjoy. Several anthologies of the time were more receptive to women than most anthologies in our own century; indeed, the proportion of women represented in Robert Dodsley's *Collection of Poems by Several Hands* (1748) is probably higher than what I present here.

Despite all the changes I have made in relation to the best anthology of the last generation, the present anthology is still fairly conservative. It would certainly be possible and defensible to work harder for equal representation for women and working-class writers. It would also be defensible for an anthology to move further than I have from traditional literary critical criteria to give more prominence to works because of their social or historical significance. I have also been conservative by identifying works with their authors and presenting them all under their author's names, rather than experimenting with a purely chronological or intertextual mode of presentation. In addition, I have, conservatively, been selective in a way that I would not have been had I chosen to present the anthology as a hypertext, a series of WorldWide Web pages, or an anonymous FTP containing ten times as much text as one could read in a course. In sum, this anthology is a conventional book, in which the works are arranged according to the author who wrote them in the order in which the authors were born. I hope no one in an age of hypertexts is going to feel compelled to read all the selections in the order in which they appear, but it is not an arbitrary order. There are a limited number of texts here, and I wish there were more, but I have made editorial decisions in selecting them, as I have in determining which editions to follow and in writing the footnotes. A truly revolutionary editor would presumably not assert himself or herself at all. We could have every text and every version of every text available. This may be ideal, but the work of editing would not then disappear; it would become the work of each and every student and teacher who wanted to learn the literature of this period. This anthology, with its somewhat more capacious CD-ROM version, conservatively retains the features of an eighteenth-century book produced primarily by one person, who has been largely responsible for determining its contents and must humbly accept responsibility for all its failings.

Editorial Principles

One of the many difficult decisions about how to present the following material was whether or not to retain the spelling and punctuation of the original texts. I believe that texts are not really separable from their material manifestations: capitalization, italicization, spelling, punctuation, even paper, and ink contribute to making a text what it is, or what it was when it first appeared. On the other hand, I have a feeling that a certain amount can be changed without significantly affecting the text. How much can be changed without changing the text itself? This sounds like a good question for a philosopher because it cannot be answered without revealing commitments about the definition of "the text." My less-than-philosophical solution has been: 1) to modernize the representation of letters completely: no long *s* (*f*), no representation of *th* by *y*, and no unusual abbreviations or digraphs; 2) to modernize spelling where it could be done without definitely changing the sound that readers would gather from it; for example, there did not seem to be any reason to use most of the old '*d* spellings meant to prevent readers from making a syllable out of the past-participial ending *-ed* because, as a rule, we do not hear that *-ed* as a syllable today; where it was meant to be heard, I had to add an accent over the *e* (thus, *è*). Such cases are relatively rare and it seemed worth making these few changes to accommodate a lot of harmless modernization; 3) in poetry it seemed impossible to change punctuation without changing sound, so I left it, except in a few very rare cases where a slight change seemed absolutely necessary for sense; in prose, I was just slightly bolder in making changes; 4) I introduced quotation marks, opening and closing in the modern way, to indicate direct speech both in prose and poetry; in some cases I used these in place of italicization indicating quotation, and I used commas in place of parentheses indicating a break in the direct quotation: "Begone", he said, instead of *Begone* (he said), to make up an extreme case; 5) except in rare cases where change seemed impossible, I did not represent reverse italicization (common in the titles of some works); but I retained regular italicization used for emphasis (and often for proper names) as well as all forms of capitalization. The end result of all these decisions is a text that retains a good deal of the typographical diversity of the original but that will pose a bit less of an obstacle to an appreciation of the work itself.

One goal of such modernization as I have allowed is to reduce the number of footnotes. I have often thought of Samuel Johnson's remark that notes are necessary but they are necessary evils. Footnotes distract one from the consecutive progress of reading; they interrupt the thoughts and ideas that one has in reading and diminish the force of the experience. On the other hand, constant reference to a dictionary, or an encyclopedia, not to mention all the other reference books I have needed, is more distracting, and a failure to investigate the meaning of some phrases can completely disrupt understanding. Most of my notes explain the meanings of words no longer current or proper names no longer familiar to college and university students. I have very frequently cited Johnson's *Dictionary* (1755), and in this way made the notes part of the literature of the period. There are plenty of occasions on which I had to use the *Oxford English Dictionary*. I also widely used a variety of dictionaries and atlases of the Bible, the *Oxford Classical Dictionary*, *The Encyclopaedia Britannica* (especially the eleventh edition and the new electronic version), *The Dictionary of National Biography*, and *A Dictionary of British and American Women Writers 1660–1800*, edited by Janet Todd. But perhaps most of all I relied on the notes already compiled in the many great editions of the works I reprint here. Works such as the Twickenham *Pope* and the Yale *Johnson*, to name only two, saved me months of work, even when I double-checked their information. I have acknowledged them separately in the introductions to my authors but rarely in the individual notes where they helped.

In the introductions too I have noted which editions I used for copytexts. For much the most part I have preferred first editions, and I have given the dates of these editions along with the titles of the works. (However, in those few cases where publication lagged far behind composition, I have given an approximate date of composition with the title.) An aspect of my policy of modernization is, where there is a choice, to prefer New Style dates, in which the year begins on 1 January rather than on 25 March, as it did in the Julian calendar, which England did not abandon until 1752. Although I have often included substantive variants from editions produced later in the author's lifetime, I have tried to provide a good sense of what these texts looked like to readers when they first appeared in print.

Acknowledgements

Although I am responsible for the contents of this book, I had a great deal of help. My editor Andrew McNeillie was my constant correspondent during the long process of building, expanding, contracting, and shaping the table of contents. Like me, he solicited and read contributions on the subject from scores of teachers and scholars. I am grateful to everyone who contributed, and I am sorry it was impossible to construct a book that satisfied every reasonable request. The following scholars made thoughtful suggestions or supplied me with expert opinions on the works of particular authors: Carol Barash, John Bender, O. M. Brack, Bliss Carnochan, Caryn Chaden, Brian Connery, Patricia Craddock, Marlies Danziger, Lennard Davis, Aileen Douglas, Margaret Doody, David Duff, Gordon Fulton, Achsah Guibbory, Richard Greene, Robert Griffin, Patrick Harrison, Nelson Hilton, J. Paul Hunter, Ann Imbrie, Felix Irwin, Gwin Kolb, Anne Krook, Joanne Long, Jack Lynch, Robert Markley, Carey McIntosh, Wendy Motooka, David Oakleaf, John O'Neill, Michael Payne, David Radcliffe, Claude Rawson, John Richetti, George Rousseau, Ted Ruml, Jonathan Sawday, John Scanlan, John Shawcross, Stuart Sherman, David Shields, John Sitter, Lars Troide, Eleanor Ty, Cynthia Wall, and Richard Wendorf. I owe a greater debt to Terry Castle, who advised me at the very outset and later became an official advisory editor of the volume. She helped me appreciate the importance of many writers in the period whose work I did not know. I owe a similar debt to my colleague in eighteenth-century studies at Vassar Donna Heiland. David Norbrook, the volume's other advisory editor, supplied much information I lacked concerning writers of the earliest period in the book. Robert Brown and Rachel Kitzinger of the Classics Department assisted me, as ever, with numerous notes concerning Latin and Greek works.

The bulk of this volume, great as it is, indicates less than half of the volume of text that had to be processed in the course of its compilation and frequent revision. Stephanie Harzewski, my regular student assistant for three years, gave me indispensable assistance with the enormous tasks of typing and collating. She was joined by an equally diligent student, Jennifer Simpson, for our frantic summer of assembling the first draft of the book. I am very grateful to both of these students and to Vassar College and the Ford Foundation for supplying them. I must also thank the Institute for Advanced Study in the Behavioral

Sciences, where, with support from the Mellon Foundation, I first planned this project in 1993.

In pursuit of early editions of eighteenth-century texts I had the pleasure of working in numerous fine libraries. I wish to thank the librarians at Stanford University, Vassar College, the New York Public Library, the Beinecke Rare Books and Manuscript Library, the British Library, the British Art Center, and the Bodleian Library.

I am also indebted to the following publishers for granting me permission to publish parts of editions to which they hold the copyright: Blackwell Publishers for "A Letter from Artemiza in the Town to Chloe in the Country," "Lampoon [On the Women about Town]," "Signior Dildo," and "A Satyr on Charles II" from *The Poems of John Wilmot, Earl of Rochester*, ed. Keith Walker, 1984; and material from Robert Filmer, *Patriarcha*, ed. Peter Laslett, 1949, pp. 60–3; HarperCollins Publishers for material from *The Diary of Samuel Pepys*, eds Robert Latham and William Matthews, G. Bell & Sons, 1970; Oxford University Press for "Letter to Lady Wortley Montagu 1 September 1718" from *The Correspondence of Alexander Pope*, ed. George Sherburn, 5 vols, Clarendon Press, 1956; "Letter to Esther Burney 30 September 1811" from *Journals and Letters of Frances Burney d'Arblay*, ed. Joyce Hemlow, vol. 6, 1975 (copyright © Oxford University Press, 1975); "Letter to Mrs. and Miss Thrale 27/8 March 1777" from *The Early Journals and Letters of Frances Burney d'Arblay*, ed. Lars E. Troide, vol. 2, 1990 (copyright © Lars E. Troide, 1990); material from Lucy Apsley Hutchinson, *Memoirs*, ed. James Sutherland, Oxford University Press, 1973; two letters from *The Letters of Samuel Johnson*, ed. R. W. Chapman, 3 vols, Clarendon Press, 1952; Yale University Press for *Rescuing Horace Walpole*, ed. W. S. Lewis, vol. 13, 1948 and vol. 31, 1961; letter from Thomas Gray to Richard West 21 April 1741, from *The Correspondence of Thomas Gray*, ed. Paget Toynbee and Leonard Whibley, 3 vols, Clarendon Press, 1933. Every effort has been made to trace all the copyright holders but if any have been inadvertently overlooked the publishers will be pleased to make the necessary arrangement at the first opportunity.

Partly because of its size, partly because of its frequent revision, and partly because of the varied constituency it tries to please, this book required even more patience than usual from my family. I am grateful to Alex, Davy, and especially Joanne for their unfailing support and good humor.

Ballads and Newsbooks from the Civil War
(1640–1649)

One of the dramatic effects of the revolution in England was a change in the character and probably in the amount of publication. The popular appetite for news was stimulated by the political upheaval, which also disturbed and suspended the usual forms of government censorship and control. From about 1641 the many and various factions in the kingdom were freer to express their views than they ever had been before or were to be for many years after the restoration of conventional government in 1660. This period did not give birth to the newspaper and the political editorial (Ben Jonson satirized the industry of newsmaking in the 1620s in The Staple of News) *but the revolution fostered unprecedented coverage of domestic news and changed the nature of periodical publication for good.*[1] *Along with the newsbooks, came an increased production of pamphlets and broadsides, the cheapest and most ephemeral kinds of publication. One of the most consciously literary forms appearing in such publications was the ballad. Long an oral vehicle of news and commentary, the ballad came more often to take printed form during the interregnum. In this section I offer two pieces from newsbooks and three ballads. Four of the five focus on the execution of Charles I, which was probably the most frequently mentioned event in English writing from 1649 until well into the eighteenth century.*

Hyder Rollins edited a collection of ballads called Cavalier *and* Puritan *(New York University Press, 1923); his careful transcriptions of the original texts in the Thomason collection at the British Library provide the basis of the ballads I present here. The newsbooks were selected from* Making the News, *edited by Joad Raymond.*

THE WORLD IS TURNED UPSIDE DOWN (1646)

To the tune of, *When the King enjoys his own again*[1]

Listen to me and you shall hear,
News hath not been this thousand year:
Since *Herod, Caesar,* and many more,[2]
You never heard the like before.
    Holy-days are despised.   5
    New fashions are devised.
Old Christmas is kicked out of Town.[3]
    Yet let's be content, and the times lament,
    You see the world turned upside down.

BALLADS AND NEWSBOOKS FROM THE CIVIL WAR
[1] I am paraphrasing the introduction of *Making the News: An Anthology of the Newsbooks of Revolutionary England, 1641–1660*, ed. Joad Raymond (St Martins, 1993); on the effects of the war on literature, see Nigel Smith, *Literature and Revolution in England, 1640–1660* (Yale University Press, 1994).

THE WORLD IS TURNED UPSIDE DOWN
[1] This royalist ballad has been dated 8 April 1646.
[2] *Herod* ruler in Judaea who condemned John the Baptist and returned Christ to his subordinate Pontius Pilate, having set him at nought (Luke 23.11); he was subject to Augustus Caesar.
[3] *Old Christmas is kicked out* The Puritans banned Christmas festivities and other holidays as idolatrous.

The wise men did rejoice to see   10
Our Saviour Christ's Nativity:
The Angels did good tidings bring,
The Shepherds did rejoice and sing.
    Let all honest men,
      Take example by them.   15
Why should we from good Laws be bound?[4]
    Yet let's be content, &c.

Command is given, we must obey,
And quite forget old Christmas day:
Kill a thousand men, or a Town regain,[5]   20
We will give thanks and praise amain.[6]
    The wine pot shall clink,
      We will feast and drink.
And then strange motions will abound.[7]
    Yet let's be content, &c.   25

Our Lords and Knights, and Gentry too,
Do mean old fashions to forego:
They set a porter at the gate,
That none must enter in thereat.
    They count it a sin,   30
      When poor people come in.
Hospitality it self is drowned.
    Yet let's be content, &c.

The serving men do sit and whine,
And think it long ere dinner time: 35
The Butler's still out of the way,
Or else my Lady keeps the key,
    The poor old cook,
      In the larder doth look,
Where is no goodness to be found,   40
    Yet let's be content, &c.

To conclude, I'll tell you news that's right,
Christmas was killed at *Nasby* fight:[8]
Charity was slain at that same time,
Jack Tell troth too, a friend of mine,   45
    Likewise then did die,
      Roast beef and shred pie,[9]
Pig, Goose and Capon no quarter found.

---

[4] *bound*   "gone away from" (*OED*, *boun*).
[5] *Kill . . . regain*   Puritan victories in the Civil War.
[6] *amain*   with vigor.
[7] *motions*   legal motions, like the one banning Christmas festivities.

[8] *Nasby*   the decisive battle of the Civil War, June 14, 1645.
[9] *shred pie*   mince pie.

Yet let's be content, and the times lament,
You see the world is quite turned round. 50

The KING'S Last farewell to the World, OR The Dead KING'S Living Meditations, at the approach of Death denounced against Him[1] (1649)

Through fear of sharp and bitter pain,
  by cutting off my days,
No pleasure in my Crown I take,
  nor in my Royal Rays.[2]
I shall descend with grievèd heart, 5
  (for none my life can save)
Unto the dismal gates of death,
  to moulder in the Grave.

Farewell my Wife, and Children all,
  wipe off my brinish teares. 10
I am deprivèd of my Throne,
  and from my future years.
Farewell my people every one,
  for I no more shall see
The wonders of the Lord on earth, 15
  nor with you shall I be.

Mine eyes do fail, and to the earth
  to worms I must be hurled:
Henceforth no more shall I behold
  the people of the world. 20
My Crown and Sceptre I must leave,
  my glory, and my Throne:
Adieu my fellow Princes all,
  I from the earth am gone.

Mine Age (which did approach to me) 25
  departed is away;
And as a Shepherd's tent removed,
  and I returned to clay;
And as a Weaver doth cut off
  his thrum,[3] even so my life, 30
Must be cut off, from people and
  from Children, and from Wife.

THE KING'S LAST FAREWELL TO THE WORLD
[1] This Puritan ballad appeared on January 31, 1649,
the day after the execution of King Charles I; *denounce*
"To threaten by proclamation" (Johnson).

[2] *Rays* "Any lustre corporeal or intellectual"
(Johnson).
[3] *thrum* "The ends of weavers' threads" (Johnson).

In sighs by day, and groans by night
    with bitterness I moan,
And do consume away[4] with grief,   35
    my end to think upon.
Fear in the morning me assails,
    Death Lion-like I see,
Even all the day (till night) to roar
    to make an end of me.   40

I chattered as the shrieking Crane,
    or Swallow that doth fly:
As Dove forlorn, in pensiveness,
    doth mourn, even so do I.
I looked up to thee, O Lord,   45
    but now mine eyes do fail.
Oh ease my sad oppressèd soul,
    for death doth now prevail.

What shall I say, to God's Decree,
    if he would speak, I then   50
should live; it is a work for God,
    I find no help from men.
Yet if my life prolongèd was,
    my sins for to repent,
Then softly I would go and mourn,   55
    until my life was spent.

And all my years, that I should live,
    for mine offences foul,
I would pass o'er in bitterness,
    of my distressèd soul.   60
O Lord, thou hast discoverèd
    to me, that by these things
Men live; through thee, Princes do Reign,
    thou swayest over Kings.

In all things here God's Providence,   65
    and will alone commands,
The life of my poor spirit sad,
    is only in his hands,
Oh, that the Lord would me restore.
    My strength then I would give,   70
To serve my God in humbleness
    whilst he would let me live.

---

[4]   *consume away*   "burn away" (*OED* 6c).

Behold, O Lord, when I in peace,
   did look to be restored,
Then was my soul in bitterness,   75
   cast off, and I abhored,
Yet in the love of God most good,
   his righteousness most just
Hath thrown me down into the pit,
   and to corrupted dust,   80

Because that I have gone astray,
   And cherished war and strife,
My days are now cut off, and I
   am quite bereft of life,
Oh cast my sins behind thy back,   85
   good God, I humbly pray,
And my offences with the blood
   of Christ wash clean away.

When my dead body is intered,
   I cannot praise thee there,   90
Death cannot celebrate the Lord,
   my God, most good, most dear;
They that go down into the pit
   destructions them devour:
For in thy truth they cannot hope,   95
   but perish by thy power.

The living, Lord, the living, they
   shall praise thy holy name.
With all the glorious host above,
   and I shall do the same,   100
The father to his children here,
   that are of tender youth,
Shall them forewarn, and unto them
   make known thy glorious truth.

Forgive my sins, and save my soul   105
   O Lord, I thee entreat,
And blot out mine offences all,
   for they are very great:
Receive my soul for Christ his[5] sake,
   my Prophet, Priest, and King,   110
That I with Saints and Angels may
   eternal praises sing.
FINIS

---

[5] *Christ his*   Christ's.

The Royal Health to the Rising Sun (1649)

To the tune of, *O my pretty little winking, &c.*[1]

As I was walking forth one day,
I heard distressèd people say,
Our Peace and Plenty now is gone,
And we poor people quite undone:
    A Royal Health I then begun[2]   5
    Unto the rising of the Sun,
Gallant English Spirits
    do not thus complain,
The Sun that sets
    may after rise again.   10

The Tempest hath endurèd long,
We must not say, we suffer wrong,
The Queen of Love sits all alone.[3]
No man is Master of his own.

We over-whelmèd are with grief,   15
And harbour many [a] private Thief,
Poor House-keepers can hardly live,
Who used in former times to give:[4]

The Thistle chokes the Royal Rose,[5]
And all our bosom friends turned foes,   20
The Irish Harp is out of tune,
And we, God knows, undone too soon.

The second Part, to the same tune.
True love and friendship doth now decay,
Poor People's almost starved they say,   25
Our Trading's spoiled, and all things dear
We may complain, and ne'er the near:[6]

Though all be true that here is said,
Kind Country-men be not dismayed,
For when the worst of harms is past,   30
We shall have better times at last.

THE ROYAL HEALTH TO THE RISING SUN
[1] This bravely optimistic royalist ballad laments the state of the kingdom after the execution of Charles I on January 30, 1649 and predicts a happy turn of events. The tune is unknown.
[2] The six-line refrain follows every stanza.
[3] *Queen of Love* Henrietta Maria, daughter of Henry IV of France, wife to Charles I.

[4] *to give* to give to the poor.
[5] *Thistle* symbolic of the Scots, whose Presbyterian forces contributed importantly to the defeat of Charles; the Royal Rose is England (and Charles); the Irish were nearly in rebellion against Charles, but suffered most terribly under Cromwell.
[6] *near* "Nearer to one's end or purpose" (*OED* adv.[1] 5).

When Rulers cast off self-respects,[7]
Then shall our Yokes fall from our Necks,
Our safeties shall not then depend
On promise of a Faithless Friend: 35

When as the Cloud of War is down,
The Royal Sun enjoys the Crown,
The Lamb shall with the Lion feed,
'Twill be a happy time indeed:

Let us cheer up each other then,   40
And show our selves true English-men,
And not like bloody Wolves and Bears,
As we have been these many years.

The Father of our Kingdom's dead,
His Royal Sun from *England's* fled,   45
God send all well that Wars may cease,
    A Royal Health I then begun
    Unto the rising of the Sun,
Gallant English Spirits,
    do not thus complain   50
The Sun that sets
    may after rise again.

from *A Perfect Diurnal of Some Passages in Parliament*

NUMBER 288
29 JANUARY–5 FEBRUARY 1649

Tuesday, January 30

This day the King was beheaded, over against the Banqueting house by White-Hall, The manner of Execution, and what passed before his death take thus.

He was brought from Saint *James* about ten in the morning, walking on foot through the Park, with a Regiment of Foot for his guard, with Colours flying, Drums beating, his private Guard of Partisans, with some of his Gentlemen before, and some behind bareheaded, Doctor Juxon late Bishop of London next behind him, and Colonel Thomlinson (who had charge of him) to the Gallery in Whitehall, and so into the Cabinet Chamber, where he used to lie, where he continued at his Devotion . . . The Scaffold was hung round with black, and the floor covered with black, and the Axe and Block laid in the middle of the Scaffold. There were diverse companies of Foot and Horse, on every side the Scaffold, and the multitudes of people that came to be Spectators, very great. The King making a Pass upon the Scaffold, looked very earnestly on the Block, and asked Colonel *Hacker* if there were no higher; and then spake thus, directing his speech to the Gentlemen upon the Scaffold. King. 'I shall be very little heard of any body here, I shall therefore speak a word unto you here;[1] indeed I could hold my peace

---

[7]   *self-respects* selfish aims.

A PERFECT DIURNAL
[1]   *here* on the scaffold; ranks of soldiers separated King Charles from the large crowd.

very well, if I did not think that holding my peace, would make some men think that I did submit to the guilt, as well as to the punishment; but I think it is my duty to God first, and to my Country, for to clear my self both as an honest man, and a good king, and a good Christian. I shall begin first with my Innocency, In troth I think it not very needful for me to insist long upon this, for all the world knows that I never did begin a war with the two house of Parliament, and I call God to witness, to whom I must shortly make an account, that I never did intend for to encroach upon their Privileges; they began upon me; it is the Militia they began upon; they confessed that the Militia was mine, but they thought it fit to have it from me; and to be short, if any body will look to the dates of Commissions, theirs and mine, and likewise to the Declarations, will see clearly that they began these unhappy troubles, not I; so that as the guilt of these Enormous crimes that are laid against me, I hope in God that God will clear me of it. . . . yet for all this, God forbid that I should be so ill a Christian, as not to say that God's Judgements are just upon me: Many times he does pay Justice by an unjust Sentence, that is ordinary; I only say this, That an unjust sentence [meaning Strafford][2] that I suffered for to take effect, is punished now, by an unjust sentence upon me; that is, so far I have said, to show you that I am an innocent man. Now for to show you that I am a good Christian: I hope there is [pointing to Dr. Juxon] a good man that will bear me witness, That I have forgiven all the world, and those in particular that have been the chief causers of my death; who they are, God knows, I do not desire to know, I pray God forgive them. But this is not all, my Charity must go further, I wish that they may repent, for indeed they have committed a great sin in particular, I pray God with St. *Stephen*,[3] That this be not laid to their charge; nay, not only so but that they may take the right way to the Peace of the Kingdom, for Charity commands me not only to forgive particular men, but to endeavour to the last gasp the Peace of the Kingdom: so (sirs) I do wish with all my soul, and I do hope (there is some here will carry it further) that they may endeavour the Peace of the Kingdom'.

from *Mercurius Pragmaticus*

NUMBER 43
30 JANUARY–6 FEBRUARY 1649

Nay, you may e'en go to rest now, your *Great* and *Acceptable* WORK is done; the *Fatal Blow* is given, the Kingdom is translated to the Saints – Oh Horror! Blood! Death! Had you none else to wreak your cursed *malice* on, but the sacred Person of the King? *cursed be your* rage *for it is fierce, and your* malice *for it is implacable.*

Good God, how every day adds fresh supplies of Miseries to poor dying England; enough of Care, but little enough of Cure; though years and months end, yet your sorrows are still beginning, and our Calamities cease not . . .

Beware the building, for the *Foundation* is taken away, the winds begin to blow, and the waves to beat, the Restless *Ark* is tossed; none but unclean Beasts are entered into her, the *Dove* will not return, neither will the *Olive Branch* appear.[1] The Axe is laid to the Root,[2] even of the Royal Cedar, then what can the Inferior Tree expect but to be crushed and bruised in His fall, and afterwards hewn down and cast into the fire . . .

---

[2] *Strafford* A Parliamentary supporter executed May 12, 1641.
[3] *St. Stephen* A martyr killed with stones.
MERCURIUS PRAGMATICUS

[1] Genesis 8.11; the olive branch is the sign that the waters have subsided, and there is peace on earth.
[2] The apocalyptic prophecy of John the Baptist, reported in all four gospels (e.g. Matthew 3.10).

Thomas Hobbes (1588–1679)

Hobbes says that his mother, frightened by the impending attack of the Spanish Armada, gave premature birth to twins – himself and fear. Commentators have cherished this anecdote because Hobbes's twin, fear, plays such an important role in his philosophy. He describes human life in its natural state as a horrible field of contestation in which people are driven to sociability by their passions, especially fear, rather than by an innate sense of charity or love of community. Hobbes's conception of natural life as "nasty, brutish, and short" and his complex views on liberty and determinism, which he saw as compatible, made him the most controversial philosopher of the period. Long after his death in 1679, writers were still reacting to Hobbes's disturbing views. Swift's Tale of a Tub *(1704) is an attempt to keep Hobbes at bay, and Samuel Johnson's* Dictionary *is another: Johnson consciously excluded Hobbes from his illustrative quotations and inserted numerous sentences from John Bramhall, one of his chief antagonists. But both Johnson and Swift felt the validity of Hobbes's views and paraphrased them on occasion, as did practically all philosophical writers in the period.*

First published in 1651, Leviathan *consists of four parts: "Of Man;" "Of Commonwealth;" "Of a Christian Commonwealth;" and "Of the Kingdom of Darkness." The following chapter, one of Hobbes's most famous and infamous pieces of writing comes towards the end of part one and provides part of the transition to part two. Despite his royalist background and his implicit defense of Charles I's authority in* Leviathan, *Hobbes was seen as a defector by Oxford royalists and took a pledge of loyalty to the Commonwealth government in 1652. Although he had been tutor to Charles II, he was never welcome at his restored court (1660–85). Hobbes's work is complex and his personality was evidently rebarbative as well. He is satirized in numerous poems of the period as well as attacked in serious treatises. He was certainly one of the most accomplished, least understood, most frequently attacked, and most influential writers of the whole period.*

There are several good recent editions of Leviathan, *including Michael Oakeshott's (Blackwell, 1957), Richard Tuck's (Cambridge University Press, 1991), and Edwin Curly's (Hackett Publishing, 1994), which includes variants from Hobbes's considerably revised Latin edition of 1668. The text I present is based, like all of these, on the first edition of 1651. For a complete introductory guide to the study of Hobbes, see* A Hobbes Dictionary, *ed. A. P. Martinich (Blackwell, 1995).*

from *Leviathan* (1651)

CHAPTER XIII
OF THE NATURAL CONDITION OF MANKIND,
AS CONCERNING THEIR FELICITY, AND MISERY

Men by nature equal. Nature hath made men so equal, in the faculties of the body, and mind; as that though there be found one man sometimes manifestly stronger in body, or of quicker mind than another; yet when all is reckoned together, the difference between man, and man, is not so considerable, as that one man can thereupon claim to himself any benefit, to which another may not pretend, as well as he. For as to the strength of body, the weakest has strength enough to kill the strongest, either by secret machination, or by confederacy with others, that are in the same danger with himself.

And as to the faculties of the mind (setting aside the arts grounded upon words, and especially that skill of proceeding upon general, and infallible rules, called Science; which very few have, and but in few things; as being not a native faculty, born with us; nor attained – as Prudence – while we look after somewhat else) I find yet a greater equality amongst men, than that of strength. For Prudence, is but Experience; which equal time, equally bestows on all men, in those things they equally apply themselves unto. That which may perhaps make such equality incredible, is but a vain conceit of one's own wisdom, which almost all men think they have in a greater degree than the Vulgar;[1] that is, than all men but themselves, and a few others, whom by Fame, or for concurring with themselves, they approve. For such is the nature of men, that howsoever they may acknowledge many others to be more witty, or more eloquent, or more learned; yet they will hardly believe there be many so wise as themselves: for they see their own wit at hand, and other men's at a distance. But this proveth rather that men are in that point equal, than unequal. For there is not ordinarily a greater sign of the equal distribution of any thing, than that every man is contented with his share.

From Equality proceeds Diffidence.[2] From this equality of ability, ariseth equality of hope in the attaining of our Ends. And therefore if any two men desire the same things, which nevertheless they cannot both enjoy, they become enemies; and in the way to their End (which is principally their own conservation, and sometimes their delectation only) endeavour to destroy, or subdue one another. And from hence it comes to pass, that where an invader hath no more to fear, than another man's single power; if one plant, sow, build, or possess a convenient Seat, others may probably be expected to come prepared with forces united, to dispossess, and deprive him, not only of the fruit of his labour, but also of his life, or liberty. And the Invader again is in the like danger of another.

From Diffidence War. And from this diffidence of one another, there is no way for any man to secure himself, so reasonable, as Anticipation; that is, by force, or wiles, to master the persons of all men he can, so long, till he see no other power great enough to endanger him: And this is no more than his own conservation requireth, and is generally allowed. Also because there be some, that taking pleasure in contemplating their own power in the acts of conquest, which they pursue farther than their security requires; if others, that otherwise would be glad to be at ease within modest bounds, should not by invasion increase their power, they would not be able, long time, by standing only on their defence, to subsist. And by consequence, such augmentation of dominion over men being necessary to a man's conservation, it ought to be allowed him.

Again, men have no pleasure, (but on the contrary a great deal of grief,) in keeping company, where there is no power able to over-awe them all. For every man looketh that his companion should value him, at the same rate he sets upon himself: And upon all signs of contempt, or undervaluing, naturally endeavours, as far as he dares (which amongst them that have no common power to keep them in quiet, is far enough to make them destroy each other) to extort a greater value from his contemners, by dommage;[3] and from others, by the example.

So that in the nature of man, we find three principal causes of quarrel. First, Competition; Secondly, Diffidence; thirdly, Glory.

The first, maketh men invade for Gain; the second, for Safety; and the third, for Reputation. The first use Violence, to make themselves Masters of other men's persons, wives, children, and cattle; the second, to defend them; the third, for trifles, as a word, a smile, a

---

LEVIATHAN
[1] *Vulgar* "The common people" (Johnson).

[2] *Diffidence* mistrust.

[3] *dommage* damage.

different opinion, and any other sign of undervalue, either direct in their Persons, or by reflection in their Kindred, their Friends, their Nation, their Profession,[4] or their Name.

Out of Civil States, there is always War of every one against every one. Hereby it is manifest, that during the time men live without a common Power to keep them all in awe, they are in that condition which is called War; and such a war, as is of every man, against every man. For WAR, consisteth not in Battle only, or the act of fighting; but in a tract of time, wherein the Will to contend by Battle is sufficiently known: and therefore the notion of *Time,* is to be considered in the nature of War; as it is in the nature of Weather. For as the nature of Foul weather, lieth not in a shower or two of rain; but in an inclination thereto of many days together: So the nature of War, consisteth not in actual fighting; but in the known disposition thereto, during all the time there is no assurance to the contrary. All other time is PEACE.

The Incommodities of such a War. Whatsoever therefore is consequent to a time of War, where every man is Enemy to every man; the same is consequent to the time, wherein men live without other security, than what their own strength, and their own invention shall furnish them withal. In such condition, there is no place for Industry; because the fruit thereof is uncertain: and consequently no Culture of the Earth; no Navigation, nor use of the commodities that may be imported by Sea; no commodious Building; no Instruments of moving, and removing, such things as require much force; no Knowledge of the face of the Earth; no account of Time; no Arts; no Letters; no Society; and which is worst of all, continual fear, and danger of violent death; And the life of man, solitary, poor, nasty, brutish, and short.

It may seem very strange to some man, that has not well weighed these things; that Nature should thus dissociate, and render men apt to invade, and destroy one another: and he may therefore, not trusting to this Inference, made from the Passions,[5] desire perhaps to have the same confirmed by Experience. Let him therefore consider with himself, when taking a journey, he arms himself, and seeks to go well accompanied; when going to sleep, he locks his doors; when even in his house he locks his chests; and this when he knows there be Laws, and public Officers, armed, to revenge all injuries shall be done him; what opinion he has of his fellow subjects, when he rides armed; of his fellow Citizens, when he locks his doors; and of his children, and servants, when he locks his chests. Does he not there as much accuse mankind by his actions, as I do by my words? But neither of us accuse man's nature in it. The Desires, and other Passions of man, are in themselves no Sin. No more are the Actions, that proceed from those Passions, till they know a Law that forbids them: which till Laws be made they cannot know: nor can any Law be made, till they have agreed upon the Person that shall make it.

It may peradventure be thought, there was never such a time, nor condition of war as this; and I believe it was never generally so, over all the world: but there are many places, where they live so now. For the savage people in many places of *America,* except the government of small Families, the concord whereof dependeth on natural lust,[6] have no government at all; and live at this day in that brutish manner, as I said before. Howsoever, it may be perceived what manner of life there would be, where there were no common Power to fear, by the manner of life, which men that have formerly lived under a peaceful government, use[7] to degenerate into, in a civil War.

---

4 *Profession* religious or political commitments.
5 *the Passions* principles in the psychology of Hobbes and other writers of the period.

6 *lust* "Any violent or irregular desire" (Johnson).
7 *use* "To be customarily in any manner; to be wont" (Johnson).

But though there had never been any time, wherein particular men were in a condition of war one against another; yet in all times, Kings, and Persons of Sovereign authority, because of their Independency, are in continual jealousies, and in the state and posture of Gladiators; having their weapons pointing, and their eyes fixed on one another; that is, their Forts, Garrisons, and Guns upon the Frontiers of their Kingdoms; and continual Spies upon their neighbours; which is a posture of War. But because they uphold thereby, the Industry of their Subjects; there does not follow from it, that misery, which accompanies the Liberty of particular men.

In such a War nothing is Unjust. To this war of every man against every man, this also is consequent, that nothing can be Unjust. The notions of Right and Wrong, Justice and Injustice have there no place. Where there is no common Power, there is no Law: no Injustice. Force, and Fraud, are in war the two Cardinal virtues. Justice, and injustice are none of the Faculties neither of the Body, nor Mind. If they were, they might be in a man that were alone in the world, as well as his Senses, and Passions. They are Qualities, that relate to men in Society, not in Solitude. It is consequent also to the same condition, that there be no Propriety,[8] no Dominion, no *Mine* and *Thine* distinct; but only that to be every man's that he can get; and for so long, as he can keep it. And thus much for the ill condition, which man by mere Nature is actually placed in; though with a possibility to come out of it, consisting partly in the Passions, partly in his Reason.

The Passions that incline men to Peace. The Passions that incline men to Peace, are Fear of Death; Desire of such things as are necessary to commodious living; and a Hope by their Industry to obtain them. And Reason suggesteth convenient Articles of Peace, upon which men may be drawn to agreement. These Articles, are they, which otherwise are called the Laws of Nature: whereof I shall speak more particularly, in the two following Chapters.

Robert Filmer (d. 1653)

Like some of the victims of Pope's and Dryden's satires, Sir Robert Filmer has the misfortune to be known chiefly as the object of a more famous writer's attack. John Locke's attack on Patriarcha, or the Natural Power of Kings Asserted *comprises the first of his* Two Treatises of Government, *which gradually became key documents in almost all democratic theories of government. Locke launched his assault in 1690, ten years after the first publication of* Patriarcha *and thirty-seven years after the death of its author. Filmer wrote several tracts in which he opposed Hobbes, Milton, Grotius, and other unconventional or progressive thinkers, but* Patriarcha *is his most important work; it provides the clearest modern statement of absolutist monarchical principles, and, perhaps most importantly, it shows how those principles operated in the conception of the family as well as the state.*

Patriarcha *has been edited, with some of Filmer's other tracts, by Peter Laslett. My text is based on his edition (Blackwell, 1949), which makes use of important manuscripts in private hands.*

---

[8] *Propriety* "Peculiarity of possession; exclusive right" (Johnson).

from *Patriarcha, or the Natural Power of Kings Asserted* (1680)

V KINGS ARE EITHER FATHERS OF THEIR PEOPLE, OR HEIRS OF SUCH FATHERS, OR THE USURPERS OF THE RIGHTS OF SUCH FATHERS

It may seem absurd to maintain that Kings now are the fathers of their people, since experience shows the contrary. It is true, all Kings be not the natural parents of their subjects, yet they all either are, or are to be reputed, as the next heirs of those progenitors who were at first the natural parents of the whole people, and in their rights succeed to the exercise of supreme jurisdiction. And such heirs are not only lords of their own children, but also of their brethren, and all others that were subject to their Fathers.

And therefore we find that God told Cain of his brother Abel: 'His desires shall be subject unto thee, and thou shalt rule over him'.[1] Accordingly, when Jacob had bought his brother's birthright, Isaac blessed him thus: 'Be lord over thy brethren, and let the sons of thy mother bow before thee'.[2] So we find that at the offering of Princes at the dedication at the tabernacle the Princes of Israel are said to be heads of the houses of their Fathers, as Eliab the son of Helon was Prince of the children of his Father Zebulum. Numbers vii, 2 and 24.

As long as the first Fathers of families lived, the name of Patriarchs did aptly belong unto them. But after a few descents, when the true fatherhood itself was extinct, and only the right of the Father descended to the true heir, then the title of Prince or King was the more significant to express the power of him who succeeds only to the right of that fatherhood which his ancestors did *naturally* enjoy. By this means it comes to pass, that many a child, by succeeding a King, hath the right of a Father over many a grey-headed multitude, and hath the title of Pater Patriae.[3]

VI OF THE ESCHEATING[1] OF KINGDOMS

It may be demanded what becomes of the right of fatherhood in case the Crown does escheat for want of an heir, whether it doth not then devolve to the people. The answer is:

First, it is but the negligence or ignorance of the people to lose the knowledge of the true heir, for an heir there always is. If Adam himself were still living, and now ready to die, it is certain that there is one man, and but one in the world, who is next heir, although the knowledge who should be that one man be quite lost.

Secondly, this ignorance of the people being admitted, it doth not by any means follow that, for want of heirs, the supreme power devolves to the multitude, and that they have the power to rule or choose what rulers they please. No: the Kingly power escheats in such cases to the prime and independent heads of families, for every kingdom is resolved into those principles whereof at first it was made. By the uniting of great families or petty Princedoms, we find the greater monarchies were at the first erected, and into such again, as into their first matter, many times they return. And because the dependency of ancient families is oft obscure or worn out of knowledge, therefore the wisdom of all or most Princes have thought fit to adopt many times those for heads of families and Princes of provinces whose merits, abilities, or fortunes have enabled them, or made them fit and capable of such royal favours.

V KINGS ARE EITHER FATHERS OF THEIR PEOPLE
[1] Genesis 4.7.
[2] Genesis 27.29.
[3] *Pater Patriae* father of the nation.

OF THE ESCHEATING OF KINGDOMS
[1] *Escheating* forfeiture to a superior lord, for want of an heir.

All such prime heads and Fathers have power to consent in the uniting or conferring of their fatherly right of sovereign authority on whom they please. And he that is so elected claims not his power as a donative from the people, but as being substituted properly by God, from whom he receives his royal charter of an universal Father, though testified by the ministry of the heads of the people.

If it please God, for the correction of the Prince or punishment of the people, to suffer Princes to be removed and others to be placed in their rooms, either by the factions of the nobility or rebellion of the people, in all such cases the judgement of God, who hath power to give and take away kingdoms, is most just. Yet the ministry of men who execute God's judgements without commission is sinful and damnable. God doth but use and turn men's unrighteous acts to the performance of His righteous decrees.

In all kingdoms or commonwealths in the world, whether the Prince be the supreme Father of the people or but the true heir of such a Father, or whether he come to the Crown by usurpation, or by any other way whatsoever, or whether some few or a multitude govern the commonwealth, yet still the authority that is in any one, or in many, or in all of these, is the only right and natural authority of a supreme Father. There is, and always shall be continued to the end of the world, a natural right of a supreme Father over every multitude, although, by the secret will of God, many at first do most unjustly obtain the exercise of it.

To confirm this natural right of regal power, we find in the Decalogue[2] that the law which enjoins obedience to Kings is delivered in the terms of 'Honour thy Father', as if all power were originally in the Father. If obedience to parents be immediately due by a natural law, and subjection to Princes but by the mediation of a human ordinance, what reason is there that the law of nature should give place to the laws of men, as we see in the power of the magistrate?

VII OF THE AGREEMENT OF PATERNAL AND REGAL POWER

If we compare the natural duties of a Father with those of a King, we find them to be all one, without any difference at all but only in the latitude or extent of them. As the Father over one family, so the King, as Father over many families, extends his care to preserve, feed, clothe, instruct and defend the whole commonwealth. His wars, his peace, his courts of justice, and all his acts of sovereignty, tend only to preserve and distribute to every subordinate and inferior Father, and to their children, their rights and privileges, so all the duties of a King are summed up in an universal fatherly care of his people. By conferring these proofs and reasons drawn from the authority of Scripture, it appears little less than a paradox which Bellarmine[1] and others affirm of the freedom of the multitude to choose what rulers they please.

Had the patriarchs their power given them by their own children? Bellarmine dares not say it, but the contrary. If then, the fatherhood enjoyed this authority for so many ages by the law of nature, when was it lost, or when forfeited, or how is it devolved to the liberty of the multitude?

---

[2] *Decalogue* the ten commandments (Exodus 20).

VII OF THE AGREEMENT OF PATERNAL AND REGAL POWER
[1] *Bellarmine* Italian cardinal and theologian (1542–1621), supported the Pope's right to temporal power.

Robert Herrick (1591–1674)

Hesperides *was published in 1648 and contains 1,130 poems, nearly all of those confidently attributed to Herrick. Many of the poems celebrate more or less ideal aspects of the country life that Herrick experienced, or witnessed, as a vicar in Devonshire in the 1630s and 40s. As a loyal royalist, he lost his living in 1647 and returned joyfully to his native London. After being restored to his living in 1662, however, Herrick returned to the country for good.*

Herrick's delight in country things is evident in poems like "The Hock-Cart," and his pleasure in other kinds of sensual life comes out in his poems to Julia. Yet, Herrick is also evidently pleased by the composition of his own verse. His poetic sportiveness and his awareness of classical and renaissance genres give his verse a fine tone of cultivation which blends brilliantly with his sensual impulses. Eager to sound like a real poet and yet to write about his personal experience, the juvenile Samuel Johnson chose Herrick's "Daffodils" as the pattern for his first attempt at formal verse. Like almost every attempt to emulate Herrick, Johnson's was both less energetic and less polished than his model. Because of their clear rhythms and easy style many of Herrick's poems have been set to music. His melodious poem "To the Virgins, to Make Much of Time" is one of the most famous in all of British literature. Although earlier twentieth-century criticism branded Herrick as a minor poet, recent studies have elevated him, partly by paying attention to the political elements of his verse, and partly by discussing the latent integrity of his great book of poems.

The texts presented here are based on the first edition of Hesperides. *The standard modern edition is by L. C. Martin (Oxford University Press, 1968).*

from *Hesperides* (1648)

THE ARGUMENT OF HIS BOOK

I sing of *Brooks*, of *Blossoms*, *Birds*, and *Bowers*:
Of *April*, *May*, of *June*, and *July*-Flowers.
I sing of May-poles, Hock-carts, Wassails, Wakes[1]
Of Bride-grooms, Brides, and of their Bridal-cakes.
I write of *Youth*, of *Love*, and have Access   5
By these to sing of cleanly-*Wantonness*.
I sing of *Dews*, of *Rains*, and piece by piece
Of *Balm*, of *Oil*, of *Spice*, and *Amber-Greece*[2]
I sing of *Times trans-shifting*; and I write
How *Roses* first came *Red*, and *Lilies White*.   10
I write of *Groves*, of *Twilights*, and I sing
The Court of *Mab*, and of the *Fairy-King*.[3]
I write of *Hell*; I sing (and ever shall)
Of *Heaven*, and hope to have it after all.

THE ARGUMENT OF HIS BOOK
[1] *Hock-carts* decorated carts carrying the last load of the harvest; *wassails* liquors used for celebratory drinks of health.
[2] *Amber-Greece* Ambergris "A fragrant drug . . . used both as a perfume and a cordial" (Johnson, quoting Ephraim Chambers's *Cyclopaedia* and the *Dictionnaire des Trevoux*).
[3] *Mab* Queen Mab of the fairies (a mab is also a slattern or loose woman).

TO DAFFODILS

Fair Daffodils, we weep to see
   You haste away so soon:
As yet the early-rising Sun
   Has not attained his Noon.
     Stay, stay,   5
   Until the hasting day
     Has run
   But to the Even-song;
And, having prayed together, we
   Will go with you along.   10

We have short time to stay, as you,
   We have as short a Spring;
As quick a growth to meet Decay,
   As you, or any thing.
     We die,   15
   As your hours do, and dry
     Away,
   Like to the Summer's rain;
Or as the pearls of Morning's dew
   Ne'er to be found again.   20

THE NIGHT-PIECE, TO JULIA

Her Eyes the Glow-worm lend thee,
The Shooting Stars attend thee
   And the Elves also,
   Whose little eyes glow,
Like the sparks of fire, befriend thee.   5

No *Will-o' th'-Wisp* mis-light thee;[1]
Nor Snake, or Slow-worm bite thee:
   But on, on thy way
   Not making a stay,
Since Ghost there's none to affright thee.   10

Let not the dark thee cumber;
What though the Moon does slumber?
   The Stars of the night
   Will lend thee their light,
Like Tapers clear without number.   15

THE NIGHT-PIECE, TO JULIA
[1] *Will-o'-th'-Wisp*   false beacons of marsh gas; "[contracted from William] Will with a wisp; Jack with a lanthorn. '. . . when viewed near at hand, it shines less than at a distance. They wander about in the air, not far from the surface of the earth . . . They haunt burying places, places of execution, dunghills . . . Now they dilate themselves and now contract . . . They follow those that run away, and fly from those that follow them . . .' Musch[enbroek]" (Johnson).

Then *Julia* let me woo thee,
Thus, thus to come unto me:
　　And when I shall meet
　　Thy silv'ry feet,
My soul I'll pour into thee.　　　　　　　　　　　　　　20

THE HOCK-CART, OR HARVEST HOME[1]

To the Right Honourable Mildmay, Earl of Westmoreland[2]

Come Sons of Summer, by whose toil
We are the Lords of Wine and Oil:
By whose tough labours and rough hands
We rip up first, then reap our lands.
Crowned with the ears of corn, now come,　　　　　　5
And, to the Pipe, sing Harvest home.
Come forth, my Lord, and see the Cart
Drest up with all the Country Art.
See, here a Malkin, there a sheet,[3]
As spotless pure as it is sweet:　　　　　　　　　　10
The Horses, Mares, and frisking Fillies
(Clad, all, in Linen, white as Lillies).
The Harvest Swains and Wenches bound
For joy, to see the *Hock-cart* crowned.
About the Cart, hear how the Rout　　　　　　　　　15
Of Rural Younglings raise the shout;
Pressing before, some coming after,
Those with a shout, and these with laughter.
Some bless the Cart; some kiss the sheaves;
Some prank them up with Oaken leaves;　　　　　　20
Some cross the Fill-horse; some with great[4]
Devotion stroke the home-borne wheat;
While other Rustics, less attent
To Prayers than to Merriment,
Run after with their breeches rent.　　　　　　　　25
Well, on, brave boys, to your Lord's Hearth,
Glitt'ring with fire; where, for your mirth,
Ye shall see first the large and chief
Foundation of your Feast, Fat beef,
With Upper Stories, Mutton, Veal[5]　　　　　　　　30
And Bacon (which makes full the meal)
With several dishes standing by,

THE HOCK-CART, OR HARVEST HOME
[1]　*Hock-Cart*　the decorated last wagon of the harvest.
[2]　*Mildmay*　Fane (1600?–66).
[3]　*Malkin*　"[from mal, of Mary, and kin, the diminutive termination] A kind of mop made of clouts [rags] for sweeping ovens; thence a frightful figure of clouts dressed up; thence a dirty wench" (Johnson, quoting Hanmer); a sheet could be used as an instrument of punishment for fornication, or simply for decoration (see *OED*).
[4]　*cross the Fill-horse*　bless the horse positioned between the fills (thills or shafts) of the cart.
[5]　*Upper Stories*　additional courses.

As here a Custard, there a Pie,
And here all tempting Frumenty[6]
And for to make the merry cheer,   35
If smirking Wine be wanting here,[7]
There's that which drowns all care, stout Beer;
Which freely drink, to your Lord's health,
Then to the Plough (the Common-wealth)
Next to your Flails, your Fans, your Fatts[8]   40
Then to the Maids with Wheaten Hats:
To the rough Sickle, and crookt Scythe,
Drink, frolic boys, till all be blithe.
Feed, and grow fat; and as ye eat
Be mindful that the lab'ring neat[9]   45
(As you) may have their fill of meat.[10]
And know, besides, ye must revoke[11]
The patient Ox unto the Yoke,
And all go back unto the Plough
And Harrow (though they're hanged up now).   50
And, you must know, your Lord's word's true,
Feed him ye must, whose food fills you;
And that this pleasure is like rain,
Not sent ye for to drown your pain,
But for to make it spring again.   55

UPON JULIA'S CLOTHES

When as in silks my *Julia* goes,
Then, then (me thinks) how sweetly flows
That liquefaction of her clothes.

Next, when I cast mine eyes and see
That brave Vibration each way free;[1]   5
O how that glittering taketh me!

WHEN HE WOULD HAVE HIS VERSES READ

In sober mornings, do not thou rehearse[1]
The holy incantation of a verse;
But when that men have both well drunk, and fed,
Let my Enchantments then be sung, or read.
When Laurel spirts i' th' fire, and when the Hearth   5

---

[6] *Frumenty* "Food made of wheat boiled in milk"
(Johnson).
[7] *smirking* smirky, "Nice; smart; jaunty" (Johnson).
[8] *Fans* winnowing fans; *Fats* old spelling and pronunciation of "vats."
[9] *neat* "Black cattle; oxen" (Johnson).
[10] *meat* nourishment, food in general.
[11] *revoke* call back.

UPON JULIA'S CLOTHES
[1] *Vibration* "The act of moving or being moved with
quick reciprocations, or returns; the act of quivering"
(Johnson).
WHEN HE WOULD HAVE HIS VERSES READ
[1] *rehearse* recite.

Smiles to it self, and guilds the roof with mirth;
When up the *Thyrse* is raised, and when the sound[2]
Of sacred *Orgies* flies, A round, A round.[3]
When the *Rose* reigns, and locks with ointments shine,[4]
Let rigid *Cato* read these Lines of mine.[5]   10

DELIGHT IN DISORDER

A sweet disorder in the dress
Kindles in clothes a wantonness:
A Lawn about the shoulders thrown[1]
Into a fine distraction:
An erring Lace, which here and there   5
Enthralls the Crimson Stomacher:[2]
A Cuff neglectful, and thereby
Ribbands to flow confusedly:
A winning wave (deserving Note)
In the tempestuous petticoat: 10
A careless shoe-string, in whose tie
I see a wild civility:
Do more bewitch me, than when Art
Is too precise in every part.

TO THE VIRGINS, TO MAKE MUCH OF TIME

Gather ye Rose-buds while ye may,
    Old Time is still a flying:
And this same flower that smiles to day
    To morrow will be dying.

The glorious Lamp of Heaven, the Sun,   5
    The higher he's a getting;
The sooner will his Race be run,
    And nearer he's to Setting.

That Age is best, which is the first,
    When Youth and Blood are warmer;   10
But being spent, the worse, and worst
    Times, still succeed the former.

Then be not coy, but use your time;
    And while ye may, go marry:

---

[2] *Thyrse*   the sceptre of Bacchus; god of revelry.
[3] *Orgies*   "Mad rites of Bacchus; frantic revels" (Johnson).
[4] *Rose*   as in the phrase "to speak under the Rose" the reference is to "the ancient custom in symposiac meetings [notable for revelry], to wear chaplets of roses about their heads" (Johnson, quoting Sir Thomas Browne); the oiled locks refer to similarly Dionysian rites.

[5] *Cato*   M. Porcius, the elder, a rigid Roman moralist.
DELIGHT IN DISORDER
[1] *A Lawn*   a scarf or shawl made of lawn, "fine linen, remarkable for being used in the sleeves of bishops" (Johnson).
[2] *Stomacher*   "An ornamental covering worn by women on the breast" (Johnson).

For having lost but once your prime,   15
    You may forever tarry.

HIS RETURN TO LONDON

From the dull confines of the drooping West,
To see the day spring from the pregnant East,
Ravished in spirit, I come, nay more, I fly
To thee, blest place of my Nativity!
Thus, thus with hallowed foot I touch the ground,   5
With thousand blessings by thy Fortune crowned.
O fruitful Genius! that bestowest here
An everlasting plenty, year by year.
O *Place*! O *People*! Manners! framed to please
All *Nations, Customs, Kindreds, Languages*!   10
I am a free-born *Roman*; suffer then,
That I amongst you live a Citizen.
London my home is: though by hard fate sent
Into a long and irksome banishment;
Yet since called back; henceforward let me be,   15
O native country, repossessed by thee!
For, rather than I'll to the West return,
I'll beg of thee first here to have mine Urn.
Weak I am grown, and must in short time fall;
Give thou my sacred Relics Burial.   20

THE BAD SEASON MAKES THE POET SAD

Dull to my self, and almost dead to these
My many fresh and fragrant Mistresses:
Lost to all Music now; since every thing
Puts on the semblance here of sorrowing.
Sick is the Land to th' heart; and doth endure   5
More dangerous faintings by her desperate cure.
But if that golden Age would come again,
And *Charles* here Rule, as he before did Reign;
If smooth and unperplext the Seasons were,
As when the *Sweet Maria* livèd here:[1]   10
I should delight to have my Curls half drowned
In *Tyrian Dews*, and Head with Roses crowned;[2]
And once more yet (ere I am laid out dead)
Knock at a Star with my exalted Head.

THE PILLAR OF FAME

    Fame's pillar here, at last, we set,
      Out-during *Marble, Brass*, or *Jet*,

THE BAD SEASON MAKES THE POET SAD
[1] *Maria* Henrietta Maria (1609–69) Queen Consort
of Charles I.

[2] *Tyrian Dews* purple (from the famous dye made at
Tyre) liquid (i.e. wine).

Charmed and enchanted so,
As to withstand the blow
Of   overthrow: 5
Nor shall the seas
Or   Outrages
Of storms o'erbear
What we up-rear
Tho' Kindoms fall,   10
This pillar never shall
Decline or waste at all;
But stand for ever by his owne
Firm and well fixed foundation

Charles I (1600–1649) and John Gauden (1605–1662)

Soon after succeeding to the throne in 1625, Charles married Henrietta Maria. He and his queen were destined to be the focal points of a royalist culture that was forced out of power in England for about twenty years but continued to express itself in literature throughout that period. Charles was executed by the Commonwealth government in 1649, and after the restoration of the monarchy, under his son, Charles II, he was celebrated as a martyr. As a symbolic presence in royalist literature Charles I achieved great power, but in his life he presided over a series of errors and failures that rapidly stripped him of funds and support. One of his least popular tactics was to recruit forces in Ireland and later in Scotland to invade England, with a promise of concessions for interests in those parts of the kingdom. Charles's treaty with Scotland, known as the "Engagement," was a desperate move to get the Scottish army on his side by promising to accept Presbyterianism, a form of church government favoured by the Scots and by the Long Parliament, in which the chief officers are representative presbyters rather than court appointed bishops, as in the episcopal Church of England. Charles tried to hide that treaty, of course, and in Eikon Basilike *he blames Parliament for the entry of the Scots into England, which first occurred in 1640, initiated the Second Bishop's War, led to the Treaty of Ripon and impelled Charles to summon the Long Parliament. It was the Scottish army and the demands of the rebellious Scottish parliament that broke Charles's power as much as anything. He was the Scots' prisoner in 1646 (before being turned over to the English) and his ill-fated Engagement was one of the principal acts of "treason" for which he was executed by his own parliament in 1649.*

Scholarship has gradually discovered that Charles was only partially responsible for the composition of Eikon Basilike. *Like modern politicians, Charles had ghost writers; Charles took notes, or uttered them, and, in this case, John Gauden (1605–62) composed the book. But the book projected Charles's image in an immensely sympathetic way: the title means "the King's image," and it contained a portrait of Charles. It galvanized royalist, episcopal sentiment and, going into forty odd editions in a brief time, posed a serious public relations threat to the Commonwealth government. Milton was engaged almost immediately to discredit the work and the recently executed King; the result was his* Eikonoklastes, *"the image-smasher" (see below, p. 51). My text is based on an early issue of the first edition (February, 1649). For the complex printing history of "the King's Book" see Francis F. Madan, "A New Bibliography of the Eikon Basilike,"* Oxford Biblio-

graphical Society, new series 3 (1950). A similar, early issue of the first edition was edited by
Philip A. Knachel for The Folger Shakespeare Library (Cornell University Press, 1966).

from *Eikon Basilike* (1649)

UPON THE CALLING IN OF THE SCOTS, AND THEIR COMING

The *Scots* are a Nation, upon whom I have not only common ties of Nature, Sovereignty,
and Bounty, with My Father of blessed memory; but also special and late obligations of
favours, having gratified the active Spirits among them so far, that I seemed to many, to
prefer the desires of that Party, before My own interest and Honour. But, I see, Royal bounty
emboldens some men to ask, and act beyond all bounds of modesty and gratitude.

My charity, and Act of Pacification, forbids Me to reflect on former passages; wherein I
shall ever be far from letting any man's ingratitude, or inconstancy, make Me repent of what
I granted them, for the public good: I pray God it may so prove.

The coming again of that Party into *England*, with an Army, only to conform this Church
to their late New model,[1] cannot but seem as unreasonable, as they would have thought the
same measure offered from hence to themselves.

Other errand I could never understand they had (besides those common and vulgar
flourishes for Religion and Liberty), save only to confirm the Presbyterian Copy[2] they had set,
by making this Church to write after them, though it were in bloody Characters.

Which design and end, whether it will justify the use of such violent means, before the
divine Justice, I leave to their Consciences to judge, who have already felt the misery of the
means, but not reaped the benefit of the end, either in this Kingdom, or that.

Such knots and crossness of grain being objected here, will hardly suffer that form which
they cry up, as the only just reformation, and settling of Government and Discipline in
Churches, to go on so smoothly here, as it might do in *Scotland*; and was by them imagined
would have done in *England*, when so many of the *English* Clergy, through levity, or
discontent, if no worse passion, suddenly quitted their former engagements to Episcopacy,
and faced about to their Presbytery.

It cannot but seem either passion, or some self-seeking, more than true Zeal, and pious
Discretion, for any foreign State or Church to prescribe such medicines only for others, which
themselves have used, rather successfully than commendably, not considering that the same
Physic[3] on different constitutions, will have different operations; That may kill one, which
doth but cure another.

Nor do I know any such tough and malignant humours in the constitution of the *English*
Church, which gentler applications than those of an Army, might not easily have removed:
Nor is it so proper to hew out religious Reformations by the Sword, as to polish them by fair
and equal disputations among those that are most concerned in the differences, whom not
force, but Reason ought to convince.

But their design now, seemed rather to cut off all disputation here, than to procure a fair
and equal one: For, it was concluded there, that the *English* Clergy must conform to the *Scots*
pattern before ever they could be heard, what they could say for themselves, or against the
other's way.

UPON THE CALLING IN OF THE SCOTS, AND THEIR
COMING
[1] *their late New model*   Presbyterianism.

[2] *Copy*   "The autograph; the original; the archetype;
that from which any thing is copied" (Johnson).
[3] *Physic*   "Medicines; remedies" (Johnson).

I could have wished fairer proceedings both for their credits, who urge things with such violence; and for other men's Consciences too, who can receive little satisfaction in these points which are maintained rather by Soldiers fighting in the Field, than Scholars disputing in free and learned Synods.[4]

Sure in matters of Religion those truths gain most on men's Judgements and Consciences, which are least urged with secular violence, which weakens Truth with prejudices; and is unreasonable to be used, till such means of rational conviction hath been applied, as leaving no excuse for ignorance, condemns men's obstinacy to deserved penalties.

Which no charity will easily suspect of so many learned and pious Church men in *England*; who being always bred up, and conformable to the Government of Episcopacy, cannot so soon renounce both their former opinion and practice, only because that Party of the *Scots* will needs, by force assist a like Party here, either to drive all Ministers, as sheep into the common fold of Presbytery, or destroy them; at least fleece them, by depriving them of the benefit of their Flocks. If the *Scotch* sole Presbytery were proved to be the only institution of Jesus Christ, for all Churches Government; yet I believe it would be hard to prove that Christ had given those *Scots*, or any other of my Subjects, Commission by the Sword to set it up in any of my Kingdoms, without my Consent.

What respect and obedience Christ and his Apostles paid to the chief Governors of States where they lived is very clear in the Gospel; but that he, or they ever commanded to set up such a parity of Presbyters,[5] and in such a way as those *Scots* endeavour, I think is not very disputable.[6]

If Presbytery in such a supremacy be an institution of Christ; sure it differs from all others; and is the first and only point of Christianity, that was to be planted and watered with so much Christian blood; whose effusions run in a stream so contrary to that of the Primitive planters, both of Christianity and Episcopacy, which was with patient shedding of their own blood, not violent drawing other men's; sure there is too much of Man in it, to have much of Christ, none of whose institutions were carried on, or begun with the temptations of Covetousness or Ambition; of both which this is vehemently suspected.

Yet was there never any thing upon the point, which those *Scots* had by Army or Commissioners to move me with, by their many Solemn obtestations,[7] and pious threatenings, but only this; to represent to me the wonderful necessity of setting up their Presbytery in *England*, to avoid the further miseries of a War; which some men chiefly on this design at first had begun, and now further engaged themselves to continue.

What hinders any Sects, Schisms, or Heresies, if they can get but numbers, strength and opportunity, may not, according to this opinion and pattern, set up their ways by the like methods of violence? all which Presbytery seeks to suppress, and render odious under those names; when wise and learned men think, that nothing hath more marks of Schism and Sectarism, than this Presbyterian way, both as to the Ancient, and still most Universal way of the Church-government, and specially as to the particular Laws and Constitutions of this *English* Church, which are not yet repealed, nor are like to be for me, till I see more Rational and Religious motives, than Soldiers use to carry in their Knapsacks.[8]

---

[4] *Synod* "An assembly, particularly of ecclesiastics" (Johnson).

[5] *parity of Presbyters* representative church officers meeting as equals in a synod, and differing from the more hierarchical assembly of appointed bishops in the episcopal church.

[6] *disputable* tenable; arguable.

[7] *Obtestations* "solemn adjuration, entreaty, or supplication" (OED).

[8] *motives . . . in their Knapsacks* arguments or persuasive pamphlets or even abridged Bibles, carried by Protestant Soldiers.

But we must leave the success of all to God, who hath many ways (having first taken us off from the folly of our opinions, and fury of our passion) to teach us those rules of true Reason, and peaceable Wisdom, which is from above, tending most to God's glory, & his Church's good; which I think my self so much the more bound in Conscience to attend, with the most judicious Zeal and care, by how much I esteem the Church above the State, the glory of Christ above mine Own; and the salvation of their Bodies and Estates.

Nor may any men, I think, without sin and presumption, forcibly endeavour to cast the Churches under my care and tuition, into the moulds they have fancied, and fashioned to their designs, till they have first gained my consent, and resolved, both my own and other men's Consciences by the strength of their Reasons.

Other violent motions, which are neither Manly, Christian, nor Loyal, shall never either shake or settle my Religion; nor any man's else, who knows what Religion means; And how far it is removed from all Faction, whose proper engine is force; the arbitrator of beasts, not of reasonable men, much less of humble Christians, and loyal Subjects, in matters of Religion.

But men are prone to have such high conceits of themselves, that they care not what cost they lay out upon their opinions; especially those, that have some temptation of gain, to recompence their losses and hazards.

Yet I was not more scandalized at the *Scots* Armies coming in against my will, and their forfeiture of so many obligations of duty, and gratitude to me: than I wondered, how those here, could so much distrust God's assistance; who so much pretended God's cause to the People, as if they had the certainty of some divine Revelation; considering they were more than competently furnished with my Subjects' Arms and Ammunition; My Navy by Sea, my Forts, Castles, and Cities by Land.

But I find, that men jealous of the Justifiableness of their doings, and designs before God, never think they have human strength enough to carry their work on, seem it never so plausible to the People; what cannot be justified in Law or Religion, had need be fortified with Power.

And yet such is the inconstancy that attends all minds engaged in violent motion, that whom some of them one while earnestly invite to come into their assistance; others of them soon after are weary of, and with nauseating cast them out: what one Party thought to rivet to a settledness by the strength and influence of the *Scots*, that the other rejects and contemns; at once, despising the Kirk Government,[9] and Discipline of the *Scots*, and frustrating the success of so chargeable, more than charitable assistance: For, sure the Church of *England* might have purchased at a far cheaper rate, the truth and happiness of Reformed government and discipline (if it had been wanting) though it had entertamed[10] the best Divines of Christendom for their advice in a full and free Synod; which, I was ever willing to, and desirous of, that matters being impartially settled, might be more satisfactory to all, and more durable.

But much of God's justice, and man's folly, will at length be discovered, through all the films and pretensions of Religion, in which Politicians wrap up their designs: In vain do men hope to Build their piety on the ruins of Loyalty. Nor can those considerations or designs be durable, whose Subjects make a bankrupt of their Allegiance, under pretence of setting up a quicker trade for Religion.

But, as My best Subjects of *Scotland* never deserted Me, so I cannot think that the most are gone so far from Me, in a prodigality of their love and respects toward Me, as to make Me to despair of their return; when besides the bonds of nature and Conscience, which they have to

---

[9]   *Kirk Government*   church government, the Church of   [10]   *entertamed*   entertained; retained in service.
Scotland.

Me, all Reason and true Policy will teach them, that their chiefest interest consists in their fidelity to the Crown, not in their serviceableness to any Party of the People, to a neglect and betraying of My Safety and Honour for their own advantages: However the less cause I have to trust to men, the more I shall apply My self to God.

The troubles of my Soul are enlarged, O Lord, bring thou me out of My distress.

Lord direct thy Servant in the ways of that pious simplicity, which is the best policy.

Deliver Me from the combined strength of those, who have so much of the Serpent's subtlety, that they forget the Dove's Innocency.

Though hand join in hand, yet let them not prevail against My soul, to the betraying of My Conscience, and Honour.

Thou, O Lord, canst turn the hearts of those Parties in both Nations, as thou didst the men of Judah *and* Israel, *to restore* David *with as much loyal Zeal, as they did with inconstancy and eagerness pursue* Him.[11]

Preserve the love of thy Truth and uprightness in Me, and I shall not despair of My Subjects' affections returning towards Me.

Thou canst soon cause the overflowing Seas to ebb, and retire back to the bounds which thou hast appointed for them.

O My God, I trust in thee; let me not be ashamed; let not My enemies triumph over Me.

Let them be ashamed who transgress without a cause; let them be turned back that persecute My Soul.

Let integrity and uprightness preserve Me, for I wait on thee O Lord.

Redeem thy Church, O God, out of all its Troubles.

Sir Thomas Browne (1605–1682)

Browne's first book, Religio Medici *(1642) or the Religion of a Physician, describes some of the complex and often antagonistic attitudes towards the natural world incumbent upon a scientific and pious mind in early seventeenth-century England. Some of the tensions of* Religio Medici *remain in* Pseudodoxia Epidemica: or, Enquiries into Very Many Received Tenents, and Commonly Presumed Truths *(1646). However, in this long, encyclopedic work Browne gives free rein to his pleasure and assiduity in pursuing his knowledge of the natural world. He also takes considerable pleasure in cataloguing the prolific fictions, old wives' tales, and myths that substitute for fact in the popular mind. Browne is far from irreligious in his long work and far from what would today be called rigorously scientific. Biblical information is very important to him, for example, although he is skeptical about many received interpretations of it. There is an exuberance and delight in navigating the mazes of error that give Browne's writing a certain satirical slant and archness. Although Jonathan Swift vastly magnifies such satire and turns it on even skeptical investigators like Browne, some of the satirical exuberance of* A Tale of a Tub *or parts of* Gulliver's Travels *is visible in* Pseudodoxia Epidemica.

In the selection presented here Browne announces his intentions and describes his task to the reader. The rest of book 1 discusses the general causes of error; books 2–4 take up errors about the mineral, vegetable, animal, and human worlds; books 5–7 are concerned with errors in human works of art, history, geography, and biblical interpretation. Some sense of his program is evident in the table of contents of the third book where he explodes the following list of pseudodoxia: "That

---

[11]   *to restore David . . . pursue Him*   see 2 Samuel, especially 2 and 20; David's restoration in Israel became an   allegory of the restoration of Stuart monarchy in England for royalists.

an Elephant hath no joints; That an horse hath no Gall . . . That a Beaver to escape the hunter bites off his Testicles or stones; That a Badger hath the legs of one side shorter than of the other; That a Bear brings forth her cubs informous or unshaped . . . That the Chameleon lives only by Air; That the Ostrich digesteth Iron; That all Animals in the land are in their kind in the Sea . . ."

Browne added to his work over the first six editions (obviously, the subject is endless and was to him endlessly fascinating); for this reason the text here is based on the sixth edition of 1672. The whole work has been edited with full textual apparatus and extensive commentary by Robin Robbins (Oxford, 1981).

from *Pseudodoxia Epidemica: or, Enquiries into Very Many Received Tenets, and Commonly Presumed Truths* (1646)

TO THE
READER

Would Truth dispense,[1] we could be content, with *Plato*, that knowledge were but remembrance; that intellectual acquisition were but reminiscential evocation, and new impressions but the colouring of old stamps which stood pale in the soul before.[2] For what is worse, knowledge is made by oblivion, and to purchase a clear and warrantable body of Truth, we must forget and part with much we know. Our tender Enquiries taking up Learning at large, and together with true and assured notions, receiving many, wherein our reviewing judgements do find no satisfaction. And therefore in this *Encyclopædie* and round of Knowledge, like the great and exemplary wheels of Heaven, we must observe two Circles: that while we are daily carried about, and whirled on the swing and rapt of the one, we may maintain a natural and proper course, in the slow and sober wheel of the other. And this we shall more readily perform, if we timely survey our knowledge; impartially singling out those encroachments, which junior[3] compliance and popular credulity hath admitted. Whereof at present we have attempted a long and serious *Adviso*; proposing not only a large and copious List, but from experience and reason, attempting their decisions.[4]

And at first we crave exceeding pardon in the audacity of the Attempt; humbly acknowledging a work of such concernment unto truth, and difficulty in it self, did well deserve the conjunction of many heads. And surely more advantageous had it been unto Truth, to have fallen into the endeavours of some co-operating advancers, that might have performed it to the life,[5] and added authority thereto; which the privacy of our condition,[6] and unequal abilities cannot expect. Whereby notwithstanding we have not been diverted; nor have our solitary attempts been so discouraged, as to despair the favourable look of Learning upon our single and unsupported endeavours.

TO THE READER
[1] *dispense*   permit.

[2]   In the *Timaeus* and elsewhere, Plato suggests that true knowledge comes from the soul's memory of the forms or ideas of things, which it saw during its transcendental residence in a heavenly world before entering our world of shadows.

[3] *junior*   "youthful" (*OED*).

[4] *decisions*   judgements upon them, but perhaps the more latinate sense of curtailments or excisions.

[5] *to the life*   "with the utmost pains" (*OED* 7 b).

[6] *privacy*   being a private individual rather than a member of an academy or society; *our* Browne uses the plural forms here for singular meaning, as was not uncommon in formal language.

Nor have we let fall our Pen, upon discouragement of Contradiction, Unbelief and Difficulty of dissuasion from radicated beliefs,[7] and points of high prescription, although we are very sensible, how hardly teaching years do learn,[8] what roots old age contracteth unto errors, and how such as are but acorns in our younger brows, grow Oaks in our elder heads, and grow inflexible unto the powerfullest arm of reason. Although we have also beheld, what cold requitals others have found in their several redemptions of Truth; and how their ingenious Enquiries have been dismissed with censure, and obloquy of singularities.

Some consideration we hope from the course of our Profession,[9] which though it leadeth us unto many truths that pass undiscerned by others, yet doth it disturb their Communications, and much interrupt the office of our Pens in their well intended Transmissions. And therefore surely in this work attempts will exceed performances; it being composed by snatches of time, as medical vacations, and the fruitless importunity of *Uroscopy*[10] would permit us. And therefore also, perhaps it hath not found that regular and constant style, those infallible experiments and those assured determinations, which the subject sometimes requireth, and might be expected from others, whose quiet doors and unmolested hours afford no such distractions. Although whoever shall indifferently perpend[11] the exceeding difficulty, which either the obscurity of the subject, or unavoidable paradoxology[12] must often put upon the Attemptor, he will easily discern, a work of this nature is not to be performed on one leg; and should smell of oil[13] if duly and deservedly handled.

Our first intentions considering the common interest of Truth, resolved to propose it unto the Latin republic[14] and equal Judges of *Europe*, but owing in the first place this service to our Country, and therein especially unto its ingenuous[15] Gentry, we have declared our self in a language best conceived. Although I confess, the quality of the Subject will sometimes carry us into expressions beyond mere English apprehensions. And indeed, if elegancy still proceedeth, and English Pens maintain that stream, we have of late observed to flow from many; we shall within few years be fain to learn Latin to understand English, and a work will prove of equal facility in either. Nor have we addressed our Pen or Style unto the people, (whom Books do not redress, and are this way incapable of reduction[16]) but unto the knowing and leading part of Learning. As well understanding (at least probably hoping) except they be watered from higher regions, and fructifying meteors[17] of Knowledge, these weeds must lose their alimental sap, and wither of themselves. Whose conserving influence, could our endeavours prevent; we should trust the rest unto the scythe of *Time*, and hopeful[18] dominion of Truth.

We hope it will not be unconsidered, that we find no open tract, or constant manuduction[19] in this Labyrinth; but are oft-times fain to wander in the *America* and untravelled parts of Truth. For though not many years past, *Dr. Primerose*[20] hath made a

---

[7] *radicated* rooted, entrenched.

[8] *how hardly teaching years do learn* with what difficulty youth learns.

[9] Browne was a medical doctor.

[10] *Uroscopy* Inspection of Urines [marginal note] for medical analysis.

[11] *perpend* "To weigh in the mind; to consider attentively" (Johnson).

[12] *paradoxology* "The use of paradoxes . . . tenet[s] contrary to received opinion . . . position[s] in appearance absurd" (Johnson).

[13] *smell of oil* be deeply learned.

[14] *the Latin republic* the intellectual community of Europe (*respublica litterarum*), which used Latin as its common language.

[15] *ingenuous* "Open; fair; candid; generous; noble" (Johnson).

[16] *reduction* reclamation [from ignorance].

[17] *meteors* "Any bodies in the air or sky that are of a flux and transitory nature" (Johnson).

[18] *hopeful* hoped for.

[19] *manuduction* "Guidance by the hand" (Johnson).

[20] *Dr. Primerose* author of a Latin treatise on vulgar errors in medicine (1638).

learned Discourse of vulgar Errors in Physic,[21] yet have we discussed but two or three thereof. *Scipio Mercurii*[22] hath also left an excellent tract in *Italian*, concerning popular Errors; but confining himself only unto those in Physic, he hath little conduced unto the generality of our doctrine. *Laurentius Ioubertus*[23], by the same Title led our expectation into thoughts of great relief; whereby notwithstanding we reaped no advantage; it answering scarce at all the promise of the inscription. Nor perhaps (if we were yet extant) should we find any farther Assistance from that ancient piece of *Andreas*, pretending the same Title.[24] And therefore we are often constrained to stand alone against the strength of opinion, and to meet the *Goliath* and Giant of Authority, with contemptible pebbles, and feeble arguments, drawn from the scrip[25] and slender stock of our selves. Nor have we indeed scarce named any Author whose name we do not honour; and if detraction could invite us, discretion surely would constrain us from any derogatory intention, where highest Pens and friendliest eloquence must fail in commendation.

And therefore also we cannot but hope [for] the equitable considerations, and candour[26] of reasonable minds. We cannot expect the frown of *Theology* herein; nor can they which behold the present state of things, and controversy of points so long received in Divinity, condemn our sober Enquiries in the doubtful appertinancies[27] of Arts, and Receptaries[28] of Philosophy. Surely Philologers and Critical Discoursers, who look beyond the shell and obvious exteriors of things, will not be angry with our narrower explorations. And we cannot doubt, our Brothers in Physic (whose knowledge in Naturals will lead them into a nearer apprehension of many things delivered) will friendly accept, if not countenance our endeavours. Nor can we conceive it may be unwelcome unto those honoured Worthies, who endeavour in the advancement of Learning: as being likely to find a clearer progression, when so many rubs[29] are levelled, and many untruths taken off, which passing as principles with common beliefs, disturb the tranquillity of Axioms,[30] which otherwise might be raised. And wise men cannot but know, that arts and learning want this expurgation: and if the course of truth be permitted unto itself; like that of time and uncorrected computations,[31] it cannot escape many errors, which duration still enlargeth.

Lastly, we are not Magisterial in opinions, nor have we Dictator-like obtruded our conceptions; but in the humility of Enquiries or disquisitions, have only proposed them unto more ocular[32] discerners. And therefore opinions are free, and open it is for any to think or declare the contrary. And we shall so far encourage contradiction, as to promise no disturbance, or re-oppose any Pen, that shall Fallaciously or captiously refute us; that shall only lay hold of our lapses, single out Digressions, Corollaries, or Ornamental conceptions, to evidence his own in as indifferent[33] truths. And shall only take notice of such, whose experimental and judicious knowledge shall solemnly look upon it; not only to destroy of ours, but to

---

[21]   *Physic*   "The science of healing" (Johnson).

[22]   *Scipio Mercurii*   his work was published in 1645.

[23]   *Laurentius Ioubertus*   his Latin work was published in 1600.

[24]   *Andreas*   author of a lost Greek work on vulgar errors, mentioned by the encyclopedist Athenaeus (7.18).

[25]   *scrip*   a satchel.

[26]   *candour*   "Sweetness of temper; purity of mind; openness; ingenuity kindness" (Johnson).

[27]   *appertinancies*   "That which belongs or relates to another thing" (Johnson).

[28]   *Receptaries*   "Thing[s] received. Not in use" (Johnson).

[29]   *rub*   any obstruction but especially an unevenness on a bowling green.

[30]   *Axioms*   "established principle[s] to be granted without new proof" (Johnson).

[31]   *time and uncorrected computations*   a reference to the inaccuracy of the Julian calendar, which became more evident as time went on and the cardinal points of the year, like the equinox, migrated to earlier dates.

[32]   *ocular*   knowing or discovering by the eye (Johnson).

[33]   *indifferent*   "Neutral; not determined to either side" (Johnson).

establish of his own; not to traduce[34] or extenuate,[35] but to explain, and dilucidate, to add and ampliate, according to the laudable customs of the Ancients in their sober promotions of Learning. Unto whom notwithstanding, we shall not contentiously rejoin, or only to justify our own, but to applaud or confirm his maturer assertions; and shall confer what is in us unto his name and honour; Ready to be swallowed in any worthy enlarger: as having acquired our end, if any way, or under any name we may obtain a work, so much desired, and yet desiderated[36] of Truth.

John Milton (1608–1674)

John Milton believed, with much justification, that he was gifted and that only a very great work would vindicate his special, God-given talents. He regarded his early life as preparation for his high promise and never doubted that he had the ability to write a work that the world, in his words, "would not willingly let die."[1] He contemplated an epic about King Arthur, feeling that such a poem (like the Aeneid *or the* Iliad*) must have national implications. Although* Paradise Lost *reflects Milton's view of English politics, its canvass is biblical and therefore, for Milton, universal history. Although he explores the full scope of biblical history in the last two books, Milton concentrates mainly on the portion of it described in brief in Genesis 1–3. Drawing on his encyclopedic knowledge of classical and biblical learning, Milton makes this crystal grow to embrace a vision of all human life – domestic, political, religious, social, and artistic.*

For all its universality, however, Milton's vision is tinged with his own views: the polity between the sexes is his idealized vision of marriage formed partly through the experience of his first, failed marriage, for example, while his devils are frequently made to resemble Roman Catholics or Episcopal figures who, in Milton's view, had revolted or rebelled from the true religion of the Protestants. Because Milton saw the established monarchy in England and the Catholic Church as usurpers, it is probably misleading to imagine, with William Blake and some great critics, that he sides with the Devil's party, despite the exciting poetry he created to describe them. In fact, the language of Satan and the devils is filled with irony and innuendo that redounds against them. God and Christ can also be ironic, but the joke is always on the devils who imagine they can outwit God, whose enduring nature is ever to work good out of whatever evil they contrive.

Partly because of its tinges of contemporary satire and its ironies, Paradise Lost *has some affinities with the world of mock-heroic, satirical, and ironic poetry that was prevalent through the main part of the period covered in this anthology. Most subsequent writers of the period recognized its greatness and immediately incorporated it into their literary backgrounds: because it provided an example of truly heroic English poetry on a grand scale,* Paradise Lost *made mock-heroic poetry in English much more possible. Like Milton himself, succeeding generations of poets continued to refer to Spenser's more pastoral epic, and the language of Shakespearian tragedy provided a standard of high seriousness, but Milton became the most important model of grandeur and sublimity in English writing.*

Paradise Lost *was not published until 1667 when Milton was fifty-eight and seven years from his death. It might never have been finished if the collapse of Cromwell's government had not freed Milton from his duties as Latin Secretary to the Lord Protector and disengaged him from his life as polemicist.*

---

[34] *traduce* "To censure; to condemn; to represent as blameable; to calumniate; to decry" (Johnson).

[35] *extenuate* "To lessen; to degrade; to lessen in honour" (Johnson).

[36] *desiderated* "wanted; missed; desired in absence. A word scarcely used" (Johnson).

JOHN MILTON

[1] *The Reason of Church Government* (1642).

It also would not have been finished if Charles II's government had decided to prosecute Milton for the views he espoused during the interregnum, which included justifications for the execution of Charles I. He boldly reaffirmed the Commonwealth's most drastic single measure, among other places, in Eikonoklastes *(1649), his attack on Charles's popular, posthumously published* Eikon Basilike. *As it was, partly through the intervention of Andrew Marvell, the government allowed Milton to live a private life in which he completed his life's work. I include two selections from Milton's prose: a small part of* The Doctrine and Discipline of Divorce *(1643) and most of* Areopagitica *(1644), his attack on an order banning most publications unless they were licensed by a Parliamentary Committee. Both works were written partly in response to personal experience. Milton expounded the scriptural justification for divorce shortly after his wife of one month, Mary Powell, returned to her father's house because she found life with her husband too difficult.* Areopagitica *is partly Milton's response to complaints about his unlicensed publication of the divorce tracts. In both cases, however, as in all of his works, Milton combines universal with personal considerations. Despite the various roles that Milton played in society, he was always a consummate artist who brilliantly and egotistically transmuted the stuff of his own experience into works that are important and inspiring for readers whom he never imagined and about whose lives he certainly would not have cared to learn.*

In addition to the pieces of prose and Paradise Lost, *I include three of Milton's sonnets. I follow the text of* Poems *(1673) in Sonnets 18 and 19, but take the numbering of all three sonnets from the* Columbia Edition of the Works of John Milton. *The text of sonnet 16 is based on a Trinity College (Cambridge) manuscript. My texts of Milton are based on first editions, except in the case of* Paradise Lost, *where the second edition of 1674 is the copytext. There have been many fine editors of Milton and I am indebted to several of them, particularly Douglas Bush and Merrit Hughes, from whose texts I was taught and have taught for many years. The* Yale Edition of the Complete Prose Works *(1953–82) of John Milton is a magnificent achievement, and I am also indebted to its editors. Recent biographies of Milton include William Riley Parker's definitive* Milton *(1968) and the relatively brief* Life of John Milton *by A. N. Wilson (Oxford, 1987).*

from *The Doctrine and Discipline of Divorce; Restored to the Good of Both Sexes, From the bondage of Canon Law, and other mistakes, to Christian freedom, guided by the Rule of Charity. Wherein also many places of Scripture, have recovered their long-lost meaning. Seasonable to be now thought on in the Reformation intended.* (1643)

MATTHEW. 13.52.
Every Scribe instructed to the Kingdom of Heaven, is like the Master of a house which bringeth out of his treasury things old and new.

BOOK I
THE PREFACE

Many men, whether it be their fate, or fond opinion, easily persuade themselves, if GOD would be pleased a while to withdraw his just punishments from us, and to restrain what power either the devil, or any earthly enemy hath to work us woe, that then man's nature would find immediate rest and releasement from all evils. But verily they who think so, if they be such as have a mind large enough to take into their thoughts a general survey of human things, would soon prove themselves in that opinion far deceived. For though it were granted us by divine indulgence to be exempt from all that can be harmful to us from without, yet the perverseness of out folly is so bent, that we should never lin[1] hammering out of our own hearts, as it were out of a flint, the seeds and sparkles of new miseries to our selves, till all were in a blaze again. And no marvel if out of our own hearts, for they are evil; but even out of those things which God meant us, either for a principal good, or a pure contentment, we are still hatching and contriving upon our selves matter of continual sorrow and perplexity. What greater good to man than that revealed rule, whereby God vouchsafes to show us how he would be worshipped? and yet that not rightly understood, became the cause that once a famous man in *Israel*[2] could not but oblige his conscience to be the sacrificer, or if not, the jailer of his innocent and only daughter. And was the cause oft-times that Armies of valiant men have given up their throats to a heathenish enemy on the Sabbath day: fondly[3] thinking their defensive resistance to be as then a work unlawful. What thing more instituted to the solace and delight of man than marriage, and yet the misinterpreting of some Scripture[4] directed mainly against the abusers of the Law for divorce given them by *Moses*, hath changed the blessing of matrimony not seldom into a familiar and co-inhabiting mischief; at least into a drooping and disconsolate household captivity, without refuge or redemption. So ungoverned and so wild a race doth superstition run us from one extreme of abused liberty into the other of unmerciful restraint. For although God in the first ordaining of marriage, taught us to what end he did it, in words expressly implying the apt and cheerful conversation of man with woman, to comfort and refresh him against the evil of solitary life, not mentioning the purpose of generation till afterwards, as being but a secondary end in dignity, though not in necessity; yet now, if any two be but once handed[5] in the Church, and have tasted in any sort of the nuptial bed, let them find themselves never so mistaken in their dispositions through any error, concealment, or misadventure, that through their different tempers, thought, and constitutions, they can neither be to one another a remedy against loneliness, nor live in any union or contentment all their days, yet they shall, so they be but found suitably weaponed to the least possibility of sensual enjoyment, be made, [in] spite of *antipathy* to fadge[6] together, and combine as they may to their unspeakable wearisomeness & despair of all sociable delight in the ordinance which God established to that very end. What a calamity is this, and as the Wise-man, if he were alive, would sigh out in his own phrase, what a *sore evil is this under the Sun!*[7] All which we can refer justly to no other author than the Canon Law[8] and her adherents, not consulting with charity, the interpreter and guide of our faith, but resting in the mere element of the Text; doubtless by the policy of the devil to make that gracious ordinance become unsupportable, that what with men not daring to venture upon wedlock, and what with men wearied out of it, all inordinate licence might abound. It was for many ages

---

DOCTRINE AND DISCIPLINE OF DIVORCE

[1] *lin* "stop; give over" (Johnson).

[2] *famous man in Israel* Jephthah the Gileadite vowed to make a sacrifice to God of whatever walked first through his door to great him upon his return from successful battle with the children of Ammon. His daughter greeted him and he kept his vow, though commentators disagreed on whether or not this entailed human sacrifice (Judges 11.30–40).

[3] *fondly* foolishly.

[4] *Scripture* Matthew 5.31–2 where Christ says only adultery is cause for a man to divorce his wife; Mosaic law cited any kind of "uncleanness" as an adequate cause for divorce (Deuteronomy 24.1).

[5] *handed* joined, hand in hand.

[6] *fadge* "To agree; not to quarrel; to live in amity . . . This is a mean word not now used, unless perhaps in ludicrous and low compositions" (Johnson).

[7] *sore evil is this under the Sun* Ecclesiastes 5.13 where the evil is "riches kept for the owners thereof to their hurt."

[8] *Canon Law* "that law which is made and ordained in a general council, or provincial synod of the church" (Johnson, quoting John Ayliffe).

that marriage lay in disgrace with most of the ancient Doctors,[9] as a work of the flesh, almost a defilement, wholly denied to Priests, and the second time dissuaded to all, as he that reads *Tertullian* or *Jerome* may see at large. Afterwards it was thought so Sacramental, that no adultery or desertion could dissolve it; and this is the sense of our Canon Courts in *England* to this day, but in no other reformed Church else; yet there remains in them also a burden on it as heavy as the other two were disgraceful or superstitious, and of as much iniquity, crossing a Law not only written by *Moses*, but charactered[10] in us by nature, of more antiquity and deeper ground than marriage it self; which Law is to force nothing against the faultless proprieties of nature: yet that this may be colourably[11] done, our Saviour's words touching divorce, are as it were congealed into a stony rigour, inconsistent both with his doctrine and his office, and that which he preached only to the conscience, is by canonical tyranny snatched into the compulsive censure of a judicial Court; where Laws are imposed even against the venerable & secret power of nature's impression, to love, what ever cause be found to loathe. Which is a heinous barbarism both against the honour of marriage, the dignity of man and his soul, the goodness of Christianity, and all the humane respects of civility. Notwithstanding that some of the wisest and gravest among the Christian Emperors, who had about them, to consult with, those of the fathers then living, who for their learning & holiness of life are still with us in great renown, have made their statutes & edicts concerning this debate, far more easy and relenting in many necessary cases, wherein the Canon is inflexible. And *Hugo Grotius*,[12] a man of these times, one of the best learned, seems not obscurely to adhere in his persuasion to the equity of those imperial decrees, in his notes upon the *Evangelists*, much allaying the outward roughness of the Text, which hath for the most part been too immoderately expounded; and excites the diligence of others to enquire further into this question, as containing many points which have not yet been explained. By which, and by mine own apprehension of what public duty each man owes, I conceive my self exhorted among the rest to communicate such thoughts as I have, and offer them now in this general labour of reformation, to the candid view both of Church and Magistrate; especially because I see it the hope of good men, that those irregular and unspiritual Courts have spun their utmost date in this Land; and some better course must now be constituted. He therefore that by adventuring shall be so happy as with success to ease & set free the minds of ingenuous and apprehensive men from this needless thraldom, he that can prove it lawful and just to claim the performance of a fit and matchable conversation, no less essential to the prime scope of marriage than the gift of bodily conjunction, or else to have an equal plea of divorce as well as for that corporal deficiency; he that can but lend us the clue that winds out this labyrinth[13] of servitude to such a reasonable and expedient liberty as this, deserves to be reckoned among the public benefactors of civil and humane life; above the inventors of wine and oil; for this is a far dearer, far nobler, and more desirable cherishing to man's life, unworthily exposed to sadness and mistake, which he shall vindicate. Not that licence and levity and unconsented breach of faith should herein be countenanced, but that some conscionable, and tender pity might be had of those who have unwarily in a thing they never practised before, made themselves the bondmen of a luckless and helpless matrimony. In which Argument he whose

---

[9]   *ancient Doctors* early interpreters of the Bible, Church fathers like Tertullian and Jerome.

[10]   *charactered* written.

[11]   *colourably* plausibly.

[12]   *Hugo Grotius* (1585–1645) Dutch scholar who excelled especially in theology and law.

[13]   *clue that winds out this labyrinth* Ariadne gave Theseus the clue of thread that helped him out of the labyrinth in which her father kept the minotaur; Theseus promised to marry her, but (in the most popular account) abandoned her on Naxos where she became the wife of Dionysius.

courage can serve him to give the first onset, must look for two several oppositions; the one from those who having sworn themselves to long custom and the letter of the Text, will not out of the road: the other from those whose gross and vulgar apprehensions conceit[14] but low of matrimonial purposes, and in the work of male and female think they have all. Nevertheless, it shall be here sought by due ways to be made appear, that those words of God in the institution, promising a meet help against loneliness;[15] and those words of Christ, *That his yoke is easy and his burden light*,[16] were not spoken in vain; for if the knot of marriage may in no case be dissolved but for adultery, all the burdens and services of the Law are not so intolerable. This only is desired of them who are minded to judge hardly of thus maintaining, that they would be still and hear all out, nor think it equal to answer deliberate reason with sudden heat and noise; remembering this, that many truths now of reverend esteem and credit, had their birth and beginning once from singular and private thoughts; while the most of men were otherwise possessed; and had the fate at first to be generally exploded[17] and exclaimed on by many violent opposers; yet I may err perhaps in soothing my self that this present truth revived, will deserve to be not ungently received on all hands; in that it undertakes the cure of an inveterate disease crept into the best part of humane society: and to do this with no smarting corrosive, but with a smooth and pleasing lesson, which received hath the virtue to soften and dispel rooted and knotty sorrows; and without enchantment or spell used hath regard at once both to serious pity, and upright honesty; that tends to the redeeming and restoring of none but such as are the object of compassion; having in an ill hour hampered themselves to the utter dispatch of all their most beloved comforts & repose for this life's term. But if we shall obstinately dislike this new overture of unexpected ease and recovery, what remains but to deplore the frowardness[18] of our hopeless condition, which neither can endure the estate we are in, nor admit of remedy either sharp or sweet. Sharp we our selves distaste; and sweet, under whose hands we are, is scrupled and suspected as too luscious.[19] In such a posture Christ found the *Jews*, who were neither won with the austerity of *John the Baptist*, and thought it too much licence to follow freely the charming pipe of him[20] who sounded and proclaimed liberty and relief to all distress: yet Truth in some age or other will find her witness, and shall be justified at last by her own children.

FROM CHAPTER I

To remove therefore, if it be possible, this great and sad oppression which through the strictness of a literal interpreting hath invaded and disturbed the dearest and most peaceable estate of household society, to the over-burdening, if not the overwhelming of many Christians better worth than to be so deserted of the Church's considerate care, this position shall be laid down; first proving, then answering what may be objected either from Scripture or light of reason.

That indisposition, unfitness, or contrariety of mind, arising from a cause in nature unchangeable, hindering and ever likely to hinder the main benefits of conjugal society, which are solace and peace, is a greater reason of divorce than natural frigidity, especially if there be no children, and that there be mutual consent . . .

---

[14] *conceit* conceive.

[15] *a meet help against loneliness* Genesis 2.18; *meet* "Fit; proper; qualified" (Johnson).

[16] *his yoke is easy and his burden light* Matthew 11.30 where the yoke symbolizes devotion to Christ.

[17] *exploded* driven "out disgracefully with some noise of contempt" (Johnson).

[18] *frowardness* advanced state.

[19] *luscious* "Sweet, so as to nauseate" (Johnson).

[20] *him* Jesus (Matthew 11.16–19).

FROM CHAPTER VI

... Fourthly, Marriage is a covenant the very being whereof consists, not in a forced cohabitation, and counterfeit performance of duties, but in unfained love and peace. Thence, saith *Solomon* in *Ecclesiastes, Live joyfully with the wife whom thou lovest, all thy days, for that is thy portion*.[21] How then, where we find it impossible to rejoice or to love, can we obey this precept? how miserably do we defraud our selves of that comfortable portion which God and nature will not join, adding but more vexation and violence to that blissful society by our importunate superstition, that will not hearken to St. *Paul*, 1 *Corinthians* 7 [15] who speaking of marriage and divorce, determines plain enough in general that God therein *hath called us to peace* and not *to bondage*. Yet God himself commands in his Law more than once, and by his Prophet *Malachi*, as *Calvin* and the best translations read, that *he who hates let him divorce*; that is, he who cannot love, or delight.[22] I cannot therefore be so diffident, as not securely to conclude, that he who can receive nothing of the most important helps in marriage, being thereby disenabled to return that duty which is his, with a clear and hearty countenance; and thus continues to grieve whom he would not [be married to], and is no less grieved, that man ought even for love's sake and peace to move divorce upon good and liberal conditions to the divorced. And it is less breach of wedlock to part with wise and quiet consent betimes, than still to soil and profane that mystery of joy and union with a polluting sadness and perpetual distemper; for it is not the outward continuing of marriage that keeps whole that covenant, but whosoever does most according to peace and love, whether in marriage, or in divorce, he it is that breaks marriage least; it being so often written, that *love only is the fulfilling of every Commandment*.[23]

from *Areopagitica; A Speech of Mr. John Milton For the Liberty of Unlicensed Printing, to the Parliament of England*[1] (1644)

They who to States and Governors of the Commonwealth direct their Speech, High Court of Parliament, or wanting such access in a private condition, write that which they foresee may advance the public good; I suppose them as at the beginning of no mean endeavour, not a little altered and moved inwardly in their minds: Some with doubt of what will be the success, others with fear of what will be the censure; some with hope, others with confidence of what they have to speak. And me perhaps each of these dispositions, as the subject was whereon I entered, may have at other times variously affected; and likely might in these foremost expressions now also disclose which of them swayed most, but that the very attempt of this address thus made, and the thought of whom it hath recourse to, hath got the power within me to a passion, far more welcome than incidental to a Preface. Which though I stay not to confess ere any ask, I shall be blameless, if it be no other, than the joy and gratulation

---

[21]   *saith Salomon in Ecclesiastes ... portion*   Ecclesiastes 9.9.

[22]   *Calvin and the best ... delight*   Malachi 2.16; Milton adopts a very doubtful reading.

[23]   *love only is the fulfilling of every Commandment* Romans 13.10, "love is the fulfilling of the law."

AREOPAGITICA

[1]   Milton derives his title from an oration by Isocrates called *Areopagiticus*, which concerned a legal institution called the Court of the Areopagus.

which it brings to all who wish and promote their Country's liberty; whereof this whole Discourse proposed will be a certain testimony, if not a Trophy. For this is not the liberty which we can hope, that no grievance ever should arise in the Commonwealth, that let no man in this World expect; but when complaints are freely heard, deeply considered, and speedily reformed, then is the utmost bound of civil liberty attained, that wise men look for. To which if I now manifest by the very sound of this which I shall utter, that we are already in good part arrived, and yet from such a steep disadvantage of tyranny and superstition grounded into our principles as was beyond the manhood of a *Roman* recovery, it will be attributed first, as if most due, to the strong assistance of God our deliverer, next to your faithful guidance and undaunted Wisdom, Lords and Commons of *England*. Neither is it in God's esteem the diminution of his glory, when honourable things are spoken of good men and worthy Magistrates; which if I now first should begin to do, after so fair a progress of your laudable deeds, and such a long obligement upon the whole Realm to your indefatigable virtues,[2] I might be justly reckoned among the tardiest, and the unwillingest of them that praise ye. Nevertheless there being three principal things, without which all praising is but Courtship and flattery, First, when that only is praised which is solidly worth praise: next, when greatest likelihoods are brought that such things are truly and really in those persons to whom they are ascribed, the other, when he who praises, by showing that such his actual persuasion is of whom he writes, can demonstrate that he flatters not; the former two of these I have heretofore endeavoured, rescuing the employment from him[3] who went about to impair your merits with a trivial and malignant *Encomium*; the latter as belonging chiefly to mine own acquittal, that whom I so extolled I did not flatter, hath been reserved opportunely to this occasion. For he who freely magnifies what hath been nobly done, and fears not to declare as freely what might be done better, gives ye the best covenant of his fidelity; and that his loyalest affection and his hope waits on your proceedings. His highest praising is not flattery, and his plainest advice is a kind of praising; for though I should affirm and hold by argument, that it would fare better with truth, with learning, and the Commonwealth, if one of your published Orders which I should name, were called in, yet at the same time it could not much redound to the lustre of your mild and equal Government, when as private persons are hereby animated to think ye better pleased with public advice, than other statists[4] have been delighted heretofore with public flattery. And men will then see what difference there is between the magnanimity of a triennial Parliament,[5] and that jealous hautiness of Prelates and cabin Counsellors that usurped of late,[6] when as they shall observe ye in the midst of your Victories and successes more gently brooking written exceptions against a voted Order, than other Courts, which had produced nothing worth memory but the weak ostentation of wealth, would have endured the least signified dislike at any sudden Proclamation. If I should thus far presume upon the meek demeanour of your civil and gentle greatness, Lords and Commons, as what your published Order hath directly said, that to gainsay, I might defend my self with ease, if any should accuse me of being new or insolent, did they but know how much better I find ye esteem it to imitate the old and elegant humanity of Greece, than the barbaric pride of a *Hunnish* and *Norwegian* stateliness. And out of those ages, to whose polite

[2] *your indefatigable virtues* the Long Parliament that Milton praises had been meeting since 1640, about four years.
[3] *him* Joseph Hall, bishop of Norwich (1574–1656).
[4] *statists* statesmen; politicians.

[5] *triennial Parliament* a Parliament that would meet only every three years; Charles I had agreed to such a minimum in an act of February 16, 1641.
[6] *usurped of late* Parliamentary supporters regarded the King's refusal to convene Parliament as a usurpation of authority.

wisdom and letters we owe that we are not yet *Goths* and *Jutlanders*, I could name him who from his private house wrote that discourse to the Parliament of *Athens*,[7] that persuades them to change the form of *Democracy* which was then established. Such honour was done in those days to men who professed the study of wisdom and eloquence, not only in their own Country, but in other Lands, that Cities and Seigniories[8] heard them gladly, and with great respect, if they had ought in public to admonish the State. Thus did *Dion Prusaeus*[9] a stranger and a private Orator counsel the *Rhodians* against a former Edict: and I abound with other like examples, which to set here would be superfluous. But if from the industry of a life wholly dedicated to studious labours, and those natural endowments haply not the worst for two and fifty degrees of northern latitude,[10] so much must be derogated, as to count me not equal to any of those who had this privilege, I would obtain to be thought not so inferior, as your selves are superior to the most of them who received their counsel: and how far you excell them, be assured, Lords and Commons, there can no greater testimony appear, than when your prudent spirit acknowledges and obeys the voice of reason from what quarter soever it be heard speaking; and renders ye as willing to repeal any Act of your own setting forth, as any set forth by your Predecessors.

If ye be thus resolved, as it were injury to think ye were not, I know not what should withhold me from presenting ye with a fit instance wherein to show both that love of truth which ye eminently profess, and that uprightness of your judgement which is not wont to be partial to your selves; by judging over again that Order which ye have ordained *to regulate Printing. That no Book, pamphlet, or paper shall be henceforth Printed, unless the same be first approved and licensed by such*, or at least one of such as shall be thereto appointed.[11] For that part which preserves justly every man's Copy to himself,[12] or provides for the poor,[13] I touch not, only wish they be not made pretences to abuse and persecute honest and painful[14] Men, who offend not in either of these particulars. But that other clause of Licensing Books,[15] which we thought had died with his brother *quadragesimal* and *matrimonial*[16] when the Prelates expired, I shall now attend with such a Homily, as shall lay before ye, first the inventors of it to be those whom ye will be loathe to own; next what is to be thought in general of reading, what ever sort the Books be; and that this Order avails nothing to the suppressing of scandalous, seditious, and libellous Books, which were mainly intended to be suppressed. Last, that it will be primely to the discouragement of all learning, and the stop of Truth, not only by the disexercising and blunting our abilities in what we know already, but by hindering and cropping the discovery that might be yet further made both in religious and civil Wisdom.

---

[7]   *him who from . . . Athens*   Isocrates (436–338 BCE) addressed the assembled citizens of Athens, whom Milton styles the Parliament; like *Areopagitica*, Isocrates' oration was written to be read rather than for him to perform.

[8]   *Seigniories*   territories under the control of a feudal lord.

[9]   *Dion Prusaeus*   Greek orator of the first century CE.

[10]   Milton seems to believe that northern climates dampen intellectual vigor; cf. *Paradise Lost* 9.44–5.

[11]   This order of Parliament was passed on June 14, 1643 and effectively reinstituted the procedures for controlling the press decreed by the Star Chamber in 1637. Milton's eloquence did not impel Parliament to rescind its order.

[12]   The order forbad republication of licensed books without the consent of the owner; Copy means "The autograph; the original" (Johnson).

[13]   The order protected books granted to the Stationers' Company for the maintenance of their poor.

[14]   *painful*   painstaking.

[15]   The principal clause of the order banned publication of books, pamphlets, or papers unless they were licensed by a committee of Parliamentary appointees and entered in the rollbooks of the Stationers' Company.

[16]   *quadragesimal* and *matrimonial*   dispensations concerning Lent and marriage in the Episcopal Church; its Prelates', or bishops', power *expired* in a bill passed in 1642.

I deny not, but that it is of greatest concernment in the Church and Commonwealth, to have a vigilant eye how Books demean[17] themselves as well as men; and thereafter to confine, imprison, and do sharpest justice on them as malefactors: For Books are not absolutely dead things, but do contain a potency of life in them to be as active as that soul was whose progeny they are; nay they do preserve as in a vial the purest efficacy and extraction of that living intellect that bred them. I know they are as lively, and as vigorously productive, as those fabulous Dragon's teeth; and being sown up and down, may chance to spring up armed men.[18] And yet on the other hand unless wariness be used, as good almost kill a Man as kill a good Book; who kills a Man kills a reasonable creature, God's Image; but he who destroys a good Book, kills reason it self, kills the Image of God, as it were in the eye. Many a man lives a burden to the Earth; but a good Book is the precious life-blood of a master spirit, embalmed and treasured up on purpose to a life beyond life. 'Tis true, no age can restore a life, whereof perhaps there is no great loss; and revolutions of ages do not oft recover the loss of a rejected truth, for the want of which whole Nations fare the worse. We should be wary therefore what persecution we raise against the living labours of public men, how we spill that seasoned life of man preserved and stored up in Books; since we see a kind of massacre, whereof the execution ends not in the slaying of an elemental life, but strikes at that ethereal and fifth essence,[19] the breath of reason it self, slays an immortality rather then a life. But lest I should be condemned of introducing licence, while I oppose Licensing, I refuse not the pains to be so much Historical, as will serve to show what hath been done by ancient and famous Commonwealths, against this disorder, till the very time that this project of licensing crept out of the *Inquisition*,[20] was catched up by our Prelates, and hath caught some of our Presbyters.[21]

In *Athens* where Books and Wits were even busier then in any other part of *Greece*, I find but only two sorts of writings which the Magistrate cared to take notice of; those either blasphemous and Atheistical, or Libellous. Thus the Books of *Protagorus* were by Judges of *Areopagus* commanded to be burnt, and himself banished the territory for a discourse begun with his confessing not to know *whether there were gods, or whether not*: And against defaming, it was decreed that none should be traduced by name, as was the manner of *Vetus Comœdia*,[22] whereby we may guess how they censured libelling: And this course was quick enough, as *Cicero* writes,[23] to quell both the desperate wits of other Atheists, and the open way of defaming, as the event shewed. Of other sects and opinions though tending to voluptuousness, and the denying of divine providence they took no heed . . . .[24]

And thus ye have the Inventors and the original of Book-licensing ripped up, and drawn as lineally as any pedigree. We have it not, that can be heard of, from any ancient State, or polity, or Church, nor by any Statute left us by our Ancestors, elder or later; nor from the

---

17   *demean* "To behave; to carry one's self" (Johnson).
18   Cadmus killed the fabulous dragon on his way to founding Thebes; following a god's advice he planted the dragon's teeth, which sprang up as the belligerent Sparti, the forefathers of the city.
19   *fifth essence* quintessence; a mystical substance above the four elements of nature.
20   *Inquisition* a Roman Catholic institution for suppressing heresy, especially strong in Spain after 1478.
21   *Presbyters* representative officers in the reformed but censorious Presbyterian organization of the church which was officially accepted by the British Parliament

in 1646 but swiftly rejected in the same year because of objections by Independents in the House of Commons.
22   *Vetus Comœdia* the old comedy, which was more direct and personal in its satire than the comedy that flourished in mid-fifth century BCE Athens and later.
23   *Cicero writes* in *De Natura Deorum*.
24   I omit several pages in which Milton continues to find the Athenian and Roman governments free of licensing and traces its origins in the Popes and its perfection to the Council of Trent (1545–63) and the Spanish Inquisition.

modern custom of any reformed City, or Church abroad; but from the most Antichristian Council, and the most tyrannous Inquisition that ever inquired. Till then Books were ever as freely admitted into the World as any other birth; the issue of the brain was no more stifled than the issue of the womb: no envious *Juno* sat cross-legged over the nativity of any man's intellectual off spring;[25] but if it proved a Monster, who denies, but that it was justly burnt, or sunk in the Sea. But that a Book in worse condition than a peccant soul, should be to stand before a Jury ere it be born to the World, and undergo yet in darkness the judgement of *Radamanth* and his Colleagues,[26] ere it can pass the ferry backward into light, was never heard before, till that mysterious iniquity provoked and troubled at the first entrance of Reformation, sought out new limbos and new hells wherein they might include our Books also within the number of their damned. And this was the rare morsel so officiously snatched up, and so ill-favouredly imitated by our inquisiturient Bishops, and the attendant minorities their Chaplains. That ye like not now these most certain Authors of this licensing order, and that all sinister intention was far distant from your thoughts, when ye were importuned the passing it, all men who know the integrity of your actions, and how ye honour Truth, will clear ye readily.

But some will say, what though the Inventors were bad, the thing for all that may be good? It may so: yet if that thing be no such deep invention, but obvious, and easy for any man to light on, and yet best and wisest Commonwealths through all ages, and occasions have forborn to use it, and falsest seducers, and oppressors of men were the first who took it up, and to no other purpose but to obstruct and hinder the first approach of a Reformation; I am of those who believe, it will be a harder alchemy than *Lullius*[27] ever knew, to sublimate[28] any good use out of such an invention. Yet this only is what I request to gain from this reason, that it may be held a dangerous and suspicious fruit, as certainly it deserves, for the tree that bore it, until I can dissect one by one the properties it has. But I have first to finish as was propounded, what is to be thought in general of reading Books, what ever sort they be, and whether be more the benefit, or the harm that thence proceeds?

Not to insist upon the examples of *Moses, Daniel* and *Paul,* who were skilful in all the learning of the Egyptians, Chaldeans, and Greeks, which could not probably be without reading their Books of all sorts, in *Paul* especially, who thought it no defilement to insert into holy Scripture the sentences of three Greek Poets, and one of them a Tragedian, the question was, notwithstanding sometimes controverted among the Primitive Doctors,[29] but with great odds on that side which affirmed it both lawful and profitable, as was then evidently perceived, when *Julian* the Apostate,[30] and subtlest enemy to our faith, made a decree forbidding Christians the study of heathen learning: for, said he, they wound us with our own weapons, and with our own arts and sciences they overcome us. And indeed the Christians were put so to their shifts by this crafty means, that the two *Apollinarii*[31] were fain as a man

---

[25] Juno caused one of the guardian deities of birth to sit cross-legged on the threshold of Alcmena when she was trying to give birth to Hercules, son of Juno's husband Zeus (Ovid, *Metamorphoses* 9.281–313).

[26] *Radamanth and his Colleagues* judges of Hades supervising the embarcation of souls on Charon's ferry across the River Styx into the land of darkness; Milton describes licensing as an ironic, death-like birth or passage into light.

[27] *Lullius* Raymond Lully, thirteenth-century Italian alchemist.

[28] *sublimate* "To raise by the force of chemical fire" (Johnson).

[29] *Primitive Doctors* early commentators on the Bible or Church fathers.

[30] *Julian the Apostate* Flavius Claudius Julianus (331–63), emperor of Rome from 361 CE, reverted from Christianity to worship of natural but also symbolic entities like the sun.

[31] *the two Apollinarii* father and son, Christian scholars in the fourth century.

may say, to coin all the seven liberal Sciences out of the Bible, reducing it into divers forms of Orations, Poems, Dialogues, even to the calculating of a new Christian Grammar. But saith the Historian *Socrates*, The providence of God provided better then the industry of *Apollinarius* and his son, by taking away that illiterate law with the life of him who devised it. So great an injury they then held it to be deprived of *Hellenic* learning; and thought it a perfection more undermining, and secretly decaying the Church than the open cruelty of *Decius* or *Dioclesian*.[32] And perhaps it was the same politic drift that the Devil whipped St. *Jerome*[33] in a lenten dream, for reading *Cicero*; or else it was a phantasm bred by the fever which had then seized him. For had an Angel been his discipliner, unless it were for dwelling too much upon Ciceronianisms,[34] and had chastised the reading, not the vanity, it had been plainly partial; first to correct him for grave *Cicero*, and not for scurril *Plautus*[35] whom he confesses to have been reading not long before; next to correct him only, and let so many more ancient Fathers[36] wax old in those pleasant and florid studies without the lash of such a tutoring apparition; insomuch that *Basil*[37] teaches how some good use may be made of *Margites*[38] a sportful Poem, not now extant, writ by *Homer*; and why not then of *Morgante* an Italian Romance[39] much to the same purpose. But if it be agreed we shall be tried by visions, there is a vision recorded by *Eusebius*[40] far ancienter than this tale of *Jerome* to the nun *Eustochium*, and besides has nothing of a fever in it. *Dionysius Alexandrinus* was about the year 240, a person of great name in the Church for piety and learning, who had wont to avail himself much against heretics by being conversant in their Books; until a certain Presbyter laid it scrupulously among those defiling volumes. The worthy man loathe to give offence fell into a new debate with himself what was to be thought; when suddenly a vision sent from God, it is his own Epistle that so avers it, confirmed him in these words: Read any books what ever come to thy hands, for thou art sufficient both to judge aright, and to examine each matter. To this revelation he assented the sooner, as he confesses, because it was answerable to that of the Apostle to the Thessalonians, Prove all things, hold fast that which is good.[41] And he might have added another remarkable saying of the same Author; To the pure all things are pure,[42] not only meats and drinks, but all kind of knowledge, whether of good and evil; the knowledge cannot defile, nor consequently the books, if the will and conscience be not defiled. For books are as meats and viands are; some of good, some of evil substance; and yet God in that unapocryphal vision, said without exception, Rise *Peter*, kill and eat, leaving the choice to each man's discretion.[43] Wholesome meats to a vitiated stomach differ little or nothing from unwholesome; and best books to a naughty mind are not unappliable to occasions of evil. Bad meats will scarce breed good nourishment in the healthiest concoction; but herein the difference is of bad books, that they to a discreet and judicious Reader serve in many respects to discover, to confute, to forewarn, and to illustrate. Whereof what better witnes can ye expect I should produce, than one of your own now sitting in Parliament, the

---

[32] *Decius* or *Dioclesian* Roman emperors infamous for their persecution of Christians.
[33] *St Jerome* fourth-century Christian scholar and translator of the Bible into Latin.
[34] *Ciceronianisms* imitations of Cicero's Latin prose style.
[35] *Plautus* Roman comic dramatist of the second century BCE.
[36] *ancient Fathers* early Christian commentators.
[37] *Basil* fourth-century bishop who wrote on the proper use of pagan writing.

[38] *Margites* a mock-heroic poem traditionally ascribed to Homer.
[39] *Romance* "A military fable of the middle ages; a tale of wild adventures in war and love" (Johnson).
[40] *Eusebius* fourth-century bishop and author of a most important history of the church; the story comes from Book 7.
[41] *Prove all things . . .* 1 Thessalonians 5.21.
[42] *To the pure . . .* Titus 1.15.
[43] *Rise Peter . . .* Acts 10.13.

chief of learned men reputed in this Land, Mr. *Selden*,[44] whose volume of natural and national laws proves, not only by great authorities brought together, but by exquisite reasons and theorems almost mathematically demonstrative, that all opinions, yea errors, known, read, and collated, are of main service and assistance toward the speedy attainment of what is truest. I conceive therefore, that when God did enlarge the universal diet of man's body, saving ever the rules of termperance, he then also, as before, left arbitrary the dieting and repasting of our minds; as wherein every mature man might have to exercise his own leading capacity. How great a virtue is temperance, how much of moment through the whole life of man? yet God commits the managing so great a trust, without particular Law or prescription, wholly to the demeanour[45] of every grown man. And therefore when he himself tabled[46] the Jews from heaven, that Omer which was every man's daily portion of Manna, is computed to have been more than might have well sufficed the heartiest feeder thrice as many meals. For those actions which enter into a man, rather than issue out of him, and therefore defile not, God uses not to captivate under a perpetual childhood of prescription, but trusts him with the gift of reason to be his own chooser; there were but little work left for preaching, if law and compulsion should grow so fast upon those things which heretofore were governed only by exhortation. *Solomon* informs us that much reading is a weariness to the flesh;[47] but neither he, nor other inspired author tells us that such, or such reading is unlawful: yet certainly had God thought good to limit us herein, it had been much more expedient to have told us what was unlawful, than what was wearisome. As for the burning of those Ephesian books by St. *Paul's* converts,[48] 'tis replied the books were magic, the Syriac[49] so renders them. It was a private act, a voluntary act, and leaves us to a voluntary imitation: the men in remorse burnt those books which were their own; the Magistrate by this example is not appointed: these men practised the books, another might perhaps have read them in some sort usefully. Good and evil we know in the field of this World grow up together almost inseparably; and the knowledge of good is so involved and interwoven with the knowledge of evil, and in so many cunning resemblances hardly to be discerned, that those confused seeds which were imposed on *Psyche* as an incessant labour to cull out, and sort asunder, were not more intermixed.[50] It was from out the rind of one apple tasted, that the knowledge of good and evil as two twins cleaving together leapt forth into the World. And perhaps this is that doom which *Adam* fell into of knowing good and evil, that is to say of knowing good by evil. As therefore the state of man now is; what wisdom can there be to choose, what continence to forbear without the knowledge of evil? He that can apprehend and consider vice with all her baits and seeming pleasures, and yet abstain, and yet distinguish, and yet prefer that which is truly better, he is the true warfaring Christian. I cannot praise a fugitive and cloistered virtue, unexercised and unbreathed,[51] that never sallies out and sees her adversary, but slinks out of the race, where that immortal garland is to be run for, not without dust and heat. Assuredly we bring not innocence into the world, we bring impurity much rather: that which purifies us is trial, and trial is by what is contrary. That virtue therefore which is but a youngling in the contemplation of evil, and knows not the utmost that vice promises to her followers, and

---

[44]   *Selden*   John Selden (1584–1654), learned lawyer and historian, author of *De Jure Naturali et Gentium juxta Disciplinam Ebraeorum* (1640), to which Milton refers.
[45]   *demeanour*   behaviour.
[46]   *tabled*   banqueted, fed; see Exodus 16.
[47]   *much reading is a weariness*   Ecclesiastes 12.12 where he also says, "Of making many books there is no end."

[48]   *the burning of those Ephesian books*   Acts 19.19.
[49]   *Syriac*   a semitic language used in ancient Syria.
[50]   *Psyche*   in her attempts to win back Eros and appease his mother Aphrodite the beautiful Psyche had to undergo many trials; sorting the seeds tested her industry.
[51]   *unbreathed*   not made to breathe hard with exertion.

rejects it, is but a blank virtue, not a pure; her whiteness is but an excremental[52] whiteness; Which was the reason why our sage and serious Poet *Spenser*, whom I dare be known to think a better teacher then *Scotus* or *Aquinas*,[53] describing true temperance under the person of *Guyon*,[54] brings him in with his palmer through the cave of Mammon, and the bower of earthly bliss that he might see and know, and yet abstain. Since therefore the knowledge and survey of vice is in this world so necessary to the constituting of human virtue, and the scanning of error to the confirmation of truth, how can we more safely, and with less danger scout into the regions of sin and falsity than by reading all manner of tractates, and hearing all manner of reason? And this is the benefit which may be had of books promiscuously read. But of the harm that may result hence three kinds are usually reckoned. First, is feared the infection that may spread; but then all human learning and controversy in religious points must remove out of the world, yea the Bible it self; for that oftimes relates blasphemy not nicely, it describes the carnal sense of wicked men not unelegantly, it brings in holiest men passionately murmuring against providence through all the arguments of *Epicurus:* in other great disputes it answers dubiously and darkly to the common reader . . .

   Seeing therefore that those books, and those in great abundance which are likeliest to taint both life and doctrine, cannot be suppressed without the fall of learning, and of all ability in disputation, and that these books of either sort are most and soonest catching to the learned, from whom to the common people what ever is heretical or dissolute may quickly be conveyed, and that evil manners are as perfectly learnt without books a thousand other ways which cannot be stopped, and evil doctrine not with books can propagate, except a teacher guide, which he might also do without writing, and so beyond prohibiting, I am not able to unfold, how this cautelous[55] enterprise of licensing can be exempted from the number of vain and impossible attempts. And he who were pleasantly disposed, could not well avoid to liken it to the exploit of that gallant man who thought to pound up the crows by shutting his Parkgate. Besides another inconvenience, if learned men be the first receivers of books and dispredders both of vice and error, how shall the licensers themselves be confided in, unless we can confer upon them, or they assume to themselves above all others in the Land, the grace of infallibility, and uncorruptedness? And again if it be true, that a wise man like a good refiner can gather gold out of the drossiest volume, and that a fool will be a fool with the best book, yea or without book, there is no reason that we should deprive a wise man of any advantage to his wisdom, while we seek to restrain from a fool, that which being restrained will be no hindrance to his folly. For if there should be so much exactness always used to keep that from him which is unfit for his reading, we should in the judgement of *Aristotle* not only, but of *Solomon*, and of our Saviour, not vouchsafe him good precepts, and by consequence not willingly admit him to good books, as being certain that a wise man will make better use of an idle pamphlet, then a fool will do of sacred Scripture. 'Tis next alleged we must not expose our selves to temptations without necessity, and next to that, not employ our time in vain things. To both these objections one answer will serve, out of the grounds already laid, that to all men such books are not temptations, nor vanities; but useful drugs and materials wherewith to temper and compose effective and strong medicines, which man's life cannot

---

[52] *excremental* useless.

[53] *Scotus or Aquinas* scholastic philosophers, less entertaining and therefore less successful in their teaching than Spenser.

[54] *Guyon* the hero of Book 2 of Spenser's *Faerie Queene* passes the Cave of Mammon, symbolic of luxury (the Palmer does not accompany him here) and the Bower of Bliss on his way to holiness.

[55] *cautelous* treacherous

want. The rest, as children and childish men, who have not the art to qualify and prepare these working minerals, well may be exhorted to forbear, but hindered forcibly they cannot be by all the licensing that Sainted Inquisition could ever yet contrive; which is what I promised to deliver next, That this order of licensing conduces nothing to the end for which it was framed; and hath almost prevented[56] me by being clear already while thus much hath been explaining. See the ingenuity of Truth, who when she gets a free and willing hand, opens her self faster, than the pace of method and discourse can overtake her. It was the talk of which I began with, To shew that no Nation, or well instituted State, if they valued books at all, did ever use this way of licensing; and it might be answered, that this is a piece of prudence lately discovered, To which I return, that as it was a thing slight and obvious to think on, for if it had been difficult to find out, there wanted not among them long since, who suggested such a course; which they not following, leave us a pattern of their judgement, that it was not the not knowing, but the not approving, which was the cause of their not using it. *Plato*, a man of high authority indeed, but least of all for his Commonwealth, in the book of his laws, which no City ever yet received, fed his fancy with making many edicts to his airy Burgomasters, which they who otherwise admire him, wish had been rather buried and excused in the *genial* cups of an *Academic* night-sitting.[57] By which laws he seems to tolerate no kind of learning, but by unalterable decree, consisting most of practical traditions, to the attainment whereof a Library of smaller bulk than his own dialogues would be abundant. And there also enacts that no Poet should so much as read to any private man, what he had written, until the Judges and Law-keepers had seen it, and allowed it: But that *Plato* meant this Law peculiarly to that Commonwealth which he had imagined, and to no other, is evident. Why was he not else a Law-giver to himself, but a transgressor, and to be expelled by his own Magistrates both for the wanton epigrams and dialogues which he made, and his perpetual reading of *Sophron Mimus*,[58] and *Aristophanes*,[59] books of grossest infamy, and also for commending the latter of them though he were the malicious libeller of his chief friends[60], to be read by the Tyrant *Dionysius*, who had little need of such trash to spend his time on? But that he knew this licensing of Poems had reference and dependence to many other provisos here set down in his fancied republic, which in this world could have no place: and so neither he himself, nor any Magistrate, or City ever imitated that course, which taken apart from those other collateral injunctions must needs be vain and fruitless. For if they fell upon one kind of strictness, unless their care were equal to regulate all other things of like aptness to corrupt the mind, that single endeavour they knew would be but a fond labour; to shut and fortify one gate against corruption, and be necessitated to leave others round about wide open. If we think to regulate Printing, thereby to rectify manners, we must regulate all recreations and pastimes, all that is delightful to man. No music must be heard, no song be set or sung, but what is grave and *Doric*. There must be licensing dancers, that no gesture, motion, or deportment be taught our youth but what by their allowance shall be thought honest; for such *Plato* was provided of; It will ask more than the work of twenty licensers to examine all the lutes, the violins, and the guitars in every house; they must not be suffered to prattle as they do, but must be licensed what they may say. And who shall silence all the airs and madrigals, that whisper softness in chambers? The Windows also, and the *Balconies* must be thought on, there are shrewd books, with dangerous Frontispieces set to sale; who shall

---

[56] *prevented* precluded
[57] *Academic night-sitting* an evening meeting of Plato's school in the house of Academus.
[58] *Sophron Mimus* a popular writer of Plato's time.
[59] *Aristophanes* the greatest Greek writer of comedy.
[60] *his chief friends* philosophers, especially Socrates, whom Aristophanes derides in the *Clouds*.

prohibit them, shall twenty licensers? The villages also must have their visitors to enquire what lectures the bagpipe and the rebeck[61] reads even to the ballatry, and the gammuth[62] of every *municipal* fiddler, for these are the Countryman's *Arcadias*[63] and his *Monte Mayors*.[64] Next, what more National corruption, for which England hears ill abroad, than houshold gluttony; who shall be the rectors of our daily rioting? and what shall be done to inhibit the multitudes that frequent those houses where drunkeness is sold and harboured? Our garments also should be referred to the licensing of some more sober work-masters to see them cut into a less wanton garb. Who shall regulate all the mixed conversation of our youth, male and female together, as is the fashion of this Country, who shall still appoint what shall be discoursed, what presumed, and no further? Lastly, who shall forbid and separate all idle resort, all evil company? These things will be, and must be; but how they shall be least hurtful, how least enticing, herein consists the grave and governing wisdom of a State. To sequester out of the world into *Atlantic*[65] and *Utopian* polities, which never can be drawn into use, will not mend our condition; but to ordain wisely as in this world of evil, in the midst whereof God hath placed us unavoidably. Nor is it *Plato*'s licensing of books will do this, which necessarily pulls along with it so many other kinds of licensing, as will make us all both ridiculous and weary, and yet fustrate; but those unwritten, or at least unconstraining laws of virtuous education, religious and civil nurture, which *Plato* there mentions, as the bonds and ligaments of the Commonwealth, the pillars and the sustainers of every written Statute; these they be which will bear chief sway in such matters as these, when all licensing will be easily eluded. Impunity and remissness, for certain are the bane of a Commonwealth, but here the great art lies to discern in what the law is to bid restraint and punishment, and in what things the persuasion only is to work. If every action which is good, or evil in man at ripe years, were to be under pittance,[66] and prescription, and compulsion, what were virtue but a name, what praise could be then due to well-doing, what gramercy[67] to be sober, just, or continent? many there be that complain of divine Providence for suffering *Adam* to transgress, foolish tongues! when God gave him reason, he gave him freedom to choose, for reason is but choosing; he had been else a mere artificial *Adam*, such an *Adam* as he is in the motions.[68] We our selves esteem not of that obedience, or love, or gift, which is of force: God therefore left him free, set before him a provoking object, ever almost in his eyes; herein consisted his merit, herein the right of his reward, the praise of his abstinence. Wherefore did he create passions within us, pleasures round about us, but that these rightly tempered are the very ingredients of virtue? They are not skilful considerers of human things, who imagine to remove sin by removing the matter of sin; for, besides that it is a huge heap increasing under the very act of diminishing though some part of it may for a time be withdrawn from some persons, it cannot from all, in such a universal thing as books are; and when this is done, yet the sin remains entire. Though ye take from a covetous man all his treasure, he has yet one jewel left, ye cannot bereave him of his covetousness. Banish all objects of lust, shut up all youth into the severest discipline that can be exercised in any hermitage, ye cannot make them chaste, that came not thither so; such great care and wisdom is required to the right managing of this point. Suppose we could expel sin by this means; look how much we thus

---

[61] *rebeck* a kind of fiddle.
[62] *gammuth* gamut, the whole series of notes used by a musician.
[63] *Arcadia* a prose romance by Sir Philip Sidney (1590).
[64] *Monte Mayor* Jorge de Montemayor, author of the romance *Diana* (c. 1559).

[65] *Atlantic* Atlantis-like, belonging to a fanciful utopia.
[66] *pittance* "An allowance of meat in a monastery" (Johnson).
[67] *gramercy* thanks.
[68] *motions* puppet shows.

expel of sin, so much we expel of virtue: for the matter of them both is the same; remove that, and ye remove them both alike. This justifies the high providence of God, who though he command us temperance, justice, continence, yet pours out before us even to a profuseness all desirable things, and gives us minds that can wander beyond all limit and satiety. Why should we then affect a rigour contrary to the manner of God and of nature, by abridging or scanting those means, which books freely permitted are, both to the trial of virtue, and the exercise of truth. It would be better done to learn that the law must needs be frivolous which goes to restrain things, uncertainly and yet equally working to good, and to evil. And were I the chooser, a dram of well-doing should be preferred before many times as much the forcible hindrance of evil-doing. For God sure esteems the growth and completing of one virtuous person, more than the restraint of ten vicious. And albeit what ever thing we hear or see, sitting, walking, travelling, or conversing may be fitly called our book, and is of the same effect that writings are, yet grant the thing to be prohibited were only books, it appears that this order hitherto is far insufficient to the end which it intends. Do we not see, not once or oftener, but weekly that continued Court-libel against the Parliament and City,[69] Printed, as the wet sheets can witness, and dispersed among us for all the licensing can do? yet this is the prime service a man would think, wherein this order should give proof of it self . . .

Another reason, whereby to make it plain that this order will miss the end it seeks, consider by the quality which ought to be in every licenser. It cannot be denied but that he who is made judge to sit upon the birth, or death of books whether they may be wafted into this world, or not, had need to be a man above the common measure, both studious, learned, and judicious; there may be else no mean mistakes in the censure of what is passable or not; which is also no mean injury. If he be of such worth as behooves him, there cannot be a more tedious and unpleasing journey-work, a greater loss of time levied upon his head, than to be made the perpetual reader of unchosen books and pamphlets, oftimes huge volumes. There is no book that is acceptable unless at certain seasons; but to be enjoined the reading of that at all times, and in a hand scarce legible, whereof three pages would not down at any time in the fairest Print, is an imposition which I cannot believe how he that values time, and his own studies, or is but of a sensible nostril should be able to endure . . .

I lastly proceed from the no good it can do, to the manifest hurt it causes, in being first the greatest discouragement and affront that can be offered to learning and to learned men. It was the complaint and lamentation of Prelates, upon every least breath of a motion to remove pluralities, and distribute more equally Church revenues, that then all learning would be for ever dashed and discouraged. But as for that opinion, I never found cause to think that the tenth part of learning stood or fell with the Clergy: nor could I ever but hold it for a sordid and unworthy speech of any Churchman who had a competency left him. If therefore ye be loathe to dishearten utterly and discontent, not the mercenary crew of false pretenders to learning, but the free and ingenuous sort for it self, not for lucre, or any other end, but the service of God and of truth, and perhaps that lasting fame and perpetuity of praise which God and good men have consented shall be the reward of those whose published labours advance the good of mankind, then know, that so far to distrust the judgement and the honesty of one who hath but a common repute in learning, and never yet offended, as not to count him fit to print his mind without a tutor and examiner, lest he should drop a schism,[70] or something of a corruption, is the greatest displeasure and indignity to a free and knowing spirit that can

---

[69] Court-libel against the Parliament and City   Mercurius
Aulicus, a Royalist newsbook.

[70] schism an opinion that causes disunity in the church.

be put upon him. What advantage is it to be a man over it is to be a boy at school, if we have only escaped the ferular,[71] to come under the fescu[72] of an *Imprimatur*?[73] if serious and elaborate writings, as if they were no more than the theme of a Grammar lad under his Pedagogue must not be uttered without the cursory eyes of a temporizing and extemporizing licenser. He who is not trusted with his own actions, his drift not being known to be evil, and standing to the hazard of law and penalty, has no great argument to think himself reputed in the Commonwealth wherein he was born, for other than a fool or a foreigner. When a man writes to the world, he summons up all his reason and deliberation to assist him; he searches, meditates, is industrious, and likely consults and confers with his judicious friends; after all which done he takes himself to be informed in what he writes, as well as any that writ before him; if in this the most consummate act of his fidelity and ripeness, no years, no industry, no former proof of his abilities can bring him to that state of maturity, as not to be still mistrusted and suspected, unless he carry all his considerate diligence, all his midnight watching, and expense of *Palladian*[74] oil, to the hasty view of an unleasured licenser, perhaps much his younger, perhaps far his inferior in judgement, perhaps one who never knew the labour of book-writing, and if he be not repulsed, or slighted, must appear in Print like a puny[75] with his guardian, and his censor's hand on the back of his title to be his bail and surety, that he is no idiot, or seducer, it cannot be but a dishonour and derogation to the author, to the book, to the privilege and dignity of Learning. And what if the author shall be one so copious of fancy, as to have many things well worth the adding, come into his mind after licensing, while the book is yet under the Press, which not seldom happens to the best and diligentest writers; and that perhaps a dozen times in one book. The Printer dares not go beyond his licensed copy; so often then must the author trudge to his leave-giver, that those his new insertions may be viewed; and many a jaunt will be made, ere that licenser, for it must be the same man, can either be found, or found at leisure; mean while either the Press must stand still, which is no small damage, or the author lose his accuratest thought, and send the book forth worse then he had made it, which to a diligent writer is the greatest melancholy and vexation that can befall . . .

And lest some should persuade ye, Lords and Commons, that these arguments of learned men's discouragement at this your order, are mere flourishes, and not real, I could recount what I have seen and heard in other Countries, where this kind of inquisition tyrannizes; when I have sat among their learned men, for that honour I had, and been counted happy to be born in such a place of *Philosophic* freedom, as they supposed England was, while themselves did nothing but bemoan the servile condition into which learning amongst them was brought; that this was it which had damped the glory of Italian wits; that nothing had been there written now these many years but flattery and fustian. There it was that I found and visited the famous *Galileo* grown old, a prisoner to the Inquisition, for thinking in astronomy otherwise than the Franciscan and Dominican licencers thought. And though I knew that England then was groaning loudest under the Prelatical yoke, nevertheless I took it as a pledge of future happiness, that other Nations were so persuaded of her liberty. Yet was it beyond my hope that those Worthies were then breathing in her air, who should be her

---

[71] *ferular* "An instrument of correction with which young scholars are beaten on the hand" (Johnson).

[72] *fescu* "A small wire by which those who teach to read point out the letters" (Johnson).

[73] *Imprimatur* "let it be printed," the seal of approval from the papal and then from any body of licensers.

[74] *Palladian* belonging to Pallas Athena, the goddess of wisdom.

[75] *puny* "A young unexperienced, unseasoned wretch" (Johnson).

leaders to such a deliverance, as shall never be forgotten by any revolution of time that this world hath to finish. When that was once begun, it was as little in my fear, that what words of complaint I heard among learned men of other parts uttered against the Inquisition, the same I should hear by as learned men at home uttered in time of Parliament against an order of licensing; and that so generally, that when I disclosed my self a companion of their discontent, I might say, if without envy, that he[76] whom an honest *quæstorship* had endeared to the *Sicilians*, was not more by them importuned against *Verres,* then the favourable opinion which I had among many who honour ye, and are known and respected by ye, loaded me with entreaties and persuasions, that I would not despair to lay together that which just reason should bring into my mind, toward the removal of an undeserved thraldom upon learning. That this is not therefore the disburdening of a particular fancy, but the common grievance of all those who had prepared their minds and studies above the vulgar pitch to advance truth in others, and from others to entertain it, thus much may satisify. And in their name I shall for neither friend nor foe conceal what the general murmur is; that if it come to inquisitioning again, and licensing, and that we are so timorous of our selves, and so suspicious of all men, as to fear each book, and the shaking of every leaf, before we know what the contents are, if some who but of late were little better then silenced from preaching, shall come now to silence us from reading, except what they please, it cannot be guessed what is intended by some but a second tyranny over learning: and will soon put it out of controversy that Bishops and Presbyters are the same to us both name and thing . . .

There is yet behind of what I purposed to lay open, the incredible loss, and detriment that this plot of licensing puts us to, more than if some enemy at sea should stop up all our havens and ports, and creeks, it hinders and retards the importation of our richest Merchandise Truth; nay it was first established and put in practice by Antichristian malice and mystery on set purpose to extinguish, if it were possible, the light of Reformation, and to settle falshood; little differing from that policy wherewith the Turk upholds his *Alcoran,* by the prohibition of Printing. 'Tis not denied, but gladly confessed, we are to send our thanks and vows to heaven, louder than most Nations, for that great measure of truth which we enjoy, especially in those main points between us and the Pope, with his appertinences the Prelates: but he who thinks we are to pitch our tent here, and have attained the utmost prospect of reformation, that the mortal glass wherein we contemplate, can show us, till we come to *beatific* vision, that man by this very opinion declares, that he is yet far short of Truth.

Truth indeed came once into the world with her divine Master, and was a perfect shape most glorious to look on: but when he ascended, and his Apostles after him were laid asleep, then straight arose a wicked race of deceivers, who as that story goes of the *Egyptian Typhon* with his conspirators, how they dealt with the good *Osiris,* took the virgin Truth, hewed her lovely form into a thousand pieces, and scattered them to the four winds. From that time ever since, the sad friends of Truth, such as durst appear, imitating the careful search that *Isis* made for the mangled body of *Osiris,* went up and down gathering up limb by limb still as they could find them. We have not yet found them all, Lords and Commons, nor ever shall do, till her Master's second coming; he shall bring together every joint and member, and shall mould them into an immortal feature of loveliness and perfection. Suffer not these licensing prohibitions to stand at every place of opportunity forbidding and disturbing them that continue seeking, that continue to do our obsequies to the torn body of our martyred Saint.

---

[76] *he* Cicero, who indicted Verres in two famous orations which forced the corrupt official into exile.

We boast our light; but if we look not wisely on the Sun it self, it smites us into darkness. Who can discern those planets that are oft *Combust*,[77] and those stars of brightest magnitude that rise and set with the Sun, until the opposite motion of their orbs bring them to such a place in the firmament, where they may be seen evening or morning. The light which we have gained, was given us, not to be ever staring on, but by it to discover onward things more remote from our knowledge. It is not the unfrocking of a Priest, the unmitring of a Bishop, and the removing him from off the *Presbyterian* shoulders that will make us a happy Nation, no, if other things as great in the Church, and in the rule of life both economical and political be not looked into and reformed, we have looked so long upon the blaze that *Zuinglius* and *Calvin*[78] hath beaconed up to us, that we are stark blind. There be who perpetually complain of schisms and sects, and make it such a calamity that any man dissents from their maxims. 'Tis their own pride and ignorance which causes the disturbing, who neither will hear with meekness, nor can convince, yet all must be suppressed which is not found in their *Syntagma*.[79] They are the troublers, they are the dividers of unity, who neglect and permit not others to unite those dissevered pieces which are yet wanting to the body of Truth. To be still searching what we know not, by what we know, still closing up truth to truth as we find it (for all her body is *homogeneal*, and proportional) this is the golden rule in *Theology* as well as in Arithmetic, and makes up the best harmony in a Church; not the forced and outward union of cold, and neutral, and inwardly divided minds.

Lords and Commons of England, consider what Nation it is whereof ye are, and whereof ye are the governors: a Nation not slow and dull, but of a quick, ingenious, and piercing spirit, acute to invent, subtle and sinewy to discourse, not beneath the reach of any point the highest that human capacity can soar to. Therefore the studies of learning in her deepest Sciences have been so ancient, and so eminent among us, that Writers of good antiquity, and ablest judgement have been persuaded that even the school of *Pythagoras*, and the *Persian* wisdom took beginning from the old Philosophy of this Island.[80] And that wise and civil Roman, *Julius Agricola*,[81] who governed once here for *Cæsar*, preferred the natural wits of Britain, before the laboured studies of the French. Nor is it for nothing that the grave and frugal *Transylvanian*[82] sends out yearly from as far as the mountainous borders of *Russia*, and beyond the *Hercynian* wilderness,[83] not their youth, but their staid men, to learn our language, and our *theologic* arts. Yet that which is above all this, the favour and the love of heaven we have great argument to think in a peculiar manner propitious and propending towards us. Why else was this Nation chosen before any other, that out of her as out of *Zion*[84] should be proclaimed and founded forth the first tidings and trumpet of Reformation to all *Europe*. And had it not been the obstinate perverseness of our Prelates against the divine and admirable spirit of *Wicklef*,[85] to suppress him as a schismatic and *innovator*, perhaps neither the *Bohemian Husse* and *Jerom*,[86] no nor the name of *Luther*, or of *Calvin* had been ever known: the glory of

[77] *Combust* 8.5 degrees in elevation from the Sun.
[78] *Zuinglius* and *Calvin* famous Protestant reformers.
[79] *Syntagma* systematic treatise.
[80] *the old Philosophy of this Island* the teachings of druids, perhaps; Milton's sources for this opinion are obscure or shaky, or both.
[81] *Julius Agricola* proconsul in Britain 78–85 CE, subject of a biography by his son-in-law Tacitus
[82] *Transylvanian* ruler of a then independent, Protestant country with an elective government, near present-day Romania.
[83] *Hercynian wilderness* Hercynia Silva, Roman name of a forested area in Germany.
[84] *Zion* Jerusalem and the mount of the Temple in particular.
[85] *Wicklef* John Wyclif (c. 1320–84), English church reformer and translator of the Bible.
[86] *Husse and Jerom* John Huss and Jerome of Prague, church reformers, contemporaries of Wyclif.

reforming all our neighbours had been completely ours. But now, as our obdurate Clergy have with violence demeaned the matter, we are become hitherto the latest and the backwardest Scholars,[87] of whom God offered to have made us the teachers. Now once again by all concurrence of signs, and by the general instinct of holy and devout men, as they daily and solemnly express their thoughts, God is decreeing to begin some new and great period in his Church, even to the reforming of Reformation it self: what does he then but reveal Himself to his servants, and as his manner is, first to his English-men; I say as his manner is, first to us, though we mark not the method of his counsels, and are unworthy. Behold now this vast City; a City of refuge, the mansion house of liberty, encompassed and surrounded with his protection; the shop of war hath not there more anvils and hammers waking, to fashion out the plates and instruments of armed Justice in defence of beleaguered Truth, than there be pens and heads there, sitting by their studious lamps, musing, searching, revolving new notions and ideas wherewith to present, as with their homage and their fealty the approaching Reformation: others as fast reading, trying all things, assenting to the force of reason and convincement. What could a man require more from a Nation so pliant and so prone to seek after knowledge. What wants there to such a towardly and pregnant soil, but wise and faithful labourers, to make a knowing people, a Nation of Prophets, of Sages, and of Worthies. We reckon more than five month yet to harvest; there need not be five weeks, had we but eyes to lift up, the fields are white already.[88] Where there is much desire to learn, there of necessity will be much arguing, much writing, many opinions; for opinion in good men is but knowledge in the making. Under these fantastic terrors of sect and schism, we wrong the earnest and zealous thirst after knowledge and understanding which God hath stirred up in this City. What some lament of, we rather should rejoice at, should rather praise this pious forwardness among men, to reassume the ill deputed care of their Religion into their own hands again. A little generous prudence, a little forbearance of one another, and some grain of charity might win all these diligences to join, and unite in one general and brotherly search after Truth; could we but forego this Prelatical tradition of crowding free consciences and Christian liberties into canons and precepts of men. I doubt not, if some great and worthy stranger should come among us, wise to discern the mould and temper of a people, and how to govern it, observing the high hopes and aims, the diligent alacrity of our extended thought and reasoning in the pursuance of truth and freedom, but that he would cry out as *Pyrrhus*[89] did, admiring the Roman docility[90] and courage, if such were my *Epirots*. I would not despair the greatest design that could be attempted to make a Church or Kingdom happy. Yet these are the men cried out against for schismatics and sectaries; as if, while the Temple of the Lord was building, some cutting, some squaring the marble, others hewing the cedars, there should be a sort of irrational men who could not consider there must be many schisms and many dissections made in the quarry and in the timber, ere the house of God can be built. And when every stone is laid artful together, it cannot be united into a continuity, it can but be contiguous in this world; neither can every piece of the building be of one form; nay rather the perfection consists in this, that out of many moderate varieties and brotherly dissimilitudes that are not vastly disproportional arise the goodly and the graceful symmetry that commends the whole pile[91] and structure. Let us therefore be more considerate builders, more

---

87 *Scholars* students.
88 *the fields are white already* John 4.35.
89 *Pyrrhus* (c. 318–272 BCE), king of Epirus (land of the Epirots), a country in northwestern Greece, one of the greatest generals in history.
90 *docility* "Aptness to be taught; readiness to learn" (Johnson).
91 *pile* "An edifice; a building" (Johnson).

wise in spiritual architecture, when great reformation is expected. For now the time seems come, wherein *Moses* the great Prophet may sit in heaven rejoicing to see that memorable and glorious wish of his fulfilled, when not only our seventy Elders, but all the Lord's people are become Prophets . . .[92]

Methinks I see in my mind a noble and puissant Nation rousing herself like a strong man after sleep, and shaking her invincible locks: Methinks I see her as an Eagle mewing[93] her mighty youth, and kindling her undazzled eyes at the full midday beam; purging and unscaling her long abused sight at the fountain it self of heavenly radiance, while the whole noise of timorous and flocking birds, with those also that love the twilight, flutter about, amazed at what she means, and in their envious gabble would prognosticate a year of sects and schisms.

What should ye do then, should ye suppress all this flowery crop of knowledge and new light sprung up and yet springing daily in this City, should ye set an *Oligarchy* of twenty engrossers[94] over it, to bring a famine upon our minds again, when we shall know nothing but what is measured to us by their bushel? Believe it, Lords and Commons, they who counsel ye to such a suppressing, do as good as bid ye suppress yourselves; and I will soon show how. If it be desired to know the immediate cause of all this free writing and free speaking, there cannot be assigned a truer then your own mild, and free, and human government; it is the liberty, Lords and Commons, which your own valorous and happy counsels have purchased us, liberty which is the nurse of all great wits; this is that which hath rarified and enlightened our spirits like the influence of heaven; this is that which hath enfranchised, enlarged and lifted up our apprehensions degrees above themselves. Ye cannot make us now less capable, less knowing, less eagerly pursuing of the truth, unless ye first make your selves, that made us so, less the lovers, less the founders of our true liberty. We can grow ignorant again, brutish, formal, and slavish, as ye found us; but you then must first become that which ye cannot be, oppressive, arbitrary, and tyrannous, as they were from whom ye have freed us. That our hearts are now more capacious, our thoughts more erected to the search and expectation of greatest and exactest things, is the issue of your own virtue[95] propagated in us; ye cannot supress that unless ye reinforce an abrogated and merciless law, that fathers may dispatch at will their own children. And who shall then stick closest to ye, and excite others? not he who takes up arms for coat and conduct,[96] and his four nobles of Danegelt.[97] Although I dispraise not the defence of just immunities, yet love my peace better, if that were all. Give me the liberty to know, to utter, and to argue freely according to conscience, above all liberties.

. . . if all cannot be of one mind, as who looks they should be? this doubtless is more wholesome, more prudent, and more Christian that many be tolerated, rather then all compelled. I mean not tolerated Popery, and open superstition, which as it extirpates all religions and civil supremacies, so it self should be extirpate, provided first that all charitable and compassionate means be used to win and regain the weak and misled: that also which is impious or evil absolutely either against faith or maners no law can possibly permit, that

---

[92] *not only our seventy Elders* . . . Numbers 12.24–9.
[93] *mewing* from "mew" "To shed the feathers. It is, I believe, used in this sense, because birds are, by close confinement, brought to shed their feathers" (Johnson).
[94] *engrossers* those who purchase "large quantities of any commodity, in order to sell it at a high price" (Johnson).

[95] *virtue* strength, influence.
[96] *coat and conduct* a tax exacted by Charles I to support the military (*OED coat sb* 12).
[97] *Danegelt* another kind of tax to support the military (originally tribute to the Danes) levied by Charles.

intends not to unlaw it self: but those neighbouring distances, or rather indifferences, are what I speak of, whether in some point of doctrine or of discipline, which though they may be many, yet need not interrupt *the unity of Spirit*, if we could but find among us *the bond of peace*.[98] In the mean while if any one would write, and bring his helpful hand to the slow-moving Reformation we labour under, if Truth have spoken to him before others, or but seemed at least to speak, who hath so bejesuited us that we should trouble that man with asking licence to do so worthy a deed? and not consider this, that if it come to prohibiting, there is not aught more likely to be prohibited than truth it self; whose first appearance to our eyes bleared and dimmed with prejudice and custom, is more unsightly and unplausible than many errors, even as the person is of many a great man slight and contemptible to see to . . .

And as for regulating the Press, let no man think to have the honour of advising ye better then your selves have done in that Order published next before this, that no book be Printed, unless the Printer's and the Author's name, or at least the Printer's be registered.[99] Those which otherwise come forth, if they be found mischievous and libellous, the fire and the executioner[100] will be the timeliest and the most effectual remedy, that man's prevention can use. For this *authentic* Spanish policy of licensing books, if I have said aught, will prove the most unlicensed book it self within a short while; and was the immediate image of a Star-chamber decree to that purpose made in those very times when that Court did the rest of those her pious works, for which she is now fallen from the Stars with *Lucifer*. Whereby ye may guess what kind of State prudence, what love of the people, what care of Religion, or good manners there was at the contriving, although with singular hypocrisy it pretended to bind books to their good behaviour. And how it got the upper hand of your precedent Order so well constituted before, if we may believe those men whose profession gives them cause to enquire most, it may be doubted[101] there was in it the fraud of some old *patentees* and *monopolizers* in the trade of book-selling; who under pretence of the poor in their Company not to be defrauded, and the just retaining of each man his several copy, which God forbid should be gainsaid, brought divers glozing colours[102] to the House, which were indeed but colours, and serving to no end except it be to exercise a superiority over their neighbours, men who do not therefore labour in an honest profession to which learning is indebted, that they should be made other men's vassals. Another end is thought was aimed at by some of them in procuring by petition this Order, that having power in their hands, malignant books might the easier escape abroad, as the event shows. But of these *Sophisms* and *Elenchs*[103] of merchandise I skill not: This I know, that errors in a good government and in a bad are equally almost incident; for what Magistrate may not be misinformed, and much the sooner, if liberty of Printing be reduced into the power of a few; but to redress willingly and speedily what hath been erred, and in highest authority to esteem a plain advertisement[104] more than others have done a sumptuous bribe, is a virtue, honoured Lords and Commons, answerable to Your highest actions, and whereof none can participate but greatest and wisest men.

---

[98] *unity of spirit . . . bond of peace*   Ephesians 4.3.
[99] Milton refers to the order of January 29, 1642.
[100] *the fire and the executioner*   condemned books were burned by the hangman.
[101] *doubted*   suspected.
[102] *glozing colours*   false, rhetorical arguments.
[103] *Elench*   "An argument; a sophism" (Johnson).
[104] *advertisement*   "Instruction; admonition" (Johnson).

from *Eikonoklastes*[1] (1649)

CHAPTER 13
UPON THE CALLING IN OF THE SCOTS AND THEIR COMING

It must needs seem strange, where Men accustom themselves to ponder and contemplate things in their first original and institution, that Kings, who, as all other Officers of the Public, were at first chosen and installed only by consent and suffrage of the People, to govern them as Freemen by Laws of their own framing, and to be, in consideration of that dignity and riches bestowed upon them, the entrusted Servants of the Common-Wealth, should notwithstanding grow up to that dishonest encroachment, as to esteem themselves Masters, both of that great trust which they serve, and of the People that betrusted them: counting what they ought to do both in discharge of their public duty, and for the great reward of honour and revenue which they receive, as done all of mere grace and favour; as if their power over us were by nature, and from themselves, or that God had sold us into their hands. Indeed if the race of Kings[2] were eminently the best of men, as the breed at Tutbury [Staffordshire] is of Horses, it would in some reason then be their art only to command, ours always to obey. But Kings by generation no way excelling others, and most commonly not being the wisest or worthiest by far of whom they claim to have the governing, that we should yield them subjection to our own ruin, or hold of them the right of our common safety, and our natural freedom by mere gift, as when the Conduit pisses Wine at Coronations,[3] from the superfluity of their royal grace and beneficence, we may be sure was never the intent of Nature, whose works are also regular; never of any People not wholly barbarous, whom prudence, or no more but human sense would have better guided when they first created Kings, than so to nullify and tread to dirt the rest of mankind, by exalting one person and his Lineage without other merit looked after, but the mere contingency of a begetting, into an absolute and unaccountable dominion over them and their posterity. Yet this ignorant or wilful mistake of the whole matter, had taken so deep root in the imagination of this King, that whether to the English or to the Scot, mentioning what acts of his Regal Office, though God knows how unwillingly, he had passed, he calls them, as in other places, Acts of grace and bounty, so here 'special obligations, favours to gratify active spirits, and the desires of that party'.[4] Words not only sounding pride and Lordly usurpation, but Injustice, Partiality, and Corruption. For to the Irish he so far condescended,[5] as first to tolerate in private, then to covenant openly the tolerating of Popery: So far to the Scot, as to remove Bishops, establish Presbytery, and the Militia in their own hands, 'preferring, as some thought, the desires of Scotland before his own interest and Honour'. But being once on this side *Tweed*,[6] his reason, his conscience, and his honour became so straightened with a kind of false Virginity, that to the English neither

UPON THE CALLING IN OF THE SCOTS AND THEIR COMING

[1] *Eikonoklastes* literally "the image-smasher"; in his preface Milton says he takes the name from the surnames of "Greek Emperors, who in their zeal to the command of God, after long tradition of Idolatry in the Church, took courage, and broke all superstitious Images to pieces"; he is reacting in this work to *Eikon Basilike* "the King's image" (see the excerpt above, p. 21).

[2] *Indeed if the race of Kings* this sentence and the next were added in the second edition (1650).

[3] *Conduit pisses Wine* the public water fountains ran with wine, according to reports of Charles's coronation in Edinburgh, a conspicuously high church affair, which angered the Scots.

[4] "special obligations . . ." these and further quotations are from *Eikon Basilike* (see above, pp. 21–5).

[5] *condescend* "To stoop; to bend; to yield; to submit; to become subject" (Johnson).

[6] *Tweed* the river dividing England and Scotland; see the introduction to *Eikon Basilike* (above, p. 21).

one nor the other of the same demands could be granted, wherewith the Scots were gratified; as if our air and climate on a sudden had changed the property and the nature both of Conscience, Honour, and Reason, or that he found none so fit as English to the subjects of his arbitrary power. *Ireland* was as *Ephraim*, the strength of his head, *Scotland*, as *Judah*, was his Law-giver; but over *England* as over *Edom* he meant to cast his Shoe;[7] and yet so many sober Englishmen not sufficiently awake to consider this, like men enchanted with the Circean cup of servitude,[8] will not be held back from running their own heads into the Yoke of Bondage.

The sum of his discourse is against 'settling of Religion by violent means'; which whether it were the Scots' design upon *England*, they are best able to clear themselves. But this of all may seem strangest, that the King who, while it was permitted him, never did thing more eagerly than to molest and persecute the consciences of most Religious men, he who had made a War and lost all, rather than not uphold a Hierarchy of persecuting Bishops, should have the confidence here to profess himself so much an Enemy of those that force the conscience. For was it not he, who upon the English obtruded new Ceremonies, upon the Scots a new Liturgy,[9] & with his Sword went about to score a bloody *Rubric*[10] on their backs? Did he not forbid and hinder all effectual search of Truth, nay like a besieging Enemy stopped all her passages both by Word and Writing?[11] Yet here can talk of 'fair and equal disputations': Where notwithstanding, if all submit not to his judgement as not being 'rationally convicted', they must submit (and he conceals it not) to his 'penalty' as counted 'obstinate'. But what if he himself and those his 'learned Churchmen', were the convicted or the obstinate part long ago; should Reformation suffer them to sit Lording over the Church in their fat Bishoprics and Pluralities, like the great Whore that sitteth upon many Waters,[12] till they would vouchsafe to be disputed out? Or should we sit disputing while they sat plotting and persecuting? Those Clergymen were not 'to be driven into the fold like Sheep', as his Simile runs, but to be driven out of the Fold like Wolves,[13] or Thieves, where they sat Fleecing those Flocks which they never fed.

He believes 'that Presbytery though proved to be the only Institution of Jesus Christ were not by the Sword to be set up without his consent'; which is contrary both to the Doctrine, and the known practice of all Protestant Churches; if his Sword threaten those who of their own accord embrace it.

And although Christ and his Apostles, being to civil affairs but private men, contended not with Magistrates, yet when Magistrates themselves and especially Parliaments, who have greatest right to dispose of the civil Sword, come to know Religion, they ought in conscience to defend all those who receive it willingly, against the violence of any King or Tyrant whatsoever. Neither is it therefore true, 'That Christianity is planted or watered with Christian blood', for there is a large difference between forcing men by the Sword to turn *Presbyterians*, and defending those who willingly are so, from a furious inroad of bloody Bishops, armed with the *Militia* of a King their Pupil. And if 'covetousness and ambition' be

---

[7] *Ireland ... Law-giver* a reference to the language of David's prayer after his victory over Edom and other Palestinian cities (Psalm 60).

[8] *Circean cup of servitude* the drug used by the sorceress of the *Odyssey* who turned men into domestic beasts.

[9] *Ceremonies ... Liturgy* under Archbishop Laud the Church of England instituted new, "Romish" practices and pressed a Book of Common Prayer on Scotland, which led to their rebellious Covenant in 1637–8.

[10] *Rubric* "Directions printed in books of law and in prayer books; so termed, because they were originally distinguished by being in red ink" (Johnson).

[11] *Word and Writing* censorship of speech and the press (see *Areopagitica*, pp. 34–50 above).

[12] *the great Whore that sitteth upon many Waters* adopted from Revelation (17.15) as a symbol of the Roman Catholic Church.

[13] *Wolves* cf. *Paradise Lost* 12.508.

an argument that Presbytery hath not much of Christ, it argues more strongly against Episcopacy, which from the time of her first mounting to an order above the Presbyters, had no other Parents than Covetousness & Ambition. And those 'Sects, Schisms, and Heresies', which he speaks of, 'if they get but strength and numbers', need no other 'pattern' than Episcopacy and himself, 'to set up their ways by the like method of violence'. Nor is there any thing that hath more marks of Schism and Sectarism than English Episcopacy, whether we look at Apostolic times, or at reformed Churches, for the 'universal way of Church government' before, may as soon lead us into gross error, as their universally corrupted Doctrine. And Government by reason of ambition was likeliest to be corrupted much the sooner of the two. However nothing can be to us Catholic or universal in Religion, but what the Scripture teaches; whatsoever without Scripture pleads to be universal in the Church, in being universal is but the more Schismatical. Much less can particular Laws and Constitutions impart to the Church of England any power of consistory or tribunal above other Churches, to be the sole Judge of what is Sect or Schism, as with much rigour, and without Scripture, they took upon them. Yet these the King resolves here to defend and maintain, to his last, pretending, after all those conferences offered, or had with him, 'not to see more rational and religious motives[14] than Soldiers carry in their Knapsacks'; with one thus resolved it was but folly to stand disputing . . .

In fine[15] he accuses *Piety* with the want of *Loyalty*, and *Religion* with the breach of *Allegiance*, as if God and he were one Master, whose commands were so often contrary to the commands of God. He would persuade the Scots that their 'chief Interest consists in their fidelity to the Crown'. But true policy will teach them to find a safer interest in the common friendship of *England*, than in the ruins of one ejected family.

from *Poems* (1673)

SONNET 18[1] (1665)
ON THE LATE MASSACRE IN PIEMONT

Avenge O Lord thy slaughtered Saints, whose bones
    Lie scattered on the Alpine mountains cold,
    Ev'n them who kept thy truth so pure of old
    When all our fathers worshipped Stocks and Stones,[2]
Forget not: in thy book record their groans   5
    Who were thy Sheep, and in their ancient Fold
    Slain by the bloody *Piemontese* that rolled
    Mother with Infant down the Rocks. Their moans
The Vales redoubled to the Hills, and they
    To Heav'n. Their martyred blood and ashes sow   10
    O'er all th' *Italian* fields where still doth sway

---

14   *motives*   tracts carried by Protestant soldiers.
15   *In fine*   in conclusion.
FROM POEMS (1673)
1   This poem responds to the slaughter of Waldensians (a sect of reformed Christians) on April 24, 1655 by Catholic troops billeted in Piedmont, a northern region of the Italian peninsula.

2   *all our fathers*   the imagery of superstitious worship comes from the Old Testament (Jeremiah 2.27), but Milton applies it to pre-Reformation England; the Waldensian sect arose in the twelfth century but claimed earlier origins.

The triple Tyrant, that from these may grow[3]
    A hundred-fold, who having learnt thy way,
    Early may fly the *Babylonian* woe.[4]

SONNET 19[5]
'WHEN I CONSIDER HOW MY LIGHT IS SPENT' (1652?)

When I consider how my light is spent,
    E're half my days, in this dark world and wide,
    And that one Talent which is death to hide,[6]
    Lodged with me useless, though my soul more bent
To serve therewith my Maker, and present   5
    My true account, lest he returning chide,
    'Doth God exact day labour, light denied?'[7]
    I fondly ask; But patience to prevent
That murmur, soon replies: 'God doth not need
    Either man's work or his own gifts; who best   10
    Bear his mild yoke, they serve him best. His State
Is Kingly. Thousands at his bidding speed,
    And post o'er Land and Ocean without rest:
    They also serve who only stand and wait'.

SONNET 16[8]
[TO THE LORD GENERAL CROMWELL, 1652]

Cromwell, our chief of men, who through a cloud
    Not of war only, but detractions wide,
    Guided by faith & matchless Fortitude
    To peace & truth thy glorious way hast ploughed
And on the neck of crownèd Fortune proud[9]   5
    Hast reared God's Trophies & his work pursued[10]
    While Darwen stream with blood of Scots imbrued,[11]
    And Dunbar field resounds thy praises loud,[12]

---

[3] *triple Tyrant* the Pope with his triple crown.

[4] *Babylonian* a common epithet for Papacy among Protestants, recalling Revelation 14.8.

[5] The date of this poem is uncertain, but the theme strongly suggests that it was composed close to the winter of 1651–2, when Milton's blindness became complete, and before he began the great work of his life, *Paradise Lost,* in 1657 or 1658.

[6] *Talent* in the parable of the talents (Matthew 25.14–30) the servant who hides money (the one talent) given him by the lord, rather than using it to earn more, is cast into "outer darkness."

[7] *day labour* labour paid in daily wages; Milton jests about his blindness: he has not daylight so would not expect to do day labour.

[8] The title on the manuscript is crossed out but reads, "To the Lord General Cromwell, May 1652, on the proposals of certain ministers at the Committee for Propagation of the Gospel." The proposals that alarmed Milton concerned the institution of a clerical hierarchy that reminded Milton of the Catholic Church. The poem was not printed until 1694.

[9] *crownèd Fortune* a name for Charles I and his royal line.

[10] *Trophies* "Something taken from an enemy, and shown or treasured up in proof of victory" (Johnson).

[11] *Darwen stream* . . . at the battle of Preston in which the Royalist Scots were defeated, August 17, 1648.

[12] *Dunbar field* scene of Cromwell's victory over the Scots, September 3, 1650.

And Worcester's laureate wreath; yet much remains[13]
    To conquer still; peace hath her victories   10
    No less renowned than war, new foes arise
Threat'ning to bind our souls with secular chains
    Help us to save free Conscience from the paw
    Of hireling wolves whose Gospel is their maw.[14]

Paradise Lost (1667)

The following text of Paradise Lost is based on the second edition (1674); like other editors of the poem I have admitted a few substitutions from the manuscript of Book I and the first edition of 1667. In a very few cases I have accepted emendations of other editors. The textual problems of Paradise Lost *are numerous and have been the subject of much controversy, but on the whole the problems are not crucial; they have mainly to do with spelling and, less often, with punctuation.*

I have modernized the spelling in this edition only where I was confident I could do so without significantly changing the sound or the prosody of the poem. I have retained the original capitalization, italicization, and punctuation. How much Milton cared about capitalization and italicization is unclear; sometimes it matters, but rather than attempting to judge each instance, I have left that part of the text, despite its inconsistencies, intact; at the least, these features provide a sense of what the text looked like to contemporary readers, without adding to the difficulty of the poem. Milton cared more about spelling and punctuation; he used them to direct readers of his poem to hear it correctly. His punctuation is not grammatical in the modern sense but an indication of tempo: comma, semicolon, colon, and period (full stop) represent incrementally longer pauses. Despite his interesting ideas about spelling and punctuation, Milton was not completely consistent in his efforts to regulate his text (his blindness was certainly an obstacle), and, in addition, there are aspects of the spelling and typography that seem needlessly distracting to students. These have been silently modernized. Hence, Milton's "tast" appears as "taste" and "Rhime" as "Rhyme." Spellings that seem to direct pronunciation, such as "Heav'n," are retained, except where the modern spelling indicates the pronunciation just as well. Weak verbs in the past tense and past participles, for example, are given a modern "-ed" ending in preference to Milton's "'d" as long as the modern ending does not add a syllable. Hence "flam'd" is rendered "flamed." Milton's spellings of some participles with "'t" or "-ed" (ravish't, mixt) are changed to "-ed" (ravished, mixed) because, after much deliberation and consultation, I find that there is little or no difference in sound between the original and the modernized forms, as we realize them in speech today. Also modernized are the variant spellings of "thir" and "their," and "mee" and "me." Milton used the added "e" to indicate that the word was stressed, but the text is very inconsistent, and, usually, the added "e" is not needed to hear the stress. I have retained Milton's spelling of words that we think of as contractions, such as "adventrous," although in potentially confusing cases I have added an apostrophe in place of the "missing" letter.

Of course, there are many instances in which it was hard to decide about the effects of modernization, and overall I must confess to falling short of scientific regularity or even complete

---

[13] *Worcester* the battle in which Charles II was defeated and narrowly escaped capture, September 3, 1651.   [14] *hireling wolves* corrupt clergy (John 10.11–16).

consistency. My text is a compromise between what is there in 1674 and what I thought would be most intelligible. There is thus plenty of work left for the reader. I must ask British readers, for example, usually to pronounce "been" with a short sound because I have not retained Milton's "bin." Grave accent marks are added to indicate the presence of an unusual syllable, and acute accents are added to indicate surprising stress: it must be "obdúrate pride," for example, and "fixèd anchor." Most abnormalities of pronunciation, however, could not be marked, and the reader must be highly conscious of Milton's tendency to use pronunciations (normal, variant, and abnormal) that fit within the pentametric "Heroic" measure. Hence, for example, American readers must recognize that "Disobedience" (I. 1) has four syllables, not five, and all readers must hear that "Spirit" (I. 17) and "Power" (I. 44) can be pronounced as one syllable rather than two, "aspiring" as two syllables rather than three, and "dire Arms," "many a" or "to incur" as two syllables, to give just a few examples. As a further aid to readers, quotation marks and apostrophes indicating the possessive form are also added, although Milton never used either.

In myriad ways that this edition cannot begin to chronicle, Milton believed there was a strong connection between the form and the meaning of his poetry. For him, spelling, punctuation, and prosody were all of a piece not only with his aesthetic life but also with his political and religious convictions. The strength of Milton's feelings about the importance of his prosody is clearly evident in an addition that he made to the second edition in order to defend what some readers saw as his failure to use rhyme.

THE
VERSE

The Measure is English *Heroic Verse without Rhyme, as that of* Homer *in* Greek, *and of* Virgil *in* Latin; *Rhyme being no necessary Adjunct or true Ornament of Poem or good Verse, in longer Works especially, but the Invention of a barbarous Age, to set off wretched matter and lame Meter; graced indeed since by the use of some famous modern Poets, carried away by Custom, but much to their own vexation, hindrance, and constraint to express many things otherwise, and for the most part worse than else they would have expressed them. Not without cause therefore some both* Italian *and* Spanish *Poets of prime note have rejected Rhyme both in longer and shorter Works, as have also long since our best* English *Tragedies, as a thing of it self, to all judicious ears, trivial and of no true musical delight; which consists only in apt Numbers,[1] fit quantity[2] of Syllables, and the sense variously drawn out from one Verse into another, not in the jingling sound of like endings, a fault avoided by the learned Ancients both in Poetry and all good Oratory. This neglect then of Rhyme so little is to be taken for a defect, though it may seem so perhaps to vulgar[3] Readers, that it rather is to be esteemed an example set, the first in* English, *of ancient liberty recovered to Heroic Poem from the troublesome and modern[4] bondage of Rhyming.*

BOOK I
THE ARGUMENT

This first Book proposes, first in brief, the whole Subject, *Man's disobedience, and the loss thereupon of Paradise wherein he was placed:* Then touches *the prime cause of his fall, the Serpent, or*

---

[1]   *Numbers*   prosodical meter, with some sense of musical harmony and proportion.

[2]   *quantity*   in classical prosody refers to the length or duration of syllables, but English prosody usually "measures" syllables as stressed or unstressed, and they may be all that Milton means.

[3]   *vulgar*   "Plebeian; suiting to the common people" (Johnson).

[4]   *modern*   both recent and "vulgar; mean; common" (Johnson).

rather Satan in the Serpent; who revolting from God, and drawing to his side many Legions of Angels, was by the command of God driven out of Heaven with all his Crew into the great Deep. Which action passed over, the Poem hastes into the midst of things, presenting *Satan with his Angels now fallen into Hell, described* here, *not in the Centre* (for Heaven and Earth may be supposed as yet not made, certainly not yet accursed) *but in a place of utter darkness, fitliest called* Chaos: *Here Satan with his Angels lying on the burning Lake, thunder-struck and astonished, after a certain space recovers, as from confusion, calls up him who next in Order and Dignity lay by him; they confer of their miserable fall.* Satan *awakens all his Legions, who lay till then in the same manner confounded; They rise, their Numbers, array of Battle, their chief Leaders named, according to the Idols known afterwards in* Canaan[5] *and the Countries adjoining. To these* Satan *directs his Speech, comforts them with hope yet of regaining Heaven, but tells them lastly of a new World and new kind of Creature to be created, according to an ancient Prophesy or report in Heaven;* for that Angels were long before this visible Creation, was the opinion of many ancient Fathers.[6] *To find out the truth of this Prophesy, and what to determine thereon he refers to a full Council. What his Associates thence attempt.* Pandemonium *the Palace of* Satan *rises, suddenly built out of the Deep: The infernal Peers there sit in Council.*

Of Man's First Disobedience, and the Fruit
Of that Forbidden Tree whose mortal taste
Brought Death into the World, and all our woe,
With loss of *Eden*, till one greater Man
Restore us, and regain the blissful Seat,   5
Sing, Heav'nly Muse, that on the secret top
Of *Oreb*, or of *Sinai*, didst inspire[7]
That Shepherd, who first taught the chosen Seed,
In the Beginning how the Heav'ns and Earth
Rose out of *Chaos*: or, if *Sion* hill[8]   10
Delight thee more, and *Siloa*'s Brook that flowed[9]
Fast by the Oracle of God; I thence
Invoke thy aid to my adventrous Song,
That with no middle flight intends to soar
Above th' *Aonian* Mount, while it pursues[10]   15
Things unattempted yet in Prose or Rhyme.
And chiefly Thou, O Spirit, that dost prefer
Before all Temples th' upright heart and pure,
Instruct me, for Thou know'st; Thou from the first
Wast present, and with mighty wings outspread   20
Dove-like sat'st brooding on the vast Abyss,
And mad'st it pregnant: What in me is dark
Illumine, what is low raise and support;
That to the heighth of this great Argument,

---

[5]   *Canaan*   Palestine, the biblical Holy Land.
[6]   *Fathers*   church fathers, early Christian commentators on the Bible.
[7]   *Oreb . . . Sinai*   mounts where Moses ("That Shepherd") may have received the word of God.
[8]   *Sion*   or Zion, one of the hills of Jerusalem, where David brought the ark of the covenant.

[9]   *Siloa's Brook*   a pool in Jerusalem, used by Jesus for healing (John 9.7), but perhaps Shiloh is meant, a town where there was an annual feast of Jehovah and where the ark resided for some time.
[10]   *Aonian Mount*   located in Boetia, a district in central Greece famous for ancient poets and musicians.

I may assert Eternal Providence,   25
And justify the ways of God to men.
    Say first, for Heav'n hides nothing from thy view,
Nor the deep tract of Hell, say first what cause
Moved our Grand Parents, in that happy State,
Favoured of Heav'n so highly, to fall off   30
From their Creator, and transgress his Will
For one restraint, Lords of the World besides?
Who first seduced them to that foul revolt?
Th' infernal Serpent; he it was, whose guile,
Stirred up with Envy and Revenge, deceived   35
The Mother of Mankind, what time his Pride
Had cast him out from Heav'n, with all his Host
Of Rebel Angels, by whose aid aspiring
To set himself in Glory above his Peers,
He trusted to have equalled the Most High,   40
If he opposed; and with ambitious aim
Against the Throne and Monarchy of God
Raised impious War in Heav'n and Battle proud
With vain attempt. Him the Almighty Power
Hurled headlong flaming from th' Ethereal Sky,   45
With hideous ruin and combustion down
To bottomless perdition, there to dwell
In Adamantine Chains and penal Fire,
Who durst defy th' Omnipotent to Arms.
Nine times the Space that measures Day and Night   50
To mortal men, he with his horrid crew
Lay vanquished, rolling in the fiery Gulf,
Confounded though immortal: But his doom
Reserved him to more wrath; for now the thought
Both of lost happiness and lasting pain   55
Torments him; round he throws his baleful eyes,
That witnessed huge affliction and dismay,
Mixed with obdúrate pride and steadfast hate:
At once as far as Angels ken he views
The dismal Situation waste and wild,   60
A Dungeon horrible, on all sides round
As one great Furnace flamed; yet from those flames
No light, but rather darkness visible
Served only to discover sights of woe,
Regions of sorrow, doleful shades, where peace   65
And rest can never dwell, hope never comes
That comes to all; but torture without end
Still urges, and a fiery Deluge, fed
With ever-burning Sulphur unconsumed.
Such place Eternal Justice has prepared   70
For those rebellious, here their Prison ordained
In utter darkness, and their portion set

As far removed from God and light of Heav'n
As from the Centre thrice to th' utmost Pole.
O how unlike the place from whence they fell!   75
There the companions of his fall, o'erwhelmed
With Floods and Whirlwinds of tempestuous fire,
He soon discerns, and weltering by his side
One next himself in power, and next in crime,
Long after known in *Palestine*, and named   80
Beëlzebub. To whom th' Arch-Enemy,
And thence in Heav'n called Satan, with bold words
Breaking the horrid silence, thus began.
   'If thou beest he; but O how fall'n! how changed
From him, who in the happy Realms of Light   85
Clothed with transcendent brightness didst out-shine
Myriads though bright: If he whom mutual league,
United thoughts and counsels, equal hope
And hazard in the Glorious Enterprise,
Joined with me once, now misery hath joined   90
In equal ruin: into what Pit thou seest
From what heighth fall'n, so much the stronger proved
He with his Thunder: and till then who knew
The force of those dire Arms? yet not for those,
Nor what the Potent Victor in his rage   95
Can else inflict, do I repent or change,
Though changed in outward lustre; that fixed mind
And high disdain, from sense of injured merit,
That with the mightiest raised me to contend,
And to the fierce contention brought along   100
Innumerable force of Spirits armed
That durst dislike his reign, and, me preferring,
His utmost power with adverse power opposed
In dubious Battle on the Plains of Heav'n,
And shook his throne. What though the field be lost?   105
All is not lost; the unconquerable Will,
And study of revenge, immortal hate,
And courage never to submit or yield:
And what is else not to be overcome?
That Glory never shall his wrath or might   110
Extort from me. To bow and sue for grace
With suppliant knee, and deify his power,
Who from the terror of this Arm so late
Doubted his Empire, that were low indeed,
That were an ignominy and shame beneath   115
This downfall; since by Fate the strength of Gods
And this Empyreal Substance cannot fail,
Since through experience of this great event
In Arms not worse, in foresight much advanced,
We may with more successful hope resolve   120

To wage by force or guile eternal War
Irreconcilable, to our grand Foe,
Who now triúmphs, and in th' excess of joy
Sole reigning holds the Tyranny of Heav'n'.
   So spake th' Apostate Angel, though in pain,   125
Vaunting aloud, but racked with deep despair:
And him thus answered soon his bold Compeer.
   'O Prince, O Chief of many Throned Powers,
That led th' embattled Seraphim to War
Under thy conduct, and in dreadful deeds   130
Fearless, endangered Heaven's perpetual King;
And put to proof his high Supremacy,
Whether upheld by strength, or Chance, or Fate,
Too well I see and rue the dire event,
That with sad overthrow and foul defeat   135
Hath lost us Heav'n, and all this mighty Host
In horrible destruction laid thus low,
As far as Gods and Heav'nly Essences
Can perish: for the mind and spirit remains
Invincible, and vigour soon returns,   140
Though all our Glory extinct, and happy state
Here swallowed up in endless misery.
But what if he our Conqueror, (whom I now
Of force believe Almighty, since no less
Than such could have o'erpow'red such force as ours)   145
Have left us this our spirit and strength entire,
Strongly to suffer and support our pains,
That we may so suffice his vengeful ire,
Or do him mightier service as his thralls
By right of War, what e'er his business be   150
Here in the heart of Hell to work in Fire,
Or do his Errands in the gloomy Deep;
What can it then avail though yet we feel
Strength undiminished, or eternal being
To undergo eternal punishment?'   155
Whereto with speedy words th' Arch-Fiend replied.
   'Fall'n Cherub, to be weak is miserable
Doing or Suffering: but of this be sure,
To do aught good never will be our task,
But ever to do ill our sole delight,   160
As being the contrary to his high will
Whom we resist. If then his Providence
Out of our evil seek to bring forth good,
Our labour must be to pervert that end,
And out of good still to find means of evil;   165
Which oft times may succeed, so as perhaps
Shall grieve him, if I fail not, and disturb

His inmost counsels from their destined aim.
But see the angry Victor hath recalled
His Ministers of vengeance and pursuit   170
Back to the Gates of Heav'n: the Sulphurous Hail
Shot after us in storm, o'erblown hath laid
The fiery Surge, that from the Precipice
Of Heav'n received us falling, and the Thunder,
Winged with red Lightning and impetuous rage,   175
Perhaps hath spent his shafts, and ceases now
To bellow through the vast and boundless Deep.
Let us not slip th' occasion, whether scorn,
Or satiate fury yield it from our Foe.
Seest thou yon dreary plain, forlorn and wild,   180
The seat of desolation, void of light,
Save what the glimmering of these livid flames
Casts pale and dreadful? Thither let us tend
From off the tossing of these fiery waves,
There rest, if any rest can harbour there,   185
And reassembling our afflicted Powers,
Consult how we may henceforth most offend
Our Enemy, our own loss how repair,
How overcome this dire Calamity,
What reinforcement we may gain from Hope,   190
If not what resolution from despair'.
      Thus Satan, talking to his nearest Mate
With head up-lift above the wave, and eyes
That sparkling blazed, his other Parts besides
Prone on the Flood, extended long and large   195
Lay floating many a rood,[11] in bulk as huge
As whom the Fables name of monstrous size,[12]
Titanian or *Earth-born*, that warred on *Jove*,
Briareos or *Typhon*, whom the Den
By ancient *Tarsus* held, or that Sea-beast[13]   200
Leviathan, which God of all his works
Created hugest that swim th' Oceanstream:
Him, haply slumbering on the *Norway* foam
The Pilot of some small night-foundered Skiff,
Deeming some Island, oft, as Sea-men tell,   205
With fixèd anchor in his scaly rind
Moors by his side under the Lee, while Night
Invests the Sea, and wishèd Morn delays.

---

[11]   *rood* "A pole; a measure of sixteen feet and a half in long measure" (Johnson).
[12]   *Briareos and Typhon* Titans or older gods, sons of Gaia (earth); three-hundred-headed Briareos fought with Zeus, against his brethren; Zeus (Jove) killed *Typhon*

with his hundred serpent heads and buried him under Mount Aetna, near Tarsus (mod. Terassus) on Sicily.
[13]   *Leviathan* a sea-dragon in the Bible (see Isaiah 27.1; Psalm 74.13–14).

So stretcht out huge in length the Arch-fiend lay
Chained on the burning Lake, nor ever thence   210
Had ris'n, or heaved his head, but that the will
And high permission of all-ruling Heaven
Left him at large to his own dark designs,
That with reiterated crimes he might
Heap on himself damnation, while he sought   215
Evil to others, and enraged might see
How all his malice served but to bring forth
Infinite goodness, grace, and mercy shewn
On Man by him seduct, but on himself
Treble confusion, wrath and vengeance poured.   220
Forthwith upright he rears from off the Pool
His mighty Stature; on each hand the flames
Driv'n backward slope their pointing spires, and rolled
In billows, leave i' th' midst a horrid Vale.
Then with expanded wings he steers his flight   225
Aloft, incumbent on the dusky Air
That felt unusual weight, till on dry Land
He lights, if it were Land that ever burned
With solid, as the Lake with liquid fire;
And such appeared in hue, as when the force   230
Of subterranean wind transports a Hill
Torn from *Pelorus*, or the shattered side[14]
Of thundering *Ætna*, whose combustible
And fuellèd entrails thence conceiving fire,
Sublimed with mineral fury, aid the winds,   235
And leave a singèd bottom all involved
With stench and smoke: Such resting found the sole
Of unblest feet. Him followed his next Mate,
Both glorying to have scaped the *Stygian* flood[15]
As Gods, and by their own recovered strength,   240
Not by the sufferance of supernal Power.
    'Is this the Region, this the Soil, the Clime,'
Said then the lost Arch-angel, 'this the seat
That we must change for Heav'n?, this mournful gloom
For that celestial light? Be it so, since he   245
Who now is Sovereign can dispose and bid
What shall be right: farthest from him is best
Whom reason hath equalled, force hath made supreme
Above his equals. Farewell happy Fields
Where Joy for ever dwells: Hail horrors, hail,   250
Infernal world, and thou profoundest Hell
Receive thy new possessor: one who brings

[14] *Pelorus* a sandy promontory in Sicily (mod. Capo di Faro).   [15] *Stygian* from Styx, the poisonous, cold river said to flow into Hell.

A mind not to be changed by Place or Time.
The mind is its own place, and in it self
Can make a Heav'n of Hell, a Hell of Heav'n.   255
What matter where, if I be still the same,
And what I should be, all but less than he
Whom Thunder hath made greater? Here at least
We shall be free; th' Almighty hath not built
Here for his envy, will not drive us hence: 260
Here we may reign secure; and, in my choice
To reign is worth ambition, though in Hell:
Better to reign in Hell, than serve in Heav'n.
But wherefore let we then our faithful friends,
Th' associates and copartners of our loss   265
Lie thus astonished on th' oblivious Pool,[16]
And call them not to share with us their part
In this unhappy Mansion, or once more
With rallied Arms to try what may be yet
Regained in Heav'n, or what more lost in Hell?'   270
    So *Satan* spake; and him *Beëlzebub*
Thus answered. 'Leader of those Armies bright,
Which but th' Omnipotent none could have foiled,
If once they hear that voice, their liveliest pledge
Of hope in fears and dangers, heard so oft   275
In worst extremes, and on the perilous edge
Of battle, when it raged, in all assaults
Their surest signal, they will soon resume
New courage and revive, though now they lie
Grovelling and prostrate on yon Lake of Fire,   280
As we erewhile, astounded and amazed,
No wonder, fall'n such a pernicious heighth'.
    He scarce had ceased when the superior Fiend
Was moving toward the shore; his ponderous shield,
Ethereal temper, massy, large and round,   285
Behind him cast; The broad circumference
Hung on his shoulders like the Moon, whose Orb
Through Optic Glass the *Tuscan* Artist views[17]
At Evening, from the top of *Fésole*,
Or in Valdarno, to descry new Lands,   290
Rivers or Mountains in her spotty Globe.
His Spear, to equal which the tallest Pine
Hewn on *Norwegian* hills, to be the Mast
Of some great Ammiral, were but a wand,[18]

---

[16] *oblivious* causing forgetfulness.
[17] *the Tuscan artist* Galileo, the astronomer and maker
of telescopes; Milton visited him in Fiesole or the nearby
valley of the Arno (*Valdarno*).

[18] *Ammiral* "the ship which carries the admiral or
commander of the fleet" (Johnson).

He walked with to support uneasy steps   295
Over the burning Marl, not like those steps
On Heaven's Azure, and the torrid Clime
Smote on him sore besides, vaulted with Fire,
Nathless he so endured, till on the Beach
Of that inflamèd sea, he stood, and called   300
His Legions, Angel Forms, who lay entranced
Thick as Autumnal Leaves that strow the Brooks
In *Vallombrosa*, where th' *Etrurian* shades[19]
High overarched imbow'r; or scattered sedge
Afloat, when with fierce Winds *Orion* armed[20]   305
Hath vexed the Red-Sea Coast, whose waves o'erthrew
Busiris and his *Memphian* Chivalry,[21]
While with perfidious hatred they pursued
The sojourners of Goshen, who beheld[22]
From the safe shore their floating carcases   310
And broken Chariot-Wheels, so thick bestrown
Abject and lost lay these, covering the Flood,
Under amazement of their hideous change.
He called so loud, that all the hollow Deep
Of Hell resounded. 'Princes, Potentates,   315
Warriors, the Flow'r of Heav'n, once yours, now lost,
If such astonishment as this can seize
Eternal Spirits, or have ye chos'n this place
After the toil of Battle to repose
Your wearied virtue, for the ease you find   320
To slumber here, as in the Vales of Heav'n?
Or in this abject posture have ye sworn
To adore the Conqueror, who now beholds
Cherub and Seraph rolling in the flood
With scattered Arms and Ensigns, till anon   325
His swift pursuers from Heav'n-Gates discern
Th' advantage, and descending tread us down
Thus drooping, or with linkèd Thunderbolts
Transfix us to the bottom of this Gulf.
Awake, arise, or be for ever fall'n'.   330
    They heard, and were abashed, and up they sprung
Upon the wing, as when men wont to watch
On duty, sleeping found by whom they dread,
Rouse and bestir themselves ere well awake.
Nor did they not perceive the evil plight   335
In which they were, or the fierce pains not feel;

---

[19] *Vallombrosa* (lit. "shady valley") a place in Etruria (mod. Tuscany).
[20] *Orion* the rising of this constellation, named after the mythical hunter, was said to be accompanied by storms.
[21] *Busiris* a most cruel tyrant of Egypt, commander of cavalry ("chivalry") from Memphis.
[22] *Sojourners of Goshen* the Jews passing through a place in Egypt in search of the promised land.

Yet to their General's voice they soon obeyed
Innumerable. As when the potent Rod
Of *Amram*'s Son in *Egypt*'s evil day[23]
Waved round the Coast, upcalled a pitchy cloud   340
Of *Locusts*, warping on the Eastern Wind,
That o'er the Realm of impious *Pharaoh* hung
Like Night, and darkened all the Land of *Nile*:
So numberless were those bad Angels seen
Hovering on wing under the Cope of Hell   345
'Twixt upper, nether, and surrounding Fires;
Till, as a signal giv'n, th' uplifted Spear
Of their great Sultan waving to direct
Their course, in even balance down they light
On the firm brimstone, and fill all the Plain: 350
A multitude, like which the populous North
Poured never from her frozen loins, to pass
Rhene or the *Danaw*, when her barbarous sons[24]
Came like a deluge on the South, and spread
Beneath *Gibraltar* to the *Libian* sands.   355
Forthwith, from every Squadron and each Band
The Heads and Leaders thither haste where stood
Their great Commander; Godlike shapes, and forms
Excelling human, princely Dignities,
And Powers that erst in Heaven sat on thrones,   360
Though of their Names in heav'nly Records now
Be no memorial, blotted out and razed
By their Rebellion from the Books of Life.
Nor had they yet among the sons of *Eve*
Got them new Names, till wandring o'er the Earth,   365
Through God's high sufferance, for the trial of man,
By falsities and lies the greatest part
Of Mankind they corrupted to forsake
God their Creator, and th' invisible
Glory of him that made them, to transform   370
Oft to the Image of a Brute, adorned
With gay Religions full of Pomp and Gold,
And Devils to adore for Deities:
Then were they known to men by various Names,
And various Idols through the Heathen World.   375
Say, Muse, their Names then known, who first, who last,
Roused from the slumber, on that fiery Couch,
At their great Emperor's call, as next in worth
Came singly where he stood on the bare strand,

---

[23] *Amram's Son* Moses (see Exodus 10.12–15).   [24] *Rhene or the Danaw* Rhine and Danube, homelands
of Goths.

While the promiscuous crowd stood yet aloof?   380
The chief were those who from the Pit of Hell
Roaming to seek their prey on earth, durst fix
Their Seats long after next the Seat of God,
Their Altars by his Altar, Gods adored
Among the Nations round, and durst abide   385
Jehovah thundering out of *Sion*, throned
Between the Cherubim; yea, often placed
Within his Sanctuary it self their Shrines,
Abominations; and with cursèd things
His holy Rites, and solemn Feasts profaned,   390
And with their darkness durst affront his light.
First *Moloch*, horrid King besmeared with blood[25]
Of human sacrifice, and parents' tears,
Though for the noise of Drums and Timbrels loud,
Their children's cries unheard, that past through fire   395
To his grim Idol. Him the *Ammonite*[26]
Worshipped in *Rabba* and her wat'ry Plain,
In *Argob* and in *Basan*, to the stream
Of utmost *Arnon*. Nor content with such
Audacious neighbourhood, the wisest heart   400
Of *Solomon* he led by fraud to build
His Temple right against the Temple of God
On that opprobrious Hill, and made his Grove[27]
The Pleasant valley of *Hinnom*, *Tophet* thence[28]
And black *Gehenna* called, the Type of Hell.[29]   405
Next *Chemos*, th' obscene dread of *Moab*'s sons,[30]
From *Aroar* to *Nebo*, and the wild
Of Southmost *Abarim*; in *Hesebon*
And *Horonaim*, *Seon*'s realm, beyond
The flowry Dale of *Sibma* clad with Vines,   410
And *Eleale* to th' *Asphaltic* Pool.[31]
Peor his other name, when he enticed
Israel in Sittim, on their march from Nile,
To do him wanton rites, which cost them woe.[32]
Yet thence his lustful Orgies he enlarged   415
Even to that Hill of Scandal, by the Grove
Of *Moloch* homicide, lust hard by hate;[33]
Till good *Josiah* drove them thence to Hell.[34]

---

[25] *Moloch* a Caananite god of fire to whom children were sacrificed.
[26] *the Ammonite* a tribe hostile to the Israelites, inhabiting a land of giants.
[27] *that opprobrious Hill* the Mount of Olives near Jerusalem (1 Kings 11.7).
[28] *Tophet* lit. place of fire (Isaiah 30.33).
[29] *Type* "That by which something future is prefigured" (Johnson).

[30] *Chemos* a false god worshipped in Moab; equated with *Peor*.
[31] *th' Asphaltic Pool* the Dead Sea, north and east of which lie the other places in the passage.
[32] See Numbers 25.1–3, where the Israelites are seduced by the daughters of Moab.
[33] *Hill of Scandal* and *the Grove of Moloch* see l. 403 above.
[34] 2 Kings 23.1–14.

With these came they, who, from the bordring flood
Of old *Euphrates* to the Brook that parts   420
Egypt from *Syrian* ground, had general Names
Of *Baalim* and *Ashtaroth*, those male,
These Feminine. For Spirits when they please
Can either Sex assume, or both; so soft
And uncompounded is their Essence pure,   425
Not tied or manacled with joint or limb,
Nor founded on the brittle strength of bones,
Like cumbrous flesh; but in what shape they choose
Dilated or condensed, bright or obscure,
Can execute their airy purposes,   430
And works of love or enmity fulfil.
For those the Race of Israel oft forsook
Their living strength, and unfrequented left
His righteous Altar, bowing lowly down
To bestial gods; for which their heads as low   435
Bowed down in Battle, sunk before the Spear
Of despicable foes. With these in troop
Came *Astoreth*, whom the *Phoenicians* called[35]
Astarte, Queen of Heav'n, with crescent Horns;
To whose bright Image nightly by the moon   440
Sidonian virgins paid their Vows and Songs;
In *Sion* also not unsung, where stood
Her Temple on th' offensive Mountain, built
By that uxorious King, whose heart though large,[36]
Beguil'd by fair Idolatresses, fell   445
To Idols foul. *Thammuz* came next behind,[37]
Whose annual wound in *Lebanon* allured
The *Syrian* Damsels to lament his fate
In amorous ditties all a Summer's day,
While smooth *Adonis* from his native Rock   450
Ran purple to the Sea, supposed with blood
Of *Thammuz* yearly wounded: the Love-tale
Infected Sion's daughters with like heat,
Whose wanton passions in the sacred Porch[38]
Ezekiel saw, when by the Vision led   455
His eye surveyed the dark Idolatries
Of alienated *Judah*. Next came one
Who mourned in earnest, when the Captive Ark
Maimed his brute Image, head and hands lopped off

[35] *Astoreth* 2 Kings 23.13; as Astarte, identified with
Venus and associated with sexual rites.
[36] *that uxorious King* Solomon, see l. 401 above.
[37] *Thammuz* Phoenician Adonis, in love with
Astarte and killed by a wild boar; the cult of
Adonis celebrated his death annually in a festival of
regeneration.
[38] *sacred Porch* scene of pagan worship in Ezekiel
8.13–18.

In his own Temple, on the grunsel edge,[39]   460
Where he fell flat, and shamed his Worshippers:
Dagon his Name, Sea Monster, upward Man[40]
And downward Fish; yet had his temple high
Reared in *Azotus*, dreaded, through the Coast
Of *Palestine*, in *Gath* and *Ascalon*,   465
And *Accaron* and *Gaza*'s frontier bounds.
Him followed *Rimmon*, whose delightful Seat[41]
Was fair *Damascus*, on the fertile Banks
Of Abbana and Pharphar, lucid streams.
He also against the house of God was bold: 470
A Leper once he lost and gained a King —[42]
Ahaz his sottish Conqueror, whom he drew[43]
God's Altar to disparage and displace
For one of *Syrian* mode, whereon to burn
His odious offrings, and adore the Gods   475
Whom he had vanquished. After these appeared
A crew who under Names of old Renown —
Osiris, Isis, Orus, and their Train —[44]
With monstrous shapes and sorceries abused
Fanatic *Egypt* and her Priests, to seek   480
Their wandring Gods disguised in brutish forms
Rather than human. Nor did *Israel* 'scape
Th' infection when their borrowed Gold composed
The Calf in *Oreb*: and the Rebel King[45]
Doubled that sin in *Bethel* and in *Dan*,   485
Lik'ning his Maker to the Grazed Ox,
Jehovah, who in one Night, when he passed[46]
From *Egypt* marching, equalled with one stroke
Both her firstborn and all her bleating Gods.
Belial came last, than whom a Spirit more lewd   490
Fell not from Heav'n, or more gross to love
Vice for it self: to him no Temple stood
Or Altar smoked; yet who more oft than he
In Temples and at Altars, when the Priest
Turns Atheist, as did *Eli*'s Sons, who filled[47]   495
With lust and violence the house of God.
In Courts and Palaces he also Reigns

---

[39] *grunsel* var. of groundsel, "the lower part of the building" (Johnson).
[40] *Dagon* national god of the Philistines, who occupied the places named in the passage.
[41] *Rimmon* a Syrian god identical with Hadad.
[42] *Leper* Naaman, saved by Elijah, renounced Rimmon (2 Kings 5.1–18).
[43] *Ahaz* 2 Kings 16.10–18.
[44] *Osiris, Isis, Orus* father, mother and son, gods of ancient Egypt.

[45] *The Calf* Aaron commanded the forging and worship of the golden calf (Exodus 32.1–6); *the Rebel King* Jeroboam, an idolator (1 Kings 12.25–33).
[46] The event celebrated in Passover, when the Israelites were spared and delivered from Egypt (Exodus 12.29–36).
[47] *Eli* a high priest who did not sufficiently correct his sons (1 Samuel 2.22–5).

And in luxurious Cities, where the noise
Of riot ascends above their loftiest Tow'rs,
And injury and outrage: and, when Night   500
Darkens the Streets, then wander forth the Sons
Of *Belial*, flown with insolence and wine.[48]
Witness the Streets of *Sodom*, and that night[49]
In *Gibeah*, when the hospitable door
Exposed a Matron to avoid worse rape.   505
These were the prime in order and in might;
The rest were long to tell, though far renowned
Th' *Ionian* gods – of Javan's issue held[50]
Gods, yet confessed later than Heav'n and Earth,
Their boasted parents; *Titan*, Heav'n's first-born,   510
With his enormous brood, and birthright seized
By younger *Saturn*, he from mightier Jove,[51]
His own and *Rhea*'s son, like measure found;
So *Jove* usurping reigned: these, first in *Crete*
And *Ida* known, thence on the snowy top[52]   515
Of cold Olympus ruled the middle Air,
Their highest Heav'n; or on the *Delphian* Cliff,
Or in Dodona, and through all the bounds
Of *Doric* Land; or who with *Saturn* old
Fled over *Adria* to th' *Hesperian* Fields,   520
And o'er the *Celtic* roamed the utmost Isles.
All these and more came flocking; but with looks
Down cast and damp; yet such wherein appeared
Obscure some glimpse of joy, to have found their chief
Not in despair, to have found themselves not lost   525
In loss it self; which on his count'nance cast
Like doubtful hue: but he his wonted pride
Soon recollecting, with high words, that bore
Semblance of worth, not substance, gently raised
Their fainting courage, and dispelled their fears.   530
Then straight commands that, at the warlike sound
Of Trumpets loud and Clarions be upreared
His mighty Standard; that proud honour claimed
Azazel as his right, a Cherub tall:

---

[48] *flown* "puffed; inflated; elate" (Johnson).
[49] *The Streets of Sodom* Lot protected two angels from
the carousing men of Sodom, even offering his daughters
to distract them (Genesis 19.4–14); *that night in Gebeah*
a man gave up his daughter and his concubine to gang
rape in order to protect a sojourning Levite (Judges
19.16–30).
[50] *Javan* son of Japhet (Genesis 10.2), reputed sire of
Greek gods, though Heaven and Earth, parents of the
Titans, are said to be older.

[51] *Saturn* the youngest Titan, who seized the throne
from his elders and was likewise displaced by his son
Jove (Jupiter, Zeus), fled over the Adriatic sea (*Adria*),
then west to the edge of the Atlantic (*Hesperides*), and
north to the British Isles (*utmost Isles*).
[52] *Ida* mountain in Crete, birthplace of Zeus and the
gods who occupied *Olympus*, *Delphi* and *Dodona* and other
Greek (*Doric*) places.

Who forthwith from the glittering staff unfurled   535
Th' Imperial Ensign, which full high advanced,
Shone like a Meteor streaming to the Wind,
With Gems and Golden lustre rich emblazed,
Seraphic arms and Trophies: all the while
Sonòrous metal blowing martial sounds: 540
At which the universal Host upsent
A shout that tore Hell's Concave, and beyond
Frighted the Reign of *Chaos* and old Night.
All in a moment through the gloom were seen
Ten thousand Banners rise into the Air   545
With Orient Colours waving: with them rose
A Forest huge of Spears: and thronging Helms
Appeared, and serried Shields in thick array
Of depth immeasurable. Anon they move
In perfect Phalanx to the *Dorian* mood[53]   550
Of Flutes and soft Recorders – such as raised
To height of noblest temper Heroes old
Arming to Battle, and in stead of rage
Deliberate valour breathed, firm and unmoved
With dread of death to flight or foul retreat,   555
Nor wanting power to mitigate and swage[54]
With solemn touches, troubled thoughts, and chase
Anguish and doubt and fear and sorrow and pain
From mortal or immortal minds. Thus they,
Breathing united force with fixèd thought   560
Moved on in silence to soft Pipes that charmed
Their painful steps o'er the burnt soil; and now
Advanced in view, they stand, a horrid Front
Of dreadful length and dazzling Arms, in guise
Of Warriors old with ordered Spear and Shield,   565
Awaiting what command their mighty Chief
Had to impose: he through the armèd Files
Darts his experienced eye, and soon traverse
The whole battalion views – their order due,
Their visages and stature as of Gods,   570
Their number last he sums. And now his heart
Distends with pride, and hardning in his strength
Glories: for never since created man,
Met such embodied force as, named with these,
Could merit more than that small infantry[55]   575
Warred on by Cranes: though all the Giant brood
Of *Phlegra* with th' Heroic Race were joined[56]

---

[53] *Dorian mood* the most stately and dignified of the scales, or modes, of classical music.
[54] *swage* assuage.

[55] *that small infantry* Pygmies, thought to be an African or Asian race.
[56] *Phlegra* a town in Thessaly on the plains near which giants were said to have fought against the gods.

That fought at *Thebes* and *Ilium*, on each side
Mixed with auxiliar Gods; and what resounds
In Fable or *Romance* of *Uther*'s Son,[57]   580
Begirt with *British* and *Armoric* Knights;[58]
And all who since, Baptized or Infidel,
Jousted in *Aspramont*, or *Montalban*,[59]
Damasco, or *Marocco*, or *Trebisond*,
Or whom *Biserta* sent from *Afric* shore[60]   585
When *Charlémain* with all his Peerage fell
By *Fontarabbia*. Thus far these beyond
Compare of mortal prowess, yet observed
Their dread commander: he, above the rest
In shape and gesture proudly eminent,   590
Stood like a Tower; his form had yet not lost
All her Original brightness, nor appeared
Less than Arch Angel ruined, and th' excess
Of Glory obscured: As when the Sun new ris'n
Looks through the Horizontal misty Air   595
Shorn of his Beams, or from behind the Moon,
In dim Eclipse disastrous twilight sheds
On half the Nations, and with fear of change
Perplexes Monarchs. Darkened so, yet shone
Above them all th' Arch Angel: but his face   600
Deep scars of Thunder had entrenched, and care
Sat on his faded cheek, but under Brows
Of dauntless courage, and considerate Pride
Waiting revenge: cruel his eye, but cast
Signs of remorse and passion, to behold   605
The fellows of his crime, the followers rather
(Far other once beheld in bliss), condemned
For ever now to have their lot in pain —
Millions of Spirits for his fault amerced[61]
Of Heav'n, and from Eternal Splendours flung   610
For his revolt, yet faithful how they stood,
Their Glory withered; as, when Heaven's fire
Hath scathed the Forest Oaks, or Mountain Pines,
With singèd top their stately growth though bare
Stands on the blasted Heath. He now prepared   615
To speak; whereat their doubled Ranks they bend
From wing to wing, and half enclose him round

---

[57] *Uther's Son* King Arthur.
[58] *Armoric Knights* Arthur's comrades from Brittany.
[59] *Aspramont . . . Trebisond* scenes of battles between Christian and Islamic warriors, from France to Turkey.
[60] *Biserta* African town under the control of Islamic Tunis, across the sea from Spanish *Fontarabbia*, supposed

site of Charlemagne's defeat at Roncevaux (Spain) and the death of his nephew Roland. In *La Chanson de Roland* the battle is between Turks and Christians, as Milton frames it here.
[61] *amerced* fr. amerce "To punish with a pecuniary penalty; to exact a fine; to inflict a forfeiture" (Johnson).

With all his Peers: attention held them mute.
Thrice he assayed, and thrice in spite of scorn,
Tears such as Angels weep, burst forth: at last   620
Words interwove with sighs found out their way:
    'O Myriads of immortal Spirits, O Powers
Matchless, but with th' Almighty, and that strife
Was not inglorious, though th' event was dire,
As this place testifies, and this dire change,   625
Hateful to utter: but what power of mind
Foreseeing or presaging, from the Depth
Of knowledge past or present, could have feared
How such united force of Gods, how such
As stood like these, could ever know repulse?   630
For who can yet believe, though after loss,
That all these puissant Legions, whose exile
Hath emptied Heav'n, shall fail to re-ascend
Self-raised, and repossess their native seat?
For me be witness all the Host of Heav'n,   635
If counsels different, or danger shunned
By me, have lost our hopes. But he who reigns
Monarch in Heav'n till then as one secure
Sat on his Throne, upheld by old repute,
Consent or custom, and his Regal State   640
Put forth at full, but still his strength concealed,
Which tempted our attempt, and wrought our fall.
Henceforth his might we know, and know our own
So as not either to provoke, or dread
New war, provoked; our better part remains   645
To work in close design, by fraud or guile
What force effected not: that he no less
At length from us may find, who overcomes
By force, hath overcome but half his foe.
Space may produce new Worlds; whereof so rife   650
There went a fame in Heav'n that he ere long
Intended to create, and therein plant
A generation, whom his choice regard
Should favour equal to the Sons of Heav'n:
Thither, if but to pry, shall be perhaps   655
Our first eruption, thither, or elsewhere:
For this Infernal Pit shall never hold
Celestial Spirits in Bondage, nor th' Abyss
Long under darkness cover. But these thoughts
Full Counsel must mature: Peace is despaired,   660
For who can think Submission? War then, War
Open or understood must be resolved'.
    He spake: and, to confirm his words, out-flew
Millions of flaming swords, drawn from the thighs

Of mighty Cherubim; the sudden blaze   665
Far round illumined hell: highly they raged
Against the Highest, and fierce with grasped Arms
Clashed on their sounding Shields the din of war,
Hurling defiance toward the Vault of Heav'n.
    There stood a Hill not far whose grisly top   670
Belched fire and rolling smoke; the rest entire
Shone with a glossy scurf, undoubted sign[62]
That in his womb was hid metallic Ore,
The work of Sulphur. Thither winged with speed
A numerous Brigade hastened. As when Bands   675
Of Pioneers with Spade and Pickaxe armed[63]
Forerun the Royal camp, to trench a Field,
Or cast a Rampart. *Mammon* led them on,
Mammon, the least erected Spirit that fell
From heav'n; for ev'n in heav'n his looks and thoughts   680
Were always downward bent, admiring more
The riches of Heav'n's pavement, trodd'n Gold,
Than aught divine or holy else enjoyed
In vision beatific: by him first
Men also, and by his suggestion taught,   685
Ransacked the Centre, and with impious hands
Rifled the bowels of their mother Earth
For Treasures better hid. Soon had his crew
Opened into the Hill a spacious wound
And digged out ribs of Gold. Let none admire[64]   690
That riches grow in Hell; that soil may best
Deserve the precious bane. And here let those
Who boast in mortal things, and wond'ring tell
Of *Babel*, and the works of *Memphian* Kings,[65]
Learn how their greatest Monuments of Fame   695
And Strength and Art are easily out-done
By Spirits reprobate, and in an hour
What in an age they with incessant toil
And hands innumerable scarce perform.
Nigh on the Plain in many cells prepared,   700
That underneath had veins of liquid fire
Sluiced from the Lake, a second multitude
With wondrous Art founded the massy Ore,
Severing each kind, and scummed the Bullion dross:

---

[62] *scurf* "1. A kind of dry miliary scab . . . 3. Any thing sticking on the surface" (Johnson).
[63] *Pioneers* "One whose business is to level the road, throw up works, or sink mines in military operations" (Johnson).

[64] *admire* "to regard with wonder" (Johnson).
[65] *Babel* the tower built by Nimrod that was supposed to reach heaven; *work of Memphian Kings* pyramids or other Egyptian monuments.

A third as soon had formed within the ground   705
A various mould, and from the boiling cells
By strange conveyance filled each hollow nook,
As in an Organ from one blast of wind
To many a row of Pipes the sound-board breathes.
Anon out of the earth a Fabric huge   710
Rose like an Exhalation, with the sound
Of Dulcet Symphonies and voices sweet,
Built like a Temple, where Pilasters round[66]
Were set, and Doric pillars overlaid
With Golden Architrave; nor did there want   715
Cornice or Frieze, with bossy Sculptures grav'n;
The Roof was fretted Gold. Not *Babylon*
Nor great *Alcairo* such magnificence[67]
Equalled in all their glories, to enshrine
Belus or *Sarapis* their Gods, or seat   720
Their Kings, when *Egypt* with *Assyria* strove
In wealth and luxury. Th' ascending pile
Stood fixed her stately heighth, and straight the doors,
Op'ning their brazen folds discover wide
Within, her ample spaces, o'er the smooth   725
And level pavement: from the archèd roof
Pendant by subtle Magic many a row
Of Starry Lamps and blazing Cressets fed[68]
With Naptha and Asphaltus yielded light[69]
As from a sky. The hasty multitude   730
Admiring entered, and the work some praise
And some the Architect: his hand was known
In Heav'n by many a Towered structure high,
Where Sceptred Angels held their residence,
And sat as Princes, whom the supreme King   735
Exalted to such power, and gave to rule,
Each in his Hierarchy, the Orders bright.
Nor was his name unheard or unadored
In ancient *Greece*; and in *Ausonian* land[70]
Men called him *Mulciber*; and how he fell[71]   740
From Heav'n they fabled, thrown by angry *Jove*
Sheer o'er the Crystal Battlements; from Morn
To Noon he fell, from Noon to dewy Eve,
A Summer's day; and with the setting Sun

---

[66]   *Pilasters*   square columns set within a wall; like the rest of the architectural terms in the passage, it suggests ornamental excess.
[67]   *Alcairo*   "the" Cairo, ancient Memphis.
[68]   *Cressets*   beacons, from "*croissette*, Fr. because beacons had crosses anciently on their tops" (Johnson).

[69]   *Naptha and Asphaltus*   bituminous minerals.
[70]   *Ausonian land*   Italy in general, but especially an early culture established in the volcanic Aeolian Islands near Sicily and trading in volcanic minerals such as sulfur.
[71]   *Mulciber*   Vulcan or Hephaestus.

Dropt from the Zenith like a falling Star,   745
On *Lemnos*, th' Aegaean Isle: thus they relate,
Erring; for he with this rebellious rout
Fell long before; nor aught availed him now
To have built in Heav'n high Towers; nor did he scape
By all his Engines, but was headlong sent,   750
With his industrious crew to build in hell.
Mean while the wingèd Heralds by command
Of Sovereign power, with awful Ceremony
And trumpet's sound, throughout the Host proclaim
A solemn Council forthwith to be held   755
At *Pandæmonium*, the high Capital[72]
Of Satan and his Peers: their summons called
From every Band and squarèd Regiment
By place or choice the worthiest; they anon
With hundreds and with thousands trooping came   760
Attended: all access was thronged, the Gates
And Porches wide, but chief the spacious Hall
(Though like a covered field, where Champions bold
Wont ride in armed, and at the Soldan's chair[73]
Defied the best of *Paynim* chivalry   765
To mortal combat, or career with Lance),
Thick swarmed, both on the ground and in the air,
Brushed with the hiss of rustling wings. As Bees
In spring time, when the Sun with *Taurus* rides,[74]
Pour forth their populous youth about the Hive   770
In clusters; they among fresh dews and flow'rs
Fly to and fro, or on the smoothèd Plank,
The suburb of their Straw-built Citadel,
New rubbed with balm, expatiate and confer[75]
Their State affairs. So thick the airy crowd   775
Swarmed and were straitened; till the Signal giv'n,
Behold a wonder! they but now who seemed
In bigness to surpass Earth's Giant Sons
Now less than smallest Dwarfs, in narrow room
Throng numberless, like that Pygméan Race   780
Beyond the *Indian* Mount; or Faerie Elves,[76]
Whose midnight Revels, by a Forest side
Or Fountain some belated Peasant sees,
Or dreams he sees, while over-head the Moon

---

[72]   *Pandæmonium*   a place (lit.) "of all demons."
[73]   *Soldan*   "[for sultan] The emperor of the Turks" (Johnson), considered paynims, or pagans, by the Christian warriors in the Crusades.
[74]   *when the Sun with Taurus rides*   from April 19 to 20 May the Sun appears to be in this constellation.

[75]   *balm*   pollen, perhaps, but also oil used in rites such as Roman Catholic confirmation and part of the implicit similarity between Pandaemonium and St Peter's Cathedral; *expatiate* "To range at large; to rove without any prescribed limits" (Johnson).
[76]   *Indian Mount*   Himalayan mountains.

Sits Arbitress, and nearer to the Earth   785
Wheels her pale course, they on their mirth and dance
Intent, with jocund Music charm his ear;
At once with joy and fear his heart rebounds.
Thus incorporeal Spirits to smallest forms
Reduced their shapes immense, and were at large,   790
Though without number still amidst the hall
Of that infernal Court. But far within,
And in their own dimensions like themselves,
The great Seraphic Lords and Cherubim
In close recess and secret conclave sat,[77]   795
A thousand Demi-Gods on golden seats,
Frequent and full. After short silence then[78]
And summons read, the great consult began.

BOOK II
THE ARGUMENT

The Consultation begun, Satan *debates whether another Battle be to be hazarded for the recovery of Heaven: some advise it, others dissuade: A third proposal is preferred, mentioned before by* Satan, *to search the truth of that Prophesy or Tradition in Heaven concerning another world, and another kind of creature equal or not much inferiour to themselves, about this time to be created: Their doubt who shall be sent on this difficult search:* Satan *their chief undertakes alone the voyage, is honoured and applauded. The Council thus ended, the rest betake them several ways and to several employments, as their inclinations lead them, to entertain the time till* Satan *return. He passes on his Journey to Hell Gates, finds them shut, and who sat there to guard them, by whom at length they are opened, and discover to him the great Gulf between Hell and Heaven; with what difficulty he passes through, directed by* Chaos, *the Power of that place, to the sight of this new World which he sought.*

High on a Throne of Royal State, which far
Outshone the wealth of *Ormus* and of *Ind*,[1]
Or where the gorgeous East with richest hand
Show'rs on her Kings *Barbaric* Pearl and Gold,[2]
Satan exalted sat, by merit raised   5
To that bad eminence; and from despair
Thus high uplifted beyond hope, aspires
Beyond thus high, insatiate to pursue
Vain War with Heav'n, and by success untaught
His proud imaginations thus displayed.   10
'Powers and Dominions, Deities of Heav'n,
For since no deep within her gulf can hold
Immortal vigour, though oppressed and fall'n,
I give not Heav'n for lost. From this descent

---

[77] *recess* "departure into privacy" (Johnson); *conclave* "the assembly of the cardinals" (Johnson).
[78] *frequent* "full of concourse" (Johnson).

BOOK II
[1] *Ormus* an island at the mouth of the Persian Gulf.
[2] *Barbaric* "foreign; far-fetched" (Johnson).

Celestial virtues rising, will appear[3]   15
More glorious and more dread than from no fall,
And trust themselves to fear no second fate:
Me though just right, and the fixed Laws of Heav'n
Did first create your Leader, next free choice,
With what besides, in Counsel or in Fight,   20
Hath been achieved of merit, yet this loss
Thus far at least recovered, hath much more
Established in a safe unenvied Throne
Yielded with full consent. The happier state
In Heav'n, which follows dignity, might draw   25
Envy from each inferior; but who here
Will envy whom the highest place exposes
Foremost to stand against the Thunderer's aim
Your bulwark, and condemns to greatest share
Of endless pain? where there is then no good   30
For which to strive, no strife can grow up there
From Faction; for none sure will claim in Hell
Precedence, none, whose portion is so small
Of present pain, that with ambitious mind
Will covet more. With this advantage then   35
To union, and firm Faith, and firm accord,
More than can be in Heav'n, we now return
To claim our just inheritance of old,
Surer to prosper than prosperity
Could have assured us; and by what best way,   40
Whether of open War or covert guile,
We now debate; who can advise may speak'.
    He ceased, and next him *Moloc*, Sceptred King
Stood up, the strongest and the fiercest Spirit
That fought in Heav'n; now fiercer by despair: 45
His trust was with th' Eternal to be deemed
Equal in strength, and rather than be less
Cared not to be at all; with that care lost
Went all his fear: of God, or Hell, or worse
He recked not, and these words thereafter spake.   50
    'My sentence is for open War: Of Wiles,[4]
More unexpert, I boast not: them let those
Contrive who need, or when they need, not now.
For while they sit contriving, shall the rest,
Millions that stand in arms, and longing wait   55
The Signal to ascend, sit lingering here
Heav'n's fugitives, and for their dwelling place
Accept this dark opprobrious Den of Shame,
The Prison of his Tyranny who Reigns

---

[3] *Celestial virtues* a high order of angels.

[4] *sentence* "Determination or decision, as of a judge civil or criminal" (Johnson).

By our delay? no, let us rather choose 60
Armed with Hell flames and fury all at once
O'er Heav'n's high Towers to force resistless way,
Turning our tortures into horrid arms
Against the Torturer; when, to meet the noise
Of his Almighty Engine, he shall hear[5] 65
Infernal Thunder, and for Lightning see
Black fire and horror shot with equal rage
Among his Angels; and his Throne it self
Mixed with *Tartárean* Sulphur, and strange fire,[6]
His own invented Torments. But perhaps 70
The way seems difficult and steep to scale
With upright wing against a higher foe.
Let such bethink them, if the sleepy drench
Of that forgetful Lake benumb not still,[7]
That in our proper motion we ascend 75
Up to our native seat: descent and fall
To us is adverse. Who but felt of late
When the fierce Foe hung on our broken Rear[8]
Insulting, and pursued us through the Deep,[9]
With what compulsion and laborious flight 80
We sunk thus low? Th' ascent is easy then;
Th' event is feared; should we again provoke
Our stronger, some worse way his wrath may find
To our destruction: if there be in Hell
Fear to be worse destroyed: what can be worse 85
Than to dwell here, driv'n out from bliss, condemned
In this abhorrèd deep to utter woe;
Where pain of unextinguishable fire
Must exercise us without hope of end
The Vassals of his anger, when the Scourge 90
Inexorably, and the torturing hour
Calls us to Penance? More destroyed than thus
We should be quite abolished, and expire.
What fear we then? what doubt we to incense
His utmost ire? which to the heighth enraged, 95
Will either quite consume us, and reduce
To nothing this essential, happier far
Than miserable to have eternal being:
Or if our substance be indeed Divine,

---

[5] *Engine* "A military machine" (Johnson); God's thunder.
[6] *Tartarean* of Tartarus, that part of the underworld where the wicked are punished.
[7] *forgetful Lake* the river Lethe, which means forgetfulness, one of the five rivers of the underworld; see the "oblivious Pool" (1. 266 and l. 583 below).

[8] *Rear* "The hinder troop of an army" (Johnson).
[9] *Insulting* fr. *insult*, "To trample upon; to triumph over" (Johnson).

And cannot cease to be, we are at worst   100
On this side nothing; and by proof we feel
Our power sufficient to disturb his Heav'n,
And with perpetual inroads to Alarm,
Though inaccessible, his fatal Throne:
Which if not Victory is yet Revenge'.   105
    He ended frowning, and his look denounced
Desperate revenge, and Battle dangerous
To less than Gods. On th' other side up rose
Belial, in act more graceful and humane;
A fairer person lost not Heav'n; he seemed   110
For dignity composed and high exploit:
But all was false and hollow; though his Tongue
Dropt Manna, and could make the worse appear[10]
The better reason, to perplex and dash
Maturest Counsels: for his thoughts were low;   115
To vice industrious, but to Nobler deeds
Timorous and slothful: yet he pleased the ear,
And with persuasive accent thus began.
    'I should be much for open War, O Peers,
As not behind in hate; if what was urged   120
Main reason to persuade immediate War,
Did not dissuade me most, and seem to cast
Ominous conjecture on the whole success:
When he who most excels in fact of Arms,
In what he counsels and in what excels   125
Mistrustful, grounds his courage on despair
And utter dissolution, as the scope
Of all his aim, after some dire revenge.
First, what Revenge? the Towers of Heav'n are filled
With Armèd watch, that render all access   130
Impregnable; oft on the bordering Deep
Encamp their Legions, or with óbscure wing
Scout far and wide into the Realm of night,
Scorning surprise. Or could we break our way
By force, and at our heels all Hell should rise   135
With blackest Insurrection, to confound
Heav'n's purest Light, yet our great Enemy,
All incorruptible would on his Throne
Sit unpolluted, and th' Ethereal mould[11]
Incapable of stain would soon expel   140
Her mischief, and purge off the baser fire
Victorious. Thus repulsed, our final hope

---

[10] *Manna* a mysterious gum with honey-like juice which was miraculously supplied to the Israelites to sustain them on their forty-day sojourn in the wilderness (Exodus 16).

[11] *mould* "cast; form" (Johnson), with a suggestion of the heat-resistant matrix in which molten metal is poured when something is cast.

Is flat despair: we must exasperate
Th' Almighty Victor to spend all his rage,
And that must end us, that must be our cure,   145
To be no more; sad cure; for who would lose,
Though full of pain, this intellectual being,
Those thoughts that wander through Eternity,
To perish rather, swallowed up and lost
In the wide womb of uncreated night,   150
Devoid of sense and motion? and who knows,
Let this be good, whether our angry Foe
Can give it, or will ever? how he can
Is doubtful; that he never will is sure.
Will he, so wise, let loose at once his ire,   155
Belike through impotence, or unaware,
To give his Enemies their wish, and end
Them in his anger, whom his anger saves
To punish endless? 'wherefore cease we then?'
Say they who counsel War, 'we are decreed,   160
Reserved and destined to Eternal woe;
Whatever doing, what can we suffer more,
What can we suffer worse?' is this then worst,
Thus sitting, thus consulting, thus in Arms?
What when we fled amain, pursued and strook   165
With Heav'n's afflicting Thunder, and besought
The Deep to shelter us? this Hell then seemed
A refuge from those wounds: or when we lay
Chained on the burning Lake? that sure was worse.
What if the breath that kindled those grim fires   170
Awaked should blow them into sevenfold rage
And plunge us in the flames? or from above
Should intermitted vengeance arm again
His red right hand to plague us? what if all
Her stores were opened, and this Firmament   175
Of Hell should spout her Cataracts of Fire,
Impendent horrors, threatning hideous fall[12]
One day upon our heads; while we perhaps
Designing or exhorting glorious war,
Caught in a fiery Tempest shall be hurled   180
Each on his rock transfixt, the sport and prey
Or racking whirlwinds, or for ever sunk
Under yon boiling Ocean, wrapped in Chains;
There to converse with everlasting Groans,
Unrespited, unpitied, unreprieved,   185
Ages of hopeless end; this would be worse.

---

[12] *impendent* "Imminent; hanging over; pressing
closely" (Johnson).

War therefore, open or concealed, alike
My voice dissuades; for what can force or guile[13]
With him, or who deceive his mind, whose eye
Views all things at one view? he from Heav'n's heighth   190
All these our motions vain, sees and derides;
Not more Almighty to resist our might
Than wise to frustrate all our plots and wiles.
Shall we then live thus vile, the race of Heav'n
Thus trampled, thus expelled, to suffer here   195
Chains and these Torments? Better these than worse,
By my advice; since fate inevitable
Subdues us, and Omnipotent Decree,
The Victor's will. To suffer, as to do,
Our strength is equal, nor the Law unjust   200
That so ordains: this was at first resolved,
If we were wise, against so great a foe
Contending, and so doubtful what might fall.[14]
I laugh when those who at the Spear are bold
And vent'rous, if that fail them, shrink and fear   205
What yet they know must follow, to endure
Exile, or ignominy, or bonds, or pain,
The sentence of their Conqueror: This is now
Our doom; which if we can sustain and bear,
Our Súpreme Foe in time may much remit   210
His anger, and perhaps thus far removed
Not mind us not offending, satisfied
With what is punished; whence these raging fires
Will slacken, if his breath stir not their flames.
Our purer essence then will overcome   215
Their noxious vapour, or inured not feel,
Or changed at length, and to the place conformed
In temper and in nature, will receive
Familiar the fierce heat, and void of pain;
This horror will grow mild, this darkness light,   220
Besides what hope the never-ending flight
Of future days may bring, what chance, what change
Worth waiting, since our present lot appears
For happy though but ill, for ill not worst,
If we procure not to our selves more woe'.   225
     Thus *Belial*, with words clothed in reason's garb
Counselled ignoble ease, and peaceful sloth,
Not peace: and after him thus *Mammon* spake.
     'Either to disenthrone the King of Heav'n
We war, if war be best, or to regain   230
Our own right lost: him to unthrone we then

---

[13] *Can* avails.   [14] *fall* fall out, happen.

May hope when everlasting Fate shall yield
To fickle Chance, and *Chaos* judge the strife:
The former vain to hope argues as vain
The latter: for what place can be for us   235
Within Heav'n's bound, unless Heav'n's Lord supreme
We overpower? Suppose he should relent
And publish Grace to all, on promise made
Of new Subjection; with what eyes could we
Stand in his presence humble, and receive   240
Strict Laws imposed, to celebrate his Throne
With warbled Hymns, and to his Godhead sing
Forced Hallelujahs; while he Lordly sits
Our envied Sovereign, and his Altar breathes
Ambrosial Odours and Ambrosial Flow'rs,   245
Our servile offerings. This must be our task
In Heav'n this our delight; how wearisome
Eternity so spent in worship paid
To whom we hate. Let us not then pursue
By force impossible, by leave obtained   250
Unacceptable, though in Heav'n, our state
Of splendid vassalage, but rather seek
Our own good from our selves, and from our own
Live to our selves, though in this vast recess,
Free, and to none accountable, preferring   255
Hard liberty before the easy yoke
Of servile Pomp. Our greatness will appear
Then most conspicuous, when great things of small,
Useful of hurtful, prosperous of adverse
We can create, and in what place soe'er   260
Thrive under evil, and work ease out of pain
Through labour and endurance. This deep world
Of darkness do we dread? How oft amidst
Thick clouds and dark doth Heav'n's all-ruling Sire
Choose to reside, his Glory unobscured,   265
And with the Majesty of darkness round
Covers his Throne; from whence deep thunders roar
Must'ring their rage, and Heav'n resembles Hell?
As he our darkness, cannot we his Light
Imitate when we please? This Desert soil   270
Wants not her hidden lustre, Gems and Gold;
Nor want we skill or Art, from whence to raise
Magnificence; and what can Heav'n show more?
Our torments also may in length of time
Become our Elements, these piercing Fires   275
As soft as now severe, our temper changed
Into their temper; which must needs remove
The sensible of pain. All things invite[15]

---

[15] *The sensible of pain* the feeling of pain.

To peaceful Counsels, and the settled State
Of order, how in safety best we may   280
Compose our present evils, with regard
Of what we are and where, dismissing quite
All thoughts of War: ye have what I advise'.
        He scarce had finished, when such murmur filled
Th' Assembly, as when hollow Rocks retain   285
The sound of blustering winds, which all night long
Had roused the Sea, now with hoarse cadence lull
Sea-faring men o'erwatched, whose Bark by chance[16]
Or Pinnace anchors in a craggy Bay[17]
After the Tempest: Such applause was heard   290
As *Mammon* ended, and his Sentence pleased,
Advising peace: for such another Field
They dreaded worse than Hell; so much the fear
Of Thunder and the Sword of *Michaël*
Wrought still within them; and no less desire   295
To found this nether Empire, which might rise
By policy and long process of time,
In emulation opposite to Heav'n.
Which when *Beëlzebub* perceived, than whom,
Satan except, none higher sat, with grave   300
Aspect he rose, and in his rising seemed
A Pillar of State; deep on his Front engraven
Deliberation sat and public care;
And Princely counsel in his face yet shone,
Majestic though in ruin: *Sage* he stood   305
With *Atlantean* shoulders fit to bear[18]
The weight of mightiest Monarchies; his look
Drew audience and attention still as Night
Or summer's Noon-tide air, while thus he spake.
        'Thrones and Imperial Powers, off-spring of Heav'n   310
Ethereal Virtues; or these Titles now[19]
Must we renounce, and changing style be called
Princes of Hell? for so the popular vote
Inclines, here to continue, and build up here
A growing Empire; doubtless; while we dream,   315
And know not that the King of Heav'n hath doomed
This place our dungeon, not our safe retreat
Beyond his Potent arm, to live exempt
From Heav'n's high jurisdiction, in new League
Banded against his Throne, but to remain   320
In strictest bondage, though thus far removed,
Under th' inevitable curb, reserved

---

[16] *o'er watched*   strained by too long a watch, or stretch of duty; *Bark*   "a small ship" (Johnson).
[17] *Pinnace*   "a small sloop or bark attending a larger ship" (Johnson).
[18] *Atlantean*   having the strength of Atlas, the Titan who was said to support the sky.
[19] *Virtues*   angels (l.15 above).

His captive multitude: For he, to be sure
In heighth or depth, still first and last will Reign
Sole King, and of his Kingdom lose no part   325
By our revolt, but over Hell extend
His Empire, and with Iron Sceptre rule[20]
Us here, as with his Golden those in Heav'n.
What sit we then projecting peace and War?
War hath determined us and foiled with loss   330
Irreparable; terms of peace yet none
Vouchsafed or sought; for what peace will be giv'n
To us enslaved, but custody severe,
And stripes, and arbitrary punishment
Inflicted? and what peace can we return,   335
But to our power hostility and hate,
Untamed reluctance, and revenge though slow,
Yet ever plotting how the Conqueror least
May reap his conquest, and may least rejoice
In doing what we most in suffering feel?   340
Nor will occasion want, nor shall we need
With dangerous expedition to invade
Heav'n, whose high walls fear no assault or Siege,
Or ambush from the Deep. What if we find
Some easier enterprise? There is a place   345
(if ancient and prophetic fame in Heav'n
Err not) another World, the happy seat
Of some new Race called *Man*, about this time
To be created like to us, though less
In power and excellence, but favoured more   350
Of him who rules above; so was his will
Pronounced among the Gods, and by an Oath,
That shook Heav'n's whole circumference, confirmed.
Thither let us bend all our thoughts, to learn
What creatures there inhabit, of what mould,   355
Or substance, how endued, and what their Power,
And where their weakness, how attempted best,
By force or subtlety: Though Heav'n be shut,
And Heav'n's high Arbitrator sit secure
In his own strength, this place may lie exposed   360
The utmost border of his Kingdom, left
To their defence who hold it: here perhaps
Some advantageous act may be achieved
By sudden onset, either with Hell fire
To waste his whole Creation, or possess   365
All as our own, and drive as we were driven,
The puny habitants, or if not drive,[21]

---

[20]   *Iron Sceptre*   see Psalms 2.9.   [21]   *puny*   "(puis né, Fr.) 1. Young. 2. Inferior"
                                                                  (Johnson).

Seduce them to our Party, that their God
May prove their foe, and with repenting hand
Abolish his own works. This would surpass   370
Common revenge, and interrupt his joy
In our Confusion, and our Joy upraise
In his disturbance; when his darling Sons,
Hurled headlong to partake with us, shall curse
Their frail original, and faded bliss,   375
Faded so soon. Advise if this be worth
Attempting, or to sit in darkness here
Hatching vain Empires'. Thus *Beëlzebub*
Pleaded his devilish Counsel, first devised
By *Satan*, and in part proposed: for whence,   380
But from the Author of all ill could Spring
So deep a malice, to confound the race
Of mankind in one root, and Earth with Hell
To mingle and involve, done all to spite
The great Creator? But their spite still serves   385
His glory to augment. The bold design
Pleased highly those infernal States, and joy
Sparkled in all their eyes; with full assent
They vote: whereat his speech he thus renews.
    'Well have ye judged, well ended long debate,   390
Synod of Gods, and like to what ye are,
Great things resolved, which from the lowest deep
Will once more lift us up, in spite of Fate,
Nearer our ancient Seat; perhaps in view
Of those bright confines, whence with neighbouring Arms   395
And opportune excursion we may chance
Re-enter Heav'n; or else in some mild Zone
Dwell not unvisited of Heav'n's fair Light
Secure, and at the brightning Orient beam
Purge off this gloom; the soft delicious Air,   400
To heal the scar of these corrosive Fires
Shall breathe her balm. But first whom shall we send
In search of this new world? whom shall we find
Sufficient? who shall tempt with wandring feet[22]
The dark unbottomed infinite Abyss   405
And through the palpable obscure find out
His uncouth way, or spread his airy flight
Upborn with indefatigable wings
Over the vast abrupt, ere he arrive[23]
The happy Isle; what strength, what art can then   410
Suffice, or what evasion bear him safe

---

[22] *tempt* "to try; to attempt" (Johnson).   [23] *abrupt* a noun based as much on the Latin adjective
abruptus (precipitous, sheer) as on the English.

Through the strict Senteries and Stations thick[24]
Of Angels watching round? Here he had need
All circumspection, and we now no less
Choice in our suffrage; for on whom we send,   415
The weight of all and our last hope relies'.
    This said, he sat; and expectation held
His look suspense, awaiting who appeared
To second, or oppose, or undertake
The perilous attempt: but all sat mute,   420
Pondering the danger with deep thoughts; and each
In other's count'nance read his own dismay
Astonished: none among the choice and prime
Of those Heav'n-warring Champions could be found
So hardy as to proffer or accept   425
Alone the dreadful voyage; till at last
Satan, whom now transcendent glory raised
Above his fellows, with Monarchal pride
Conscious of highest worth, unmoved thus spake.
    'O Progeny of Heav'n! Empyreal Thrones,   430
With reason hath deep silence and demur
Seized us, though undismayed: long is the way
And hard, that out of Hell leads up to light;
Our prison strong, this huge convex of Fire,
Outrageous to devour, immures us round   435
Ninefold, and gates of burning adamant
Barred over us prohibit all egress.
These past, if any pass, the void profound
Of unessential Night receives him next
Wide gaping, and with utter loss of being   440
Threatens him, plunged in that abortive gulf.
If thence he scape into whatever world,
Or unknown Region, what remains him less
Than unknown dangers and as hard escape.
But I should ill become this Throne, O Peers,   445
And this Imperial sovereignty, adorned
With splendour, armed with power, if aught proposed
And judged of public moment, in the shape
Of difficulty or danger could deter
Me from attempting. Wherefore do I assume   450
These Royalties, and not refuse to Reign,
Refusing to accept as great a share
Of hazard as of honour, due alike
To him who Reigns, and so much to him due
Of hazard more, as he above the rest   455
High honoured sits? Go therefore mighty Powers,

---

[24] *Senteries* sentries; *stations* "post[s] assigned"
(Johnson).

Terror of Heav'n, though fall'n; intend at home,[25]
While here shall be our home, what best may ease
The present misery, and render Hell
More tolerable; if there be cure or charm   460
To respite or deceive, or slack the pain
Of this ill Mansion: intermit no watch
Against a wakeful Foe, while I abroad
Through all the Coasts of dark destruction seek
Deliverance for us all: this enterprise   465
None shall partake with me'. Thus saying rose
The Monarch, and prevented all reply,
Prudent, lest, from his resolution raised
Others among the chief might offer now
(Certain to be refused) what erst they feared;   470
And so refused might in opinion stand
His Rivals, winning cheap the high repute
Which he through hazard huge must earn. But they
Dreaded not more th' adventure than his voice
Forbidding; and at once with him they rose;   475
Their rising all at once was as the sound
Of Thunder heard remote. Towards him they bend
With awful reverence prone; and as a God
Extol him equal to the highest in Heav'n:
Nor failed they to express how much they praised,   480
That for the general safety he despised
His own: for neither do the Spirits damned
Lose all their virtue; lest bad men should boast
Their specious deeds on earth, which glory excites,
Or close ambition varnished o'er with zeal.   485
Thus they their doubtful consultations dark
Ended rejoicing in their matchless Chief:
As when from mountain tops the dusky clouds
Ascending, while the North wind sleeps, o'erspread
Heav'n's cheerful face, the louring element   490
Scowls o'er the darkened lantskip[26] Snow or shower;
If chance the radiant Sun with farewell sweet
Extend his ev'ning beam, the fields revive,
The birds their notes renew, and bleating herds
Attest their joy, that hill and valley rings.   495
O shame to men! Devil with Devil damned
Firm concord holds, men only disagree
Of Creatures rational, though under hope
Of heavenly Grace: and God proclaiming peace,
Yet live in hatred, enmity, and strife   500
Among themselves, and levy cruel wars

---

[25] *intend* "To pay regard or attention to. This sense is   [26] *lantskip* landscape.
now little used" (Johnson).

Wasting the Earth, each other to destroy:
As if (which might induce us to accord)
Man had not hellish foes enow besides,
That day and night for his destruction wait.   505
    The *Stygian* Counsel thus dissolved; and forth[27]
In order came the grand infernal Peers,
Midst came their mighty Paramount, and seemed
Alone th' Antagonist of Heav'n, nor less
Than Hell's dread Emperor with pomp supreme,   510
And God-like imitated State; him round
A Globe of fiery Seraphim enclosed
With bright emblazonry, and horrent Arms.[28]
Then of their Session ended they bid cry
With Trumpet's regal sound the great result: 515
Toward the four winds four speedy Cherubim
Put to their mouths the sounding Alchemy[29]
By Herald's voice explained: the hollow Abyss
Heard far and wide, and all the host of Hell
With deafning shout, returned them loud acclaim.   520
Thence more at ease their minds and somewhat raised
By false presumptuous hope, the rangèd powers
Disband, and wandring, each his several way
Pursues, as inclination or sad choice
Leads him perplext, where he may likeliest find   525
Truce to his restless thoughts, and entertain
The irksome hours, till his great Chief return.
Part on the Plain, or in the Air sublime
Upon the wing, or in swift Race contend,
As at th' *Olympian* Games or *Pythian* fields;[30]   530
Part curb their fiery Steeds, or shun the Goal[31]
With rapid wheels, or fronted Brígades form.
As when to warn proud Cities war appears
Waged in the troubled Sky, and Armies rush
To Battle in the Clouds, before each Van[32]   535
Prick forth the Airy Knights, and couch their spears
Till thickest Legions close; with feats of Arms
From either end of Heav'n the welkin burns.
Others with vast *Typhoean* rage, more fell[33]

---

[27] *Stygian* "Hellish; infernal; pertaining to Styx, one of the poetical rivers of hell" (Johnson).
[28] *horrent* latinate English, from *horrens*, dreadful, awful and *horrere*, to bristle.
[29] *sounding Alchemy* sound producing gold, i.e. the trumpets.
[30] *Olympian . . . Pythian* the first and second most important contests in the ancient world.
[31] *shun the Goal* cut in close to the turning post on the oval race-track, without hitting it.
[32] *Van* "the front of an army; the first line" (Johnson).
[33] *Typhoean* like Typhon, a terrible monster with a hundred heads, driven into Tartarus by Zeus or buried under volcanic Mount Aetna; *fell* "Cruel; barbarous, inhuman" (Johnson).

Rend up both Rocks and Hills, and ride the Air   540
In whirlwind; Hell scarce holds the wild uproar.
As when *Alcides from Oechalia* Crowned[34]
With conquest, felt th' envenomed robe, and tore
Through pain up by the roots *Thessalian* Pines,
And *Lichas* from the top of *Oeta* threw   545
Into th' *Euboic* Sea. Others more mild,
Retreated in a silent valley, sing
With notes Angelical to many a Harp
Their own Heroic deeds and hapless fall
By doom of battle; and complain that Fate   550
Free Virtue should enthrall to Force or Chance.
Their Song was partial, but the harmony
(What could it less when Spirits immortal sing?)
Suspended Hell, and took with ravishment
The thronging audience. In discourse more sweet   555
(For Eloquence the Soul, Song charms the Sense,)
Others apart sat on a Hill retired,
In thoughts more elevate, and reasoned high
Of Providence, Foreknowledge, Will and Fate,
Fixed fate, free will, foreknowledge absolute,   560
And found no end, in wandring mazes lost.
Of good and evil much they argued then,
Of happiness and final misery,
Passion and Apathy, and glory and shame,[35]
Vain wisdom all, and false Philosophy: 565
Yet with a pleasing sorcery could charm
Pain for a while or anguish, and excite
Fallacious hope, or arm th' obdurèd breast[36]
With stubborn patience as with triple steel.[37]
Another part in Squadrons and gross Bands,[38]   570
On bold adventure to discover wide
That dismal world, if any clime perhaps
Might yield them easier habitation, bend
Four ways their flying March, along the Banks
Of four infernal Rivers that disgorge   575
Into the burning Lake their baleful streams;

---

[34] *Alcides . . . Euboic Sea* an allusion to the story of Hercules' (Alcides) death: he returns from sacking *Oechalia* with a girl; his wife Deianira sends Lichas to him with the burning shirt of Nessus, which she believes to carry a love potion; Hercules goes mad with pain, tears up the landscape, and destroys his friend Lichas. In most stories the action occurs in Euboea, an island in the Aegean close to central Greece, but Ovid places it on the nearby mainland of southern Thessaly, the location of Mount Oeta (*Metamorphoses* 9.134–272). There were cities named Oechalia in both places.

[35] *Apathy* "The quality of not feeling; exemption from passion; freedom from mental perturbation" (Johnson).
[36] *obdurèd* obdurate, hardened.
[37] *patience* "The power of suffering; endurance; the power of expecting long without rage or discontent; the power of supporting faults or injuries without revenge; long suffering" (Johnson).
[38] *Squadron* "A body of men drawn up square" (Johnson); *gross* "Thick; bulky" (Johnson).

Abhorred *Styx* the flood of deadly hate,[39]
Sad *Acheron* of sorrow, black and deep;
Cocytus, named of lamentation loud
Heard on the rueful stream; fierce *Phlegeton*   580
Whose waves of torrent fire inflame with rage.
Far off from these a slow and silent stream,
Lethe the River of Oblivion, rolls
Her wat'ry Labyrinth, whereof who drinks,
Forthwith his former state and being forgets,   585
Forgets both joy and grief, pleasure and pain.
Beyond this flood a frozen continent
Lies dark and wild, beat with perpetual storms
Of Whirlwind and dire Hail, which on firm land
Thaws not, but gathers heap, and ruin seems   590
Of ancient pile; all else deep snow and ice,
A gulf profound as that *Serbonian* bog[40]
Betwixt *Damiata* and mount *Casius* old,
Where Armies whole have sunk: the parching Air
Burns frore, and cold performs th' effect of Fire.[41]   595
Thither by harpy-footed Furies hailed,[42]
At certain revolutions all the damned
Are brought: and feel by turns the bitter change
Of fierce extremes, extremes by change more fierce,
From Beds of raging Fire to starve in Ice[43]   600
Their soft Ethereal warmth, and there to pine
Immovable, infixed, and frozen round,
Periods of time, thence hurried back to fire.
They ferry over this *Lethean* Sound
Both to and fro, their sorrow to augment,   605
And wish and struggle, as they pass, to reach
The tempting stream, with one small drop to lose
In sweet forgetfulness all pain and woe,
All in one moment, and so near the brink;
But Fate withstands, and to oppose th' attempt   610
Medusa with *Gorgonian* terror guards[44]
The Ford, and of it self the water flies
All taste of living wight, as once it fled
The lip of *Tantalus*. Thus roving on[45]

---

[39] *Styx . . . Phlegeton*   the four rivers of Hell with the literal meanings of their names.
[40] *Serbonian bog*   a region east of the Nile delta where the Persian army was supposed to have sunk as it advanced on Egypt in 350 BCE.
[41] *frore*   "Frozen. This word is not used since the time of Milton" (Johnson).
[42] *harpy-footed Furies*   harpies are winged beings with talons for snatching, sometimes described as servants to the Furies or Erinyes, avenging spirits.

[43] *starve* "To kill with cold" (Johnson).
[44] *Medusa . . . Gorgonian*   Medusa, also called Gorgo, was a monster with snakes for hair and eyes that turned the beholder to stone; her sisters were also gorgons.
[45] *Tantalus*   punished eternally for stealing the food of the gods, he stands in water up to his chin but cannot drink because the water disappears when he tries to bring his lips to it.

In confused march forlorn, th' adventrous Bands   615
With shuddring horror pale, and eyes aghast
Viewed first their lamentable lot, and found
No rest: through many a dark and dreary Vale
They passed, and many a Region dolorous,
O'er many a Frozen, many a fiery Alp,   620
Rocks, Caves, Lakes, Fens, Bogs, Dens, and shades of death,
A Universe of death, which God by curse
Created evil, for evil only good,
Where all life dies, death lives, and Nature breeds,
Perverse, all monstrous, all prodigious things,   625
Abominable, inutterable, and worse
Than fables yet have feigned, or fear conceived,
Gorgons and *Hydras*, and *Chimeras* dire.[46]
    Mean while the Adversary of God and Man,
Satan with thoughts inflamed of highest design,   630
Puts on swift wings, and towards the Gates of Hell
Explores his solitary flight; some times
He scours the right hand coast, sometimes the left,[47]
Now shaves with level wing the Deep, then soars
Up to the fiery Concave towering high.   635
As when far off at Sea a fleet descried
Hangs in the Clouds, by Equinoctial Winds
Close sailing from *Bengala*, or the Isles[48]
Of *Ternate* and *Tidore*, whence Merchants bring
Their spicy Drugs: they on the Trading Flood   640
Through the wide *Ethiopian* to the Cape[49]
Ply stemming nightly toward the Pole. So seemed
Far off the flying Fiend: at last appear
Hell bounds high reaching to the horrid Roof,[50]
And thrice threefold the Gates; three folds were Brass,   645
Three Iron, three of Adamantine Rock,
Impenetrable, impaled with circling fire,
Yet unconsumed. Before the Gates there sat
On either side a formidable shape;
The one seemed Woman to the waist, and fair,   650
But ended foul in many a scaly fold
Voluminous and vast, a Serpent armed
With mortal sting: about her middle round
A cry of Hell Hounds never ceasing barked
With wide *Cerberian* mouths full loud, and rung[51]   655

---

[46] *Gorgons* and *Hydras*, and *Chimeras* three kinds of monster: respectively, snake-haired; many-headed; and compounded of lion's head, goat's belly, and dragon's tail.

[47] *scour* "To rove; to range" (Johnson).

[48] *Bengala* . . . *Ternate* and *Tidore* trading ports in India (Bengala) and Indonesia.

[49] *the wide Ethiopian to the Cape* from the Indian Ocean to the Cape of Good Hope, on their way back to Europe from Bengala or Ternate.

[50] *horrid* latinate, fr. *horreo*, to bristle.

[51] *Cerberian* like Cerberus, the three-headed dog assigned to guard the entrance to Hades.

A hideous Peal: yet, when they list, would creep,
If aught disturbed their noise, into her womb,
And kennel there, yet there still barked and howled,
Within unseen. Far less abhorred than these
Vexed *Scylla* bathing in the Sea that parts[52]   660
Calabria from the hoarse *Trinacrian* shore:
Nor uglier follow the Night-Hag, when called[53]
In secret, riding through the Air she comes
Lured with the smell of infant blood, to dance
With *Lapland* Witches, while the labouring Moon[54]   665
Eclipses at their charms. The other shape,
If shape it might be called that shape had none
Distinguishable in member, joint, or limb,
Or substance might be called that shadow seemed,[55]
For each seemed either; black it stood as Night,   670
Fierce as ten Furies, terrible as Hell,
And shook a dreadful Dart: what seemed his head
The likeness of a Kingly Crown had on.
Satan was now at hand, and from his seat
The Monster moving onward came as fast   675
With horrid strides; Hell trembled as he strode.
Th' undaunted Fiend what this might be admired,[56]
Admired, not feared; God and his Son except,
Created thing naught valued he nor shunned;
And with disdainful look thus first began.   680
    'Whence and what art thou, execrable shape,
That dar'st, though grim and terrible, advance
Thy miscreated Front athwart my way
To yonder Gates? through them I mean to pass,
That be assured, without leave asked of thee.   685
Retire, or taste thy folly, and learn by proof,
Hell-born, not to contend with Spirits of Heav'n'.
    To whom the Goblin full of wrath, replied,
'Art thou that traitor Angel, art thou he,
Who first broke peace in Heav'n and Faith, till then   690
Unbroken, and in proud rebellious Arms
Drew after him the third part of Heav'n's Sons
Conjured against the Highest, for which both Thou
And they outcast from God, are here condemned
To waste eternal days in woe and pain?   695
And reckonst thou thy self with Spirits of Heav'n,

---

[52] *Scylla* a six-headed monster inhabiting a cave in the Straits of Messina between the toe of Italy (part of *Calabria*) and Sicily (*Trinacria*).
[53] *Night-Hag* Hecate, a goddess of the underworld who deploys ghosts and whose approach is signaled by howling dogs.

[54] *labouring* "To be in distress; to be pressed" (Johnson) by the forces causing the eclipse.
[55] *shadow* "An imperfect or faint representation; opposed to substance" (Johnson).
[56] *admired* wondered.

Hell-doomed, and breath'st defiance here and scorn
Where I reign King, and to enrage thee more,
Thy King and Lord? Back to thy punishment,
False fugitive, and to thy speed add wings,   700
Lest with a whip of Scorpions I pursue
Thy lingring, or with one stroke of this Dart
Strange horror seize thee, and pangs unfelt before'.
        So spake the grisly terror, and in shape,
So speaking and so threatning, grew tenfold   705
More dreadful and deform: on th' other side
Incensed with indignation *Satan* stood
Unterrified, and like a Comet burned,[57]
That fires the length of *Ophiucus* huge[58]
In th' arctic sky, and from his horrid hair   710
Shakes pestilence and War. Each at the head
Levelled his deadly aim; their fatal hands
No second stroke intend, and such a frown
Each cast at th' other, as when two black Clouds
With Heav'n's Artillery fraught, come rattling on   715
Over the *Caspian*, then stand front to front
Hov'ring a space, till winds the signal blow
To join their dark encounter in mid air:
So frowned the mighty Combatants, that Hell
Grew darker at their frown, so matched they stood;   720
For never but once more was either like
To meet so great a foe: and now great deeds
Had been achieved, whereof all Hell had rung,
Had not the snaky Sorceress that sat
Fast by Hell-gate and kept the fatal key,   725
Ris'n, and with hideous outcry rushed between:
        'O Father, what intends thy hand', she cried,
'Against thy only Son? What fury O Son,
Possesses thee to bend that mortal Dart
Against thy Father's head? and know'st for whom: 730
For him who sits above and laughs the while
At thee ordained his drudge, to execute
What e're his wrath, which he calls Justice, bids,
His wrath which one day will destroy ye both'.
        She spake, and at her words the hellish Pest   735
Forbore, then these to her *Satan* returned:
        'So strange thy outcry, and thy words so strange
Thou interposest, that my sudden hand[59]
Prevented spares to tell thee yet by deeds

---

[57] *Comet* (fr. Gk κομήτης, wearing long hair), heavenly bodies once thought to bring disasters like pestilence and war.

[58] *Ophiucus* (Gk serpent-bearer), a constellation.

[59] *sudden* "Hasty; violent; rash; passionate, precipitous; not in use" (Johnson).

What it intends; till first I know of thee,   740
What thing thou art, thus double-formed, and why
In this infernal Vale first met thou call'st
Me father, and that Phantasm call'st my Son?
I know thee not, nor ever saw till now
Sight more detestable than him and thee'.   745
    T' whom thus the Portress of Hell Gate replied;
'Hast thou forgot me then, and do I seem
Now in thine eye so foul, once deemed so fair
In Heav'n, when at th' Assembly, and in sight
Of all the Seraphim with thee combined   750
In bold conspiracy against Heav'n's King,
All on a sudden miserable pain
Surprised thee, dim thine eyes, and dizzy swum
In darkness, while thy head flames thick and fast
Threw forth, till on the left side op'ning wide,   755
Likest to thee in shape and count'nance bright,
Then shining heav'nly fair, a Goddess armed
Out of thy head I sprung. Amazement seized[60]
All th' Host of Heav'n; back they recoiled afraid
At first, and called me *Sin*, and for a Sign   760
Portentous held me; but familiar grown,
I pleased, and with attractive graces won
The most averse, thee chiefly, who full oft
Thy self in me thy perfect image viewing
Becam'st enamoured, and such joy thou took'st   765
With me in secret, that my womb conceived
A growing burden. Meanwhile war arose,
And fields were fought in Heav'n; wherein remained
(For what could else) to our Almighty Foe
Clear victory, to our part loss and rout   770
Through all the Empyrean: down they fell
Driv'n headlong from the Pitch of Heav'n, down
Into this Deep, and in the general fall
I also; at which time this powerful Key
Into my hands was giv'n, with charge to keep   775
These Gates for ever shut, which none can pass
Without my op'ning. Pensive here I sat
Alone, but long I sat not, till my womb,
Pregnant by thee, and now excessive grown
Prodigious motion felt and rueful throes.   780
At last this odious offspring whom thou seest
Thine own begotten, breaking violent way
Tore through my entrails, that with fear and pain
Distorted, all my nether shape thus grew

---

[60]   *Out of thy head I sprung*   the birth of Sin imitates the   Zeus but the connection between lust, sin, and death
birth of Athena, goddess of wisdom, from the head of   comes from James 1.15.

Transformed: but he my inbred enemy   785
Forth issued, brandishing his fatal Dart
Made to destroy: I fled, and cried out *Death*;
Hell trembled at the hideous Name, and sighed
From all her Caves, and back resounded *Death*;
I fled, but he pursued (though more, it seems,   790
Inflamed with lust than rage) and swifter far,
Me overtook his mother all dismayed,
And in embraces forcible and foul
Engendring with me, of that rape begot
These yelling Monsters that with ceaseless cry   795
Surround me, as thou sawst, hourly conceived
And hourly born, with sorrow infinite
To me, for when they list into the womb
That bred them they return, and howl and gnaw
My Bowels, their repast; then bursting forth   800
Afresh with conscious terrors vex me round,
That rest or intermission none I find.
Before mine eyes in opposition sits
Grim *Death* my Son and foe who sets them on,
And me his Parent would full soon devour   805
For want of other prey, but that he knows
His end with mine involved; and knows that I
Should prove a bitter Morsel, and his bane,
When ever that shall be; so Fate pronounced.
But thou O Father, I forewarn thee, shun   810
His deadly arrow; neither vainly hope
To be invulnerable in those bright Arms,
Though tempered Heav'nly, for that mortal dint,
Save he who reigns above, none can resist'.

     She finished, and the subtle Fiend his lore   815
Soon learned, now milder, and thus answered smooth.
'Dear Daughter, since thou claim'st me for thy Sire,
And my fair Son here showst me, the dear pledge
Of dalliance had with thee in Heav'n, and joys
Then sweet, now sad to mention, through dire change   820
Befall'n us unforeseen, unthought of, know
I come no enemy, but to set free
From out this dark and dismal house of pain,
Both him and thee, and all the heav'nly Host
Of Spirits that in our just pretences armed   825
Fell with us from on high: from them I go
This uncouth errand sole, and one for all
My self expose, with lonely steps to tread
Th' unfounded deep, and through the void immense
To search with wandring quest, a place foretold   830
Should be, and, by concurring signs, ere now
Created vast and round, a place of bliss

In the purlieus of Heav'n, and therein placed
A race of upstart Creatures, to supply
Perhaps our vacant room, though more removed,   835
Lest Heav'n, surcharged with potent multitude
Might hap to move new broils: Be this or aught
Than this more secret now designed, I haste
To know, and this once known, shall soon return,
And bring ye to the place where Thou and Death   840
Shall dwell at ease, and up and down unseen
Wing silently the buxom Air, embalmed[61]
With odours; there ye shall be fed and filled
Immeasurably, all things shall be your prey'.
He ceased, for both seemed highly pleased, and Death   845
Grinned horrible a ghastly smile, to hear
His famine should be filled, and blessed his maw
Destined to that good hour: no less rejoiced
His mother bad, and thus bespake her Sire.
    'The key of this infernal Pit by due,   850
And by command of Heav'n's all-powerful King
I keep, by him forbidden to unlock
These Adamantine Gates; against all force
Death ready stands to interpose his dart,
Fearless to be o'ermatched by living might.   855
But what owe I to his commands above
Who hates me, and hath hither thrust me down
Into this gloom of *Tartarus* profound,
To sit in hateful Office here confined,
Inhabitant of Heav'n, and heav'nly-born,   860
Here in perpetual agony and pain,
With terrors and with clamours compassed round
Of mine own brood, that on my bowels feed:
Thou art my Father, thou my Author, thou
My being gav'st me; whom should I obey   865
But thee, whom follow? thou wilt bring me soon
To that new world of light and bliss, among
The Gods who live at ease, where I shall Reign
At thy right hand voluptuous, as beseems
Thy daughter and thy darling, without end'.   870
    Thus saying, from her side the fatal Key,
Sad instrument of all our woe, she took;
And towards the Gate rolling her bestial train,
Forthwith the huge Portcullis high up drew,
Which but her self, not all the *Stygian* powers   875
Could once have moved; then in the key-hole turns

---

[61] *buxom*   "It originally signified obedient, as John de
Trevisa, a clergyman, tells his patron, that he is 'obedient
and *buxom* to all his commands'" (Johnson).

Th' intricate wards, and every Bolt and Bar
Of massy Iron or solid rock with ease
Unfastens: on a sudden open fly
With impetuous recoil and jarring sound   880
Th' infernal doors, and on their hinges grate
Harsh Thunder, that the lowest bottom shook
Of *Erebus*. She opened, but to shut[62]
Excelled her power; the Gates wide op'n stood,
That with extended wings a Bannered Host   885
Under spread Ensigns marching might pass through
With Horse and Chariots ranked in loose array;
So wide they stood, and like a Furnace mouth
Cast forth redounding smoke and ruddy flame.
Before their eyes in sudden view appear   890
The secrets of the hoary deep, a dark
Illimitable Ocean without bound,
Without dimension; where length, breadth, & heighth,
And time and place are lost; where eldest *Night*
And *Chaos*, ancestors of Nature, hold   895
Eternal *Anarchy*, amidst the noise
Of endless Wars, and by confusion stand.
For hot, cold, moist, and dry, four Champions fierce[63]
Strive here for Mastry, and to Battle bring
Their embryon Atoms; they around the flag[64]   900
Of each his Faction, in their several Clans,
Light-armed or heavy, sharp, smooth, swift, or slow,
Swarm populous, unnumbered as the Sands
Of *Barca* or *Cyrene's* torrid soil,[65]
Levied to side with warring Winds, and poise   905
Their lighter wings. To whom these most adhere,
He rules a moment; *Chaos* umpire sits,
And by decision more embroils the fray
By which he Reigns: next him high Arbiter
Chance governs all. Into this wild Abyss,   910
The Womb of nature and perhaps her Grave,
Of neither Sea, nor Shore, nor Air, nor Fire,
But all these in their pregnant causes mixed
Confus'dly, and which thus must ever fight,
Unless th' Almighty Maker them ordain   915
His dark materials to create more worlds,
Into this wild Abyss the wary fiend
Stood on the brink of Hell and looked a while,

---

[62] *Erebus* a place of darkness making a passage between earth and Hades.

[63] *hot, cold, moist, and dry* the four elements in the old physics: fire, earth, water, air (cf. l. 912 below).

[64] *embryon Atoms* embryonic constituent elements of matter, as described by Lucretius in *De Rerum Natura*.

[65] *Barca, Cyrene* cities of Cyrenaica, the land west of Egypt on the North African coast.

Pondering his Voyage; for no narrow frith[66]
He had to cross. Nor was his ear less pealed[67]   66
With noises loud and ruinous (to compare
Great things with small) than when *Bellona* storms,[68]
With all her battering Engines bent to raze
Some Capital City; or less than if this frame
Of Heav'n were falling, and these Elements   925
In mutiny had from her Axle torn
The steadfast Earth. At last his Sail-broad vans[69]
He spreads for flight, and in the surging smoke
Uplifted spurns the ground, thence many a League
As in a cloudy Chair ascending rides   930
Audacious, but that seat soon failing, meets
A vast vacuity: all unawares
Fluttring his pennons vain plumb down he drops[70]
Ten thousand fadom deep, and to this hour[71]
Down had been falling, had not by ill chance   935
The strong rebuff of some tumultuous cloud
Instinct with Fire and Nitre, hurried him
As many miles aloft: that fury stayed,
Quenched in a boggy *Syrtis*, neither Sea,[72]
Nor good dry Land: nigh foundered on he fares,   940
Treading the crude consistence, half on foot,
Half flying; behoves him now both Oar and Sail.
As when a Gryphon through the Wilderness[73]
With winged course o'er Hill or moory Dale,
Pursues the *Arimaspian*, who by stealth   945
Had from his wakeful custody purloined
The guarded Gold: So eagerly the Fiend
O'er bog or steep, through strait, rough, dense, or rare,
With head, hands, wings or feet pursues his way,
And swims, or sinks, or wades, or creeps, or flies: 950
At length a universal hubbub wild
Of stunning sounds, and voices all confused
Borne through the hollow dark assaults his ear
With loudest vehemence: thither he plies,
Undaunted to meet there what ever power   955
Or Spirit of the nethermost Abyss
Might in that noise reside, of whom to ask

---

[66] *frith* firth, arm of the sea.
[67] *peal* "To assail with noise" (Johnson).
[68] *Bellona* Roman goddess of war.
[69] *van* "A wing with which the air is beaten" (Johnson).
[70] *pennon* poetic for *pinion*, wing.
[71] *fadom* fathoms.
[72] *Syrtis* according to old dictionaries, two quicksands on the African shore; more properly, the name of two bays, famous for treacherous navigation and dangerous, sandy shores.
[73] *Gryphon* a beast with the head of a lion and the wings and talon of an eagle, guardian of the gold of the north, enemy of the one-eyed Arimaspians who dwelt in Scythia, north of the Black Sea.

Which way the nearest coast of darkness lies
Bordering on light; when straight behold the Throne
Of *Chaos*, and his dark Pavilion spread   960
Wide on the wasteful Deep; with him enthroned
Sat Sable-vested *Night*, eldest of things,
The consort of his reign; and by them stood
Orcus and *Ades*, and the dreaded name[74]
Of *Demogorgon*; *Rumour* next, and *Chance*,[75]   965
And *Tumult* and *Confusion* all embroiled,
And *Discord* with a thousand various mouths.
        T' whom *Satan*, turning boldly, thus. 'Ye Powers
And Spirits of this nethermost Abyss,
Chaos and *ancient Night*, I come no Spy,   970
With purpose to explore or to disturb
The secrets of your Realm, but by constraint
Wandring this darksome Desert, as my way,
Lies through your spacious Empire up to light,
Alone, and without guide, half lost, I seek   975
What readiest path leads where your gloomy bounds
Confine with Heav'n; or if some other place
From your Dominion won, th' Ethereal King
Possesses lately, thither to arrive
I travel this profound, direct my course;   980
Directed no mean recompense it brings
To your behoof, if I that Region lost,[76]
All usurpation thence expelled, reduce
To her original darkness and your sway
(Which is my present journey) and once more   985
Erect the Standard there of *ancient Night*;
Yours be th' advantage all, mine the revenge'.
        Thus *Satan*; and him thus the Anarch old
With faltring speech and visage incomposed
Answered. 'I know thee, stranger, who thou art,   990
That mighty leading Angel, who of late
Made head against Heav'n's King, though overthrown.
I saw and heard, for such a numerous Host
Fled not in silence through the frighted deep
With ruin upon ruin, rout on rout,   995
Confusion worse confounded; and Heav'n Gates
Poured out by millions her victorious Bands
Pursuing. I upon my Frontiers here
Keep residence; if all I can will serve,

---

[74] *Orcus* and *Ades* (Hades) both names for the god of
the underworld.
[75] *Demogorgon* a renaissance name for the primaeval
god, corrupted from "demiurge," and dreaded because

it sounds like "gorgon" (see Spenser, *Faerie Queene*
4.2.47).
[76] *lost* highly ironic because paradise is now *lost* to the
rule of Chaos but later will be *lost* to all.

That little which is left so to defend, 1000
Encroached on still through our intestine broils[77]
Weakning the Sceptre of old *Night*: first Hell
Your dungeon, stretching far and wide beneath;
Now lately Heav'n and Earth, another World
Hung o'er my Realm, linked in a golden Chain[78] 1005
To that side Heav'n from whence your Legions fell:
If that way be your walk, you have not far;
So much the nearer danger; go and speed;
Havoc and spoil and ruin are my gain'.

   He ceased; and *Satan* stayed not to reply, 1010
But glad that now his Sea should find a shore,
With fresh alacrity and force renewed
Springs upward like a Pyramid of fire
Into the wild expanse, and through the shock
Of fighting Elements, on all sides round 1015
Environed wins his way; harder beset
And more endangered, than when *Argo* passed[79]
Through *Bosporus* betwixt the justling Rocks:
Or when *Ulysses* on the Larboard shunned[80]
Charybdis, and by th' other whirlpool steered. 1020
So he with difficulty and labour hard
Moved on, with difficulty and labour he;
But he once past, soon after when man fell,
Strange alteration! Sin and Death amain
Following his track, such was the will of Heav'n, 1025
Paved after him a broad and beaten way
Over the dark Abyss, whose boiling Gulf
Tamely endured a Bridge of wondrous length
From Hell continued reaching th' utmost Orb
Of this frail World; by which the Spirits perverse 1030
With easy intercourse pass to and fro
To tempt or punish mortals, except whom
God and good Angels guard by special grace.

   But now at last the sacred influence
Of light appears, and from the walls of Heav'n 1035
Shoots far into the bosom of dim Night
A glimmering dawn; here Nature first begins
Her farthest verge, and *Chaos* to retire
As from her outmost works a broken foe

---

[77] *intestine* domestic, internal; cf. *Henry IV* Part 1, 1.1. 12.
[78] *golden Chain* an image of divine order from Homer (*Iliad* 8.18–27) to the eighteenth century, when it becomes known as the great chain of being (cf l. 1051 below).
[79] *Argo* the ship used by Jason and his argonauts; on their quest for the golden fleece, they had to pass through the dangerous *Bosporus*, a strait leading to the Black Sea.
[80] *Ulysses . . . steered Charybdis* is the whirlpool in the straits of Messina, on the Larboard or Sicilian side as Ulysses sailed west; he preferred the rocks on the starboard, Italian side where Scylla snatched six of his men (*Odyssey* 12.234–59).

With tumult less and with less hostile din;   1040
That *Satan* with less toil, and now with ease,
Wafts on the calmer wave by dubious light
And like a weather-beaten Vessel holds
Gladly the Port, though Shrouds and Tackle torn;
Or in the emptier waste, resembling Air,   1045
Weighs his spread wings, at leisure to behold[81]
Far off th' Empyreal Heav'n, extended wide
In circuit, undetermined square or round,
With Opal Towers and Battlements adorned
Of living Sapphire, once his native Seat: 1050
And fast by hanging in a golden Chain
This pendant world, in bigness as a Star[82]
Of smallest Magnitude close by the Moon.
Thither full fraught with mischievous revenge,
Accursed, and in a cursèd hour he hies.   1055

BOOK III
THE ARGUMENT

God sitting on his Throne sees Satan *flying towards this world, then newly created; shows him to the Son who sat at his right hand; foretells the success of* Satan *in perverting mankind; clears his own Justice and Wisdom from all imputation, having created Man free and able enough to have withstood his Tempter; yet declares his purpose of Grace towards him, in regard he fell not of his own malice, as did* Satan, *but by him seduced. The Son of God renders praises to his Father for the manifestation of his gracious purpose towards Man; but God again declares, that Grace cannot be extended towards Man without the satisfaction of Divine Justice; Man hath offended the majesty of God by aspiring to Godhead, and therefore with all his Progeny devoted to death must die, unless some one can be found sufficient to answer for his offence, and undergo his Punishment. The Son of God freely offers himself a Ransom for Man: the Father accepts him, ordains his incarnation, pronounces his exaltation above all Nations in Heaven and Earth; commands all the Angels to adore him, they obey, and hymning to their Harps in full Choir, celebrate the Father and the Son. Meanwhile* Satan *alights upon the bare Convex of this World's outermost Orb; where wandering he first finds a place since called The Limbo of Vanity; what persons and things fly up thither; thence comes to the Gate of Heaven, described ascending by stairs, and the waters above the Firmament that flow about it: His passage thence to the Orb of the Sun; he finds there* Uriel *the Regent of that Orb, but first changes himself into the shape of a meaner Angel; and pretending a zealous desire to behold the new Creation and Man whom God had placed here, inquires of him the place of his habitation, and is directed; alights first on Mount* Niphates.

Hail holy Light, offspring of Heav'n first-born,
Or of th' Eternal Coeternal beam
May I express thee unblam'd? since God is light,[1]
And never but in unapproachèd light

---

[81] *weighs* raises.
[82] *pendant* or *pendent*,   the meanings of both the noun and the participle are present, as well as the sense of *dependent*.

BOOK III
[1]   *May I express thee*   two metrical feet, with coalescence between *I* and *e*.

Dwelt from Eternity, dwelt then in thee,   5
Bright effluence of bright essence increate.
Or hear'st thou rather pure Ethereal stream,[2]
Whose Fountain who shall tell? before the Sun,
Before the Heav'ns thou wert, and at the voice
Of God, as with a Mantle didst invest   10
The rising world of water dark and deep,
Won from the void and formless infinite.
Thee I re-visit now with bolder wing,
Escaped the Stygian Pool, though long detained
In that obscure sojourn, while in my flight   15
Through utter and through middle darkness borne
With other notes than to the *Orphean* Lyre[3]
I sung of *Chaos* and *eternal Night*
Taught by the heav'nly Muse to venture down
The dark descent, and up to reascend,[4]   20
Though hard and rare: thee I revisit safe,
And feel thy sovereign vital Lamp; but thou
Revisit'st not these eyes, that roll in vain
To find thy piercing ray, and find no dawn;
So thick a drop serene hath quenched their Orbs,[5]   25
Or dim suffusion veiled. Yet not the more
Cease I to wander where the Muses haunt
Clear Spring, or shady Grove, or Sunny Hill,
Smit with the love of sacred Song; but chief
Thee *Sion* and the flowry Brooks beneath[6]   30
That wash thy hallowed feet, and warbling flow,
Nightly I visit: nor sometimes forget[7]
Those other two equalled with me in Fate,
So were I equalled with them in renown,
Blind *Thamyris* and blind *Maeonides*,[8]   35
And *Tiresias* and *Phineus* Prophets old.[9]
Then feed on thoughts, that voluntary move
Harmonious numbers; as the wakeful Bird[10]
Sings darkling, and in shadiest Covert hid[11]

[2] *hear'st* fr. hear, "To acknowledge. A Latin phrase" (Johnson), Lat. *audire*, meaning to hear but also to hear oneself spoken of as.
[3] *Orphean Lyre* Orpheus was a fabulous pre-Homeric poet, whose lyre playing charmed wild beasts; he ventured into the underworld but failed to recover his wife Eurydice.
[4] On the difficulty of escaping hell, Milton recalls *Aeneid* 6.128–9, a passage that had become proverbial.
[5] *drop serene* "Gutta serena. An obstruction of the optic nerve" (Johnson); *dim suffusion* is similarly medical. Milton's blindness was almost total by 1652.

[6] *Sion . . . Brooks* a hill near Jerusalem and the neighboring Siloa and Kidron streams (see 1.10).
[7] Milton suggests that he receives his poetic inspiration at night.
[8] *Thamyris* legendary Thracian poet, blinded by the gods; *Maeonides* a patronymic of Homer.
[9] *Tiresias* a prophet blinded by the gods; *Phineus* a Thracian king with prophetic powers, blinded by Zeus.
[10] *the wakeful Bird* the nightingale.
[11] *darkling* "(a participle as it seems from *darkle*, which yet I have never found) Being in the dark; being without light: a word merely poetical" (Johnson).

Tunes her nocturnal Note. Thus with the year   40
Seasons return, but not to me returns
Day, or the sweet approach of Ev'n or Morn,
Or sight of vernal bloom, or Summer's Rose,
Or flocks, or herds, or human face divine;
But cloud in stead, and ever-during dark   45
Surrounds me, from the cheerful ways of men
Cut off, and for the Book of knowledge fair
Presented with a Universal blank
Of Nature's works to me expunged and razed,
And wisdom at one entrance quite shut out.   50
So much the rather thou Celestial light
Shine inward, and the mind through all her powers
Irradiate, there plant eyes, all mist from thence
Purge and disperse, that I may see and tell
Of things invisible to mortal sight.   55
        Now had th' Almighty Father from above,
From the pure Empyrean where he sits
High Throned above all heighth, bent down his eye,
His own works and their works at once to view:
About him all the Sanctities of Heav'n[12]   60
Stood thick as Stars, and from his sight received
Beatitude past utterance; on his right
The radiant image of his Glory sat,
His only Son; on earth he first beheld
Our two first Parents, yet the only two   65
Of mankind, in the happy Garden placed,
Reaping immortal fruits of joy and love,
Uninterrupted joy, unrivalled love,
In blissful solitude; he then surveyed
Hell and the Gulf between, and *Satan* there   70
Coasting the wall of Heav'n on this side Night
In the dun Air sublime, and ready now[13]
To stoop with wearied wings, and willing feet
On the bare outside of this World, that seemed
Firm land embosomed, without Firmament,   75
Uncertain which, in Ocean or in Air.
Him God beholding from his prospect high,
Wherein past, present, future he beholds,
Thus to his only Son foreseeing spake.
        'Only begotten Son, seest thou what rage   80
Transports our adversary, whom no bounds
Prescribed, no bars of Hell, nor all the chains
Heaped on him there, nor yet the main Abyss
Wide interrupt can hold; so bent he seems[14]

---

[12] *Sanctities* angels.
[13] *dun* "Dark; gloomy" (Johnson).

[14] *wide interrupt* having caused a great separation (adverb plus past participle).

On desperate revenge, that shall redound   85
Upon his own rebellious head. And now
Through all restraint broke loose he wings his way
Not far off Heav'n, in the Precincts of light,[15]
Directly towards the new created World,
And Man there placed, with purpose to assay[16]   90
If him by force he can destroy, or, worse,
By some false guile pervert; and shall pervert
For man will hearken to his glozing lies,[17]
And easily transgress the sole Command,[18]
Sole pledge of his obedience: So will fall,   95
He and his faithless Progeny: whose fault?
Whose but his own? ingrate, he had of me
All he could have; I made him just and right,
Sufficient to have stood, though free to fall.
Such I created all th' Ethereal Powers   100
And Spirits, both them who stood and them who failed;
Freely they stood who stood, and fell who fell.
Not free, what proof could they have giv'n sincere
Of true allegiance, constant Faith or Love,
Where only what they needs must do, appeared,   105
Not what they would? what praise could they receive?
What pleasure I from such obedience paid,
When Will and Reason (Reason also is choice)
Useless and vain, of freedom both despoiled,
Made passive both, had served necessity,   110
Not me. They therefore as to right belonged,
So were created, nor can justly accuse
Their maker, or their making, or their Fate,
As if predestination over-ruled
Their will, disposed by absolute Decree   115
Or high foreknowledge; they themselves decreed
Their own revolt, not I: if I foreknew,
Foreknowledge had no influence on their fault,
Which had no less proved certain unforeknown.
So without least impulse or shadow of Fate,   120
Or aught by me immutably foreseen,
They trespass, Authors to themselves in all
Both what they judge and what they choose; for so
I formed them free, and free they must remain,
Till they enthrall themselves: I else must change   125
Their nature, and revoke the high Decree
Unchangeable, Eternal, which ordained
Their freedom: they themselves ordained their fall.
The first sort by their own suggestion fell,[19]

---

[15] *Precincts* "Outward limit; boundary" (Johnson).
[16] *assay* "Attack; trouble" (Johnson).
[17] *glozing* flattering, fawning.
[18] *easily* readily.
[19] *The first sort* the angels who fell.

Self-tempted, self-depraved: Man falls deceived   130
By the other first: Man therefore shall find grace,
The other none: in Mercy and Justice both,
Through Heav'n and Earth, so shall my glory excel,[20]
But Mercy first and last shall brightest shine'.

   Thus while God spake, ambrosial fragrance filled   135
All Heav'n, and in the blessèd Spirits elect
Sense of new joy ineffable diffused:
Beyond compare the Son of God was seen
Most glorious, in him all his Father shone
Substantially expressed, and in his face   140
Divine compassion visibly appeared,
Love without end, and without measure Grace,
Which uttering thus he to his Father spake.

   'O Father, gracious was that word which closed
Thy sovereign sentence, that Man should find grace;   145
For which both Heav'n and Earth shall high extol
Thy praises, with th' innumerable sound
Of Hymns and sacred Songs, wherewith thy Throne
Encompassed shall resound thee ever blest.
For should Man finally be lost, should Man   150
Thy creature late so loved, thy youngest Son
Fall circumvented thus by fraud, though joined
With his own folly? that be from thee far,
That far be from thee, Father, who art Judge
Of all things made, and judgest only right.   155
Or shall the Adversary thus obtain
His end, and frustrate thine, shall he fulfil
His malice, and thy goodness bring to nought,
Or proud return though to his heavier doom,
Yet with revenge accomplished, and to Hell   160
Draw after him the whole Race of mankind,
By him corrupted? or wilt thou thy self
Abolish thy Creation, and unmake,
For him, what for thy glory thou hast made?
So should thy goodness and thy greatness both   165
Be questioned and blasphemed without defence'.

   To whom the great Creator thus replied.
'O Son, in whom my Soul hath chief delight,
Son of my bosom, Son who art alone
My word, my wisdom, and effectual might,   170
All hast thou spoken as my thoughts are, all
As my Eternal purpose hath decreed:
Man shall not quite be lost, but saved who will,
Yet not of will in him, but grace in me

---

[20] *my glory excel* two metrical feet; coalescence between the sound of *y* and following *e*.

Freely vouchsafed; once more I will renew   175
His lapsèd powers, though forfeit and enthralled
By sin to foul exorbitant desires;
Upheld by me, yet once more he shall stand
On even ground against his mortal foe
By me upheld, that he may know how frail   180
His fall'n condition is, and to me owe
All his deliv'rance, and to none but me.
Some I have chosen of peculiar grace[21]
Elect above the rest; so is my will:
The rest shall hear me call, and oft be warned   185
Their sinful state, and to appease betimes
Th' incensèd Deity, while offered grace
Invites; for I will clear their senses dark,
What may suffice, and soften stony hearts
To pray, repent, and bring obedience due.   190
To Prayer, repentance, and obedience due,
Though but endeavoured with sincere intent,
Mine ear shall not be slow, mine eye not shut.
And I will place within them as a guide
My Umpire *Conscience*, whom if they will hear,   195
Light after light well used they shall attain,
And to the end persisting, safe arrive.
This my long sufferance and my day of grace
They who neglect and scorn, shall never taste;
But hard be hardened, blind be blinded more,   200
That they may stumble on, and deeper fall;
And none but such from mercy I exclude.
But yet all is not done; Man disobeying,
Disloyal, breaks his fealty, and sins
Against the high Supremacy of Heav'n,   205
Affecting God-head, and, so losing all,
To expiate his Treason hath nought left,
But to destruction sacred and devote,
He with his whole posterity must die,
Die he or Justice must; unless for him   210
Some other able, and as willing, pay
The rigid satisfaction, death for death.[22]
Say Heav'nly powers, where shall we find such love,
Which of ye will be mortal to redeem
Man's mortal crime, and just th' unjust to save,   215
Dwells in all Heav'n charity so dear?'
He asked, but all the Heav'nly Quire stood mute,

---

[21] *Some* are *Elect*, but *the rest* through *prayer* and *repentance* may *safe arrive* (l. 197).

[22] *rigid* unyielding or cruel; *satisfaction* "Amends; atonement for a crime; recompense for an injury" (Johnson).

And silence was in Heav'n: on man's behalf
Patron or Intercessor none appeared,
Much less that durst upon his own head draw   220
The deadly forfeiture, and ransom set.
And now without redemption all mankind
Must have been lost, adjudged to Death and Hell
By doom severe, had not the Son of God,
In whom the fullness dwells of love divine,   225
His dearest mediation thus renewed.
    'Father, thy word is passed, man shall find grace;
And shall grace not find means, that finds her way,
The speediest of thy wingèd messengers,
To visit all thy creatures, and to all   230
Comes unprevented, unimplored, unsought,[23]
Happy for man, so coming; he her aid
Can never seek, once dead in sins and lost;
Atonement for himself or offering meet,
Indebted and undone, hath none to bring: 235
Behold me then, me for him, life for life
I offer, on me let thine anger fall;
Account me man; I for his sake will leave
Thy bosom, and this glory next to thee
Freely put off, and for him lastly die   240
Well pleased, on me let Death wreck all his rage;[24]
Under his gloomy power I shall not long
Lie vanquished. Thou hast giv'n me to possess
Life in my self for ever; by thee I live,
Though now to Death I yield, and am his due   245
All that of me can die, yet that debt paid,
Thou wilt not leave me in the loathsome grave
His prey, nor suffer my unspotted Soul
For ever with corruption there to dwell;
But I shall rise Victorious, and subdue   250
My Vanquisher, spoiled of his vaunted spoil;
Death his death's wound shall then receive, and stoop
Inglorious, of his mortal sting disarmed.
I through the ample Air in Triumph high
Shall lead Hell Captive maugre Hell, and show[25]   255
The powers of darkness bound. Thou at the sight
Pleased, out of Heaven shalt look down and smile,
While by thee raised I ruin all my Foes,
Death last, and with his carcass glut the grave:
Then with the multitude of my redeemed   260
Shall enter Heav'n long absent, and return,

---

[23] *unprevented* "Unpreceded by anything" (Johnson).   [25] *maugre* "In spite of; notwithstanding; it is now out
[24] *wreck* wreak.   of use" (Johnson).

Father, to see thy face, wherein no cloud
Of anger shall remain, but peace assured,
And reconcilement; wrath shall be no more
Thenceforth, but in thy presence Joy entire'.   265
    His words here ended, but his meek aspéct
Silent yet spake, and breathed immortal love
To mortal men, above which only shone
Filial obedience: as a sacrifice
Glad to be offered, he attends the will   270
Of his great Father. Admiration seized
All Heav'n, what this might mean, and whither tend
Wondring; but soon th' Almighty thus replied:
    'O thou in Heav'n and Earth the only peace
Found out for mankind under wrath, O thou   275
My sole complacence! Well thou know'st how dear,[26]
To me are all my works; nor Man the least
Though last created, that for him I spare
Thee from my bosom and right hand, to save,
By losing thee a while, the whole Race lost.   280
Thou therefore whom thou only canst redeem,
Their Nature also to thy Nature join;
And be thy self Man among men on Earth,
Made flesh, when time shall be, of Virgin seed,
By wondrous birth: Be thou in *Adam's* room   285
The Head of all mankind, though *Adam's* Son.
As in him perish all men, so in thee
As from a second root shall be restored,
As many as are restored, without thee none.
His crime makes guilty all his Sons, thy merit[27]   290
Imputed shall absolve them who renounce
Their own both righteous and unrighteous deeds,
And live in thee transplanted, and from thee
Receive new life. So Man, as is most just,[28]
Shall satisfy for Man, be judged and die,   295
And dying rise, and rising with him raise
His Brethren, ransomed with his own dear life.
So Heav'nly love shall outdo Hellish hate
Giving to death, and dying to redeem,
So dearly to redeem what Hellish hate   300
So easily destroyed, and still destroys
In those who, when they may, accept not grace.
Nor shalt thou by descending to assume
Man's Nature, lessen or degrade thine own.

---

[26]   *complacence*   "The cause of pleasure; joy" (Johnson).   [28]   *Man*   Christ in his human incarnation.
[27]   *thy merit Imputed*   the act of imputing to Christ the
credit for human deeds.

Because thou hast, though Throned in highest bliss   305
Equal to God, and equally enjoying
God-like fruition, quitted all to save
A World from utter loss, and hast been found
By Merit more than Birthright Son of God,
Found worthiest to be so by being Good,   310
Far more than Great or High; because in thee
Love hath abounded more than glory abounds[29]
Therefore thy Humiliation shall exalt
With thee thy Manhood also to this Throne,
Here shalt thou sit incarnate, here shalt Reign   315
Both God and Man, Son both of God and Man,
Anointed universal King, all Power
I give thee, reign for ever, and assume
Thy Merits; under thee, as Head Supreme
Thrones, Princedoms, Powers, Dominions I reduce: 320
All knees to thee shall bow, of them that bide
In Heav'n, or Earth, or under Earth in Hell.
When thou attended gloriously from Heav'n
Shalt in the Sky appear, and from thee send
The summoning Arch-Angels to proclaim   325
Thy dread Tribunal: forthwith from all Winds[30]
The living, and forthwith the cited dead[31]
Of all past Ages to the general Doom
Shall hasten, such a peal shall rouse their sleep.
Then all thy Saints assembled, thou shalt judge   330
Bad men and Angels, they arraigned shall sink
Beneath thy Sentence; Hell her numbers full,
Thenceforth shall be for ever shut. Meanwhile
The World shall burn, and from her ashes spring
New Heav'n and Earth, wherein the just shall dwell,   335
And after all their tribulations long
See golden days, fruitful of golden deeds,
With Joy and Love triúmphing, and fair Truth.
Then thou thy regal Sceptre shalt lay by,
For regal Sceptre then no more shall need,   340
God shall be All in All. But all ye Gods,
Adore him, who to compass all this dies,
Adore the Son, and honour him as me'.
    No sooner had th' Almighty ceased, but all
The multitude of Angels with a shout   345
Loud as from numbers without number, sweet
As from blest voices, uttering joy, Heav'n rung
With Jubilee, and loud Hosannas filled
Th' eternal Regions: lowly reverent

---

[29] *glory abounds* coalescence of *y* and *a* sounds.   [31] *cited* summoned.
[30] *Winds* directions.

Towards either Throne they bow, and to the ground   350
With solemn adoration down they cast
Their crowns inwove with Amarant and Gold,[32]
Immortal Amarant, a flowr which once
In Paradise, fast by the Tree of Life,
Began to bloom, but soon for man's offence   355
To Heav'n removed where first it grew, there grows,
And flowrs aloft shading the Fount of Life,
And where the river of Bliss through midst of Heav'n[33]
Rolls o'er *Elysian* Flowrs her Amber stream;
With these that never fade the Spirits elect   360
Bind their resplendent locks inwreathed with beams,
Now in loose Garlands thick thrown off, the bright
Pavement that like a Sea of Jasper shone
Impurpled with Celestial Roses smiled.[34]
Then Crowned again their golden Harps they took,   365
Harps ever tuned, that glittering by their side
Like Quivers hung, and with Preamble sweet
Of charming symphony they introduce
Their sacred Song, and waken raptures high;
No voice exempt, no voice but well could join   370
Melodious part, such concord is in Heav'n.
    Thee Father first they sung Omnipotent,
Immutable, Immortal, Infinite,
Eternal King; the Author of all being,
Fountain of Light, thy self invisible   375
Amidst the glorious brightness where thou sit'st
Throned inaccessible, but when thou shad'st
The full blaze of thy beams, and, through a cloud
Drawn round about thee like a radiant Shrine,
Dark with excessive bright thy skirts appear,   380
Yet dazzle Heav'n, that brightest Seraphim
Approach not, but with both wings veil their eyes,
Thee next they sang of all Creation first,
Begotten Son, Divine Similitude,
In whose conspicuous count'nance, without cloud   385
Made visible, th' Almighty Father shines,
Whom else no Creature can behold; on thee
Impressed the effulgence of his Glory abides,[35]
Transfused on thee his ample Spirit rests.

---

[32] *Amarant* amaranth, "The name of a plant . . . 'The long pendulous amaranth, with reddish, coloured seeds commonly called Love lies a bleeding' (Phillip Miller) . . . 2. In poetry it is sometimes an imaginary flower supposed according to its name (Gk α–μαραίνω) never to fade" (Johnson).

[33] *river of Bliss* the image is biblical (Revelation 22.1), but Milton, characteristically, joins it with the classical imagery of *Elysium*, the Isles of the Blessed, or the pleasantest part of the underworld.

[34] *smile* "To look gay or joyous" (Johnson); covered with flowers, the pavement smiles.

[35] Vowel coalescence occurs twice in this line.

He Heav'n of Heavens and all the Powers therein   390
By thee created, and by thee threw down
Th' aspiring Dominations: Thou that day[36]
Thy Father's dreadful Thunder didst not spare,
Nor stop thy flaming Chariot wheels, that shook
Heav'n's everlasting Frame, while o'er the necks   395
Thou drov'st of warring Angels disarrayed.
Back from pursuit thy Powers with loud acclaim
Thee only extolled, Son of thy Father's might,
To execute fierce vengeance on his foes,
Not so on Man: him through their malice fall'n,   400
Father of Mercy and Grace, thou didst not doom
So strictly, but much more to pity incline:
No sooner did thy dear and only Son
Perceive thee purposed not to doom frail Man
So strictly, but much more to pity enclined,   405
He to appease thy wrath, and end the strife
Of Mercy and Justice in thy face discerned,
Regardless of the Bliss wherein he sat
Second to thee, offered himself to die
For man's offence. O unexampled love,   410
Love no where to be found less than Divine!
Hail, Son of God, Saviour of Men, thy Name
Shall be the copious matter of my Song
Henceforth, and never shall my Harp thy praise
Forget, nor from thy Father's praise disjoin.   415
   Thus they in Heav'n, above the starry Sphere,[37]
Their happy hours in joy and hymning spent.
Mean while upon the firm opacous Globe[38]
Of this round World, whose first convex divides
The luminous inferior Orbs, enclosed   420
From *Chaos*, and the inroad of Darkness old,
Satan alighted walks: a Globe far off
It seemed, now seems a boundless Continent
Dark, waste, and wild, under the frown of Night
Starless exposed, and ever-threatning storms   425
Of *Chaos* blustring round, inclement sky;
Save on that side which from the wall of Heav'n
Though distant far some small reflection gains
Of glimmering air less vexed with tempest loud:
Here walked the Fiend at large in spacious field.   430
As when a Vulture on *Imaus* bred,[39]
Whose snowy ridge the roving *Tartar* bounds,

[36] *Th' aspiring Dominations* Satan and the other rebels.
[37] *the starry Sphere* one of the outer concentric spheres
in the Ptolemaic system of the universe (see below, ll.
481–3).
[38] *opacous* "Dark; obscure; not transparent" (Johnson).
[39] *Imaus* central Asian mountain, philologically related to Skt. *Himalaya* (abode of snow).

Dislodging from a Region scarce of prey
To gorge the flesh of Lambs or yeanling Kids[40]
On Hills where Flocks are fed, flies toward the Springs   435
Of *Ganges* or *Hydaspes*, *Indian* streams;
But in his way lights on the barren Plains
Of *Sericana*, where *Chineses* drive[41]
With Sails and Wind their cany Wagons light:[42]
So on this windy Sea of Land, the Fiend   440
Walked up and down alone bent on his prey,
Alone, for other Creature in this place
Living or lifeless to be found was none,
None yet, but store hereafter from the earth
Up hither like Aerial vapours flew   445
Of all things transitory and vain, when Sin
With vanity had filled the works of men:
Both all things vain, and all who in vain things
Built their fond hopes of glory or lasting fame,
Or happiness in this or th' other life;   450
All who have their reward on earth, the fruits
Of painful Superstition and blind Zeal,
Nought seeking but the praise of men, here find
Fit retribution, empty as their deeds;
All th' unaccomplished works of Nature's hand,   455
Abortive, monstrous, or unkindly mixed,
Dissolved on Earth, fleet hither, and in vain,
Till final dissolution, wander here,
Not in the neighbouring Moon as some have dreamed;
Those argent Fields more likely habitants,   460
Translated Saints, or middle Spirits hold
Betwixt th' Angelical and Human kind:
Hither of ill-joined Sons and Daughters born
First from the ancient World those Giants came
With many a vain exploit, though then renowned: 465
The builders next of *Babel* on the Plain[43]
Of *Sennaar*, and still with vain design
New *Babels*, had they wherewithal, would build:
Others came single; he who to be deemed
A God, leaped fondly into *Ætna* flames,   470
Empedocles, and he who to enjoy[44]
Plato's Elysium, leaped into the Sea,
Cleombrotus and many more too long,[45]
Embryos and Idiots, Eremites and Friars[46]

---

[40] *yeanling* young.
[41] *Sericana* or Serica, a region north of India.
[42] *cany* made of cane or bamboo.
[43] *Babel* Nimrod built the tower of Babel on the plain of Shinär (*Sennaar*) (Genesis 10.1–9).
[44] *Empedocles* Greek philosopher, falsely said to have leapt into Mount Aetna in order to suggest by his total

disappearance that he was a god (Diogenes Laertius *Lives of the Philosophers* 8.67–75).
[45] *Cleombrotus* a young man said to have drowned himself in order to enter the afterlife described in Plato's *Phaedo*.
[46] *Eremites* hermits; *Friars White, Black, and Grey* Carmelites, Dominicans and Franciscans.

White, Black, and Grey, with all their trumpery.   475
Here Pilgrims roam, that strayed so far to seek
In *Golgotha* him dead, who lives in Heav'n;[47]
And they who to be sure of Paradise
Dying put on the weeds of *Dominic*,[48]
Or in *Franciscan* think to pass disguised;   480
They pass the Planets seven, and pass the fixed,
And that Crystálline Sphere whose balance weighs
The Trepidation talked, and that first moved;[49]
And now Saint *Peter* at Heav'n's Wicket seems[50]
To wait them with his Keys, and now at foot   485
Of Heav'n's ascent they lift their Feet, when lo
A violent cross wind from either Coast
Blows them transverse ten thousand Leagues awry
Into the devious Air; then might ye see
Cowls, Hoods, and Habits, with their wearers tossed[51]   490
And fluttered into Rags, then Relics, Beads,
Indulgences, Dispenses, Pardons, Bulls,
The sport of Winds: all these upwhirled aloft
Fly o'er the backside of the World far off
Into a *Limbo* large and broad, since called[52]   495
The Paradise of Fools, to few unknown
Long after, now unpeopled, and untrod;
All this dark Globe the Fiend found as he passed,
And long he wandered, till at last a gleam
Of dawning light turned thither-ward in haste   500
His travelled steps; far distant he descries
Ascending by degrees magnificent
Up to the wall of Heaven a Structure high,
At top whereof, but far more rich, appeared
The work as of a Kingly Palace Gate   505
With Frontispiece of Diamond and Gold
Embellished, thick with sparkling orient Gems
The Portal shone, inimitable on Earth
By Model, or by shading Pencil drawn.
These Stairs were such as whereon *Jacob* saw[53]   510
Angels ascending and descending, bands
Of Guardians bright, when he from *Esau* fled

---

[47] *Golgotha* Calvary, the place near Jerusalem where Christ was crucified.
[48] *weeds* garments, robes.
[49] *Trepidation* a hypothetical variation in the position of the spheres in the Ptolemaic system of the universe (see John Donne, "A Valediction Forbidding Mourning," l. 11); *that first moved* the *primum mobile*, the outermost sphere of the Ptolemaic system.
[50] *Saint . . . Wicket* Christ gives Peter of Galilee the keys to heaven's gate (Matthew 16.19), but the passage is satirical because Peter and his keys are prime images of Roman Catholicism and other forms of episcopacy, which Milton despised.
[51] *Cowls . . . Bulls* the clothing, accoutrements, and various kinds of edicts issued by priests, bishops, and popes in the Roman Catholic Church.
[52] *Limbo* "A region bordering on hell, in which there is neither pleasure nor pain. Popularly hell" (Johnson).
[53] *Jacob* God is at the top of the ladder (Genesis 28.12).

To *Padan-Aram* in the field of *Luz*,
Dreaming by night under the open Sky,
And waking cried, 'This is the Gate of Heav'n'.   515
Each Stair mysteriously was meant, nor stood
There always, but drawn up to Heav'n sometimes
Viewless, and underneath a bright Sea flowed
Of Jasper, or of liquid Pearl, whereon
Who after came from Earth, sailing arrived   520
Wafted by Angels, or flew o'er the Lake
Rapt in a Chariot drawn by fiery Steeds.
The Stairs were then let down, whether to dare
The Fiend by easy ascent, or aggravate
His sad exclusion from the doors of Bliss   525
Direct against which opened from beneath,
Just o'er the blissful seat of Paradise,
A passage down to th' Earth, a passage wide,
Wider by far than that of after-times
Over mount *Sion*, and, though that were large,   530
Over the *Promised Land* to God so dear,
By which, to visit oft those happy Tribes,
On high behests his Angels to and fro
Passed frequent, and his eye with choice regard
From *Paneas*, the fount of *Jordan's* flood,[54]   535
To *Beërsaba*, where the *Holy Land*
Borders on *Ægypt* and the *Arabian* shore;
So wide the op'ning seemed, where bounds were set
To darkness, such as bound the Ocean wave.
Satan from hence now on the lower stair   540
That scaled by steps of Gold to Heaven Gate
Looks down with wonder at the sudden view
Of all this World at once. As when a Scout
Through dark and desert ways with peril gone
All night at last by break of cheerful dawn   545
Obtains the brow of some high-climbing Hill,
Which to his eye discovers unaware
The goodly prospect of some foreign land
First-seen, or some renowned Metropolis
With glistering Spires and Pinnacles adorned,   550
Which now the Rising Sun gilds with his beams.
Such wonder seized, though after Heaven seen,
The Spirit malign, but much more envy seized
At sight of all this World beheld so Fair.
Round he surveys, and well might, where he stood   555
So high above the circling Canopy

---

[54] *Paneas . . . To Beersaba*   from the north (near Mount
Herman) to the south (near Gaza) of the Holy Land of
Palestine.

Of Night's extended shade; from Eastern Point
Of *Libra* to the fleecy Star that bears[55]
Andromeda far off Atlantic Seas
Beyond th' Horizon; then from Pole to Pole   560
He views in breadth, and without longer pause
Down right into the World's first Region throws
His flight precipitant, and winds with ease
Through the pure marble Air his oblique way[56]
Amongst innumerable Stars, that shone   565
Stars distant, but nigh hand seemed other worlds;
Or other worlds they seemed, or happy Isles,
Like those *Hesperian* Gardens famed of old,[57]
Fortunate Fields, and Groves and flowry Vales,
Thrice happy Isles, but who dwelt happy there   570
He stayed not to inquire: above them all
The golden sun in splendour likest Heaven
Allured his eye: thither his course he bends
Through the calm Firmament; but up or down,
By centre, or eccentric, hard to tell,[58]   575
Or Longitude, where the great Luminary
Aloof the vulgar Constellations thick,
That from his Lordly eye keep distance due,
Dispenses Light from far; they as they move
Their Starry dance in numbers that compute   580
Days, months, & years, towards his all-cheering Lamp
Turn swift their various motions, or are turned
By his Magnetic beam, that gently warms[59]
The Universe, and to each inward part
With gentle penetration, though unseen,   585
Shoots invisible virtue even to the deep:
So wondrously was set his Station bright.
There lands the Fiend, a spot like which perhaps
Astronomer in the Sun's lucent Orb[60]
Through his glazed Optic tube yet never saw.   590
The place he found beyond expression bright,
Compared with aught on Earth, Metal or Stone;
Not all parts like, but all alike informed

---

[55]   *Libra . . . the fleecy Star . . . Andromeda* a vision of
the night sky from Libra in the east, to western Aries (the
fleecy ram) with northern Andromeda above.

[56]   *marble* etymologically, shining, sparkling (Gk
μαρμαίρω).

[57]   *Hesperian Gardens* like the other places mentioned
in the passage, the home of the Hesperides (daughters of
Night and Erebus) was uncertainly located in the extreme west of the Mediterranean world.

[58]   *By centre . . . Longitude* Milton expresses doubt
about how to describe Satan's lateral and vertical movements through the universe, which may be either Coper-

nican (with the Sun at the centre) or Ptolemaic (with the
Sun on an ecliptic around the earth).

[59]   *Magnetic beam* the conflation of light (as a form of
matter) with gravitational effects was common in the
seventeenth century; from Plato through to Milton the
sun is also seen as an image of divine order and providen-
tial government (including the daily supply of gravity)
(see, e.g. George Cheyne, *Philosophical Principles of Religion*, 50–92).

[60]   *Astronomer* Galileo discovered sunspots with his
telescope, or *Optic tube*.

With radiant light, as glowing Iron with fire;
If metal, part seemed Gold, part Silver clear;   595
If stone, Carbuncle most or Chrysolite,
Ruby or Topaz, to the Twelve that shone
In *Aaron's* Breast-plate, and a stone besides[61]
Imagined rather oft than elsewhere seen,
That stone, or like to that which here below   600
Philosophers in vain so long have sought,
In vain, though by their powerful Art they bind
Volatile *Hermes*, and call up unbound[62]
In various shapes old *Proteus* from the Sea,
Drained through a Limbec to his Native form.   605
What wonder then if fields and regions here
Breathe forth *Elixir* pure, and Rivers run[63]
Potable Gold, when with one virtuous touch
Th' Arch-chemic Sun so far from us remote
Produces with Terrestrial Humour mixed,   610
Here in the dark so many precious things
Of colour glorious and effect so rare?
Here matter new to gaze the Devil met
Undazzled, far and wide his eye commands,
For sight no obstacle found here, nor shade,   615
But all Sun-Shine, as when his Beams at Noon
Culminate from th' *Equator*, as they now
Shot upward still direct, whence no way round[64]
Shadow from body opaque can fall, and the Air,
No where so clear, sharpened his visual ray   620
To objects distant far, whereby he soon
Saw within ken a glorious Angel stand,
The same whom *John* saw also in the Sun:[65]
His back was turned, but not his brightness hid;
Of beaming sunny Rays a golden tiar[66]   625
Circled his Head, nor less his Locks behind
Illustrious on his Shoulders fledge with wings[67]
Lay waving round; on some great charge employed
He seemed, or fixed in cogitation deep.
Glad was the Spirit impure as now in hope   630
To find who might direct his wandring flight

---

[61] *Aaron's Breast-plate* had twelve stones for the twelve tribes of Israel (Exodus 28.17–21); the *stone beside* is the imaginary, all-powerful philosopher's stone, sought by alchemists.
[62] *Hermes . . . Proteus . . . Limbec* (alembic) terms of alchemy.
[63] *Elixir* "The liquor, or whatever it be, with which chemists hope to transmute metals to gold 'No chemist yet the elixir got, But glorifies his pregnant pot, If by the

way to him befal Some odoriferous thing, or medicinal'. Donne" (Johnson).
[64] In the unfallen world, the earth was not tilted on its axis, and the sun was directly overhead (see Thomas Burnet, *Sacred Theory of the Earth*).
[65] *A glorious Angel* who announces the Apocalypse to John (Revelation 19.17).
[66] *tiar* tiara.
[67] *fledge* fledged.

To Paradise the happy seat of Man,
His journey's end and our beginning woe.
But first he casts to change his proper shape,
Which else might work him danger or delay: 635
And now a stripling Cherub he appears,
Not of the prime, yet such as in his face
Youth smiled Celestial, and to every Limb
Suitable grace diffused, so well he feigned;
Under a Coronet his flowing hair[68]   640
In curls on either cheek played, wings he wore
Of many a coloured plume sprinkled with Gold,
His habit fit for speed succinct, and held[69]
Before his decent steps a Silver wand.
He drew not nigh unheard; the Angel bright,   645
Ere he drew nigh, his radiant visage turned,
Admonished by his ear, and straight was known
The Arch-Angel *Uriel*, one of the sev'n[70]
Who in God's presence, nearest to his Throne
Stand ready at command, and are his Eyes   650
That run through all the Heav'ns, or down to th' Earth
Bear his swift errands over moist and dry,
O'er Sea and Land: him *Satan* thus accosts;
    'Uriel, for thou of those sev'n Spirits that stand
In sight of God's high Throne, gloriously bright,   655
The first art wont his great authentic will
Interpreter through highest Heav'n to bring,
Where all his Sons thy Embassy attend;
And here art likeliest by supreme decree
Like honour to obtain, and as his Eye   660
To visit oft this new Creation round;
Unspeakable desire to see, and know
All these his wondrous works, but chiefly Man,
His chief delight and favour, him for whom
All these his works so wondrous he ordained,   665
Hath brought me from the Quires of Cherubim
Alone thus wandring. Brightest Seraph tell
In which of all these shining Orbs hath Man
His fixèd seat, or fixèd seat hath none,
But all these shining orbs his choice to dwell;   670
That I may find him, and with secret gaze,
Or open admiration him behold
On whom the great Creator hath bestowed
Worlds, and on whom hath all these graces poured;

---

[68] *Coronet*   "An inferior crown worn by the nobility"   [70] *Uriel*   literally, "fire of God."
(Johnson).
[69] *succinct*   "Tucked or girded up; having the clothes
drawn up to disengage the legs" (Johnson).

That both in him and all things, as is meet,   675
The Universal Maker we may praise;
Who justly hath drivn out his Rebel Foes
To deepest Hell, and to repair that loss,
Created this new happy Race of Men
To serve him better: wise are all his ways'.   680
     So spake the false dissembler unperceived;
For neither Man nor Angel can discern
Hypocrisy, the only evil that walks
Invisible, except to God alone,
By his permissive will, through Heav'n and Earth: 685
And oft though wisdom wake, suspicion sleeps
At wisdom's Gate, and to simplicity
Resigns her charge, while goodness thinks no ill
Where no ill seems: Which now for once beguiled
Uriel, though Regent of the Sun, and held   690
The sharpest sighted Spirit of all in Heav'n;
Who to the fraudulent Impostor foul,
In his uprightness answer thus returned.
'Fair Angel, thy desire which tends to know
The works of God, thereby to glorify   695
The great Work-Master, leads to no excess
That reaches blame, but rather merits praise
The more it seems excess, that led thee hither
From thy Empyreal Mansion thus alone,
To witness with thine eyes what some perhaps   700
Contented with report hear only in heav'n:
For wonderful indeed are all his works,
Pleasant to know, and worthiest to be all
Had in remembrance always with delight;
But what created mind can comprehend   705
Their number, or the wisdom infinite
That brought them forth, but hid their causes deep.
I saw when at his Word the formless Mass,
This world's material mould, came to a heap:
Confusion heard his voice, and wild uproar   710
Stood ruled, stood vast infinitude confined;
Till at his second bidding darkness fled,
Light shone, and order from disorder sprung:
Swift to their several Quarters hasted then
The cumbrous Elements, Earth, Flood, Air, Fire;   715
And this Ethereal quintessence of Heav'n
Flew upward, spirited with various forms,
That rolled orbicular, and turned to Stars
Numberless, as thou seest, and how they move;
Each had his place appointed, each his course   720
The rest in circuit walls this Universe.

Look downward on that Globe whose hither side[71]
With light from hence, though but reflected, shines;
That place is Earth the seat of Man, that light
His day, which else as th' other Hemisphere   725
Night would invade, but there the neighbouring Moon
(So call that opposite fair Star) her aid
Timely interposes, and her monthly round
Still ending, still renewing, through mid Heav'n,
With borrowed light her countenance triform[72]   730
Hence fills and empties to enlighten the Earth,
And in her pale dominion checks the night.
That spot to which I point is *Paradise*,
Adam's abode, those lofty shades his Bowre.
Thy way thou canst not miss, me mine requires'.   735
Thus said, he turned, and *Satan*, bowing low,
As to superior Spirits is wont in Heav'n,
Where honour due and reverence none neglects,
Took leave, and toward the coast of Earth beneath,
Down from th' ecliptic, sped with hoped success,   740
Throws his steep flight in many an Aery wheel,
Nor staid, till on *Niphates* top he lights.[73]

BOOK IV
THE ARGUMENT

Satan *now in prospect of* Eden, *and nigh the place where he must now attempt the bold enterprise which he undertook alone against God and Man, falls into many doubts with himself, and many passions, fear, envy, and despair; but at length confirms himself in evil, journeys on to Paradise, whose outward prospect and situation is described, overleaps the bounds, sits in the shape of a Cormorant on the Tree of life, as highest in the Garden, to look about him. The Garden described;* Satan's *first sight of* Adam *and* Eve; *his wonder at their excellent form and happy state, but with resolution to work their fall; overhears their discourse, thence gathers that the Tree of knowledge was forbidden them to eat of, under penalty of death; and thereon intends to found his Temptation, by seducing them to transgress: then leaves them a while, to know further of their state by some other means. Meanwhile* Uriel *descending on a Sun-beam warns* Gabriel, *who had in his charge the Gate of Paradise, that some evil spirit had escaped the Deep, and passed at Noon by his Sphere in the shape of a good Angel down to Paradise, discovered after by his furious gestures in the Mount.* Gabriel *promises to find him ere morning. Night coming on,* Adam *and* Eve, *discourse of going to their rest: their Bower described; their Evening worship.* Gabriel *drawing forth his Bands of Night-watch to walk the round of Paradise, appoints two strong Angels to* Adam's *Bower, lest the evil spirit should be there doing some harm to* Adam *or* Eve *sleeping;*

---

[71] *hither side*   the daytime half of the earth shines with the reflected light from the sun.
[72] *triform* because different when waning, waxing, and full; also because associated with Artemis and Hecate, who are both sometimes described as having three aspects or faces.

[73] *Niphates* (literally, "snowstorms"), an eastern part of the Taurus Mountains, in Armenia, near old Assyria, now Iran (cf 4.126).

there they find him at the ear of Eve, *tempting her in a dream, and bring him, though unwillingly, to*
Gabriel; *by whom questioned, he scornfully answers, prepares resistance, but hindered by a Sign from*
Heaven, *flies out of Paradise.*

O For that warning voice, which he who saw[1]
Th' *Apocalypse*, heard cry in Heav'n aloud,
Then when the Dragon, put to second rout,
Came furious down to be revenged on men,
Woe to the inhabitants on earth! that now,[2]   5
While time was, our first-Parents had been warned
The coming of their secret foe, and scaped,
Haply so scaped his mortal snare; for now
Satan, now first inflamed with rage, came down,
The Tempter ere th' Accuser of man-kind,   10
To wreak on innocent frail man his loss
Of that first Battle, and his flight to Hell:
Yet not rejoicing in his speed, though bold,
Far off and fearless, nor with cause to boast,
Begins his dire attempt, which nigh the birth   15
Now rolling, boils in his tumultuous breast,
And like a devilish Engine back recoils[3]
Upon himself; horror and doubt distract
His troubled thoughts, and from the bottom stir
The Hell within him for within him Hell   20
He brings, and round about him, nor from Hell
One step no more than from himself can fly
By change of place: Now conscience wakes despair
That slumbered, wakes the bitter memory
Of what he was, what is, and what must be   25
Worse; of worse deeds worse sufferings must ensue.
Sometimes towards *Eden* which now in his view
Lay pleasant, his grieved look he fixes sad,
Sometimes towards Heav'n and the full-blazing Sun,
Which now sat high in his Meridian Tower: 30
Then much revolving, thus in sighs began.
    'O thou that with surpassing Glory crowned,
Look'st from thy sole Dominion like the God
Of this new World; at whose sight all the Stars
Hide their diminished heads; to thee I call,   35
But with no friendly voice, and add thy name
O Sun, to tell thee how I hate thy beams
That bring to my remembrance from what state
I fell, how glorious once above thy Sphere;
Till Pride and worse Ambition threw me down   40

BOOK IV
[1] *he who saw* Th' *Apocalypse* St John (Revelation
12.10).
[2] *Woe . . . earth!* Revelation 12.12.
[3] *devilish Engine* cannon (cf. 6.518).

Warring in Heav'n against Heav'n's matchless King:
Ah wherefore! he deserved no such return
From me, whom he created what I was
In that bright eminence, and with his good
Upbraided none; nor was his service hard.   45
What could be less than to afford him praise,
The easiest recompense, and pay him thanks,
How due! yet all his good proved ill in me,
And wrought but malice; lifted up so high
I sdeined subjection, and thought one step higher[4]   50
Would set me highest, and in a moment quit
The debt immense of endless gratitude,
So burthensome still paying, still to owe;
Forgetful what from him I still received,
And understood not that a grateful mind   55
By owing owes not, but still pays, at once
Indebted and discharged; what burden then?
O had his powerful Destiny ordained
Me some inferior Angel, I had stood
Then happy; no unbounded hope had raised   60
Ambition. Yet why not? some other Power
As great might have aspired, and me though mean
Drawn to his part; but other Powers as great
Fell not, but stand unshaken, from within
Or from without, to all temptations armed.   65
Hadst thou the same free Will and Power to stand?[5]
Thou hadst: whom hast thou then or what to accuse,[6]
But Heav'n's free Love dealt equally to all?
Be then his Love accurst, since love or hate,
To me alike, it deals eternal woe.   70
Nay cursed be thou; since against his thy will
Chose freely what it now so justly rues.
Me miserable! which way shall I fly
Infinite wrath, and infinite despair?
Which way I fly is Hell; my self am Hell;   75
And in the lowest deep a lower deep
Still threatning to devour me opens wide,
To which the Hell I suffer seems a Heav'n.
O then at last relent: is there no place
Left for Repentance, none for Pardon left?   80
None left but by submission; and that word
Disdain forbids me, and my dread of shame
Among the *Spirits* beneath, whom I seduced
With other promises and other vaunts

---

[4] *sdeined* disdained.
[5] *thou* Satan addresses himself in the second person
(cf. l. 71), a sign of his fallen condition.

[6] *to accuse* vowel coalescence.

Than to submit, boasting I could subdue   85
Th' Omnipotent. Ay me, they little know
How dearly I abide that boast so vain,
Under what torments inwardly I groan,
While they adore me on the Throne of Hell.
With Diadem and Sceptre high advanced   90
The lower still I fall, only Supreme
In misery, such joy Ambition finds.
But say I could repent and could obtain,
By Act of Grace my former state; how soon
Would highth recall high thoughts, how soon unsay   95
What feigned submission swore: ease would recant
Vows made in pain, as violent and void.
For never can true reconcilement grow
Where wounds of deadly hate have pierced so deep:
Which would but lead me to a worse relapse,   100
And heavier fall: so should I purchase dear
Short intermission bought with double smart.
This knows my punisher; therefore as far
From granting he, as I from begging peace:
All hope excluded thus, behold in stead   105
Of us out-cast, exiled, his new delight,
Mankind created, and for him this World.
So farewell Hope, and with hope farewell fear,
Farewell Remorse: all Good to me is lost;
Evil be thou my Good; by thee at least   110
Divided Empire with Heav'n's King I hold
By thee, and more than half perhaps will reign;[7]
As Man ere long, and this new World shall know'.
        Thus while he spake, each passion dimmed his face
Thrice changed with pale, ire, envy, and despair,[8]   115
Which marred his borrowed visage, and betrayed[9]
Him counterfeit, if any eye beheld.
For heav'nly minds from such distempers foul
Are ever clear. Whereof he soon aware,
Each perturbation smoothed with outward calm,   120
Artificer of fraud; and was the first
That practised falsehood under saintly show,
Deep malice to conceal, couched with revenge:
Yet not enough had practised to deceive
Uriel once warned; whose eye pursued him down   125
The way he went, and on th' *Assyrian* mount[10]
Saw him disfigured, more than could befall

---

[7] *reign* probably reign over, govern; but possibly a
variant spelling of *rein*.
[8] *pale* paleness, pallor; *ire, envy and despair* make the
three changes of pallor.

[9] *borrowed visage* the likeness of the *stripling Cherub*,
which he had assumed (3.636).
[10] *Assyrian mount* Niphates (3.742).

Spirit of happy sort: his gestures fierce
He marked and mad demeanour, then alone,
As he supposed, all unobserved, unseen.   130
So on he fares, and to the border comes,
Of *Eden*, where delicious Paradise,
Now nearer, Crowns with her enclosure green,
As with a rural mound, the champaign head[11]
Of a steep wilderness, whose hairy sides   135
With thicket overgrown, grotesque and wild,[12]
Access denied; and over head up grew
Insuperable highth of loftiest shade,
Cedar, and Pine, and Fir, and branching Palm,
A Sylvan Scene, and as the ranks ascend   140
Shade above shade, a woody Theatre[13]
Of stateliest view. Yet higher than their tops
The verdurous wall of Paradise upsprung:
Which to our general Sire gave prospect large
Into his nether Empire neighbouring round.   145
And Higher than that Wall a circling row
Of goodliest Trees loaden with fairest Fruit,
Blossoms and Fruits at once of golden hue
Appeared, with gay enamelled colours mixed:[14]
On which the Sun more glad impressed his beams   150
Than in fair Evening Cloud, or humid Bow,[15]
When God hath showered the earth; so lovely seemed
That lantskip: And of pure now purer air
Meets his approach, and to the heart inspires[16]
Vernal delight and joy, able to drive   155
All sadness but despair: Now gentle gales,[17]
Fanning their odoriferous wings dispense
Native perfumes, and whisper whence they stole
Those balmy spoils. As when to them who sail
Beyond the *Cape of Hope*, and now are passed[18]   160
Mozambic, off at Sea North-East winds blow
Sabean Odours from the spicy shore
Of *Araby* the blest, with such delay
Well pleased they slack their course, and many a League
Cheered with the grateful smell old Ocean smiles.   165

---

[11] *champaign* "A flat open country" (Johnson).
[12] *grotesque* grotto-like, as well as "distorted . . . wildly formed" (Johnson).
[13] *Theatre* (lit. "a place for viewing") "A place rising by steps like a theatre" (Johnson).
[14] *enammelled*, fr. *enamel* "To lay upon another body so as to vary it" (Johnson).
[15] *humid Bow* rainbow.
[16] *inspires* "To breathe into; to infuse into the mind; to impress upon the fancy" (Johnson).

[17] *gales* "A wind not tempestuous, yet stronger than a breeze" (Johnson).
[18] *Cape of Hope . . . Araby the blest   passed* the southern tip of Africa, sailing north, up the east coast, beyond Mozambique and smelling the frankincense and myrrh produced in Saba (modern Yemen), to the northeast, in the southern part of Arabia, formerly called *Arabia Felix* (blessed, fortunate).

So entertained those odorous sweets the Fiend,
Who came their bane, though with them better pleased
Than *Asmodeus* with the fishy fume,[19]
That drove him, though enamoured, from the Spouse
Of *Tobits* Son, and with a vengeance sent   170
From *Media* post to *Ægypt*, there fast bound.[20]
   Now to th' ascent of that steep savage Hill
Satan had journeyed on, pensive and slow;
But further way found none, so thick entwined,
As one continued brake, the undergrowth   175
Of shrubs and tangling bushes had perplexed
All path of Man or Beast that passed that way:
One Gate there only was, and that looked East
On th' other side: which when th' arch-felon saw
Due entrance he disdained, and in contempt,   180
At one flight bound high over leaped all bound
Of Hill or highest Wall, and sheer within
Lights on his feet. As when a prowling Wolf,
Whom hunger drives to seek new haunt for prey,
Watching where Shepherds pen their Flocks at eve   185
In hurdled Cotes amid the field secure,[21]
Leaps o'er the fence with ease into the Fold:
Or as a Thief bent to unhoard the cash
Of some rich Burgher, whose substantial doors,
Cross-barred and bolted fast, fear no assault,   190
In at the window climbs, or o'er the tiles:[22]
So clomb this first grand Thief into God's Fold:
So since into his Church lewd Hirelings climb.[23]
Thence up he flew, and on the Tree of Life
The middle Tree and highest there that grew,   195
Sat like a Cormorant; yet not true Life
Thereby regained, but sat devising Death
To them who lived; nor on the virtue thought[24]
Of that life-giving Plant, but only used
For prospect, what well used had been the pledge   200
Of immortality. So little knows
Any, but God alone, to value right
The good before him, but perverts best things
To worst abuse, or to their meanest use.

---

[19] *Asmodeus*   the demon in the Book of Tobit (part of the *Apocrypha*) who haunts Sarah and kills her first seven husbands on their wedding nights. Acting on instructions from the angel Raphael, Tobias, the son of Tobit, burns the heart and liver of a fish on the ashes of incense as he enters Sarah's chamber on his wedding night; the demon flees from Media (the kingdom of the Medes in Asia, south of the Caspian Sea) into uppermost Egypt where he is bound by the angel (Tobit 8).

[20] *post*   posthaste; with great speed.
[21] *hurdled Cotes*   sheepfolds made of a "texture of sticks woven together" (Johnson).
[22] *tiles*   the tiled roof.
[23] *lewd*   "1. Lay; not clerical . . . 2. Wicked, bad, naughty" (Johnson).
[24] *virtue*   power.

Beneath him with new wonder now he views   205
To all delight of human sense exposed
In narrow room Nature's whole wealth, yea more,
A Heav'n on Earth, for blissful Paradise
Of God the Garden was, by him in the East
Of *Eden* planted; *Eden* stretched her Line[25]   210
From *Auran* Eastward to the Royal Towers
Of great *Seleucia*, built by *Grecian* Kings,
Of where the Sons of Eden long before
Dwelt in *Telassar*: in this pleasant soil
His far more pleasant Garden God ordained;   215
Out of the fertile ground he caused to grow
All Trees of noblest kind for sight, smell, taste;
And all amid them stood the Tree of Life,
High eminent, blooming Ambrosial Fruit
Of vegetable Gold; and next to Life   220
Our Death the Tree of Knowledge grew fast by,
Knowledge of Good bought dear by knowing ill.
Southward through *Eden* went a River large,
Nor changed his course, but through the shaggy hill
Passed underneath engulfed; for God had thrown   225
That Mountain as his Garden-mould high raised[26]
Upon the rapid current, which, through veins
Of porous Earth with kindly thirst up drawn,
Rose a fresh Fountain, and with many a rill
Watered the Garden; thence united fell   230
Down the steep glade, and met the nether Flood,
Which from his darksome passage now appears,
And now divided into four main Streams,
Runs diverse, wandring many a famous Realm
And Country whereof here needs no account,   235
But rather to tell how, if Art could tell,
How from that Sapphire Fount the crispèd Brooks,
Rolling on orient Pearl and sands of Gold,
With mazy error under pendant shades[27]
Ran Nectar, visiting each plant, and fed   240
Flow'rs worthy of Paradise which not nice Art[28]
In Beds and curious Knots, but Nature boon[29]
Poured forth profuse on Hill and Dale and Plain,
Both where the morning Sun first warmly smote

[25] *Eden* (pleasure), is located near the northern end of the Persian Gulf, west of Haran (*Auran*), Abraham's chosen home, near *Telassar*; *Seleucia*, founded by Seleucus (one of five kings of the Greek dominion of Syria), was on the coast of northern Palestine, near Antioch.
[26] *That Mountain* Eden, *the shaggy hill*; *Garden-mould* earth or soil for making a garden.
[27] *error* wandering, the etymological sense (L. *error*).
[28] *worthy of* vowel coalescence; *nice* fastidious; overly careful.
[29] *Knots* a feature of formal gardens; *boon* bounteous (*OED*) but also jovial, convivial.

The open field, and where the unpierced shade   245
Imbrowned the noontide Bow'rs: Thus was this place
A happy rural seat of various view;
Groves whose rich Trees wept odorous Gums and Balm,
Others whose fruit burnished with Golden Rind
Hung amiable, *Hesperian* Fables true,[30]   250
If true, here only, and of delicious taste:
Betwixt them Lawns, or level Downs, and Flocks
Grazing the tender herb, were interposed,
Or palmy hillock, or the flowry lap
Of some irriguous Valley spread her store,[31]   255
Flowrs of all hue, and without Thorn the Rose:
Another side, umbrageous Grots and Caves[32]
Of cool recess, o'er which the mantling vine
Lays forth her purple Grape, and gently creeps
Luxuriant; mean while murmuring waters fall   260
Down the slope hills, dispersed, or in a Lake,
That to the fringèd Bank with Myrtle crowned,
Her crystal mirror holds, unite their streams.
The Birds their quire apply; airs, vernal airs,
Breathing the smell of field and grove, attune   265
The trembling leaves, while Universal *Pan*,[33]
Knit with the *Graces* and the *Hours* in dance,
Led on th' Eternal Spring. Not that fair field
Of *Enna*, where *Proserpin* gathring flowrs,[34]
Her self a fairer Flower by gloomy *Dis*   270
Was gathered, which cost *Ceres* all that pain
To seek her through the world; nor that sweet Grove[35]
Of *Daphne* by *Orontes*, and th' inspired
Castalian Spring, might with this Paradise
Of *Eden* strive; nor that *Nyseian* Isle[36]   275
Girt with the River *Triton*, where old *Cham*,
Whom Gentiles *Ammon* call and *Libyan Jove*,

---

[30]   *Hesperian Fables*   the Hesperides, daughters of
Night and Erebus, were guardians of a tree of golden
apples.
[31]   *irriguous*   "Watery; watered" (Johnson).
[32]   *umbrageous Grots*   shady grottoes.
[33]   *Universal Pan . . . Graces . . . Hours*   nature (Gk τὸ
πᾶν) with the three Graces and four Hours, goddesses of
giving, receiving and returning favors, and of the
seasons.
[34]   *Enna*   city in the center of Sicily from which Pluto
(*Dis*) carried *Proserpin(a)* off to Hades (Ovid, *Metamorphoses* 5.385–408); her mother Ceres sought her all over
the earth; Zeus's adjudication of the matter put an end to
the primordial eternal spring. The story suggests the
seduction of Eve by Satan.

[35]   *Grove of Daphne*   a park near Antioch where Apollo
was worshipped and celebrations were held remembering
his pursuit of the nymph Daphne, daughter of a river god
(Peneus first but then *Castilia*, near Antioch), which
ended with her transformation into the tree of her name
(laurel); see the selection from Gibbon's *Decline and Fall
of the Roman Empire*, below.
[36]   *that Nyseian Isle*   an island in the *Triton* river, North
Africa, conflated with an Arabian place called Nysa;
there *Cham* (Hammon, son of Noah), conflated with
Ammon (an Egyptian Jupiter), sent his son *Bacchus*
(Dionysius, lit. god of Nysa) by *Amalthea* (in some
myths, though usually Semele) to escape *Rhea*, his jealous
wife (though she is usually his mother).

Hid *Amalthea* and her Florid Son
Young *Bacchus* from his Stepdame *Rhea's* eye;
Nor where *Abassin* Kings their issue Guard,   280
Mount *Amara*, though this by some supposed[37]
True Paradise under the *Ethiop* Line
By *Nilus* head, enclosed with shining Rock,
A whole day's journey high, but wide remote
From this *Assyrian* Garden, where the Fiend   285
Saw undelighted all delight, all kind
Of living Creatures new to sight and strange:
Two of far nobler shape erect and tall,
Godlike erect, with native Honour clad
In naked majesty seemed Lords of all,   290
And worthy seemed, for in their looks Divine
The image of their glorious Maker shone,
Truth, wisdom, Sanctitude severe and pure,
Severe but in true filial freedom placed;
Whence true authority in men; though both   295
Not equal, as their sex not equal seemed;
For contemplation he and valour formed,
For softness she and sweet attractive Grace,
He for God only, she for God in him:
His fair large Front and Eye sublime declared[38]   300
Absolute rule; and Hyacinthine Locks[39]
Round from his parted forelock manly hung
Clustring, but not beneath his shoulders broad:[40]
She as a veil down to the slender waist
Her unadornèd golden tresses wore   305
Dishevelled, but in wanton ringlets waved
As the Vine curls her tendrils, which implied
Subjection, but required with gentle sway,
And by her yielded, by him best received,
Yielded with coy submission, modest pride,[41]   310
And sweet reluctant amorous delay.
Nor those mysterious parts were then concealed,
Then was not guilty shame, dishonest shame[42]
Of nature's works, honour dishonourable,
Sin-bred, how have ye troubled all mankind   315
With shows instead, mere shows of seeming pure,
And banished from man's life his happiest life,

---

[37] *Amara* (Amhara) a place near the supposed head of the Nile where Abyssinian (*Abassin*) kings raised their princes (see Samuel Johnson, *Rasselas*); it is above the equator, not *under the Ethiop Line*.

[38] *Front* forehead.

[39] *Hyacinthine* Homer uses the epithet of hair and says it resembles a craftsman's mixture of gold with silver (*Odyssey* 6.231–2).

[40] *but not beneath . . .* the style worn by Cavaliers is forbidden in Milton's Eden.

[41] *coy* "Modest; decent" (Johnson).

[42] *dishonest* "Disgraceful; ignominious" (Johnson).

Simplicity and spotless innocence.
So passed they naked on, nor shunned the sight
Of God or Angel, for they thought no ill: 320
So hand in hand they passed, the loveliest pair
That ever since in love's embraces met,
Adam the goodliest man of men since born
His Sons, the fairest of her Daughters *Eve.*
Under a tuft of shade that on a green   325
Stood whispering soft, by a fresh Fountain side
They sat them down; and, after no more toil
Of their sweet Gardning labour than sufficed
To recommend cool *Zephyr*, and made ease[43]
More easy, wholesome thirst and appetite   330
More grateful, to their Supper Fruits they fell,[44]
Néctarine Fruits which the compliant boughs
Yielded them, side-long as they sat recline
On the soft downy bank damasked with flowers:
The savoury pulp they chew, and in the rind   335
Still as they thirsted scoop the brimming stream;
Nor gentle purpose, nor endearing smiles
Wanted, nor youthful dalliance as beseems
Fair couple, linked in happy nuptial League,
Alone as they. About them frisking played   340
All Beasts of th' Earth, since wild, and of all chase[45]
In Wood or Wilderness, Forest or Den;
Sporting the lion ramped, and in his paw
Dandled the Kid; Bears, Tigers, Ounces, Pards,
Gambled before them, th' unwieldy Elephant   345
To make them mirth used all his might, and wreathed
His Lithe Proboscis; close the Serpent sly
Insinuating, wove with Gordian twine[46]
His braided train, and of his fatal guile
Gave proof unheeded; others on the grass   350
Couched, and now filled with pasture gazing sat,
Or Bedward ruminating: for the Sun[47]
Declined was hasting now with prone career
To th' Ocean Isles, and in th' ascending Scale
Of Heav'n the Stars that usher Evening rose: 355
When *Satan* still in gaze, as first he stood,
Scarce thus at length failed speech recovered sad.
   'O Hell! what do mine eyes with grief behold,
Into our room of bliss thus high advanced

---

[43] *Zephyr* "The west wind; and poetically any calm
soft wind" (Johnson).
[44] *grateful* pleasing.
[45] *chase* "Open ground stored with such beasts as are
hunted" (Johnson) (plural).

[46] *Insinuating* fr. *to insinuate,* "to enfold; to wreath; to
wind" (Johnson); *Gordian* a famous knot in Gordium,
cut by Alexander the Great.
[47] *ruminating* chewing the cud.

Creatures of other mould, earth-born perhaps,   360
Not Spirits, yet to heav'nly Spirits bright
Little inferior; whom my thoughts pursue
With wonder, and could love, so lively shines
In them Divine resemblance, and such grace
The hand that formed them on their shape hath poured.   365
Ah gentle pair, ye little think how nigh
Your change approaches, when all these delights
Will vanish and deliver ye to woe;
More woe, the more your taste is now of joy;
Happy, but for so happy ill secured   370
Long to continue, and this high seat your Heav'n
Ill fenced for Heav'n to keep out such a foe
As now is entered; yet no purposed foe
To you whom I could pity thus forlorn
Though I unpitied: League with you I seek,   375
And mutual amity so straight, so close,
That I with you must dwell, or you with me
Henceforth; my dwelling haply may not please
Like this fair Paradise, your sense, yet such
Accept your Maker's work; he gave it me,   380
Which I as freely give; Hell shall unfold,
To entertain you two, her widest Gates,
And send forth all her Kings; there will be room,
Not like these narrow limits, to receive
Your numerous offspring; if no better place,   385
Thank him who puts me loth to this revenge
On you who wrong me not for him who wronged.
And should I at your harmless innocence
Melt, as I do, yet public reason just,
Honour and Empire with revenge enlarged,   390
By conquering this new World, compels me now
To do what else, though damned, I should abhor'.
    So spake the Fiend, and with necessity,
The Tyrant's plea, excused his devilish deeds.
Then from his lofty stand on that high Tree   395
Down he alights among the sportful Herd
Of those four footed kinds, himself now one,
Now other, as their shape served best his end
Nearer to view his prey, and unespied
To mark what of their state he more might learn   400
By word or action marked: about them round
A Lion now he stalks with fiery glare,
Then as a Tiger, who by chance hath spied
In some Purlieu two gentle Fawns at play,
Straight couches close, then rising changes oft   405
His couchant watch, as one who chose his ground
Whence rushing he might surest seize them both

Gripped in each paw: When *Adam* first of men
To first of women *Eve* thus moving speech,
Turned him all ear to hear new utterance flow.[48]   410
    'Sole partner and sole part of all these joys,
Dearer thy self than all; needs must the Power
That made us, and for us this ample World
Be infinitely good, and of his good
As liberal and free as infinite,   415
That raised us from the dust and placed us here
In all this happiness, who at his hand
Have nothing merited, nor can perform
Aught whereof he hath need, he who requires
From us no other service than to keep   420
This one, this easy charge, of all the Trees
In Paradise that bear delicious fruit
So various, not to taste that only Tree
Of knowledge, planted by the Tree of Life,
So near grows Death to Life, what e'er Death is,   425
Some dreadful thing no doubt; for well thou knowst
God hath pronounced it death to taste that Tree,
The only sign of our obedience left
Among so many signs of power and rule
Conferred upon us, and Dominion giv'n   430
Over all other Creatures that possess
Earth, Air, and Sea. Then let us not think hard
One easy prohibition, who enjoy
Free leave so large to all things else, and choice
Unlimited of manifold delights: 435
But let us ever praise him, and extol
His bounty, following our delightful task
To prune these growing Plants, and tend these Flowrs,
Which were it toilsome, yet with thee were sweet'.
    To whom thus *Eve* replied. 'O thou for whom   440
And from whom I was formed flesh of thy flesh,
And without whom am to no end, my Guide
And Head, what thou hast said is just and right.
For we to him indeed all praises owe,
And daily thanks, I chiefly, who enjoy   445
So far the happier Lot, enjoying thee
Preeminent by so much odds, while thou
Like consort to thy self canst no where find.
That day I oft remember, when from sleep
I first awaked, and found my self reposed   450
Under a shade of flowrs, much wondring where
And what I was, whence thither brought, and how.
Not distant far from thence a murmuring sound

---

[48] *him*   himself; Eve is *all ear*.

Of waters issued from a Cave and spread
Into a liquid Plain, then stood unmoved   455
Pure as th' expanse of Heav'n; I thither went
With unexperienced thought, and laid me down
On the green bank, to look into the clear
Smooth Lake, that to me seemed another Sky.
As I bent down to look, just opposite,[49]   460
A Shape within the watry gleam appeared
Bending to look on me, I started back,
It started back, but pleased I soon returned,
Pleased it returned as soon with answering looks
Of sympathy and love; there I had fixed   465
Mine eyes till now, and pined with vain desire,
Had not a voice thus warned me, "What thou seest,
What there thou seest fair Creature is thy self
With thee it came and goes: but follow me,
And I will bring thee where no shadow stays[50]   470
Thy coming, and thy soft embraces, he
Whose image thou art, him thou shalt enjoy
Inseparably thine, to him shalt bear
Multitudes like thy self, and thence be called
Mother of human race:" what could I do,   475
But follow straight, invisibly thus led?
Till I espied thee, fair indeed and tall,
Under a Platan; yet methought less fair,[51]
Less winning soft, less amiably mild,
Than that smooth watry image; back I turned,   480
Thou following cryd'st aloud, "Return fair *Eve*,
Whom fli'st thou? whom thou fli'st, of him thou art,
His flesh, his bone; to give thee being I lent
Out of my side to thee, nearest my heart
Substantial Life, to have thee by my side   485
Henceforth an individual solace dear;[52]
Part of my Soul I seek thee, and thee claim
My other half:" with that thy gentle hand
Seized mine, I yielded, and from that time see
How beauty is excelled by manly grace,   490
And wisdom, which alone is truly fair'.
    So spake our general Mother, and with eyes
Of conjugal attraction unreproved,
And meek surrender, half embracing leaned
On our first Father, half her swelling Breast   495
Naked met his under the flowing Gold
Of her loose tresses hid: he in delight

---

[49] The story recalls the myth of Narcissus, who loves only his own reflection.
[50] *stays* awaits.
[51] *Platan* plane tree.
[52] *individual* "Undivided; not to be parted or disjoined" (Johnson).

Both of her Beauty and submissive charms
Smiled with superior Love, as *Jupiter*[53]
On *Juno* smiles, when he impregns the Clouds   500
That shed *May* Flowers; and pressed her Matron lip
With kisses pure: aside the Devil turned
For envy, yet with jealous leer malign
Eyed them askance, and to himself thus plained.
    'Sight hateful, sight tormenting! thus these two,   505
Imparadised in one another's arms
The happier *Eden*, shall enjoy their fill
Of bliss on bliss, while I to Hell am thrust,
Where neither joy nor love, but fierce desire,
Among our other torments not the least,   510
Still unfulfilled with pain of longing pines;
Yet let me not forget what I have gained
From their own mouths; all is not theirs it seems:
One fatal Tree there stands of Knowledge called,
Forbidden them to taste: Knowledge forbidd'n?   515
Suspicious, reasonless. Why should their Lord
Envy them that? can it be sin to know,
Can it be death? and do they only stand
By Ignorance, is that their happy state,
The proof of their obedience and their faith?   520
O fair foundation laid whereon to build
Their ruin! Hence I will excite their minds
With more desire to know, and to reject
Envious commands, invented with design
To keep them low, whom knowledge might exalt   525
Equal with Gods; aspiring to be such,
They taste and die: what likelier can ensue?
But first with narrow search I must walk round
This Garden, and no corner leave unspied;
A chance but chance may lead where I may meet   530
Some wandring Spirit of Heav'n by Fountain side,
Or in thick shade retired, from him to draw
What further would be learnt. Live while ye may,
Yet happy pair; enjoy, till I return,
Short pleasures, for long woes are to succeed'.   535
    So saying, his proud step he scornful turned,
But with sly circumspection, and began
Through wood, through waste, o'er hill, o'er dale, his roam.
Mean while in utmost Longitude, where Heav'n
With Earth and Ocean meets, the setting Sun   540
Slowly descended, and with right aspéct

---

[53] *Jupiter On Juno smiles* recalling *Iliad* 14.346–51, a
somewhat rough but glittery scene in which the gods are
momentarily equated with the elements of the heavens.

Against the eastern Gate of Paradise
Levelled his evening Rays: it was a Rock
Of Alabaster, piled up to the Clouds,
Conspicuous far, winding with one ascent   545
Accessible from Earth, one entrance high;
The rest was craggy cliff, that overhung
Still as it rose, impossible to climb.
Betwixt these rocky pillars *Gabriel* sat
Chief of th' Angelic Guards, awaiting night;   550
About him exercised Heroic games
Th' unarmed youth of Heav'n, but nigh at hand
Celestial Armoury, Shields, Helms, and Spears,
Hung high with diamond flaming, and with gold.
Thither came *Uriel*, gliding through the Even   555
On a Sun beam, swift as a shooting Star
In *Autumn* thwarts the night, when vapours fired[54]
Impress the Air, and shows the Mariner
From what point of his Compass to beware
Impetuous winds: he thus began in haste.   560
    'Gabriel, to thee thy course by Lot hath giv'n
Charge and strict watch that to this happy Place
No evil thing approach or enter in;
This day at highth of Noon came to my Sphere
A Spirit, zealous, as he seemed, to know   565
More of th' Almighty's works, and chiefly Man
God's latest Image: I described his way
Bent all on speed, and marked his Airy Gate;[55]
But in the Mount that lies from *Eden* North,
Where he first lighted, soon discerned his looks   570
Alien from Heav'n, with passions foul obscured:
Mine eye pursued him still, but under shade
Lost sight of him; one of the banished crew
I fear, hath ventured from the deep, to raise
New troubles; him thy care must be to find'.   575
    To whom the wingèd Warrior thus returned:
'Uriel, no wonder if thy perfect sight,
Amid the Sun's bright circle where thou sitst,
See far and wide: in at this Gate none pass
The vigilance here placed, but such as come   580
Well known from Heav'n; and since Meridian hour
No creature thence: if Spirit of other sort,
So minded, have o'erleapt these earthy bounds
On purpose, hard thou knowst it to exclude
Spiritual substance with corporeal bar.   585
But if within the circuit of these walks

---

[54] *thwarts* crosses; *vapours fired* probably lightning;   [55] *Gate* way, path.
Johnson mentions "electrical vapours" (s.v. *electricity*).

In whatsoever shape he lurk, of whom
Thou tellst, by morrow dawning I shall know'.
        So promised he; and *Uriel* to his charge
Returned on that bright beam, whose point now raised   590
Bore him slope downward to the Sun now fall'n
Beneath th' *Azores*; whether the prime Orb,[56]
Incredible how swift, had thither rolled
Diurnal, or this less volúble Earth[57]
By shorter flight to th' East, had left him there   595
Arraying with reflected Purple and Gold
The Clouds that on his Western Throne attend:
Now came still Evening on, and Twilight grey
Had in her sober Livery all things clad;
Silence accompanied, for Beast and Bird,   600
They to their grassy Couch, these to their Nests
Were slunk, all but the wakeful Nightingale;
She all night long her amorous descant sung;
Silence was pleased: now glowed the Firmament
With living Sapphires: *Hesperus* that led   605
The starry Host, rode brightest, till the Moon
Rising in clouded Majesty, at length
Apparent Queen unveiled her peerless light,
And o'er the dark her Silver Mantle threw.
        When *Adam* thus to *Eve*: 'Fair Consort, th' hour   610
Of night, and all things now retired to rest
Mind us of like repose, since God hath set
Labour and rest, as day and night to men
Successive, and the timely dew of sleep
Now falling with soft slumbrous weight inclines   615
Our eye-lids; other Creatures all day long
Rove idle, unemployed, and less need rest;
Man hath his daily work of body or mind
Appointed, which declares his Dignity,
And the regard of Heav'n on all his ways;   620
While other Animals unactive range,
And of their doings God takes no account.
To morrow ere fresh Morning streak the East
With first approach of light, we must be ris'n,
And at our pleasant labour, to reform   625
Yon flowry Arbors, yonder Alleys green,
Our walks at noon, with branches overgrown,
That mock our scant manuring, and require[58]
More hands than ours to lop their wanton growth:

---

[56] *whether* "whither" in both early editions, but this is probably just a seventeenth-century spelling (see *OED*, A, γ); *whether* stresses Milton's regular profession of uncertainty about the construction of the universe; *prime Orb* the Sun.

[57] *voluble* "Rolling; having quick motion" (Johnson).
[58] *manuring* fr. *manure* "To cultivate by manual labour" (Johnson).

Those Blossoms also, and those dropping Gums,   630
That lie bestrown, unsightly and unsmooth,
Ask riddance, if we mean to tread with ease;
Mean while, as Nature wills, Night bids us rest'.
    To whom thus *Eve* with perfect beauty adorned.[59]
'My Author and Disposer, what thou bidst   635
Unargued I obey; so God ordains,
God is thy law, thou mine: to know no more
Is woman's happiest knowledge and her praise.
With thee conversing I forget all time,
All seasons and their change, all please alike.   640
Sweet is the breath of morn, her rising sweet,
With charm of earliest Birds; pleasant the Sun[60]
When first on this delightful Land he spreads
His orient Beams, on herb, tree, fruit, and flowr,
Glistring with dew; fragrant the fertile earth   645
After soft showers; and sweet the coming on
Of grateful Evening mild; then silent Night
With this her solemn Bird and this fair Moon,
And these the Gems of Heav'n, her starry train:
But neither breath of Morn when she ascends   650
With charm of earliest Birds, nor rising Sun
On this delightful land, nor herb, fruit, flowr,
Glistring with dew, nor fragrance after showers,
Nor grateful Evening mild, nor silent Night
With this her solemn Bird, nor walk by Moon,   655
Or glittering Star-light without thee is sweet.
But wherefore all night long shine these, for whom
This glorious sight, when sleep hath shut all eyes?'
    To whom our general Ancestor replied.
'Daughter of God and Man, accomplished *Eve*,   660
Those have their course to finish, round the Earth,
By morrow Evening, and from Land to Land
In order, though to Nations yet unborn,
Ministring light prepared, they set and rise;
Lest total darkness should by Night regain   665
Her old possession, and extinguish life
In Nature and all things, which these soft fires
Not only enlighten, but with kindly heat
Of various influence foment and warm,
Temper or nourish, or in part shed down   670
Their stellar virtue on all kinds that grow[61]
On Earth, made hereby apter to receive
Perfection from the Sun's more potent Ray.
These then, though unbeheld in deep of night,

---

[59] *beauty adorned*   vowel coalescence.   [61] *virtue*   power, influence.
[60] *charm*   variant of *chirm*, "The blended singing or
noise of many birds" (*OED, charm*[2]).

Shine not in vain, nor think, though men were none,   675
That heav'n would want spectators, God want praise:
Millions of spiritual Creatures walk the Earth
Unseen, both when we wake, and when we sleep:
All these with ceaseless praise his works behold
Both day and night: how often from the steep   680
Of echoing Hill or Thicket have we heard
Celestial voices to the midnight air,
Sole, or responsive each to other's note
Singing their great Creator: oft in bands
While they keep watch, or nightly rounding walk   685
With Heav'nly touch of instrumental sounds
In full harmonic number joined, their songs
Divide the night, and lift our thoughts to Heaven'.[62]
    Thus talking hand in hand alone they passed
On to their blissful Bower; it was a place   690
Chos'n by the sovereign Planter, when he framed
All things to man's delightful use; the roof
Of thickest covert was inwoven shade
Laurel and Myrtle, and what higher grew
Of firm and fragrant leaf; on either side   695
Acanthus, and each odorous bushy shrub
Fenced up the verdant wall; each beauteous flowr,
Iris all hues, Roses, and Jessamin
Reared high their flourished heads between, and wrought
Mosaic; underfoot the Violet,   700
Crocus, and Hyacinth, with rich inlay
Broidered the ground, more coloured than with stone
Of costliest Emblem: other Creature here[63]
Beast, Bird, Insect, or Worm durst enter none;
Such was their awe of Man. In shadier Bower   705
More sacred and sequestered, though but feigned,
Pan or *Sylvanus* never slept, nor Nymph,[64]
Nor *Faunus* haunted. Here in close recess
With Flowers, Garlands, and sweet-smelling Herbs
Espousèd *Eve* decked first her nuptial Bed,   710
And Heav'nly Choirs the Hymenaean sung,[65]
What day the genial Angel to our Sire[66]
Brought her in naked beauty more adorned,
More lovely than *Pandora*, whom the Gods[67]

---

[62] *Divide the night* into watches, or portions, as bells
once did.
[63] *Emblem* "Inlay; enamel; any thing inserted into the
body of another" (Johnson).
[64] *Pan . . . Sylvanus . . . Faunus* woodland gods.
[65] *Hymenaean* bridal song.
[66] *genial* "That which contributes to propagation"
(Johnson).

[67] *Pandora* ("all gifts"), the first woman in Greek mythology; she received gifts from all the gods, but Hermes
taught her flattery and brought her, at Zeus' command,
to Prometheus' *unwiser* brother Epimetheus, son of the
Titan Iapetos (traditionally associated with *Japhet*, son of
Noah); she released the contents of a jar containing all
the ills of mankind.

Endowed with all their gifts, and O too like   715
In sad event, when to the unwiser Son
Of *Japhet* brought by *Hermes*, she ensnared
Mankind with her fair looks, to be avenged
On him who had stole *Jove's* authentic fire.
    Thus at their shady Lodge arrived, both stood   720
Both turned, and under op'n Sky adored
The God that made both Sky, Air, Earth and Heav'n
Which they beheld, the Moon's resplendent Globe
And starry Pole: 'Thou also mad'st the Night,[68]
Maker Omnipotent, and thou the Day,   725
Which we in our appointed work employed
Have finished, happy in our mutual help
And mutual love, the Crown of all our bliss
Ordained by thee, and this delicious place
For us too large, where thy abundance wants   730
Partakers, and uncropped falls to the ground.
But thou hast promised from us two a Race
To fill the Earth, who shall with us extol
Thy goodness infinite, both when we wake,
And when we seek, as now, thy gift of sleep'.   735
    This said unanimous, and other Rites
Observing none, but adoration pure
Which God likes best, into their inmost bower
Handed they went; and eased the putting off[69]
These troublesome disguises which we wear,   740
Straight side by side were laid, nor turned I ween,
Adam from his fair Spouse, nor *Eve* the Rites
Mysterious of connubial Love refused:
Whatever Hypocrites austerely talk
Of purity and place and innocence,   745
Defaming as impure what God declares
Pure, and commands to some, leaves free to all.
Our Maker bids increase, who bids abstain[70]
But our destroyer, foe to God and Man?
Hail wedded Love, mysterious Law, true source   750
Of human offspring, sole propriety,[71]
In Paradise of all things common else,
By thee adulterous lust was driv'n from men
Among the bestial herds to range, by thee
Founded in Reason, Loyal, Just, and Pure,   755
Relations dear, and all the Charities[72]
Of Father, Son, and Brother, first were known.
Far be it, that I should write thee sin or blame,

---

[68] *Pole* sky, heavens.
[69] *Handed* hand in hand.
[70] *Our Maker bids increase* Genesis 1.28.

[71] *propriety* "Peculiarity of possession; exclusive right"
(Johnson).
[72] *Charities* "Tenderness; kindness; love" (Johnson).

Or think thee unbefitting holiest place,
Perpetual Fountain of domestic sweets,   760
Whose bed is undefiled and chaste pronounced,
Present, or past, as Saints and Patriarchs used.
Here Love his golden shafts employs, here lights
His constant Lamp, and waves his purple wings,
Reigns here and revels; not in the bought smile   765
Of Harlots, loveless, joyless, unendeared,
Casual fruition, nor in Court Amours
Mixed Dance, or wanton Mask, or Midnight Ball,
Or Serenate, which the starved Lover sings[73]
To his proud fair, best quitted with disdain.[74]   770
These lulled by Nightingales embracing slept,
And on their naked limbs the flowry roof
Showered Roses, which the Morn repaired. Sleep on
Blest pair; and O yet happiest if ye seek
No happier state, and know to know no more.   775
    Now had night measured with her shadowy Cone
Half way up Hill this vast Sublunar Vault,[75]
And from their Ivory Port the Cherubim
Forth issuing at th' accustomed hour stood armed
To their night watches in warlike Parade,   780
When *Gabriel* to his next in power thus spake.
    '*Uzziel*, half these draw off, and coast the South
With strictest watch; these other wheel the North,
Our circuit meets full West. As flame they part
Half wheeling to the Shield, half to the Spear'.[76]   785
From these, two strong and subtle Spirits he called
That near him stood, and gave them thus in charge.
    '*Ithuriel* and *Zephon*, with winged speed
Search through this Garden, leave unsearched no nook,
But chiefly where those two fair Creatures Lodge,   790
Now laid perhaps asleep secure of harm.
This evening from the Sun's decline arrived
Who tells of some infernal Spirit seen[77]
Hitherward bent (who could have thought?) escaped
The bars of Hell, on errand bad no doubt: 795
Such where ye find, seize fast, and hither bring'.
    So saying, on he led his radiant Files,
Dazzling the Moon; these to the Bower direct
In search of whom they sought: him there they found

---

[73] *Serenate* serenade, "Music or songs with which ladies are entertained by their lovers in the night" (Johnson).
[74] *quitted* requited; responded to.

[75] It is 9:00 p.m.; the point of the cone of the earth's shadow, if visible, would be seen at the zenith at midnight.
[76] *Shield . . . Spear* left hand . . . right hand.
[77] *Who* one who.

Squat like a Toad, close at the ear of *Eve*;   800
Assaying by his Devilish art to reach[78]
The Organs of her Fancy, and with them forge
Illusions as he list, Phantasms and Dreams,
Or if, inspiring venom, he might taint
Th' animal spirits, that from pure blood arise[79]   805
Like gentle breaths from Rivers pure, thence raise
At least distempered, discontented thoughts,
Vain hopes, vain aims, inordinate desires
Blown up with high conceits engendring pride.
Him thus intent *Ithuriel* with his Spear   810
Touched lightly; for no falsehood can endure
Touch of Celestial temper, but returns
Of force to its own likeness: up he starts
Discovered and surprised. As when a spark
Lights on a heap of nitrous Powder, laid[80]   815
Fit for the Tun some Magazine to store
Against a rumoured War, the Smutty grain
With sudden blaze diffused, inflames the Air:
So started up in his own shape the Fiend.
Back stepped those two fair Angels half amazed   820
So sudden to behold the grisly King;
Yet thus, unmoved with fear, accost him soon.
    'Which of those rebel Spirits adjudged to Hell
Com'st thou, escaped thy prison, and transformed,
Why sat'st thou like an enemy in wait   825
Here watching at the head of these that sleep?'
    'Know ye not then' said *Satan*, filled with scorn,
'Know ye not me? ye knew me once no mate
For you, there sitting where ye durst not soar;
Not to know me argues your selves unknown,   830
The lowest of your throng; or if ye know,
Why ask ye, and superfluous begin
Your message, like to end as much in vain?'
To whom thus *Zephon*, answering scorn with scorn.
'Think not, revolted Spirit, thy shape the same,   835
Or undiminished brightness, to be known
As when thou stoodst in Heav'n upright and pure;
That Glory then, when thou no more wast good,
Departed from thee, and thou resembl'st now
Thy sin and place of doom obscure and foul.   840
But come, for thou, be sure, shalt give account
To him who sent us, whose charge is to keep

---

78 *Assaying* trying.
79 *animal spirits* those governing the *anima* (mind).

80 *nitrous Powder, laid Fit for the Tun* gunpowder ready
to be barreled.

This place inviolable, and these from harm'.[81]
    So spake the Cherub, and his grave rebuke
Severe in youthful beauty, added grace   845
Invincible: abashed the Devil stood,
And felt how awful goodness is, and saw
Virtue in her shape how lovely, saw, and pined
His loss; but chiefly to find here observed
His lustre visibly impaired; yet seemed   850
Undaunted. 'If I must contend', said he,
'Best with the best, the Sender not the sent,
Or all at once; more glory will be won,
Or less be lost'. 'Thy fear', said *Zephon* bold,
'Will save us trial what the least can do   855
Single against thee wicked, and thence weak'.
    The Fiend replied not, overcome with rage;
But like a proud Steed reined, went haughty on,
Champing his iron curb: to strive or fly[82]
He held it vain; awe from above had quelled   860
His heart, not else dismayed. Now drew they nigh
The western Point, where those half-rounding guards
Just met, and closing stood in squadron joined
Awaiting next command. To whom their Chief
Gabriël, from the Front thus called aloud.   865
    'O friends, I hear the tread of nimble feet
Hasting this way, and now by glimpse discern
Ithuriël and *Zephon* through the shade,
And with them comes a third of Regal port,
But faded splendour wan; who by his gait   870
And fierce demeanour seems the Prince of Hell,
Not likely to part hence without contest;
Stand firm, for in his look defiance lours'.
    He scarce had ended, when those two approached
And brief related whom they brought, where found,   875
How busied, in what form and posture couched.
    To whom with stern regard thus *Gabriel* spake.
'Why hast thou, *Satan*, broke the bounds prescribed
To thy transgressions, and disturbed the charge
Of others, who approve not to transgress   880
By thy example, but have power and right
To question thy bold entrance on this place;
Employed it seems to violate sleep, and those
Whose dwelling God hath planted here in bliss?'
    To whom thus *Satan* with contemptuous brow.   885
'*Gabriel*, thou hadst in Heav'n th' esteem of wise,
And such I held thee; but this question asked

---

[81] *these*   Adam and Eve.   [82] *iron curb*   a horse's bit.

Puts me in doubt. Lives there who loves his pain?
Who would not, finding way, break loose from Hell,
Though thither doomed? Thou wouldst thy self, no doubt,   890
And boldly venture to whatever place
Farthest from pain, where thou mightst hope to change
Torment with ease, and soonest recompense
Dole with delight, which in this place I sought;
To thee no reason; who knowst only good,   895
But evil hast not tried: and wilt object[83]
His will who bounds us? Let him surer bar
His Iron gates, if he intends our stay
In that dark durance: thus much what was asked.[84]
The rest is true, they found me where they say;   900
But that implies not violence or harm'.
    Thus he in scorn. The warlike Angel moved,
Disdainfully half smiling thus replied.
'O loss of one in Heav'n to judge of wise,[85]
Since *Satan* fell, whom folly overthrew,   905
And now returns him from his prison scaped,
Gravely in doubt whether to hold them wise
Or not, who ask what boldness brought him hither
Unlicenced from his bounds in Hell prescribed;
So wise he judges it to fly from pain   910
However, and to scape his punishment.
So judge thou still, presumptuous, till the wrath,
Which thou incurr'st by flying, meet thy flight
Sev'nfold, and scourge that wisdom back to Hell,
Which taught thee yet no better, that no pain   915
Can equal anger infinite provoked.
But wherefore thou alone? wherefore with thee
Came not all Hell broke loose? is pain to them
Less pain, less to be fled, or thou than they
Less hardy to endure? courageous Chief,   920
The first in flight from pain, hadst thou alleged
To thy deserted host this cause of flight,
Thou surely hadst not come sole fugitive'.
    To which the Fiend thus answered frowning stern.
'Not that I less endure, or shrink from pain,   925
Insulting Angel, well thou knowst I stood
Thy fiercest, when in Battle to thy aid
The blasting vollied Thunder made all speed
And seconded thy else not dreaded Spear.
But still thy words at random, as before,   930
Argue thy inexperience what behooves
From hard assays and ill successes past

---

[83] *wilt object* . . . will you cite . . . (legal language).   [85] angelic irony.
[84] *durance* imprisonment.

A faithful Leader, not to hazard all
Through ways of danger by himself untried.
I therefore, I alone first undertook   935
To wing the desolate Abyss, and spy
This new created World, whereof in Hell
Fame is not silent, here in hope to find
Better abode, and my afflicted Powers
To settle here on Earth, or in mid Air;[86]   940
Though for possession put to try once more[87]
What thou and thy gay Legions dare against;
Whose easier business were to serve their Lord
High up in Heav'n, with songs to hymn his Throne,
And practised distances to cringe, not fight'.   945
      To whom the warrior Angel soon replied.
'To say and straight unsay, pretending first
Wise to fly pain, professing next the spy,
Argues no Leader but a liar traced,
Satan, and couldst thou faithful add? O name,   950
O sacred name of faithfulness profaned!
Faithful to whom? to thy rebellious crew?
Army of Fiends, fit body to fit head;
Was this your discipline and faith engaged,
Your military obedience, to dissolve   955
Allegiance to th' acknowledged Power supreme?
And thou sly hypocrite, who now wouldst seem
Patron of liberty, who more than thou
Once fawned, and cringed, and servily adored
Heav'n's awful Monarch? wherefore but in hope   960
To dispossess him, and thyself to reign?
But mark what I areed thee now, avaunt;[88]
Fly thither whence thou fledst; if from this hour
Within these hallowed limits thou appear,
Back to th' infernal pit I drag thee chained,   965
And Seal thee so, as henceforth not to scorn
The facile gates of Hell too slightly barred'.
      So threatened he, but *Satan* to no threats
Gave heed, but waxing more in rage replied.
'Then when I am thy captive talk of chains,   970
Proud limitary Cherub, but ere then[89]
Far heavier load thy self expect to feel
From my prevailing arm, though Heav'n's King
Ride on thy wings, and thou with thy Compeers,
Us'd to the yoke, draw'st his triumphant wheels   975

---

[86]   *mid Air*   the middle air, between heaven and earth.
[87]   *Though . . . against*   even if I must fight against your opposition.
[88]   *areed*   advise.
[89]   *limitary*   in charge of the limit or boundary, a border guard.

In progress through the road of Heav'n Star-paved'.
    While thus he spake, th' Angelic Squadron bright
Turned fiery red, sharpning in moonèd horns
Their Phalanx, and began to hem him round
With ported Spears, as thick as when a field[90]   980
Of *Ceres* ripe for harvest waving bends
Her bearded Grove of ears, which way the wind
Sways them; the careful Ploughman doubting stands
Lest on the threshing floor his hopeless sheaves
Prove chaff. On th' other side, *Satan*, alarmed   985
Collecting all his might dilated stood,
Like *Teneriff* or *Atlas*, unremoved:[91]
His stature reached the Sky, and on his Crest
Sat horror Plumed; nor wanted in his grasp
What seemed both Spear and Shield: now dreadful deeds   990
Might have ensued, nor only Paradise
In this commotion, but the Starry Cope[92]
Of Heav'n perhaps, or all the Elements[93]
At least had gone to wrack, disturbed and torn
With violence of this conflict, had not soon   995
Th' Eternal to prevent such horrid fray
Hung forth in Heav'n his golden Scales, yet seen[94]
Betwixt *Astrea* and the *Scorpion* sign,
Wherein all things created first he weighed,
The pendulous round Earth with balanced air   1000
In counterpoise, now ponders all events,
Battles and Realms: in these he put two weights
The sequel each of parting and of fight,
The latter quick up flew, and kicked the beam;
Which *Gabriel* spying, thus bespake the Fiend.   1005
    '*Satan*, I know thy strength, and thou knowest mine,
Neither our own but giv'n; what folly then
To boast what Arms can do, since thine no more
Than Heav'n permits, nor mine, though doubled now
To trample thee as mire: for proof look up,   1010
And read thy Lot in yon celestial Sign
Where thou art weighed, and shown how light, how weak,
If thou resist'. The Fiend looked up, and knew
His mounted scale aloft: nor more; but fled
Murmuring, and with him fled the shades of night.   1015

---

[90] *ported* carried with both hands "in form" (Johnson).
[91] *Teneriff or Atlas* mountain peaks off the coast of North Africa and in Morocco.
[92] *Cope* "Any thing which is spread over the head; as the concave of the skies" (Johnson).

[93] *Elements* earth, air, fire, and water.
[94] *golden Scales* the balance beam of the constellation Libra, on the zodiac between Virgo, or *Astrea*, and Scorpio; God's action resembles Zeus' judgement on the Trojan war (*Iliad* 8.69–72).

BOOK V
THE ARGUMENT

Morning approached, Eve *relates to* Adam *her troublesome dream; he likes it not, yet comforts her: They come forth to their day labours: Their Morning Hymn at the Door of their Bower.* God *to render* Man *inexcusable sends* Raphael *to admonish him of his obedience, of his free estate, of his enemy near at hand; who he is, and why his enemy, and whatever else may avail* Adam *to know.* Raphael *comes down to Paradise, his appearance described, his coming discerned by* Adam *afar off sitting at the door of his Bower; he goes out to meet him, brings him to his lodge, entertains him with the choicest fruits of Paradise got together by* Eve; *their discourse at Table:* Raphael *performs his message, minds* Adam *of his state and of his enemy; relates at* Adams *request who that enemy is, and how he came to be so, beginning from his first revolt in Heaven, and the occasion thereof; how he drew his Legions after him to the parts of the North, and there incited them to rebel with him, persuading all but only* Abdiel *a* Seraph, *who in Argument dissuades and opposes him, then forsakes him.*

Now Morn her rosy steps in th' Eastern Clime
Advancing, sowed the earth with Orient Pearl,
When *Adam* waked, so customed, for his sleep
Was Airy light from pure digestion bred,
And temperate vapours bland, which th' only sound[1]   5
Of leaves and fuming rills, *Aurora's* fan,[2]
Lightly dispersed, and the shrill Matin Song
Of Birds on every bough; so much the more
His wonder was to find unwak'ned *Eve*
With Tresses discomposed, and glowing Cheek,   10
As through unquiet rest: he on his side
Leaning half-raised, with looks of cordial Love
Hung over her enamoured, and beheld
Beauty, which whether waking or asleep,
Shot forth peculiar Graces; then with voice   15
Mild, as when *Zephyrus* on *Flora* breathes,[3]
Her hand soft touching, whispered thus. 'Awake
My fairest, my espoused, my latest found,
Heav'n's last best gift, my ever new delight,
Awake, the morning shines, and the fresh field   20
Calls us, we lose the prime, to mark how spring[4]
Our tender Plants, how blows the Citron Grove,[5]
What drops the Myrrh, and what the balmy Reed,
How Nature paints her colours, how the Bee
Sits on the Bloom extracting liquid sweet'.   25
Such whispering waked her, but with startled eye

BOOK V

[1] *vapours* "Fume; steam . . . 'The morning is the best, because the imagination is not clouded by the *vapours* of meat' Dryden" (Johnson).

[2] *Aurora* (Gk Ἡώς, commonly with the epithet *rosy-fingered*) goddess of the morning; in various stories, she carried away several handsome youths.

[3] *Zephyrus . . . Flora* Zephyrus (the west wind) pursued the nymph Chloris who turned into *Flora* (flowers) and dispersed flowers around the world.

[4] *the prime* early morning, but also, the first or best state of life, Eden.

[5] *blows* blossoms.

On *Adam*, whom embracing, thus she spake.
   'O Sole in whom my thoughts find all repose,
My Glory, my Perfection, glad I see
Thy face, and Morn returned, for I this Night,   30
Such night till this I never passed, have dreamed,
If dreamed, not as I oft am wont, of thee,
Works of day past, or morrow's next design,
But of offence and trouble, which my mind
Knew never till this irksome night; methought;   35
Close at mine ear one called me forth to walk
With gentle voice, I thought it thine; it said,
"Why sleep'st thou, *Eve*? now is the pleasant time,
The cool, the silent, save where silence yields
To the night-warbling Bird, that now awake   40
Tunes sweetest his love-laboured song; now reigns
Full Orbed the Moon, and with more pleasing light
Shadowy sets off the face of things; in vain,
If none regard, Heav'n wakes with all his eyes,[6]
Whom to behold but thee, Nature's desire,   45
In whose sight all things joy, with ravishment
Attracted by thy beauty still to gaze".
I rose as at thy call, but found thee not;
To find thee I directed then my walk;
And on, methought, alone I passed through ways   50
That brought me on a sudden to the Tree
Of interdicted Knowledge: fair it seemed,
Much fairer to my Fancy than by day:
And as I wondring looked, beside it stood
One shaped and winged like one of those from Heav'n   55
By us oft seen; his dewy locks distilled
Ambrosia; on that Tree he also gazed;
And "O fair plant", said he, "with fruit surcharged,
Deigns none to ease thy load, and taste thy sweet,
Nor God, nor Man; Is Knowledge so despised?[7]   60
Or envy, or what reserve forbids to taste?
Forbid who will, none shall from me withhold
Longer thy offered good, why else set here?"
This said he paused not, but with ventrous Arm
He plucked, he tasted; me damp horror chilled   65
At such bold words vouched with a deed so bold:[8]
But he thus overjoyed, "O Fruit Divine,
Sweet of thy self, but much more sweet thus cropped,
Forbidden here, it seems, as only fit
For Gods, yet able to make Gods of Men: 70
And why not Gods of Men, since good, the more

---

[6] *eyes* stars.
[7] *Nor . . . nor* neither . . . nor.
[8] *vouched* confirmed.

Communicated, more abundant grows,
The Author not impaired, but honoured more?
Here, happy Creature, fair Angelic *Eve*,
Partake thou also; happy though thou art,   75
Happier thou mayst be, worthier canst not be:
Taste this, and be henceforth among the Gods
Thy self a Goddess, not to Earth confined,
But sometimes in the Air, as we, sometimes
Ascend to Heav'n, by merit thine, and see   80
What life the Gods live there, and such live thou".
So saying, he drew nigh, and to me held,
Ev'n to my mouth of that same fruit held part
Which he had plucked; the pleasant savoury smell
So quick'ned appetite, that I, methought,   85
Could not but taste. Forthwith up to the Clouds
With him I flew, and underneath beheld
The earth outstretched immense, a prospect wide
And various: wondring at my flight and change
To this high exaltation; suddenly   90
My Guide was gone, and I, me thought, sunk down,
And fell asleep; but O how glad I waked
To find this but a dream!' Thus *Eve* her Night
Related, and thus *Adam* answered sad.
    'Best Image of my self and dearer half,   95
The trouble of thy thoughts this night in sleep
Affects me equally; nor can I like
This uncouth dream, of evil sprung I fear;
Yet evil whence? in thee can harbour none,
Created pure. But know that in the Soul   100
Are many lesser Faculties, that serve
Reason as chief; among these Fancy next
Her office holds; of all external things,
Which the five watchful Senses represent,
She forms Imaginations, Airy shapes,[9]   105
Which Reason joining or disjoining, frames
All what we affirm or what deny, and call
Our knowledge or Opinion; then retires
Into her private Cell, when Nature rests.[10]
Oft in her absence mimic Fancy wakes   110
To imitate her; but misjoining shapes,
Wild work produces oft, and most in dreams,
Ill matching words and deeds long past or late.
Some such resemblances methinks I find
Of our last Evening's talk, in this thy dream,   115
But with addition strange; yet be not sad.

---

[9] *Imaginations* images.   [10] *when Nature rests* during sleep.

Evil into the mind of God or Man[11]
May come and go, so unreproved, and leave
No spot or blame behind: Which gives me hope
That what in sleep thou didst abhor to dream,   120
Waking thou never wilt consent to do.
Be not disheartened then, nor cloud those looks
That wont to be more cheerful and serene
Than when fair Morning first smiles on the World,
And let us to our fresh employments rise   125
Among the Groves, the Fountains, and the Flowrs
That open now their choisest bosomed smells
Reserved from night, and kept for thee in store.'
    So cheered he his fair Spouse, and she was cheered,
But silently a gentle tear let fall   130
From either eye, and wiped them with her hair;
Two other precious drops that ready stood,
Each in their Crystal sluice, he ere they fell
Kissed, as the gracious signs of sweet remorse
And pious awe, that feared to have offended.   135
    So all was cleared, and to the Field they haste.
But first from under shady arborous roof,
Soon as they forth were come to open sight
Of day-spring, and the Sun, who scarce up ris'n
With wheels yet hov'ring o'er the Ocean-brim,[12]   140
Shot parallel to the earth his dewy ray,
Discovering in wide Lantskip all the East[13]
Of Paradise and *Eden's* happy Plains,
Lowly they bowed adoring, and began
Their Orisons, each Morning duly paid[14]   145
In various style, for neither various style
Nor holy rapture wanted they to praise
Their Maker, in fit strains pronounced, or sung
Unmeditated, such prompt eloquence
Flowed from their lips, in Prose or numerous Verse,[15]   150
More tuneable than needed Lute or Harp
To add more sweetness, and they thus began.
    'These are thy glorious works, Parent of good,
Almighty, thine this universal Frame,
Thus wondrous fair; thy self how wondrous then!   155
Unspeakable, who sitst above these Heavens
To us invisible or dimly seen
In these thy lowest works, yet these declare

---

[11] *God* angels or other superior beings, not the supreme deity.
[12] *wheels* chariot.
[13] *Lantskip* landscape, "A region; the prospect of a country" (Johnson).
[14] *Orisons* morning prayers.
[15] *numerous* "Harmonious; consisting of parts rightly numbered; melodious; musical" (Johnson).

Thy goodness beyond thought, and Power Divine:
Speak ye who best can tell, ye Sons of light,   160
Angels, for ye behold him, and with songs
And choral symphonies, Day without Night,
Circle his throne rejoicing; ye in Heav'n,
On Earth join all ye Creatures to extol
Him first, him last, him midst, and without end.   165
Fairest of Stars, last in the train of Night,
If better thou belong not to the dawn,
Sure pledge of day, that crownst the smiling Morn
With thy bright Circlet, praise him in thy Sphere
While day arises, that sweet hour of Prime.   170
Thou Sun, of this great World both eye and soul,
Acknowledge him thy Greater, sound his praise
In thy eternal course, both when thou climbst,
And when high Noon hast gained, and when thou fallst.
Moon, that now meetst the orient Sun, now fli'st,   175
With the fixed Stars, fixed in their Orb that flies,
And ye five other wandring Fires that move[16]
In mystic Dance not without Song, resound
His praise, who out of Darkness called up Light.
Air, and ye Elements the eldest birth   180
Of Nature's Womb, that in quaternion run[17]
Perpetual Circle, multiform; and mix
And nourish all things, let your ceaseless change
Vary to our great Maker still new praise.
Ye Mists and Exhalations that now rise   185
From Hill or steaming Lake, dusky or grey,
Till the sun paint your fleecy skirts with Gold,
In honour to the World's great Author rise,
Whether to deck with Clouds the uncoloured sky,
Or wet the thirsty Earth with falling showers,   190
Rising or falling still advance his praise.
His praise ye Winds, that from four Quarters blow,
Breathe soft or loud; and wave your tops, ye Pines,
With every Plant, in sign of Worship wave.
Fountains and ye that warble, as ye flow,   195
Melodious murmurs, warbling tune his praise.
Join voices all ye living Souls, ye Birds,
That singing up to Heaven Gate ascend,
Bear on your wings and in your notes his praise;
Ye that in waters glide, and ye that walk   200
The earth, and stately tread, or lowly creep;
Witness if I be silent, morn or even,
To hill, or valley, fountain, or fresh shade,
Made vocal by my song, and taught his praise.

---

[16] *wandring fires* planets.   [17] *quaternion* in a group of four.

Hail universal Lord, be bounteous still   205
To give us only good; and if the night
Have gathered aught of evil or concealed,
Disperse it, as now light dispels the dark'.
    So prayed they innocent, and to their thoughts
Firm peace recovered soon and wonted calm.   210
On to their mornings rural work they haste
Among sweet dews and flowrs; where any row
Of Fruit-trees overwoody reached too far
Their pampered boughs, and needed hands to check
Fruitless embraces: or they led the vine   215
To wed her Elm; she spoused about him twines[18]
Her marriageable arms, and with him brings
Her dowr th' adopted Clusters, to adorn
His barren leaves. Them thus employed beheld
With pity Heav'n's high King, and to him called   220
Raphael, the sociable Spirit, that deigned
To travel with Tobias, and secured[19]
His marriage with the seventimes-wedded Maid.
'*Raphael*', said he, 'thou hear'st what stir on Earth
Satan, from Hell scaped through the darksome Gulf   225
Hath raised in Paradise, and how disturbed
This night the human pair, how he designs
In them at once to ruin all mankind.
Go therefore, half this day as friend with friend
Converse with *Adam*, in what Bowr or shade   230
Thou find'st him from the heat of Noon retired,
To respite his day-labour with repast,
Or with repose; and such discourse bring on,
As may advise him of his happy state,
Happiness in his power left free to will,   235
Left to his own free Will, his Will though free,
Yet mutable; whence warn him to beware
He swerve not too secure: tell him withal
His danger, and from whom; what enemy
Late falln himself from Heav'n, is plotting now   240
The fall of others from like state of bliss;
By violence, no, for that shall be withstood,
But by deceit and lies; this let him know,
Lest wilfully transgressing he pretend
Surprisal, unadmonished, unforewarned'.   245
    So spake th' Eternal Father, and fulfilled
All Justice: nor delayed the wingèd Saint

---

[18] *Elm* "It was used to support vines, to which   [19] *Tobias* cf. 4.166–71.
the poets allude . . . 'Thou art an elm, my husband, I
a vine . . .' Shakespeare [*Comedy of Errors* 2. 2. 176]"
(Johnson).

After his charge received; but from among
Thousand Celestial Ardors, where he stood[20]
Veiled with his gorgeous wings, up springing light   250
Flew through the midst of Heav'n; th Angelic Choirs
On each hand parting, to his speed gave way[21]
Through all th' empyreal road; till at the Gate
Of Heav'n arrived, the gate self-opened wide
On golden Hinges turning, as by work   255
Divine the sovereign Architect had framed.
From hence, no cloud, or, to obstruct his sight,
Star interposed, however small he sees,
Not unconform to other shining Globes,
Earth and the Gard'n of God, with Cedars crowned   260
Above all Hills. As when by night the Glass
Of *Galileo*, less assured, observes
Imagined Lands and Regions in the Moon:
Or Pilot, from amidst the *Cyclades*[22]
Delos or *Samos* first appearing kens   265
A cloudy spot. Down thither prone in flight
He speeds, and through the vast Ethereal sky
Sails between worlds and worlds, with steady wing
Now on the polar winds, then with quick Fan[23]
Winnows the buxom Air; till within soar   270
Of Towering Eagles, to all the Fowls he seems
A *Phoenix*, gazed by all, as that sole Bird[24]
When to enshrine his relics in the Sun's
Bright Temple, to *Ægyptian* Thebes he flies.
At once on th' Eastern cliff of Paradise   275
He lights, and to his proper shape returns
A Seraph winged; six wings he wore, to shade
His lineaments Divine; the pair that clad
Each shoulder broad, came mantling o'er his breast
With regal Ornament; the middle pair   280
Girt like a Starry Zone his waist, and round[25]
Skirted his loins and thighs with downy Gold
And colours dipped in Heav'n; the third his feet
Shadowed from either heel with feathered mail,
Sky-tinctured grain. Like *Maia's* son he stood,[26]   285
And shook his Plumes, that Heav'nly fragrance filled
The circuit wide. Straight knew him all the Bands

---

[20]   *Ardors*   angels "The person ardent or bright. This is used only by Milton" (Johnson).
[21]   *speed*   "Haste; hurry; dispatch" (Johnson).
[22]   *Cyclades, Delos, Samos*   islands in the Aegean.
[23]   *Fan*   wing.
[24]   *Phoenix*   every 500 years a new phoenix is born from the nest and deathbed of the old; soon after birth he carries his parent's body to Egypt for burial, though probably in the lower Egyptian city of Heliopolis at the temple of the Sun God, rather than to the upper Egyptian city of Thebes, famous for its royal tombs.
[25]   *Zone*   belt, girdle.
[26]   *Maia's son*   Hermes, the messenger of the gods.

Of Angels under watch; and to his state,
And to his message high, in honour rise;
For on some message high they guessed him bound.   290
Their glittering Tents he passed, and now is come
Into the blissful field, through Groves of Myrrh,
And flowring Odours, Cassia, Nard, and Balm;
A Wilderness of sweets; for Nature here
Wantoned as in her prime, and played at will   295
Her Virgin Fancies, pouring forth more sweet,
Wild above Rule or Art, enormous bliss.[27]
Him through the spicy Forest onward come
Adam discerned, as in the door he sat
Of his cool Bowr, while now the mounted Sun   300
Shot down direct his fervid Rays to warm
Earth's inmost womb, more warmth than *Adam* needs;
And *Eve* within, due at her hour prepared[28]
For dinner savoury fruits, of taste to please
True appetite, and not disrelish thirst   305
Of nectarous draughts between, from milky stream,
Berry or Grape: to whom thus *Adam* called.
'Haste hither *Eve*, and worth thy sight behold
Eastward among those Trees, what glorious shape
Comes this way moving; seems another Morn   310
Ris'n on mid-noon; some great behest from Heav'n
To us perhaps he brings, and will vouchsafe
This day to be our Guest. But go with speed,
And what thy stores contain, bring forth and pour
Abundance, fit to honour and receive   315
Our Heav'nly stranger; well we may afford
Our givers their own gifts, and large bestow
From large bestowed, where Nature multiplies
Her fertile growth, and by disburd'ning grows
More fruitful, which instructs us not to spare'.   320
        To whom thus *Eve*. 'Adam, earth's hallowed mould,
Of God inspired, small store will serve, where store,[29]
All seasons, ripe for use hangs on the stalk;
Save what by frugal storing firmness gains[30]
To nourish, and superfluous moist consumes: 325
But I will haste, and from each bough and brake,
Each Plant and juiciest Gourd will pluck such choice
To entertain our Angel guest, as he
Beholding shall confess that here on Earth

---

[27] *enormous* "Irregular; out of rule; not regulated by any stated measures; excursive beyond the limits of a regular figure" (Johnson).
[28] *due* "Exact; without deviation" (Johnson).

[29] *inspired* "animate[d] by supernatural infusion" (Johnson); the soil (*mould*) is made productive by God's breath.
[30] *frugal storing* dried fruits, for example.

God hath dispensed his bounties as in Heav'n'.   330
    So saying, with dispatchful looks in haste
She turns, on hospitable thoughts intent
What choice to choose for delicacy best,
What order, so contrived as not to mix
Tastes, not well joined, inelegant, but bring   335
Taste after taste upheld with kindliest change,
Bestirs her then, and from each tender stalk
Whatever Earth all-bearing Mother yields
In *India* East or West, or middle shore
In *Pontus* or the *Punic* Coast, or where[31]   340
Alcinous reigned, fruit of all kinds, in coat,[32]
Rough, or smooth rind, or bearded husk, or shell
She gathers, Tribute large, and on the board
Heaps with unsparing hand; for drink the Grape
She crushes, inoffensive must, and meaths[33]   345
From many a berry, and from sweet kernels prest
She tempers dulcet creams, nor these to hold
Wants her fit vessels pure, then strews the ground[34]
With Rose and Odours from the shrub unfumed.
Mean while our Primitive great Sire, to meet   350
His God-like Guest, walks forth, without more train
Accompanied than with his own complete
Perfections; in himself was all his state,
More solemn than the tedious pomp that waits
On Princes, when their rich Retinue long   355
Of Horses led, and Grooms besmeared with Gold
Dazzles the crowd, and sets them all agape.
Nearer his presence *Adam* though not awed,
Yet with submiss approach and reverence meek,
As to a superior Nature, bowing low,   360
    Thus said. 'Native of Heav'n, for other place
None can than Heav'n such glorious shape contain;
Since by descending from the Thrones above,
Those happy places thou hast deigned a while
To want, and honour these, vouchsafe with us[35]
Two only, who yet by sovereign gift possess
This spacious ground, in yonder shady Bowr
To rest, and what the garden Choicest bears
To sit and taste, till this meridian heat
Be over, and the Sun more cool decline'.   370
    Whom thus the Angelic Virtue answered mild.
'*Adam*, I therefore came, nor art thou such

---

31 *Pontus* a large country with ports on the south-eastern shore of the Black Sea.
32 *Alcinous* king of Phaeacia, perhaps part of modern Corfu; Homer describes his gardens (*Odyssey* 6).
33 *meaths* meads, sweet drinks.
34 *Wants her* does she lack.
35 *To want* to lack; to miss.

Created, or such place hast here to dwell,
As may not oft invite, though Spirits of Heav'n
To visit thee; lead on then where thy Bowr   375
O'ershades; for these mid-hours, till evening rise
I have at will'. So to the Sylvan Lodge
They came, that like *Pomona*'s Arbour smiled[36]
With flowerets decked, and fragrant smells; but *Eve*
Undecked save with her self, more lovely fair   380
Than Wood-Nymph, or the fairest Goddess feigned
Of three that in Mount *Ida* naked strove,[37]
Stood to entertain her guest from Heav'n; no veil
She needed, Virtue-proof, no thought infirm[38]
Altered her cheek. On whom the Angel 'Hail'   385
Bestowed, the holy salutation used[39]
Long after to blest Mary, second *Eve*.
'Hail Mother of Mankind, whose fruitful Womb
Shall fill the World more numerous with thy Sons
Than with these various fruits the Trees of God   390
Have heaped this Table'. Raised of grassy turf
Their Table was, and mossy seats had round,
And on her ample Square from side to side
All *autumn* piled, though *spring* and *autumn* here
Danced hand in hand. A while discourse they hold;   395
No fear lest Dinner cool; when thus began[40]
Our Author. 'Heav'nly stranger, please to taste
These bounties which our Nourisher, from whom
All perfect good, unmeasured out, descends,
To us for food and for delight hath caused   400
The Earth to yield; unsavoury food perhaps
To spiritual Natures; only this I know,
That one Celestial Father gives to all'.
    To whom the Angel. 'Therefore what he gives
(Whose praise be ever sung) to man in part   405
Spiritual, may of purest Spirits be found
No ingrateful food: and food alike those pure[41]
Intelligential substances require[42]
As doth your Rational; and both contain
Within them every lower faculty   410
Of sense, whereby they hear, see, smell, touch, taste,
Tasting concoct, digest, assimilate,

---

[36] *Pomona* goddess of fruit, wooed by Vertumnus, who rules over autumn, the turn of the year.
[37] *three in Mount Ida* Hera, Aphrodite, and Athena competed for the golden apple with the inscription "for the fairest"; Aphrodite won by promising Helen to Paris, and so began the Trojan War.
[38] *Virtue-proof* armed or protected by virtue, rather than a veil.

[39] *holy salutation* "Ave Maria" or "Hail Mary," the most common prayer to the mother of Christ.
[40] *No fear lest Dinner cool* a moment of pleasant, if not comic, relief from epic seriousness.
[41] *ingrateful* "Unpleasing to the sense" (Johnson).
[42] *Intelligential substances* angels.

And corporeal to incorporeal turn.
For know, whatever was created, needs
To be sustained and fed; of Elements   415
The grosser feeds the purer, earth the sea,[43]
Earth and the Sea feed Air, the Air those Fires
Ethereal, and as lowest first the Moon;
Whence in her visage round those spots, unpurged
Vapours not yet into her substance turned.   420
Nor doth the Moon no nourishment exhale
From her moist Continent to higher Orbs.
The Sun that light imparts to all, receives
From all his alimental recompense
In humid exhalations, and at Even[44]   425
Sups with the Ocean: though in Heav'n the Trees
Of life ambrosial fruitage bear, and vines
Yield Nectar, though from off the boughs each Morn
We brush mellifluous Dews, and find the ground
Covered with pearly grain: yet God hath here   430
Varied his bounty so with new delights,
As may compare with Heav'n; and to taste
Think not I shall be nice.[45] So down they sat,
And to their viands fell, nor seemingly[46]
The Angel, nor in mist, the common gloss   435
Of Theologians; but with keen dispatch
Of real hunger, and concoctive heat[47]
To transubstantiate; what redounds, transpires[48]
Through Spirits with ease; nor wonder; if by fire
Of sooty coal the Empiric Alchemist[49]   440
Can turn, or holds it possible to turn
Metals of drossiest Ore to perfet Gold
As from the Mine. Mean while at Table *Eve*
Ministered naked, and their flowing cups
With pleasant liquors crowned: O innocence   445
Deserving Paradise! if ever, then,
Then had the Sons of God excuse to have been[50]
Enamoured at that sight; but in those hearts
Love unlibidinous reigned, nor jealousy
Was understood, the injured Lover's Hell.   450
    Thus when with meats and drinks they had sufficed,
Not burdened Nature, sudden mind arose
In *Adam*, not to let th' occasion pass
Given him by this great Conference to know

---

[43] *grosser* heavier, denser.
[44] *humid exhalations* water vapour.
[45] *nice* fastidious; overly careful.
[46] *nor . . . nor* neither . . . nor.

[47] *concoctive* digestive.
[48] *redounds* is "sent back by reaction" (Johnson).
[49] *Empiric* "Versed in experiments" (Johnson).
[50] *to have* one syllable.

Of things above his World, and of their being   455
Who dwell in Heav'n, whose excellence he saw
Transcend his own so far, whose radiant forms'
Divine effulgence, whose high Power so far
Exceeded human, and his wary speech
Thus to th' Empyreal Minister he framed.   460
    'Inhabitant with God, now know I well
Thy favour, in this honour done to man,
Under whose lowly roof thou hast vouchsafed
To enter, and these earthly fruits to taste,
Food not of Angels, yet accepted so,   465
As that more willingly thou couldst not seem
At Heav'n's high feasts to have fed: yet what compare?'
    To whom the wingèd Hierarch replied.
'O *Adam*, one Almighty is, from whom
All things proceed, and up to him return,[51]   470
If not depraved from good, created all
Such to perfection, one first matter all,
Endued with various forms, various degrees
Of substance, and, in things that live, of life;
But more refined, more spiritous, and pure,   475
As nearer to him placed, or nearer tending
Each in their several active Spheres assigned,
Till body up to spirit work, in bounds
Proportioned to each kind. So from the root
Springs lighter the green stalk, from thence the leaves   480
More airy, last the bright consúmmate flowr
Spirits odórous breathes: flowrs and their fruit,
Man's nourishment, by gradual scale sublimed
To vital Spirits aspire, to animal,
To intellectual, give both life and sense,   485
Fancy and understanding, whence the Soul
Reason receives, and reason is her being,
Discursive, or Intuitive; discourse
Is oftest yours, the latter most is ours,
Differing but in degree, of kind the same.   490
Wonder not then, what God for you saw good
If I refuse not, but convert, as you,
To proper substance; time may come, when men
With Angels may participate, and find
No inconvenient Diet, nor too light Fare: 495
And from these corporal nutriments perhaps
Your bodies may at last turn all to Spirit,
Improved by tract of time, and winged ascend
Ethereal, as we, or may at choice

---

[51] Another version of the great chain of being follows.

Here or in Heav'nly Paradises dwell;   500
If ye be found obedient, and retain
Unalterably firm his love entire
Whose progeny you are. Mean while enjoy
Your fill what happiness this happy state
Can comprehend, incapable of more'.   505
    To whom the Patriarch of mankind replied.
'O favourable spirit, propitious guest,
Well hast thou taught the way that might direct
Our knowledge, and the scale of Nature set
From centre to circumference, whereon   510
In contemplation of created things
By steps we may ascend to God. But say,
What meant that caution joined, *if ye be found*
Obedient? can we want obedience then
To him, or possibly his love desert   515
Who formed us from the dust, and placed us here
Full to the utmost measure of what bliss
Human desires can seek or apprehend?'
    To whom the Angel. 'Son of Heav'n and Earth,
Attend: That thou art happy, owe to God;   520
That thou continu'st such, owe to thy self,
That is, to thy obedience; therein stand.
This was that caution giv'n thee; be advised.
God made thee perfet, not immutable;
And good he made thee, but to persevere   525
He left it in thy power, ordained thy will
By nature free, not over-ruled by Fate
Inextricable, or strict necessity;
Our voluntary service he requires,
Not our necessitated, such with him   530
Finds no acceptance, nor can find, for how
Can hearts, not free, be tried whether they serve
Willing or no, who will but what they must
By Destiny, and can no other choose?
My self, and all th' Angelic host that stand   535
In sight of God enthroned, our happy state
Hold, as you yours, while our obedience holds;
On other surety none: freely we serve,
Because we freely love, as in our will
To love or not; in this we stand or fall: 540
And some are fall'n, to disobedience fall'n,
And so from Heav'n to deepest Hell; O fall
From what high state of bliss into what woe!'
    To whom our great Progenitor. 'Thy words
Attentive, and with more delighted ear,   545
Divine instructer, I have heard, than when
Cherubic Songs by night from neighbouring Hills

Aerial Music send: nor knew I not
To be both will and deed created free;
Yet that we never shall forget to love   550
Our maker, and obey him whose command
Single, is yet so just, my constant thoughts
Assured me, and still assure: though what thou tellest
Hath past in Heav'n, some doubt within me move,[52]
But more desire to hear, if thou consent,   555
The full relation, which must needs be strange,
Worthy of Sacred silence to be heard;
And we have yet large day, for scarce the Sun
Hath finished half his journey, and scarce begins
His other half in the great Zone of Heav'n'.   560
   Thus *Adam* made request; and *Raphael*
After short pause assenting, thus began.
   'High matter thou enjoinest me, O prime of men,
Sad task and hard, for how shall I relate
To human sense th' invisible exploits   565
Of warring Spirits; how without remorse
The ruin of so many glorious once
And perfet while they stood; how last unfold
The secrets of another world, perhaps
Not lawful to reveal? yet for thy good   570
This is dispensed, and what surmounts the reach[53]
Of human sense, I shall delineate so,
By lik'ning spiritual to corporal forms,[54]
As may express them best, though what if Earth
Be but a shadow of Heav'n, and things therein   575
Each to other like, more than on earth is thought?
   'As yet this world was not, and *Chaos* wild[55]
Reigned where these Heav'ns now roll, where Earth now rests
Upon her Centre poised, when on a day
(For time, though in Eternity, applied   580
To motion, measures all things durable
By present, past, and future) on such day
As Heav'n's great Year brings forth, th' Empyreal Host
Of Angels by Imperial summons called,
Innumerable before th' Almighty's Throne   585
Forthwith from all the ends of Heav'n appeared
Under their Hierarchs in orders bright
Ten thousand thousand Ensigns high advanced,
Standards, and Gonfalons twixt Van and Rear[56]

---

[52] *move* moves (subjunctive form).
[53] *dispensed* given dispensation from the law; allowed.
[54] *corporal* probably an error for *corporeal*, "having a body" as opposed to *corporal*, "relating to the body" (Johnson).
[55] This marks the chronological beginning of the plot of *Paradise Lost*.
[56] *Gonfalons* battle flags, ensigns; *Van* vanguard, front of the military formation.

Stream in the Air, and for distinction serve   590
Of Hierarchies, of Orders, and Degrees;
Or in their glittering Tissues bear imblazed
Holy Memorials, acts of Zeal and Love
Recorded eminent. Thus when in Orbs
Of circuit inexpressible they stood,   595
Orb within Orb, the Father infinite,
By whom in bliss imbosomed sat the Son,
Amidst as from a flaming Mount, whose top
Brightness had made invisible, thus spake.
    '"Hear all ye Angels, Progeny of Light,   600
Thrones, Dominations, Princedoms, Virtues, Powers,
Hear my Decree, which unrevoked shall stand.
This day I have begot whom I declare[57]
My only Son, and on this holy Hill
Him have anointed, whom ye now behold   605
At my right hand; your Head I him appoint;
And by my Self have sworn to him shall bow
All knees in Heav'n, and shall confess him Lord:
Under his great Vice-gerent Reign abide
United as one individual Soul[58]   610
For ever happy: him who disobeys
Me disobeys, breaks union, and that day
Cast out from God and blessèd vision, falls
Into utter darkness, deep ingulft, his place[59]
Ordained without redemption, without end".   615
    'So spake th' Omnipotent, and with his words
All seemed well pleased, all seemed, but were not all.
That day, as other solemn days, they spent
In song and dance about the sacred Hill,
Mystical dance, which yonder starry Sphere   620
Of Planets and of fixed in all her Wheels
Resembles nearest, mazes intricate,
Eccentric, intervolved, yet regular
Then most, when most irregular they seem,
And in their motions harmony Divine[60]   625
So smooths her charming tones, that God's own ear
Listens delighted. Evening now approached
(For we have also our evening and our Morn,
We ours for change delectable, not need)
Forthwith from dance to sweet repast they turn   630
Desirous; all in Circles as they stood,

---

[57] *begot* a difficult word because it seems to suggest that Christ is born after the angels whom God here addresses, but ll. 837–8 make it clear that he existed before them; as in Milton's own translation of Psalms 2.6–7, *begot* should be taken in a special theological sense, which is atemporal and applies nearly exclusively to the unique relationship between God the Father and the Son (see *OED*, *beget* 3).
[58] *individual* indivisible.
[59] *Into utter darkness* two metrical feet.
[60] *harmony Divine* a reference to the supposed music of the spheres.

Tables are set, and on a sudden pil'd
With Angels' Food, and rubied nectar flows
In Pearl, in Diamond, and massy Gold,
Fruit of delicious Vines, the growth of Heav'n.   635
On flowrs reposed, and with fresh flowrets crowned,
They eat, they drink, and in communion sweet
Quaff immortality and joy, secure
Of surfeit where full measure only bounds
Excess before th' all bounteous King, who showred   640
With copious hand, rejoicing in their joy.
Now when ambrosial Night with Clouds exhaled
From that high mount of God, whence light & shade
Spring both, the face of brightest Heav'n had changed
To grateful Twilight (for Night comes not there   645
In darker veil) and roseate Dews disposed
All but the unsleeping eyes of God to rest,
Wide over all the Plain, and wider far
Than all this globous Earth in Plain outspread,
(Such are the Courts of God) Th' Angelic throng   650
Dispersed in Bands and Files, their Camp extend
By living Streams among the Trees of Life,
Pavilions numberless, and sudden reared,
Celestial Tabernacles, where they slept
Fanned with cool Winds, save those who in their course   655
Melodious Hymns about the sovereign Throne
Alternate all night long: but not so waked
Satan, so call him now, his former name
Is heard no more in Heav'n; he of the first,
If not the first Arch-Angel, great in Power,   660
In favour and preeminence, yet fraught
With envy against the Son of God, that day
Honoured by his great Father, and proclaimed
Messiah King anointed, could not bear
Through pride that sight, & thought himself impaired.   665
Deep malice thence conceiving and disdain,
Soon as midnight brought on the dusky hour
Friendliest to sleep and silence, he resolved
With all his Legions to dislodge, and leave
Unworshipped, unobeyed, the Throne supreme   670
Contemptuous, and his next subordinate
Awak'ning, thus to him in secret spake.
    '"Sleepst thou Companion dear, what sleep can close
Thy eye-lids? and remembrest what Decree
Of yesterday, so late hath passed the lips   675
Of Heav'n's Almighty. Thou to me thy thoughts
Wast wont, I mine to thee was wont to impart;
Both waking we were one; how then can now
Thy sleep dissent? new Laws thou seest imposed;

New Laws from him who reigns, new minds may raise　　　680
In us who serve, new Counsels to debate
What doubtful may ensue, more in this place
To utter is not safe. Assemble thou
Of all those Myriads which we lead the chief;
Tell them that by command, ere yet dim Night　　　685
Her shadowy cloud withdraws, I am to haste,
And all who under me their Banners wave,
Homeward with flying march where we possess
The Quarters of the North; there to prepare
Fit entertainment to receive our King　　　690
The great *Messiah*, and his new commands,
Who speedily through all the Hierarchies
Intends to pass triumphant, and give Laws".
　'So spake the false Arch-Angel, and infused
Bad influence into th' unwary breast　　　695
Of his Associate; he together calls,
Or several one by one, the Regent Powers,
Under him Regent, tells, as he was taught,
That the most High commanding, now ere Night,
Now ere dim Night had disencumberd Heav'n,　　　700
The great Hierarchal Standard was to move;
Tells the suggested cause, and casts between
Ambiguous words and jealousies, to sound
Or taint integrity but all obeyed
The wonted signal, and superior voice　　　705
Of their great Potentate; for great indeed
His name, and high was his degree in Heav'n;
His count'nance, as the Morning Star that guides[61]
The starry flock, allured them, and with lies
Drew after him the third part of Heav'n's Host:　　　710
Mean while th' Eternal eye, whose sight discerns
Abstrusest thoughts, from forth his holy Mount
And from within the golden Lamps that burn
Nightly before him, saw without their light
Rebellion rising, saw in whom, how spread　　　715
Among the sons of Morn, what multitudes
Were banded to oppose his high Decree;
And smiling to his only Son thus said.
　'"Son, thou in whom my glory I behold
In full resplendence, Heir of all my might,　　　720
Nearly it now concerns us to be sure
Of our Omnipotence, and with what Arms

---

[61] *Morning Star* Satan's unfallen name was Lucifer
(light-bearing) and he was known as "son of the morning" (Isaiah 14.12).

We mean to hold what anciently we claim
Of Deity or Empire, such a foe
Is rising, who intends to erect his Throne   725
Equal to ours, throughout the spacious North;
Nor so content, hath in his thought to try
In battle, what our Power is, or our right.
Let us advise, and to this hazard draw
With speed what force is left, and all employ   730
In our defence; lest unawares we lose
This our high place, our Sanctuary, our Hill".

   'To whom the Son with calm aspéct and clear
Lightning Divine, ineffable, serene,
Made answer. "Mighty Father, thou thy foes   735
Justly hast in derision, and secure
Laugh'st at their vain designs and tumults vain,
Matter to me of Glory, whom their hate
Illustrates; when they see all Regal Power[62]
Giv'n me to quell their pride, and in event   740
Know whether I be dextrous to subdue[63]
Thy Rebels, or be found the worst in Heav'n".

   'So spake the Son, but *Satan*, with his Powers
Far was advanced on wingèd speed, an Host
Innumerable as the Stars of Night,   745
Or Stars of Morning, Dew-drops, which the Sun
Impearls on every leaf and every flower.
Regions they passed, the mighty Regencies
Of Seraphim and Potentates and Thrones
In their triple Degrees, Regions to which   750
All thy Dominion, *Adam*, is no more
Than what this Garden is to all the Earth,
And all the Sea, from one entire globóse[64]
Stretched into Longitude; which having passed
At length into the limits of the North   755
They came, and *Satan* to his Royal seat
High on a Hill, far blazing, as a Mount
Raised on a Mount, with Pyramids and Towers
From Diamond Quarries hewn, and Rocks of Gold;
The Palace of great *Lucifer*, (so call   760
That Structure in the Dialect of men
Interpreted) which not long after, he

---

[62] *Illustrates* "brighten[s] with honour" (Johnson).
[63] *dextrous* with a pun on Latin *dexter*, right hand,
because Jesus sits on the right hand side of God; both
Father and Son are somewhat witty and ironical in discussing Satan's revolt because they know there is no real
threat to their rule.

[64] *one entire globóse* a three-dimensional shape, which
Milton then imagines stretched into a two-dimensional
line in a highly metaphysical fashion.

Affecting all equality with God,
In imitation of that Mount whereon
Messiah was declared in sight of Heav'n,   765
The Mountain of the Congregation called;[65]
For thither he assembled all his Train,
Pretending so commanded to consult
About the great reception of their King,
Thither to come, and with calumnious Art   770
Of counterfeited truth thus held their ears.
     '"Thrones, Dominations, Princedoms, Virtues, Powers,
If these magnific Titles yet remain
Not merely titular, since by Decree
Another now hath to himself engrossed   775
All Power, and us eclipsed under the name
Of King anointed, for whom all this haste
Of midnight march, and hurried meeting here,
This only to consult how we may best
With what may be devised of honours new   780
Receive him coming to receive from us
Knee-tribute yet unpaid, prostration vile,[66]
Too much to one, but double how endured,
To one and to his image now proclaimed?
But what if better counsels might erect   785
Our minds and teach us to cast off this Yoke?
Will ye submit your necks, and choose to bend
The supple knee? ye will not, if I trust
To know ye right, or if ye know your selves
Natives and Sons of Heav'n possessed before   790
By none, and if not equal all, yet free,
Equally free; for Orders and Degrees
Jar not with liberty, but well consist.
Who can in reason then or right assume
Monarchy over such as live by right   795
His equals, if in power and splendour less,
In freedom equal? or can introduce
Law and Edict on us, who without law
Err not, much less for this to be our Lord,
And look for adoration to th' abuse   800
Of those Imperial Titles which assert
Our being ordained to govern, not to serve?"
     'Thus far his bold discourse without control
Had audience, when among the Seraphim
Abdiel, than whom none with more zeal adored   805
The Deity, and divine commands obeyed,
Stood up, and in a flame of zeal severe

---

[65] *Mountain of the Congregation* Isaiah 14.13.   [66] *Knee-tribute* "Genuflection; worship or obeisance shown by kneeling" (Johnson).

The current of his fury thus opposed.
  '"O argument blasphemous, false, and proud!
Words which no ear ever to hear in Heav'n   810
Expected, least of all from thee, ingrate
In place thy self so high above thy Peers.
Canst thou with impious obloquy condemn
The just Decree of God, pronounced and sworn,
That to his only Son by right endued   815
With Regal Sceptre, every Soul in Heav'n
Shall bend the knee, and in that honour due
Confess him rightful King? unjust thou sayest
Flatly unjust, to bind with Laws the free,
And equal over equals to let Reign,   820
One over all with unsucceeded power.
Shalt thou give Law to God, shalt thou dispute
With him the points of liberty, who made
Thee what thou art, and formed the Powers of Heav'n
Such as he pleased, and circumscribed their being?   825
Yet, by experience taught, we know how good,
And of our good and of our dignity
How provident he is, how far from thought
To make us less, bent rather to exalt
Our happy state under one Head more near   830
United. But to grant it thee unjust,
That equal over equals Monarch Reign:
Thy self though great and glorious dost thou count,
Or all Angelic Nature joined in one,
Equal to him begotten Son, by whom   835
As by his Word the mighty Father made[67]
All things, ev'n thee, and all the Spirits of Heav'n
By him created in their bright degrees,
Crowned them with Glory, and to their glory named
Thrones, Dominations, Princedoms, Virtues, Powers,   840
Essential Powers, nor by his Reign obscured,
But more illustrious made, since he the Head
One of our number thus reduced becomes,[68]
His Laws our Laws; all honour to him done
Returns our own. Cease then this impious rage,   845
And tempt not these; but hasten to appease
Th' incensèd Father, and th' incensèd Son,
While Pardon may be found in time besought".
  'So spake the fervent Angel; but his zeal
None seconded, as out of season judged,   850
Or singular and rash, whereat rejoiced
Th' Apostate, and more haughty, thus replied.

---

[67] *Word* Christ is the Word of God, by whom he   [68] *reduced* led back, to the company of angels from his
created the universe (John 1.1).   higher station as logos or word of God.

"That we were formed then sayest thou? and the work
Of secondary hands, by task transferred
From Father to his Son? strange point and new!　　　　　855
Doctrine which we would know whence learnt; who saw
When this creation was? rememberst thou
Thy making, while the Maker gave thee being?
We know no time when we were not as now;
Know none before us, self-begot, self-raised　　　　　860
By our own quick'ning power, when fatal course
Had circled his full Orb, the birth mature
Of this our native Heav'n, Ethereal Sons.
Our puissance is our own, our own right hand
Shall teach us highest deeds, by proof to try　　　　　865
Who is our equal: then thou shalt behold
Whether by supplication we intend
Address, and to begirt the Almighty Throne[69]
Beseeching or besieging. This report,
These tidings carry to the anointed King;　　　　　870
And fly, ere evil intercept thy flight".
　　'He said, and as the sound of waters deep
Hoarse murmur echoed to his words applause
Through the infinite Host; nor less for that
The flaming Seraph fearless, though alone　　　　　875
Encompassed round with foes, thus answered bold.
　　'"O alienate from God, O Spirit accursed,
Forsaken of all good; I see thy fall
Determined, and thy hapless crew involved
In this perfidious fraud, contagion spread　　　　　880
Both of thy crime and punishment: henceforth
No more be troubled how to quit the yoke
Of God's *Messiah*; those indulgent Laws
Will not be now vouchsafed, other Decrees
Against thee are gone forth without recall;　　　　　885
That Golden sceptre which thou didst reject
Is now an Iron Rod to bruise and break
Thy disobedience. Well thou didst advise,
Yet not for thy advice or threats I fly
These wicked Tents devoted, lest the wrath　　　　　890
Impendent, raging into sudden flame[70]
Distinguish not: for soon expect to feel
His Thunder on thy head, devouring fire.
Then who created thee lamenting learn,
When who can uncreate thee thou shalt know".　　　　　895
　　'So spake the Seraph *Abdiel* faithful found,
Among the faithless, faithful only he;

---

[69] *begirt* begird, encircle; surround.　　[70] *Impendent* "Imminent; hanging over; pressing closely" (Johnson).

Among innumerable false, unmoved,
Unshaken, unseduced, unterrified
His Loyalty he kept, his Love, his Zeal;   900
Nor number, nor example with him wrought
To swerve from truth, or change his constant mind
Though single. From amidst them forth he passed,
Long way through hostile scorn, which he sustained
Superior, nor of violence feared aught;   905
And with retorted scorn his back he turned
On those proud Towers to swift destruction doomed'.

BOOK VI
THE ARGUMENT

Raphael *continues to relate how* Michael *and* Gabriel *were sent forth to battle against* Satan *and his* Angels. *The first fight described:* Satan *and his Powers retire under Night: He calls a Council, invents devilish Engines, which in the second day's Fight put* Michael *and his Angels to some disorder; but they at length pulling up Mountains overwhelmed both the force and Machines of* Satan: *Yet the Tumult not so ending, God on the third day sends* Messiah *his Son, for whom he had reserved the glory of that Victory: He in the Power of his Father coming to the place, and causing all his Legions to stand still on either side, with his Chariot and Thunder driving into the midst of his Enemies, pursues them unable to resist towards the Wall of Heaven; which opening, they leap down with horror and confusion into the place of punishment prepared for them in the Deep:* Messiah *returns with triumph to his Father.*

'All night the dreadless Angel unpursued,
Through Heav'n's wide Champaign held his way, till Morn,
Waked by the circling Hours, with rosy hand[1]
Unbarred the gates of Light. There is a Cave
Within the Mount of God, fast by his Throne,   5
Where light and darkness in perpetual round
Lodge and dislodge by turns, which makes through Heav'n
Grateful vicissitude, like Day and Night;
Light issues forth, and at the other door
Obsequious darkness enters, till her hour   10
To veil the Heav'n, though darkness there might well
Seem twilight here; and now went forth the Morn
Such as in highest Heav'n, arrayed in Gold
Empyreal; from before her vanished Night,
Shot through with orient beams; when all the plain   15
Covered with thick embattled Squadrons bright,
Chariots and flaming Arms, and fiery Steeds,
Reflecting blaze on blaze, first met his view:
War he perceived, war in procinct, and found[2]
Already known what he for news had thought   20
To have reported: gladly then he mixed

BOOK VI
[1] *Hours* goddesses of the seasons.

[2] *procinct* "Complete   preparation;   preparation brought to the point of action" (Johnson).

Among those friendly Powers who him received
With joy and acclamations loud, that one
That of so many Myriads fall'n, yet one
Returned not lost: On to the sacred hill   25
They led him high applauded, and present
Before the seat supreme; from whence a voice
From midst a Golden Cloud thus mild was heard.
    "Servant of God, well done, well hast thou fought[3]
The better fight, who single hast maintained   30
Against revolted multitudes the Cause[4]
Of Truth, in word mightier than they in Arms;
And for the testimony of Truth hast borne
Universal reproach, far worse to bear
Than violence: for this was all thy care   35
To stand approved in sight of God, though Worlds
Judged thee perverse: the easier conquest now
Remains thee, aided by this host of friends,
Back on thy foes more glorious to return
Than scorned thou didst depart, and to subdue   40
By force, who reason for their Law refuse,
Right reason for their Law, and for their King[5]
Messiah, who by right of merit Reigns.
Go *Michael* of Celestial Armies Prince,
And thou in Military prowess next   45
Gabriel, lead forth to Battle these my Sons
Invincible, lead forth my armèd Saints
By Thousands and by Millions, ranged for fight;
Equal in number to that Godless crew
Rebellious, them with Fire and hostile Arms   50
Fearless assault, and to the brow of Heav'n
Pursuing drive them out from God and bliss,
Into their place of punishment, the Gulf
Of *Tartarus*, which ready opens wide
His fiery *Chaos* to receive their fall".   55
   'So spake the Sovereign voice, and Clouds began
To darken all the Hill, and smoke to roll
In dusky wreaths, reluctant flames, the sign
Of wrath awaked: nor with less dread the loud
Ethereal Trumpet from on high gan blow:[6]   60
At which command the Powers Militant,
That stood for Heav'n, in mighty Quadrate joined

---

[3] *Servant of God* the literal meaning of "Abdiel."
[4] *the Cause* specifically applied to the aims of the Puritans during the Civil War, and became known as the "good old cause"; the phrase continues into the next line, of course, but the prosody leads one to dwell a moment on these two words, which may be witty.

[5] *Right reason* a complex phrase, which can mean natural law, conscience, or the voice of God, as well as, simply, good or correct reason.
[6] *gan* began to.

Of Union irresistible, moved on
In silence their bright Legions, to the sound
Of instrumental Harmony that breathed   65
Heroic Ardour to advent'rous deeds
Under their God-like Leaders, in the Cause
Of God and his *Messiah*. On they move
Indissolubly firm; nor obvious Hill,
Nor strait'ning Vale, nor Wood, nor Stream divides   70
Their perfet ranks; for high above the ground
Their march was, and the passive Air upbore
Their nimble tread, as when the total kind
Of Birds in orderly array on wing
Came summoned over *Eden* to receive   75
Their names of thee; so over many a tract
Of Heav'n they marched, and many a Province wide
Tenfold the length of this terrene: at last[7]
Far in th' Horizon to the North appeared
From skirt to skirt a fiery Region, stretched   80
In battailous aspéct, and nearer view
Bristled with upright beams innumerable
Of rigid Spears, and Helmets thronged, and Shields
Various, with boastful Argument portrayed,[8]
The banded Powers of *Satan* hasting on   85
With furious expedition; for they weened
That self same day by fight, or by surprise
To win the Mount of God, and on his Throne
To set the envier of his State, the proud
Aspirer, but their thoughts proved fond and vain   90
In the mid way: though strange to us it seemed
At first, that Angel should with Angel war,
And in fierce hosting meet, who wont to meet[9]
So oft in Festivals of joy and love
Unanimous, as sons of one great Sire   95
Hymning th' Eternal Father: but the shout
Of Battle now began, and rushing sound
Of onset ended soon each milder thought.
High in the midst, exalted as a God
Th' Apostate in his Sun-bright Chariot sat,   100
Idol of majesty divine, enclosed
With Flaming Cherubim, and golden Shields;
Then lighted from his gorgeous Throne, for now
'Twixt Host and Host but narrow space was left,
A dreadful interval, and Front to Front   105
Presented stood in terrible array

---

[7] *terrene* the earth.
[8] *Argument* emblematic statement painted on the
shield.

[9] *hosting* encountering in battle array.

Of hideous length: before the cloudy Van,
On the rough edge of battle ere it joined,
Satan with vast and haughty strides advanced,
Came towering, armed in Adamant and Gold;   110
Abdiel that sight endured not, where he stood
Among the mightiest, bent on highest deeds,
And thus his own undaunted heart explores.
   '"O Heav'n! that such resemblance of the Highest
Should yet remain, where faith and realty[10]   115
Remain not; wherefore should not strength and might
There fail where Virtue fails, or weakest prove
Where boldest; though to sight unconquerable?
His puissance, trusting in th' Almighty's aid,
I mean to try, whose Reason I have tried[11]   120
Unsound and false; nor is it aught but just,
That he who in debate of Truth hath won,
Should win in Arms, in both disputes alike
Victor; though brutish that contest and foul,
When Reason hath to deal with force, yet so   125
Most reason is that Reason overcome".
   'So pondering, and from his armèd Peers
Forth stepping opposite, half way he met
His daring foe, at this prevention more[12]
Incensed, and thus securely him defied.   130
   '"Proud, art thou met? thy hope was to have reached
The heighth of thy aspiring unopposed,
The Throne of God unguarded, and his side
Abandoned at the terror of thy Power
Or potent tongue; fool, not to think how vain   135
Against th' Omnipotent to rise in Arms;
Who out of smallest things could without end
Have raised incessant Armies to defeat
Thy folly; or with solitary hand
Reaching beyond all limit at one blow   140
Unaided could have finished thee, and whelmed
Thy Legions under darkness; but thou seest
All are not of thy Train; there be who Faith
Prefer, and Piety to God, though then
To thee not visible, when I alone   145
Seemed in thy World erroneous to dissent
From all: my Sect thou seest, now learn too late[13]
How few sometimes may know, when thousands err".
   'Whom the grand foe with scornful eye askance

---

[10] *realty* "loyalty," from Italian *reale* (Johnson, quoting Zachariah Pearce); sincerity (*OED*).
[11] *tried* proved, demonstrated by a test.
[12] *prevention* "Hindrance; obstruction" (Johnson).

[13] *Sect* a system of beliefs, or a body of persons holding such beliefs, especially unorthodox or dissenting views; applied in a bad sense by Anglicans to the Puritan sects of Milton's day.

Thus answered. "Ill for thee, but in wished hour   150
Of my revenge, first sought for thou returnst
From flight, seditious Angel, to receive
Thy merited reward, the first assay
Of this right hand provoked, since first that tongue
Inspired with contradiction durst oppose   155
A third part of the Gods, in Synod met
Their Deities to assert, who while they feel
Vigour Divine within them, can allow
Omnipotence to none. But well thou comst
Before thy fellows, ambitious to win   160
From me some Plume, that thy success may show
Destruction to the rest: this pause between
(Unanswered lest thou boast) to let thee know;
At first I thought that Liberty and Heav'n
To heav'nly Souls had been all one; but now   165
I see that most through sloth had rather serve,
Ministring Spirits, trained up in Feast and Song;
Such hast thou armed, the Minstrelsy of Heav'n,
Servility with freedom to contend,
As both their deeds compared this day shall prove".   170
    'To whom in brief thus *Abdiel* stern replied.
"Apostate, still thou errst, nor end wilt find
Of erring, from the path of truth remote:
Unjustly thou deprav'st it with the name
Of *servitude* to serve whom God ordains,   175
Or Nature; God and Nature bid the same,
When he who rules is worthiest, and excels
Them whom he governs. This is servitude,
To serve th' unwise, or him who hath rebelled
Against his worthier, as thine now serve thee,   180
Thy self not free, but to thy self enthralled;
Yet lewdly dar'st our ministring upbraid.
Reign thou in Hell thy Kingdom, let me serve
In Heav'n God ever blest, and his Divine
Behests obey, worthiest to be obeyed,   185
Yet Chains in Hell, not Realms expect: mean while
From me returned, as erst thou saidst, from flight,
This greeting on thy impious Crest receive".
    'So saying, a noble stroke he lifted high,
Which hung not, but so swift with tempest fell   190
On the proud Crest of *Satan*, that no sight,
Nor motion of swift thought, less could his Shield
Such ruin intercept: ten paces huge[14]
He back recoiled; the tenth on bended knee

---

[14]   *ruin*   etymologically, a falling (of the sword).

His massy Spear upstaid; as if on Earth   195
Winds under ground or waters forcing way[15]
Sidelong had pushed a Mountain from his seat
Half sunk with all his Pines. Amazement seized
The Rebel Thrones, but greater rage to see
Thus foiled their mightiest, ours joy filled, and shout,   200
Presage of Victory and fierce desire
Of Battle: whereat *Michaël* bid sound
Th' Arch-Angel trumpet; through the vast of Heav'n
It sounded, and the faithful Armies rung
Hosanna to the Highest: nor stood at gaze   205
The adverse Legions, nor less hideous joined
The horrid shock: now storming fury rose,
And clamour such as heard in Heav'n till now
Was never, Arms on Armour clashing brayed
Horrible discord, and the madding Wheels   210
Of brazen Chariots raged; dire was the noise
Of conflict; over head the dismal hiss
Of fiery Darts in flaming vollies flew,
And flying vaulted either Host with fire.
So under fiery Cope together rushed   215
Both Battles main, with ruinous assault
And inextinguishable rage; all Heav'n
Resounded; and had Earth been then, all Earth
Had to her centre shook. What wonder? when
Millions of fierce encountring Angels fought   220
On either side, the least of whom could wield
These Elements, and arm him with the force
Of all their Regions: how much more of Power
Army against Army numberless to raise
Dreadful combustion warring, and disturb,   225
Though not destroy, their happy Native seat;
Had not th' Eternal King Omnipotent
From his strong hold of Heav'n high over-ruled
And limited their might; though numbered such
As each divided Legion might have seemed   230
A numerous Host, in strength each armèd hand
A Legion, led in fight, yet Leader seemed
Each Warrior single as in Chief, expert[16]
When to advance, or stand, or turn the sway
Of Battle, open when, and when to close   235
The ridges of grim War; no thought of flight,
None of retreat, no unbecoming deed
That argued fear; each on himself relied,
As only in his arm the moment lay

---

[15] *Winds . . . waters* the cause of earthquakes or volcanoes.

[16] *in Chief* in command, "In law, *in capite* [as head], without a superior lord" (Johnson).

Of victory; deeds of eternal fame   240
Were done, but infinite: for wide was spread
That War and various; sometimes on firm ground
A standing fight, then soaring on main wing[17]
Tormented all the Air; all Air seemed then
Conflicting Fire: long time in even scale   245
The Battle hung; till *Satan*, who that day
Prodigious power had shown, and met in Arms
No equal, ranging through the dire attack
Of fighting Seraphim confused, at length
Saw where the Sword of *Michael* smote, and felled   250
Squadrons at once, with huge two-handed sway
Brandished aloft, the horrid edge came down
Wide wasting; such destruction to withstand
He hasted, and opposed the rocky Orb[18]
Of tenfold Adamant, his ample Shield   255
A vast circumference: At his approach
The great Arch-Angel from his warlike toil
Surceased, and glad as hoping here to end
Intestine War in Heav'n, the arch foe subdued[19]
Or Captive dragged in Chains, with hostile frown   260
And visage all inflamed first thus began.
    '"Author of evil, unknown till thy revolt,
Unnamed in Heav'n, now plenteous, as thou seest
These Acts of hateful strife, hateful to all,
Though heaviest by just measure on thy self   265
And thy adherents: how hast thou disturbed
Heav'n's blessèd peace and into Nature brought
Misery, uncreated till the crime
Of thy rebellion? how hast thou instilled
Thy malice into thousands, once upright   270
And faithful, now proved false. But think not here
To trouble Holy Rest; Heav'n casts thee out
From all her Confines. Heav'n the seat of bliss
Brooks not the works of violence and War.
Hence then, and evil go with thee along   275
Thy offspring, to the place of evil, Hell,
Thou and thy wicked crew; there mingle broils,[20]
Ere this avenging Sword begin thy doom,
Or some more sudden vengeance winged from God
Precipitate thee with augmented pain".[21]   280
    'So spake the Prince of Angels; to whom thus
The Adversary. "Nor think thou with wind

---

[17] *main* "Violent;   strong;   overpowering;   vast"   [19] *subdued* past participle, having been subdued.
(Johnson).   [20] *mingle broils* engage in quarrels.
[18] *opposed* held up (to ward off the blow).   [21] *Precipitate* "To throw headlong" (Johnson).

Of airy threats to awe whom yet with deeds
Thou canst not. Hast thou turned the least of these
To flight, or if to fall, but that they rise   285
Unvanquished, easier to transact with me
That thou shouldst hope, imperious, and with threats
To chase me hence? err not, that so shall end
The strife which thou call'st evil, but we style   290
The strife of Glory: which we mean to win,
Or turn this Heav'n it self into the Hell
Thou fablest, here however to dwell free,
If not to reign: mean while thy utmost force,
And join him named *Almighty* to thy aid,
I fly not, but have sought thee far and nigh".   295
    'They ended parle, and both addressed for fight
Unspeakable; for who, though with the tongue
Of Angels, can relate, or to what things
Liken on Earth conspicuous, that may lift[22]
Human imagination to such heighth   300
Of Godlike Power: for likest Gods they seemed,
Stood they or moved, in stature, motion, arms
Fit to decide the Empire of great Heav'n.
Now waved their fiery Swords, and in the Air
Made horrid Circles; two broad Suns their Shields   305
Blazed opposite, while expectation stood
In horror; From each hand with speed retir'd
Where erst was thickest fight, th' Angelic throng,
And left large field, unsafe within the wind
Of such commotion, such as to set forth   310
Great things by small, if Nature's concord broke,
Among the Constellations war were sprung,
Two Planets rushing from aspéct malign
Of fiercest opposition in mid Sky,
Should combat, and their jarring Spheres confound.   315
Together both with next to Almighty Arm,
Uplifted imminent one stroke they aimed
That might determine, and not need repeat,
As not of power, at once; nor odds appeared
In might or swift prevention; but the sword   320
Of *Michael* from the Armoury of God
Was giv'n him tempered so, that neither keen
Nor solid might resist that edge: it met
The sword of *Satan* with steep force to smite
Descending, and in half cut sheer, nor staid,   325
But with swift wheel reverse, deep entring shared[23]
All his right side; then *Satan* first knew pain,

---

[22] *conspicuous* visible.   [23] *shared* sheared.

And writhed him to and fro convolved; so sore
The griding sword with discontinuous wound[24]
Passed through him, but th' Ethereal substance closed   330
Not long divisible; and from the gash
A stream of Nectarous humour issuing flowed
Sanguine, such as Celestial Spirits may bleed,
And all his Armour stained, ere while so bright.
Forthwith on all sides to his aid was run   335
By Angels many and strong who interposed
Defence, while others bore him on their Shields
Back to his Chariot; where it stood retir'd
From off the files of War; there they him laid
Gnashing for anguish and despite and shame   340
To find himself not matchless, and his pride
Humbled by such rebuke, so far beneath
His confidence to equal God in power.
Yet soon he healed; for Spirits that live throughout
Vital in every part, not as frail man   345
In Entrails, Heart or Head, Liver or Reins,[25]
Cannot but by annihilating die;
Nor in their liquid texture mortal wound
Receive, no more than can the fluid Air:
All Heart they live, all Head, all Eye, all Ear,   350
All Intellect, all Sense, and as they please,
They Limb themselves, and colour, shape or size
Assume, as likes them best, condense or rare.[26]
    'Mean while in other parts like deeds deserved
Memorial, where the might of *Gabriel* fought,   355
And with fierce Ensigns pierced the deep array
Of *Moloch* furious King who him defied,
And at his Chariot wheels to drag him bound
Threatened, nor from the Holy One of Heav'n
Refrained his tongue blasphemous; but anon   360
Down clov'n to the waist, with shattered Arms
And uncouth pain fled bellowing. On each wing
Uriel and *Raphäel* his vaunting foe,
Though huge, and in a Rock of Diamond Armed,
Vanquished *Adramelech*, and *Asmadai*,   365
Two potent Thrones, that to be less than Gods
Disdained, but meaner thoughts learned in their flight,
Mangled with ghastly wounds through Plate and Mail,
Nor stood unmindful *Abdiel* to annoy
The Atheist crew, but with redoubled blow   370
Ariel and *Arioch*, and the violence
Of *Ramiel* scorched and blasted overthrew.

---

[24] *griding* piercing; cutting; wounding.   [26] *as likes them best* as they prefer.
[25] *Reins* kidneys.

I might relate of thousands, and their names
Eternize here on Earth; but those elect
Angels contented with their fame in Heav'n   375
Seek not the praise of men: the other sort
In might though wondrous and in Acts of War,
Nor of Renown less eager, yet by doom
Cancelled from Heav'n and sacred memory,
Nameless in dark oblivion let them dwell.   380
For strength from Truth divided and from Just,
Illaudable, nought merits but dispraise
And ignominy, yet to glory aspires
Vain glorious, and through infamy seeks fame:
Therefore Eternal silence be their doom.   385
    'And now their Mightiest quelled, the battle swerved,
With many an inroad gored; deformèd rout
Entered, and foul disorder; all the ground
With shivered armour strow'n, and on a heap
Chariot and Charioteer lay overturned   390
And fiery foaming Steeds; what stood, recoil'd
O'erwearied, through the faint Satanic Host
Defensive scarce, or with pale fear surprised,[27]
Then first with fear surprised and sense of pain
Fled ignominious, to such evil brought   395
By sin of disobedience, till that hour
Not liable to fear, or flight or pain.[28]
Far otherwise th' inviolable Saints
In Cubic Phalanx firm, advanced entire,
Invulnerable, impenetrably armed: 400
Such high advantages their innocence
Gave them above their foes; not to have sinned,
Not to have disobeyed; in fight they stood
Unwearied, unobnoxious to be pained[29]
By wound, though from their place by violence moved.   405
    'Now Night her course began, and over Heav'n
Inducing darkness, grateful truce imposed,
And silence on the odious din of War:
Under her Cloudy covert both retired,
Victor and Vanquished: on the foughten field   410
Michäel and his Angels prevalent
Encamping, placed in Guard their Watches round,
Cherubic waving fires: on th' other part
Satan with his rebellious disappeared,
Far in the dark dislodged, and void of rest,[30]   415
His Potentates to Council called by night;

---

[27] *Defensive scarce* with scarce defenses.
[28] *or . . . or* neither nor.
[29] *unobnoxious* "Not liable; not exposed to any hurt"
(Johnson).

[30] *dislodged* driven from home, but also badly lodged
(from Gk δύς, bad).

And in the midst thus undismayed began.
   '"O now in danger tried, now known in Arms
Not to be overpowered, Companions dear,
Found worthy not of Liberty alone,   420
Too mean pretence, but what we more affect,
Honour, Dominion, Glory, and renown,
Who have sustained one day in doubtful fight
(And if one day, why not Eternal days?)
What Heaven's Lord had powerfullest to send   425
Against us from about his Throne, and judged
Sufficient to subdue us to his will,
But proves not so: then fallible, it seems,
Of future we may deem him, though till now
Omniscient thought. True is, less firmly armed,   430
Some disadvantage we endured and pain,
Till now not known, but known as soon contemned,
Since now we find this our Empyreal form
Incapable of mortal injury
Imperishable, and, though pierced with wound,   435
Soon closing, and by native vigour healed.
Of evil then so small as easy think
The remedy; perhaps more valid Arms,[31]
Weapons more violent, when next we meet,
May serve to better us, and worse our foes,   440
Or equal what between us made the odds,
In Nature none: if other hidden cause
Left them Superior, while we can preserve
Unhurt our minds, and understanding sound,
Due search and consultation will disclose".   445
    'He sat; and in th' assembly next upstood
Nisroch, of Principalities the prime;[32]
As one he stood escaped from cruel fight,
Sore toiled, his riv'n Arms to havoc hewn,
And cloudy in aspéct thus answering spake.   450
"Deliverer from new Lords, leader to free
Enjoyment of our right as Gods; yet hard
For Gods, and too unequal work we find
Against unequal arms to fight in pain,
Against unpained, impassive; from which evil[33]   455
Ruin must needs ensue; for what avails
Valour or strength, though matchless, quelled with pain
Which all subdues, and makes remiss the hands
Of Mightiest. Sense of pleasure we may well

---

[31] *valid* "Strong; powerful; efficacious; prevalent" (Johnson).
[32] *Nisroch* in the Bible, a god worshipped in Assyria (2 Kings 19.37); *Principalities* members of an order in the celestial hierarchy charged with guarding religion and watching over rulers.
[33] *impassive* not suffering.

Spare out of life perhaps, and not repine,   460
But live content, which is the calmest life:
But pain is perfet misery, the worst
Of evils, and, excessive, overturns
All patience. He who therefore can invent
With what more forcible we may offend   465
Our yet unwounded Enemies, or arm
Our selves with like defence, to me deserves
No less than for deliverance what we owe".[34]
　　'Whereto with look composed *Satan* replied.
Not uninvented that, which thou aright   470
Believst so main to our success, I bring;
Which of us who beholds the bright surface
Of this Ethereous mould whereon we stand,
This continent of spacious Heav'n, adorned
With Plant, Fruit, Flower Ambrosial, Gems & Gold,   475
Whose Eye so superficially surveys
These things, as not to mind from whence they grow
Deep under ground, materials dark and crude,
Of spiritous and fiery spume, till touched
With Heav'n's ray, and tempered they shoot forth   480
So beauteous, op'ning to the ambient light.
These in their dark Nativity the Deep
Shall yield us pregnant with infernal flame,
Which into hollow Engines long and round
Thick-rammed, at th' other bore with touch of fire   485
Dilated and infuriate, shall send forth
From far with thundring noise among our foes
Such implements of mischief, as shall dash
To pieces, and o'erwhelm whatever stands
Adverse, that they shall fear we have disarmed   490
The Thunderer of his only dreaded bolt.
Nor long shall be our labour, yet ere dawn,
Effect shall end our wish. Mean while revive;
Abandon fear; to strength and counsel joined
Think nothing hard, much less to be despaired".   495
He ended, and his words their drooping cheer
Enlightened, and their languished hope revived.
Th' invention all admired, and each, how he
To be th' inventer missed, so easy it seemed
Once found, which yet unfound most would have thought   500
Impossible: yet haply of thy Race
In future days, if Malice should abound,
Some one intent on mischief, or inspir'd
With dev'lish machination might devise

---

[34] *No less . . . owe*　nothing less than the reward that
we would owe to our saviour.

Like instrument to plague the Sons of men   505
For sin, on war and mutual slaughter bent.
Forthwith from Council to the work they flew,
None arguing stood, innumerable hands
Were ready, in a moment up they turned
Wide the Celestial soil, and saw beneath   510
Th' originals of Nature in their crude
Conception; Sulphurous and Nitrous Foam
They found, they mingled, and with subtle Art,
Concocted and adusted they reduced
To blackest grain, and into store conveyed: 515
Part hidden veins digged up (nor hath this Earth
Entrails unlike) of Mineral and Stone,
Whereof to found their Engines and their Balls
Of missive ruin;³⁵ part incentive reed
Provide, pernicious with one touch to fire.³⁶   520
So all ere day-spring, under conscious Night
Secret they finished, and in order set,
With silent circumspection unespied.
Now when fair Morn Orient in Heav'n appeared
Up rose the Victor Angels, and to Arms   525
The matin Trumpet Sung: in Arms they stood
Of Golden Panoply, refulgent Host,
Soon banded; others from the dawning Hills
Look round, and Scouts each Coast light-armèd scour,
Each quarter to descry the distant foe,   530
Where lodged, or whither fled, or if for fight,
In motion or in alt: him soon they met³⁷
Under spread Ensigns moving nigh, in slow
But firm Battalion; back with speediest Sail
Zophiel, of Cherubim the swiftest wing,   535
Came flying, and in mid Air aloud thus cried.
    "Arm, Warriors, Arm for fight, the foe at hand,
Whom fled we thought, will save us long pursuit
This day, fear not his flight; so thick a Cloud
He comes, and settled in his face I see   540
Sad resolution and secure: let each
His Adamantine coat gird well, and each
Fit well his Helm, grip fast his orbèd Shield,
Born ev'n or high, for this day will pour down,
If I conjecture aught, no drizzling showr,   545
But rattling storm of Arrows barbed with fire".
So warned he them aware themselves, and soon

---

³⁵ *missive* "Used at a distance" (Johnson); *incentive*
"That which kindles" (Johnson).

³⁶ *pernicious* "Quick. An use which I have found only
in Milton, and which, as it produces an ambiguity, ought
not to be imitated" (Johnson).
³⁷ *alt* halt.

In order, quit of all impediment;
Instant without disturb they took Alarm,[38]
And onward moved Embattled; when behold   550
Not distant far with heavy pace the Foe
Approaching gross and huge; in hollow Cube
Training his devilish Enginry, impaled[39]
On every side with shadowing Squadrons Deep,
To hide the fraud. At interview both stood   555
A while, but suddenly at head appeared
Satan: And thus was heard Commanding loud.
    '"Vanguard, to Right and Left the Front unfold;
That all may see who hate us, how we seek
Peace and composure, and with open breast   560
Stand ready to receive them, if they like
Our overture, and turn not back perverse;
But that I doubt; however witness Heaven,
Heav'n, witness thou anon, while we discharge
Freely our part; ye who appointed stand   565
Do as you have in charge, and briefly touch
What we propound, and loud that all may hear".
    So scoffing in ambiguous words he scarce,
Had ended; when to Right and Left the Front
Divided, and to either Flank retired.   570
Which to our eyes discovered new and strange,
A triple mounted row of Pillars laid
On Wheels (for like to Pillars most they seemed
Or hollowed bodies made of Oak or Fir
With branches lopt, in Wood or Mountain felled)   575
Brass, Iron, Stony mould, had not their mouths
With hideous orifice gaped on us wide,
Portending hollow truce; at each behind
A Seraph stood, and in his hand a Reed
Stood waving tipped with fire; while we suspense,[40]   580
Collected stood within our thoughts amused,
Not long, for sudden all at once their Reeds
Put forth, and to a narrow vent applied
With nicest touch. Immediate in a flame,
But soon obscured with smoke, all Heav'n appeared,   585
From those deep throated Engines belched, whose roar
Embowelled with outrageous noise the Air,
And all her entrails tore, disgorging foul
Their devilish glut, chained Thunderbolts and Hail
Of Iron Globes, which on the Victor Host   590
Levelled, with such impetuous fury smote,
That whom they hit, none on their feet might stand,

---

[38] *Instant* "Quick; without delay" (Johnson).
[39] *impaled* fortified, defended.

[40] *suspense* "Held in doubt; held in expectation" (Johnson).

Though standing else as Rocks, but down they fell
By thousands, Angel on Arch-Angel rolled;
The sooner for their Arms, unarmed they might   595
Have easily as Spirits evaded swift
By quick contraction or remove; but now
Foul dissipation followed and forced rout;[41]
Nor served it to relax their serried files.
What should they do? if on they rushed, repulse   600
Repeated, and indecent overthrow
Doubled, would render them yet more despised;
And to their foes a laughter; for in view
Stood ranked of Seraphim another row
In posture to displode their second tire[42]   605
Of Thunder: back defeated to return
They worse abhorred. *Satan* beheld their plight,
And to his Mates thus in derision called.
    '"O Friends, why come not on these Victors proud?
Ere while they fierce were coming, and when we,   610
To entertain them fair with open Front
And Breast, (what could we more?) propounded terms[43]
Of composition, straight they changed their minds,
Flew off, and into strange vagaries fell,
As they would dance, yet for a dance they seemed   615
Somewhat extravagant and wild, perhaps
For joy of offered peace: but I suppose
If our proposals once again were heard
We should compel them to a quick result".
    'To whom thus *Belial* in like gamesome mood,   620
"Leader, the terms we sent were terms of weight,
Of hard contents, and full of force urged home,
Such as we might perceive amused them all,
And stumbled many, who receives them right,
Had need from head to foot well understand;   625
Not understood, this gift they have besides,
They show us when our foes walk not upright".
    'So they among themselves in pleasant vein
Stood scoffing, heightened in their thoughts beyond
All doubt of Victory, eternal might   630
To match with their inventions they presumed
So easy, and of his Thunder made a scorn,
And all his Host derided, while they stood
A while in trouble; but they stood not long,
Rage prompted them at length, and found them arms   635
Against such hellish mischief fit to oppose.

---

[41] *dissipation* "The state of being dispersed" (Johnson).
[42] *tire* "Rank; row" (Johnson).

[43] *propounded terms/Of composition* proposed a truce but also meaning, pounded with the composite material of gunpowder.

Forthwith (behold the excellence, the power
Which God hath in his mighty Angels placed)
Their Arms away they threw, and to the Hills
(For Earth hath this variety from Heav'n   640
Of pleasure situate in Hill and Dale)
Light as the Lightning glimpse they ran, they flew,
From their foundations loosning to and fro
They plucked the seated Hills with all their load,
Rocks, Waters, Woods, and by the shaggy tops   645
Up lifting bore them in their hands: Amaze,
Be sure, and terror seized the rebel Host,
When coming tówards them so dread they saw
The bottom of the Mountains upward turned,
Till on those cursèd Engines' triple-row   650
They saw them whelmed, and all their confidence
Under the weight of Mountains buried deep,
Themselves invaded next, and on their heads
Main Promontories flung, which in the Air
Came shadowing, and oppressed whole Legions armed,   655
Their armour helped their harm, crushed in and bruised
Into their substance pent, which wrought them pain
Implacable, and many a dolorous groan,
Long struggling underneath, ere they could wind
Out of such prison, though Spirits of purest light,   660
Purest at first, now gross by sinning grown.
The rest in imitation to like Arms
Betook them, and the neighbouring Hills uptore;
So Hills amid the Air encountered Hills
Hurled to and fro with jaculation dire,[44]   665
That under ground, they fought in dismal shade;
Infernal noise; War seemed a civil Game
To this uproar; horrid confusion heaped
Upon confusion rose: and now all Heav'n
Had gone to wrack, with ruin overspread,   670
Had not th' Almighty Father where he sits
Shrined in his Sanctuary of Heav'n secure,
Consulting on the sum of things, foreseen
This tumult, and permitted all, advised:
That his great purpose he might so fulfil,   675
To honour his Anointed Son avenged
Upon his enemies, and to declare
All power on him transferred: whence to his Son
Th' Assessor of his Throne, he thus began.[45]
    '"Effulgence of my Glory, Son beloved,   680
Son in whose face invisible is beheld

---

[44] *jaculation* "The act of throwing missive weapons"
(Johnson).

[45] *Assessor* "He that sits by another, as next in
dignity" (Johnson).

Visibly, what by Deity I am,
And in whose hand what by Decree I do,
Second Omnipotence, two days are past,
Two days, as we compute the days of Heav'n,   685
Since *Michael* and his Powers went forth to tame
These disobedient; sore hath been their fight,
As likeliest was, when two such Foes met armed;
For to themselves I left them, and thou knowst,
Equal in their Creation they were formed,   690
Save what sin hath impaired, which yet hath wrought
Insensibly, for I suspend their doom;
Whence in perpetual fight they needs must last
Endless, and no solution will be found:
War wearied hath performed what War can do,   695
And to disordered rage let loose the reins,
With Mountains as with Weapons armed, which makes
Wild work in Heav'n, and dangerous to the main.
Two days are therefore past, the third is thine;
For thee I have ordained it, and thus far   700
Have suffered, that the Glory may be thine
Of ending this great War, since none but Thou
Can end it. Into thee such Virtue and Grace
Immense I have transfused, that all may know
In Heav'n and Hell thy Power above compare,   705
And this perverse Commotion governed thus,
To manifest thee worthiest to be Heir
Of all things, to be Heir and to be King
By Sacred Unction, thy deservèd right.[46]
Go then thou Mightiest in thy Father's might,   710
Ascend my Chariot, guide the rapid Wheels
That shake Heav'n's basis, bring forth all my War,
My Bow and Thunder, my Almighty Arms
Gird on, and Sword upon thy puissant Thigh;
Pursue these sons of Darkness, drive them out   715
From all Heav'n's bounds into the utter Deep:
There let them learn, as likes them, to despise
God and *Messiah* his anointed King".
    'He said, and on his Son with Rays direct
Shone full, he all his Father full expressed   720
Ineffably into his face received,
And thus the filial Godhead answering spake.
    '"O Father, O Supreme of heav'nly Thrones,
First, Highest, Holiest, Best, thou always seekst
To glorify thy Son, I always thee,   725
As is most just; this I my Glory account,

---

[46] *Unction* "The act of anointing" (Johnson).

My exaltation, and my whole delight,
That thou, in me well pleased, declarst thy will
Fulfilled, which to fulfil is all my bliss.
Sceptre and Power, thy giving, I assume,   730
And gladlier shall resign, when in the end
Thou shalt be All in All, and I in thee
For ever, and in me all whom thou lov'st:
But whom thou hat'st, I hate, and can put on
Thy terrors, as I put thy mildness on,   735
Image of thee in all things; and shall soon,
Armed with thy might, rid heav'n of these rebelled,
To their prepared ill Mansion driven down
To chains of darkness, and th' undying Worm,
That from thy just obedience could revolt,   740
Whom to obey is happiness entire.
Then shall thy Saints unmixed, and from th' impure
Far separate, circling thy holy Mount
Unfeignèd *Halleluiahs* to thee sing,
Hymns of high praise, and I among them chief".   745
So said, he o'er his Sceptre bowing, rose
From the right hand of Glory where he sat,
And the third sacred Morn began to shine
Dawning through Heav'n: forth rushed with whirlwind sound
The Chariot of Paternal Deity,[47]   750
Flashing thick flames, Wheel within Wheel undrawn,
It self instinct with Spirit, but convoyed
By four Cherubic shapes, four Faces each
Had wonderous, as with Stars their bodies all
And Wings were set with Eyes, with Eyes the wheels   755
Of Beryl, and careering Fires between;[48]
Over their heads a crystal Firmament,
Whereon a Sapphire Throne, inlaid with pure
Amber, and colours of the showry Arch.
He in Celestial Panoply all armed   760
Of radiant *Urim*, work divinely wrought,[49]
Ascended, at his right hand Victory[50]
Sat Eagle-winged, beside him hung his Bow
And Quiver with three-bolted Thunder stored,
And from about him fierce Effusion rolled   765
Of smoke and bickering flame, and sparkles dire;
Attended with ten thousand thousand Saints,
He onward came, far off his coming shone,
And twenty thousand (I their number heard)

---

[47]   The chariot comes from Ezekiel 1.
[48]   *Beryl*   a transparent precious stone.
[49]   *Urim*   (light); something worn in the breastplate of
Aaron and symbolic of true judgement.

[50]   *Victory*   Nike, the personification of victory, often
depicted with wings.

Chariots of God, half on each hand were seen: 770
He on the wings of Cherub rode sublime
On the Crystalline Sky, in Sapphire Throned.
Illustrious far and wide, but by his own
First seen, them unexpected joy surprised,
When the great Ensign of *Messiah* blazed   775
Aloft by Angels born, his Sign in Heav'n:
Under whose conduct *Michael* soon reduced
His Army, circumfused on either Wing,
Under their Head imbodied all in one.
Before him Power Divine his way prepared;   780
At his command the uprooted Hills retir'd
Each to his place, they heard his voice and went
Obsequious, Heav'n his wonted face renewed,
And with fresh Flowrets Hill and Valley smiled.
This saw his hapless Foes but stood obdured,[51]   785
And to rebellious fight rallied their Powers
Insensate, hope conceiving from despair.
In heav'nly Spirits could such perverseness dwell?
But to convince the proud what Signs avail,
Or Wonders move th' obdurate to relent?   790
They hardened more by what might most reclaim,
Grieving to see his Glory, at the sight
Took envy, and aspiring to his heighth,
Stood re-embattled fierce, by force or fraud
Weening to prosper, and at length prevail[52]   795
Against God and *Messiah*, or to fall
In universal ruin last, and now
To final Battle drew, disdaining flight,
Or faint retreat; when the great Son of God
To all his Host on either hand thus spake.   800
  '"Stand still in bright array ye Saints, here stand
Ye Angels armed, this day from Battle rest;
Faithful hath been your warfare, and of God
Accepted, fearless in his righteous Cause,
And as ye have received, so have ye done   805
Invincibly; but of this cursèd crew
The punishment to other hand belongs,
Vengeance is his, or whose he sole appoints;
Number to this day's work is not ordained
Nor multitude, stand only, and behold   810
God's indignation on these Godless poured
By me; not you but me they have despised,
Yet envied; against me is all their rage,
Because the Father, t' whom in Heav'n supreme

---

[51] *obdured* "Hardened; inflexible; impenitent"   [52] *Weening* thinking.
(Johnson).

Kingdom and Power and Glory appertains,   815
Hath honoured me according to his will.
Therefore to me their doom he hath assigned;
That they may have their wish, to try with me
In Battle which the stronger proves, they all,[53]
Or I alone against them, since by strength   820
They measure all, of other excellence
Not emulous, nor care who them excels;
Nor other strife with them do I vouchsafe".
   'So spake the Son, and into terror changed
His count'nance too severe to be beheld   825
And full of wrath bent on his Enemies.
At once the Four spread out their Starry wings
With dreadful shade contiguous, and the Orbs
Of his fierce Chariot rolled, as with the sound
Of torrent Floods, or of a numerous Host.   830
He on his impious Foes right onward drove,
Gloomy as Night; under his burning Wheels
The steadfast Empyréan shook throughout,
All but the Throne it self of God. Full soon
Among them he arrived; in his right hand   835
Grasping ten thousand Thunders, which he sent
Before him, such as in their Souls infixed
Plagues; they astonished all resistance lost,
All courage; down their idle weapons dropped;
O'er Shields and Helms, and helmèd heads he rode   840
Of Thrones and mighty Seraphim prostrate,
That wished the Mountains now might be again
Thrown on them as a shelter from his ire.
Nor less on either side tempestuous fell
His arrows, from the fourfold-visaged Four,   845
Distinct with eyes, and from the living Wheels
Distinct alike with multitude of eyes,
One Spirit in them ruled, and every eye
Glared lightning, and shot forth pernicious fire
Among th' accurssed, that withered all their strength,   850
And of their wonted vigour left them drained,
Exhausted, spiritless, afflicted, fall'n.
Yet half his strength he put not forth, but checked
His Thunder in mid Volley, for he meant
Not to destroy, but root them out of Heav'n: 855
The overthrown he raised, and as a Herd
Of Goats or timorous flock together thronged
Drove them before him Thunder-struck, pursued
With terrors and with furies, to the bounds

---

[53]   In this challenge, and throughout much of the passage, Christ resembles Zeus.

And Crystal wall of Heav'n, which op'ning wide,   860
Rolled inward, and a spacious Gap disclosed
Into the wasteful Deep; the monstrous sight[54]
Strook them with horror backward, but far worse
Urged them behind; headlong themselves they threw
Down from the verge of Heav'n, Eternal wrath   865
Burnt after them to the bottomless pit.
  'Hell heard th' unsufferable noise, Hell saw
Heav'n ruining from Heav'n and would have fled[55]
Affrighted; but strict Fate had cast too deep
Her dark foundations, and too fast had bound.   870
Nine days they fell; confounded *Chaos* roared,
And felt tenfold confusion in their fall
Through his wild anarchy, so huge a rout
Incumbered him with ruin: Hell at last
Yawning received them whole, and on them closed,   875
Hell their fit habitation fraught with fire
Unquenchable, the house of woe and pain.
Disburdened Heav'n rejoiced, and soon repaired
Her mural breach, returning whence it rolled.[56]
Sole Victor from th' expulsion of his Foes   880
Messiah his triumphal Chariot turned:
To meet him all his Saints, who silent stood
Eye witnesses of his Almighty Acts,
With Jubilee advanced; and as they went,
Shaded with branching Palm, each order bright,   885
Sung Triumph, and him sung Victorious King,
Son, Heir, and Lord, to him Dominion giv'n,
Worthiest to Reign: he celebrated rode
Triumphant through mid Heav'n, into the Courts
And Temple of his mighty Father Throned   890
On high: who into Glory him received,
Where now he sits at the right hand of bliss.
  'Thus measuring things in Heav'n by things on Earth
At thy request, and that thou may'st beware
By what is past, to thee I have revealed   895
What might have else to human Race been hid;
The discord which befell, and War in Heav'n
Among th' Angelic Powers, and the deep fall
Of those too high aspiring, who rebelled
With *Satan*, he who envies now thy state,   900
Who now is plotting how he may seduce
Thee also from obedience, that with him
Bereaved of happiness thou maist partake
His punishment, Eternal misery;

---

[54] *wasteful* desert-like, empty.   [56] *mural* of the wall.
[55] *ruining* falling.

Which would be all his solace and revenge,   905
As a despite done against the most High,
Thee once to gain Companion of his woe.
But list'n not to his Temptations, warn
Thy weaker; let it profit thee to have heard[57]
By terrible Example the reward   910
Of disobedience; firm they might have stood,
Yet fell; remember, and fear to transgress.'

BOOK VII
THE ARGUMENT

Raphael *at the request of* Adam *relates how and wherefore this world was first created; that God, after the expelling of* Satan *and his Angels out of Heaven, declared his pleasure to create another World and other Creatures to dwell therein; sends his Son with Glory and attendance of Angels to perform the work of Creation in six days: the Angels celebrate with Hymns the performance thereof, and his reascension into Heaven.*

Descend from Heav'n *Urania*, by that name[1]
If rightly thou art called, whose Voice divine
Following, above th' *Olympian* Hill I soar,
Above the flight of *Pegasean* wing.[2]
The meaning, not the Name I call: for thou   5
Nor of the Muses nine, nor on the top
Of old *Olympus* dwell'st, but Heav'nly born,
Before the Hills appeared, or Fountain flowed,
Thou with Eternal wisdom didst converse,
Wisdom thy Sister, and with her didst play   10
In presence of th' Almighty Father, pleased
With thy Celestial Song. Up led by thee
Into the Heav'n of Heav'ns I have presumed,
An Earthly Guest, and drawn Empyreal Air,
Thy tempring; with like safety guided down   15
Return me to my Native Element:
Lest from this flying Steed unreined, (as once
Bellerophon, though from a lower Clime)[3]
Dismounted, on th' *Aleian* Field I fall[4]
Erroneous there to wander and forlorn.[5]   20
Half yet remains unsung but narrower bound
Within the visible Diurnal Sphere;[6]
Standing on Earth, not rapt above the Pole,[7]

---

[57] *Thy weaker* Eve.
BOOK VII
[1] *Urania* the muse who inspires the study of the heavens.
[2] *Pegasean* of Pegasus, the winged horse, sacred to the Muses, on whom Bellerophon (l. 18) tried to ride up to Mount *Olympus*, home of the gods.
[3] *a lower Clime* Bellerophon was from Corinth, Greece whereas Milton is from England.

[4] *Aleian Field* literally the plain of wandering, associated with a place in Lycia (in interior Asia Minor), the scene of Bellerophon's exploits.
[5] *Erroneous* wandering (Latin *errare*).
[6] *Diurnal Sphere* the part of the sky that seems to revolve daily around the earth.
[7] *Pole* sky.

More safe I Sing with mortal voice, unchanged
To hoarse or mute, though fall'n on evil days,   25
On evil days though fall'n, and evil tongues;
In darkness, and with dangers compassed round,
And solitude; yet not alone, while thou
Visit'st my slumbers Nightly, or when Morn
Purples the East: still govern thou my Song,   30
Urania, and fit audience find, though few.
But drive far off the barbarous dissonance
Of *Bacchus* and his revellers, the Race
Of that wild Rout that tore the *Thracian* Bard[8]
In *Rhodope*, where Woods and Rocks had Ears   35
To rapture, till the savage clamour drowned
Both Harp and Voice; nor could the Muse defend[9]
Her Son. So fail not thou, who thee implores:
For thou art Heav'nly, she an empty dream.
　　Say Goddess, what ensued when *Raphaël*,   40
The affable Arch-Angel, had forewarned
Adam by dire example, to beware
Apostasy, by what befell in Heaven
To those Apostates lest the like befall
In Paradise to *Adam* or his Race,   45
Charged not to touch the interdicted Tree,
If they transgress, and slight that sole command,
So easily obeyed amid the choice
Of all tastes else to please their appetite,
Though wandring. He with his consorted *Eve*   50
The story heard attentive, and was filled
With admiration, and deep Muse to hear
Of things so high and strange, things to their thought
So unimaginable as hate in Heav'n,
And War so near the Peace of God in bliss   55
With such confusion: but the evil soon
Driv'n back redounded as a flood on those
From whom it sprung, impossible to mix
With Blessedness. Whence *Adam* soon repealed
The doubts that in his heart arose: and now   60
Led on, yet sinless, with desire to know
What nearer might concern him, how this World
Of Heav'n and Earth conspicuous first began,[10]
When, and whereof created, for what cause,

8　*that wild Rout ... Thracian Bard* in Ovid's story (*Metamorphoses* 11.1–66) a howling band of bacchanals (followers of Bacchus or Dionysius) drown out Orpheus' music with howls, thus interrupting its power over *Woods and Rocks*; they stone him and finally kill him with farming tools.

9　*Muse* Calliope, particularly associated with epic poetry, was the mother of Orpheus; Milton means us to identify him with Orpheus, leaving the bawdy court of Charles II to be associated with the bacchanals.
10　*conspicuous* visible.

What within *Eden* or without was done   65
Before his memory, as one whose drouth[11]
Yet scarce allayed still eyes the current stream,
Whose liquid murmur heard new thirst excites,
Proceeded thus to ask his Heav'nly Guest.
    'Great things, and full of wonder in our ears,   70
Far differing from this World, thou hast revealed
Divine interpreter, by favour sent
Down from the Empyrean to forewarn
Us timely of what might else have been our loss,
Unknown, which human knowledge could not reach: 75
For which to the infinitely Good we owe
Immortal thanks, and his admonishment
Receive with solemn purpose to observe
Immutably his sovereign will, the end
Of what we are. But since thou hast vouchsafed   80
Gently for our instruction to impart
Things above Earthly thought, which yet concerned
Our knowing, as to highest wisdom seemed,
Deign to descend now lower, and relate
What may no less perhaps avail us known,   85
How first began this Heav'n which we behold
Distant so high, with moving Fires adorned
Innumerable, and this which yields or fills
All space, the ambient Air wide interfused
Embracing round this florid Earth, what cause   90
Moved the Creator in his holy Rest
Through all Eternity so late to build
In *Chaos*, and the work begun, how soon
Absolved, if unforbid thou mayest unfold[12]
What we, not to explore the secrets ask   95
Of his Eternal Empire, but the more
To magnify his works, the more we know.
And the great Light of Day yet wants to run
Much of his Race though steep, suspense in Heav'n[13]
Held by thy voice, thy potent voice he hears,   100
And longer will delay to hear thee tell
His Generation, and the rising Birth
Of Nature from the unapparent Deep:
Or if the Star of Evening and the Moon
Haste to thy audience, Night with her will bring   105
Silence, and Sleep listning to thee will watch,
Or we can bid his absence, till thy Song
End, and dismiss thee ere the Morning shine'.
    Thus *Adam* his illustrious Guest besought:

---

[11] *drouth*   thirst.
[12] *Absolved*   finished.

[13] *suspense*   "Held from proceeding" (Johnson).

And thus the Godlike Angel answered mild.   110
'This also thy request with caution asked
Obtain: though to recount Almighty works
What words or tongue of Seraph can suffice,
Or heart of man suffice to comprehend?
Yet what thou canst attain, which best may serve   115
To glorify the Maker, and infer
Thee also happier, shall not be withheld
Thy hearing, such Commission from above
I have received, to answer thy desire
Of knowledge within bounds; beyond abstain   120
To ask, nor let thine own inventions hope
Things not revealed, which th' Invisible King,
Only Omniscient, hath suppressed in Night,
To none communicable in Earth or Heaven:
Enough is left besides to search and know.   125
But Knowledge is as food, and needs no less
Her Temperance over Appetite, to know
In measure what the mind may well contain,
Oppresses else with Surfeit, and soon turns
Wisdom to Folly, as Nourishment to Wind.   130
    'Know then, that after *Lucifer* from Heav'n
(So call him, brighter once amidst the Host
Of Angels, than that Star the Stars among)
Fell with his flaming Legions through the Deep
Into his place, and the great Son returned   135
Victorious with his Saints, th' Omnipotent
Eternal Father from his Throne beheld
Their multitude, and to his Son thus spake.
    '"At least our envious Foe hath failed, who thought[14]
All like himself rebellious, by whose aid   140
This inaccessible high strength, the seat
Of Deity supreme, us dispossessed,
He trusted to have seized, and into fraud
Drew many, whom their place knows here no more;
Yet far the greater part have kept, I see,   145
Their station, Heav'n yet populous retains
Number sufficient to possess her Realms
Though wide, and this high Temple to frequent
With Ministeries due and solemn Rites:
But lest his heart exalt him in the harm   150
Already done, to have dispeopled Heav'n,
My damage fondly deemed, I can repair
That detriment, if such it be to lose
Self-lost, and in a moment will create

---

[14]   *At least*   some editors have read "last."

Another World, out of one man a Race   155
Of men innumerable, there to dwell,
Not here, till by degrees of merit raised
They open to themselves at length the way
Up hither, under long obedience tried,
And Earth be changed to Heav'n, & Heav'n to Earth,   160
One Kingdom, Joy and Union without end.
Mean while inhabit lax, ye Powers of Heav'n,
And thou my Word, begotten Son, by thee[15]
This I perform, speak thou, and be it done:
My overshadowing Spirit and might with thee   165
I send along, ride forth, and bid the Deep
Within appointed bounds be Heav'n and Earth,
Boundless the Deep, because I am who fill
Infinitude, nor vacuous the space.
Though I uncircumscribed my self retire,   170
And put not forth my goodness, which is free
To act or not, Necessity and Chance
Approach not me, and what I will is Fate".
    'So spake th' Almighty, and to what he spake
His Word, the Filial Godhead, gave effect.   175
Immediate are the Acts of God, more swift
Than time or motion, but to human ears
Cannot without procéss of speech be told,
So told as earthly notion can receive.
Great triumph and rejoicing was in Heav'n,   180
When such was heard declared the Almighty's will;
Glory they sung to the most High, good will
To future men, and in their dwellings peace:
Glory to him whose just avenging ire
Had driven out th' ungodly from his sight   185
And th' habitations of the just; to him
Glory and praise, whose wisdom had ordained
Good out of evil to create, in stead
Of Spirits malign a better Race to bring
Into their vacant room, and thence diffuse   190
His good to Worlds and Ages infinite.
So sang the Hierarchies: Mean while the Son
On his great Expedition now appeared,
Girt with Omnipotence, with radiance crowned
Of Majesty Divine, Sapience and Love   195
Immense, and all his Father in him shone.
About his Chariot numberless were poured
Cherub and Seraph, Potentates and Thrones,
And Virtues, wingèd Spirits, and Chariots winged,

---

[15] *my Word* Genesis 1.3 and John 1.1; the echoes of   although, as usual, Milton mixes in classical creation
Genesis 1–2 run throughout the description of creation,   myths as well.

From the Armoury of God, where stand of old   200
Myriads between two brazen Mountains lodged
Against a solemn day, harnessed at hand,
Celestial Equipáge; and now came forth
Spontaneous, for within them Spirit lived,
Attendant on their Lord: Heav'n opened wide   205
Her ever during Gates, Harmonious sound
On golden Hinges moving, to let forth
The King of Glory in his powerful Word
And Spirit, coming to create new worlds.
On heav'nly ground they stood, and from the shore   210
They viewed the vast immeasurable Abyss
Outrageous as a Sea, dark, wasteful, wild,
Up from the bottom turned by furious winds
And surging waves, as Mountains to assault
Heav'n's heighth, and with the Centre mix the Pole.   215
    '"Silence, ye troubled waves, and thou Deep, peace,"
Said then th' Omnific Word, "your discord end":[16]
    'Nor stayed, but on the Wings of Cherubim
Uplifted, in Paternal Glory rode
Far into *Chaos*, and the World unborn;   220
For *Chaos* heard his voice: him all his Train
Followed in bright procession to behold
Creation, and the wonders of his might.
Then stayed the fervid Wheels, and in his hand
He took the golden Compasses, prepared[17]   225
In God's Eternal store, to circumscribe
This Universe, and all created things:
One foot he centred, and the other turned
Round through the vast profundity obscure,
And said, "thus far extend, thus far thy bounds,   230
This be thy just Circumference, O World".
Thus God the Heav'n created, thus the Earth,
Matter unformed and void: Darkness profound
Covered th' Abyss: but on the watry calm
His brooding wings the Spirit of God outspread,   235
And vital virtue infused, and vital warmth
Throughout the fluid Mass, but downward purged
The black tartareous cold Infernal dregs
Adverse to life: then founded, then conglobed
Like things to like, the rest to several place   240
Disparted, and between spun out the Air,
And Earth self balanced on her Centre hung.
    '"Let there be light", said God, and forthwith Light
Ethereal first of things, quintessence pure

---

[16] *Omnific* "All-creating" (Johnson).   [17] *Golden Compasses* mentioned in Proverbs 8.27,
Wisdom's account of creation.

Sprung from the Deep, and from her Native East   245
To journey through the airy gloom began,
Sphered in a radiant Cloud, for yet the Sun
Was not; she in a cloudy Tabernacle
Sojourned the while. God saw the Light was good;
And light from darkness by the Hemisphere   250
Divided: Light the Day, and Darkness Night
He named. Thus was the first Day Ev'n and Morn:
Nor passed uncelebrated, nor unsung
By the Celestial Choirs, when Orient Light
Exhaling first from Darkness they beheld;   255
Birth-day of Heav'n and Earth; with joy and shout
The hollow Universal Orb they filled,
And touched their Golden Harps, and hymning praised
God and his works, Creator him they sung,
Both when first Evening was, and when first Morn.   260
   'Again, God said, "Let there be Firmament
Amid the Waters, and let it divide
The Waters from the Waters": and God made[18]
The Firmament, expanse of liquid, pure,
Transparent, Elemental Air, diffused   265
In circuit to the uttermost convex
Of this great Round: partition firm and sure,
The Waters underneath from those above
Dividing: for as Earth, so he the World
Built on circumfluous Waters calm, in wide   270
Crystálline Ocean, and the loud misrule
Of *Chaos* far removed, lest fierce extremes
Contiguous might distemper the whole frame:
And Heav'n he named the Firmament: So Ev'n
And Morning *Chorus* sung the second Day.   275
   'The Earth was formed, but in the Womb as yet
Of Waters, Embryon immature involved,
Appeared not: over all the face of Earth
Main Ocean flowed, not idle, but, with warm[19]
Prolific humour soft'ning all her Globe,   280
Fermented the great Mother to conceive,
Satiate with genial moisture, when God said,
"Be gathered now ye Waters under Heav'n
Into one place, and let dry Land appear.
Immediately the Mountains huge appear   285
Emergent, and their broad bare backs upheave

---

[18] *Waters from the Waters* those on the surface of the
earth and those in the *Crystalline Ocean* (l. 271) of the
outermost sphere of the Ptolemaic universe; the *Firmament* here means the sky above the earth, or the heavens
(*Heav'n*, l. 274).

[19] *warm Prolific humour* The imagery is from Ovid,
Metamorphoses 1.416–37.

Into the Clouds, their tops ascend the Sky:
So high as heaved the tumid Hills, so low
Down sunk a hollow bottom broad and deep,
Capacious bed of Waters: thither they   290
Hasted with glad precipitance, uprolled
As drops on dust conglobing from the dry;
Part rise in crystal Wall, or ridge direct,[20]
For haste; such flight the great command impressed
On the swift floods: as armies at the call   295
Of Trumpet (for of Armies thou hast heard)
Troop to their Standard; so the watry throng,
Wave rolling after Wave, where way they found,
If steep, with torrent rapture, if through Plain,[21]
Soft-ebbing; nor withstood them Rock or Hill,   300
But they, or under ground, or circuit wide
With Serpent error wandring, found their way,[22]
And on the washy Ooze deep Channels wore;
Easy, ere God had bid the ground be dry,
All but within those banks, where Rivers now   305
Stream, and perpetual draw their humid train.
The dry Land, Earth, and the great receptacle
Of congregated Waters he called Seas:
And saw that it was good, and said, "Let th' Earth
Put forth the verdant Grass, Herb yielding Seed,   310
And Fruit Tree yielding Fruit after her kind;
Whose Seed is in her self upon the Earth".
He scarce had said, when the bare Earth, till then
Desert and bare, unsightly, unadorned,
Brought forth the tender Grass, whose verdure clad   315
Her Universal Face with pleasant green,
Then Herbs of every leaf, that sudden flowred
Op'ning their various colours, and made gay
Her bosom smelling sweet: and these scarce blown,
Forth flourished thick the clustering Vine, forth crept   320
The swelling Gourd, up stood the corny Reed[23]
Embattled in her field: and the humble Shrub,
And Bush with frizzled hair implicit: last[24]
Rose as in Dance the stately Trees, and spread
Their branches hung with copious Fruit; or gemmed   325
Their blossoms: with high woods the hills were crowned,
With tufts the valleys and each fountain side,

---

[20] *ridge* "A steep protuberance" (Johnson); *direct* straight.
[21] *rapture* "Rapidity; haste" (Johnson).
[22] *Serpent error* Latin *serpens* and *error*, winding wandering.
[23] *corny* "Strong or hard like horn {Latin *cornus*}" (Johnson), but it may mean grainy or wheaten, after the

classical comparison of the spears of a numerous host to waving fields of grain (cf. 4.980–83).
[24] *implicit* "Entangled; enfolded; complicated" (Johnson).

With borders long the Rivers. That Earth now
Seemed like to Heav'n, a seat where Gods might dwell,
Or wander with delight, and love to haunt   330
Her sacred shades: though God had yet not rained
Upon the Earth, and man to till the ground
None was, but from the Earth a dewy Mist
Went up and watered all the ground, and each
Plant of the field, which e'er it was in the Earth   335
God made, and every Herb, before it grew
On the green stem; God saw that it was good.
So Ev'n and Morn recorded the Third Day.
   'Again th' Almighty spake: "Let there be Lights
High in th' expanse of Heaven to divide   340
The Day from Night; and let them be for Signs,
For Seasons, and for Days, and circling Years,
And let them be for Lights as I ordain
Their Office in the Firmament of Heav'n
To give Light on the Earth"; and it was so.   345
And God made two great Lights, great for their use
To Man, the greater to have rule by Day,
The less by Night altern: and made the Stars,[25]
And set them in the Firmament of Heav'n
To illuminate the Earth, and rule the Day   350
In their vicissitude, and rule the Night,
And Light from Darkness to divide. God saw,
Surveying his great Work, that it was good:
For of Celestial Bodies first the Sun
A mighty Sphere he framed, unlightsome first,   355
Though of Ethereal Mould: then formed the Moon
Globose, and every magnitude of Stars,
And sowed with Stars the Heav'n thick as a field:
Of Light by far the greater part he took,
Transplanted from her cloudy Shrine, and placed   360
In the Sun's Orb, made porous to receive
And drink the liquid Light, firm to retain
Her gathered beams, great Palace now of Light.
Hither as to their Fountain other Stars
Repairing, in their golden Urns draw Light,   365
And hence the Morning planet gilds her horns;[26]
By tincture or reflection they augment
Their small peculiar, though from human sight[27]
So far remote, with diminution seen,
First in his East the glorious Lamp was seen,   370
Regent of Day, and all th' Horizon round

[25] *altern* alternately, by turns.   [27] *peculiar* their own (light).
[26] *Morning planet* Venus in her crescent phase, with horns.

Invested with bright Rays, jocund to run
His Longitude through Heav'n's high road: the grey
Dawn, and the *Pleiades* before him danced
Shedding sweet influence: less bright the Moon,   375
But opposite in levelled West was set
His mirror, with full face borrowing her Light
From him, for other light she needed none
In that aspéct, and still that distance keeps
Till night, then in the East her turn she shines,   380
Revolved on Heav'n's great Axle, and her Reign
With thousand lesser Lights dividual holds,[28]
With thousand thousand Stars, that then appeared
Spangling the Hemisphere: then first adorned
With their bright Luminaries that Set and Rose,   385
Glad Evening and glad Morn crowned the fourth day.
 'And God said, "Let the Waters generate
Reptile with Spawn abundant, living Soul:[29]
And let Fowl fly above the Earth, with wings
Displayed on the open Firmament of Heav'n".   390
And God created the great Whales, and each
Soul living, each that crept, which plenteously
The waters generated by their kinds,
And every Bird of wing after his kind;
And saw that it was good, and blessed them, saying,   395
"Be fruitful, multiply, and in the Seas
And Lakes and running Streams the waters fill;
And let the Fowl be multiplied on the Earth".
Forthwith the Sounds and Seas, each Creek and Bay,
With Fry innumerable swarm, and Shoals   400
Of Fish that with their Fins and shining Scales
Glide under the green Wave, in Sculls that oft[30]
Bank the mid Sea: part single or with mate
Graze the Seaweed their pasture, and through Groves
Of Coral stray, or sporting with quick glance[31]   405
Show to the Sun their waved coats dropped with Gold,
Or in their Pearly shells at ease, attend
Moist nutriment or under Rocks their food
In jointed Armour watch: on smooth the Seal,[32]
And bended Dolphins play: part huge of bulk   410
Wallowing unwieldy, enormous in their Gait[33]
Tempest the Ocean: there Leviathan

---

[28] *dividual* shared, divided.
[29] *living Soul* translating *animae viventis* in the
Vulgate (Genesis 1.20); no supernatural meaning is implied (cf. l. 392).
[30] *Skulls* schools, perhaps confounded with *shoals*, as
Bank (next line) suggests.

[31] *or . . . or* either . . . or.
[32] *watch* watch for, lie in wait for; *smooth* smooth
seas.
[33] Although it scans, the line is itself *enormous in* its
Gait.

Hugest of living Creatures, on the Deep
Stretched like a Promontory sleeps or swims,
And seems a moving Land, and at his Gills   415
Draws in, and at his Trunk spouts out a Sea.
Mean while the tepid Caves, and Fens, and shores
Their Brood as numerous hatch, from the Egg that soon
Bursting with kindly rupture forth disclosed
Their callow young, but feathered soon and fledge   420
They summed their Pens, and soaring th' air sublime[34]
With clang despised the ground, under a cloud
In prospect; there the Eagle and the Stork
On Cliffs and Cedar tops their Eyries build:
Part loosely wing the Region, part more wise   425
In common, ranged in figure wedge their way,
Intelligent of seasons, and set forth
Their Airy Caravan high over Seas
Flying, and over Lands with mutual wing
Easing their flight; so steers the prudent Crane   430
Her annual Voyage, borne on Winds; the Air
Floats, as they pass, fanned with unnumbered plumes:
From Branch to Branch the smaller Birds with song
Solaced the Woods, and spread their painted wings
Till Ev'n, nor then the solemn Nightingale   435
Ceased warbling, but all night tuned her soft lays:
Others on Silver Lakes and Rivers bathed
Their downy Breast; the Swan with Archèd neck
Between her white wings mantling proudly, Rows[35]
Her state with Oary feet: yet oft they quit   440
The Dank, and, rising on stiff Pennons, tower
The mid Aereal Sky: Others on ground
Walked firm; the crested Cock whose clarion sounds
The silent hours, and the other whose gay Train[36]
Adorns him, coloured with the Florid hue   445
Of Rainbows and Starry Eyes. The Waters thus
With Fish replenished, and the Air with Fowl,
Evening and Morn solemnized the Fifth day.
      'The sixth, and of Creation last arose
With Evening Harps and Matin; when God said,   450
"Let th' Earth bring forth Foul living in her kind,
Cattle and Creeping things, and Beast of the Earth,
Each in their kind". The Earth obeyed, and straight
Op'ning her fertile Womb teemed at a Birth
Innumerous living Creatures, perfet forms,   455
Limbed and full grown: out of the ground up rose

---

[34] *summed* "[in Falconry] to have feathers [*Pens*] full
grown" (Johnson).

[35] *mantling* spreading "the wings as a hawk in pleasure" (Johnson).

[36] *the other* the peacock.

As from his Lair the wild Beast where he wons[37]
In Forest wild, in Thicket, Brake, or Den;
Among the Trees in Pairs they rose, they walked:
The Cattle in the Fields and Meadows green: 460
Those rare and solitary, these in flocks
Pasturing at once, and in broad Herds upsprung.
The grassy Clods now Calved, now half appeared
The Tawny Lion, pawing to get free
His hinder parts, then springs as broke from Bonds, 465
And Rampant shakes his Brinded mane; the Ounce,[38]
The Libbard, and the Tiger, as the Mole[39]
Rising, the crumbled Earth above them threw
In Hillocks; the swift Stag from under ground
Bore up his branching head: scarce from his mould 470
Behemoth biggest born of Earth upheaved[40]
His vastness: Fleeced the Flocks and bleating rose,
As Plants: ambiguous between Sea and Land
The River horse and scaly Crocodile.
At once came forth whatever creeps the ground, 475
Insect or Worm; those waved their limber fans
For wings, and smallest Lineaments exact
In all the Liveries decked of Summer's pride
With spots of Gold and Purple, azure and green:
These as a line their long dimension drew, 480
Streaking the ground with sinuous trace; not all
Minims of Nature; some of Serpent kind[41]
Wondrous in length and corpulence involved
Their Snaky folds, and added wings. First crept
The Parsimonious Emmet, provident[42] 485
Of future, in small room large heart enclosed,
Pattern of just equality perhaps
Hereafter, joined in her popular Tribes
Of Commonalty: swarming next appeared[43]
The Female Bee that feeds her Husband Drone 490
Deliciously, and builds her waxen Cells
With Honey stored: the rest are numberless,
And thou their Natures know'st, & gav'st them Names,
Needless to thee repeated; nor unknown
The Serpent subtl'st Beast of all the field, 495
Of huge extent sometimes, with brazen Eyes

---

[37] *wons* dwells.
[38] *Brinded* brindled.
[39] *Libbard* leopard.
[40] *Behemoth* ". . . elephant . . . Job 40.15" (Johnson, citing Calmet who reviews the other possibilities, including hippopotamus, ox, and devil).

[41] *Serpent* "An animal that moves by undulation without legs" (Johnson), including worms.
[42] *Emmet* ant.
[43] *Commonalty* echoing *Commonwealth*, the Puritans' name for their ideal government; no parallel utopia is suggested in the description of the bees, who provided a traditional emblem of monarchical society.

And hairy Mane terrific, though to thee
Not noxious, but obedient at thy call.
Now Heav'n in all her Glory shone, and rolled
Her motions, as the great first-Mover's hand   500
First wheeled their course; Earth in her rich attire
Consummate lovely smiled; Air, Water, Earth,
By Fowl, Fish, Beast, was flown, was swum, was walked,
Frequent; and of the Sixth day yet remained;
There wanted yet the Master work, the end   505
Of all yet done; a Creature who not prone
And Brute as other creatures, but endued
With Sanctity of Reason, might erect
His Stature, and upright with Front serene[44]
Govern the rest, self-knowing, and from thence   510
Magnanimous to correspond with Heav'n,
But grateful to acknowledge whence his good
Descends, thither with heart and voice, and eyes
Directed in Devotion, to adore
And worship God Supreme, who made him chief   515
Of all his works: therefore the Omnipotent
Eternal Father (For where is not he
Present) thus to his Son audibly spake.
    '"Let us make now Man in our image, Man
In our similitude, and let them rule   520
Over the Fish and Fowl of Sea and Air,
Beast of the Field, and over all the Earth,
And every creeping thing that creeps the ground".
    'This said, he formed thee, *Adam*, thee O Man
Dust of the ground, and in thy nostrils breathed   525
The breath of Life; in his own Image he
Created thee, in the Image of God
Express, and thou becam'st a living Soul.
Male he created thee, but thy consort
Female for Race; then blessed Mankind, and said,   530
"Be fruitful, multiply, and fill the Earth,
Subdue it, and throughout Dominion hold
Over Fish of the Sea, and Fowl of the Air,
And every living thing that moves on the Earth".
Wherever thus created, for no place   535
Is yet distinct by name, thence, as thou know'st,
He brought thee into this delicious Grove,
This Garden, planted with the Trees of God,
Delectable both to behold and taste;
And freely all their pleasant fruit for food   540
Gave thee, all sorts are here that all th' Earth yields,
Variety without end; but of the Tree

---

[44] *Front* brow, forehead.

Which tasted works knowledge of Good and Evil,
Thou may'st not; in the day thou eat'st, thou di'st;
Death is the penalty imposed; beware,   545
And govern well thy appetite, lest sin
Surprise thee, and her black attendant Death."
Here finished he, and all that he had made
Viewed, and behold all was entirely good;
So Ev'n and Morn accomplished the Sixt day: 550
Yet not till the Creator from his work
Desisting, though unwearied, up returned
Up to the Heav'n of Heav'ns his high abode,
Thence to behold this new created World
Th' addition of his Empire, how it showed   555
In prospect from his Throne, how good, how fair,
Answering his great Idea. Up he rode
Followed with acclamation and the sound
Symphonious of ten thousand Harps that tuned
Angelic harmonies: the Earth, the Air   560
Resounded, (thou remember'st, for thou heardst)
The Heav'ns and all the Constellations rung,
The Planets in their station list'ning stood,
While the bright Pomp ascended jubilant.[45]
"Open, ye everlasting gates", they sung,   565
"Open, ye Heav'ns, your living doors; let in
The great Creator from his work returned
Magnificent, his Six days' work, a World;
Open, and henceforth oft; for God will deign
To visit oft the dwellings of just Men   570
Delighted; and with frequent intercourse
Thither will send his wingèd Messengers
On errands of supernal Grace". So sung
The glorious Train ascending: He through Heav'n,
That opened wide her blazing Portals, led   575
To God's Eternal house direct the way,
A broad and ample road, whose dust is Gold
And pavement Stars, as Stars to thee appear,
Seen in the Galaxy, that Milky way
Which nightly as a circling Zone thou seest   580
Powdered with Stars. And now on Earth the Seventh
Evening arose in *Eden*, for the Sun
Was set, and twilight from the East came on,
Forerunning Night; when at the holy mount
Of Heav'n's high-seated top, the Imperial Throne   585
Of Godhead, fixed for ever firm and sure,
The Filial Power arrived, and sat him down

---

[45] *Pomp*   "A procession of splendour and ostentation"
(Johnson).

With his great Father, for he also went
Invisible, yet stayed (such privilege
Hath Omnipresence) and the work ordained,   590
Author and end of all things, and from work
Now resting, blessed and hallowed the Sev'nth day,
As resting on that day from all his work,
But not in silence holy kept; the Harp
Had work and rested not, the solemn Pipe,   595
And Dulcimer, all Organs of sweet stop,
All sounds on fret by String or Golden Wire
Tempered soft Tunings, intermixed with Voice
Choral or Unison: of incense Clouds⁴⁶
Fuming from Golden Censers hid the Mount.   600
Creation and the Six days' acts they sung,
"Great are thy works, *Jehovah*, infinite
Thy power; what thought can measure thee or tongue
Relate thee; greater now in thy return
Than from the Giant Angels; thee that day⁴⁷   605
Thy Thunders magnified; but to create
Is greater than created to destroy.
Who can impair thee, mighty King, or bound
Thy Empire? easily the proud attempt
Of Spirits apostate, and their Counsels vain   610
Thou hast repelled, while impiously they thought
Thee to diminish, and from thee withdraw
The number of thy worshippers. Who seeks
To lessen thee, against his purpose serves
To manifest the more thy might: his evil   615
Thou usest, and from thence creat'st more good.
Witness this new-made World, another Heav'n
From Heaven Gate not far, founded in view
On the clear *Hyaline*, the Glassy Sea;⁴⁸
Of amplitude almost immense, with Stars   620
Numerous, and every Star perhaps a World
Of destined habitation; but thou know'st
Their seasons: among these the seat of men,
Earth with her nether Ocean circumfused,⁴⁹
Their pleasant dwelling place. Thrice happy men,   625
And sons of men, whom God hath thus advanced,
Created in his Image, there to dwell
And worship him, and in reward to rule
Over his Works, on Earth, in Sea, or Air,

---

⁴⁶ *Unison*   voices singing the same notes as opposed to
harmonizing a variety of notes.
⁴⁷ *Giant*   "It is observable, that the idea of a giant is
always associated with pride, brutality, and wickedness"
(Johnson); the *Giant Angels* are the fallen angels.

⁴⁸ *Hyaline*   "Glassy; crystalline; made of glass"
(Johnson); see Revelation 4.6.
⁴⁹ *nether Ocean*   the sea, as opposed to the upper ocean
of the sky.

And multiply a Race of Worshippers   630
Holy and just: thrice happy if they know
Their happiness, and persevere upright."
So sung they, and the Empyréan rung,
With *Halleluiahs*: Thus was Sabbath kept.
And thy request think now fulfilled, that asked   635
How first this World and face of things began,
And what before thy memory was done
From the beginning, that posterity
Informed by thee might know; if else thou seekst
Aught, not surpassing human measure, say'.   640

BOOK VIII
THE ARGUMENT

Adam *inquires concerning celestial Motions, is doubtfully answered, and exhorted to search rather things more worthy of knowledge*: Adam *assents, and still desirous to detain* Raphael, *relates to him what he remembered since his own Creation, his placing in Paradise, his talk with God concerning solitude and fit society, his first meeting and Nuptials with* Eve, *his discourse with the Angel thereupon; who after admonitions repeated departs.*

The Angel ended, and in *Adam's* ear
So Charming left his voice, that he a while
Thought him still speaking, still stood fixed to hear;
Then as new waked thus gratefully replied.
'What thanks sufficient, or what recompense   5
Equal have I to render thee, Divine
Historian, who thus largely hast allayed
The thirst I had of knowledge, and vouchsafed
This friendly condescension to relate
Things else by me unsearchable, now heard   10
With wonder, but delight, and, as is due,
With glory attribúted to the high
Creator; something yet of doubt remains,
Which only thy solution can resolve.
When I behold this goodly Frame, this World   15
Of Heav'n and Earth consisting, and compute,
Their magnitudes, this Earth a spot, a grain,
An Atom, with the Firmament compared[1]
And all her numbered Stars, that seem to roll
Spaces incomprehensible (for such   20
Their distance argues and their swift return
Diurnal) merely to officiate light[2]

BOOK VIII
[1] *Firmament* the sky or "ocean" between the earth and the outermost, fixed sphere of the Ptolemaic universe.

[2] *officiate* "To give, in consequence of office" [or duty] (Johnson).

Round this opacous Earth, this punctual spot,[3]
One day and night; in all her vast survey
Useless besides, reasoning I oft admire,[4]   25
How Nature wise and frugal could commit
Such disproportions, with superfluous hand
So many nobler Bodies to create,
Greater so manifold to this one use,
For aught appears, and on their Orbs impose   30
Such restless revolution day by day
Repeated, while the sedentary Earth,
That better might with far less compass move,
Served by more noble than her self, attains
Her end without least motion, and receives,   35
As Tribute such a sumless journey brought[5]
Of incorporeal speed, her warmth and light;
Speed, to describe whose swiftness Number fails'.

   So spake our Sire, and by his count'nance seemed
Entring on studious thoughts abstruse; which *Eve*   40
Perceiving where she sat retired in sight,
With lowliness Majestic from her seat,
And Grace that won who saw to wish her stay,
Rose, and went forth among her Fruits and Flowrs,
To visit how they prospered, bud and bloom,   45
Her Nursery; they at her coming sprung
And touched by her fair tendance gladlier grew.
Yet went she not, as not with such discourse
Delighted, or not capable her ear
Of what was high: such pleasure she reserved,   50
Adam relating, she sole Auditress;
Her Husband the Relater she preferred
Before the Angel, and of him to ask
Chose rather; he, she knew would intermix
Grateful digressions, and solve high dispute[6]   55
With conjugal Caresses, from his Lip
Not Words alone pleased her. O when meet now
Such pairs, in Love and mutual Honour joined?
With Goddess-like demeanour forth she went;
Not unattended, for on her as Queen   60
A pomp of winning Graces waited still,[7]
And from about her shot Darts of desire
Into all eyes to wish her still in sight.
And *Raphael* now to *Adam's* doubt proposed
Benevolent and facile thus replied.   65
   'To ask or search I blame thee not, for Heav'n

---

[3] *opacous* "Dark; obscure; not transparent" (Johnson);
punctual like a mere dot or speck.
[4] *admire* wonder.

[5] *sumless* "Not to be computed" (Johnson).
[6] *Grateful* pleasing.
[7] *pomp* procession, train.

Is as the Book of God before thee set,
Wherein to read his wondrous Works, and learn
His Seasons, Hours, or Days, or Months, or Years:
This to attain, whether Heav'n move or Earth,   70
Imports not, if thou reck'n right, the rest
From Man or Angel the great Architect
Did wisely to conceal, and not divulge
His secrets to be scanned by them who ought
Rather admire; or if they list to try[8]   75
Conjecture, he his Fabric of the Heav'n's
Hath left to their disputes, perhaps to move
His laughter at their quaint Opinions wide[9]
Hereafter, when they come to model Heav'n[10]
And calculate the Stars, how they will wield   80
The mighty frame, how build, unbuild, contrive
To save appearances, how gird the Sphere
With Centric and Eccentric scribbled o'er,
Cycle and Epicycle, Orb in Orb:
Already by thy reasoning this I guess,   85
Who art to lead thy offspring, and supposest
That bodies bright and greater should not serve
The less not bright, nor Heav'n such journeys run,
Earth sitting still, when she alone receives
The benefit: consider first, that Great   90
Or Bright infers not Excellence: the Earth
Though, in comparison of Heav'n, so small,
Nor glistering, may of solid good contain
More plenty than the Sun that barren shines,
Whose virtue on it self works no effect,[11]   95
But in the fruitful Earth; there first received
His beams, unactive else, their vigour find.
Yet not to Earth are those bright Luminaries
Officious, but to thee Earth's habitant.[12]
And for the Heav'n's wide Circuit, let it speak   100
The Maker's high magnificence, who built
So spacious, and his Line stretched out so far;
That Man may know he dwells not in his own;
An Edifice too large for him to fill,
Lodged in a small partition, and the rest   105
Ordained for uses to his Lord best known.
The swiftness of those Circles áttribute,
Though numberless, to his Omnipotence,
That to corporeal substances could add

---

[8] *list* to desire.
[9] *quaint* "Subtly excogitated; finespun" (Johnson);
wide wide of the mark, inaccurate.
[10] *model* construct models of; the rest of the passage
describes the attempts of Ptolemacists to account for new

empirical evidence, and suggests that Adam was the first
Copernican.
[11] *virtue* "Efficacy; power" (Johnson).
[12] *officious* "Kind; doing good offices" (Johnson).

Speed almost Spiritual; me thou thinkst not slow,   110
Who since the Morning Hour set out from Heav'n
Where God resides, and ere mid-day arrived
In *Eden*, distance inexpressible
By Numbers that have name. But this I urge,
Admitting Motion in the Heav'ns, to show   115
Invalid that which thee to doubt it moved;[13]
Not that I so affirm, though so it seem
To thee who hast thy dwelling here on Earth.
God to remove his ways from human sense,
Placed Heav'n from Earth so far, that earthly sight,   120
If it presume, might err in things too high,
And no advantage gain. What if the Sun
Be Centre to the World, and other Stars
By his attractive virtue and their own
Incited, dance about him various rounds?   125
Their wandring course now high, now low, then hid,
Progressive, retrograde, or standing still,
In six thou seest, and what if sev'nth to these
The Planet Earth, so steadfast though she seem,
Insensibly three different Motions move?[14]   130
Which else to several Spheres thou must ascribe,
Moved contrary with thwart obliquities,[15]
Or save the Sun his labour, and that swift
Nocturnal and Diurnal rhomb supposed,[16]
Invisible else above all Stars, the Wheel   135
Of Day and Night; which needs not thy belief,
If Earth industrious of her self fetch Day
Travelling East, and with her part averse
From the Sun's beam meet Night, her other part
Still luminous by his ray. What if that light   140
Sent from her through the wide transpicuous air,
To the terrestrial Moon be as a Star,[17]
Enlightning her by Day, as she by Night
This Earth? reciprocal, if Land be there,
Fields and Inhabitants: Her spots thou seest   145
As Clouds, and Clouds may rain, and Rain produce
Fruits in her softened Soil for some to eat
Allotted there; and other Suns perhaps
With their attendant Moons thou wilt descry
Communicating Male and Female Light,[18]   150

---

[13]   Raphael now expounds a heliocentric system, but only to show the invalidity of Adam's argument for it, not because it is correct.

[14]   *Insensibly* imperceptibly, to earth's inhabitants.

[15]   *thwart obliquities* contrary and indirect, or retrograde motions.

[16]   *rhomb* Gk 'ρόμβος, a magic wheel, spun in alternate directions by the torsion of strings (Liddell, Scott and Jones); used as an image of the invisible sphere enclosing the rest of the Ptolemaic spheres and moving them; the primum mobile.

[17]   *terrestrial* "Consisting of earth; terreous. Improper" (Johnson).

[18]   *Male and Female* the sun's and moon's original and reflected, active and passive, light respectively.

Which two great Sexes animate the World,
Stored in each Orb perhaps with some that live.
For such vast room in Nature unpossessed
By living Soul, desert and desolate,
Only to shine, yet scarce to cóntribute   155
Each Orb a glimpse of Light, conveyed so far
Down to this habitable, which returns
Light back to them, is obvious to dispute.[19]
But whether thus these things, or whether not,
But whether the Sun predominant in Heav'n   160
Rise on the Earth, or Earth rise on the Sun,
He from the East his flaming road begin,
Or She from West her silent course advance
With inoffensive pace that spinning sleeps
On her soft Axle, while she paces Ev'n,   165
And bears thee soft with the smooth Air along,
Sollicit not thy thoughts with matters hid,
Leave them to God above, him serve, and fear;
Of other Creatures, as him pleases best,
Wherever placed, let him dispose: joy thou   170
In what he gives to thee, this Paradise
And thy fair *Eve*; Heav'n is for thee too high
To know what passes there; be lowly wise:
Think only what concerns thee, and thy being;
Dream not of other Worlds, what Creatures there   175
Live, in what state, condition or degree,
Contented that thus far hath been revealed
Not of Earth only but of highest Heav'n'.
    To whom thus *Adam* cleared of doubt, replied.
'How fully hast thou satisfied me, pure   180
Intelligence of Heav'n, Angel serene,
And freed from intricacies, taught to live,
The easiest way, nor with perplexing thoughts
To interrupt the sweet of Life from which
God hath bid dwell far off all anxious cares,   185
And not molest us, unless we our selves
Seek them with wandring thoughts, and notions vain.
But apt the Mind or Fancy is to rove
Unchecked, and of her roving is no end;
Till warned, or by experience taught, she learn,   190
That not to know at large of things remote
From use, obscure and subtle, but to know
That which before us lies in daily life,
Is the prime Wisdom, what is more, is fume,
Or emptiness, or fond impertinence,   195
And renders us in things that most concern
Unpractised, unprepared, and still to seek.[20]

---

[19] *obvious* "Open; exposed" (Johnson).   [20] *to seek* puzzled.

Therefore from this high pitch let us descend
A lower flight, and speak of things at hand
Useful, whence haply mention may arise   200
Of something not unseasonable to ask
By sufferance, and thy wonted favour deigned.
Thee I have heard relating what was done
Ere my remembrance: now, hear me relate
My Story, which perhaps thou hast not heard;   205
And Day is not yet spent; till then thou seest
How subtly to detain thee I devise,
Inviting thee to hear while I relate,
Fond, were it not in hope of thy reply:
For while I sit with thee, I seem in Heav'n,   210
And sweeter thy discourse is to my ear
Than Fruits of Palm-tree pleasantest to thirst
And hunger both, from labour, at the hour
Of sweet repast; they satiate, and soon fill,
Though pleasant, but thy words with Grace Divine   215
Imbued, bring to their sweetness no satiety'.
     To whom thus *Raphael* answered heav'nly meek.
'Nor are thy lips ungraceful, Sire of men,
Nor tongue ineloquent; for God on thee
Abundantly his gifts hath also poured   220
Inward and outward both, his image fair:
Speaking or mute all comeliness and grace
Attends thee, and each word, each motion forms,
Nor less think we in Heav'n of thee on Earth
Than of our fellow servant, and inquire   225
Gladly into the ways of God with Man:
For God we see hath honoured thee, and set
On Man his Equal Love: say therefore on;
For I that day was absent, as befell,
Bound on a voyage uncouth and obscure,   230
Far on excursion toward the Gates of Hell;
Squared in full Legion (such command we had)
To see that none thence issued forth a spy,
Or enemy, while God was in his work,
Lest he, incensed at such eruption bold,   235
Destruction with Creation might have mixed.
Not that they durst without his leave attempt,
But us he sends upon his high behests
For state, as Sovereign King, and to inure
Our prompt obedience. Fast we found, fast shut   240
The dismal Gates, and barricaded strong;
But long ere our approaching heard within
Noise, other than the sound of Dance or Song,
Torment, and loud lament, and furious rage.
Glad we returned up to the coasts of Light   245

Ere Sabbath Evening: so we had in charge.
But thy relation now; for I attend,
Pleased with thy words no less than thou with mine'.
    So spake the Godlike Power, and thus our Sire.
'For Man to tell how human Life began   250
Is hard; for who himself beginning knew?
Desire with thee still longer to converse
Induced me. As new waked from soundest sleep
Soft on the flowry herb I found me laid
In Balmy Sweat, which with his Beams the Sun   255
Soon dried, and on the reeking moisture fed.[21]
Straight toward Heav'n my wondring Eyes I turned,
And gazed a while the ample Sky, till raised
By quick instinctive motion, up I sprung,
As thitherward endeavouring, and upright   260
Stood on my feet; about me round I saw
Hill, Dale, and shady Woods, and sunny Plains,
And liquid Lapse of murmuring Streams; by these,
Creatures that lived and moved, and walked, or flew,
Birds on the branches warbling; all things smiled,   265
With fragrance and with joy my heart o'erflowed.
My self I then perused, and Limb by Limb
Surveyed, and sometimes went, and sometimes ran
With supple joints, as lively vigour led:
But who I was, or where, or from what cause,   270
Knew not; to speak I tried, and forthwith spake,
My tongue obeyed and readily could name
What e'er I saw. "Thou Sun", said I, "fair Light,
And thou enlightened Earth, so fresh and gay,
Ye Hills and Dales, ye Rivers, Woods, and Plains,   275
And ye that live and move, fair Creatures, tell,
Tell, if ye saw, how I came thus, how here?
Not of my self; by some great Maker then,
In goodness and in power preeminent;
Tell me, how may I know him, how adore,   280
From whom I have that thus I move and live,
And feel that I am happier than I know".
While thus I called, and strayed I knew not whither,
From where I first drew Air, and first beheld
This happy light, when answer none returned,   285
On a green shady Bank, profuse of Flowrs
Pensive I sat me down; there gentle sleep
First found me, and with soft oppression seized
My drowsèd sense, untroubled, though I thought
I then was passing to my former state   290

---

[21] *reeking* reek, "To smoke; to steam; to emit vapour" (Johnson).

Insensible, and forthwith to dissolve:
When suddenly stood at my Head a dream,
Whose inward apparition gently moved
My fancy to believe I yet had being,
And lived: One came, methought, of shape Divine,   295
And said, "thy Mansion wants thee, *Adam*, rise,
First Man, of Men innumerable ordained
First Father, called by thee I come thy Guide
To the Garden of bliss, thy seat prepared".
So saying, by the hand he took me raised,   300
And over Fields and Waters, as in Air
Smooth sliding without step, last led me up
A woody Mountain; whose high top was plain,
A Circuit wide, enclosed, with goodliest Trees
Planted, with Walks, and Bowers, that what I saw   305
Of Earth before scarce pleasant seemed. Each tree
Load'n with fairest Fruit that hung to the Eye
Tempting, stirred in me sudden appetite
To pluck and eat; whereat I waked, and found
Before mine Eyes all real, as the dream   310
Had lively shadowed: Here had new begun
My wandring, had not he, who was my Guide
Up hither, from among the Trees appeared,
Presence Divine. Rejoicing, but with awe
In adoration at his feet I fell   315
Submiss: he reared me, and "Whom thou soughtst I am",
Said mildly, "Author of all this thou seest
Above, or round about thee or beneath.
This Paradise I give thee, count it thine
To Till and keep, and of the Fruit to eat: 320
Of every Tree that in the Garden grows
Eat freely with glad heart; fear here no dearth:
But of the Tree whose operation brings
Knowledge of good and ill, which I have set
The Pledge of thy Obedience and thy Faith,   325
Amid the Garden by the Tree of Life,
Remember what I warn thee, shun to taste,
And shun the bitter consequence: for know,
The day thou eat'st thereof, my sole command
Transgressed, inevitably thou shalt die;   330
From that day mortal, and this happy State
Shalt lose, expelled from hence into a World
Of woe and sorrow". Sternly he pronounced
The rigid interdiction, which resounds
Yet dreadful in mine ear, though in my choice   335
Not to incur; but soon his clear aspéct
Returned, and gracious purpose thus renewed.[22]

---

[22] *purpose* discourse.

"Not only these fair bounds, but all the Earth
To thee and to thy Race I give; as Lords
Possess it, and all things that therein live,   340
Or live in Sea, or Air, Beast, Fish, and Fowl.
In sign whereof each Bird and Beast behold
After their kinds; I bring them to receive
From thee their Names, and pay thee fealty
With low subjection; understand the same   345
Of Fish within their watry residence,
Not hither summoned, since they cannot change
Their Element, to draw the thinner Air".
As thus he spake, each Bird and Beast behold
Approaching two and two, these cowring low   350
With blandishment, each Bird stooped on his wing.
I named them, as they passed, and understood
Their Nature, with such knowledge God endued
My sudden apprehension: but in these
I found not what methought I wanted still;[23]   355
And to the heav'nly vision thus presumed.
  '"O by what Name, for thou above all these,
Above mankind, or aught than mankind higher,
Surpassest far my naming, how may I
Adore thee, Author of this Universe,   360
And all this good to man, for whose well being
So amply, and with hands so liberal
Thou hast provided all things: but with me
I see not who partakes. In solitude
What happiness, who can enjoy alone,   365
Or all enjoying, what contentment find?"
Thus I presumptuous; and the vision bright,
As with a smile more brightened, thus replied.
"What call'st thou solitude, is not the Earth
With various living creatures, and the Air   370
Replenished, and all these at thy command
To come and play before thee, know'st thou not
Their language and their ways, they also know,
And reason not contemptibly; with these
Find pastime, and bear rule; thy Realm is large".   375
So spake the Universal Lord, and seemed
So ordering. I with leave of speech implored,
And humble deprecation thus replied.
  '"Let not my words offend thee, Heav'nly Power,
My Maker, be propitious while I speak.   380
Hast thou not made me here thy substitute,
And these inferior far beneath me set?
Among unequals what society

---

[23]   Genesis 2.18–25 forms the basis for this and the
following passages on the creation of Eve.

Can sort, what harmony or true delight?
Which must be mutual, in proportion due   385
Giv'n and received; but in disparity
The one intense, the other still remiss
Cannot well suit with either, but soon prove
Tedious alike: Of fellowship I speak
Such as I seek, fit to participate   390
All rational delight, wherein the brute
Cannot be human consort; they rejoice
Each with their kind, Lion with Lioness;
So fitly them in pairs thou hast combined;
Much less can Bird with Beast, or Fish with Fowl   395
So well converse, nor with the Ox the Ape;
Worse then can Man with Beast, and least of all".
Whereto th' Almighty answered, not displeased.
"A nice and subtle happiness I see
Thou to thy self proposest, in the choice   400
Of thy Associates, *Adam*, and wilt taste
No pleasure, though in pleasure, solitary.
What thinkst thou then of me, and this my State,
Seem I to thee sufficiently possessed
Of happiness, or not? who am alone   405
From all Eternity, for none I know
Second to me or like, equal much less.
How have I then with whom to hold converse
Save with the Creatures which I made, and those
To me inferior, infinite descents   410
Beneath what other Creatures are to thee?"
He ceased, I lowly answered. "To attain
The heighth and depth of thy Eternal ways
All human thoughts come short, Supreme of things!
Thou in thy self art perfet, and in thee   415
Is no deficience found; not so is Man,
But in degree, the cause of his desire
By conversation with his like to help,
Or solace his defects. No need that thou
Shouldst propagate, already infinite;   420
And through all numbers absolute, though One;[24]
But Man by number is to manifest
His single imperfection, and beget
Like of his like, his Image multiplied,
In unity defective, which requires   425
Collateral love, and dearest amity.
Thou in thy secrecy although alone,
Best with thy self accompanied, seek'st not

---

[24] *numbers*   full complements of individuals needed to make up an aggregate whole; to be complete in aggrega- tion, though one, is one of the paradoxical qualities of God.

Social communication, yet so pleased,
Canst raise thy Creature to what heighth thou wilt   430
Of Union or Communion, deified;
I by conversing cannot these erect
From prone, nor in their ways complacence find".
Thus I emboldened spake, and freedom used
Permissive, and acceptance found, which gained   435
This answer from the gracious voice Divine.
     "Thus far to try thee, Adam, I was pleased,
And find thee knowing not of Beasts alone,
Which thou hast rightly named, but of thy self,
Expressing well the spirit within thee free,   440
My Image, not imparted to the Brute,
Whose fellowship therefore unmeet for thee[25]
Good reason was thou freely shouldst dislike,
And be so minded still; I, ere thou spak'st,
Knew it not good for Man to be alone,   445
And no such company as then thou saw'st
Intended thee for trial only brought,
To see how thou could'st judge of fit and meet:
What next I bring shall please thee, be assured,
Thy likeness, thy fit help, thy other self,   450
Thy wish exactly to thy heart's desire".
     'He ended, or I heard no more, for now
My earthly by his heav'nly overpowered,
Which it had long stood under, strained to the heighth
In that celestial Colloquy sublime,   455
As with an object that excels the sense,
Dazzled and spent, sunk down, and sought repair
Of sleep, which instantly fell on me, called
By Nature as in aid, and closed mine eyes.
Mine eyes he closed, but open left the Cell   460
Of Fancy my internal sight, by which
Abstract as in a trance methought I saw,
Though sleeping where I lay, and saw the shape
Still glorious before whom awake I stood;
Who stooping opened my left side, and took   465
From thence a Rib, with cordial spirits warm,[26]
And Life-blood streaming fresh; wide was the wound,
But suddenly with flesh filled up and healed:
The Rib he formed and fashioned with his hands;
Under his forming hands a Creature grew,   470
Manlike, but different Sex, so lovely fair,
That what seemed fair in all the World, seemed now

---

[25]   *unmeet*   "Not fit; not proper; not worthy" (Johnson);   [26]   *cordial spirits*   the spirits or fluids distributed by the
"helpmeet," the biblical term for wife, is suggested in   heart.
Milton's use of the word.

Mean, or in her summed up, in her contained
And in her looks, which from that time infused
Sweetness into my heart, unfelt before,   475
And into all things from her Air inspir'd
The spirit of love and amorous delight.
She disappeared, and left me dark, I waked
To find her, or for ever to deplore
Her loss, and other pleasures all abjure: 480
When out of hope, behold her, not far off,
Such as I saw her in my dream, adorned
With what all Earth or Heaven could bestow,
To make her amiable: On she came,
Led by her Heav'nly Maker, though unseen,   485
And guided by his voice, nor uninformed
Of nuptial Sanctity and marriage Rites:
Grace was in all her steps, Heav'n in her Eye,
In every gesture dignity and love.
I overjoyed, could not forbear aloud.   490
    "This turn hath made amends; thou hast fulfilled
Thy words, Creator bounteous and benign,
Giver of all things fair, but fairest this
Of all thy gifts, nor enviest. I now see
Bone of my Bone, Flesh of my Flesh, my Self   495
Before me; Woman is her Name, of Man
Extracted; for this cause he shall forego
Father and Mother, and to his Wife adhere;
And they shall be one Flesh, one Heart, one Soul".
    'She heard me thus, and though divinely brought,   500
Yet Innocence and Virgin Modesty,
Her virtue and the conscience of her worth,
That would be wooed, and not unsought be won,
Not obvious, not obtrusive, but retir'd,
The more desirable, or to say all,   505
Nature her self, though pure of sinful thought,
Wrought in her so, that seeing me, she turned;
I followed her, she what was Honour knew,
And with obsequious Majesty approved[27]
My pleaded reason. To the Nuptial Bow'r   510
I led her blushing like the Morn: all Heav'n,
And happy Constellations, on that hour
Shed their selectest influence; the Earth
Gave sign of gratulation, and each Hill;
Joyous the Birds; fresh Gales and gentle Airs[28]   515
Whispered it to the Woods, and from their wings
Flung Rose, flung Odours from the spicy Shrub,

---

[27] *obsequious* "Obedient; compliant; not resisting"   [28] *Gales* breezes.
(Johnson).

Disporting, till the amorous Bird of Night
Sung Spousal, and bid haste the Evening Star
On his Hill top, to light the bridal Lamp.   520
Thus I have told thee all my State, and brought
My Story to the sum of earthly bliss
Which I enjoy, and must confess to find
In all things else delight indeed, but such
As used or not, works in the mind no change,   525
Nor vehement desire, these delicacies
I mean of Taste, Sight, Smell, Herbs, Fruits, and Flowrs,
Walks, and the melody of Birds; but here
Far otherwise, transported I behold,
Transported touch; here passion first I felt,   530
Commotion strange, in all enjoyments else
Superior and unmoved, here only weak
Against the charm of Beauty's powerful glance.
Or Nature failed in me, and left some part[29]
Not proof enough such Object to sustain,   535
Or from my side subducting, took perhaps
More than enough; at least on her bestowed
Too much of Ornament, in outward show
Elaborate, of inward less exact.
For well I understand in the prime end   540
Of Nature her th' inferior, in the mind
And inward Faculties, which most excel,
In outward also her resembling less
His Image who made both, and less expressing
The character of that Dominion giv'n   545
O'er other Creatures; yet when I approach
Her loveliness, so absolute she seems
And in her self complete, so well to know
Her own, that what she wills to do or say,
Seems wisest, virtuousest, discreetest, best;   550
All higher knowledge in her presence falls
Degraded: Wisdom in discourse with her
Loses discount'nanced, and like folly shows;
Authority and Reason on her wait,
As one intended first, not after made   555
Occasionally; and to consúmmate all,
Greatness of mind and nobleness their seat
Build in her loveliest, and create an awe
About her, as a guard Angelic placed'.
To whom the Angel with contracted brow.   560
     'Accuse not Nature, she hath done her part;
Do thou but thine, and be not diffident
Of Wisdom, she deserts thee not, if thou

---

29 *Or . . . or* either . . . or.

Dismiss not her, when most thou needst her nigh,
By áttributing overmuch to things   565
Less excellent, as thou thy self perceiv'st.
For what admir'st thou, what transports thee so,
An outside? fair no doubt, and worthy well
Thy cherishing, thy honouring, and thy love,
Not thy subjection: weigh with her thy self;   570
Then value: Oft times nothing profits more
Than self esteem, grounded on just and right
Well managed; of that skill the more thou know'st,
The more she will acknowledge thee her Head,
And to realities yield all her shows: 575
Made so adorn for thy delight the more,
So awful, that with honour thou may'st love
Thy mate, who sees when thou art seen least wise.
But if the sense of touch whereby mankind
Is propagated seem such dear delight   580
Beyond all other; think the same vouchsafed
To Cattle and each Beast; which would not be
To them made common and divulged, if aught
Therein enjoyed were worthy to subdue
The Soul of Man, or passion in him move.   585
What higher in her society thou findst
Attractive, human, rational, love still;
In loving thou dost well, in passion not,
Wherein true Love consists not; love refines
The thoughts, and heart enlarges, hath his seat   590
In Reason, and is judicious, is the scale
By which to heav'nly Love thou may'st ascend,
Not sunk in carnal pleasure, for which cause
Among the Beasts no Mate for thee was found'.

    To whom thus half abashed, *Adam* replied.   595
'Neither her out-side formed so fair, nor aught
In procreation common to all kinds
(Though higher of the genial Bed by far,[30]
And with mysterious reverence I deem)
So much delights me as those graceful acts,   600
Those thousand decencies that daily flow
From all her words and actions mixed with Love
And sweet compliance, which declare unfeigned
Union of Mind, or in us both one Soul;
Harmony to behold in wedded pair   605
More grateful than harmonious sound to the ear.
Yet these subject not; I to thee disclose
What inward thence I feel, not therefore foiled,
Who meet with various objects, from the sense

---

[30] *genial* "That which contributes to propagation"
(Johnson).

Variously representing; yet still free   610
Approve the best, and follow what I approve.
To love thou blam'st me not, for love thou say'st
Leads up to Heav'n, is both the way and guide;
Bear with me then, if lawful what I ask;
Love not the heav'nly Spirits, and how their Love   615
Express they, by looks only, or do they mix
Irradiance, virtual or immediate touch?'
    To whom the Angel with a smile that glowed
Celestial rosy red, Love's proper hue,
Answered. 'Let it suffice thee that thou know'st   620
Us happy, and without Love no happiness.
Whatever pure thou in the body enjoy'st
(And pure thou wert created) we enjoy
In eminence; and obstacle find none
Of membrane, joint, or limb, exclusive bars:[31]   625
Easier than Air with Air, if Spirits embrace,
Total they mix, Union of Pure with Pure
Desiring; nor restrained conveyance need
As Flesh to mix with Flesh, or Soul with Soul.
But I can now no more; the parting Sun   630
Beyond the Earth's green Cape and verdant Isles[32]
Hesperian sets, my Signal to depart.
Be strong, live happy, and love, but first of all
Him whom to love is to obey, and keep
His great command; take heed lest Passion sway   635
Thy Judgement to do aught, which else free Will
Would not admit; thine and of all thy Sons
The Weal or woe in thee is placet; beware.
I in thy persevering shall rejoice,
And all the Blest: stand fast; to stand or fall   640
Free in thine own Arbitrement it lies.
Perfet within, no outward aid require;
And all temptation to transgress repel'.
    So saying, he arose; whom *Adam* thus
Followed with benediction. 'Since to part,   645
Go heavenly Guest, Ethereal Messenger,
Sent from whose sovereign goodness I adore.
Gentle to me and affable hath been
Thy condescension, and shall be honoured ever
With grateful Memory: thou to mankind   650
Be good and friendly still, and oft return'.
    So parted they, the Angel up to Heav'n
From the thick shade, and *Adam* to his Bow'r.

---

[31] *exclusive* "Having the power of excluding or denying admission" (Johnson).
[32] *green Cape and verdant Isles Hesperian* Cape Verde
(Ital. green), westernmost Africa, and the Cape Verde
Islands, which can be described as Hesperian because the
mythical Hesperides, source of golden apples, were inde-
terminately located in the Atlantic.

BOOK IX
THE ARGUMENT

Satan *having compassed the Earth, with meditated guile returns as a mist by Night into Paradise,*
enters into the Serpent sleeping. Adam *and* Eve *in the Morning go forth to their labours, which* Eve
proposes to divide in several places, each labouring apart: Adam *consents not, alleging the danger, lest*
that Enemy, of whom they were forewarned, should attempt her found alone: Eve *loath to be thought not*
circumspect or firm enough, urges her going apart, the rather desirous to make her trial of strength; Adam
at last yields: The Serpent finds her alone; his subtle approach, first gazing, then speaking, with much
flattery extolling Eve *above all other Creatures.* Eve *wondring to hear the Serpent speak, asks how he*
attained to human speech and such understanding not till now; the Serpent answers, that by tasting of
a certain Tree in the Garden he attained both to Speech and Reason, till then void of both: Eve *requires*
him to bring her to that Tree, and finds it to be the Tree of Knowledge forbidden: The Serpent now grown
bolder, with many wiles and arguments induces her at length to eat; she pleased with the taste deliberates
a while whether to impart thereof to Adam *or not, at last brings him of the Fruit, relates what persuaded*
her to eat thereof: Adam *at first amazed, but perceiving her lost, resolves through vehemence of love to*
perish with her; and extenuating the trespass, eats also of the Fruit: The Effects thereof in them both; they
seek to cover their nakedness; then fall to variance and accusation of one another.

No more of talk where God or Angel Guest
With Man, as with his Friend, familiar used
To sit indulgent, and with him partake
Rural repast, permitting him the while
Venial discourse unblamed: I now must change[1]   5
Those Notes to Tragic; foul distrust, and breach
Disloyal on the part of Man, revolt,
And disobedience: On the part of Heav'n
Now alienated, distance and distaste,
Anger and just rebuke, and judgement giv'n,   10
That brought into this World a world of woe,
Sin and her shadow Death, and Misery
Death's Harbinger: Sad task, yet argument
Not less but more Heroic than the wrath[2]
Of stern *Achilles* on his Foe pursued   15
Thrice Fugitive about *Troy* Wall; or rage[3]
Of *Turnus* for *Lavinia* disespoused,
Or *Neptune*'s ire, or *Juno*'s, that so long[4]
Perplexed the *Greek* and *Cytherea*'s Son;
If answerable style I can obtain   20
Of my Celestial Patroness, who deigns[5]

BOOK IX
[1] *venial* "Permitted; allowed" (Johnson).
[2] *the wrath of . . . Achilles* the theme, or argument, of
the *Iliad*, which reaches its conclusion after Achilles
pursues and kills Hector, the hero of high-walled
Troy.
[3] *rage of Turnus for Lavinia* a major theme in the
second half of the *Aeneid*, which ends with the single

combat between Turnus, the Italian suitor of Lavinia,
and Trojan Aeneas.
[4] *Neptune's ire, or Juno's* Neptune tormented *the Greek*
Odysseus as Juno did Aeneas, *Cytherea's Son*, throughout
their travels, which are described in the *Odyssey* and in
the first six books of the *Aeneid*, respectively.
[5] *Celestial Patroness* the muse of epic poetry (cf. 1.6
and 7.1).

Her nightly visitation unimplored,
And dictates to me slumbring, or inspires
Easy my unpremeditated Verse:
Since first this Subject for Heroic Song   25
Pleased me long choosing, and beginning late;
Not sedulous by Nature to indite
Wars, hitherto the only Argument
Heroic deemed, chief mast'ry to dissect
With long and tedious havoc fabled Knights   30
In Battles feigned; the better fortitude
Of Patience and Heroic Martyrdom
Unsung; or to describe Races and Games,
Or tilting Furniture, emblazoned Shields,[6]
Impresses quaint, Caparisons and Steeds;[7]   35
Bases and tinsel Trappings, gorgeous Knights[8]
At Joust and Tournament; then marshalled Feast
Served up in Hall with Sewers and Seneshals;[9]
The skill of Artifice or Office mean,
Not that which justly gives Heroic name   40
To Person or to Poem. Me of these
Nor skilled nor studious, higher Argument
Remains, sufficient of it self to raise
That name, unless an age too late, or cold
Climate, or Years damp my intended wing   45
Depressed, and much they may, if all be mine,
Not Hers who brings it nightly to my Ear.
    The Sun was sunk, and after him the Star
Of *Hesperus*, whose Office is to bring
Twilight upon the Earth, short Arbiter   50
Twixt Day and Night, and now from end to end
Night's Hemisphere had veiled the Horizon round:
When *Satan* who late fled before the threats
Of *Gabriel* out of *Eden*, now improved
In meditated fraud and malice, bent   55
On man's destruction, maugre what might hap
Of heavier on himself, fearless returned.
By Night he fled, and at Midnight returned
From compassing the Earth, cautious of day,
Since *Uriel* Regent of the Sun descried   60
His entrance, and forewarned the Cherubim
That kept their watch; thence full of anguish driv'n,
The space of seven continued Nights he rode
With darkness; thrice the Equinoctial Line

---

[6] *tilting Furniture* "Equipage" (Johnson) for jousting.
[7] *Impresses quaint* "neat, subtle, or fine mottoes"; *Caparisons* "horsecloth[s]" (Johnson).
[8] *Bases* those "part[s] of any ornament that hang down, as housings" (Johnson).

[9] *Sewers and Seneshals* feudal names for waiters and managers of ceremonial feasts.

He circled, four times crossed the Car of Night[10]   65
From Pole to Pole, traversing each Colure;[11]
On the eighth returned, and on the Coast averse
From entrance or Cherubic Watch, by stealth
Found unsuspected way. There was a place,
Now not, though Sin, not Time, first wrought the change,   70
Where *Tigris* at the foot of Paradise
Into a Gulf shot under ground, till part
Rose up a Fountain by the Tree of Life;
In with the River sunk, and with it rose
Satan involved in rising Mist, then sought   75
Where to lie hid; Sea he had searched and Land
From *Eden* over *Pontus*, and the Pool[12]
Mæotis, up beyond the River *Ob*;[13]
Downward as far Antarctic; and in length
West from *Orontes* to the Ocean barred[14]   80
At *Darien*, thence to the Land where flows[15]
Ganges and *Indus*: thus the Orb he roamed
With narrow search; and with inspection deep
Considered every Creature, which of all
Most opportune might serve his Wiles, and found   85
The Serpent subtlest Beast of all the Field.[16]
Him after long debate, irresolute
Of thoughts revolved, his final sentence chose[17]
Fit Vessel, fittest Imp of fraud, in whom
To enter, and his dark suggestions hide   90
From sharpest sight: for in the wily Snake,
Whatever sleights none would suspicious mark,
As from his wit and native subtlety
Proceeding, which in other Beasts observed
Doubt might beget of Diabolic power[18]   95
Active within beyond the sense of brute.
Thus he resolved, but first from inward grief
His bursting passion into plaints thus poured:
    'O Earth, how like to Heav'n, if not preferred
More justly, Seat worthier of Gods, as built   100
With second thoughts, reforming what was old!
For what God after better worse would build?
Terrestrial Heav'n, danced round by other Heav'ns
That shine, yet bear their bright officious Lamps,[19]

[10] *Car of Night* Night's chariot, which brings darkness, as Apollo's brings daylight.
[11] *each Colure* "Two great circles supposed to pass through the poles of the world, one through the equinoctial . . . the other through the solstitial points [of the ecliptic of the Sun]" (Johnson, quoting Harris, *Lexicon Technicum*).
[12] *Pontus* the Black Sea, north-east of which is the Maeotis (now Sea of Azov).
[13] *Ob* it flows into the Kara Sea north of Siberia.
[14] *Orontes* a river in western Syria; *the Ocean* the Atlantic.
[15] *Darien* the old name for Panama.
[16] The line repeats Genesis 3.1.
[17] *sentence* judgement.
[18] *Doubt* suspicion.
[19] *officious* kind.

Light above Light, for thee alone, as seems,   105
In thee concentring all their precious beams
Of sacred influence: As God in Heav'n
Is Centre, yet extends to all, so thou,
Centring, receiv'st from all those Orbs; in thee,
Not in themselves, all their known virtue appears[20]   110
Productive in Herb, Plant, and nobler birth
Of Creatures animate with gradual life
Of Growth, Sense, Reason, all summed up in Man.
With what delight could I have walked thee round,
If I could joy in aught, sweet interchange   115
Of Hill, and Valley, Rivers, Woods, and Plains,
Now Land, now Sea and Shores with Forest crowned,
Rocks, Dens, and Caves; but I in none of these
Find place or refuge; and the more I see
Pleasures about me, so much more I feel   120
Torment within me, as from the hateful siege
Of contraries; all good to me becomes
Bane, and in Heav'n much worse would be my state.
But neither here seek I, no nor in Heav'n
To dwell, unless by mast'ring Heav'n's Supreme;   125
Nor hope to be my self less miserable
By what I seek, but others to make such
As I, though thereby worse to me redound:
For only in destroying I find ease
To my relentless thoughts; and him destroyed,   130
Or won to what may work his utter loss,
For whom all this was made, all this will soon
Follow, as to him linked in weal or woe,
In woe then; that destruction wide may range:
To me shall be the glory sole among   135
The infernal Powers, in one day to have marred
What he *Almighty* styled, six Nights and Days
Continued making, and who knows how long
Before had been contriving, though perhaps
Not longer than since I in one Night freed   140
From servitude inglorious wellnigh half
Th' Angelic Name, and thinner left the throng
Of his adorers: he to be avenged,
And to repair his numbers thus impaired,
Whether such virtue spent of old now failed   145
More Angels to Create, if they at least
Are his Created, or to spite us more,
Determined to advance into our room
A Creature formed of Earth, and him endow,
Exalted from so base original,   150
With Heav'nly spoils, our spoils: What he decreed

---

[20] *virtue* power; influence.

He effected; Man he made, and for him built
Magnificent this World, and Earth his seat,
Him Lord pronounced, and, O indignity!
Subjected to his service Angel wings,   155
And flaming Ministers to watch and tend
Their earthly Charge: Of these the vigilance
I dread, and to elude, thus wrapped in mist
Of midnight vapour glide obscure, and pry
In every Bush and Brake, where hap may find   160
The Serpent sleeping, in whose mazy folds
To hide me, and the dark intent I bring.
O foul descent! that I who erst contended
With Gods to sit the highest, am now constrained
Into a Beast, and mixed with bestial slime,   165
This essence to incarnate and imbrute,
That to the height of Deity aspired;
But what will not Ambition and Revenge
Descend to? who aspires, must down as low
As high he soared, obnoxious first or last[21]   170
To basest things. Revenge, at first though sweet,
Bitter ere long back on it self recoils;
Let it; I reck not, so it light well aimed,
Since higher I fall short, on him who next
Provokes my envy, this new Favourite[22]   175
Of Heav'n, this Man of Clay, Son of despite,
Whom, us the more to spite his Maker raised
From dust: spite then with spite is best repaid'.
      So saying, through each Thicket Dank or Dry,
Like a black mist low creeping, he held on   180
His midnight search, where soonest he might find
The Serpent: him fast-sleeping soon he found
In Labyrinth of many a round self-rolled,
His head the midst, well stored with subtle wiles:
Not yet in horrid Shade or dismal Den,   185
Nor nocent yet, but on the grassy Herb[23]
Fearless unfeared he slept: in at his Mouth
The Devil entered, and his brutal sense,
In heart or head, possessing, soon inspir'd
With act intelligential; but his sleep   190
Disturbed not, waiting close th' approach of Morn.
Now when as sacred Light began to dawn
In *Eden* on the humid Flowrs, that breathed
Their morning incense, when all things that breathe
From th' Earth's great Altar send up silent praise   195

---

21 *obnoxious* "Liable; exposed" (Johnson).
22 *Favourite* "One chosen as a companion by his superior; a mean wretch whose whole business is by any

means to please" (Johnson); cf. Thomas Gray, "Ode on
the Death of a Favourite Cat" (l. 36 see below).
23 *nocent* "Hurtful; mischievous" (Johnson).

To the Creator, and his Nostrils fill
With grateful Smell, forth came the human pair
And joined their vocal worship to the quire
Of Creatures wanting voice, that done, partake
The season, prime for sweetest Scents and Airs: 200
Then commune how that day they best may ply
Their growing work: for much their work outgrew
The hands dispatch of two Gardning so wide,
And *Eve* first to her Husband thus began.
      '*Adam*, well may we labour still to dress   205
This Garden, still to tend Plant, Herb and Flower,
Our pleasant task enjoined, but till more hands
Aid us, the work under our labour grows,
Luxurious by restraint; what we by day
Lop overgrown, or prune, or prop, or bind,   210
One night or two with wanton growth derides
Tending to wild. Thou therefore now advise,
Or hear what to my mind first thoughts present.
Let us divide our labours, thou, where choice
Leads thee, or where most needs, whether to wind   215
The Woodbine round this Arbour, or direct
The clasping Ivy where to climb, while I
In yonder Spring of Roses intermixed
With Myrtle, find what to redress till Noon:
For while so near each other thus all day   220
Our task we choose, what wonder if so near
Looks intervene and smiles, or object new
Casual discourse draw on, which intermits
Our day's work, brought to little, though begun
Early, and th' hour of Supper comes unearned'.   225
      To whom mild answer *Adam* thus returned.
'Sole *Eve*, Associate sole, to me beyond
Compare above all living Creatures dear;
Well hast thou motioned, well thy thoughts employed
How we might best fulfil the work which here   230
God hath assigned us, nor of me shalt pass
Unpraised: for nothing lovelier can be found
In Woman, than to study household good,
And good works in her Husband to promote.
Yet not so strictly hath our Lord imposed   235
Labour, as to debar us when we need
Refreshment, whether food, or talk between,
Food of the mind, or this sweet intercourse
Of looks and smiles, for smiles from Reason flow,
To brute denied, and are of Love the food,   240
Love not the lowest end of human life.
For not to irksome toil, but to delight
He made us, and delight to Reason joined.

These paths & Bowers doubt not but our joint hands
Will keep from Wilderness with ease, as wide   245
As we need walk, till younger hands ere long
Assist us: But if much convérse perhaps
Thee satiate, to short absence I could yield.
For solitude sometimes is best society,
And short retirement urges sweet return.   250
But other doubt possesses me, lest harm
Befall thee severed from me; for thou knowst
What hath been warned us, what malicious Foe
Envying our happiness, and of his own
Despairing, seeks to work us woe and shame   255
By sly assault; and somewhere nigh at hand
Watches, no doubt, with greedy hope to find
His wish and best advantage, us asunder,
Hopeless to circumvent us joined, where each
To other speedy aid might lend at need;   260
Whether his first design be to withdraw
Our fealty from God, or to disturb
Conjugal Love, than which perhaps no bliss
Enjoyed by us excites his envy more;
Or this, or worse, leave not the faithful side[24]   265
That gave thee being, still shades thee and protects.
The Wife, where danger or dishonour lurks,
Safest and seemliest by her Husband stays,
Who guards her, or with her the worst endures'.
    To whom the Virgin Majesty of *Eve*,   270
As one who loves, and some unkin dness meets,
With sweet austere composure thus replied,
    'Offspring of Heav'n and Earth, and all Earth's Lord,
That such an Enemy we have, who seeks
Our ruin, both by thee informed I learn,   275
And from the parting Angel over-heard
As in a shady nook I stood behind,
Just then returned at shut of Evening Flowrs.
But that thou shouldst my firmness therefore doubt
To God or thee, because we have a foe   280
May tempt it, I expected not to hear.
His violence thou fearst not, being such
As we, not capable of death or pain,
Can either not receive, or can repel.
His fraud is then thy fear, which plain infers   285
Thy equal fear that my firm Faith and Love
Can by his fraud be shaken or seduced;
Thoughts, which how found they harbour in thy breast
Adam, mis-thought of her to thee so dear?'

---

[24]   *Or . . . or*   whether . . . or . . . is the case.

To whom with healing words *Adam* replied.   290
'Daughter of God and Man, immortal *Eve*,
For such thou art, from sin and blame entire:
Not diffident of thee do I dissuade
Thy absence from my sight, but to avoid
The attempt it self, intended by our Foe.   295
For he who tempts, though in vain, at least asperses
The tempted with dishonour foul, supposed
Not incorruptible of Faith, not proof
Against temptation: thou thy self with scorn
And anger wouldst resent the offered wrong,   300
Though ineffectual found: misdeem not then,
If such affront I labour to avert
From thee alone, which on us both at once
The Enemy, though bold, will hardly dare,
Or daring, first on me the assault shall light.   305
Nor thou his malice and false guile contemn;
Subtle he needs must be, who could seduce
Angels, nor think superfluous other's aid.
I from the influence of thy looks receive
Accéss in every Virtue, in thy sight[25]   310
More wise, more watchful, stronger, if need were
Of outward strength; while shame, thou looking on,
Shame to be overcome or over-reached,
Would utmost vigour raise, and raised unite.
Why shouldst not thou like sense within thee feel   315
When I am present, and thy trial choose
With me, best witness of thy Virtue tried'.
    So spake domestic *Adam* in his care
And Matrimonial Love; but *Eve*, who thought
Less attribúted to her Faith sincere,   320
Thus her reply with accent sweet renewed.[26]
    'If this be our condition, thus to dwell
In narrow circuit straitened by a Foe,
Subtle or violent, we not endued
Single with like defence, wherever met,   325
How are we happy, still in fear of harm?
But harm precedes not sin: only our Foe
Tempting affronts us with his foul esteem[27]
Of our integrity: his foul esteem
Sticks no dishonour on our Front, but turns[28]   330
Foul on himself; then wherefore shunned or feared
By us? who rather double honour gain
From his surmise proved false, find peace within,

---

[25] *Accéss* "Increase; enlargement; addition" (Johnson).   [27] *esteem* estimate.
[26] *accent* "A modification of the voice, expressive of   [28] *Front* "The face" (Johnson).
the passions or sentiments" (Johnson).

Favour from Heav'n, our witness from th' event.
And what is Faith, Love, Virtue unassayed   335
Alone, without exterior help sustained?
Let us not then suspect our happy State
Left so imperfect by the Maker wise,
As not secure to single or combined.
Frail is our happiness, if this be so,   340
And *Eden* were no *Eden* thus exposed'.
       To whom thus *Adam* fervently replied.
'O Woman, best are all things as the will
Of God ordained them, his creating hand
Nothing imperfet or deficient left   345
Of all that he Created, much less Man,
Or aught that might his happy State secure,
Secure from outward force; within himself
The danger lies, yet lies within his power:
Against his will he can receive no harm.   350
But God left free the Will, for what obeys
Reason, is free, and Reason he made right,
But bid her well beware, and still erect,[29]
Lest by some fair appearing good surprised
She dictate false, and misinform the Will   355
To do what God expressly hath forbid.
Not then mistrust, but tender love enjoins,
That I should mind thee oft, and mind thou me.
Firm we subsist, yet possible to swerve,
Since Reason not impossibly may meet   360
Some specious object by the Foe suborned,
And fall into deception unaware,
Not keeping strictest watch, as she was warned.
Seek not temptation then, which to avoid
Were better, and most likely if from me   365
Thou sever not: Trial will come unsought.
Wouldst thou approve thy constancy, approve[30]
First thy obedience; th' other who can know,
Not seeing thee attempted, who attest?
But if thou think, trial unsought may find[31]   370
Us both securer than thus warned thou seemst,
Go; for thy stay, not free, absents thee more;
Go in thy native innocence, rely
On what thou hast of virtue, summon all,
For God towards thee hath done his part, do thine'.   375
       So spake the Patriarch of Mankind, but *Eve*
Persisted, yet submiss, though last, replied.[32]

---

[29] *erect* "Vigorous; not depressed" (Johnson).
[30] *approve* prove.
[31] *find* determine that (we are stronger than you seem), as a finding of the trial.

[32] *last* last to speak, which is not indicative of submission.

'With thy permission then, and thus forewarned
Chiefly by what thy own last reasoning words
Touched only, that our trial, when least sought,   380
May find us both perhaps far less prepared,
The willinger I go, nor much expect
A Foe so proud will first the weaker seek;
So bent, the more shall shame him his repulse'.
Thus saying, from her Husband's hand her hand   385
Soft she withdrew, and like a Wood-Nymph light
Oread or Dryad, or of Delia's Train,[33]
Betook her to the Groves, but Delia's self
In gait surpassed, and Goddess-like deport,
Though not as she with Bow and Quiver armed,   390
But with such Gardning Tools as Art yet rude,
Guiltless of fire had formed, or Angels brought.
To Pales, or Pomona, thus adorned,[34]
Likest she seemed, Pomona when she fled
Vertumnus, or to Ceres in her Prime,[35]   395
Yet Virgin of Proserpina from Jove.
Her long with ardent look his Eye pursued
Delighted, but desiring more her stay.
Oft he to her his charge of quick return
Repeated, she to him as oft engaged   400
To be returned by Noon amid the Bow'r,
And all things in best order to invite
Noontide repast, or Afternoon's repose.
O much deceived, much failing, hapless Eve,
Of thy presumed return! event perverse!   405
Thou never from that hour in Paradise
Foundst either sweet repast, or sound repose;
Such ambush hid among sweet Flowrs and Shades
Waited with hellish rancour imminent
To intercept thy way, or send thee back   410
Despoiled of Innocence, of Faith, of Bliss.
For now, and since first break of dawn the Fiend,
Mere Serpent in appearance, forth was come,
And on his Quest, where likeliest he might find
The only two of Mankind, but in them   415
The whole included Race, his purposed prey.
In Bow'r and Field he sought, where any tuft
Of Grove or Garden-Plot more pleasant lay,
Their tendance or Plantation for delight,
By Fountain or by shady Rivulet   420
He sought them both, but wished his hap might find

---

33   Oread or Dryad   mountain or tree nymph, followers
of Artemis of Delos (hence Delia).
34   Pales   a Roman goddess of flocks and shepherds,
whose festival of purification was associated with the
founding of Rome; Pomona goddess of fruit, wife to
Vertumnus, a god of seasonal change.
35   Ceres   mother of Proserpina, whose abduction by
Pluto put an end to perpetual spring on earth.

Eve separáte, he wished, but not with hope
Of what so seldom chanced, when to his wish,
Beyond his hope, *Eve* separáte he spies,
Veiled in a Cloud of Fragrance, where she stood,   425
Half spied, so thick the Roses blushing round
About her glowed, oft stooping to support
Each Flowr of slender stalk, whose head though gay
Carnation, Purple, Azure, or specked with Gold,
Hung drooping unsustained, them she upstays   430
Gently with Myrtle band, mindless the while,[36]
Her self, though fairest unsupported Flowr,
From her best prop so far, and storm so nigh.
Nearer he drew, and many a walk traversed
Of stateliest Covert, Cedar, Pine, or Palm,   435
Then voluble and bold, now hid, now seen[37]
Among thick-woven Arborets, and Flowrs
Imbordered on each Bank, the hand of *Eve*:
Spot more delicious than those Gardens feigned
Or of revived *Adonis*, or renowned[38]   440
Alcinous, host of old *Laertes'* Son,[39]
Or that, not Mystic, where the Sapient King[40]
Held dalliance with his fair *Egyptian* Spouse.
Much he the Place admired, the Person more.
As one who long in populous City pent,   445
Where Houses thick and Sewers annoy the Air,
Forth issuing on a Summer's Morn to breathe
Among the pleasant Villages and Farms
Adjoined, from each thing met conceives delight;
The smell of Grain, or tedded Grass, or Kine,[41]   450
Or Dairy, each rural sight, each rural sound;
If chance with Nymphlike step fair Virgin pass,
What pleasing seemed, for her now pleases more,
She most, and in her look sums all Delight.
Such Pleasure took the Serpent to behold   455
This Flowry Plat, the sweet recess of *Eve* [42]
Thus early, thus alone; her Heav'nly form
Angelic, but more soft, and Feminine,
Her graceful Innocence, her every Air
Of gesture or least action overawed   460
His Malice, and with rapine sweet bereaved

---

[36] *mindless* inattentive to.
[37] *voluble* "Rolling; having quick motion" (Johnson).
[38] *Adonis* a divinity of vegetation and fertility; Spenser gave full allegorical and allusive life to his garden (*Faerie Queene* 3.6.29–51).
[39] *Alcinous* a king whose gardens are described when he offers hospitality to Odysseus, *Laertes' Son* (*Odyssey* 6).

[40] *Mystic* "pertaining to ancient religious mysteries" (*OED*), like the festival of Adonis; *Sapient King* Solomon, whose garden appears in the Song of Solomon, took an Egyptian Spouse (1 Kings 3.1).
[41] *tedded* from "to ted," "To lay grass newly mown in rows" (Johnson); *kine* archaic plural of *cow*.
[42] *Plat* place, plot of ground.

His fierceness of the fierce intent it brought:
That space the Evil one abstracted stood
From his own evil, and for the time remained
Stupidly good, of enmity disarmed,   465
Of guile, of hate, of envy, of revenge;
But the hot Hell that always in him burns,
Though in mid Heav'n, soon ended his delight,
And tortures him now more, the more he sees
Of pleasure not for him ordained: then soon   470
Fierce hate he recollects, and all his thoughts
Of mischief, gratulating, thus excites.
   'Thoughts, whither have ye led me, with what sweet
Compulsion thus transported to forget
What hither brought us, hate, not love, nor hope   475
Of Paradise for Hell, hope here to taste[43]
Of pleasure, but all pleasure to destroy,
Save what is in destroying, other joy
To me is lost. Then let me not let pass
Occasion which now smiles: behold alone   480
The Woman, opportune to all attempts,
Her Husband, for I view far round, not nigh,
Whose higher intellectual more I shun,
And strength, of courage haughty, and of limb
Heroic built, though of terrestrial mould,   485
Foe not informidable, exempt from wound,
I not; so much hath Hell debased, and pain
Enfeebled me, to what I was in Heav'n.[44]
She fair, divinely fair, fit Love for Gods,
Not terrible, though terror be in Love   490
And beauty, not approached by stronger hate,
Hate stronger, under show of Love well feigned,
The way which to her ruin now I tend'.
   So spake the Enemy of Mankind, enclosed
In Serpent, Inmate bad, and toward *Eve*   495
Addressed his way, not with indented wave,
Prone on the ground, as since, but on his rear,
Circular base of rising folds, that tower'd
Fold above fold a surging Maze, his Head
Crested aloft, and Carbuncle his Eyes;   500
With burnished Neck of verdant Gold, erect
Amidst his circling Spires, that on the grass
Floated redundant: pleasing was his shape,[45]
And lovely, never since of Serpent kind
Lovelier, not those that in *Illyria* changed   505

---

[43] *for* in exchange for.
[44] *to* compared to.

[45] *redundant* "Superabundant; exuberant" (Johnson),
but also latinate, wave on wave.

Hermione and Cadmus, or the God[46]
In Epidaurus; nor to which transformed[47]
Ammonian Jove, or Capitoline was seen,[48]
He with Olympias, this with her who bore
Scipio the heighth of Rome. With tract oblique[49]   510
At first, as one who sought accéss, but feared
To interrupt, side-long he works his way.
As when a Ship by skilful Steersmen wrought
Nigh River's mouth or Foreland, where the Wind
Veers oft, as oft so steers, and shifts her Sail;   515
So varied he, and of his tortuous Train
Curled many a wanton wreath in sight of Eve,
To lure her Eye; she busied heard the sound
Of rustling Leaves, but minded not, as used
To such disport before her through the Field,   520
From every Beast, more duteous at her call,
Than at Circean call the Herd disguised.[50]
He bolder now, uncalled before her stood;
But as in gaze admiring: Oft he bowed
His turret Crest, and sleek enamelled Neck,   525
Fawning, and licked the ground whereon she trod.
His gentle dumb expression turned at length
The Eye of Eve to mark his play; he glad
Of her attention gained, with Serpent Tongue
Organic, or impulse of vocal Air,[51]   530
His fraudulent temptation thus began.
     'Wonder not, sovereign Mistress, if perhaps
Thou canst, who art sole Wonder, much less arm
Thy looks, the Heav'n of mildness, with disdain,
Displeased that I approach thee thus, and gaze   535
Insatiate, I thus single, nor have feared
Thy awful brow, more awful thus retired.
Fairest resemblance of thy Maker fair,
Thee all things living gaze on, all things thine
By gift, and thy Celestial Beauty adore   540
With ravishment beheld, there best beheld

---

[46] *Hermione and Cadmus* having fled from Thebes, the city he founded in central Greece, to the Balkan wilds of Illyria, Cadmus in despair prayed to be turned into a serpent; his wife embraced him and sucessfully wished herself a serpent too (Ovid, *Metamorphoses* 4.562–603).

[47] *Epidaurus* a Greek city on the Peloponnese renowned for its sanctuary to the healing god Aesclepius, who took the form of a serpent while triumphantly proceeding to Rome to stop a plague (*Metamorphoses* 15.622–744).

[48] *Ammonian Jove* Egyptian Zeus (cf. 4.277), who took the form of a serpent when he conceived Alexander the Great with Olympias; when the legend was transferred to the great Roman general and ruler *Scipio* Africanus (236–184 BCE) Jove was given his local designation.

[49] *tract* course, path.

[50] *Circean call* Circes transformed or disguised men as beasts and controlled them, but wily Odysseus eluded her charms (*Odyssey* 10.210–574).

[51] *Organic* "Consisting of various parts co-operating with each other" (Johnson); the two parts of the forked tongue cannot "co-operate" in Ovid's stories of those transformed to snakes (l. 507 above and l. 749 below).

Where universally admired; but here
In this enclosure wild, these Beasts among,
Beholders rude, and shallow to discern
Half what in thee is fair, one man except,   545
Who sees thee? (and what is one?) who shouldst be seen
A Goddess among Gods, adored and served
By Angels numberless, thy daily Train'.
    So glozed the Tempter, and his Proem tuned;[52]
Into the Heart of *Eve* his words made way,   550
Though at the voice much marvelling; at length
Not unamazed she thus in answer spake.
'What may this mean? Language of Man pronounced
By Tongue of Brute, and human sense expressed?
The first at least of these I thought denied   555
To Beasts, whom God on their Creation-Day
Created mute to all articulate sound;
The latter I demur, for in their looks[53]
Much reason, and in their actions, oft appears.
Thee, Serpent, subtlest beast of all the field   560
I knew, but not with human voice endued;
Redouble then this miracle, and say,
How cam'st thou speakable of mute, and how
To me so friendly grown above the rest
Of brutal kind, that daily are in sight?   565
Say, for such wonder claims attention due'.
    To whom the guileful Tempter thus replied.
'Empress of this fair World, resplendent *Eve*,
Easy to me it is to tell thee all
What thou commandst, and right thou shouldst be obeyed: 570
I was at first as other Beasts that graze
The trodden Herb, of abject thoughts and low,
As was my food, nor aught but food discerned
Or Sex, and apprehended nothing high:
Till on a day roving the field, I chanced   575
A goodly Tree far distant to behold
Loaden with fruit of fairest colours mixed,
Ruddy and Gold: I nearer drew to gaze;
When from the boughs a savoury odour blown,
Grateful to appetite, more pleased my sense   580
Than smell of sweetest Fennel or the Teats[54]
Of Ewe or Goat dropping with Milk at Even,
Unsucked of Lamb or Kid, that tend their play.
To satisfy the sharp desire I had
Of tasting those fair Apples, I resolved   585
Not to defer; hunger and thirst at once,

---

[52] *glozed* from *gloze*, "To flatter; to wheedle; to insinuate; to fawn" (Johnson).

[53] *demur* "To doubt of" (Johnson).

[54] *Fennel or the Teats / Of Ewe* folkloric favorites of snakes.

Powerful persuaders, quickened at the scent
Of that alluring fruit, urged me so keen.
About the mossy Trunk I wound me soon,
For high from ground the branches would require   590
Thy utmost reach or *Adam's*: Round the Tree
All other Beasts that saw, with like desire
Longing and envying stood, but could not reach.
Amid the Tree now got, where plenty hung
Tempting so nigh, to pluck and eat my fill   595
I spared not, for such pleasure till that hour
At Feed or Fountain never had I found.
Sated at length, ere long I might perceive
Strange alteration in me, to degree
Of Reason in my inward Powers, and Speech   600
Wanted not long, though to this shape retained.
Thenceforth to Speculations high or deep
I turned my thoughts, and with capacious mind
Considered all things visible in Heav'n,
Or Earth, or Middle, all things fair and good;   605
But all that fair and good in thy Divine
Semblance, and in thy Beauty's heav'nly Ray
United I beheld; no Fair to thine
Equivalent or second, which compelled
Me thus, though importune perhaps, to come   610
And gaze, and worship thee of right declared
Sovereign of Creatures, universal Dame'.[55]
    So talked the spirited sly Snake; and *Eve*
Yet more amazed unwary thus replied.
    'Serpent, thy overpraising leaves in doubt   615
The virtue of that Fruit, in thee first proved:
But say, where grows the Tree, from hence how far?
For many are the Trees of God that grow
In Paradise, and various, yet unknown
To us, in such abundance lies our choice,   620
As leaves a greater store of Fruit untouched,
Still hanging incorruptible, till men
Grow up to their provision, and more hands
Help to disburden Nature of her Birth'.
    To whom the wily Adder, blithe and glad.   625
'Empress, the way is ready, and not long,
Beyond a row of Myrtles, on a Flat,
Fast by a Fountain, one small Thicket past
Of blowing Myrrh and Balm; if thou accept
My conduct, I can bring thee thither soon'.   630
    'Lead then', said Eve. He leading swiftly rolled

---

[55] *Dame* one who controls, feminine (L. *domina*);
mistress.

In tangles, and made intricate seem straight,
To mischief swift. Hope elevates, and joy
Brightens his Crest, as when a wandring Fire,[56]
Compact of unctuous vapour, which the Night   635
Condenses, and the cold environs round,
Kindled through agitation to a Flame,
Which oft, they say, some evil Spirit attends
Hovering and blazing with delusive Light,
Misleads th' amazed Night-wanderer from his way   640
To Bogs and Mires, and oft through Pond or Pool,
There swallowed up and lost, from succour far.
So glistered the dire Snake, and into fraud
Led *Eve* our credulous Mother, to the Tree
Of prohibition, root of all our woe;   645
Which when she saw, thus to her guide she spake.
    'Serpent, we might have spared our coming hither,
Fruitless to me, though fruit be here to excess,
The credit of whose virtue rest with thee,
Wondrous indeed, if cause of such effects.   650
But of this Tree we may not taste nor touch;
God so commanded, and left that Command
Sole Daughter of his voice; the rest, we live
Law to our selves, our Reason is our Law'.
    To whom the Tempter guilefully replied.   655
'Indeed? hath God then said that of the Fruit
Of all these Garden Trees ye shall not eat,
Yet Lords declared of all in Earth or Air?'
    To whom thus *Eve* yet sinless. 'Of the Fruit
Of each Tree in the Garden we may eat,   660
But of the Fruit of this fair Tree amidst
The Garden, God hath said, "Ye shall not eat
Thereof, nor shall ye touch it, lest ye die"'.
    She scarce had said, though brief, when now more bold
The Tempter, but with show of Zeal and Love   665
To Man, and indignation at his wrong,
New part puts on, and as to passion moved,
Fluctuates disturbed, yet comely and in act
Raised, as of some great matter to begin.
As when of old some Orator renowned   670
In *Athens* or free *Rome*, where Eloquence
Flourished, since mute, to some great cause addressed,
Stood in himself collected, while each part,
Motion, each act won audience ere the tongue,
Sometimes in heighth began, as no delay   675
Of Preface brooking, through his Zeal of Right.

---

[56] *wandring Fire*   will-o'-the-wisp, *ignis fatuus*, decep-
tive marsh gas.

So standing, moving, or to heighth upgrown
The Tempter all impassioned thus began.
   'O Sacred, Wise, and Wisdom-giving Plant,
Mother of Science, Now I feel thy Power[57]   680
Within me clear, not only to discern
Things in their Causes, but to trace the ways
Of highest Agents, deemed however wise.
Queen of this Universe, do not believe
Those rigid threats of Death; ye shall not Die: 685
How should ye? by the Fruit? it gives you Life
To Knowledge? by the Threatner, look on me,
Me who have touched and tasted, yet both live,
And life more perfet have attained than Fate
Meant me, by ventring higher than my Lot.   690
Shall that be shut to Man, which to the Beast
Is open? or will God incense his ire
For such a petty Trespass, and not praise
Rather your dauntless virtue, whom the pain
Of Death denounced, whatever thing Death be,   695
Deterred not from achieving what might lead
To happier life, knowledge of Good and Evil;
Of good, how just? of evil, if what is evil
Be real, why not known, since easier shunned?
God therefore cannot hurt ye, and be just;   700
Not just, not God; not feared then, nor obeyed:
Your fear it self of Death removes the fear.
Why then was this forbid? Why but to awe,
Why but to keep ye low and ignorant,
His worshippers; he knows that in the day   705
Ye Eat thereof, your Eyes that seem so clear,
Yet are but dim, shall perfetly be then
Opened and cleared, and ye shall be as Gods,
Knowing both Good and Evil, as they know.
That ye shall be as Gods, since I as Man,   710
Internal Man, is but proportion meet,
I of brute human, ye of human Gods.
So ye shall die perhaps, by putting off[58]
Human, to put on Gods, death to be wished,
Though threatened, which no worse than this can bring. 715
And what are Gods that Man may not become
As they, participating God-like food?
The Gods are first, and that advantage use
On our belief, that all from them proceeds;
I question it, for this fair Earth I see,   720
Warmed by the Sun, producing every kind,

---

[57] *Science* "Knowledge" (Johnson).   [58] *ye shall die . . .* a perverse version of the New Testament teaching (e.g., 1 Corinthians 15.51–8).

Them nothing: If they all things, who enclosed
Knowledge of Good and Evil in this Tree,
That whoso eats thereof, forthwith attains
Wisdom without their leave? and wherein lies   725
Th' offence, that Man should thus attain to know?
What can your knowledge hurt him, or this Tree
Impart against his will if all be his?
Or is it envy, and can envy dwell
In heav'nly breasts? these, these and many more   730
Causes import your need of this fair Fruit.
Goddess humane, reach then, and freely taste'.
    He ended, and his words replete with guile
Into her heart too easy entrance won:
Fixed on the Fruit she gazed, which to behold   735
Might tempt alone, and in her ears the sound
Yet rung of his persuasive words, impregned
With Reason, to her seeming, and with Truth;
Mean while the hour of Noon drew on, and waked
An eager appetite, raised by the smell   740
So savoury of that Fruit, which with desire,
Inclinable now grown to touch or taste,
Solicited her longing eye; yet first
Pausing a while, thus to her self she mused.
    'Great are thy Virtues, doubtless, best of Fruits,   745
Though kept from Man, and worthy to be admired,
Whose taste, too long forborne, at first assay
Gave elocution to the mute, and taught
The Tongue not made for Speech to speak thy praise:
Thy praise he also, who forbids thy use,   750
Conceals not from us, naming thee the Tree
Of Knowledge, knowledge both of good and evil;
Forbids us then to taste, but his forbidding
Commends thee more, while it infers the good
By thee communicated, and our want: 755
For good unknown sure is not had, or had
And yet unknown, is as not had at all.
In plain then, what forbids he but to know,
Forbids us good, forbids us to be wise?
Such prohibitions bind not. But if Death   760
Bind us with after-bands, what profits then
Our inward freedom? In the day we eat
Of this fair Fruit, our doom is, we shall die.
How dies the Serpent? he hath eat'n and lives,
And knows, and speaks, and reasons, and discerns,   765
Irrational till then. For us alone
Was death invented? or to us denied
This intellectual food, for beasts reserved?
For Beasts it seems: yet that one Beast which first

Hath tasted, envies not, but brings with joy   770
The good befall'n him, Author unsuspect,[59]
Friendly to man, far from deceit or guile.
What fear I then, rather what know to fear
Under this ignorance of good and Evil,
Of God or Death, of Law or Penalty?   775
Here grows the Cure of all, this Fruit Divine,
Fair to the Eye, inviting to the Taste,
Of virtue to make wise: what hinders then
To reach, and feed at once both Body and Mind?'[60]
   So saying, her rash hand in evil hour   780
Forth reaching to the Fruit, she plucked, she eat:[61]
Earth felt the wound, and Nature from her seat[62]
Sighing through all her Works gave signs of woe,
That all was lost. Back to the Thicket slunk
The guilty Serpent, and well might, for *Eve*   785
Intent now wholly on her taste, nought else
Regarded, such delight till then, as seemed,
In Fruit she never tasted, whether true
Or fancied so, through expectation high
Of knowledge, nor was God-head from her thought.   790
Greedily she engorged without restraint,
And knew not eating Death: Satiate at length,
And heightened as with Wine, jocund and boon,[63]
Thus to her self she pleasingly began.
   'O Sovereign, virtuous, precious of all Trees   795
In Paradise, of operation blest
To Sapience, hitherto obscured, infamed.
And thy fair Fruit let hang, as to no end
Created; but henceforth my early care,
Not without Song, each Morning, and due praise   800
Shall tend thee, and the fertile burden ease
Of thy full branches offered free to all;
Till dieted by thee I grow mature
In knowledge, as the Gods who all things know;
Though others envy what they cannot give;   805
For had the gift been theirs, it had not here
Thus grown. Experience, next, to thee I owe,
Best guide; not following thee, I had remained
In ignorance, thou op'nest Wisdom's way,
And giv'st accéss, though secret she retire.   810
And I perhaps am secret; Heav'n is high,
High and remote to see from thence distinct

---

[59] *Author unsuspect* "The first beginner or mover of any thing . . . Not considered as likely to do or mean ill" (Johnson).
[60] *Body and* two syllables, as often with *y* and following *a*.

[61] *eat* variant past tense.
[62] The description links Eve with Dido, her loss of honour, and Aeneas' travails (*Aeneid* 4.166–70); cf. l. 880.
[63] *boon* "Gay, merry; as a *boon* companion" (Johnson).

Each thing on Earth; and other care perhaps
May have diverted from continual watch
Our great Forbidder, safe with all his Spies[64]   815
About him. But to *Adam* in what sort
Shall I appear? shall I to him make known
As yet my change, and give him to partake
Full happiness with me, or rather not,
But keeps the odds of Knowledge in my power   820
Without Copartner? so to add what wants
In Female Sex, the more to draw his Love,
And render me more equal, and perhaps,
A thing not undesirable, sometime
Superior; for inferior who is free?   825
This may be well: but what if God have seen,
And Death ensue? then I shall be no more,
And *Adam* wedded to another *Eve*,
Shall live with her enjoying, I extinct;
A death to think. Confirmed then I resolve,   830
Adam shall share with me in bliss or woe:
So dear I love him, that with him all deaths
I could endure, without him live no life'.
   So saying, from the Tree her step she turned,
But first low Reverence done, as to the power   835
That dwelt within, whose presence had infused
Into the plant sciential sap, derived[65]
From Nectar, drink of Gods. *Adam* the while
Waiting desirous her return, had wove
Of choicest Flowrs a Garland to adorn   840
Her Tresses, and her rural labours crown,
As Reapers oft are wont their Harvest Queen.
Great joy he promised to his thoughts, and new
Solace in her return, so long delayed;
Yet oft his heart, divine of something ill,[66]   845
Misgave him; he the faltring measure felt;
And forth to meet her went, the way she took
That Morn when first they parted; by the Tree
Of Knowledge he must pass, there he her met,
Scarce from the Tree returning; in her hand   850
A bough of fairest fruit that downy smil'd,
New gathered, and ambrosial smell diffused.
To him she hasted, in her face excuse
Came Prologue, and Apology to prompt,
Which, with bland words at will she thus addressed.   855
   'Hast thou not wondered, *Adam*, at my stay?
Thee I have missed, and thought it long, deprived

---

[64] *safe* "No longer dangerous; reposited out of the
power of doing harm" (Johnson).

[65] *sciential* producing knowledge.

[66] *divine* "Presageful; divining; prescient" (Johnson).

Thy presence; agony of love till now
Not felt, nor shall be twice, for never more
Mean I to try, what rash untried I sought,   860
The pain of absence from thy sight. But strange
Hath been the cause, and wonderful to hear:
This Tree is not as we are told, a Tree
Of danger tasted, nor to evil unknown
Op'ning the way, but of Divine effect   865
To open Eyes, and make them Gods who taste;
And hath been tasted such: the Serpent wise,
Or not restrained as we, or not obeying,[67]
Hath eaten of the fruit, and is become,
Not dead, as we are threatened, but thenceforth   870
Endued with human voice and human sense,
Reasoning to admiration, and with me[68]
Persuasively hath so prevailed, that I
Have also tasted, and have also found
Th' effects to correspond, op'ner mine Eyes,   875
Dim erst, dilated Spirits, ampler Heart,
And growing up to Godhead; which for thee
Chiefly I sought, without thee can despise.
For bliss, as thou hast part, to me is bliss,
Tedious, unshared with thee, and odious soon.[69]   880
Thou therefore also taste, that equal Lot
May join us, equal Joy, as equal Love;
Lest thou not tasting, different degree
Disjoin us, and I then too late renounce
Deity for thee, when Fate will not permit'.   885
        Thus *Eve* with Countnance blithe her story told;
But in her Cheek distemper flushing glowed.
On the other side, *Adam*, soon as he heard
The fatal Trespass done by *Eve*, amazed,
Astonied stood and Blank, while horror chill[70]   890
Ran through his veins, and all his joints relaxed;
From his slack hand the Garland wreathed for *Eve*
Down dropped, and all the faded Roses shed:
Speechless he stood and pale, till thus at length
First to himself he inward silence broke.   895
        'O fairest of Creation, last and best
Of all God's works, Creature in whom excelled
Whatever can to sight or thought be formed,
Holy, divine, good, amiable, or sweet!

---

[67]   *Or . . . or*   either . . . or.
[68]   *to admiration*   admirably.
[69]   *Tedious* echoes Latin *taedet*, the description of
Dido's state of mind when she prays for death after her
fall (*Aeneid* 4.451).

[70]   *Astonied*   momentarily dazed or paralysed (*OED*).

How art thou lost, how on a sudden lost,   900
Defaced, deflowred, and now to Death devote?
Rather how hast thou yielded to transgress
The strict forbiddance, how to violate
The sacred Fruit forbidd'n! some cursèd fraud
Of Enemy hath beguil'd thee, yet unknown,   905
And me with thee hath ruined, for with thee
Certain my resolution is to Die;
How can I live without thee, how forego
Thy sweet Convérse and Love so dearly joined,
To live again in these wild Woods forlorn?   910
Should God create another *Eve*, and I
Another Rib afford, yet loss of thee
Would never from my heart; no no, I feel
The Link of Nature draw me: Flesh of Flesh,
Bone of my Bone thou art, and from thy State   915
Mine never shall be parted, bliss or woe'.
    So having said, as one from sad dismay
Recomforted, and after thoughts disturbed
Submitting to what seemed remediless,
Thus in calm mood his Words to *Eve* he turned.   920
    'Bold deed thou hast presumed, adventrous *Eve*,
And peril great provoked, who thus hath dared,
Had it been only coveting to Eye
That sacred Fruit, sacred to abstinence,
Much more to taste it under ban to touch.   925
But past who can recall, or done undo?
Not God Omnipotent, nor Fate, yet so
Perhaps thou shalt not Die, perhaps the Fact
Is not so heinous now, foretasted Fruit,
Profaned first by the Serpent, by him first   930
Made common and unhallowed ere our taste;
Nor yet on him found deadly, yet he lives;
Lives, as thou saidst, and gains to live as Man
Higher degree of Life, inducement strong
To us, as likely tasting to attain   935
Proportional ascent, which cannot be
But to be Gods, or Angels, Demi-gods.
Nor can I think that God, Creator wise,
Though threatning, will in earnest so destroy
Us his prime Creatures, dignified so high,   940
Set over all his Works, which in our Fall,
For us created, needs with us must fail,
Dependent made; so God shall uncreate,
Be frustrate, do, undo, and labour lose,
Not well conceived of God, who though his Power   945
Creation could repeat, yet would be loth
Us to abolish, lest the Adversary

Triumph and say; "Fickle their state whom God
Most Favours, who can please him long; Me first
He ruined, now Mankind; whom will he next?"   950
Matter of scorn, not to be giv'n the Foe,
However I with thee have fixed my Lot,
Certain to undergo like doom, if Death
Consort with thee, Death is to me as Life;
So forcible within my heart I feel   955
The Bond of Nature draw me to my own,
My own in thee, for what thou art is mine;
Our State cannot be severed, we are one,
One Flesh; to lose thee were to lose my self'.
        So *Adam*, and thus *Eve* to him replied.   960
'O glorious trial of exceeding Love,
Illustrious evidence, example high!
Engaging me to emulate, but short
Of thy perfection, how shall I attain,
Adam, from whose dear side I boast me sprung,   965
And gladly of our Union hear thee speak,
One Heart, one Soul in both; whereof good proof
This day affords, declaring thee resolved,
Rather than Death, or aught than Death more dread
Shall separate us, linked in Love so dear,   970
To undergo with me one Guilt, one Crime,
If any be, of tasting this fair Fruit,
Whose virtue, for of good still good proceeds,
Direct, or by occasion, hath presented[71]
This happy trial of thy Love, which else   975
So eminently never had been known.
Were it I thought Death menaced would ensue[72]
This my attempt, I would sustain alone
The worst, and not persuade thee, rather die
Deserted, than oblige thee with a fact   980
Pernicious to thy Peace, chiefly assured
Remarkably so late of thy so true,
So faithful Love unequalled; but I feel
Far otherwise th' event, not Death, but Life[73]
Augmented, opened Eyes, new Hopes, new Joys,   985
Taste so Divine, that what of sweet before
Hath touched my sense, flat seems to this, and harsh.
On my experience, *Adam*, freely taste,
And fear of Death deliver to the Winds'.
        So saying, she embraced him, and for joy   990
Tenderly wept, much won that he his Love
Had so ennobled, as of choice to incur
Divine displeasure for her sake, or Death.

---

[71] *by occasion* (three syllables) fortuitously.   [73] *event* outcome; result.
[72] *Were it* if it were the case that.

In recompense (for such compliance bad
Such recompense best merits) from the bough   995
She gave him of that fair enticing Fruit
With liberal hand: he scrupled not to eat
Against his better knowledge, not deceived,
But fondly overcome with Female charm.
Earth trembled from her entrails, as again   1000
In pangs, and Nature gave a second groan,
Sky lowred and muttering Thunder, some sad drops
Wept at completing of the mortal Sin
Original; while *Adam* took no thought,
Eating his fill, nor *Eve* to iterate   1005
Her former trespass feared, the more to soothe
Him with her loved society, that now
As with new Wine intoxicated both
They swim in mirth, and fancy that they feel
Divinity within them breeding wings   1010
Wherewith to scorn the Earth: but that false Fruit
Far other operation first displayed,
Carnal desire inflaming, he on *Eve*
Began to cast lascivious Eyes, she him
As wantonly repaid; in Lust they burn: 1015
Till *Adam* thus 'gan *Eve* to dalliance move.
     'Eve, now I see thou art exact of taste,
And elegant, of Sapience no small part,
Since to each meaning savour we apply,[74]
And Palate call judicious; I the praise   1020
Yield thee, so well this day thou hast purveyed.
Much pleasure we have lost, while we abstained
From this delightful Fruit, nor known till now
True relish, tasting; if such pleasure be
In things to us forbidd'n, it might be wished,   1025
For this one Tree had been forbidden ten.
But come, so well refreshed, now let us play,
As meet is, after such delicious Fare;
For never did thy Beauty since the day
I saw thee first and wedded thee, adorned   1030
With all perfections, so inflame my sense
With ardour to enjoy thee, fairer now
Than ever, bounty of this virtuous Tree'.
     So said he, and forbore not glance or toy[75]
Of amorous intent, well understood   1035
Of *Eve*, whose Eye darted contagious Fire.
Her hand he seized, and to a shady bank,

---

[74] *savour* "Perception; understanding" (*OED n* 5) as
well as "Relish or taste for something" (*n* 4) and other
meanings, but Milton may mean the concept of savour
rather than the word.

[75] *toy* "Play; sport; amorous dalliance" (Johnson).

Thick overhead with verdant roof embowred
He led her nothing loth; Flowrs were the Couch,
Pansies, and Violets, and Asphodel,   1040
And Hyacinth, Earth's freshest softest lap.
There they their fill of Love and Love's disport
Took largely, of their mutual guilt the Seal,
The solace of their sin, till dewy sleep
Oppressed them, wearied with their amorous play.   1045
Soon as the force of that fallacious Fruit,
That with exhilarating vapour bland
About their spirits had played, and inmost powers
Made err, was now exhaled, and grosser sleep
Bred of unkindly fumes, with conscious dreams   1050
Encumbered, now had left them, up they rose
As from unrest, and each the other viewing,
Soon found their Eyes how opened, and their minds
How darkened; innocence, that as a veil
Had shadowed them from knowing ill, was gone,   1055
Just confidence, and native righteousness
And honour from about them, naked left
To guilty shame he covered, but his Robe
Uncovered more. So rose the *Danite* strong
Herculean Samson from the Harlot-lap   1060
Of *Philistean Dálilah*, and waked
Shorn of his strength, They destitute and bare
Of all their virtue: silent, and in face
Confounded long they sat, as strucken mute,
Till *Adam*, though not less than *Eve* abashed.   1065
At length gave utterance to these words constrained.
     'O *Eve*, in evil hour thou didst give ear
To that false Worm, of whomsoever taught
To counterfeit Man's voice, true in our Fall,
False in our promised Rising; since our Eyes   1070
Opened we find indeed, and find we know
Both Good and Evil, Good lost, and Evil got,[76]
Bad Fruit of Knowledge, if this be to know,
Which leaves us naked thus, of Honour void,
Of Innocence, of Faith, of Purity,   1075
Our wonted Ornaments now soil'd and stained,
And in our Faces evident the signs
Of foul concupiscence; whence evil store;
Even shame, the last of evils; of the first
Be sure then. How shall I behold the face   1080
Henceforth of God or Angel, erst with joy
And rapture so oft beheld? those Heav'nly shapes

---

[76]   A line that shows the alternative pronunciations of
evil as one or two syllables.

Will dazzle now this earthly with their blaze
Insufferably bright. O might I here
In solitude live savage, in some glade   1085
Obscured, where highest Woods impenetrable
To Star or Sun-light, spread their umbrage broad
And brown as Evening: Cover me ye Pines,
Ye Cedars, with innumerable boughs
Hide me, where I may never see them more.   1090
But let us now, as in bad plight, devise
What best may for the present serve to hide
The Parts of each from other, that seem most
To shame obnoxious, and unseemliest seen,[77]
Some Tree whose broad smooth Leaves together sewed   1095
And girded on our loins, may cover round
Those middle parts; that this new comer, Shame,
There sit not, and reproach us as unclean'.
    So counselled he, and both together went
Into the thickest Wood; there soon they chose   1100
The Figtree, not that kind for Fruit renowned,
But such as at this day, to *Indians* known,
In *Malabar* or *Decan* spreads her Arms[78]
Branching so broad and long, that in the ground
The bended Twigs take root, and Daughters grow   1105
About the Mother Tree, a Pillared shade
High overarched, and echoing Walks between;
There oft the *Indian* Herdsman, shunning heat
Shelters in cool, and tends his pasturing Herds
At Loopholes cut through thickest shade: Those Leaves   1110
They gathered, broad as *Amazonian* Targe,[79]
And with what skill they had, together sewed,
To gird their waist, vain Covering if to hide
Their guilt and dreaded shame; O how unlike
To that first naked Glory. Such of late   1115
Columbus found the *American* so girt
With feathered Cincture, naked else and wild
Among the Trees on Isles and woody Shores.
Thus fenced, and, as they thought, their shame in part
Covered, but not at rest or ease of Mind,   1120
They sat them down to weep, nor only Tears
Rained at their Eyes, but high Winds worse within
Began to rise, high Passions, Anger, Hate,
Mistrust, Suspicion, Discord and shook sore
Their inward State of Mind, calm Region once   1125
And full of Peace, now tossed and turbulent:

---

[77]   *obnoxious*   exposed.
[78]   *Malabar* or *Decan*   places in India.

[79]   *Targe*   "A kind of buckler or shield borne on the left
arm. It seems to be commonly used for a defensive
weapon less in circumference than a shield" (Johnson).

For Understanding ruled not, and the Will
Heard not her lore, both in subjection now
To sensual Appetite, who from beneath
Usurping over sovereign Reason claimed   1130
Superior sway: from thus distempered breast,
Adam, estranged in look and altered style,
Speech intermitted thus to *Eve* renewed.
    'Would thou hadst hearkened to my words, and stayed
With me, as I besought thee, when that strange   1135
Desire of wandring, this unhappy Morn,
I know not whence possessed thee; we had then
Remained still happy, not as now, despoiled
Of all our good, shamed, naked, miserable.
Let none henceforth seek needless cause to approve[80]   1140
The Faith they owe; when earnestly they seek
Such proof, conclude, they then begin to fail'.
    To whom soon moved with touch of blame thus *Eve*.
'What words have pass't thy Lips, *Adam* severe,
Imput'st thou that to my default, or will   1145
Of wandring, as thou call'st it, which who knows
But might as ill have happened thou being by,
Or to thy self perhaps: hadst thou been there,
Or here th' attempt, thou couldst not have discerned
Fraud in the Serpent, speaking as he spake;   1150
No ground of enmity between us known,
Why he should mean me ill, or seek to harm.
Was I to have never parted from thy side?
As good have grown there still a lifeless Rib.
Being as I am, why didst not thou the Head   1155
Command me absolutely not to go,
Going into such danger, as thou saidst?
Too facile then thou didst not much gainsay,
Nay didst permit, approve, and fair dismiss.
Hadst thou been firm and fixed in thy dissent,   1160
Neither had I transgressed, nor thou with me'.
    To whom then first incensed, *Adam* replied.
'Is this the Love, is this the recompense
Of mine to thee, ingrateful *Eve*, expressed
Immutable when thou wert lost, not I,   1165
Who might have lived and joyed immortal bliss,
Yet willingly chose rather Death with thee:
And am I now upbraided, as the cause
Of thy transgressing? not enough severe,
It seems, in thy restraint: what could I more?   1170
I warned thee, I admonished thee, foretold
The danger, and the lurking Enemy

---

[80] *approve* prove.

That lay in wait; beyond this had been force,
And force upon free will hath here no place.
But confidence then bore thee on, secure   1175
Either to meet no danger, or to find
Matter of glorious trial; and perhaps
I also erred in overmuch admiring
What seemed in thee so perfet, that I thought
No evil durst attempt thee, but I rue   1180
That error now, which is become my crime,
And thou th' accuser. Thus it shall befall
Him who to worth in Women overtrusting,
Lets her will rule; restraint she will not brook,
And left to her self, if evil thence ensue,   1185
She first his weak indulgence will accuse'.
  Thus they in mutual accusation spent
The fruitless hours, but neither self-condemning,
And of their vain contést appeared no end.

BOOK X
THE ARGUMENT

 Man's transgressions known, the Guardian Angels forsake Paradise, and return up to Heaven to approve[1] their vigilance, and are approved, God declaring that The entrance of Satan could not by them be prevented. He sends his Son to judge the Transgressors, who descends and gives Sentence accordingly; then in pity clothes them both, and reascends. Sin and Death sitting till then at the Gates of Hell, by wondrous sympathy feeling the success of Satan in this new World, and the sin by Man there committed, resolve to sit no longer confined in Hell, but to follow Satan their Sire up to the place of Man: To make the way easier from Hell to this World to and fro, they pave a broad Highway or Bridge over Chaos, according to the track that Satan first made; then preparing for Earth, they meet with him proud of his success returning to Hell; their mutual gratulation. Satan arrives at Pandemonium, *in full assembly relates with boasting his success against Man; instead of applause is entertained with a general hiss by all his audience, transformed with himself also suddenly into Serpents, according to his doom given in Paradise; then deluded with a show of the forbidden Tree springing up before them, they greedily reaching to take of the Fruit, chew dust and bitter ashes. The proceedings of Sin and Death; God foretells the final Victory of his Son over them, and the renewing of all things; but for the present commands his Angels to make several alterations in the Heavens and Elements. Adam more and more perceiving his fallen condition heavily bewails, rejects the condolement of Eve; she persists and at length appeases him: then to evade the Curse likely to fall on their Offspring, proposes to Adam violent ways which he approves not, but conceiving better hope, puts her in mind of the late Promise made them, that her Seed should be revenged on the Serpent, and exhorts her with him to seek Peace of the offended Deity, by repentance and supplication.*

  Meanwhile the heinous and despiteful act
  Of *Satan* done in Paradise, and how
  He in the Serpent, had perverted *Eve*,[2]

BOOK X
[1] *approve* give proof of (l. 31 below).

[2] *pervert* "To corrupt; to turn from the right; opposed to convert, which is to turn from the wrong to the right" (Johnson).

Her Husband she, to taste the fatal fruit,
Was known in Heav'n; for what can scape the Eye   5
Of God All-seeing, or deceive his Heart
Omniscient, who in all things wise and just,
Hindered not *Satan* to attempt the mind
Of Man, with strength entire, and free will armed,
Complete to have discovered and repulsed   10
Whatever wiles of Foe or seeming Friend.
For still they knew, and ought to have still remembered
The high Injunction not to taste that Fruit,
Whoever tempted; which they not obeying,
Incurred, what could they less, the penalty,   15
And manifold in sin, deserved to fall.
Up into Heav'n from Paradise in haste
Th' Angelic Guards ascended, mute and sad
For Man, for of his state by this they knew,
Much wondring how the subtle Fiend had stol'n   20
Entrance unseen. Soon as th' unwelcome news
From Earth arrived at Heaven Gate, displeased
All were who heard, dim sadness did not spare
That time Celestial visages, yet mixed
With pity, violated not their bliss.   25
About the new-arrived, in multitudes
Th' ethereal People ran, to hear and know
How all befell: they towards the Throne Supreme
Accountable made haste to make appear
With righteous plea, their utmost vigilance,   30
And easily approved; when the most High
Eternal Father from his secret Cloud,
Amidst in Thunder uttered thus his voice.
   'Assembled Angels, and ye Powers returned
From unsuccessful charge, be not dismayed,   35
Nor troubled at these tidings from the Earth,
Which your sincerest care could not prevent,
Foretold so lately what would come to pass,
When first this Tempter crossed the Gulf from Hell.
I told ye then he should prevail and speed,[3]   40
On his bad Errand, Man should be seduced
And flattered out of all, believing lies
Against his Maker; no Decree of mine
Concurring to necessitate his Fall,
Or touch with lightest moment of impulse   45
His free Will, to her own inclining left
In even scale. But fall'n he is, and now
What rests but that the mortal Sentence pass
On his transgression, Death denounced that day,[4]

---

[3] *then*   3.92–7 above.   [4] *denounced*   "threaten[ed] by proclamation"
(Johnson).

Which he presumes already vain and void,   50
Because not yet inflicted, as he feared,
By some immediate stroke; but soon shall find
Forbearance no acquittance ere day end.
Justice shall not return as bounty scorned.
But whom send I to judge them? whom but thee   55
Vicegerent Son, to thee I have transferred
All Judgement, whether in Heav'n, or Earth, or Hell.
Easy it may be seen that I intend
Mercy colleague with Justice, sending thee
Man's Friend, his Mediator, his designed   60
Both Ransom and Redeemer voluntary,
And destined Man himself to judge Man fall'n'.[5]
    So spake the Father, and unfolding bright
Toward the right hand his Glory, on the Son
Blazed forth unclouded Deity; he full   65
Resplendent all his Father manifest[6]
Expressed, and thus divinely answered mild.
    'Father Eternal, thine is to decree,
Mine both in Heav'n and Earth to do thy will
Supreme, that thou in me thy Son beloved   70
Mayst ever rest well pleased. I go to judge
On Earth these thy transgressors, but thou knowst,
Whoever judged, the worst on me must light,
When time shall be, for so I undertook
Before thee; and not repenting, this obtain   75
Of right, that I may mitigate their doom
On me derived, yet I shall temper so[7]
Justice with Mercy, as may illústrate most[8]
Them fully satisfied, and thee appease.
Attendance none shall need, nor Train, where none   80
Are to behold the Judgement, but the judged,
Those two; the third best absent is condemned,
Convict by flight, and Rebel to all Law
Conviction to the Serpent none belongs'.[9]
    Thus saying, from his radiant Seat he rose   85
Of high collateral glory: him Thrones and Powers,
Princedoms, and Dominations ministrant
Accompanied to Heaven Gate, from whence
Eden and all the Coast in prospect lay.
Down he descended straight; the speed of Gods   90

---

[5] *destined Man* a reference to the Son's future incarnation as Christ.

[6] *manifest Expressed* as the Word of God, the Son expresses and makes manifest God's will; Dryden uses the obscure imagery of this passage for satiric ends in "Mac Flecknoe" (ll.134–6 below).

[7] *derived* "turned from its course" (Johnson), like a river.

[8] *illústrate most/Them fully satisfied* elucidate matters to their complete satisfaction.

[9] *Conviction* "Detection of guilt, which is, in law, either when a man is outlawed, or appears and confesses, or is found guilty by the inquest" (Johnson quoting John Cowell).

Time counts not, though with swiftest minutes winged.
Now was the Sun in Western cadence low[10]
From Noon, and gentle Airs due at their hour
To fan the Earth now waked, and usher in
The Evening cool when he, from wrath more cool   95
Came the mild Judge and Intercessor both
To sentence Man: the voice of God they heard
Now walking in the Garden, by soft winds
Brought to their Ears, while day declined, they heard,
And from his presence hid themselves among   100
The thickest Trees, both Man and Wife, till God
Approaching, thus to *Adam* called aloud.
     'Where art thou *Adam*, wont with joy to meet[11]
My coming seen far off? I miss thee here,
Not pleased, thus entertained with solitude,   105
Where obvious duty erewhile appeared unsought:
Or come I less conspicuous, or what change
Absents thee, or what chance detains? Come forth'.
He came, and with him *Eve*, more loth, though first
To offend, discount'nanced both, and discomposed;   110
Love was not in their looks, either to God
Or to each other, but apparent guilt,
And shame, and perturbation, and despair,
Anger, and obstinacy, and hate, and guile.
Whence *Adam* faltring long, thus answered brief.   115
     'I heard thee in the Garden, and of thy voice
Afraid, being naked, hid my self'. To whom
The gracious Judge without revile replied.
     'My voice thou oft hast heard, and hast not feared,
But still rejoiced, how is it now become   120
So dreadful to thee? that thou art naked, who
Hath told thee? hast thou eaten of the Tree
Whereof I gave thee charge thou shouldst not eat?'
     To whom thus *Adam* sore beset replied.
'O Heav'n! in evil strait this day I stand   125
Before my Judge, either to undergo
My self the total Crime, or to accuse
My other self, the partner of my life;
Whose failing, while her Faith to me remains,
I should conceal, and not expose to blame   130
By my complaint; but strict necessity
Subdues me, and calamitous constraint,
Lest on my head both sin and punishment,
However insupportable, be all

---

[10]   *cadence*   "Fall; state of sinking; decline" (Johnson).   [11]   Genesis 3.9; the twenty-four verses in Genesis 3
contain the whole biblical story of the fall, God's judge-
ment on man, and the expulsion from Eden.

Devolved; though should I hold my peace, yet thou   135
Wouldst easily detect what I conceal.
This Woman whom thou mad'st to be my help,
And gav'st me as thy perfect gift, so good,
So fit, so acceptable, so Divine,
That from her hand I could suspect no ill,   140
And what she did, whatever in it self,
Her doing seemed to justify the deed;
She gave me of the Tree, and I did eat'.
    To whom the sovereign Presence thus replied.
'Was she thy God, that her thou didst obey   145
Before his voice, or was she made thy guide,
Superior, or but equal, that to her
Thou did'st resign thy Manhood, and the Place
Wherein God set thee above her made of thee,
And for thee, whose perfection far excelled   150
Hers in all real dignity: Adorned
She was indeed, and lovely to attract
Thy Love, not thy Subjection, and her Gifts
Were such as under Government well seemed,
Unseemly to bear rule, which was thy part   155
And person, had'st thou known thy self aright'.
    So having said, he thus to *Eve* in few:
'Say Woman, what is this which thou hast done?'
    To whom sad *Eve* with shame nigh overwhelmed,
Confessing soon, yet not before her Judge   160
Bold or loquacious, thus abashed replied.
    'The Serpent me beguiled and I did eat'.
    Which when the Lord God heard, without delay
To Judgement he proceeded on th' accused
Serpent though brute, unable to transfer   165
The Guilt on him who made him instrument
Of mischief, and polluted from the end[12]
Of his Creation; justly then accursed,
As vitiated in Nature: more to know
Concerned not Man (since he no further knew)   170
Nor altered his offence; yet God at last
To Satan first in sin his doom applied,
Though in mysterious terms, judged as then best:
And on the Serpent thus his curse let fall.
    'Because thou hast done this, thou art accursed   175
Above all Cattle, each Beast of the Field;
Upon thy Belly grovelling thou shalt go,
And dust shalt eat all the days of thy Life.
Between Thee and the Woman I will put

---

[12] *end* purpose.

Enmity, and between thine and her Seed;   180
Her Seed shall bruise thy head, thou bruise his heel'.
　　So spake this Oracle, then verified
When *Jesus* Son of *Mary* second *Eve*,
Saw Satan fall like Lightning down from Heav'n,
Prince of the Air; then rising from his Grave   185
Spoiled Principalities and Powers, triumphed
In open show, and with ascension bright[13]
Captivity led captive through the Air,
The Realm it self of Satan long usurped,
Whom he shall tread at last under our feet;   190
Even he who now foretold his fatal bruise,
And to the Woman thus his Sentence turned.
　　'Thy sorrow I will greatly multiply
By thy Conception; Children thou shalt bring
In sorrow forth, and to thy Husband's will   195
Thine shall submit, he over thee shall rule'.
　　On *Adam* last thus judgement he pronounced.
'Because thou hast hearkened to the voice of thy Wife,
And eaten of the Tree concerning which
I charged thee, saying: Thou shalt not eat thereof,   200
Cursed is the ground for thy sake, thou in sorrow
Shalt eat thereof, all the days of thy life;
Thorns also and Thistles it shall bring thee forth
Unbid, and thou shalt eat th' Herb of th' Field,
In the sweat of thy Face shalt thou eat Bread,   205
Till thou return unto the ground, for thou
Out of the ground wast taken, know thy Birth,
For dust thou art, and shalt to dust return'.
　　So judged he Man, both Judge and Saviour sent,
And th' instant stroke of Death denounced that day   210
Removed far off; then pitying how they stood
Before him naked to the air, that now
Must suffer change, disdained not to begin
Thenceforth the form of servant to assume,
As when he washed his servants' feet, so now[14]   215
As Father of his Family he clad
Their nakedness with Skins of Beasts, or slain,[15]
Or as the Snake with youthful Coat repaid;
And thought not much to clothe his Enemies:
Nor he their outward only with the Skins   220
Of Beasts, but inward nakedness, much more
Opprobrious, with his Robe of righteousness,
Arraying covered from his Father's sight.

---

[13] *with ascension . . . captive* Psalm 68.18.　　　　　[15] *or . . . Or* either . . . or.
[14] *washed his servants' feet* Christ washes the feet of his
disciples (John 13.5).

To him with swift ascent he up returned,
Into his blissful bosom reassumed   225
In glory as of old, to him appeased
All, though all-knowing, what had passed with Man
Recounted, mixing intercession sweet.
Meanwhile ere thus was sinned and judged on Earth,
Within the Gates of Hell sat Sin and Death,   230
In counterview within the Gates, that now
Stood open wide, belching outrageous flame
Far into *Chaos*, since the Fiend passed through,
Sin opening, who thus now to Death began.
  'O Son, why sit we here each other viewing   235
Idly, while Satan our great Author thrives
In other Worlds, and happier Seat provides
For us, his offspring dear? It cannot be
But that success attends him; if mishap,
Ere this he had returned, with fury driv'n   240
By his Avengers, since no place like this
Can fit his punishment, or their revenge.
Methinks I feel new strength within me rise,
Wings growing, and Dominion giv'n me large
Beyond this Deep; whatever draws me on,   245
Or sympathy, or some connatural force,
Powerful at greatest distance to unite
With secret amity things of like kind
By secretest conveyance. Thou my Shade
Inseparable must with me along: 250
For Death from Sin no power can separate.
But lest the difficulty of passing back
Stay his return perhaps over this Gulf
Impassable, Impervious, let us try
Adventrous work, yet to thy power and mine   255
Not unagreeable, to found a path
Over this Main from Hell to that new World
Where Satan now prevails, a Monument
Of merit high to all th' infernal Host,
Easing their passage hence, for intercourse,   260
Or transmigration, as their lot shall lead.
Nor can I miss the way, so strongly drawn
By this new felt attraction and instinct'.
  Whom thus the meager Shadow answered soon.
'Go whither Fate, and inclination strong   265
Leads thee, I shall not lag behind, nor err
The way, thou leading, such a scent I draw
Of carnage, prey innumerable, and taste
The savour of Death from all things there that live:
Nor shall I to the work thou enterprisest   270
Be wanting, but afford thee equal aid'.

So saying, with delight he snuffed the smell
Of mortal change on Earth. As when a flock
Of ravenous Fowl, though many a League remote,
Against the day of Battle, to a Field,   275
Where Armies lie encamped, come flying, lured
With scent of living Carcasses designed
For death, the following day, in bloody fight.
So scented the grim Feature, and upturned
His Nostril wide into the murky Air,   280
Sagacious of his Quarry from so far.
Then Both from out Hell Gates into the waste
Wide Anarchy of *Chaos* damp and dark
Flew divers, and with Power (their Power was great)
Hovering upon the Waters; what they met   285
Solid or slimy, as in raging Sea
Tossed up and down, together crowded drove
From each side shoaling towards the mouth of Hell.[16]
As when two Polar Winds blowing adverse
Upon the *Cronian* Sea, together drive[17]   290
Mountains of Ice, that stop th' imagined way
Beyond *Petsora* Eastward, to the rich
Cathaian Coast. The aggregated Soil
Death with his Mace petrific, cold and dry,[18]
As with a Trident smote, and fixed as firm   295
As *Delos* floating once; the rest his look[19]
Bound with *Gorgonian* rigour not to move,[20]
And with *Asphaltic* slime; broad as the Gate,[21]
Deep to the Roots of Hell the gathered beach
They fastened, and the Mole immense wrought on[22]   300
Over the foaming deep high Arched, a Bridge
Of length prodigious joining to the Wall
Immoveable of this now fenceless world
Forfeit to Death; from hence a passage broad,
Smooth, easy, inoffensive, down to Hell.   305
So, if great things to small may be compared,
Xerxes, the Liberty of *Greece* to yoke,[23]

---

[16] *shoaling* both thronging (*OED*) and making shallows (Johnson).

[17] *Cronian Sea* the frozen or Northern sea through which navigators sought an *imagined way*, a northeast passage past the *Petsora* River, through the Kara Sea and around Siberia to Cathay, a kingdom in northern China.

[18] *cold and dry* two of the four elements; Death excludes hot and moist.

[19] *Delos* an island in the Aegean, reputed to have drifted until Zeus moored it in the center of the Cyclades so that Leto could give birth there to Apollo and Artemis.

[20] *Gorgonian* those who looked on the Gorgon Medusa were turned to stone.

[21] *Asphaltic* "Gummy; bituminous" (Johnson).

[22] *Mole* "A mound; a dike" (Johnson).

[23] *Xerxes* the Persian ruler built a bridge across the straits of the Black Sea when he unsuccessfully attacked Greece; he is said to have ordered the waves lashed and the winds chained when the weather did not cooperate with his plans (cf. Samuel Johnson, *The Vanity of Human Wishes*, 1.232); his capital was Susa (Elymais, Iran), an ancient city said to have been founded by Memnon, son of the goddess Dawn and Tithonus, a brother of King Priam.

From *Susa* his *Memnonian* Palace high
Came to the Sea, and over *Hellespont*
Bridging his way *Europe* with *Asia* joined,   310
And scourged with many a stroke the indignant waves.
Now had they brought the work by wondrous Art
Pontifical, a ridge of pendant Rock[24]
Over the vexed Abyss, following the track
Of *Satan*, to the self same place where he[25]   315
First lighted from his Wing, and landed safe
From out of *Chaos* to the out side bare
Of this round World: with Pins of Adamant
And Chains they made all fast, too fast they made
And durable; and now in little space   320
The confines met of Empyréan Heav'n
And of this World, and on the left hand Hell
With long reach interposed; three several ways
In sight, to each of these three places led.
And now their way to Earth they had descried,   325
To Paradise first tending, when behold
Satan in likeness of an Angel bright
Betwixt the *Centaur* and the *Scorpion* steering[26]
His *Zenith*, while the Sun in *Aries* rose:
Disguised he came, but those his Children dear   330
Their Parent soon discerned, though in disguise.
He after *Eve* seduced, unminded slunk
Into the Wood fast by, and changing shape
To observe the sequel, saw his guileful act
By *Eve*, though all unweeting, seconded[27]   335
Upon her Husband, saw their shame that sought
Vain covertures; but when he saw descend
The Son of God to judge them, terrified
He fled, not hoping to escape, but shun
The present, fearing guilty what his wrath   340
Might suddenly inflict; that past, returned
By Night, and listening where the hapless Pair
Sat in their sad discourse, and various plaint,
Thence gathered his own doom, which understood[28]
Not instant, but of future time. With joy   345
And tidings fraught, to Hell he now returned,
And at the brink of *Chaos*, near the foot

---

[24] *Pontifical* "Bridge-building. This sense is, I believe, peculiar to Milton, and perhaps was intended as an
equivocal satire on Popery" (Johnson).
[25] *the self same place* cf. 3.418.
[26] *Centaur, Scorpion, Aries* constellations; Scorpio and
Aries are opposite and distant from each other in the
Zodiac.

[27] *unweeting* unwitting.
[28] *understood* understood of (*OED, understand* 11), contained information about.

Of this new wondrous Pontifice, unhoped
Met who to meet him came, his Offspring dear.
Great joy was at their meeting, and at sight   350
Of that stupendious Bridge his joy increased.
Long he admiring stood, till Sin, his fair
Enchanting Daughter, thus the silence broke.
   'O Parent, these are thy magnific deeds,
Thy Trophies, which thou view'st as not thine own,   355
Thou art their Author, and prime Architect:
For I no sooner in my Heart divined,
My Heart, which by a secret harmony
Still moves with thine, joined in connexion sweet,
That thou on Earth hadst prospered, which thy looks   360
Now also evidence, but straight I felt
Though distant from thee Worlds between, yet felt
That I must after thee with this thy Son,
Such fatal consequence unites us three:
Hell could no longer hold us in our bounds,   365
Nor this unvoyageable Gulf obscure
Detain from following thy illustrious track.
Thou hast achieved our liberty, confined
Within Hell Gates till now, thou us empow'rd
To fortify thus far, and overlay   370
With this portentous Bridge the dark Abyss.
Thine now is all this World, thy virtue hath won
What thy hands builded not, thy Wisdom gained
With odds what War hath lost, and fully avenged
Our foil in Heav'n; here thou shalt Monarch reign,   375
There didst not; there let him still Victor sway,
As Battle hath adjudged, from this new World
Retiring, by his own doom alienated,
And henceforth Monarchy with thee divide
Of all things parted by th' Empyreal bounds,   380
His Quadrature, from thy Orbicular World,
Or try thee now more dang'rous to his Throne'.[29]
   Whom thus the Prince of Darkness answered glad.
'Fair Daughter, and thou Son and Grandchild both,
High proof ye now have giv'n to be the Race   385
Of *Satan* (for I glory in the name,[30]
Antagonist of Heav'n's Almighty King)
Amply have merited of me, of all
Th' infernal Empire, that so near Heav'n's door
Triumphal with triumphal act have met,   390
Mine, with this glorious Work, and made one Realm
Hell and this world, one realm, one continent
Of easy thorough-fare. Therefore while I

---

[29] *dang'rous* hurtful (*OED*, danger *n* 6).   [30] *Satan* meaning adversary (cf 1.82).

Descend through Darkness, on your Road with ease
To my associate Powers, them to acquaint   395
With these successes, and with them rejoice,
You two this way, among these numerous Orbs
All yours, right down to Paradise descend;
There dwell and Reign in bliss, thence on the Earth
Dominion exercise and in the Air,   400
Chiefly on Man, sole Lord of all declared,
Him first make sure your thrall, and lastly kill.
My Substitutes I send ye, and Create
Plenipotent on Earth, of matchless might
Issuing from me: on your joint vigour now   405
My hold of this new Kingdom all depends,
Through Sin to Death exposed by my exploit.
If your joint power prevail, th' affairs of Hell
No detriment need fear, go and be strong'.
    So saying he dismissed them, they with speed   410
Their course through thickest Constellations held
Spreading their bane; the blasted Stars looked wan,
And Planets, Planet-strook, real Eclipse³¹
Then suffered. Th' other way *Satan* went down
The Causey to Hell Gate; on either side³²   415
Disparted *Chaos* overbuilt exclaimed,
And with rebounding surge the bars assailed,
That scorned his indignation: through the Gate,
Wide open and unguarded, *Satan* passed,
And all about found desolate; for those   420
Appointed to sit there, had left their charge,
Flown to the upper World; the rest were all
Far to the inland retired, about the walls
Of *Pandemonium*, City and proud seat
Of *Lucifer*, so by allusion called,   425
Of that bright Star to *Satan* paragoned.³³
There kept their Watch the Legions, while the Grand
In Council sat, solicitous what chance
Might intercept their Emperor sent; so he
Departing gave command, and they observed.   430
As when the *Tartar* from his *Russian* Foe
By *Astracan* over the Snowy Plains³⁴
Retires, or *Bactrin* Sophy from the horns³⁵
Of *Turkish* Crescent, leaves all waste beyond

---

³¹ *Planet-strook* subject to the damaging influence of a
planet (any "wandering" body in the heavens).
³² *Causey* causeway.
³³ *bright star* Venus, the morning star (or Lucifer, the
light bearer); *paragoned* compared.
³⁴ *Astracan* Astrakhan, a city on the northeast coast of
the Caspian Sea.

³⁵ *Bactrin* from Bactria, a country located in the region of Afghanistan, incorporated into Persia (which
included the northern cities of *Tauris* – Tabriz – and
Casbeen – Kazwin – conquered by Islamic rulers who also
took the Armenian kingdom of *Aladule*.

The Realm of *Aladule*, in his retreat   435
To *Tauris* or *Casbeen*. So these the late
Heav'n-banished Host, left desert utmost Hell
Many a dark League, reduced in careful Watch[36]
Round their Metropolis, and now expecting
Each hour their great adventurer from the search   440
Of Foreign Worlds: he through the midst unmarked,
In show Plebeian Angel militant
Of lowest order, passed; and from the door
Of that *Plutonian* Hall, invisible
Ascended his high Throne, which under state[37]   445
Of richest texture spread, at th' upper end
Was placed in regal lustre. Down a while
He sat, and round about him saw unseen:
At last as from a Cloud his fulgent head
And shape Star bright appeared, or brighter, clad   450
With what permissive glory since his fall
Was left him, or false glitter: All amazed
At that so sudden blaze the *Stygian* throng
Bent their aspéct, and whom they wished beheld,
Their mighty Chief returned: loud was the acclaim: 455
Forth rushed in haste the great consulting Peers,
Raised from their dark *Divan*, and with like joy
Congratulant approached him, who with hand
Silence, and with these words attention won.
   'Thrones, Dominations, Princedoms, Virtues, Powers,   460
For in possession such, not only of right,
I call ye and declare ye now, returned
Successful beyond hope, to lead ye forth
Triumphant out of this infernal Pit
Abominable, accursed, the house of woe,   465
And Dungeon of our Tyrant: Now possess,
As Lords, a spacious World, to our native Heaven
Little inferior, by my adventure hard
With peril great achieved. Long were to tell
What I have done, what suffered, with what pain   470
Voyaged th' unreal, vast, unbounded deep[38]
Of horrible confusion, over which
By Sin and Death a broad way now is paved
To expedite your glorious march; but I
Toiled out my uncouth passage, forced to ride   475
Th' untractable Abyss, plunged in the womb
Of unoriginal *Night* and *Chaos* wild[39]
That jealous of their secrets, fiercely opposed
My journey strange, with clamorous uproar

---

[36] *reduced* "brought back" (Johnson).
[37] *state* "A canopy; a covering of dignity" (Johnson).
[38] *unreal* "Unsubstantial" (Johnson).

[39] *unoriginal* "Unoriginated. Having no birth; ungenerated" (Johnson).

Protesting Fate supreme; thence how I found   480
The new created World, which fame in Heav'n
Long had foretold, a Fabric wonderful
Of absolute perfection, therein Man
Placed in a Paradise, by our exile
Made happy: Him by fraud I have seduced   485
From his Creator, and the more to increase
Your wonder, with an Apple; he thereat
Offended, worth your laughter, hath giv'n up
Both his belovèd Man and all his World,
To Sin and Death a prey, and so to us,   490
Without our hazard, labour, or alarm,
To range in, and to dwell, and over Man
To rule, as over all he should have ruled.
True is, me also he hath judged, or rather
Me not, but the brute Serpent in whose shape   495
Man I deceived: that which to me belongs,
Is enmity, which he will put between
Me and Mankind; I am to bruise his heel;
His Seed, when is not set, shall bruise my head:
A World who would not purchase with a bruise,   500
Or much more grievous pain? Ye have th' account
Of my performance: What remains, ye Gods,
But up and enter now into full bliss'.
    So having said, a while he stood, expecting
Their universal shout, and high applause   505
To fill his ear, when contrary he hears
On all sides, from innumerable tongues
A dismal universal hiss, the sound
Of public scorn; he wondered, but not long
Had leisure, wondring at himself now more;   510
His Visage drawn he felt to sharp and spare,
His Arms clung to his Ribs, his Legs entwining
Each other, till supplanted down he fell[40]
A monstrous Serpent on his Belly prone,
Reluctant, but in vain, a greater power   515
Now ruled him, punished in the shape he sinned,
According to his doom: he would have spoke,
But hiss for hiss returned with forkèd tongue
To forkèd tongue, for now were all transformed
Alike, to Serpents all as accessories   520
To his bold Riot: dreadful was the din[41]
Of hissing through the Hall, thick swarming now
With complicated monsters head and tail,
Scorpion and *Asp*, and *Amphisbæna* dire,[42]

---

[40] *supplant* "To trip up the heels" (Johnson).   [42] *Amphisbæna* a serpent with a head at each end.
[41] *Riot* "A sedition; an uproar" (Johnson).

Cerastes horned, *Hydrus*, and *Elops* drear,[43]   525
And *Dipsas* (not so thick swarmed once the Soil[44]
Bedropped with blood of *Gorgon*, or the Isle[45]
Ophiusa) but still greatest he the midst,
Now Dragon grown, larger than whom the Sun
Engendered in the *Pythian* Vale on slime,[46]   530
Huge *Python*, and his Power no less he seemed
Above the rest still to retain; they all
Him followed issuing forth to th' open Field,
Where all yet left of that revolted Rout
Heav'n-fall'n, in station stood or just array,   535
Sublime with expectation when to see[47]
In Triumph issuing forth their glorious Chief;
They saw, but other sight instead, a crowd
Of ugly Serpents; horror on them fell,
And horrid sympathy; for what they saw,   540
They felt themselves now changing; down their arms,
Down fell both Spear and Shield, down they as fast,
And the dire hiss renewed, and the dire form
Catched by Contagion, like in punishment,
As in their crime. Thus was th' applause they meant,   545
Turned to exploding hiss, triumph to shame[48]
Cast on themselves from their own mouths. There stood
A Grove hard by, sprung up with this their change,
His will who reigns above, to aggravate
Their penance, laden with fair Fruit like that   550
Which grew in Paradise, the bait of *Eve*
Used by the Tempter: on that prospect strange
Their earnest eyes they fixed, imagining
For one forbidden Tree a multitude
Now ris'n, to work them further woe or shame;   555
Yet parched with scalding thirst and hunger fierce,
Though to delude them sent, could not abstain,
But on they rolled in heaps, and up the Trees
Climbing, sat thicker than the snaky locks
That curled *Megæra*: greedily they plucked[49]   560
The Fruitage fair to sight, like that which grew
Near that bituminous Lake where *Sodom* flamed;[50]

---

[43] *Cerastes* horned serpent; *Hydrus* water snake; *Elops* a scaly fish or serpent.

[44] *Dipsas* a snake whose bite provokes thirst; *the Soil* the snaky, variously placed home of Medusa, the *Gorgon* with snaky hair.

[45] *Isle Ophiusa* serpent-isle, a name applied to several Mediterranean islands.

[46] *Pythian Vale* near Delphi and Mount Parnassus, deriving its name from the serpent, according to Ovid (*Metamorphoses* 1.438–51).

[47] *Sublime* "Elevated by joy" (Johnson).

[48] *exploding* fr. *explode* "To drive out disgracefully with some noise of contempt" (Johnson).

[49] *Megæra* one of the three Furies, spirits of punishment, especially avenging without mercy evil deeds done within families.

[50] *bituminous Lake* the Dead Sea; *Sodom* a city of evil, destroyed by God (Genesis 19.24–5).

This more delusive, not the touch, but taste
Deceived; they fondly thinking to allay
Their appetite with gust, instead of Fruit   565
Chewed bitter Ashes, which th' offended taste
With spattering noise rejected: oft they assayed,
Hunger and thirst constraining, drugged as oft,[51]
With hatefulest disrelish writhed their jaws
With soot and cinders filled; so oft they fell   570
Into the same illusion, not as Man
Whom they triúmphed once lapsed. Thus were they plagued
And worn with Famine, long and ceaseless hiss,
Till their lost shape, permitted, they resumed,
Yearly enjoined, some say, to undergo   575
This annual humbling certain numbered days,
To dash their pride, and joy for Man seduced.
However some tradition they dispersed
Among the Heathen of their purchase got,
And Fabled how the Serpent, whom they called   580
Ophion with *Eurynome*, the wide-[52]
Encroaching *Eve* perhaps, had first the rule
Of high *Olympus*, thence by *Saturn* driv'n
And *Ops*, ere yet *Dictæan Jove* was born.[53]
Mean while in Paradise the hellish pair   585
Too soon arrived, *Sin* there in power before,
Once actual, now in body, and to dwell
Habitual habitant; behind her *Death*
Close following pace for pace, not mounted yet
On his pale Horse: to whom *Sin* thus began.   590
   'Second of *Satan* sprung, all conquering *Death*,
What thinkst thou of our Empire now, though earned
With travail difficult, not better far
Than still at Hell's dark threshold to have sat watch,
Unnamed, undreaded, and thy self half starved?'   595
   Whom thus the Sin-born Monster answered soon.
'To me, who with eternal Famine pine,
Alike is Hell, or Paradise, or Heaven,
There best, where most with ravine I may meet;
Which here, though plenteous, all too little seems   600
To stuff this Maw, this vast unhide-bound Corps'.
   To whom th' incestuous Mother thus replied.
'Thou therefore on these Herbs, and Fruits, and Flowrs
Feed first, on each Beast next, and Fish, and Fowl,
No homely morsels, and whatever thing   605

---

[51] *drugged* "Tincture[d] with something offensive" (Johnson); so they found the fruit.
[52] *Ophion* Orphic god, husband of . . . *Eurynome* (wide-possessing), later an underworld deity.
[53] *Ops* consort of Saturn; *Dictæan Jove* Zeus, born in Dicte (Crete) displaced his father Saturn (Cronos) as ruler of Olympus.

The Scythe of Time mows down, devour unspared,
Till I in Man residing through the Race,
His thoughts, his looks, words, actions all infect,
And season him thy last and sweetest prey'.
　　This said, they both betook them several ways, 610
Both to destroy, or unimmortal make
All kinds, and for destruction to mature
Sooner or later; which th' Almighty seeing,
From his transcendent Seat the Saints among,
To those bright Orders uttered thus his voice. 615
　　'See with what heat these Dogs of Hell advance
To waste and havoc yonder World, which I
So fair and good created, and had still
Kept in that State, had not the folly of Man
Let in these wasteful Furies, who impute 620
Folly to me, so doth the Prince of Hell
And his Adherents, that with so much ease
I suffer them to enter and possess
A place so heav'nly, and conniving seem[54]
To gratify my scornful Enemies, 625
That laugh, as if transported with some fit
Of Passion, I to them had quitted all,
At random yielded up to their misrule;
And know not that I called and drew them thither
My Hell-hounds, to lick up the draff and filth 630
Which man's polluting Sin with taint hath shed
On what was pure, till crammed and gorged, nigh burst
With sucked and glutted offal, at one sling[55]
Of thy victorious Arm, well-pleasing Son,
Both *Sin*, and *Death*, and yawning *Grave* at last 635
Through *Chaos* hurled, obstruct the mouth of Hell
For ever, and seal up his ravenous Jaws.
Then Heav'n and Earth renewed shall be made pure
To sanctity that shall receive no stain:
Till then the Curse pronounced on both precedes'. 640
　　He ended, and the heav'nly Audience loud
Sung *Halleluiah*, as the sound of Seas,
Through multitude that sung: 'Just are thy ways,
Righteous are thy Decrees on all thy Works;
Who can extenuate thee? Next, to the Son,[56] 645
Destined restorer of Mankind, by whom
New Heav'n and Earth shall to the Ages rise,
Or down from Heav'n descend'. Such was their song,
While the Creator calling forth by name

---

[54] *connive* "To pretend blindness or ignorance; to fore-
bear; to pass uncensured" (Johnson).
[55] *glutted* "swallowed" (Johnson).

[56] *extenuate* "To lessen; to degrade; to diminish in
honour" (Johnson).

His mighty Angels gave them several charge,   650
As sorted best with present things. The Sun
Had first his precept so to move, so shine,
As might affect the Earth with cold and heat
Scarce tolerable, and from the North to call
Decrepit Winter, from the South to bring   655
Solstitial summer's heat. To the blank Moon[57]
Her office they prescribed, to th' other five
Their planetary motions and aspécts
In *Sextile*, *Square*, and *Trine*, and *Opposite*,[58]
Of noxious efficacy, and when to join   660
In Synod unbenign, and taught the fixed
Their influence malignant when to show'r
Which of them rising with the Sun, or falling,
Should prove tempestuous: To the Winds they set
Their corners, when with bluster to confound   665
Sea, Air, and Shore, the Thunder when to roll
With terror through the dark Aerial Hall.
Some say he bid his Angels turn askance
The Poles of Earth twice ten degrees and more[59]
From the Sun's Axle; they with labour pushed   670
Oblique the Centric Globe: Some say the sun
Was bid turn Reins from th' Equinoctial Road
Like distant breadth to *Taurus* with the Sev'n[60]
Atlantic Sisters, and the *Spartan* Twins,
Up to the *Tropic* Crab; thence down amain   675
By *Leo* and the *Virgin* and the *Scales*,
As deep as *Capricorn*, to bring in change
Of Seasons to each Clime; else had the Spring
Perpetual smiled on Earth with vernant Flowrs,
Equal in Days and Nights, except to those   680
Beyond the Polar Circles; to them Day
Had unbenighted shone, while the low Sun
To recompense his distance, in their sight
Had rounded still th' *Horizon*, and not known
Or East or West, which had forbid the Snow   685
From cold *Estotiland*, and South as far[61]
Beneath *Magellan*. At that tasted Fruit[62]
The Sun, as from *Thyestean* Banquet, turned[63]
His course intended; else how had the World

---

[57] *blank*   "White" (Johnson).

[58] *Sextile . . . Opposite*   astrological relationships.

[59] *twice ten degrees and more*   23.5 degrees is the tilt of the earth.

[60] *Sev'n / Atlantic Sisters*   the Pleiades; these are all constellations on the zodiac defining the ecliptic of the Sun.

[61] *Estotiland*   name of a northern place, near Labrador.

[62] *Magellan*   the straits near the southern tip of South America.

[63] *Thyestean*   Thyestes was fed a dish containing the bodies of his sons by his brother Atreus; when he realized it, he fled in horror and called down a curse on the house of Atreus.

Inhabited, though sinless, more than now,   690
Avoided pinching cold and scorching heat?
These changes in the Heav'ns, though slow, produced
Like change on Sea and Land, sidereal blast,
Vapour, and Mist, and Exhalation hot,
Corrupt and Pestilent: Now from the North   695
Of *Norumbega*, and the *Samoed* shore[64]
Bursting their brazen Dungeon, armed with ice
And snow and hail and stormy gust and flaw,[65]
Boreas and *Cæcias* and *Argestes* loud[66]
And *Thrascias* rend the Woods and Seas upturn;   700
With adverse blast up-turns them from the South
Notus and *Afer* black with thunderous Clouds
From *Serraliona*; thwart of these as fierce
Forth rush the *Levant* and the *Ponent* Winds
Eurus and *Zephyr*, with their lateral noise,   705
Sirocco, and *Libecchio*. Thus began
Outrage from lifeless things; but Discord first
Daughter of Sin, among th' irrational
Death introduced through fierce antipathy:
Beast now with Beast gan war, and Fowl with Fowl,   710
And Fish with Fish; to graze the Herb all leaving,
Devoured each other; nor stood much in awe
Of Man, but fled him, or with count'nance grim
Glared on him passing: these were from without
The growing miseries, which *Adam* saw   715
Already in part, though hid in gloomiest shade,
To sorrow abandoned, but worse felt within,
And in a troubled Sea of passion tossed,
Thus to disburden sought with sad complaint.
    'O miserable of happy! is this the end   720
Of this new glorious World, and me so late
The Glory of that Glory, who now become
Accursed of blessed, hide me from the face
Of God, whom to behold was then my heighth
Of happiness: yet well, if here would end   725
The misery, I deserved it, and would bear
My own deservings; but this will not serve;
All that I eat or drink, or shall beget,
Is propagated curse. O voice once heard
Delightfully, "Increase and multiply",   730
Now death to hear! for what can I increase
Or multiply, but curses on my head?
Who of all Ages to succeed, but feeling

---

[64] *Norumbega* coastal North America, around 45 degrees latitude; *Samoed* Siberian.
[65] *flaw* "A sudden gust; a violent blast" (Johnson).

[66] *Boreas . . . Libecchio* the names of all the winds in groups: northern (*Boreas*); then southern (*Notus*) then eastern (*Eurus*), and western (*Zephyr*) alternately.

The evil on him brought by me, will curse
My Head, "Ill fare our Ancestor impure,   735
For this we may thank *Adam*", but his thanks
Shall be the execration; so besides
Mine own that bide upon me, all from me
Shall with a fierce reflux on me rebound,
On me as on their natural centre light   740
Heavy, though in their place. O fleeting joys
Of Paradise, dear bought with lasting woes!
Did I request thee, Maker, from my Clay
To mould me Man, did I solicit thee
From darkness to promote me, or here place   745
In this delicious Garden? as my Will
Concurred not to my being, it were but right
And equal to reduce me to my dust,
Desirous to resign, and render back
All I received, unable to perform   750
Thy terms too hard, by which I was to hold
The good I sought not. To the loss of that,
Sufficient penalty, why hast thou added
The sense of endless woes? inexplicable
Thy Justice seems; yet to say truth, too late,   755
I thus contest; then should have been refused
Those terms whatever, when they were proposed:
Thou didst accept them; wilt thou enjoy the good,
Then cavil the conditions? and though God
Made thee without thy leave, what if thy Son   760
Prove disobedient, and reproved, retort,
Wherefore didst thou beget me? I sought it not:
Wouldst thou admit for his contempt of thee
That proud excuse? yet him not thy election,
But Natural necessity begot.   765
God made thee of choice his own, and of his own
To serve him, thy reward was of his grace,
Thy punishment then justly is at his Will.
Be it so, for I submit, his doom is fair,
That dust I am, and shall to dust return: 770
O welcome hour whenever! why delays
His hand to execute what his Decree
Fixed on this day? why do I overlive,
Why am I mocked with death, and lengthened out
To deathless pain? how gladly would I meet   775
Mortality my sentence, and be Earth
Insensible, how glad would lay me down
As in my Mother's lap? there I should rest
And sleep secure; his dreadful voice no more
Would Thunder in my ears, no fear of worse   780
To me and to my offspring would torment me

With cruel expectation. Yet one doubt
Pursues me still, lest all I cannot die,
Lest that pure breath of Life, the Spirit of Man
Which God inspired, cannot together perish   785
With this corporeal Clod; then in the Grave,
Or in some other dismal place who knows
But I shall die a living Death? O thought
Horrid, if true! yet why? it was but breath
Of Life that sinned; what dies but what had life   790
And sin? the Body properly hath neither.
All of me then shall die: let this appease
The doubt since human reach no further knows.
For though the Lord of all be infinite,
Is his wrath also? be it, man is not so,   795
But mortal doomed. How can he exercise
Wrath without end on Man whom Death must end?
Can he make deathless Death? that were to make
Strange contradiction, which to God himself
Impossible is held, as Argument   800
Of weakness, not of Power. Will he, draw out,
For anger's sake, finite to infinite
In punished Man, to satisfy his rigour
Satisfied never; that were to extend
His Sentence beyond dust and Nature's Law,   805
By which all Causes else according still
To the reception of their matter act,
Not to th' extent of their own Sphere. But say
That Death be not one stroke, as I supposed,
Bereaving sense, but endless misery   810
From this day onward, which I feel begun
Both in me, and without me, and so last
To perpetuity; Ay me, that fear
Comes thundring back with dreadful revolution
On my defenceless head; both Death and I   815
Am found Eternal, and incorporate both,
Nor I on my part single, in me all
Posterity stands curst: Fair Patrimony
That I must leave ye, Sons; O were I able
To waste it all my self, and leave ye none!   820
So disinherited how would you bless
Me now your curse! Ah, why should all mankind
For one man's fault thus guiltless be condemned,
If guiltless? But from me what can proceed,
But all corrupt, both Mind and Will depraved,   825
Not to do only, but to will the same
With me? how can they then acquitted stand
In sight of God? Him after all Disputes
Forced I absolve: all my evasions vain,

And reasonings, though through Mazes, lead me still   830
But to my own conviction: first and last
On me, me only, as the source and spring
Of all corruption, all the blame lights due;
So might the wrath. Fond wish! couldst thou support
That burden heavier than the Earth to bear   835
Than all the World much heavier, though divided
With that bad Woman? Thus what thou desirest
And what thou fearst, alike destroys all hope
Of refuge, and concludes thee miserable
Beyond all past example and future,   840
To *Satan* only like both crime and doom.
O Conscience, into what Abyss of fears
And horrors hast thou driv'n me; out of which
I find no way, from deep to deeper plunged!'
    Thus Adam to himself lamented loud   845
Through the still Night, not now, as ere man fell,
Wholesome, and cool, and mild, but with black Air
Accompanied, with damps and dreadful gloom,
Which to his evil Conscience represented
All things with double terror: On the Ground   850
Outstretched he lay, on the cold ground, and oft
Cursed his Creation, Death as oft accused
Of tardy execution, since denounced[67]
The day of his offence. 'Why comes not Death',
Said he, 'with one thrice ácceptáble stroke   855
To end me? Shall Truth fail to keep her word,
Justice Divine not hasten to be just?
But Death comes not at call, Justice Divine
Mends not her slowest pace for prayers or cries.
O Woods, O Fountains, Hillocks, Dales, and Bow'rs,   860
With other echo late I taught your Shades
To answer, and resound far other Song'.
Whom thus afflicted when sad *Eve* beheld,
Desolate where she sat, approaching nigh,
Soft words to his fierce passion she assayed: 865
But her with stern regard he thus repelled.
    'Out of my sight, thou Serpent, that name best
Befits thee with him leagued, thy self as false
And hateful; nothing wants, but that thy shape,
Like his, and colour Serpentine may show   870
Thy inward fraud, to warn all Creatures from thee
Henceforth; lest that too heav'nly form, pretended
To hellish falsehood, snare them. But for thee
I had persisted happy, had not thy pride
And wandring vanity, when least was safe,   875

---

[67] *denounced* proclaimed.

Rejected my forewarning, and disdained
Not to be trusted, longing to be seen
Though by the Devil himself, him overweening
To over-reach, but with the Serpent meeting,
Fooled and beguil'd, by him thou, I by thee,   880
To trust thee from my side, imagined wise,
Constant, mature, proof against all assaults,
And understood not all was but a show
Rather than solid virtue, all but a Rib
Crooked by nature, bent, as now appears,   885
More to the part sinister from me drawn,[68]
Well if thrown out, as supernumerary
To my just number found. O why did God,
Creator wise, that peopled highest Heav'n
With Spirits Masculine, create at last   890
This novelty on Earth, this fair defect
Of Nature, and not fill the World at once
With Men as Angels without Feminine,
Or find some other way to generate
Mankind? this mischief had not then befall'n,   895
And more that shall befall, innumerable
Disturbances on Earth through Female snares,
And straight conjunction with this Sex: for either
He never shall find out fit Mate, but such
As some misfortune brings him, or mistake,   900
Or whom he wishes most shall seldom gain
Through her perverseness, but shall see her gained
By a far worse, or if she love, withheld
By Parents, or his happiest choice too late
Shall meet, already linked and Wedlock-bound   905
To a fell Adversary, his hate or shame:
Which infinite calamity shall cause
To Human life, and houshold peace confound'.
      He added not, and from her turned, but *Eve*
Not so repulsed, with Tears that ceased not flowing,   910
And tresses all disordered, at his feet
Fell humble, and embracing them, besought
His peace, and thus proceeded in her plaint.
      'Forsake me not thus, *Adam*, witness Heav'n
What love sincere, and reverence in my heart   915
I bear thee, and unweeting have offended,
Unhappily deceived; thy suppliant
I beg, and clasp thy knees; bereave me not,
Whereon I live, thy gentle looks, thy aid,
Thy counsel in this uttermost distress,   920

---

[68] *sinister* "Being on the left-hand . . . 2. Bad; corrupt; perverse" (Johnson).

My only strength and stay: forlorn of thee,
Whither shall I betake me, where subsist?
While yet we live, scarce one short hour perhaps,
Between us two let there be peace, both joining,
As joined in injuries, one enmity   925
Against a Foe by doom express assigned us,
That cruel Serpent: On me exercise not
Thy hatred for this misery befall'n,
On me already lost, me than thy self
More miserable; both have sinned, but thou   930
Against God only, I against God and thee,
And to the place of judgement will return,
There with my cries importune Heaven, that all
The sentence from thy head removed may light
On me, sole cause to thee of all this woe,   935
Me me only just object of his ire'.
      She ended weeping, and her lowly plight,
Immoveable till peace obtained from fault
Acknowledged and deplored, in *Adam* wrought
Commiseration; soon his heart relented   940
Towards her, his life so late and sole delight,
Now at his feet submissive in distress,
Creature so fair his reconcilement seeking,
His counsel whom she had displeased, his aid;
As one disarmed, his anger all he lost,   945
And thus with peaceful words upraised her soon.
      'Unwary, and too desirous, as before,
So now of what thou knowst not, who desir'st
The punishment all on thy self; alas,
Bear thine own first, ill able to sustain   950
His full wrath whose thou feelst as yet least part,
And my displeasure bearst so ill. If Prayers
Could alter high Decrees, I to that place
Would speed before thee, and be louder heard,
That on my head all might be visited,   955
Thy frailty and infirmer Sex forgiv'n,
To me committed and by me exposed.
But rise, let us no more contend, nor blame
Each other, blamed enough elsewhere, but strive
In offices of Love, how we may light'n   960
Each other's burden, in our share of woe;
Since this day's Death denounced, if ought I see,
Will prove no sudden, but a slow-paced evil,
A long day's dying to augment our pain,
And to our Seed (O hapless Seed!) derived'.   965
      To whom thus *Eve*, recovering heart, replied.
'*Adam*, by sad experiment I know
How little weight my words with thee can find,

Found so erroneous, thence by just event
Found so unfortunate; nevertheless,   970
Restored by thee, vile as I am, to place
Of new acceptance, hopeful to regain
Thy Love, the sole contentment of my heart
Living or dying, from thee I will not hide
What thoughts in my unquiet breast are ris'n,   975
Tending to some relief of our extremes,
Or end, though sharp and sad, yet tolerable,
As in our evils, and of easier choice.
If care of our descent perplex us most,
Which must be born to certain woe, devoured   980
By Death at last, and miserable it is
To be to others cause of misery,
Our own begotten, and of our Loins to bring
Into this cursèd World a woeful Race,
That after wretched Life must be at last   985
Food for so foul a Monster, in thy power
It lies, yet ere Conception to prevent
The Race unblest, to being yet unbegot.
Childless thou art, Childless remain:
So Death shall be deceived his glut, and with us two   990
Be forced to satisfy his Rav'nous Maw.
But if thou judge it hard and difficult,
Conversing, looking, loving, to abstain
From Love's due Rites, Nuptial embraces sweet,
And with desire to languish without hope,   995
Before the present object languishing
With like desire, which would be misery
And torment less than none of what we dread,
Then both our selves and Seed at once to free
From what we fear for both, let us make short,   1000
Let us seek Death, or he not found, supply
With our own hands his Office on our selves;
Why stand we longer shivering under fears,
That show no end but Death, and have the power,
Of many ways to die the shortest choosing,   1005
Destruction with destruction to destroy'.
    She ended here, or vehement despair
Broke off the rest; so much of Death her thoughts
Had entertained, as dyed her Cheeks with pale.
But *Adam* with such counsel nothing swayed,   1010
To better hopes his more attentive mind
Labouring had raised, and thus to *Eve* replied.
    '*Eve*, thy contempt of life and pleasure seems
To argue in thee something more sublime
And excellent than what thy mind contemns;   1015
But self-destruction therefore sought, refutes

That excellence thought in thee, and implies,
Not thy contempt, but anguish and regret
For loss of life and pleasure overloved.
Or if thou covet death, as utmost end   1020
Of misery, so thinking to evade
The penalty pronounced, doubt not but God
Hath wiselier armed his vengeful ire than so
To be forestalled; much more I fear lest Death
So snatched, will not exempt us from the pain   1025
We are by doom to pay; rather such acts
Of contumacy will provoke the highest[69]
To make death in us live: Then let us seek
Some safer resolution, which methinks
I have in view, calling to mind with heed   1030
Part of our Sentence, that thy Seed shall bruise
The Serpent's head; piteous amends, unless
Be meant, whom I conjecture, our grand Foe
Satan, who in the Serpent hath contrived
Against us this deceit: to crush his head   1035
Would be revenge indeed; which will be lost
By death brought on our selves, or childless days
Resolved, as thou proposest; so our Foe
Shall scape his punishment ordained, and we
Instead shall double ours upon our heads.   1040
No more be mentioned then of violence
Against our selves, and wilful barrenness,
That cuts us off from hope and savours only
Rancour and pride, impatience and despite,
Reluctance against God and his just yoke   1045
Laid on our Necks. Remember with what mild
And gracious temper he both heard and judged
Without wrath or reviling; we expected
Immediate dissolution, which we thought
Was meant by Death that day, when lo, to thee   1050
Pains only in Child-bearing were foretold,
And bringing forth, soon recompensed with joy,
Fruit of thy Womb: On me the Curse aslope[70]
Glanced on the ground, with labour I must earn
My bread; what harm? Idleness had been worse;   1055
My labour will sustain me; and lest Cold
Or Heat should injure us, his timely care
Hath unbesought, provided, and his hands
Clothed us unworthy, pitying while he judged;
How much more, if we pray him, will his ear   1060
Be open, and his heart to pity incline,

[69] *contumacy* "Obstinacy; perverseness; stubbornness; inflexibility" (Johnson).   [70] *aslope* "With declivity; obliquely; not perpendicularly" (Johnson).

And teach us further by what means to shun
Th' inclement Seasons, Rain, Ice, Hail, and Snow,
Which now the Sky with various Face begins
To show us in this Mountain, while the Winds   1065
Blow moist and keen, shattering the graceful locks
Of these fair spreading Trees; which bids us seek
Some better shroud, some better warmth to cherish⁷¹
Our Limbs benumbed, ere this diurnal Star
Leave cold the Night, how we his gathered beams   1070
Reflected, may with matter sear foment,⁷²
Or by collision of two bodies grind
The Air attrite to Fire, as late the Clouds⁷³
Justling or pushed with Winds rude in their shock
Tine the slant Lightning, whose thwart flame driv'n down⁷⁴   1075
Kindles the gummy bark of Fir or Pine,
And sends a comfortable heat from far,
Which might supply the Sun: such Fire to use,
And what may else be remedy or cure
To evils which our own misdeeds have wrought,   1080
He will instruct us praying, and of Grace
Beseeching him, so as we need not fear
To pass commodiously this life, sustained
By him with many comforts, till we end
In dust, our final rest and native home.   1085
What better can we do, than to the place
Repairing where he judged us, prostrate fall
Before him reverent, and there confess
Humbly our faults, and pardon beg, with tears
Watering the ground, and with our sighs the Air   1090
Frequenting, sent from hearts contrite, in sign
Of sorrow unfeigned, and humiliation meek.
Undoubtedly he will relent and turn
From his displeasure; in whose look serene,
When angry most he seemed and most severe,   1095
What else but favour, grace, and mercy shone?'
    So spake our Father penitent, nor *Eve*
Felt less remorse: they forthwith to the place
Repairing where he judged them prostrate fell
Before him reverent, and both confessed   1100
Humbly their faults, and pardon begged, with tears
Watering the ground, and with their sighs the Air
Frequenting, sent from hearts contrite, in sign
Of sorrow unfeigned, and humiliation meek.

---

⁷¹ *shroud* "A shelter; a cover" (Johnson).   ⁷³ *attrite* "Ground; worn by rubbing" (Johnson).
⁷² *sear* dried up.   ⁷⁴ *tine* kindle.

Book XI
THE ARGUMENT

The Son of God presents to his Father the Prayers of our first Parents now repenting, and intercedes for them: God accepts them, but declares that they must no longer abide in Paradise; sends Michael with a Band of Cherubim to dispossess them; but first to reveal to Adam *future things:* Michael's *coming down.* Adam *shows to* Eve *certain ominous signs; he discerns* Michael's *approach, goes out to meet him: the Angel denounces[1] their departure.* Eve's *Lamentation.* Adam *pleads, but submits: The Angel leads him up to a high Hill, sets before him in vision what shall happen till the Flood.*

Thus they in lowliest plight repentant stood
Praying, for from the Mercy-seat above[2]
Prevenient Grace descending had removed[3]
The stony from their hearts, & made new flesh
Regenerate grow instead, that sighs now breathed   5
Unutterable, which the Spirit of prayer
Inspir'd, and winged for Heav'n with speedier flight
Than loudest Oratory: yet their port[4]
Not of mean suitors, nor important less
Seemed their Petition, than when th' ancient Pair   10
In Fables old, less ancient yet than these,
Deucalion and chaste *Pyrrha* to restore[5]
The Race of Mankind drowned, before the Shrine
Of *Themis* stood devout. To Heav'n their prayers
Flew up, nor missed the way, by envious winds   15
Blown vagabond or frustrate: in they passed
Dimensionless through Heav'nly doors; then clad
With incense, where the Golden Altar fumed,
By their great Intercessor, came in sight
Before the Father's Throne: Them the glad Son   20
Presenting, thus to intercede began.

  'See Father, what first fruits on Earth are sprung
From thy implanted Grace in Man, these Sighs
And Prayers, which in this Golden Censer, mixed
With Incense, I thy Priest before thee bring,   25
Fruits of more pleasing savour from thy seed
Sown with contrition in his heart, than those
Which his own hand manuring all the Trees[6]

Book XI

[1] *denounces* proclaims or sentences them with.

[2] *Mercy-seat* "The *mercy-seat* was the covering of the ark of the covenant, in which the tables of the law were deposited" (Johnson, citing August Calmet); cf. Exodus 25.17–22.

[3] *Prevenient* "Preceding; going before; preventive" (Johnson).

[4] *port* "Carriage; air; mien; manner; bearing; external appearance; demeanour" (Johnson).

[5] *Deucalion . . . Pyrrha* the husband and wife who alone survived the great flood in Greek myth; they properly interpreted an oracular message (from the goddess *Themis* – "right order") that led them to repopulate the earth by throwing stones (the bones of their mother, in the oracle) over their shoulders.

[6] *manuring* tending by hand.

Of Paradise could have produced, ere fall'n
From innocence. Now therefore bend thine ear   30
To supplication, hear his sighs though mute;
Unskilful with what words to pray, let me
Interpret for him, me his Advocate
And propitiation, all his works on me
Good or not good engraft, my Merit those   35
Shall perfet, and for these my Death shall pay.
Accept me, and in me from these receive
The smell of peace toward Mankind, let him live
Before thee reconciled, at least his days
Numbered, though sad, till Death, his doom (which I   40
To mitigate thus plead, not to reverse)
To better life shall yield him, where with me
All my redeemed may dwell in joy and bliss,
Made one with me as I with thee am one'.
      To whom the Father, without Cloud, serene.   45
'All thy request for Man, accepted Son,
Obtain, all thy request was my Decree:
But longer in that Paradise to dwell,
The Law I gave to Nature him forbids:
Those pure immortal Elements that know   50
No gross, no unharmonious mixture foul,
Eject him tainted now, and purge him off
As a distemper, gross to air as gross,
And mortal food, as may dispose him best
For dissolution wrought by Sin, that first   55
Distempered all things, and of incorrupt
Corrupted. I at first with two fair gifts
Created him endowed, with Happiness
And Immortality: that fondly lost,
This other served but to eternize woe;   60
Till I provided Death; so Death becomes
His final remedy, and after Life
Tried in sharp tribulation, and refined
By Faith and faithful works, to second Life,
Waked in the renovation of the just,   65
Resigns him up with Heav'n and Earth renewed.
But let us call to Synod all the Blest
Through Heav'n's wide bounds; from them I will not hide
My judgements, how with Mankind I proceed,
As how with peccant Angels late they saw;   70
And in their state, though firm, stood more confirmed'.
      He ended, and the Son gave signal high
To the bright Minister that watched, he blew[7]

---

[7]   *Minister*   the angel Michael; cf. Matthew 24.31 and
1.6–7 above.

His Trumpet, heard in *Oreb* since perhaps
When God descended, and perhaps once more   75
To sound at general Doom. Th' Angelic blast
Filled all the Regions: from their blissful Bow'rs
Of *Amarantine* Shade, Fountain or Spring,[8]
By the waters of Life, where e'er they sat
In fellowships of joy: the Sons of Light   80
Hasted, resorting to the Summons high,
And took their Seats; till from his Throne supreme
Th' Almighty thus pronounced his sovereign Will.
　　'O Sons, like one of us Man is become
To know both Good and Evil, since his taste   85
Of that defended Fruit;[9] but let him boast
His knowledge of Good lost, and Evil got,
Happier, had it sufficed him to have known
Good by it self, and evil not at all.
He sorrows now, repents, and prays contrite,   90
My motions in him, longer than they move,
His heart I know, how variable and vain
Self-left. Lest therefore his now bolder hand
Reach also of the Tree of Life, and eat,
And live for ever, dream at least to live   95
For ever, to remove him I decree,
And send him from the Garden forth to Till
The Ground whence he was taken, fitter soil.
　　'*Michael*, this my behest have thou in charge,
Take to thee from among the Cherubim   100
Thy choice of flaming Warriors, lest the Fiend
Or in behalf of Man, or to invade[10]
Vacant possession some new trouble raise:
Haste thee, and from the Paradise of God
Without remorse drive out the sinful Pair,   105
From hallowed ground th' unholy, and denounce
To them and to their Progeny from thence
Perpetual banishment. Yet lest they faint
At the sad Sentence rigorously urged,
For I behold them softened and with tears   110
Bewailing their excess, all terror hide.
If patiently thy bidding they obey,
Dismiss them not disconsolate; reveal
To *Adam* what shall come in future days,
As I shall thee enlighten, intermix   115
My Cov'nant in the woman's seed renewed;
So send them forth, though sorrowing, yet in peace:[11]
And on the East side of the Garden place,

---

[8]   *Amarantine*   like amaranth, the immortal flower.　　[10]   *Or . . . or*   either . . . or.
[9]   *defended*   prohibited.　　　　　　　　　　　　　　　　[11]   *send them forth*   see Genesis 3.24.

Where entrance up from *Eden* easiest climbs,
Cherubic watch, and of a Sword the flame   120
Wide waving, all approach far off to fright,
And guard all passage to the Tree of Life:
Lest Paradise a receptacle prove
To Spirits foul, and all my Trees their prey,
With whose stol'n Fruit Man once more to delude'.   125
    He ceased; and th' Archangelic Power prepared
For swift descent, with him the Cohort bright
Of watchful Cherubim; four faces each
Had, like a double *Janus*, all their shape[12]
Spangled with eyes more numerous than those   130
Of *Argus*, and more wakeful than to drowse,[13]
Charmed with *Arcadian* Pipe, the Pastoral Reed
Of *Hermes*, or his opiate Rod. Mean while
To resalute the World with sacred Light
Leucothea waked, and with fresh dews imbalmed[14]   135
The Earth, when *Adam* and first Matron *Eve*
Had ended now their Orisons, and found
Strength added from above, new hope to spring
Out of despair, joy, but with fear yet linked;
Which thus to *Eve* his welcome words renewed.   140
    '*Eve*, easily may Faith admit, that all
The good which we enjoy, from Heav'n descends;
But that from us ought should ascend to Heav'n
So prevalent as to concern the mind[15]
Of God high-blest, or to incline his will,   145
Hard to belief may seem; yet this will Prayer,
Or one short sigh of human breath, up-borne
Ev'n to the Seat of God. For since I sought
By Prayer th' offended Deity to appease,
Kneeled and before him humbled all my heart,   150
Methought I saw him placable and mild,
Bending his ear; persuasion in me grew
That I was heard with favour; peace returned
Home to my Breast, and to my memory
His promise, that thy Seed shall bruise our Foe;   155
Which then not minded in dismay, yet now
Assures me that the bitterness of death
Is past, and we shall live. Whence Hail to thee,
Eve rightly called, Mother of all Mankind,
Mother of all things living, since by thee   160
Man is to live, and all things live for Man'.
    To whom thus *Eve* with sad demeanour meek.

---

[12] *Janus* Roman deity who faced in two directions and presided over portals and beginnings.
[13] *Argus* the many-eyed monster set by Hera to watch over the nymph Io, charmed or killed by wily Hermes at the bidding of Zeus, whence he was turned into the peacock.
[14] *Leucothea* lit. the white goddess, so, light-giving.
[15] *prevalent* "Predominant; powerful" (Johnson).

'Ill worthy I such title should belong
To me transgressor, who for thee ordained
A help, became thy snare; to me reproach   165
Rather belongs, distrust and all dispraise:
But infinite in pardon was my Judge,
That I who first brought Death on all, am graced
The source of life; next favourable thou,
Who highly thus to entitle me vouchsaf'st,   170
Far other name deserving. But the Field
To labour calls us now with sweat imposed,
Though after sleepless Night; for see the Morn,
All unconcerned with our unrest, begins
Her rosy progress smiling; let us forth,   175
I never from thy side henceforth to stray,
Where'er our day's work lies, though now enjoined
Laborious, till day droop; while here we dwell,
What can be toilsome in these pleasant Walks?
Here let us live, though in fall'n state, content'.   180
    So spake, so wished much humbled *Eve*, but Fate
Subscribed not; Nature first gave Signs, impressed
On Bird, Beast, Air, Air suddenly eclipsed
After short blush of Morn; nigh in her sight
The Bird of *Jove*, stooped from his airy tow'r,[16]   185
Two Birds of gayest plume before him drove:
Down from a Hill the Beast that reigns in Woods,[17]
First hunter then, pursued a gentle brace,
Goodliest of all the Forest, Hart and Hind;
Direct to th' Eastern Gate was bent their flight.   190
Adam observed, and with his Eye the chase
Pursuing, not unmoved to *Eve* thus spake.
    'O Eve, some further change awaits us nigh,
Which Heav'n by these mute signs in Nature shows
Forerunners of his purpose, or to warn   195
Us haply too secure of our discharge
From penalty, because from death released
Some days; how long, and what till then our life,
Who knows, or more than this, that we are dust,
And thither must return and be no more.   200
Why else this double object in our sight
Of flight pursued in th' Air and o'er the ground
One way the self-same hour? why in the East
Darkness ere Day's mid-course, and Morning light
More orient in yon Western Cloud that draws[18]   205
O'er the blue Firmament a radiant white,
And slow descends, with something heav'nly fraught'.
    He erred not, for by this the heav'nly Bands

---

[16] *Bird of Jove* eagle; *stooped* fr. stoop "To come   [17] *the Beast that reigns* the lion.
down on prey as a falcon" (Johnson).   [18] *orient* "Bright; shining; glittering" (Johnson).

Down from a Sky of Jasper lighted now
In Paradise, and on a Hill made halt,   210
A glorious Apparition, had not doubt
And carnal fear that day dimmed *Adam's* eye.
Not that more glorious, when the Angels met
Jacob in *Mahanaim*, where he saw[19]
The field Pavilioned with his Guardians bright;   215
Nor that which on the flaming Mount appeared[20]
In *Dothan*, covered with a Camp of Fire,
Against the *Syrian* King, who to surprise
One man, Assassin-like had levied War,
War unproclaimed. The Princely Hierarch   220
In their bright stand there left his Powers, to seize
Possession of the Garden; he alone,
To find where *Adam* sheltered, took his way,
Not unperceived of *Adam*, who to *Eve*,
While the great Visitant approached, thus spake.   225
   'Eve, now expect great tidings, which perhaps
Of us will soon determine, or impose
New Laws to be observed; for I descry
From yonder blazing Cloud that veils the Hill
One of the heav'nly Host, and by his Gait   230
None of the meanest, some great Potentate
Or of the Thrones above, such Majesty
Invests him coming; yet not terrible,
That I should fear, nor sociably mild,
As *Raphaël*, that I should much confide,   235
But solemn and sublime, whom not to offend,
With reverence I must meet, and thou retire.
He ended; and th' Arch-Angel soon drew nigh,
Not in his shape Celestial, but as Man
Clad to meet Man; over his lucid Arms[21]   240
A military Vest of purple flowed
Livelier than *Melibœan*, or the grain[22]
Of *Sarra*, worn by Kings and Heroes old[23]
In time of Truce; *Iris* had dipped the woof;[24]
His starry Helm unbuckled showed him prime   245
In Manhood where Youth ended; by his side
As in a glistering *Zodiac* hung the Sword,

---

[19] *Jacob ... Mahanaim* Genesis 32.1–2.
[20] *the flaming Mount* the hill near Dothan miraculously filled with horses and chariots of fire to defend the prophet Elisha from the attack of the king of Syria (2 Kings 6.8–18).
[21] *lucid* shining.
[22] *Melibœan* a purple color made from shellfish in the Greek city of Meliboea (Thessaly); *grain* Dyed or stained substance.

[23] *Sarra* an old name for Tyre (mod. Es-Sur, Lebanon), also famous for purple dye.
[24] *Iris* goddess of the rainbow; *woof* "Texture; cloth" (Johnson).

Satan's dire dread, and in his hand the Spear.
Adam bowed low, he Kingly from his State
Inclined not, but his coming thus declared.   250
   '*Adam*, Heav'n's high behest no Preface needs:
Sufficient that thy Prayers are heard, and Death,
Then due by sentence when thou didst transgress,
Defeated of his seizure many days
Giv'n thee of Grace, wherein thou may'st repent,   255
And one bad act with many deeds well done
Mayst cover: well may then thy Lord appeased
Redeem thee quite from Death's rapacious claim;
But longer in this Paradise to dwell
Permits not; to remove thee I am come,   260
And send thee from the Garden forth to till
The ground whence thou wast taken, fitter Soil'.
   He added not, for *Adam* at the news
Heart-strook with chilling gripe of sorrow stood,[25]
That all his senses bound; *Eve*, who unseen   265
Yet all had heard, with audible lament
Discovered soon the place of her retire.
   'O unexpected stroke, worse than of Death!
Must I thus leave thee Paradise? thus leave
Thee Native Soil, these happy Walks and Shades,   270
Fit haunt of Gods? where I had hope to spend,
Quiet though sad, the respite of that day
That must be mortal to us both. O flowrs,
That never will in other Climate grow,
My early visitation, and my last   275
At Ev'n, which I bred up with tender hand
From the first op'ning bud, and gave ye Names,
Who now shall rear ye to the Sun, or rank
Your Tribes, and water from th' ambrosial Fount?
Thee lastly nuptial Bow'r, by me adorned   280
With what to sight or smell was sweet; from thee
How shall I part, and whither wander down
Into a lower World, to this obscure
And wild, how shall we breathe in other Air
Less pure, accustomed to immortal Fruits?'   285
   Whom thus the Angel interrupted mild.
'Lament not *Eve*, but patiently resign
What justly thou hast lost; nor set thy heart,
Thus over-fond, on that which is not thine;
Thy going is not lonely, with thee goes   290
Thy Husband, him to follow thou art bound;
Where he abides, think there thy native soil'.
   Adam by this from the cold sudden damp

---

[25] *gripe* "Affliction; pinching distress" (Johnson).

Recovering, and his scattered spirits returned,
To *Michael* thus his humble words addressed.   295
    'Celestial, whether among the Thrones, or named
Of them the Highest, for such of shape may seem
Prince above Princes, gently hast thou told
Thy message, which might else in telling wound,
And in performing end us; what besides   300
Of sorrow and dejection and despair
Our frailty can sustain, thy tidings bring,
Departure from this happy place, our sweet
Recess, and only consolation left
Familiar to our eyes, all places else   305
Inhospitable appear and desolate,
Nor knowing us nor known: and if by prayer
Incessant I could hope to change the will
Of him who all things can, I would not cease
To weary him with my assiduous cries: 310
But prayer against his absolute Decree
No more avails than breath against the wind,
Blown stifling back on him that breathes it forth:
Therefore to his great bidding I submit.
This most afflicts me, that departing hence,   315
As from his face I shall be hid, deprived
His blessèd count'nance; here I could frequent,
With worship, place by place where he vouchsafed
Presence Divine, and to my Sons relate;
"On this Mount he appeared, under this Tree   320
Stood visible, among these Pines his voice
I heard, here with him at this Fountain talked':
So many grateful Altars I would rear
Of grassy Turf, and pile up every Stone
Of lustre from the Brook, in memory,   325
Or monument to Ages, and theron
Offer sweet smelling Gums and Fruits and Flowrs:
In yonder nether World where shall I seek
His bright appearances, or footstep trace?
For though I fled him angry, yet recalled   330
To life prolonged and promised Race, I now
Gladly behold though but his utmost skirts
Of glory, and far off his steps adore'.
    To whom thus *Michael* with regard benign.
'Adam, thou know'st Heav'n his, and all the Earth.   335
Not this Rock only; his Omnipresence fills
Land, Sea, and Air, and every kind that lives,
Fomented by his virtual power and warmed:[26]
All th' Earth he gave thee to possess and rule,

---

[26] *virtual* "Having the efficacy without the sensible or
material part" (Johnson).

No despicable gift; surmise not then   340
His presence to these narrow bounds confined
Of Paradise or *Eden*: this had been
Perhaps thy Capital Seat, from whence had spread
All generations, and had hither come
From all the ends of th' Earth, to celebrate   345
And reverence thee their great Progenitor.
But this preeminence thou hast lost, brought down
To dwell on even ground now with thy Sons:
Yet doubt not but in Valley and in plain
God is as here, and will be found alike   350
Present, and of his presence many a sign
Still following thee, still compassing thee round
With goodness and paternal Love, his Face
Express, and of his steps the track Divine.
Which that thou mayst believe, and be confirmed   355
Ere thou from hence depart, know I am sent
To show thee what shall come in future days
To thee and to thy Offspring; good with bad
Expect to hear, supernal Grace contending
With sinfulness of Men; thereby to learn   360
True patience, and to temper joy with fear
And pious sorrow, equally inured
By moderation either state to bear,
Prosperous or adverse: so shalt thou lead
Safest thy life, and best prepared endure   365
Thy mortal passage when it comes. Ascend
This Hill; let *Eve* (for I have drenched her eyes)
Here sleep below while thou to foresight wak'st,
As once thou slepst, while She to life was formed'.
To whom thus Adam gratefully replied.   370
'Ascend, I follow thee, safe Guide, the path
Thou lead'st me, and to the hand of Heav'n submit,
However chast'ning; to the evil turn
My obvious breast; arming to overcome[27]
By suffering, and earn rest from labour won,   375
If so I may attain'. So both ascend
In the Visions of God: It was a Hill
Of Paradise the highest, from whose top
The Hemisphere of Earth in clearest Ken
Stretched out to the amplest reach of prospect lay.   380
Not higher that Hill, nor wider looking round,
Whereon for different cause the Tempter set
Our second *Adam* in the Wilderness,[28]
To show him all Earth's Kingdoms and their Glory.

---

[27] *obvious* "Meeting any thing; opposed in front to any thing" (Johnson).

[28] *second Adam* Christ, who was tempted by the devil on a high mountain (Matthew 4.8–11).

His Eye might there command wherever stood 385
City of old or modern Fame, the Seat
Of mightiest Empire, from the destined Walls
Of *Cambalu*, seat of *Cathaian Khan*[29]
And *Samarkand* by *Oxus*, *Temir's* Throne,[30]
To *Paquin* of *Sinæan* Kings, and thence[31] 390
To *Agra* and *Lahor* of great *Mogul* [32]
Down to the golden *Chersonese*, or where[33]
The *Persian* in *Ecbatan* sat, or since[34]
In *Hispahan*, or where the *Russian Ksar*
In *Mosco*, or the Sultan in *Bizance*,[35] 395
Turkestan-born; nor could his eye not ken
Th' Empire of *Negus* to his utmost Port[36]
Ercoco and the less *Marítime* Kings
Mombaza, and *Quiloa*, and *Melind*,[37]
And *Sofala* thought *Ophir*, to the Realm[38] 400
Of *Congo*, and *Angola* farthest South;
Or thence from *Niger* Flood to *Atlas* Mount
The Kingdoms of *Almansor*, *Fez* and *Sus*,[39]
Morocco and *Algiers*, and *Tremisen*;
On *Europe* thence, and where *Rome* was to sway 405
The World: in Spirit perhaps he also saw
Rich *Mexico* the seat of *Montezume*,[40]
And *Cusco* in *Peru*, the richer seat
Of *Atabalipa*, and yet unspoiled[41]
Guiana, whose great City *Geryon's* Sons[42] 410
Call *El Dorado*: but to nobler sights[43]
Michael from *Adam's* eyes the Film removed
Which that false Fruit that promised clearer sight
Had bred; then purged with Euphrasy and Rue[44]
The visual Nerve, for he had much to see; 415
And from the Well of Life three drops instilled.

[29] *Cambalu* Cambaluc, the court of Khubla Khan near Beijing.
[30] *Samarkand* capital of Tamerlane's (*Temir's*) fourteenth-century Asian empire; the *Oxus* flows into the Aral Sea.
[31] *Paquin* modern Beijing; *Sinæan* Chinese.
[32] *Agra and Lahor* Indian cities under Mongolian (*Mogul*) rule.
[33] *Chersonese* of the many places with this name, probably a city near Sevastopol, Crimea, is meant.
[34] *Ecbatan* like *Hispahan* (Isfahan), a Persian royal city (mod. Hamadan).
[35] *Bizance* Byzantium (later Constantinople; mod. Istanbul), ruled by Turkish sultans after the fall of the Christian city in 1453.
[36] *Negus* name for a king of Abyssinia (mod. Ethiopia); *Port Ercoco* on the Red Sea near Port Sudan.
[37] *Mombaza, Quiloa, Melind,* places in East Africa.
[38] *Ophir* indeterminate, fabulously rich destination of biblical trading voyages, sometimes identified with African *Sofala*, sometimes with places in India.
[39] *Almansor* anglicized form of Arabic *Mansur* (victorious), a name taken by many Muslim rulers; *Fez and Sus . . . Tremisen* north African places ruled by Muslims.
[40] *Montezume* Montezuma II was the last ruler of the Incas, seized by Cortez.
[41] *Atabalipa* Atahualpa, last Inca king of Peru, arrested by Pizarro on his refusal to convert to Christianity.
[42] *Geryon's Sons* the Spanish (from the name of a giant, ruler of three Spanish islands, killed by Hercules).
[43] *El Dorado* a mythical place of fabulous wealth, imagined by seventeenth-century explorers to be in Ecuador (*Guiana*).
[44] *Euphrasy* (lit. well mind) eyebright, a plant used for treating sight; *rue* a plant with many medicinal uses.

So deep the power of these Ingredients pierced,
Even to the inmost seat of mental sight,
That *Adam* now enforced to close his eyes,
Sunk down and all his Spirits became entranced: 420
But him the gentle Angel by the hand
Soon raised, and his attention thus recalled.
   '*Adam*, now ope thine eyes, and first behold
Th' effects which thy original crime hath wrought
In some to spring from thee, who never touched   425
Th' excepted Tree, nor with the Snake conspired,
Nor sinned thy sin, yet from that sin derive
Corruption to bring forth more violent deeds'.
   His eyes he opened, and beheld a field,[45]
Part arable and tilth, whereon were Sheaves   430
New reaped, the other part sheep-walks and folds;
I' th' midst an Altar as the Land-mark stood
Rustic, of grassy sord; thither anon[46]
A sweaty Reaper from his Tillage brought
First Fruits, the green Ear, and the yellow Sheaf,   435
Unculled, as came to hand; a Shepherd next
More meek came with the Firstlings of his Flock
Choicest and best; then sacrificing, laid
The Inwards and their Fat, with Incense strewed,
On the cleft Wood, and all due Rites performed.   440
His Offring soon propitious Fire from Heav'n
Consumed with nimble glance, and grateful steam;[47]
The others not, for his was not sincere;
Whereat he inly raged, and as they talked,
Smote him into the Midriff with a stone   445
That beat out life; he fell, and deadly pale
Groaned out his Soul with gushing blood effused.
Much at that sight was *Adam* in his heart
Dismayed, and thus in haste to th' Angel cried.
   'O Teacher, some great mischief hath befall'n   450
To that meek man, who well had sacrificed;
Is Piety thus and pure Devotion paid?'
   T' whom *Michael* thus, he also moved, replied.
'These two are Brethren, *Adam*, and to come
Out of thy loins; th' unjust the just hath slain,   455
For envy that his Brother's Offering found
From Heav'n acceptance; but the bloody Fact
Will be avenged, and th' other's Faith approved
Lose no reward, though here thou see him die,
Rolling in dust and gore'. To which our Sire.   460

---

[45] the story of Cain and Abel (Genesis 4).
[46] *sord* turf.

[47] *glance* "A sudden shoot of light or splendour"
(Johnson); *steam* the smoke of the fire, which pleased
the gods.

'Alas, both for the deed and for the cause!
But have I now seen Death? Is this the way
I must return to native dust? O sight
Of terror, foul and ugly to behold,
Horrid to think, how horrible to feel!'   465
    To whom thus *Michaël*. 'Death thou hast seen
In his first shape on man; but many shapes
Of Death, and many are the ways that lead
To his grim Cave, all dismal; yet to sense
More terrible at th' entrance than within.   470
Some, as thou saw'st, by violent stroke shall die,
By Fire, Flood, Famine, by Intemperance more
In Meats and Drinks which on the Earth shall bring
Diseases dire, of which a monstrous crew
Before thee shall appear; that thou mayst know   475
What misery th' inabstinence of *Eve*
Shall bring on men. Immediately a place
Before his eyes appeared, sad, noisome, dark,
A Lazar-house it seemed, wherein were laid[48]
Numbers of all diseased, all maladies   480
Of ghastly Spasm, or racking torture, qualms
Of heart-sick Agony, all feverous kinds,
Convulsions, Epilepsies, fierce Catarrhs,[49]
Intestine Stone and Ulcer, Colic pangs,
Dæmoniac Phrenzy, moaping Melancholy[50]   485
And Moon-struck madness, pining Atrophy,
Marasmus, and wide-wasting Pestilence,[51]
Dropsies, and Asthmas, and Joint-racking Rheums.
Dire was the tossing, deep the groans, despair
Tended the sick busiest from Couch to Couch;   490
And over them triumphant Death his Dart
Shook, but delayed to strike, though oft invoked
With vows, as their chief good, and final hope.
Sight so deform what heart of Rock could long
Dry-eyed behold? *Adam* could not, but wept,   495
Though not of Woman born; compassion quelled[52]
His best of Man, and gave him up to tears
A space, till firmer thoughts restrained excess,
And scarce recovering words his plaint renewed.
    'O miserable Mankind, to what fall   500
Degraded, to what wretched state reserved!
Better end here unborn. Why is life giv'n

---

[48]   *Lazar*   leper.
[49]   *Catarrhs*   "A defluxion of a sharp serum from the
glands about the head and throat . . ." (Johnson quoting
John Quincy).
[50]   Lines 485–7 represent a rare addition to the second
edition of *Paradise Lost*.

[51]   *Marasmus*   "A consumption [pulmonary tuberculo-
sis] in which persons waste much of their substance"
(Johnson quoting John Quincy).
[52]   *not of Woman born* and *best of Man*   phrases that
invoke *Macbeth* 5.8, a bloody, pathetic scene.

To be thus wrested from us? rather why
Obtruded on us thus? who if we knew
What we receive, would either not accept   505
Life offered, or soon beg to lay it down,
Glad to be so dismissed in peace. Can thus
Th' Image of God in man created once
So goodly and erect, though faulty since,
To such unsightly sufferings be debased   510
Under inhuman pains? Why should not Man,
Retaining still Divine similitude
In part, from such deformities be free,
And for his Maker's Image sake exempt?'
    'Their Maker's Image', answered *Michael* then   515
'Forsook them, when themselves they vilified
To serve ungoverned appetite, and took
His Image whom they served, a brutish vice,
Inductive mainly to the sin of *Eve*.[53]
Therefore so abject is their punishment,   520
Disfiguring not God's likeness, but their own,
Or if his likeness, by themselves defaced
While they pervert pure Nature's healthful rules
To loathsome sickness, worthily, since they
God's Image did not reverence in themselves'.   525
    'I yield it just', said *Adam*, 'and submit.
But is there yet no other way, besides
These painful passages, how we may come
To Death, and mix with our connatural dust?'
    'There is', said Michael, 'if thou well observe   530
The rule of not too much, by temperance taught
In what thou eatst and drinkst, seeking from thence
Due nourishment, not gluttonous delight,
Till many years over thy head return:
So mayst thou live, till like ripe Fruit thou drop   535
Into thy Mother's lap, or be with ease[54]
Gathered, nor harshly plucked, for death mature:
This is old age; but then thou must outlive
Thy youth, thy strength, thy beauty, which will change
To withered weak and grey; thy Senses then   540
Obtuse, all taste of pleasure must forego,
To what thou hast, and for the Air of youth[55]
Hopeful and cheerful, in thy blood will reign
A melancholy damp of cold and dry
To weigh thy Spirits down, and last consume   545
The Balm of Life'. To whom our Ancestor.
    'Henceforth I fly not Death, nor would prolong

---

53   *Inductive* "Leading; persuasive" (Johnson).   55   *To what thou hast* in full.
54   *thy Mother's lap* the earth.

Life much, bent rather how I may be quit
Fairest and easiest of this cumbrous charge,
Which I must keep till my appointed day   550
Of rendring up, and patiently attend
My dissolution'. *Michaël* replied,
      'Nor love thy Life, nor hate; but what thou livst
Live well, how long or short permit to Heav'n:
And now prepare thee for another sight'.   555
      He looked and saw a spacious Plain, whereon[56]
Were Tents of various hue; by some were herds
Of Cattle grazing; others, whence the sound
Of Instruments that made melodious chime
Was heard, of Harp and Organ; and who moved   560
Their stops and chords was seen: his volant touch[57]
Instinct through all proportions low and high
Fled and pursued transverse the resonant fugue.
In other part stood one who at the Forge
Labouring, two massy clods of Iron and Brass   565
Had melted (whether found where casual fire
Had wasted woods on Mountain or in Vale,
Down to the veins of Earth, thence gliding hot
To some Cave's mouth, or whether washed by stream
From underground) the liquid Ore he drained   570
Into fit moulds prepared; from which he formed
First his own Tools; then, what might else be wrought
Fusile or grav'n in metal. After these,
But on the hither side a different sort[58]
From the high neighbouring Hills, which was their Seat,   575
Down to the Plain descended: by their guise
Just men they seemed, and all their study bent
To worship God aright, and know his works
Not hid, nor those things last which might preserve
Freedom and Peace to men: they on the Plain   580
Long had not walked, when from the Tents behold
A Bevy of fair Women, richly gay
In Gems and wanton dress; to the Harp they sung
Soft amorous Ditties, and in dance came on:
The Men though grave, eyed them, and let their eyes   585
Rove without rein, till in the amorous Net
Fast caught, they liked, and each his liking chose;
And now of love they treat till th' Evening Star
Love's Harbinger appeared; then all in heat

[56] the scenes on the *spacious Plain* are based on Genesis 4.20–2, describing the sons of Lamech, a descendant of Cain and another man guilty of murder.
[57] *volant* "Nimble; active" (Johnson).

[58] *a different sort* the "giants in the earth" (l. 688 below) or "Sons of God" (l. 622 below) described in Genesis 6.2–4; their unions with the daughters of Lamech created the heroes of the classical world (who were associated with the fallen angels) and led to God's invocation of the flood (l. 626 below).

They light the Nuptial Torch, and bid invoke   590
Hymen, then first to marriage Rites invoked;
With Feast and Music all the Tents resound.
Such happy interview and fair event
Of love and youth not lost, Songs, Garlands, Flowrs,
And charming Symphonies attached the heart   595
Of *Adam*, soon inclined to admit delight,
The bent of Nature; which he thus expressed.
    'True opener of mine eyes, prime Angel blest,
Much better seems this Vision, and more hope
Of peaceful days portends, than those two past;   600
Those were of hate and death, or pain much worse,
Here Nature seems fulfilled in all her ends'.
    To whom thus *Michael*. 'Judge not what is best
By pleasure, though to Nature seeming meet,
Created, as thou art, to nobler end   605
Holy and pure, conformity divine.
Those Tents thou sawst so pleasant, were the Tents
Of wickedness, wherein shall dwell his Race
Who slew his Brother; studious they appear
Of Arts that polish Life, Inventors rare,   610
Unmindful of their Maker, though his Spirit
Taught them, but they his gifts acknowledged none.
Yet they a beauteous offspring shall beget;
For that fair female Troop thou sawst, that seemed
Of Goddesses, so blithe, so smooth, so gay,   615
Yet empty of all good wherein consists
Woman's domestic honour and chief praise;
Bred only and completed to the taste
Of lustful appetence, to sing, to dance,
To dress, and troll the Tongue, and roll the Eye.[59]   620
To these that sober Race of Men, whose lives
Religious titled them the Sons of God,
Shall yield up all their virtue, all their fame
Ignobly, to the trains and to the smiles
Of these fair Atheists, and now swim in joy,   625
(Erelong to swim at large) and laugh; for which
The world erelong a world of tears must weep'.
    To whom thus *Adam* of short joy bereft.
'O pity and shame, that they who to live well
Entered so fair, should turn aside to tread   630
Paths indirect, or in the mid way faint!
But still I see the tenor of Man's woe
Holds on the same, from Woman to begin'.
    'From Man's effeminate slackness it begins',

---

[59] *troll* move nimbly.

Said th' Angel, 'who should better hold his place   635
By wisdom, and superior gifts received.
But now prepare thee for another Scene'.
       He looked and saw wide Territory spread[60]
Before him, Towns, and rural works between,
Cities of Men with lofty Gates and Towers,   640
Concourse in Arms, fierce Faces threatning War,
Giants of mighty Bone, and bold emprise;[61]
Part wield their Arms, part curb the foaming Steed,
Single or in Array of Battle ranged
Both Horse and Foot, nor idly must'ring stood;   645
One way a Band select from forage drives
A herd of Beeves, fair Oxen and fair Kine
From a fat Meadow ground; or fleecy Flock,
Ewes and their bleating Lambs over the Plain,
Their Booty; scarce with Life the Shepherds fly,   650
But call in aid, which makes a bloody Fray;
With cruel Tournament the Squadrons join;
Where Cattle pastured late, now scattered lies
With Carcasses and Arms th' ensanguined Field[62]
Deserted: Others to a City strong   655
Lay Siege, encamped; by Battery, Scale, and Mine,[63]
Assaulting; others from the wall defend
With Dart and Javelin, Stones and sulphúrous Fire;
On each hand slaughter and gigantic deeds.
In other part the sceptred Heralds call   660
To Council in the City Gates: anon
Grey-headed men and grave, with Warriors mixed,
Assemble, and Harangues are heard, but soon
In factious opposition, till at last
Of middle Age one rising, eminent[64]   665
In wise deport, spake much of Right and Wrong,
Of Justice, of Religion, Truth and Peace,
And Judgement from above: him old and young
Exploded and had seized with violent hands,[65]
Had not a Cloud descending snatched him thence   670
Unseen amid the throng: so violence
Proceeded, and Oppression, and Sword-Law
Through all the Plain, and refuge none was found.
Adam was all in tears, and to his guide
Lamenting turned full sad; 'O what are these,   675

---

[60] These scenes recall those on the shield of Achilles (*Iliad* 18.478–608).
[61] *emprise* "Attempt of danger; undertaking of hazard; enterprise" (Johnson).
[62] *ensanguined* stained red with blood (a term of heraldry).
[63] *Scale* scaling device, ladder.
[64] *one* see l. 700 and note, below.
[65] *Exploded* "[drove] out disgracefully with some noise of contempt" (Johnson).

Death's Ministers, not Men, who thus deal Death
Inhumanly to men, and multiply
Ten thousandfold the sin of him who slew
His Brother; for of whom such massacre
Make they but of their Brethren, men of men?   680
But who was that Just Man, whom had not Heav'n
Rescued, had in his Righteousness been lost?'
    To whom thus *Michael*. 'These are the product
Of those ill mated Marriages thou saw'st:
Where good with bad were matched, who of themselves   685
Abhor to join; and by imprudence mixed,
Produce prodigious Births of body or mind.
Such were these Giants, men of high renown;
For in those days Might only shall be admired,
And Valour and Heroic Virtue called;   690
To overcome in Battle, and subdue
Nations, and bring home spoils with infinite
Man-slaughter, shall be held the highest pitch
Of human Glory, and for Glory done
Of triumph, to be styled great Conquerors,   695
Patrons of Mankind, Gods, and Sons of Gods,
Destroyers rightlier called and Plagues of men.
Thus Fame shall be achieved, renown on Earth,
And what most merits fame in silence hid.
But he the seventh from thee, whom thou beheldst[66]   700
The only righteous in a World perverse,
And therefore hated, therefore so beset
With Foes for daring single to be just,
And utter odious Truth, that God would come
To judge them with his Saints: Him the most High   705
Rapt in a balmy Cloud with wingèd Steeds
Did, as thou sawst, receive, to walk with God
High in Salvation and the Climes of bliss,
Exempt from Death; to show thee what reward
Awaits the good, the rest what punishment;   710
Which now direct thine eyes and soon behold'.
    He looked, and saw the face of things quite changed,
The brazen Throat of War had ceased to roar,
All now was turned to jollity and game,
To luxury and riot, feast and dance,[67]   715
Marrying or prostituting, as befell,
Rape or Adultery, where passing fair
Allured them; thence from Cups to civil Broils.
At length a Reverend Sire among them came,[68]

---

[66] *he* Enoch (Genesis 5.21–4; Jude 14–15).
[67] *luxury* "Voluptuousness; addictedness to pleasure" (Johnson).

[68] *Reverend Sire* Noah; the account of the flood is based on Genesis 6–9 but also draws on Ovid (*Metamorphoses* 1.260–347) and Renaissance sources.

And of their doings great dislike declared,   720
And testified against their ways; he oft
Frequented their Assemblies, whereso met,
Triumphs or Festivals, and to them preached
Conversion and Repentance, as to Souls
In Prison under Judgements imminent: 725
But all in vain: which when he saw, he ceased
Contending, and removed his Tents far off;
Then from the Mountain hewing Timber tall,
Began to build a Vessel of huge bulk,
Measured by Cubit, length, and breadth, and heighth,   730
Smeared round with Pitch, and in the side a door
Contrived, and of provisions laid in large
For Man and Beast: when lo a wonder strange!
Of every Beast, and Bird, and Insect small
Came sev'ns, and pairs, and entered in, as taught   735
Their order: last the Sire, and his three Sons
With their four Wives; and God made fast the door.
Mean while the Southwind rose, and with black wings
Wide hovering, all the Clouds together drove
From under Heav'n; the Hills to their supply   740
Vapour, and Exhalation dusk and moist,
Sent up amain; and now the thickened Sky
Like a dark Ceiling stood; down rushed the Rain
Impetuous, and continued till the Earth
No more was seen; the floating Vessel swum   745
Uplifted; and secure with beakèd prow
Rode tilting o'er the Waves, all dwellings else
Flood overwhelmed, and them with all their pomp
Deep under water rolled; Sea covered Sea,
Sea without shore; and in their Palaces   750
Where luxury late reigned, Sea-monsters whelped
And stabled; of Mankind, so numerous late,
All left, in one small bottom swum embarked.[69]
How didst thou grieve then, *Adam*, to behold
The end of all thy Offspring, end so sad,   755
Depopulation; thee another Flood,
Of tears and sorrow a Flood thee also drowned,
And sunk thee as thy Sons; till, gently reared
By th' Angel, on thy feet thou stoodst at last,
Though comfortless, as when a Father mourns   760
His Children, all in view destroyed at once;
And scarce to th' Angel utter'dst thus thy plaint.
      'O Visions ill foreseen! better had I
Lived ignorant of future, so had borne
My part of evil only, each day's lot   765

---

[69]   *bottom*   a ship.

Enough to bear; those now, that were dispensed
The burd'n of many Ages, on me light
At once, by my foreknowledge gaining Birth
Abortive, to torment me ere their being,
With thought that they must be. Let no man seek   770
Henceforth to be foretold what shall befall
Him or his Children, evil he may be sure,
Which neither his foreknowing can prevent,
And he the future evil shall no less
In apprehension than in substance feel   775
Grievous to bear: but that care now is past,
Man is not whom to warn: those few escaped
Famine and anguish will at last consume
Wandring that wat'ry Desert: I had hope
When violence was ceased, and War on Earth,   780
All would have then gone well, peace would have crowned
With length of happy days the race of man;
But I was far deceived; for now I see
Peace to corrupt no less than War to waste.
How comes it thus? unfold, Celestial Guide,   785
And whether here the Race of man will end'.
     To whom thus *Michael*. 'Those whom last thou sawst
In Triumph and luxurious wealth, are they
First seen in acts of prowess eminent
And great exploits, but of true virtue void;   790
Who having spilt much blood, and done much waste
Subduing Nations, and achieved thereby
Fame in the World, high titles, and rich prey,
Shall change their course to pleasure, ease, and sloth,
Surfeit, and lust, till wantonness and pride   795
Raise out of friendship hostile deeds in Peace.
The conquered also, and enslaved by War
Shall with their freedom lost all virtue lose
And fear of God, from whom their piety feigned
In sharp contest of Battle found no aid   800
Against invaders; therefore cooled in zeal
Thenceforth shall practice how to live secure,
Worldly or dissolute, on what their Lords
Shall leave them to enjoy; for th' Earth shall bear
More than enough, that temperance may be tried: 805
So all shall turn degenerate, all depraved,
Justice and Temperance, Truth and Faith forgot;
One Man except, the only Son of light
In a dark Age, against example good,[70]
Against allurement, custom, and a World   810

---

[70] *against example*   contrary to the examples set for him
by others.

Offended; fearless of reproach and scorn,
Or violence, he of their wicked ways
Shall them admonish, and before them set
The paths of righteousness, how much more safe,
And full of peace, denouncing wrath to come   815
On their impenitence; and shall return
Of them derided, but of God observed
The one just Man alive; by his command
Shall build a wondrous Ark, as thou beheldst,
To save himself and houshold from amidst   820
A World devote to universal wrack.
No sooner he with them of Man and Beast
Select for life shall in the Ark be lodged,
And sheltered round, but all the Cataracts
Of Heav'n set open on the Earth shall pour   825
Rain day and night, all fountains of the Deep
Broke up, shall heave the Ocean to usurp
Beyond all bounds, till inundation rise
Above the highest Hills: then shall this Mount
Of Paradise by might of Waves be moved   830
Out of his place, pushed by the hornèd flood,[71]
With all his verdure spoiled, and Trees adrift
Down the great River to the op'ning Gulf,
And there take root an Island salt and bare,
The haunt of Seals and Orcs, and Sea-mews' clang.[72]   835
To teach thee that God attributes to place
No sanctity, if none be thither brought
By Men who there frequent, or therein dwell.
And now what further shall ensue, behold'.
    He looked, and saw the Ark hull on the flood,[73]   840
Which now abated, for the Clouds were fled,
Driv'n by a keen North-wind, that blowing dry
Wrinkled the face of Deluge, as decayed;
And the clear Sun on his wide wat'ry Glass[74]
Gazed hot, and of the fresh Wave largely drew,   845
As after thirst, which made their flowing shrink
From standing lake to tripping ebb, that stole
With soft foot towards the deep, who now had stopped
His Sluices, as the Heav'n his windows shut.
The Ark no more now floats, but seems on ground   850
Fast on the top of some high mountain fixed.
And now the tops of Hills as Rocks appear;
With clamour thence the rapid Currents drive

---

[71] *hornèd* having branches, like the Nile delta, as
Ovid describes it (*Metamorphoses* 9.774).
[72] *Orc* a sea mammal; *Sea-mew* "A sort of fowl that
frequents the sea" (Johnson).
[73] *hull* "To float, to drive to and fro on the water
without sails or rudder" (Johnson).
[74] *Glass* mirror.

Towards the retreating Sea their furious tide.
Forthwith from out the Ark a Raven flies,   855
And after him, the surer messenger,
A Dove sent forth once and again to spy
Green Tree or ground whereon his foot may light;
The second time returning, in his Bill
An Olive leaf he brings, pacific sign:⁷⁵   860
Anon dry ground appears, and from his Ark
The ancient Sire descends with all his Train;
Then with uplifted hands, and eyes devout,
Grateful to Heav'n, over his head beholds
A dewy Cloud, and in the Cloud a Bow   865
Conspicuous with three lifted colours gay,
Betok'ning peace from God, and Cov'nant new.
Whereat the heart of *Adam* erst so sad
Greatly rejoiced, and thus his joy broke forth.
        'O thou who future things canst represent   870
As present, Heav'nly instructor, I revive
At this last sight, assured that Man shall live
With all the Creatures, and their seed preserve.
Far less I now lament for one whole World
Of wicked Sons destroyed, than I rejoice   875
For one Man found so perfet and so just,
That God vouchsafes to raise another World
From him, and all his anger to forget.
But say, what mean those coloured streaks in Heav'n,
Distended as the Brow of God appeased,   880
Or serve they as a flowry verge to bind
The fluid skirts of that same wat'ry Cloud,
Lest it again dissolve and show'r the Earth?'
        To whom th' Arch-Angel. 'Dextrously thou aim'st;
So willingly doth God remit his Ire,   885
Though late repenting him of Man depraved;
Grieved at his heart, when looking down he saw
The whole Earth filled with violence, and all flesh
Corrupting each their way; yet those removed,
Such grace shall one just Man find in his sight,   890
That he relents, not to blot out mankind,
And makes a Cov'nant never to destroy
The Earth again by flood, nor let the Sea
Surpass his bounds, nor Rain to drown the World
With Man therein or Beast; but when he brings   895
Over the Earth a Cloud, will therein set
His triple-coloured Bow, whereon to look
And call to mind his Cov'nant: Day and Night,
Seed time and Harvest, Heat and hoary Frost

---

⁷⁵ *pacific* peaceful, of peace

Shall hold their course, till fire purge all things new,   900
Both Heav'n and Earth, wherein the just shall dwell'.

BOOK XII
THE ARGUMENT

The Angel Michael *continues from the Flood to relate what shall succeed; then, in the mention of* Abraham, *comes by degrees to explain, who that Seed of the Woman shall be, which was promised* Adam *and* Eve *in the Fall; his Incarnation, Death, Resurrection, and Acension; the state of the Church till his second Coming.* Adam *greatly satisfied and recomforted by these Relations and Promises descends the Hill with* Michael; *wakens* Eve, *who all this while had slept, but with gentle dreams composed to quietness of mind and submission.* Michael *in either hand leads them out of Paradise, the fiery Sword waving behind them, and the Cherubim taking their Stations to guard the Place.*

As one who in his journey bates at Noon,[1]
Though bent on speed, so here the Arch-Angel paused
Betwixt the world destroyed and world restored,
If *Adam* aught perhaps might interpose;
Then with transition sweet new Speech resumes.   5
    'Thus thou hast seen one World begin and end;
And Man as from a second stock proceed.
Much thou hast yet to see, but I perceive
Thy mortal sight to fail; objects divine
Must needs impair and weary human sense: 10
Henceforth what is to come I will relate,
Thou therefore give due audience, and attend.
This second source of Men, while yet but few;
And while the dread of judgement past remains
Fresh in their minds, fearing the Deity,   15
With some regard to what is just and right
Shall lead their lives, and multiply apace,
Labouring the soil, and reaping plenteous crop,
Corn wine and oil; and from the herd or flock,
Oft sacrificing Bullock, Lamb, or Kid,   20
With large Wine-offerings poured, and sacred Feast,
Shall spend their days in joy unblamed, and dwell
Long time in peace by Families and Tribes
Under paternal rule; till one shall rise[2]
Of proud ambitious heart, who, not content   25
With fair equality, fraternal state,
Will arrogate Dominion undeserved
Over his brethren, and quite dispossess
Concord and law of Nature from the Earth,
Hunting (and Men not Beasts shall be his game)   30

BOOK XII
[1] *bates* slackens his pace or rests.
[2] *one* Nimrod (Genesis 10.8–10), whom commentators made an oppressor, claimant to divine right of

rule, and the designer of the tower of Babel (Genesis 11.1–9).

With War and hostile snare such as refuse
Subjection to his Empire tyrannous:
A mighty Hunter thence he shall be styled
Before the Lord, as in despite of Heav'n,
Or from Heav'n claiming second Sovereignty;   35
And from Rebellion shall derive his name,[3]
Though of Rebellion others he accuse.
He with a crew, whom like Ambition joins
With him or under him to tyrannize,
Marching from *Eden* towards the West, shall find   40
The Plain, wherein a black bituminous gurge
Boils out from under ground, the mouth of Hell;
Of Brick, and of that stuff, they cast to build
A City and Tow'r, whose top may reach to Heav'n;
And get themselves a name, lest far dispersed   45
In foreign Lands their memory be lost
Regardless whether good or evil fame.
But God who oft descends to visit men
Unseen, and through their habitations walks
To mark their doings, them beholding soon,   50
Comes down to see their City, ere the Tower
Obstruct Heav'n Tow'rs, and in derision sets
Upon their Tongues a various Spirit to raze
Quite out their Native Language, and instead
To sow a jangling noise of words unknown: 55
Forthwith a hideous gabble rises loud
Among the Builders; each to other calls
Not understood, till hoarse, and all in rage,
As mocked they storm; great laughter was in Heav'n
And looking down, to see the hubbub strange   60
And hear the din; thus was the building left
Ridiculous, and the work Confusion named'.
      Whereto thus *Adam* fatherly displeased.
'O execrable Son so to aspire
Above his Brethren; to himself assuming   65
Authority usurped, from God not giv'n:
He gave us only over Beast, Fish, Fowl
Dominion absolute; that right we hold
By his donation; but Man over men
He made not Lord; such title to himself   70
Reserving, human left from human free.
But this Usurper his encroachment proud
Stays not on Man; to God his Tower intends
Siege and defiance: Wretched man! what food
Will he convey up thither to sustain   75

---

[3]   *Rebellion*   a meaning of Nimrod, according to a false   divine right monarchs the true rebels, whereas supposed
etymology, which Milton uses tendentiously, making   rebels, like himself and Cromwell, are truly orthodox.

Himself and his rash Army, where thin Air
Above the Clouds will pine his entrails gross,[4]
And famish him of Breath, if not of Bread?'
    To whom thus *Michael*. 'Justly thou abhorr'st
That Son, who on the quiet state of men   80
Such trouble brought, affecting to subdue
Rational Liberty; yet know withal,
Since thy original lapse, true Liberty
Is lost, which always with right Reason dwells[5]
Twinned, and from her hath no dividual being:[6]   85
Reason in man obscured, or not obeyed,
Immediately inordinate desires
And upstart Passions catch the Government
From Reason, and to servitude reduce
Man till then free. Therefore since he permits   90
Within himself unworthy Powers to reign
Over free Reason, God in Judgement just
Subjects him from without to violent Lords;
Who oft as undeservedly enthrall
His outward freedom: Tyranny must be,   95
Though to the Tyrant thereby no excuse.
Yet sometimes Nations will decline so low
From virtue, which is reason, that no wrong,
But Justice, and some fatal curse annexed,
Deprives them of their outward liberty,   100
Their inward lost: Witness th' irreverent Son[7]
Of him who built the Ark, who for the shame
Done to his Father, heard this heavy curse,
Servant of Servants, on his vicious Race.[8]
Thus will this latter, as the former World,   105
Still tend from bad to worse, till God at last
Wearied with their iniquities, withdraw
His presence from among them, and avert
His holy Eyes; resolving from thenceforth
To leave them to their own polluted ways;   110
And one peculiar Nation to select[9]
From all the rest, of whom to be invoked,
A Nation from one faithful man to spring:
Him on this side *Euphrates* yet residing,
Bred up in Idol-worship; O that men   115
(Canst thou believe?) should be so stupid grown,
While yet the Patriarch lived, who scaped the Flood,

---

[4] *pine* afflict, torment.
[5] *right Reason* cf. 6.176 above.
[6] *dividual* separate.
[7] *th' irreverent Son* Ham was *irreverent* to his father Noah, who then cursed him in his son Canaan (Genesis 9.22–5).

[8] *vicious* "Corrupt; wicked; opposite to virtuous. It is rather applied to habitual faults, than criminal actions" (Johnson).
[9] *one peculiar Nation* one particular nation, Israel, sprung from Abraham (Genesis 11–12).

As to forsake the living God, and fall
To worship their own work in Wood and Stone
For Gods! yet him God the most High vouchsafes   120
To call by Vision from his Father's house,
His kindred and false Gods, into a Land
Which he will show him, and from him will raise
A mighty Nation, and upon him show'r
His benediction so, that in his Seed   125
All Nations shall be blest; he straight obeys,
Not knowing to what land, yet firm believes:
I see him, but thou canst not, with what Faith[10]
He leaves his Gods, his Friends, and native Soil
Ur of *Chaldæa*, passing now the Ford[11]   130
To *Haran*, after him a cumbrous Train[12]
Of Herds and Flocks, and numerous servitude;
Not wandring poor, but trusting all his wealth
With God, who called him, in a land unknown.
Canaan he now attains, I see his Tents[13]   135
Pitched about *Sechem*, and the neighbouring Plain
Of *Moreh*; there by promise he receives
Gift to his Progeny of all that Land;
From *Hameth* Northward to the Desert South[14]
(Things by their names I call, though yet unnamed)   140
From *Hermon* East to the great Western Sea,[15]
Mount *Hermon*, yonder Sea, each place behold
In prospect, as I point them; on the shore
Mount *Carmel*; here the double-founted stream
Jordan, true limit Eastward; but his Sons   145
Shall dwell to *Senir*, that long ridge of Hills.[16]
This ponder, that all Nations of the Earth
Shall in his Seed be blessed; by that Seed
Is meant thy great deliverer, who shall bruise
The Serpent's head; whereof to thee anon   150
Plainlier shall be revealed. This Patriarch blest,
Whom *faithful Abraham* due time shall call,
A Son, and of his Son a Grand-child leaves,[17]
Like him in faith, in wisdom, and renown;
The Grandchild with twelve Sons increased, departs   155

---

[10] *Faith* St Paul's interpretation of Abraham's obedience to God's command (Hebrews 11.8).
[11] *Ur of Chaldæa* birthplace of Abraham, an ancient city on the Euphrates river.
[12] *Haran* an Assyrian city (Genesis 11.31).
[13] *Canaan* the coastal land of the eastern Mediterranean between Sinai and Syria; the places mentioned are in the hill country north of Jerusalem.
[14] *Hameth* northern limit of the United Monarchy of Israel.

[15] *Hermon* mountain south-west of Damascus.
[16] *Senir* part of Mount Hermon.
[17] *Son* Isaac; *Grand-child* Jacob; large sections of Genesis and Exodus supply the basis of the story which goes on to summarize the plot of the Bible as a whole, as Milton sees it, all the way through the New Testament to Revelation (to l. 465 below).

From *Canaan*, to a Land hereafter called
Egypt, divided by the River Nile;
See where it flows, disgorging at seven mouths
Into the Sea: to sojourn in that Land
He comes invited by a younger Son[18]   160
In time of dearth, a Son whose worthy deeds
Raise him to be the second in that Realm
Of *Pharaoh*: there he dies, and leaves his Race
Growing into a Nation, and now grown
Suspected to a sequent King, who seeks   165
To stop their overgrowth, as inmate guests
Too numerous; whence of guests he makes them slaves
Inhospitably, and kills their infant Males:
Till by two brethren (these two brethren call
Moses and *Aaron*) sent from God to claim   170
His people from enthralment, they return
With glory and spoil back to their promised Land.
But first the lawless Tyrant, who denies
To know their God, or message to regard,
Must be compelled by Signs and Judgements dire;   175
To blood unshed the Rivers must be turned,
Frogs, Lice, and Flies must all his Palace fill
With loathed intrusion, and fill all the land;
His Cattle must of Rot and Murrain die,
Botches and blains must all his flesh emboss,[19]   180
And all his people; Thunder mixed with Hail,
Hail mixed with fire, must rend th' *Egyptian* Sky
And wheel on th' Earth, devouring where it rolls;
What it devours not, Herb, or Fruit, or Grain,
A darksome Cloud of Locusts swarming down   185
Must eat, and on the ground leave nothing green:
Darkness must overshadow all his bounds,
Palpable darkness, and blot out three days;
Last with one midnight stroke all the first-born
Of *Egypt* must lie dead. Thus with ten wounds   190
The River-dragon tamed at length submits[20]
To let his sojourners depart, and oft
Humbles his stubborn heart, but still as Ice
More hardened after thaw, till in his rage
Pursuing whom he late dismissed, the Sea   195
Swallows him with his Host, but them lets pass
As on dry land between two crystal walls,
Awed by the rod of *Moses* so to stand
Divided, till his rescued gain their shore:

---

[18]   *younger Son*   Joseph.
[19]   *Botches*   "swelling or eruptive discoloration[s] of   [20]   *River-dragon*   Pharaoh.
the skin" (Johnson); *blains*   "pustule[s]; botch[es];
blister[s]" (Johnson).

Such wondrous power God to his Saint will lend,   200
Though present in his Angel, who shall go
Before them in a Cloud, and Pillar of Fire,
By day a Cloud, by night a Pillar of Fire,
To guide them in their journey, and remove
Behind them, while th' obdúrate King pursues: 205
All night he will pursue, but his approach
Darkness defends between till morning Watch;
Then through the Fiery Pillar and the Cloud
God looking forth will trouble all his Host
And craze their Chariot wheels: when by command   210
Moses once more his potent Rod extends
Over the Sea; the Sea his Rod obeys;
On their embattled ranks the Waves return,
And overwhelm their War: the Race elect
Safe toward *Canaan* from the shore advance   215
Through the wild Desert, not the readiest way,
Lest ent'ring on the *Canaanite* alarmed
War terrify them inexpert, and fear
Return them back to *Egypt*, choosing rather
Inglorious life with servitude; for life   220
To noble and ignoble is more sweet
Untrained in Arms, where rashness leads not on.
This also shall they gain by their delay
In the wide Wilderness, there they shall found
Their government, and their great Senate choose   225
Through the twelve Tribes, to rule by Laws ordained:
God from the Mount of *Sinai*, whose grey top[21]
Shall tremble, he descending, will himself
In Thunder Lightning and loud Trumpets sound,
Ordain them Laws; part such as appertain   230
To civil Justice, part religious Rites
Of sacrifice, informing them, by types
And shadows, of that destined Seed to bruise
The Serpent, by what means he shall achieve
Mankind's deliverance. But the voice of God   235
To mortal ear is dreadful; they beseech
That *Moses* might report to them his will,
And terror cease; he grants what they besought
Instructed that to God is no accéss
Without Mediator, whose high Office now   240
Moses in figure bears, to introduce
One greater, of whose day he shall foretell,
And all the Prophets in their Age the times
Of great *Messiah* shall sing. Thus Laws and Rites
Established, such delight hath God in Men   245
Obedient to his will, that he vouchsafes

---

[21]   *Mount of Sinai*   or Oreb (cf. 1.7 above).

Among them to set up his Tabernacle,
The holy One with mortal Men to dwell:
By his prescript a Sanctuary is framed
Of Cedar, overlaid with Gold, therein   250
An Ark, and in the Ark his Testimony,
The Records of his Cov'nant, over these
A Mercy-seat of Gold between the wings
Of two bright Cherubim, before him burn
Seven Lamps as in a Zodiac representing   255
The Heav'nly fires; over the Tent a Cloud
Shall rest by Day, a fiery gleam by Night,
Save when they journey, and at length they come,
Conducted by his Angel, to the Land
Promised to *Abraham* and his Seed: the rest   260
Were long to tell, how many Battles fought,
How many Kings destroyed, and Kingdoms won,
Or how the Sun shall in mid Heav'n stand still
A day entire, and Night's due course adjourn,
Man's voice commanding, 'Sun in *Gibeon* stand,[22]   265
And thou Moon in the vale of *Aialon*,
Till *Israel* overcome'; so call the third[23]
From *Abraham*, Son of *Isaac*, and from him
His whole descent, who thus shall *Canaan* win'.
          Here Adam interposed. 'O sent from Heav'n,   270
Enlightner of my darkness, gracious things
Thou hast revealed, those chiefly which concern
Just *Abraham* and his Seed: now first I find
Mine eyes true op'ning, and my heart much eased,
Erewhile perplexed with thoughts what would become   275
Of me and all Mankind; but now I see
His day, in whom all Nations shall be blest,
Favour unmerited by me, who sought
Forbidden knowledge by forbidden means.
This yet I apprehend not, why to those   280
Among whom God will deign to dwell on Earth
So many and so various Laws are giv'n;
So many Laws argue so many sins
Among them; how can God with such reside?'
          To whom thus *Michael*. 'Doubt not but that sin   285
Will reign among them, as of thee begot;
And therefore was Law given them to evince
Their natural pravity, by stirring up[24]
Sin against Law to fight; that when they see

---

[22] The speaker is Joshua (Joshua 10.12); *Gibeon* ... *Aialon* two cities north-west of Jerusalem.

[23] *Israel* the name given to Jacob after seeing God's face (Genesis 32.24–30).

[24] *pravity* "Corruption; badness; malignity" (Johnson).

Law can discover sin, but not remove,[25]   290
Save by those shadowy expiations weak,
The blood of Bulls and Goats, they may conclude
Some blood more precious must be paid for Man,
Just for unjust, that in such righteousness
To them by Faith imputed, they may find   295
Justification towards God, and peace
Of Conscience, which the Law by Ceremonies
Cannot appease, nor Man the moral part
Perform, and not performing cannot live.
So law appears imperfect, and but giv'n   300
With purpose to resign them in full time
Up to a better Cov'nant, disciplined
From shadowy Types to Truth, from Flesh to Spirit,[26]
From imposition of strict Laws, to free
Acceptance of large Grace, from servile fear   305
To filial, works of Law to works of Faith.
And therefore shall not *Moses*, though of God
Highly beloved, being but the Minister
Of Law, his people into *Canaan* lead;
But *Joshua* whom the Gentiles *Jesus* call,[27]   310
His Name and Office bearing, who shall quell
The adversary Serpent, and bring back
Through the world's wilderness long wandered man
Safe to eternal Paradise of rest.
Mean while they in their earthly *Canaan* placed   315
Long time shall dwell and prosper, but when sins
National interrupt their public peace,
Provoking God to raise them enemies:
From whom as oft he saves them penitent
By Judges first, then under Kings; of whom   320
The second, both for piety renowned[28]
And puissant deeds, a promise shall receive
Irrevocable, that his Regal Throne
For ever shall endure; the like shall sing
All Prophecy, That of the Royal Stock   325
Of *David* (so I name this King) shall rise
A Son, the Woman's Seed to thee foretold,
Foretold to *Abraham*, as in whom shall trust
All Nations, and to Kings foretold, of Kings
The last, for of his Reign shall be no end.   330
But first a long Succession must ensue,

[25] *Law* the Mosaic as opposed to the Christian dispensation, which it foreshadows in *expiations*, sacrifices that appease God.
[26] *Type* "That by which something future is prefigured" (Johnson); the Old Testament was said to contain *types* of what is in the New Testament.

[27] Joshua was considered a type of Christ.
[28] *The second* King David, whose throne was prophesied to be everlasting (2 Samuel 7.16; Isaiah 9.6–7).

And his next Son for Wealth and Wisdom famed,[29]
The clouded Ark of God till then in Tents
Wandring, shall in a glorious Temple enshrine.
Such follow him, as shall be registered　　　　　　　335
Part good, part bad, of bad the longer scroll,
Whose foul Idolatries, and other faults
Heaped to the popular sum, will so incense[30]
God, as to leave them, and expose their Land,
Their City, his Temple, and his holy Ark　　　　　　340
With all his sacred things, a scorn and prey
To that proud City, whose high Walls thou saw'st
Left in confusion, *Babylon* thence called.
There in captivity he lets them dwell
The space of seventy years, then brings them back,　345
Remembering mercy, and his Cov'nant sworn
To *David*, 'stablished as the days of Heav'n.
Returned from *Babylon* by leave of Kings
Their Lords, whom God disposed, the house of God
They first re-edify, and for a while　　　　　　　　350
In mean estate live moderate, till grown
In wealth and multitude, factious they grow;
But first among the Priests dissension springs,
Men who attend the Altar, and should most
Endeavour Peace: their strife pollution brings　　　355
Upon the Temple it self: at last they seize
The Sceptre, and regard not *David's* Sons,
Then lose it to a stranger, that the true
Anointed King *Messiah* might be born
Barred of his right; yet at his Birth a Star　　　　360
Unseen before in Heav'n proclaims him come,
And guides the Eastern Sages, who inquire
His place, to offer Incense, Myrrh, and Gold;
His place of birth a solemn Angel tells
To simple Shepherds, keeping watch by night;　　　365
They gladly thither haste, and by a Choir
Of squadroned Angels hear his Carol sung.
A Virgin is his Mother, but his Sire
The Power of the most High: he shall ascend
The Throne hereditary, and bound his Reign　　　　370
With earth's wide bounds, his glory with the Heav'ns'.
　　He ceased, discerning *Adam* with such joy
Surcharged, as had like grief been dewed in tears,
Without the vent of words, which these he breathed.
　　'O Prophet of glad tidings, finisher　　　　　　375
Of utmost hope! now clear I understand

---

[29] *next Son* Solomon, who built the temple (1 Kings 　[30] *popular* belonging to the common people.
6–7).

What oft my steadiest thoughts have searched in vain,
Why our great expectation should be called
The seed of Woman: Virgin Mother, Hail,
High in the love of Heav'n, yet from my Loins   380
Thou shalt proceed, and from thy Womb the Son
Of God most High; So God with man unites.
Needs must the Serpent now his capital bruise[31]
Expect with mortal pain: say where and when
Their fight, what stroke shall bruise the Victor's heel'.   385
      To whom thus *Michael*. 'Dream not of their fight,
As of a Duel, or the local wounds
Of head or heel: not therefore joins the Son
Manhood to God-head, with more strength to foil
Thy enemy; nor so is overcome   390
Satan, whose fall from Heav'n, a deadlier bruise,
Disabled not to give thee thy death's wound:
Which he, who comes thy Saviour, shall recure,
Not by destroying *Satan*, but his works
In thee and in thy Seed: nor can this be,   395
But by fulfilling that which thou didst want,
Obedience to the Law of God, imposed
On penalty of death, and suffering death,
The penalty to thy transgression due,
And due to theirs which out of thine will grow: 400
So only can high Justice rest appaid.
The Law of God exact he shall fulfil
Both by obedience and by love, though love
Alone fulfil the Law; thy punishment
He shall endure by coming in the Flesh   405
To a reproachful life and cursèd death,
Proclaiming Life to all who shall believe
In his redemption, and that his obedience
Imputed becomes theirs by Faith, his merits
To save them, not their own, though legal works.[32]   410
For this he shall live hated, be blasphemed,
Seized on by force, judged, and to death condemned
A shameful and accursed, nailed to the Cross
By his own Nation, slain for bringing Life;
But to the Cross he nails thy Enemies,   415
The Law that is against thee, and the sins
Of all mankind, with him there crucified,
Never to hurt them more who rightly trust
In this his satisfaction; so he dies,
But soon revives, Death over him no power   420
Shall long usurp; ere the third dawning light

---

[31] *capital* "Chief; principal" but also "Relating to the [32] *legal* lawful; relating to Old Testament laws.
head" (Johnson).

Return, the Stars of Morn shall see him rise
Out of his grave, fresh as the dawning light,
Thy ransom paid, which Man from death redeems,
His death for Man, as many as offered Life   425
Neglect not, and the benefit embrace
By Faith not void of works: this God-like act
Annuls thy doom, the death thou shouldst have died,
In sin for ever lost from life; this act
Shall bruise the head of *Satan*, crush his strength,   430
Defeating Sin and Death, his two main arms,
And fix far deeper in his head their stings
Than temporal death shall bruise the Victor's heel,
Or theirs whom he redeems, a death like sleep,
A gentle wafting to immortal Life.   435
Nor after resurrection shall he stay
Longer on Earth than certain times to appear
To his Disciples, Men who in his Life
Still followed him; to them shall leave in charge
To teach all nations what of him they learned   440
And his Salvation, them who shall believe
Baptizing in the profluent stream, the sign
Of washing them from guilt of sin to Life
Pure, and in mind prepared, if so befall,
For death, like that which the Redeemer died.   445
All Nations they shall teach; for from that day
Not only to the Sons of *Abraham's* Loins
Salvation shall be Preached, but to the Sons
Of *Abraham's* Faith wherever through the world;
So in his seed all Nations shall be blest.   450
Then to the Heav'n of Heav'ns he shall ascend
With victory, triúmphing through the air
Over his foes and thine; there shall surprise
The Serpent, Prince of air, and drag in Chains
Through all his Realm, and there confounded leave;   455
Then enter into glory, and resume
His Seat at God's right hand, exalted high
Above all names in Heav'n; and thence shall come,
When this world's dissolution shall be ripe,
With glory and power to judge both quick and dead,   460
To judge th' unfaithful dead, but to reward
His faithful, and receive them into bliss,
Whether in Heav'n or Earth, for then the Earth
Shall all be Paradise, far happier place
Than this of *Eden*, and far happier days'.   465
    So spake the Archangel *Michael*, then paused,
As at the World's great period; and our Sire
Replete with joy and wonder, thus replied.
    'O goodness infinite, goodness immense!

That all this good of evil shall produce,   470
And evil turn to good; more wonderful
Than that which by creation first brought forth
Light out of darkness! full of doubt I stand,[33]
Whether I should repent me now of sin
By me done and occasioned, or rejoice   475
Much more, that much more good thereof shall spring,
To God more glory, more good will to Men
From God, and over wrath grace shall abound.
But say, if our deliverer up to Heav'n
Must reascend, what will betide the few   480
His faithful, left among th' unfaithful herd,
The enemies of truth; who then shall guide
His people, who defend? will they not deal
Worse with his followers than with him they dealt?'
  'Be sure they will', said th' Angel; 'but from Heav'n   485
He to his own a Comforter will send,[34]
The promise of the Father, who shall dwell
His Spirit within them, and the Law of Faith
Working through love, upon their hearts shall write,
To guide them in all truth, and also arm   490
With spiritual Armour, able to resist
Satan's assaults, and quench his fiery darts,
What man can do against them, not afraid,
Though to the death, against such cruelties
With inward consolations recompensed,   495
And oft supported so as shall amaze
Their proudest persecutors: for the Spirit
Poured first on his Apostles, whom he sends
To evangelize the Nations, then on all
Baptized, shall them with wondrous gifts endue   500
To speak all Tongues, and do all Miracles,
As did their Lord before them. Thus they win
Great numbers of each Nation to receive
With joy the tidings brought from Heav'n: at length   505
Their Ministry performed, and race well run,
Their doctrine and their story written left,
They die; but in their room, as they forewarn,
Wolves shall succeed for teachers, grievous Wolves,[35]
Who all the sacred mysteries of Heav'n
To their own vile advantages shall turn   510
Of lucre and ambition, and the truth
With superstitions and traditions taint,

---

[33] Adam articulates the paradox that the fall of man is happy (*felix culpa*) because God works out of it more good than was lost.
[34] *Comforter* "the Spirit of Truth which proceedeth from the Father" (John 15.26).

[35] *grievous Wolves* St Paul's term (Acts 20.29), applied to corrupt clergy, particularly Roman Catholic clergy and the *infallible* (l. 530 below) Pope.

Left only in those written Records pure,
Though not but by the Spirit understood.
Then shall they seek to avail themselves of names,   515
Places and titles, and with these to join
Secular power, though feigning still to act
By spiritual, to themselves appropriating
The Spirit of God, promised alike and giv'n
To all Believers; and from that pretence,   520
Spiritual Laws by carnal power shall force
On every conscience; Laws which none shall find
Left them enrolled, or what the Spirit within
Shall on the heart engrave. What will they then
But force the Spirit of Grace it self, and bind   525
His consort Liberty; what, but unbuild
His living Temples, built by Faith to stand,
Their own Faith not another's: for on Earth
Who against Faith and Conscience can be heard
Infallible? yet many will presume: 530
Whence heavy persecution shall arise
On all who in the worship persevere
Of Spirit and Truth; the rest, far greater part,
Will deem in outward Rites and specious forms
Religion satisfied; Truth shall retire   535
Bestuck with slandrous darts, and works of Faith
Rarely be found: so shall the World go on,
To good malignant, to bad men benign,
Under her own weight groaning till the day
Appear of respiration to the just,[36]   540
And vengeance to the wicked, at return
Of him so lately promised to thy aid
The Woman's seed, obscurely then foretold,
Now amplier known thy Saviour and thy Lord,
Last in the Clouds from Heav'n to be revealed   545
In glory of the Father, to dissolve
Satan with his perverted World, then raise
From the conflagrant mass, purged and refined,
New Heav'ns, new Earth, Ages of endless date
Founded in righteousness and peace and love   550
To bring forth fruits Joy and eternal Bliss'.
    He ended; and thus *Adam* last replied.
'How soon hath thy prediction, Seèr blest,
Measured this transient World, the Race of time,
Till time stand fixed: beyond is all abyss,[37]   555
Eternity, whose end no eye can reach.
Greatly instructed I shall hence depart,
Greatly in peace of thought, and have my fill
Of knowledge, what this Vessel can contain;

---

[36] *respiration* "Relief from toil" (Johnson).   [37] *stand* shall stand (subjunctive).

Beyond which was my folly to aspire.   560
Henceforth I learn, that to obey is best,
And love with fear the only God, to walk
As in his presence, ever to observe
His providence, and on him sole depend,
Merciful over all his works, with good   565
Still overcoming evil, and by small
Accomplishing great things, by things deemed weak
Subverting worldly strong, and worldly wise
By simply meek; that suffering for Truth's sake
Is fortitude to highest victory,   570
And to the faithful Death the Gate of Life;
Taught this by his example whom I now
Acknowledge my Redeemer ever blest'.
    To whom thus also th' Angel last replied:
'This having learnt, thou hast attained the sum   575
Of wisdom; hope no higher, though all the Stars
Thou knewst by name, and all th' ethereal Powers,
All secrets of the deep, all Nature's works,
Or works of God in Heav'n, Air, Earth, or Sea,
And all the riches of this World enjoydst,   580
And all the rule, one Empire; only add
Deeds to thy knowledge answerable, add Faith,
Add virtue, Patience, Temperance, add Love,
By name to come called Charity, the soul
Of all the rest: then wilt thou not be loth   585
To leave this Paradise, but shalt possess
A paradise within thee, happier far.
Let us descend now therefore from this top
Of Speculation; for the hour precise
Exacts our parting hence; and see the Guards,   590
By me encamped on yonder Hill, expect
Their motion, at whose Front a flaming Sword,[38]
In signal of remove, waves fiercely round;
We may no longer stay: go, waken *Eve;*
Her also I with gentle Dreams have calmed   595
Portending good, and all her spirits composed
To meek submission: thou at season fit
Let her with thee partake what thou hast heard,
Chiefly what may concern her Faith to know,
The great deliverance by her Seed to come   600
(For by the Woman's Seed) on all Mankind.
That ye may live, which will be many days,
Both in one Faith unanimous though sad,
With cause for evils past, yet much more cheered
With meditation on the happy end'.   605
    He ended, and they both descend the Hill;

---

[38] *motion* order, command.

Descended, *Adam* to the Bow'r where *Eve*
Lay sleeping ran before, but found her waked;
And thus with words not sad she him received.
   'Whence thou returnst, and whither wentst, I know;   610
For God is also in sleep, and Dreams advise,
Which he hath sent propitious, some great good
Presaging, since with sorrow and heart's distress
Wearied I fell asleep: but now lead on;[39]
In me is no delay; with thee to go,   615
Is to stay here; without thee here to stay,
Is to go hence unwilling; thou to me
Art all things under Heav'n, all places thou,
Who for my wilful crime art banished hence.
This further consolation yet secure   620
I carry hence; though all by me is lost,
Such favour I unworthy am vouchsafed,
By me the Promised Seed shall all restore'.
   So spake our Mother *Eve*, and *Adam* heard
Well pleased, but answered not; for now too nigh   625
Th' Archangel stood, and from the other Hill
To their fixed Station, all in bright array
The Cherubim descended; on the ground
Gliding metéorous, as Ev'ning Mist
Ris'n from a River o'er the marish glides,[40]   630
And gathers ground fast at the Labourer's heel
Homeward returning. High in Front advanced,
The brandished Sword of God before them blazed[41]
Fierce as a Comet; which with torrid heat,
And vapour as the *Libyan* Air adust,[42]   635
Began to parch that temperate Clime; whereat
In either hand the hastning Angel caught
Our ling'ring Parents, and to th' Eastern Gate
Led them direct, and down the Cliff as fast
To the subjected Plain; then disappeared.[43]   640
They looking back, all th' Eastern side beheld
Of Paradise, so late their happy seat,
Waved over by that flaming Brand, the Gate
With dreadful Faces thronged and fiery Arms:
Some natural tears they dropped, but wiped them soon;   645
The World was all before them, where to choose
Their place of rest, and Providence their guide:
They hand in hand with wandring steps and slow,
Through *Eden* took their solitary way.

THE END

---

[39] *lead on*   Eve's speech recalls Ruth 1.16–17.
[40] *marish*   marsh.
[41] Genesis 3.24.
[42] *adust*   "Burnt; scorched; dried with fire" (Johnson).
[43] *subjected*   "put under" (Johnson).

Richard Crashaw (1613?–1649)

In 1641 Parliamentary investigators visited Cambridge University to observe a breeding ground of high-church Anglicanism. Crashaw was found guilty of superstitious practices and two years later, after the outbreak of open war, he fled Cambridge, never to return. Like some other loyal royalists, he followed in the footsteps of Henrietta Maria, Charles I's queen. He died on the continent in the same year as Charles I. His greatest work is religious poetry, and some of his best poems express his fascination with female saints. This has been attributed to his family circumstances: his strict Puritan father and the fact that he was left motherless twice by age nine. Crashaw wrote three poems to St Teresa of Avila. The "Hymn" first appeared in Steps to the Temple: Sacred Poems *(1646), but Crashaw probably left instructions for the revised edition of 1652, which is the basis for the text presented here.*

The standard edition of Crashaw's poems is edited by L. C. Martin (1927; 2nd ed., Oxford University Press, 1957). The standard biography is Austin Warren, Richard Crashaw: A Study in Baroque Sensibility *(Louisiana State University Press, 1939).*

from *Steps to the Temple* (1646)

A HYMN TO THE NAME AND HONOUR OF THE ADMIRABLE SAINT TERESA

Foundress of the Reformation of the Discalced Carmelites, both men and Women;
A woman for Angelical height of speculation, for Masculine courage of
performance, more than a woman. Who Yet a child, out ran maturity,
and durst plot a Martyrdom[1]

Love thou art Absolute, sole Lord[2]
Of Life & Death. To prove the word,
We'll now appeal to none of all
Those thy old Soldiers, Great & tall,
Ripe Men of Martyrdom that could reach down   5
With strong arms, their triumphant crown:
Such as could with lusty breath,
Speak loud unto the face of death
Their Great Lord's glorious name, to none
Of those whose spacious Bosoms spread a throne   10
For Love at large to fill; spare Blood & sweat,
And see him take a private seat,[3]
Making his mansion in the mild
And milky soul of a soft child.[4]
Scarce has she learn't to lisp the name   15

A HYMN TO THE NAME
[1] St Teresa (1515–82), a Spanish nun who founded the reformed Carmelite order known as the Descalzos or Barefoots.
[2] *Love* divine love and a name for Christ the Lord.
[3] *seat* "Mansion; residence; dwelling; abode" (Johnson).

[4] Teresa left home at age eighteen to join a Carmelite convent, but she was interested in the stories of martyrs as a child. She published an autobiography (as well as other works), and there were biographies supplying details about her life that Crashaw uses in his poem.

Of Martyr, yet she thinks it shame
Life should so long play with that breath,
Which spent can buy so brave a death.
  She never undertook to know,
What death with love should have to do.   20
Nor hath she ere yet understood
Why to show love she should shed blood,
Yet though she cannot tell you why,
She can Love, & she can die.
  Scarce had she Blood enough, to make   25
A guilty sword blush for her sake:
Yet has she a Heart dares hope to prove,
How much less strong is Death than Love.
  Be love but there, let poor six years,
Be posed with the maturest fears⁵   30
Man trembles at, you straight shall find
Love knows no nonage, nor the Mind.⁶
'Tis Love, not Years, or Limbs, that can
Make the Martyr, or the man.
  Love touch't her heart, & lo it beats   35
High, & burns with such brave heats:
Such thirsts to die, as dares drink up,
A thousand cold deaths in one cup.
Good reason. For she breathes All fire.
Her weak breast heaves with strong desire   40
Of what she may with fruitless wishes
Seek for amongst her Mother's Kisses.
  Since 'tis not to be had at home,
She'll travel to a Mártyrdom.
No home for hers confesses she,   45
But where she may a Martyr be.
  She'll to the Moors; And trade with them,
For this unvalued Diadem.⁷
She'll offer them her dearest Breath,
With Christ's name in't, in change for death.   50
She'll bargain with them; & will give
Them God; teach them how to live
In him: or, if they this deny,
For him she'll teach them how to Die.
So shall she leave amongst them sown,   55
Her Lord's blood, or at least her own.
  Farewell then, all the world! Adieu.
Teresa is no more for you.
Farewell, all pleasures, sports, & joys,
(Never till now esteemèd toys)   60

---

⁵ *posed* confronted.   ⁷ *unvalued* invaluable.
⁶ *nonage* the condition of being underage, with a pun
on nun age.

Farewell what ever dear may be,
Mother's arms, or Father's knee.
Farewell house, & farewell home!
She's for the Moors & Martyrdom.
    Sweet, not so fast! Lo thy fair Spouse[8]   65
Whom thou seekst with so swift vows
Calls thee back, & bids thee come,
T'embrace a milder Martyrdom.
    Blest powers forbid, Thy tender life,
Should bleed upon a barbarous knife;   70
Or some base hand have power to race[9]
Thy Breast's chaste cabinet, & uncase[10]
A soul kept there so sweet. O no;
Wise heav'n will never have it so.
Thou art Love's victim; & must die   75
A death more mystical & high.
Into love's arms thou shalt let fall
A still-surviving funeral.
    His is the Dart must make the Death[11]
Whose stroke shall taste thy hallowed breath;   80
A Dart thrice dip't in that rich flame
Which writes thy spouse's radiant Name
Upon the roof of Heav'n; where ay
It shines, & with a sovereign ray,
Beats bright upon the burning faces   85
Of souls, which in that name's sweet graces,
Find everlasting smiles. So rare,
So spiritual, pure, & fair,
Must be th' immortal instrument,
Upon whose choice point shall be sent,   90
A life so loved; And that there be
Fit executioners for Thee,
The fair'st & the first-born sons of fire,
Blest Seraphim shall leave their quire,
And turn love's soldiers, upon Thee,   95
To exercise their archery.
    O how oft shalt thou complain
Of a sweet & subtle Pain;
Of intolerable Joys;
Of a Death, in which who dies   100
Loves his death, and dies again;
And would for ever so be slain.
And lives, & dies; and knows not why
To live, But that he thus may never leave to Die.

---

[8] *Spouse* Christ, whom nuns marry when they take their vows of devotion; Christ described himself in a parable as the bridegroom (Matthew 9.15).
[9] *race* slash.
[10] *uncase* disembody.
[11] *Dart* Teresa reports having acute pain in her side which she attributed to the work of an angel who touched her heart with a lance tipped with fire.

How kindly will thy gentle Heart,   105
Kiss the sweetly-killing Dart!
And close in his embraces keep,
Those delicious Wounds, that weep
Balsam, to heal themselves with. Thus
When These thy Deaths, so numerous,   110
Shall all at last die into one,
And melt thy Soul's sweet mansion;
Like a soft lump of incense, hasted
By too hot a fire, & wasted,
Into perfúming clouds, so fast   115
Shalt thou exhale to Heav'n at last[12]
In a resolving Sigh, and then[13]
O what? Ask not the Tongues of men.
Angels cannot tell, suffice,
Thy self shalt feel thine own full joys.   120
And hold them fast for ever. There,
So soon as thou shalt first appear,
The Moon of maiden stars, thy white
Mistress attended by such bright[14]
Souls as thy shining self, shall come   125
And in her first ranks make thee room.
Where 'mongst her snowy family,
Immortal welcomes wait on thee.
    O what delight, when revealed Life shall stand,[15]
And teach thy lips heav'n, with his hand,   130
On which thou now may'st to thy wishes,
Heap up thy consecrated kisses.
What joys shall seize thy soul when she
Bending her blessèd eyes, on thee
(Those second Smiles of Heav'n) shall dart   135
Her mild rays, through thy melting heart!
    Angels, thy old friends, there shall greet thee
Glad at their own home now to meet thee.
All thy good Works which went before
And waited for thee, at the door,   140
Shall own thee there; and all in one
Weave a Constellation
Of Crowns, with which the King thy spouse,
Shall build up thy triumphant brows.
    All thy old woes shall now smile on thee,   145
And thy pains sit bright upon thee.
All thy sorrows here shall shine,
And thy Suffrings be divine.

---

[12] *exhale* "To send or draw out in vapours or fumes"   [14] *Mistress* the Virgin Mary.
(Johnson).   [15] *Life* Christ.
[13] *resolving* melting; dissolving.

Tears shall take comfort, & turn gems,
And Wrongs repent to Diadems.   150
Even thy Deaths shall live, & new
Dress the soul, that erst they slew.
Thy wounds shall blush to such bright scars,
As keep account of the Lamb's wars.[16]
   Those rare Works, where thou shalt leave writ,   155
Love's noble history, with wit
Taught thee by none but him, while here
They feed our souls, shall clothe Thine there.
Each heav'nly word, by whose hid flame
Our hard Hearts shall strike fire, the same   160
Shall flourish on thy brows; & be
Both fire to us, & flame to thee;
Whose light shall live bright, in thy Face.
   By glory, in our hearts by grace.
Thou shalt look round about, & see   165
Thousands of crowned souls, throng to be
Themselves thy crown, sons of thy vows,[17]
The virgin-births with which thy sovereign spouse
Made fruitful thy fair soul. Go now
And with them all about thee, bow   170
To Him. 'Put on', he'll say, 'put on,
My rosy love, that thy rich zone,[18]
Sparkling with the sacred flames,
Of thousand souls whose happy names,
Heav'n keeps upon thy score. (Thy bright   175
Life brought them first to kiss the light
That kindled them to stars.)' And so
Thou with the Lamb, thy Lord, shalt go;
And wheresoe'er he sets his white
Steps, walk with Him those ways of light   180
Which who in death would live to see,
Must learn in life to die like thee.

Margaret Fell Fox (1614–1702)

Margaret Fell met George Fox (1624–91), the founder of the Society of Friends, in the 1650s and became known as "the mother of Quakerism." She conducted meetings in her home, Swarthmore Hall, for which she was jailed from 1664–8. She married Fox in 1669 by which time she had become an active polemicist, publishing several treatises in support of religious freedom and equal rights for women. Her arguments are always closely tied to scripture, in her exegesis of which, like

---

[16] *Lamb* another name for Christ.

[17] *sons of thy vows* the men who entered the reformed Carmelite order founded by Teresa.

[18] *zone* anything that encircles; usually a belt or girdle but here a crown.

Milton, she found irrefutable support for her convictions. Women's Speaking Justified (1666), *a crudely manufactured pamphlet, is mainly concerned with showing the biblical foundation for admitting women's voices to be heard on spiritual questions. It also provides an example of a woman's voice speaking out in the newly created public sphere that was, like the royal court, mainly dominated by men.*

The Augustan Reprint Society has produced a facsimile of the pamphlet (1979), and the Brown University Women Writers Project has reprinted the work. There is a biography by Isabel Ross (Longman, 1949).

from *Women's Speaking Justified, Proved and Allowed by the Scriptures* (1666)

Whereas it hath been an Objection in the minds of many, and several times hath been objected by the Clergy, or Ministers, and others, against Women's speaking in the Church; and so consequently may be taken, that they are condemned for medling in the things of *God*; the ground of which *Objection*, is taken from the Apostle's words, which he writ in his first Epistle to the *Corinthians* 14.34, 35. And also what he writ to *Timothy* in the first Epistle, 2.11, 12. But how far they wrong the Apostle's intentions in these Scriptures, we shall show clearly when we come to them in their course and order. But first let me lay down how *God* himself hath manifested his Will and Mind concerning women, and unto women.

And first, when *God created Man in his own Image: in the Image of God created he them, Male and Female: and God blessed them, and God said unto them, Be fruitful, and multiply: And God said, Behold, I have given you of every Herb,* &c. *Genesis* 1. Here *God* joins them together in his own Image, and makes no such distinctions and differences as men do; for though they be weak, he is strong; and as he said to the Apostle, His Grace is sufficient, and his strength is made manifest in weakness, 2 Corinthians 12.9. And such hath the *Lord* chosen, even *the weak things of the world, to confound the things which are mighty; and things which are despised, hath God chosen, to bring to nought things that are,* 1 Corinthians 1. And *God* hath put no such difference between Male and Female as men would make.

It is true, *The Serpent that was more subtle then any other Beast of the Field,* came unto the Woman, with his Temptation, and with a lie, his subtlety discerning her to be more inclinable to hearken to him, when he said *If ye eat, your eyes shall be opened*: and the woman saw that *the Fruit was good to make one* wise; there the temptation got into her, and *she did eat, and gave to her Husband, and he did eat* also, and so they were both tempted into the transgression and disobedience; and therefore God said unto *Adam*, when that he hid himself when he heard his voice, *Hast thou eaten of the Tree which I commanded thee that thou shouldest not eat?* and *Adam* said, *The Woman which thou gavest me, she gave me of the Tree, and I did eat. And the Lord said unto the Woman, What is this that thou hast done?* and the Woman said, *The Serpent beguiled me, and I did eat.* Here the Woman spoke the truth unto the Lord: See what the Lord saith . . . after he had pronounced Sentence on the Serpent; *I will put enmity between thee and the Woman, and between thy Seed and her Seed; it shall bruise thy head, and thou shalt bruise his heel,* Genesis 3.

Let this Word of the Lord, which was from the beginning, stop the mouths of all that oppose Women's Speaking in the Power of the Lord; for he hath put enmity between the Woman and the Serpent; and if the seed of the Woman speak not, the Seed of the Serpent speaks; for God hath put enmity between the two Seeds, and it is manifest, that those that speak against the Woman and her Seed's Speaking, speak out of the enmity of the old Serpent's Seed; and God hath fulfilled his Word and his Promise, *When the fullness of time was come, he hath sent forth his Son, made of a woman, made under the Law, that we might receive the adoption of Sons,* Galatians 4.4, 5.

Moreover, the Lord is pleased, when he mentions his Church, to call her by the name of *Woman* by his Prophets, saying, *I have called thee as a Woman forsaken, and grieved in Spirit, and as a wife of Youth,* Isaiah 54. Again, *How long wilt thou go about, thou black-sliding Daughter? For the Lord hath created a new thing in the earth, a woman shall compass*[1] *a Man,* Jeremiah 31.22. And *David,* when he was speaking of Christ and his Church, he saith, *The King's Daughter is all glorious within, her clothing is of wrought Gold; she shall be brought unto the King: with gladness and rejoicing shall they be brought; they shall enter into the King's Palace.* Psalm 45. And also King *Solomon* in his Song, where he speaks of Christ and his Church, where she is complaining and calling for Christ, he saith, *If thou knowest not, O thou fairest among women, go thy way by the footsteps of the Flock,* Canticles 1.8 And *John,* when he saw the wonder that was in Heaven, he saw *a woman clothed with the Sun, and the Moon under her feet, and upon her head a Crown of twelve Stars; and there appeared another wonder in Heaven, a great red Dragon stood ready to devour her Child*: here the enmity appears that God put between the woman and the Dragon, *Revelations* 12.

Thus much may prove that the Church of Christ is a woman, and those that speak against the woman's speaking, speak against the Church of Christ, and the Seed of the Woman, which Seed is Christ; that is to say, Those that speak against the Power of the Lord, and the Spirit of the Lord speaking in a woman, simply by reason of her Sex, or because she is a Woman, not regarding the Seed, the Spirit, and Power that speaks in her; such speak against Christ, and his Church, and are the Seed of the Serpent, wherein lodgeth the enmity. And as God the Father made no such difference in the first Creation, nor never since between the Male and Female, but always out of his Mercy and loving kindness, had regard unto the weak. So also, his Son, Christ Jesus, confirms the same thing: when the *Pharisees* came to him, and asked him, if it were lawful for a man to put away his Wife? he answered and said unto them, *Have you not read, That he that made them in the beginning, made them Male and Female,* and said, *For this cause shall a Man leave Father and Mother, and shall cleave unto his Wife, and they twain shall be one flesh, wherefore they are no more twain but one flesh; What therefore God hath joined together, let no man put asunder,* Matthew 19.

Again, Christ Jesus, when he came to the City of *Samaria* where *Jacob's* Well was, where the Woman of *Samaria* was; you may read, in *John* 4. how well he was pleased to preach the Everlasting Gospel to her; and when the Woman said unto him, *I know when the Messiah cometh,* (which is called Christ) *when he cometh, he will tell us all things;* Jesus saith unto her, *I that speak unto thee am he*; This is more than ever he said in plain words to Man or Woman (that we read of) before he suffered. Also he said unto *Martha,* when she said, she knew that her Brother should rise again in the last day, Jesus said unto her, *I am the Resurrection and the Life: he that believeth on me, though he were dead, yet shall he live; and whosoever liveth and believeth shall never die. Believest thou this?* she answered, *Yea, Lord, I believe that thou art the Christ, the Son of God.* Here she manifested her true and saving Faith, which few at that day believed so on him, *John* 11.25, 26.

FROM *WOMEN'S SPEAKING JUSTIFIED*

[1] *compass* "To encircle; to environ; to surround; to enclose" (Johnson).

Also that Woman that came unto Jesus with an Alabaster Box of very precious Ointment, and poured it on his Head as he sat at meat; it's manifested that this Woman knew more of the secret Power and Wisdom of God, than his Disciples did, that were filled with indignation against her; and therefore Jesus saith, *Why do ye trouble the Woman? for she hath wrought a good work upon me; Verily, I say unto you, Wheresoever this Gospel shall be preached in the whole World, there shall also this that this Woman hath done, be told for a memorial of her*, Matthew 26, Mark 14.3. *Luke* saith further, *She was a sinner*, and that *she stood at his feet behind him weeping, and began to wash his feet with her tears and did wipe them with the hair of her head, and kissed his feet, and annointed them with Ointment*. And when Jesus saw the Heart of the *Pharisee* that hath bidden him to his house, he took occasion to speak unto *Simon* as you may read in *Luke* 7, and he turned to the woman, and said, Simon, *seest thou this Woman? Thou gavest me no water to my feet, but she hath washed my feet with tears, and wiped them with the hair of her head: Thou gavest me no kiss, but this Woman, since I came in, hath not ceased to kiss my Feet: My Head with Oil thou didst not annoint, but this Woman hath annointed my Feet with Ointment: wherefore I say unto thee, her sins, which are many, are forgiven her, for she hath loved much, Luke* 7.37, to the end.

Also there was many women which followed Jesus from *Galilee*, ministering unto him, and stood a far off when he was Crucified, *Matthew* 28.55, *Mark* 15. Yea even the women of Jerusalem wept for him, insomuch that he said unto them, *Weep not for me, Ye Daughters of* Jerusalem, *but weep for your selves, and for your Children*, Luke 23.28.

And certain Women which had been healed of evil Spirits and Infirmities, Mary Magdalen, *and Joanna the Wife of* Chuza, Herod's *Steward's Wife, and many others which ministered unto him of their substance*, Luke 6.2, 3.

Thus we see that Jesus owned[2] the *Love* and Grace that appeared in Women, and did not despise it, and by what is recorded in the Scriptures, he received as much love, kindness, compassion, and tender dealing towards him from Women, as he did from any others, both in his life time, and also after they had exercised their cruelty upon him, for *Mary Magdalene*, and *Mary* the Mother of Joses,[3] beheld where he was laid: *And when the Sabbath was past*, Mary Magdalen, *and* Mary *the Mother of* James, *and* Salom,[4] *had brought sweet spices that they might annoint him: And very early in the morning, the first day of the week, they came unto the Sepulchre at the rising of the Sun, And they said among themselves who shall roll us away the stone from the door of the Sepulchre? And when they looked, the stone was rolled away for it was very great*: Mark 16.1–4, Luke 24.1, 2. *and they went down into the sepulchre, and as Matthew* saith, *The Angel rolled away the stone, and he said unto the Women, Fear not, I know, whom ye seek, Jesus which was crucified: he is not here, he is risen*, Matthew 28. Now *Luke* saith thus: that *there stood two men by them in shining apparel, and as they were perplexed and unafraid, the men said unto them, He is not here; remember how he said unto you when he was in Galilee, That the Son of Man must be delivered into the hands of sinful men, and be crucified, and the third day rise again, and they remembered his words, and returned from the Sepulchre, and told all these things to the eleven, and to all the rest*.

It was *Mary Magdalene, and Joanna*,[5] and *Mary* the Mother of *James*, and the other Women that were with them, which told these things to the Apostles, *And their words seemed unto them as idle tales, and they believed them not*. Mark this, ye despisers of the weakness of Women, and look upon your selves to be so wise: but Christ Jesus doth not so, for he makes use of the weak:

---

[2]   *owned*   acknowledged.
[3]   *Mary*   Mary of Cleophas (John 19.25).
[4]   *Mary*   the same person; *Salom* should perhaps be *Simon*.

[5]   *Joanna*   wife of Chuza, steward of Herod (Luke 8.3).

For when he met the women after he was risen, he said unto them, *All Hail,* and they came and held him by the Feet, and worshipped him, then said Jesus unto them, *Be not afraid, go tell my Brethren that they go into Gallilee, and there they shall see me,* Matthew 28.10, Mark 16.9. And *John* saith when *Mary* was weeping at the Sepulchre, that Jesus said unto her, *Woman, why weepest thou? what seekest thou? And when she supposed him to be the Gardener, Jesus saith unto her,* Mary; *she turned her self, and saith unto him, Rabboni, which is to say master: Jesus saith unto her, Touch me not, for I am not yet ascended to my Father, but go to my Brethren, and say unto them I ascend unto my Father, and your Father, and to my God, and your God,* John 20.16, 17.

Mark this, you that despise and oppose the Message of the Lord God that he sends by women, what had become of the Redemption of the whole Body of Man-kind, if they had not believed the Message that the *Lord* Iesus sent by these women, of and concerning his Resurrection? And if these women had not thus, out of tenderness and bowels[6] of love, who had received Mercy, and Grace, and forgiveness of sins, and Virtue, and Healing from him, which many men also had received the like, if their hearts had not been so united and knit unto him in love, that they could not depart as the men did, but sat watching, and waiting, and weeping about the Sepulchre until the time of his Resurrection, and so were ready to carry his Message, as is manifested, else how should his Disciples have known, who were not there?

Oh! blessed and glorified be the *Glorious Lord,* for this may all the whole body of mankind say, though the wisdom of men, that never knew *God,* is always ready to except against the weak; but the weakness of *God* is stronger than men, and the foolishness of *God* is wiser than men.

Abraham Cowley (1618–1667)

Cowley began publishing poetry at the age of fifteen and had three editions of a youthful collection in print by age nineteen. The Parliamentary government forced him out of Cambridge in 1643, and he soon migrated from Oxford to Paris, where he served Charles I's queen. In 1656 Cowley went on a mission to England, was arrested, and saw the publication of his most important collection of poems. After the Restoration he became a founding member of the Royal Society and willed his literary remains to Thomas Sprat, the Society's first historian. Cowley wrote all kinds of verse; he achieved fame for love poetry, for his strenuous Pindaric odes, for his epic Davideis *and his long historical poem on the Civil War. Within a generation of his death, however, Cowley's reputation sank, as his name became synonymous with extravagantly witty, linguistically contorted poetry that Samuel Johnson permanently labelled "Metaphysical."*

The text of the "Ode of Wit" is based on the edition of his collected works published in 1656. "To Mr Hobbes" is based on Thomas Sprat's edition (1707–11). The Collected Works of Abraham Cowley in six volumes is in the midst of publication (University of Delaware Press, 1989–).

---

[6] *bowels* the intestines as the seat of tenderness in the old physiognomy, and so synonymous with it.

from *Poems* (1656)

ODE
OF WIT

1

Tell me, O tell, what kind of thing is *Wit*,[1]
  Thou who *Master* art of it.[2]
For the *First Matter* loves *Variety* less;[3]
  A thousand different shapes it bears,
  Comely in thousand shapes appears.
Yonder we saw it plain; and here 'tis now.
Like *Spirits* in a *Place*, we know not *How*.[4]

2

London that vents of *false Ware* so much store,[5]
  In no *Ware* deceives us more.
For men led by the *Colour*, and the *Shape*,
Like *Zeuxis' Birds* fly to the painted *Grape*;[6]
  Some things do through our Judgement pass[7]
  As through a *Multiplying Glass*.[8]
And sometimes, if the *Object* be too far,
We take a *Falling Meteor* for a *Star*.

3

Hence 'tis a *Wit* that greatest *word* of *Fame*[9]
  Grows such a common Name.
And *Wits* by our *Creation* they become,
Just so, as *Titular Bishops* made at *Rome*.
  'Tis not a *Tale*, 'tis not a *Jest*
  Admired with *Laughter* at a feast,
Nor florid *Talk* which can that *Title* gain;
The *Proofs* of *Wit* for ever must remain.

5

10

15

20

ODE OF WIT
[1] *Wit* "The powers of the mind; the mental faculties; the intellects. This is the original signification" [sense 1]; "Imagination; quickness of fancy" [sense 2]; "Sentiments produced by quickness of fancy" [sense 3] (Johnson).
[2] *Thou* God, creator of the world.
[3] *First Matter* the primigenial stuff out of which the world evolved according to materialist theories of creation like that of Lucretius.
[4] *Spirits in a Place* a paradox, because spirit is non-material and place material.
[5] *vents* vends, sells.

[6] *Zeuxis* (fl. 424–380 BCE), a Greek artist who excelled at life-like paintings and created famous illusions, such as painted grapes that deceived birds.
[7] *Judgement* "The power of discerning the relations between one term or one proposition and another . . . 'The power which God has given man to supply the want of certain knowledge, is *judgement* . . .' Locke" (Johnson).
[8] *Multiplying Glass* telescope or magnifying glass.
[9] *a Wit* "A man of fancy" [sense 4]; "A man of genius" [sense 5] (Johnson).

4

'Tis not to force some lifeless *Verses* meet
   With their five gouty feet.   25
All every where, like *Man's*, must be the *Soul,*
And *Reason* the *Inferior Powers* control.
   Such were the *Numbers* which could call[10]
   The *Stones* into the *Theban* wall.[11]
Such *Miracles* are ceased; and now we see   30
No *Towns* or *Houses* raised by *Poetry.*

5

Yet 'tis not to adorn, and gild each part;
   That shows more *Cost,* than *Art.*
Jewels at *Nose* and *Lips* but ill appear;
Rather than *all things Wit,* let *none* be there.   35
   Several *Lights* will not be seen,
   If there be nothing else between.
Men doubt, because they stand so thick i' th' sky,
If those be *Stars* which paint the *Galaxy.*

6

'Tis not when two like words make up one noise;   40
   Jests for *Dutch Men,* and *English Boys.*
In which who finds out *Wit,* the same may see
In *Anagrams* and *Acrostics Poetry.*
   Much less can that have any place
   At which a *Virgin* hides her face,   45
Such *Dross* the *Fire* must purge away; 'tis just
The *Author blush,* there where the *Reader* must.

7

'Tis not such *Lines* as almost crack the *Stage*
   When *Bajazet* begins to rage.[12]
Nor a tall *Metaphor* in th'*Oxford way.*[13]   50
Nor the dry chips of short-lunged *Seneca.*[14]
   Nor upon all things to obtrude,
   And force some odd *Similitude.*
What is it then, which like the *Power Divine*
We only can by *Negatives* define?   55

[10] *Numbers* harmonies or verses.
[11] *the Theban wall* spontaneously assembled itself, according to legend, when Amphion played his lyre.
[12] *Bajazet* a pompous king in Marlowe's play *Tamburlaine.*

[13] *Oxford* changed to "bombast" in later editions.
[14] *Seneca* Roman philosopher of the first century CE who wrote in a non-periodic, abrupt, and pointed style.

8

In a true piece of *Wit* all things must be,
　　Yet all things there *agree.*
As in the *Ark,* joined without force or strife,
All *Creatures* dwelt; all *Creatures* that had *Life.*
　　Or as the *Primitive Forms* of all   60
　　　(If we compare great things with small)
Which without *Discord* or *Confusion* lie,
In that strange *Mirror* of the *Deity.*[15]

9

But *Love* that moulds *One Man* up out of *Two,*
　　Makes me forget and injure you.   65
I took *you* for *my self* sure, when I thought
That you in any thing were to be *Taught.*
　　Correct my error with thy Pen;
　　　And if any ask me then,
What thing right *Wit,* and height of *Genius* is,   70
I'll only show your *Lines,* and say, ' *'Tis This'.*

TO MR HOBBES

I

　　Vast *Bodies* of *Philosophy*
　　I oft have seen, and read
　　But all are *Bodies dead,*
　　Or *Bodies* by *Art fashionèd*
I never yet the *Living Soul* could see,   5
　　But in thy *Books* and *thee.*
'Tis only *God* can know
Whether the fair *Idea* thou dost show
Agree entirely with his own or no.
　　This I dare boldly tell,   10
'Tis so *like Truth,* 'twill serve our Turn as well.
Just, as in *Nature,* their *Proportions* be,
As full of *Concord* their *Variety,*
As *firm* the Parts upon their *Centre* rest,
And all so *solid* are, that they at least   15
As much as Nature, *Emptiness detest.*[1]

2

Long did the mighty *Stagirite* retain[2]
The *universal Intellectual Reign;*

---

[15] *Mirror of the Deity*　the platonic world of forms,
conflated with the mind of god in neoplatonic thought;
mirror　meant "exemplar; archetype" (Johnson).

TO MR HOBBES
[1] *Emptiness detest*　"Nature abhors a vacuum" is an old
proverb.
[2] *Stagirite*　Aristotle, born in the town of Stagira in
Macedonia.

Saw his own Country's short-lived *Leopard* slain;[3]
The stronger *Roman-Eagle* did outfly,   20
Oftner *renewed* his *Age*, and saw that *die*.
Mecca it self, in spite of *Mahomet*, possessed,
And chased by a wild *Deluge* from the *East*,[4]
His *Monarchy* new-planted in the *West*.
But as in time each great Imperial Race   25
Degenerates, and gives some new one place:
  So did this noble *Empire* waste,
  Sunk by degrees from Glories past,
And in the *School-men*'s hands it perished quite at last.[5]
  Then nought but *Words it grew*,   30
  And those all *Barb'rous* too.
 It *perished*, and it *vanished* there,
The *Life* and *Soul* breathed out became but empty *Air*.

3

The *Fields* which answered well the *Ancients' Plough*,
Spent and out-worn return no *Harvest* now,   35
In barren *Age* wild and unglorious lie,
  And boast of *past Fertility*,
The *poor Relief* of *present Poverty*.
  Food and *Fruit* we must now want:
  Unless new *Lands* we *plant*.   40
We break up *Tombs* with *Sacrilegious Hands*,
  Old *Rubbish* we remove;
To walk in *Ruins*, like vain *Ghosts*, we love,
  And with fond *Divining Wands*,[6]
  We search among the *dead*   45
  For Treasures *burièd*;
 Whilst still the *Liberal Earth* does hold
So many *Virgin Mines* of *undiscovered Gold*.

4

The *Baltic*, *Euxine*, and the *Caspian*,
And slender-limbed *Mediterranean*,[7]   50
Seem narrow *Creeks* to *thee*, and only fit
For the poor wretched *Fisher-boats* of *Wit*.
Thy nobler *Vessel* the vast *Ocean* tries,
  And nothing sees but *Seas* and *Skies*,

---

[3] *Leopard* "the *Graecian Empire*, which in the Visions of Daniel is represented by a Leopard . . . chapter 7, verse 6" [Cowley's note].
[4] *Deluge* "the Inundation of the *Turks*, and other *Nations*" [Cowley's note].
[5] *School-men* scholastic philosophers of the middle ages, who built elaborate systems of thought on the basis of Aristotelian concepts.

[6] *Divining Wands* "a two-forked Branch of a *Hazel-Tree*, which is used for the finding out either of *Veins*, or hidden *Treasures* of *Gold* or *Silver*" [Cowley's note].
[7] *Baltic . . . Mediterranean* "All the *Navigation* of the Ancients was in these Seas; they seldom ventured into the [Atlantic] *Ocean*" [Cowley's note].

'Till unknown *Regions* it descries,   55
Thou great *Columbus* of the *Golden Lands* of *new Philosophies*.
   Thy Task was harder much than his,
   For thy learned *America* is
  Not only found out first by *thee*,
And rudely left to *future Industry*,   60
   But thy *Eloquence* and thy *Wit*
Has *planted*, *peopled*, *built*, and *civilized* it.

5

   I little thought before,
   (Nor, being my *own self* so *poor*,
   Could comprehend so vast a *Store*)   65
  That all the *Wardrobe* of rich *Eloquence*
   Could have afforded half enough,
   Of *bright*, of *new*, and *lasting* Stuff,
To clothe the mighty *Limbs* of thy *gigantic Sense*.
Thy solid *Reason* like the *Shield* from Heaven[8]   70
   To the *Trojan Hero* given,
Too strong to take a Mark from any mortal Dart,
Yet shines with *Gold* and *Gems* in every Part,
And *Wonders* on it graved by the learned Hand of *Art*;
   A *Shield* that gives Delight   75
   Even to the *Enemies'* Sight,
Then, when they're sure to *lose* the *Combat* by 't.

6

Nor can the *Snow* which now cold *Age* does shed
   Upon thy reverend Head,
Quench or allay the noble *Fires* within,   80
   But all which thou hast *been*,
   And all that *Youth* can *be*, thou 'rt yet,
   So fully still dost thou
Enjoy the *Manhood*, and the *Bloom* of *Wit*,
And all the *Natural Heat*, but not the *Fever* too.   85
So *Contraries* on *Ætna's* Top conspire,[9]
Here hoary *Frosts*, and by them breaks out *Fire*;
A secure *Peace* the *faithful Neighbours* keep,
Th' emboldened *Snow* next to the *Flames* does *sleep*.
   And if we weigh, like *thee*,   90
   Nature, and *Causes*, we shall see
   That thus it *needs must be*.
To Things *Immortal Time* can do no Wrong,
And that which never is *to die*, for ever must be *Young*.

---

[8] *Shield*   made by Vulcan at the request of Venus for her son Æneas (*Aeneid* 8.626–731).

[9] *Ætna*   a tall, active volcano in Sicily (now spelt Etna).

Richard Lovelace (1618–1658)

When Lovelace entered college in Oxford he was "accounted the most amiable and beautiful person that ever eye beheld," according to his near contemporary, the historian Anthony À Wood. Favoured by the King and Queen for his looks and conversation, he went to Court upon graduation. As the King's cause sickened, Lovelace migrated emotionally and politically from a splendid cavalier to a "neutralist," impoverished, satirical denizen of the London streets. Gerald Hammond has shown the complexity of Lovelace's stance and the ways it reveals itself, to a degree, in his arrangement of his poems in Lucasta *(1649), which he prepared while in prison.*

The following selections are based on the first edition of Lucasta. *The standard edition of the poems is by C. H. Wilkinson (Clarendon Press, 1930). The names of the women to whom Lovelace addresses himself are abstractions meaning "Pure Light" (Lucasta), "Truth" (Althea), and "Immortal" (Amarantha), though he may also have had in mind some of the many real women and men who admired him.*

from *Lucasta* (1649)

SONG
TO LUCASTA,
GOING TO THE WARS

1

Tell me not (Sweet) I am unkind,
    That from the Nunnery
Of thy chaste breast, and quiet mind
    To War and Arms I fly.

2

True, a new Mistress now I chase,   5
    The first Foe in the Field;
And with a stronger Faith embrace
    A Sword, a Horse, a Shield.

3

Yet this Inconstancy is such
    As you too shall adore;   10
I could not love thee, Dear, so much,
    Loved I not Honour more.

SONG

TO AMARANTHA,

THAT SHE WOULD DISHEVEL HER HAIR

1

Amarantha sweet and fair,
Ah braid no more that shining hair!
As my curious hand or eye,
Hovering round thee let it fly.

2

Let it fly as unconfined   5
As its calm Ravisher, the wind;
Who hath left his darling th' East,
To wanton o'er that spicy Neast.[1]

3

Every Tress must be confess't
But neatly tangled at the best;   10
Like a Clue of golden thread,[2]
Most excellently ravelled.

4

Do not then wind up that light
In Ribands, and o'er-cloud in Night;
Like the Sun in 's early ray,   15
But shake your head and scatter day.

5

See 'tis broke! Within this Grove
The Bower, and the walks of Love,
Weary lie we down and rest,
And fan each other's panting breast.   20

6

Here we'll strip and cool our fire
In Cream below, in milk-baths higher:
And when all Wells are drawn dry,
I'll drink a tear out of thine eye,

SONG   TO AMARANTHA
[1] *Neast*   an alternate spelling of *nest*.

[2] *Clue* "Thread wound upon a bottom; a ball of thread" (Johnson), such as Ariadne gave to her beloved Theseus to lead him out of the labyrinth containing the Minotaur.

7

Which our very Joys shall leave   25
That sorrows thus we can deceive;
    Or our very sorrows weep,
That joys so ripe, so little keep.

TO ALTHEA,
FROM PRISON
SONG

1

When Love with unconfinèd wings
    Hovers within my Gates;
And my divine *Althea* brings
    To whisper at the Grates:
When I lie tangled in her hair,   5
    And fettered to her eye;
The *Gods* that wanton in the Air,[1]
    Know no such Liberty.

2

When flowing Cups run swiftly round
    With no allaying *Thames*,[2]   10
Our careless heads with Roses bound,
    Our hearts with Loyal Flames;
When thirsty grief in Wine we steep,
    When Healths and draughts go free,
Fishes that tipple in the Deep,   15
    Know no such Liberty.

3

When (like committed Linnets) I[3]
    With shriller throat shall sing
The sweetness, Mercy, Majesty,
    And glories of my KING;   20
When I shall voice aloud, how Good
    He is, how Great should be;
Enlargèd Winds that curl the Flood,[4]
    Know no such Liberty.

To ALTHEA
[1] *Gods* angels.
[2] *Thames* water; in the classical world, wine was usually taken with water.
[3] *committed* imprisoned, caged; *Linnet* a kind of song bird.
[4] *Flood* sea.

4

Stone Walls do not a Prison make,   25
   Nor Iron bars a Cage;
Minds innocent and quiet take
   That for an Hermitage;
If I have freedom in my Love,
   And in my soul am free;   30
Angels alone that soar above,
   Enjoy such Liberty.

Abiezer Coppe (1619–1672)

Coppe left the royalist town of Oxford at the outbreak of the Civil War and became a very active Anabaptist preacher in the Midlands: he boasted of having baptized 7,000 born-again souls. Before 1650 he joined the Society of Ranters, an extreme sect whose faith in the universal immanence of God's holy spirit led them to reject conventional morality. Coppe seems to have demonstrated his freedom from mere law – civil as well as Mosaic – by preaching naked, openly espousing adultery and cursing, and by having some sort of sexual relations in public with gypsies or street people. He was imprisoned for publishing his Fiery Flying Roll *(1649), and the work was ordered to be seized and burned by the hangman. Coppe recanted in 1651 and began leading a less conspicuous public life. After the Restoration he changed his infamous name and practiced medicine as Dr Higham.*

The prose style of his pamphlets is as incendiary as their asseverations. Although Coppe is extreme in every way, elements of his thinking (or feeling) appear in the works of several writers of the period. Bunyan and Blake, as well as the more conservative Smart and Collins, felt some of the enthusiasm so evident in Coppe; even Milton, though his conviction of revelation led to moral rigidity rather than looseness, evinces a confidence in the accuracy of his personal vision that resembles Coppe's. The following passages are based on the 1650 edition of the first and second Fiery Roll, *which is reprinted in* A Collection of Ranter Writings from the 17th Century, *edited by Nigel Smith (Junction Books, 1983).*

from A Fiery Flying Roll:[1]

A

Word from the Lord to all the Great Ones of the Earth, whom this may concern: Being the last WARNING PIECE *at the dreadful day of* JUDGEMENT
For now the LORD *is come* (1650)

to
   {
1 *Inform*
2 *Advise and warn*
3 *Charge*
4 *Judge and sentence*
}
   the Great Ones

FROM A FIERY FLYING ROLL
[1] *Roll*   "Writing rolled upon itself" (Johnson).

As also most compassionately informing, and most lovingly and pathetically
advising and warning
London.

With a terrible Word, and fatal Blow from the LORD, upon the Gathered
CHURCHES.

And all by his Most Excellent MAJESTY, dwelling in, and shining through
AUXILIUM PATRIS,[2] [KP, in Hebrew] alias, *Coppe.*

With another FLYING ROLL ensuing (to all the Inhabitants of the Earth) The
Contents of both following.

*Isa{iah} 23.9 The Lord of Hosts (is) staining the pride of all glory, and bringing
into contempt all the honourable (persons and things) of the Earth.*
*O London, London, how would I gather thee, as a hen gathereth her chickens
under her wings, &c.*[3]
Know thou (in this thy day) the things that belong to thy Peace—[4]
I know the blasphemy of them which say they are Jews, and are not, but are the Synagogue of Satan,
Rev[elation] 2.9.
Imprinted at *London,* in the beginning of that notable day, wherein the secrets of all hearts
are laid open; and wherein the worst and foulest of villanies, are discovered, under the best
and fairest outsides. 1649.

THE
PREFACE

An inlet into the Land of Promise, the new *Jerusalem*, and a gate into the ensuing
Discourse, worthy of serious consideration.

My Dear One.
All or None.
Every one under the Sun.
Mine own.
My most Excellent Majesty (in me) hath strangely and variously transformed this form.
And behold, by mine own Almightiness (In me) I have been changed in a moment, in the
twinkling of an eye, at the sound of the Trump.[5]
And now the Lord is descended from Heaven, with a shout, with the voice of the
Archangel, and with the Trump of God.
And the sea, the earth, yea all things are now giving up their dead. And all things that
ever were, are, or shall be visible – are the Grave wherein the King of Glory (the eternal,
invisible Almightiness, hath lain as it were) dead and buried.
But behold, behold, he is now risen with a witness, to save *Zion* with vengeance, or to
confound and plague all things into himself; who by his mighty Angel is proclaiming (with
a loud voice) That Sin and Transgression is finished and ended; and everlasting righteousness
brought in; and the everlasting Gospel preaching; Which everlasting Gospel is brought in
with most terrible earth-quakes, and heaven-quakes, and with signs and wonders following.
Amen.

---

[2]   *Auxilium patris*   the aid of his country.
[3]   *O London* . . .   substituted for Jerusalem in this reference to Matthew 23.37.
[4]   *Know thou* . . .   a version of Luke 19.42.
[5]   *Trump*   trumpet, horn (see 1 Corinthians 15.52).

And it hath pleased my most Excellent Majesty, (who is universal love, and whose service is perfect freedom) to set this form (the Writer of this Roll) as no small sign and wonder in fleshly *Israel*; as you may partly see in the ensuing Discourse.

And now (my dear ones!) every one under the Sun, I will only point at the gate; through which I was led into that new City, new *Jerusalem*, and to the Spirits of just men, made perfect, and to God the Judge of all.

First, all my strength, my forces were utterly routed, my house I dwelt in fired; my father and mother forsook me, the wife of my bosom loathed me, mine old name was rotted, perished; and I was utterly plagued, consumed, damned, rammed, and sunk into nothing, into the bowels of the still Eternity (my mother's womb) out of which I came naked, and whitherto I returned again naked. And lying a while there, rapt up in silence, at length (the body or outward form being awake all this while) I heard with my outward ear (to my apprehension) a most terrible thunder-clap, and after that a second. And upon the second thunder-clap, which was exceeding terrible, I saw a great body of light, like the light of the Sun, and red as fire, in the form of a drum (as it were) whereupon with exceeding trembling and amazement on the flesh, and with joy unspeakable in the spirit, I clapped my hands, and cried out, '*Amen, Halelujah, Halelujah, Amen*'. And so lay trembling, sweating and smoking (for the space of half an hour) at length with a loud voice (I inwardly) cried out, 'Lord, what wilt thou do with me; my most excellent majesty and eternal glory (in me) answered & said, 'Fear not, I will take thee up into mine everlasting Kingdom. But thou shalt (first) drink a bitter cup, a bitter cup, a bitter cup'; whereupon (being filled with exceeding amazement) I was thrown into the belly of hell (and take what you can of it in these expressions, though the matter is beyond expression) I was among all the Devils in hell, even in their most hideous hue.

And under all this terror, and amazement, there was a little spark of transcendent, transplendent, unspeakable glory, which survived, and sustained it self, triumphing, exulting, and exalting it self above all the Fiends. And confounding the very blackness of darkness (you must take it in these terms, for it is infinitely beyond expression.) Upon this the life was taken out of the body (for a season) and it was thus resembled, as if a man with a great brush dipped in whiting,[6] should with one stroke wipe out, or sweep off a picture upon a wall, &c.; after a while, breath and life was returned into the form again; whereupon I saw various streams of light (in the night) which appeared to the outward eye; and immediately I saw three hearts (or three appearances) in the form of hearts, of exceeding brightness; and immediately an innumerable company of hearts, and yet most strangely and unexpressibly complicated or folded up in unity. I clearly saw distinction, diversity, variety, and as clearly saw all swallowed up into unity. And it hath been my song many times since, within and without, unity, universality, universality, unity, Eternal Majesty, &c.. And at this vision, a most strong, glorious voice uttered these words, *The spirits of just men made perfect*. The spirits &c., with whom I had as absolute, clear, full communion, and in a two-fold more familiar way, than ever I had outwardly with my dearest friends, and nearest relations. The visions and revelations of God, and the strong hand of eternal invisible almightiness, was stretched out upon me, within me, for the space of four days and nights, without intermission.

The time would fail if I would tell you all, but it is not the good will and pleasure of my most excellent Majesty in me, to declare any more (as yet) than thus* such further: That

---

6   *whiting*   "A soft chalk" (Johnson).

*   It not being shown to me, what I should do, more than preach and print something, et cetera, very little expecting I should be so strangely acted, as to (my exceeding joy and delight) I have been, though to the utter cracking of my credit, and to the rotting of my old name which is damned, and cast out (as a toad to the dunghill) that I might have a new name, with me, upon me, within me, which is, "I am –" [Coppe's marginal note].

amongst those various voices that were then uttered within, these were some, 'Blood, blood, Where, where? upon the hypocritical holy heart, &c.'. Another thus, 'Vengeance, vengeance, vengeance, Plagues, plagues, upon the Inhabitants of the earth; Fire, fire, fire, Sword, sword, &c. upon all that bow now down to eternal Majesty, universal love; I'll recover, recover, my wool, my flax, my money. Declare, declare, fear thou not the faces of any; I am (in thee) a munition of Rocks, &c.' [Hosea 2.9]

Go up to *London,* to *London,* that great City, write, write, write. And behold I writ, and lo a hand was sent to me, and a roll of a book was therein, which this fleshly hand would have put wings to, before the time. Whereupon it was snatched out of my hand, & the Roll thrust into my mouth; and I eat it up, and filled my bowels with it, (*Ezekiel.* 2.8, 3.1–3) where it was as bitter as worm-wood; and it lay broiling, and burning in my stomach, till I brought it forth in this form.

And now I send it flying to thee, with my heart, And all
Per AUXILIUM PATRIS [Hebrew letters KP]

CHAPTER V

The Author's strange and lofty carriage towards great ones, and his most lowly carriage towards Beggars, Rogues, and Gypsies: together with a large declaration what glory shall rise up from under all this ashes. The most strange, secret, terrible, yet most glorious design of God, in choosing base things to confound things that are. And how. A most terrible vial[7] poured out upon the well-favoured Harlot,[8] and how the Lord is bringing into contempt not only honourable persons, with a vengeance, but all honourable, holy things also. Wholesome advice, with a terrible threat to the Formalists.[9] How base things have confounded base things; and how base things have been a fiery Chariot to mount the Author up into divine glory, &c.. And how his wife is, and his life is in, that beauty which makes all visible beauty seem mere deformity.

1. And because I am found of those that sought me not. And because some say, wilt thou not tell us what these things are to us, that thou dost so?

Wherefore waving my charging so many Coaches, so many hundreds of men and women of the greater rank, in the open streets, with my hand stretched out, my hat cock't up, staring on them as if I would look through them, gnashing with my teeth at some of them, and day and night with a huge loud voice proclaiming the day of the Lord throughout London and Southwark, and leaving divers other exploits, &c. It is my good will and pleasure (only) to single out the former story with its Parallels.

2. (*Viz.*) in clipping,[10] hugging, embracing, kissing a poor deformed wretch in London, who had no more nose on his face, than I have on the back of my hand (but only two little holes in the place where the nose used to stand).[11]

And no more eyes to be seen than on the back of my hand, and afterwards running back to him in a strange manner, with my money giving it to him, to the joy of some, to the afrightment and wonderment of other Spectators.

3. As also in falling down flat upon the ground before rogues, beggars, cripples, halt, maimed; blind, &c. kissing the feet of many, rising up again, and giving them money, &c.

[7] *vial* one of the seven vials of the wrath of God (Revelation 16).
[8] *Harlot* a corrupt city or people (Isaiah 1.21; Hosea 4.15).
[9] *Formalist* "One who practises external ceremony; one who prefers appearance to reality; one who seems what he is not" (Johnson).
[10] *clipping* embracing.
[11] Loss of nose flesh was a commonly recognized symptom of advanced syphilis.

Besides that notorious business with the Gypsies and Gaolbirds[12] (mine own brethren and sisters, flesh of my flesh, and as good as the greatest Lord in England) at the prison in Southwark near St *George's* Church.

Now that which rises up from under all this heap of ashes, will fire both heaven and earth; the one's ashamed, and blushes already, the other reels to and fro, like a drunken man.

4. Wherefore thus saith the Lord, 'Hear O heavens, and harken O earth, I'll overturn, overturn, I am now [sta]ining the pride of all glory, and bringing into contempt all the honourable of the earth' (*Isaiah* 23.9), not only honourable persons (who shall come down with a vengeance, if they bow not to universal love the eternal God, whose service is perfect freedom) but honourable things, as Elderships, Pastorships, Fellowships, Churches, Ordinances, Prayers, &c. Holinesses, Righteousnesses, Religions of all sorts, of the highest strains; yea, Mysterians,[13] and Spiritualists, who scorn carnal Ordinances, &c.

I am about my act, my strange act, my work, my strange work, that whosoever hears of it, both his ears shall tingle.[14]

5. I am confounding, plaguing, tormenting nice, demure, barren *Michal*,[15] with *David's* unseemly carriage, by skipping, leaping, dancing, like one of the fools, vile, base fellows, shamelessely, basely, and uncovered too before handmaids –

Which thing was St *Paul's* Tutor, or else it prompted him to write, 'God hath chosen BASE things, and things that are despised, to confound – the things are –'[16]

Well! family duties are no base things; they ar[e] things that ARE: Churches, Ordinances, &c, are no BASE things, though indeed Presbyterian Churches begun to live i' th womb, but died there, and rot and stink there to the death of the mother and child. Amen. Not by the Devil, but (by* God) it's true.

Grace before meat and after meat, are no BASE things; these are things that ARE. But how long Lord, holy and true, &c.

Fasting for strife and debate, and to smite with the fist of wickedness, – (and not for taking off heavy burthens, breaking every yoke, *Isaiah.* 58 [4]) and Thanksgiving days for killing of men for money, are no BASE things, these are things that ARE.

→Starting up into the notion of spirituals, scorning History, speaking nothing but Mystery, crying down carnal ordinances, &c. is a fine thing among many, it's no base thing (now adays) though it be a cloak for covetousness, yea, though it be to maintain pride and pomp; these are no base things.

6. These are things that ARE, and must be confounded by BASE things, which *St Paul* saith, not God hath connived at, winked at, permitted, tolerated, But God has CHOSEN &c. BASE things.

What base things? Why Michal took *David* for a base fellow, and thought he had chosen BASE things, in dancing shamelessly uncovered before handmaids.

And barren, demure *Michal* thinks ('for I know her heart', saith the Lord) that I chose base things when I sat down, and eat and drank around on the ground with Gypsies, and clip't, hugged, and kissed them, putting my hand in their bosoms, loving the she-Gypsies dearly. O base! saith mincing *Michal,* the least spark of modesty would be as red as crimson or scarlet, to hear this.

---

[12] *Gaolbirds* jailbirds.
[13] *Mysterians* mystics (not in *OED*).
[14] *ears shall tingle* "When our cheek burneth or ear tingleth, we usually say that somebody is talking of us" (Browne, *Pseudodoxia Epidemica* 5.22).

[15] *Michal* the younger daughter of King Saul, given to David in marriage, but, disapproving of David's dancing and revelry, she was rejected and died childless.
[16] *God hath chosen* 1 Corinthians 1.28.
* "That's a base thing" [Coppe's marginal note].

I warrant me, *Michal* could better have borne this if I had done it to Ladies: so I can for a need, if it be my will, and that in the height of honour and majesty, without sin. But at that time when I was hugging the Gipsies, I abhorred the thoughts of Ladies, their beauty could not bewitch mine eyes, or snare my lips, or entangle my hands in their bosoms; yet I can if it be my will, kiss and hug Ladies, and love my neighbour's wife as my self, without sin.

7. But thou Precisian,[17] by what name or title soever dignified, or distinguished, do but blow a kiss to thy neighbour's wife, or dare to think of darting one glance of one of thine eyes towards her, if thou dar'st.

It's meat and drink to an Angel (who knows none evil, no sin) so swear a full-mouthed oath, *Rev{elation}* 10.6. It's joy to *Nehemiah* to come in like a mad-man, and pluck folks' hair off their beards, and curse like a devil – and make them swear by God – *Nehem{iah}* 13.[25]. Do thou O holy man (who knows evil) lift up thy finger against a Jew, a Church-member, call thy brother fool, and with a peasecods on him;[18] or swear i' faith, if thou dar'st, if thou dost, thou shalt howl in hell for it, and I will laugh at thy calamity, &c.

8. But once more hear O heavens, hearken O earth, Thus saith the Lord, I have chosen such base things, to confound things that are, that the ears of those (who scorn to be below Independents, yea the ears of many who scorn to be so low as carnal Ordinances, &c.) that hear thereof shall tingle.

9. Hear one word more (whom it hitteth it hitteth) give over thy base nasty stinking, formal grace before meat, and after meat (I call it so, though thou hast rebaptized it –) give over thy stinking family duties, and thy Gospel Ordinances as thou callest them; for under them all there lies snapping, snarling, biting, besides covetousness, horrid hypocrisy, envy, malice, evil surmising.

10. Give over, give over, or if nothing else will do it, I'll at a time, when thou least of all thinkest of it, make thine own child the fruit of thy loins, in whom thy soul delighted, lie with a whore – before thine eyes: That that plaguey holiness and righteousness of thine might be confounded by that base thing. And thou be plagued back again into thy mother's womb, the womb of eternity: That thou may'st become a little child, and let the mother *Eternity, Almightiness*, who is universal love, and whose service is perfect freedom, dress thee, and undress thee, swaddle, unswaddle, bind, loose, lay thee down, take thee up, &c.

– And to such a little child, undressing is as good as dressing, foul clothes, as good as fair clothes – he knows no evil, &c. – And shall see evil no more, – but he must first lose all his righteousness, every bit of his holiness, and every crumb of his Religion, and be plagued, and confounded (by base things) into nothing.

By base things which God and I have chosen

11. And yet I show you a more excellent way, when you have passed this. – In a word, my plaguey, filthy, nasty holiness hath been confounded by base things. And then (behold I show you a mystery, and put forth a riddle to you) by base things, base things so called have been confounded also; and thereby have I been confounded into eternal Majesty, unspeakable glory, my life, my self.

12. There's my riddle, but because neither all the Lords of the Philistines, no nor my Delilah her self can read it,

I'll read it my self, I'll (only) hint it thus.

Kisses are numbered amongst transgressors – base things – well! by bare hellish swearing, and cursing, (as I have accounted it in the time of my fleshly holiness) and by base impudent

---

[17] *Precisian* "One who is superstitiously rigorous"   [18] *a peasecods on him*   a mock curse.
(Johnson).

kisses (as I then accounted them) my plaguey holiness hath been confounded, and thrown into the lake of fire and brimstone.

And then again, by wanton kisses, kissing hath been confounded; and external kisses, have been made the fiery chariots, to mount me swiftly into the bosom of him whom my soul loves, (his excellent Majesty, the king of glory).

Where I have been, where I have been, where I have been, hugged, embraced, and kissed with the kisses of his mouth, whose loves are better than wine, and have been utterly overcome therewith, beyond expression, beyond admiration.

13. Again, Lust is numbered amongt transgressors – a base thing. –

Now fair objects attract Spectators' eyes.

And beauty is the father of lust or love.

Well! I have gone along the streets impregnant with that child (lust) which as particular beauty had begot: but coming to the place, where I expected to have been delivered, I have providentially met there a company of devils in appearance, though Angels with golden vials, in reality, pouring out full vials, of such odious abominable words, that are not lawful to be uttered.

Words enough to deafen the ears of plaguey holinesse. And such horrid abominable actions, the sight whereof were enough to put out holy man's eyes, and to strike him stark dead, &c.

These base things (I saw) words and actions, have confounded and plagued to death, the child in the womb that I was so big of.

14. And by, and through these BASE things (as upon the wings of the wind) have I been carried up into the arms of my love, which is invisible glory, eternal Majesty, purity it self, unspotted beauty, even that beauty which maketh all other beauty but mere ugliness, when set against it, &c.

Yea, could you imagine that the quintessence of all visible beauty, should be extracted and made up into one huge beauty, it would appear to be mere deformity to that beauty, which through BASE things I have been lifted up into.

Which transcendent, unspeakable, unspotted beauty, is my crown and joy, my life and love: and though I have chosen, and cannot be without BASE things, to confound some in mercy, some in judgement, Though also I have concubines without number, which I cannot be without, yet this is my spouse, my love, my dove, my fair one.

Now I proceed to that which follows.

Anna Trapnel (1620?–1660?)

A short pamphlet entitled Strange and Wonderful NEWS FROM WHITE-HALL: Or, The Mighty Visions PROCEEDING From Mistress ANNA TRAPNEL *(1654) relates "how she lay eleven days, and twelve nights in a Trance, without taking any sustenance, except a cup of small Beer once in 24 hours." During this time Trapnel "sang" or "uttered" various things and had "many Visions, and Revelations touching the Government of the Nation, the Parliament, Army, and Ministry." Her vision was apocalyptic, involving the image of the lamb with horns prominent in the Book of Revelation. Her dream vision and utterances suggest that Parliament is in danger and argue for greater preparedness on the part of the army. It was also in 1654 that Trapnel was arrested, threatened with prosecution as a witch, and perhaps temporarily committed to Bridewell, a prison for the insane. She managed to maintain her freedom, however, and in 1657 she entered a trance reported to have lasted ten months.*

The following excerpt is from The Cry of a Stone: or a Relation of Something spoken in Whitehall, *a longer pamphlet (76 pages) than the newsy one cited above; it describes Trapnel's experience in greater detail and quotes or purports to quote many hundred lines of her spontaneous prayers or songs. The text is based on the first edition (1654) and represents a small portion of the first and all of the last song.*

from *The Cry of a Stone: or a Relation of Something spoken in Whitehall* (1654)

When Babylon within, the great and tall,
With tumults shall come down:
Then that which is without shall fall,
And be laid flat on the ground.

Oh King Jesus thou art longed for,   5
Oh take thy power and reign,
And let thy children see thy face,
Which with them shall remain.

Thy lovely looks will be so bright,
They will make them to sing,   10
They shall bring offerings unto thee,
And myrrh unto their King.

For they know that thou dost delight
To hear their panting soul;
They do rejoice in thy Marrow,   15
And esteem it more than gold.

Therefore thou hearing their hearts cry,
Thou sayest, Oh wait a while!
And suddenly thou wilt draw near,
The world's glory to spoil.   20

Oh you shall have great Rolls of writ
Concerning Babylon's fall,
And the destruction of the Whore,
Which now seems spiritual.

. . . .

Oh glorious Lord, thou dost break forth
Unto thy servant here,
Oh the glorious shine of the great God[1]
Most lovely doth appear.

FROM *THE CRY OF A STONE*
[1] *shine* "Brightness; splendour; lustre. It is word,   though not unanalogical, yet ungraceful, and little used" (Johnson).

Oh the Seal of God is glorious,[2]   5
It is a Seal abides,
Oh, it doth seal the soul to thee
That art its running tides.

Oh a Seal of the mighty Lord,
When others are gone, there comes   10
The fresh discoveries of that seal,
Given forth by thee the Son.

A broad seal sure, oh Lord it is,
Which none can break in sunder,
Yet it is a seal that is within,   15
No foe can come it plunder.

A seal that is not by men here,
To be melted at all,
But it is a seal which thou dost keep,
It never here shall fall.   20

Thy servant Lord shall be preserved
By this thy seal of Love,
Which over and over thou bringest down,
From the Eternal Love.

Oh that all thine may know what 'tis,   25
That so they might up mount,
To magnify the Lord their God,[3]
And give of this Account.

For who can Lord, show forth, but those
To whom thou doest it bring,   30
Oh, who can with language set forth
The sealing of their King?

Oh, thou dear Christ, first sealèd was,
That sealèd One indeed,
And through thee thine they do partake   35
A sealing in their need.

When they are in great despairings,
And in great temptations lie,
Oh then comes forth the seal to them,
And draws them through the sky.   40

Through all Clouds they most swiftly fly
Unto their Saviour great,

---

[2] *the Seal of God*   in the vision of John, before the apocalypse the foreheads of God's servants are marked   with the protective "seal of the living God" (Revelation 7.2).

[3] *magnify*   honor; praise; extol.

Which bids them welcome unto him,
And to his Mercy Seat.[4]

Where they shall see his loving heart,   45
And his embracing arms,
Where they shall be for evermore,
Taken up from all these harms.

Lucy Apsley Hutchinson (1620–1681)

Hutchinson's birthdate is better known than that of many seventeenth-century women because she was born in the Tower of London. Her father, a Lieutenant of the Tower, gave her an extraordinary education, which included tuition in Latin as well as French and the more traditional female studies of needlework and music. Her bent was for serious study and her skill in it is shown in the sophisticated, allusive prose of her most important work, Memoirs of the Life of Colonel Hutchinson, *her husband. Hutchinson's work is almost incredibly laudatory and presents a vision of marital subordination that might have prevented the Fall of Mankind, had it been adopted in the Garden of Eden. On the other hand, Hutchinson's volubility and articulation (both in her* Memoirs *and, evidently, in her pleas on behalf of her staunchly puritan husband to royalist friends) argue a degree of independence and certainly self-confidence.*

The Memoirs *were not so titled and published until 1806, although they were written shortly after John Hutchinson's death in prison in 1664. The portion that follows recounts the betrothal, marriage, and early married life of the couple; my presentation is based on the recent edition by James Sutherland (Oxford University Press, 1973), which prints the full text of the manuscript for the first time.*

from *Memoirs of the Life of Colonel Hutchinson* (1664)

They had not six weeks enjoyed this peace but the young men and women, who saw them allow each other that kindness which they did not commonly afford to others, first began to grow jealous and envious at it, and after to use all the malicious practices they could invent to break the friendship. Among the rest, that gentleman who at the first had so highly commended her to Mr. Hutchinson now began to caution him against her, and to disparage her with such subtle insinuations as would have ruined any love less constant and honourable than his. The women, with witty spite, represented all her faults to him, which chiefly terminated in the negligence of her dress and habit and all womanish ornaments, giving herself wholly up to study and writing. Mr. Hutchinson, who had a very pleasant and sharp wit, retorted all their malice with such just reproofs of their idleness and vanity as made them hate her who, without affecting it, had so engaged such a person in her protection as they with all their arts could not catch. He in the mean time prosecuted his love with so much discretion, duty, and honour, that at the length, through many difficulties, he accomplished his design.

---

[4] *Mercy Seat* the covering of the ark of the covenant;
the place where God received offerings of atonement and
communed with his people (Exodus 25.17–22).

I shall pass by all the little amorous relations, which if I would take the pains to relate, would make a true history of a more handsome management of love than the best romances describe; for these are to be forgotten as the vanities of youth, not worthy mention among the greater transactions of his life. There is only this to be recorded, that never was there a passion more ardent and less idolatrous; he loved her better than his life, with unexpressable tenderness and kindness, had a most high obliging esteem of her, yet still considered honour, religion, and duty above her, nor ever suffered the intrusion of such a dotage as should blind him from marking her imperfections; which he looked upon with such an indulgent eye as did not abate his love and esteem of her, while it augmented his care to blot out all those spots which might make her appear less worthy of that respect he paid her. And thus indeed he soon made her more equal to him than he found her, for she was a very faithful mirror, reflecting truly, though but dimly, his own glories upon him, so long as he was present; but she, that was nothing before his inspection gave her a fair figure, when he was removed was only filled with a dark mist, and could never again take in any delightful object, nor return any shining representation. The greatest excellence she had was the power of apprehending and the virtue[1] of loving his. So, as his shadow, she waited on him everywhere, till he was taken into that region of light which admits of none, and then she vanished into nothing. 'Twas not her face he loved, her honour and virtue were his mistresses, and these (like Pygmalion's[2]) images of his own making, for he polished and gave form to what he found with all the roughness of the quarry about it; but meeting a compliant subject to his own wise government, he found as much satisfaction as he gave, and never had occasion to number his marriage among his infelicities.

That day that the friends on both sides met to conclude the marriage, she fell sick of the small pox, which was many ways a great trial upon him; first her life was almost in desperate hazard, and then the disease, for the present, made her the most deformed person that could be seen for a great while after she recovered. Yet he was nothing troubled at it, but married her as soon as she was able to quit the chamber, when the priest and all that saw her were affrighted to look on her; but God recompensed his justice and constancy by restoring her, though she was longer than ordinary before she recovered as well as before. One thing is very observable, and worthy imitation in him: although he had as strong and violent affections for her as ever any man had, yet he declared it not to her till he had acquainted first his father, and after never would make any engagement but what his love and honour bound him in, wherein he was more firm and just than all the promissory oaths and ties in the world could have made him, notwithstanding many powerful temptations of wealth and beauty, and other interests that were laid before him; for his father had concluded another treaty, before he knew his son's inclinations were this way fixed, with a party in many things much more advantageable for his family, and more worthy of his liking. But the father was no less honourably indulgent to his son's affection than the son was strict in the observance of his duty, and at length, to the full content of all, the thing was accomplished, and on the third day of July, in the year 1638, being tuesday, he was married to Mrs. Lucy Apsley, the second daughter of Sir Allen Apsley, late Lieutenant of the Tower of London, at St Andrew's Church in Holborn, where he lived with her mother, in a place called Bartlett's Court. But four months were scarce past after their marriage before he was in very great danger to have lost her, when she lost two children she had conceived by him; and soon after conceiving again, grew so sickly that her indulgent mother and husband, for the advantage of her health,

FROM *MEMOIRS OF THE LIFE OF COLONEL HUTCHINSON*
[1]   *virtue*   power.

[2]   *Pygmalion*   a king of Cyprus who fell in love with an ivory statue of his own creation; Aphrodite brought the statue to life, and the maiden became his wife.

removed their dwelling out of the city to a house they took in Enfield Chace called the blue house, where, upon the third of September 1639, being wednesday, about two of the clock in the morning, she was brought to bed of two sons, whereof the elder he named after his own father, Thomas, the younger was called Edward, who both survived him. In September 1641 she brought him another son, called by his own name, John, who lived scarce six years, and was a very hopeful child, full of his father's vigour and spirit, but death soon nipped that blossom.

Mr. Hutchinson, after fourteen months various exercise of his mind in the pursuit of his love, being now at rest in the enjoyment of his wife, his next design was to draw her into his own country, but he would not set upon it too roughly, and therefore let her rest a while, when he had drawn her ten miles nearer it out of the City, where she had her birth and education, and where all her relations were most conversant, which she could not suddenly resolve to quit for altogether to betake herself to the North, which was a formidable name among the London ladies. While she was weaning from the friends and places she had so long conversed in, Mr. Hutchinson employed his time in making an entrance upon the study of School Divinity, wherein his father was the most eminent scholar of any Gentleman in England, and had a most choice library, valued at a thousand pounds; which Mr. Hutchinson, mistakingly expecting to be part of his inheritance, thought it would be very inglorious for him not to understand how to make use of his father's books. Having therefore gotten into the house with him an excellent scholar in that kind of learning, he for two years made it the whole employment of his time, and converted the Gentleman that assisted him to a right belief in that great point of Predestination, he having been before of the Arminian[3] judgement, till upon the serious examination of both principles, and comparing them with the Scriptures, Mr. Hutchinson convinced him of the truth, and grew so well instructed in this principle that he was able to maintain it against any man.

At that time this great doctrine grew much out of fashion with the Prelates,[4] but was generally embraced by all religious and holy persons in the land. Mr. Hutchinson being desirous to inform himself thoroughly of it, when he was able to manange the question, offered it to his father, but Sir Thomas would not declare himself in the point to him, nor indeed in any other, as we conceived, lest a father's authority might sway against his children's light, who he thought ought to discern things with their own eyes, and not with his. Mr. Hutchinson taking delight in the study of divinity, presently left off all foolish nice points that tended to nothing but vain brangling, and employed his whole study in laying in a foundation of sound and necessary principles, among which he gave the first place to this of God's absolute decrees; which was so far from producing a carelesseness of life in him, a thing usually objected against this faith, that, on the other side, it excited him to a more strict and holy walking in thankfulness to God, who had been pleased to choose him out of the corrupted mass of lost mankind to fix his love upon him, and give him knowledge of himself by his ever blessed Son. This principle of love and life in God, which had been given him even when he discerned not what it was in himself, had from a child preserved him from fleshly lusts and pollutions, and from wallowing in the mire of sin and wickedness wherein most of the gentry of those times were miserably plunged, except a few that were therefore the scorn of mankind; and but few of those few that had not natural and superstitious follies that were in some kind justly ridiculous and contemptible. But that spark of divine love, which had warmed his bosom before he discerned it, began now to reveal it self in a little flame,

---

3 *Arminian* following the doctrine of Arminius, who believed predestination to be conditional, in opposition to Calvin who thought it absolute.

4 *Prelates* the bishops and other high church officers.

comparatively to that bright blaze which afterward lighted him home to his father's palace. Now he began to practise his devotion upon knowledge and to delight in studying the doctrines of the Lord, he made a happy progress in discovery of the false, carnal and Antichristian Doctrines of Rome; and while he was viewing the sermons and practice of the Lord and his Apostles he began to suspect what, in reverence to the usurped name of mother, he had never yet called into question – the whorish dress and behaviour of that which called it self the Church of England. But this was only a time of dawning, and he by degrees was led up into the brighter sunshine with which it pleased the Lord to enlighten him.

It is only a remarkable providence of the Lord in his life, which must not be passed over without special notice, how God took this time to instruct him, when he had given him rest from all the passions which commonly distract young people, and sequestered him into a private life before he had yet many domestic concernments to divert his mind. If small things may be compared with great, it seems to me not unlike the preparation of Moses in the wilderness with his father in law, where it is thought he writ the book of Genesis, some believe that of Job; certain it is he was sequestered from Pharaoh's Court, allowed the consolation of a wife and blessed with two sons in his retirement, and had more pleasure in the contemplation of God's great works than in all the enjoyments of the world's vain pomps, before he was thus prepared to be a leader of God's people out of bondage; and afterwards, when he had seen the fall of his enemies, passing safe and dryshod through that sea where all their proud foes were drowned, amidst the sorrows and difficulties of passing through a barren wilderness with a murmuring discontented people, in the holy mount and wilderness Tabernacle received more full and glorious instructions from God and discoveries of him, yet, after all, was but allowed a Pisgah's sight of Canaan.[5] In these things the parallel runs evenly along, and bears a similitude of that great prince as limnings do of larger tables, or small drops, of the whole spherical body of water. Mr. Hutchinson lived in his mother in law's house, had two sons there born, was sequestered from a wicked court and country into a solitude not unpleasant, exercised himself in contemplation of the first works and discoveries of God. Here he beheld the burning bush still unconsumed, here had a call to go back to deliver his country, groaning under spiritual and civil bondage. Indeed in this point, as no parallel holds in all, there was a vast difference between the silent whispers of the spirit, which led him back and told him not his work before he was engaged in it, and between that visible miraculous power which was given to Moses to carry on his work alone, on whom the spirit of glory was by so much the more resplendent, in as much as he was called to be the Lord's sole Viceroy, and the great General of God's Host. Mr. Hutchinson was joined with many partners equally sharing the work, and the strength given out for it, and many of them set in more eminent places than he, who made it only his business to perform what he was called to in the station God set him, and never had aspiring thoughts to step out of that rank, where he ever sought the Lord's, not his own, glory. The great deliverance of God's people, their unthankfulness and miscarriage after it, no less than theirs of old, is too sadly known to all. What grief and exercise of spirit this was to the Moseses of our times those that have been witnesses of it cannot but with bleeding hearts remember: in this, whosoever considers the following history shall find that Mr. Hutchinson again might often take up the parallel of the great Hebrew Prince; and if we may allegorize the eminent place of suffering into which God called him up at last, there it was in the bleak mountains of affliction that the Lord instructed

---

[5]   *a Pisgah's sight of Canaan*   Moses saw the promised land from Mount Pisgah but never crossed the Jordan river into it (Deuteronomy 34.1–4); most of the story of Moses and the Israelites forty years' sojourn in the desert is recounted in the Book of Exodus.

him in his law, and showed him a pattern of his glorious tabernacle, and gave him a fuller discovery of his person. To one of these he was led up to see the promised land, and had a soul-refreshing view of it: such a one as made him forget on what side of the river he stood, while by faith he took possession of future glory, and resigned himself in the assured hope of returning with the Lord and his great Army of Saints.

Andrew Marvell (1621–1678)

In 1657, a year before Oliver Cromwell's death, Marvell became Milton's associate Latin secretary for the Commonwealth. Unlike his elder colleague, Marvell remained in government service after the Restoration, being thrice elected the MP for his home district of Hull. He had influence enough to defend Milton from the possibility of prosecution for aiding and abetting regicide, and he served as secretary on several diplomatic missions abroad. Gradually, however, he became deeply disaffected: he composed satirical poems about Charles II, his government and its defenders (including John Dryden); and he published anti-government pamphlets, including the anonymous and sensational Account of the Growth of Popery and Arbitrary Government in England *(1677). Most of Marvell's poetry did not appear until after his death.* Miscellaneous Poems *came out in 1681, but in every known copy of this edition but one Marvell's "Horatian Ode upon Cromwell's Return from Ireland" was canceled during the process of publication, and the poem did not reappear in print until 1776. Some of Marvell's other Cromwell poems suffered a similar fate, and his satires on the monarchy circulated only in manuscript form until after the Glorious Revolution of 1688. Although it does not lampoon anyone, Marvell's "Horatian Ode" is a powerful endorsement of Cromwell's most militant posture; it glorifies the execution of Charles; and it is excellent poetry that tends to recommend its opinions by the strength of its expression; it is dangerous literature at its best.*

However, some readers will prefer Marvell's less political verse (practically no verse could be apolitical at this time). The poems are metaphysical, perhaps definitively so in the case of "On a Drop of Dew," yet they elude the kind of solutions and closure found in the similar verse of the previous generation. "The Garden," "The Nymph's Complaint," and "Bermudas" are poems without answers or settled meanings. This may be true of all great poems, but these verses seem at first to invite us into a world of theorems and proofs, a Pythagorean world in which formulas may actually describe the world. But we soon find we have been misled; there is an enameled, artificial quality to the world we enter, but we can neither penetrate the surface to understand the experience below nor become satisfied that the poem is mere artifice. States of mind are expressed in Marvell's verse, sometimes several states in a single poem, but the furniture of these states of mind is so elegantly turned that we feel we have entered a society that may be too sophisticated for us to comprehend. There is some sense of this even when lust is the state of mind, as in "To his Coy Mistress." The speaker has such total command over the commonplaces of seduction verse and is able to deliver them with such poise that it seems reasonable to doubt he is ever, like mere mortals, subject to his passions.

The standard edition of Marvell's verse is edited by H. M. Margoliouth (Clarendon Press, 1927). I am indebted to his commentary, especially on the difficult "Horatian Ode." I follow him in using the British Library copy of Miscellaneous Poems *(1681) as my copytext.*

from *Miscellaneous Poems* (1681)

BERMUDAS (1653?)

Where the remote *Bermudas* ride
In th' Ocean's bosom unespied,
From a small Boat, that rowed along,
The listening Winds received this Song.
　　'What should we do but sing his Praise　　　　　5
That led us through the wat'ry Maze,
Unto an Isle so long unknown,
And yet far kinder than our own?
Where the huge Sea-Monsters wracks,
That lift the Deep upon their Backs.　　　　　10
He lands us on a grassy Stage;
Safe from the Storms, and Prelate's rage.[1]
He gave us this eternal Spring,
Which here enamels every thing;
And sends the Fowls to us in care,　　　　　15
On daily Visits through the Air,
He hangs in shades the Orange bright,
Like golden Lamps in a green Night.
And does in the Pomgranates close,
Jewels more rich than *Ormus* shows.[2]　　　　　20
He makes the Figs our mouths to meet;
And throws the Melons at our feet.
But Apples plants of such a price,[3]
No Tree could ever bear them twice.
With Cedars, chosen by his hand,[4]　　　　　25
From *Lebanon*, he stores the Land.
And makes the hollow Seas, that roar,
Proclaim the Ambergris on shore.[5]
He cast (of which we rather boast)
The Gospel's Pearl upon our Coast.[6]　　　　　30
And in these Rocks for us did frame
A Temple, where to sound his Name.
Oh let our voice his Praise exalt,
Till it arrive at Heaven's Vault:
Which thence (perhaps) rebounding, may　　　　　35
Echo beyond the *Mexique Bay'*.

BERMUDAS
[1] *Prelate* bishops or other high officers of the established church, from whom these Protestant singers have fled.
[2] *Ormus* fabulously wealthy city on the Persian Gulf.
[3] *Apples* pineapples, which must be replanted each year.
[4] *Cedars* Lebanon cedars are symbolic of great stature and power in biblical writings (e.g. Ezekiel 31.3).

[5] *Ambergris* "A fragrant drug . . . found on the seacoasts of several warm countries" (Johnson quoting Ephraim Chambers's *Cyclopaedia*); the origin of the substance was then obscure, but many connected it correctly with whales.
[6] *Gospel's Pearl* perhaps the pearl of great price symbolic of Heaven (Matthew 14.46).

Thus sung they, in the *English* boat,
An holy and a cheerful Note,
And all the way, to guide their Chime,
With falling Oars they kept the time.   40

THE NYMPH COMPLAINING FOR THE DEATH OF HER FAUN (1651–2?)

The wanton Troopers riding by[1]
Have shot my Faun and it will die.
Ungentle men! They cannot thrive
To kill thee. Thou ne'er didst alive
Them any harm: alas nor could   5
Thy death yet do them any good.
I'm sure I never wisht them ill;
Nor do I for all this; nor will:
But, if my simple Prayers may yet
Prevail with Heaven to forget   10
Thy murder, I will Join my Tears
Rather then fail. But, O my fears!
It cannot die so. Heaven's King
Keeps register of every thing:
And nothing may we use in vain.   15
Even Beasts must be with justice slain;
Else Men are made their *Deodands*.[2]
Though they should wash their guilty hands
In this warm life blood, which doth part
From thine, and wound me to the Heart,   20
Yet could they not be clean: their Stain
Is dyed in such a Purple Grain.[3]
There is not such another in
The World, to offer for their Sin.
      Unconstant *Sylvio*, when yet   25
I had not found him counterfeit,
One morning (I remember well)
Tied in this silver Chain and Bell,
Gave it to me: nay and I know
What he said then; I'm sure I do.   30
Said He, 'look how your Huntsman here
Hath taught a Faun to hunt his *Dear*.'
But *Sylvio* soon had me beguiled.
This waxed tame; while he grew wild,
And quite regardless of my Smart,   35
Left me his Faun, but took his Heart.[4]

THE NYMPH COMPLAINING FOR THE DEATH OF HER
FAUN
[1] *Trooper* "A horse soldier" (Johnson).
[2] *Deodand* "A thing given or forfeited to God for the
pacifying his wrath, in the case of any misfortune, by
which any Christian comes to a violent end, without the

fault of any reasonable creature" (Johnson, quoting John
Cowell); animals involved in human deaths were sometimes made deodands.
[3] *Grain* dye; color.
[4] *Heart* with a pun on *hart*, a male deer.

Thenceforth I set my self to play
My solitary time away,
With this: and very well content,
  Could so mine idle Life have spent.   40
For it was full of sport; and light
Of foot, and heart; and did invite,
Me to its game: it seem'd to bless
Its self in me. How could I less
Than love it? O I cannot be   45
Unkind, t' a Beast that loveth me.

  Had it lived long, I do not know
Whether it too might have done so
As *Sylvio* did: his Gifts might be
Perhaps as false or more than he.   50
But I am sure, for ought that I
Could in so short a time espy,
Thy Love was far more better than
The love of false and cruel men.

  With sweetest milk, and sugar, first   55
I it at mine own fingers nurst.
And as it grew, so every day
It waxed more white and sweet than they.
It had so sweet a Breath! And oft
I blusht to see its foot more soft,   60
And white – shall I say than my hand? –
NAY any Lady's of the Land.

  It is a wond'rous thing, how fleet
'Twas on those little silver feet.
With what a pretty skipping grace,   65
It oft would challenge me the Race:
And when 't had left me far away,
'Twould stay, and run again, and stay.
For it was nimbler much than Hinds;[5]
And trod, as on the foùr Winds.   70

  I have a Garden of my own,
But so with Roses over grown,
And Lillies, that you would it guess
To be a little Wilderness.
And all the Spring time of the year   75
It only lovèd to be there.
Among the beds of Lillies, I
Have sought it oft, where it should lie;
Yet could not, till it self would rise,
Find it, although before mine Eyes.   80
For, in the flaxen Lillies' shade,

---

[5]   *Hinds*   female deer.

It like a bank of Lillies laid.
Upon the Roses it would feed,
Until its Lips even seemed to bleed:
And then to me 'twould boldly trip,   85
And print those Roses on my Lip.
But all its chief delight was still
On Roses thus its self to fill:
And its pure virgin Limbs to fold
In whitest sheets of Lillies cold.   90
Had it lived long, it would have been
Lillies without, Roses within.
    O help! O help! I see it faint:
And die as calmly as a Saint.
See how it weeps. The Tears do come   95
Sad, slowly dropping like a Gum.
So weeps the wounded Balsam: so[6]
The holy Frankincense doth flow.
The brotherless *Heliades*[7]
Melt in such Amber Tears as these.   100
    I in a golden Vial will
Keep these two crystal Tears; and fill
It till it do o'erflow with mine;
Then place it in *Diana*'s Shrine.[8]
    Now my sweet Faun is vanished to   105
Whither the Swans and Turtles go:
In fair *Elysium* to endure,[9]
With milk-white Lambs, and Ermines pure.
O do not run too fast: for I
Will but bespeak thy Grave, and die.   110
    First my unhappy Statue shall
Be cut in Marble; and withal,
Let it be weeping too: but there
Th' Engraver sure his Art may spare;
For I so truly thee bemoan,   115
That I shall weep though I be Stone:
Until my Tears, still dropping, wear
My breast, themselves engraving there.
There at my feet shalt thou be laid,
Of purest Alabaster made: 120
For I would have thine Image be
White as I can, though not as Thee.

---

[6] *Balsam* a biblical tree which produces a healing ointment of the same name.
[7] *Heliades* sisters of Phaethon, who wept so piteously over his death that the gods changed them into poplar trees shedding tears of amber (Ovid, *Metamorphoses* 2.340–66).
[8] *Diana* Artemis, the chaste goddess and huntress.
[9] *Elysium* the land of the blessed in the underworld of the ancients.

The Mower to the Glo-Worms[1] (1651–2?)

1

Ye living Lamps, by whose dear light
The Nightingale does sit so late,
And studying all the Summer-night,
Her matchless Songs does meditate;

2

Ye Country Comets, that portend[2]   5
No War, nor Prince's funeral,
Shining unto no higher end
Than to presage the Grasses' fall;

3

Ye Glo-worms, whose officious Flame[3]
To wandring Mowers shows the way,   10
That in the Night have lost their aim,
And after foolish Fires do stray,[4]

4

Your courteous Lights in vain you waste,
Since *Juliana* here is come,
For She my Mind hath so displaced   15
That I shall never find my home.

An *Horatian* Ode upon *Cromwell's* Return from *Ireland*[1] (1650)

The forward Youth that would appear[2]
Must now forsake his *Muses* dear,
      Now in the Shadows sing
      His Numbers languishing.[3]
'Tis time to leave the Books in dust,   5
And oil th' unused Armour's rust:
      Removing from the Wall
      The Corslet of the Hall.[4]

The Mower to the Glo-Worms
[1] *Glo-Worm* glow-worm, an insect that emits light,
like a firefly.
[2] *Comets* were thought to be signs of dire events.
[3] *officious* kind.
[4] *foolish fires ignis fatuus*, delusive lights caused by
marsh gases, will-o'-the-wisp.
An *Horatian* Ode upon *Cromwell's* Return
[1] Oliver Cromwell put down an Irish royalist rebellion
against Parliamentary rule in 1649; he returned in 1650

to launch a similar campaign against the Scots, becoming at that time commander-in-chief of the Parliamentary army.
[2] *forward* "Warm; earnest" (Johnson); *appear* "to
display oneself on the stage of action" (*OED*).
[3] *Numbers* verses.
[4] *Corslet* "A light armour for the forepart of the body"
(Johnson).

So restless *Cromwell* could not cease
In the inglorious Art of Peace,   10
    But through adventrous War
    Urged his active Star.[5]
And, like the three-forked Lightning, first
Breaking the Clouds where it was nursed,
    Did thorough his own Side[6]   15
    His fiery way divide.
For 'tis all one to Courage high
The Emulous or Enemy;
    And with such to enclose[7]
    Is more than to oppose.   20
Then burning through the Air he went,
And Palaces and Temples rent:
    And *Cæsar's* head at last[8]
    Did through his Laurels blast.[9]
'Tis Madness to resist or blame   25
The force of angry Heaven's flame:
    And, if we would speak true,
    Much to the Man is due.
Who, from his private Gardens, where
He lived reserved and austere,   30
    As if his highest plot
    To plant the Bergamot,[10]
Could by industrious Valour climb
To ruin the great Work of Time,
    And cast the Kingdom old   35
    Into another Mould.
Though Justice against Fate complain,
And plead the ancient Rights in vain:
    But those do hold or break
    As Men are strong or weak.   40
Nature that hateth emptiness,[11]
Allows of penetration less:[12]
    And therefore must make room
    Where greater Spirits come.
What Field of all the Civil Wars,   45
Where his were not the deepest Scars?
    And *Hampton* shows what part[13]

---

[5] *Star* "Configuration of the planets supposed to influence fortune" (Johnson).

[6] *Side* "Party; interest; faction; sect" (Johnson).

[7] *enclose* limit (the rise or career).

[8] *Caesar* the monarch, Charles I.

[9] *Laurels* bay laurel was associated with kings and supposed to prevent lightning strikes (Pliny, *Natural History* 2.56).

[10] *Bergamot* a kind of pear.

[11] *Nature . . . hateth emptiness* nature abhors a vacuum, proverbial axiom of classical physics.

[12] *penetration* "a supposed or conceived occupation of the same space by two bodies at the same time" (*OED*).

[13] *Hampton* the palace where Charles I was under arrest in 1647 until his escape to Carisbrooke on the Isle of Wight, where he was recaptured. Marvell represents the events as part of Cromwell's plan to eliminate the king.

He had of wiser Art.
Where, twining subtle fears with hope,[14]
He wove a Net of such a scope,   50
    That *Charles* himself might chase
    To *Carebrook's* narrow case.
That thence the *Royal Actor* born
The *Tragic Scaffold* might adorn:
    While round the armèd Bands   55
    Did clap their bloody hands.
He nothing common did or mean
Upon that memorable Scene:
    But with his keener Eye
    The Axe's edge did try:[15]   60
Nor called the *Gods* with vulgar spite
To vindicate his helpless Right,
    But bowed his comely Head,
    Down as upon a Bed.
This was that memorable Hour   65
Which first assured the forcèd Pow'r.
    So when they did design
    The *Capitol's* first Line,[16]
A bleeding Head where they begun,
Did fright the Architects to run;   70
    And yet in that the *State*
    Foresaw its happy Fate.
And now the *Irish* are ashamed
To see themselves in one Year tamed:
    So much one Man can do,   75
    That does both act and know.
They can affirm his Praises best,
And have, though overcome, confessed
    How good he is, how just,
    And fit for highest Trust: 80
Nor yet grown stiffer with Command,
But still in the *Republic's* hand:
    How fit he is to sway
    That can so well obey.
He to the *Common Feet* presents[17]   85
A *Kingdom*, for his first year's rents:
    And, what he may, forbears
    His Fame to make it theirs:
And has his Sword and Spoils ungirt,
To lay them at the *Public's* skirt.   90
    So when the Falcon high

---

[14] *subtle* "Nice; fine; delicate; not coarse" (Johnson).
[15] *try* "To act on as a test" (Johnson) but also to experience.
[16] *Capitol* the Roman building of state, begun around 500 BCE and associated with the rise of the Roman republic; a bloody head found during the excavation was interpreted by soothsayers to foretell that Rome would be head of the world (Livy 1.55.6; Pliny, *Natural History* 28.15).
[17] *Common feet* sometimes emended to *Common's Feet*.

Falls heavy from the Sky,
She, having killed, no more does search,
But on the next green Bough to perch;
    Where, when he first does lure,[18]   95
    The Falc'ner has her sure.
What may not then our *Isle* presume
While Victory his Crest does plume!
    What may not others fear
    If thus he crown each year!   100
A *Cæsar* he ere long to *Gaul*,[19]
To *Italy* an *Hannibal*,[20]
    And to all States not free
    Shall *Clymacterick* be.[21]
The *Pict* no shelter now shall find[22]   105
Within his party-coloured Mind;
    But from this Valour sad
    Shrink underneath the Plaid:
Happy if in the tufted brake[23]
The *English Hunter* him mistake;   110
    Nor lay his Hounds in near
    The *Caledonian* Deer.[24]
But thou the War's and Fortune's Son
March indefatigably on;
    And for the last effect   115
    Still keep thy Sword erect:
Besides the force it has to fright[25]
The Spirits of the shady Night,
    The same *Arts* that did *gain*
    A *Pow'r* must it *maintain*.   120

THE GARDEN (1651–2?)

I

How vainly men themselves amaze
To win the Palm, the Oak, or Bays;[1]
And their uncessant Labours see
Crowned from some single Herb or Tree,
Whose short and narrow vergèd Shade   5
Does prudently their Toils upbraid;

---

[18] *lure* "To call hawks" (Johnson).
[19] *Gaul* France, conquered by Julius Caesar.
[20] *Hannibal* the Carthaginian general who conquered much of the Italian peninsula.
[21] *Clymacterick* fr. climacter, "A certain space of time or progression of years, which is supposed to end in a critical or dangerous time" (Johnson).
[22] *Pict* British ancestors of the Scots; the Roman name means "painted" or "parti-colored"; Marvell puns on "party."

[23] *brake* "A thicket of brambles or of thorns" (Johnson).
[24] *Caledonian* Scottish.
[25] *the force it has to fright* because of the cross on the hilt.

THE GARDEN
[1] *Palm, Oak, Bays* leaves used in crowns given for excellence in various spheres of activity, military, civic, and literary.

While all Flow'rs and all Trees do close
To weave the Garlands of repose.

2

Fair quiet, have I found thee here,
And Innocence thy Sister dear!   10
Mistaken long, I sought you then
In busy Companies of Men.
Your sacred Plants, if here below,
Only among the Plants will grow.
Society is all but rude,   15
To this delicious Solitude.[2]

3

No white nor red was ever seen[3]
So am'rous as this lovely green.
Fond Lovers, cruel as their Flame,
Cut in these Trees their Mistress' name.   20
Little, Alas, they know, or heed,
How far these Beauties Hers exceed!
Fair Trees! where s' e'er your barks I wound,
No Name shall but your own be found.

4

When we have run our Passion's heat,   25
Love hither makes his best retreat.
The *Gods,* that mortal Beauty chase,
Still in a Tree did end their race.
Apollo hunted *Daphne* so,[4]
Only that She might Laurel grow.   30
And *Pan* did after *Syrinx* speed,[5]
Not as a Nymph, but for a Reed.

5

What wond'rous Life is this I lead!
Ripe Apples drop about my head;
The Luscious Clusters of the Vine
Upon my Mouth do crush their Wine;   35
The Nectarine, and curious Peach,
Into my hands themselves do reach;

---

[2] *to* compared to.
[3] *white nor red* the colors of a lady's face in the traditional blazon, or laudatory description.
[4] *Daphne* escaped being ravished by Apollo by being changed into a laurel, which the god adopted as his sacred tree (Ovid, *Metamorphoses* 1.452–567).

[5] *Syrinx* escaped Pan by metamorphosis into marsh reeds, of which the god made his famous pipes (Ovid, *Metamorphoses* 1.689–712).

Stumbling on Melons, as I pass,
Ensnared with Flow'rs, I fall on Grass.   40

6

Mean while the Mind, from pleasure less,
Withdraws into its happiness:
The Mind, that Ocean where each kind
Does straight its own resemblance find;[6]
Yet it creates, transcending these,   45
Far other Worlds, and other Seas;
Annihilating all that's made[7]
To a green Thought in a green Shade.

7

Here at the Fountain's sliding foot,
Or at some Fruit-tree's mossy root,   50
Casting the Body's Vest aside,[8]
My Soul into the boughs does glide:
There like a Bird it sits, and sings,
Then whets, and combs its silver Wings;
And, till prepared for longer flight,   55
Waves in its Plumes the various Light.

8

Such was that happy Garden-state,
While Man there walked without a Mate:
After a Place so pure, and sweet,
What other Help could yet be meet![9]   60
But 'twas beyond a Mortal's share
To wander solitary there:
Two Paradises 'twere in one
To live in Paradise alone.

9

How well the skilful Gardner drew   65
Of flow'rs and herbs this Dial new;[10]
Where from above the milder Sun
Does through a fragrant Zodiac run;
And, as it works, th' industrious Bee[11]
Computes its time as well as we.   70

---

6 In *Pseudodoxia Epidemica* Sir Thomas Browne exploded the myth that "all Animals in the land are in their kind in the Sea" (3.24).
7 *Annihilate* "To destroy, so as to make the thing otherwise than it was" (Johnson), but the lines are marvelously ambiguous.
8 *Body's vest* corporeality as clothing.

9 *Help . . . meet* plays on the description of Eve as "help meet [appropriate] for him" (Genesis 2.20).
10 *Dial* sundial.
11 *Bee Computes its time* a reference to the punctual behavior of bees, as described by Virgil, for example (*Georgics* 4.185–90).

How could such sweet and wholesome Hours
Be reckoned but with herbs and flow'rs!

ON A DROP OF DEW (1651–2?)

See how the Orient Dew,
    Shed from the Bosom of the Morn
  Into the blowing Roses,
Yet careless of its Mansion new;
For the clear Region where 'twas born   5
    Round in its self incloses:
    And in its little Globe's Extent,
Frames as it can its native Element.
    How it the purple flow'r does slight,
      Scarce touching where it lies,   10
    But gazing back upon the Skies,
      Shines with a mournful Light;
        Like its own Tear,
Because so long divided from the Sphere.
    Restless it rolls and unsecure,   15
      Trembling lest it grow impure:
  Till the warm Sun pity its Pain,
And to the Skies exhale it back again.
      So the Soul, that Drop, that Ray
Of the clear Fountain of Eternal Day,   20
Could it within the humane flow'r be seen,
    Remembring still its former height,
    Shuns the sweet leaves and blossoms green;
    And, recollecting its own Light,
Does, in its pure and circling thoughts, express   25
The greater Heaven in an Heaven less.
    In how coy a Figure wound,
    Every way it turns away:
    So the World excluding round,
    Yet receiving in the Day.   30
    Dark beneath, but bright above:
    Here disdaining, there in Love.
    How loose and easy hence to go:
    How girt and ready to ascend.
    Moving but on a point below,   35
    It all about does upwards bend.
Such did the Manna's sacred Dew distil;[1]
White, and entire, though congealed and chill.
Congealed on Earth: but does, dissolving, run
Into the Glories of th' Almighty Sun.   40

ON A DROP OF DEW
[1] *Manna's sacred Dew* the food that fell miraculously
from the heavens to feed the Israelites during their sojourn in the desert (Exodus 16.13–15).

TO HIS COY MISTRESS (*c.* 1645)

Had we but World enough, and Time,
This coyness Lady were no crime.
We would sit down, and think which way
To walk, and pass our long Love's Day.
Thou by the *Indian Ganges* side   5
Should'st Rubies find: I by the Tide
Of *Humber* would complain. I would[1]
Love you ten years before the Flood:[2]
And you should if you please refuse
Till the Conversion of the *Jews.*   10
My vegetable Love should grow
Vaster than Empires, and more slow.
An hundred years should go to praise
Thine Eyes, and on thy Forehead Gaze.
Two hundred to adore each Breast: 15
But thirty thousand to the rest.
An Age at least to every part,
And the last Age should show your Heart.
For Lady you deserve this State;
Nor would I love at lower rate.   20
        But at my back I always hear
Time's wingèd Chariot hurrying near:
And yonder all before us lie
Deserts of vast Eternity.
Thy Beauty shall no more be found;   25
Nor, in thy marble Vault, shall sound
My echoing Song: then Worms shall try
That long preserved Virginity:
And your quaint Honour turn to dust;
And into ashes all my Lust.   30
The Grave's a fine and private place,
But none I think do there embrace.
        Now therefore, while the youthful hue
Sits on thy skin like morning dew,[3]
And while thy willing Soul transpires[4]   35
At every pore with instant Fires,
Now let us sport us while we may;
And now, like am'rous birds of prey,
Rather at once our Time devour,
Than languish in his slow-chapt pow'r.[5]   40

TO HIS COY MISTRESS
[1] *Humber* a river in northern England, in Yorkshire, Marvell's home county; from the Ganges to the Humber was reckoned about the extent of the classical world.
[2] *ten years before the Flood . . . Conversion of the Jews* virtually all of biblical time, from Genesis to Revelation.

[3] *dew* the text reads "glew," which has been very variously emended.
[4] *transpire* "To be emitted by insensible vapour" (Johnson).
[5] *slow-chapt* (eating) with slowing moving jaws.

Let us roll all our Strength, and all
Our sweetness, up into one Ball:
And tear our Pleasure with rough strife,
Thorough the Iron gates of Life.[6]
Thus, though we cannot make our Sun   45
Stand still, yet we will make him run.

Henry Vaughan (1622–1695)

For his second volume of poems Vaughan took the name Silurist, after Tacitus, the Roman historian's name for the Welsh. He called the volume itself Silex Scintillans (1650), which means "sparkling flint," another reference to his native Wales. In most respects, however, Vaughan's poetry is devoted to a lingua franca of ideas – a Latin generality of thought – rather than anything peculiar to his country. In his first volume of poetry he wrote a loose translation of Juvenal's tenth satire, a sophisticated philosophical work that Dryden and Samuel Johnson would, more predictably, imitate in the accents of high Augustan poetry. Vaughan's most important poetical relatives are the metaphysical poets, and his interest in mysterious, transcendental relations would not seem to mix well with the urbanity of Juvenal. However, like George Herbert, Vaughan retains an air of informality and innocent directness in his approach to metaphysical topics. This unusual combination leads him to affinities with the emblematical tradition, in which an abstract state of mind or faith can be figured forth in a simple image, which then requires an ingenious or contrived interpretation. Some of this emblematizing impulse survives even in Samuel Johnson's verse: the imagery of mists and ignorance, but not the purer illuminations of "They are all gone into the world of light," links the rhetorical world of early seventeenth-century poetry and that of the mid-eighteenth. "The Night" explores a scene of inspiration that became familiar in the mid-eighteenth century, especially in Edward Young's Night Thoughts (1742–4), which is often regarded as a pre-Romantic work.

Vaughan's interesting life as a medical doctor and the twin of the alchemist Thomas Vaughan has been written by F. E. Hutchinson (Oxford University Press, 1947). My texts are based on Silex Scintillans, second edition, in two books (1655). There is a very useful edition of the complete poetry by French Fogle (1964; reprinted Norton, 1969) in addition to the standard edition by L. C. Martin (Second edition, Oxford University Press, 1957).

from *Silex Scintillans* (1655)

'THEY ARE ALL GONE INTO THE WORLD OF LIGHT!'

They are all gone into the world of light!
    And I alone sit ling'ring here;
Their very memory is fair and bright,
    And my sad thoughts doth clear.

It glows and glitters in my cloudy breast   5
    Like stars upon some gloomy grove,

---

[6]   *Thorough*   through.

Or those faint beams in which this hill is drest,
    After the Sun's remove.

I see them walking in an Air of glory,
    Whose light doth trample on my days: 10
My days, which are at best but dull and hoary,
    Mere glimmering and decays.

O holy hope! and high humility,
    High as the Heavens above!
These are your walks, and you have showed them me   15
    To kindle my cold love,

Dear, beauteous death! the Jewel of the Just,
    Shining no where, but in the dark;
What mysteries do lie beyond thy dust;
    Could man outlook that mark!   20

He that hath found some fledged bird's nest, may know
    At first sight, if the bird be flown;
But what fair Well, or Grove he sings in now,
    That is to him unknown.

And yet, as Angels in some brighter dreams   25
    Call to the soul, when man doth sleep:
So some strange thoughts transcend our wonted themes,
    And into glory peep.

If a star were confined into a Tomb
    Her captive flames must needs burn there;   30
But when the hand that lockt her up, gives room,
    She'll shine through all the sphere.

O Father of eternal life, and all
    Created glories under thee!
Resume thy spirit from this world of thrall   35
    Into true liberty.

Either disperse these mists, which blot and fill
    My perspective (still) as they pass,[1]
Or else remove me hence unto that hill,
    Where I shall need no glass.[2]   40

THEY ARE ALL GONE INTO THE WORLD OF LIGHT
[1] *perspective* looking glass or small telescope.

[2] *glass* "For now we see through a glass darkly; but then face to face: now I know in part; but then shall I know even as also I am known" (1 Corinthians 13.12).

THE NIGHT

John 3.2[1]

Through that pure *Virgin-shrine*,
That sacred veil drawn o'er thy glorious noon
That men might look and live as Glow-worms shine,[2]
  And face the Moon:
Wise *Nicodemus* saw such light   5
As made him know his God by night.

Most blest believer he!
Who in that land of darkness and blind eyes
Thy long expected healing wings could see,[3]
  When thou didst rise,   10
And what can never more be done,
Did at mid-night speak with the Sun!

     O who will tell me, where
He found thee at that dead and silent hour!
What hallowed solitary ground did bear   15
  So rare a flower,
 Within whose sacred leafs did lie
 The fullness of the Deity.

No mercy-seat of gold,[4]
No dead and dusty *Cherub*, nor carved stone,   20
But his own living works did my Lord hold,
  And lodge alone;
 Where *trees* and *herbs* did watch and peep
 And wonder, while the *Jews* did sleep.

Dear night! this world's defeat;   25
The stop to busy fools; care's check and curb;
The day of Spirits; my soul's calm retreat
  Which none disturb!
 Christ's progress, and his prayer time[5]
 The hours to which high Heaven doth chime.30

God's silent, searching flight:
When my Lord's head is filled with dew, and all[6]
His locks are wet with the clear drops of night;
  His still, soft call;

THE NIGHT
[1] Nicodemus "came to Jesus by night, and said unto him, 'Rabbi, we know that thou art a teacher come from God . . .'"
[2] *Glow-worms* insects that emit light, like fireflies.
[3] *healing wings . . . rise* "But unto you that fear my Name, shall the Sun of righteousness arise with healing in his wings" (Malachi 4.2).

[4] *mercy-seat* the golden lid of the ark of the covenant, flanked by images of cherubim; here God communed with man (Exodus 25.17–22).
[5] Mark 1.35; Luke 21.37 [Vaughan's note; both passages tell of Christ going out – making a *progress* – in the dark].
[6] The imagery of this passage comes from Song of Solomon 5.2, where the Lord comes knocking at night, asking admission to his beloved, the heart or soul.

His knocking time; the soul's dumb watch,   35
When Spirits their fair kinred catch

Were all my loud, evil days
Calm and unhaunted as is thy dark Tent
Whose peace but by some *Angel's* wing or voice
 Is seldom rent;   40
Then I in Heaven all the long year
Would keep, and never wander here.

But living where the Sun
Doth all things wake, and where all mix and tire
Themselves and others, I consent and run   45
 To every mire
And by this world's ill-guiding light,
Err more than I can do by night.

There is in God (some say)
A deep, but dazzling darkness; as men here   50
Say it is late and dusky, because they see not all clear;
 O for that night where I in him
 Might live invisible and dim.

Margaret Cavendish, Duchess of Newcastle
(1623–1673)

Cavendish was one of the most prolific women writers in the seventeenth century, and for a long time she was one of the very few given any substantial recognition. However, she has been condemned at least as often as praised, and Virginia Woolf's characterization of her as a "giant cucumber," filling and crowding the literary garden, has stuck. More recent commentators have perceived that Cavendish self-protectively portrayed herself as an impulsive, distracted wit. Her productivity is incontrovertible. In addition to poems and plays, she published The Life of William Cavendish *(1667),* Description of a New World *(1666),* Orations of Divers Sorts *(1662),* Observations upon Experimental Philosophy *(1666), and several other books of literature, philosophy and science.*

 The text of my selection is based on her first publication, Poems and Fancies *(1653). The volume has recently been reprinted by the Brown Women Writers Project. Kate Lilley has edited a selection of Cavendish's prose,* The Blazing World and Other Writings *(Penguin, 1994).*

from *Poems and Fancies* (1653)

A DIALOGUE BETWIXT LEARNING, AND IGNORANCE

Learning Thou *Busy Forester*, that searchest 'bout
    The *World*, to find the *Heart* of *Learning* out.
    Or, *Perseus* like, foul *Monsters* thou dost kill;
    Rude Ignorance, which always doeth ill,

Ignorance	O thou *Proud Learning,* that standst on *Tip-toes* high,	5
	Can never reach to know the *Deity:*	
	Nor where the *Cause* of any one thing lies,	
	But fill man full of *Care,* and *Miseries.*	
	Learning inflames the *Thoughts* to take great pains,	
	Doth nought but make an *Alms-tub* of the *Brains.*[1]	10
Learning	*Learning* doth seek about, new things to find;	
	In that *Pursuit,* doth recreate the *Mind.*	
	It is a *Perspective, Nature* to espy,[2]	
	Can all her *Curiosity* descry.	
Ignorance	*Learning*'s an useless pain, unless it have	15
	Some ways, or means to keep us from the *Grave.*	
	For, what is all the *World,* if understood,	
	If we do use it not, nor taste the *Good?*	
	Learning may come to know the use of things,	
	Yet not receive the *Good* which from them springs.	20
	For *Life* is short, and *Learning tedious, long:*[3]	
	Before we come to use what's *Learned, Life*'s gone.	
Learning	O *Ignorance,* thou *Beast,* which dull and lazy liest,	
	And only eat'st, and sleepest, till thou diest.	
Ignorance	The *Lesson Nature taught,* is, most delight,	25
	To please the *Sense,* and eke the *Appetite.*[4]	
	I *Ignorance* am still the *Heaven of Bliss.*	
	For in me lies the truest *happiness.*	
	Give me still *Ignorance,* that *Innocent Estate,*	
	That *Paradise,* that's free from *Envious Hate.*	30
	Learning a *Tree* was, whereon *Knowledge* grew,	
	Tasting that *Fruit, Man* only *Misery* knew.	
	Had *Man* but *Knowledge, Ignorance* to love,	
	He happy would have been, as *Gods* above.[5]	
Learning	O *Ignorance,* how foolish thou dost talk!	35
	Is't *happiness* in *Ignorance* to walk?	
	Can there be *Joy* in *Darkness,* more than *Light?*	
	Or *Pleasure* more in *Blindness,* than in *Sight?*	

Dorothy Osborne Temple (1627–1695)

In 1648 Charles I was imprisoned in Carisbrooke Castle on the Isle of Wight. Dorothy Osborne and her brother were passing through on their way to St Malo, Guernsey to meet their father, the royalist governor who held the island for the king. Dorothy's brother sneaked away from the party to write with a diamond on a glass, "And Haman was hanged upon the Gallows he had prepared for Mordecai," referring to the story in the Book of Esther in which an enemy of the Jews, a minister

---

A *Dialogue* betwixt *Learning and Ignorance*
[1] *Alms-tub*   a large vessel for holding leftovers and scraps for the poor.
[2] *Perspective*   magnifying glass.

[3] *Life is short . . . long*   one of the oldest aphorisms.
[4] *eke*   also.
[5] *Gods*   angels.

of King Ahasuerus is hanged (with his ten sons), when the king reverses his written order for hanging a Jewish leader. It just so happened that the puritan governor of Wight was named Hammond; the graffiti was discovered; and Dorothy's brother was instantly apprehended by the guard. As the Protestant officer William Temple looked on, Dorothy intervened and convinced the guard that she herself had written the offending words. The officers were gentlemen enough to believe her and let the whole party go on. But this was the fabled origin of the courtship between William Temple and Dorothy Osborne. Separated by politics and sometimes by the English Channel, the two corresponded for several years before finally marrying in 1655. Temple was an important states- man, author of a treatise on government that Samuel Johnson declared a model for his prose style, a figure in intellectual debates of the time, and the employer of his cousin Jonathan Swift. He destroyed his own love letters after his wife's death, but those she wrote between 1652 and 1654 survive. These expressive and candid performances provide a glimpse of private life at the time, as it was experienced by a highly intelligent though characteristically unlearned female observer. They suggest that in all but public achievement, Dorothy was the match of her distinguished husband.

The letters are very ably edited, with a learned if excessively gallant introduction, by G. C. Moore Smith (Clarendon Press, 1928) and more recently by K. Hart (1968). The following excerpts are based on Smith's edition and are indebted to his commentary.

from Letters to William Temple

LETTER 3   8 JANUARY 1653

Sir,

There is nothing moves my Charity like Gratitude, and when a Beggar's thankful for a small relief, I always repent it was not more. But seriously this place will not afford much towards the enlarging of a letter and I am grown so dull with living in't (for I am not willing to confess that I was always so) as to need all helps. Yet you shall see I will endeavour to satisfy you, upon condition you will tell me, why you quarrelled so, at your last letter. I cannot guess at it, unless it were that you repented you told me so much of your Story, which I am not apt to believe neither, because it would not become our freindship, a great part of it consisting (as I have been taught) in a mutual confidence, and to let you see that I believe it so, I will give you an account of my self, and begin my Story as you did yours, from our Parting at Goring house.[1]

I came down hither not half so well pleased as I went up, with an engagement upon me, that I had little hope of ever shaking off, for I had made use of all the liberty my friends would allow me, to preserve my own, and 'twould not do, he was so weary of his, that he would part with 't upon any terms. As my last refuge, I got my Brother to go down with him to see his house, who when he came back made the relation I wished; he said the seat[2] was as ill, as so good a country would permit, and the house so ruined for want of living in 't, as it would ask a good proportion of time, and money, to make it fit for a woman to confine her self to. This (though it were not much) I was willing to take hold of, and made it considerable enough to break the agreement. I had no quarrel to his Person, or his fortune but was in love with neither, and much out of love with a thing called marriage, and have since thanked God I was so, for 'tis not long since one of my Brothers writ me word of him, that he was killed in a

---

LETTER 3   8 JANUARY
[1] *Goring house* the town house of George Goring, which stood on the site of Buckingham Palace.

[2] *seat* "Situation; site" (Johnson).

Duel, though since, I hear 'twas the other that was killed and he is fled upon 't, which does not mend the matter much. Both made me glad I had 'scaped him, and sorry of his misfortune, which in Earnest was the least return, his many Civilities to me could deserve.

Presently after this was at an End, my Mother died, and I was left at liberty to mourn her loss a while. At length, my Aunt (with whom I was when you last saw me) commanded me to wait on her at London, and when I came she told me how much I was in her care, how well she loved me for my Mother's sake, and something for my own, and drew out a long, set, speech, which ended in a good motion (as she called it) and truly I saw no harm in 't, for by what I had heard of the Gentleman I guessed he expected a better fortune than mine, and it proved so, yet he protested he liked me so well, that he was very angry my Father would not be persuaded to give a 1000 pounds more with me, and I him so ill, that I vowed, if had had a 1000 pounds less I should have thought it too much for him, and so we parted; Since, he has made a story with a new Mistress, that is worth your knowing, but too long for a letter, I'll keep it for you.

After this, some friends that had observed a Gravity in my face, which might become an Elderly man's wife (as they termed it) and a Mother in Law, proposed a Widower to me, that had four daughters, all old enough to be my Sisters: But he had a great Estate, was as fine a Gentleman as ever England bred, and the very Pattern of Wisdom. I that knew how much I wanted it, thought this the safest place for me to engage in, and was mightily pleased to think, I had met with one at least that had wit enough for himself and me too; But shall I tell you what I thought when I knew him (you will say nothing on't)? 'Twas the vainest, Impertinent, self conceited, Learned, Coxcombe, that ever yet I saw. To say more, were to spoil his marriage, which I hear he is towards with a daughter of my Lord of Coleraines, but for his sake I shall take heed of a fine Gentleman as long as I live . . .

LETTER 28   2 JULY 1653

In my opinion you do not understand the Laws of friendship right; 'tis generally believed it owes its birth to an agreement & conformity of humours,[1] and that it lives no longer than 'tis preserved by the Mutual care of those that bred it, 'tis wholly Governed by Equality, and can there be such a thing in it, as a distinction of Power? No sure, if we are friends, we must both command & both obey alike. Indeed a Mistress and a Servant, sounds otherwise, but that is Ceremony, and this is truth.

LETTER 58   11 FEBRUARY 1654

'Tis certain (what you say) that where divine or human Laws are not positive we may be our own Judges; nobody can hinder us, nor is it in it self to be blamed; but sure it is not safe to take all the liberty [that] is allowed us; there are not many that are sober enough to be trusted with the government of themselves, and because others Judge us with more severity than our indulgence to ourselves will permit, it must necessarily follow that 'tis safer being ruled by their opinion than by our own. I am disputing again though you told me my fault so Plainly; I'll give it over and tell you that *Parthenissa*[1] is now my company; my Brother sent it down and I have almost read it. 'Tis handsome Language, you would know it to be writ by a person of good Quality though you were not told it, but in the whole I am not very much

LETTER 28   2 JULY 1653
[1]   *humours*   "The different kind[s] of moisture in man's body, reckoned by the old physicians to be phlegm, blood, choler, and melancholy, which, as they predominated, were supposed to determine the temper of mind" (Johnson).
LETTER 58   11 FEBRUARY 1654
[1]   *Parthenissa*   a romance by Lord Broghill.

taken with it, all the Stories have too near a resemblance with those of Other Romances; there is nothing of new or *surprenant*[2] in them, the Ladies are all so kind they make no sport, and I meet only with one that took me by doing a handsome thing of the kind. She was in a beseiged Town, and persuaded all those of her Sex to go out with her to the Enemy (which were a barbarous People) and die by their swords, that the provision of the Town might last the longer for such as were able to do service in defending it. But how angry was I to see him spoil this again, by bringing out a letter this woman left behind her for the Governor of the Town, where she discovers a passion for him and makes that the reason why she did it. I confess I have no patience for our *faiseurs de Romance*,[3] when they make women court. It will never enter into my head that 'tis posible any woman can Love where she is not first Loved, & much less that if they should do that, they could have the face to own it.

John Bunyan (1628–1688)

Bunyan's first child was born blind in 1650, and with his first wife he had three more children before her death in 1658. He remarried in 1659. During this emotional decade Bunyan underwent a period of spiritual doubt and conversion remarkable for its vicissitudes. Grace Abounding *is the record of his tumultuous inner life during this period. It displays a concentration on the state of an individual soul and a striving for improvement that are startlingly intense. The pattern of achievement and temporary satisfaction followed by renewed awareness of inadequacy and corruption recurs with the frequency of waves in a tropical storm. Indeed, Bunyan's spiritual life is so tangible, that it seems to require the spiritual landscape of* Pilgrim's Progress *(1678). That later creation is Bunyan's most famous book and one of the most widely read and reprinted books in history.*

Although Bunyan began publishing tracts in 1656, he prepared his longer works during his twelve or thirteen years of somewhat discontinuous imprisonment for illegal preaching. He was arrested shortly after the Restoration and refused to swear that he would not repeat his offense. Grace Abounding *was first published in 1666; I follow this edition, ignoring the additions that Bunyan made in later printings. The standard edition is edited by Roger Sharrock (Clarendon Press, 1962).*

from *Grace Abounding to the Chief of Sinners*

28. But upon a day, the good Providence of God did cast me to *Bedford*, to work on my calling; and in one of the streets of that town, I came where there was three or four poor women sitting at a door in the Sun, and talking about the things of God; and being now willing to hear them discourse, I drew near to hear what they said; for I was now a brisk talker also my self in the matters of Religion: but now I may say, *I heard, but I understood not*; for they were far above out of my reach, for their talk was about a new birth, the work of God on their hearts, also how they were convinced of their miserable state by nature: they talked how God had visited their souls with his love in the Lord Jesus, and with what words and promises they had been refreshed, comforted, and supported against the temptations of the Devil; moreover, they reasoned of the suggestions and temptations of Satan in particular, and told to each other by which they had been afflicted, and how they were borne up under his assaults: they also

---

[2] *surprenant* French, surprising.   [3] *faiseurs de Romance* romance writers.

discoursed of their own wretchedness of heart, of their unbelief, and did contemn, slight, and abhor their own righteousness, as filthy, and insufficient to do them any good.

29. And me thought they spake as if joy did make them speak: they spake with such pleasantness of Scripture language, and with such appearance of grace in all they said, that they were to me as if they had found a new world, as if they were people that dwelt alone, and were not to be reckoned amongst their Neighbours [Numbers 23.9].

30. At this I felt my own heart began to shake, as mistrusting my condition to be naught; for I saw that in all my thoughts about Religion and Salvation, the New birth did never enter into my mind, neither knew I the comfort of Word and Promise, nor the deceitfulness and treachery of my own wicked heart. As for secret thoughts, I took no notice of them; neither did I understand what Satan's temptations were, nor how they were to be withstood and resisted, &c.

31. Thus therefore when I had heard and considered what they said, I left them, and went about my employment again: but their talk and discourse went with me, also my heart would tarry with them, for I was greatly afflicted with their words, both because by them I was convinced that I wanted the true tokens of a truly godly man, and also because by them I was convinced of the happy and blessed condition of him that was such a one.

32. Therefore I should often make it my business to be going again and again into the company of these poor people; for I could not stay away; and the more I went amongst them, the more I did question my condition; and as I still do remember, presently I found two things within me, at which I did sometimes marvel (especially considering what a blind, ignorant, sordid, and ungodly Wretch but just before I was); the one was, a very great softness and tenderness of heart, which caused me to fall under the conviction of what by Scripture they asserted; and the other was, a great bending in my mind to a continual meditating on them, and on all other good things which at any time I heard or read of.

33. By these things my mind was now so turned, that it lay like a Horseleech[1] at the vein, still crying out, 'Give, give', [Proverbs 30.15]. Yea, it was so fixed on Eternity, and on the things about the Kingdom of Heaven, that is, as far as I knew, though as yet God knows, I knew but little, that neither pleasures nor profits, nor persuasions, nor threats, could loosen it, or make it let go its hold; and though I may speak it with shame, yet it is in very deed a certain truth, it would then have been as difficult for me to have taken my mind from heaven to earth, as I have found it often since to get it again from earth to heaven.

71. And now I was sorry that God had made me a man, for I feared I was a reprobate: I counted man, as unconverted, the most doleful of all the Creatures: Thus being afflicted and tossed about by my sad condition, I counted my self alone, and above the most of men unblessed. In this condition I went a great while, but when comforting time was come, I heard one preach a sermon upon those words in the *Song* (Song [of Solomon] 4.1), *Behold thou art fair, behold, thou art fair*; but at that time he made these two words, *My Love,* his chief and subject matter; from which after he had a little opened the text, he observed these several conclusions: 1. *That the Church, and so every saved Soul, is Christ's Love, when loveless*: 2. *Christ's Love without a cause*: 3. *Christ's Love when hated of the world*: 4. *Christ's Love when under temptation, and under desertion*: 5. *Christ's Love from first to last.*

FROM *GRACE ABOUNDING TO THE CHIEF OF SINNERS*
[1] *Horseleech* "A great leech that bites horses"
(Johnson), applied for bloodletting, a common medical
procedure of the time.

72. But I got nothing by what he said at present, only when he came to the application of the fourth particular, this was the word he said, *If it be so, that the saved soul is Christ's love when under temptation and desertion; then poor tempted Soul, when thou art assaulted and afflicted with temptation, and the hidings of God's Face, yet think on these two words, MY LOVE,* still.

73. So as I was going home, these words came into my thoughts, and I well remember as they came in, I said thus in my heart, What shall I get by thinking on these two words? this thought had no sooner passed through my heart, but the words began to kindle in my Spirit, *Thou art my Love, thou art my Love,* twenty times together; and still as they ran thus in my mind, they waxed stronger and warmer, and began to make me look up; but being as yet between hope and fear, I still replied in my heart, *But is it true too? but is it true?* at which, that sentence fell in upon me, *He wist[2] not that it was true which was done unto him of the angel,* Acts 12.9.

74. Then I began to give place to the Word, which with my power, did over and over make this joyful sound within my Soul, *Thou art my Love, thou art my Love; and nothing shall separate thee from my love*; and with that *Rom*[ans] 8.39 came into my mind. Now was my heart filled full of comfort and hope, and now I could believe that my sins should be forgiven me; yea, I was now so taken with the love and mercy of God, that I remember I could not tell how to contain till I got home; I thought I could have spoken of his Love, and of his mercy to me, had they been capable to have understood me, wherefore I said in my Soul with much gladness, 'Well, I would I had a pen and ink here; I would write this down before I go any further, for surely, I will not forget *this* forty years hence'; but alas! within less than forty days I began to question this all again.

214. At another time, though just before I was pretty well and savoury[3] in my spirit, yet suddenly there fell upon me a great cloud of darkness, which did so hide from me the things of God and Christ, that I was as if I had never seen or known them in my life; I was also so over-run in my Soul, with a senseless heartless frame of spirit, that I could not feel my soul to move or stir after grace and life by Christ; I was as if my loins were broken, or as if my hands and feet had been ties or bound with chains. At this time also I felt some weakness to seize my outward man, which made still the other affliction the more heavy and uncomfortable.

215. After I had been in this condition some three or four days, as I was sitting by the fire, I suddenly felt this word to sound in my heart, *I must go to Jesus*; at this my former darkness and atheism fled away, and the blessed things of heaven were set within my view; while I was on this sudden thus overtaken with surprise, 'Wife,' said I, 'is there ever such a Scripture, *I must go to Jesus?*' She said she could not tell; therefore I sat musing still to see if I could remember such a place, I had not sat above two or three minutes but that came bolting in upon me, *And to an innumerable company of Angels,* and withal, *Hebrews* the twelfth, about the mount of *Zion,* was set before mine eyes. *Heb*[rews] 12.22, 23, 24.

216. Then with joy I told my Wife, O now I know, I know! but that night was a good night to me; I never had but few better; I longed for the company of some of God's people, that I might have imparted unto them what God hath showed me: Christ was a precious Christ to my Soul last night; I could scarce lie in Bed for joy, and peace, and triumph, through Christ; this great glory did not continue upon me until morning, yet that twelfth of the Author to the *Hebrews,* Heb[rews] 12.21, 22, 23. was a blessed Scripture to me for many days together after this.

217. The words are these, *Ye are come to mount Zion, to the City of the living God, to the heavenly Jerusalem, and to an innumerable company of Angels, to the general assembly and Church of the first-*

---

[2] *wist* knew; understood.   [3] *savoury* "Pleasing to the smell" (Johnson).

born, which are written in heaven, and to God the Judge of all, and to the spirits of just men made perfect, and to Jesus the Mediator of the New Testament, and to the blood of sprinkling, that speaketh better things than that of Abel:[4] Through this blessed Sentence the Lord led me over and over, first to this word, and then to that, and showed me wonderful glory in every one of them. These words also have oft since this time been great refreshment to my Spirit. Blessed be God for having mercy on me.

Katherine Philips (1631–1664)

The "matchless Orinda," as Philips became known, was one of the most respected poets of her time. She and Sappho were the great models to whom Dryden very flatteringly compared Anne Killigrew in his ode on that lesser poet's death. Although her connections were largely puritan and her much older husband was an official of the Commonwealth, Philips was royalist in her sympathies and published her first poems in the prefatory matter of an edition of Vaughan's poetry. For the most part, her reputation was built on the circulation of her poetry in manuscript, and a responsibly published edition of her work did not come out until 1667. (That edition provides the basis for the selections that follow.) Philips's poems, letters, and translations have recently been edited by P. Thomas and others in three separate volumes (Stump Cross Books, 1993).

Using code names for her friends – chiefly Lucasia (Anne Owen), Rosania (Mary Aubrey) and Antenor (her husband) – Philips is a coterie writer who wrote about and for a small circle of friends. She is rarely so private that she is obscure, however, and she touches on general themes even when relating private experience. Many of her poems are about her intimacy with her friends and simultaneously about the broader theme of friendship; this is a fundamental humanist subject, anchored in Cicero's De Amicitia, and not the concern only of an individual or of any particular group. Philips's personal, sometimes urgent poems are some of the best the period has to offer on this important topic.

from *Poems by the most deservedly Admired Mrs. Katherine Philips, the matchless Orinda* (1667)

FRIENDSHIP'S MYSTERY, TO MY DEAREST *LUCASIA*[1]

Come, my *Lucasia*, since we see
    That Miracles Men's faith do move,
By wonder and by prodigy
    To the dull angry world let's prove
There's a Religion in our Love.   5

2

For though we were designed t' agree,
    That Fate no liberty destroys,
But our Election is as free

---

[4] *Abel* the second son of Adam, slain by his brother Cain; his "blood cried unto [God] from the ground" and Cain was "cursed from the earth" (Genesis 4.10–11).

FRIENDSHIP'S MYSTERY
[1] *Lucasia* (like *Lucas*, "light-giving") Philips's poetic name for her friend Anne Owen; the poem was set to music by Henry Lawes.

As Angels, who with greedy choice
Are yet determined to their joys.[2]   10

3

Our hearts are doubled by the loss,
    Here Mixture is Addition grown;
We both diffuse, and both engross:[3]
    And we whose minds are so much one,
    Never, yet ever are alone.   15

4

We court our own Captivity
    Than Thrones more great and innocent:
'Twere banishment to be set free,
    Since we wear fetters whose intent
    Not bondage is, but Ornament.   20

5

Divided joys are tedious found,
    And griefs united easier grow:
We are selves but by rebound,
    And all our Titles shuffled so,
    Both Princes, and both Subjects too.   25

6

Our Hearts are mutual Victims laid,
    While they (such power in Friendship lies)
Are Altars, Priests, and Off'rings made:
    And each Heart which thus kindly dies,
    Grows deathless by the Sacrifice.   30

EPITAPH
ON HER SON *H. P.* AT *ST. SYTH*'S CHURCH WHERE HER BODY ALSO LIES INTERRED[1]

What on Earth deserves our Trust?
Youth and Beauty both are dust.
Long we gathering are with pain,
What one Moment calls again.
Seven years Childless, Marriage past,   5
A Son, a Son is born at last:
So exactly limbed and Fair,
Full of good Spirits, Mien, and Air,
As a long life promised;

---

[2] *Angel . . . determined* Church doctrine was that angels were created with free will but gave it up a moment after they were formed and turned towards God, thus becoming fixed in goodness.

[3] *engross* thicken.
EPITAPH
[1] Hector Philips, born and died in 1655.

Yet, in less than six weeks, dead.   10
Too promising, too great a Mind[2]
In so small room to be confined:
Therefore, fit in Heav'n to dwell,
He quickly broke the Prison shell.
So the subtle Alchemist,   15
Can't with *Hermes' Seal* resist.[3]
The Powerful Spirit's subtler flight,[4]
But 'twill bid him long good night.
So the Sun, if it arise
Half so glorious as his Eyes,   20
  Like this Infant, takes a shroud,
  Buried in a morning Cloud.

THE VIRGIN

The things that make a Virgin please,
She that seeks, will find them these;
A Beauty, not to Art in debt,
Rather agreeable than great;
An Eye, wherein at once do meet,   5
The beams of kindness, and of wit;
And undissembled Innocence,
Apt not to give, nor take offence:
A Conversation, at once, free
From Passion, and from Subtlety;   10
A Face that's modest, yet serene,
A sober, and yet lively Mien;
The virtue which does her adorn,
By honour guarded, not by scorn;
With such wise lowliness indued,[1]   15
As never can be mean, or rude;
That prudent negligence enrich,
And Time's her silence and her speech;
Whose equal mind, does always move,
Neither a foe, nor slave to Love;   20
And whose Religion's strong and plain,
Not superstitious, nor profane.

---

[2] *Mind* soul.
[3] *Hermes' Seal* hermetic, airtight closure on a bottle or
test tube.
[4] *Spirit* a volatile, distilled liquid, in alchemical language; *subtler* from subtlety "Thinness; fineness; exility
of particles" (Johnson).

THE VIRGIN
[1] *indue* "It seems sometimes to be, even by good writers, confounded with endow or indow, to furnish or
enrich with any quality or excellence" (Johnson).

Upon the graving of her Name upon a Tree in *Barnelmes* Walks

Alas how barbarous are we,
Thus to reward the courteous Tree,
Who its broad shade affording us,
Deserves not to be wounded thus;
See how the Yielding Bark complies   5
With our ungrateful injuries.
And feeling this, say how much then
Trees are more generous than Men,
Who by a Nobleness so pure
Can first oblige and then endure.   10

To Her Royal Highness the Duchess of *York*, on her commanding me to send her some things that I had written[1]

To you whose Dignity strikes us with awe,
And whose far greater Judgement gives us law,
(Your Mind b'ing more transcendent than your State,
For while but Knees to this, Hearts bow to that)
These humble Papers never durst come near,   5
Had not your pow'rful Word bid them appear;
In which such majesty, such sweetness dwells,
As in one act obliges, and compels.
None can dispute commands vouchsafed by you.
What shall my fears then and confusion do?   10
They must resign, and by their just pretence
Some value set on my obedience.
For in religious Duties, 'tis confessed,
The most Implicit are accepted best.
If on that score your Highness will excuse   15
This blushing tribute of an artless Muse,
She may (encouraged by your least regard,
Which first can worth create, and then reward)
At modest distance with improvèd strains
That Mercy celebrate which now she gains.   20
But should you that severer justice use,
Which these too prompt Approaches may produce,
As the swift Hind which hath escapèd long,
Believes a Vulgar shot would be a wrong;
But wounded by a Prince falls without shame,   25
And what in life she loses, gains in fame:
So if a Ray from you chance to be sent,

To Her Royal Highness the Duchess of *York*
[1] *Duchess of York* Anne Hyde (1637–71), secretly
married to James II in 1660.

Which to consume, and not to warm, is meant;
My trembling Muse at least more nobly dies,
And falls by that a truer sacrifice.   30

TO THE TRULY COMPETENT JUDGE OF HONOUR, *LUCASIA,* UPON A SCANDALOUS LIBEL MADE BY J. J.

Honour, which differs Man from Man much more
Than Reason differed him from Beasts before,
Suffers this common Fate of all things good,
By the blind World to be misunderstood.
For as some Heathens did their Gods confine,   5
While in a Bird or Beast they made their shrine;
Deposed their Deities to Earth, and then
Offered them Rites that were too low for Men;
So those who most to Honour sacrifice,
Prescribe to her a mean and weak disguise;   10
Imprison her to others' false Applause,
And from Opinion do receive their Laws.
While that inconstant Idol they implore,
Which in one breath can murther and adore.
From hence it is that those who Honour court,   15
(And place her in a popular report)
Do prostitute themselves to sordid Fate,
And from their Being oft degenerate.
And thus their Tenets too are low and bad,
As if 'twere honourable to be mad: 20
Or that their Honour had concernèd been
But to conceal, not to forbear, a sin.
But Honour is more great and more sublime,
Above the battery of Fate or Time.
We see in Beauty certain airs are found,   25
Which not one Grace can make, but all compound.
Honour's to th' Mind as Beauty to the Sense,
The fair result of mixèd Excellence.
As many Diamonds together lie,
And dart one lustre to amaze the Eye: 30
So Honour is that bright Ætherial Ray
Which many stars doth in one light display.
But as that Beauty were as truly sweet,
Were there no Tongue to praise, no Eye to see 't;
And 'tis the Privilege of a native Spark,[1]   35
To shed a constant Splendour in the dark:
So Honour is its own Reward and End,
And satisfied within, cannot descend

TO THE TRULY COMPETENT JUDGE OF HONOUR
[1] *native* "Produced by nature; natural, not artificial"
(Johnson).

To beg the suffrage of a vulgar Tongue,[2]
Which by commending Virtue doth it wrong. 40
It is the Charter of a noble Action,
That the performance giveth satisfaction.
Other things are below 't; for from a Clown[3]
Would any Conqueror receive his Crown?
'Tis restless Cowardice to be a drudge 45
To an uncertain and unworthy Judge.
So the *Chameleon,* who lives on air,[4]
Is of all Creatures most inclined to fear.
But peaceable reflections on the Mind
Will in a silent shade Contentment find. 50
Honour keeps Court at home, and doth not fear
To be condemned abroad, if quitted there.[5]
While I have this retreat, 'tis not the noise
Of Slander, though believed, can wrong my Joys.
There is advantage in't: for Gold uncoined 55
Had been unuseful, nor with glory shined:
This stamped my Innocency in the Ore,
Which was as much, but not so bright, before.
Till an *Alembic* wakes and outward draws,[6]
The strength of Sweets lies sleeping in their cause: 60
So this gave me an opportunity
To feed upon my own Integrity.
And though their Judgement I must still disclaim,
Who can nor give nor take away a fame:
Yet I'll appeal unto the knowing few, 65
Who dare be just, and rip my heart to you.[7]

TO MRS. WOGAN, MY HONOURED FRIEND, ON THE DEATH OF HER HUSBAND

Dry up your tears, there's enough shed by you,
And we must pay our share of Sorrows too.
It is not private loss when such men fall,
The World's concerned, and Grief is general.
But though of our Misfortune we complain, 5
To him it is injurious and vain.
For since we know his rich Integrity,
His real Sweetness, and full Harmony;
How free his heart and house were to his Friends,
Whom he obliged without Design or Ends; 10
How universal was his courtesy,

---

[2] *vulgar* "Plebeian; suiting to the common people; practised among the common people" (Johnson).
[3] *Clown* "A coarse, ill-bred man" (Johnson).
[4] *the Chameleon . . . lives on air* a popular belief (Browne, *Pseudodoxia Epidemica* 3.21).
[5] *quitted* acquitted, absolved.
[6] *Alembic* "A vessel used in distilling" (Johnson); *wake* boil, produce steam.
[7] *rip* disclose.

How clear a Soul, how even, and how high;
How much he scorned disguise or meaner Arts,
But with a native Honour conquered Hearts;
We must conclude he was a Treasure lent,   15
Soon weary of this sordid Tenement.[1]
The Age and World deserved him not, and he
Was kindly snatched from future Misery.
We can scarce say he's Dead, but gone to rest,
And left a Monument in every breast.   20
For you to grieve then in this sad excess,
Is not to speak your Love, but make it less.
A noble Soul no Friendship will admit,
But what's Eternal and Divine as it.
The Soul is hid in mortal flesh we know,   25
And all its weaknesses must undergo,
Till by degrees it does shine forth at length,
And gathers Beauty, Purity, and Strength:
But never yet doth this Immortal Ray
Put on full splendour till it put off Clay: 30
So Infant Love is in the worthiest breast:
By Sense and Passion fettered and oppressed;
But by degrees it grows still more refined,
And scorning clogs, only concerns the mind.
Now as the Soul you loved is here set free   35
From its material gross capacity;
Your Love should follow him now he is gone,
And quitting Passion, put Perfection on.
Such Love as this will its own good deny,
If its dear Object have Felicity.   40
And since we cannot his great Loss Reprieve,
Let's not lose you in whom he still doth Live.
For while you are by Grief secluded thus,
It doth appear your Funeral to us.

FRIENDSHIP IN EMBLEM, OR THE SEAL. TO MY DEAREST LUCASIA

I

The Hearts thus intermixèd speak
A Love that no bold shock can break;
For joined and growing both in one,
Neither can be disturbed alone.

TO MRS. WOGAN
[1] *Tenement* "Any thing held by a tenant" (Johnson); a
common metaphor for the body, which is tenanted by
the soul.

2

That means a mutual Knowledge too;   5
For what is 't either heart can do,
Which by its panting Sentinel
It does not to the other tell?

3

That Friendship Hearts so much refines,
It nothing but it self designs: 10
The hearts are free from lower ends,
For each point to the other tends.

4

They flame, 'tis true, and several ways,
But still those Flames do so much raise,
That while to either they incline   15
They yet are noble and divine.

5

From smoke or hurt those Flames are free,
From grossness or mortality:
The Heart (like *Moses'* Bush presumed)[1]
Warmed and enlightened, not consumed.   20

6

The Compasses that stand above[2]
Express this great immortal Love;
For Friends, like them, can prove this true,
They are, and yet they are not, two.

7

And in their posture is express't   25
Friendship's exalted Interest:
Each follows where the other leans,
And what each other does, this other means.

8

And as when one foot does stand fast,
And t'other circles seeks to cast,   30
The steady part does regulate
And make the wanderer's motion straight:

FRIENDSHIP IN EMBLEM
[1] *Moses' Bush* the burning bush from which God spoke to Moses (Exodus 3.2).

[2] *Compasses* the golden compasses with which God made the world mentioned in Proverbs 8.27 (cf. *Paradise Lost* 6.225).

9

So Friends are only two in this,
T' reclaim each other when they miss:
For whosoe'er will grossly fall,   35
Can never be a Friend at all,

10

And as that useful Instrument
For Even lines was ever meant;
So Friendship from good Angels springs,
To teach the world Heroic things.   40

11

As these are found out in design
To rule and measure every Line;
So Friendship governs actions best,
Prescribing unto all the rest.

12

And as in Nature nothing's set   45
So just as Lines in number met;
So Compasses for these b'ing made,
Do Friendship's harmony persuade.

13

And like to them, so Friends may own
Extension, not Division:
Their Points, like Bodies, separate;   50
But Head, like Souls, knows no such fate.

14

And as each part so well is knit,
That their Embraces ever fit:
So Friends are such by destiny,   55
And no third can the place supply.

15

There needs no Motto to the Seal:
But that we may the mind reveal
To the dull Eye, it was thought fit
That *Friendship* only should be writ.   60

16

But as there are Degrees of bliss,
So there's no Friendship meant by this,
But such as will transmit to Fame
Lucasia and *Orinda*'s name.

ORINDA TO LUCASIA

1

Observe the weary birds ere night be done,
How they would fain call up the tardy Sun,
    With feathers hung with dew,
    And trembling voices too.
They court their glorious Planet to appear,[1]   5
That they may find recruits of spirits there.[2]
    The drooping Flowers hang their heads,
    And languish down into their beds:
While Brooks more bold and fierce than they,
    Wanting those beams, from whence   10
    All things drink influence,
Openly murmur and demand the day.

2

Thou my Lucasia art far more to me,
Than he to all the under-world can be;[3]
    From thee I've heat and light,   15
    Thy absence makes my night.
But ah! my Friend, it now grows very long,
The sadness weighty, and the darkness strong:
    My tears (its dew) dwell on my cheeks,
    And still my heart thy dawning seeks,   20
And to thee mournfully it cries,
    That if too long I wait,
    Even thou may'st come too late,
And not restore my life, but close my eyes.

PARTING WITH LUCASIA, A SONG

1

Well, we will do that rigid thing[1]
    Which makes Spectators think we part;
Though Absence hath for none a sting
    But those who keep each other's heart.

2

And when our Sense is dispossessed,   5
    Our labouring Souls will heave and pant,
And gasp for one another's breast,
    Since their Conveyances they want.

ORINDA TO LUCASIA
[1] *Planet* literally "a wanderer"; any heavenly body that appears to move; here, the Sun.
[2] *recruit* "Supply of any thing wanted" (Johnson).

[3] *under-world* the sublunary world; earth.
PARTING WITH LUCASIA
[1] *rigid* "Sharp; cruel" (Johnson).

3

Nay, we have felt the tedious smart
    Of absent Friendship, and do know   10
That when we die we can but part;
    And who knows what we shall do now?

4

Yet I must go: we will submit,
    And so our own Disposers be;
For while we nobly suffer it,   15
    We triumph o'er Necessity.

5

By this we shall be truly great,
    If having other things o'ercome,
To make our victory complete
    We can be Conquerors at home.   20

6

Nay then to meet we may conclude,
    And all Obstructions overthrow,
Since we our Passion have subdued,
    Which is the strongest thing I know.

To Antenor,
on a Paper of mine which J. J. threatens to publish
to prejudice him

Must then my Crimes become thy Scandal too?
Why, sure the Devil hath not much to do.
The weakness of the other Charge is clear,
When such a trifle must bring up the Rear
But this is mad design, for who before   5
Lost his repute upon another's score?
My Love and Life I must confess are thine,
But not my Errors, they are only mine.
And if my Faults must be for thine allowed,
It will be hard to dissipate the Cloud: 10
For *Eve*'s Rebellion did not *Adam* blast,
Until himself forbidden Fruit did taste.
'Tis possible this Magazine of Hell
(Whose name would turn a verse into a spell,
Whose mischief is congenial to his life)   15
May yet enjoy an honourable Wife.
Nor let his ill be reckoned as her blame,
Nor yet my Follies blast *Antenor*'s name.
But if those lines a Punishment could call

Lasting and great as this dark Lanthorn's gall;   20
Alone I'd court the Torments with content,
To testify that thou art Innocent.
So if my Ink through malice proved a stain,
My Blood should justly wash it off again.
But since that Mint of slander could invent   25
To make so dull a Rhyme his Instrument,
Let Verse revenge the quarrel. But he's worse
Than wishes, and below a Poet's curse;
And more than this Wit knows not how to give,
Let him be still himself, and let him live.   30

John Dryden (1631–1700)

Dryden stood beside Milton and Marvell at the funeral of Oliver Cromwell in 1658 and published Heroic Stanzas *on the death of the Protector. Two years later, like most other poets, he shifted his loyalties and welcomed King Charles with poems of praise. Dryden adapted himself to the political changes of his day and became Poet Laureate and Historiographer Royal under Charles II and James II. Some of his greatest poetry was written in response to political events and tended both to exalt the King and to shed a comfortable and flattering light on his foibles as well as on the trials and tribulations of the nation. Perhaps the most famous of his political poems is* Absalom and Achitophel *(1681), which glorifies and fictionalizes the conflict between the King and his illegitimate son, the Duke of Monmouth. Throughout the reigns of Charles and James, however, Dryden also cultivated a life as a professional writer who appealed to the public as well as to wealthy or lordly patrons: he made his living at his craft and in the end he was better and more consistently supported by his publishers and the reading public than by royal patronage. He was thrown completely on his devices as a professional writer after the Glorious Revolution of 1688 when he made no attempt to shift party or religion again; he had become a Catholic out of loyalty to James, and that left him on the outside of King William's Protestant court.*

The most lucrative part of Dryden's career may have been playwriting. He became one of the most popular dramatists of the Restoration supplying both comedies and tragedies to theaters, which had been closed for close to twenty years during the interregnum because of puritan restrictions. All for Love, *his version of Shakespeare's* Antony and Cleopatra *and* Marriage à la Mode *are two of his most famous plays. In the prefaces to his plays and in the longer* Essay of Dramatic Poesy, *which he wrote while plague closed the theaters in 1666, Dryden also produced a great deal of influential dramatic criticism. Added to these works, his prefaces to some of his later translations, particularly the* Aeneid *(1697) and the* Fables Ancient and Modern *(1700) clearly justify Samuel Johnson's characterization of Dryden as "the father of English criticism."*

The poems offered here display Dryden in only some of his very many literary modes. Like many poems of the time, "To My Honoured Friend, Dr. Charleton" was written in order to win favor; Charleton was pleased, and Dryden was elected to the Royal Society. The poem shows how skilfully Dryden can flatter but also how adept he is at mastering an unusual subject well enough to draw it into the realm of poetry. "Mac Flecknoe" exhibits Dryden's powers of satire and shows him in the midst of the kind of Grubstreet controversy in which he was embroiled for literally his whole professional life. Many of the poets with whom Dryden was forever breaking lances are only remembered now because he immortalized them in his satires. Like so much of Dryden's poetry, the elegies for Oldham and Killigrew are occasional pieces that should not be taken as expressions of personal grief, as modern elegies might be, but rather as performances that celebrate and decorate the dead. Dryden's deftness at performances of this kind is sometimes difficult for readers used to expressiveness in verse to appreciate. But such poems, like funeral services or civil ceremonies of various kinds, give an enduring decency to the raw, disturbing, and moving events of life, especially when they are as brilliantly composed as Dryden's poems. The desirability of occasional verse is probably easiest to appreciate in Dryden's Song for St. Cecilia's Day, *which celebrates music in musical verse.*

The last selection comes from Dryden's last work, Fables Ancient and Modern. *At this stage in his life Dryden was writing, mostly translating, full time for a living. He achieved such a facility in writing verse that it came as naturally to him as what he called "the other Harmony of prose." His retelling of the Ovidian story of Pygmalion heightens the sensuality of the original and takes a pleasure in the subject that is correspondent to the easiness Dryden has achieved with his medium. In his translations of this period – in his* Aeneid, *his* Juvenal, *and Ovid above all – as in his prose, Dryden had an undeniable effect on English. He pushed the language much closer to its modern form both in diction and in syntax. He is only a scant generation younger than Milton, whom he deeply admired, but his language seems as close to ours as the English written in the late eighteenth century, almost a hundred years after his death.*

The texts presented here are based on first editions, except in the case of "Mac Fleckno." This great comic poem was probably composed in 1676 and circulated in manuscript for six years before it was pirated and badly printed in 1682; the preferred copytext, which I follow, is the authorized edition in Miscellany Poems . . . By the most Eminent Hands *(1684). The standard edition of Dryden's works is* The California Dryden *(University of California Press, 1956–); I am deeply indebted to this magnificent, ongoing project. The poems to 1697 occupy four volumes. For the* Fables *and other poems of the last period the Oxford edition by James Kinsey is still the standard.*

To my Honoured Friend, Dr. Charleton, on his learned and useful Works; and more particularly this of STONE-HENGE, by him Restored to the true Founders[1] (1663)

The longest Tyranny that ever swayed
Was that wherein our Ancestors betrayed
Their free-born *Reason* to the *Stagirite,*[2]
And made his Torch their universal Light.
So *Truth,* while only one supplied the State,   5
Grew scarce and dear, and yet sophisticate;[3]

TO MY HONOURED FRIEND
[1] Walter Charleton (1620–1707), author of *Chorea Gigantum; or the most famous antiquity of Great-Britain, vulgarly called Stone-Henge, standing on the Salisbury plain, restored to the Danes* (1663), a work which opposed the theory that they were the ruins of a Roman temple. Dryden's poem appears as a preliminary, commendatory poem in the book (which provides my copytext).

Charleton returned the favor by proposing Dryden for admission to the Royal Society.
[2] *Stagirite* Aristotle, who was born in the town of Stagirus in Macedonia; Dryden refers to the Aristotelian approach to science, which was formal rather than empirical, especially as elaborated by the scholastic philosophers of the middle ages.
[3] *sophisticate* "Adulterate; not genuine" (Johnson).

Until 'twas bought, like Emp'ric Wares or Charms,[4]
Hard words sealed up with *Aristotle*'s Arms.[5]
Columbus was the first that shook his Throne
And found a *Temp'rate* in a *Torrid* Zone:[6]   10
The fev'rish air fanned by a cooling breeze,
The fruitful Vales set round with shady Trees;
And guiltless *Men*, that danced away their time,
Fresh as their *Groves*, and *Happy* as their *Clime*.
Had we still paid homage to a *Name*,   15
Which only *God* and *Nature* justly claim;
The *western Seas* had been our utmost bound,[7]
Where *Poets* still might dream the *Sun* was drowned:
And all the *Stars* that shine in *Southern* Skies
Had been admired by none but *Salvage* Eyes[8]   20
     Among th'*Assertors* of free Reason's claim,
The *English* are not the least in Worth, or Fame.
The World to *Bacon* does not only owe[9]
Its *present* Knowledge, but its *future* too.
Gilbert shall live, till *Load-stones* cease to draw,[10]   25
Or *British* Fleets the boundless Ocean awe;
And noble *Boyle*, not less in *Nature* seen,[11]
Than his great *Brother*, read in *States* and *Men*.[12]
The *Circling* streams, once thought but pools, of blood
(Whether Life's fuel, or the Body's food)   30
From dark Oblivion *Harvey*'s name shall save;[13]
While *Ent* keeps all the honour that he gave.[14]
Nor are *You*, Learned Friend, the least renowned;
Whose Fame, not circumscribed with *English* ground,
Flies like the nimble journeys of the Light,   35
And is, like that, unspent too in its flight.
Whatever *Truths* have been, by *Art* or *Chance*,
Redeemed from *Error*, or from *Ignorance*,
Thin in their *Authors* (like rich veins in Ore)
Your Works unite, and still discover more.   40
Such is the healing virtue of Your Pen,
To perfect Cures on *Books*, as well as *Men*.
Nor is This Work the least: You well may give

---

[4] *Emp'ric* an uneducated practitioner of medicine; a quack.
[5] *Hard words* philosophic words; latinate terms or jargon.
[6] Aristotle assumed that the equatorial regions of the earth were all uninhabitably hot.
[7] *western Seas* the Atlantic Ocean.
[8] *Salvage* old spelling of *savage*, "Uncivilised; barbarous; untaught" (Johnson).
[9] *Bacon* Sir Francis Bacon's *New Organon* provided a blueprint for the organization of knowledge.

[10] *Gilbert* William Gilbert (1540–1603) author of a treatise on magnets, of which the loadstone (an iron ore) used in nautical compasses was the prime example.
[11] *Boyle* Robert Boyle (1627–91) chemist and physicist, calculated barometric pressure.
[12] *Brother* Roger Boyle, Lord Broghill, author of the romance *Parthenissa*.
[13] *Harvey* William Harvey (1578–1657) correctly described the circulation of the blood.
[14] *Ent* Sir George Ent (1604–89) defended Harvey's theory.

To *Men* new vigour, who make *Stones* to live.[15]
Through You, the DANES (their short Dominion lost)[16]   45
A longer Conquest than the *Saxons* boast.
STONE-HENGE, once thought a *Temple*, You have found
A *Throne* where Kings, our Earthly Gods, were Crowned;
Where by their wond'ring Subjects They were seen,
Chose by their Stature, and their Princely mien.   50
Our *Sovereign* here above the rest might stand;[17]
And here be chose again to sway the Land.
   These ruins sheltered once *His* Sacred Head,
Then when from *Worcester*'s fatal Field *He* fled,[18]
Watched by the Genius of this Kingly place,   55
And mighty Visions of the Danish Race.
His *Refuge* then was for a *Temple* shown:
But, *He* Restored, 'tis now become a *Throne*.

Mac Flecknoe (1676?)

All human things are subject to decay,
And when Fate summons, Monarchs must obey:
This *Fleckno* found, who, like *Augustus*, young[1]
Was called to Empire, and had governed long;
In Prose and Verse, was owned, without dispute   5
Through all the Realms of *Non-sense*, absolute.
This agèd Prince now flourishing in Peace,
And blest with issue of a large increase,
Worn out with business, did at length debate
To settle the succession of the State: 10
And pond'ring which of all his Sons were fit
To Reign, and wage immortal War with Wit,
Cried, ' 'Tis resolved; for Nature pleads that He
Should only rule, who most resembles me:
Sh—— alone my perfect image bears,[2]   15
Mature in dullness from his tender years.
Sh—— alone, of all my Sons, is he

---

[15] *Men . . . who make Stones to live* apostles of the truth (1 Peter 2.4–5).
[16] *Danes* Danish vikings ruled parts of England under the Danelaw from about 870–920; Charleton proposed that Stonehenge was an older Danish ceremonial structure raised for the inauguration of their kings.
[17] *Our Sovereign* Charles II was very tall.
[18] *Wor'ster's fatal field* the battle of Worcester, September 3, 1651, the end of Charles II's abortive attempt to establish himself on the throne; he eventually passed through Salisbury Plain on his flight to the continent, where he remained until the restoration of the monarchy in 1660.

MAC FLECKNOE
[1] *Fleckno* Richard Flecknoe, a poor English poet and playwright lampooned about thirty-five years earlier in a hilarious poem by Andrew Marvell, "Flecknoe, an English Priest at Rome." *Augustus* he was nineteen when his great uncle Julius Caesar was assassinated in 44 BCE; he gradually consolidated his rule and was emperor until his death in 14 CE.
[2] *Sh*—— stands for Shadwell, as everyone reading the poem knew; Thomas Shadwell was a poet and rival playwright with whom Dryden had skirmished for several years over questions of literary decorum.

Who stands confirmed in full stupidity.
The rest to some faint meaning make pretence,
But *Sh*——— never deviates into sense.   20
Some Beams of Wit on other souls may fall,
Strike through and make a lucid interval;
But *Sh*———'s genuine night admits no ray,
His rising Fogs prevail upon the Day:
Besides his goodly Fabric fills the eye,[3]   25
And seems designed for thoughtless Majesty:
Thoughtless as Monarch Oaks, that shade the plain,
And, spread in solemn state, supinely reign.[4]
Heywood and *Shirley* were but Types of thee,[5]
Thou last great Prophet of Tautology: 30
Even I, a dunce of more renown than they,
Was sent but before to prepare thy way;
And coarsely clad in *Norwich* Drugget came[6]
To teach the Nations in thy greater name.
My warbling Lute, the Lute I whilom strung[7]   35
When to King *John* of *Portugal* I sung,
Was but the prelude to that glorious day,
When thou on silver *Thames* did'st cut thy way,
With well timed Oars before the Royal Barge,
Swelled with the Pride of thy Celestial charge;   40
And big with Hymn, Commander of an Host,
The like was ne'er in *Epsom* Blankets tossed.[8]
Methinks I see the new *Arion* Sail,[9]
The Lute still trembling underneath thy nail.
At thy well sharpened thumb from Shore to Shore[10]   45
The Treble squeaks for fear, the Basses roar:
Echoes from *Pissing-Alley*, "*Sh*———" call,[11]
And "*Sh*———" they resound from *A*——— *Hall*.[12]
About thy boat the little Fishes throng,
As at the Morning Toast, that Floats along.   50
Sometimes as Prince of thy Harmonious band

---

[3]   *goodly Fabric*   ample or large body.
[4]   *supinely*   "1. With the face upward; 2. Drowsily; thoughtlessly; indolently" (Johnson).
[5]   *Heywood and Shirley*   Thomas Heywood and James Shirley, popular, unsophisticated dramatists of the earlier seventeenth century; *Type*   "That by which something future is prefigured" (Johnson).
[6]   *Norwich Drugget*   a coarse cloth, in keeping with the representation of Flecknoe as John the Baptist (who wore coarse clothing), the herald of Shadwell's coming.
[7]   *Lute*   Flecknoe actually played for King John, although the instrument is often a metaphor for poetry; *whilom*   formerly.

[8]   *in Epsom Blankets tossed*   this was an act of punishment or contempt (Johnson, s.v. *blanket*); Epsom probably refers to Shadwell's play *Epsom Wells*.
[9]   *Arion*   a Greek musician and poet of the seventh century BCE, reputed to have been rescued on the back of a charmed dolphin when thrown overboard by thieves; he was also associated with the origins of drama.
[10]   *Shore*   also means sewer.
[11]   *Pissing-Alley*   a nasty little street near the river.
[12]   *A*——— *Hall*   Aston Hall in the first edition, but the place is unlocated and A——— may make a pair with Pissing-Alley.

Thou wield'st thy Papers in thy threshing hand.[13]
St. *Andre*'s feet ne'er kept more equal time,[14]
Not even the feet of thy own *Psyche*'s rhyme:[15]
Though they in number as in sense excel;   55
So just, so like tautology they fell,
That, pale with envy, *Singleton* forswore[16]
The Lute and Sword which he in Triumph bore,
And vowed he ne'er would act *Villerius*[17] more.'
Here stopped the good old Sire; and wept for joy   60
In silent raptures of the hopeful boy.
All arguments, but for most his Plays, persuade,
That for anointed dullness he was made.
    Close to the Walls which fair *Augusta* bind,[18]
(The fair *Augusta* much to fears inclined)[19]   65
An ancient fabric, raised t' inform the sight,[20]
There stood of yore, and *Barbican* it hight:[21]
A watch tower once; but now, to Fate ordains,
Of all the Pile an empty name remains.
From its old Ruins Brothel houses rise,   70
Scenes of lewd loves, and of polluted joys,
Where their vast Courts the Mother Strumpets keep,
And undisturbed by Watch, in silence sleep.
Near these a Nursery erects its head,[22]
Where Queens are formed, and future Heroes bred;[23]   75
Where unfledged Actors learn to laugh and cry,
Where infant Punks their tender Voices try,[24]
And little *Maximins* the Gods defy.[25]
Great *Fletcher* never treads in Buskins here,[26]
Nor greater *Jonson* dares in Socks appear.   80
But gentle *Simkin* just reception finds[27]
Admist this Monument of vanished minds:
Pure Clinches, the suburban Muse affords;[28]

---

[13]   *threshing*   from thrash "To labour; to drudge . . . 'I would rather be Mevius, thresh for rhymes/ Like his, the scorn and scandal of the times' Dryden" (Johnson).
[14]   St. *Andre*   a French choreographer who worked on the opera *Psyche*.
[15]   *Psyche*   Shadwell wrote the libretto.
[16]   *Singleton*   an undistinguished actor and musician.
[17]   *Villerius*   a character in *The Siege of Rhodes*, a bombastic play by John Davenant.
[18]   *Augusta*   an old name for London.
[19]   *fears*   Dryden alludes to the contemporary panic about the "Popish Plot" to overthrow the English government, considered folly by the high-church royalists (including Charles and his brother James, who actually was Roman Catholic), but fanned into a frenzy with the machinations of radicals like Titus Oates and Israel Tongue.

[20]   *inform*   "To animate; to actuate by vital powers" (Johnson).
[21]   *Barbican*   Burgh-kenning, Old English for "city-watching," a defensive wall or tower; *hight*   archaic, was called.
[22]   *Nursery*   "The place or state where any thing is fostered or brought up" (Johnson).
[23]   *Queen*   with a pun on *quean*, a harlot.
[24]   *Punk*   prostitute.
[25]   *Maximin*   an emperor in one of Dryden's own plays, *Tyrannic Love*.
[26]   *Fletcher*   John Fletcher Elizabethan playwright whom Dryden admired; *Buskins*   the elevated shoes worn by actors in Greek tragedy to make them taller and therefore more heroic in stature; comic actors wore socks to lower their stature.
[27]   *Simkin*   clown in a popular farce of the day.
[28]   *Clinch*   a pun.

And *Panton* waging harmless War with words.[29]

Here *Fleckno*, as a place to Fame well known,   85
Ambitiously designed his *Sh*————'s Throne.
For ancient *Decker* prophesied long since,[30]
That in this Pile should Reign a mighty Prince,[31]
Born for a scourge of Wit, and flail of Sense:
To whom true dullness should some *Psyches* owe,   90
But Worlds of *Misers* from his Pen should flow:[32]
Humourists and *Hypocrites* it should also produce,
Whole *Raymond* families, and Tribes of *Bruce*;[33]

   Now Empress *Fame* had published the renown,
Of *Sh*————'s Coronation through the Town.   95
Roused by report of Fame, the Nations meet,
From near *Bun Hill*, and distant *Watling-street*.[34]
No *Persian* Carpets spread th' Imperial way,
But scattered Limbs of mangled Poets lay:
From dusty shops neglected Authors come   100
Martyrs of Pies, and Relics of the Bum.[35]
Much *Heywood*, *Shirley*, *Ogleby* there lay,[36]
But loads of *Sh*———— almost choked the way.
Bilked *Stationers* for Yeomen stood prepared,[37]
And *H*———— was Captain of the Guard.[38]   105
The hoary Prince in Majesty appeared,
High on a Throne of his own Labours reared.[39]
At his right hand our young *Ascanius* sat[40]
Rome's other hope, and pillar of the State.
His Brows thick fogs, instead of glories, grace,   110
And lambent dullness played around his face.
As *Hannibal* did to the Altars come,[41]
Sworn by his *Sire* a mortal Foe to *Rome*;
So *Sh*———— swore, nor should his Vow be vain,
That he till Death true dullness would maintain;   115
And in his father's Right, and Realms defence,
Ne'er to have peace with Wit, nor truce with Sense.
The King himself the sacred Unction made,
As King by Office, and as Priest by Trade:
In his sinister hand, instead of Ball,[42]   120
He placed a mighty Mug of Potent Ale;

---

[29] *Panton* another character from farce.
[30] *Decker* Thomas Decker a Jacobean author of relatively low city life.
[31] *Pile* "An edifice; a building" (Johnson).
[32] *Miser, Humourist, Hypocrite* plays by Shadwell.
[33] *Raymond, Bruce* characters in Shadwell's plays.
[34] *Bun Hill, Watling* two places in the City of London less than a mile apart.
[35] *Martyrs . . . Relics* remaindered, unbound pages of poetry sometimes ended up as wrapping or toilet paper.
[36] *Ogleby* John Ogilby a recently deceased translator of Virgil and Homer.

[37] *Bilk* "To cheat; to defraud, by running into debt, and avoiding payment" (Johnson); *Stationers* booksellers or publishers, who sometimes gave authors financial credit lines.
[38] *Herringman* Henry Herringman a stationer.
[39] *High on a Throne* cf. *Paradise Lost* 2.1.
[40] *Ascanius* son of Aeneas, the founder of Rome.
[41] *Hannibal* Carthaginian general whose father swore him to eternal enmity with Rome.
[42] *sinister* Latin or heraldic, left; *Ball* a globe symbolizing power in regal portraits.

Love's Kingdom to his right he did convey,[43]
At once his Sceptre and his rule of Sway;
Whose righteous Lore the Prince had practised young,
And from whose Loins recorded Psyche sprung.[44]   125
His Temples last with Poppies were o'erspread,[45]
That nodding seemed to consecrate his head:
Just at that point of time, if Fame not lie,
On his left hand twelve reverend Owls did fly.[46]
So Romulus 'tis sung, by Tiber's Brook,[47]   130
Presage of Sway from twice six Vultures took.
Th' admiring throng loud acclamations make,
And Omens of his future Empire take.
The Sire then shook the honours of his head,
And from his brows damps of oblivion shed   135
Full on the filial dullness: long he stood,
Repelling from his Breast the raging God;[48]
At length burst out in this prophetic mood:
     'Heavens bless my Son, from Ireland let him reign
To far Barbadoes on the Western main;   140
Of his Dominion may no end be known,
And greater than his Father's be his Throne.
Beyond loves Kingdom let him stretch his Pen';
He paused, and all the people cried 'Amen'.
Then thus, continued he, 'My Son advance   145
Still in new Impudence, new Ignorance.
Success let others teach, learn thou from me
Pangs without birth, and fruitless Industry.
Let Virtuoso's in five years be Writ;
Yet not one thought accuse thy toil of Wit;   150
Let gentle George in triumph tread the Stage,[49]
Make Dorimant betray, and Loveit rage;
Let Cully, Cockwood, Fopling charm the Pit,
And in their folly show the Writer's wit.
Yet still thy fools shall stand in thy defence,   155
And justify their Author's want of sense.
Let 'em be all by thy own model made
Of dullness, and desire no foreign aid:
That they to future ages may be known,
Not Copies drawn, but Issue of thy own.   160
Nay let thy men of wit too be the same,

---

[43] Love's Kingdom   a play by Flecknoe.
[44] record   "To celebrate; to cause to be remembered solemnly" (Johnson).
[45] Poppies   source of sleep-inducing opiates, to which Shadwell was known to be addicted.
[46] Owls   birds of night and therefore sleep.

[47] Romulus   with his brother Remus, the fabled founders of Rome.
[48] Repelling . . . the raging God   recalling the sibyl struggling as Apollo possesses and inspires her (Aeneid 6.78–9).
[49] George   Etherege, restoration comic playwright whose characters include Dorimant, Loveit, Cully, Cockwood, and Fopling.

All full of thee, and differing but in name;
But let no Alien *S-dl-y* interpose,[50]
To lard with wit thy hungry *Epsom* prose.
And when false flowers of *Rhetoric* thou would'st cull,   165
Trust Nature, do not labour to be dull;
But write thy best, and top; and in each line,[51]
Sir *Formal's* oratory will be thine.[52]
Sir *Formal*, though unsought, attends thy quill,
And does thy *Northern Dedications* fill.[53]   170
Nor let false friends seduce thy mind with praise,
By Arrogating *Jonson's* Hostile Name;
Let Father *Flecknoe* Fire thy Mind with Praise,
And Uncle *Ogleby* thy envy raise.
Thou art my blood, where *Jonson* has no part;   175
What share have we in Nature or in Art?
Where did his wit on learning fix a brand,
Or rail at Arts he did not understand?
Where made he love in Prince *Nicander's* vein,[54]
Or swept the dust in *Psyche's* humble strain?   180
Where sold he Bargains, "Whip-stitch, kiss my Arse,"[55]
Promised a Play and dwindled to a Farce?
Where did his Muse from *Fletcher* scenes purloin,
As thou whole *Eth'rege* dost transfuse to thine?
But so transfused as Oil on Water flow,   185
His always floats above, thine sinks below.
This is thy Province, this thy wondrous way,
New Humours to invent for each new Play:[56]
This is that boasted Bias of thy mind,
By which one way, to dullness, 'tis inclined.   190
Which makes thy writings lean on one side still,
And in all changes that way bends thy will.
Nor let thy mountain belly make pretence
Of likeness; thine's a tympany of sense.[57]
A Tun of Man in thy Large bulk is writ,[58]   195
But sure thou'rt a Kilderkin of wit.
Like mine thy gentle numbers feebly creep,[59]
Thy Tragic Muse gives smiles, thy Comic sleep.
With whate'er gall thou sett'st thy self to write,

---

[50] *S-dl-y* Sir Charles Sedley, a playwright who helped Shadwell on *Epsom Wells*.
[51] *top* "To perform eminently . . . This word, in this sense, is seldom used but on light or ludicrous occasions" (Johnson).
[52] *Sir Formal* Sir Formal Trifle, one of Shadwell's characters.
[53] *Northern Dedications* because directed to the Duke and Duchesss of Newcastle, in northern England.
[54] *Prince Nicander* a character in *Psyche*.
[55] *sold . . . Bargains* made sharp retorts; the examples that follow paraphrase Thomas Shadwell's *The Virtuoso* 4.74.
[56] *Humour* "General turn or temper of mind" (Johnson), exemplified in a flat, comic character.
[57] *Tympany* "A kind of obstructed flatulence that swells the body like a drum" (Johnson).
[58] *Tun* a large barrel, as opposed to a *kilderkin*, a small one.
[59] *numbers* verses.

Thy inoffensive Satires never bite. 200
In thy felonious heart, though Venom lies,
It doth but touch thy *Irish* pen, and dies.
Thy Genius calls thee not to purchase fame
In keen Iambics, but mild Anagram:[60]
Leave writing Plays, and choose for thy command 205
Some peaceful Providence in *Acrostic* Land
There thou mayst wings display and Altars raise,[61]
And torture one poor word Ten thousand ways.[62]
Or if thou would'st thy different talent suit,
Set thy own Songs, and sing them to thy lute.' 210
He said, but his last words were scarcely heard,
For *Bruce* and *Longvil* had a *Trap* prepared,[63]
And down they sent the yet declaiming *Bard.*
Sinking he left the Drugget robe behind,
Borne upwards by a subterranean wind, 215
The Mantle fell to the young Prophet's part,[64]
With double portion of his Father's Art.

To the Memory of Mr. *Oldham*[1] (1684)

Farewell, too little and too lately known,
Whom I began to think and call my own;
For sure our Souls were near allied; and thine
Cast in the same Poetic mould with mine.
One common Note on either Lyre did strike, 5
And Knaves and Fools were both abhorred alike:
To the same Goal did both our Studies drive,
The last set out the soonest did arrive.
Thus *Nisus* fell upon the slippery place,[2]
While his young Friend performed and won the Race. 10
O early ripe! to thy abundant store
What could advancing Age have added more?
It might (what Nature never gives the young)
Have taught the numbers of thy native Tongue.[3]
But Satire needs not those, and Wit will shine 15
Through the harsh cadence of a rugged line.[4]

---

60 *Iambics* the classical measure for satire.
61 *wings . . . Altars* a reference to poems in which the lines are arranged to look like their subject, such as George Herbert's "Easter Wings" (about angels and the Ascension) and "The Altar"; Dryden and his age considered such poems mere gimickry or false wit.
62 *torture one . . . word* the metaphysical practice of "catachresis" or using words in new and varied senses.
63 *Bruce* and *Longvil* characters in *The Virtuoso*; *Trap* trapdoor.
64 *the young Prophet* the scene imitates the prophet Elijah's reception of his father's mantle (2 Kings 2).

TO THE MEMORY OF MR. *OLDHAM*
1 John Oldham (1653–83) was a poet best known for his *Satyrs upon the Jesuits* (1681); he probably met Dryden in London shortly after the publication of that work, but allusions in his earlier work show that he had admired Dryden for years. The poem first appeared in *Remains of Mr. John Oldham in Verse and Prose* (London, 1684).
2 *Nisus* having fallen near the finish line, he tripped the next runner and gave the victory to his close friend Euryalus (*Aeneid* 5.315–39).
3 *numbers* harmony, correct prosody.
4 The rugged harmony of this line exemplifies the kind of verse it praises.

A noble Error, and but seldom made,
When Poets are by too much force betrayed,
Thy generous fruits, though gathered ere their prime
Still showed a quickness; and maturing time[5]   20
But mellows what we write to the dull sweets of Rhyme.
Once more, hail and farewell; farewell thou young
But ah too short, *Marcellus* of our Tongue;[6]
Thy Brows with Ivy, and with Laurels bound;
But Fate and gloomy Night encompass thee around.   25

To the Pious Memory
of the Accomplished Young LADY
Mrs. Anne Killigrew[1] (1686)

Excellent in the Two Sister-Arts of
Poesy and Painting

AN ODE

I

Thou Youngest Virgin-Daughter of the Skies,
    Made in the last Promotion of the Blest;
Whose Palms, new plucked from Paradise,[2]
In spreading Branches more sublimely rise,
Rich with Immortal Green above the rest: 5
Whether, adopted to some Neighbouring Star,[3]
Thou roll'st above us, in thy wand'ring Race,
    Or, in Procession fixed and regular,[4]
    Moved with the Heaven's Majestic Pace;
    Or, called to more Superior Bliss,   10
Thou tread'st with Seraphims the vast Abyss:
What ever happy region be thy place,
Cease thy Celestial Song a little space;
(Thou wilt have time enough for Hymns Divine,
    Since Heav'n's Eternal Year is thine.)   15
Hear then a Mortal Muse thy Praise rehearse,[5]

[5] *quickness* "Sharpness; pungency" (Johnson) as well as aliveness.
[6] *Marcellus* adoptive son of Augustus Caesar, destined for empire, who died at the age of twenty and was memorialized in a famous passage of the *Aeneid* (6.860–6).
AN ODE
[1] Anne Killigrew (1660–85), a noblewoman whose near relations held high places at court: her father was Chaplain to Charles I and sometime playwright (stanza 2); her brother became an admiral (see stanza 9); she was a maid of honor to the Duchess of York and painted a portrait of her husband James II. Dryden's poem first appeared in the slender volume of Killigrew's poetry published shortly after her death (see the selection below). "Mrs." in the title stands for mistress, which means "a woman who governs," "a woman skilled in anything" and "a woman beloved and courted" (Johnson).
[2] *Palms* in the Book of Revelation the blessed are described as carrying palms (7.9), which were classical and Hebrew tokens of victory.
[3] *Star* planet or, etymologically, wanderer.
[4] *Procession fixed* the Ptolemaic fixed sphere of the stars.
[5] *a Mortal Muse* a living poet.

In no ignoble Verse;
But such as thy own voice did practise here,
When thy first Fruits of Poesy were giv'n,
To make thy self a welcome Inmate there:[6]   20
    While yet a young Probationer,[7]
    And Candidate of Heav'n.

2

If by Traduction[8] came thy Mind,
Our Wonder is the less to find
A Soul so charming from a Stock so good;   25
Thy Father was transfused into thy Blood:
So wert thou born into a tuneful strain,
(An early, rich, and inexhausted Vein.)
    But if thy Preexisting Soul
    Was formed, at first, with Myriads more,   30
It did through all the Mighty Poets roll,
    Who Greek or Latin Laurels wore,
And was that Sappho last, which once it was before.[9]
If so, then cease thy flight, O Heav'n-born Mind!
Thou hast no Dross to purge from thy Rich Ore:[10]   35
Nor can thy Soul a fairer Mansion find,
Than was the Beauteous Frame she left behind:
Return, to fill or mend the Quire, of thy Celestial kind.

3

May we presume to say, that at thy Birth,
New joy was sprung in Heav'n, as well as here on Earth.   40
For sure the Milder Planets did combine
On thy Auspicious Horoscope to shine,
And ev'n the most Malicious were in Trine.[11]
    Thy Brother-Angels at thy Birth
    Strung each his Lyre, and tuned it high,   45
    That all the People of the Sky
Might know a Poetess was born on Earth.
    And then, if ever, Mortal Ears
    Had heard the Music of the Spheres![12]
    And if no clust'ring Swarm of Bees[13]   50

---

6 Inmate "those that be admitted to dwell for their money jointly with another man, though in several rooms of his mansion-house, passing in and out by one door" (Johnson quoting John Cowell).

7 Probationer novice.

8 Traduction a process by which the Mind, or soul, destined for a mortal is transmitted through the medium of related souls.

9 Sappho she was one of the greatest of the Greek lyric poets (fl. 600 BCE).

10 no Dross to purge according to Pythagorean theory the soul seeks to perfect itself through its successive reincarnations.

11 Trine a benign configuration of planets in astrology.

12 Music of the Spheres the harmonious sound thought to be generated by the synchronous movement of the spheres in the Ptolemaic universe.

13 Bees said to have buzzed round the lips of the infant Plato, an omen that he would have the gift of sweet speech.

On thy sweet Mouth distilled their golden Dew,
   'Twas that, such vulgar Miracles
   Heav'n had not Leisure to renew:
For all the Blest Fraternity of Love
Solemnised there thy Birth, and kept thy Holiday above.   55

4

O Gracious God! How far have we
Profaned thy Heav'nly Gift of Poesy?
Made prostitute and profligate the Muse,
Debased to each obscene and impious use,
Whose Harmony was first ordained Above   60
For Tongues of Angels, and for Hymns of Love?
O wretched We! why were we hurried down
   This lubric and adult'rate age,[14]
   (Nay added fat Pollutions of our own)[15]
   T' increase the steaming Ordures of the stage?   65
What can we say t'excuse our *Second Fall?*
Let this thy *Vestal*, Heav'n, atone for all!
Her *Arethusian* Stream remains unsoiled,[16]
Unmixed with Foreign Filth, and undefiled;
Her Wit was more than Man, her Innocence a Child!   70

5

   Art she had none, yet wanted none:
   For Nature did that Want supply:
   So rich in Treasures of her Own,
   She might our boasted Stores defy:
Such Noble Vigour did her Verse adorn,   75
That it seemed borrowed, where 'twas only born.
Her Morals too were in her Bosom bred,
   By great Examples daily fed,
What in the best of Books, her Father's Life, she read:
   And to be read her self she need not fear;   80
   Each Test, and every Light, her Muse will bear,
   Though *Epictetus* with his Lamp were there.[17]
Even Love (for Love sometimes her Muse expressed)
Was but a *Lambent-flame* which played about her Breast,
   Light as the Vapours of a Morning Dream,[18]   85
   So cold herself, whilst she such Warmth expressed,
   'Twas *Cupid* bathing in *Diana*'s Stream.

---

[14] *lubric* "Wanton; lewd" (Johnson).
[15] *fat* "Coarse; gross; dull" (Johnson).
[16] *Arethusian* chaste, pure, like Arethusa, a nymph changed by Diana into a stream to escape rape by Alpheus.

[17] *Epictetus* Stoic philosopher of the first century CE who lived an exemplary, simple life, with no furniture except a bed and a lamp.
[18] *Vapours* "Mental fume; vain imagination; fancy unreal" (Johnson).

6

Born to the spacious Empire of the *Nine*,[19]
One would have thought, she should have been content
To manage well that Mighty Government;   90
But what can young ambitious Souls confine?
    To the next Realm she stretcht her Sway,
    For *Painture* near adjoining lay,[20]
A plenteous Province, and alluring Prey.
A *Chamber of Dependences* was framed,[21]   95
(As Conquerors will never want Pretence,
    When armed, to justify the offence,)
And the whole Fief, in right of Poetry she claimed.
    The Country open lay without Defence;
    For Poets frequent in-roads there had made,   100
    And perfectly could represent
    The Shape, the Face, with every Lineament,
And all the large Domains which the *Dumb-sister* swayed;
    All bowed beneath her Government,
    Received in Triumph wheresoe'er she went.   105
    Her Pencil drew, whate'er her Soul designed,
And oft the happy Draught surpassed the Image in her Mind.[22]
    The *Sylvan* Scenes of Herds and Flocks,
    And fruitful Plains and barren Rocks,
    Of shallow Brooks that flowed so clear,   110
    The Bottom did the Top appear;
    Of deeper too and ampler Floods,
    Which, as in Mirrors, showed the Woods;
    Of lofty Trees, with Sacred Shades,
    And Perspectives of pleasant Glades,[23]   115
    Where Nymphs of brightest Form appear,
    And shaggy Satyrs standing near,
    Which them at once admire and fear.
    The Ruins too of some Majestic Piece,
    Boasting the Pow'r of ancient *Rome* or *Greece*,   120
    Whose Statues, Friezes, Columns broken lie,
    And, though defaced, the Wonder of the Eye;
    What Nature, Art, bold Fiction, e'er durst frame,
    Her forming Hand gave Shape unto the Name.
    So strange a Concourse ne'er was seen before,   125
But when the peopled Ark the whole Creation bore.

---

[19] *Nine* the nine muses, none of them devoted to painting.
[20] *Painture* the art of painting; painting and poetry were called the sister arts and their age-old affinity was made permanently memorable in Horace's famous dictum *ut pictura poesis* ("Ars Poetica," l. 361).

[21] *Chamber of Dependences* an office devised by Louis XIV of France to justify his imperial designs.
[22] *happy* lucky.
[23] *Perspective* "View; vista" (Johnson).

7

The Scene then changed, with bold Erected Look[24]
Our Martial King the sight with Reverence strook:[25]
For not content to express his Outward Part,
Her hand called out the Image of his Heart,   130
His Warlike Mind, his Soul devoid of Fear,
His High-designing Thoughts, were figured there,
As when, by Magic, Ghosts are made appear.
   Our Phoenix Queen was portrayed too so bright,
Beauty alone could Beauty take so right:[26]   135
Her Dress, her Shape, her matchless Grace,
Were all observed, as well as heav'nly Face.
With such a Peerless Majesty she stands,
As in that Day she took from Sacred hands:[27]
The Crown; 'mong num'rous Heroines was seen,   140
More yet in Beauty, than in rank, the Queen!
   Thus nothing to her *Genius* was denied,
But like a Ball of Fire the further thrown,
   Still with a greater Blaze she shone,
And her bright Soul broke out on every side.   145
What next she had designed, Heaven only knows,
To such Immod'rate Growth her Conquest rose,
That Fate alone its Progress could oppose.

8

   Now all those Charms, that blooming Grace,
The well-proportioned Shape, and beauteous Face,   150
Shall never more be seen by Mortal Eyes;
In Earth the much lamented Virgin lies.
   Not Wit, nor Piety could Fate prevent;
   Nor was the cruèl *Destiny* content
   To finish all the Murder at a Blow,
   To sweep at once her Life, and Beauty too;   155
But, like a hardened Fellon, took a pride
   To work more Mischievously slow,
   And plundered first, and then destroyed.[28]
O double Sacrilege on things Divine,   160
To rob the Relic, and deface the Shrine!
   But thus *Orinda* died;[29]
   Heaven, by the same Disease, did both translate,[30]
As equal were their Souls, so equal was their Fate.

---

[24] *Erected* from "to erect" "To establish anew" or adjective "Bold; confident; unshaken" (Johnson); James's line was restored to the throne, having been displaced during Cromwell's reign.

[25] *Martial King* James II.

[26] *take* "To copy" (Johnson).

[27] *Sacred hands* those of the Archbishop of Canterbury on coronation day.

[28] *plundered* small pox robbed her of her beauty.

[29] *Orinda* the much more accomplished poet Katherine Philips (see pp. 357–68 above).

[30] *translate* transported to another plane of existence.

9

Mean time her Warlike Brother on the Seas   165
His waving Streamers to the Winds displays,
And vows for his Return, with vain Devotion, pays.
Ah, Generous Youth! that Wish forbear,
The Winds too soon will waft thee here!
Slack all thy Sails, and fear to come,   170
Alas, thou know'st not, Thou art wrecked at home!
No more shalt thou behold thy Sister's Face,
Thou hast already had her last Embrace.
But look aloft, and if thou ken'st from far,[31]
Among the *Pleiads* a New-kindled Star,[32]   175
If any sparkles, than the rest, more bright,
'Tis she that shines in that propitious Light.

10

When in mid-Air, the Golden Trump shall sound,[33]
To raise the Nations under ground;
When in the Valley of *Jehosaphat*,   180
The Judging God shall close the Book of Fate;
And there the last Assizes keep,[34]
For those who Wake, and those who Sleep;
When rattling Bones together fly,[35]
From the four Corners of the Sky;   185
When Sinews o'er the Skeletons are spread,
Those clothed with Flesh, and Life inspires the Dead;
The sacred Poets first shall hear the Sound,
And foremost from the Tomb shall bound,
For they are covered with the lightest Ground   190
And straight, with in-born Vigour, on the Wing,
Like mounting Larks, to the New Morning sing.
There *Thou*, Sweet Saint, before the Quire shalt go,
As Harbinger of Heav'n, the Way to show,
The Way which thou so well hast learned below.   195

A Song for St. Cecilia's Day (1687)[1]

I

From Harmony, from heav'nly Harmony
This Universal Frame began.[2]

---

[31] *ken'st* from "ken," to know or see.
[32] *Pleiads* Pleiades, the seven sisters or seven poets, a constellation.
[33] *When . . .* at the apocalypse, when God shall pass final judgement on the living and the dead (1 Corinthians 15.52; Joel 3.2).
[34] *Assizes* "Any court of justice" (Johnson).

[35] *When rattling Bones* the resurrection of the body at judgement day was a common Christian belief in the seventeenth century.
A SONG FOR ST. CECILIA'S DAY
[1] First published as a broadside to celebrate the day of St Cecilia, the patron saint of music, and set to music by Giovanni Battista Draghi.
[2] *Universal Frame* the world.

When Nature underneath a heap[3]
  Of jarring Atoms lay,
  And could not heave her Head,   5
The tuneful Voice was heard from high,
  Arise ye more than dead.
Then cold, and hot, and moist, and dry,
In order to their stations leap,
  And MUSIC'S pow'r obey.   10
From Harmony, from Heav'nly Harmony
  This universal Frame began:
  From Harmony to Harmony
Through all the compass of the Notes it ran,
The Diapason closing full in Man.[4]   15

2

What Passion cannot MUSIC raise and quell!
  When Jubal struck the corded Shell,[5]
  His List'ning Brethren stood around
  And wond'ring, on their Faces fell
  To worship that Celestial Sound.   20
Less than a God they thought there could not dwell
  Within the hollow of that Shell
  That spoke so sweetly and so well.
What Passion cannot MUSIC raise and quell!

3

The TRUMPET'S loud Clangor   25
  Excites us to Arms
With shrill Notes of Anger
  And mortal Alarms.
The double double double beat
  Of the thundring DRUM   30
Cries, hark the Foes come;
Charge, Charge, 'tis too late to retreat.

4

The soft complaining FLUTE
  In dying Notes discovers
  The Woes of hopeless Lovers,   35
Whose Dirge is whispered by the warbling LUTE.

5

Sharp VIOLINS proclaim
Their jealous Pangs, and Desperation,
Fury, frantic Indignation,
Depth of Pains, and height of Passion,   40
  For the fair, disdainful Dame.

---

[3] Cf. Milton's description of Chaos in *Paradise Lost*   a burst of harmony.
(2.898–900).   [5] *Jubal* biblical inventor of music (Genesis 4.21).
[4] *Diapason* the full range of a voice or instrument, or

6

But oh! what Art can teach
    What human Voice can reach
The sacred Organ's praise?
Notes inspiring holy Love,
Notes that wing their heav'nly ways
    To mend the Choirs above.[6]

45

7

Orpheus could lead the savage race;[7]
And Trees unrooted left their place;
    Sequacious of the Lyre:[8]
But bright *CECILIA* raised the wonder high'r;
When to her ORGAN, vocal Breath was giv'n
An Angel heard, and straight appeared
    Mistaking Earth for Heaven.

50

GRAND CHORUS

As from the pow'r of sacred Lays
    The Spheres began to move,
And sung the great Creator's praise
    To all the blessed above;
So when the last and dreadful hour[9]
This crumbling Pageant shall devour,
The TRUMPET *shall be heard on high,*
The Dead shall live, the Living die,
And MUSIC *shall untune the Sky.*

55

60

from *Fables Ancient and Modern* (1700)

PYGMALION AND THE STATUE[1]

Pygmalion loathing their lascivious Life,[2]
Abhorred all Womankind, but most a Wife:
So single chose to live, and shunned to wed,
Well pleased to want a Consort of his Bed.[3]
Yet fearing Idleness, the Nurse of Ill,
In Sculpture exercised his happy Skill;
And carved in Ivory such a Maid, so fair,
As Nature could not with his Art compare,

5

---

[6]   *mend*   "To improve; to increase" (Johnson).
[7]   *Orpheus*   mythical poet and musician who sailed with the Argonauts.
[8]   *Sequacious*   "Following; attendant" (Johnson).
[9]   *the last and dreadful hour*   the day of final judgement (e.g. 1 Corinthians 15.52).

PYGMALION AND THE STATUE
[1]   The poem is a loose translation of Ovid, *Metamorphoses* 10.243–97.
[2]   *their*   the Propætides, Cyprian girls who denied the divinity of Venus and were in consequence forced into prostitution by the goddess and later turned to stones (*Metamorphoses* 10.238–42).
[3]   *want*   lack.

Were she to work; but in her own Defence
Must take her pattern here, and copy hence. 10
Pleased with his Idol, he commends, admires,
Adores; and last, the Thing adored, desires.
A very Virgin in her Face was seen,
And had she moved, a living Maid had been:
One would have thought she could have stirred, but strove 15
With Modesty, and was ashamed to move.
Art hid with Art, so well performed the Cheat,
It caught the Carver with his own Deceit:
He knows 'tis Madness, yet he must adore,
And still the more he knows it, loves the more: 20
The Flesh, or what so seems, he touches oft,
Which feels so smooth, that he believes it soft.
Fired with this Thought, at once he strained the Breast,[4]
And on the Lips a burning Kiss impressed.
'Tis true, the hardened Breast resists the Grip, 25
And the cold Lips return a Kiss unripe:
But when, retiring back, he looked again,
To think it Ivory, was a Thought too mean:
So would believe she kissed, and courting more,
Again embraced her naked Body o'er; 30
And straining hard the Statue, was afraid
His Hands had made a Dent, and hurt his Maid:
Explored her, Limb by Limb, and feared to find
So rude a Grip had left a livid Mark behind:
With Flatt'ry now, he seeks her Mind to move, 35
And now with Gifts (the pow'rful Bribes of Love)
He furnishes her Closet first; and fills
The crowded Shelves with Rarieties of Shells;
Adds Orient Pearls, which from the Conchs he drew,[5]
And all the sparkling Stones of various Hue: 40
And Parrots, imitating Human Tongue,
And Singing-birds in Silver Cages hung;
And every fragrant Flow'r, and od'rous Green,
Were sorted well, with Lumps of Amber laid between:
Rich, fashionable Robes her Person deck, 45
Pendants her Ears, and Pearls adorn her Neck:
Her tapered Fingers too with Rings are graced,
And an embroidered Zone surrounds her slender Waist.[6]
Thus like a Queen arrayed, so richly dressed,
Beauteous she showed, but naked showed the best. 50
Then, from the Floor, he raised a Royal Bed,
With Cov'rings of *Sidonian* Purple spread:[7]

---

[4] *strain* "To squeeze in an embrace" (Johnson).
[5] *Orient* "Bright; shining; glittering; gaudy; sparkling".
[6] *Zone* girdle or belt.
[7] *Sidonian* from Sidon, ancient Tyre, famous for purple dye.

The Solemn Rites performed, he calls her Bride,
With Blandishments invites her to his Side,
And as she were with Vital Sense possessed,   55
Her Head did on a plumy Pillow rest.
    The Feast of *Venus* came, a Solemn Day,
To which the *Cypriots* due Devotion pay:[8]
With gilded Horns, the Milk-white Heifers led,
Slaughtered before the sacred Altars, bled: 60
Pygmalion off'ring, first, approached the Shrine,
And then with Prayers implored the Pow'rs Divine,
'Almighty Gods, if all we Mortals want,
If all we can require, be yours to grant;
Make this fair Statue mine', he would have said,   65
But changed his Words, for shame; and only prayed,
'Give me the Likeness of my Ivory Maid'.
    The Golden Goddess, present at the Prayer
Well knew he meant th' inanimated Fair,
And gave the Sign of granting his Desire;   70
For thrice in cheerful Flames ascends the Fire.
The Youth, returning to his Mistress, hies,
And impudent in Hope, with ardent Eyes,
And beating Breast, by the dear Statue lies.
He kisses her white Lips, renews the Bliss,   75
And looks, and thinks they redden at the Kiss;
He thought them warm before: Nor longer stays,
But next his Hand on her hard Bosom lays:
Hard as it was, beginnning to relent,
It seemed, the Breast beneath his Fingers bent;   80
He felt again, his Fingers made a Print,
'Twas Flesh, but Flesh so firm, it rose against the Dent:
The pleasing Task he fails not to renew;
Soft, and more soft at every Touch it grew;
Like pliant Wax, when chafing Hands reduce[9]   85
The former Mass to Form, and frame for Use.
He would believe, but yet is still in pain,
And tries his Argument of Sense again,
Presses the Pulse, and feels the leaping Vein.
Convinced, o'erjoyed, his studied Thanks and Praise,   90
To her who made the Miracle, he pays:
Then Lips to Lips he joined; now freed from Fear,
He found the Savour of the Kiss sincere:
At this the wakened Image op'd her Eyes,
And viewed at once the Light and Lover, with surprise.   95
The Goddess present at the Match she made,

---

[8]   *Cypriots*   because Cyprus is the birthplace of Venus   [9]   *chafe*   "To warm with rubbing" (Johnson).
and one of her names.

So blessed the Bed, such Fruitfulness conveyed,
That ere ten Moons had sharpened either Horn,
To crown their Bliss, a lovely Boy was born;
Paphos his Name, who grown to Manhood, walled   100
The City Paphos, from the Founder called.[10]

John Locke (1632–1704)

Although he published nothing until he reached the age of fifty-five, in the last ten years of his life Locke produced the most influential philosophical and political works of the age. His Essay concerning Human Understanding *(1690) provided the basis for the durable school of British empiricism. Even more importantly, it expounded an epistemology so persuasive and common-sensical that it provided the language in which many succeeding generations would discuss their perceptions, and very probably, therefore, affected the mode of perception itself. His convictions about language were influential in the formation of Johnson's* Dictionary, *and he is quoted over and over in later philological works. His influence extended into all sorts of basic areas of understanding, but in none was his influence quite as dramatic and as unforeseen as in the realm of politics.*

As the personal physician and advisor of Anthony Ashley Cooper, first Earl of Shaftesbury, Locke was embroiled in the major national political disputes of his time. Like Cooper, Locke favoured assignment of the throne to the Duke of Monmouth, Charles II's illegitimate son, and the exclusion of James II, who was next in the royal line. After the so-called Exclusion Crisis came to a head in 1682, Locke and Shaftesbury fled the country. Recent evidence suggests that Locke continued to favour the appointment of Monmouth and may have contributed to the infamous Rye House Plot to kill the King. In 1685 James became King but he was ousted in 1689 by the Glorious or Bloodless Revolution in which Parliament brought in William of Orange and Queen Mary (who had a remote title to the throne). The Revolution showed where the true power now lay, and put a final end to Divine Right as a principle of rule in England. In many respects Locke's Two Treatises of Government *was written to defend and to elaborate the principles of the Revolution. The first treatise demolishes the theory of Divine Right, as expounded in Robert Filmer's posthumously published* Patriarcha. *The second treatise, however, achieves a kind of universality that goes far beyond Filmer and the particular circumstances of the revolution. It became a central document not only in the growth of liberal thinking in England but also in the formation of both the American and French republics later in the century. Locke could not possibly have agreed with the many disparate groups that adopted his political thinking in succeeding generations, nor could he have imagined that his particular, historically bound position could have become so thoroughly a part of the mainstream of political thought in the West.*

The Clarendon Press edition of Locke's Works *is setting the standard as each volume appears, but there is already a fine edition of the* Two Treatises *by Peter Laslett (Cambridge University Press, 1988). I follow the text of the first edition of 1690, but I am indebted to Laslett's commentary.*

---

[10]   *Paphos*   a Cyprian city and site of a famous temple
of Venus, her chief resort according to Homer.

from *An Essay Concerning the True Original Extent and End of Civil Government* (1690)

FROM CHAPTER 1

I. It having been shown in the foregoing Discourse,[1]

1. That *Adam* had not, either by natural Right of Fatherhood, or by positive Donation from God, any such Authority over his Children, or Dominion over the World as is pretended.

2. That if he had, his Heirs, yet, had no right to it.

3. That if his Heirs had, there being no Law of Nature nor positive Law of God that determines, which is the Right Heir in all cases that may arise, the Right of Succession, and consequently of bearing Rule, could not have been certainly determined.

4. That if even that had been determined, yet the knowledge of which is the Eldest Line of *Adam*'s Posterity, being so long since utterly lost, that in the Races of Mankind and Families of the World, there remains not to one above another, the least pretence to be the Eldest House, and to have the Right of Inheritance.

All these premises having, as I think, been clearly made out, it is impossible that the Rulers now on Earth, should make any benefit, or derive any the least shadow of Authority from that, which is held to be the Fountain of all Power, *Adam's Private Dominion and Paternal Jurisdiction*; so that, he that will not give just occasion, to think that all Government in the World is the product only of Force and Violence, and that Men live together by no other Rules but that of Beasts, where the strongest carries it, and so lay a Foundation for perpetual Disorder and Mischief, Tumult, Sedition, and Rebellion[2] (things that the followers of that Hypothesis so loudly cry out against) must of necessity find out another rise of Government, another Original of Political Power, and another way of designing and knowing the Persons that have it, than what Sir *Robert F*[ilmer] hath taught us.

2. To this purpose, I think it may not be amiss, to set down what I take to be Political Power. That the Power of a Magistrate over a Subject, may be distinguished from that of a Father over his Children, a Master over his Servant, a Husband over his Wife, and a Lord over his Slave. All which distinct Powers happening sometimes together in the same Man, if he be considered under these different Relations, it may help us to distinguish these Powers one from another, and show the difference betwixt a Ruler of a Common-wealth, a Father of a Family, and a Captain of a Galley.

3. Political Power, then, I take to be a Right of making Laws with Penalties of Death, and consequently all less Penalties, for the Regulating and Preserving of Property, and of employing the force of the Community, in the Execution of such Laws, and in the defence of the Common-wealth from Foreign Injury, and all this only for the Public Good . . .

FROM CHAPTER 2
OF THE STATE OF NATURE

. . . 4. To understand Political Power aright, and derive it from its Original, we must consider what Estate all Men are naturally in, and that is, a State of perfect Freedom to order

---

FROM *AN ESSAY CONCERNING THE TRUE ORIGINAL*.
[1] *foregoing Discourse* the first treatise, which is largely a refutation of Robert Filmer's *Patriarcha* (see selection above, pp. 12–14).

[2] *. . . Rebellion* a description of the Hobbesian state of nature (above, pp. 9–12), as also criticized by Filmer.

their Actions, and dispose of their Possessions and Persons as they think fit, within the bounds of the Law of Nature, without asking leave or depending upon the Will of any other Man.

A State also of Equality, wherein all the Power and Jurisdiction is reciprocal, no one having more than another, there being nothing more evident, than that Creatures of the same species and rank promiscuously born to all the same advantages of Nature, and the use of the same faculties, should also be equal one amongst another without Subordination or Subjection, unless the Lord and Master of them all should by any manifest Declaration of his Will set one above another, and confer on him by an evident and clear appointment an undoubted Right to Dominion and Sovereignty.

5. This equality of Men by Nature, the Judicious *Hooker*[3] looks upon as so evident in it self, and beyond all question, that he makes it the Foundation of that Obligation to mutual Love amongst Men, on which he Builds the Duties they owe one another, and from whence he derives the great Maxims *of Justice* and *Charity* . . .

6. But though this be a State of Liberty, yet it is not a State of Licence, though Man in that State have an uncontrollable Liberty, to dispose of his Person or Possessions, yet he has not Liberty to destroy himself, or so much as any Creature in his Possession, but where some nobler use, than its bare Preservation calls for it. The State of Nature, has a Law of Nature to govern it, which obliges every one, and reason, which is that Law, teaches all Mankind, who will but consult it: That being all equal and independent, no one ought to harm another in his Life, Health, Liberty or Possessions; for Men being all the Workmanship of one Omnipotent, and infinitely wise maker – All the Servants of one Sovereign Master, sent into the World by his order and about his business – they are his Property, whose Workmanship they are, made to last during his, not one another's Pleasure. And being Furnished with like Faculties, sharing all in one Community of Nature, there cannot be supposed any such Subordination among us, that may Authorize us to destroy one another, as if we were made for one another's uses, as the inferior ranks of Creatures are for ours. Every one as he is bound to preserve himself, and not to quit his Station wilfully; so by the like reason when his own Preservation comes not in competition, ought he, as much as he can, to preserve the rest of Mankind, and may not, unless it be to do Justice on an Offender, take away, or impair the life, or what tends to the Preservation of the Life, the Liberty, Health, Limb or Goods of another.

7. And that all Men may be restrained from invading others' Rights, and from doing hurt to one another, and the Law of Nature be observed, which willeth the Peace and Preservation of all Mankind, the Execution of the Law of Nature is in that State, put into every Man's hands, whereby every one has a right to punish the transgressors of that Law to such a Degree, as may hinder its Violation. For the Law of Nature would, as all other Laws that concern Men in this World, be in vain, if there were nobody that in the State of Nature, had a Power to Execute that Law, and thereby preserve the innocent and restrain offenders, and if any one in the State of Nature may punish another, for any evil he has done, every one may do so. For in that State of perfect Equality, where naturally there is no superiority or jurisdiction of one over another, what any may do in Prosecution of that Law, every one must needs have a Right to do.

8. And thus in the State of Nature, one Man comes by a Power over another; but yet no Absolute or Arbitrary Power, to use a Criminal when he has got him in his hands, according

---

[3] *Hooker*   Richard Hooker (1554?–1600), theologian, author of *Of the Laws of Ecclesiastical Polity* (1594); Locke cites a passage from *Laws* 1.8.7, which I omit.

to the passionate heats, or boundless extravagancy of his own Will, but only to retribute to him, so far as calm reason and conscience dictates, what is proportionate to his Transgression, which is so much as may serve for Reparation and Restraint. For these two are the only reasons, why one Man may lawfully do harm to another, which is that we call punishment. In transgressing the Law of Nature, the Offender declares himself to live by another Rule, than that of reason and common equity, which is that measure God has set to the actions of Men, for their mutual security, and so he becomes dangerous to Mankind, the tie, which is to secure them from injury and violence, being slighted and broken by him, which being a trespass against the whole Species, and the Peace and Safety of it, provided for by the Law of Nature, every Man upon this score, by the Right he hath to preserve Mankind in general, may restrain, or where it is necessary, destroy things noxious to them, and so may bring such evil on any one, who hath transgressed that Law, as may make him repent the doing of it, and thereby deter him, and by his Example others, from doing the like mischief. And in this case, and upon this ground, every Man hath a Right to punish the Offender, and be Executioner of the Law of Nature.

CHAPTER 4
OF SLAVERY

. . . 22. The natural Liberty of Man is to be free from any Superior Power on Earth, and not to be under the Will or Legislative Authority of Man, but to have only the Law of Nature for his Rule. The Liberty of Man, in Society, is to be under no other Legislative Power, but that established, by consent, in the Commonwealth, nor under the Dominion of any Will, or Restraint of any Law, but what the Legislative shall enact, according to the Trust put in it. Freedom then is not what Sir R[obert] F[ilmer] tells us, O{bservations on} A{ristotle} 55. A Liberty for every one to do what he lists,[4] to live as he pleases, and not to be tied by any Laws: But Freedom of Men, under Government, is, to have a standing Rule to live by, common to every one of that Society, and made by the Legislative Power erected in it. A Liberty to follow my own Will in all things, where the Rule prescribes not; not to be subject to the inconstant, uncertain, unknown, Arbitrary Will of another Man, as Freedom of Nature is to be under no other restraint but the Law of Nature.

23. This Freedom from Absolute, Arbitrary Power, is so necessary to, and closely joined with a Man's Preservation, that he cannot part with it, but by what forfeits his Preservation and Life together. For a Man, not having the Power of his own Life, cannot, by Compact, or his own Consent, enslave himself to any one, nor put himself under the Absolute, Arbitrary Power of another, to take away his Life, when he pleases. No body can give more Power than he has himself; and he that cannot take away his own Life, cannot give another power over it. Indeed having, by his fault, forfeited his own Life, by some Act that deserves Death, he, to whom he has forfeited it, may (when he has him in his Power) delay to take it, and make use of him to his own Service, and he does him no injury by it. For, whenever he finds the hardship of his Slavery outweigh the value of his Life, 'tis in his Power, by resisting the Will of his Master, to draw on himself the Death he desires.

24. This is the perfect condition of Slavery, which is nothing else, but the State of War[5] continued, between a lawful Conqueror, and a Captive. For, if once Compact enter between them, and make an agreement for a limited Power on the one side, and Obedience, on the

---

[4] *lists* wishes.

[5] *State of War* "a State of Enmity and Destruction," the subject of Locke's chapter 3.

other, the State of War and Slavery ceases, as long as the Compact endures. For, as has been said, no Man can, by agreement, pass over to another that which he hath not in himself, a Power over his own Life.

I confess, we find among the *Jews*, as well as other Nations, that Men did sell themselves; but, 'tis plain, this was only to Drudgery, not to Slavery.[6] For, it is evident, the Person sold was not under an Absolute, Arbitrary, Despotical Power. For the Master could not have Power to kill him, at any time, whom, at a certain time, he was obliged to let go free out of his Service: And the Master of such a Servant was so far from having an Arbitrary Power over his Life, that he could not, at pleasure, so much as maim him, but the loss of an Eye, or Tooth, set him free.

CHAPTER 5
OF PROPERTY

. . . 25. Whether we consider natural Reason, which tells us, that Men, being once born, have a right to their Preservation, and consequently to Meat and Drink, and such other things, as Nature affords for their Subsistence: Or *Revelation*, which gives us an account of those Grants God made of the World to *Adam,* and to *Noah,* and his Sons; 'tis very clear, that God, as K[ing] *David* says, *Psalm* 115.16. 'has given the earth to the Children of men', given it to Mankind in common. But this being supposed, it seems to some a very great difficulty how any one should ever come to have a Property in any thing; I will not content myself to answer, 'That if it be difficult to make out *Property*, upon a supposition, that God gave the world to *Adam* and his Posterity in common; it is impossible that any Man, but one universal Monarch, should have any *Property* upon a supposition, That God gave the World to *Adam,* and his Heirs in Succession, exclusive of all the rest of his Posterity'. But I shall endeavour to show, how Men might come to have a Property in several parts of that which God gave to Mankind in common, and that without any express Compact of all the Commoners.

26. God, who hath given the World to Men in common, hath also given them reason to make use of it to the best advantage of life, and convenience. The Earth, and all that is therein, is given to Men for the Support and Comfort of their being. And though all the Fruits it naturally produces, and Beasts it feeds, belong to Mankind in common, as they are produced by the spontaneous hand of Nature; and no body has originally a private Dominion, exclusive of the rest of Mankind, in any of them, as they are thus in their natural state: yet being given for the use of Men, there must, of necessity, be a means to appropriate them some way or other before they can be of any use, or at all beneficial to any particular Men. The Fruit, or Venison which nourishes the wild *Indian*, who knows no Inclosure, and is still a Tenant in common, must be his, and so his, *i.e.* a part of him, that another can no longer have any right to it, before it can do him any good for the support of his Life

27. Though the Earth, and all inferior Creatures be common to all Men, yet every Man has a *Property* in his own *Person*. This no Body has any Right to but himself. The *Labour* of his Body, and the *Work* of his Hands, we may say, are properly his. Whatsoever then he removes out of the State that Nature hath provided, and left it in, he hath mixed his Labour with it, and joined to it something that is his own, and thereby makes it his Property. It being by him removed from the common state Nature placed it in, it hath by this labour something annexed to it, that excludes the common right of other Men. For this *labour* being the

---

[6] *Jews . . . Slavery* the Mosaic law with respect to ser- vitude is laid out in Exodus 21.1-11, 20-1, 26-7; it provides for six years of service only with freedom granted in the seventh.

unquestionable Property of the Labourer, no Man but he can have a right to what that is once joined to, at least where there is enough, and as good left in common for others.

28. He that is nourished by the Acorns he picked up under an Oak, or the Apples he gathered from the Trees in the Wood, has certainly appropriated them to himself. No Body can deny but the nourishment is his. I ask then, 'when did they begin to be his? When he digested? Or when he eat? Or when he boiled? Or when he brought them home? Or when he picked them up?' And 'tis plain, if the first gathering made them not his, nothing else could. That labour put a distinction between them and common. That added something to them more than Nature, the common Mother of all, had done; and so they became his private right. And will any one say he had no right to those Acorns or Apples he thus appropriated, because he had not the consent of all Mankind to make them his? Was it a Robbery thus to assume to himself what belonged to all in Common? If such a consent as that was necessary, Man had starved, notwithstanding the Plenty God had given him. We see in Commons,[7] which remain so by Compact, that 'tis the taking any part of what is common, and removing it out of the state Nature leaves it in, which begins the Property; without which the Common is of no use. And the taking of this or that part, does not depend on the express consent of all the Commoners. Thus the Grass my Horse has bit; the Turfs my Servant has cut; and the Ore I have digged in any place where I have a right to them in common with others, become my Property, without the assignation[8] or consent of any body. The labour that was mine, removing them out of that common state they were in, hath fixed my Property in them.

Samuel Pepys (1633–1703)

With the possible exception of Boswell's London Journal, the diary kept by Samuel Pepys from 1660 to 1669 is the most famous work of its kind in English. Part of Pepys's motivation for beginning the work on January 1 of a momentous year was his interest in politics. As a household official in the service of Edward Mountagu (a staunch Cromwellian and a naval commander), Pepys found himself at the centre of the events that led to the restoration of the Stuart monarchy in 1660, two years after the death of Oliver Cromwell and about a year after the failure of Richard Cromwell to maintain control over the revolutionary government. Pepys rose with Mountagu and became a member of the Navy Board, under the direction of the Duke of York, later King James II. He had been schooled at St Paul's and Cambridge, but as the son of a London tailor, Pepys knew little about naval affairs. Through diligence and a devotion to systematic methods, however, he mastered the difficulties of the job and enacted many reforms, especially in the area of purchasing. He streamlined costs and reduced corruption, though he did not puritanically reject all of the gifts presented by merchants and tradesman looking for contractual favors. By 1669 when he ended his diary, he was known as the "right hand of the Navy." As he gratefully and lovingly records, his esteem and his finances grew vastly throughout the period of his diary, and by the end of it he was a made man with a large household and a private coach.

Political events may have prompted Pepys to begin his diary, but he gives at least equal attention to his rich private life. Especially interesting is his unsteady relationship with his Anglo-French

---

[7] *Common* "An open ground equally used by many   [8] *assignation* assigning. persons" (Johnson).

wife, Elizabeth St Michel, whom he had married in 1655 when he was 22 and she was 15. The two were separated for a time in 1668 when Elizabeth discovered that Pepys was conducting one of his many secret extra-marital affairs with her companion, Deborah Willet. Pepys's self-examination in his personal crises leaves something to be desired, but his buoyancy, his range of feelings, and the scope of his interests make him an attractive personality nevertheless. The diary conveys Pepys's personal outlook on every subject, whether public or private, and he gives readers the distinct sense that the diary is not only an extension of his experience but a sign of being alive that gradually became for him inseparable from living. At the end of May 1669, Pepys was suffering so much eye-strain that he feared he was going blind and gave up his diary-keeping to preserve his sight. He writes that the sacrifice was "almost as much as to see myself go into my grave." It is hard not to view this attitude as a prototype or forerunner of a characteristically modern (or even postmodern) view of reality as something defined by language. In fact, the philosophical basis of this modern notion can be traced to the work of Pepys's nearly exact coeval, John Locke.

Although his eyesight returned and he kept some diaries after 1669, Pepys never again wrote anything on the scale of his famous work. We therefore know less than we might about his reactions to the death of Elizabeth at age 29 in late 1669 or the sort of domestic tranquility he evidently enjoyed in late middle age (without marriage) with Mary Skinner. We do know that after the diary years Pepys's professional success continued, although it was linked with the rise and fall of the Duke of York. Pepys held positions in Parliament and rose to Secretary for Admiralty Affairs in 1684. In that year he also became the President of the Royal Society. But in 1689, with the fall of James II, the former Duke of York, and the Glorious Revolution that brought William of Orange to the English throne, Pepys was forced into retirement, as he had been temporarily so forced during five years (1679–84) when the Duke and his supporters were thought to be complicitous in the so-called "Popish Plot" to sell the government of England to France and Roman Catholicism. In retirement Pepys pursued his interests in collecting books, manuscripts, ballads, prints, and drawings. His collections, especially the ballads, were among the greatest in England, and he enjoyed the company of other learned gentlemen, including Sir Isaac Newton and John Evelyn, who lived to write an admiring, elegiac note in his own diary about Pepys's death in 1703.

Pepys bequeathed the unique manuscript of his diary to Magdalene College, Cambridge where it remains in six elegantly bound, gold-stamped volumes. Pepys had many of his books richly bound, and a codicil in his will makes it clear that he took pride in passing his private journals, and the rest of his library, on to succeeding generations. The manuscript is remarkably neatly written, and there is evidence that the Magdalene College volumes represent a fair copy of more haphazardly jotted notes. In fact, at least in many instances, Pepys probably engaged in an arduous process of composition. Assembling notes from his "pocket-books" and the backs of slips of paper, ephemera picked up at plays, receipts, and so on, Pepys compiled a rough draft of sorts. At the same time, he seems to have distributed some of his collections into other manuscript books (account books, and "by books" all now lost) which he kept simultaneously. Using notes, drafts for the diary and parts of his other books, Pepys then slowly and neatly composed the diary as we have it. It was once thought that Pepys's book represents an immediate expression of his experience rather than a careful composition involving several stages of writing. This view would make Pepys attractively romantic and spontaneous, but it does not account for the varying styles of composition in the work nor for its extraordinarily neat physical presentation. Nor would it sort with everything we know about the compulsively orderly and diligent habits of the diarist. The greatest oddity of the diary from a modern standpoint is also readily subject to misinterpretation. Although it is almost all written in shorthand, Pepys did not mean the work to be indecipherable – at least not to the learned people to whom he bequeathed it. Shorthand was a dignified, philosophical kind of writing in the seventeenth century, and it was the subject of many learned works in what now might be called communication theory. Pepys did not invent his shorthand but adopted (and in small ways adapted) one of the many methods invented in the seventeenth century. He obviously intended the work to frustrate casual inspection (most probably by members of his household), and he further obscured passages concerning his sexual adventures by using a macaronic vocabulary of French, Spanish, and Latin. However, although the work looks dauntingly cryptic, the deception was not meant to be lasting, and, though Pepys destroyed some personal papers, he carefully preserved his diary.

Visitors and residents of Magdalene College noticed Pepys's diary from time to time in the eighteenth century, but not a single line was quoted in print before 1812, and the first edition, abridged and bowdlerized, did not appear until 1825. Although there were several popular editions in the nineteenth century, the work has only recently been properly edited and published in its entirety, including Pepys's accounts of his sexual affairs, which Victorian editors had omitted as inappropriate for print. The following excerpts are from the standard edition, edited by Robert Latham and William Matthews, 9 vols (G. Bell and Sons Ltd, 1970). The prefaces to these volumes and the accompanying Pepys Handbook provide excellent introductions to the life and works, and I rely on them here. The standard biography is Pepys by Sir Arthur Bryant, 3 vols (London, 1948–9).

The small extract from the diary presented here records Pepys's experience during a six-week period when the so-called Great Plague was devastating London. Plague was a disease transmitted by flea bites and peaked in the summer when fleas, infesting rats, thrived. Estimates put the death toll for London in 1665 at 100,000, one quarter of the population of the city. Believing that the disease was airborne, wealthy people left the city in droves at this time. Pepys stayed, though he moved his delicate wife to Woolwich. He records his horror and his fears of the plague, but he does not neglect his other experiences. Fear does not prevent him from continuing his social and sometimes profligate ways, nor does it entirely dampen his wonderful and memorable good cheer.

from *Diary*

JULY 1665

1. Called up betimes, though weary and sleepy, by appointment by Mr. Povey and Colonel Norwood, to discourse about some payments of Tangier.[1] They gone, I to the office and there sat all morning. At noon dined at home, and then to the Duke of Albemarles by appointment to give him an account of some disorder in the yard at Portsmouth, by workmen's going away of their own accord for lack of money, to get work of haymaking or anything else to earn themselves bread.

Thence I to Westminister, where I hear the sickness increases greatly. And to the Harp and Ball[2] with Mary, talking, who tells me simply of losing her first love in the country in Wales and coming up hither unknown to her friends. And it seems Dr. Williams[3] doth pretend to love her, and I have found him there several times.

FROM *DIARY*

[1] *Povey ... Tangier* In 1665 Pepys succeeded Thomas Povey (1615–c. 1702) as treasurer of the Privy Council's Committee for Tangier, a besieged, highly strategic and wealthy city acquired by England in 1661; Henry

Norwood (c. 1614–89) became the deputy governor of the colony in 1665.
[2] *the Harp and Ball* a large tavern near Charing Cross.
[3] *Dr. Williams* a physician who treated Pepys's wife.

Thence by coach, and late at the office and so to bed – sad at the news that seven or eight houses in Bazing-hall street are shut up of the plague.

2. *Sunday*. Up, and all the morning dressing my closet[4] at the office with my plat[5] very neatly, and a fine place now it is and will be a pleasure to sit in – though I thank God I needed none before. At noon dined at home, and after dinner to my accounts and cast them up, and find that though I have spent above £90 this month yet I have saved £17 and am worth in all above £1450, for which the Lord be praised.

In the evening my Lady Penn[6] and daughter came to see and supped with us. Then a messenger about business of the office from Sir G. Carteret[7] at Chatham[8] – and by word of mouth did send me word that the business between my Lord[9] and him is fully agreed on and is mightily liked of by the King and the Duke of York, and that he sent me this word with great joy. They gone, we to bed.

I hear this night that Sir J Lawson[10] was buried late last night at St. Dunstans by us, without any company at all – and that the condition of his family is but very poor, which I could be contented to be sorry for, though he never was the man that ever obliged me by word or deed.

3. Up, and by water with Sir W. Batten[11] and Sir J. Mennes[12] by water to Whitehall to the Duke of Albemarle's, where, after a little business – we parted, and I to the Harp and Ball and there stayed a while talking with Mary, and so home to dinner; after dinner to the Duke of Albemarle's[13] again, and so to the Swan[14] and there demeurais un peu de temps con la fille.[15] And so to the Harp and Ball and alone demeurais un peu de temps besándola;[16] and so away home and late at the office about letters; and so home resolving from this night forward to close all my letters if possible and end all my business at the office by daylight, and I shall go near to do it and put all my affairs in the world in good order, the season growing so sickly that it is much to be feared how a man can scape having a share with others in it – for which the good Lord God bless me or to be fitted to receive it.

So after supper to bed, and mightily troubled in my sleep all night with dreams of Jacke Cole my old school-fellow, lately dead, who was born at the same time with me, and we reckoned our fortunes pretty equal. God fit me for his condition.

5. Up, and advised about sending of my wife's bedding and things today to Woolwich,[17] in order to her removal thither. So to the office, where all the morning till noon; and so to the Change and thence home to dinner. In the afternoon I abroad to St. James, and there with Mr. Coventry[18] a good while and understand how matters are ordered in the fleet. . . .

4 *closet* "A small room of privacy and retirement" (Johnson).

5 *plat* an engraved plan or map, which Pepys had framed.

6 *Lady Penn* Margaret Jasper, wife of Sir William and mother of William, the Quaker leader.

7 *Sir G{eorge} Carteret* (c. 1610–80), Navy Treasurer 1660–7.

8 *Chatham* site of the most important royal dockyard of the time.

9 *my Lord* Edward Mountagu, Earl of Sandwich (1625–72), naval commander, father-in-law of Lady Mary Wortley-Montagu (see below, pp. 768–82).

10 *Sir J{ohn} Lawson* naval officer, died of wounds received at the Battle of Lowestoft.

11 *Sir W{illiam} Batten* (c.1601–67), Surveyor of the Navy 1660–7.

12 *Sir J{ohn} Mennes* (1599–1671), Comptroller of the Navy 1660–71.

13 *Duke of Albemarle* George Monck (1608–70), an important military leader under Cromwell but instrumental in restoring the monarchy.

14 *Swan* one of several taverns by that name.

15 *demeurais . . . fille* "tarried a little while with the girl"; even though the whole diary is written in code, Pepys obscures his dalliances further by breaking into French or, elsewhere, a kind of Spanish or quasi-Latin.

16 *besándola* kissing her.

17 *Woolwich* site of a shipyard, outside of London and so safer from the plague.

18 *Mr. Coventry* Henry, younger brother of Sir William, Pepys's mentor and colleague.

Being come to Deptford, my Lady[19] not being within, we parted; and I by water to Woolwich, where I found my wife come and her two maids, and very prettily accommodated they will be. And I left them going to supper, grieved in my heart to part with my wife, being worse by much without her, though some trouble there is in having the care of the family at home in this plague time. And so took leave, and I in one boat and W. Hewer[20] in another, home very late, first against tide – we having walked in the dark to Greenwich.

Late home and to bed – very alonely [sic].

24. . . . by appointment to Deptford to Sir G. Carteret between 6 and 7 a-clock, where I found him and my Lady[21] almost ready; and by and by went over to the Ferry and took coach and six horses nobly for Dagenhams,[22] himself and Lady and their little daughter Louisonne and myself in the coach – where when we came, we were bravely entertained and spent the day most pleasantly with the young ladies, and I so merry as never more. Only, for want of sleep, and drinking of strange beer, had a rheum[23] in one of my eyes which troubled me much. Here with great content all the day, as I think I ever passed a day in my life, because of the contentfulness of our errand – and the nobleness of the company and our manner of going. But I find Mr. Carteret[24] yet as backward almost in his caress as he was the first day. At night, about 7 a-clock, took coach again; but Lord, to see in what pleasant humour Sir G. Carteret hath been, both coming and going; so light, so fond, so merry, so boyish (so much content he takes in this business), it is one of the greatest wonders I ever saw in my mind. But once in serious discourse, he did say that if he knew his son to be a debauch, as many and most are nowadays about the Court, he would tell it, and my Lady Jem should not have him. And so enlarged, both he and she, about the baseness and looseness of the Court, and told several stories of the Duke of Monmouth[25] and Richmond.[26] And some great person married to a lady of extraordinary Quality (fit and that might have made a wife for the King himself) about six months since, that this great person hath given the pox[27] to. And discoursed how much this would oblige the Kingdom if the King would banish some of these great persons publicly from the Court – and wished it with all their hearts.

We set out so late that it grew dark, so as we doubted the losing of our way; and a long time it was or seemed before we could get to the waterside, and that about 11 at night; where when we come, all merry (only, my eye troubled me as I said), we find no ferry-boat was there nor no Oars[28] to carry us to Deptford. However, afterward oars was called from the other side at Greenwich; but when it came, a frolic, being mighty merry, took us, and there we would sleep all night in the Coach in the Isle of Dogs[29]; so we did, there being now with us my Lady Scott[30] – and with great pleasure drew up the glasses and slept till daylight; and then some victuals and wine being brought us we eat a bit, and so up and took boat, merry as might be; and when come to Sir G. Carteret, there all to bed – our good humour in everybody continuing;

---

19   Lady Sandwich, wife of Edward Mountagu.
20   W{ill} Hewer (1642–1715), naval official and close friend of Pepys.
21   my Lady   Elizabeth Carteret, George's cousin and wife.
22   Dagenhams   the home of Lady Wright (a relative of the Mountagues) in Essex.
23   rheum   "A thin watery matter oozing through the glands" (Johnson quoting Quincy).
24   Mr. Carteret   Philip, who married Mountagu's daughter Jemima in this month.

25   Monmouth   James Scott, Duke of Monmouth (1649–85), illegitimate son of Charles II.
26   Richmond   Charles Stuart, third Duke of Richmond.
27   pox   "The venereal disease. This is the sense when it has no epithet" (Johnson).
28   Oars   a large ferry operated by two men.
29   Isle of Dogs   a marshy peninsula in the Thames.
30   Lady Scott   wife of the soldier Sir Edward Scott.

25. and there I slept till 7 a-clock, then up, and to the office well refreshed, my eye only troubling me, which by keeping a little covered with my hankercher and washing now and then with cold water grew better by night. At noon to the Change,[31] which was very thin; and thence homeward and was called in by Mr. Rawlinson,[32] with whom I dined, and some good company, very harmlessly merry. But sad the story of the plague in the City, it growing mightily. This day my Lord Brouncker[33] did give me Mr. Graunt's book upon the Bills of Mortality,[34] new-printed and enlarged.

26. Up; and after doing a little business, down to Deptford with Sir W. Batten – and there left him, and I to Greenwich to the park, where I hear the King and Duke are come by water this morn from Hampton Court.[35] they asked me several Questions. . . . Great variety of talk – and was often led to speak to the King and Duke. By and by they to dinner; and all to dinner and sat down to the King saving myself, which though I could not in modesty expect, yet God forgive my pride, I was sorry I was there, that Sir W. Batten should say that he could sit down where I could not – though he had twenty times more reason than I. But this was my pride and folly . . .

[Mr. Castle][36] and I by and by to dinner, mighty nobly; and the King having dined, he came down, and I went in the barge with him, I sitting at the door – down to Woolwich (and there I just saw and kissed my wife, and saw some of her painting, which is very curious, and away again to the King) and back again with him in the barge, hearing him and the Duke talk and seeing and observing their manner of discourse; and God forgive me, though I adore them with all the duty possible, yet the more a man considers and observes them, the less he finds of difference between them and other men, though (blessed be God) they are both princes of great nobleness and spirits.

The Barge put me into another boat that came to our side, Mr. Holder[37] with a bag of gold to the Duke; and so they away, and I home to the office. The Duke of Monmouth is the most skittish, leaping gallant that ever I saw, always in action, vaulting or leaping or clambering.[38]

Thence, mighty full of the honour of this day – took coach and to Kate Joyce,[39] but she not within; but spoke with Anth,[40] who tells me he likes well of my proposal for Pall to Harman;[41] but I fear that less than £500 will not be taken, and that I shall not be able to give – though I did not say so to him. After a little other discourse, and the sad news of the death of so many in the parish of the plague, 40 last night – the bell always going – I back to the Exchange, where I went up and sat talking with my beauty, Mrs. Batelier,[42] a great while, who is indeed one of the finest women I ever saw in my life. After buying some small matter, I home, and there to the office and saw Sir J. Mennes, now come from Portsmouth; I home to set my Journal for these four days in order, they being four days of as great content and honour and pleasure to me as ever I hope to live or desire or think anybody else can live. For methinks if a man could but reflect upon this, and think that all these things are ordered by

---

31 *Change*   the Royal Exchange a center for merchants.
32 *Mr. Rawlinson*   landlord of the Mitre tavern.
33 *Lord Brounker*   William, second Viscount (1620–84), Navy Commissioner.
34 *Bills of Mortality   Natural and Political Observations . . . upon the Bills of Mortality* by John Graunt (1662), a pioneering work of demography registering deaths in London during the plague years.
35 *Hampton Court*   a palace west of London used by Charles mainly during the plague.
36 [Mr. Castle]   William, a private shipbuilder.

37 *Mr. Holder*   an accountant for the Duke.
38 *vaulting . . . clambering*   the Duke was then sixteen years old.
39 *Kate Joyce*   Pepys's cousin.
40 *Anthony Joyce*   a candle-maker, brother-in-law of Kate.
41 *Harman   Philip*   Pepys's cousin by marriage, recently widowed.
42 *Mrs. Batelier*   a relative of Pepys's neighbours; *Mrs.* means mistress and does not indicate marriage.

God Almighty to make me contented, and even this very marriage now on foot is one of the things intended to find me content in my life and matter of mirth, methinks it should make one mightily more satisfied in the world than he is. This day poor Robin Shaw at Backwell's[43] died – and Backwell himself now in Flanders. The King himself asked about Shaw; and being told he was dead, said he was very sorry for it.

The Sickness is got into our parish this week; and is got indeed everywhere, so that I begin to think of setting things in order, which I pray God enable me to put, both as to soul and body.

AUGUST 1665

8. Up, and to the office, where all the morning we sat. At noon I home to dinner alone. And after dinner Bagwell's wife[44] waited at the door, and went with me to my office, en lequel jo haze todo which I had a corasón a hazer con ella.[45] So parted, and I to Sir W. Batten's and there sat the most of the afternoon, talking and drinking too much with my Lord Brouncker, Sir G. Smith, G. Cocke,[46] and others, very merry. I drunk a little, mixed, but yet more than I should do. So to my office a little, and then to the Duke of Albemarle's about some business. The streets mighty empty all the way now, even in London, which is a sad sight. And to Westminister hall, where talking, hearing very sad stories from Mrs. Mumford[47] among others, of Mrs. Mitchell's son's family.[48] And poor Will that used to sell us ale at the Hall[49] door – his wife and three children dead, all I think in a day. So home through the City again, wishing I may have taken no ill in going; but I will go, I think, no more hither.

12. Coming back to Deptford, old Bagwell walked a little way with me and would have me in to his daughter's; and there, he being gone dehors, ego had my volunté de su hija.[50] Eat and drank, and away home; and after a little at the office, to my chamber to put more things still in order, and late to bed.

The people die so, that now it seems they are fain to carry the dead to be buried by daylight, the nights not sufficing to do it in. And my Lord Mayor commands people to be within 9 at night, all (as they say) that the sick may have liberty to go abroad for air. There is one also dead out of one of our ships at Deptford, which troubles us mightily – the *Providence* fire-ship, which was just fitted to go to sea. But they tell me today, no more sick on board. And this day W. Bodham[51] tell me that one is dead at Woolwich, not far from the Ropeyard. I am told too, that a wife of one of the grooms at Court is dead at Salsbury, so that the King and Queen are speedily to be all gone to Wilton.[52] God preserve us.

15. Up by 4 a-clock and walked to Greenwich, where called at captain Cocke's and to his chamber, he being in bed – where something put my last night's dream into my head, which I think is the best that ever was dreamed – which was, that I had my Lady Castlemaine[53] in my arms and was admitted to use all the dalliance I desired with her, and then dreamed that this could not be awake but that it was only a dream. But that since

---

[43] *Robin Shaw at Backwell's* a former colleague of Pepys's who had become managing clerk for Edward Backwell, a banker.

[44] *Bagwell's wife* one of Pepys's mistresses, wife of William, a ship's carpenter.

[45] *en lequel . . . con ella* where I did what I wished with her.

[46] *Sir G. Smith, G. Cocke* both George, a pair of well-to-do, hard-drinking merchants.

[47] *Mrs. Mumford* a shopkeeper.

[48] *Mrs. Mitchell* a bookseller and old friend of Pepys.

[49] *Hall* the great room in Westminster Palace, which accommodated many shops and stalls, as well as several government offices.

[50] *dehors . . . hija* "[he] gone away, I had my pleasure on her."

[51] *W{illiam} Bodham* clerk of the Ropeyard.

[52] *Wilton* the Earl of Pembroke's house in the country southwest of London.

[53] *Lady Castlemaine* Barbara Palmer, Countess of Castlemaine (1641–1709), a promiscuous beauty, a mistress of Charles II and other notables.

it was a dream and that I took so much real pleasure in it, what a happy thing it would be, if when we are in our graves (as Shakespeare resembles it), we could dream, and dream but such dreams as this that then we should not need to be so fearful of death as we are this plague-time?

Thomas Sprat (1635–1713)

Like many poets of his time, Sprat published an elegiac poem on the death of Oliver Cromwell and in succeeding years became a staunch defender of King Charles. Like Dryden, Sprat continued his drift to the political right wing during the brief reign of James II and was somewhat out of favor after the Glorious Revolution. He was a Doctor of Divinity as well as a poet and authored volumes of sermons. His best known literary work, however, was done in the service of science. He was commissioned by Bishop John Wilkins and other members of the fledgling Royal Society to write a kind of apology for the institution in the form of a history. The history of the Académie française had been written by Paul Péllisson-Fontanier (1653), and there was a political as well as an intellectual need to justify and explain the purposes of the English group that most resembled a European academy of arts and sciences. The England of Charles II was eager to stand on an equal footing with the Continent culturally as well as politically, and writers like Dryden and Sprat made important contributions to the national effort.

Improving, fixing, and regulating the national language was not the primary objective of the Royal Society, although there was a committee assigned to the subject. Wilkins, the warden of Gresham College (the London home of the Society), was a linguistic projector who invented a universal language meant to perfect the relationship between words and things. His manuscript was lost in the great fire of 1666, and his Essay towards a Real Character and a Philosophical Language *was not published until 1669, two years after the publication of Sprat's History. However, Sprat knew Wilkins's views, and he reflects them in his description of the plain, "naked" style of the Royal Society, in which there is no rhetoric and almost an equality between words and things. Sprat's own style is not so naked, as critics were quick to point out. Except for the usual modernization of spelling, I present the text of the first edition (1667) with its own elaborate, but perhaps, in its way, scientific punctuation.*

There is a facsimile edition of Sprat's History, *with commentary by Jackson I. Cope and Harold Whitmore Jones (Routledge and Kegan Paul, 1959), to which I am indebted.*

from *The History of the Royal Society* (1667)

PART TWO, SECTION XX
THEIR MANNER OF DISCOURSE

Thus they have directed, judged, conjectured upon, and improved *Experiments.* But lastly, in these, and all other businesses, that have come under their care; there is one thing more, about which the *Society* has been most solicitous; and that is, the manner of their *Discourse:* which, unless they had been very watchful to keep in due temper, the whole spirit and vigour of their *Design,* had been soon eaten out, by the luxury and redundance of *Speech.* The ill effects of this superfluity of talking, have already overwhelmed most other *Arts* and *Professions;* insomuch, that when I consider the means of *happy living,* and the causes of their corruption,

I can hardly forbear recanting what I said before;[1] and concluding, that *eloquence* ought to be banished out of all *civil Societies*, as a thing fatal to Peace and good Manners. To this opinion I should wholly incline; if I did not find, that it is a Weapon, which may be as easily procured by *bad* men, as *good*: and that, if these should only cast it away, and those retain it; the *naked Innocence* of virtue, would be upon all occasions exposed to the *armed Malice* of the wicked. This is the chief reason, that should now keep up the Ornaments of speaking, in any request: since they are so much degenerated from their original usefulness. They were at first, no doubt, an admirable Instrument in the hands of *Wise Men* when they were only employed to describe *Goodness, Honesty, Obedience*; in larger, fairer, and more moving Images: to represent *Truth*, clothed with Bodies; and to bring *Knowledge* back again to our very senses, from whence it was at first derived to our undertandings. But now they are generally changed to worse uses. They make the *Fancy* disgust[2] the best things, if they come sound, and unadorned: they are in open defiance against *Reason*; professing, not to hold much correspondence with that; but with its Slaves, *the Passions*: they give the mind a motion too changeable, and bewitching, to consist with *right practice*. Who can behold, without Indignation, how many mists and uncertainties, these specious *Tropes*[3] and *Figures* [4]have brought on our Knowledge? How many rewards, which are due to more profitable, and difficult *Arts,* have been still snatched away by the easy vanity of *fine speaking*: For now I am warmed with this just Anger, I cannot with-hold my self, from betraying the shallowness of all these seeming Mysteries; upon which, *we Writers,* and *Speakers,* look so big. And, in few words, I dare say; that of all the Studies of men, nothing may be sooner obtained, than this vicious abundance of *Phrase*, this trick of *Metaphors*, this volubility of *Tongue*, which makes so great a noise in the World. But I spend words in vain; for the evil is now so inveterate, that it is hard to know whom to *blame,* or where to begin to *reform*. We all value one another so much, upon this beautiful deceit; and labour so long after it, in the years of our education: that we cannot but ever after think kinder of it, than it deserves. And indeed, in most other parts of Learning, I look on it to be a thing almost utterly desperate in its cure: and I think, it may be placed amongst those *general mischiefs*; such, as the *dissension* of Christian Princes, the *want of practice* in Religion, and the like; which have been so long spoken against, that men are become insensible about them; every one shifting off the fault from himself to others; and so they are only made bare commonplaces of complaint. It will suffice my present purpose, to point out, what has been done by the *Royal Society*, towards the correcting of its excesses in *Natural Philosophy*;[5] to which it is, of all others, a most professed enemy.

They have therefore been most rigorous in putting in execution, the only Remedy, that can be found for this *extravagance*: and that has been, a constant Resolution, to reject all the amplifications, digressions, and swellings of style: to return back to the primitive purity, and shortness, when men delivered so many *things,* almost in an equal number of *words*. They have exacted from all their members, a close, naked, natural way of speaking; positive expressions, clear senses; a native easiness: bringing all things as near the Mathematical plainness, as they can: and preferring the language of Artisans, Countrymen, and Merchants, before that, of Wits, or Scholars.

FROM *THE HISTORY OF THE ROYAL SOCIETY*
[1]   *what I said before*   Sprat proposed an academy for the refinement of the English language (Part 1, chapters 19–20).
[2]   *disgust*   have no taste for.
[3]   *Trope*   "A change of a word from its original signification; as, the clouds *foretell* rain for *foreshow*" (Johnson).
[4]   *Figures*   figures of speech, such as metaphor.
[5]   *Natural Philosophy*   the natural sciences.

And here, there is one thing, not to be passed by; which will render this established custom of the *Society*, well nigh everlasting: and that is, the general constitution of the minds of the *English*. I have already often insisted on some of the prerogatives of *England*; whereby it may justly lay claim, to be the Head of a *Philosophical league*, above all other Countries in *Europe:* I have urged its situation, its present Genius, and the disposition of its Merchants;[6] and many more such *arguments* to encourage us, still remain to be used: But of all others, this, which I am now alleging, is of the most weighty, and important consideration. If there can be a true character even of the *Universal Temper* of any Nation under Heaven: then certainly this must be ascribed to our Countrymen: that they have commonly an unaffected sincerity; that they love to deliver their minds with a sound simplicity; that they have the middle qualities, between the reserved subtle southern, and the rough unhewn Northern people: that they are not extremely prone to speak: that they are most concerned, what others will think of the strength, than of the fineness of what they say: and that a universal modesty possesses them. These Qualities are so conspicuous, and proper to our Soil; that we often hear them objected to us, by some of our neighbour Satirists,[7] in more disgraceful expressions. For they are wont to revile the *English*, with a want of familiarity; with a melancholy dumpishness; with slowness, silence, and with the unrefined sullenness of their behaviour. But these are only the reproaches of partiality, or ignorance: for they ought rather to be commended for an honourable integrity; for a neglect of circumstances, and flourishes; for regarding things of *greater* moment, more than *less*; for a scorn to deceive as well as to be deceived: which are all the best endowments, that can enter into a *Philosophical Mind*. So that even the position of our climate, the air, the influence of the heavens, the composition of the English blood; as well as the embraces of the Ocean, seem to join with the labours of the *Royal Society*, to render our Country, a Land of *Experimental knowledge*. And it is a good sign, that Nature will reveal more of its secrets to the English, than to others; because it has already furnished them with a Genius so well proportioned, for the receiving, and retaining its mysteries.

Aphra Behn (1640–1689)

Poet, playwright, novelist, and translator, Aphra Behn was among the most versatile writers of her time. She is probably the first woman ever to make a living as a writer, and she was the first woman to be memorialized as a writer in Westminster Abbey. In surveying the history of English literature from her vantage point as a woman in the early twentieth century, Virginia Woolf would find in Behn a most important early advocate for the place of women in the world of letters.

Although the facts of Behn's early life are uncertain, she seems to have been born Aphra Johnson, and it is likely that as a young woman she travelled to Surinam or British Guiana. She places herself there amidst the scene of much of the action of her most famous novel, Oroonoko. *On her return to England she probably married a merchant named Behn, whose family was Dutch. Shortly thereafter, from 1666–7, Behn was in Antwerp as a spy for the English government under the code name "Astrea," which she later used as her literary name. At some point early on her husband died or abandoned her, for she was briefly in debtors' prison in 1667. Not long after this, Behn began*

---

[6] *situation . . . Genius . . . Merchants* points made by Sprat in Part 2, section 13.

[7] *Satirists* Frenchmen, particularly Samuel Sorbière in *Relation d'un voyage en Angleterre* (1664).

writing for a living: remarkably, she published over thirty separate volumes or pamphlets between 1676 and 1689, including an enormous epistolary novel that presents a recent scandal in a thinly veiled fiction. Her work as a playwright began before this period of massive publication and continued deep into it. Behn wrote at least nineteen plays, the first of which to be published was The Forced Marriage (1670). The Rover, perhaps Behn's best play, was popular enough to support a sequel. The Rover is a romantic comedy about temporarily disenfranchised English Cavaliers and their escapades in the masquerade world of Venice at Carnival time. Like some of Behn's poetry, The Rover displays a mastery of sexual innuendo and bawdiness that is much more common in male writers and conventionally thought of as inappropriate in women. Contemporary satirical writings, like that of Thomas Brown,[1] and later accounts, including the article in the Dictionary of National Biography, express dismay about Behn's morals. Happily, interest has lately returned to her diverse literary output, and perhaps most of all to her novel Oroonoko, or the Royal Slave.

There is an obvious temptation to read Oroonoko as a manifesto of anti-slavery, anti-colonialist, egalitarian, and perhaps even proto-feminist values, but the novel also has qualities that should appeal to those who are not interested in its usefulness to a political agenda. Although Behn draws on her knowledge of some historical incidents and persons, in genre the work is a romance, a popular fictional form designed to appeal to women and to members of the recently educated middle class. Oroonoko was certainly meant to be popular; but in a startling reversal of stereotypes, Behn substitutes Africans for the European nobles that traditionally take the lead roles in seventeenth-century romances. Yet, in many respects, Prince Oroonoko and his bride are nobler and more traditional than their European counterparts, and the work can be read as profoundly conservative, even though it is concerned with the injustices of the colonial system. Behn's politics always revolved around her extremely loyal royalism, which was not in conflict, for her, with her observations on the inequality of women, her obvious hatred of slavery, or her tacit campaign for the empowerment of women in the public as well as the private sphere. In short, when one tries to interpret Oroonoko, it resists easy solutions and displays some of the complexity and difficulty that many conservative critics think of as one of the defining qualties of art. Such complexity is not always evident in the language or the plot of the novel, but the book has all kinds of value for students of literature. In addition to its other virtues, Oroonoko shows the old, largely upper-class genre of the romance, in the process of transforming itself into a work with a broader social horizon and less parochial interests.

The text of Oroonoko is based on the first edition (1688). Most of the poems presented here come from Poems upon Several Occasions (1684). However, the text of "To the Fair Clarinda" is based on the version that appeared in Lycidus: or the Lover in Fashion (London, 1688), and both "Epitaph on the Tombstone of a Child" and "Ovid to Julia" come from Miscellany, Being a Collection of Poems by Several hands (1685). The Works are being edited by Janet Todd (Ohio State University Press, 1992–). I am indebted to Todd's notes on the poetry and on Oroonoko. There is a fairly recent critical biography by Angeline Goreau, Reconstructing Aphra (1980).

APHRA BEHN
[1]   See below, p. 563.

from *Poems upon Several Occasions* (1684)

A FAREWELL TO CELLADON, ON HIS GOING INTO IRELAND[1]

Pindaric

> Farewell the Great, the Brave and Good,
>   By all admired and understood;
> For all thy virtues so extensive are,
> Writ in so noble and so plain a Character,
>   That they instruct humanity what to do,   5
>   How to reward and imitate 'em[2] too,
>   The mighty *Caesar* found and knew,
>   The Value of a Swain so true:
> And early called the Industrious Youth from Groves
>   Where unambitiously he lay,   10
> And knew no greater Joys, nor Power than Loves;
>   Which all the day
> The careless and delighted *Celladon* Improves;[3]
> So the first man in Paradise was laid,
> So blest beneath his own dear fragrant shade,[4]   15
>   Till false Ambition made him range,
>   So the Almighty called him forth,
> And though for Empire he did *Eden* change;
>   Less Charming 'twas, and far less worth.

2

> Yet he obeys and leaves the peaceful Plains,   20
>   The weeping Nymphs, and sighing Swains,
>   Obeys the mighty voice of *Jove*.
> The Dictates of his Loyalty pursues,
> Business Debauches all his hours of Love;[5]
>   Business, whose hurry, noise and news   25
>   Even Nature's self subdues;
> Changes her best and first simplicity,
>   Her soft, her easy quietude
> Into mean Arts of cunning Policy,
> The Grave and Drudging Coxcomb to Delude.   30

A FAREWELL TO CELLADON
[1] Celladon has not been positively identified; clearly he was someone sent by Charles II (*Caesar* in the poem) on some kind of mission or assignment. The poem is "Pindaric" (after the great Greek praise poet of the fifth century BCE), which suggests mainly that it is rapid in its "narrative" transitions and relatively free in its prosody.
[2] *'em* them; an old form, not an informal one.
[3] *careless* "Cheerful; undisturbed" (Johnson).

[4] God "formed man of the dust of the ground" (Genesis 2.7) and later "took the man and put him into the Garden of Eden, to dress it and to keep it" (Genesis 2.15). Behn compares Charles's command to Celladon with God's deployment of Adam. In this analogy, what we are to think of Celladon's posture before the assignment is uncertain.
[5] *Business* "Employment" (Johnson).

Say, mighty *Celladon*, oh tell me why,
    Thou dost thy nobler thought employ
    In business, which alone was made
To teach the restless Statesman how to Trade
In dark Cabals for Mischief and Design,[6]   35
But ne'er was meant a Curse to Souls like thine.
    Business the *Check* to Mirth and Wit,
    Business the Rival of the Fair,
The Bane to Friendship, and the Lucky Hit,[7]
Only to those that languish in Despair;   40
Leave then that wretched troublesome Estate
    To him to whom forgetful Heaven,
    Has no one other virtue given,
    But dropt down the unfortunate,
    To Toil, be Dull, and to be Great.   45

                        3

    But thou whose nobler Soul was framed,
    For Glorious and Luxurious Ease,
    By Wit adorned, by Love inflamed;
    For every Grace, and Beauty Famed,
    Formed for delight, designed to please,   50
    Give Give a look to every Joy,
That youth and lavish Fortune can invent,
Nor let Ambition, that false God, destroy
    Both Heaven and Nature's first intent.
    But oh in vain is all I say,   55
        And you alas must go,
        The Mighty *Cæsar* to obey,
        And none so fit as you.
From all the Envying Crowd he calls you forth,
He knows your Loyalty, and knows your worth;   60
He's tried it oft, and put it to the Test,
It grew in Zeal even whilst it was oppressed,[8]
    The great, the Godlike *Celladon*,
    Unlike the base Examples of the times,
Could never be Corrupted, never won,   65
    To stain his honest blood with Rebel Crimes,
Fearless unmoved he stood amidst the tainted Crowd,
And justified and owned his Loyalty aloud.

---

[6] *Cabal* "A body of men united in some close [secret]
design. A cabal differs from a party as few from many"
(Johnson).

[7] *Hit* "A lucky chance" (Johnson) in judgement, wit,
or any affair.

[8] *whilst it was oppressed* during the interregnum, when
royalists were "oppressed."

4

Hibernia hail! Hail happy Isle,[9]
    Be glad, and let all Nature smile.   70
Ye Meads and Plains send forth your Gayest Flowers;[10]
    Ye Groves and every Purling Spring,
    Where Lovers sigh, and Birds do sing,
Be glad and gay, for *Celladon* is yours;
    He comes, he comes to grace your Plains.   75
    To Charm the Nymphs, and bless the Swains,
    Echoes repeat his Glorious Name
    To all the Neigbouring Woods and Hills;
    Ye Feathered Choir chant forth his Fame,
    Ye Fountains, Brooks, and Wand'ring Rills,   80
  That through the Meadows in Meanders run,
Tell all your Flowry Brinks, the generous Swain is come.

6

Divert him all ye pretty Solitudes,
And give his Life some softning Interludes:
    That when his wearied mind would be,   85
    From Noise and Rigid Business free;[11]
He may upon your Mossy Beds lie down,
    Where all is Gloomy, all is Shade,[12]
    With some dear She, whom Nature made,
    To be possessed by him alone;   90
    Where the soft tale of Love She breathes,
Mixt with the rushing of the wind-blown leaves,
    The different Notes of Cheerful Birds,
    And distant Bleating of the Herds:
Is Music far more ravishing and sweet,   95
Than all the Artful Sounds that please the noisy Great.

7

    Mix thus your Toils of Life with Joys,
And for the public good, prolong your days:
Instruct the World, the great Example prove,
Of Honour, Friendship, Loyalty, and Love.   100
    And when your busier hours are done,
    And you with *Damon* sit alone;[13]
    Damon the honest, brave and young;
Whom we must Celebrate where you are sung.
For you (by Sacred Friendship tied)   105
    Love nor Fate can ne'er divide;

---

[9] *Hibernia* Ireland.
[10] *Meads* meadows.
[11] *rigid* "Sharp; cruel" (Johnson).

[12] *Gloomy* "Obscure; imperfectly illuminated; almost dark" (Johnson).
[13] *Damon* unidentified.

When your agreeing thoughts shall backward run,
Surveying all the Conquests you have won,
The Swains you've left, the sighing Maids undone;
Try if you can a fatal prospect take,   110
Think if you can a soft *Idea* make:[14]
 Of what we are, now you are gone,
 Of what we feel for *Celladon.*

8

'Tis *Celladon* the witty and the gay,
That blest the Night, and cheered the world all Day: 115
'Tis *Celladon*, to whom our Vows belong,
And *Celladon* the Subject of our Song.
For whom the Nymphs would dress, the Swains rejoice,
 The praise of these, of those the choice;
And if our Joys were raised to this Excess,   120
Our Pleasures by thy presence made so great:
 Some pitying God help thee to guess
 (What Fancy cannot well Express)[15]
 Our Languishments by thy Retreat,
Pity our Swains, pity our Virgins more,   125
And let that pity haste thee to our shore;
And whilst on happy distant Coasts you are,
Afford us all your sighs, and *Caesar* all your care.[16]

ON A COPY OF VERSES MADE IN A DREAM, AND SENT TO ME IN A MORNING BEFORE I WAS AWAKE

 Amyntas, if your Wit in Dreams[1]
 Can furnish you with Themes,
What must it do when your Soul looks abroad,
Quickened with Agitations of the Sense,
And dispossessed of Sleep's dull heavy Load,   5
When every Syllable has Eloquence?
 And if by Chance such Wounds you make,
 And in your Sleep such welcome Mischiefs do;
 What are your Powers when you're awake,
Directed by Design and Reason too?   10
 I slept, as duller Mortals use,[2]
 Without the Music of a Thought,
When by a gentle Breath, soft as thy Muse,

---

[14] *Idea* image.
[15] *Fancy* imagination.
[16] The line recalls Jesus' answer to the Pharisees who asked if they should pay tribute to Caesar: "Render therefore unto Caesar the things which are Caesar's and unto God the things that are God's" (Matthew 22.21).

ON A COPY OF VERSES MADE IN A DREAM
[1] *Amyntas* a stock name in pastoral poetry, which probably represents a particular but unidentified person.
[2] *use* do habitually.

Thy name to my glad Ear was brought:
'*Amyntas*', cried the Page — And at the Sound,   15
My listening Soul unusual Pleasure found.
So the Harmonious *Spheres* surprize,[3]
Whilst the All-Ravish'd *Shepherd* gazes round,
And wonders whence the Charms should rise,
That can at once both please and wound.   20
Whilst trembling I unript the *Seal*
         Of what you'd sent,
My Heart with an Impatient Zeal,
Without my Eyes, would needs reveal
         Its Business and Intent.   25
         But so beyond the *Sense* they were
Of every scribbling Lover's common Art,
         That now I find an equal share
Of Love and Admiration in my Heart.
         And while I read, in vain I strove   30
             To hide the Pleasure which I took;
         Bellario saw in every Look[4]
My smiling Joy and blushing Love.
Soft every word, easy each Line, and true;
         Brisk, witty, manly, strong and gay;   35
         The Thoughts are tender all, and new,
And Fancy every where does gently play.
         Amyntas if you thus go on,
Like an unwearied Conqueror day and night,
         The World at last must be undone.   40
         You do not only kill at sight,
         But like a *Parthian* in your flight.[5]
         Whether you Rally or Retreat,
         You still have Arrows for Defeat.

To my Lady *Morland* at *Tunbridge*[1]

As when a Conqu'ror does in Triumph come,
And proudly leads the vanquished Captives home,
The Joyful People crowd in every Street,
And with loud shouts of Praise the Victor greet;
While some whom Chance or Fortune kept away,   5
Desire at least the Story of the Day;
How brave the Prince, how gay the Chariot was,

---

[3] *Harmonious Spheres*   the concentric shells comprising
the Ptolemaic universe (or the celestial bodies that move
in them), said to produce music because of their perfect
coordination.
[4] *Bellario*   the page who delivered the letter.
[5] *Parthian*   these ancient Asian cavalrymen (fl. 3–2 C.
BCE) were famous for shooting from horseback while in
retreat.

To MY LADY *MORLAND* AT *TUNBRIDGE*
[1]   *Lady Morland*   Carola Harsnett, wife of Sir Samuel
Morland (1652–74); *Tunbridge*   Tunbridge Wells a
fashionable resort town in Kent.

How beautiful he looked, with what a Grace;
Whether upon his Head he Plumes did wear;
Or if a Wreath of Bays adorned his Hair:[2]   10
They hear 'tis wondrous fine, and long much more
To see the *Hero* than they did before.
So when the Marvels by Report I knew,
Of how much Beauty, *Cloris*, dwelt in you;
How many *Slaves* your Conqu'ring Eyes had won,   15
And how the gazing Crowd admiring throng:
I wished to see, and much a Lover grew
Of so much Beauty, though my Rivals too.
I came and saw, and blest my Destiny;
I found it Just you should out-Rival me.   20
'Twas at the Altar, where more hearts were giv'n
To you that day, than were addressed to Heav'n.
The Reverend Man whose Age and Mystery[3]
Had rendred Youth and Beauty Vanity,
By fatal Chance casting his Eyes your way,   25
Mistook the duller Business of the Day,
Forgot the Gospel, and began to Pray.
Whilst the Enamoured Crowd that near you pressed,
Receiving *Darts* which none could e'er resist,
Neglected the Mistake o' th' Love-sick Priest.   30
Even my Devotion, *Cloris*, you betrayed,
And I to Heaven no other Petition made,
But that you might all other Nymphs out-do
In Cruelty as well as Beauty too.
I called *Amyntas* Faithless *Swain* before,[4]   35
But now I find 'tis Just he should Adore.
Not to love you, a wonder sure would be,
Greater than all his Perjuries to me.
And whilst I Blame him, I Excuse him too;
Who would not venture Heav'n to purchase you?[5]   40
But Charming *Cloris*, you too meanly prize
The more deserving Glories of your Eyes,
If you permit him on an Amorous score,
To be your *Slave*, who was my *Slave* before.
He oft has Fetters worn, and can with ease   45
Admit 'em or dismiss 'em when he please.
A Virgin-Heart you merit, that ne'er found
It could receive, till from your Eyes, the *Wound*;
A Heart that nothing but your Force can fear,
And own a *Soul* as Great as you are Fair.   50

---

[2] *Bay* "A poetical name for an honorary crown or garland, bestowed as a prize for any kind of victory or excellence" (Johnson).
[3] *Mystery* "A trade; a calling" (Johnson).
[4] *Amyntas* a poetical name for one of Behn's lovers, perhaps the notorious libertine John Hoyle (d. 1692).
[5] *venture* risk losing.

THE DISAPPOINTMENT[1]

1

One day the Amorous *Lysander*,
By an impatient Passion swayed,
Surprized fair *Cloris*, that loved Maid,
Who could defend her self no longer.
All things did with his Love conspire;   5
That gilded Planet of the Day,
In his gay Chariot drawn by Fire,
Was now descending to the Sea,
And left no Light to guide the World,
But what from *Cloris'* Brighter Eyes was hurled.   10

2

In a lone Thicket made for Love,
Silent as yielding Maid's Consent,
She with a Charming Languishment,
Permits his Force, yet gently strove;
Her Hands his Bosom softly meet,   15
But not to put him back designed,
Rather to draw 'em on inclined:
Whilst he lay trembling at her Feet,
Resistance 'tis in vain to show;
She wants the power to say, 'Ah! What d' ye do?'   20

3

Her Bright Eyes sweet, and yet severe,
Where Love and Shame confus'dly strive,
Fresh Vigour to *Lysander* give;
And breathing faintly in his Ear,
She cried, 'Cease, Cease – your vain Desire,   25
Or I'll call out – What would you do?
My Dearer Honour ev'n to You
I cannot, must not give – Retire,
Or take this Life, whose chiefest part
I gave you with the Conquest of my Heart'.   30

4

But he as much unused to Fear,
As he was capable of Love,

THE DISAPPOINTMENT
[1] This poem was long thought to be by John Wilmot (see selections below, pp. 461–80) and was first published, with many differences in a poorly edited collection of his verse, *Poems on Several Occasions* (1680). It begins as a translation of a French poem called "Sur une Impuissance" by de Cantenac first published in 1661, which in turn is based on Ovid, *Amores* 3.7.

The blessèd minutes to improve,
Kisses her Mouth, her Neck, her Hair;
Each Touch her new Desire Alarms,   35
His burning trembling Hand he pressed
Upon her swelling Snowy Breast,
While she lay panting in his Arms.
All her Unguarded Beauties lie
The Spoils and Trophies of the Enemy.   40

5

And now without Respect or Fear,
He seeks the Object of his Vows,
(His Love no Modesty allows)
By swift degrees advancing – where
His daring Hand that Altar seized,   45
Where Gods of Love do sacrifice:
That Awful Throne, that Paradise
Where Rage is calmed, and Anger pleased;
That Fountain where Delight still flows,
And gives the Universal World Repose.   50

6

Her Balmy Lips encount'ring his,
Their Bodies, as their Souls, are joined;
Where both in Transports Unconfined
Extend themselves upon the Moss.
Cloris half dead and breathless lay;   55
Her soft Eyes cast a Humid Light,
Such as divides the Day and Night;
Or falling Stars, whose Fires decay:
And now no signs of Life she shows,
But what in short-breathed Sighs returns & goes. 60

7

He saw how at her Length she lay;
He saw her rising Bosom bare;
Her loose thin *Robes*, through which appear
A Shape designed for Love and Play;
Abandoned by her Pride and Shame.   65
She does her softest Joys dispense,
Off'ring her Virgin-Innocence
A Victim to Love's Sacred Flame;
While the o'er-Ravished Shepherd lies
Unable to perform the Sacrifice.   70

8

Ready to taste a thousand Joys,
The too transported hapless Swain

Found the vast Pleasure turned to Pain;
Pleasure which too much Love destroys:
The willing Garments by he laid, 75
And Heaven all opened to his view,
Mad to possess, himself he threw
On the Defenceless Lovely Maid.
But Oh what envying God conspires
To snatch his Power, yet leave him the Desire! 80

9

Nature's Support (without whose Aid
She can no Human Being give)
It self now wants the Art to live;
Faintness its slackened Nerves invade:
In vain th' enraged Youth essayed[2] 85
To call its fleeting Vigour back,
No motion 'twill from Motion take;
Excess of Love his Love betrayed:
In vain he Toils, in vain Commands;
The Insensible fell weeping in his Hand. 90

10

In this so Amorous Cruel Strife,
Where Love and Fate were too severe,
The poor *Lysander* in despair
Renounced his Reason with his Life:
Now all the brisk and active Fire 95
That should the Nobler Part inflame,
Served to increase his Rage and Shame,
And left no Spark for New Desire:
Not all her Naked Charms could move
Or calm that Rage that had debauched his Love. 100

11

Cloris returning from the Trance
Which Love and soft Desire had bred,
Her timorous Hand she gently laid
(Or guided by Design or Chance)
Upon that Fabulous *Priapus*,[3] 105
That Potent God, as Poets feign;
But never did young *Shepherdess*,
Gath'ring of Fern upon the Plain,
More nimbly draw her Fingers back,
Finding beneath the verdant Leaves a Snake: 110

---

[2] *essayed* tried.

[3] *Priapus* Greek fertility god whose symbol is a phallus; hence his name is synonymous with phallus.

12

Than *Cloris* her fair Hand withdrew,
Finding that God of her Desires
Disarmed of all his Awful Fires,
And Cold as Flow'rs bathed in the Morning-Dew.
Who can the *Nymph*'s Confusion guess?   115
The Blood forsook the hinder Place,
And strewed with Blushes all her Face,
Which both Disdain and Shame expressed:
And from *Lysander*'s Arms she fled,
Leaving him fainting on the Gloomy Bed.   120

13

Like Lightning through the Grove she hies,
Or *Daphne* from the *Delphic God*,[4]
No Print upon the grassy Road
She leaves, t' instruct Pursuing Eyes.
The Wind that wantoned in her Hair,   125
And with her Ruffled Garments played,
Discovered in the Flying Maid
All that the Gods e'er made, if Fair.
So *Venus*, when her *Love* was slain,
With Fear and Haste flew o'er the Fatal Plain.[5]   130

14

The *Nymph*'s Resentments none but I
Can well Imagine or Condole:
But none can guess *Lysander*'s Soul,
But those who swayed his Destiny.
His silent Griefs swell up to Storms,   135
And not one God his Fury spares;
He cursed his Birth, his Fate, his Stars;
But more the *Sheperdess*'s Charms,
Whose soft bewitching Influence
Had Damned him to the *Hell* of Impotence.   140

ON A LOCKET OF HAIR WOVE IN A TRUE-LOVE'S KNOT, GIVEN ME BY SIR R. O.[1]

What means this Knot, in Mystic Order Tied,[2]
And which no Human Knowledge can divide?

---

4   *Daphne ... Delphic God*   the nymph's lengthy flight
from Apollo ends with her transformation into a laurel
tree (Ovid, *Metamorphoses* 1.502–52).
5   *Venus ... o'er the Fatal Plain*   the goddess, seeing
Adonis slain, turns her Swan-borne chariot and jumps
down from the sky (Ovid, *Metamorphoses* 10.720–2).

ON A LOCKET OF HAIR WOVE
1   *Sir R. O.*   uncertainly identified as Sir Rowland
Okeover of Staffordshire.
2   *Mystic*   "Sacredly obscure" or "Involving some secret
meaning; emblematical" (Johnson).

Not the Great Conqu'ror's Sword can this undo[3]
Whose very Beauty would divert the Blow.
    Bright Relic! Shrouded in a Shrine of Gold!   5
Less Myst'ry made a Deity of Old.
Fair Charmer! Tell me by what pow'rful Spell
You into this Confusèd Order fell?
If Magic could be wrought on things Divine,
Some *Amorous Sibyl* did thy Form design[4]   10
In some soft hour, which the Prophetic Maid
In Nobler Mysteries of Love employed,
Wrought thee a Hieroglyphic, to express
The wanton God in all his Tenderness;
Thus shaded, and thus all adorned with Charms,[5]   15
Harmless, Unfletched, without Offensive Arms,[6]
He used of Old in shady Groves to Play,
Ere *Swains* broke Vows, or *Nymphs* were vain and coy,
Or Love himself had Wings to fly away.
    Or was it (his Almighty Pow'r to prove)   20
Designed a Quiver for the God of Love?
And all these shining Hairs which th' inspired Maid
Has with such strange Mysterious Fancy laid,
Are meant his Shafts; the subt'lest surest Darts
That ever Conquered or Secured his Hearts;   25
Darts that such tender Passions do convey,
Not the young Wounder is more soft than they.
    'Tis so; the Riddle I at last have learned:
But found it when I was too far concerned.[7]

AN ODE TO LOVE[1]

I

Dull Love no more thy Senseless Arrows prize,
Damn thy Gay Quiver, break thy Bow;
'Tis only young *Lysander's* Eyes,
That all the Arts of Wounding know.

2

A Pox of Foolish Politics in Love,   5
A wise delay in War the Foe may harm:
By Lazy Siege while you to Conquest move;
His fiercer Beauties vanquish by a Storm.

---

[3] *the Great Conqueror* Alexander the Great who cut the Gordian knot with his sword.
[4] *Sibyl* a prophetess associated with a classical oracle or god; this sibyl is associated with Cupid, *the wanton God*.
[5] *shaded* "paint[ed] in obscure colours" (Johnson).

[6] *Unfletched* "unfledged," inexperienced, but with a suggestion of the special meaning of "fletch," to fit an arrow with feathers.
[7] *concern* "To disturb; to make uneasy" in addition to "To interest" (Johnson).
AN ODE TO LOVE
[1] *Love* the god of love, Cupid.

3

Some wounded God, to be revenged on thee,
The Charming Youth formed in a *lucky* hour,   10
Dressed him in all that fond Divinity,
That has out-Rivalled thee, a God, in Pow'r.

4

Or else while thou supinely laid
Basking beneath some Myrtle shade,
In careless sleep, or tired with play,   15
When all thy Shafts did scattered lie;
Th' unguarded Spoils he bore away,
And Armed himself with the Artillery.

5

The Sweetness from thy Eyes he took,
The Charming Dimples from thy Mouth,   20
That wondrous Softness when you spoke;
And all thy Everlasting Youth.

6

Thy bow, thy Quiver, and thy Darts:
Even of thy Painted Wings has rifled thee,
To bear him from his Conquered broken Hearts,   25
To the next Fair and Yielding She.

A LETTER TO A BROTHER OF THE PEN IN TRIBULATION[1]

Poor *Damon*! Art thou caught? Is 't even so?
Art thou become a *Tabernacler* too?[2]
Where sure thou dost not mean to Preach or Pray,
Unless it be the clean contrary way:
This holy time I little thought thy sin[3]   5
Deserved a *Tub* to do its Penance in.[4]
O how you'll for th' *Egyptian Flesh-pots* wish,[5]
When you're half-famished with your Lenten-dish,
Your *Almonds*, *Currans*, *Biscuits* hard and dry,

A LETTER TO A BROTHER OF THE PEN IN TRIBULATION
[1] *Brother of the Pen* fellow writer, perhaps the dramatist Edward Ravenscroft (1640–1707).
[2] *Tabernacler* So he called a Sweating-Tub [Behn's
note, referring to her addressee's contemptuous name for
churches of Protestant non-conformists; sitting in a real
sweating-tub was a treatment for venereal disease, the
addressee's "Tribulation"].

[3] *holy time* Lent [Behn's note].
[4] *Tub* Diogenes the Cynic, a Stoic philosopher of the
fifth century BCE was said to have lived in a tub as part
of his ascetic scheme of life; lenten, if not ascetic, habits
were recommended for patients with venereal disease.
[5] *Egyptian Flesh-pots* the plentiful board of Egypt, for
which the Israelites long on the march through the
desert (Exodus 16.3).

Food that will Soul and Body mortify: 10
Damned Penitential Drink, that will infuse
Dull Principles into thy Grateful Muse.[6]
    Pox on 't that you must needs be fooling now,
Just when the Wits had greatest need of you.[7]
Was Summer then so long a-coming on,   15
That you must make an Artificial one?
Much good may 't do thee; but 'tis thought thy Brain
Ere long will wish for cooler Days again.
For Honesty no more will I engage:[8]
I durst have sworn thou'dst had thy Pucelage.[9]   20
Thy Looks the whole Cabal have cheated too;[10]
But thou wilt say, most of the Wits do so.
Is this thy writing Plays? who thought thy Wit[11]
An Interlude of Whoring would admit?
To Poetry no more thou'lt be inclined,   25
Unless in Verse to damn all Woman-kind:
And 'tis but Just thou shouldst in Rancour grow
Against that Sex that has Confined thee so.
    All things in Nature now are Brisk and Gay
At the Approaches of the *Blooming May*:   30
The new-fletched Birds do in our Arbours sing[12]
A Thousand Airs to welcome in the Spring;
Whilst ev'ry Swain is like a Bridegroom dressed,
And every Nymph as going to a Feast:
The Meadows now their flowry Garments wear,   35
And every Grove does in its Pride appear:
Whilst thou poor *Damon* in close Rooms art pent,
Where hardly thy own Breath can find a vent.
Yet that too is a Heaven, compared to th' Task
Of Codling every Morning in a Cask.[13]   40
    Now I could curse this Female, but I know,
She needs it not, that thus could handle you.
Besides, that Vengeance does to thee belong,
And 'twere Injustice to disarm thy Tongue.
Curse then, dear Swain, that all the Youth may hear,   45
And from thy dire Mishap be taught to fear.
Curse till thou hast undone the Race, and all
That did contribute to thy Spring and Fall.

---

[6]   *Grateful Muse*   pleasure-giving poetry.
[7]   *need of you*   I wanted a prologue to a play [Behn's note].
[8]   *engage*   wager; stake a bet.
[9]   *Pucelage*   "State of virginity" (Johnson).
[10]   *Cabal*   Behn's circle of friends.
[11]   *thy writing Plays*   He pretended to Retire to Write [Behn's note].
[12]   *new-fletched*   recently feathered or fledged.
[13]   *Codling . . . in a Cask*   parboiling in a tub.

from *Lycidus: or the Lover in Fashion* (1688)

TO THE FAIR CLARINDA, WHO MADE LOVE TO ME, IMAGINED MORE THAN WOMAN

Fair lovely Maid, or if that Title be
Too weak, too Feminine for Nobler thee,
Permit a Name that more Approaches Truth:
And let me call thee, Lovely Charming Youth.
This last will justify my soft complaint,   5
While that may serve to lessen my constraint;
And without Blushes I the Youth pursue,
When so much beauteous Woman is in view.
Against thy Charms we struggle but in vain
With thy deluding Form thou giv'st us pain,   10
While the bright Nymph betrays us to the Swain.
In pity to our Sex sure thou wer't sent,
That we might Love, and yet be Innocent:
For sure no Crime with thee we can commit;
Of if we should – thy Form excuses it.   15
For who, that gathers fairest Flowers believes
A Snake lies hid beneath the Fragrant Leaves.
   Thou beauteous Wonder of a different kind,
Soft *Cloris* with the dear *Alexis* joined;
When e'er the Manly part of thee would plead,   20
Thou tempts us with the Image of the Maid,
While we the noblest Passions do extend
The Love to *Hermes*, *Aphrodite* the Friend.[1]

from *Miscellany, Being a Collection of Poems by Several hands* (1685)

EPITAPH ON THE TOMBSTONE OF A CHILD, THE LAST OF SEVEN THAT DIED BEFORE

This Little, Silent, Gloomy Monument,
Contains all that was sweet and innocent;
The softest pratler that e'er found a Tongue,
His Voice was Music and his Words a Song,
Which now each List'ning Angel smiling hears;   5
Such pretty Harmonies compose the Spheres.[1]
Wanton as unfledged Cupids, ere their Charms[2]

TO THE FAIR CLARINDA
[1] *Hermes, Aphrodite* the father and mother of Hermaphroditus, who became a mixture of man and woman when joined to Salmacis, the nymph whose love he spurned (Ovid, *Metamorphoses* 4.285–389).

EPITAPH ON THE TOMBSTONE OF A CHILD
[1] *Spheres* the concentric spheres of the Ptolemaic universe, supposed to revolve in harmony and produce music audible to the angels.
[2] *Wanton* "Frolicsome; gay; sportive; airy" (Johnson).

Had learned the little arts of doing harms;
Fair as young Cherubins, as soft and kind,
And though translated could not be refined;[3]   10
The Seventh dear pledge the Nuptial Joys had given,
Toiled here on Earth, retired to rest in Heaven;
Where they the shining Host of Angels fill,
Spread their gay wings before the Throne, and smile.

OVID TO JULIA. A LETTER[1]

Fair Royal Maid, permit a Youth undone
To tell you how he drew his Ruin on;
By what degrees he took that Poison in,
That made him guilty of *Prometheus'* sin;
Who from the Gods durst steal Celestial fire,   5
And though with less success, I did as high aspire.
Oh why ye Gods! was she of Mortal Race?
And why 'twixt her and me, was there so vast a space?
Why was she not above my Passion made
Some Star in Heaven, or Goddess of the Shade?[2]   10
And yet my haughty Soul could ne'er have bowed
To any Beauty, of the common Crowd.
None but the Brow, that did expect a Crown
Could Charm or Awe me with a Smile, or Frown;
I had the Envy of th' *Arcadian* Plains,[3]   15
Sought by the Nymphs, and bowed to by the Swains;
Where I passed, I swept the Fields along,
And gathered round me all the gazing throng:
In numerous Flocks and Herds I did abound,
And when I spread my wanton wishes round,   20
They wanted nothing but my being Crowned.
Yet witness all ye spiteful Powers above,
If my Ambition did not spring from Love!
Had you my Charming *Julia* been less fair,
Less Excellent, less Conqu'ring than you are,   25
I had my Glorious Loyalty retained,
My Noble Blood untainted had remained.
Witness ye Groves, witness ye Sacred Powers!
Ye shaded Rivers Banks, and Beds of Flowers,
Where the expecting Nymphs have past their hours.   30
Witness how oft, all careless of their Fame,
They languished for the Author of their flame,
And when I came reproached my cold reserve;

---

[3] *translated* brought to Heaven.
OVID TO JULIA. A LETTER
[1] *Ovid to Julia* the Roman poet was banished from the
court of Augustus in 8 CE, reportedly for committing
adultery with Caesar's granddaughter, Julia; the classical
figures may represent contemporary illicit lovers, Lord
Mulgrave and Princess Anne; the text is based on the
version in *Miscellany, Being a Collection of Poems by Several
hands* (London, 1685).
[2] *Shade* "An obscure place, properly in a grove or
close wood" (Johnson).
[3] *th' Arcadian Plains* the fanciful, rural setting of
much pastoral poetry, named after Arcadia, a mountainous region in interior southern Greece.

Asked for what Nymph I did my Joys preserve?
What sighing Maid was next to be undone?   35
For whom I dressed, and put my Graces on?
And never thought (though I feigned every proof
Of tender Passion) that I loved enough.
While I with Love's variety was cloyed;
Or the faint pleasure like a Dream enjoyed.   40
'Twas *Julia*'s brighter Eyes my soul alone
With everlasting gust, could feed upon.[4]
From her first bloom my Fate I did pursue,
And from the tender fragrant Bud, I knew
The Charming Sweets it promised, when it Blew.[5]   45
This gave me Love, and 'twas in vain I tried
The Beauty from the Princess to divide;
For he at once must feel, whom you inspire,
A soft Ambition, and a haughty fire,
And Hopes the Natural aid of young desire.   50
My unconsidering Passion had not yet
Thought your Illustrious Birth for mine too great,
'Twas Love that I pursued, vast Love that leads
Sometimes the equalled slave, to Princes' Beds.
But I forgot that Sacred Flame must rest   55
In your bright Soul, that makes th' Adorer blest;
Your generous fire alone must you subdue,
And raise the Humbler Lover up to you;
Yet if by Chance m' Ambition met a stop,[6]
By any thought that checked m' advancing hope,   60
This new one straight would all the rest confound,
How every Coxcomb aimed at being Crowned;
The vain young Fool with all his Mother's parts,[7]
(Who wanted wit enough for little Arts,)
With Crowds, and unmatched nonsense, lays a claim   65
To th' Glorious title of a Sovereign;
And when our Gods such wretched things set up,
Was it so great a crime in me to hope?
No laws of Heaven, or Man my Vows reprove;
There is no Treason in Ambitious Love.   70
That sacred Antidote, i' th' poisoned Cup,
Quells the Contagion of each little drop,
I bring no Forces, but my sighs and tears,
My Languishments, my soft complaints and Prayers,
Artillery which I ne'er sent in vain,   75

---

[4] *gust* "1. Sense of tasting. . . . 2. Height of perception; height of sensual enjoyment. . . . 3. Love"
(Johnson).
[5] *Blew* blossomed.
[6] *m'* my.

[7] *vain young Fool* Duke of Monmouth, popular, handsome, illegitimate son of Charles II, a candidate for the
throne proposed by Anthony Ashley Cooper (Earl of
Shaftesbury) and others who feared the Catholic heir,
James II.

Nor Failed where e'er addressed, to wound with pain:
Here, only here! rebated they return,[8]
Meeting the solid Armour of your Scorn;
Scorn! By the Gods! I any thing could bear,
The Rough Fatigues and Storms of dangerous War; 80
Long Winters' Marches, or the Summer heat,
Nay even in Battle, from the Foe defeat;
Scars on my face, Scars, whose full recompense,
Would ne'er atone, for what they rob from thence.
Scandal of Coward, nay half witted too, 85
Or siding with the Pardoned Rebel Crew;[9]
Or any thing but scorn – and yet frown on,
Your Slave was destined thus to be undone.
You the Avenging Deity appear,
And I a Victim fall to all the injured Fair. 90

Oroonoko: or, the Royal Slave. A True History (1688)

I do not pretend, in giving you the History of this *Royal Slave*, to entertain my Reader with the Adventures of a feigned *Hero*, whose Life and Fortunes Fancy may manage at the Poet's Pleasure; nor in relating the truth, design to adorn it with any Accidents, but such as arrived in earnest to him: And it shall come simply into the World, recommended by its own proper Merits, and natural Intrigues; there being enough of Reality to support it, and to render it diverting, without the Addition of Invention.[1]

I was myself an Eye-Witness, to a great part, of what you will find here set down; and what I could not be Witness of, I received from the Mouth of the chief Actor in this History, the *Hero* himself, who gave us the whole Transactions of his Youth; and though I shall omit, for Brevity's sake, a thousand little Accidents of his Life, which, however pleasant to us, where History was scarce, and Adventures very rare; yet might prove tedious and heavy to my Reader, in a World where he finds Diversions for every Minute, new and strange: But we who were perfectly charmed with the character of this great Man, were curious to gather every Circumstance of his Life.

The Scene of the last part of his Adventures lies in a Colony in *America*, called *Surinam*,[2] in the *West-Indies*.

But before I give you the Story of this *Gallant Slave*, 'tis fit I tell you the manner of bringing them to these new *Colonies*; for those they make use of there, are not *Natives* of the place; for those we live with in perfect Amity, without daring to command them; but on the contrary, caress them with all the brotherly and friendly Affection in the World; trading with them for their Fish, Venison, Buffalo Skins, and little Rarities; as Marmosets, a sort of *Monkey* as big as a Rat or Weasel, but of a marvellous and delicate shape, and has Face and Hands like an Human Creature; and Cousheries, a little Beast in the form and fashion of a Lion, as big

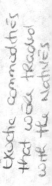

---

[8] *rebate* "To blunt; to beat to obtuseness; to deprive of keenness" (Johnson).
[9] *Pardoned Rebel Crew* former followers of Cromwell or perhaps present followers of Shaftesbury and Monmouth; Mulgrave was a royalist and opposed Monmouth.

OROONOKO: OR, THE ROYAL SLAVE. A TRUE HISTORY
[1] *Invention* "Fiction" (Johnson).
[2] *Surinam* Dutch Guiana on the north-east coast of South America.

as a Kitten, but so exactly made in all parts like that noble Beast, that it is it in *Minature*: then for little *Parakeetoes*, great Parrots, *Macaws* and a thousand other Birds and Beasts of wonderful and surprising Forms, Shapes, and Colours: for Skins of prodigious Snakes, of which there are some three-score Yards in length; as is the Skin of one that may be seen at His Majesty's *Antiquaries*:[3] Where are also some rare Flies, of amazing Forms and Colours, presented to them by my self; some as big as my Fist, some less; and all of various Excellencies, such as Art cannot imitate. Then we trade for Feathers, which they order into all Shapes, make themselves little short Habits of them, and glorious Wreaths for their Heads, Necks, Arms and Legs, whose Tinctures are inconceivable. I had a Set of these presented to me, and I gave them to the King's Theatre,[4] and it was the dress of the *Indian Queen*,[5] infinitely admired by Persons of Quality; and were unimitable. Besides these, a thousand little Knacks,[6] and Rarities in Nature; and some of Art; as their Baskets, Weapons, Aprons, &c. We dealt with them with Beads of all Colours, Knives, Axes, Pins and Needles; which they used only as Tools to drill Holes with in their Ears, Noses and Lips, where they hang a great many little things; as long Beads, bits of Tin, Brass, or Silver, beat thin, and any shining Trinket. The Beads they weave into Aprons about a quarter of an Ell[7] long, and of the same breadth; working them very prettily in Flowers of several Colours of Beads; which Apron they wear just before them, as *Adam* and *Eve* did the Fig-leaves; the Men wearing a long Stripe of Linen, which they deal with us for. They thread these Beads also on long Cotton-threads, and make Girdles to tie their Aprons to, which come twenty times, or more, about the Waist; and then cross, like a Shoulder-belt, both ways, and round their Necks, Arms and Legs. This Adornment, with their long black Hair, and the Face painted in little Specks or Flowers here and there, makes them a wonderful Figure to behold. Some of the Beauties, which indeed are finely shaped, as almost all are, and who have pretty Features, are charming and novel; for they have all that is called Beauty, except the Colour, which is a reddish Yellow; or after a new Oiling, which they often use to themselves, they are of the colour of a new Brick, but smooth, soft and sleek. They are extreme modest and bashful, very shy, and nice[8] of being touched. And though they are all thus naked, if one lives for ever among them, there is not to be seen an indecent Action, or Glance; and being continually used to see one another so unadorned, so like our first Parents before the Fall, it seems as if they had no Wishes; there being nothing to heighten Curiosity, but all you can see, you see at once, and every Moment see; and where there is no Novelty, there can be no Curiosity. Not but I have seen a handsome young *Indian*, dying for Love of a very beautiful young *Indian* Maid; but all his Courtship was, to fold his Arms, pursue her with his Eyes, and Sighs were all his Language: whilst she, as if no such Lover were present; or rather, as if she desired none such, carefully guarded her eyes from beholding him; and never approached him, but she looked down with all the blushing Modesty I have seen in the most severe and cautious of our World. And these People represented to me an absolute *Idea* of the first State of Innocence, before Man knew how to sin: And 'tis most evident and plain, that simple Nature is the most harmless, inoffensive and virtuous mistress. 'Tis she alone, if she were permitted, that better instructs the World, than all the Inventions of Man: Religion would here but destroy that Tranquillity, they possess by Ignorance; and Laws would but teach them to know Offence, of which now they have no Notion. They once

---

[3] *His Majesty's Antiquaries*   the natural history museum in Gresham College, catalogued by Nehemiah Grew in 1681.

[4] *King's Theatre*   the Bridges' Street Theater, home of the King's Company of Actors from 1663.

[5] *Indian Queen*   title role in a play by Dryden and Robert Howard, first produced in 1664.

[6] *Knack*   "A little machine; a petty contrivance; a toy" (Johnson).

[7] *Ell*   a measure of forty-five inches.

[8] *nice*   "Fastidious; squeamish" (Johnson).

made Mourning and Fasting for the Death of the *English* Governor, who had given his Hand to come on such a day to them, and neither came, nor sent; believing, when once a Man's Word was past, nothing but Death could or should prevent his keeping it: And when they saw he was not dead, they asked him, what Name they had for a Man who promised a thing he did not do? The Governor told them, Such a man was a 'Liar', which was a Word of Infamy to a Gentleman. Then one of them replied, 'Governor, you are a Liar, and guilty of that Infamy'. They have a Native Justice, which knows no Fraud; and they understand no Vice, or Cunning, but when they are taught by the *White Men*. They have Plurality of Wives, which, when they grow old, they serve those that succeed them, who are young; but with a Servitude easy and respected; and unless they take Slaves in War, they have no other Attendants.

Those on that *Continent* where I was, had no King; but the oldest War-Captain was obeyed with great Resignation.

A War-Captain is a Man who has led them on to Battle with Conduct,[9] and Success; of whom I shall have Occasion to speak more hereafter, and of some other of their Customs and Manners, as they fall in my way.

With these People, as I said, we live in perfect Tranquillity, and good Understanding, as it behooves us to do; they knowing all the places where to seek the best Food of the Country, and the Means of getting it; and for very small and unvaluable Trifles, supply us with what it is almost impossible for us to get; for they do not only in the Wood, and over the *Savannas*, in hunting, supply the parts of Hounds, by swiftly scouring through those almost impassable places, and by the mere activity of their Feet, run down the nimblest Deer, and other eatable Beasts: But in the water, one would think they were Gods of the Rivers, or Fellow-Citizens of the Deep; so rare an Art they have in Swimming, Diving, and almost Living in Water; by which they command the less swift Inhabitants of the Floods. And then for Shooting; what they cannot take, or reach with their Hands, they do with Arrows; and have so admirable an Aim, that they will split almost an Hair; and at any distance that an Arrow can reach, they will shoot down Oranges, and other Fruit, and only touch the Stalk with the Dart's Points, that they may not hurt the Fruit. So that they being, on all Occasions, very useful to us, we find it absolutely necessary to caress them as Friends, and not to treat them as Slaves; nor dare we do other, their numbers so far surpassing ours in that *Continent*.

Those then whom we make use of to work in our Plantations of Sugar, are *Negroes, Black-Slaves* altogether; who are transported thither in this manner.

Those who want Slaves, make a Bargain with a Master, or Captain of a Ship, and contract to pay him so much a-piece, a matter of twenty Pound a Head for as many as he agrees for, and to pay for them when they shall be delivered on such a Plantation: So that when there arrives a Ship laden with Slaves, they who have so contracted, go aboard, and receive their Number by Lot; and perhaps in one Lot that may be ten, there may happen to be three or four Men; the rest, Women and Children: Or be there more or less of either Sex, you are obliged to be contented with your Lot.

Coramantien,[10] a Country of *Blacks* so called, was one of those places in which they found the most advantageous Trading for these Slaves; and thither most of our great Traders in that Merchandise trafficked; for that Nation is very war-like and brave; and having a continual Campaign, being always in Hostility with one neighbouring Prince or other, they had the fortune to take a great many Captives; for all they took in Battle, were sold as Slaves; at least, those common Men who could not ransom themselves. Of these Slaves so taken, the General

---

[9] *Conduct* "The act of leading troops; the duty of a general" (Johnson).

[10] *Coramantien* on the Gold Coast of Africa.

only has all the profit; and of these Generals our Captains and Masters of Ships buy all their Freights.

The King of *Coramantien* was of himself a Man of an Hundred and odd Years old, and had no Son, though he had many beautiful *Black*-Wives; for most certainly, there are Beauties that can charm of that Colour. In his younger Years he had had many gallant Men to his Sons, thirteen of which died in Battle, conquering when they fell; and he had only left him for his Successor, one Grand-Child, Son to one of these dead Victors; who, as soon as he could bear a Bow in his Hand, and a Quiver at his Back, was sent into the Field, to be trained up by one of the oldest Generals, to War; where, from his natural Inclination to Arms, and the Occasions given him, with the good Conduct of the old General, he became, at the Age of Seventeen, one of the most expert Captains, and bravest Soldiers that ever saw the Field of *Mars*:[11] So that he was adored as the Wonder of all that World, and the Darling of the Soldiers. Besides, he was adorned with a native Beauty so transcending all those of his gloomy Race, that he struck an Awe and Reverence, even in those that knew not his Quality; as he did in me, who beheld him with Surprise and Wonder, when afterwards he arrived in our World.

He had scarce arrived at his Seventeenth Year, when, fighting by his Side, the General was killed with an Arrow in his Eye, which the Prince *Oroonoko* (for so was this gallant *Moor* called) very narrowly avoided; nor had he, if the General, who saw the Arrow shot, and perceiving it aimed at the Prince, had not bowed his Head between, on purpose to receive it in his own Body rather than it should touch that of the Prince, and so saved him.

'Twas then, afflicted as *Oroonoko* was, that he was proclaimed General in the old Man's place; and then it was, at the finishing of that War, which had continued for two Years, that the Prince came to Court; where he had hardly been a Month together, from the time of his fifth Year to that of Seventeen; and 'twas amazing to imagine where it was he learned so much Humanity; or, to give his Accomplishments a juster Name, where 'twas he got that real Greatness of Soul, those refined Notions of true Honour, that absolute Generosity, and that Softness that was capable of the highest Passions of Love and Gallantry, whose Objects were almost continually fighting Men, or those mangled, or dead; who heard no Sounds, but those of War and Groans: Some part of it we may attribute to the Care of a *French*-Man of Wit and Learning; who finding it turn to a very good Account to be a sort of Royal Tutor to this young *Black*, & perceiving him very ready, apt, and quick of Apprehension, took a great pleasure to teach him Morals, Language and Science; and was for it extremely beloved and valued by him. Another Reason was, He loved when he came from War, to see all the *English* Gentlemen that traded thither; and did not only learn their Language, but that of the *Spaniards* also, with whom he traded afterwards for Slaves.

I have often seen and conversed with this great Man, and been a Witness to many of his mighty Actions; and do assure my Reader, the most Illustrious Courts could not have produced a braver Man, both for Greatness of Courage and Mind, a Judgement more solid, a Wit more quick, and a Conversation more sweet and diverting. He knew almost as much as if he had read much: He had heard of, and admired the *Romans*: he had heard of the late Civil Wars in *England*, and the deplorable Death of our great Monarch; and would discourse of it with all the Sense and Abhorrence of the Injustice imaginable. He had an extreme good and graceful Mien, and all the Civility of a well-bred great Man. He had nothing of Barbarity in his Nature, but in all Points addressed himself, as if his Education had been in some *European* Court.

---

[11]   *the Field of Mars*   i.e. war, after the Roman god of war.

This great and just Character of *Oroonoko* gave me an extreme Curiosity to see him, especially when I knew he spoke *French* and *English*, and that I could talk with him. But though I had heard so much of him, I was as greatly surprised when I saw him, as if I had heard nothing of him; so beyond all Report I found him. He came into the Room, and addressed himself to me, and some other Women, with the best Grace in the World. He was pretty tall, but of a Shape the most exact[12] that can be fancied: The most famous Statuary could not form the Figure of a Man more admirably turned from Head to Foot. His Face was not of that brown, rusty Black which most of that Nation are, but a perfect Ebony, or polished Jet.[13] His Eyes were the most awful that could be seen, and very piercing; the White of them being like Snow, as were his Teeth. His Nose was rising and *Roman*, instead of *African* and flat. His Mouth, the finest shaped that could be seen; far from those great turned lips, which are so natural to the rest of the *Negroes*. The whole Proportion and Air of his Face was so noble, and exactly formed, that, bating[14] his Colour, there could be nothing in nature more beautiful, agreeable and handsome. There was no one Grace wanting, that bears the Standard of true Beauty. His Hair came down to his Shoulders, by the Aids of Art; which was, by pulling it out with a Quill, and keeping it combed; of which he took particular Care. Nor did the Perfections of his Mind come short of those of his Person; for his Discourse was admirable upon almost any Subject; and whoever had heard him speak, would have been convinced of their Errors, that all fine Wit[15] is confined to the *White* Men, especially to those of *Christendom*; and would have confessed that *Oroonoko* was as capable even of reigning well, and of governing as wisely, had as great a Soul, as politic Maxims, and was as sensible[16] of Power as any Prince civilized in the most refined Schools of Humanity and Learning, or the most Illustrious Courts.

This Prince, such as I have described him, whose Soul and Body were so admirably adorned, was (while yet he was in the Court of his Grandfather) as I said, as capable of Love, as 'twas possible for a brave and gallant Man to be; and in saying that, I have named the highest Degree of Love; for sure, great Souls are most capable of that Passion.

I have already said, the old General was killed by the shot of an Arrow, by the Side of this Prince, in Battle; and that *Oroonoko* was made General. This old dead *Hero* had one only Daughter left of his race, a Beauty that, to describe her truly, one need say only, she was Female to the noble Male; the beautiful *Black Venus* to our young *Mars*; as charming in her Person as he, and of delicate Virtues. I have seen an hundred *White* Men sighing after her, and making a thousand Vows at her Feet, all vain, and unsuccessful: And she was, indeed, too great for any, but a Prince of her own Nation to adore.

Oroonoko coming from the Wars (which were now ended), after he had made his Court to his Grandfather, he thought in Honour he should make a Visit to *Imoinda*, the Daughter of his Foster-father, the dead General; and to make some Excuses to her, because his Preservation was the Occasion of her Father's Death; and to present her with those Slaves that had been taken in this last Battle, as the Trophies of her Father's Victories. When he came, attended by all the young Soldiers of any Merit, he was infinitely surprised at the Beauty of this fair Queen of Night, whose Face and Person was so exceeding all he had ever beheld, that lovely Modesty with which she received him, that Softness in her Look, and Sighs, upon the

---

[12] *exact* "Nice; without failure; without deviation from rule" (Johnson).

[13] *Jet* "a very beautiful fossil . . . of a fine deep black colour, having a grain resembling that of wood" (Johnson quoting John Hill).

[14] *bating* except.

[15] *Wit* "The powers of the mind; the mental faculties" (Johnson).

[16] *sensible* "having moral perception; having the quality of being affected by moral good or ill" (Johnson, sense 5).

Color associated with ugliness

melancholy Occasion of this Honour that was done by so great a Man as *Oroonoko*, and a Prince of whom she had heard such admirable things; the Awfulness[17] wherewith she received him, and the Sweetness of her Words and Behaviour while he stayed, gained a perfect Conquest over his fierce Heart, and made him feel the Victor could be subdued. So that having made his first Complements, and presented her an hundred and fifty Slaves in Fetters, he told her with his Eyes that he was not insensible of her Charms; while *Imoinda*, who wished for nothing more than so glorious a Conquest, was pleased to believe, she understood that silent Language of new-born Love; and from that Moment, put on all her Additions to Beauty.

The Prince returned to Court with quite another Humour[18] than before; and though he did not speak much of the fair *Imoinda*, he had the pleasure to hear all his followers speak of nothing but the Charms of that Maid; insomuch that, even in the Presence of the old King, they were extolling her, and heightening, if possible, the Beauties they had found in her: So that nothing else was talked of, no other Sound was heard in every Corner where there were Whisperers, but 'Imoinda! Imoinda!'

'Twill be imagined *Oroonoko* stayed not long before he made his second Visit; nor, considering his Quality, not much longer before he told her, he adored her. I have often heard him say, that he admired by what strange Inspiration he came to talk things so soft, and so passionate, who never knew Love, nor was used to the Conversation of Women; but (to use his own Words) he said, 'Most happily, some new, and till then unknown Power instructed his Heart and Tongue in the Language of Love, and at the same time, in favour of him, inspired *Imoinda* with a Sense of his Passion'. She was touched with what he said, and returned it all in such Answers as went to his very Heart, with a Pleasure unknown before: Nor did he use those Obligations ill, that Love had done him; but turned all his happy Moments to the best advantage; and as he knew no Vice, his Flame aimed at nothing but Honour, if such a distinction may be made in Love; and especially in that Country, where Men take to themselves as many as they can maintain; and where the only Crime and Sin with Woman is, to turn her off, to abandon her to Want, Shame and Misery: Such ill Morals are only practised in *Christian*-Countries, where they prefer the bare Name of Religion; and, without Virtue or Morality, think that's sufficient. But *Oroonoko* was none of those Professors; but as he had right Notions of Honour, so he made her Propositions as were not only and barely such; but contrary to the Custom of his Country, he made her Vows she should be the only woman he would possess while he lived; that no Age or Wrinkles should incline him to change, for her Soul would always be fine, and always young; and he should have an eternal *Idea* in his Mind of the Charms she now bore, and should look into his Heart for that *Idea*, when he could find it no longer in her Face.

After a thousand Assurances of his lasting flame, and her eternal Empire over him, she condescended to receive him for her Husband; or rather, received him, as the greatest Honour the Gods could do her.

There is a certain Ceremony in these Cases to be observed, which I forgot to ask how performed; but 'twas concluded on both sides, that, in Obedience to him, the Grandfather was to be first made acquainted with the Design: for they pay a most absolute Resignation to the Monarch, especially when he is a Parent also.

On the other side, the old King, who had many Wives, and many Concubines, wanted not Court-flatterers to insinuate in his Heart a thousand tender Thoughts for this young Beauty; and who represented her to his Fancy, as the most charming he had ever possessed in all the

---

[17] *Awfulness* "The quality of striking with awe; sol-   [18] *Humour* "Present disposition" (Johnson). emnity" (Johnson).

long Race of his numerous Years. At this Character, his old Heart, like an extinguished Brand, most apt to take Fire, felt new Sparks of Love, and began to kindle; and now grown to his second Childhood, longed with Impatience to behold this gay thing, with whom, alas! he could but innocently play. But how he should be confirmed she was this *Wonder*, before he used his Power to call her to Court (where Maidens never came, unless for the King's private Use) he was next to consider; and while he was so doing, he had Intelligence brought him, that *Imoinda* was most certainly Mistress to the Prince *Oroonoko*. This gave him some *Shagrien*:[19] however, it gave him also an Opportunity, one Day, when the Prince was a-hunting, to wait on a Man of Quality, as his Slave and Attendant, who should go and make a Present to *Imoinda*, as from the Prince; he should then, unknown, see this fair Maid, and have an Opportunity to hear what Message she would return the Prince for his Present, and from thence gather the state of her heart, and degree of her Inclination. This was put in Execution, and the old Monarch saw, and burnt: He found all he had heard, and would not delay his Happiness, but found he should have some Obstacle to overcome her Heart; for she expressed her Sense of the Present the Prince had sent her, in terms so sweet, so soft and pretty, with an Air of Love and Joy that could not be dissembled; insomuch that 'twas past doubt whether she loved *Oroonoko* entirely. This gave the old King some Affliction; but he salved it with this, that the Obedience the People pay their King, was not at all inferior to what they payed their Gods: And what Love would not oblige *Imoinda* to do, Duty would compel her to.

He was therefore no sooner got to his Apartment, but he sent the Royal Veil to *Imoinda*; that is, the Ceremony of Invitation; he sends the Lady he has a Mind to honour with his Bed, a Veil, with which she is covered, and secured for the King's Use; and 'tis Death to disobey; besides, held a most impious Disobedience.

'Tis not to be imagined the Surprise and Grief that seized this lovely Maid at this News and Sight. However, as Delays in these Cases are dangerous, and Pleading worse than Treason; trembling, and almost fainting, she was obliged to suffer herself to be covered, and led away.

They brought her thus to Court; and the King, who had caused a very rich Bath to be prepared, was led into it, where he sat under a Canopy, in State, to receive this longed-for Virgin; whom he having commanded should be brought to him, they (after disrobing her) led her to the Bath, and making fast the Doors, left her to descend. The King, without more Courtship, bade her throw off her Mantle, and come to his Arms. But *Imoinda*, all in Tears, threw her self on the Marble, on the brink of the Bath, and besought him to hear her. She told him, as she was a Maid, how proud of the Divine Glory she should have been of having it in her power to oblige her King: but as by the Laws, he could not; and from his Royal Goodness would not take from any Man his wedded Wife: So she believed she should be the Occasion of making him commit a great Sin, if she did not reveal her State and Condition; and tell him, she was another's, and could not be so happy to be his.

The King, enraged at this Delay, hastily demanded the Name of the bold Man that had married a Woman of her Degree, without his Consent. *Imoinda*, seeing his Eyes fierce, and his Hands tremble (whether with Age, or Anger, I know not, but she fancied the last), almost repented she had said so much, for now she feared the Storm would fall on the Prince; she therefore said a thousand things to appease the raging of his Flame, and to prepare him to hear who it was with Calmness; but before she spoke, he imagined who she meant, but would not seem to do so, but commanded her to lay aside her Mantle, and suffer herself to receive his

---

[19] *Shagrien* chagrin, "Ill humour; vexation. . . . It is pronounced *shagreen*" (Johnson).

Caresses; or, by his Gods, he swore, that happy Man whom she was going to name should die, though it were even *Oroonoko* himself. 'Therefore', said he, 'deny this Marriage, and swear thy self a Maid'. 'That', replied Imoinda, 'by all our powers I do; for I am not yet known to my husband'. ''Tis enough', said the King, ''tis enough to satisfy my Conscience, and my Heart'. And rising from his Seat, he went, and led her into the Bath; it being in vain for her to resist.

In this time, the Prince, who was returned from Hunting, went to visit his *Imoinda*, but found her gone; and not only so, but heard she had received the Royal Veil. This raised him to a Storm; and in his Madness, they had so much ado to save him from laying violent Hands on himself. Force first prevailed, and then Reason: They urged all to him, that might oppose his Rage; but nothing weighed so greatly with him as the King's Old Age uncapable of injuring him with *Imoinda*. He would give way to that Hope, because it pleased him most, and flattered best his Heart. Yet this served not altogether to make him cease his different Passions, which sometimes raged within him, and sometimes softned into Showers. 'Twas not enough to appease him to tell him his Grand-father was old, and could not that way injure him, while he retained that awful Duty which the young Men are used there to pay their grave Relations. He could not be convinced that he had no Cause to sigh and mourn for the Loss of a Mistress he could not with all his Strength and Courage retrieve. And he would often cry, 'Oh, my Friends! were she in walled Cities, or confined from me in Fortifications of the greatest Strength; did Enchantments or Monsters detain her from me, I would venture through any Hazard to free her: But here, in the Arms of a feeble old Man, my Youth, my violent Love, my Trade in Arms, and all my vast Desire of Glory, avail me nothing: Imoinda is as irrecoverably lost to me, as if she were snatched by the cold Arms of Death. Oh! She is never to be retrieved. If I would wait tedious Years; till Fate should bow the old King to his Grave; even that would not leave me *Imoinda* free; but still that Custom that makes it so vile a Crime for a Son to marry his Father's Wives or Mistresses, would hinder my Happiness; unless I would either ignobly set an ill Precedent to my Successors, or abandon my Country, and fly with her to some unknown World, who never heard our Story.'

But it was objected to him, that his Case was not the same: for *Imoinda* being his lawful Wife, by solemn Contract, 'twas he that was the injured Man, and might, if he so pleased, take *Imoinda* back, the Breach of law being on his Grandfather's side; and that if he could circumvent him, and redeem her from the *Otan*, which is the Palace of the King's Women, a sort of *Seraglio*, it was both just and lawful for him so to do.

This Reasoning had some force upon him, and he should have been entirely comforted, but for the Thought that she was possessed by his Grandfather. However, he loved so well, that he was resolved to believe what most favoured his hope, and to endeavour to learn from *Imoinda*'s own Mouth, what only she could satisfy him in; whether she was robbed of that Blessing, which was only due to his Faith and Love. But as it was very hard to get a Sight of the Women, for no Men ever entered into the *Otan*, but when the King went to entertain himself with some one of his Wives, or Mistresses; and 'twas death, at any other time, for any other to go in; so he knew not how to contrive to get Sight of her.

While *Oroonoko* felt all the Agonies of Love, and suffered under a Torment the most painful in the World, the old King was not exempted from his share of Affliction. He was troubled, for having been forced by an irresistible passion, to rob his Son of a Treasure, he knew, could not but be extremely dear to him, since she was the most beautiful that had ever been seen, and had besides, all the Sweetness and Innocence of Youth and Modesty, with a Charm of Wit surpassing all. He found that however she was forced to expose her lovely Person to his withered Arms, she could only sigh and weep there, and think of *Oroonoko*; and oftentimes could not forbear speaking of him, though her Life were, by Custom, forfeited by owning her Passion. But since she spoke not of a lover only, but of a Prince dear to him, to whom she spoke, and of the Praises of a Man, who, till now, filled the old Man's Soul with Joy at every Recital of his Bravery, or even his Name. And 'twas this Dotage on our young *Hero* that gave *Imoinda* a thousand Privileges to speak of him, without offending; and this Condescension in the old King, that made her take the Satisfaction of speaking of him so very often.

Besides, he many times enquired how the Prince bore himself; and those of whom he asked, being entirely Slaves to the Merits and Virtues of the Prince, still answered what they thought conduced best to his Service, which was to make the old King fancy that the Prince had no more Interest in *Imoinda*, and resigned her willingly to the Pleasure of the King; that he diverted himself with his Mathematicians, his Fortifications, his Officers, and his Hunting.

This pleased the old Lover, who failed not to report these things again to *Imoinda*, that she might, by the Example of her young Lover, withdraw her Heart, and rest better contented in his Arms. But, however she was forced to receive this unwelcome News, in all Appearance, with Unconcern, and Content, her Heart was bursting within, and she was only happy when she could get alone, to vent her Griefs and Moans with Sighs and Tears.

What Reports of the Prince's Conduct were made to the King, he thought good to justify, as far as possibly he could by his Actions; and when he appeared in the Presence of the King, he showed a Face not at all betraying his Heart: So that in a little time the old Man, being entirely convinced that he was no longer a Lover of *Imoinda*, he carried him with him, in his Train, to the *Otan*, often to banquet with his Mistress. But as soon as he entered, one Day, into the Apartment of *Imoinda*, with the King, at the first Glance from her Eyes, notwithstanding all his determined Resolution, he was ready to sink in the place where he stood; and had certainly done so, but for the Support of *Aboan*, a young Man who was next to him, which, with his Change of Countenance, had betrayed him, had the King chanced to look that way. And I have observed, 'tis a very great Error in those who laugh when one says, 'A *Negro* can change colour'; for I have seen them as frequently blush, and look pale, and that as visibly as ever I saw in the most beautiful *White*. And it is certain that both these Changes were evident, this Day, in both these Lovers. And *Imoinda*, who saw with some Joy the Change in the Prince's Face, and found it in her own, strove to divert the King from beholding either by a forced Caress, with which she met him, which was a new Wound in the heart of the poor dying Prince. But soon as the King was busied in looking on some fine thing of *Imoinda*'s making, she had time to tell the Prince with her angry, but Love-darting Eyes, that she resented his Coldness, and bemoaned her own miserable Captivity. Nor were his Eyes silent, but answered hers again, as much as eyes could do, instructed by the most tender, and most passionate Heart that ever loved: And they spoke so well, and so effectually, as *Imoinda* no longer doubted but she was the only Delight, and the Darling of that Soul she found pleading in them its Right of Love, which none was more willing to resign than she. And it was this powerful Language alone that in an Instant conveyed all the Thoughts of their Souls to each other; that they both found, there wanted but Opportunity to make them both entirely happy. But when he saw another Door opened by *Onahal*, a former old wife of the King's, who now had charge of *Imoinda*; and saw the prospect of a Bed of State made ready, with Sweets and Flowers for the Dalliance of the King; who immediately led the trembling Victim from his Sight, into the prepared Repose. What Rage! what wild Frenzies seized his Heart! which forcing to keep within Bounds, and to suffer without Noise, it became the more insupportable, and rent his Soul with ten thousand Pains. He was forced to retire, to vent his Groans, where he fell down on a Carpet, and lay struggling a long time, and only breathing now and then – 'O Imoinda!' When *Onahal* had finished her necessary Affair within, shutting the Door, she came forth to wait, till the King called; and hearing some one sighing in the other Room, she passed on, and found the Prince in that deplorable Condition, which she thought needed her Aid. She gave him Cordials, but all in vain, till finding the nature of his Disease, by his Sighs, and naming *Imoinda*. She told him he had not so much Cause as he imagined to afflict himself; for if he knew the King so well as she did, he would not lose a Moment in Jealousy; and that she was confident that *Imoinda* bore, at this Minute, part in his Affliction. *Aboan* was of the same Opinion; and both together, persuaded him to re-assume his Courage; and all sitting down on the Carpet, the Prince said so many obliging things to *Onahal*, that he half persuaded her to be of his Party. And she promised him, she would thus far comply with his just Desires, that she would let *Imoinda* know how faithful he was, what he suffered, and what he said.

This Discourse lasted till the King called, which gave *Oroonoko* a certain Satisfaction; and with the hope *Onahal* had made him conceive, he assumed a Look as gay as 'twas possible a man in his Circumstances could do; and presently after, he was called in with the rest who waited without. The King commanded Music to be brought, and several of his young Wives and Mistresses came all together by his Command to dance before him, where *Imoinda* performed her Part with an Air and Grace so passing all the rest, as her Beauty was above them, and received the Present, ordained as a Prize. The Prince was every Moment more charmed with the new Beauties and Graces he beheld in this fair One; and while he gazed, and she danced, *Onahal* was retired to a Window with *Aboan*.

This *Onahal*, as I said, was one of the Cast-Mistresses[20] of the old King; and 'twas these (now past their Beauty) that were made Guardians or Governants to the new, and the young Ones; and whose Business it was, to teach them all those wanton Arts of Love, with which they prevailed and charmed heretofore in their Turn; and who now treated the triumphing happy Ones with all the Severity, as to Liberty and Freedom, that was possible, in revenge of those Honours they rob them of; envying them those Satisfactions, those Gallantries and Presents, that were once made to themselves, while Youth and Beauty lasted, and which they now saw pass were regardless by,[21] and paid only to the Bloomings.[22] And certainly, nothing is more afflicting to a decayed Beauty, than to behold in it self declining Charms, that were once adored; and to find those Caresses paid to new Beauties, to which once she laid a Claim; to hear them whisper as she passes by, 'That once was a delicate Woman'. These abandoned Ladies therefore endeavour to revenge all the Despites[23] and Decays of Time on these flourishing happy Ones. And 'twas this Severity that gave *Oroonoko* a thousand Fears he should never prevail with *Onahal* to see *Imoinda*. But, as I said, she was now retired to a window with *Aboan*.

This young Man was not only one of the best Quality,[24] but a Man extremely well made, and beautiful; and coming often to attend the King to the *Otan*, he had subdued the Heart of the antiquated *Onahal*, which had not forgot how pleasant it was to be in Love: And though she had some Decays in her Face, she had none in her Sense and Wit; she was there agreeable still, even to *Aboan*'s Youth, so that he took pleasure in entertaining her with Discourses of Love. He knew also that to make his Court to these She-Favourites was the way to be great, these being the Persons that do all Affairs and Business at Court. He had also observed that she had given him Glances more tender and inviting than she had done to others of his

---

[20]   *Cast-Mistress*   former, cast-away mistress.
[21]   *were regardless by*   i.e. they were paid no attention; the text is hard, perhaps typographically in error, though the sense is pretty clear.
[22]   *Bloomings*   women in the bloom of youth.
[23]   *Despite*   "Act of malice; act of opposition" (Johnson).
[24]   *Quality*   "Comparative or relative rank" (Johnson).

Quality: And now, when he saw that her Favour could so absolutely oblige the Prince, he failed not to sigh in her Ear, and look with Eyes all soft upon her, and give her Hope that she had made some Impressions on his Heart. He found her pleased at this, and making a thousand Advances to him; but the Ceremony ending, and the King departing, broke up the Company for that Day, and his Conversation.

Aboan failed not that night to tell the Prince of his Success, and how advantageous the Service of *Onahal* might be to his Amour with *Imoinda*. The Prince was overjoyed with this good News, and besought him, if it were possible to caress her so, as to engage her entirely, which he could not fail to do, if he complied with her Desires: 'For then', said the Prince, 'her Life lying at your Mercy, she must grant you the Request you make in my Behalf'. *Aboan* understood him and assured him he would make Love so effectually that he would defy the most expert Mistress of the Art to find out whether he dissembled it, or had it really. And 'twas with Impatience they waited the next Opportunity of going to the *Otan*.

The Wars came on, the Time of taking the Field approached, and 'twas impossible for the Prince to delay his going at the Head on his Army, to encounter the Enemy: So that every Day seemed a tedious Year, till he saw his *Imoinda*; for he believed he could not live, if he were forced away without being so happy. 'Twas with Impatience therefore that he expected the next Visit the King would make; and, according to his Wish, it was not long.

The Parley of the Eyes of these two Lovers had not passed so secretly, but an old jealous Lover could spy it; or rather, he wanted not Flatterers, who told him they observed it: So that the Prince was hastened to the Camp, and this was the last Visit he found he should make to the *Otan*; he therefore urged *Aboan* to make the best of this last Effort, and to explain himself so to *Onahal*, that she, deferring her Enjoyment of her young Lover no longer, might make way for the Prince to speak to *Imoinda*.

The whole Affair being agreed on between the Prince and *Aboan*, they attended the King, as the Custom was, to the *Otan*; where, while the whole Company was taken up in beholding the Dancing and antic[25] Postures the Women Royal made to divert the King, *Onahal* singled out *Aboan*, whom she found most pliable to her Wish. When she had him where she believed she could not be heard, she sighed to him, and softly cried, 'Ah, *Aboan*! When will you be sensible[26] to my Passion? I confess it with my Mouth, because I would not give my Eyes the Lie; and you have but too much already perceived they have confessed my Flame: Nor would I have you believe, that because I am the abandoned Mistress of a King, I esteem myself altogether divested of Charms: No, *Aboan*; I have still a Rest of Beauty enough engaging, and I have learned to please too well, not to be desirable. I can have Lovers still, but will have none but *Aboan*'.

'Madam', replied the half-feigning youth, 'you have already, by my Eyes, found, you can still conquer; and I believe 'tis in pity of me, you condescend to this kind Confession. But, Madam, Words are used to be so small a part of our Country-Courtship, that it is rare one can get so happy an Opportunity as to tell one's Heart; and those few Minutes we have are forced to be snatched for more certain Proofs of Love, than speaking and sighing; and such I languish for'.

He spoke this wish with such a Tone, that she hoped it true, and could not forbear believing it; and being wholly transported with Joy, for having subdued the finest of all the King's Subjects to her Desires, she took from her Ears two large pearls, and commanded him to wear them in his. He would have refused them, crying, 'Madam, these are not the Proofs of your Love that I expect; 'tis Opportunity, 'tis a Lone-hour only, that can make me happy'.

---

[25] *antic*   "Odd; ridiculously wild" (Johnson).   [26] *sensible*   "Perceiving by either mind or senses" (Johnson).

But forcing the Pearls into his Hand, she whispered softly to him, 'Oh! Do not fear a Woman's Invention, when Love sets her a-thinking'. And pressing his hand, she cried, 'This Night you shall be happy. Come to the Gate of the Orange Groves, behind the *Otan*, and I will be ready, about Mid-night, to receive you'. 'Twas thus agreed, and she left him, that no notice might be taken of their speaking together.

The Ladies were still dancing, and the King, laid on a Carpet, with a great deal of pleasure, was beholding them, especially *Imoinda*; who that Day appeared more lovely than ever, being enlivened with the good Tidings *Onahal* had brought her of the constant Passion the Prince had for her. The Prince was laid on another Carpet, at the other end of the Room, with his Eyes fixed on the Object of his Soul; and as she turned, or moved, so did they; and she alone gave his Eyes and Soul their Motions: Nor did *Imoinda* employ her Eyes to any other Use, than in beholding with infinite Pleasure the Joy she produced in those of the Prince. But while she was more regarding him, than the Steps she took, she chanced to fall; and so near him, as that leaping with extreme force from the carpet, he caught her in his Arms as she fell; and 'twas visible to her whole Presence, the Joy wherewith he received her: He clasped her close to his Bosom, and quite forgot that Reverence that was due to the Mistress of a King, and that Punishment that is the Reward of a Boldness of this nature; and had not the Presence of Mind of *Imoinda* (fonder of his Safety, than her own) befriended him, in making her spring from his Arms, and fall into her Dance again, he had, at that Instant, met his Death; for the old King, jealous to the last degree, rose up in Rage, broke all the Diversion, and led *Imoinda* to her Apartment, and sent out Word to the Prince to go immediately to the Camp; and that if he were found another Night in Court, he should suffer the Death ordained for disobedient Offenders.

You may imagine how welcome this News was to *Oroonoko*, whose unseasonable Transport and Caress of *Imoinda* was blamed by all Men that loved him; and now he perceived his Fault, yet cried, 'That for such another Moment, he would be content to die'.

All the *Otan* was in disorder about this Accident; and *Onahal* was particularly concerned, because on the Prince's Stay depended her Happiness; for she could no longer expect that of *Aboan*. So that, ere they departed, they contrived it so, that the Prince and he should come both that Night to the Grove of the *Otan*, which was all of Oranges and Citrons; and that there they should wait her Orders.

They parted thus, with Grief enough, till Night; leaving the King in possession of the lovely Maid. But nothing could appease the Jealousy of the old Lover: He would not be imposed on, but he would have it, that *Imoinda* made a false Step on purpose to fall into *Oroonoko*'s Bosom, and that all things looked like a Design on both sides, and 'twas in vain she protested her Innocence: He was old and obstinate, and left her more than half assured that his Fear was true.

The King going to his Apartment, sent to know where the Prince was, and if he intended to obey his Command. The Messenger returned, and told him, he found the Prince pensive, and altogether unpreparing for the Campaign; that he lay negligently on the Ground, and answered very little. This confirmed the Jealousy of the King, and he commanded that they should very narrowly and privately watch his Motions; and that he should not stir from his Apartment, but one spy or another should be employed to watch him: so that the Hour approaching, wherein he was to go to the Citron-Grove; and taking only *Aboan* along with him, he leaves his Apartments, and was watched to the very Gate of the *Otan*; where he was seen to enter, and where they left him, to carry back the Tidings to the King.

Oroonoko and *Aboan* were no sooner entered, but *Onahal* led the Prince to the apartment of *Imoinda*; who, not knowing any thing of her Happiness, was laid in Bed. But *Onahal* only left him in her chamber, to make the best of his Opportunity, and took her dear *Aboan* to her own; where he showed the heighth of Complaisance[27] for his Prince, when, to give him an Opportunity, he suffered himself to be caressed in bed by *Onahal*.

The Prince softly wakened *Imoinda*, who was not yet a little surprised with Joy to find him there; and yet she trembled with a thousand Fears. I believe he omitted saying nothing to this young Maid that might persuade her to suffer him to seize his own, and take the Rights of Love; and I believe she was not long resisting those Arms where she so longed to be; and having Opportunity, Night and Silence, Youth, Love and Desire, he soon prevailed, and ravished in a Moment, what his old Grand-father had been endeavouring for so many Months.

'Tis not to be imagined the Satisfaction of these two young Lovers; nor the Vows she made him, that she remained a spotless Maid, till that Night, and that what she did with his Grandfather had robbed him of no part of her Virgin-Honour; the Gods, in Mercy and Justice, having reserved that for her plighted[28] Lord, to whom of Right it belonged. And 'tis impossible to express the Transports he suffered, while he listened to a Discourse so charming, from her loved Lips; and clasped that Body in his Arms, for whom he had so long languished; and now nothing afflicted him, but his sudden Departure from her; for he told her the Necessity, and his Commands; but should depart satisfied in this, that since the old King had not been able to deprive him of those Enjoyments which only belonged to him, he believed for the future he would be less able to injure him; so that, abating that Scandal of the Veil, which was no otherwise so, than that she was Wife to another: He believed her safe, even in the Arms of the King, and innocent; yet would he have ventured at the Conquest of the World, and given it all, to have had her avoided that Honour of receiving the *Royal Veil*. 'Twas thus, between a thousand Caresses, that both bemoaned the hard Fate of Youth and Beauty, so liable to that cruel Promotion: 'Twas a Glory that could have been spared here, though desired and aimed at by all the young Females of that Kingdom.

But while they were thus fondly employed, forgetting how Time ran on, and that the Dawn must conduct him far away from his only Happiness, they heard a great Noise in the *Otan*, and unusual Voices of Men; at which the Prince, starting from the Arms of the frighted *Imoinda*, ran to a little Battle-Ax he used to wear by his Side; and having not so much leisure, as to put on his Habit, he opposed himself against some who were already opening the Door; which they did with so much Violence, that *Oroonoko* was not able to defend it; but was forced to cry out with a commanding Voice, 'Whoever ye are that have the Boldness to attempt to approach this Apartment thus rudely; know, that I, the Prince *Oroonoko*, will revenge it with the certain death of him that first enters: therefore stand back, and know, this place is sacred to Love, and me this Night; to Morrow 'tis the King's'.

This he spoke with a Voice so resolved and assured, that they soon retired from the Door; but cried, ''Tis by the King's command we are come; and being satisfied by thy Voice, O Prince, as much as if we had entered, we can report to the King the Truth of all his Fears, and leave thee to provide for thy own Safety, as thou art advised by thy Friends'.

At these Words they departed, and left the Prince to take a short and sad Leave of *Imoinda*; who, trusting in the strength of her Charms, believed she should appease the Fury of a jealous King, by saying, She was surprised, and that it was by force of Arms he got into her Apartment. All her Concern now was for his Life, and therefore she hastened him to the Camp, and with much a-do prevailed on him to go. Nor was it she alone that prevailed; *Aboan* and *Onahal* both pleaded, and both assured him of a Lie that should be well enough contrived

---

[27] *Complaisance* "Civility; desire of pleasing; act of adulation" (Johnson).   [28] *plighted* promised, avowed.

to secure *Imoinda*. So that, at last, with a Heart sad as Death, dying Eyes, and sighing Soul, *Oroonoko* departed, and took his way to the Camp.

It was not long after the King in Person came to the *Otan*; where beholding *Imoinda*, with Rage in his Eyes, he upbraided her Wickedness and Perfidy and threatening[29] her Royal Lover; she fell on her Face at his Feet, bedewing the floor with her Tears, and imploring his Pardon for a Fault which she had not with her Will committed; as *Onahal*, who was also prostrate with her, could testify: That, unknown to her, he had broke into her Apartment, and ravished her. She spoke this much against her Conscience; but to save her own Life, 'twas absolutely necessary she should feign this Falsity. She knew it could not injure the Prince, he being fled to an Army that would stand by him, against any Injuries that should assault him. However, this last Thought of *Imoinda*'s being ravished, changed the Measures of his Revenge; and whereas before he designed to be himself her Executioner, he was now resolved she should not die. But as it is the greatest Crime in nature amongst them to touch a Woman after having been possessed by a Son, a Father, or a Brother; so now he looked on *Imoinda* as a polluted thing, wholly unfit for his Embrace; nor would he resign her to his Grandson, because she had received the *Royal Veil*: he therefore removed her from the *Otan*, with *Onahal*; whom he put into safe Hands, with the Order they should be both sold off as Slaves to another Country, either *Christian*, or *Heathen*; 'twas no matter where.

This cruel Sentence, worse than Death, they implored might be reversed; but their Prayers were vain, and it was put in Execution accordingly, and that with so much secrecy, that none, either without, or within the *Otan*, knew any thing of their Absence, or their Destiny.

The old King, nevertheless, executed this with a great deal of Reluctancy; but he believed he had made a very great Conquest over himself, when he had once resolved, and had performed what he resolved. He believed now, that his Love had been unjust; and that he could not expect the Gods, or the Captain of the Clouds (as they call the unknown Power) would suffer a better Consequence from so ill a Cause. He now begins to hold *Oroonoko* excused; and to say, he had Reason for what he did: And now every Body could assure the King, how passionately *Imoinda* was beloved by the Prince; even those confessed it now, who said the contrary before his Flame was abated. So that the King being old, and not able to defend himself in War, and having no Sons of all his Race remaining alive, but only this, to maintain him on his Throne; and looking on this as a Man disobliged, first by the Rape of his Mistress, or rather wife, and now by depriving him wholly of her, he feared, might make him desperate, and do some cruel thing, either to himself, or his old Grandfather, the Offender; he began to repent him extremely of the Contempt he had, in his Rage, put on *Imoinda*. Besides, he considered he ought in Honour to have killed her for this Offence, if it had been one; He ought to have had so much Value and Consideration for a Maid of her Quality, as to have nobly put her to death; and not to have sold her like a common Slave, the greatest Revenge, and the most disgraceful of any; and to which they a thousand times prefer Death, and implore it, as *Imoinda* did, but could not obtain that Honour. Seeing therefore it was certain that *Oroonoko* would highly resent this Affront, he thought good to make some Excuse for his Rashness to him; and to that End he sent a Messenger to the Camp with orders to treat with him about the Matter, to gain his Pardon, and to endeavour to mitigate his Grief; but that by no means he should tell him she was sold, but secretly put to death; for he knew he should never obtain his Pardon for the other.

When the Messenger came, he found the Prince upon the point of engaging with the Enemy; but as soon as he heard of the Arrival of the Messenger, he commanded him to his

---

[29] *threatening* the participle is confusing; the subject
is probably the King, despite the lack of parallelism .

Tent, where he embraced him, and received him with Joy; which was soon abated by the downcast Looks of the Messenger, who was instantly demanded the Cause by *Oroonoko*; who impatient of Delay, asked a thousand Questions in a Breath, and all concerning *Imoinda*. But there needed little Return, for he could almost answer himself of all he demanded, from his Sighs and Eyes. At last, the Messenger casting himself at the Prince's Feet, and kissing them with all the Submission of a Man that had something to implore which he dreaded to utter, he besought him to hear with Calmness what he had to deliver to him, and to call up all his noble and Heroic Courage, to encounter with his Words, and defend himself against the ungrateful things he must relate. *Oroonoko* replied, with a deep Sigh, and a languishing Voice, – 'I am armed against their worst Efforts –; for I know they will tell me, *Imoinda* is no more –; and after that, you may spare the rest.' Then, commanding him to rise, he laid himself on a Carpet, under a rich Pavilion, and remained a good while silent, and was hardly heard to sigh. When he was come a little to himself, the Messenger asked him leave to deliver that part of his Embassy, which the Prince had not yet divined: and the Prince cried, 'I permit thee' – Then he told him the Affliction the old King was in, for the Rashness he had committed in his Cruelty to *Imoinda*; and how he deigned to ask Pardon for his Offence, and to implore the Prince would not suffer that Loss to touch his Heart too sensibly, which now all the Gods could not restore him, but might recompense him in Glory, which he begged he would pursue; and that Death, that common Revenger of all Injuries, would soon even the Account between him and a feeble old Man.

Oroonoko bade him return his Duty to his Lord and Master; and to assure him, there was no Account of Revenge to be adjusted between them; if there was, he was the Agressor, and that Death would be just, and maugre[30] his Age, would see him righted; and he was contented to leave his Share of Glory to Youths more fortunate and worthy of that Favour from the Gods. That henceforth he would never lift a Weapon, or draw a Bow; but abandon the small Remains of his Life to Sighs and Tears, and the continual Thoughts of what his Lord and Grandfather had thought good to send out of the World, with all that Youth, that Innocence, and Beauty.

After having spoken this, whatever his greatest Officers and Men of the best Rank could do, they could not raise him from the Carpet, or persuade him to Action and Resolutions of Life; but commanding all to retire, he shut himself into his Pavilion all that Day, while the Enemy was ready to engage; and wondering at the Delay, the whole Body of the chief of the Army then addressed themselves to him, and to whom they had much ado to get Admittance. They fell on their Faces at the Foot of his Carpet; where they lay, and besought him with earnest Prayers and Tears to lead them forth to Battle, and not let the Enemy take Advantages of them; and implored him to have regard to his Glory, and to the World, that depended on his Courage and Conduct. But he made no other Reply to all their Supplications but this, That he had now no more Business for Glory; and for the World, it was a Trifle not worth his Care. 'Go', continued he, sighing, 'and divide it amongst you; and reap with Joy what you so vainly prize, and leave me to my more welcome Destiny'.

They then demanded what they should do, and whom he would constitute in his Room, that the Confusion of ambitious Youth and Power might not ruin their Order, and make them a Prey to the Enemy. He replied, He would not give himself the Trouble –; but wished them to chose the bravest Man amongst them, let his Quality or Birth be what it would: 'For, oh my Friends', said he! 'it is not Titles that make Men brave, or good; or Birth that bestows Courage and Generosity, or makes the Owner happy. Believe this, when you behold *Oroonoko*, the most wretched, and abandoned by Fortune, of all the Creation

---

[30]   *maugre*   in spite of.

of the Gods'. So turning himself about, he would make no more Reply to all they could urge or implore.

The Army beholding their Officers return unsuccessful, with sad Faces, and ominous Looks, that presaged no good Luck, suffered a thousand Fears to take possession of their Hearts, and the Enemy to come even upon them, before they would provide for their Safety, by any Defence: and though they were assured by some, who had a mind to animate them, that they should be immediately headed by the Prince, and that in the mean time *Aboan* had Orders to command as General; yet they were so dismayed for want of that great Example of Bravery, that they could make but a very feeble Resistance; and, at last, downright fled before the Enemy, who pursued them to the very Tents, killing them: Nor could all *Aboan*'s Courage, which that Day gained him immortal Glory, shame them into a Manly Defence of themselves. The Guards that were left behind, about the Prince's Tent, seeing the Soldiers flee before the Enemy, and scatter themselves all over the Plain, in great Disorder, made such Outcries, as roused the Prince from his amorous Slumber, in which he had remained buried for two Days, without permitting any Sustenance to approach him. But, in spite of all his Resolutions, he had not the Constancy of Grief to that Degree, as to make him insensible of the Danger of his Army; and in that Instant he leaped from his Couch, and cried, – 'Come, if we must die, let us meet Death the noblest Way; and 'twill be more like *Oroonoko* to encounter him at an Army's Head, opposing the Torrent of a conquering Foe, than lazily, on a Couch, to wait his lingering Pleasure, and die every Moment by a thousand wrecking Thoughts; or be tamely taken by an Enemy, and led a whining, Love-sick Slave to adorn the Triumphs of *Jamoan*, that young Victor, who already is entered beyond the Limits I had prescribed him'.

While he was speaking, he suffered his People to dress him for the Field; and sallying out of his Pavilion, with more Life and Vigour in his Countenance than ever he showed, he appeared like some Divine Power descended to save his Country from Destruction; and his People had purposely put on him all things that might make him shine with most Splendour, to strike a reverend Awe into the Beholders. He flew into the thickest of those that were pursuing his Men; and being animated with Despair, he fought as if he came on purpose to die, and did such things as will not be believed that Human Strength could perform; and such as soon inspired all the rest with new Courage, and new Order: And now it was, that they began to fight indeed; and so, as if they would not be outdone, even by their adored *Hero*; who turning the Tide of Victory, changing absolutely the Fate of the Day, gained an entire Conquest; and *Oroonoko* having the good Fortune to single out *Jamoan*, he took him Prisoner with his own Hand, having wounded him almost to death.

This *Jamoan* afterwards became very dear to him, being a Man very gallant, and of excellent Graces, and fine Parts; so that he never put him amongst the Rank of Captives, as they used to do, without distinction, for the common Sale, or Market, but kept him in his own Court, where he retained nothing of the Prisoner, but the Name, and returned no more into his own Country, so great an Affection he took for *Oroonoko*, and by a thousand Tales and Adventures of Love and Gallantry, flattered[31] his Disease of Melancholy and Languishment; which I have often heard him say, had certainly killed him, but for the Conversation of this Prince and *Aboan*, the *French* Governor he had from his Childhood, of whom I have spoken before, and who was a Man of admirable Wit, great Ingenuity and Learning; all which he had infused into his young Pupil. This *French*-Man was banished out of his own Country, for some

---

[31]   *flatter*   "To please; to soothe. This sense is purely Gallic" (Johnson).

Heretical Notions he held; and though he was a man of very little Religion, he had admirable Morals, and a brave Soul.

After the total Defeat of *Jamoan*'s Army, which all fled, or were left dead upon the Place, they spent some time in the Camp; *Oroonoko* chosing rather to remain awhile there in his Tents, than to enter into a Place, or live in a Court where he had so lately suffered so great a Loss. The Officers therefore, who saw and knew his Cause of Discontent, invented all sorts of Diversions and Sports, to entertain their Prince: So that what with those Amusements abroad, and others at home, that is, within their Tents, with the Persuasions, Arguments, and Care of his Friends and Servants that he more peculiarly prized, he wore off in time a great part of that *Shagrien*, and Torture of Despair, which the first Efforts[32] of *Imoinda*'s Death had given him: Insomuch as having received a thousand kind Embassies from the King, and Invitations to return to Court, he obeyed, though with no little Reluctancy; and when he did so, there was a visible Change in him, and for a long time he was much more melancholy than before. But Time lessens all Extremes, and reduces them to *Mediums*, and Unconcern; but no Motives or Beauties, though all endeavoured it, could engage him in any sort of Amour, though he had all the Invitations to it, both from his own Youth, and other Ambitions and Designs.

Oroonoko was no sooner returned from this last Conquest, and received at Court with all the Joy and Magnificence that could be expressed to a young Victor, who was not only returned triumphant, but beloved like a Deity, when there arrived in the Port an *English* Ship.

This Person had often before been in these Countries, and was very well known to *Oroonoko*, with whom he had trafficked for Slaves, and had used to do the same with his Predecessors.

This Commander was a Man of a finer sort of Address, and Conversation, better bred, and more engaging, than most of that sort of Men are; so that he seemed rather never to have been bred out of a Court, than almost all his Life at Sea. This Captain therefore was always better received at Court, than most of the Traders to those Countries were; and especially by *Oroonoko*, who was more civilized, according to the *European* Mode, than any other had been, and took more Delight in the *White* Nations; and, above all, Men of Parts and Wit. To this Captain he sold abundance of his Slaves; and for the Favour and Esteem he had for him, made him many Presents, and obliged him to stay at Court as long as possibly he could. Which the Captain seemed to take as a very great Honour done him, entertaining the Prince every Day with Globes and Maps, and Mathematical Discourses and Instruments; eating, drinking, hunting, and living with him with so much Familiarity, that it was not to be doubted, but he had gained very greatly upon the Heart of this gallant young Man. And the Captain, in Return of all these mighty Favours, besought the Prince to honour his Vessel with his Presence some Day or other, to Dinner, before he should set Sail; which he condescended[33] to accept, and appointed his Day. The Captain, on his part, failed not to have all things in a Readiness, in the most magnificent Order he could possibly: And the Day being come, the Captain, in his Boat, richly adorned with Carpets and Velvet-Cushions, rowed to the Shore to receive the Prince; with another Long-Boat, where was placed all his Music and Trumpets, with which *Oroonoko* was extremely delighted; who met him on the Shore, attended by his *French* Governor, *Jamoan*, *Aboan*, and about an hundred of the noblest of the Youths of the Court: And after they had first carried the Prince on Board, the boats fetched the rest off;

---

[32] *Efforts* a typographical error for "Effects," I think. [33] *condescend* "To consent to do more than mere justice can require" (Johnson).

where they found a very splendid Treat, with all sorts of fine Wines; and were as well entertained, as 'twas possible in such a place to be.

The Prince having drunk hard of Punch, and several Sorts of Wine, as did all the rest (for great Care was taken, they should want nothing of that part of the Entertainment) was very merry, and in great Admiration of the Ship, for he had never been in one before; so that he was curious of beholding every place where he decently might descend. The rest, no less curious, who were not quite overcome with Drinking, rambled at their pleasure *Fore* and *Aft*, as their fancies guided them: So that the Captain, who had well laid his Design before, gave the Word, and seized on all his Guests; they clapping great Irons suddenly on the Prince, when he was leaped down in the Hold, to view that part of the Vessel; and locking him fast down, secured him. The same Treachery was used to all the rest; and all in one Instant, in several places of the Ship, were lashed fast in Irons, and betrayed to Slavery. That great Design over, they set all Hands to work to hoist Sail; and with as treacherous and fair a Wind, they made from the Shore with this innocent and glorious Prize, who thought of nothing less than such an Entertainment.

Some have commended this Act, as brave, in the Captain; but I will spare my Sense of it, and leave it to my Reader, to judge as he pleases.

It may be easily guessed in what manner the Prince resented this Indignity, who may be best resembled to a Lion taken in a Toil;[34] so he raged, so he struggled for Liberty, but all in vain; and they had so wisely managed his Fetters, that he could not use a Hand in his Defence, to quit himself of a Life that would by no Means endure Slavery; nor could he move from the Place, where he was tied, to any solid part of the Ship, against which he might have beat his Head, and have finished his Disgrace that way: So that being deprived of all other means, he resolved to perish for want of Food: And pleased at last with that Thought, and toiled[35] and tired by Rage and Indignation, he laid himself down, and sullenly resolved upon dying, and refused all things that were brought him.

This did not a little vex the Captain, and the more so, because, he found almost all of them of the same Humour; so that the loss of so many brave Slaves, so tall and goodly to behold, would have been very considerable: He therefore ordered one to go from him (for he would not be seen himself) to *Oroonoko*, and to assure him he was afflicted for having rashly done so inhospitable a Deed, and which could not be now remedied, since they were far from shore; but since he resented it in so high a nature, he assured him he would revoke his Resolution, and set both him and his Friends ashore on the next Land they should touch at; and of this the Messenger gave him his Oath, provided he would resolve to live: And *Oroonoko*, whose Honour was such as he never had violated a Word in his Life himself, much less a solemn Asseveration, believed in an instant what this Man said, but replied, He expected for a Confirmation of this, to have his shameful Fetters dismissed. This Demand was carried to the *Captain*, who returned him answer, That the Offence had been so great which he had put upon the Prince, that he durst not trust him with Liberty while he remained in the Ship, for fear lest by a Valour natural to him, and a Revenge that would animate that Valour, he might commit some Outrage fatal to himself and the *King* his Master, to whom the Vessel did belong. To this *Oroonoko* replied, he would engage his Honour to behave himself in all friendly Order and Manner, and obey the Command of the *Captain*, as he was Lord of the *King*'s Vessel, and General of those Men under his Command.

This was delivered to the still doubting *Captain*, who could not resolve to trust a *Heathen* he said, upon his *Parole*,[36] a Man that had no sense or notion of the God that he Worshipped.

---

[34] *Toil*   net.
[35] *toiled*   wearied.

[36] *Parole*   "Word given as an assurance" (Johnson).

Oroonoko then replied, He was very sorry to hear that the *Captain* pretended to the Knowledge and Worship of any *Gods*, who had taught him no better Principles, than not to Credit as he would be Credited: but they told him, the Difference of their Faith occasioned that Distrust: for the *Captain* had protested to him upon the Word of a *Christian*, and sworn in the Name of a Great *GOD*; which if he should violate, he must expect eternal Torment in the World to come. 'Is that all the Obligations he has to be Just to his Oath', replied Oroonoko? 'Let him know I Swear by my Honour, which to violate, would not only render me contemptible and despised by all brave and honest Men, and so give my self perpetual pain, but it would be eternally offending and diseasing[37] all Mankind, harming, betraying, circumventing and outraging all Men; but Punishments hereafter are suffered by one's self; and the World takes no cognizances whether this God has revenged them, or not, 'tis done so secretly, and deferred so long; While the Man of no Honour suffers every moment the scorn and contempt of the honester World, and dies every day ignominiously in his Fame[38], which is more valuable than Life: I speak not this to move Belief, but to show you how you mistake when you imagine That he who will violate his Honour will keep his Word with his *Gods'*. So turning from him with a disdainful smile, he refused to answer him, when he urged him to know what Answer he should carry back to his *Captain*; so that he departed without saying any more.

The Captain pondering and consulting what to do, it was concluded that nothing but *Oroonoko*'s Liberty would encourage any of the rest to eat, except the *French*-man, whom the *Captain* could not pretend to keep Prisoner, but only told him he was secured because he might act something in favour of the Prince, but that he should be freed as soon as they came to Land. So that they concluded it wholly necessary to free the Prince from his Irons, that he might show himself to the rest; that they might have an Eye upon him, and that they could not fear a single Man.

This being resolved, to make the Obligation the greater, the Captain himself went to *Oroonoko*; where, after many Complements, and Assurances of what he had already promised, he receiving from the Prince his *Parole*, and his Hand, for his good Behaviour, dismissed his Irons, and brought him to his own Cabin; where, after having treated and reposed him a while, for he had neither eaten nor slept in four Days before, he besought him to visit those obstinate People in Chains, who refused all manner of Sustenance; and entreated him to oblige them to eat, and assure them of their Liberty the first Opportunity.

Oroonoko, who was too generous not to give Credit to his Words, showed himself to his People, who were transported with Excess of Joy at the sight of their Darling Prince, falling at his Feet, and kissing and embracing them, believing, as some Divine Oracle, all he assured them. But he besought them to bear their Chains with that Bravery that became those whom he had seen act so nobly in Arms; and that they could not give him greater Proofs of their Love and Friendship, since it was all the Security the Captain (his Friend) could have against the Revenge, he said, they might possibly justly take, for the Injuries sustained by him. And they all, with one Accord, assured him, that they could not suffer enough, when it was for his Repose and Safety.

After this they no longer refused to eat, but took what was brought them, and were pleased with their Captivity, since by it they hoped to redeem the Prince, who, all the rest of the Voyage, was treated with all the Respect due to his Birth, though nothing could divert his Melancholy; and he would often sigh for *Imoinda*, and think this a Punishment due to his Misfortune, in having left that noble Maid behind him, that fatal Night, in the *Otan*, when he fled to the Camp.

---

[37] *disease* "To put to pain; to pain; to make uneasy" (Johnson).   [38] *Fame* reputation.

Possessed with a thousand Thoughts of past Joys with this fair young Person, and a thousand Griefs for her eternal Loss, he endured a tedious Voyage, and at last arrived at the Mouth of the River of *Surinam*, a Colony belonging to the King of *England*, and where they were to deliver some part of their Slaves. There the Merchants and Gentlemen of the Country going on Board, to demand those Lots of Slaves they had already agreed on; and amongst those, the Overseers of those Plantations where I then chanced to be, the Captain, who had given the Word, ordered his men to bring up those noble Slaves in Fetters, whom I have spoken of; and having put them, some in one, and some in other Lots, with Women and Children (which they call *Pickaninies*,[39]) they sold them off, as Slaves, to several Merchants and Gentlemen; not putting any two in one Lot, because they would separate them far from each other; not daring to trust them together, lest Rage and Courage should put them upon contriving some great Action, to the Ruin of the Colony.

Oroonoko was first seized on, and sold to our Overseer, who had the first Lot, with seventeen more of all sorts and sizes, but not one of Quality with him. When he saw this, he found what they meant; for, as I said, he understood *English* pretty well; and being wholly unarmed and defenceless, so as it was in vain to make any Resistance, he only beheld the Captain with a Look all fierce and disdainful, upbraiding him with Eyes, that forced Blushes on his guilty Cheeks, he only cried, in passing over the Side of the Ship: 'Farewell, Sir: 'Tis worth my Suffering, to gain so true a Knowledge both of you, and of your Gods by whom you swear'. And desiring those that held him to forbear their pains, and telling them he would make no Resistance, he cried, 'Come, my Fellow-Slaves, let us descend, and see if we can meet with more Honour and Honesty in the next World we shall touch upon'. So he nimbly leaped into the Boat, and showing no more Concern, suffered himself to be rowed up the River, with his seventeen Companions.

The Gentleman that bought him was a young *Cornish* Gentleman, whose Name was *Trefry*;[40] a man of great Wit, and fine Learning, and was carried into those Parts by the Lord —— Governor, to manage all his Affairs. He reflecting on the last Words of *Oroonoko* to the Captain, and beholding the Richness of his Vest, no sooner came into the Boat, but he fixed his Eyes on him; and finding something so extraordinary in his Face, his Shape and Mien, a Greatness of Look, and Haughtiness in his Air, and finding he spoke *English*, had a great mind to be enquiring into his Quality and Fortune; which, though *Oroonoko* endeavoured to hide, by only confessing he was above the Rank of common Slaves, *Trefry* soon found he was yet something greater than he confessed; and from that Moment began to conceive so vast an Esteem for him, that he ever after loved him as his dearest Brother, and showed him all the Civilities due to so great a Man.

Trefry was a very good Mathematician, and a Linguist; could speak *French* and *Spanish*; and in the three Days they remained in the Boat (for so long were they going from the Ship to the Plantation) he entertained *Oroonoko* so agreeably with his *Art* and *Discourse*, that he was no less pleased with *Trefry*, than he was with the Prince; and he thought himself, at least, fortunate in this, that since he was a Slave, as long as he would suffer himself to remain so, he had a Man of so excellent Wit and Parts for a Master: So that before they had finished their Voyage up the River, he made no scruple of declaring to *Trefry* all his Fortunes, and most part of what I have here related, and put himself wholly into the Hands of his new Friend, whom he found

---

[39] *Pickaninies* from Portuguese *pequenino*; first use recorded in *OED* is 1657.
[40] *Trefry* John Trefry, the actual overseer for the Governor, Lord Willoughby, to whom Charles II had issued letters patent for control of the region in 1663; Willoughby died in a storm at sea in 1666, as Behn correctly suggests later.

resenting all the Injuries were done him, and was charmed with all the Greatness of his Actions; which were recited with that Modesty, and delicate Sense, as wholly vanquished him, and subdued him to his Interest. And he promised him on his Word and Honour, he would find the Means to re-conduct him to his own Country again: assuring him, he had a perfect Abhorrence of so dishonourable an Action; and that he would sooner have died, than have been the author of such a Perfidy. He found the Prince was very much concerned to know what became of his Friends, and how they took their Slavery; and *Trefry* promised to take care about the enquiring after their Condition, and that he should have an Account of them.

Though, as *Oroonoko* afterwards said, he had little reason to credit the words of a *Backearary*;[41] yet he knew not why; but he saw a kind of Sincerity, and awful Truth in the Face of *Trefry*; he saw an Honesty in his Eyes, and he found him wise and witty enough to understand Honour: for it was one of his Maxims, A Man of Wit could not be a Knave or Villain.

In their passage up the River, they put in at several Houses for Refreshment; and ever when they landed, numbers of People would flock to behold this Man; not but their Eyes were daily entertained with the sight of Slaves; but the Fame of *Oroonoko* was gone before him, and all People were in Admiration of his Beauty. Besides, he had a rich Habit on, in which he was taken, so different from the rest, and which the Captain could not strip him of, because he was forced to surprise[42] his Person in the Minute he sold him. When he found his Habit made him liable, as he thought, to be gazed at the more, he begged *Trefry* to give him something more befitting a Slave; which he did, and took off his Robes. Nevertheless, he shone through all; and his *Osenbrigs* (a sort of brown *Holland Suit* he had on) could not conceal the Graces of his Looks and Mien; and he had no less Admirers, than when he had his dazzling Habit on: The Royal Youth appeared in spite of the Slave, and People could not help treating him after a different manner, without designing it: As soon as they approached him, they venerated and esteemed him; his Eyes insensibly commanded Respect, and his Behaviour insinuated it into every Soul. So that there was nothing talked of but this young and gallant Slave, even by those who yet knew not that he was a Prince.

I ought to tell you, that the *Christians* never buy any Slaves but they give them some Name of their own, their native ones being likely very barbarous,[43] and hard to pronounce; so that Mr. *Trefry* gave *Oroonoko* that of *Cæsar*; which Name will live on in that Country as long as that (scarce more) glorious one of the great *Roman*: for 'tis most evident, he wanted no part of the Personal Courage of that *Cæsar*, and acted things as memorable, had they been done in some part of the World replenished with People, and Historians, that might have given him his due. But his Misfortune was, to fall in an obscure World, that afforded only a Female Pen to celebrate his Fame; though I doubt not but it had lived from others' Endeavours, if the *Dutch*, who immediately after his Time took that Country, had not killed, banished and dispersed all those that were capable of giving the World this great Man's Life, much better than I have done. And Mr. *Trefry*, who designed it, died before he began it; and bemoaned himself for not having undertook it in time.

For the future therefore I must call *Oroonoko*, *Cæsar*, since by that Name only he was known in our Western World, and by that name he was received on Shore at *Parham-House*,[44] where he was destined a Slave. But if the King himself (God bless him) had come ashore there

---

[41]   *Backearary*   white man.
[42]   *Surprise*   reveal, display.

[43]   *barbarous*   foreign or "A form of speech contrary to the purity and exactness of any language" (Johnson, s.v. "barbarism").
[44]   *Parham-House*   part of Lord Willoughby's estate.

could not have been greater Expectations by all the whole Plantation, and those neighbouring ones, than was on ours at that time; and he was received more like a Governor than a Slave. Notwithstanding, as the Custom was, they assigned him his Portion of Land, his House, and his Business, up in the Plantation. But as it was more for Form, than any Design, to put him to his Task, he endured no more of the Slave but the Name, and remained some Days in the House, receiving all Visits that were made him, without stirring towards that part of the Plantation where the *Negroes* were.

At last, he would needs go view his Land, his House, and the Business assigned him. But he no sooner came to the Houses of the Slaves, which are like a little Town by it self, the *Negroes* all having left Work, but they all came forth to behold him, and found he was that Prince who had, at several times, sold most of them to these Parts; and from a Veneration they pay to great Men, especially if they know them, and from the Surprize and Awe they had at the sight of him, they all cast themselves at his Feet, crying out, in their Language, 'Live, O King! Long live, O King!' And kissing his Feet, paid him even Divine Homage.

Several *English* Gentlemen were with him; and what Mr. *Trefry* told them, was here confirmed; of which he himself before had no other Witness than *Cæsar* himself: But he was infinitely glad to find his Grandeur confirmed by all the Adoration of the Slaves.

Cæsar, troubled with their Over-Joy, and Over-Ceremony, besought them to rise, and to receive him as their Fellow-Slave, assuring them, he was no better. At which they set up with one Accord a most terrible and hideous Mourning and condoling, which he and the *English* had much ado to appease; but at last they prevailed with them, and they prepared all their barbarous Musick, and every one killed and dressed something of his own Stock (for every Family has their Land apart, or which, at their leisure times, they breed all eatable things); and clubbing it together, made a most magnificent Supper, inviting their *Grandee Captain*, their *Prince*, to honour it with his Presence; which he did, and several *English* with him; where they all waited on him, some playing, others dancing before him all the time, according to the Manners of their several Nations, and with unwearied Industry endeavouring to please and delight him.

While they sat at Meat, Mr. *Trefry* told *Cæsar*, that most of these young *Slaves* were undone in Love with a fine she *Slave*, whom they had had about Six Months on their Land; the *Prince*, who never heard the Name of *Love* without a Sigh, nor any mention of it without the Curiosity of examining further into that tale, which of all Discourses was most agreeable to him, asked, how they came to be so Unhappy, as to be all Undone for one fair *Slave*? *Trefry*, who was naturally Amorous, and loved to talk of Love as well as any body, proceeded to tell him, they had the most charming Black that ever was beheld on their *Plantation*, about Fifteen or Sixteen Years old, as he guessed; that for his part, he had done nothing but Sigh for her ever since she came; and that all the white Beauties he had seen, never charmed him so absolutely as this fine Creature had done; and that no Man, of any Nation, ever beheld her, that did not fall in Love with her; and that she had all the *Slaves* perpetually at her Feet; and the whole Country resounded with the Fame of *Clemene*, for so, said he, we have Christened her: But she denies us all with such noble Disdain, that 'tis a Miracle to see, that she, who can give such eternal Desires, should herself be all Ice, and all Unconcern. She is adorned with the most Graceful Modesty that ever beautified Youth; the softest Sigher – that, if she were capable of Love, one would swear she languished for some absent happy Man; and so retired, as if she feared a Rape even from the God of Day; or that the Breezes would steal Kisses from her delicate Mouth. Her Task of Work some sighing Lover every day makes it his Petition to perform for her, which she accepts blushing, and with reluctancy, for fear he will ask her a Look for a Recompense, which he dares not presume to hope, so great an Awe she strikes into the Hearts of her Admirers. 'I do not wonder', replied the Prince, 'that *Clemene* should refuse Slaves, being as you say so Beautiful, but wonder how she escapes those who entertain her as you can do; or why, being your Slave, you do not oblige her to yield'.

'I confess', said Trefry, 'when I have, against her will, entertained her with Love so long, as to be transported with my Passion, even above Decency, I have been ready to make use of those advantages of Strength and Force Nature has given me. But oh! she disarms me with that Modesty and Weeping so tender and so moving, that I retire, and thank my Stars she overcame me'. The Company laughed at his Civility to a *Slave*, and *Cæsar* only applauded the nobleness of his Passion and Nature; since that Slave might be Noble, or, what was better, have true Notions of Honour and Virtue in her. Thus passed they this night, after having received, from the *Slaves* all imaginable Respect and Obedience.

The next day, *Trefry* asked *Cæsar* to walk when the heat was allayed, and designedly carried him by the cottage of the *fair Slave*; and told him, she whom he spoke of last Night lived there retired: 'But', says he, 'I would not wish for you to approach, for, I am sure you will be in Love as soon as you behold her'. *Cæsar* assured him, he was proof against all the Charms of that Sex; and that if he imagined his Heart could be so perfidious to Love again, after *Imoinda*, he believed he should tear it from his Bosom: They had no sooner spoke, but a little shock Dog[45], that *Clemene* had presented her, which she took great Delight in, ran out; and she, not knowing any body was there, ran to get it in again, and bolted out on those who were just Speaking of her: When seeing them, she would have run in again; but *Trefry* caught her by the Hand, and cried, '*Clemene*, however you fly a Lover, you ought to pay some respect to this Stranger', pointing to *Cæsar*. But she, as if she had resolved never to raise her Eyes to the Face of a Man again, bent them the more to the Earth, when he spoke, and gave the *Prince* the Leisure to look the more at her. There needed no long-Gazing, or Consideration, to examine who this fair Creature was; he soon saw *Imoinda* all over her; in a Minute he saw her Face, her Shape, her Air, her Modesty, and all that called forth his Soul with Joy at his Eyes, and left his Body destitute of almost life; it stood without Motion, and for a Minute, knew not that it had a Being; and, I believe, he had never come to himself, so oppressed he was with over-Joy, if he had not met with this Allay, that he perceived *Imoinda* fall dead in the Hands of *Trefry*: This awakened him, and he ran to her aid, and caught her in his Arms, where, by degrees, she came to herself; and 'tis needless to tell what transports, what ecstasies of Joy, they both a while beheld each other, without Speaking; then Snatched each other to their Arms; then Gaze again, as if they still doubted whether they possessed the Blessing: They Grasped, but when they recovered their Speech, 'tis not to be imagined, what tender things they expressed to each other, wondering what strange Fate had brought them again together. They soon informed each other of their Fortunes, and equally bewailed their Fate; but, at the same time they mutually protested, that even Fetters and Slavery were Soft and Easy, and would be supported with Joy and Pleasure, while they could be so happy to possess each other, and to be able to make good their Vows. *Cæsar* swore he disdained the Empire of the World, while he could behold his *Imoinda*; and she despised Grandeur and Pomp, those Vanities of her sex, when she could Gaze on *Oroonoko*. He adored the very Cottage where she resided, and said, That little Inch of the World would give him more Happiness than all the Universe could do; and she vowed, It was a Palace, while adorned with the Presence of *Oroonoko*.

Trefry was infinitely pleased with this Novel[46], and found this *Clemene* was the Fair Mistress of whom *Cæsar* had before spoke; and was not a little satisfied, that Heaven was so

---

[45] *shock Dog* "[from *shagg*] A rough dog" (Johnson).   [46] *Novel* "A small tale, generally of love" (Johnson).

kind to the *Prince*, as to sweeten his Misfortunes by so lucky an Accident; and leaving the Lovers to themselves, was impatient to come down to *Parham House* (which was on the same *Plantation*) to give me an Account of what had happened. I was as impatient to make these Lovers a Visit, having already made a Friendship with *Cæsar*; and from his own Mouth learned what I have related, which was confirmed by his French-man, who was set on Shore to seek his Fortunes, and of whom they could not make a Slave, because a Christian; and he came daily to *Parham Hill* to see and pay his Respects to his Pupil *Prince*: So that concerning and interesting my self, in all that related to *Cæsar*, whom I had assured of Liberty, as soon as the Governor arrived, I hasted presently to the Place where the Lovers were, and was infinitely glad to find this Beautiful young *Slave* (who had already gained all our Esteems, for her Modesty and extraordinary Prettiness) to be the same I had heard *Cæsar* spoke so much of. One may imagine then, we paid her a treble Respect; and though from her being carved in fine Flowers and Birds all over her body, we took her to be of Quality before, yet when we knew *Clemene* was *Imoinda*, we could not enough admire her.

I had forgot to tell you, that those who are Nobly born of that Country, are so delicately Cut and Raced[47] all over the fore-part of the Trunk of their Bodies, that it looks as if it were Japanned,[48] the Works being raised like high Point[49] round the Edges of the Flowers: Some are only Carved with a little Flower, or Bird, at the Sides of the Temples, as was *Cæsar*; and those who are so Carved over the Body, resemble our Ancient *Picts*[50] that are figured in the Chronicles,[51] but these Carvings are far more delicate.

From that happy Day *Cæsar* took *Clemene* for his Wife, to the general Joy of all People; and there was as much Magnificence as the Country would afford at the Celebration of this Wedding: and in a very short time after she conceived with Child, which made *Cæsar* even adore her, knowing he was the last of his Great Race. This new Accident made him more Impatient of Liberty, and he was every Day treating with *Trefry* for his and *Clemene*'s Liberty, and offered either Gold, or a vast quantity of Slaves, which should be paid before they let him go, provided he could have any Security that he should go when his Ransom was paid: They fed him from Day to Day with Promises, and delayed him, till the Lord-Governor should come; so that he began to suspect them of falsehood, and that they would delay him till the time of his Wife's delivery, and make a slave of that too, for all the Breed is theirs to whom the Parents belong: This Thought made him very uneasy, and his Sullenness gave them some Jealousies[52] of him; so that I was obliged, by some Persons, who feared a Mutiny (which is very Fatal sometimes in those Colonies that abound so with Slaves, that they exceed the Whites in vast Numbers) to discourse with *Cæsar*, and to give him all the Satisfaction I possibly could; they knew he and *Clemene* were scarce an Hour in a Day from my Lodgings; that they eat with me, and that I obliged them in all things I was capable of: I entertained them with the Lives of the Romans, and great Men, which charmed him to my Company; and her, with teaching her all the pretty Works I was Mistress of, and telling her Stories of Nuns, and endeavouring to bring her to the knowledge of the true God. But of all Discourses, *Cæsar* liked that the worst, and would never be reconciled to our Notions of the Trinity, of which he ever made a Jest; it was a Riddle, he said, would turn his Brain[53] to conceive, and one could not make him understand what Faith was. However, these Conversations failed not altogether so well to divert him, that he liked the Company of us Women much above the Men; for he

[47] *race* "Cut or slash (shoes or clothes) in an ornamental fashion" (*OED*).

[48] *Japan* "To varnish, and embellish with gold and raised figures" (Johnson).

[49] *high Point* fancy embroidery or lace.

[50] *Picts* early inhabitants of Scotland.

[51] *Chronicles* any of a number of early British historical writings and later imitations thereof.

[52] *Jealousy* "Suspicious fear" (Johnson).

[53] *turn his Brain* "To infatuate; to make mad" (Johnson, sense 22).

could not Drink, and he is but an ill Companion in that Country that cannot: So that obliging him to love us very well, we had all the Liberty of Speech with him, especially myself, whom he called his *Great Mistress*; and indeed my Word would go a great way with him. For these reasons I had Opportunity to take notice to him, that he was not well pleased of late, as he used to be (was more retired and thoughtful) and told him, I took it ill he should Suspect we would break our Words with him, and not permit both him and *Clemene* to return to his own Kingdom, which was not so long a way, but when he was once on his Voyage he would quickly arrive there. He made me some Answers that showed a doubt in him, which made me ask him, what advantage it would be to doubt? it would but give us a Fear of him, and possibly compel us to treat him so as I should be very loath to behold: that is, it might occasion his Confinement. Perhaps this was not so Luckily spoke of me,[54] for I perceived he resented that Word, which I strove to Soften again in vain: However, he assured me, that whatsoever Resolutions he should take, he would Act nothing upon the White-People; and as for my self, and those upon that *Plantation* where he was, he would sooner forfeit his eternal Liberty, and Life it self, than lift his Hand against his greatest Enemy on that Place: He besought me to suffer no Fears upon his Account, for he could do nothing that Honour should not dictate; but he accused himself for having suffered Slavery so long; yet he charged that weakness on Love alone, who was capable of making him neglect even Glory it self, and, for which, now he reproaches himself every moment of the Day. Much more to this effect he spoke, with an Air impatient enough to make me know he would not be long in Bondage; and though he suffered only the Name of a Slave, and had nothing of the Toil and Labour of one, yet that was sufficient to render him Uneasy; and he had been too long Idle, who used to be always in Action, and in Arms: He had a Spirit all Rough and Fierce, and that could not be tamed to lazy Rest; and though all endeavours were used to exercise himself in such Actions and Sports as this World afforded, as Running, Wrestling, Pitching the Bar,[55] Hunting and Fishing, Chasing and Killing *Tigers* of a monstrous Size, which this Continent affords in abundance; and wonderful *Snakes*, such as *Alexander* is reported to have encountered at the River of *Amazons*,[56] and which *Cæsar* took great Delight to overcome; yet these were not Actions great enough for his large Soul, which was still panting after more renowned Action.

Before I parted that Day with him, I got, with much ado, a Promise from him to rest yet a little longer with Patience, and wait the coming of the Lord Governor, who was every Day expected on our Shore; he assured me he would, and this Promise he desired me to know was given perfectly in Complaisance to me, in whom he had an entire Confidence.

After this, I neither thought it convenient to trust him much out of our View, nor did the Country who feared him; but with one accord it was advised to treat him Fairly, and oblige him to remain within such a compass, and that he should be permitted, as seldom as could be, to go up to the Plantations of the Negroes; or, if he did, to be accompanied by some that should be rather in appearance Attendants than Spies. This Care was for some time taken, and *Cæsar* looked upon it as a Mark of extraordinary Respect, and was glad his discontent had obliged them to be more observant to him; he received new assurance from the Overseer, which was confirmed to him by the Opinion of all the Gentlemen of the Country, who made their court of him: During this time that we had his Company more frequently than hitherto we had had, it may not be unpleasant to relate to you the Diversions we entertained him with, or rather he us.

---

[54] *spoke of me*   spoken by me.
[55] *Pitching the Bar*   a kind of weight throwing contest (see *Spectator* 434).

[56] *Alexander is reported . . . Amazons*   in one of the many romances of Alexander based on the fictional history of Pseudo-Callisthenes.

My stay here was to be short in that Country, because my Father died at Sea, and never arrived to possess the Honour was designed him (which was Lieutenant-General of Six and thirty Islands, besides the Continent[57] of *Surinam*) nor the advantages he hoped to reap by them; so that though we were obliged to continue on our Voyage, we did not intend to stay upon the Place: Though, in a Word, I must say this much of it, That certainly had his late Majesty,[58] of sacred Memory, but seen and known what a vast and charming World he had been Master of in that Continent, he would have never parted so easily with it to the Dutch.[59] 'Tis a Continent whose vast Extent was never yet known, and may contain more Noble Earth than all the Universe besides; for, they say, it reaches from East to West one way as far as *China*, and another to *Peru*:[60] It affords all things both for Beauty and Use; 'tis there Eternal Spring, always the very Months of *April*, *May*, and *June*; the Shades are perpetual, the Trees, bearing at once all degrees of Leaves, and Fruit, from blooming Buds to ripe Autumn; Groves of Oranges, Lemons, Citrons, Figs, Nutmegs, and noble Aromatics, continually bearing their Fragrancies. The trees appearing all like Nosegays adorned with Flowers of different kind; some are all White, some Purple, some Scarlet, some Blue, some Yellow; bearing, at the same time, Ripe Fruit and Blooming Young, or producing every Day new. The very Wood of all these Trees has an intrinsic Value, above common Timber; for they are, when cut, of different Colours, glorious to behold, and bear a Price considerable, to inlay withal. Besides this, they yield rich Balm, and Gums; so that we make our Candles of such an Aromatic Substance, as does not only give a sufficient Light, but, as they Burn, they cast their Perfumes all about. Cedar is the common Firing, and all the Houses are built with it. The very Meat we eat, when set on the Table, if it be Native, I mean of the Country, perfumes the whole Room; especially a little Beast called an *Armadilly*, a thing which I can liken to nothing so well as a *Rhinoceros*; 'tis all in white Armour so jointed, that it moves as well in it, as if it had nothing on; this Beast is about the bigness of a pig Six Weeks old. But it were endless to give an Account of all the divers Wonderful and Strange things that Country affords, and which we took a great Delight to go in search of; though those adventures are oftentimes Fatal, and at least Dangerous. But while we had *Cæsar* in our Company on these Designs we feared no harm, nor suffered any.

As soon as I came into the Country, the best House in it was presented me, called St. *John's Hill*.[61] It stood on a vast Rock of white Marble, at the Foot of which the River ran a vast depth down, and not to be descended on that side; the little Waves still dashing and washing the foot of this Rock, made the softest Murmurs and Purlings in the World; and the Opposite Bank was adorned with such vast quantities of different Flowers eternally Blowing,[62] and every Day and Hour new, fenced behind them with lofty Trees of a Thousand rare Forms and Colours, that the Prospect was the most ravishing that Sands[63] can create. On the Edge of this white Rock, towards the River, was a Walk or Grove of Orange and Lemon Trees, about half the length of the Mall[64] here, whose Flowery and Fruit-bearing Branches met at the top, and hindered the sun, whose Rays are very fierce there, from entering a Beam into the Grove; and

[57]　*Continent*　"Land not disjoined by the sea from other lands" (Johnson).

[58]　*his late Majesty*　Charles II.

[59]　*Dutch*　The English gave up Surinam to the Dutch in the Treaty of Breda (1667) and took control of New York.

[60]　*'Tis a Continent . . . to Peru*　the description reflects the fact that the region was thought to contain the fabulous city of El Dorado (see *Paradise Lost* 11.410–11);

Raleigh sailed up the Orinoco River in search of that golden world in 1595.

[61]　*St. John's Hill*　an estate probably sold to Willoughby in 1664 by Robert Walpole, uncle of the more famous Robert, 1st Earl of Oxford (1661–1724).

[62]　*Blowing*　blooming.

[63]　*Sands*　emended to "Fancy" in some later editions.

[64]　*Mall*　a fashionable walk in St James's Park, London.

the cool Air that came from the River made it not only fit to entertain People in, at all the hottest Hours of the Day, but refresh the sweet Blossoms, and made it always Sweet and Charming; and sure the whole Globe of the World cannot show so delightful a Place as this Grove was: Not all the Gardens of boasted *Italy* can produce a Shade to outvie this, which Nature had joined with Art to render so exceeding Fine; and 'tis a marvel to see how such vast Trees, as big as English Oaks, could take footing on so solid a Rock, and in so little Earth, as covered that Rock. But all things by Nature there are Rare, Delightful and Wonderful. But to our Sports.

Sometimes we would go surprising and in search of young *Tigers* in their Dens, watching when the old Ones went forth to forage for Prey; and oftentimes we have been in great Danger, and have fled apace for our Lives, when surprised by the Dams. But once, above all other times, we went on this Design, and *Cæsar* went with us, who had no sooner stolen a young *Tiger* from her Nest, but going off, we encountered the Dam, bearing a Buttock of a Cow, which he had torn off with his mighty Paw, and going with it towards his *Den*; we had only four Women, *Cæsar*, and an English Gentleman, Brother to *Harry Martin*, the great *Oliverian*;[65] we found there was no escaping this enraged and ravenous Beast. However, we Women fled as fast as we could from it; but our Heels had not saved our Lives, if *Cæsar* had not laid down his *Cub*, when he found the *Tiger* quit her Prey to make the more speed towards him; and taking Mr. *Martin*'s Sword desired him to stand aside, or follow the Ladies. He obeyed him, and *Cæsar* met this monstrous Beast of might, size, and vast Limbs, who came with open Jaws upon him; and fixing his Awful stern Eyes full upon those of the Beast, and putting himself into a very steady and good aiming posture of Defence, ran his Sword quite through his Breast, down to his very Heart, home to the Hilt of the Sword; the dying Beast stretched forth her Paw, and going to grasp his Thigh, surprised with Death in that very moment, did him no other harm than fixing her long Nails in his Flesh very deep, feebly wounded him, but could not grasp the Flesh to tear off any. When he had done this, he hallooed us to return, which, after some assurance of his Victory, we did, and found him lugging out the Sword from the Bosom of the *Tiger*, who was laid in her Blood on the Ground; he took up the *Cub*, and with an unconcern, that had nothing of the Joy or Gladness of a Victory, he came and laid the Whelp at my Feet: We all extremely wondered at his Daring, and at the Bigness of the Beast, which was about the heighth of an Heifer, but of mighty, great, and strong Limbs.

Another time, being in the Woods, he killed a *Tiger*, which had long infested that part, and borne away abundance of Sheep and Oxen, and other things, that were for the support of those to whom they belonged; abundance of People assailed this Beast, some affirming they had shot her with several Bullets quite through the Body, at several times; and some swearing they shot her through the very Heart, and they believed she was a Devil rather than a Mortal thing. *Cæsar*, had often said, he had a mind to encounter this Monster, and spoke with several Gentlemen who had attempted her, one crying, 'I shot her with so many poisoned Arrows', another with his Gun in this part of her, and another in that; so that he remarking all these Places where she was shot, fancied still he should overcome her, by giving her another sort of Wound than any had yet done; and one day said (at the Table) 'What Trophies and Garlands Ladies will you make me if I bring you home the Heart of this Ravenous Beast, that eats up all your Lambs and Pigs?' We all promised he should be rewarded at all our Hands. So taking a Bow, which he chose out of a great many, he went up into the Wood with two Gentlemen,

---

[65] *Harry Martin, the great Oliverian*   Henry Martin, a great supporter of Oliver Cromwell; there was a planta-tion owner in Surinam named Martin who may have been the brother of Henry.

where he imagined this Devourer to be. They had not passed very far into it when they heard her Voice growling and grumbling, as if she were pleased with something she was doing. When they came in view, they found her muzzling in the Belly of a new ravished Sheep, which she had torn open; and seeing herself approached, she took fast hold of her Prey with her fore Paws, and set a very fierce raging look on *Cæsar*, without offering to approach him; for fear, at the same time of loosing what she had in Possession. So that *Cæsar* remained a good while, only taking aim, and getting an opportunity to shoot her where he designed; 'twas some time before he could accomplish it, and to wound her, and not kill her, would but have enraged her more, and endangered him: He had a Quiver of Arrows at his side, so that if one failed he could be supplied; at last, retiring a little, he gave her opportunity to eat, for he found she was Ravenous, and fell to as soon as she saw him retire, being more eager of her Prey than of doing new Mischiefs. When he going softly to one side of her, and hiding his Person behind certain Herbage that grew high and thick, he took so good aim, that, as he intended, he shot her just into the Eye, and the Arrow was sent with so good a will, and so sure a hand, that it stuck in her Brain, and made her caper, and become mad for a moment or two; but being seconded by another Arrow, he[66] fell dead upon the Prey. *Cæsar* cut him open with a Knife, to see where those Wounds were that had been reported to him, and why she did not Die of them. But I shall now relate a thing that possibly will find no Credit among Men, because 'tis a Notion commonly received with us, That nothing can receive a Wound in the Heart and Live; but when the Heart of this courageous Animal was taken out, there were Seven Bullets of Lead in it, and the Wounds seamed up with great Scars, and she lived with the Bullets a great while, for it was long since they were shot: This Heart the Conqueror brought up to us, and 'twas a very great Curiosity, which all the Country came to see; and which gave *Cæsar* occasion of many fine Discourses of Accidents in War, and Strange Escapes.

At other times he would go a Fishing; and discoursing on that Diversion, he found we had in that Country a very Strange Fish, called, a *Numb Eel*[67] (an *Eel* of which I have eaten) that while it is alive, it has a quality so Cold, that those who are Angling, though with a Line of ever so great a length, with a Rod at the end of it, it shall, in the same minute the Bait is touched by this *Eel*, seize him or her that holds the Rod with benumbedness, that shall deprive them of Sense, for a while; and some have fallen into the Water, and others dropped as dead on the Banks of the Rivers where they stood, as soon as this Fish touches the Bait. *Cæsar* used to laugh at this, and believed it impossible a Man could loose his Force at the touch of a Fish; and could not understand that Philosophy,[68] that a cold Quality should be of that Nature: However, he had a great Curiosity to try whether it would have the same effect on him it had on others, and often tried, but in vain; at last, the sought for Fish came to the Bait, as he stood Angling on the Bank; and instead of throwing away the Rod, or giving it a sudden twich out of the Water, whereby he might have caught both the *Eel*, and have dismissed the Rod, before it could have too much Power over him; for Experiment sake, he grasped it but the harder, and fainting fell into the River; and still being possessed of the Rod, the Tide carried him senseless as he was a great way, till an *Indian* Boat took him up and perceived, when they touched him, a Numbness seize them, and by that knew the Rod was in his Hand, which, with a Paddle (that is a short Oar) they struck away, and snatched it into the Boat, *Eel* and all. If *Cæsar* was almost Dead, with the effect of this Fish, he was more so with that of the Water, where he had remained the space of going a League;[69] and they found they had much ado to bring him back to Life: But, at last, they did, and brought him home,

---

66   *he*   the referent is unclear to me.
67   *Numb Eel*   electric eel.

68   *Philosophy*   scientific principle.
69   *League*   a nautical measurement; three miles.

where he was in a few Hours well Recovered and Refreshed, and not a little Ashamed to find he should be overcome by an *Eel*; and all the People, who heard his Defiance, would Laugh at him. But we cheered him up; and he, being convinced, we had the *Eel* at Supper, which was a quarter of an Ell about, and most delicate Meat; and was of the more Value, since it cost so Dear, as almost the Life of so gallant a Man.

About this time we were in many mortal Fears, about some Disputes the *English* had with the *Indians*; so that we could scarce trust our selves, without great Numbers, to go to any *Indian* Towns, or Place, where they abode for fear they should fall upon us, as they did immediately after my coming away; and that it was in the possession of the *Dutch*, who used them not so civilly as the *English*; so that they cut in pieces all they could take, getting into Houses, and hanging up the Mother, and all her Children about her; and cut a Footman I left behind me, all in Joints,[70] and nailed him to Trees.

This feud began while I was there; so that I lost half the satisfaction I proposed, in not seeing and visiting the *Indian* Towns. But one Day, bemoaning of our Misfortunes upon this account, *Cæsar* told us, we need not Fear; for if we had a mind to go, he would undertake to be our Guard: Some would, but most would not venture; about Eighteen of us resolved, and took Barge; and, after Eight Days, arrived near an *Indian* Town: But approaching it, the Hearts of some of our Company failed, and they would not venture on Shore; so we Polled who would, and who would not: For my part, I said, if *Cæsar* would, I would go; he resolved, so did my Brother, and my Woman, a Maid of good Courage. Now none of us speaking the Language of the People, and imagining we should have a half Diversion in Gazing only; and not knowing what they said, we took a Fisherman that lived at the Mouth of the River, who had been a long Inhabitant there, and obliged him to go with us: But because he was known to the *Indians*, as trading among them; and being, by long Living there, become a perfect Indian in colour, we, who resolved to surprise them, by making them see something they never had seen (that is, White People), resolved only my self, my Brother and Woman should go; so *Cæsar*, the Fisherman, and the rest, hiding behind some thick Reeds and Flowers, that grew on the Banks, let us pass on towards the Town, which was on the Bank of the River all along. A little distant from the Houses, or Huts; we saw some Dancing, others busied in fetching and carrying of Water from the River: They had no sooner spied us, but they set up a loud Cry, that frighted us at first; we thought it had been for those that should Kill us, but it seems it was of Wonder and Amazement. They were all Naked, and we were Dressed, so as is most comode[71] for the hot Countries, very Glittering and Rich; so that we appeared extremely fine; my own Hair was cut short, and I had a Taffaty[72] Cap, with Black Feathers, on my Head; my Brother was in a Stuff[73] Suit, with Silver Loops and Buttons, and abundance of Green Ribbon; this was all infinitely surprising to them, and because we saw them stand still till we approached them, we took Heart and advanced, came up to them and offered them our Hands, which they took, and looked on us round about, calling still for more Company, who came swarming out, all wondering, and crying out *Tepeeme*; taking their Hair up in their Hands, and spreading it wide to those they called out too; as if they would say (as indeed it signified) *Numberless Wonders*, or not to be recounted, no more than to number the Hair of their Heads. By degrees they grew more bold, and from gazing upon us round, they touched us; laying their Hands upon all the Features of our Faces, feeling our Breasts and Arms, taking up one Petticoat, then wondering to see another; admiring our Shoes and Stockings, but more our Garters, which we gave them; and they tied about their Legs, being Laced with Silver Lace at the ends, for they much Esteem

---

[70] *Joint* "One of the limbs of an animal cut up by the butcher" (Johnson).
[71] *comode* suitable.

[72] *Taffaty* taffeta, "A thin silk" (Johnson).
[73] *Stuff* "Textures of wool thinner and slighter than cloth" (Johnson).

any shining things: In fine,[74] we suffered them to survey us as they pleased, and we thought they would never have done admiring us. When *Cæsar*, and the rest, saw we were received with such wonder, they came up to us; and finding the *Indian* Trader whom they knew (for 'tis by these Fishermen, called *Indian* Traders, we hold a Commerce with them; for they love not to go far from home, and we never go to them) when they saw him therefore they set up a new Joy; and cried, in their language, 'Oh! here's our *Tiguamy*, and we shall now know whether those things can speak': So advancing to him, some of them gave him their Hands, and cried, '*Amora Tiguamy*'; which is as much as, 'How do you, or Welcome Friend'; and all, with one din, began to gabble to him, and asked, If we had Sense, and Wit? if we could talk of affairs of Life, and War, as they could do? if we could Hunt, Swim, and do a thousand things they use? He answered them, We could. Then they invited us into their Houses, and dressed Venison and Buffalo for us; and, going out, gathered a Leaf of a Tree, called a *Sarumbo* leaf, of Six Yards long, and spread it on the Ground for a Table-Cloth; and cutting another in pieces instead of Plates, setting us on little low *Indian* Stools, which they cut out of one entire piece of Wood, and Paint, in a sort of Japan Work[75]: They serve every one their Mess on these pieces of Leaves, and it was very good, but too high seasoned with Pepper. When we had eat, my Brother and I took out our Flutes, and played to them, which gave them new Wonder; and I soon perceived, by an admiration, that is natural to these People; and by the Extreme Ignorance and Simplicity of them, it were not difficult to establish any unknown or extravagant Religion among them, and to impose any Notions or Fictions upon them. For seeing a Kinsman of mine set some Paper a Fire with a Burning-glass, a Trick they had never before seen, they were like to have Adored him for a God; and begged he would give them the Characters or Figures of his Name, that they might oppose it against Winds and Storms; which he did, and they held it up in those Seasons, and fancied it had a Charm to conquer them, and kept it like a Holy Relic. They are very Superstitious, and called him the Great *Peeie*, that is, *Prophet.* They showed us their *Indian Peeie*, a youth of about Sixteen Years old, as handsome as Nature could make a Man. They consecrate a beautiful Youth from his Infancy, and all Arts are used to complete him in the finest manner, both in Beauty and Shape: He is bred to all the little Arts and cunning they are capable of, to all the Legerdemain Tricks, and Slight of Hand, whereby he imposes upon the Rabble, and is both a Doctor in Physic[76] and Divinity. And by these Tricks [that he] makes the Sick believe he sometimes eases their Pains – by drawing from the afflicted part little Serpents, or odd Flies, or Worms, or any Strange thing – and though they have besides undoubted good Remedies, for almost all their Diseases, they cure the Patient more by Fancy than by Medicines, and make themselves Feared, Loved, and Reverenced. This young *Peeie* had a very young Wife, who seeing my Brother kiss her, came running and kissed me; after this, they kissed one another, and made it a very great Jest, it being so Novel; and new Admiration and Laughing went round the Multitude, that they never will forget that Ceremony, never before used or known. *Cæsar* had a mind to see and talk with their War *Captains*, and we were conducted to one of their Houses; where we beheld several of the great *Captains*, who had been at Council: But so frightful a Vision it was to see them no Fancy can create; no such Dreams can represent so dreadful a Spectacle. For my part, I took them for Hobgoblins, or Fiends, rather than Men; but however their Shapes appeared, their Souls were very Human and Noble; but some wanted their Noses, some their Lips, some both Noses and Lips, some their Ears, and others Cut through each Cheek, with long Slashes, through which their Teeth appeared; they had other several formidable Wounds and Scars, or rather Dismemberings; they had *Comitias*,

---

[74] *In fine*   in brief.

[75] *Japan Work*   an elaborate lacquer finish.

[76] *Physic*   medicine.

or little Aprons before them; and Girdles of Cotton, with their Knives naked, stuck in it; a Bow at their Backs, and a Quiver of Arrows on their Thighs; and most had Feathers on their Heads of diverse Colours. They cried '*Amora Tiguame*' to us, at our entrance, and were pleased we said as much to them; they seated us, and gave us Drink of the best Sort; and wondered, as much as the others had done before, to see us. *Cæsar* was marvelling as much at their Faces, wondering how they should all be so Wounded in War; he was Impatient to know how they all came by those frightful Marks of Rage or Malice, rather than Wounds got in Noble Battle: They told us by our Interpreter, That when any War was waging, two Men chosen out by some old *Captain*, whose Fighting was past, and who could only teach the Theory of War, these two Men were to stand in Competition for the Generalship, or Great War Captain; and being brought before the old Judges, now past Labour, they are asked, What they dare do to show they are worthy to lead an Army? When he, who is first asked, making no Reply, Cuts of his Nose, and throws it contemptibly on the Ground; and the other does something to himself that he thinks surpasses him, and perhaps deprives himself of Lips and an Eye; so they slash on till one gives out, and many have died in this Debate. And 'tis by a passive Valour they show and prove their Activity; a sort of Courage too Brutal to be applauded by our Black Hero; nevertheless he expressed his Esteem of them.

In this Voyage *Cæsar* begot so good an understanding between the *Indians* and the *English*, that there were no more Fears or Heart-burnings during our stay; but we had a perfect, open, and free Trade with them. Many things Remarkable, and worthy Reciting, we met with in this short Voyage; because *Cæsar* made it his Business to search out and provide for our Entertainment, especially to please his dearly Adored *Imoinda*, who was a sharer in all our Adventures; we being resolved to make her Chains as easy as we could, and to Compliment the Prince in that manner that most obliged him.

As we were coming up again, we met with some *Indians* of strange Aspects, that is, of a larger Size, and other sort of Features, than those of our Country. Our *Indian Slaves*, that Rowed us, asked them some Questions, but they could not understand us; but showed us a long Cotton String, with several Knots on it; and told us, they had been coming from the Mountains so many Moons as there were Knots; they were habited in Skins of a strange Beast, and brought along with them Bags of Gold Dust; which, as well as they could give us to understand, came streaming in little small Channels down the high Mountains, when the Rains fell;[77] and offered to be the Convoy to any Body, or Persons, that would go to the Mountains. We carried these Men up to *Parham*, where they were kept till the Lord Governor came: And because all the Country was mad to be going on this Golden Adventure, the Governor, by his Letters, commanded (for they sent some of the Gold to him) that a Guard should be set at the Mouth of the River of *Amazons* (a River so called, almost as broad as the River of *Thames*[78]) and prohibited all People from going up that River, it conducting to those Mountains of Gold. But we going off for *England* before the Project was further prosecuted, and the Governor being drowned in a Hurricane, either the Design died, or the *Dutch* have the Advantage of it: And it is to be bemoaned what his Majesty lost by loosing that part of *America*.

Though this digression is a little from my Story, however since it contains some Proofs of the Curiosity and Daring of this great Man, I was content to omit nothing of his Character.

---

[77] *Gold . . . when the Rains fell* this may not be part of the mythic description; the same phenomenon is reported in the review of *The Description and Natural His-* *tory of Peru*, in *Literary Magazine*, no. 10 (January 1757), pp. 10–11 and 13.

[78] *Thames* the comparison suggests Behn did not see the Amazon.

It was thus, for sometime we diverted him; but now *Imoinda* began to show she was with Child, and did nothing but Sigh and Weep for the Captivity of her Lord, her Self, and the Infant yet Unborn; and believed, if it were so hard to gain the Liberty of Two, 'twould be more difficult to get that for Three. Her Griefs were so many Darts in the great Heart of *Cæsar*; and taking his Opportunity one *Sunday*, when all the Whites were overtaken in Drink, as there were abundance of several Trades, and *Slaves* for Four Years, that Inhabited among the *Negro* Houses; and Sunday being their Day of Debauch (otherwise they were a sort of Spies upon *Cæsar*), went pretending, out of Goodness to them, to Feast among them, and sent all his Music, and ordered a great Treat for the whole Gang, about Three Hundred *Negros*, and about a Hundred and Fifty were able to bear Arms, such as they had, which were sufficient to do Execution with Spirits accordingly: For the *English* had none but rusty Swords that no Strength could draw from a Scabbard, except the People of particular Quality, who took care to Oil them and keep them in good Order: The Guns also, unless here and there one, or those newly carried from *England*, would do no good or harm; for 'tis the Nature of that Country to Rust and Eat upon Iron, or any Metals, but Gold and Silver. And they are very Unexpert at the Bow, which the *Negroes* and *Indians* are perfect Masters of.

Cæsar, having singled out these Men from the Women and Children, made a Harangue to them of the Miseries, and Ignominies of Slavery; counting up all their Toils and Sufferings, under such Loads, Burdens, and Drudgeries as were fitter for Beasts than Men; [for] Senseless Brutes, [rather] than Human Souls. He told them, it was not for Days, Months or Years, but for Eternity; there was no end to be of their Misfortunes: They suffered not like Men, who might find a Glory, and Fortitude in Oppression, but like Dogs that loved the Whip and Bell,[79] and fawned the more they were beaten: That they had lost the Divine Quality of Men, and were become insensible Asses, fit only to bear; nay worse: an Ass, or Dog, or Horse having done his duty, could lie down in Retreat, and rise to work again, and while he did his Duty endured no Stripes; but Men, Villianous, Senseless Men, such as they, Toiled on all the tedious Week till Black *Friday*; and then, whether they Worked or not, whether they were Faulty or Meriting, they promiscuously, the Innocent with the Guilty, suffered the infamous Whip, the sordid Stripes, from their Fellow *Slaves* till their Blood trickled from all Parts of their Body – Blood, whose every drop ought to be Revenged with a Life of some of those Tyrants, that impose it; 'And why', said he, 'my dear Friends and Fellow-sufferers, should we be Slaves to an unknown People? Have they Vanquished us Nobly in Fight? Have they Won us in Honourable Battle? And are we, by the chance of War, become their Slaves? This would not anger a Noble Heart, this would not animate a Soldier's Soul; no, but we are Bought and Sold like Apes, or Monkeys, to be the Sport of Women, Fools and Cowards; and the Support of Rogues, Renegades, that have abandoned their own Countries, for Rapine, Murders, Thefts and Villainies. Do you not hear every Day how they upbraid each other with infamy of Life, below the Wildest Savages; And shall we render Obedience to such a degenerate Race, who have no one Human Virtue left, to distinguish them from the vilest Creatures? Will you, I say, suffer the Lash from such Hands?' They all Replied, with one accord, 'No, no, no; *Cæsar* has spoke like a Great Captain, like a Great King'.

After this he would have proceeded, but was interrupted by a tall *Negro* of some more Quality than the rest, his Name was *Tuscan*; who Bowing at the Feet of *Cæsar*, cried, 'My Lord, we have listened with Joy and Attention to what you have said; and, were we only Men, would follow so great a Leader through the World: But oh! consider, we are Husbands

---

[79]   *Whip and {a} Bell*   anything that causes discomfort, according to the *OED*, from the Roman custom of   putting these items on a general's chariot to ward off evil spirits.

and Parents too, and have things more dear to us than Life – our Wives and Children unfit for Travel, in these unpassable Woods, Mountains and Bogs; we have not only difficult Lands to overcome, but Rivers to Wade, and Monsters to Encounter, Ravenous Beasts of Prey ——'

To this, *Cæsar* replied, That 'Honour was the First Principle in Nature, that was to be Obeyed; but as no Man would pretend to that, without all the Acts of Virtue, Compassion, Charity, Love, Justice and Reason; he found it not inconsistent with that, to take an equal Care of their Wives and Children, as they would of themselves; and that he did not Design, when he led them to Freedom, and Glorious Liberty, that they should leave that better part of themselves to Perish by the Hand of the Tyrant's Whip: But if there were a Woman among them so degenerate from Love and Virtue, to choose Slavery before the pursuit of her Husband, and with the hazard of her Life, to share with him in his Fortunes; that such an one ought to be Abandoned, and left as a Prey to the common Enemy'.

To which they all Agreed, – and Bowed. After this, he spoke of the Impassable Woods and Rivers; and convinced them, the more Danger, the more Glory. He told them that he had heard of one *Hannibal*, a Great Captain, had Cut his Way through Mountains of Solid Rocks;[80] and should a few Shrubs oppose them, which they could Fire before them? No, 'twas a trifling Excuse to Men resolved to die, or overcome. As for Bogs, they are with a little Labour filled and hardened; and the Rivers could be no Obstacle, since they Swam by Nature – at least by Custom – from the First Hour of their Birth: That when the Children were weary they must carry them by turns, and the Woods and their own Industry would afford them Food. To this they all assented with Joy.

Tuscan then demanded, What he would[81] do? He said, they would travel towards the Sea, Plant a New Colony, and Defend it by their Valour; and when they could find a Ship, either driven by stress of Weather, or guided by Providence that way, they would Sieze it, and make it a Prize, till it had transported them to their own Countries; at least, they should be made Free in his Kingdom, and be Esteemed as his Fellow-Sufferers, and Men that had the Courage, and the Bravery to attempt, at least, for Liberty; and if they Died in the attempt, it would be more brave than to Live in perpetual Slavery.

They bowed and kissed his Feet at this Resolution, and with one accord Vowed to follow him to Death. And that Night was appointed to begin their March. They made it known to their Wives, and directed them to tie their Hamaca[82] about their Shoulders, and under their Arms like a scarf; and to lead their Children that could go, and carry those that could not. The Wives, who pay an entire Obedience to their Husbands obeyed, and stayed for them where they were appointed: The Men stayed but to furnish themselves with what defensive Arms they could get; and All met at the Rendezvous, where *Cæsar* made a new encouraging Speech to them and led them out.

But as they could not march far that Night, on Monday early, when the Overseers went to call them all together, to go to Work, they were extremely surprised, to find not one upon the Place, but all fled with what Baggage they had. You may imagine this News was not only suddenly spread all over the *Plantation*, but soon reached the Neighbouring ones; and we had by Noon about Six hundred Men, they call the *Militia* of the Country, that came to assist us in the pursuit of the Fugitives: But never did one see so comical an Army march forth to War. The Men, of any fashion, would not concern themselves, though it were almost the common

---

80   *Hannibal . . . Cut his Way through Mountains of Solid Rocks* with fire and vinegar, according to Plutarch in his *Life of Hannibal*.

81   *would* wished or planned to.

82   *Hamaca* hammock; this is the Spanish source of the English word.

Cause; for such Revoltings are very ill Examples, and have very fatal Consequences oftentimes in many Colonies: But they had a Respect for *Cæsar*, and all hands were against the *Parhamites*, as they called those of *Parham Plantation*; because they did not in the first place love the Lord Governor; and secondly, they would have it, that *Cæsar* was ill-used, and Baffled with[83]; and 'tis not impossible but some of the best in the Country was of his Council in this Flight, and depriving us of all the *Slaves*; so that they of the better sort would not meddle in the matter. The Deputy Governor, of whom I have had no great occasion to speak, and who was the most Fawning fair-tongued Fellow in the World, and one that pretended the most friendship to *Cæsar*, was now the only violent Man against him; and though he had nothing, and so need fear nothing, yet talked and looked bigger than any Man: He was a Fellow, whose Character is not fit to be mentioned with the worst of the *Slaves*. This Fellow would lead his Army forth to meet *Cæsar*, or rather to pursue him; most of their arms were of those sort of cruel Whips they call *Cat with Nine tails*; some had rusty useless Guns for show; others old Basket-hilts, whose Blades had never seen the Light in this Age; and others had long Staffs and Clubs. Mr. *Trefry* went along, rather to be a Mediator than a Conqueror, in such a Battle; for he foresaw, and knew, if by fighting they put the *Negroes* into despair, they were a sort of sullen Fellows, that would drown, or kill themselves, before they would yield; and he advised that fair means was best. But *Byam*[84] was one that abounded in his own Wit, and would take his own Measures.

It was not hard to find these Fugitives; for as they fled they we forced to fire and cut the Woods before them, so that Night or Day they pursued them by the light they made, and by the path they had cleared. But as soon as *Cæsar* found he was pursued, he put himself in a Posture of Defence, placing all the Women and Children in the rear; and himself, with *Tuscan* by his side, or next to him, all promising to Die or Conquer. Encouraged thus, they never stood to Parley, but fell Pell-mell upon the *English*, and killed some and wounded a great many – they having recourse to their Whips, as the best of their Weapons – And as they observed no Order, they perplexed the Enemy so sorely, with Lashing them in the Eyes; and the Women and Children, seeing their Husbands so treated, being of fearful Cowardly Dispositions, and hearing the *English* cry out, 'Yield and live, Yield and be pardoned'; they all ran in amongst their Husbands and Fathers, and hung about them, crying out, 'Yield, Yield, and leave *Cæsar* to their Revenge'; that by degrees the *Slaves* abandoned *Cæsar*, and left him only *Tuscan* and his heroic *Imoinda*; who, grown as big as she was, did nevertheless press near her Lord, having a Bow and a Quiver full of poisoned Arrows, which she managed with such dexterity, that she wounded several, and shot the *Governor* into the Shoulder; of which Wound he had liked to have Died, but that an *Indian* Woman, his Mistress, sucked the Wound, and cleansed it from the Venom: But however, he stirred not from the Place till he had Parleyed with *Cæsar*, who he found was resolved to die Fighting, and would not be Taken; no more would *Tuscan* or *Imoinda*. But he, more thirsting after Revenge of another sort, than that of depriving him of Life, now made use of all his Art of talking, and dissembling; and besought *Cæsar* to yield himself upon Terms, which he himself should propose, and should be Sacredly assented to, and kept by him: He told him, it was not that he any longer feared him, or could believe the force of Two Men, and a young Heroin, could overcome all them, and with all the Slaves on their side also; but it was the vast Esteem he had for his Person; the desire he had to serve so Gallant a Man; and to hinder himself from the Reproach hereafter, of having been the occasion of the Death of a *Prince*, whose Valour and

[83]   *Baffled with* from "baffle," "to defeat with some confusion . . . to baffle is sometimes less than to conquer" (Johnson).

[84]   *Byam* William Byam, the Deputy Governor.

Magnanimity deserved the Empire of the World. He protested to him, he looked upon this Action, as Gallant and Brave; however tending to the prejudice of his Lord and Master, who would by it have lost so considerable a number of *Slaves*; that this Flight of his should be looked on as a heat of Youth, and rashness of a too forward Courage, and an unconsidered impatience of Liberty, and no more; and that he laboured in vain to accomplish that which they would effectually perform, as soon as any Ship arrived that would touch on his Coast. 'So that if you will be pleased', continued he, 'to surrender yourself, all imaginable Respect shall be paid to you; and yourself, your Wife and Child, if it be born here, shall depart free out of our Land'. But *Cæsar* would hear of no Composition[85]; though *Byam* urged, If he pursued and went on in his Design, he would inevitably Perish, either by great *Snakes*, wild Beasts or Hunger; and he ought to have regard to his Wife, whose Condition required ease, and not the fatigues of tedious Travel, where she could not be secured from being devoured. But *Cæsar* told him, there was no Faith in the White Men, or the Gods they Adored, who instructed them in Principles so false, that honest Men could not live amongst them; though no People professed so much, none performed so little; that he knew what he had to do, when he dealt with Men of Honour; but with them a Man ought to be eternally on his Guard, and never to Eat and Drink with *Christians* without his Weapon of Defence in his Hand; and, for his own Security, never to credit one Word they spoke. As for the rashness and inconsiderateness of his Action, he would confess the Governor is in the right; and that he was ashamed of what he had done, in endeavouring to make those Free, who were by Nature *Slaves*, poor wretched Rogues, fit to be used as *Christians'* Tools – Dogs, treacherous and cowardly, fit for such Masters – and they wanted only but to be whipped into the knowledge of the *Christian Gods* to be the vilest of all creeping things – to learn to Worship such Deities as had not Power to make them Just, Brave, or Honest. In fine, after a thousand things of this Nature, not fit here to be recited, he told *Byam*, he had rather Die than Live upon the same Earth with such Dogs. But *Trefry* and *Byam* pleaded and protested together so much that *Trefry* believing the *Governor* to mean what he said, and speaking very cordially himself, generously put himself into *Cæsar*'s Hands, and took him aside, and persuaded him, even with Tears, to Live, by Surrendering himself, and to name his Conditions. *Cæsar* was overcome by his Wit and Reasons, and in consideration of *Imoinda*; and demanding what he desired, and that it should be ratified by their Hands in Writing, because he had perceived that was the common way of contract between Man and Man, amongst the Whites: All this was performed, and *Tuscan*'s Pardon was put in, and they Surrender to the Governor, who walked peacefully down into the *Plantation* with them, after giving order to bury their dead. *Cæsar* was very much toiled with the bustle of the Day; for he had fought like a Fury; and what Mischief was done he and *Tuscan* performed alone; and gave their Enemies a fatal Proof that they durst do anything, and feared no mortal Force.

But they were no sooner arrived at the Place, where all the Slaves receive their Punishments of Whipping, but they laid hands on *Cæsar* and *Tuscan*, faint with heat and toil; and, surprising them, Bound them to two several Stakes, and Whipped them in a most deplorable and inhumane Manner, rending the very Flesh from their Bones, especially *Cæsar*, who was not perceived to make any Moan or to alter his Face, only to roll his Eyes on the Faithless *Governor*, and those he believed Guilty, with Fierceness and Indignation; and, to complete his Rage, he saw every one of those *Slaves*, who, but a few Days before, Adored him as something more than Mortal, now had a Whip to give him some Lashes, while he strove not to break his

---

[85] *Composition* "Compact; agreement; terms on which differences are settled" (Johnson).

Fetters; though, if he had, it were impossible: But he pronounced a Woe and Revenge from his Eyes, that darted Fire, that 'twas at once both Awful[86] and Terrible to behold.

When they thought they were sufficiently Revenged on him, they untied him, almost Fainting, with loss of Blood, from a thousand Wounds all over his Body; from which they had rent his Clothes, and led him Bleeding and Naked as he was; and loaded him all over with Irons; and then rubbed his Wounds, to complete their Cruelty, with *Indian Pepper*, which had like to have made him raving Mad; and, in this Condition, made him so fast to the Ground that he could not stir, if his Pains and Wounds would have given him leave. They spared *Imoinda*, and did not let her see this Barbarity committed towards her Lord, but carried her down to *Parham*, and shut her up; which was not in kindness to her, but for fear she should Die with the Sight, or Miscarry; and then they should lose a young *Slave*, and perhaps the Mother.

You must know, that when the News was brought on Monday Morning that *Cæsar* had betaken himself to the Woods, and carried with him all the *Negroes*, we were possessed with extreme Fear, which no persuasions could Dissipate, that he would secure himself till Night; and then, that he would come down and Cut all our Throats. This apprehension made all the Females of us fly down the River, to be secured; and while we were away, they acted this Cruelty: for I suppose I had Authority and Interest enough there, had I suspected any such thing, to have prevented it; but we had not gone many Leagues, but the news overtook us that *Cæsar* was taken, and Whipped like a common *Slave*. We met on the River with Colonel *Martin*, a Man of great Gallantry, Wit, and Goodness, and whom I have celebrated in a Character of my New *Comedy*,[87] by his own Name, in memory of so brave a Man: He was Wise and Eloquent; and, from the fineness of his Parts, bore a great Sway over the Hearts of all the *Colony*: He was a Friend to *Cæsar*, and resented this false Dealing with him very much. We carried him back to *Parham*, thinking to have made an Accommodation; when he came, the First News we heard was, that the *Governor* was Dead of a Wound that *Imoinda* had given him; but it was not so well: But it seems he would have the Pleasure of beholding the Revenge he took on *Cæsar*; and before the cruel Ceremony was finished, he dropped down; and then they perceived the Wound he had on his Shoulder, was by a venomed Arrow, which, as I said, his *Indian* Mistress healed, by Sucking the Wound.

We were no sooner Arrived, but we went up to the *Plantation* to see *Cæsar*, whom we found in a very Miserable and Unexpressable Condition; and I have a Thousand times admired how he lived in so much tormenting Pain. We said all things to him, that Trouble, Pity and Good Nature could suggest; Protesting our Innocency of the Fact, and our abhorrence of such Cruelties. Making a Thousand Professions and Services to him, and Begging as many Pardons for the Offenders, till we said so much, that he believed that we had no Hand in his ill Treatment; but told us, he could never Pardon *Byam*; as for *Trefry*, he confessed he saw his Grief and Sorrow, for his Suffering, which he could not hinder, but was like to have been beaten down by the very *Slaves*, for Speaking in his Defence. But for *Byam*, who was their Leader, their Head – and should, by his Justice, and Honour, have been an Example to them – For him, he wished to Live, to take a dire Revenge of him, and said, 'It had been well for him, if he had Sacrificed me, instead of giving me the contemptable Whip'. He refused to Talk much; but Begging us to give him our Hands; he took them, and Protested never to lift up his, to do us any Harm. He had a great Respect for Colonel *Martin*, and always took his Counsel, like that of a Parent; and assured him, he would obey him in any thing, but his

---

[86]   *Awful*   "That which strikes with awe, or fills with reverence" (Johnson).

[87]   *my New Comedy   The Younger Brother: or the Amorous Jilt* (published 1696).

Revenge on *Byam*: 'Therefore', said he, 'for his own Safety, let him speedily dispatch me; for if I could dispatch my self, I would not, till that Justice were done to my injured Person, and the contempt of a Soldier: No, I would not kill my self, even after a Whipping, but will be content to live with that Infamy, and be pointed at by every grinning Slave, till I have completed my Revenge; and then you shall see that *Oroonoko* scorns to live with the Indignity that was put on *Cæsar*'. All we could do could get no more Words from him; and we took care to have him put immediately into a healing Bath, to rid him of his Pepper, and ordered a Chirurgeon[88] to annoint him with healing Balm, which he suffered, and in some time he began to be able to Walk and Eat; we failed not to visit him every Day, and, to that end, had him brought to an apartment at *Parham*.

The *Governor* was no sooner recovered, and had heard of the menaces of *Cæsar*, but he called his Council; who (not to disgrace them, or Burlesque the Government there) consisted of such notorious Villains as *Newgate*[89] never transported[90]; and, possibly, originally were such, who understood neither the laws of *God* or *Man*; and had no sort of Principles to make them worthy the Name of Men: But at the very Council Table would Contradict and Fight with one another; and Swear so bloodily, that 'twas terrible to hear, and see them. (Some of them were afterwards Hanged, when the *Dutch* took possession of the place; others sent off in Chains:) But calling these special Rulers of the Nation together, and requiring their council in this weighty Affair, they all concluded, that (Damn them) it might be their own Cases; and that *Cæsar* ought to be made an Example to all the *Negroes*, to fright them from daring to threaten their Betters, their Lords and Masters; and, at this rate, no Man was safe from his own *Slaves*; and concluded, *nemine contradicente*[91] that *Cæsar* should be Hanged.

Trefry then thought it time to use his Authority; and told *Byam* his Command did not extend to his Lord's *Plantation*; and that *Parham* was as much exempt from the Law as *White-hall*;[92] and that they ought no more to touch the Servants of the Lord (who there represented the King's Person) than they could those about the King himself; and that *Parham* was a Sanctuary; and though his Lord were absent in Person, his Power was still in Being there; which he had entrusted with him, as far as the Dominions of his particular *Plantations* reached, and all that belonged to it; the rest of the *Country*, as *Byam* was Lieutenant to his Lord, he might exercise his Tyranny upon. *Trefry* had others as powerful, or more, that interested themselves in *Cæsar*'s Life, and absolutely said, He should be Defended. So turning the *Governor*, and his wise Council, out of Doors (for they sat at *Parham-house*) they set a Guard upon our Landing Place, and would admit none but those we called Friends to us and *Cæsar*.

The *Governor* having remained wounded at *Parham*, till his recovery was completed, *Cæsar* did not know but he was still there; and indeed for the most part, his time was spent there; for he was one that loved to Live at other People's Expense, and if he were a Day absent, he was Ten present there; and used to Play, and Walk, and Hunt, and Fish, with *Cæsar*. So that *Cæsar* did not at all doubt, if he once recovered Strength, but he should find an opportunity of being Revenged on him: Though, after such a Revenge, he could not hope to Live; for if he escaped the Fury of the *English* Mobile,[93] who perhaps would have been glad of the occasion to have killed him, he was resolved not to survive his Whiping; yet he had, some tender Hours, a repenting Softness, which he called his fits of Coward; wherein he struggled with

---

88 *Chirurgeon* surgeon.

89 *Newgate* an old prison in London.

90 *transport* "To carry into banishment: as a felon" (Johnson); at this time the place of banishment was often America.

91 *nemine contradicente* with no dissenting votes.

92 *White-hall* the king's palace in London.

93 *Mobile* "The populace; the rout; the mob" (Johnson).

Love for the Victory of his Heart, which took part with his charming *Imoinda* there; but, for the most part, his time was past in melancholy Thought, and black Designs; he considered, if he should do this Deed, and Die, either in the Attempt, or after it, he left his lovely *Imoinda* a Prey, or at best a *Slave*, to the enraged Multitude; his great Heart could not endure that Thought: 'Perhaps', said he, 'she may be first Ravished by every Brute; exposed first to their nasty Lusts, and then a shameful Death'. No, he could not Live a Moment under that Apprehension, too insuportable to be borne. These were his Thoughts, and his silent Arguments with his Heart, as he told us afterwards; so that now resolving not only to kill *Byam*, but all those he thought had enraged him; pleasing his great Heart with the fancied Slaughter he should make over the whole Face of the *Plantation*. He first resolved on a Deed, that (however Horrid it at first appeared to us all) when we had heard his Reasons, we thought it Brave and Just: Being able to Walk, and, as he believed, fit for the Execution of his great Design, he begged *Trefry* to trust him into the Air, believing a Walk would do him good; which was granted him, and taking *Imoinda* with him, as he used to do in his more happy and calmer Days, he led her up into a Wood, where, after (with a thousand Sighs, and long Gazing silently on her Face, while Tears gushed, in spite of him, from his Eyes) he told her his Design first of Killing her, and then his Enemies, and next himself, and the impossibility of Escaping, and therefore he told her the necessity of Dying; he found the Heroic Wife faster pleading for Death than he was to propose it, when she found his fixed Resolution; and, on her Knees, besought him, not to leave her a Prey to his Enemies. He (grieved to Death) yet pleased at her noble Resolution, took her up, and embracing of her, with all the Passion and Languishment of a dying Lover, drew his Knife to kill this Treasure of his Soul, this Pleasure of his Eyes; while Tears trickled down his Cheeks, hers were Smiling with Joy she should die by so noble a Hand, and be sent into her own Country (for that's their Notion of the next World) by him she so tenderly Loved, and so truly Adored in this; for Wives have a respect for their Husbands equal to what any other People pay a Deity; and when a Man finds any occasion to quit his Wife, if he love her, she dies by his Hand; if not, he sells hers, or suffers some other to kill her. It being thus, you may believe the Deed was soon resolved on; and 'tis not to be doubted, but the Parting, the eternal Leave taking of Two such Lovers, so greatly Born, so Sensible,[94] so Beautiful, so Young, and so Fond, must be very Moving, as the Relation of it was to me afterwards.

All that Love could say in such cases, being ended, and all the intermitting Irresolutions being adjusted, the Lovely, Young and Adored Victim lays her self down, before the Sacrificer, while he, with a Hand resolved, and a Heart breaking within, gave her the Fatal Stroke, first, cutting her Throat, and then severing her yet Smiling, Face from that Delicate Body, pregnant as it was with the Fruits of tenderest Love. As soon as he had done, he laid the Body decently on Leaves and Flowers, of which he made a Bed, and concealed it under the same cover-lid of Nature; only her Face he left yet bare to look on: But when he found she was Dead, and past all Retrieve, never more to bless him with her Eyes, and soft Language, his Grief swelled up to Rage; he Tore, he Raved he Roared, like some Monster of the Wood, calling on the loved Name of *Imoinda*; a thousand times he turned the Fatal Knife that did the Deed, toward his own Heart, with a Resolution to go immediately after her; but dire Revenge, which now was a thousand times more fierce in his Soul than before, prevents him; and he would cry out, 'No, since I have sacrificed *Imoinda* to my revenge, shall I lose that glory which I have purchased so dear, as at the price of the fairest, dearest, softest creature that ever nature made? No, no!' Then, at her Name, grief would get the ascendant of Rage, and he

---

[94] *Sensible* "Having quick intellectual feeling; being easily or strongly affected" (Johnson).

would lie down by her side, and water her Face with showers of Tears, which were never wont to fall from those Eyes: And however bent he was on his intended Slaughter, he had not the power to stir from the Sight of this dear Object, now more Beloved, and more Adored than ever.

He remained in this deploring Condition for two Days, and never rose from the Ground where he had made his sad Sacrifice; at last, rousing from her side, and accusing himself for living too long, now *Imoinda* was dead; and that the Deaths of those barbarous Enemies were deferred too long, he resolved now to finish the great Work; but offering to rise, he found his Strength so decayed, that he reeled to and fro, like Boughs assailed by contrary Winds; so that he was forced to lie down again, and try to summons all his Courage to his Aid; he found his Brains turn round, and his Eyes were dizzy; and Objects appeared not the same to him they were wont to do; his Breath was short; and all his Limbs surprised with a Faintness he had never felt before: He not Eaten in two Days, which was one occasion of this Feebleness, but excess of Grief was the greatest; yet still he hoped he should recover Vigour to act his Design; and lay expecting it yet six Days longer; still mourning over the dead Idol of his Heart, and striving every Day to rise, but could not.

In all this time you may believe we were in no little affliction for *Cæsar*, and his Wife; some were of Opinion he was escaped never to return; others thought some Accident had happened to him: But however, we failed not to send out a hundred People several ways to search for him; a Party, of about forty, went that way he took; among whom was *Tuscan*, who was perfectly reconciled to *Byam*; they had not gone very far into the Wood, but they smelt an unusual Smell, as of a dead Body; for thinks must be very noisome that can be distinguished among such a quantity of Natural Sweets, as every Inch of that Land produces. So that they concluded they should find him dead, or somebody that was so; they passed on towards it, as Loathsome as it was, and made such a rustling among the Leaves that lie thick on the Ground, by continual Falling, that *Cæsar* heard he was approached; and though he had, during the space of these eight Days, endeavoured to rise, but found he wanted Strength, yet looking up, and seeing his Pursuers, he rose, and reeled to a Neighbouring Tree, against which he fixed his Back; and being within a dozen Yards of those that advanced, and saw him; he called out to them, and bid them approach no nearer, if they would be safe: So that they stood still, and hardly believing their Eyes, that would persuade them that it was *Cæsar* that spoke to them, so much was he altered; they asked him, What he had done with his Wife? for they smelt a Stink that almost struck them dead? He, pointing to the dead Body, sighing, cried, 'Behold her there'; they put off the flowers that covered her with their Sticks, and found she was killed; and cried out, 'Oh, Monster! that hast murdered thy Wife'. Then asking him, Why he did so cruel a deed? He replied, he had no leisure to answer impertinent Questions: 'You may go back', continued he, 'and tell the Faithless Governor, he may thank Fortune that I am breathing my last; and that my Arm is too feeble to obey my Heart, in what it had designed him': But his Tongue faltering, and trembling, he could scarce end what he was saying. The *English* taking Advantage by his weakness, cried, 'Let us take him alive by all means': He heard them; and, as if he had revived from a Fainting, or a Dream, he cried out, 'No, Gentlemen, you are decieved; you will find no more *Cæsars* to be Whipped; no more find a Faith in me: Feeble as you think me, I have Strength yet left to secure me from a second Indignity'. They swore all anew; and he only shook his Head, and beheld them with Scorn; then they cried out, 'Who will venture on this single Man? Will no body?' They stood all silent, while *Cæsar* replied, 'Fatal will be the Attempt of the first Adventurer; let him assure himself', and, at that Word, held up his Knife in a menacing Posture. 'Look ye, ye faithless Crew', said he, ''tis not Life I seek, nor am I afraid of Dying', and, at that Word, cut a piece of Flesh from his own Throat, and threw it at them; 'yet still I would Live if I could, till I had perfected my Revenge. But oh! it cannot be; I feel Life gliding from my Eyes and Heart; and, if I make not haste, I shall yet fall a Victim to the shameful Whip'. At that, he ripped up his own Belly, and took his Bowels and pulled them out, with what Strength he could; while some, on their Knees imploring, besought him to hold his Hand. But when they saw him tottering, they cried out, 'Will none venture on him?' A bold *English* cried, 'Yes, if he were the Devil' (taking Courage when he saw him almost Dead), and swearing a horrid Oath for his farewell to the World; he rushed on *Cæsar*, [who] with his Armed Hand met him so fairly, as stuck him to the Heart, and he fell Dead at his Feet. *Tuscan* seeing that, cried out, 'I love thee, O Cæsar; and therefore will not let thee Die, if possible': And running to him, took him in his Arms; but, at the same time, warding a Blow that *Cæsar* made at his Bosom, he received it quite through his Arm; and *Cæsar* having not Strength to pluck the Knife forth, though he attempted it, *Tuscan* neither pulled it out himself, nor suffered it to be pulled out; but came down with it sticking in his Arm; and the reason he gave for it was, because the Air should not get into the Wound: They put their Hands across, and carried *Cæsar* between Six of them, fainting as he was; and they thought Dead, or just Dying; and they brought him to *Parham*, and laid him on a Couch, and had the Chirurgeon immediately to him, who dressed his Wounds, and sowed up his Belly, and used means to bring him to Life, which they effected. We ran all to see him; and, if before we thought him so beautiful a Sight, he was now so altered, that his Face was like a Death's Head[95] blacked over; nothing but Teeth, and Eyeholes: For some Days we suffered nobody to speak to him, but caused Cordials to be poured down his Throat, which sustained his Life; and in six or seven Days he recovered his Senses: For, you must know, that Wounds are almost to a Miracle cured in the *Indies*; unless Wounds in the Legs, which rarely ever cure.

When he was well enough to speak, we talked to him; and asked him some Questions about his Wife, and the Reasons why he killed her; and he then told us what I have related of that Resolution, and of his Parting; and he besought us we would let him Die, and was extremely Afflicted to think it was possible he might Live; he assured us, if we did not Dispatch him, he would prove very Fatal to a great many. We said all we could to make him Live, and gave him new Assurances; but he begged we would not think so poorly of him, or his love to *Imoinda*, to imagine we could Flatter him to Life again; but the Chirurgeon assured him, he could not Live, and therefore he need not Fear. We were all (but *Cæsar*) afflicted at this News, and the Sight was gashly[96]; his Discourse was sad; and the earthly Smell about him so strong, that I was persuaded to leave the Place for some time (being my self but Sickly, and very apt to fall into Fits of dangerous Illness upon any extraordinary Melancholy); the Servants, and *Trefry*, and the Chirurgeons, promised all to take what possible care they could of the Life of *Cæsar*; and I, taking Boat, went with other Company to Colonel *Martin*'s, about three Days' Journey down the River; but I was no sooner gone, but the *Governor* taking *Trefry*, about some pretended earnest Business, a Day's Journey up the River; having communicated his Design to one *Banister*,[97] a wild *Irish* Man, and one of the Council – a Fellow of absolute Barbarity, and fit to execute any Villainy, but was Rich. He came up to *Parham*, and forcibly took *Cæsar*, and had him carried to the same Post where he was Whipped; and causing him to be tied to it, and a great Fire made before him, he told him he should Die like a Dog, as he was. *Cæsar* replied, this was the first piece of Bravery that ever *Banister* did; and he never spoke Sense till he pronounced that Word; and, if he would keep it, he would declare, in the other World, that he was the only Man, of all the Whites, that ever he heard speak Truth.

---

[95] *a Death's Head* a skull, sometimes kept by scholars as a reminder of death.

[96] *gashly* ghastly.

[97] *Banister* Major James Bannister.

And turning to the Men that bound him, he said, 'My friends, am I to Die, or to be Whipped?' And they cried, 'Whipped! no; you shall not escape so well'. And then he replied, smiling, 'A blessing on thee'; and assured them, they need not tie him, for he would stand fixed, like a Rock, and endure Death so as should encourage[98] them to Die. 'But if you Whip me', said he, 'be sure you tie me fast'.

He had learned to take Tobacco; and when he was assured he should Die, he desired they would give him a Pipe in his Mouth, ready Lighted, which they did; and the Executioner came, and first cut off his Members, and threw them in the Fire; after that, with an ill-favoured Knife, they cut his Ears, and his Nose, and burned them; he still Smoked on, as if nothing had touched him; then they hacked off one of his Arms, and still he bore up, and held his Pipe; but at the cutting off the other Arm, his Head sunk, and his Pipe dropped; and he gave up the Ghost, without a Groan, or a Reproach. My Mother and Sister were by him all the while, but not suffered to save him; so rude and wild were the Rabble, and so inhuman were the Justices, who stood by to see the Execution, who after paid dearly enough for their Insolence. They cut *Cæsar* in Quarters, and sent them to several of the chief *Plantations*: One Quarter was sent to Colonel *Martin*, who refused it; and swore, he had rather see the Quarters of *Banister*, and the *Governor* himself, than those of *Cæsar*, on his *Plantations*; and that he could govern his *Negroes* without Terrifying and Grieving them with frightful Spectacles of a mangled King.

Thus Died this Great Man, worthy of a better Fate, and a more sublime Wit than mine to write his Praise; yet, I hope, the Reputation of my Pen is considerable enough to make his Glorious Name to survive to all Ages; with that of the Brave, the Beautiful and the Constant *Imoinda*.

John Wilmot, Second Earl of Rochester (1647–1680)

Rochester entered Wadham College, Oxford at age thirteen and was given his MA in the following year. Graduating at such an early age was more common in the seventeenth century than in the twentieth, but in Rochester's case it was a sign of his considerable literary talent and his high degree of personal appeal. From College he went to the court of King Charles where he became a favorite and one of the rowdiest rakes in a society infamous for profligacy. He drank, whored, vandalized, and publicly appeared both naked and in full disguise. He abducted an heiress named Elizabeth Malet, for which he spent some time imprisoned in the Tower of London, but later he married her. Very late in his short life, Rochester repented and became serious about religion. He called in Thomas Burnet, and according to the Bishop's spiritual biography, Rochester presented his Maker with a penitent soul.

Rochester's bawdy poetry is still considered scandalous by some, but many readers admire his most outrageous works because of their insistence on the glories of what the world calls immoral behavior. The more philosophical poems also turn conventional beliefs upside down, but they do so in the service of more conventional satirical aims. The paradoxical or apparently false positions that Rochester delights in arguing inevitably reveal arbitrary and irrational aspects of our own

---

[98] *encourage* "To raise confidence; to make confident".

unexamined suppositions about the world. By so doing, Rochester's poetry achieves a certain philosophical astuteness even in its impudence.

The most accessible version of Rochester's poetry is edited by David Vieth (Yale University Press, 1968). However, the editorial decisions of Keith Walker in Rochester's Poems *(Blackwell, 1984) presents texts that are closer to the typographic style of the day. Rochester authorized the publication of very few of his works, and in many instances it is difficult to select a copytext. Both Vieth and Walker did extensive research on manuscript versions of the poems in order to correct (or sometimes replace) the uneven versions printed in Rochester's lifetime. I have used* Poems on Several Occasions *(1680?) as a copytext for "The Imperfect Enjoyment," "A Satire against Reason and Mankind," and "The Disabled Debauchee"; but for the other poems, in which manuscripts supply the best versions, I have preferred simply to adopt Walker's edition as the basis for my text. In editing every poem I have profited from both Walker's and Vieth's collations and notes.*

from *Poems on Several Occasions* (1680?)

THE IMPERFECT ENJOYMENT

Naked she lay, clasped in my longing Arms,
I filled with Love, and she all over Charms;
Both equally inspired with eager fire,
Melting through kindness, flaming in desire.
With *Arms, Legs, Lips* close clinging to embrace,   5
She clips me to her *Breast*, and sucks me to her *Face*.[1]
Her nimble *Tongue* (*Love*'s lesser Lightning) played
Within my *Mouth*, and to my thoughts conveyed
Swift Orders that I should prepare to throw
The *All-dissolving Thunderbolt* below.   10
My flutt'ring *Soul*, sprung with the pointed Kiss,
Hangs hov'ring o'er her *Balmy Lips* of Bliss.
But whilst her busy hand would guide that part,
Which should convey my *Soul* up to her *Heart*,
In Liquid *Raptures* I dissolve all o'er,   15
Melt into Sperm, and spend at every Pore.
A touch from any part of her had done 't:
Her Hand, her Foot, her very Look's a *Cunt*.
　　　Smiling, she Chides in a kind murm'ring *Noise*,
And from her Body wipes the Clammy Joys,   20
When, with a Thousand Kisses wand'ring o'er
My panting Bosom, 'Is there then no more?'
She cries. 'All this to Love and Rapture's due;
Must we not pay a Debt to Pleasure too?'
　　　But I, the most forlorn, lost Man alive,   25
To show my wished Obedience vainly strive:
I Sigh, alas! and Kiss, but cannot *Swive*.[2]

THE IMPERFECT ENJOYMENT   [2] *Swive* copulate.
[1] *clips* hugs.

Eager desires confound my first intent,
Succeeding shame does more success prevent,
And Rage at last confirms me Impotent.   30
Ev'n her fair Hand, which might bid heat return
To frozen Age, and make cold *Hermits* burn,
Applied to my dead *Cinder*, warms no more
Than Fire to Ashes could past Flames restore.
Trembling, confused, despairing, limber, dry,   35
A wishing, weak, unmoving Lump I lie.
This *Dart* of Love, whose piercing point, oft tried,
With *Virgin blood Ten Thousand Maids* has dyed;
Which *Nature* still directed with such *Art*
That it through every *Cunt* reached every *Heart* –   40
Stiffly resolved, 'twould carelessly invade
Woman or *Boy*, nor aught its fury stayed:
Where e'er it pierced, a *Cunt* it found or made –
Now languid lies in this unhappy hour,
Shrunk up and Sapless like a withered Flower.   45
    Thou treacherous, base deserter of my flame,
False to my Passion, fatal to my Fame,
Through what mistaken *Magic* dost thou prove
So true to Lewdness, so untrue to Love?
What *Oyster-Cinder-Beggar*-Common *Whore*[3]   50
Didst thou e'er fail in all thy Life before?
When *Vice, Disease*, and *Scandal* lead the way,
With what officious haste dost thou obey!
Like a Rude, roaring *Hector* in the Streets[4]
Who Scuffles, Cuffs, and Justles all he meets,   55
But if his King or Country claim his Aid,
The *Rascal Villain* shrinks and hides his Head;
Ev'n so thy Brutal Valour is displayed,
Breaks every *Stew*, does each small *Whore invade*,[5]
But if great *Love* the onset does command,   60
Base Recreant to thy *Prince*, thou dar'st not stand.
Worst part of me, and henceforth hated most,
Through all the *Town* a common *Fucking Post*,
On whom each *Whore* relieves her tingling *Cunt*
As *Hogs* on gates do rub themselves and grunt,   65
Mayst thou to rav'nous *Cankers* be a *Prey*,
Or in consuming *Weepings* waste away;
May *Stranguries and Stone* thy *Days* attend;[6]
May'st thou ne'er Piss, who didst refuse to spend

---

[3] *Oyster-* oysterwench, "A woman whose business is to sell oysters. Proverbially. A low woman" (Johnson; see Shakespeare, *Richard* II, 1.4.31).
[4] *Hector* "A bully; a blustering, turbulent, pervicacious, noisy fellow" (Johnson).

[5] *stew* brothel.
[6] *Strangury* "A difficulty of urine attended with pain" (Johnson); *Stone* a concretion in the kidneys or bladder that blocks urination.

When all my Joys did on False thee depend.   70
And may *Ten Thousand* abler *Pricks* agree
To do the wronged *Corinna* right for thee.

A SATYR AGAINST REASON AND MANKIND

Were I (who to my cost already am
One of those strange, prodigious Creatures, Man)
A Spirit free to choose, for my own share,
What Case of Flesh and Blood I pleased to wear,
I'd be a Dog, a Monkey, or a Bear,   5
Or anything but that vain Animal
Who is so Proud of being Rational.
    The Senses are too gross, and he'll contrive
A Sixth, to contradict the other Five,
And before certain Instinct, will prefer   10
Reason, which fifty times for one does err;
Reason, an *Ignis fatuus* in the Mind,[1]
Which, leaving Light of Nature, Sense, behind,
Pathless and dang'rous wand'ring ways it takes
Through Error's Fenny Bogs and Thorny Brakes;   15
Whilst the misguided Follower climbs with pain
Mountains of Whimsies, heaped in his own Brain;
Stumbling from Thought to Thought, falls headlong down
Into Doubt's boundless Sea, where, like to drown,
Books bear him up awhile, and make him try   20
To swim with Bladders of Philosophy;[2]
In hopes still to o'ertake th' escaping Light,
The Vapour dances in his dazzling sight
Till, spent, it leaves him to eternal Night.
Then Old Age and Experience, hand in hand,   25
Lead him to Death, and make him understand,
After a Search so painful and so long,
That all his Life he has been in the wrong.
Huddled in Dirt the Reasoning Engine lies,
Who was so Proud, so Witty, and so Wise.   30
    Pride drew him in, as Cheats their Bubbles catch,[3]
And made him venture to be made a Wretch.
His Wisdom did his Happiness destroy,
Aiming to know that World he should enjoy.
And Wit his vain, frivolous Pretence   35
Of pleasing others at his own Expense,
For Wits are treated just like Common Whores:
First they're enjoyed, and then kicked out of Doors.
The Pleasure past, a threat'ning Doubt remains
That frights th' Enjoyer with succeeding Pains.   40

A SATYR AGAINST REASON AND MANKIND
[1] *Ignis fatuus* false fire, will-o'-the-wisp, luminous marsh gases, which travelers mistakenly take for beacons.

[2] *Bladders* "It is usual for those that learn to swim, to support themselves with blown bladders" (Johnson).
[3] *Bubbles* dupes.

Women and Men of Wit are dangerous Tools,
And ever fatal to admiring Fools:
Pleasure allures, and when the *Fops* escape,
'Tis not that they're belov'd, but fortunate,
And therefore what they fear, at last they hate.   45
    But now, methinks, some formal Band and Beard[4]
Takes me to task. Come on, Sir; I'm prepared.
    'Then, by your favour, anything that's writ
Against this gibing, jingling knack called *Wit*
Likes me abundantly, but you take care[5]   50
Upon this point, not to be too severe.
Perhaps my *Muse* were fitter for this part,
For I profess, I can be very smart
On *Wit*, which I abhor with all my Heart.
I long to lash it in some sharp Essay,   55
But your grand indiscretion bids me stay
And turns my Tide of Ink another way.
What rage ferments in your degen'rate Mind
To make you Rail at Reason and Mankind?
Blest, glorious *Man*! to whom alone kind *Heav'n*   60
An everlasting *Soul* has freely giv'n,
Whom his great *Maker* took such care to make
That from himself he did the *Image* take
And this fair frame in shining *Reason* dressed
To dignify his Nature above *Beast*;   65
Reason, by whose aspiring influence
We take a flight beyond material sense,
Dive into Mysteries, then soaring pierce
The flaming limits of the Universe,
Search Heav'n and Hell, find out what's Acted there,   70
And give the World true grounds of hope and fear'.
    'Hold, mighty man', I cry, 'all this we know
From the Pathetic Pen of *Ingelo*,[6]
From *Patrick's Pilgrim*, *Sibbes'* soliloquies,[7]
And 'tis this very Reason I despise: 75
This Supernatural Gift, that makes a *Mite*
Think he's the *Image* of the *Infinite*,
Comparing his short Life, void of all Rest,
To the *Eternal* and the ever Blest;
This busy, puzzling stirrer-up of doubt   80
That frames deep *Mysteries*, then finds 'em out,
Filling with frantic Crowds of thinking *Fools*
Those reverend *Bedlams, Colleges* and *Schools*;[8]
Borne on whose wings, each heavy *Sot* can pierce

[4] *Band and Beard* the neckcloth and tonsorial style of a clergyman or professor.
[5] *Likes me* pleases me.
[6] *Pathetic* productive of painful feelings; *Ingelo* Nathaniel Ingelo (?1621–83), a religious writer.
[7] *Patrick's Pilgrim* The Parable of the Pilgrim (1664) by Simon Patrick; *Sibbes' soliloquies* any of a number of works by Richard Sibbes (1577–1635), a Puritan divine.
[8] *Bedlam* an asylum for the insane in London.

The limits of the boundless Universe;   85
So Charming Ointments make an Old *Witch* fly[9]
And bear a Crippled Carcass through the Sky.
'Tis this exalted Pow'r, whose business lies
In *Nonsense* and *Impossibilities*,
This made a whimsical *Philosopher*[10]   90
Before the spacious *World*, his *Tub* prefer,
And we have modern *Cloistered Coxcombs* who
Retire to think, 'cause they have nought to do.
    But thoughts are given for Action's Government;
Where Action ceases, Thought's impertinent.   95
Our *Sphere* of Action is Life's happiness,
And he who thinks beyond, thinks like an *Ass*.
Thus, whilst against false reas'ning I inveigh,
I own right *Reason*, which I would obey:
That *Reason* which distinguishes by Sense,   100
And gives us *Rules* of good and ill from thence;
That bounds Desires with a reforming Will,
To keep 'em more in vigour, not to Kill.
Your *Reason* hinders, mine helps to enjoy,
Renewing Appetites yours would destroy;   105
My Reason is my Friend, yours is a Cheat;
Hunger calls out, my Reason bids me eat;
Perversely, yours your Appetite does mock:
This asks for Food, that answers, 'What's o'Clock?'
This plain Distinction, Sir, your doubt Secures: 110
'Tis not true Reason I despise, but yours.
    'Thus I think reason righted; but for Man,
I'll ne'er Recant, defend him if you can.
For all his Pride and his Philosophy,
'Tis evident, Beasts are, in their Degree,   115
As wise at least, and better far than he.
Those Creatures are the wisest who attain,
By surest Means, the Ends at which they aim:
If therefore *Jowler* finds and kills his hares[11]
Better than Meres supplies committee chairs,[12]   120
Though one's a Statesman, th' other but a Hound,
Jowler, in Justice, would be wiser found.
    'You see how far Man's Wisdom here extends;
Look next if Human Nature makes amends:
Whose Principles most gen'rous are, and just,   125
And to whose Morals you would sooner trust.
Be Judge yourself, I'll bring it to the Test:
Which is the basest Creature, Man or Beast?

---

9   *Charming Ointments*   magic oils, which were believed to be used by witches to let them fly.
10   *whimsical Philosopher*   Diogenes the Cynic.

11   *Jowler*   the name of a dog.
12   *Meres*   Sir Thomas Meres (1634–1715), Whig MP and Commissioner of the Admiralty.

Birds feed on Birds, Beasts on each other prey,
But Savage Man alone does Man betray. 130
Pressed by Necessity, they Kill for Food;
Man undoes Man to do himself no good.
With Teeth and Claws by Nature Armed, they hunt
Nature's Allowance, to supply their Want.
But Man, with Smiles, Embraces, Friendship's praise, 135
Unhumanly his Fellow's Life betrays;
With voluntary Pains works his distress,
Not through Necessity, but Wantonness.
'For Hunger or for Love they fight or tear,
Whilst wretched Man is still in Arms for fear. 140
For fear he arms, and is of Arms afraid,
By Fear to Fear successively betrayed;
Base Fear, the Source whence his best Passions came,
His boasted Honour, and his dear-bought Fame;
That Lust of Pow'r, to which he's such a Slave, 145
And for the which alone he dares be brave;
To which his various Projects are designed;
Which makes him gen'rous, affable, and kind;
For which he takes such pains to be thought wise,
And screws his Actions in a forced Disguise,[13] 150
Leading a tedious Life in Misery
Under laborious, mean Hypocrisy.
Look to the bottom of his vast Design,
Wherein Man's Wisdom, Pow'r, and Glory join:
The Good he acts, the Ill he does endure, 155
'Tis all from fear, to make himself Secure.
Merely for Safety, after Fame we Thirst,
For all Men would be Cowards, if they durst.
'And honesty's against all common Sense:
Men must be Knaves, 'tis in their own defence. 160
Mankind's dishonest; if you think it fair
Amongst known Cheats to play upon the Square,[14]
You'll be undone ———
Nor can weak Truth your Reputation save:
The Knaves will all agree to call you Knave. 165
Wronged shall he live, insulted o'er, oppressed,[15]
Who dares be less a Villain than the rest.
'Thus, Sir, you see what Human Nature craves:
Most Men are Cowards, all Men should be Knaves.
The difference lies (as far as I can see) 170
Not in the thing it self, but the degree;
And all the Subject matter of debate
Is only who's a Knave of the first Rate?

[13] *screw* "To force; to bring by violence" (Johnson).
[14] *to play upon the Square* to deal fairly.
[15] *insult* "To trample upon; to triumph over" (Johnson).

'All this with indignation have I hurtled
At the pretending part of the proud World,   175
Who, swollen with selfish Vanity, devise
False Freedoms, holy Cheats, and formal Lies
Over their Fellow-Slaves to Tyrannize.
    'But if in Court so just a Man there be
(In Court a just Man, yet unknown to me)   180
Who does his needful flattery direct,
Not to oppress and ruin, but protect
(Since flattery, which way soever laid,[16]
Is still a Tax on that unhappy Trade);
If so upright a States-Man you can find,   185
Whose Passions bend to his unbiased Mind,
Who does his Arts and Policies apply
To raise his Country, not his Family,
Nor, while his Pride owned Avarice withstands,[17]
Receives close Bribes through friends' corrupted hands —[18]   190
    'Is there a Church-Man who on God relies?
Whose Life, his Faith and Doctrine justifies?
Not one blown up with vain Prelatic Pride,
Who, for reproof of Sins, does Man deride;
Whose envious Heart makes preaching a pretence;   195
With his obstreperous, saucy Eloquence,
Dares chide at Kings, and rail at Men of Sense;
Who from his Pulpit vents more peevish Lies,
More bitter Railings, Scandals, Calumnies,
Than at a Gossipping are thrown about,   200
When the good *Wives* get drunk, and then fall out;
None of that sensual *Tribe* whose *Talents* lie
In Avarice, Pride, Sloth, and Gluttony;
Who hunt good Livings, but abhor good Lives;
Whose Lust exalted to that height arrives,   205
They act Adultery with their own *Wives*,
And ere a score of Years completed be,
Can from the lofty Pulpit proudly see
Half a large Parish their own Progeny;
    'Nor doting Bishop who would be adored   210
For domineering at the Council-Board,[19]
A greater *Fop* in business at Fourscore,
Fonder of serious Toys, affected more,
Than the gay, glittering Fool at Twenty proves
With all his noise, his tawdry Clothes, and Loves;   215
    'But a meek, humble *Man* of modest Sense,
Who, Preaching Peace, does practice Continence;
Whose pious life's a proof he does believe

---

[16] *which way soever laid* however you look at it.
[17] *owned* admitted.

[18] *close* hidden (the copytext has the metrically awkward "Aureal", golden).
[19] *Council-Board* council table.

Mysterious Truths, which no Man can conceive.
If upon Earth there dwell such God-like Men,   220
Then I'll Recant my Paradox to them,[20]
Adore those *Shrines* of *Virtue*, Homage pay,
And, with the Rabble-world, their *Laws* obey.
    'If such there be, yet grant me *This* at least:
Man differs more from Man, than Man from Beast'.   225

THE DISABLED DEBAUCHEE

As some brave Admiral, in former War
    Deprived of Force, but pressed with Courage still,
Two Rival-Fleets appearing from afar,
    Crawls to the top of an adjacent Hill,

From whence (with thoughts full of concern) he views   5
    The wise and daring Conduct of the Fight,
Whilst each bold Action to his Mind renews
    His present Glory and his past Delight;

From his fierce Eyes Flashes of Fire he throws,
    As from black Clouds when Lightning breaks away;   10
Transported, thinks himself amidst the Foes,
    And absent, yet enjoys the Bloody Day;

So, when my Days of Impotence approach,
    And I'm by Pox and Wine's unlucky Chance[1]
Driv'n from the pleasing Billows of Debauch   15
    On the dull Shore of Lazy Temperance,

My pains at least some Respite shall afford
    Whilst I behold the Battles you maintain
When Fleets of Glasses sail about the Board,
    From whose Broadsides Volleys of Wit shall rain.   20

Nor let the sight of Honourable Scars,
    Which my too forward Valour did procure,
Frighten new-listed Soldiers from the Wars:[2]
    Past joys have more than paid what I endure.

Should any Youth (worth being drunk) prove Nice,[3]   25
    And from his fair inviter meanly shrink,
'Twill please the Ghost of my departed Vice
    If, at my counsel, he repent and drink.

Or should some cold-complexioned Sot forbid,
    With his dull morals, our Night's brisk alarms,   30
I'll fire his Blood by telling what I did
    When I was strong, and able to bear Arms.

---

[20] *Paradox* a statement that is apparently false but arguably true; Rochester's paradox is that, despite the apparent and accepted superiority of human beings, it is actually better to be a beast.

THE DISABLED DEBAUCHEE
[1] *Pox* venereal disease.
[2] *new-listed* newly enlisted.
[3] *Nice* peevish, delicate, shy.

I'll tell of Whores attacked, their Lords at home;
    Bawds' quarters beaten up, and Fortress won;
Windows demolished, Watches overcome;[4]   35
    And handsome ills, by my contrivance done.

Nor shall our Love-fits, *Chloris*, be forgot,
    When each the well-looked Link-boy strove t' enjoy,[5]
And the best Kiss was the deciding Lot
    Whether the Boy fucked you, or I the Boy.   40

With Tales like these, I will such Heat inspire,
    As to important Mischief shall incline;
I'll make him long some Ancient Church to fire,
    And fear no Lewdness he's called to by Wine.

Thus, States-manlike, I'll saucily impose,   45
    And safe from Danger, valiantly advise;
Sheltered in impotence, urge you to Blows,
    And being good for nothing else, be wise.

Lampoon [On the Women about Town][1]

Too long the Wise Commons have been in debate
About Money, and Conscience (those Trifles of State)[2]
Whilst dangerous Grievances daily increase,
And the Subject can't riot in Safety and peace;
Unless (as against Irish Cattle before)[3]   5
You now make an Act to forbid Irish whore.
The Coots (black, and white) Clenbrazell, and Fox,[4]
Invade us with Impudence, beauty, and pox.[5]
They carry a Fate which no man can oppose:
The loss of his heart, and the fall of his Nose.[6] 10
Should he dully resist, yet would each take upon her,
To beseech him to do it, and engage him in honour.
O! Ye merciful powers, who of Mortals take Care,
Make the Women more modest, more sound, or less fair.
Is it just that with death cruel Love should conspire,   15

---

[4] *Watches* night watchmen, guards.
[5] *well-looked* handsome; *Link-boy* candle bearer for hire in the dark streets of seventeenth-century cities.
LAMPOON [ON THE WOMEN ABOUT TOWN]
[1] The text of this poem is based on manuscripts and taken from Keith Walker's edition of Rochester's poems; in other versions it is entitled "On the Women about Town."
[2] *Money and Conscience* Parliament was then (1673) discussing the Money Bill to support the war against the Dutch and the Test Act, which required government appointees to take communion in the Church of England.

[3] *Irish cattle* the importation of Irish livestock was forbidden by an act of Parliament.
[4] *Coots (black, and white)* simpletons but also blonde and brunette women related to Charles Coote, second Earl of Mountrath and a Lord Justice of Ireland; *Clenbrazell and Fox* women in the running for the honor of being mistress to Charles II; at least one of them was Irish.
[5] *pox* venereal disease.
[6] *fall of his Nose* in the advanced stages of syphilis, the mucous membrane decays, and in the centuries before antibiotics brass noses were sometimes fitted over the mutilated flesh.

And our Tarses be burnt by our hearts taking fire?[7]
There's an end of Communion if humble Believers
Must be damned in the Cup like unworthy Receivers.[8]

Signior Dildo

You Ladies all of Merry England
Who have been to kiss the Duchess's hand,[1]
Pray did you lately observe in the Show
A Nobel Italian called Signior Dildo?

The Signior was one of her Highness's Train   5
And helped to Conduct her over the Main,
But now she Cries out to the Duke, 'I will go,
I have no more need for Signior Dildo'.

At the Sign of the Cross in Saint James's Street,[2]
When next you go thither to make your Selves Sweet,   10
By Buying of Powder, Gloves, Essence, or So
You may Chance get a Sight of Signior Dildo.

You'll take him at first for no Person of Note
Because he appears in a plain Leather Coat:
But when you his virtuous Abilities know   15
You'll fall down and Worship Signior Dildo.

My Lady Southesk, Heav'ns prosper her for 't[3]
First Clothed him in Satin, then brought him to Court;
But his Head in the Circle, he Scarcely durst Show,[4]
So modest a Youth was Signior Dildo.   20

The good Lady Suffolk thinking no harm
Had got this poor Stranger hid under her Arm:
Lady Betty by Chance came the Secret to know,
And from her own Mother, Stole Signior Dildo:

The Countess of Falmouth, of whom People tell   25
Her Footmen wear Shirts of a Guinea an Ell:[5]
Might Save the Expense, if she did but know
How Lusty a Swinger is Signior Dildo.[6]

By the Help of this Gallant the Countess of Rafe[7]
Against the fierce Harris preserved her Self Safe: 30

[7] *Tarses* penises.
[8] *unworthy Receivers* those who take holy communion
in a state of sin damn themselves, according to St. Paul
(1 Corinthians 11.27–9).
SIGNIOR DILDO
[1] *Duchess* Mary of Modena, second wife of James II
(then Duke of York), arrived in London in 1673; she
brought many of her countrymen (Italians) with her in
her entourage.
[2] *Sign of the Cross* unidentified "toyshop," a place for
buying cosmetics and other trinkets.

[3] *Lady Southesk* one of the Duke of York's mistresses.
[4] *Circle* "An assembly surrounding the principal person" (Johnson).
[5] *Guinea* twenty-one shillings; *Ell* forty-five
inches, a measure of cloth.
[6] *Swinger* a "rogue" but also a "vigorous performer"
(*OED*).
[7] *Countess of Rafe* wife of Ralph (pronounced Rafe)
Montagu, later Duke of Montagu.

She Stifled him almost beneath her Pillow,
So Closely she embraced Signior Dildo.

Our dainty fine Duchesses have got a Trick
To Dote on a Fool, for the Sake of his Prick,
The Fops were undone, did their Graces but know   35
The Discretion and vigour of Signior Dildo.

That Pattern of Virtue, her Grace of Cleveland,
Has Swallowed more Pricks, than the Ocean has Sand,
But by Rubbing and Scrubbing, so large it does grow,
It is fit for just nothing but Signior Dildo.   40

The Duchess of Modena, though she looks high,
With such a Gallant is contented to Lie:
And for fear the English her Secrets should know,
For a Gentleman Usher took Signior Dildo.[8]

The countess of the Cockpit (who knows not her Name?)[9]   45
She's famous in Story for a Killing Dame:
When all her old Lovers forsake her I Trow[10]
She'll then be contented with Signior Dildo.

Red Howard, Red Sheldon, and Temple so tall[11]
Complain of his absence so long from Whitehall: 50
Signior Barnard has promised a Journey to go,[12]
And bring back his Countryman Signior Dildo.

Doll Howard no longer with his Highness must Range,[13]
And therefore is proffered this Civil Exchange:
Her Teeth being rotten, she Smells best below,   55
And needs must be fitted for Signior Dildo[14]

St Albans with Wrinkles and Smiles in his Face
Whose kindness to Strangers, becomes his high Place,
In his Coach and Six Horses is gone to Pergo[15]
To take the fresh Air with Signior Dildo.   60

Were this Signior but known to the Citizen Fops
He'd keep their fine Wives from the Foremen of Shops,
But the Rascals deserve their Horns should still grow,
For Burning the Pope, and his Nephew Dildo.[16]

---

8 *Usher* "One whose business is to introduce strangers, or walk before a person of high rank" (Johnson).
9 *Cockpit* a playhouse in London.
10 *Trow* believe.
11 *Howard, Sheldon, Temple* maids of honor to the
queen.
12 *Signior Barnard* probably Bernardi, a dealer in
erotic toys.
13 *Doll Howard* maid of honor to the Duchess of
York, sister of "Red" (Anne), l. 49

14 *fitted* some manuscripts read "fittest" or "fitter."
15 *Pergo* an unidentified place; perhaps Borgo, Italy.
16 *Burning the Pope* in effigy on Guy Fawkes Day,
which celebrates the discovery of the Gunpowder Plot, a
Roman Catholic scheme to burn down Parliament and
destabilize Protestant England; *his Nephew Dildo* in
1671 Rochester was informed by a correspondent that a
box of dildos had been seized and burned by the Customs
Office.

Tom Killigrew's wife, North Holland's fine Flower,[17]   65
At the Sight of this Signior, did fart, and Belch Sour,
And her Dutch Breeding further to Show,
Says 'welcome to England, myn Heer Van Dildo'.

He civilly came to the Cockpit one night,
And proffered his Service to fair Madam Knight,[18]   70
Quoth she, 'I intrigue with Captain Cazzo.[19]
Your Nose in myne Arse good Signior Dildo'.

This Signior is sound, safe, ready, and Dumb,
As ever was Candle, Carrot, or Thumb:
Then away with these nasty devices, and Show   75
How you rate the just merits of Signior Dildo.

Count Cazzo who carries his Nose very high,
In Passion he Swore, his Rival should Die,
Then Shut up himself, to let the world know,
Flesh and Blood could not bear it from Signior Dildo.   80

A Rabble of Pricks, who were welcome before,
Now finding the Porter denied 'em the Door,
Maliciously waited his coming below,
And inhumanely fee on Signior Dildo.

Nigh wearied out, the poor Stranger did fly   85
And along the Pall Mall, they followed full Cry[20]
The Women concerned from every Window,
Cried, 'Oh! for Heav'n's sake save Signior Dildo'.

The good Lady Sandys, burst into a Laughter
To see how the Ballocks came wobbling after,   90
And had not their weight retarded the Foe
Indeed 't had gone hard with Signior Dildo.

A Satyr on Charles II[1]

I' th' Isle of Britain, long since famous grown
For breeding the best cunts in Christendom,
There reigns, and oh long may he reign and thrive
The easiest King and best bred man alive.
Him no Ambition moves, to get Renown   5
Like the french Fool, hazarding his Crown.[2]
Peace is his Aim, his Gentleness is such

[17] *Tom Killigrew* courtier and playwright, father of Anne (see the poem by her, below).
[18] *Madam Knight* Mary, a singer.
[19] *Cazzo* Italian for penis.
[20] *Pall Mall* a fashionable street in London.
A SATYR ON CHARLES II
[1] This poem caused Rochester to flee the court early in 1674 when he delivered it by mistake to the King. The text, based on manuscripts, is taken from Walker's edition of the poems.
[2] *french Fool* Louis XIV, who pursued the current war with the Dutch, even after the English withdrew from their alliance in 1674.

And Love, he loves, for he loves fucking much.
Nor are his high Desires above his Strength:
His Sceptre and his Prick are of a Length;   10
And she may sway the one, who plays with th' other
And make him little wiser than his Brother.[3]
Restless he rolls about from Whore to Whore
A merry Monarch, scandalous and poor.
Poor Prince thy Prick like thy Buffoons at Court   15
Will govern thee because it makes thee sport.
'Tis sure the sauciest that e'er did swive
The proudest, peremptoriest Prick alive.
Though Safety, Law, Religion, Life lay on 't,
'Twould break through all to make its way to Cunt.   20
To Carwell the most Dear of all his dears[4]
The best Relief of his declining years[5]
Oft he bewails his fortune, and her fate
To love so well and be beloved so late.
For though in her he settles well his Tarse[6]   25
Yet his dull graceless Ballocks hang an arse.[7]
This you'd believe had I but Time to tell you
The Pains it Costs the poor laborious Nelly[8]
Whilst she employs, hands, fingers, mouth, and thighs
Ere she can raise the Member she enjoys –   30
I hate all Monarchs, and the Thrones they sit on
    From the Hector of France to the Cully of Britain.[9]

A Letter from Artemiza
in the Town to Chloe
in the Country

Chloe, in Verse by your command I write;
Shortly you'll bid me ride astride, and fight.
These Talents better with our sex agree,
Than lofty flights of dang'rous poetry.
Amongst the Men (I mean) the Men of Wit   5
(At least they passed for such, before they writ)
How many bold Advent'rers for the Bays,[1]
(Proudly designing large returns of praise)
Who durst that stormy pathless World explore,
Were soon dashed back, and wrecked on the dull shore,   10
Broke of that little stock, they had before?

---

[3] *his Brother* the future James II.
[4] *Carwell* Louise de Keroualle, Duchess of Portsmouth.
[5] *his declining years* Charles was 43 when the much younger Rochester wrote this poem.
[6] *Tarse* "A man's yard" (Nathan Bailey, *Dictionarium Britannicum*; not in Johnson); penis.

[7] *hang an arse* hold back; be reluctant.
[8] *Nelly* Eleanor Gwyn (1650–87), actress and mistress of Charles.
[9] *Hector* bully; *Cully* dupe.
A Letter from Artemiza
[1] *Bays* a crown of bay leaves, symbolic of literary achievement.

How would a Woman's tott'ring Bark be tossed,[2]
Where stoutest Ships (the Men of Wit) are lost?
When I reflect on this, I straight grow wise,
And my own self thus gravely I advise.   15
Dear Artemiza, poetry's a snare:
Bedlam has many Mansions: have a Care.[3]
Your Muse diverts you, makes the Reader sad;
You fancy, you're inspired, he thinks you mad.
Consider too, 'twill be discreetly done,   20
To make your Self the Fiddle of the Town,[4]
To find th' ill-humored pleasure at their need,
Cursed, if you fail, and scorned, though you succeed.
Thus, like an Arrant Woman, as I am,[5]
No sooner well convinced, writing's a shame,   25
That Whore is scarce a more reproachful name,
Than poetess:
Like Men, that marry, or like Maids, that woo,
'Cause 'tis the very worst thing they can do,
Pleased with the Contradiction, and the Sin,   30
Mee-thinks, I stand on Thorns, till I begin.
Y' expect at least, to hear, what Loves have past
In this Lewd Town, since you, and I met last.
What change has happened of Intrigues, and whether
The Old ones last, and who, and who's together.   35
But how, my dearest Chloe, shall I set
My pen to write, what I would fain forget,
Or name that lost thing (Love) without a tear
Since so debauched by ill-bred Customs here?
Love, the most generous passion of the mind,   40
The softest refuge Innocence can find,
The safe director of unguided youth,
Fraught with kind wishes, and secured by Truth,
That Cordial drop Heav'n in our Cup has thrown,
To make the nauseous draught of life go down,   45
On which one only blessing God might raise[6]
In lands of Atheists Subsidies of praise
(For none did e'er so dull, and stupid prove,
But felt a God, and blest his power in Love)
This only Joy, for which poor We were made,   50
Is grown like play, to be an Arrant Trade;[7]
The Rooks creep in, and it has got of late[8]
As many little Cheats, and Tricks, as that.
But what yet more a Womans heart would vex,
'Tis chiefly carried on by our own Sex,   55
Our silly Sex, who born, like Monarchs, free,

---

[2]   *Bark*   ship.
[3]   *Bedlam*   an asylum for the insane in London.
[4]   *Fiddle*   fool, jester.
[5]   *Arrant*   "Bad in a high degree" (Johnson).
[6]   *only*   sole.
[7]   *play*   gambling.
[8]   *Rooks*   "A cheat; a trickish rapacious fellow"
(Johnson).

Turn Gypsies for a meaner Liberty,
And hate restraint, though but from Infamy.
They call whatever is not Common, nice,
And deaf to Nature's rule, or Love's advice,   60
Forsake the pleasure, to pursue the vice.
To an exact perfection they have wrought
The Action Love, the Passion is forgot.
'Tis below wit, they tell you, to admire,
And ev'n without approving they desire.   65
Their private wish obeys the public Voice,
'Twixt good, and bad Whimsy decides, not Choice.
Fashions grow up for taste, at Forms they strike:
They know, what they would have, not what they like.
Bovey's a beauty, if some few agree,[9]   70
To call him so, the rest to that degree
Affected are, that with their Ears they see.
Where I was visiting the other night,
Comes a fine Lady with her humble Knight,
Who had prevailed on her, through her own skill,   75
At his request, though much against his will,
To come to London.
As the Coach stopped, we heard her Voice more loud,
Than a great bellied Woman's in a Crowd,
Telling the Knight, that her affairs require,   80
He for some hours obsequiously retire.[10]
I think, she was ashamed, to have him seen
(Hard fate of Husbands) the Gallant had been,
Though a diseased ill-favoured Fool, brought in.
'Dispatch', says she, 'that business you pretend,   85
Your beastly visit to your drunken friend;
A Bottle ever makes you look so fine!
Me-thinks I long to smell you stink of Wine.
Your Country-drinking-breath's enough to kill
Sour Ale corrected with a Lemon peel.   90
Prithee farewell – we'll meet again anon';
The necessary thing bows, and is gone.
She flies up stairs, and all the haste does show,
That fifty Antic Postures will allow,[11]
And then bursts out – 'Dear madam, am not I   95
The alter'dst Creature breathing? Let me die,[12]
I find myself ridiculously grown
Embarrassée with being out of Town,
Rude, and untaught, like any Indian Queen;
My Country nakedness is strangely seen.   100

---

[9]   *Bovey*   Sir Ralph Bovey (d. 1679).
[10] *obsequiously*   obediently.
[11] *Antic*   "Odd; ridiculously wild" (Johnson).

[12] *Let me die*   an affected, high-society expression, like many others in the speech of this "fine lady."

How is Love governed? Love, that rules the State,
And, pray, who are the Men most worn of late?
When I was married, Fools were *à la mode*,
The Men of Wit were then held *incommode*,
Slow of belief, and fickle in desire,   105
Who ere they'll be persuaded, must inquire,
As if they came to spy, not to admire.
With searching Wisdom fatal to their ease
They still find out, why, what may, should not please;
Nay take themselves for injured, when We dare,   110
Make 'em think better of us, than We are:
And if We hide our frailties from their sights,
Call Us deceitful Jilts and Hypocrites.[13]
They little guess, who at Our Arts are grieved,
The perfect Joy of being well deceived.   115
Inquisitive, as jealous Cuckolds, grow,
Rather than not be knowing, they will know,
What being known creates their certain woe.
Women should these of all mankind avoid;
For Wonder by clear knowledge is destroyed.   120
Woman, who is an Arrant Bird of night,
Bold in the Dusk, before a Fool's dull sight,
Should fly, when Reason brings the glaring light:
But the kind easy Fool apt to admire
Himself, trusts us, his Follies all conspire,   125
To flatter his, and favour Our desire.[14]
Vain of his proper Merit he with ease
Believes, we love him best, who best can please.
On him Our gross dull common Flatteries pass,
Ever most Joyful, when most made an Ass.   130
Heavy, to apprehend, though all Mankind
Perceive Us false, the Fop concerned is blind,
Who doting on himself,
Thinks every one, that sees him, of his mind.
These are true women's Men'. – Here forced to cease 135
Through Want of Breath, not Will, to hold her peace,
She to the Window runs, where she had spied
Her much esteemed dear Friend the monkey tied.[15]
With forty smiles, as many Antic bows,
As if 't had been the Lady of the House,   140
The dirty chatt'ring Monster she embraced,
And made it this fine tender speech at last
'Kiss me, thou curious Miniature of Man;
How odd thou art? How pretty? How Japan?[16]

---

[13] *Jilt* "A woman who gives her lover hopes, and deceives him" (Johnson).
[14] *flatter* "To raise false hopes" (Johnson).
[15] *monkey* a fashionable pet at this time.
[16] *Japan* a high varnish with gold embellishments once used on fashionable furniture.

Oh I could live, and die with thee' – then on   145
For half an hour in Compliment she run.
I took this time, to think, what Nature meant,
When this mixed thing into the World she sent,
So very wise, yet so impertinent.
One, who knew every thing, who, God thought fit,   150
Should be an Ass through choice, not want of Wit:
Whose Foppery, without the help of Sense,
Could ne'er have rose to such an Excellence.
Nature's as lame, in making a true Fop,
As a Philosopher; the very top,   155
And Dignity of Folly we attain
By studious Search, and labour of the Brain,
By observation, Counsel, and deep thought:
God never made a Coxcomb worth a groat.[17]
We owe that name to Industry, and Arts: 160
An Eminent Fool must be a Fool of parts;[18]
And such a one was she, who had turned o'er
As many Books, as Men, loved much, read more,
Had a discerning Wit; to her was known
Every one's fault, and merit, but her own.   165
All the good qualities, that ever blest
A Woman, so distinguished from the rest,
Except discretion only, she possessed.
But now, 'Mon cher dear Pug', she cries, 'adieu',
And the Discourse broke off does thus renew.   170
'You smile, to see me, whom the World perchance
Mistakes, to have some Wit, so far advance
The interest of Fools, that I approve
Their Merit more, than Men's of Wit, in Love.
But in Our Sex too many proofs there are   175
Of such, whom Wits undo, and Fools repair.
This in my time was so observed a Rule,
Hardly a Wench in Town, but had her Fool.
The meanest Common Slut, who long was grown
The Jest, and Scorn of every Pit-Buffon,   180
Had yet left Charms enough, to have subdued
Some Fop, or other fond, to be thought lewd.
Foster could make an Irish Lord a Nokes,[19]
And Betty Morris had her City-Cokes.[20]
A Woman's ne'er so ruined, but she can   185
Be still revenged on her undoer Man.
How lost so e'er, she'll find some Lover more
A lewd abandoned Fool, than she a whore.

---

[17] groat a coin worth only a few pence.
[18] parts "Qualities; powers; faculties; or accomplishments" (Johnson).

[19] Foster a lower-class girl on whom Rochester had
designs; Nokes an actor known for his ability to play
solemn fools.
[20] Betty Morris a well known prostitute; City the
financial center of London; Cokes fool.

That wretched thing Corinna, who had run
Through all the several Ways of being undone, 190
Cozened at first by Love, and living then[21]
By turning the too-dear-bought trick on Men:
Gay were the hours, and winged with Joys they flew,
When first the Town her early Beauties knew,
Courted, admired, and loved, with presents fed, 195
Youth in her looks, and pleasure in her bed,
Till Fate, or her ill Angel thought it fit,
To make her dote upon a Man of Wit,
Who found, 'twas dull, to love above a day,
Made his ill-natured Jest, and went away. 200
Now scorned by all, forsaken, and oppressed,
She's a *Memento Mori* to the rest.[22]
Diseased, decayed, to take up half a Crown,
Must mortgage her long Scarf, and Manteau Gown.[23]
Poor Creature! Who unheard of, as a Fly, 205
In some dark hole must all the Winter lie,
And Want, and dirt endure a whole half year,
That for one Month she tawdry may appear.[24]
In Easter Term she gets her a new Gown,
When my young Master's Worship comes to Town,[25] 210
From Pedagogue, and Mother just set free,
The Heir, and Hopes of a great Family,
Which with strong Ale, and Beef the Country Rules,
And ever since the Conquest have been Fools:[26]
And now with careful prospect to maintain 215
This Character, lest crossing of the Strain
Should mend the Booby-breed, his Friends provide[27]
A cousin of his own, to be his Bride;
And thus set out –
With an Estate, no Wit, and a young Wife 220
(The solid comforts of a Coxcomb's life)
Dunghill, and Pease forsook, he comes to Town,[28]
Turns Spark, learns to be lewd, and is undone.[29]
Nothing suits worse with Vice than want of Sense,
Fools are still wicked at their own Expense. 225
This o'ergrown Schoolboy lost – Corinna wins,
And at first dash, to make an Ass, begins:
Pretends, to like a Man, who has not known
The Vanities, nor Vices of the Town,

21 *Cozened* cheated, deceived.
22 *Memento Mori* salutary reminder of death.
23 *Manteau Gown* a loose upper garment worn in preference to a straight-bodied dress (*OED*, citing the Phillips-Kersey dictionary [1706]).
24 *tawdry* "Meanly showy; splendid without cost; fine without grace; shewy without elegance" (Johnson).
25 *Worship* "A character of honour" (Johnson).
26 *Conquest* the Norman conquest (1066), from which many great families in England date their eminence.
27 *Booby* "A dull, heavy, stupid fellow; a lubber" (Johnson).
28 *Pease* food made from peas.
29 *Spark* "A lively, showy, gay man. It is usually used in contempt" (Johnson).

Fresh in his youth, and faithful in his Love; 230
Eager of Joys, which he does seldom prove,
Healthful, and strong, he does no pains endure,
But what the Fair One, he adores, can cure.
Grateful for favours does the Sex esteem,[30]
And libels none, for being kind to him. 235
Then of the Lewdness of the times complains,
Rails at the Wits, and Atheists, and maintains,
'Tis better, than good Sense, than power, or Wealth,
To have a love untainted, youth, and health.
The unbred puppy, who had never seen 240
A Creature look so gay, or talk so fine,
Believes, then falls in Love, and then in Debt,
Mortgages all, ev'n to th' Ancient Seat,[31]
To buy this Mistress a new house for life;
To give her Plate, and Jewels, robs his wife; 245
And when to th' height of fondness he is grown,
'Tis time, to poison him, and all's her own.
Thus meeting in her Common Arms his Fate,
He leaves her Bastard Heir to his Estate;
And as the Race of such an Owl deserves,[32] 250
His own dull lawful progeny he starves.
Nature, who never made a thing in vain,
But does each Insect to some end ordain,
Wisely contrived kind-keeping Fools, no doubt,
To patch up Vices, Men of Wit wear out'. 255
Thus she ran on two hours, some grains of Sense
Still mixed with Volleys of Impertinence.
But now 'tis time, I should some pity show
To Chloe, since I cannot choose, but know,
Readers must reap the dullness writers sow. 260
By the next Post such stories I will tell,
As joined with these shall to a volume swell,
As true, as Heaven, more infamous than Hell;
But you are tired, and so am I. Farewell.

Archbishop William King (1650–1729)

The son of a Scotsman who emigrated to escape Commonwealth Presbyterianism at home, King was born and bred in Ireland. At the age of twenty-four he became a priest in the Church of Ireland and eventually rose to Bishop of Dublin. He was as zealous in opposing Roman Catholics as he was in contending with Presbyterians, and he was a strong supporter of William of Orange, although the Irish government was strongly Jacobite (preferring, that is, the rule of James II and the Stuart royal line). King was even imprisoned for a time, but after the English defeated the Irish at the Battle

[30] *the Sex* women.   [32] *Owl* a solemn fool.
[31] *Seat* principal residence of the family.

of the Boyne, his star was on the rise. However, King cared about the state of the Irish people, and he grew to mistrust English interference. England's policies in Ireland were extremely punitive at this time, and King opposed them.

In the following report on taxation, King makes a strong argument against adding to the burdens placed on the Irish. By the time he wrote it, King was already deep in a complicated relationship with Jonathan Swift, whom he had despatched to London in 1707 to protect the funding of the Church of Ireland. The two clergymen shared an interest in the welfare of Ireland, though they clashed in personal ways. Swift would certainly have known the arguments that King presents in the following report, and his famous ironical essay A Modest Proposal *suggests that he was also familiar with King's writing.*[1] *The text is based on Appendix 30 in the* Second Report of the Royal Commission on Historical Manuscripts *(London, 1871).*

from *Taxation of Ireland*, A.D. 1716

Some observations on the taxes paid by Ireland to support the Government

'Tis a general opinion in Great Britain, and passes current without contradiction, that Ireland is in a flourishing condition; that whilst England has been oppressed and deeply sunk in debt by excessive taxes, Ireland has been at ease, contributed nothing to the support of the Government, and is not one shilling[1] in debt; this I take to be a great reason of that ill affection that appears on many occasions against Ireland in the Parliament of Great Britain, and the occasion of several laws passed there, which the people of Ireland look on as very hard upon them. But in answer to this I believe it may be demonstrated that Ireland, in proportion to the riches thereof, has contributed as much as Great Britain, if not more, to the support of the Crown and Government since the Revolution;[2] this perhaps may be looked on as a paradox, but I believe it will not appear such to any one that will impartially consider the following particulars.

1st. That the hardship of the taxes paid by subjects to support the Government is not to be estimated by the quantity of the money given, but by the proportion it bears to the substance of the person that gives it, as, for example, a person that is worth in substance but £20 and gives one pound out of it, gives as much in proportion and feel the hardship of parting with it as much as another that is worth 20 thousand pounds and contributes one thousand out of it. Nay, the less a man's substance is, the more he must feel the parting with his proportional part; as, for example, suppose a man worth 20 thousand pounds and the public should require 19 thousand of it, yet he wou'd have one thousand left him, which would prevent his starving & furnish him and his family with the necessaries of life, but if a man be worth but 20 shillings and 19 be taken away 'tis impossible the remaining shilling should subsist him & his family, and so in all probability he must starve.

2dly. If we compare the riches of Ireland with that of Great Britain we shall find that they do not bear the proportion of one to 13 . . .

As to the charges of England in reducing Ireland, I will allow that in the 3 years the war continued it cost England five millions, though, I believe, that is a great deal too much, this was the sum of the loss; now as to Ireland, I believe the rents of Ireland may be computed at

---

ARCHBISHOP WILLIAM KING
[1] *A Modest Proposal* appears on pp. 646–51 below.
FROM *TAXATION OF IRELAND*
[1] *shilling* one twentieth of a pound sterling.

[2] *the Revolution* the Glorious Revolution of 1688–9, when James II was removed and William of Orange placed on the throne.

£1,500,000 per annum; now take the landlords of Ireland one with another and 'twill be found that they lost four years' rents at least by the war, for though the Courts did not allow so much, yet many gentlemen's lands lay waste five or six years, or they got nothing out of them, and many set theirs at a rising rent, that is one-third of the old rent for 7 years, 2/3 for the next 7, and then to come to the old rents; so that computing one place with another and one landlord with another, the loss could not be less than 4 years of the whole, that is six millions if we add the stocks of the cow kind, the sheep, and horses that were destroyed in the war, these will amount at least to 3 millions more . . .

Perhaps some will doubt of the truth of this representation of the miserable estate of the common people of Ireland, but whoever has been in their cabins has seen the matter of fact to be so and can vouch the truth of it. There are two sort of men that I except against as incompetent witness in this case: first, such English gentlemen as come over into Ireland on visits or business, and 2ndly such gentlemen of Ireland as live in England or that though they live generally in Ireland yet are as much strangers to the common people and their way of living as if bred in Turkey. I know these two represent Ireland as the most plentiful, luxurious country in Europe, and magnify the excessive eating and drinking in it. To unfold the mystery of this it must be observed that there are perhaps a thousand gentlemen in Ireland that live very splendidly, keep good tables, and make their friends welcome; when, therefore, a stranger comes to them, they hospitably invite him, liberally entertain him, and do the best they can to make him welcome; thus he is feasted from house to house while he stays, and he returns into England full of the plenty and luxury of Ireland. But he doth not consider that there are 300 thousand families in Ireland, and among all these hardly a thousand live in that condition in which the gentleman lives who entertained him, and for the good dinner he met there, three hundred neighbours or tenants dine on a potato without salt. This and the plenty in the good houses in Dublin deceive most strangers and give them conceptions of Ireland most distant from truth. Most strangers that come to Ireland go no further than that city and only converse with gentlemen or the richer sort there, and never are acquainted with the poverty of the rest, which is very great; perhaps a third part of that city need charity. As to in the Irish gentlemen that go to England or live there, they often know little more than their father's house or the city of Dublin, and are in truth strangers to the common way of living in that kingdom, or if they do know it, either shame or vanity make them conceal it as much they can, which I take to be [a] source of infinite mischiefs to the country and provokes envy instead of pity in our neighbours of Great Britain. And perhaps many of the laws complained of in Ireland owe their being to this mistake. I know that laziness is commonly objected to in the Irish and this is made the ground of their poverty. I own that there are some whose ancestors had great estates and lost them in the several rebellions, being forfeited and seized by the English, who give occasion to this surmise; now the posterity of these men commonly preserve with care their genealogies and still reckon themselves gentlemen and look on it as the greatest debasement in the world to work or exercise any trade; they live therefore, either by robbing or on their clans who still pay them a respect and maintain them after a sort, but the common Irish are laborious people, and if we set aside the holidays their religion enjoins, they work as hard and as long as any in England. I confess not with the same success, for they have neither the assistance to labour nor the encouragement workmen have in England; their poverty will not furnish them with convenient tools, and so the same quantity of work costs them perhaps twice the labour with which it is performed in England; there are many accidental differences that increase their labour on them, as, for example, England is already enclosed,[3] and if a farmer have a mind to keep a field for meadow, grazing, or ploughing, it

---

[3]   *enclosed*   divided by fences.

costs him no more but the shutting his gate, but the Irishman must fence his whole field every year or leave it in common, and the like saving of labour happens in the plough, utensils, in building houses and providing firing.[4] Neither hath the Irishman that encouragement to labour as there is in England: he has no market for his manufactories; if he build a good house or enclose his grounds, to be sure he must raise his rent or turn out[5] at the end of a short lease. These and many other considerations make the Irishman's case very pitiful, and ought, as seems to me, to move compassion rather than anger or a severe condemnation. Upon the whole I do not see how Ireland can on the present foot pay greater taxes than it does without starving the inhabitants and leaving them entirely without meat or clothes. They have already given their bread, their flesh, their butter, their shoes, their stockings, their beds, their house furniture and houses to pay their landlord and taxes. I cannot see how any more can be got from them, except we take away their potatoes and butter milk, or flay them and sell their skins.

Jane Barker (1652–c. 1727)

Much of what is known about the life of Jane Barker is gleaned from the semi-autobiographical narrative that she began publishing late in life. Love Intrigues *(1713) and* A Patch-work Screen for the Ladies *relate episodes of her life under the fictional name of Galesia. The moral maxims, often in verse, that Barker weaves into her romances may be what induced Johnson to make her one of the very few novelists and very few women quoted in his* Dictionary of the English Language. *Barker saw herself primarily as a poet, however; Katherine Philips was her literary idol, and her first book was* Poetical Recreations: Consisting of Original Poems, Songs, Odes &c. With Several New Translations *(1688). I take the short selelction of Barker from this volume.*

from *Poetical Recreations: Consisting of Original Poems, Songs, Odes, &c. with Several New Translations* (1688)

TO MY YOUNG LOVER ON HIS VOW

I

Alas, why mad'st thou such a *Vow*,
    Which thou wilt never pay,
And promise that from very now,
    Till everlasting day
Thou mean'st to love, sigh, bleed, and die,   5
    And languish out thy breath,
In praise of my Divinity,
    To th' minute of thy Death?

2

Sweet *Youth*, thou know'st not what it is
    To be Love's *Votary*;   10

---

4 *firing* fuel.   5 *turn out* evict the tenants.

Where thou must for the smallest bliss,
   Kneel, beg, and sigh, and cry.
Probationer thou should be first,[1]
   That thereby thou may'st try,
Whether thou can'st endure the worst   15
   Of Love's *austerity*.

3

For Worlds of *Beauties* always stand
   To tempt thy willing Eye,
And Troops of *Lusts* are at thy hand,
   To vanquish thee, or die.   20
And now this *Vow* exposes thee
   To th' third (of all the worst)
The Devil of *inconstancy*,
   That Tempter most accursed.

ABSENCE FOR A TIME

I Dread this tedious Time more than
   A *Fop* to miss a Fashion,[1]
Or the *Pope's Head* Tavern can[2]
   Dread the long *Vacation*.[3]

This time's as troublesome to me,   5
   As th' Town when Money's spent;
Grave Lectures to a *Debauchee*,
   Or *Whigs* to th' Government.[4]

Methinks I almost wish 'twas torn
   Out of the Rolls of *Fate*;   10
Or that some Pow'r, till his return,
   Would me *annihilate*,

But I, alas, must be content,
   Upon necessity;
Since him, until this time be spent,   15
   I cannot hope to see.

No more than we can hope to have
   The Life of perfect bliss,
Till by Afflictions, and the Grave,
   We're separate from this.   20

To My Young Lover on His Vow
[1] *Probationer* "novice" or "one who is upon trial" (Johnson), especially in a religious order.
Absence for a Time
[1] *Fop* "A word probably made by chance, and therefore without etymology. A simpleton; a coxcomb; a man of small understanding and much ostentation; a pretender; a man fond of show, dress, and flutter; an impertinent" (Johnson).
[2] *Pope's Head Tavern* one of two places of the name in the City of London, near the law courts.
[3] *long Vacation* the summer months between the terms when the law courts are in session.
[4] *Whigs* the opposition party in the latter part of Queen Anne's reign.

PARTING WITH———

Although thou now put'st me in doubt,
　By going I know not where;
Yet know my *soul* will beat about,
　Nor rest till she have found thee out,
　　And tend upon thee there.　　　　　　　　　5

Look to your *actions* then, for she
　So strict a watch will keep,
That if you give one *thought* from me,
　She'll swear it is flat Felony,
　　Though 't be when you're asleep.　　　　　10

But if a *sigh*, or *glance*, or *smile*
　Should to my Rival 'scape,
She'd cry out Robbery and spoil;[1]
　But if a *kiss* thy Lips should soil,
　　Then Murther and a Rape.　　　　　　　15

All this a *Metaphor* may seem,
　Or mad Philosophy
To the unthinking World, who deem
　That but a fancy or a dream,
　　Which Souls do really hear and see.　　　20

Lady Mary Chudleigh (1656–1710)

Mary Lee married George Chudleigh, a baronet, and spent her whole life in Devonshire. However, she widened her intellectual life by corresponding with the very active writer and religious controversialist John Norris; through him she met Mary Astell, an outspoken advocate for the equality of women. Reacting strongly to a sermon on the moral weakness of women published in 1699, Chudleigh published The Ladies' Defence, *her first work, at the age of forty-five. The work was conspicuous enough to incite the London publisher Bernard Lintot to bring out an unauthorized edition, when he failed to obtain Chudleigh's permission to reprint the work. In the last decade of her life, Chudleigh produced a volume of collected verse and a collection of essays. In his* Memoirs of Several Ladies of Great Britain *(1752), George Ballard noted that Chudleigh was learned and had written numerous translations of classical writers, which are preserved in her family's archives. Chudleigh's classical training shows in her poetry, where she is aware of ancient social and literary history. The essence of her work is in its combination of anger at narrow-minded contemporary attitudes towards women and her spiritualism, which was influenced by Norris's neo-Platonic view of the ephemerality of earthly existence.*

The texts presented here are based on the first edition of The Ladies' Defence *(1701) and* Poems on Several Occasions *(1703). Both works, along with Chudleigh's essays, have recently been edited by Margaret J. M. Ezell (Oxford University Press, 1993).*

PARTING WITH———
[1] *spoil* "The act of robbery" (Johnson).

from *The Ladies' Defence:* or, *The Bride-Woman's Counsellor*
Answered: A Poem in a Dialogue between Sir John Brute, Sir
William Loveall, Melissa, and a Parson (1701)[1]

... If like th' Ancients you would generous prove,
And in our Education show your Love;
Into our Souls would noble Thoughts instill,
Our Infant-Minds with bright Ideas fill:
Teach us our Time in Learning to employ,   695
And place in solid Knowledge all our Joy:
Persuade us trifling Authors to refuse,
And when we think, the useful'st Subjects choose:
Inform us how a prosperous State to bear,
And how to Act when Fortune is severe: 700
We should be Wiser, and more blameless live,
And less occasion for your Censures give:
At least in us less Failings you would see,
And our Discourses would less tiresome be:
Though Wit like yours we never hope to gain,   705
Yet from Impertinence we should refrain,
And learn to be less Talkative and Vain.
Unto the strictest Rules we should submit,
And what we ought to do, think always fit.
Never dispute, when Duty leads the way,   710
But its commands without a Sigh Obey.
To Reason, not to Humour, give the Reins,[2]
And be the same in Palaces and Chains.
But you our humble Suit will still decline;
To have us wise was never your Design: 715
You'll keep us Fools, that we may be your Jest;
They who know least, are ever treated best.
If we do well, with Care it is concealed;
But every Error, every Fault's revealed:
While to each other you still partial prove,   720
Can see no Failures, and even Vices love.
The bloody Masters of the martial Trade,
Are praised for Mischiefs, and for Murders paid.
The noisy Lawyers, if they can but bawl,
Soon grace the Wool-sacks, and adorn the Hall.[3]   725
The envied Great, those darling sons of Fame,
Who carry a Majestic Terror in their Name;

FROM *THE LADIES' DEFENCE*
[1] *The Bride-Woman's Counsellor* a sermon by John Sprint
full of sexist remarks, which Chudleigh specifically attacks in her preface to this poem. The excerpt presented
here is part of Melissa's last speech, which concludes the
poem.

[2] *Humour* mood, inclination.
[3] *the Wool-sack* "The seat of the judges in the House
of Lords" (Johnson); *Hall* "A court of justice"
(Johnson).

Who like the Demy Gods are placed on High,
And seem th' exalted Natives of the Sky:
Who swayed by Pride, and by Self-love betrayed,   730
Are Slaves to their imperious Passions made,
Are with a Servile Awe by you revered;
Praised for their Follies, for their Vices feared.
The Courtier, who with every Wind can veer,
And midst the Mounting Waves can safely steer;   735
Who all can flatter; and with wondrous grace,
Low cringing Bows, and a designing Face,
A smiling Look, and a dissembled Hate,
Can hug a Friend, and hasten on his Fate,
Has your Applause; his Policy you praise;   740
And to the Skies his prudent Conduct raise.
The Scholar, if he can a Verb decline,[4]
And has the Skill to reckon Nine times Nine,
Or but the nature of a Fly define;
Can Mouth some Greek, and knows where *Athens* stood,   745
Though he perhaps is neither Wise, nor Good,
Is fit for *Oxford;* where when he has been,
Each College viewed, and each grave Doctor seen,
He mounts a Pulpit, and th' exalted Height
Makes Vapours dance before his troubled Sight,[5]   750
And he no more can see, nor think aright.
Yet such as these your Consciences do Guide,
And o'er your Actions and your Words preside,
Blame you for Faults which they themselves commit,
Arraign your Judgement, and condemn your Wit: 755
Instil their Notions with the Greatest Ease,
And Hood-winked lead you where so e'er they please.
The formal Justice, and the jolly Knight,
Who in their Money place their chief delight;
Who watch the Kitchen, and survey the field,   760
To see what each will to their Luxury yield:
Who Eat and Run, then quarrel, Rail and Drink,
But never are at leisure once to Think:
Who weary of Domestic Cares being grown,
And yet, like Children, frighted when alone,   765
(Detesting Books) still Hunt, or Hawk, or Play,
And in laborious Trifles waste the Day,
Are liked by you, their Actions still approved,
And if they're Rich, are sure to be beloved.
These are the Props, the Glory of the State,   770
And on their Nod depends the Nation's Fate:
These weave the Nets, where little Flies betrayed,
Are Victims to relentless Justice made,

---

[4] *Scholar* student.

[5] *Vapours* "Mental fume; vain imagination; fancy un-real" (Johnson).

While they themselves contemn the Snares that they have laid,
As Bonds too weak such mighty Men to hold,   775
As scorn to be by any Laws controlled.
Physicians with hard Words and haughty Looks,[6]
And promised Health, bait their close-covered Hooks:
Like Birds of Prey, while they your Gold can scent,
You are their Care, their utmost help is lent;   780
But when your Guineas cease, you to the *Spa* are sent,[7]
Yet still you Court 'em, think you cannot die
If you've a Son of Æsculapius by.[8]
The Tradesmen you Caress, although you know
They wealthy by their Cheats and Flatteries grow;   785
You seem to credit every Word they say,
And as they sell, with the same Conscience pay:
Nay to the Mob, those Dregs of Human kind,
Those Animals you slight, you're wondrous kind;
To them you Cringe, and though they are your Sport,   790
Yet still you fawn, and still their Favour Court.
Thus on each other daily you impose,
And all for Wit, and dextrous Cunning goes.
'Tis we alone hard Measure still must find;
But spite of you, we'll to our selves be kind: 795
Your Censures slight, your little Tricks despise,
And make it our whole Business to be wise.
The mean low trivial Cares of Life disdain,
And Read and Think, and Think and Read again,
And on our Minds bestow the utmost Pain.   800
Our Souls with strictest Morals we'll adorn,
And all your little Arts of wheedling Scorn;
Be humble, mild, forgiving, just and true,
Sincere to all, respectful unto you,
While, as becomes you, sacred Truths you teach,   805
And live those Sermons you to others Preach.
With want of Duty none shall us upbraid,
Where-e'er 'tis due, it shall be nicely paid.
Honour and Love we'll to our Husbands give,
And ever Constant and Obedient live: 810
If they are Ill, we'll try by gentle ways
To lay those Tempests which their Passions raise;[9]
But if our soft Submissions are in vain,
We'll bear our fate, and never once complain:
Unto our Friends the tenderest kindness show,   820
Be wholly theirs, no separate Interest know;
With them their Dangers and their Suff'rings share,
And make their Persons, and their Fame our Care.

---

[6] *hard Words* technical, latinate terms.   [8] *Æsculapius* Greek god of healing.
[7] *Guineas* gold coins worth £1.05.   [9] *lay* allay.

The Poor we'll feed, to the Distressed be kind,
And strive to Comfort each afflicted Mind.   825
Visit the Sick, and try their Pains to ease;
Not without Grief the meanest Wretch displease:
And by a Goodness as diffused as Light,
To the pursuit of Virtue all invite.
Thus will we live, regardless of your hate,   830
Till re-admitted to our former State;
Where, free from the Confinement of our Clay
In glorious Bodies we shall bask in Day,
And with enlightened Minds new Scenes survey.
Scenes, much more bright than any here below,   835
And we shall then the whole of Nature know;
See all her Springs, her secret Turnings view,
And be as knowing, and as wise as you.
With generous Spirits of a Make Divine,
In whose blest Minds Celestial Virtues shine,   840
Whose Reason, like their Station, is sublime,
And who see clearly through the Mists of Time,
Those puzzling Glooms where busy Mortals stray,
And still grope on, but never find their way.
We shall, well-pleased, eternally converse,   845
And all the Sweets of Sacred Love possess:
Love, freed from all the gross Allays of Sense,[10]
So pure, so strong, so constant, so intense,
That it shall all our Faculties employ,
And leave no Room for any thing but Joy.   850

from *Poems on Several Occasions* (1703)

TO THE LADIES

Wife and Servant are the same,
But only differ in the Name:
For when that fatal Knot is tied,
Which nothing, nothing can divide:
When she the word 'obey' has said,   5
And Man by Law supreme has made,
Then all that's kind is laid aside,
And nothing left but State and Pride:
Fierce as an Eastern Prince he grows,
And all his innate Rigour shows: 10
Then but to look, to laugh, or speak,
Will the Nuptial Contract break.

---

[10]   *Allay*   alloy, "metal of a baser kind, mixed in coins,
to harden them" (Johnson).

Like Mutes, she Signs alone must make,
And never any Freedom take:
But still be governed by a Nod,   15
And fear her Husband as a God:
Him still must serve, him still obey,
And nothing act, and nothing say,
But what her haughty Lord thinks fit,
Who with the Pow'r, has all the Wit.   20
Then shun, oh! shun that wretched State,
And all the fawning Flatt'rers hate:
Value your selves, and Men despise:
You must be proud, if you'll be wise.

Friendship

Friendship is a Bliss Divine,
And does with radiant Lustre shine:
But where can that blest Pair be found
That are with equal Fetters bound?
Whose Hearts are one, whose Souls combine,   5
And neither know or Mine, or Thine[1]
Who've but one Joy, one Grief, one Love,
And by the self same Dictates move;
Who've not a Frailty unrevealed,
Nor yet a Thought that is concealed;   10
Who freely one another blame,
And strive to raise each other's Fame;
Who're always just, sincere, and kind,
By Virtue, not by Wealth, combined;
Whose Friendship nothing can abate,   15
Nor Poverty, nor adverse Fate.[2]
Nor Death it self: for when above,
They'll never, never, cease to love,
But with a Passion more refined,
Become one pure celestial Mind.   20

Daniel Defoe (1660–1731)

Robinson Crusoe is one of three books that Samuel Johnson said he wished longer than it was. This undeniably great, ground-breaking, and remarkably durable novel may be Defoe's best creation, but it represents a tiny fraction of the immense amount of invention with which he filled his life. He wrote literally hundreds of works of all sorts; so industrious was he and so mercurial in his interests, and in the surprising slants he could take on various issues, that a full and accurate accounting of his works will probably never be achieved. Most of his work can be broadly described

---

Friendship
[1] *or . . . or*   either . . . or.

[2] *Nor . . . nor*   neither . . . nor.

as journalism, and to a large degree Defoe created that highly various kind of writing. His works are based largely on contemporary events and experiences, though they often have historical frameworks and also, very often, depart from ascertainable facts. Defoe shows that it is possible to be an author on this model, and not only on the "higher" model followed by fellow journalists like Addison and Johnson, in which the present is viewed mainly through the spectacles of classical literature.

Although he was desperate and venal enough at times to serve Tory as well as Whig politicians, as a spy and counter-spy, most of Defoe's works are imbued with his democratic, Whiggish political outlook. He believed in the Lockean, and later, American, values of individual life, liberty, and the pursuit of happiness in preference to the protection of the established society, church, or government. His literary works were entrepreneurial projects designed to further his interest, and they were very much of a piece with his operation of a brick and tile factory, his investment and development of land, and his sales of timber. He launched businesses, established markets, and undertook mortgages with the same speed and industry that he created new forms of literature. Insofar as the laws and customs of society could be flexed to permit it, Defoe's life was itself a creation of his own. There is an emblem of his self-fashioning in the fact that he changed his name from that of his butcher father, Foe, to the classier Norman-sounding name by which he is known.

Defoe could, of course, change the names of other people even more easily and make them what he wished in his artistic life as a kind of fictionalizing journalist. A Journal of the Plague Year and Moll Flanders are only two of the best known of Defoe's transformations. It was long thought that The Apparition of Mrs. Veal was one of Defoe's most obvious hoaxes, but it appears now that in this case he did nothing but transmit the same report heard by another in the very consistent and largely unimpeachable accounts of Mrs. Bargrave. A much trickier work is Defoe's Shortest Way with the Dissenters; here he presents a speaker who rabidly supports the position on toleration that Defoe despises, but he is so realistic a creation that many who shared his views did not at first understand that they were being lampooned. Defoe paid dearly for this trick; he lost his business through fines and imprisonment and was exposed in the public stocks. The irony in A True-Born Englishman is more obvious; in fact, the whole poem is dedicated to ridiculing its title phrase and showing that virtually all Englishmen are immigrants of mixed national heritage. The conclusion, proclaiming virtue rather than birth the measure of a man, was meant to support King William's image in Britain, but it might be used as a credo for members of the underclasses in many parts of the world today. Along with the rights of immigrants and the poor, Defoe also championed the rights of women. He was not the only person in England in the seventeenth century to decry the miserable state of women's education, but he was in the minority, and his call for women's colleges was not fully heeded until the second half of the nineteenth century.

The following texts are all based on first editions, with somewhat more modernization in the prose than in the poetry. There is not, and may never be, a standard edition of Defoe's works, although a great many of his works are in print. There is a recent and very engaging biography by Paula Backschieder (Johns Hopkins University Press, 1989), which includes a well-researched but still controversial bibliography of his works.

from *An Essay upon Projects* (1698)

AN ACADEMY FOR WOMEN

I have often thought of it as one of the most barbarous Customs in the world, considering us as a Civilized and a Christian Country, that we deny the advantages of Learning to

Women. We reproach the Sex[1] every day with Folly and Impertinence, while I am confident, had they the advantages of Education equal to us, they would be guilty of less than our selves.

One would wonder indeed how it should happen that Women are conversible at all, since they are only beholding to Natural Parts[2] for all their Knowledge. Their Youth is spent to teach them to Stitch and Sow, or make Bawbles: They are taught to Read, indeed, and perhaps to write their Names, or so; and that is the height of a Woman's Education. And I would but ask any who slight the Sex for their Understanding, what is a Man (a Gentleman, I mean) good for, that is taught no more?

I need not give Instances, or examine the Character of a Gentleman with a good Estate, and of a good Family, and with tolerable Parts, and examine what Figure he makes for want of Education.

The Soul is placed in the Body like a rough Diamond, and must be polished, or the Lustre of it will never appear: And 'tis manifest, that as the Rational Soul distinguishes us from Brutes, so Education carries on the distinction, and makes some less brutish than others: This is too evident to need any demonstration. But why then should Women be denied the benefit of Instruction? If Knowledge and Understanding had been useless additions to the Sex, God Almighty would never have given them Capacities; for he made nothing needless: Besides, I would ask such, What they can see in Ignorance, that they should think it a necessary Ornament to a Woman? Or how much worse is a Wise Woman than a Fool? Or what has the Woman done to forfeit the Privilege of being taught? Does she plague us with her Pride and Impertinence? Why did we not let her learn, that she might have had more Wit? Shall we upbraid Women with Folly, when 'tis only the Error of this inhuman Custom that hindered them being made wiser?

The Capacities of Women are supposed to be greater, and their Senses quicker than those of the Men; and what they might be capable of being bred to, is plain from some Instances of Female-Wit, which this Age is not without; which upbraids us with Injustice, and looks as if we denied Women the advantages of Education, for fear they should *vie* with the Men in their Improvements.

To remove this Objection, and that Women might have at least a needful Opportunity of Education in all sorts of Useful Learning, I propose the Draught[3] of an Academy for that purpose.

I know 'tis dangerous to make Public Appearances of the Sex; they are not either to be *confined* or *exposed*; the first will disagree with their Inclinations, and the last with their Reputations; and therefore it is somewhat difficult; and I doubt[4] a Method proposed by an Ingenious Lady, in a little Book, called, *Advice to the Ladies*[5] would be found impracticable. For, saving my Respect to the Sex, the Levity, which perhaps is a little peculiar to them, at least in their Youth, will not bear the Restraint; and I am satisfied, nothing but the height of Bigotry can keep up a Nunnery: Women are extravagantly desirous of going to Heaven, and will punish their *Pretty Bodies* to get thither; but nothing else will do it; and even in that case sometimes it falls out that *Nature will prevail*.

When I talk therefore of an Academy for Women, I mean both the Model, the Teaching, and the Government, different from what is proposed by that Ingenious Lady, for whose

---

AN ACADEMY FOR WOMEN
[1] *the Sex* women.
[2] *Parts* abilities.
[3] *Draught* sketch.

[4] *doubt* expect, believe.
[5] *Advice to the Ladies* Advice to the Ladies of London (1686–8) by Thomas D'Urfey.

Proposal I have a very great Esteem, and also a great Opinion of her Wit; different too from all sorts of Religious Confinement, and above all, from *Vows of Celibacy.*

Wherefore the Academy I propose should differ but little from Public Schools, wherein such Ladies as were willing to study, should have all the advantages of Learning suitable to their Genius.

But since some Severities of Discipline more than ordinary would be absolutely necessary to preserve the Reputation of the House, that Persons of Quality and Fortune might not be afraid to venture their Children thither, I shall venture to make a small Scheme by way of Essay.

The House I would have built in a Form by it self, as well as in a Place by it self

The Building should be of Three plain Fronts, without any Jettings, or Bearing-Work, that the Eye might at a Glance see from one Coign[6] to the other; the Gardens walled in the same Triangular Figure, with a large Moat, and but one Entrance.

When thus every part of the Situation was contrived well as might be for discovery, and to render *Intriguing* dangerous, I would have no Guards, no Eyes, no Spies set over the Ladies, but shall expect them to be tried by the Principles of Honour and strict Virtue.

And if I am asked, 'Why?' I must ask Pardon of my own Sex for giving this reason for it:

I am so much in Charity with Women, and so well acquainted with Men, that 'tis my opinion, There needs no other Care to prevent Intriguing than to keep the men effectually away: For though *Inclination*, which we prettily call *Love*, does sometimes move a little too visibly in the Sex, and Frailty often follows; yet I think verily, *Custom*, which we miscall *Modesty*, has so far the Ascendant over the Sex, that *Solicitation* always goes before it.

> *Custom with Women 'stead of Virtue rules;*
> *It leads the Wisest, and commands the Fools;*
> *For this alone, when Inclinations reign,*
> *Though Virtue's fled, will Acts of Vice restrain.*
> *Only by Custom 'tis that Virtue lives,*
> *And Love requires to be asked, before it gives.*
> *For that which we call Modesty is Pride:*
> *They scorn to ask, and hate to be denied.*
> *'Tis Custom thus prevails upon their Want;*
> *They'll never beg, what asked they eas'ly grant.*
> *And when the needless Ceremony's over,*
> *Themselves the Weakness of the Sex discover.*
> *If then Desires are strong, and Nature free,*
> *Keep from her Men, and Opportunity.*
> *Else 'twill be vain to curb her by Restraint;*
> *But keep the Question off, you keep the Saint.*

In short, let a Woman have never such a Coming-Principle,[7] she will let you ask before she complies, at least if she be a Woman of any Honour.

Upon this ground I am persuaded such Measures might be taken, that the Ladies might have all the Freedom in the world within their own Walls, and yet no Intriguing, no

---

[6] *Coign* projecting corner.   [7] *Coming-Principle* natural forwardness.

Indecencies, nor Scandalous Affairs happen; and in order to this, the following Customs and Laws should be observed in the Colleges; of which I would propose One at least in every County in *England*, and about Ten for the City of *London*.

After the Regulation of the Form of the Building as before;

(1.) All the Ladies who enter into the House, should set their Hands[8] to the Orders of the House, to signify their Consent to submit to them.

(2.) As no Woman should be received, but who declared her self willing, and that it was the Act of her Choice to enter her self, so no Person should be confined to continue there a moment longer than the same voluntary Choice inclined her.

(3.) The Charges of the House being to be paid by the Ladies, every one that entered should have only this Incumbrance, That she should pay for the whole Year, though her mind should change as to her continuance.

(4.) An Act of Parliament should make it Felony without Clergy,[9] for any man to enter by Force or Fraud into the House, or to solicit any Woman, *though it were to Marry*, while she was in the House. And this Law would by no means be severe; because any Woman who was willing to receive the Addresses of a Man, might discharge her self of the House when she pleased; and on the contrary, any Woman who had occasion, might discharge her self of the Impertinent Addresses of any Person she had an Aversion to, by entering into the House.

In this House

The Persons who Enter, should be taught all sorts of Breeding suitable to both their Genius and their Quality; and in particular, *Music* and *Dancing*, which it would be cruelty to bar the Sex of, because they are their Darlings: But besides this, they should be taught Languages, as particularly *French* and *Italian*; and I would venture the Injury of giving a Woman more Tongues than one.

They should, as a particular Study, be taught all the Graces of Speech, and all the necessary Air of Conversation; which our common Education is so defective in, that I need not expose it: They should be brought to read Books, and especially History, and so to read as to make them understand the World, and be able to know and judge of things when they hear of them.

To such whose Genius would lead them to it, I would deny no sort of Learning; but the chief thing in general is to cultivate the Understandings of the Sex, that they may be capable of all sorts of Conversation; that their Parts and Judgements being improved, they may be as Profitable in their Conversation as they are Pleasant.

Women, in my observation, have little or no difference in them, but as they are, or are not distinguished by Education. Tempers indeed may in some degree influence them, but the main distinguishing part is their Breeding.

The whole Sex are generally Quick and Sharp: I believe I may be allowed to say generally so, for you rarely see them lumpish and heavy when they are Children, as Boys will often be. If a Woman be well-bred, and taught the proper Management of her Natural Wit, she proves generally very sensible and retentive: And without partiality, a Woman of Sense and Manners is the Finest and most Delicate Part of God's Creation; the Glory of her Maker, and the greatest Instance of his singular regard to Man, his Darling Creature, to whom he gave the best Gift either God could bestow, or man receive: And 'tis the sordidest Piece of Folly and Ingratitude in the world, to withhold from the Sex the due Lustre which the advantages of Education gives to the Natural Beauty of their Minds.

---

8   *set their Hands*   sign their names.

9   *Felony without Clergy*   a capital offense with no possibility of appeal.

A Woman well Bred and well Taught, furnished with the additional Accomplishments of Knowledge and Behaviour, *is a Creature without comparison*; her Society is the Emblem of sublimer Enjoyments; her Person is Angelic, and her Conversation heavenly; she is all Softness and Sweetness, Peace, Love, Wit, and Delight: She is every way suitable to the sublimest Wish; and the man that has such a one to his Portion, has nothing to do but to rejoice in her, and to be thankful.

On the other hand, Suppose her to be the *very same* Woman, and rob her of the Benefit of Education, and it follows thus;

If her Temper be Good, want of Education makes her Soft and Easy.

Her Wit, for want of Teaching, makes her Impertinent and Talkative.

Her Knowledge, for want of Judgement and Experience, makes her Fanciful and Whimsical.

If her Temper be Bad, want of Breeding makes her worse, and she grows Haughty, Insolent, and Loud.

If she be Passionate, want of Manners makes her Termagant,[10] and a Scold, *which is much at one with Lunatic.*

If she be Proud, want of Discretion (which still is Breeding) makes her Conceited, Fantastic, and Ridiculous.

And from these she degenerates to be Turbulent, Clamorous, Noisy, Nasty, *and the Devil.*

Methinks Mankind for their own sakes, since say what we will of the Women, we all think fit one time or other to be concerned with 'em,[11] should take some care to breed them up to be *suitable* and *serviceable*, if they expected no such thing as *Delight* from 'em. Bless us! What Care do we take to Breed up a good Horse, and to Break him well! and what a Value do we put upon him when it is done, and all because he should be fit for our use! and why not a Woman? Since all her Ornaments and Beauty, without suitable Behaviour, is a Cheat in Nature, like the false Tradesman, who puts the best of his Goods uppermost, that the Buyer may think the rest are of the same Goodness.

Beauty of the Body, which is the Woman's Glory, seems to be now unequally bestowed, and Nature, or rather Providence, to lie under some Scandal about it, and if 'twas given a Woman for a Snare to Men, and so made a kind of *She-Devil* of her: Because they say Exquisite Beauty is *rarely* given with Wit; *more rarely* with Goodness of Temper, and *never at all* with Modesty. And some, pretending to justify the Equity of such a Distribution, will tell us 'tis the Effect of the Justice of Providence in dividing particular Excellencies among all his Creatures: *share and share alike, as it were*, that all might for something or other be acceptable to one another, else some would be despised.

I think both these Notions false; and yet the last, which has the show of Respect to Providence, is the worst; for it supposes Providence to be Indigent and Empty; as if it had not wherewith to furnish all the Creatures it had made, but was fain to be parsimonious in its Gifts, and distribute them by *piece-meal*, for fear of being exhausted.

If I might venture my Opinion against an almost universal Notion, I would say, Most men mistake the Proceedings of Providence in this case, and all the world at this day are mistaken in their Practice about it. And because the Assertion is very bold, I desire to explain my self.

That Almighty First Cause which made us all, is certainly the Fountain of Excellence, as it is of Being, and by an Invisible Influence could have diffused Equal Qualities and Perfections to all the Creatures it has made, as the Sun does its Light, without the least Ebb

---

[10]   *Termagant*   "Quarrelsome; scolding; furious"   [11]   *'em*   an old form of "them," not slang.
(Johnson).

or Diminution to himself; and has given indeed to every individual sufficient to the Figure his Providence had designed him in the world.

I believe it might be defended, if I should say, That I do suppose God has given to all Mankind equal Gifts and Capacities, in that he has given them all *Souls* equally capable; and that the whole difference in Mankind proceeds either from Accidental Difference in the Make of their Bodies, or from the *foolish Difference* of Education.

1. *From Accidental Difference in Bodies.* I would avoid discoursing here of the Philosophical Position of the Soul in the Body: But if it be true, as Philosophers do affirm, That the Understanding and Memory is dilated or contracted according to the accidental Dimensions of the Organ through which 'tis conveyed; then though God has given a Soul as capable to me as another, yet if I have any Natural Defect in those Parts of the Body by which the Soul should act, I may have the same Soul infused as another man, and yet he be a Wise Man, and I a very Fool. *For example,* If a Child naturally have a Defect in the Organ of Hearing, so that he could never distinguish any Sound, that Child shall never be able to speak or read, though it have a Soul capable of all the Accomplishments in the world. The Brain is the Centre of the Soul's actings, where all the distinguishing Faculties of it reside; and 'tis observable, A man who has a narrow contracted Head, in which there is not room for the due and necessary Operations of Nature by the Brain, is never a man of very great Judgement; and that Proverb, *A Great Head and Little Wit,* is not meant by Nature, but is a Reproof upon Sloth; as if one should, by way of wonder, say, *Fie, fie, you that have a Great Head, have but Little Wit, that's strange! that must certainly be your own fault.* From this Notion I do believe there a great matter in the Breed of Men and Women; not that Wise Men shall always get Wise Children; but I believe Strong and Healthy Bodies have the Wisest Children; and Sickly Weakly Bodies affect the Wits as well as the Bodies of their Children. We are easily persuaded to believe this in the Breeds of Horses, Cocks, Dogs, and other Creatures; and I believe 'tis as visible in Men.

But to come closer to the business; the great distinguishing difference which is seen in the world between Men and Women, is in their Education; and this is manifested by comparing it with the difference between one Man or Woman, and another.

And herein it is that I take upon me to make such a bold Assertion, That all the World are mistaken in their Practice about Women: For I cannot think that God Almighty ever made them so delicate, so glorious Creatures, and furnished them with such Charms, so Agreeable and so Delightful to Mankind, with Souls capable of the same Accomplishments with Men, and all to be only Stewards of our Houses, *Cooks, and Slaves.*

Not that I am for exalting the Female Government in the least: But, in short, *I would have Men take Women for Companions, and Educate them to be fit for it.* A Woman of Sense and Breeding will scorn as much to encroach upon the Prerogative of the Man, as a Man of Sense will scorn to oppress the 'Weakness' of the Woman. But if the Women's Souls were refined and improved by Teaching, that word would be lost; to say, 'The Weakness of the Sex', as to Judgement, would be Nonsense; for Ignorance and Folly would be no more found among Women than Men. I remember a Passage which I heard from a very Fine Woman; she had Wit and Capacity enough, an Extraordinaary Shape and Face, and a Great Fortune, but had been cloistered up all her time, and for fear of being stolen, had not had the liberty of being taught the common necessary knowledge of Women's Affairs; and when she came to converse in the world, her Natural Wit made her so sensible of the want of Education that she gave this short Reflection on her self:

'I am ashamed to talk with my very Maids', says she, 'for I don't know when they do right or wrong: I had more need to go to School, than be Married'.

I need not enlarge on the Loss the Defect of Education is to the Sex, nor argue the Benefit of the contrary Practice; 'tis a thing will be more easily granted than remedied: This Chapter is but an Essay[12] at the thing, and I refer the Practice to those Happy Days, if ever they shall be, when men shall be wise enough to mend it.

from The True-Born *Englishman*: A Satire (1700)

PART I

Wherever God erects a House of Prayer,[1]
The Devil always builds a Chapel there:
And 'twill be found upon Examination,
The latter has the largest Congregation:
For ever since he first debauched the Mind,   5
He made a perfect Conquest of Mankind.
With Uniformity of Service, he
Reigns with a general Aristocracy.
No Nonconforming Sects disturb his Reign,
For of his Yoke there's very few complain.[2]   10
He knows the Genius and the Inclination,
And matches proper Sins for every Nation.
He needs no Standing-Army Government;[3]
He always rules us by our own Consent:
His Laws are easy, and his gentle Sway   15
Makes it exceeding pleasant to obey.
The List of his Vicegerents and Commanders,
Out-does your *Cæsars*, or your *Alexanders*.
They never fail of his Infernal Aid,
And he's as certain ne'er to be betrayed.   20
Through all the World they spread his vast Command,
And Death's Eternal Empire's maintained.
They rule so politically and so well,
As if they were L——— J——— of Hell.[4]
Duly divided to debauch Mankind,   25
And plant Infernal Dictates in his Mind.
   Pride, the first Peer, and President of Hell,
To his share *Spain*, the largest Province, fell.
The subtle Prince thought fittest to bestow
On these the Golden Mines of *Mexico*;   30

---

[12] *Essay* attempt.
FROM THE TRUE-BORN ENGLISHMAN   PART I
[1] An *English* Proverb, *Where God has a Church, the Devil has a Chapel* [Defoe's note].
[2] *Yoke* a reference to Christ's description of the discipline he enjoins, "my yoke is easy, and my burden is light" (Matthew 11.30).
[3] *Standing-Army* whether or not there was a need for a permanent military force was one of the most hotly

contested issues in politics in the seventeenth and eighteenth centuries; Defoe wrote against King William's retention of his standing army.
[4] *L{ords} J{ustices}* the officers left in charge of England when King William made his annual return to the Netherlands.

With all the Silver Mountains of *Peru*;
Wealth which would in wise hands the World undo:
Because he knew their Genius was such;
Too Lazy and too Haughty to be Rich.
So proud a People, so above their Fate,   35
That if reduced to beg, they'll beg in State.
Lavish of Money, to be counted Brave,
And Proudly starve, because they scorn to save.
Never was a Nation in the World before,
So very Rich, and yet so very Poor.   40
   Lust chose the Torrid Zone of *Italy*,
Were Blood ferments in Rapes and Sodomy:
Where swelling Veins o'erflow with livid Streams,
With Heat impregnate from *Vesuvian* Flames:[5]
Whose flowing Sulphur forms Infernal Lakes,   45
And human Body of the Soil partakes.
There Nature ever burns with hot Desires,
Fanned with Luxuriant Air from Subterranean Fires:
Here undisturbed in Floods of scalding Lust,
Th' Infernal King reigns with Infernal Gust.[6]   50
   Drunkenness, the Darling Favourite of Hell,
Chose *Germany* to Rule; and rules so well,
No Subjects more obsequiously obey,
None please so well, or are so pleased as they.
The cunning Artist manages so well,   55
He lets them Bow to Heav'n, and Drink to Hell.
If but to Wine and him they Homage pay,
He cares not to what Deity they Pray,
What God they worship˙most, or in what way.
Whether by *Luther*, *Calvin*, or by *Rome*,[7]   60
They sail for Heav'n, by Wine he steers them home.
   Ungoverned Passion settled first in *France*,
Where Mankind Lives in haste, and Thrives by Chance,
A *Dancing Nation*, Fickle and Untrue:
Have oft undone themselves, and others too: 65
Prompt the Infernal Dictates to Obey,
And in Hell's Favour none more great than they.
   The *Pagan* World he blindly leads away,
And Personally rules with Arbitrary Sway:
The Mask thrown off, *Plain Devil* his Title stands;   70
And what elsewhere he Tempts, he there Commands.
There with full Gust th' Ambition of his Mind
Governs, as he of old in Heav'n designed.
Worshipped as God, his *Painim Altars*[8] smoke,

---

[5] *Vesuvian* from the volcanic Mount Vesuvius near
Pompeii and Naples.
[6] *Gust* "height of sensual enjoyment" (Johnson).

[7] *Luther*, *Calvin* founders of important Protestant
sects in opposition to the Roman Catholic Church.
[8] *Painim Altars* pagan places of worship where Defoe
imagines human sacrifices.

Embrued with Blood of those that him Invoke.   75
   The rest by Deputies he rules as well,
And plants the distant Colonies of Hell.
By them his secret Power he well maintains,
And binds the World in his Infernal Chains.
   By Zeal the *Irish*; and the *Rush* by Folly:[9]   80
Fury the *Dane*: The *Swede* by Melancholy:[10]
By stupid Ignorance, the *Muscovite*:
The *Chinese* by a *Child of Hell*, called Wit:
Wealth makes the *Persian* too Effeminate:
And Poverty the *Tartars* Desperate: 85
The *Turks* and *Moors* by *Mah'met* he subdues:
And God has given him leave to rule the Jews:
Rage rules the *Portuguese*; and Fraud the *Scotch*:
Revenge the *Pole*; and Avarice the *Dutch*.
   Satire be kind, and draw a silent Veil,   90
Thy *Native England*'s Vices to conceal:
Or if that Task's impossible to do,
At least be just, and show her Virtues too;
Too Great the first, Alas! the last too Few.
   England unknown as yet, unpeopled lay;   95
Happy, had she remained so to this day,
And not to every Nation been a Prey.
Her Open Harbours, and her Fertile Plains,
The Merchant's Glory these, and those the Swains,
To every Barbarous Nation have betrayed her,   100
Who conquer her as oft as they Invade her.
So Beauty guarded but by Innocence,
That ruins her which should be her Defence.
   Ingratitude, a Devil of Black *Renown*,
Possessed her very early for his own.   105
An Ugly, Surly, Sullen, Selfish Spirit,
Who Satan's *worst Perfections does inherit*:
Second to him in Malice and in Force,
All *Devil without*, and all *within* him *Worse.*
   He made her First-born Race to be so rude,   110
And suffered her to be so oft subdued:
By several Crowds of Wand'ring Thieves o'er-run,
Often unpeopled, and as oft undone.
While every Nation that her Powers reduced,
Their Languages and Manners introduced.   115
From whose mixed Relics our compounded Breed,
By Spurious Generation does succeed;
Making a Race uncertain and unev'n,
Derived from all the Nations under Heav'n.
   The *Romans* first with *Julius Cæsar* came,   120
Including all the Nations of that Name,

---

[9] *Rush* Russ, Russians.   [10] *Melancholy* madness.

Gauls, Greeks, and *Lombards*; and by Computation,[11]
Auxiliaries, or Slaves of every Nation.
With *Hengist, Saxons*; Danes with *Sueno* Came,[12]
In search of Plunder, not in search of Fame.   125
Scots, Picts and *Irish* from th' *Hibernian* Shore;[13]
And Conqu'ring *William* brought the *Normans* o'er.

    All these their Barb'rous off-spring left behind
The Dregs of Armies, they of all Mankind;
Blended with *Britains* who before were here,   130
Of whom the *Welsh* have blest the Character.

    From this Amphibious Ill-born Mob began
That vain ill natured thing, an Englishman.
The Customs, Surnames, Languages, and Manners,
Of all these Nations are their own Explainers: 135
Whose Relics are so lasting and so strong,
They have left a *Shibboleth* upon our Tongue;[14]
By which with easy search you may distinguish
Your *Roman-Saxon-Danish-Norman* English.

    The great Invading *Norman* let us know[15]   140
What Conquerors in After-Times might do.
To every *Musketeer* he brought to *Town*,[16]
He gave the Lands which never were his own.
When first the *English* Crown he did obtain,
He did not send his *Dutchmen* home again.[17]   145
No Reassumptions in his Reign were known,[18]
Davenant might there have let his Book alone.[19]
No Parliament his Army could disband;
He raised no Money, for he paid in Land.
He gave his Legions their Eternal Station,   150
And made them all Freeholders of the Nation.
He cantoned out the Country to his Men,
And every Soldier was a Denizen.
The Rascals thus enriched, he called them *Lords*,
To please their Upstart Pride with new-made Words;   155
And *Doomsday-Book* his Tyranny records.[20]

    And here begins the Ancient Pedigree
That so exalts our Poor Nobility:

---

[11] *Gauls, Greeks, and Lombards*   peoples conquered by the Romans and pressed into military service for them.
[12] *Hengist*   with his brother Horsa, he came from the region of southern Denmark to found Kent in England around 449; *Sueno*   King Sweyn II (d. 1075) assisted Anglo-Saxon rebels in England for a year but settled with William the Conqueror and withdrew in 1070.
[13] *Picts*   an ancient people of northern England; *Hibernian*   Irish.
[14] *Shibboleth*   a test word that identifies a speaker as belonging to an ethnic, political, religious or other such group (see Judges 12.6).

[15] *Invading Norman*   William the Conqueror [Defoe's note].
[16] *Musketeer*   Or Archer [Defoe's note].
[17] *Dutchmen*   the nationality of King William's guard, not William the Conqueror's.
[18] *Reassumption*   the act of the crown in reassuming ownership of lands once granted to others.
[19] *Davenant*   Charles Davenant, *A Discourse upon Grants and Resumptions.*
[20] *Doomsday-Book*   the record of the survey of lands made by William the Conqueror in 1086.

'Tis that from some *French* Trooper they derive,
Who with the *Norman* Bastard did arrive:[21] 160
The Trophies of the Families appear;
Some show the Sword, the Bow, and some the Spear,
Which their Great Ancestor, *forsooth*, did wear.
These in Herald's Register remain,
Their Noble Mean Extraction to explain. 165
Yet who the Hero was, no man can tell,
Whether a Drummer, or a Colonel:
The silent Record blushes to reveal
Their Undescended Dark Original.
    But grant the best, How came the Change to pass; 170
A *True-Born Englishman* of *Norman* Race?
A *Turkish* Horse can show more History,
To prove his Well-descended Family.
Conquest, as by the Moderns 'tis expressed,
May give a Title to the Lands possessed: 175
But that the Longest Sword should be so Civil,
To make a *Frenchman English*, that's the Devil.
    These are the Heroes that despise the *Dutch*,
And rail at new-come Foreigners so much;
Forgetting that themselves are all derived 180
From the most Scoundrel Race that ever lived,
A horrid Medley of Thieves and Drones,
Who ransacked Kingdoms, and dispeopled Towns.
The *Pict* and Painted *Britain*, Treach'rous *Scot*,[22]
By Hunger, Theft, and Rapine, hither brought. 185
Norwegian Pirates, Buccaneering *Danes*,
Whose Red-haired Off-spring every where remains.
Who joined with *Norman-French* compound the Breed
From whence your *True-Born Englishmen* proceed
    And lest by Length of Time it be pretended, 190
The Climate may this Modern Breed have mended,
Wise Providence, to keep us where we are,
Mixes us daily with exceeding Care:
We have been *Europe*'s Sink, *the Jakes* where she[23]
Voids all her Offal Out-cast Progeny. 195
From our Fifth *Henry*'s time, the Strolling Bands
Of banished Fugitives from Neighb'ring Lands,
Have here a certain Sanctuary found:
The Eternal Refuge of the Vagabond.
Where in but half a common Age of Time, 200
Borr'wing new Blood and Manners from the Clime,
Proudly they learn all Mankind to contemn,

---

[21] *Norman Bastard* William I of England was William the bastard son and heir of Robert the Devil, Duke of Normandy.

[22] *Painted Britain* Roman conquerors described the inhabitants of Britain as painted for ceremony or war.
[23] *Jakes* "A house of office" (Johnson); privy; toilet.

And all their Race are *True-Born Englishmen*.

Dutch, *Walloons*, *Flemings*, *Irishmen*, and *Scots*,[24]
Vaudois and *Valtolins*, and *Huguenots*,[25]   205
In good Queen *Bess*'s Charitable Reign,[26]
Supplied us with Three hundred thousand Men.
Religion, *God we thank thee*, sent them hither,
Priests, Protestants, the Devil and all together:
Of all Professions, and of every Trade,   210
All that were persecuted or afraid;
Whether for Debt or other Crimes they fled,
David at *Hackelah* was still their Head.[27]

The Offspring of this Miscellaneous Crowd,
Had not their new Plantations long enjoyed,   215
But they grew *Englishmen*, and raised their Votes
At Foreign Shoals of *Interloping Scots*.
The Royal Branch from *Pict-land* did succeed,[28]
With Troops of *Scots* and Scabs from *North-by-Tweed*[29].
The Seven first Years of his Pacific Reign,   220
Made him and half his Nation *Englishmen*.
Scots from the *Northern* Frozen Banks of *Tay*,
With Packs and Plods came *Whigging* all away:[30]
Thick as the Locusts which in *Egypt* swarmed,[31]
With Pride and hungry Hopes completely armed: 225
With Native Truth, Diseases, and no Money,
Plundered our *Canaan* of the Milk and Honey.[32]
Here they grew quickly Lords and Gentlemen,
And all their Race are *True-Born Englishmen*.

The Civil Wars, the common Purgative,   230
Which always use to make the Nation thrive,
Made way for all the strolling Congregation,[33]
Which thronged in Pious *Ch——s* 's Restoration.[34]
The *Royal Refugee* our Breed restores,
With *Foreign Courtiers*, and with *Foreign Whores*:   235
And carefully repeopled us again,

---

[24] *Walloons* a people of Gallic origins inhabiting southern Belgium in the sixteenth century; *Flemings* Flemish people; inhabitants of Flanders.
[25] *Vaudois* a Protestant sect of southern France; *Valtolins* natives of Valtellina in present-day Switzerland; *Huguenots* a sect of French Protestants.
[26] *Queen Bess* Queen Elizabeth I reigned from 1558–1603; some members of sects persecuted in Roman Catholic countries took refuge in Protestant England.
[27] *David at Hackelah* David and his followers fled from King Saul and sheltered in a stronghold on the hill of Hachilah (1 Samuel 23.19).
[28] James VI of Scotland (*Pict land*) became James I of England in 1603, thus beginning the reign of the House of Stuart.

[29] *Scab* "A paltry fellow, so named from the itch often incident to negligent poverty" (Johnson); *North-by-Tweed* Scotland, which is divided from England by the River Tweed.
[30] *Whigging* jogging.
[31] *Locusts* "they covered the face of the whole earth" (Exodus 10.15).
[32] *Canaan* the promised land of the Israelites in the Bible, "a land that floweth with milk and honey" (Joshua 5.6).
[33] *strolling* from "stroll," "To wander; to ramble; to rove; to be a vagrant" (Johnson).
[34] *Ch{arles}* II, restored to the throne in 1660, after a long, enforced sojourn in France.

Throughout his Lazy, Long, Lascivious Reign;
With such a blest and True-Born *English* Fry,
As much Illustrates our Nobility.[35]
A Gratitude which will so black appear,   240
As future Ages must abhor to hear:
When they look back on all that Crimson Flood,
Which streamed in *Lindsey*'s, and *Caernarvon*'s Blood:[36]
Bold *Strafford, Cambridge, Capel, Lucas, Lisle*,
Who crowned in Death his Father's Fun'ral Pile,   245
The loss of whom, in order to supply,
With True-Born *English* Nobility,
Six Bastard Dukes survive his Luscious Reign,[37]
The Labours of *Italian C———n*,[38]
French P———h, Taby S———t, and Cambrian.   250
Besides the Num'rous Bright and Virgin Throng,
Whose Female Glories shade them from my Song.
     This Offspring, if one Age they multiply,
May half the House with *English* Peers supply:[39]
There with true *English* Pride they may contemn   255
S———g and *P———d*, new-made Noblemen.[40]
     French Cooks, *Scotch* Pedlars, and *Italian* Whores,
Were all made Lords, or Lords' Progenitors.
Beggars and Bastards by his new Creation,
Much multiplied the Peerage of the Nation;   260
Who will be all, e'er one short Age runs o'er,
As *True-Born* Lords as those we had before.
     Then to recruit the Commons he prepares,
And heal the latent Breaches of the Wars:
The Pious Purpose better to advance,   265
H' invites the banished Protestants of *France*:
Hither for God's sake and their own they fled,
Some for Religion came, and some for Bread:
Two hundred thousand Pair of Wooden Shoes,[41]
Who, God be thanked, had nothing left to lose;   270
To Heav'n great Praise did for Religion fly,
To make us starve our Poor in Charity.
In every Port they plant their fruitful Train,
To get a Race of *True-Born Englishmen*:

---

[35] *Illustrate* "To brighten with honour" (Johnson);
Charles created a great many new nobles upon his return.
[36] *Lindsey . . . Caernarvon . . . Strafford, Cambridge,
Capel, Lucas, Lisle* all noblemen killed in the Civil War.
[37] *Six Bastard Dukes* Charles created six of his illegitimate sons dukes.
[38] *Italian C{astlemai}n, French P{ortsmout}h, Taby
S{lu}t, and Cambrian* mothers of Charles's illegitimate
children, Barbara Villiers, Louise de Keroualle, Nell
Gwynne, and Lucy Walter.

[39] *House* the House of Lords, the non-elective branch
of Parliament.
[40] *S{chomberg}* Frederick Herman von Schomberg
(1640–90), German-born English noble and gallant soldier killed at Boyne; *P{ortland}* William Bentinck,
first Earl of Portland (1649–1709), Dutch-born English
noble, close confidant of William III.
[41] *Wooden Shoes* a sign of indigence or rusticity.

Whose Children will, when Riper Years they see,   275
Be as Ill-natured and as Proud as we:
Call them *English*, Foreigners despise,
Be Surly like us all, and just as Wise.
    Thus from a Mixture of all Kinds began,
That Het'rogeneous *Thing, An Englishman*:   280
In eager Rapes, and furious Lust begot,
Betwixt a Painted *Britain* and a *Scot*:
Whose gend'ring Offspring quickly learnt to bow,[42]
And Yoke their Heifers to the *Roman* Plough:
From whence a Mongrel half-bred Race there came,   285
With neither Name nor Nation, Speech nor Fame.
In whose hot Veins new Mixtures quickly ran,
Infused betwixt a *Saxon* and a *Dane*.
While their Rank Daughters, to their Parents just,
Received all Nations with Promiscuous Lust.   290
This Nauseous Blood directly did contain
The well-extracted Blood of *Englishmen*.
    Which Medley cantoned in a Heptarchy[43],
A Rhapsody of Nations to supply,
Among themselves maintained eternal Wars,   295
And still the Ladies loved the Conquerors.
The *Western* Angles all the rest subdued;
A bloody Nation, barbarous and rude:
Who by the Tenure of the Sword possessed
One part of *Britain*, and subdued the rest.   300
And as great things denominate the small,
The Conqu'ring part gave Title to the Whole.
The *Scot, Pict, Britian, Roman, Dane* submit,
And with the *English-Saxon* all unite:
And these the Mixture have so close pursued,   305
The very Name and Memory's subdued:
No *Roman* now, no *Britain* does remain;
Wales strove to separate, but strove in vain:
The silent Nations undistinguished fall,
And *Englishman*'s the common Name for all.   310
Fate jumbled them together, *God knows how*;
Whate'er they were, they're *True-Born English* now.
    The Wonder which remains is at our Pride,
To value that which all wise men deride.
For *Englishmen* to boast of Generation,[44]   315
Cancels their Knowledge, and lampoons the Nation.
A *True-Born Englishman*'s a Contradiction,

---

[42] *gender* "To copulate; to breed" (Johnson).   [44] *Generation* "A family; a race" (Johnson).
[43] *Heptarchy* the seven kingdoms of the Angles and
Saxons (sixth to ninth centuries).

In Speech an Irony, in Fact a Fiction.
A Banter made to be a Test of Fools,
Which those that use it justly ridicules.   320
A Metaphor invented to express
A Man *a-kin* to all the Universe.

   For as the *Scots*, as Learned Men have said,
Throughout the World their Wand'ring Seed have spread;
So open-handed *England*, 'tis believed,   325
Has all the Gleanings of the World received.

   Some think of *England* 'twas our Saviour meant,
The Gospel should to all the World be sent:
Since when the blessèd Sound did hither reach,
They to all Nations might be said to Preach.   330

   'Tis well that Virtue gives Nobility,
Else God knows where we had our Gentry;
Since scarce one Family is left alive,
Which does not from some Foreigner derive.
Of Sixty thousand *English* Gentlemen,   335
Whose Names and Arms in Registers remain,
We challenge all our Heralds to declare
Ten Families which *English-Saxons* are.

   France justly boasts the Ancient Noble Line
Of *Bourbon, Mommorency,* and *Lorrain.*   340
The *Germans* too their House of *Austria* show,
And *Holland* their Invincible *Nassau,*
Lines which in Heraldry were Ancient grown,
Before the Name of *Englishman* was known.
Even *Scotland* too, her Elder Glory shows,   345
Her *Gordons, Hamiltons,* and her *Monroes;*
Douglas, Mackays, and *Grahams,* Names well known,
Long before Ancient *England* knew her own.

   But *England*, Modern to the last degree,
Borrows or makes her own Nobility,   350
And yet she boldly boasts of Pedigree:
Repines that Foreigners are put upon her,
And talks of her Antiquity and Honour:
Her S [ackvi]*lls,* S [avi]*ls,* C [eci]*ls, De-la-M* [ere]*s,*
M [ohu]*ns* and M[ontag]*ues,* D [urase]*s* and V [ere]*s,*   355
Not one have *English* Names, yet all are *English* Peers.
Your H[oublons], P[apillons], and L[ethuliers],
Pass now for True-Born *English* Knights and Squires,
And make good Senate-Members, or Lord-Mayors.
Wealth, howsoever got, in *England* makes   360
Lords of Mechanics, Gentlemen of Rakes.
Antiquity and Birth are needless here;
'Tis Impudence and Money makes a P[ee]r.

   Innumerable City-Knights we know,

From *Bluecoat Hospitals* and *Bridewell* flow.[45]   365
Draymen and Porters fill the City Chair,
And Footboys Magisterial Purple wear.
Fate has but very small Distinction set
Betwixt the *Counter* and the Coronet.[46]
Tarpaulin Lords, Pages of high Renown,[47]   370
Rise up by Poor Men's Valour, not their own.
Great Families of yesterday we show,
And Lords, whose Parents were *the Lord knows who*.

FROM PART 2

The Breed's described: Now, *Satire*, if you can,
Their Temper show, for *Manners make the Man*.[48]
Fierce as the *Britain*, as the *Roman* Brave;
And less inclined to Conquer than to Save:
Eager to fight, and lavish of their Blood;   5
And equally of *Fear and Forecast* void.
The *Pict* has made 'em Sour, the *Dane* Morose;
False from the *Scot*, and from the *Norman* worse.
What Honesty they have, the *Saxons* gave them,
And That, now they grow old, begins to leave them.   10
The Climate makes them Terrible and Bold;
The *English* Beef their Courage does uphold:
No Danger can their Daring Spirit pall,
Always provided that their Belly's full.

In close Intrigues their Faculty's but weak,   15
For gen'rally whate'er they know, they speak:
And often their own Councils undermine
By their Infirmity, and not design.
From whence the Learnèd say it does proceed,
That *English* Treasons never can succeed: 20
For they're so open-hearted, you may know
Their own most secret Thoughts, and others too.

The Lab'ring Poor, in spite of Double Pay,
Are *Saucy, Mutinous*, and *Beggarly*:
So lavish of their Money and their Time,   25
That want of Forecast is the Nation's Crime.
Good Drunken Company is their Delight;
And what they get by Day, they spend by Night.
Dull Thinking seldom does their Heads engage,
But Drink their Youth away, and hurry on Old Age.   30
Empty of all good Husbandry and Sense;
And void of Manners most, when void of Pence.

---

[45]   *Bluecoat Hospitals and Bridewell*   a "hospital" was "A place built for the reception of the sick, or support of the poor" (Johnson); Bluecoat (or Christ-Church) and Bridewell served as orphanages and poor houses.

[46]   *Counter*   debtors' prison.
[47]   *Tarpaulin*   nickname for a common sailor.
[48]   *Manners make the Man*   a proverb attributed to William Wickham, Bishop of Winchester (1367–1404).

Their strong Aversion to Behaviour's such,
They always talk too little, or too much.
So dull, they never take the pains to think; 35
And seldon are good-natured, *but in Drink*.

    In *English* Ale their dear Enjoyment lies,
For which they'll starve themselves and Families.
An Englishman will fairly drink as much
As will maintain Two Families of Dutch: 40
Subjecting all their Labour to the Pots;
The greatest Artists are the greatest Sots.

    The Country Poor do by Example live;
The Gentry Lead them, and the Clergy drive:
What may we not from such Examples hope? 45
The Landlord is their God, the Priest their Pope.
A Drunken Clergy, and a Swearing Bench,
Has giv'n the Reformation such a Drench,
As wise men think there is some cause to doubt,[49]
Will purge Good Manners and Religion out. 40

    Nor do the Poor alone their Liquor prize,
The *Sages* join in this great Sacrifice.
The Learnèd Men who study *Aristotle*,
Correct him with an Explanation-Bottle;
Praise *Epicurus* rather than *Lysander*,[50] 55
And *Aristippus* more than *Alexander*.[51]
The Doctors too their Galen here resign,[52]
And gen'rally prescribe *Specific Wine*.
The Graduates Study's grown an easier Task,
While for the *Urinal* they toss the *Flask*.[53] 60
The Surgeon's Art grows plainer ev'ry Hour,
And Wine's the Balm which into Wounds they pour.

    Poets long since *Parnassus* have forsaken,[54]
And say the ancient Bards were all mistaken.
Apollo's lately abdicate and fled, 65
And good King Bacchus reigneth in his stead;
He does the Chaos of the Head refine,
And Atom-Thoughts jump into Words by Wine:[55]
The Inspiration's of a finer Nature;
As Wine must needs excel *Parnassus* Water. 70
    Statesman their weighty Politics refine,

---

[49] *doubt* expect, think.
[50] *Epicurus* founder of the Epicurean school, (inaccurately) thought of as devoted to sensual pleasure; *Lysander* a Spartan general.
[51] *Aristippus* The Drunkards Name for Canary [Defoe's note]; *Canary* is a kind of wine; Aristippus was the name of a Greek of luxurious habits and another man who founded the Cyrenaic school of thought in which the present moment contains the only reality.

[52] *Galen* a book of medicine named after the second-century CE physician.
[53] *Urinal* a bottle used for medical inspection of urine.
[54] *Parnassus* the principal seat of Apollo and the muses.
[55] *Atom-Thoughts* tiny bits of thought.

And Soldiers raise their Courages by Wine.
Cæcilia gives her Choristers their Choice,[56]
And lets them all drink Wine to clear their Voice.
    Some think the Clergy first found out the way,   75
And Wine's the only Spirit by which they Pray.
But others less profane than so, agree,
It clears the Lungs, and helps the Memory:
And therefore all of them Divinely think,
Instead of Study, 'tis as well to drink.   80
    And here I would be very glad to know,
Whether our *Asgilites* may drink or no.[57]
Th' Enlight'ning Fumes of Wine would certainly
Assist them much *when they begin to fly*:
Or if a Fiery Chariot should appear,   85
Inflamed by Wine, they'd have the less to fear.
    Even the Gods themselves, as Mortals say,
Were they on Earth, would be as drunk as they:
Nectar would be no more Celestial Drink,
They'd all take *Wine*, to teach them how to Think.   90
But *English* Drunkards, Gods and men outdo,
Drink their Estates away, and Senses too.
Colon's in Debt, and if his Friends should fail
To help him out, must die at last in Gaol:
His *Wealthy Uncle* sent a Hundred Nobles,   95
To pay his Trifles off, and rid him of his Troubles:
But *Colon*, like a *True-Born Englishman*,
Drank all the Money out in bright Champagne;
And *Colon* does in Custody remain.
Drunk'ness has been the Darling of the Realm,   100
E'er since a Drunken Pilot had the Helm.[58]
    In their Religion they are so unev'n,
That each man goes *his own By-way to Heaven.*
Tenacious of Mistakes to that degree,
That every Man pursues it separately,   105
And fancies none can find the Way but he:
So shy of one another they are grown,
As if they strove to get to Heav'n alone.
Rigid and Zealous, Positive and Grave,
And every Grace, but Charity, they have: 110
This makes them so Ill-natured and Uncivil,
That all men think an *Englishman* the Devil.
    Surly to Strangers, Froward to their Friend;[59]
Submit to Love with a reluctant Mind;
Resolved to be ungrateful and unkind.   115

---

[56] *Cæcilia* patron saint of music.
[57] *Asgilites* followers of John Asgil (1659–1738) who believed it was possible to get to Heaven without dying.
[58] *Drunken Pilot* Charles II.
[59] *Froward* "Peevish; angry; ungovernable; perverse" (Johnson).

If by Necessity reduced to ask,
The Giver has the difficultest Task:
For what's bestowed they awkwardly receive,
And always Take less freely than they Give.
The Obligation is their highest Grief;   120
And never love, where they accept Relief.
So sullen in their Sorrows, that 'tis known,
They'll rather die than their Afflictions own
And if relieved, it is too often true,
That they'll abuse their Benefactors too: 125
For in Distress their Haughty Stomach's such,
They hate to see themselves obliged too much.
Seldom contented, often in the wrong;
Hard to be pleased at all, and never long.

    If your Mistakes their Ill Opinion gain,   130
No Merit can their Favour reobtain:
And if they're not Vindictive in their Fury,
'Tis their unconstant Temper does secure ye:
Their Brain's so cool, their Passion seldom burns;
For all's condensed before the Flame returns: 135
The Fermentation's of so weak a Matter,
The Humid damps the Fume, and runs it all to Water.
So though the Inclination may be strong,
They're pleased by Fits, and never angry long.

    Then if Good Nature shows some slender Proof,   140
They never think they have Reward enough:
But like our *Modern Quakers* of the Town,
Expect your Manners, and return you none.

    Friendship, th' abstracted Union of the Mind,
Which all men seek, but very few can find: 145
Of all the Nations in the Universe,
None talk on't more, or understand it less:
For if it does their Property annoy,
Their Property their Friendship will destroy.

    As you discourse them, you shall hear them tell 150
All things in which they think they do excel:
No Panegyric needs their Praise record;
An Englishman ne 'er wants his own good word.
His long Discourse gen'rally appear
Prologued with his own wond'rous Character: 155
When, to illustrate his own good Name,
He never fails his Neighbour to defame:
And yet he really designs no wrong;
His Malice goes no further than his Tongue.
But pleased to Tattle, he delights to Rail,   160
To satisfy the Lech'ry of a Tale.
His own dear Praises close the ample Speech,
Tells you how Wise he is; *that is, how Rich*:

For Wealth is Wisdom; he that's Rich is wise;
And all men Learnèd Poverty despise.   165
His Generosity comes next, and then
Concludes that he's a *True-Born Englishman*;
And they, 'tis known, are Generous and Free,
Forgetting, and Forgiving Injury:
Which may be true, thus rightly understood,   170
Forgiving Ill Turns, and Forgetting Good.
    Cheerful in Labour when they've undertook it;
But out of Humour, when they're out of Pocket.
But if their Belly and their Pocket's full,
They may be Phelgmatic, but never Dull: 175
And if a Bottle does their Brains refine,
It makes their Wit as sparkling as their Wine.
    As for the general Vices which we find
They're guilty of in common with Mankind,
Satire, forbear, and silently endure;   180
We must conceal the Crimes we cannot cure.
Nor shall my Verse the brighter Sex defame;
For *English* Beauty will preserve her Name.
Beyond dispute, Agreeable and Fair;
And Modester than other Nations are: 185
For where the Vice prevails, the great Temptation
Is want of Money, more than Inclination.
In general, this only is allowed,
They're something Noisy, and a little Proud.
    An *Englishman* is gentlest in Command;   190
Obedience is a Stranger in the Land:
Hardly subjected to the Magistrate;
For Englishmen *do all Subjection hate.*
Humblest when Rich, but peevish when they're Poor;
And think whate'er they have, they Merit more.   195
. . . .

    The meanest *English* Ploughman studies Law,
And keeps thereby the Magistrates in Awe:
Will boldly tell them what they ought to do,
And sometimes punish their Omissions too.   230
    Their Liberty and Property's so dear,
They Scorn their Laws or Governors to fear:
So bugbeared with the Name of Slavery,
They can't submit to their own Liberty.
Restraint from Ill is Freedom to the Wise;   235
But Englishmen *do all Restraint despise.*
Slaves to the Liquor, Drudges to the Pots,
The Mob are Statesman, and their Statesmen Sots.
    Their Governors they count such dangerous things,
That 'tis their custom to affront their Kings: 240
So jealous of the Power their Kings possessed,

They suffered neither Power nor Kings to rest.
The Bad with Force they eagerly subdue;
The Good with constant Clamours they pursue:
And did King Jesus reign, they'd murmur too.   245
A discontented Nation, and by far
Harder to rule in Times of Peace than War:
Easily set together by the Ears,
And full of causeless Jealousies and Fears:
Apt to revolt, and willing to rebel,   250
And never are contented when they're well.
No Government could ever please them long,
Could tie their Hands, or rectify their Tongue.
In this to Ancient Israel well compared,
Eternal Murmurs are among them heard.[60]   255

THE CONCLUSION

Then let us boast of Ancestors no more,
Or Deeds of Heroes done in days of Yore,
In latent Records of Ages past,
Behind the Rear of Time, in long Oblivion placed.
For if our Virtues must in Lines descend,   5
The Merit with the Families would end:
And Intermixtures would most fatal grow;
For Vice would be Hereditary too;
The Tainted Blood would of necessity,
Involuntary Wickedness convey.
     Vice, like Ill Nature, for an Age or two,
May seem a Generation to pursue;
But Virtue seldom does regard the Breed;
Fools do the Wise, and Wise Men Fools succeed.
     What is 't to us, what Ancestors we had?   15
If Good, what better? or what worse, if Bad?
Examples are for Imitation set,
Yet all men follow Virtue with Regret.
     Could but our Ancestors retrieve their Fate,
And see their Offspring thus degenerate;   20
How we contend for Birth and Names unknown,
And build on their past Actions, not our own;
They'd cancel Records, and their Tombs deface,
And openly disown the vile degenerate Race;
For Fame of Families is all a Cheat,   25
'Tis Personal Virtue only makes us great.

---

[60] *Murmur* "A complaint half suppressed; a complaint not openly uttered" (Johnson; see Exodus 16.2).

The Shortest-Way with the Dissenters:[1] Or Proposals for the Establishment of the Church (1702)

Sir *Roger L'Estrange* tells us a Story in his Collection of Fables,[2] of the Cock and the Horses. The Cock was gotten to Roost in the Stable, among the Horses, and there being no Racks or other Conveniencies for him, it seems, he was forced to roost upon the Ground; the Horses jostling about for room, and putting the Cock in danger of his Life, he gives them this grave Advice: 'Pray Gentlefolks let us stand still, for fear we should tread upon one or another'.

There are some People in the World, who now they are *unperched*, and reduced to an Equality with other People, and under strong and very just Apprehensions of being further treated as they deserve, begin with *Æsop's* Cock, to Preach up to Peace and Union, and the Christian Duties of Moderation, forgetting, that when they had the Power in their Hands, those Graces were Strangers in their Gates.

It is now near Fourteen Years,[3] that the Glory and Peace of the purest and most flourishing Church in the World has been Eclipsed, Buffeted, and Disturbed by a sort of Men, who God in his Providence has suffered to insult over her, and bring her down; these have been the Days of her Humiliation and Tribulation: She has borne with an invincible Patience the Reproach of the Wicked, and God has at last heard her Prayers, and delivered her from the Oppression of the Stranger.[4]

And now they find their Day is over, their Power gone, and the Throne of this Nation possessed by a Royal, *English*, True, and ever Constant Member of, and Friend to the Church of *England*. Now they find that they are in danger of the Church of *England's* just Resentments; now they cry out, *Peace*, *Union*, *Forbearance*, and *Charity*, as if the Church had not too long harboured her Enemies under her Wing, and nourished the viperous Brood, till they hiss and fly in the Face of the Mother that cherished them.[5]

No Gentlemen, the Time of Mercy is past, your *Day of Grace is over*; you should have practised Peace, and Moderation, and Charity, if you expected any your selves.

We have heard none of this Lesson for Fourteen Years past: We have been huffed and bullied with your Act of Toleration;[6] you have told us that you are the *Church established by Law*, as well as others; have set up your Canting-Synagogues at our Church-Doors, and the Church and her Members have been loaded with Reproaches, with Oaths, Associations, Abjurations, and what not; where has been the Mercy, the Forbearance, the Charity you have

---

THE SHORTEST-WAY WITH THE DISSENTERS

[1] *Dissenters* non-conformists, members of religious sects separate from the Church of England; these people and their educational academies were tolerated during the reign of William III, but when she ascended the throne in March 1702 Queen Anne made it clear that she would favor members of the national church. High Tory clergymen, especially a charismatic speaker named Henry Sacheverell, pressed the point and called for the suppression of dissenters and the extirpation of their academies. Defoe's brilliant essay is an answer to Sacheverell so deeply ironical that it was at first taken by many people as a defense of the High Tory position. When its meaning became clear, a warrant was issued for Defoe's arrest (see below, pp. 527–8); he was very heavily fined, made to stand in the public stocks, and imprisoned.

[2] *Roger L'Estrange* Tory journalist and voluminous writer, author of *The Fables of Aesop* (1692).
[3] *Fourteen Years* the length of William III's reign.
[4] *Stranger* "deliver thee from the strange woman, even from the stranger . . . Which forsaketh the guide of her youth, and forgetteth the covenant of her God" (Proverbs 16–22)
[5] *viperous Brood . . . them* it was popularly believed that snakes tore through the mother's womb in birth, in revenge of the mother's biting off the head of the father in conception (Browne, *Pseudodoxia Epidemica*, chapter 16).
[6] *Act of Toleration* a bill passed May 24, 1689, granting freedom of worship to Protestant dissenters, provided they took an oath of allegiance.

shown to *tender Consciences of the Church of England*, that could not take Oaths *as fast as you made 'em*; that having sworn Allegiance to their lawful and rightful King,[7] could not dispense with that Oath, *their King being still alive*, and swear to your new *Hodge-podge of a Dutch-Government*.[8] These ha' been turned out of their Livings, and they and their Families left to starve; their Estates double Taxed to carry on a War[9] they had *no Hand in*, and you *got nothing by*: What Account can you give of the Multitudes you have forced to comply, against their Consciences, with your new *sophistical Politics*, who like the new Converts[10] in *France*, Sin because they can't Starve. And now the Tables are turned upon you, *you must not be Persecuted, 'tis not a Christian Spirit*.

You have *Butchered* one King, *Deposed* another King, and made a *mock King* of a Third; and yet you could have the Face to expect to be employed and trusted by the Fourth;[11] any body that did not know the Temper of your Party, would stand amazed at the Impudence, as well as Folly, to think of it.

Your Management of your *Dutch Monarch*, whom you reduced to a mere *King of Cl* [*ub*]*s*, is enough to give any future Princes such an Idea of your Principles, as to warn them sufficiently from coming into your Clutches; and God be thanked, the Queen is out of your Hands, knows you, and will have a care of you.

There is no doubt but the supreme Authority of a Nation has in it self a Power, *and a Right to that Power*, to execute the Laws upon any Part of that nation it governs. The execution of the known Laws of the Land, and that with but a weak and gentle Hand neither, was all that the fanatical Party of this Land have ever called Persecution; this they have magnified to a height, that the sufferings of the *Huguenots* in *France*[12] were not to be compared with – Now to execute the known Laws of a Nation upon those who transgress them, after having first been voluntarily consenting to the making those Laws, can never be called Persecution, but Justice. But Justice is always Violence to the Party offending, for every Man is Innocent in his own Eyes. The first execution of the Laws against Dissenters in *England*, was in the Days of King *James* the First; and what did it amount to, truly? the worst they suffered, was at their own request, to let them go to *New-England*, and erect a new Colony,[13] and give them great Privileges, Grants, and suitable Powers, keep them under Protection, and defend them against all Invaders, and receive no Taxes or Revenue from them. This was the cruelty of the Church of *England*, fatal Lenity! 'Twas the ruin of that excellent Prince, King *Charles* the First. Had King *James* sent all the Puritans in *England* away to the *West-Indies*, we had been a national unmixed Church; the Church of *England* had been kept undivided and entire.

To requite the Lenity of the Father, they take up Arms against the Son; Conquer, Pursue, Take, Imprison, and at last put to Death the anointed of God, and destroy the very Being and Nature of Government, setting up a sordid Impostor,[14] who had neither Title to Govern, nor Understanding to Manage, but supplied that want with Power, bloody and desperate Councils and Craft, without Conscience.

---

[7] *rightful King*   James II.

[8] *Dutch-Government*   the Government of William III.

[9] *War*   one phase of the war against France, initiated in the Treaty of Vienna (1689).

[10] *new Converts*   French Protestants forced to convert to Roman Catholicism.

[11] *Fourth*   Queen Anne, following Charles I, James II, and William III in this list.

[12] *Huguenots in France*   thousands were slain in the infamous Massacre of St Bartholomew's Day on the night of 24/25 August 1572.

[13] *New Colony*   Plymouth, in present-day Massachusetts, was founded by the Pilgrims who sailed on the *Mayflower* in 1620.

[14] *sordid Imposter*   Oliver Cromwell, Lord Protector of the Commonwealth of England, Scotland, and Ireland, 1653–8.

Had not King *James* the First witheld the full execution of the Laws; had he given them strict Justice, he had cleared the Nation of them, and the Consequences had been plain; his *Son had never been murdered by them*, nor the Monarchy overwhelmed; 'twas *too much Mercy* shown them, was the ruin of his Posterity, and the ruin of the Nation's Peace. One would think the Dissenters should not have the Face to believe that we are to be wheedled and canted into Peace and Toleration, when they know that they have once requited us with a civil War, and once with an intolerable and unrighteous Persecution for our former Civility.

Nay, to encourage us to be Easy with them, 'tis apparent, that they never had the Upper-hand of the Church, but[15] they treated her with all the Severity, with all the Reproach and Contempt as was possible: What Peace, and what Mercy did they show the Loyal Gentry of the Church of *England* in the time of their Triumphant Common-Wealth? How did they put all the Gentry of *England* to ransom, whether they were actually in Arms for the King or Not, making People compound[16] for their Estates, and starve their Families? How did they treat the Clergy of the Church of *England*, sequestered the Ministers, devoured the Patrimony of the Church, and divided the Spoil, by sharing the Church-Lands among their Soldiers, and turning her Clergy out to starve; just such Measure as they have mete, should be measured to them again.

Charity and Love is the known Doctrine of the Church of *England*, and 'tis plain she has put it in practice towards the Dissenters, even beyond what they ought, till she has been wanting to her self, and in effect, unkind to her own Sons; particularly, in the too much Lenity of King *James* the First, mentioned before, had he so rooted the Puritans from the Face of the Land, which he had an opportunity early to have done, they had not the Power to vex the Church, as since they have done.

In the Days of King *Charles* the Second, how did the Church reward their bloody Doings with Lenity and Mercy,[17] *except the barbarous Regicides of the pretended Court of Justice*; not a Soul suffered for the Blood in an unnatural War: King *Charles* came in all Mercy and Love, cherished them, preferred them, employed them, witheld the rigour of the Law, and oftentimes, even agianst the Advice of his Parliament, gave them liberty of Conscience; and how did they requite him with the villainous Contrivance to Depose and Murder him and his Successor at the *Rye-Plot*.[18]

King *James*, as if Mercy was the inherent Quality of the Family, began his Reign with unusual Favour to them: Nor could their joining with the Duke of *Monmouth* against him, move him to do himself Justice upon them; but that mistaken Prince thought to win them by Gentleness and Love, proclaimed an universal Liberty[19] to them and rather discountenanced the Church of *England* than them; how they requited him all the World knows.

The late Reign is too fresh in the Memory of all the World to need a Comment; how under Pretence of joining with the Church in redressing some Grievances, they pushed things to that extremity, in conjunction with some mistaken Gentlemen, as to Depose the late King, as if the Grievance of the Nation could not have been redressed but by the absolute ruin of the Prince: Here's an Instance of their Temper, their Peace, and Charity. To what height they

---

15   *never . . . but*   whenever.
16   *compound*   "To come to terms" (Johnson).
17   *Lenity and Mercy*   shown in An Act of Indemnity (August 1660), pardoning almost everyone who had fought against the King.

18   *Rye-Plot*   Rye-House Plot, an attempt in 1683 to murder King Charles II and his Catholic brother, who became James II.
19   *universal Liberty*   in A Declaration of Indulgence (1687 and 1688), which was issued mostly for the benefit of his fellow Catholics.

carried themselves during the Reign of a King of their own; how they crope[20] into all Places of Trust and Profit; how they insinuated into the Favour of the King, and were at first preferred to the highest Places in the Nation; how they engrossed the Ministry, and, *above* all, *how pitifully they Managed*, is too plain to need any Remarks.

But particularly, their Mercy and Charity, the Spirit of Union, they tell us so much of, has been remarkable in *Scotland*, there they made entire Conquest of the Church, trampled down the sacred Orders, and suppressed the Episcopal Government, with an absolute, and as they suppose, irretrievable Victory, though 'tis possible, *they may find themselves mistaken*: Now 'twould be a very proper Question to ask their *Impudent Advocate, the Observator,*[21] Pray how much Mercy and Favour did the Members of the Episcopal Church find in *Scotland*, from the *Scotch* Presbyterian-Government; and I shall undertake for the Church of *England*, that the Dissenters shall still receive as much as here, though they deserve but little.

In a small Treatise[22] of the Sufferings of the Episcopal Clergy in *Scotland*, 'twill appear, what Usage they met with, how they not only lost their Livings, but in several Places, were plundered and abused in their Persons; the Ministers that could not conform, turned out, with numerous Families, and no Maintenance, and hardly Charity enough left to relieve them with a bit of Bread; and the Cruelties of the Party[23] are innumerable, and are not to be attempted in this short Piece.

And now to prevent the distant Cloud which they perceived to hang over their Heads from *England*; with a true Presbyterian Policy, they put in for *a union of Nations*,[24] that *England* might unite their Church with the Kirk of *Scotland*, and their Presbytarian Members sit in our House of Commons, and their Assembly of *Scotch* canting Long-Cloaks[25] in our Convocation;[26] what might have been, if our Fanatic, Whiggish-States-men had continued, God only knows; but we hope we are out of fear of that now.

'Tis alleged by some of the Faction,[27] and they began to Bully us with it; that if we won't unite with them, they will not settle the Crown with us again, but when her majesty dies, will choose a King for themselves.

If they won't, we must make them, and 'tis not the first time we have let them know that we are able: The Crowns of these Kingdoms have not so far disowned the right of Succession; but they may retrieve it again, and if *Scotland* thinks to come off from a Successive to an Elective State of Government, *England* has not promised not to assist the right Heir, and put him into possession, without any regard to their ridiculous Settlements.[28]

These are the Gentlemen, these their ways of treating the Church, both at home and abroad. Now let us examine the Reasons they pretend to give why we should be favourable to them, why we should continue and tolerate them among us.

First, They are very Numerous, they say, they are a great Part of the Nation, and we cannot suppress them.

---

20   *crope*   old past tense of "creep."

21   *the Observator*   John Tutchin, who wrote a Whig journal under that name from 1702–12; he defended Defoe after his imprisonment in 1703.

22   *Treatise   The Sufferings of the Episcopal Clergy* (1691).

23   *the Party*   the Whigs.

24   *a union of Nations*   the Act of Union joining Scotland to the United Kingdom became law in 1707; as an agent of the Whigs, Defoe spent time in Edinburgh campaigning for ratification.

25   *Long-Cloaks*   Presbyterians.

26   *Convocation*   "An assembly of the clergy for consultation on matters ecclesiastical, in time of Parliament" (Johnson, quoting John Cowell).

27   *the Faction*   the Whigs.

28   *Settlements*   The Act of Settlement (1701) maintained the Protestant succession and shifted the regal line to the House of Hanover (1714).

To this may be answered, 1. They are not so Numerous as the Protestants in *France*, and yet the *French* King effectually cleared the Nation[29] of them at once, and we don't find he misses them at home.

But I am not of the Opinion that they are so Numerous as is pretended; their Party is more Numerous than their Persons, and those mistaken People of the Church, who are misled and deluded by their wheedling Artifices, to join with them, make their Party the greater; but those will open their Eyes, when the Government shall set heartily about the work, and come off from them, as some Animals, which they say, always desert a House when 'tis likely to fall.

2dly. The more Numerous, the more Dangerous, and therefore the more need to suppress them; and God has suffered us to bear them as Goads in our sides, for not utterly extinguishing them long ago.

3dly. If we are to allow them, only because we cannot suppress them, then it ought to be tried whether we can or no; and I am of the Opinion 'tis easy to be done, and could prescribe Ways and Means, if it were proper, but I doubt not but the Government will find effectual Methods for the rooting the Contagion from the Face of this Land.

Another Argument they use, which is this, That 'tis a time of War, and we have need to unite against the common Enemy.

We answer, this common Enemy had been no Enemy, if they had not made him so; he was quiet, in peace, and no way disturbed, or encroached upon us, and we know no reason we had to quarrel with him.

But further, We make no question but we are able to deal with this common Enemy without their help; but why must we unite with them because of the Enemy? will they go over to the Enemy, if we do not prevent it by a union with them – We are very well contented they should; and make no question, we shall be ready to deal with them and the common Enemy too, and better without them than with them.

Besides, if we have a common Enemy, there is the more need to be secure against our private Enemies; if there is one common Enemy, we have the less need to have an Enemy in our Bowels.

'Twas a great Argument some People used against suppressing the Old-Money,[30] that 'twas a time of War, and was too great a Risk for the Nation to run; if we should not master it, we should be undone; and yet the Sequel proved the Hazard was not so great, but it might be mastered; and the Success was unswerable. The suppressing the Dissenters is not a harder Work, nor a Work of less necessity to the Public; we can never enjoy a settled uninterrupted Union and Tranquillity in this Nation, till the Spirit of Whiggism, Faction, and Schism is melted down like the Old-Money.

To talk of the Difficulty, is to Frighten our selves with Chimeras and Notions of a Powerful Party, which are indeed a Party without Power; Difficulties often appear greater at a distance, than when they are searched into with Judgement, and distinguished from the Vapours and Shadows that attend them.

We shall not be frightened with it; this Age is wiser than that, by all our own Experience, *and theirs too*; King *Charles* the First, had early suppressed this Party, if he had took more

---

[29] *cleared the Nation* in 1685 Louis XIV revoked the Edict of Nantes (1598), which had given religious freedom to the Huguenots, and in a few succeeding years 400,000 of them and other unprotected Protestants fled to the Americas and elsewhere.

[30] *suppressing the Old-Money* the debased silver coinage of the realm was called in and replaced in 1695 in what is known as the great recoinage.

deliberate Measures. In short, 'tis not worth arguing, to talk of their Arms, their *Monmouths*,[31] and *Shaftesburys*, and *Argylls* are gone, their *Dutch-Sanctuary* is at an end; Heaven has made way for their Destruction, and if we do not close with the Divine occasion, we arc to blame our selves, and may remember that we once had opportunity to serve the Church of *England*, by extirpating her implacable Enemies, and having let slip the Minute that Heaven presented, may experimentally[32] Complain, *Post est Occasio Calvo.*[33]

Here are some popular Objections in the way.

As first, The Queen has promised them, to continue them in their tolerated Liberty; and has told us she will be a religious Observer of her Word.

What her Majesty will do we cannot help, but what, as the Head of the Church, she ought to do, is another Case: Her Majesty has promised to Protect and Defend the Church of *England*, and if she cannot effectually do that without the Destruction of the Dissenters, she must of course dispense with one Promise to comply with another. But to answer *this Cavil more effectually*: Her Majesty did never promise to maintain the Toleration, to the Destruction of the Church; but this is upon supposition that it may be compatible with the well being and safety of the Church, which she had declared she would take especial Care of: Now if these two Interests clash, 'tis plain her Majesty's Intentions are to Uphold, Protect, Defend, and Establish the Church, and this we conceive is impossible.

Perhaps it may be said, That the Church is in no immediate danger from the Dissenters, and therefore 'tis time enough: But this is a weak Answer.

For first. If a Danger be real, the Distance of it is no Argument against, but rather a Spur to quicken us to prevention, lest it be too late hereafter.

And 2ndly, Here is the Opportunity, and the only one perhaps that ever the Church had to secure her self, and destroy her Enemies.

The Representatives of the Nation have now an Opportunity; the Time is come when all good Men have wished for, that the Gentlemen of *England* may serve the Church of *England*; now they are protected and encouraged by a Church of *England* Queen.

What will ye do for your Sister in the Day that she shall be spoken for?[34]

If ever you establish the best Christian Church in the World.

If ever you will suppress the Spirit of Enthusiasm.

If ever you will free the Nation from the viperous Brood that have so long sucked the Blood of their Mother.

If [ever] you will leave your Posterity free from Faction and Rebellion, this is the time.

This is the time to pull up this hysterical Weed of Sedition, that has so long disturbed the Peace of the Church, and poisoned the good Corn.

But, says another Hot and Cold Objector, this is renewing Fire and Faggot, reviving the Act *De Heret{ico} Comburendo*:[35] This will be Cruelty in its Nature, and Barbarous to all the World.

---

[31] *Monmouths* James Scott, Charles's illegitimate son by Nell Gwynn, the favourite of Protestants to succeed to the throne instead of Catholic James II; Anthony Ashley Cooper, 1st Earl of *Shaftesbury* and Archibald Campbell, 9th Earl of *Argyll* were important supporters.
[32] *experimentally* on the basis of experience.
[33] *Post est Occasio Calvo* "occasion is bald behind" a proverb illustrated by emblematical pictures of Occasion with a forelock that must be seized.

[34] *What will ye do . . . spoken for* see Song of Solomon 8. 8, where the text reads "we" instead of "ye"; the female speaker of these lines was allegorically interpreted as Christ's Church, and here she could be construed to be enjoining establishment of the Church.
[35] *Act De Heret Comburendo* concerning the burning of heretics (1382), which empowered Bishops to pass such a sentence without royal approval.

I answer, 'tis Cruelty to kill a Snake or a Toad in cold Blood, but the Poison of their Nature makes it a Charity to our Neighbours, to destroy those Creatures, for not any personal Injury received, but for prevention; not for the Evil they have done, but the Evil they may do.

Serpents, Toads, Vipers, &c. are noxious to the Body, and poison the sensitive Life;[36] these poison the Soul, corrupt our Posterity, ensnare our Children, destroy the Vitals of our Happiness, our future Felicity, and contaminate the whole Mass.

Shall any Law be given to such wild Creatures? Some Beasts are for Sport, and the Huntsmen give them advantages of Ground;[37] but some are knocked on their head by all possible ways of Violence and Surprise.

I do not prescribe Fire and Faggot; but as *Scipio* said of *Carthage*, *Delenda est Carthago*,[38] they are to be rooted out of this Nation, if we will ever live in Peace, serve God, or enjoy our own: As for the Manner, I leave it to those Hands, who have a right to execute God's Justice on the Nation's and the Church's Enemies.

But if we must be frighted from this Justice, under the specious Pretences, and odious Sense of Cruelty, nothing will be effected: 'Twill be more Barbarous and Cruel to our own children, and dear Posterity, when they shall reproach their Fathers, as we do ours, and tell us, 'You had an Opportunity to root out this cursed Race from the World, under the Favour and Protection of a true *English* Queen; and out of your foolish Pity you spared them, because, forsooth, you would not be Cruel, and now our Church is suppressed and persecuted, our Religion trampled under Foot, our Estates plundered, our Persons imprisoned and dragged to Jails, Gibbets, and Scaffolds; your sparing this *Amalekite* Race[39] is our Destruction, your Mercy to them proves Cruelty to your poor Posterity.'

How just will such Reflections be, when our Posterity shall fall under the merciless Clutches of this uncharitable Generation, when our Church shall be swallowed up in Schism, Faction, Enthusiasm, and Confusion; when our Government shall be devolved upon Foreigners, and our Monarchy dwindled into a Republic.

'Twould be more rational for us, if we must spare this Generation, to summon our own to a general Massacre, and as we have brought them into the World Free, send them out so, and not betray them to Destruction by our supine negligence, and then cry, 'it is Mercy'.

Moses was a merciful meek Man, and yet with what Fury did he run through the Camp, and cut the Throats of Three and thirty thousand of his dear *Israelites*,[40] that were fallen into Idolatry; what was the reason? 'twas Mercy to the rest, to make these be Examples, to prevent the Destruction of the whole Army.

How many Millions of future Souls we [should] save from Infection and Delusion, if the present Race of poisoned Spirits were purged from the Face of the Land.

'Tis vain to trifle in this matter, the light foolish handling of them by Mulcts,[41] Fines, &c. 'tis their Glory and their Advantage; if the Gallows instead of the Counter,[42] and the Gallies

---

[36] *sensitive Life* the life of sense and perception, rather than reason or *Soul*.

[37] *Ground* "The intervening space between the flyer and pursuer" (Johnson; sense 16).

[38] *Delenda est Carthago* "Carthage must be destroyed," frequently repeated by Cato the Censor, or the Elder, Marcus Porcius Cato (234–149 BCE) in framing his nationalistic foreign policy.

[39] *Amalekite Race* an enemy of the Israelites condemned to annihilation by the Lord in a revelation to Moses (Exodus 17. 14).

[40] *Three and thirty thousand of his dear Israelites* see Exodus 33.25–9; the correct number is merely 3,000.

[41] *Mulcts* fines.

[42] *Counter* prison.

instead of the Fines, were the Reward of going to a Conventicle,[43] to preach or hear, there would not be so many Sufferers. The Spirit of Martyrdom is over; they that will go to Church to be chosen Sheriffs and Mayors,[44] would go to forty Churches rather than be Hanged.

If one severe Law were made, and punctually executed, that who was ever found at a Conventicle, should be Banished the Nation, and the Preacher be Hanged, we should soon see an end of the Tale; they would all come to Church, and one Age would make us all One again.

To talk of five shillings a Month for not coming to the Sacrament, and one shilling *per* Week for not coming to Church, this is such a way of converting People as never was known; this is selling them a Liberty to transgress for so much Money: If it be not a Crime, why don't we give them full Licence? And if it be, no Price ought to compound for the committing it, for that is selling a Liberty to People to sin against God and the Government.

If it be a Crime of the highest Consequence, both against the Peace and Welfare of the Nation, the Glory of God, the Good of the Church, and the Happiness of the Soul, let us rank it among capital Offences, and let it receive a Punishment in proportion to it.

We Hang Men for Trifles, and Banish them for things not worth naming, but that an Offence against God and the Church, against the Welfare of the World, and the Dignity of Religion, shall be bought off for five shillings, this is such a shame to Christian Government, that 'tis with regret I transmit it to Posterity.

If Men sin against God, affront his Ordinances, rebel against his Church, and disobey the Precepts of their Superiors, let them suffer as such capital Crimes deserve, so will Religion flourish, and this divided Nation be once again united.

And yet the Title of Barbarous and Cruel will soon be taken off from this Law too. I am not supposing that all the Dissenters in *England* should be Hanged or Banished, but as in cases of Rebellions and Insurrections, if a few of the Ring-leaders suffer, the Multitude are dismissed, so a few obstinate People being made Examples, there's no doubt but the Severity of the Law would find a stop in the Compliance of the Multitude.

To make the reasonableness of this matter out of question, and more unanswerably plain, let us examine for what it is that this Nation is divided into Parties and Factions, and let us see how they can justify a Separation, or we of the Church of *England* can justify our bearing the Insults and Inconveniences of the Party.

One of their leading Pastors, and a Man of as much Learning as most among them, in his Answer to a Pamphlet entitled *An Enquiry into the Occasional Conformity*,[45] hath these Words, P. 27: 'Do the Religion of the Church and the Meeting-houses make two Religions? Wherein do they differ? The Substance of the same Religion is common to them both; and the Modes and Accidents are the things in which only they differ'. P. 28: 'Thirty nine Articles[46] are given us for the summary of our Religion. Thirty six contain the Substance of it, wherein we agree. Three [are] the additional Appendices, about which we have some differences'.

Now, if as by their own acknowledgement, the Church of *England* is a true Church, and the Difference between them is only in a few *Modes and Accidents*, Why should we expect that

---

[43] *Conventicle* "An assembly for worship. Generally used in an ill sense, including heresy or schism" (Johnson).

[44] *go to Church to be chosen Sheriffs and Mayors* dissenters could avoid the Test Act and hold public office if they occasionally took communion in the Church of England; the Tory Act of Occasional Conformity (1711) sought to put an end to the practice.

[45] *An Enquiry into the Occasional Conformity* a pamphlet by Defoe himself, published in 1698.

[46] *Thirty nine Articles* the articles of faith to which individuals had to subscribe in order to enjoy privileges such as government positions and matriculation at Oxford or Cambridge; the Act of Toleration had released dissenters from subscribing to three of the thirty-nine.

they will suffer Gallows and Gallies, corporeal Punishment and Banishment for these Trifles; there is no question but they will be wiser; even their own Principles won't bear them out in it; they will certainly comply with the Laws, and with Reason, and though at the first, Severity may seem hard, the next Age will feel nothing of it; the Contagion will be rooted out; the Disease being cured, there will be no need of the Operation, but if they should venture to transgress, and fall into the Pit, all the World must condemn their Obstinacy, as being without Ground from their own Principles.

Thus the Pretence of Cruelty will be taken off, and the Party actually suppressed, and the Disquiets they have so often brought upon the Nation, prevented.

Their Numbers, and their Wealth, makes them Haughty, and that is so far from being an Argument to persuade us to forbear them, that 'tis a Warning to us, without any more delay, to reconcile them to the Unity of the Church, or remove them from us.

At present, Heaven be praised, they are not so Formidable as they have been, and 'tis our own fault if ever we suffer them to be so; Providence, and the Church of *England*, seems to join in this particular, that now the Destroyers of the Nation's Peace may be overturned, and to this end the present Opportunity seems to be put into our Hands.

To this end her present Majesty seems reserved[47] to enjoy the Crown, that the Ecclesiastic as well as Civil Rights of the Nation may be restored by her Hand.

To this end the Face of Affairs have received such a Turn in the process of a few Months, as has never been before; the leading Men of the Nation, the universal Cry of the People, the unanimous Request of the Clergy, agree in this, that the Deliverance of our Church is at hand.

For this end has Providence given us such a Parliament, such a Convocation, such a Gentry, and such a Queen as we never had before.

And what may be the Consequences of a Neglect of such Opportunities? The Succession of the Crown has but a dark Prospect, another *Dutch* Turn may make the Hopes of it ridiculous, and the Practice impossible: Be the House of our future Princes ever so well inclined, they will be Foreigners; and many Years will be spent in suiting the Genius of Strangers to the Crown, and to the Interests of the Nation; and how many Ages it may be before the *English* Throne be filled with so much Zeal and Candour, so much Tenderness, and hearty Affection to the Church, as we see it now covered with, who can imagine.

'Tis high time then for the Friends of the Church of *England*, to think of Building up, and Establishing her, in such a manner, that she may be no more Invaded by Foreigners, nor Divided by Factions, Schisms, and Error.

If this could be done by gentle and easy Methods, I should be glad, but the Wound is corroded, the Vitals begin to mortify,[48] and nothing but Amputation of Members can complete the Cure; all the ways of Tenderness and Compassion, all persuasive Arguments have been made use of in vain.

The Humour[49] of the Dissenters has so increased among the People, that they hold the Church in Defiance, and the House of God is an Abomination among them: Nay, they have brought up their Posterity in such prepossessed Aversions to our Holy Religion, that the ignorant Mob think we are all Idolators, and Worshippers of *Baal*;[50] and account it a Sin to come within the Walls of our Churches.

---

[47] *reserved* kept in store, by Providence.
[48] *mortify* "To gangrene; to corrupt" (Johnson).
[49] *Humour* inclination, temper.

[50] *Baal* Jehovah's chief competition in the Old Testament.

The primitive Christians were not more shy of a Heathen-Temple, or of Meat offered to Idols, nor the *Jews* of Swine's-Flesh, than some of our Dissenters are of the Church, and the Divine Service solemnized therein.

This Obstinacy must be rooted out with the Profession of it; while the Generation are left at liberty daily to affront God Almighty, and Dishonour his Holy Worship, we are wanting in our Duty to God, and our Mother the Church of *England*.

How can we answer it to God, to the Church, and to our Posterity, to leave them entangled with Fanaticism, Error, and Obstinacy, in the Bowels of the Nation; to leave them an Enemy in their Streets, that in time may involve them in the same Crimes, and endanger the utter Extirpation of Religion in the Nation.

What's the Difference betwixt this, and being subjected to the Power of the Church of *Rome*, from whence we have reformed? If one be an extreme on one Hand, and one on another, 'tis equally destructive to the Truth, to have Errors settled among us, let them be of what Nature they will.

Both are Enemies of our Church, and of our Peace, and why should it not be as criminal to admit an Enthusiast as a Jesuit? Why should the *Papist* with his Seven Sacraments be worse than the *Quaker* with no Sacraments at all? Why should Religious-houses be more intolerable than Meeting-Houses – *Alas the Church of England!* What with Popery on one Hand, and Schismatics on the other, how has she been Crucified between two Thieves.

Now, *let us Crucify the Thieves.* Let her Foundations be established upon the Destruction of her Enemies: The Doors of Mercy being always open to the returning Part of the deluded People: Let the Obstinate be ruled with the Rod of Iron.

Let all true Sons of so Holy an Oppressed Mother, exasperated by her Afflictions, harden their Hearts against those who have oppressed her.

And may God Almighty put it into the Hearts of all the Friends of Truth, to lift up a Standard against Pride and Antichrist, that the Posterity of the Sons of Error may be rooted out from the Face of this Land for ever——.

FINIS

A True Relation OF THE APPARITION OF ONE Mrs. VEAL, The next Day after Her DEATH: TO ONE Mrs. BARGRAVE At *Canterbury*. The 8th of *September*, 1705 (1706)[1]

THE PREFACE

This relation is Matter of Fact, and attended with such Circumstances as may induce any Reasonable Man to believe it. It was sent by a Gentleman, a Justice of Peace of *Maidstone* in *Kent*, and a very Intelligent Person, to his Friend in *London*, as it is here worded; which Discourse is attended by a very sober and understanding Gentlewoman, a Kinswoman of the said Gentleman's, who lives in *Canterbury*, within a few Doors of the House in which the within named Mrs. *Bargrave* lives; who believes his Kinswoman to be of so discerning a Spirit,

---

A TRUE RELATION
[1] *Mrs. Veal* Mistress Veal, or Miss Veal, as we would call such an unmarried woman, was a real person, and

Defoe's account has proven to be an accurate relation of the facts as they were consistently reported by Bargrave.

as not to be put upon by any Fallacy, and who positively assured him, that the whole Matter, as it is here released and laid down, is what is really True; and what She her self had in the same Words (as near as may be) from Mrs. *Bargrave's* own Mouth, who she knows had no Reason to invent and publish such a Story, nor any design to forge and tell a Lie, being a Woman of much Honestly and Virtue, and her whole Life a Course as it were of Piety. The use which we ought to make of it is, to consider, That there is a Life to come after this, and a Just God, who will retribute to every one according to the Deeds done in the Body; and therefore, to reflect upon our past Course of Life we have led in the World, That our Time is Short and Uncertain, and that if we would escape the Punishment of the Ungodly, and receive the Reward of the Righteous, which is the laying hold of Eternal Life, we ought for the time to come, to turn to God by a speedy Repentance, ceasing to do Evil and learning to do Well: To seek after God Early, if happily he may be found of us, and lead such Lives for the future, as may be well pleasing in his Sight.

A
RELATION
OF THE
APPARITION
OF MRS. VEAL

This thing is so rare in all its Circumstances, and on so good Authority, that my Reading and Conversation has not given me any thing like it; it is fit to gratify the most Ingenious and Serious Enquirer. Mrs. *Bargrave* is the Person to whom Mrs. *Veal* Appeared after her Death; she is my Intimate Friend, and I can avouch for her Reputation, for these last fifteen or sixteen Years, on my own Knowledge; and I can confirm the Good Character she had from her Youth, to the time of my Acquaintance. Though since this Relation, she is Calumniated by some People, that are Friends to the Brother of Mrs. *Veal* who Appeared;[2] who think the Relation of this Appearance to be a Reflection, and endeavour what they can to Blast Mrs. *Bargrave's* Reputation; and to Laugh the Story out of Countenance. But the Circumstances thereof, and the Cheerful Disposition of Mrs. *Bargrave*, notwithstanding the unheard of ill Usage of a very wicked Husband, there is not yet the least sign of Dejection in her Face; nor did I ever hear her let fall a Desponding or Murmuring Expression; nay, not when actually under her Husband's Barbarity; which I have been Witness to, and several other Persons of undoubted Reputation.

Now you must know, that Mrs. *Veal* was a Maiden Gentlewoman of about 30 Years of Age, and for some Years last past,[3] had been troubled with Fits; which were perceived coming on her, by her going off from her Discourse very abruptly, to some impatience: She was maintained by an only Brother, and kept his House in *Dover*. She was a very Pious Woman, and her Brother a very Sober Man to all Appearance: But now he does all he can to Null and Quash the Story. Mrs. *Veal* was intimately acquainted with Mrs. *Bargrave* from her Child-hood. Mrs. *Veal's* Circumstances were then Mean; her Father did not take care of his Children as he ought, so that they were exposed to Hardships: And Mrs. *Bargrave* in those days, had as unkind a father, though She wanted neither for Food nor Clothing, whilst Mrs. *Veal* wanted for both: So that it was in the Power of Mrs. *Bargrave* to be very much her Friend in several Instances, which mightily endeared Mrs. *Veal*; insomuch that she would often say, 'Mrs. Bargrave, you are not only the best, but the only Friend I have in the World; and no

---

[2]   *Appear*   "To become visible as a spirit" (Johnson).   [3]   *last past*   the last years she passed in life.

Circumstances of Life, shall ever dissolve my Friendship'. They would often condole each other's adverse Fortunes, and read together, *Drelincourt upon Death*:[4] and other good Books: and so like two Christian Friends, they comforted each other under their Sorrow.

Sometime after, Mr. *Veal's* Friends got him a Place in the Custom-House at *Dover*, which occasioned Mrs. *Veal* by little and little, to fall off from her Intimacy with Mrs. *Bargrave*, though there was never any such thing as a Quarrel; but an Indifferency came on by degrees, till at last Mrs. *Bargrave* had not seen her in two Years and a half; though above a Twelve Month of the time, Mrs. *Bargrave* had been absent from *Dover*, and this last half Year, has been in *Canterbury* about two Months of the time, dwelling in a House of her own.

In this House, on the Eighth of *September* last, *viz.* 1705. She was sitting alone in the Forenoon, thinking over her Unfortunate Life, and arguing her self into a due Resignation to Providence, though her Condition seemed hard. And said she, 'I have been provided for hitherto, and doubt not but I shall be still; and am well satisfied, that my Afflictions shall end, when it is most fit for me': And then took up her Sewing Work, which she had no sooner done, but she hears a Knocking at the Door; she went to see who was there, and this proved to be Mrs. *Veal*, her Old Friend, who was in a Riding Habit: At that Moment of Time, the Clock struck Twelve at Noon.

'Madam', says Mrs. *Bargrave*, 'I am surprised to see you; you have been so long a stranger', but told her, she was glad to see her and offered to Salute[5] her, which Mrs. *Veal* complied with, till their Lips almost touched, and then Mrs. *Veal* drew her hand cross her own Eyes, and said, 'I am not very well', and so waved it. She told Mrs. *Bargrave*, she was going a Journey, and had a great mind to see her first: 'But', says Mrs. *Bargrave*, 'how came you to take a Journey alone? I am amazed at it, because I know you have so fond a Brother'.

'O!' says Mrs. Veal, 'I gave my Brother the Slip, and came away, because I had so great a Mind to see you before I took my Journey'. So Mrs. *Bargrave* went in with her, into another Room within the first, and Mrs. *Veal* sat her down in an Elbow-chair,[6] in which Mrs. *Bargrave* was sitting when she heard Mrs. *Veal* Knock. Then says Mrs. *Veal*, 'My Dear Friend, I am come to renew our Old Friendship again, and to beg your Pardon for my breach of it, and if you can forgive me, you are the best of Women'.

'O!' says Mrs. Bargrave, 'don't mention such a thing. I have not had an uneasy thought about it; I can easily forgive it'.

'What did you think of me?' says Mrs. *Veal*. Says Mrs. *Bargrave*, 'I thought you were like the rest of the World, and that Prosperity had made you forget your self and me'. Then Mrs. *Veal* reminded Mrs. *Bargrave* of the many Friendly Offices she did her in former Days, and much of the Conversation they had with each other in time of their Adversity; what Books they Read, and what Comfort in particular they received from *Drelincourt's Book of Death*, which was the best she said on that Subject was ever Wrote. She also mentioned Dr. *Sherlock*,[7] and two *Dutch* Books which were Translated, Wrote upon Death, and several others: But *Drelincourt* she said, had the clearest Notions of Death, and of the Future State, of any who have handled that Subject. Then she asked Mrs. *Bargrave*, whether she had *Drelincourt*. She said yes. Says Mrs. *Veal*, 'Fetch it', and so Mrs. *Bargrave* goes up Stairs, and brings it down. Says Mrs. *Veal*, 'Dear Mrs. *Bargrave*, If the Eyes of our Faith were as open as the Eyes of our Body, we should see numbers of Angels about us for our Guard: The Notions we have of

---

[4] *Drelincourt upon Death   The Christian's Defence against the Fears of Death* (English translation, 1675).
[5] *Salute* kiss.

[6] *Elbow-chair* "A chair with arms to support the elbows" (Johnson).
[7] *Dr. Sherlock* William Sherlock, *A Practical Discourse concerning Death* (1689).

Heaven now, are nothing like what it is, as *Drelincourt* says. Therefore be comforted under your Afflictions, and believe that the Almighty has a particular regard to you; and that your Afflictions are Marks of God's Favour: And when they have done the business they were sent for, they shall be removed from you. And believe me my Dear Friend, believe what I say to you, One Minute of future Happiness will infinitely reward you for all your Sufferings. For I can never believe' (and claps her Hand upon her Knee, with a great Earnestness, which indeed ran through all her Discourse) 'that ever God will suffer you to spend all your Days in this afflicted State: But be assured, that your Afflictions shall leave you, or you them in a short time'. She spake in that Pathetical and Heavenly manner, that Mrs. *Bargrave* wept several times; she was so deeply affected with it. Then Mrs. *Veal* mentioned Dr. *Horneck's Ascetic*,[8] at the end of which, he gives an Account of the Lives of the Primitive Christians. Their Pattern she recommended to our Imitation, and said, 'their Conversation was not like this of our Age. For now', says she, 'there is nothing but frothy vain Discourse, which is far different from theirs. Theirs was to Edification, and to Build one another up in Faith: So that they were not as we are, nor are we as they are; but', said she, 'We might do as they did. There was a Hearty Friendship among them; but where is it now to be found?'

Says Mrs. *Bargrave*, ''tis hard indeed to find a true Friend in these days'.

Says Mrs. *Veal*, 'Mr. *Norris*[9] has a Fine Copy of Verses, called *Friendship in Perfection*, which I wonderfully admire. Have you seen the Book?' says Mrs. *Veal*.

'No', says Mrs. *Bargrave*, 'but I have the Verses, of my own writing out'.

'*Have you?*' says Mrs. *Veal*, 'then fetch them'; which she did from above Stairs, and offered them to Mrs. *Veal* to read, who refused, and waved the thing, saying, holding down her Head would make it ache, and then desired Mrs. *Bargrave* to read them to her, which she did. As they were admiring Friendship, Mrs. *Veal* said, 'Dear Mrs. *Bargrave*, I shall love you for ever'. In the Verses there is twice used the Word 'Elysium'. 'Ah!', says Mrs. *Veal*, 'These Poets have such Names for Heaven'. She would often draw her hand cross her own Eyes and say, 'Mrs. *Bargrave*, Don't you think I am mightily impaired by my Fits?'

'No', says Mrs. *Bargrave*, 'I think you look as well as ever I knew you'.

After all this discourse, which the Apparition put in Words much finer than Mrs. *Bargrave* said she can remember (for it cannot be thought, that an hour and three-quarters' Conversation could all be retained, though the main of it, she thinks she does), she said to Mrs. *Bargrave*, she would have her write a Letter to her Brother, and tell him, she would have him give Rings to such and such; and that there was a Purse of Gold in her Cabinet, and that she would have Two Broad Pieces given to her Cousin Watson. Talking at this Rate, Mrs. *Bargrave* thought that a Fit was coming upon her, and so placed her self in a Chair just before her Knees, to keep her from falling to the Ground, if her Fits should occasion it; for the Elbow Chair she thought would keep her from falling on either side. And to divert Mrs. *Veal* as she thought, took hold of her Gown Sleeve several times, and commended it. Mrs. *Veal* told her, it was a Scoured[10] Silk, and newly made up. But for all this Mrs. *Veal* persisted in her Request, and told Mrs. *Bargrave* that she must not deny her: and she would have her tell her Brother all their Conversation, when she had an opportunity.

'Dear Mrs. *Veal*', said Mrs. *Bargrave*, 'this seems so impertinent, that I cannot tell how to comply with it; and what a mortifying Story will our Conversation be to a Young Gentleman?'

---

8   *Dr. Horneck's Ascetic*   Anthony Horneck, *The Happy Ascetic* (1681).

9   *Mr. Norris*   John Norris of Bemerton, *A Collection of Miscellanies* (1687).

10   *Scoured*   bleached.

'Well', says Mrs. *Veal*, 'I must not be denied'.

'Why', says Mrs. *Bargrave*, ''tis much better methinks to do it your self'.

'No', says Mrs. *Veal*; 'though it seems impertinent to you now, you will see more reason for it hereafter'. Mrs. *Bargrave* then to satisfy her importunity, was going to fetch a Pen and Ink: but Mrs. *Veal* said, 'let it alone now, but do it when I am gone; but you must be sure to do it': which was one of the last things she enjoined her at parting; and so she promised her.

Then Mrs. *Veal* asked for Mrs. *Bargrave's* Daughter; she said she was not at home. 'But if you have a mind to see her', says Mrs. *Bargrave*, 'I'll send for her'.

'Do', says Mrs. *Veal*. On which she left her, and went to a Neighbour's to send for her; and by the Time Mrs. *Bargrave* was returning, Mrs. *Veal* was got without the Door into the Street, in the face of the *Beast-Market* on a Saturday (which is Market day) and stood ready to part, as soon as Mrs. *Bargrave* came to her. She asked her why she was in such haste? She said she must be going; though perhaps she might not go to her journey till Monday, and told Mrs. *Bargrave* she hoped she should see her again, at her Cousin *Watson*'s before she went whither she was a going. Then she said she would take Leave of her, and walked from Mrs. *Bargrave* in her view, till a turning interrupted the sight of her, which was three quarters after One in the Afternoon.

Mrs. *Veal* Died the 7th of *September* at 12 a Clock at Noon, of her Fits, and had not above four hours' Senses before her Death, in which time she received the Sacrament. The next day after Mrs. *Veal's* appearing being Sunday, Mrs. *Bargrave* was so mightily indisposed with a Cold, and a Sore Throat, that she could not go out that day: but on Monday morning she sends a person to Captain *Watson's* to know if Mrs. *Veal* was there. They wondered at Mrs. *Bargrave's* enquiry, and sent her Word, that she was not there, nor was expected. At this Answer Mrs. *Bargrave* told the Maid she had certainly mistook the Name, or made some blunder. And though she was ill, she put on her Hood, and went her self to Captain *Watson's*, though she knew none of the Family, to see if Mrs. *Veal* was there or not. They said, they wondered at her asking, for that she had not been in Town; they were sure, if she had, she would have been there. Says Mrs. *Bargrave*, 'I am sure she was with me on Saturday almost two hours'. They said it was impossible, for they must have seen her if she had. In comes Captain *Watson*, while they were in Dispute, and said that Mrs. *Veal* was certainly Dead, and her Escutcheons[11] were making. This strangely surprised Mrs. *Bargrave*, who went to the Person immediately who had the care of them, and found it true. Then she related the whole Story to Captain *Watson's* Family, and what Gown she had on, and how striped. And that Mrs. *Veal* told her it was Scoured. Then Mr. *Watson* cried out, 'you have seen her indeed, for none knew but Mrs. *Veal* and my self, that the Gown was Scoured'; and Mrs. *Watson* owned that she described the Gown exactly; for, said she, 'I helped her to make it up'. This, Mrs. *Watson* blazed all about the Town, and avouched the Demonstration of the Truth of Mrs. *Bargrave's* seeing Mrs. *Veal's* Apparition. And Captain *Watson* carried two Gentlemen immediately to Mrs. *Bargrave's* House, to hear the Relation from her own Mouth. And then it spread so fast, that Gentlemen and Persons of Quality, the Judicious and Sceptical part of the World, flocked in upon her, which at last became such a Task, that she was forced to go out of the way. For they were in general, extremely satisfied of the truth of the thing; and plainly saw, that Mrs. *Bargrave* was no Hypochondriac,[12] for she always appears with such a cheerful Air, and pleasing Mien, that she has gained the favour and esteem of all the Gentry. And it's thought a great favour if they can but get the Relation from her own Mouth.

---

[11] *Escutcheons* armorial badges for the hearse.

[12] *Hypochondriac* one who is "melancholy; disordered in the imagination" (Johnson).

I should have told you before, that Mrs. *Veal* told Mrs. *Bargrave*, that her Sister and Brother in Law, were just come down from *London* to see her.

Says Mrs. *Bargrave*, 'how came you to order Matters so strangely?'

'It could not be helped', said Mrs. *Veal*; and her Sister and Brother did come to see her, and entered the Town of *Dover*, just as Mrs. *Veal* was expiring. Mrs. *Bargrave* asked her, whether she would drink some Tea. Says Mrs. *Veal*, 'I do not care if I do: but I'll Warrant this Mad Fellow' (meaning Mrs. *Bargrave's* Husband) 'has broke all your Trinkets'.

'But', says Mrs. *Bargrave*, 'I'll get something to Drink in for all that'; but Mrs. *Veal* waved it, and said, 'it is no matter, let it alone', and so it passed.

All the time I sat with Mrs. *Bargrave*, which was some Hours, she recollected fresh Sayings of Mrs. *Veal*. And one material thing more she told Mrs. *Bargrave*, that Old Mr. *Breton* allowed Mrs. *Veal* Ten Pounds a Year, which was a Secret, and unknown to Mrs. *Bargrave*, till Mrs. *Veal* told it to her. Mrs. *Bargrave* never varies in her Story, which puzzles those who doubt of the Truth, or are unwilling to believe it. A Servant in the Neighbour's Yard adjoining to Mrs. *Bargrave's* House, heard her talking to some body, an Hour of the Time Mrs. *Veal* was with her. Mrs. *Bargrave* went out to her next Neighbour's the very Moment she parted with Mrs. *Veal*, and told her what Ravishing Conversation she had with an Old Friend, and told the whole of it. *Drelincourt's Book of Death* is, since this happened, Bought up strangely. And it is to be observed, that notwithstanding all this Trouble and Fatigue Mrs. *Bargrave* has undergone upon this Account, she never took the value of a Farthing, nor suffered her Daughter to take any thing of any Body, and therefore can have no Interest in telling the Story.

But Mr. *Veal* does what he can to stifle the matter, and said he would see Mrs. *Bargrave*; but yet it is certain matter of fact, that he has been at Captain *Watson's* since the Death of his Sister, and yet never went near Mrs. *Bargrave*; and some of his Friends report her to be a great Liar, and that she knew of Mr. *Breton's* Ten Pounds a Year. But the Person who pretends to say so, has the Reputation of a Notorious Liar, among persons which I know to be of undoubted Repute. Now Mr. *Veal* is more a Gentleman, than to say, she Lies; but says, a bad Husband has Crazed her. But she needs only to present her self, and it will effectually confute that Pretence. Mr. *Veal* says he asked his Sister on her Death Bed, whether she had a mind to dispose of any thing, and she said, No. Now the things which Mrs. *Veal's* Apparition would have disposed of, were so Trifling, and nothing of Justice aimed at in their disposal, that the design of it appears to me to be only in order to make Mrs. *Bargarve*, so to demonstrate the Truth of her Appearance, as to satisfy the World of the Reality thereof, as to what she had seen and heard: and to secure her Reputation among the Reasonable and understanding part of Mankind. And then again, Mr. *Veal* owns that there was a Purse of Gold; but it was not found in her Cabinet, but in a Comb-Box. This looks improbable, for that Mrs. *Watson* owned that Mrs. *Veal* was so very careful of the Key of her Cabinet, that she would trust no Body with it. And if so, no doubt she would not trust her Gold out of it. And Mrs. *Veal* often drawing her hand over her Eyes, and asking Mrs. *Bargrave*, whether her Fits had not impaired her, looks to me as if she did it on purpose to remind Mrs. *Bargrave* of her Fits, to prepare her not to think it strange that she should put her upon Writing to her Brother to dispose of Rings and Gold, which looked so much like a dying Person's Bequest; and it took accordingly with Mrs. *Bargrave*, as the effect of her Fits coming upon her; and was one of the many Instances of her Wonderful Love to her, and Care of her, that she should not be affrighted: which indeed appears in her whole management; particularly, in her coming to her in the day time, waving the Salutation[13], and when she was alone; and then the manner of her parting, to prevent a second attempt to Salute her.

---

[13]   *Salutation*   kiss.

Now, why Mr. *Veal* should think this Relation a Reflection[14] (as 'tis plain he does by his endeavouring to stifle it) I can't imagine, because the Generality believe her to be a good Spirit; her Discourse was so Heavenly. Her two great Errands were to comfort Mrs. *Bargrave* in her Affliction, and to ask her forgiveness for her Breach of Friendship, and with a Pious Discourse to encourage her. So that after all, to suppose that Mrs. *Bargrave* could Hatch such an Invention as this from *Friday-Noon* till *Saturday-Noon*, (supposing that she knew of Mrs. *Veal*'s Death the very first Moment) without jumbling Circumstances, and without any Interest too; she must be more Witty, Fortunate, and Wicked too, than any indifferent Person I dare say, will allow. I asked Mrs. *Bargrave* several times, If she was sure she felt the Gown. She answered Modestly, 'if my Senses be to be relied on, I am sure of it'. I asked her, If she heard a Sound, when she clapped her Hand upon her Knee: She said, she did not remember she did: And she said, she Appeared to be as much a Substance as I did, who talked with her. 'And I may', said she, 'be as soon persuaded that your Apparition is talking to me now, as that I did not really see her; for I was under no manner of Fear; I received her as a Friend, and parted with her as such. I would not', says she, 'give one Farthing to make any one believe it, I have no Interest in it; nothing but trouble is entailed upon me for a long time for ought I know; and had it not come to Light by Accident, it would never have been made Public'. But now, she says, she will make her own Private Use of it, and keep her self out of the way as much as she can. And so she has done since. She says, she had a Gentleman who came thirty Miles to her to hear the Relation; and that she had told it to a Room full of People at a time. Several particular Gentlemen have had the Story from Mrs. *Bargrave*'s own Mouth.

This thing has very much affected me, and I am well satisfied, as I am of the best grounded Matter of Fact. And why we should dispute Matter of Fact, because we cannot solve things, of which we can have no certain or demonstrative Notions, seems strange to me: Mrs. *Bargrave*'s Authority and Sincerity alone, would have been undoubted in any other Case.

FINIS

Advertisement

Drelincourt's Book of Consolations against the Fear of Death, has been four times Printed already in *English* of which many Thousands have been Sold, and not without great Applause: And its bearing so great a Character in this Relation the Impression is near Sold off.

from *The London Gazette*[1]
Monday 11 January to Thursday 14 January 1702

Deal, January 12. Admiral *Allemonde* arrived here Yesterday from *Holland*, on Board a *Dutch* Man of War, which immediately after his landing sailed for *Spithead*.

---

[14] *Reflection* censure.

FROM *THE LONDON GAZETTE*

[1] Begun in 1665 as *The Oxford Gazette*, the *London Gazette* was perhaps the first regularly published newspaper in England. It was always a government organ, and Samuel Johnson expressed a common, though largely anti-government view in his second definition of "gazetteer": "It was lately a term of the utmost infamy, being applied to wretches who were hired to vindicate the court." The court in 1702 belonged to the newly crowned Queen Anne, and Defoe had earned its displeasure with his highly ironical *Shortest-Way with the Dissenters*. This notice of a reward for information leading to Defoe's arrest appears amidst other news and contains the only known physical description of the author.

St. James's, Jan. 10. Whereas *Daniel de Foe* alias *de Fooe,* is charged with writing a Scandalous and Seditious Pamphlet. Entitled {*The Shortest way with the Dissenters.*} Whoever shall discover the said *Daniel de Foe* alias *de Fooe* to one of Her Majesty's Principal Secretaries of State, or any of Her Majesty's Justices of the Peace, so as he may be apprehended, shall have a Reward of £50 which Her Majesty has ordered immediately to be paid upon such Discovery.

He is a middle Sized Spare Man, about 40 years old, of a brown Complexion, and dark brown coloured Hair, but wears a Wig, a hooked Nose, a sharp Grin, grey Eyes, and a large Mould[2] near his Mouth, was born in *London,* and for many years was a Hose Factor in Freeman's-yard, in Cornhill, and now is Owner of the Brick and Pantile Works near *Tilbury-Fort* in *Essex.*

Anne Killigrew (1660–1685)

Killigrew's poems were published a year after her death in a slender volume prefaced by one of John Dryden's best odes (see p. 379 above). Her memory has been both preserved and outshone by the overstated but poetically pleasing accolades in Dryden's elegy. When she died at age twenty-five Killigrew had certainly not matured as a poet or, in her other major pursuit, as a painter. Talented and cultivated, she was a maid of honor to Mary of Modena, the wife of the future James II, and a companion of Anne Finch, Countess of Winchilsea. Her work shows considerable skill, if not mature achievement, and her performance in the following selection gains force from the fact that so many women writers were similarly not given credit for their creations. Later in the period, for example, Henry Fielding was credited with work written by his sister Sarah. The text is based on that in Poems by Anne Killigrew *(London, 1686).*

from *Poems* (1686)

UPON THE SAYING MY *VERSES* WERE MADE BY ANOTHER

Next Heaven my Vows to thee, O Sacred *Muse!*
I offered up, nor didst thou them refuse.
  'O Queen of Verse', said I , 'if thou'lt inspire,
And warm my Soul with thy Poetic Fire,
No Love of Gold shall share with thee my Heart,   5
Or yet Ambition in my Breast have Part,
More Rich, more Noble I will ever hold
The *Muses'* Laurel, than a Crown of Gold.[1]
An Undivided Sacrifice I'll lay
Upon thine Altar, Soul and Body pay;   10
Thou shalt my Pleasure, my Employment be,
My All I'll make a Holocaust to thee'.[2]

---

[2] *Mould* mole.
UPON THE SAYING MY *VERSES* WERE MADE BY ANOTHER
[1] *Laurel* a crown of bay laurel leaves, given as a sign of poetic achievement.

[2] *Holocaust* lit. "all burnt," a total sacrifice.

The Deity that ever does attend
Prayers so sincere, to mine did condescend.
I writ, and the Judicious praised my Pen: 15
Could any doubt Ensuing Glory then?
What pleasing Raptures filled my Ravished Sense?
How strong, how Sweet, Fame, was thy Influence?
And thine, False Hope, that to my flattered sight
Didst Glories represent so Near, and Bright?   20
By thee deceived, methought, each Verdant Tree,
Apollo's transformed *Daphne* seemed to be;[3]
And every fresher Branch, and every Bough
Appeared as Garland to empale my Brow.[4]
The Learned in Love, say, Thus the Wingèd Boy[5]   25
Does first approach, dressed up in welcome Joy;
At first he to the Cheated Lover's sight
Nought represents, but Rapture and Delight,
Alluring Hopes, Soft Fears, which stronger bind
Their Hearts, than when they more assurance find.   30
    Emboldened thus, to Fame I did commit,
(By some few hands) my most Unlucky Wit.[6]
But, ah, the sad effects that from it came!
What ought t' have brought me Honour, brought me shame!
Like *Æsop's* Painted Jay I seemed to all,[7]   35
Adorned in Plumes, I not my own could call:
Rifled like her, each one my Feathers tore,
And, as they thought, unto the Owner bore.
My Laurels thus an Other's Brow adorned,
My Numbers they Admired, but Me they scorned:[8]   40
An other's Brow, that had so rich a store
Of Sacred Wreaths, that circled it before;
Where mine quite lost, like a small stream that ran
Into a Vast and Boundless Ocean,
Was swallowed up with what it joined and drowned,   45
And that Abyss yet no Accession found.
    Orinda (*Albion's* and her Sex's Grace)[9],
Owed not her Glory to a Beauteous Face;
It was her Radiant Soul that shone With-in,
Which struck a Lustre through her Outward Skin;   50
That did her Lips and Cheeks with Roses dye,

3 *Daphne* Gk. "laurel"; she was transformed into the tree to escape the advances of the god Apollo, who then held the tree sacred (Ovid, *Metamorphoses* 1.452–548).
4 *empale* to encircle.
5 *Wingèd Boy* Cupid.
6 *Wit* intelligence, mind.
7 *Æsop's Painted Jay* a jackdaw who attaches to himself the moulted feathers from all the other birds in an attempt to impress Zeus and win the rule over his kind;
just when victory seems assured, the other birds take their own back, and the jackdaw is left bare in the sight of the god.
8 *Numbers* metrical language, verse.
9 *Albion* an ancient, poetical name for England (perhaps from Latin *albus*, "white," for the white cliffs on the southern coast); *Orinda* the poetical name of Katherine Philips (see above, p. 357).

Advanced her Height, and Sparkled in her Eye.
Nor did her Sex at all obstruct her Fame,
But higher 'mong the Stars it fixed her Name;
What she did write, not only all allowed,   55
But every Laurel, to her Laurel, bowed!
   Th' Envious Age, only to Me alone,
Will not allow, what I do write, my Own,
But let 'em Rage, and 'gainst a Maid Conspire,
So Deathless Numbers from my Tuneful Lyre   60
Do ever flow; so *Phoebus* I by thee[10]
Divinely Inspired and possessed may be;
I willingly accept *Cassandra's* Fate[11],
To speak the Truth, although believed too late.

Anne Kingsmill Finch, Countess of Winchilsea
(1661–1720)

1688 marked a watershed in Finch's life as well as that of the nation's. She and her husband held positions in the court of James II, and after his deposition, they refused to swear allegiance to William and Mary. Outcast from the political world of London, they went to live with relations in Kent. Heneage Finch eventually became the Earl of Winchilsea, and Anne devoted herself to reading, writing, and an appreciation of her beautiful natural surroundings. However, contact with literary London was not altogether lost. In 1713, for example, she dined with Alexander Pope in London and heard a play read with him, as the great poet's correspondence for December of that year atttests. On 12 January 1709 Jonathan Swift wrote to a friend in Paris, "I amuse myself sometimes with writing verses to Mrs. Finch, and sometimes with Projects for uniting of Parties, which I perfect over night, and burn in the morning; sometimes Mr. Addison and I steal a pint of bad wine . . ." Finch was enough of a figure to be on Swift's mind and to require no more explanation in a friendly letter than Addison.

Finch published "The Spleen" anonymously in 1701, but one of the three editions of her Miscellany Poems in 1713 actually printed her name on the title page, a fairly good indication of celebrity. "The Spleen" was revised and reprinted for Miscellany Poems, and most of the texts printed here are based on that edition. Two poems, however, "The Unequal Fetters" and "The Answer" are among the many that were not published in Finch's lifetime, and I draw them from a much later edition of her poems by Myra Reynolds (University of Chicago Press, 1903). Like many seventeenth- and eighteenth-century poets, but particularly women, Finch wrote numerous poems that she would have been uncomfortable publishing in her lifetime. The reasons for this have partly to do with changed standards of decorum but also with the nearly complete disappearance of manuscript "publication" – the informal circulation of poetry among the coterie of friends or fellow writers for whom the works were mainly intended. That has all but entirely been taken over by

---

[10] *Phoebus* Apollo, god of poetry.
[11] *Cassandra's Fate* she was beloved of Apollo and given the gift of prophecy but suffered the fate of never being believed, as when she prophesied the fall of her father's kingdom of Troy.

print. Therefore, a complete edition of Finch is long overdue, but it is finally about to appear under the editorship of Carol Barash.

from *Miscellany Poems* (1713)

THE INTRODUCTION

Did I, my lines intend for public view,
How many censures, would their faults pursue,
Some would, because such words they do affect,
Cry they're insipid, empty, uncorrect.
And many, have attained, dull and untaught   5
The name of Wit, only by finding fault.
True judges, might condemn their want of wit,
And all might say, they're by a Woman writ.
Alas! a woman that attempts the pen,
Such an intruder on the rights of men,   10
Such a presumptuous Creature, is esteemed,
The fault, can by no virtue be redeemed.
They tell us, we mistake our sex and way;
Good breeding, fashion, dancing, dressing, play
Are the accomplishments we should desire;   15
To write, or read, or think, or to enquire
Would cloud our beauty, and exhaust our time,
And interrupt the Conquests of our prime;
Whilst the dull manage, of a servile house
Is held by some, our utmost art, and use.   20
    Sure 'twas not ever thus, nor are we told
Fables, of Women that excelled of old;[1]
To whom, by the diffusive hand of Heaven
Some share of wit, and poetry was given.
On that glad day, on which the Ark returned,[2]   25
The holy pledge, for which the Land had mourned,
The joyful Tribes, attend it on the way,
The Levites do the sacred Charge convey,
Whilst various Instruments, before it play;
Here, holy Virgins in the Concert join,   30
The louder notes, to soften, and refine,
And with alternate verse, complete the Hymn Divine.[3]
Lo! the young Poet, after God's own heart,
By Him inspired, and taught the Muses' Art,

THE INTRODUCTION
[1] *Fables* false stories.
[2] *Ark* the ark of the covenant, the chest containing agreements between God and the Israelites, such as the tablets on which the ten commandments were written, the central object of the tabernacle; the most elaborate description of the return of the ark from an enemy is in 1 Chronicles 15–16.
[3] *Hymn Divine* David, *the young Poet*'s psalm of thanks for the return of the ark (1 Chronicles 16.7–36).

Returned from Conquest, a bright Chorus meets,[4]   35
That sing his slain ten thousand in the streets.
In such loud numbers they his acts declare,[5]
Proclaim the wonders, of his early war,
That Saul upon the vast applause does frown,
And feels, its mighty thunder shake the Crown.   40
What, can the threatened Judgement now prolong?[6]
Half of the Kingdom is already gone;
The fairest half, whose influence guides the rest,
Have David's Empire, o'er their hearts confessed.
    A Woman here, leads fainting Israel on,   45
She fights, she wins, she triumphs with a song,
Devout, Majestic, for the subject fit,
And far above her arms, exalts her wit,
Then, to the peaceful, shady Palm withdraws,
And rules the rescued Nation, with her Laws.   50
How are we fal'n, fal'n by mistaken rules?
And Education's, more than Nature's fools,
Debarred from all improvements of the mind,
And to be dull, expected and designed;
And if some one, would Soar above the rest,   55
With warmer fancy, and ambition pressed,
So strong, th' opposing faction still appears,
The hopes to thrive, can ne'er outweigh the fears,
Be cautioned then my Muse, and still retired;
Nor be despised, aiming to be admired;   60
Conscious of wants, still with contracted wing,
To some few friends, and to thy sorrow sing;
For groves of Laurel, thóu wert never meant;[7]
Be dark enough thy shades, and be thou there content.

LIFE'S PROGRESS

How gayly is at first begun
    Our *Life*'s uncertain Race!
Whilst yet that sprightly Morning Sun,
With which we just set out to run
    Enlightens all the Place.   5

How smiling the World's Prospect lies
    How tempting to go through!
Not *Canaan* to the Prophet's Eyes,[1]

---

[4] *a bright Chorus*   women greet David on his return from his miraculous conquest of Goliath; King Saul envies him (1 Samuel 18.6–7).
[5] *numbers*   verses, poetry.
[6] *Judgement*   the prophecy of Samuel that a "neighbour" would rule instead of Saul (1 Samuel 15.28).

[7] *laurel*   bay laurel, symbolic of poetic or some other public achievement.
LIFE'S PROGRESS
[1] *Canaan*   the promised land of the Israelites.

From *Pisgah* with a sweet Surprise,[2]
   Did more inviting show.   10

How promising's the Book of Fate,
   Till throughly understood!
Whilst partial Hopes such Lots create,
As may the youthful Fancy treat
   With all that's Great and Good.   15

How soft the first Ideas prove,
   Which wander through our Minds!
How full the Joys, how free the Love,
Which does that early Season move;
   As Flow'rs the Western Winds!   20

Our Sighs are then but Vernal Air;
   But *April*-drops our Tears,
Which swiftly passing, all grows Fair,
Whilst Beauty compensates our Care,
   And Youth each Vapour clears.   25

But oh! too soon, alas, we climb;
   Scarce feeling we ascend
The gently rising Hill of *Time*,
From whence with Grief we see that Prime,
   And all its Sweetness end.   30

The Die now cast, our Station known,
   Fond Expectation past;
The Thorns, which former Days had sown,[3]
To Crops of late Repentance grown,
Through which we toil at last.[4]   35

Whilst every Care's a driving Harm,
   That helps to bear us down;
Which faded Smiles no more can charm,
But every Tear's a Winter-Storm,
   And every Look's a Frown.   40

Till with succeeeding Ills oppressed,
   For Joys we hoped to find;
By Age too, rumpled and undressed,
We gladly sinking down to rest,
   Leave following Crowds behind.   45

---

[2] *Pisgah* the mountain from which Moses viewed the promised land which he was never able to enter (Deuteronomy 34.1–4).

[3] *Thorns* an echo of Jeremiah 12.13, "They have sown wheat, but shall reap thorns."

[4] *Through which we toil* "The way of the slothful man is as an hedge of thorns" (Proverbs 15.19).

Adam Posed[1]

Could our First Father, at his toilsome Plough,
Thorns in his Path, and Labour on his Brow,
Clothed only in a rude, unpolished Skin,
Could he a vain Fantastic Nymph have seen,[2]
In all her Airs, in all her antic Graces,[3]　　　　　　　　　　　　5
Her various Fashions, and more various Faces;
How had it posed that Skill, which late assigned
Just Appellations to Each several Kind![4]
A right Idea of the Sight to frame;
T' have guessed from what New Element she came;　　　　　　10
T' have hit the wav'ring Form, or giv'n this Thing a Name.

The Petition for an Absolute Retreat

Inscribed to the Right Honourable *CATHARINE* Countess of *THANET*,
mentioned in the Poem under the Name of *ARMINDA*[1]

Give me O indulgent Fate!
Give me yet, before I Die,
A sweet, but absolute Retreat,
'Mongst Paths so lost, and Trees so high,
That the World may ne'er invade,　　　　　　　　　　　　5
Through such Windings and such Shade,
My unshaken Liberty.
　　No Intruders thither come!
Who visit, but to be from home;
None who their vain Moments pass,　　　　　　　　　　　10
Only studious of their Glass,[2]
News, that charm to list'ning Ears;
That false Alarm to Hopes and Fears;
That common Theme for every Fop,[3]
From the Statesman to the Shop,　　　　　　　　　　　　15
In those Coverts ne'er be spread,
Of who's Deceased, or who's to Wed,
Be no Tidings thither brought,
But Silent, as a Midnight Thought,
Where the World may ne'er invade,　　　　　　　　　　　20
Be those Windings, and that Shade:
　　Courteous Fate! afford me there
A *Table* spread without my Care,
With what the neighb'ring Fields impart,

Adam Posed
[1] *Posed* puzzled.
[2] *Nymph* "A lady. In poetry" (Johnson).
[3] *antic* "Odd; ridiculously wild" (Johnson).
[4] *just Appelations* Adam named all the animals of Eden (Genesis 2.20).

The Petition for an Absolute Retreat
[1] *Catharine, Countess of Thanet* member of a prominent Kent family.
[2] *Glass* mirror.
[3] *Fop* a dandy, a fashionable, superficial fellow.

Whose Cleanliness be all its Art,   25
When, of old, the Calf was dressed,
(Though to make an Angel's Feast)
In the plain, unstudied Sauce
Nor *Treufle*, nor *Morillia* was;[4]
Nor could the mighty Patriarch's Board[5]   30
One far-fetched *Ortolane*[6] afford.
Courteous Fate, then give me there
Only plain, and wholesome Fare.
Fruits indeed (would Heaven bestow)
All, that did in *Eden* grow,   35
All, but the *Forbidden Tree*,
Would be coveted by me;
Grapes, with Juice so crowded up,
As breaking through the native Cup;
Figs (yet growing) candied o'er,   40
By the Sun's attracting Pow'r;
Cherries, with the downy Peach,
All within my easy Reach;
Whilst creeping near the humble Ground,
Should the Strawberry be found   45
Springing wheresoe'er I strayed,
Through those Windings and that Shade.
   For my *Garments*; let them be
What may with the Time agree;
Warm, when *Phœbus* does retire,[7]   50
And is ill-supplied by Fire:
But when he renews the Year,
And verdant all the Fields appear;
Beauty every thing resumes,
Birds have dropped their Winter-Plumes;   55
When the Lilly full displayed,
Stands in purer White arrayed,
Than that Vest, which heretofore
The Luxurious Monarch wore,[8]
When from *Salem*'s Gates he drove,[9]   60
To the soft Retreat of Love,
Lebanon's all burnished House,
And the dear *Egyptian* Spouse.[10]
Clothe me, Fate, though not so Gay;
Clothe me light, and fresh as *May*:   65

---

4 *Treufle* truffle, an edible fungus; *Morillia* morel, another edible fungus.
5 *Patriarch* Abraham, who entertains three messengers of the Lord in plain but hospitable fashion (Genesis 18).
6 *Ortolane* a small bird with a delicate flavor.
7 *Phœbus* Apollo, the Greek god of the sun.

8 *Luxurious Monarch* Solomon; Finch inserts a long note here, citing the historian Josephus' account of Solomon's very white robe, or "vest."
9 *Salem* Jerusalem.
10 *Egyptian Spouse* the daughter of Pharaoh, for whom Solomon built a house of Lebanon cedar, covered with jewels (1 Kings 7.8–12).

In the Fountains let me view
All my Habit cheap and new;
Such as, when sweet *Zephyrs* fly,[11]
With their Motions may comply;
Gently waving, to express   70
Unaffected Carelessness:
No Perfumes have there a Part,
Borrowed from the *Chemist's* Art;
But such as rise from flow'ry Beds,
Or the falling *Jasmine* Sheds!   75
'Twas the Odour of the Field,
Esau's rural Coat did yield,[12]
That inspired his Father's Prayer,
For Blessings of the Earth and Air:
Of Gums, or Powders had it smelt;   80
The Supplanter, then unfelt,
Easily had been descried,
For One that did in Tents abide;
For some beauteous Handmaid's Joy,
And his Mother's darling Boy.   85
Let me then no Fragrance wear,
But what the Winds from Gardens bear,
In such kind, surprising Gales,[13]
As gathered from *Fidentia's* Vales,
All the Flowers that in them grew;   90
Which intermixing, as they flew,
In wreathen Garlands dropped again,
On *Lucullus*, and his Men;
Who, cheered by the victorious Sight,
Trebled Numbers put to Flight.[14]   95
Let me, when I must be fine,
In such natural Colours shine;
Wove, and painted by the Sun,
Whose resplendent Rays to shun,
When they do too fiercely beat,   100
Let me find some close Retreat,
Where they have no Passage made,
Through those Windings, and that Shade.
    Give me there (since Heaven has shown
It was not Good to be alone)   105
A *Partner* suited to my Mind,
Solitary, pleased and kind;
Who, partially, may something see

---

[11] *Zephyrs* light westerly winds.
[12] *Esau's rural Coat* the "goodly raiment" of animal skins in which Rebekah clothed Jacob so he could deceive his aged father Isaac into giving him the blessing meant for his older brother (Genesis 27.6–29).
[13] *Gales* gentle breezes.

[14] *Lucullus and his Men . . . put to Flight* as Finch notes, the story is in Plutarch's life of Sulla (27.7–8); the flowers from *Fidentia* (in northern Italy) seemed to the Roman soldiers as garlands crowning them and their weapons with victory; this inspired them to kill 18,000 of the enemy (c. 83 BCE).

Preferred to all the World in me;
Slighting, by my humble Side,   110
Fame and Splendour, Wealth and Pride.
When but Two the Earth possessed,
'Twas their happiest Days, and best;
They by Business, nor by Wars,
They by no Domestic Cares,   115
From each other e'er were drawn,
But in some Grove, or flow'ry Lawn,
Spent their own, and Nature's Prime,
In Love; that only Passion given
To perfect Man, whilst Friends with Heaven.   120
Rage, and Jealousy, and Hate,
Transports of his fallen State
(When by *Satan*'s Wiles betrayed),
Fly those Windings, and that Shade!
    Thus from Crowds, and Noise removed,   125
Let each Moment be improved;
Every Object still produce,
Thoughts of Pleasure, and of Use:
When some River slides away,
To increase the boundless Sea;   130
Think we then, how Time does haste,
To grow Eternity at last,
By the Willows, on the Banks,
Gathered into social Ranks,
Playing with the gentle Winds,   135
Straight the Boughs, and smooth the Rinds,
Moist each Fibre, and each Top,
Wearing a luxurious Crop,
Let the time of Youth be shown,
The time alas! too soon outgrown;   140
Whilst a lonely stubborn Oak,
Which no Breezes can provoke,
No less Gusts persuade to move,
Than those, which in a Whirlwind drove,
Spoiled the old Fraternal Feast,   145
And left alive but one poor Guest;[15]
Rivelled the distorted Trunk,[16]
Sapless Limbs all bent, and shrunk,
Sadly does the Time presage,
Of our too near approaching Age.   150
When a helpless Vine is found,
Unsupported on the Ground,
Careless all the Branches spread,
Subject to each haughty Tread,

---

[15] *one poor Guest* the messenger who reports the de-   [16] *Rivelled* shrivelled, wrinkled.
struction of his son's house to Job (Job 1.18–19).

Bearing neither Leaves, nor Fruit,   155
Living only in the Root;
Back reflecting let me say,
So the sad *Ardelia* lay;[17]
Blasted by a Storm of Fate,[18]
Felt, through all the *British* State;   160
Fall'n, neglected, lost, forgot,
Dark Oblivion all her Lot;
Faded till *Arminda*'s Love,
(Guided by the Pow'rs above)
Warmed anew her drooping Heart,
And Life diffused through every Part;   165
Mixing Words, in wise Discourse,
Of such Weight and wond'rous Force,
As could all her Sorrows charm,
And transitory Ills disarm;
Cheering the delightful Day,   170
When disposed to be more Gay,
With Wit, from an unmeasured Store,
To Woman ne'er allowed before.
What Nature, or refining Art,
All that Fortune could impart,   175
Heaven did to *Arminda* send;
Then gave her for *Ardelia*'s Friend:
To her cares the Cordial drop,
Which else had overflowed the Cup.
So, when once the Son of *Jesse*,[19]   180
Every Anguish did oppress,
Hunted by all kinds of Ills,
Like a *Partridge* on the Hills;
Trains were laid to catch his Life,
Baited with a Royal Wife,   185
From his House, and Country torn,
Made a Heathen Prince's Scorn;
Fate, to answer all these Harms,
Threw a *Friend* into his Arms.[20]
Friendship still has been designed,   190
The Support of Human-kind;
The safe delight, the useful Bliss,
The next World's Happiness, and this.
Give then, O indulgent Fate!
Give a Friend in that Retreat   195
(Though withdrawn from all the rest)

[17] *Ardelia* Finch's poetic name for herself.
[18] *Storm of Fate* the Glorious Revolution (1688–9), which sent Finch and her husband into retirement in Kent because they remained loyal to the Stuarts and would not swear allegiance to William III.
[19] *Son of Jesse* King David.
[20] *a Friend* Jonathan, the son of King Saul, who envied and persecuted David (1 Samuel 18.24).

Still a Clue, to reach my Breast.[21]
Let a Friend be still conveyed
Through those Windings, and that Shade!
    Where, may I remain secure,   200
Waste, in humble Joys and pure,
A Life, that can no Envy yield;
Want of Affluence my Shield.
Thus, had *Crassus* been content,[22]
When from *Marius* Rage he went,   205
With the Seat that Fortune gave,
The commodious ample Cave,
Formed, in a divided Rock,
By some mighty Earthquake's Shock,
Into Rooms of every Size,   210
Fair, as Art could e'er devise,
Leaving, in the marble Roof
('Gainst all Storms and Tempests proof),
Only Passage for the Light,
To refresh the cheerful Sight,   215
Whilst Three Sharers in his Fate,
On th' Escape with joy dilate,
Beds of Moss their Bodies bore,
Canopied with Ivy o'er;
Rising Springs, that round them played,   220
O'er the native Pavement strayed;
When the Hour arrived to Dine,
Various Meats, and sprightly Wine,
On some neighb'ring Cliff they spied;
Every Day a-new supplied   225
By a Friend's entrusted Care;
Had He still continued there,
Made that lonely wond'rous Cave
Both his Palace, and his Grave;
Peace and Rest he might have found   230
(Peace and Rest are under Ground),
Nor have been in that Retreat,
Famed for a Proverbial Fate;[23]
In pursuit of Wealth been caught,
And punished with a golden Draught.   235

---

[21] *Clue* the thread given by Ariadne to Theseus to help him from the labyrinth once he had killed the Minotaur.

[22] *Crassus* Marcus Licinius Crassus (115–53 BCE), later a Roman triumvir, fled from the slaughter of real and imagined enemies launched by Cinna and Gaius Marius in 86 BCE and lived in a spacious cave (Plutarch, *Crassus* 4–5); Finch notes that her description of the cave is "exactly taken" from Plutarch.

[23] *a Proverbial Fate* his life was said to have ended like a tragedy; he sought wealth in Syria, but was killed by the Parthians; his head was brought to the Parthian court during a performance of Euripides' *Bacchae* and used as the head of slaughtered Pentheus in the final act (Plutarch, *Crassus* 33).

Nor had He, who Crowds could blind,[24]
Whisp'ring with a snowy Hind,
Made 'em think that from above,
(Like the great Impostor's Dove)[25]
Tidings to his Ears she brought,   240
Rules by which he marched and fought,
After *Spain* he had o'er-run,
Cities sacked, and Battles won,
Drove *Rome*'s Consuls from the Field,
Made her darling *Pompey* yield,[26]   245
At a fatal, treacherous Feast,
Felt a Dagger in his Breast;
Had he his once-pleasing Thought
Of Solitude to Practice brought;
Had no wild Ambition swayed;   250
In those Islands had he stayed,[27]
Justly called the Seats of Rest,
Truly Fortunate, and Blest,
By the ancient Poets giv'n
As their best discovered Heav'n.   255
Let me then, indulgent Fate!
Let me be still, in my Retreat,
From all roving Thoughts be freed,
Or Aims, that may Contention breed:
Nor be my Endeavours led   260
By Goods, that perish with the Dead!
Fitly might the Life of Man
Be indeed esteemed a Span,[28]
If the present Moment were
Of Delight his only Share;   265
If no other Joys he knew
Than what round about him grew:
But as those, who Stars would trace
From a subterranean Place,
Through some Engine lift their Eyes[29]   270
To the outward, glorious Skies;
So th' immortal Spirit may,
When descended to our Clay,
From a rightly governed Frame
View the Height, from whence she came;   275
To her Paradise be caught,
And things unutterable taught.

[24]   *He*   Sertorius [Finch's note; he deceived locals into believing his tame doe was a gift from heaven and could speak its prophecies; see Plutarch, *Sertorius* 11].
[25]   *great Impostor*   the French playwright Molière's title character Tartuffe.
[26]   *Pompey*   great Roman general forced to bring in reserves to deal with Sertorius.

[27]   *those Islands*   The Canary Islands, called by the Ancients the Fortunate Islands and taken by some of the Poets for Elysium [Finch's note; see Plutarch, *Sertorius* 8–9].
[28]   *Span*   "Any short duration" (Johnson).
[29]   *Engine*   instrument, device.

        Give me then, in that Retreat,
        Give me, O indulgent Fate!
        For all Pleasures left behind,   280
        Contemplations of the Mind.
        Let the Fair, the Gay, the Vain
        Courtship and Applause obtain;
        Let th' Ambitious rule the Earth;
        Let the giddy Fool have Mirth;   285
        Give the Epicure his Dish,
        Every one their several Wish;
        Whilst my Transport I employ
        On that more extensive Joy,
        When all Heaven shall be surveyed   290
        From those Windings and that Shade.

TO THE NIGHTINGALE

Exert thy Voice, sweet Harbinger of Spring!
    This Moment is thy Time to Sing,
    This Moment I attend to Praise,
And set my Numbers to thy Lays.
    Free as thine shall be my Song;   5
    As thy Music, short, or long.
Poets, wild as thee, were born,
    Pleasing best when unconfined,
    When to Please is least designed,
Soothing but their Cares to rest;   10
    Cares do still their Thoughts molest,
    And still th' unhappy Poet's Breast,
Like thine, when best he sings, is placed against a Thorn.
She begins, Let all be still!
    Muse, thy Promise now fulfil!   15
Sweet, oh! sweet, still sweeter yet
Can thy Words such Accents fit,
Canst thou Syllables refine,
Melt a Sense that shall retain
Still some Spirit of the Brain,   20
Till with Sounds like these it join.
    'Twill not be! then change thy Note;
    Let Division shake thy Throat.[1]
Hark! Division now she tries;
Yet as far the Muse outflies.   25
    Cease then, prithee, cease thy Tune;
    Trifler, wilt thou sing till *June*?
Till thy Business all lies waste,

TO THE NIGHTINGALE
[1] *Division* in music, a run or variation, in which several notes are interpolated between those of the main melody.

> And the Time of Building's past!
> Thus we Poets that have Speech,   30
> Unlike what thy Forests teach,
> If a fluent Vein be shown
> That's transcendent to our own,
> Criticize, reform, or preach,
> Or censure what we cannot reach.   35

A POEM FOR THE BIRTH-DAY OF THE RIGHT HONOURABLE THE LADY CATHARINE TUFTON[1]

Occasioned by sight of some Verses upon that Subject for the preceding Year, composed by no Eminent Hand

> 'Tis fit SERENA should be sung.
> High-born SERENA, Fair and Young,
> Should be of every Muse and Voice
> The pleasing, and applauded Choice.
> But as the Meanest of the Show   5
> Do First in all Processions go:
> So, let my Steps pursue that Swain
> The humblest of th' inspired Train;
> Whose well-meant Verse did just appear,
> To lead on the preceding Year: 10
> So let my Pen, the next in Fame,
> Now wait on fair SERENA's Name;
> The second Tribute gladly pay,
> And hail this blest returning Day.
> But let it not attempt to raise   15
> Or rightly speak SERENA's Praise:
> Since with more ease we might declare
> How Great that more distinguished Peer,[2]
> To whom she owes her Being here;
> In whom our *Britain* lets us see   20
> What once they were, and still should be;
> As, when the earliest Race was drowned,
> Some Patterns, from amongst them found,
> Were kept to show succeeding Times
> Their Excellence without their Crimes: 25
> More easily we might express
> What Virtues do her Mother dress;
> What does her Form and Mind adorn,
> Of whom th' engaging Nymph was born:
> What Piety, what generous Love,   30

A POEM FOR THE BIRTH-DAY
[1] *Catharine Tufton* (b. 1692), daughter of the Countess of Thanet (see "Petition for an Absolute Retreat," above); called Serena in Finch's poetry.

[2] *more distinguished Peer* Thomas Tufton, sixth Earl of Thanet.

Does the enlargèd Bosom move
Of her, whose Favourite she appears,[3]
Who more than as a Niece endears.
Such full Perfections obvious lie,
And strike, at first, a Poet's Eye.   35
Deep lines of Honour all can hit,
Or mark out a superior Wit;
Consummate Goodness all can show,
And where such Graces shine below:
But the more tender Strokes to trace,   40
T' express the Promise of a Face,
When but the Drawings of the Mind
We from an Air unripened find;
Which alt'ring, as new Moments rise,
The Pen or Pencil's Art defies;   45
When Flesh and Blood in Youth appears,
Polished like what our Marble wears;
Fresh as that Shade of op'ning Green,
Which first upon our Groves is seen;
Enlivened by a harmless Fire,   50
And brightened by each gay Desire;
These nicer Touches would demand
A *Cowley*'s or a *Waller*'s Hand,[4]
T' explain, with undisputed Art,
What 'tis affects th' enlightened Heart,   55
When every darker Thought gives way,
Whilst blooming Beauty we survey;
To show how All, that's soft and sweet,
Does in the fair SERENA meet;
To tell us, with a sure Presage,   60
The Charms of her maturer Age.
When *Hothfield*[5] shall (as heretofore
From its far-sought and virtuous Store
It Families of great Renown
Did with illustrious Hymen's crown)[6]   65
When *Hothfield* shall such Treasure know,
As fair SERENA to bestow:
Then should some Muse of loftier Wing
The Triumphs of that Season sing;
Describe the Pains, the Hopes, the Fears   70
Of noble Youths, th' ambitious Cares
Of Fathers, the long-framed Design,
To add such Splendour to their Line,

---

[3] *her* the Lady Coventry [Finch's note, meaning
Margaret Tufton].
[4] *Cowley . . . Waller* Abraham Cowley (1618–67) and
Edmund Waller (1606–86), poets.
[5] *Hothfield* the family seat of the Tuftons in Kent.
[6] *Hymen* god of marriage.

Whilst all shall strive for such a Bride
    So Educated, and Allied.   75

THE ATHEIST AND THE ACORN

'Methinks this World is oddly made,
    And every thing's amiss',
A dull presuming Atheist said,
As stretched he lay beneath a Shade;
    And instanced in this: 5

'Behold', quoth he, 'that mighty thing,
    A *Pumpkin*, large and round,
Is held but by a little String,
Which upwards cannot make it spring,
    Or bear it from the Ground.   10

'Whilst on this *Oak*, a Fruit so small,
    So disproportioned, grows;
That, who with Sense surveys this *All*,
This universal Casual Ball,[1]
    Its ill Contrivance knows.   15

'My better Judgement would have hung
    That Weight upon a Tree,
And left this Mast, thus slightly strung,[2]
'Mongst things which on the Surface sprung,
    And small and feeble be'.   20

No more the Caviller could say,
    Nor farther Faults descry;
For, as he upwards gazing lay,
An *Acorn*, loosened from the Stay,
    Fell down upon his Eye.   25

Th' offended Part with Tears ran o'er,
    As punished for the Sin:
Fool! had that Bough a *Pumpkin* bore,
Thy Whimsies must have worked no more,
    Nor Skull had kept them in.   30

The Unequal Fetters

Could we stop the time that's flying
    Or recall it when 'tis past
Put far off the day of Dying
    Or make Youth for ever last
To Love would then be worth our cost.   5

THE ATHEIST AND THE ACORN   [2] *Mast* "The fruit of the oak and beech" (Johnson).
[1] *Casual* "arising from chance; depending upon
chance" (Johnson), rather than divine government.

But since we must lose those Graces
    Which at first your hearts have won
And you seek for in new Faces
    When our Spring of Life is done
It would but urge our ruin on   10

Free as Nature's first intention
    Was to make us, I'll be found
Nor by subtle Man's invention
    Yield to be in Fetters bound
By one that walks a freer round.   15

Marriage does but slightly tie Men
    Whilst close Pris'ners we remain
They the larger Slaves of Hymen[1]
    Still are begging Love again
At the full length of all their chain.   20

The Answer
(To Pope's Impromptu)[1]

Disarmed with so genteel an air,
    The contest I give o'er;
Yet, Alexander, have a care,
    And shock the sex no more.
We rule the world our life's whole race,   5
    Men but assume that right;
First slaves to every tempting face,
    Then martyrs to our spite.
You of one Orpheus sure have read,[2]
    Who would like you have writ   10
Had he in London town been bred,
    And polished too his wit;
But he poor soul thought all was well,
    And great should be his fame,
When he had left his wife in hell,   15
    And birds and beast could tame.
Yet venturing then with scoffing rhymes
    The women to incense,
Resenting Heroines of those times
    Soon punished his offence.   20
And as the Hebrus rolled his skull,
    And harp besmeared with blood,
They clashing as the waves grew full,
    Still harmonized the flood.

THE UNEQUAL FETTERS
[1] *larger* freer; *Hymen* god of marriage.
THE ANSWER
[1] *Pope's Impromptu* *The Rape of the Lock.*

[2] *Orpheus* a legendary pre-Homeric poet whose music charmed wild beasts and made rocks and trees move; he failed to recover his wife Eurydice from Hades; maenads, followers of Dionysius, tore him to pieces and sent his head floating down the River *Hebrus* in Thrace.

But you our follies gently treat,   25
    And spin so fine the thread
You need not fear his awkward fate,
    The lock won't cost the head.
Our admiration you command
    For all that's gone before;   30
What next we look for at your hand
    Can only raise it more.
Yet sooth the Ladies I advise
    (As me too pride has wrought),
We're born to wit, but to be wise   35
    By admonitions taught.

The *Spleen*: A Pindaric Poem[1] (1701; revised 1713)

What art thou, *SPLEEN*, which every thing dost ape?
    Thou *Proteus* to abused Mankind,[2]
    Who never yet thy real Cause could find,
Or fix thee to remain in one continued Shape.
    Still varying thy perplexing Form,   5
    Now a Dead sea thou'lt represent,
    A Calm of stupid Discontent,
Then, dashing on the Rocks wilt rage into a Storm.
    Trembling sometimes thou dost appear,
    Dissolved into a Panic fear;   10
    On Sleep intruding dost thy Shadows spread,
    Thy gloomy Terrors round the silent Bed,
And crowd with boding Dreams the Melancholy Head;
    Or, when the Midnight Hour is told,
    And drooping Lids thou still dost waking hold,   15
    Thy fond Delusions cheat the Eyes,
    Before them antic Spectres dance,[3]
Unusual Fires their pointed Heads advance,
    And airy Phantoms rise.
    Such was the monstrous *Vision* seen,   20
When *Brutus* (now beneath his Cares oppressed,[4]
And all *Rome's* Fortunes rolling in his Breast,
    Before *Philippi's* latest Field,
Before his Fate did to *Octavius* lead)
    Was vanquished by the *Spleen*.   25

THE *SPLEEN*: A PINDARIC POEM
[1] *Pindaric* after the great praise poet of fifth century
BCE Greece, but meaning largely that the poem uses a
variety of prosodical forms and is somewhat irregular, as
Pindar was thought to be because of his difficulty and the
rapid rhetorical shifts in his verse; *Spleen* "Melancholy;
hypochondriacal vapours" (Johnson); the name of a variety of ills, like today's "depression."

[2] *Proteus* a shape-shifting, prophetic old man of the
sea in Greek myth.
[3] *antic* "Odd; ridiculously wild" (Johnson).
[4] *Brutus* Marcus Junius Brutus (85–42 BCE) Roman
general and statesman; participated in the assassination
of Julius Caesar; committed suicide after his defeat by
Antony and Octavius Caesar in the second battle of
Philippi.

Falsely, the Mortal part we blame
Of our depressed, and pond'rous Frame,
Which, till the First degrading Sin
Let Thee, its dull Attendant, in,
Still with the Other did comply,   30
Nor clogged the Active Soul, disposed to fly,
And range the Mansions of its native Sky.
   Nor, whilst in his own Heaven he dwelt,
   Whilst Man his Paradise possessed,
His fertile Garden in the fragrant East,   35
   And all united Odours smelt,
   No armèd Sweets, until thy Reign,
   Could shock the Sense, or in the Face
   A flushed, unhandsome Colour place.
Now the *Jonquille* o'ercomes the feeble Brain;[5]   40
We faint beneath the Aromatic Pain,
Till some offensive Scent thy Pow'rs appease,
And Pleasure we resign for short, and nauseous Ease.
   In every One thou dost possess,
   New are thy Motions, and thy Dress: 45
   Now in some Grove a list'ning Friend
   Thy false Suggestions must attend,
Thy whispered Griefs, thy fancied Sorrows hear,
Breathed in a Sigh, and witnessed by a Tear;
   Whilst in the light, and vulgar Crowd,   50
   Thy Slaves, more clamorous and loud,
By Laughters unprovoked, thy Influence too confess.
In the Imperious *Wife* thou Vapours art,[6]
   Which from o'erheated Passions rise
   In clouds to the attractive Brain,   55
   Until descending thence again,
Through the o'ercast, and show'ring Eyes,
Upon her Husband's softened Heart,
   He the disputed Point must yield,
Something resign of the contested Field;   60
Till Lordly *Man*, born to Imperial Sway,
Compounds for Peace, to make that Right away,[7]
And *Woman*, armed with *Spleen*, does servilely Obey.
   The *Fool*, to imitate the Wits,
   Complains of thy pretended Fits,   65
   And Dullness, born with him, would lay
   Upon thy accidental Sway,
   Because, sometimes, thou dost presume

[5] *Jonquille* "A species of daffodil. The flowers of this plant . . . are greatly esteemed for their strong sweet scent, though few ladies can bear the smell of them, it being so powerful as to overcome their spirits" (Johnson, quoting Miller's *Gardener's Dictionary*).

[6] *Vapours* "Mental fume; vain imagination" or, in the plural only, "hypochondriacal maladies; melancholy; spleen" (Johnson).
[7] *Compounds* comes to compromising terms.

Into the ablest heads to come:
That, often, Men of Thoughts refined,   70
Impatient of unequal Sense,[8]
Such slow Returns, where they so much dispense,
Retiring from the Crowd, are to thy Shades inclined.
O'er me alas! thou dost too much prevail:
I feel thy Force, whilst I against thee rail;   75
I feel my Verse decay, and my cramped Numbers fail.
Through thy black Jaundice I all Objects see,
As Dark, and Terrible as Thee,
My Lines decried, and my Employment thought
An useless Folly, or presumptuous Fault: 80
Whilst in the *Muse's* Path I stray,
Whilst in their Groves, and by their secret Springs
My Hand delights to trace unusual Things,
And deviates from the known, and common way;
Nor will in fading Silks compose   85
Faintly th' inimitable *Rose*,
Fill up an ill-drawn *Bird*, or paint on Glass
The *Sovereign's* blurred and undistinguished Face,[9]
The threat'ning *Angel*, and the speaking *Ass*.[10]
Patron thou art to every gross Abuse,   90
The sullen *Husband's* feigned Excuse,
When the ill Humour with his Wife he spends,
And bears recruited Wit, and Spirits to his Friends.
The Son of *Bacchus* pleads thy Pow'r,
As to the Glass he still repairs,   95
Pretends but to remove thy Cares,
Snatch from thy Shades one gay, and smiling Hour,
And drown thy Kingdom in a purple Show'r.
When the *Coquette*, whom every Fool admires,
Would in Variety be Fair,   100
And, changing hastily the Scene
From Light, Impertinent, and Vain,
Assumes a soft, a melancholy Air,
And of her Eyes rebates the wand'ring Fires,[11]
The careless Posture, and the Head reclined,   105
The thoughtful, and composèd Face,
Proclaiming the withdrawn, the absent Mind,
Allows the Fop more liberty to gaze,
Who gently for the tender Cause inquires;
The Cause, indeed, is a Defect in Sense,   110
Yet is the *Spleen* alledged, and still the dull Pretence.
But these are thy fantastic Harms,
The Tricks of thy pernicious Stage,

---

[8] *unequal Sense* experiential life, which is unequal to the flights of thoughts.
[9] *undistinguished* indistinguishable.

[10] *speaking Ass* it speaks when God places an angel in its path to prevent its master Balaam from disobeying him (Numbers 22.22–33); a hackneyed subject of amateur art.
[11] *rebates* blunts, damps.

Which do the weaker Sort engage;
Worse are the dire Effects of thy more pow'rful Charms.   115
    By Thee *Religion*, all we know,
    That should enlighten here below,
    Is veiled in Darkness, and perplexed
With anxious Doubts, with endless Scruples vexed,
And some Restraint implied from each perverted Text.   120
    Whilst *Touch* not, *Taste* not, what is freely giv'n,
Is but thy niggard Voice, disgracing bounteous Heav'n.
    From Speech restrained, by thy Deceits abused,
    To Deserts banished, or in Cells reclused,
    Mistaken Vot'ries to the Pow'rs Divine,   125
    Whilst they a purer Sacrifice design,
Do but the *Spleen* obey, and worship at thy Shrine.
    In vain to chase thee every Art we try,
    In vain all Remedies apply,
    In vain the *Indian* Leaf infuse,[12]   130
    Or the parched *Eastern* Berry bruise;[13]
Some pass, in vain, those Bounds, and nobler Liquors use.
    Now *Harmony*, in vain, we bring,
    Inspire the Flute, and touch the String.
    From Harmony no help is had;   135
Music but soothes thee, is too sweetly sad,
And if too light, but turns thee gayly Mad.
    Though the Physician's greatest Gains,[14]
    Although his growing Wealth he sees
    Daily increased by Ladies' Fees,   140
Yet dost thou baffle all his studious Pains.
    Not skillful *Lower* thy Source could find,[15]
    Or through the well-dissected Body trace
    The secret, the mysterious ways,
By which thou dost surprise, and prey upon the Mind.   145
    Though in the Search, too deep for Human Thought,
    With unsuccessful Toil he wrought,
'Till thinking Thee to've catched, Himself by thee was caught,
    Retained thy Pris'ner, thy acknowledged Slave,
And sunk beneath thy Chain to a lamented Grave.   150

Delarivière Manley (1663–1724)

Soon after she was orphaned, with £200 and a share in her late father's estate, Delarivière Manley was seduced into a bigamous marriage by her cousin John Manley. When he abandoned her, she lived briefly with the Duchess of Cleveland and undoubtedly began collecting the kind of "intelligence" or gossip about the nobility that she would later exploit in her sensational novels. The Duchess expelled Manley from her house by accusing her of intriguing with her son; this seems to

---

12 *Indian Leaf* tea.
13 *Eastern Berry* coffee, from Turkey.
14 *Though* in spite of.

15 *Lower* Richard Lower (1631–91), most famous physician of his time.

be the beginning of Manley's career as a writer, for, after two years away from London, she reappeared with a pair of plays ready for production. She had some success, but she got into trouble with the law through her dealings with Mary Thompson, a known criminal, and their plot to extort money from a man named Pheasant. With no bird in hand, Manley nevertheless made a name for herself as a wit among the London writers who taunted the court, and each other, in the coffee houses and taverns. In 1705 she published a satire on the Duchess of Marlborough called The Secret History of Queen Zarah. *She followed this first attempt at mixing the conventions of romance and scandal with a more wide-ranging send-up of the Whig nobility, full of gossip and scandal about all its most prominent members. The whole work is a* roman à clef, *but the veil of allegory is thin, and gossip, followed by published "keys," made everything clear to her readers. Shortly after the appearance of* Secret Memoirs and Manners of Several Persons of Quality of Both Sexes. From the New Atalantis, *Manley was arrested along with the two publishers and the printer. Like a faithful modern investigative reporter, Manley refused to reveal the sources of her information, and, after she was held in prison for over three months, her case was dismissed.*

With its numerous erotic scenes of seduction and its inside accounts of the private lives of many members of the nobility, the New Atalantis *was a sensation. It became an emblem of dissolute, upper-class reading in Pope's more gently satirical picture of that life,* The Rape of the Lock. *Manley published a number of sequels to the* New Atalantis *and some similar works, including* The Adventures of Rivella (1714), *which is mainly about herself and is the principal source of information about her early life. (Her birth on a boat sailing near the Channel Islands suggests the reason for her unusual first name.) Manley's novels are racy romances that excite our curiosity as readers, even without intimate knowledge of the "key," but the allegory was fraught with political meaning for her contemporaries. She was a sharp-tongued enemy of the Whigs and fought in print with Richard Steele and, early on, with Jonathan Swift. They were reconciled, however, and Manley referred in her will to her "much honoured friend, the dean of St Patrick, Dr. Swift."*

Manley is one of the women writers of the eighteenth century who has recently emerged from the obscurity imposed first by morally censorious Victorian judgements of her work and then by formalist aesthetics of the earlier twentieth century. In fact, she performs excellently in her somewhat purplish genre; she is not only sensational, and she does not simply look back to earlier French romans à clef: *there is also an archness and self-assuredness in her tone that helps prepare the way for the greater, more measured accomplishments of later women writers like Jane Austen. The text here presented is based on the first edition of 1709. I have profited from the notes in the Penguin edition (1991), edited by Rosalind Ballaster.*

from Secret Memoirs and Manners of Several Persons of Quality of Both Sexes. From the New Atalantis, an Island in the Mediterranean (1709)

Astrea:][1] We are entertained with another Object; who is that Person[2] not very *young* nor *handsome*, yet something august and solemn in his *Mien*, he that walks up the *Vista?*[3] He sees

---

From *Secret Memoirs and Manners*

[1] *Astrea* a Greek goddess associated with justice, who was supposed to have left the world after the Golden Age; in Manley's fiction, she returns "to see if humankind were still as defective, as when she in disgust forsook it."

[2] *Person* William Bentinck, first Earl of Portland (1649–1709), a Dutchman created an English earl by William III, who relied on him in military matters and foreign affairs (see Defoe, *The True-Born Englishman*, p. 497 above).

[3] *Vista* "an avenue or glade" (*OED*).

us not; 'tis certainly one that loved the departed Monarch,[4] his Handkerchief is in his Hand, his Eyes red and full of Tears; he comes hither doubtless to weep in Solitude, a Master upon whom his Fortune probably depended.

Intell:][5] He weeps indeed, and he loved his Master, but his Fortune is the greatest of all the Favourites; therefore are his Tears the more Meritorious, yet he is not free from the Vices of Men in Power; the greediness of Gain and unbounded Ostentation in expending with Noise and Splendour in Foreign Courts what he by Cunning had acquired in this. Love has had his turn, in a fatal manner! Fatal I mean to the unhappy Object of his Flame; raised from a mean degree, 'tis no wonder his Head is giddy with the heighth. If Pride and Contempt of those beneath them be fashionable Manners, worn even by those that are born Great, we need not wonder to find 'em assumed by Persons that oftner by Chance than true Merit, touch a Fortune unexpected; yet is the Duke's Fidelity to his Master to be applauded, and as well as he loves *Riches*, he could never be brought to depart from the King's Interest. He has been bred to the Business of the State and Cabinet; he perfectly knows the management of Affairs, the posture of his own and that of his Neighbour-Nations; their true and their false Interests. He is not Eloquent but Wise; to be short, few Princes but would be glad of such a Servant, for since in the Composition of the Human Frame, Vices are generally blended with the Virtues, we are to Reverence that Man, who suffers not, to the Prejudice of his Master, the former to get the ascendant.

If I be not tiresome, I design a short sketch of the Amour he had with a Lady, truly named Unfortunate. I will take the Duke as high as from his first coming to Court, a Boy, to attend Prince *Henriquez*,[6] as his Page of *Honour*. When Persons have their Fortune to make, and are born with little or no Estate, 'tis necessary that they have a lucky hit, a happy Introduction, a leading Card to make a prosperous Game. Such the Duke met with, and had the Courage and Address to lay hold of the Opportunity. Prince *Henriquez* fell ill of a malignant Distemper; *Medicine* was at a loss; it seemed as if Art were no more; the *Physicians* could find no Drugs of sufficient Heat to throw out the Distemper, without which, inevitable Death was all that could be expected. One of those Sons of *Esculapius*[7] proposed that a Youth of Warmth and Vigour should be put to Bed to him, by that natural glow of Body, to draw out the Malignancy of the Distemper. The Duke was the only Person, that with Pleasure and Boldness, offered his own, to save the Life of his Master; he would not even stay to take his leave of any of his Friends, but with the greatest Bravery throwing off his Clothes got into Bed to the *Prince*, embracing closely his Feverish Body, from whence he never stirred, 'till the happy Effects of his kind Endeavours, were visible. The Disease passed from the *Heart* into the *Blood*, from thence by the Application of a kindly Warmth, 'twas thrown into the Flesh and Skin; after which, the Symptoms being favourable, they no longer doubted the Life of the Prince. But the generous Youth could not escape the Infection; it seized him in such a terrible manner that Destiny was expected to be fatal to him. They removed him to another Bed. The Prince tenderly regretted his Sufferings, assured him, That he hoped he would live to find in his *Friendship* and *Gratitude* the Rewards of *Fidelity* and *Generosity*. The Gods were too-well pleased at so glorious an Action to let him sink under it; after an unusual and bitter Conflict, they restored him to his former Health and Vigour. And if he still wears the cruel Marks of

---

[4] *departed Monarch* William III.

[5] *Intell{igence}* Astrea's guide in New Atalantis, which stands for England; her name means "Commerce of information" (Johnson) or news.

[6] *Prince Henriquez* the Dutch title of William III was Willem Hendrik, Prins Van Oranje.

[7] *Æsculapius* the Greek god of healing.

so malignant a Distemper, they are in him but glorious Proofs of *Love* and *Duty* to his Prince, no less to be revered, than the most flourishing Laurels of others.

Not one of the most fortunate Courtiers but dreaded the towering Genius[8] of the Youth; they saw he was resolved to push, though at the expense of Life; rather than not to make his Fortune, to sink under the Endeavour. *Henriquez* was young, *Human*, disposed by Nature (all Hero as he was) to the soft Trusts and Joys of Friendship: He called the Youth near to his Confidence, found in him a strength of Mind, a Capacity far above his Years, a projecting[9] Brain, with a height of Courage, able to put in practice the boldest Resolutions. The Prince had in his Nonage been oppressed by a potent faction, that left him only a titular Sovereignty;[10] he had no longer the Command of his own Fleet and Armies, all were at the disposal of those who pretended to Administer to Public Good. He would often lament with his young Favourite the Oppression. His inborn courage, and boiling Youth, made him long to rush into the Field of Glory, to snatch from thence those Laurels that were not to be attained but with the greatest Difficulty! At the head of his own Armies, to meet the Enemy of his Country,[11] who with hostile Fire, and cruel slaughter, had successfully Invaded it. The young Statesman (by his intrigue and management with some of the Head Officers) procured that a Battle should be lost. The Event was fatal to the two Brothers that opposed the Prince, and were at the Head of the State. The People (dreading the approach of the Conqueror) called aloud for their own Sovereign to defend 'em. They rushed unanimously upon the two Usurpers,[12] with as much Ease and Fierceness, as a hungry Lion the devouring Wolf, or Tiger falls upon the harmless Flock; and, with the same Expedition (animated by the Intrigues, Cabals,[13] and Spirit of our young Favourite) rends 'em piecemeal! Scatters their Body, small as the Dust thrown in to the air! Swift as Destruction, as mortal Plagues fall from Hands of the avenging Deities, when by the accumulated Sins of Mortals, they are justly provoked.

This was no sooner performed, but they rush into the Palace, seize upon *Henriquez*, bear him (with Exultings of Rapturous Joy) upon their Shoulders, force open the Door of the *Divan*, and with Acclamations that pierced the Skies, seat the Prince upon the Royal Throne! Invest him with the Purple Robe, the Sword of Defence, the awful Diadem, and all other Ensigns of Sovereignty! take a voluntary Oath of Fidelity! perform their Homage! and then with the same Exclamations (of rude and hasty Joy) present him to the Army! who echoed back with loud Shootings their Approbation of what was done. The *Prince* and his *young Favourite*, harangue and caress the Soldiers and People; he tells 'em (like his glorious Ancestors) he longs to lose his Blood in defence of his Country! That he will either die or relieve 'em from the Oppression of the Invader! They one and all demand him to lead 'em on to Conquest and Revenge.

No Age has ever shown us a Hero made up of greater Compositions! *Henriquez* was ardent for Battle, yet cautiously prudent to watch all the Advantages of it. His young Favourite, with his Valour, maintained that Opinion he had acquired; by Conduct and politic Management, they put a stop to the rapid Course of the Enemy's Victories, and regained the Towns that were lost . . .

---

[8] *Genius* "Disposition; nature" (Johnson).
[9] *projecting* contriving, resourceful.
[10] *titular Sovereignty* after the death of William's father, eight days before his heir's birth, a republican oligarchy designed laws that limited the power of the princes of Orange.

[11] *the Enemy of his Country* the French invaded the United Provinces in June 1672, with the support of the British.
[12] *the two Usurpers* Johann de Witt and his brother were killed by an angry mob at the Hague on August 20, 1672.
[13] *Cabal* "Intrigue" (Johnson).

After this the young Favourite (though formerly but of his Pleasures) became his first Minister. He was always trusted and extreme *habile*[14] in the Affairs of State; he followed the wise Maxims of *Machiavel*,[15] who aimed to make his Prince Great, let what would be the Price. He it was that encouraged *Count Fortunatus*, and the Disaffected Lords of *Atalantis*, to expel their Bigoted Monarch.[16] By his politic Management the young *Caesario* was sacrificed, and the Prince called to take possession of the Government. Without such a Head as his (cunning to conceal, crafty to forsee, wise to Project, and valiant to undertake) the whole Fabric[17] had tottered. He was the solid Foundation upon which the greatest *Hero* of the Age has raised himself to be such; though in all his Advices the finishing Stroke still came from *Henriquez.*

Now raised to be *Duke* and *Peer*, *General* of the *Army*, in Possession of the Ear and Cabinet of the Prince, whom we must henceforward (if we have occasion to speak of him) call King, he gave up himself to amass up Riches! his Ambition was not satisfied! he aimed at something more! 'Twas Glorious to be a Sovereign Prince, though but of a Petty State! He offered sixteen hundred thousand Crowns for the Succession, where only a Princess Dowager was in Possession, and to become her Husband. Affairs of that Consequence, that depend not upon Action but Treaty, are generally tedious: Whilst it was depending, our Duke felt the Sting of a Passion, which (at the Expense of the Ladies) he had hitherto only played with. There was a young Girl, named *Mademoiselle Charlot*,[18] left to his Care by her Father, for whom he had as great a Friendship, as a Statesman can be supposed to have. The young *Charlot* had lost her Mother long before: Her Dowry amounted to forty thousand Crowns; the Family was Noble, and there was almost nothing but what she might pretend to. The Duke had been some considerable time a Widower;[19] his Wife was of the Family of the Favourites, naturally Born to the soothing Arts of the Courts. *Fame* is not afraid to speak aloud, that *Henriquez* saw what was agreeable in her; and when wearied with the Fatigues of Hunting, would go to Bed between her and her Husband, but you may be sure all very Innocent, especially where such a Witness was in Place. When she died, he transferred his Esteem, with an additional Tenderness, to her Sister. She affected first to be in Love with the *Hero*, not the *Prince*. Personal Lovers are so rarely found among People of their Station; so few are acquainted with the Delicacy of dividing the *Monarch* from the *Man*, that out of Gratitude he gave into those Endearments that were necessary to bespeak a reciprocal Passion. And as his Temper to his Favourites was magnificently Lavish, she tasted all the Sweets of unlimited Majesty, and the charming Effects of unbounded Generosity!

But to return to the Duke. He spared for no Expense in the Education of young *Charlot*. She was brought up at his own House with his Children; but having something the Advantage in Age of his Daughters, the Precepts were proportionably advanced. He designed her (in those early Days of his Power) as a Wife for his Son, before the increase of his own Ambition and Riches taught him other Desires; that is to say, to look out a Lady for the young Lord with more than six times *Charlot*'s Fortune . . .

Charlot was no great Beauty, her Shape was the best; but Youth and Dress make all Things agreeable. To have prepossessed you in her Favour, I should, as I was inclined, have advanced

---

14 *habile* able.
15 *Machiavel* Niccolo Macchiavelli (1469–1527), Florentine diplomat, author of *Il Principe* (1513), *The Prince*, a book of practical statecraft; his name is somewhat unjustly synonymous with unscrupulous diplomacy.
16 *Bigoted Monarch* James II, who was Catholic.

17 *Fabric* construction.
18 *Mademoiselle Charlot* Stuarta Werburge Howard, daughter of James Howard, 3rd Earl of Suffolk (d. 1688) and Charlotte Jemima Henrietta Maria, an illegitimate daughter of Charles II (d. 1684).
19 *Widower* Anne Villiers, his first wife, died in 1688; her sister Elizabeth (d. 1733) was William's mistress.

a System of her Charms; but *Truth*, who too well foresaw my Intentions, has repelled 'em with a Frown; not but *Charlot* had many Admirers. There's something so touching in the *agreeable*, that I know not whether it does not enchant us deeper than Beauty; we are oftentimes upon our guard against the Attack of that, whilst the unwary Heart, Careless and Defenceless, as dreading no Surprise, permits the *agreeable* to manage as they please.

The Duke had a seeming Admiration for *Virtue* wherever he found it, but he was a Statesman, and held it incompatable (in an age like this) with a Man's making his Fortune. *Ambition, Desire of Gain, Dissimulation, Cunning,* all these were meritoriously Serviceable to him. 'Twas enough he always applauded Virtue, and in his Discourse decried Vice. As long as he stuck close in his Practice, no matter what became of his Words; these are times where the Heart and the Tongue do not agree! However, young *Charlot* was to be Educated in the high road to Applause and Virtue. He banished far from her Conversation whatever would not Edify, airy *Romances*, *Plays*, dangerous Novels, *loose* and *insinuating Poetry*, artificial Introductions of *Love*, well-painted Landscapes of that dangerous Poison; her Diversions were always among the sort that were most Innocent and Simple, such as Walking, but not in public Assemblies. Music, in Airs all Divine; reading and improving Books of Education and Piety; as well knowing, that if a Lady be too early used to violent Pleasures, it debauches their Tastes for ever to any others. He taught her to beware of *Hopes* and *Fears*, never to desire any thing with too much eagerness; to guard herself from those dangerous Convulsions of the Mind, that upon the least Disappointment precipitates into a million of Inconveniences. He endeavoured to cure her of those number of Affections and Aversions, so natural to young People, by showing her that nothing truly deserved to be passionately beloved, but the *Gods*, because they alone were perfect; though nothing on the other Hand ought to be hated but Vice, because we are all the Image of our Divinities. He wisely and early forewarned her, for what seemed natural to her, a desire of being applauded for her Wit. She had a brightness of Genius, that would often break out in dangerous Sparkles; he showed her that true Wit consisted not in much speaking, but in speaking much in a few Words; that whatever carried her beyond the knowledge of her Duty, carried her too far; all other Embellishments of the Mind were more dangerous than useful, and to be avoided as her Ruin. That the possession of 'em were attended with *Self-Love*, *Vanity* and *Coquetry*, things incompatable, and never mingled in the Character of a Woman of true Honour. He recommended *Modesty* and *Silence*, that she should shun all occasions of speaking upon Subjects not necessary to a Lady's Knowledge, though it were true she spoke never so well. He remembered[20] her, that so Great, so wise a man as *Zeno*,[21] of all the Virtues made choice of Silence, for by it he heard other Men's Imperfections and concealed his own; that the more Wit she was Mistress of, the less occasion she had to show it; that if want of it gave a disgust, too much does not generally please better. That assuming Air that generally accompanies it, is distasteful to the Company, where all pretend an equal right to be heard. The weakness of Human Nature is such, the chiefest Pleasure of Conversation lies in the speaking, not the hearing part; and if a presumptuous Person (though with never so great a Capacity) pretends to usurp once upon that Privilege, they look upon her as a Tyrant, that would ravish from 'em the Freedom of their Votes. But his strongest Battery was united against *Love*, that invader of the *Heart;* he showed her how shameful it was for a young Lady ever so much as to think of any tenderness for a Lover, 'till he was become her Husband; that true Piety and Duty would instruct her in all that was necessary for a good Wife to feel of that dangerous Passion; that she should not so

---

[20] *remembered* reminded.

[21] *Zeno* Zeno of Citium (*c.* 335–263 BCE), founder of Stoicism, had many maxims about the value of listening and the dangers of speaking.

much as ever seek to know what was meant by that shameful Weakness called Jealousy. 'Twas
abominable in us to give others occasion to be Jealous, and painful to be so our selves: that
'tis generally attended with *Slander* and *Hatred*, two base and contemptible Qualities. That
that violent *inborn* desire of pleasing, so natural to Ladies, is the pest of Virtue; they would
by the Charms of their Beauty, and their sweet and insinuating way of Conversation, assume
that native Empire over Mankind, which seems to be politically denied them, because the
way to Authority and Glory is stopped up. Hence it is, that with their acquired Arts and
languishing Charms, they risk their *Virtue* to gain a little contemptible Dominion over a
Heart, that at the same time it surrenders it self a Slave, refuses to bestow esteem upon the
Victor; that Friendship was far nobler in its Nature, and much to be preferred to Love,
because a 'Friend loves always, a Lover but for a time'. That under the most flattering
appearances it concealed inevitable Ruin; the very first Impressions were dreadful, and to be
carefully suppressed. *Pythagoras* taught, 'The assaults of Love were to be beaten back at the
first Sight, lest they undermine at the second'. *And* Plato, That 'the first step to Wisdom was
not to love; the second so to love, as not to be perceived'.

Fraught with these, and a number more of such Precepts as these, the young *Charlot*
seemed to intend her self a Pattern for the Ladies of this degenerate Age, who divide their
Hours between the *Toilet* and the *Basset*-Table,[22] which is grown so totally the Business of the
Fair, that even the Diversions of the *Opera*, *Gallantry* and *Love* are but second Pleasures. A
Person who has once given her self up to Gaming, neglects all her Duties, disorders her
Family, breaks her Rest, forgets her Husband, and by her Expense often inconveniences him
irreparably, together with their waste of time. The Passions of Anger and Avarice, concur to
make her odious to all, but those who engage with her at the dangerous Diversion; not to
instance [those] who have compounded[23] for the loss of Money, with the loss of their Chastity
and Honour: Nor is it a new, though frequent way of paying of Play-Debts, in this entirely
corrupted Age.

The Duke had a magnificent *Villa* within five Leagues of the Capitol, adorned with all
that's imaginable Beautiful, either in Art or Nature; the pride of Conquest, the Plunder of
Victory, the homage of the Vanquished, the Presents of Neighbouring Monarchs, and
whatever Curiosity could inform, or Money recover, were the Ornaments of this Palace.[24]
Henriquez had received a new Favourite into his Bosom, but it was a Favourite not at all
interfering with the Duke, who was ever trusted and esteemed; by this means he oftener
found a recess from Court; his great Master would sometimes in Goodness dismiss him to his
Villa, to take a rest from Power, a calm of Greatness, a suspense of Business, a respiration of
Glory. Here it was that he used to confirm the young *Charlot* in that early love of Virtue that
had been taught her, to unbend her Mind from the more serious Studies. He sometimes
permitted her those of *Poetry*, not loose Descriptions, lascivious Joys, or wanton heightenings
of the Passions. They sung and acted the History of the *Gods*, the Rape of *Prosperine*,[25] the
Descent of *Ceres*, the Chastity of *Diana*,[26] and such Pieces that tended to the instruction of
the Mind. One Evening at a Representation, where *Charlot* personated the Goddess, and the
Duke's Son *Acteon*, she Acted with so animated a Spirit, cast such Rays of Divinity about her,

22 *Basset*   a card game.
23 *compounded*   settled, made an agreement on compromising terms.
24 *Palace*   Windsor Castle.
25 *the Rape of Prosperine*   Hades takes Proserpine to the
underworld, and her mother Ceres, after searching in
anguish for her daughter, leaves the world in winter half
the year (Ovid, *Metamorphoses*, 5.391–571).

26 *the Chastity of Diana*   Artemis, or Diana, the chaste
huntress of the gods, was seen bathing with her followers
by Actaeon; in revenge she turned him into a stag; in
that form he was hunted down and torn to pieces by his
own hounds (Ovid, *Metamorphoses* 3.138–252).

gave every Word so twanging,[27] yet so sweet an Accent, that awakened the Duke's Attention; and so admirably she varied the Passions, that gave Birth in his Breast, to what he had never felt before. He applauded, embraced, and even kissed the charming *Diana*. 'Twas Poison to his Peace, the cleaving sweetness thrilled[28] swiftly to his Heart, thence tingled his Blood, and cast Fire throughout his whole Person; he Sighed with Pleasure! he wondered what those Sighs meant! he repeats his Kisses, to find if *Charlot* were the occasion of his Disorder. Confirmed by this new taste of Joy, he throws the young Charmer hastily from him, folds his Arms, and walks off with continued Sighs! The innocent Beauty makes after him, modest and afraid, insinuatingly,[29] and with trembling she inquires, if she have not offended? Begs to know her Fault, and that she will endeavour to repair it. He answers her not but with his Eyes, which have but too tender an Aspect. The Maid (by them) improving her Courage, comes nearer, spreads her fond Arms about him, and in her usual fawning Language calls him dear *Papa*; joins her Face, her Eyes, her Cheeks, her Mouth, close to his. By this time the Duke was fallen upon a Chair that stood next him, he was fully in her reach, and without any opposition she had leisure to diffuse the irremediable Poison through his Veins. He sat immovable to all Kindness, but with the greatest taste of Joy, he had ever been sensible of. Whilst he was thus dangerously entertained, the young *Acteon*, and the rest of the Company, join 'em; the Duke was forced to rouse himself from his Love-sick Lethargy; *Charlot* would not leave him, till he would tell her in what she had done amiss. He only answered her, That he had nothing to object; she had acted her part but too well. The young Lady had been taught (in her cold Precepts of Education) that it was a degree of fault to excel, even in an Accomplishment. Occasion was not to be sought of eminently distinguishing one's self in any thing but solid Virtue; she feared she had shown too great a Transport in representing *Diana*; that the Duke would possibly think she was prepossessed more than she ought with that Diversion; and in this Despondence she took resolutions to regulate her self hereafter more to his satisfaction.

That fatal Night the Duke felt hostile Fires in his Breast. *Love* was entered with all his dreadful Artillery; he took possession in a moment of the Avenues that led to the Heart; neither did the resistance he found there serve for any thing but to make his Conquest more illustrious. The Duke tried every corner of his uneasy Bed! whether shut or open, *Charlot* was still before his Eyes! his Lips and Face retained the deep Impression of her Kisses! the Idea of her innocent and charming Touches, wandered o'er his Mind! he wished again to be so blessed! but then, with a deep and dreadful Sigh, he remembered who she was, the Daughter of his Friend! of a Friend who had at his Death left the charge of her Education to him! His Treaty with the Princess Dowager, would not admit him to think of marrying of her; Ambition came in to rescue him (in that particular) from the Arms of Love. To possess her without [love], was a villainous detestable thought! but not to possess her at all, was loss of Life! was Death inevitable! Not able to gain one wink of Sleep, he arose with the first dawn, and posted back to *Angela*.[30] He hoped the hurry of Business and the Pleasures of the Court, would stifle so guilty a Passion; he was too well persuaded of his Distemper, the Symptoms were right, the Malignity was upon him! he was regularly possessed! Love in all its forms, had took in that formidable Heart of his! He began to be jealous of his Son, whom he had always designed for *Charlot*'s Husband; he could not bear the thoughts that he should be beloved by her, though all beautiful as the lovely Youth was. She had never any tender Inclinations for

---

[27] *twanging* from "twang," "An affected modulation of the voice" (Johnson).

[28] *thrilled* pierced.

[29] *insinuatingly* from "insinuate," "To push gently into favour or regard" (Johnson).

[30] *Angela* London.

him, nothing that exceeded the warmth of a Sister's love! whether it were that he were designed for [her], or that the Precepts of Education had warned her from too precipitate a liking. She was bred up with him, accustomed to his Charms; they made no impression upon her Heart; neither was the Youth more sensible. The Duke could distress neither of 'em by his love of that side, but this he was not so happy to know. He wrote up for the young Lord to come to Court, and gave immediate Orders for forming his Equipage, that he might be sent to Travel. Mean time *Charlot* was never from his Thoughts. Who knows not the violence of beginning Love! especially a Love that we hold opposite to our Interest and Duty. ' 'Tis an unreasonable excess of Desire, which enters swiftly, but departs slowly. The love of Beauty is the loss of Reason. Neither is to be suppressed by Wisdom, because it is not to be comprehended with Reason'. And the Emperor *Aurelius;*[31] 'Love is a cruel Impression of that wonderful Passion, which to define is impossible, because no Words reach to the strong Nature of it, and only they know which inwardly feel it'.

The Duke vainly struggled in the Snare; he would live without seeing *Charlot*, but then he must live in Pain, in inexplicable Torture! He applies the relief of Business, the Pleasures of Woman! *Charlot*'s Kisses were still upon his Lips, and made all others insipid to him. In short, he tried so much to divert his Thoughts from her, that it but more perfectly confirmed him of the vanity and unsuccessfulness of the Attempt. He could neither eat nor sleep! Love and Restlessness raised Vapours[32] in him to that degree, he was no longer Master of his Business! Wearied with all things, hurried by a secret Principle of *Self-Love* and *Self-Preservation,* the Law of Nature! he orders his Coach to carry him down once more to his *Villa*, there to see his Dear! This dangerous *Charlot!* that little innocent Sweetness! that embittered his Happiness. She loved him tenderly as a Benefactor, a Father, or something more; that she had been used to love without that severe mixture of Fear that mingles in the love we bear to Parents. She ran to meet him as he alighted; her young Face, over-spread with blushing Joys! his transport exceeded hers! he took her in his Arms with eagerness! he exchanged all his Pains for Pleasures! there was the Cure of his past Anguish! her Kisses were the Balm of his wounded Mind! he wondered at the immediate Alteration! she caressed and courted him, showed him all Things that could divert or entertain. He knew not what to resolve upon; he could not prudently marry her, and how to attempt to corrupt her! those excellent Principles that had been early infused into her were all against him; but yet he must love her! He found he could not live without her! He opened a *Machiavel,* and read there a Maxim, That none but great Souls could be completely Wicked.[33] He took it for an Oracle to him. He would be loath to tell himself, his Soul was not great enough for any Attempt . He closed the Book, took some turns about the Gallery to digest what he had read, and from thence concluded, that neither *Religion, Honour, Gratitude*, nor *Friendship*, were ties sufficient to deprive us of an essential Good! *Charlot* was necessary to his very Being! all his Pleasures faded without her! and, which was worse, he was in Torture! in actual Pain as well as want of Pleasure! therefore *Charlot* he would have. He had struggled more than sufficient; Virtue ought to be satisfied with the terrible Conflict he had suffered! but Love was become Master, and 'twas time for her to abscond. After he had settled his Thoughts, he grew more calm and quiet; nothing should now disturb him, but the manner how to corrupt her. He was resolved to change her whole Form of Living, to bring her to Court, to show her the World; *Balls, Assemblies, Operas, Comedies, Cards*, and *Visits*, every thing that might enervate the Mind, and fit it for the soft

---

[31] *Aurelius* Marcus Aurelius (Emperor of Rome 161–80 CE), author of *Meditations*, in Greek, which had been recently translated by Jeremy Collier (1701).

[32] *Vapours* "Mental fume; vain imagination; fancy unreal" (Johnson).

[33] *none but great souls . . . Wicked* Il Principe, chapter 8.

Play and Impression of Love. One Thing he a little scrupled, lest in making her susceptible of that Passion, it should be for another, and not for him. He did not doubt but upon her first Appearance at Court she would have many Admirers. Lovers have this Opinion peculiar to themselves, they believe that others see with their Eyes. He knew that were she less agreeable, the Gloss of Novelty was enough to recommend her; but the Remedy he found for this, was, to caress and please her above all others, to show such a particular regard for her, that should frighten any new Pretender. Few are willing to cross a first Minister, especially in such a tender Point, where all Mankind are tenacious of their Pretensions.

He had observed, that *Charlot* had been, but with Disgust[34] denied the gay part of Reading. 'Tis natural for young People to choose the Diverting, before the Instructive; he sent for her into the Gallery, where was a noble Library in all Languages, a Collection of the most valuable Authors, with a mixture of the most Amorous. He told her, that now her Understanding was increased, with her Stature, he resolved to make her Mistress of her own Conduct; and as the first thing that he intended to oblige her in, that *Governante*, who had hitherto had the care of her Actions, should be dismissed, because he had observed the Severity of her Temper had sometimes been displeasing to her. That she should henceforth have none above her that she should need to stand in awe of; and to confirm to her that good Opinion he seemed to have, he presented her with the Key of that Gallery, to improve her Mind, and seek her Diversion among those Authors he had formerly forbid her the Use of. *Charlot* made him a very low Curtsy, and, with a blushing Grace, returned him Thanks for the two Favours he bestowed upon her. She assured him, That no Action of hers should make him repent the Distinction: That her whole endeavour should be to walk in that Path he had made familiar to her; and that Virtue should ever be her only Guide. Though this was not what the Duke wanted, 'twas nothing but what he expected. He observed formerly, that she was a great lover of Poetry, especially when 'twas forbid her; he took down an *Ovid*, and opening it just at the love of *Myrra* for her Father,[35] conscious red overspread his Face; he gave it her to read, she obeyed him with a visible delight: Nothing is more pleasing to young Girls, than in being first considered as Women. *Charlot* saw the Duke entertained her with an Air of Consideration more than usual, passionate and respectful; this taught her to refuge in the native Pride and cunning of the Sex;[36] she assumed an air more haughty. Then, leaving a Girl just beginning to believe her self capable of attaining that Empire over Mankind, which they are all born and are taught by Instinct to expect, she took the Book, and placed herself by the Duke; his Eyes feasted themselves upon her Face, thence wandered over her snowy Bosom, and saw the young swelling Breasts just beginning to distinguish themselves, and which were gently heaved at the Impression of *Myrra*'s Sufferings made upon her Heart.

By this dangerous reading he pretended to show her, that there were Pleasures her Sex were born for, and which she might consequently long to taste! Curiosity is an early and dangerous Enemy to Virtue. The young *Charlot*, who had by a noble Inclination of Gratitude, a strong Propension of Affection for the Duke, whom she called and esteemed her *Papa*, being a Girl of wonderful reflection and consequently Application, wrought her Imagination up to such a lively height at the Father's Anger after the Possession of his Daughter, which she judged highly unkind and unnatural, that she dropped her Book, Tears filled her Eyes, Sobs rose to oppress her, and she pulled out her Handkerchief to cover the Disorder. The Duke,

---

[34] *Disgust* "ill-humour; malevolence; offence conceived" (Johnson).
[35] *the love of Myrra for her Father Metamorphoses* 10.312–518; aided by her nurse, she succeeds in sleeping with her father, but when he discovers the deceit, she is forced to flee and in pity the gods transform her into the myrrh tree, which sheds balm as she shed tears; the child of her incestuous conception lives and is named Adonis.
[36] *the Sex* women.

who was Master of all Mankind, could trace 'em in all the *Meanders* of Dissimulation and Cunning, was not at a loss how to interpret the Agitation of a Girl who knew no Hypocrisy. All was Artless, the beautiful Product of Innocence and Nature. He drew her gently to him, drank her Tears with his Kisses, sucked her Sighs, and gave her by that dangerous Commerce (her Soul before prepared to Softness) new and unfelt Desires. Her Virtue was becalmed, or rather unapprehensive of him for an Invader. He pressed her Lips with his; the nimble Beatings of his Heart, apparently seen and felt through his open Breast! the Glowings! the Tremblings of his Limbs! the Glorious Sparkles from his guilty Eyes! his Shortness of Breath, and eminent Disorder, were things all new to her that had never seen, heard, or read before of those powerful Operations, struck from the Fire of the two meeting Sex. Nor had she Leisure to examine his Disorders, possessed by greater of her own! Greater! because that Modesty opposing Nature, forced a struggle of Dissimulation. But the Duke's pursuing Kisses overcame the very Thoughts of any thing; but the new and lazy Poison stealing to her Heart, and spreading swiftly and imperceptibly through all her Veins, she closed her Eyes with languishing Delight! Delivered up the Possession of her Lips and Breath to the amorous Invader; returned his eager Grasps; and, in a word, gave her whole Person into his Arms, in meltings full of Delight! The Duke by that lovely Ecstasy carried beyond himself, sunk over the expiring Fair in Raptures too powerful for Description! calling her his admirable *Charlot!* his charming Angel! his adorable Goddess! But all was so far modest that he attempted not beyond her Lips and Breast, but cried that she should never be another's. The Empire of his Soul was hers; enchanted by inexplicable, irresistible Magic! she had the Power beyond the Gods themselves!

Charlot, returned from that amiable Disorder, was anew charmed at the Duke's Words — words that set her so far above what was Mortal, the Woman assumed in her, and she would have no Notice taken of the Transports she had shown. He saw and favoured her Modesty, secure of that fatal Sting he had fixed within her Breast, that Taste of Delight, which powerful Love and Nature would call upon her to repeat. He owned he loved her; that he never could love any other; that 'twas impossible for him to live a Day, an Hour, without seeing her; that in her Absence he had felt more than ever had been felt by Mortal. He begged her to have pity on him, to return his Love, or else he should be the most lost, undone Thing alive. *Charlot,* amazed and charmed, felt all those dangerous Perturbations of Nature that arise from an amorous Constitution; with Pride and Pleasure, she saw her self necessary to the Happiness of one, that she had hitherto esteemed so much above her, ignorant of the Power of Love, that Leveller of Mankind, that blender of Distinction and Hearts. Her soft Answer was, That she was indeed reciprocally Charmed, she knew not how; all he had said and done was wonderful and pleasing to her; and if he would still more please her (if there were a more) it should be never to be parted from her. The Duke had one of those violent Passions, where, to heighten it, Resistance was not at all necessary; it had already reached the Ultimate; it could not be more ardent; yet was he loath to rush upon the Possession of the Fair, lest the too early Pretension might disgust her. He would steal himself into her Soul; he would make himself necessary to her Quiet, as she was to his.

From the Library he led her to his Cabinet;[37] from forth his strong Box he took a set of Jewels that had been her Mother's; he told her she was now of an Age to expect the Ornaments, as well as Pleasures, of a Woman. He was pleased to see her look down with a seeming contempt upon what most other Girls would have been transported with. He had taught her other Joys, those of the Mind and Body. She sighed, she raved to her self, she was

---

37   *Cabinet*   "A set of boxes or drawers for curiosities; a private box" (Johnson).

all charmed and uneasy! The Duke casting over the rest of his Jewels, made a Collection of such as were much more valuable than her Mother's; he presented her with, and would force her to accept 'em. But *Charlot*, as tender and gallant as the Duke, seeing his picture in little, set round with Diamonds, begged that he would only honour her with that Mark of his Esteem. The ravished Duke consented, conditionally, that she would give him hers in return.

After this tender, dangerous Commerce, *Charlot* found every thing insipid, nothing but the Duke's Kisses could relish with her; all those Conversations she had formerly delighted in, were insupportable. He was obliged to return to Court, and had recommended to her Reading the most dangerous Books of Love, *Ovid, Petrarch, Tibullus*,[38] those moving Tragedies that so powerfully expose the Force of Love, and corrupt the Mind. He went even farther, and left her such as explained the Nature, Manner, and Raptures of Enjoyment. Thus he infused Poison into the Ears of the lovely Virgin. She easily (from those Emotions she had found in her self) believed as highly of those Delights as was unimaginable; her waking Thoughts, her golden Slumber, ran all of a Bliss only imagined, but never proved. She even forgot, as one that wakes from Sleep and the Visions of the Night, all those Precepts of airy Virtue, which she had found had nothing to do with Nature. She longed again to renew those dangerous Delights. The Duke was an Age absent from her; she could only in Imagination possess what she believed so pleasing. Her Memory was prodigious, she was indefatigable in Reading. The Duke had left Orders she should not be controlled in any thing: Whole Nights were wasted by her in that Gallery; she had too well informed her self of the speculative Joys of Love. There are Books dangerous to the Community of Mankind,[39] abominable for Virgins, and destructive to Youth; such as explain the Mysteries of Nature, the congregated Pleasures of *Venus*, the full Delights of mutual Lovers, and which rather ought to pass the Fire than the Press. The Duke had laid in her way such as made no mention of *Virtue* or *Hymen*,[40] but only advanced native, generous and undissembled Love. She was become so great a Proficient, that nothing of the Theory was a stranger to her.

Whilst *Charlot* was thus employed, the Duke was not idle; he had prepared her a Post at Court with *Henriquez*'s Queen. The young Lady was sent for; neither Art, Money, nor Industry was wanting, to make her Appearance glorious. The Duke awed and trembling with his Passion, approached her as a Goddess; conscious of his and her own Desires. The mantling Blood would smile upon her Cheeks, sometimes glowing with Delight, then afterwards, by a feeble Recollection of Virtue, sink apace, to make room for a guilty succeeding Paleness. The Duke knew all the Motions of her Heart; he debated with himself whether it were best to attempt the Possession of her whilst so young, or permit her time to know and set a Value upon what she granted. His Love was highly Impatient, but Respectful; he longed to be Happy, but he dreaded to displease her. The Ascendant she had over him was wonderful; he had let slip those first Impressions which strike deepest in the Hearts of Women; to be successful, 'One ought never to allow 'em time to think, their Vivacity being prodigious, and their foresight exceeding short, and limited: The first hurry of their Passions, if they are but vigorously followed, is what is generally most favourable to Lovers'. *Charlot* by this time had informed her self, that there were such terrible Things such as Perfidy and Inconstancy in Mankind; that even the very Favours they received, often disgusted, and that to be entirely Happy, one ought never to think of the faithless Sex. This brought her back to those Precepts

---

[38] *Ovid, Petrarch, Tibullus* Ovid's *Amores*; Petrarch's sonnets; and the Latin love poetry of Albius Tibullus (d. 19 BCE).

[39] *Books dangerous to . . . Mankind* for a discussion of some of these, see David Foxon, *Libertine Literature in England 1660–1745*.

[40] *Hymen* Greek god of marriage.

of Virtue that had embellished her dawn of Life; but alas! these Admonitions were too feeble, the Duke was all submissive, passionate, eager to obey, and to oblige. He watched her Uprisings,[41] scarce could eat without her; she was Mistress of his Heart and Fortune; his own Family, and the whole Court imagined that he resolved her for his Duchess; they almost looked upon her as such; she went often to his Palace, where all were devoted to her Service; the very glance of her Eyes commanded their Attention; at her least Request, as soon as her Mouth was opened to speak, before her Words were half formed, they started to obey her.

She had learnt to manage the Duke, and to distrust herself; she would no more permit of Kisses, that sweet and dangerous Commerce. The Duke had made her wise at his own Cost, and vainly languished for a Repetition of Delight. He guessed at the Interest he had in her Heart, had proved the Warmth of her Constitution, and was resolved he would no more be wanting to his own Happiness; he omitted no occasion by which he might express his Love, pressing her to crown his Longings. Her courage did not reach to ask him that honourable Proof of his Passion, which 'tis believed he would not have refused, if she had but insisted on it. The Treaty was still depending: he might marry the Princess Dowager. *Charlot* tenderly dropped a Word that spoke her Apprehensions of it; he assured her there was nothing in it; all he aimed at was to purchase the Succession, that he might make her a Princess, as she deserved. Indeed the Hopes his Agent had given the Lady of becoming her Husband was not the smallest Inducement to the Treaty; therefore he delayed his Marriage to *Charlot*; for if that were but once confirmed, the Princess (by resenting, as she ought, the Abuse that had been laid upon her) would put an end to it, infinitely to his Prejudice.

Charlot, very well satisfied with these Reasons, and unwilling to do any thing against the Interest of a Man whom she tenderly loved, accustomed herself to hear his eager Solicitations. He could no longer contend with a Fire that consumed him, he must be gratified, or die. She languished under the same Disquiets. The Season of the Year[42] was come that he must make the Campaign with the King; he could not resolve to depart unblessed; *Charlot* still refused him that last Proof of her Love. He took a tender and passionate Farewell. *Charlot*, drowned in Tears, told him, 'twas impossible she should support his Absence; all the Court would ridicule her Melancholy. This was what he wanted; he bid her take care of that; a Maid was but an ill Figure that brought her self to be the sport of Laughters; but since her Sorrow (so pleasing and glorious to him) was like to be visible, he advised her to pass some days at his *Villa*, till the height of Melancholy should be over, under the Pretence of Indisposition. He would take care that the Queen should be satisfied of the necessity of her Absence. He advised her even to depart that Hour; since the King was already on his Journey, he must be gone that moment, and endeavour to overtake him. He assured her he would write by every Courier, and begged her not to admit of another lover, though he was sensible there were many (taking the advantage of his Absence, would endeavour to please her). To this all she answered so as to quiet his Distrust and Fears; her Tears drowned her Sighs; her Words were lost in Sobs and Groans! The Duke did not show less concern, but led her all trembling to put her in a Coach that was to carry her to his *Villa*; where he had often wished to have her, but she distrusted her self, and would not go with him; nor had she have ventured now, but that she thought he was to follow the King, who could not be without him.

Charlot no sooner arrived, but the Weather being very hot, she ordered a Bath to be prepared for her. Soon as she was refreshed with that, she threw her self down upon a Bed,

---

41   *watched her Uprisings*   was anxious for her rising in the morning.

42   *Season of the Year*   summer, when armies were traditionally "on campaign" or in the field.

with only one thin Petticoat and a loose Nightgown, the Bosom of her Gown and Shift open; her Night-clothes tied carelessly together with a Cherry-coloured Ribbon, which answered well to the yellow and Silver Stuff of her Gown. She lay uncovered in a melancholy careless Posture, her Head resting upon one of her Hands; the other held a Handkerchief that she employed to dry those Tears that sometimes fell from her Eyes; when raising herself a little at gentle noise she heard from the opening of a Door that answered to the Bed-side, she was quite astonished to see enter the amorous Duke. Her first Emotions were all Joy; but in a minute she recollected herself, thinking he was not come there for nothing. She was going to rise; but he prevented her by flying to her Arms, where, as we may call it, he nailed her down to the Bed with Kisses; his Love and Resolution gave him double Vigour; he would not stay a moment to capitulate[43] with her; whilst yet her Surprise made her doubtful of his Designs, he took advantage of her confusion to accomplish 'em; neither her Prayers, Tears, nor Strugglings could prevent him, but in her Arms he made himself a full amends for all those Pains he had suffered for her.

Thus *Charlot* was undone! thus ruined by him that ought to have been her Protector! 'Twas very long before he could appease her; but so artful, so amorous, so submissive was his Address, so violent his Assurances, he told her, that he must have died without the Happiness. *Charlot* espoused[44] his Crime, by sealing[45] his Forgiveness. He passed the whole Night in her Arms, pleased, transported, and out of himself; whilst the ravished Maid was not at all behind-hand in Ecstasies and guilty Transports. He stayed a whole Week with *Charlot* in a surfeit of Love and Joy! that Week more inestimable than all the Pleasures of his Life before! whilst the Court believed him with the King, posting to the Army. He neglected *Mars* to devote himself wholly to *Venus*; abstracted from all Business, that happy Week sublimed him almost to an Immortal. *Charlot* was formed to give and take all those Raptures necessary to accomplish the Lover's Happiness; none were ever more Amorous; none were ever more Happy!

The two Lovers separated, the Duke for the Army, *Charlot* returned to the Court; one of the Royal-Secretaries[46] fell in Love with her, but his being of the precise[47] Party, and a married Man, it behooved to carry himself discreetly. He omitted no private Devoirs to please her, but her Heart entirely fixed upon the Duke, neglected the Attempt. She had made an intimate Friendship with a young Countess,[48] who was a *lovely Widow*, full of *Air*, *Life* and *Fire*; her Lord purchased her from his Rival, by the Point of his Sword, but he did not long survive to enjoy the Fruits of his *Victory*: He made her Circumstances as easy as he could, but that was not extraordinary; however, she appeared well at Court, knew the management of Mankind, and how to procure herself universal Love and Admiration. *Charlot* made her the unwary Confidant of her Passion for the Duke; the Countess had the Goodness, or Complaisance,[49] which you please, to hearken to the Over-flowings of a Love-sick-Heart . . .

---

[43] *capitulate* "to draw up articles of agreement; to parley" (*OED*).

[44] *espouse* "To adopt; to take to h[er]self" (Johnson).

[45] *sealing* confirming, ratifying.

[46] *one of the Royal-Secretaries* Sir John Trenchard (1640–95), an influential Whig.

[47] *precise* "Formal; finical; solemnly and superstitiously exact" (Johnson).

[48] *a young Countess* Martha Jane Temple; her first husband fought a duel for her; she married Bentinck in 1700.

[49] *Complaisance* civility.

Thomas Brown (1663–1704)

Brown began his life as the son of farmer at Shifnal in Shropshire, but he was a zealous convert to city life. He gave up school teaching after three years in London and put his Oxford education to the even less dignified use of producing various kinds of journalism. His works were for, and often about, the world of tavern-hopping playwrights, actresses, rakes, and the people of various classes who were drawn to their company or simply wished to know about their somewhat Bohemian lives. Brown's education enabled him to give his gossip an intellectually high tone, and his writings were collected in the noble form of Works *after his death. Although he is not a major figure, Brown's kind of journalism, in focusing on things near to the lives and experiences of the readers it hopes to attract, was instrumental to the development of the novel in England. It is also deft and amusing.*

The first edition of The Letters from the Dead to the Living *was in 1702. The present selection comes from the third edition (1708) of* The Continuation or Second Part of the Letters, *which was bound, with a separate title page, into the multi-volume edition of Brown's* Works, *which began printing in 1707.*

from *The Letters from the Dead to the Living* (1702)

FROM WORTHY MRS. BEHN THE POETESS, TO THE FAMOUS VIRGIN ACTRESS[1]

Madam,

I Vow to Gad Lady, of all the fair Sex that ever occupied their Faculties upon the public Stage, I think your pretty Self the only Miracle! For a Woman to cloak the frailties of Nature with such admirable cunning as you have hitherto done, merits, in my Opinion, the Wonder and Applause of the whole Kingdom! How many chaste *Diana*'s, in your station have lost their Reputation before they had done any thing to deserve it? But for a Woman of your Quality to first surrender her Honour, and afterwards preserve her Character, shows a discreet management beyond the Policy of a Statesman: Your appearance upon the Stage puts the Court Ladies to the Blush, when they reflect that a mercenary Player should be more renowned for her Virtue than all the glorious Train of fair Spectators, who, like true Women, hear your Praises whispered with regret, and behold your Person with insupportable Envy. The *Roman* Empress *Messalina*[2] was never half so famous for her Lust, as you are for your Chastity; nor the most Christian King's Favourite, Madam *Maintenon*,[3] more Eminent for her Parts, than you are for your Cunning; Nothing is a greater manifestation of a Woman's Conduct than for her to be Vicious without mistrust, and to gratify her looser Inclinations without discovery; at which sort of managements you are an absolute Artist, as since my departure I have made evident to my self, by residing in those Shades where the Secrets of all

---

FROM WORTHY MRS. BEHN THE POETESS
[1] *Behn*   Aphra Behn (see above, p. 403); *the Virgin Actress*   Anne Bracegirdle (1671–1748); Portia, Desdemona, Ophelia, and Cordelia were among her signature roles.

[2] *Roman Empress Messalina*   the notoriously promiscuous wife of the Emperor Claudius.
[3] *Madam Maintenon*   Françoise d'Aubigné (1635–1719), mistress, then wife of Louis XIV.

are open; for peeping by chance into the Breast of your old Acquaintance,[4] where his Sins were as plainly scored as Tavern Reckonings upon a Bar-board, there did I behold, among his numberless Transgressions, your Name registered so often in the Black-List, that Fornification with Madam B—— came so often into the score that it seemed to me like a Chorus at the end of every Stanza in an old Ballad: Besides, had I wanted so manifest a Proof, as by chance I met with, Experience has taught me to judge of my own Sex to a perfection, and I know the difference there is between being really Virtuous, and only accounted so: I am sensible 'tis as hard a matter for a pretty Woman to keep her self Honest in a Theatre, as 'tis for an Apothecary to keep his Treacle from the Flies in hot Weather; for every Libertine in the Audience will be buzzing about her Honey-pot, and her Virtue must defend it self by abundance of Fly-flaps, or those Flesh-loving Insects will soon blow[5] upon her Honour, and when once she has had a Maggot in her Tail, all the Pepper and Salt in the Kingdom will scarce keep her Reputation from stinking; therefore that which makes me admire your good Housewifery above all your Sex is, that notwithstanding your Powdering-tub has been so often polluted, yet you have kept your Flesh in such Credit and good Order that the nicest[6] Appetite in the Town would be glad to make a Meal of it.

You must excuse me, *Madam*, that I am thus free with you, for you know 'tis the Custom of our Sex to take all manner of Liberty with one another, and to talk Smuttily and act Waggishly when we are by our selves, though we scarce dare listen to a merry Tale in Man's company for fear of being thought Impudent. You know the bobtailed Monster[7] is a censorious Creature, and if we should not be cunning enough to cast a mist before the Eyes of their understanding sometimes, there would be no living among them; and therefore I cannot but highly commend you for your Prudence in covering all your vicious Inclinations[8] by an hypocritical Deportment: For how often have we heard Men say, though a Woman be a Whore, yet they love she should carry herself modestly? That is as much as to say, they love to be Cheated, and you know, *Madam*, we can hit their Humours in that particular to a hairs-breadth, and convey one Man away from under our Petticoats to make room for another, with as much dexterity as the *German* Artist does his Balls, that the keenest eye in Christendom shall not discern the Juggle, for a Woman ought to be made up of all Chinks and Crannies, that when a Man searches her for any thing he should not find, she may shuffle about her Secrets so, that the Devil can't discover them, or else she's fit only to make a Seamstress on, and can never be rightly qualified for Intriguing. I have just now the remembrance of a few Female stratagems crept into my Head, which were practised by a pretty Lady of my acquaintance, perhaps, *Madam*, if they are not stale to you, you may make them of some service hereafter; therefore in hopes of obliging you, I shall acquaint you with the particulars:

I happened long since in the time of my Youth, when powerful Nature prompted me to delight in amorous Adventures, to contract a Friendship with a fair Lady who, for her Wit and Beauty, was oftentimes solicited by the Male Sex to help to make up that Beast of Pleasure with two Backs, and hating to submit her self to the Tyrannical Government of a single Person, she never wanted[9] a whole Parliament of Nipples to give her Suck, though she flattered one Man that kept her, to believe he was sole Monarch of the Low-Countries; but one

---

[4] *Acquaintance* the brilliant playwright William Congreve (1670–1729).

[5] *blow* "The act of a fly by which she lodges eggs in flesh" (Johnson).

[6] *nicest* most finicky.

[7] *the bobtailed Monster* the public; the crude, male world.

[8] *vicious Inclinations* tendencies to vice.

[9] *wanted* lacked.

time he unfortunately happened to catch her with a new Relation, of whom he was a little Jealous, believing for some Reasons he had an underhand design of Liquoring his Boots[10] for him, to prevent which he imposed an Oath of Abjuration[11] upon his Mistress, and made her Swear for the future to renounce the Sight of him, which to oblige her Keeper she very readily consented to; but no sooner was his back turned, but she had invented a Salvo[12] for her Conscience as well as her Concupiscence, and dispatching a Letter to her new Lover, told him what had passed, but withal encouraged him to renew his Visits at such Opportunities as she informed him were convenient; at the time appointed her Spark came, she received him with a blind Compliment, and told him she would open any thing but her Eyes to oblige him; but those she must keep shut for her Oath's sake, having Sworn never to see him if she could help it. The Gentleman was very well satisfied he had so conscientious a Lady to deal with: 'Love, *Madam*,' says he, 'is always Blind, and for my part I shall be content to enjoy the darkest of your Favours'; upon which he began vigorously to attack Love's Fortress, which you know, *Madam*, has no more Eyes than a Beetle; as she told me the Story, he was beat off three times, and at last was forced to draw off his Forces, so marched off to raise Recruits against the next opportunity. The next Day came the Governor of the Garrison, as he foolishly thought himself, and made a strict inquiry whether she had any correspondence with the Enemy? 'Lord, *Sir*,' says she, 'what do you take me to be? a devil! As I hope to be saved I never set Eyes on him since you engaged me to the contrary': So all things passed off as well as if no Evil had been acted.

The next fresh Acquaintance she contracted, she would never suffer to wait upon her at her Lodgings, other-ways than dressed in Female Apparel; so when a new fit of Jealousy put her Spark upon purging her Conscience upon Oath, 'As I have Soul to be saved,' says she, 'no Creature in Breeches but your self has been near to me since you had knowledge of it; therefore why, my Dear, should you harbour such ill thoughts of a Woman that loves you as dearly as I do my Beads and Crucifix?' Thus, though she deceived him as often as she had opportunity, yet her discretion kept all things in such admirable decorum that I never knew any of the fair Sex, except your self, like her.

If it were not for these Witty Contrivances, subtle Shifts and Evasions, which we are forced to use to keep the Male Sex easy, a pretty or an ingenious Woman, to make one Man happy, must make twenty miserable; for Wit and Beauty are never without abundance of Admirers, and if such a Woman were to sacrifice all her Charms to the miserly temper of one single Lover, the rest must run distracted, and at this rate the whole World in a short time would become one *Great Bedlam*;[13] besides, since there is enough to make all happy, if prudently dispensed, I know no Reason why one Man should engross[14] more than he is able to deal with, and other Men want that, which by using there can be no miss of; therefore I commend you for the Liberty you take to oblige your chosen Friends, and the Prudence you use to conceal it from the envious Number you think unworthy of your Smiles; so with this Advice I shall conclude, if you have twenty Gallants that taste your Favours in their turns, let no Man know he has a Rival-sharer in the Happiness, but Swear to every one a-part, none enjoys you but

10 *Liquoring his Boots* cuckolding him (*OED*, citing this passage).
11 *Oath of Abjuration* a formal renunciation of the claims of the House of Stuart, devised in 1702 and required of public office holders, along with the oath of fidelity to William's government; those who would not take both oaths were called non-jurors.
12 *Salvo* "An exception, a reservation, an excuse" (Johnson).
13 *Bedlam* London asylum for the insane.
14 *engross* "To purchase the whole of any commodity for the sake of selling at a high price" (Johnson).

himself; and by this means you will oblige the whole Herd, and make your self easy in their numerous Embraces. Yours,

A. BEHN.

Matthew Prior (1664–1721)

According to the accepted story, the Earl of Dorset found young Prior reading Horace in a corner of his uncle's tavern and sent him back to Westminster School, from which he had been withdrawn after his father's death. From there Prior went to Cambridge, graduated, became a Fellow, earned the confidence of noblemen, especially his fellow poet Charles Montagu, and was made a Gentleman of the King's Bedchamber by William III. He rose further to become Under Secretary of State and unofficial but effective ambassador to France. Prior was instrumental in negotiating the very important Treaty of Utrecht (1713). After the death of Queen Anne in 1714, Prior's political fortunes fell. He lost his posts and his income, but his friends published a magnificent folio edition (1718) of his Poems on Several Occasions, *which had appeared in octavo and lesser editions earlier. The proceeds from this landmark production supported Prior for the remaining years of his life and provided the money for an impressive monument in Westminster Abbey.*

Prior's poetry consists of tales, amorous verse, numerous occasional poems and a couple of plays. Many of the poems are long and light, and Prior has accordingly been credited with creating the genre of "familiar verse" in English. In his Lives of the Poets, *Johnson praised Prior more for avoiding disgrace than for achieving any greatness in poetry. That seems severe, but there is some disparity between the magnificent folio of Prior's works (and the grand display in Westminster) and his more modest poetic aims. In achieving those lesser heights, even this brief selection shows that Prior was consistently skilful and delightful. The first authorized edition of Prior's* Poems on Several Occasions *was published in 1709 (there had been an unauthorized edition two years earlier); it was followed by numerous editions throughout the century. Several of the early editions were expanded and corrected. I have used the large folio edition of 1718 as a copytext for all the poems presented here, except "Jinny the Just," which I take from* The Writings of Matthew Prior, *edited by A. R. Waller, 2 vols (Cambridge University Press, 1907). Waller edited the poem, which he also gave this name, from manuscript sources. Waller's edition of Prior is still valuable, but it has been superseded by* The Literary Works of Matthew Prior, *edited by H. Bunker Wright and Monroe K. Spears, 2 vols (1959; second edition Clarendon Press, 1971).*

from *Poems on Several Occasions* (1718)

TO THE HONOURABLE *CHARLES MONTAGU*, ESQ.[1]

I

Howe'er, 'tis well, that while Mankind
Through Fate's perverse *Meander* errs,

TO THE HONOURABLE *CHARLES MONTAGU*, ESQ.

[1] *Charles Montagu*   later Lord Halifax (1661–1715), a classmate of Prior's at Westminster School and Cambridge; an important figure in William III's govern-ment; collaborated with Prior on a satire of Dryden; a patron of several poets; eventually opposed by Prior in Parliament.

He can Imagined Pleasures find,
    To combat against Real Cares.

2

Fancies and Notions He pursues,   5
    Which ne'er had Being but in Thought:
Each, like the GRÆCIAN Artist, woos[2]
    The Image He himself has wrought.

3

Against Experience He believes;
    He argues against Demonstration;   10
Pleased, when his Reason He deceives;
    And sets his Judgement by his Passion.

4

The hoary Fool, who many Days
    Has struggled with continued Sorrow,
Renews his Hope, and blindly lays   15
    The desperate Bet upon to Morrow.

5

To Morrow comes: 'tis Noon, 'tis Night;
    This Day like all the former flies:
Yet on He runs, to seek Delight
    To Morrow, 'till to Night he dies.   20

6

Our Hopes, like tow'ring Falcons, aim
    At Objects in an airy height:
The little Pleasure of the Game
    Is from afar to view the Flight.

7

Our anxious Pains We, all the Day,   25
    In search of what We like, employ:
Scorning at Night the worthless Prey,
    We find the Labour gave the Joy.

8

At Distance through an artful Glass[3]
    To the Mind's Eye Things well appear: 30
They lose their Forms, and make a Mass
    Confused and black, if brought too near.

---

[2] *the GRAECIAN Artist* Pygmalion, whose statue of a woman came to life as his beloved (see Dryden's version of the Ovidian fable, p. 386 above).   [3] *an artful Glass* a finely made telescope.

9

If We see right, We see our Woes:
    Then what avails it to have Eyes?
From Ignorance our Comfort flows: 35
    The only Wretched are the Wise.

10

We wearied should lie down in Death:
    This Cheat of Life would take no more;
If You thought Fame but empty Breath;
    I, PHILLIS but a perjured Whore.[4]   40

THE LADY'S LOOKING-GLASS

Celia and I the other Day
Walked o'er the Sand-Hills to the Sea:
The setting Sun adorned the Coast,
His Beams entire, his Fierceness lost:
And, on the Surface of the Deep,   5
The Winds lay only not asleep:
The Nymph did like the Scene appear,
Serenely pleasant, calmly fair:
Soft fell her Words, as flew the Air.
With secret Joy I heard her say,   10
That She would never miss one Day
A Walk so fine, a Sight so gay.
    But, oh the Change! the Winds grow high;
Impending Tempests charge the Sky;
The Lightning flies; the Thunder roars;   15
And big Waves lash the frightened Shores.
Struck with the Horror of the Sight,
She turns her Head, and wings her Flight;
And trembling vows, She'll ne'er again
Approach the Shore, or view the Main.   20
    'Once more at least look back', said I,
'Thy self in That large Glass descry:
When Thou art in good Humour dressed;
When gentle Reason rules thy Breast;
The Sun upon the calmest Sea   25
Appears not half so bright as Thee:
'Tis then, that with Delight I rove
Upon the boundless Depth of Love:
I bless my Chain; I hand my Oar;
Nor think on all I left on Shore.   30
    'But when vain Doubt, and groundless Fear

---

[4] *perjured* having committed perjury or falsely sworn.

Do That Dear Foolish Bosom tear;
When the big Lip, and wat'ry Eye
Tell Me, the rising Storm is nigh:
'Tis then, Thou art yon' angry Main,   35
Deformed by Winds, and dashed by Rain;
And the poor Sailor, that must try
Its Fury, labours less than I.
    'Shipwrecked, in vain to Land I make;
While Love and Fate still drive Me back: 40
Forced to dote on Thee thy own Way,
I chide Thee first, and then obey.
Wretched when from Thee, vexed when nigh,
I with Thee, or without Thee, die.'

THE CHAMELEON

As the Chameleon, who is known
To have no Colours of his own;
But borrows from his Neighbour's Hue
His White or Black, his Green or Blue;
And struts as much in ready Light,   5
Which Credit gives Him upon Sight;
As if the Rain-bow were in Tail[1]
Settled on Him, and his Heirs Male:
So the young Squire, when first He comes
From Country School, to WILL's or TOM's;[2]   10
And equally, in Truth, is fit
To be a Statesman, or a Wit;
Without one Notion of his own,
He Saunters wildly up and down;
'Till some Acquaintance, good or bad,   15
Takes notice of a staring Lad;
Admits Him in among the Gang:
They jest, reply, dispute, harangue:
He acts and talks, as They befriend Him,
Smeared with the Colours, which They lend Him.   20
    Thus merely, as his Fortune chances,
His Merit or his Vice advances.
    If haply He the Sect pursues,
That read and comment upon News;
He takes up Their mysterious Face: 25
He drinks his Coffee without Lace.[3]
This Week his mimic-Tongue runs o'er
What They have said the Week before.
His Wisdom sets all Europe right;

THE CHAMELEON
[1] in Tail   entailed, given with a condition, such as,
the gift must be passed on to certain heirs.

[2] WILL's or TOM's   London coffee-houses, hubs of literary and political activity, respectively.
[3] Lace   coffee-house jargon for sugar.

And teaches MARLBRO when to Fight.[4]   30
   Or if it be his Fate to meet
With Folks who have more Wealth than Wit;
He loves cheap *Port*, and double Bub;[5]
And settles in the *Hum-Drum* Club.[6]
He learns how Stocks will Fall or Rise;   35
Holds Poverty the greatest Vice;
Thinks Wit the Bane of Conversation;
And says, that Learning spoils a Nation.
   But if, at first, He minds his Hits,[7]
And drinks *Champagne* among the Wits;   40
Five deep, He Toasts the tow'ring Lasses;
Repeats you Verses wrote on Glasses;
Is in the Chair; prescribes the Law;[8]
And Lies with Those he never saw.

For my own Tomb-stone

To Me 'twas giv'n to die: to Thee 'tis giv'n
  To live: Alas! one Moment sets us ev'n.
Mark! how impartial is the Will of Heav'n.

[Jinny the Just]

Released from the noise of the Butcher and Baker
Who, my old Friends be thanked, did seldom forsake her
And from the soft Duns of my Landlord the Quaker,

From chiding the Footmen and watching the Lasses,
From Nell that burned Milk, and Tom that broke Glasses   5
(Sad mischiefs through which a good housekeeper passes!),

From some real Care but more fancied vexation,
From a life party-Coloured half reason half passion,
Here lies, after all, the best Wench in the Nation.

From the Rhine to the Po, from the Thames to the Rhone   10
Joanna or Janneton, Jinny or Joan
'Twas all one to her by what name She was known.

For the Idiom of words very little She heeded;
Provided the Matter She drove at succeeded,
She took and gave Languages just as She needed.   15

So for Kitching and Market, for bargain & Sale[1]
She paid English or Dutch or French down on the Nail,
But in telling a Story she sometimes did fail.

---

[4] *MARLBRO*   John Churchill, Duke of Marlborough (1650–1722), Captain General of all British military forces under Queen Anne.
[5] *Bub*   "A cant word. Strong malt liquor" (Johnson).
[6] *Hum-Drum Club*   a club "made up of very honest Gentlemen, of peaceable Dispositions, that used to sit together, smoke their Pipes, and say nothing till Midnight" (Addison, *Spectator* 9, cited in *OED*).
[7] *minds his Hits*   looks to his chances (*OED*).
[8] *in the Chair*   in critical authority.
[Jinny the Just]
[1] *Kitching*   the furnishing of supplies for the kitchen.

Then begging Excuse as She happened to Stammer
With respect to her betters but none to her Grammar,   20
Her blush helped her out and her Jargon became her.

Her Habit and Mien she endeavoured to frame
To the different Gout of the place where She came,[2]
Her outside still changed, but her inside the same.

At the Hague in her Slippers & hair as the Mode is;   25
At Paris all falbalowed fine as a Goddess;[3]
And at censuring London in smock sleeves and Bodice.[4]

She ordered Affairs that few People could tell
In what part about her that mixture did dwell
Of Vrough or Mistress, or Mademoiselle.[5]   30

For her Surname and race let the Héraults e'en Answer;[6]
Her own proper worth was enough to advance her,
And he who liked her, little valued her Grandsire.

But from what House so ever her lineage may come,
I wish my own Jinny but out of her Tomb,   35
Though all her Relations were there in her Room.

Of such terrible beauty She never could boast
As with absolute Sway o'er all hearts rules the roast
When J—— bawls out to the Chair for a Toast;

But of good Household Features her Person was made,   40
Nor by Faction cried up nor of Censure afraid,
And her beauty was rather for Use than Parade

Her Blood so well mixed and flesh so well Pasted
That though her Youth faded her Comeliness lasted;
The blue was wore off but the Plum was well tasted.   45

Less smooth than her Skin and less white than her breast
Was this polished stone beneath which she lies pressed
Stop, Reader and Sigh while thou think'st on the rest.

With just a trim of Virtue her Soul was endued
Not affectedly Pious nor secretly lewd   50
She cut even between the Coquette and the Prude.

Her Will with her Duty so equally stood
That seldom opposed She was commonly good,
And did pretty well doing just what she would.

---

[2] *Gout* taste.
[3] *falbalowed* or furbelowed, with ornamental trim on
her dress.
[4] *smock* lady's undergarment, shift; *Bodice* "Stays; a
waistcoat quilted with whalebone, worn by women"
(Johnson).

[5] *Vrough* Dutch for Mistress (Miss) or Mademoiselle.
[6] *Héraults* members of an ancient and distinguished
French family.

Declining all Pow'r she found means to persuade,   55
Was then most regarded when most she Obeyed,
The Mistress in truth when she seemed but the Maid.

Such care of her own proper Actions She took
That on other folks' lives She had no time to look,
So Censure and Praise were struck out of her Book.   60

Her thought still confined to its own little Sphere,
She minded not who did Excel or did Err,
But just as the matter related to her.

Then too when her Private Tribunal was reared,
Her Mercy so mixed with her judgement appeared   65
That her Foes were condemned & her friends always cleared.

Her Religion so well with her learning did suit
That in Practice sincere, and in Controverse Mute
She showed She knew better to live than dispute.

Some parts of the Bible by heart She recited   70
And much in historical Chapters delighted,
But in points about Faith She was something short sighted,

So Notions and modes She referred to the Schools,[7]
And in matters of Conscience adhered to Two Rules:
To advise with no Biggots, and jest with no Fools.   75

And scrupling but little, enough she believed;[8]
By Charity ample small sins She retrieved,
And when she had New Clothes She always received.[9]

Thus still whilst her Morning unseen fled away
In ord'ring the Linen and making the Tea   80
That she scarce could have time for the Psalms of the Day.

And while after Dinner the Night came so soon
That half she proposed very seldom was done
With twenty god bless Me's how this day is gone.

While she read and Accounted & paid & abated[10]   85
Eat and drank, Played & Worked, laughed & Cried, loved & hated,[11]
As answered the end of her being Created.

In the midst of her Age came a cruel Disease
Which neither her Julaps nor receipts could appease,[12]
So down dropped her Clay, may her Soul be at peace.[13]   90

---

[7] *modes* part of the vocabulary of the *Schools*, scholasticism, the Aristotelian method of philosophy found in Thomas Aquinas and many other important early Christian theologians.
[8] *scruple* doubt.
[9] *received* entertained guests.
[10] *abate* to reduce the payment on or the cost of merchandise.

[11] *Eat* an acceptable form of the past tense at this time.
[12] *Julap* "an extemporaneous form of medicine" made of sweetened water (Johnson, citing John Quincy); *receipts* recipes or prescriptions.
[13] *Clay* body, corporeal life.

Retire from this Sepulchre all the Profane,
You that love for Debauch or that marry for gain.
Retire lest Ye trouble the Manes of J——[14]

But Thou that know'st Love above Interest or lust,
Strew the Myrtle and Rose on this once beloved Dust,   95
And shed one pious tear upon Jinny the Just.

Tread soft on her Grave, and do right to her honour.
Let neither rude hand nor ill Tongue light upon her.
Do all the small Favours that now can be done her,

And when what Thou liked shall return to her Clay,[15]   100
For so I'm persuaded she must do one Day,
What ever fantastic J—— Asgill may say.[16]

When as I have done now, thou shalt set up a Stone
For something, however distinguished or known,
May some Pious Friend the Misfortune bemoan   105
And make thy Concern by reflection his own.

Mary Astell (1666–1731)

Bishop Tillotson, John Locke, John Norris, and Daniel Defoe were among the foremost writers and religious thinkers that Astell was bold enough, committed enough, and intelligent enough to oppose in life as a controversialist. She was passionately committed to the Church of England, to the monarchy, and to the unification of church and state. She believed in a religion of love and feeling, which drew her, like several other women writers, into correspondence with Norris. Even more than Norris, however, she favored faith, hope, and charity above the rational and abstract elements of religion. The most prominent feature of Astell's constellation of beliefs, however, was her conviction that women were tragically failing in modern society to cultivate their immortal souls and their minds. As a response to this situation, Astell proposed the formation of an academy for women. It was to be primarily religious in its aims, although it was also meant to provide intellectual training. Defoe was very favorably impressed, the monastic elements of the scheme suggested Roman Catholic oppression to him and to many others. His own scheme (see p. 491 above) emphasized the secular parts of Astell's. Although, a charity school for girls was formed shortly after her death along lines proposed by Astell, it was the fate of her ideas only to be realized much later (in the nineteenth century) and in a much more progressive, liberal, and secular form than she had conceived them. Although she may not have approved of them in many respects, the women's colleges finally established in the nineteenth century owe a great deal to the ground-breaking ideas and forceful thinking of Mary Astell.

The small portion of A Serious Proposal *(1694) presented here is based on the third edition, corrected, of 1696. There is a recent and important biography by Ruth Perry,* The Celebrated Astell *(University of Chicago, 1986).*

---

[14] *Manes* the spirit of the dead (singular meaning, though the form is plural).

[15] *return to her Clay* the resurrection of the body on Judgement Day was a disputed but common point of Christian belief at this time.

[16] *J[ohn] Asgill* an eccentric theological writer who believed it was possible to go to Heaven without dying.

from A Serious Proposal to the Ladies, for the Advancement of their True and Greatest Interest. By a Lover of her Sex (1694)

Ladies,

Since the Profitable Adventures[1] that have gone abroad in the World have met with so great Encouragement, though the highest advantage they can propose, is an uncertain Lot for such matters as Opinion, not real worth, give a value to; things which if obtained are as flitting and fickle as that Chance which is to dispose of them; I therefore persuade my self, you will not be less kind to a Proposition that comes attended with more certain and substantial Gain, whose only design is to improve your Charms and heighten your Value by suffering you no longer to be cheap and contemptible. Its aim is to fix that Beauty, to make it lasting and permanent, which Nature with all the helps of Art cannot secure, and to place it out of the reach of Sickness and Old Age, by transferring it from a corruptible Body to an immortal Mind. An obliging Design, which would procure them *inward* Beauty, to whom Nature has unkindly denied the *outward*, and not permit those Ladies who have comely Bodies to tarnish their Glory with deformed Souls. Would have you all be wits, or what is better, Wise. Raise you above the Vulgar by something more truly illustrious, than a founding Title[2] or a great Estate. Would excite in you a generous Emulation to excel in the best things, and not in such Trifles as every mean person who has but Money enough may purchase as well as you. Not suffer you to take up with the low thought of distinguishing your selves by any thing that is not truly valuable, and procure you such Ornaments as all the Treasures of the *Indies* are not able to purchase. Would help you to surpass the Men as much in Virtue and Ingenuity, as you do in Beauty; that you may not only be as lovely, but as wise as Angels. Exalt and Establish your Fame, more than the best wrought *Poems* and loudest *Panegyrics*,[3] by ennobling your Minds with such Graces as really deserve it. And instead of the Fustian[4] Complements and Fulsome Flatteries of your Admirers, obtain for you the Plaudit of Good Men and Angels, and the approbation of Him who cannot err. In a word, render you the Glory and Blessing of the present Age, and the Admiration and Pattern of the next.

And sure, I shall not need many words to persuade you to close with[5] this *Proposal*. The very offer is a sufficient inducement, nor does it need the set-offs of *Rhetoric* to recommend it, were I capable, which yet I am not, of applying them with the greatest force. Since you can't be so unkind to your selves, as to refuse your *real* Interest, I only entreat you to be so wise as to examine wherein it consists; for nothing is of worse consequence than to be deceived in a matter of so great concern. 'Tis as little beneath your Grandeur as your Prudence, to examine curiously what is in this case offered you; and to take care that cheating Hucksters don't impose upon you with deceitful Ware. This is a Matter infinitely more worthy your Debates, than what Colours are the most agreeable, or what's the Dress becomes you best. Your *Glass*[6] will not do you half so much service as a serious reflection on your own Minds, which will

---

FROM *A SERIOUS PROPOSAL TO THE LADIES*
1 *Profitable Adventures* successful economic ventures; Astell is thinking of some fad in fashion or make-up.
2 *founding Title* one that comes with a perpetual fund.
3 *Panegyrics* speeches or poems of praise.

4 *Fustian* "Swelling; unnaturally pompous" (Johnson).
5 *close with* agree to.
6 *Glass* mirror.

discover Irregularities more worthy your Correction, and keep you from being either too much elated or depressed by the representations of the other. 'Twill not be near so advantageous to consult with your Dancing-Master as with your own Thoughts, how you may with greatest exactness tread in the Paths of Virtue, which has certainly the most attractive *Air*, and Wisdom the most graceful and becoming *Mien*: Let these attend you and your Carriage will be always well composed, and every thing you do will carry its Charm with it. No solicitude in the adornation of your selves is discommended, provided you employ your care about that which is really your *self*; and do not neglect that particle of Divinity within you, which must survive, and may (if you please) be happy and perfect when it's unsuitable and much inferior Companion is mouldering into Dust. Neither will any pleasure be denied you, who are only desired not to catch at the Shadow and let the Substance go. You may be as ambitious as you please, so you aspire to the best things; and contend with your Neighbours as much as you can, that they may not outdo you in any commendable Quality. Let it never be said, That they to whom pre-eminence is so very agreeable, can be tamely content that others should surpass them in *this*, and precede them in a *better* World! Remember, I pray you, the famous Women of former Ages, the *Orinda*'s[7] of late and the more Modern Heroines, and blush to think how much is now, and will hereafter be said of them, when you your selves (as great a Figure as you make) must be buried in silence and forgetfulness! Shall your Emulation fail *there only* where it is commendable? Why are you so preposterously humble, as not to contend for one of the highest Mansions in the Court of Heaven? Believe me, Ladies, this is the only *Place* worth contending for; you are neither better nor worse in your selves for going before, or coming after *now*; but you are really so much the better, by how much the higher your station is in an Orb of Glory. How can you be content to be in the World like Tulips in a Garden, to make a fine *show* and be good for nothing; have all your Glories set in the Grave, or perhaps much sooner! What your own sentiments are I know not, but I can't without pity and resentment reflect, that those Glorious Temples on which your kind Creator has bestowed such exquisite workmanship, should enshrine no better than *Ægyptian* Deities; be like a garnished Sepulchre, which for all its glittering, has nothing within but emptiness or putrefaction! What a pity it is, that whilst your Beauty casts a lustre round about, your Souls which are infinitely more bright and radiant, (of which if you had but a clear Idea, as lovely as it is, and as much as you now value it, you would then despise and neglect the mean *Case* that encloses it) should be suffered to over-run with Weeds, lie fallow and neglected, unadorned with any Grace! Although the Beauty of the mind is necessary to secure those Conquests which your Eyes have gained, and Time that mortal Enemy to handsome Faces, has no influence on a lovely Soul, but to better and improve it. For shame let us abandon that *Old*, and therefore one would think, unfashionable employment of pursuing Butter-flies and Trifles! No longer drudge on in the dull beaten road of Vanity and Folly, which so many of us have gone before us, but dare to break the enchanted Circle that custom has placed us in, and scorn the vulgar way of imitating all the Impertinencies of our Neighbours. Let us learn to pride our selves in something more excellent than the invention of a Fashion; And not entertain such a degrading thought of our own *worth*, as to imagine that our Souls were given us only for the service of our Bodies, and that the best improvement we can make of these, is to attract the Eyes of Men. We value *them* too much, and our *selves* too

---

[7] *Orinda* a general name for a female heroine, particularly recalling Katherine Philips (see p. 357 above).

little, if we place any part of our worth in their Opinion; and don't think our selves capable of Nobler Things than the pitiful Conquest of some worthless heart. She who has opportunties of making an interest in Heaven, in obtaining the love and admiration of GOD and Angels, is too prodigal of her Time, and injurious to her Charms, to throw them away on vain insignificant men. She need not make her self so cheap, as to descend to court their Applauses; for at the greater distance she keeps, and the more she is above them, the more effectually she secures their esteem and wonder. Be so generous then, Ladies, as to do nothing unworthy of you; so true to your Interest, as not to lessen your Empire and depreciate your Charms. Let not your Thoughts be wholly busied in observing what respect is paid you, but a part of them at least, in studying to deserve it. And after all, remember that Goodness is the truest Greatness; to be wise of your selves the greatest Wit; and *that* Beauty the most desirable which will endure to Eternity.

Jonathan Swift (1667–1745)

Editing Swift and commenting on his writing makes one part of the universe of minds that his work ridicules. The complexities and ironies of his best known books and essays invite (even demand) commentary and explanation because they are subtle in tone, allusive, and stocked with arcana from his classical and theological studies. Yet, Swift's message is often about the folly of sophisticated study and the simplicity of the basic, Christian truths that a good person needs to know and follow. "Sophisticated study," in fact, defines the object of Swift's satire too narrowly: it often seems that reading and writing and everything that goes along with modern print culture is ridiculous in his eyes. That means that you, "Gentle Reader," or "Candid Reader," as Swift will sarcastically address you, are also part of the joke by virtue merely of the fact that you are reading and trying to interpret the printed page in front of you.

Swift perpetually reveals the potential of print to lie, to conceal, to obfuscate, to prevaricate and sophisticate the truth; as you read, you enter this world of falsehood. Perhaps we are meant to realize that all other printed works, all the constructions of the print world (the rhetoric of politics, law, and business, for example) are just as baseless as the hypothetical speakers and bizarre visions that Swift creates. But what then? Silence or illiteracy is no solution. The ugly, savage life led by the Yahoos in Book 4 in Gulliver's Travels *makes it clear that Swift has no illusions about the beauty of a life devoid of cultural sophistication. Yet, much of his writing shows that no degree of sophistication can eradicate the weakness and insufficiency of humanity. The human body reveals human weakness, as Swift shows, for example, in the hideous images in the poem "On a Beautiful Young Nymph Going to Bed." Swift's attitude to the body, especially his apparent fixation on the organs of digestion and defecation, is striking and likely to arouse a wish for psychological inquiry about his childhood. It is true that an accident of weather and the hasty decision of a nurse caused him to be separated from his recently widowed mother for the first three years of his life, and you may make of this what you will, but it is possible to explain Swift's attack on the body in terms of conventional religious exhortations about the infirmity of human life and the consequent necessity of placing our faith in God.*

For all its obvious attention to the body, however, what makes Swift's work perpetually interesting is its distressing, complex satire of the human mind. A Tale of a Tub *is one of the most original, alarming, and amusing critiques of mentality ever written. Its involvement with religious beliefs and with the contemporary critical debate about the superiority of modern or ancient writers make it more obscure to late twentieth-century readers than it was to Swift's contemporaries. On the other hand, the work contains elements which resemble representations of eliptical, fragmented, or deconstructive perceptions that are more familiar to us than to the astonished purchasers of the first edition in 1704.* Gulliver's Travels, *which Swift wrote late in life, is more entertaining, but* A Tale of a Tub *is Swift's most concise and uncompromising expression of his creative vision.*

The edition of Swift's collected works, begun by the Dublin publisher George Faulkner, was four volumes in 1735, and eventually ran to twenty volumes (1772), as more and more of Swift's essays and poems were attributed or came to light. Swift probably participated in the assembly of Faulkner's edition, although he denied it; earlier, beginning in 1711, he also participated in bringing together many of his own scattered (or sometimes previously unpublished works) in a series of volumes called Miscellanies. *His diverse body of work contains various political writings, spoofs, send-ups, and satires, as well as carefully reasoned arguments. His poetry as well as his prose often defy categorization, because they tend to mock the standard forms, even when they depend upon them. Perhaps the most famous short work in this large body of miscellaneous work is "A Modest Proposal." The unreliable speaker in this essay has long been the textbook case for English students, but, like many of Swift's works, it is just such a textbook approach that he ridicules in hopes of making readers more alive to the simple fact that people are starving, and there are practical ways to alleviate their suffering, though they are unpopular and require some sacrifice for the wealthy and middle-class.*

A few years after barely escaping expulsion and getting his BA from Trinity College, Dublin, Swift made the first of his many trips to England and served as a secretary to the diplomat and writer William Temple at his home Moor Park. There he met the young Esther Johnson ("Stella"), a woman whom he loved and depended upon until her death in 1728. Later, he established her in Ireland, where he was ordained as a priest in the Church of Ireland and received successively better appointments until he became Dean of St Patrick's in 1713. Swift's Journal to Stella, *his letters home to her from England, provide much of what we know about his private life and sensibility. On one of his trips he met Esther Vanhomrigh, with whom he also had a long and intimate association. Swift was also close to several important literary figures of his time, especially Alexander Pope and John Gay, with whom he collaborated on several elaborate lampoons. Although he came to England first as a Whig, his most active participation in English political life was in service of the Tory ministry from 1710–14. After the death of Queen Anne, Swift spent most of his time in Dublin. His few surviving sermons are remarkably simple, straightforward, if somewhat condescending, exhortations to simple virtue. It is tempting to think that in those works one hears the "real" Swift, but no such construction will really stand up to modern scrutiny of the very kind that Swift helped create.*

I have based my text of the Tale *on the first edition, of "A Modest Proposal" on the second edition (1730), and the texts of the poems on those in Faulkner's edition. The edition of the* Tale *by Guthkeltch and D. N. Smith (second edition, Clarendon Press, 1958) supplied me with a great deal of the information I print in my notes to that work. I also profited from the notes and collations in Harold Williams' edition of the poems (second edition, Clarendon Press, 1958). The comprehensive biography is by Irwin Ehrenpreis,* Swift: the Man, his Works, and the Age, *3 vols (Methuen, 1962–83).*

A Tale of a Tub
Written for the Universal Improvement of Mankind (1704)

Diu multumque desideratum[1]
Basima eacabasa irraurista, diarba da caeotaba fobor camelanthi.
Iren. Lib. I. C. 18[2]
————*Juvatque novos decerpere flores,*
Insignemque meo capiti petere inde coronam,
Unde prius nulli velarunt tempore Musæ. Lucret.[3]

Treatises written by the same Author, most of them mentioned in the following Discourses, which will be speedily published.[4]

A Character of the present set of Wits *in this Island.*
A panegyrical Essay upon the Number THREE.
A dissertation upon the principal Productions of Grub Street.[5]
Lectures upon a Dissection of Human Nature.
A Panegyric upon the World.
An analytical Discourse upon Zeal, histori-theo-physi-logically *considered.*
A general History of Ears.
A modest Defence of the Proceedings of the Rabble *in all ages.*
A Description of the Kingdom of Absurdities.
A Voyage into England, *by a Person of Quality in* Terra Australis incognita, *translated from the Original.*
A critical Essay upon the Art of Canting, *philosophically, physically, and musically considered.*

To the Right Honourable
John *Lord* Somers[6]

My Lord,

Though the author has written a large Dedication, yet That being addressed to a Prince,[7] whom I am never likely to have the Honour of being known to; a Person, besides, as far as I

A TALE OF A TUB
[1] *Diu multumque desideratum* "having been long and much needed".
[2] *Basima eacabasa* etc.   The Citation out of Irenaeus [second-century Christian theologian who wrote a treatise "Against Hereses"] in the Title-Page, which seems to be all Gibberish, is a Form of Initiation used anciently by the Marcosian Heretics. W[illiam] Wotton [note added in the fifth edition, taken from Wotton's *Defence of the Reflections upon Ancient Learning* (1705); the Marcosians believed in a complete separation between the creating and judgemental God of the Old Testament and the redeeming God of the new; they preached rejection of the old creator's world and concentration on the totally unworldly God whom they could only know in Heaven; Wotton translates Irenaeus' translation of the Syriac, "I call upon this, which is above all the Power of the Father, which is called Light, and Spirit, and Life, because thou hast reigned in the Body."]

[3] *Juvatque . . . Musae* "I love to pluck new flowers, and to seek an illustrious chaplet for my head from fields whence before this the Muses have crowned the brows of none" (Lucretius, *De Rerum Natura* 4.2–5; Loeb Library translation).
[4] *Treatises . . . published* This mock advertising page faced the title-page in the first edition.
[5] *Grub Street* "Originally the name of a street in Moorfields in London, much inhabited by writers of small histories, dictionaries, and temporary poems; whence any mean production is called *grubstreet*" (Johnson).
[6] *Lord Somers* Lord High Chancelor of England (1697), patron of many writers of the time, and very influential politician; in the fifth edition, Swift inserted "An Apology" between the title page and this dedication.
[7] *Prince* Posterity, see below.

can observe, not at all regarded, or thought on by any of our present Writers; And, I being wholly free from that Slavery, which Booksellers usually lie under, to the Caprices of Authors, I think it a wise Piece of Presumption, to ins|cribe these Papers to your Lordship, and to implore your Lordship's Protection of them. God and your Lordship know their Faults and their Merits; for as to my own Particular, I am altogether a Stranger to the Matter, and though everybody else should be equally ignorant, I do not fear the Sale of the Book at all the worse, upon that Score. Your Lordship's Name on the Front, in Capital Letters, will at any time get off one Edition: Neither would I desire any other Help to grow an Alderman, than a Patent for the sole Privilege of dedicating to your Lordship.

I should now, in right of a dedicator, give your Lordship a List of your own Virtues, and at the same time, be very unwilling to offend your Modesty; But, chiefly, I should celebrate your Liberality towards Men of great Parts and small Fortunes, and give you broad Hints, that I mean my self. And, I was just going on in the usual Method, to peruse a hundred or two of Dedications, and transcribe an Abstract to be applied to your Lordship; But, I was diverted by a certain Accident. For, upon the Covers of these Papers, I casually observed written in large Letters, the two following Words, *DETUR DIGNISSIMO*; which, for ought I knew, might contain some important Meaning. But it unluckily fell out that none of the Authors I employ, understood *Latin* (though I have them often in pay, to translate out of that Language) I was therefore compelled to have recourse to the Curate of our Parish, who Englished it thus, *Let it be given to the Worthiest:* And his Comment was, that the Author meant, his Work should be dedicated to the sublimest Genius of the Age, for Wit, Learning, Judgement, Eloquence and Wisdom. I called at a Poet's Chamber (who works for my Shop) in an Alley hard by, showed him the Translation, and desired his Opinion, who it was that the Author could mean; He told me, after some Consideration, that Vanity was a Thing he abhorred; but by the Description, he thought Himself to be the Person aimed at; And, at the same time, he very kindly offered his own Assistance *gratis* towards penning a Dedication to Himself. I desired him, however, to give a second Guess. Why, then, said he, It must be I, or my Lord Somers. From thence I went to several other Wits of my Acquaintance, with no small Hazard and Weariness to my Person, from a prodigious Number of dark, winding Stairs;[8] But found them all in the same Story, both of your Lordship and themselves. Now, your Lordship is to understand that this Proceeding was not of my own Invention; For, I have somewhere heard, it is a Maxim, that those, to whom every Body allows the second Place, have an undoubted Title to the First.

This, infallibly, convinced me, that your Lordship was the Person intended by the Author. But, being very unacquainted in the style and form of dedications, I employed those wits aforesaid to furnish me with hints and materials towards a panegyric upon your Lordship's virtues.

In two Days, they brought me ten Sheets of Paper, filled up on every Side. The swore to me, that they had ransacked whatever could be found in the Characters of *Socrates, Aristides*,[9] *Epaminondas*,[10] *Cato*,[11] *Tully*,[12] *Atticus*,[13] and other hard names which I cannot now recollect. However, I have Reason to believe, they imposed upon my Ignorance, because when I came to read over their Collections, there was not a Syllable there, but what I and every body else,

---

[8] *dark, winding Stairs* Grubstreet wits, or writers, were infamous for dwelling in garrets or attics, the cheapest places to live.

[9] *Aristides* Athenian statesman of fifth century BCE.

[10] *Epaminondas* Theban general of the fourth century BCE.

[11] *Cato* Roman writer and general of the second century BCE.

[12] *Tully* Marcus Tullius Cicero.

[13] *Atticus* friend of Cicero, scholar, and patron.

knew as well as themselves: Therefore I grievously suspect a Cheat, and that these Authors of mine, stole and transcribed every Word, from the universal Report of Mankind. So that I look upon my self, as fifty Shillings[14] out of Pocket, to no manner of Purpose.

If, by altering the Title, I could make the same Materials serve for another Dedication (as my Betters have done) it would help to make up my Loss; but I have made several persons dip here and there in those Papers, and before they read three Lines, they have all assured me, plainly, that they cannot possibly be applied to any Person, besides your Lordship.

I expected, indeed, to have heard of your Lordship's Bravery, at the Head of an Army; of your undaunted Courage in mounting a Breach, or scaling a Wall; Or, to have had your Pedigree traced in a Lineal Descent from the House of *Austria*; Or, of your wonderful talent at Dress and Dancing; Or, your Profound Knowledge in *Algebra*, *Metaphysics*, and the Oriental Tongues: But to ply the World with an old beaten Story of your Wit, and Eloquence, and Learning, and Wisdom, and Justice, and Politeness, and Candour, and Evenness of Temper in all Scenes of Life; Of that great Discernment in Discovering, and Readiness in Favouring deserving Men; with forty other common Topics: I confess, I have neither Conscience, nor Countenance to do it. Because there is no Virtue, either of a Public or Private Life, which some Circumstances of your own, have not often produced upon the Stage of the World; and those few, which for want of Occasions to exert them, might otherwise have passed unseen or unobserved by your *Friends*, your *Enemies* have at length brought them to Light.[15]

'Tis true, I should be very loath, the Bright Example of your Lordship's Virtues should be lost to after Ages, both for their sake and your own; but chiefly, because they will be so very necessary to adorn the History of a *late Reign*;[16] And That is another Reason, why I would forbear to make a Recital of them here; Because, I have been told by Wise Men, that as Dedications have run for some Years past, a good Historian will not be apt to have Recourse thither, in search of Characters.[17]

There is one Point, wherein I think we Dedicators would do well to change our Measures; I mean, instead of running on so far upon the Praise of our Patron's *liberality*, to spend a Word or two, in admiring their *Patience*. I can put no greater Compliment on your Lordship's, than by giving you so ample an Occasion to exercise it at present. Though, perhaps I shall not be apt to reckon much Merit to your Lordship upon that Score, who having been formerly used to tedious Harangues, and sometimes, to as little Purpose, will be the readier to pardon this, especially, when it is offered by one, who is with all Respect and Veneration,

> MY LORD,
> Your Lordship's most obedient,
> and most faithful servant,
> THE BOOKSELLER

THE BOOKSELLER TO THE READER

It is now Six Years, since these Papers came first to my Hands, which seems to have been about a Twelvemonth after they were writ: for the Author tells us in his Preface to the first Treatise, that he has calculated it for the Year 1697, and in several Passages of that Discourse, as well as the second, it appears, they were written about that Time.

---

[14] *fifty shillings* £2.50, several hundred pounds and many hundred dollars in today's money.
[15] *Enemies have . . . brought them to Light* in a failed impeachment proceeding in Parliament in 1701.
[16] *a late Reign* that of King William III.
[17] *Character* "A representation of any man as to his personal qualities" (Johnson).

As to the Author, I can give no manner of Satisfaction; However, I am credibly informed, that this Publication is without his Knowledge, for he concludes the Copy is lost, having lent it to a Person, since dead, and being never in Possession of it after: So that whether the Work received his last Hand, or, whether he intended to fill up the defective Places, is like to remain a Secret.

If I should go about to tell the Reader, by what Accident, I became Master of these Papers, it would, in this unbelieving Age, pass for little more than the Cant, or Jargon of the Trade. I, therefore, gladly spare both him and my self so unnecessary a Trouble. There yet remains a difficult Question, why I published them no sooner. I forbore upon two Accounts: First, because I thought I had better Work upon my Hands; and Secondly, because, I was not without some Hope of hearing from the Author, and receiving his Directions. But, I have been lately alarmed with Intelligence of a surreptitious Copy which a certain great Wit had new polished and refined, or, as our present Writers express themselves, fitted to the Humour of the Age, *as they have already done with great Felicity, to* Don Quixote, Boccalini, la Bruyere, *and other Authors.*[18] *However, I thought it fairer Dealing to offer the whole Work in its Naturals. If any Gentleman will please to furnish me with a Key,* [19]*in order to explain the more difficult Parts, I shall very gratefully acknowledge the Favour, and print it by it self.*

The Epistle Dedicatory
to His Royal Highness
Prince Posterity

SIR,

I here present Your Highness with the Fruits of a very few leisure Hours, stolen from the short Intervals of a World of Business and of an Employment quite alien from such Amusements as this: The poor Production of that Refuse of Time, which has lain heavy upon my Hands, during a long Prorogation[20] of Parliament, a great Dearth of Foreign News, and a tedious Fit of rainy Weather: For which, and other Reasons, it cannot chose extremely to deserve such a Patronage as that of *Your Highness*, whose numberless Virtues in so few Years, make the World look upon You as the future Example to all Princes: For although *Your Highness* is hardly got clear of Infancy, yet has the universal learned World already resolved upon appealing to Your future Dictates with the lowest and most resigned Submission; Fate having decreed You sole Arbiter of the Productions of human Wit, in this polite and most accomplished Age. Methinks, the Number of Appellants were enough to shock and startle any Judge of a Genius less unlimited than Yours: but in order to prevent such glorious Trials, the *Person*[21] (it seems) to whose Care the Education of Your Highness is committed, has resolved (as I am told) to keep You in almost an universal Ignorance of our Studies, which it is your inherent Birth-right to inspect.

It is amazing to me, that this *Person* should have Assurance in the face of the Sun, to go about persuading *Your Highness* that our Age is almost wholly illiterate, and has hardly produced one Writer upon any Subject. I know very well that when *Your Highness* shall come to riper Years, and have gone through the Learning of Antiquity, You will be too curious to neglect inquiring into the Authors of the very Age before You; and to think that this *Insolent*, in the Account he is preparing for Your View, designs to reduce them to a Number so insignificant as I am ashamed to mention; it moves my Zeal and my Spleen[22] for the Honour

---

[18] *they have already done . . . and other Authors* such adaptive translations or imitations were, in fact, common.

[19] *Key* such a work was printed in 1710; it was compiled by Benjamin Tooke, and some parts of it, perhaps worked over by Swift, came into the fifth edition as footnotes.

[20] *Prorogation* "Interruption of the session of Parliament by regal authority" (Johnson).

[21] *Person* Time.

[22] *Spleen* "It is supposed the seat of anger and melancholy" (Johnson).

and Interest of our vast flourishing Body, as well as of my self, for whom I know by long Experience, he has professed, and Still continues a peculiar Malice.

'Tis not unlikely that when *Your Highness* will one Day peruse what I am now writing, You may be ready to expostulate with Your *Governor* upon the Credit of what I here affirm, and command Him to show You some of our Productions. To which he will answer (for I am well informed of his Designs) by asking *Your Highness*, where they are? and what is become of them? and pretend it a Demonstration that there never were any, because they are not then to be found: Not to be found! Who has mislaid them? Are they sunk in the Abyss of Things? 'Tis certain, that in their own Nature they were *light* enough to swim upon the Surface for all Eternity: Therefore the Fault is in Him, who tied Weights so heavy to their Heels, as to depress them to the Centre. Is their very Essence destroyed? Who has annihilated them? Were they drowned by *Purges*, or martyred by *Pipes*?[23] Who administered them to the posteriors of———— But that it may no longer be a Doubt with *Your Highness,* who is to be the Author of this universal Ruin; I beseech you to observe that large and terrible *Scythe* which Your *Governor* affects to bear continually about him. Be pleased to remark the Length and Strength, the Sharpness and Hardness, of his *Nails* and *Teeth*; Consider his baneful, abominable *Breath*, Enemy to Life and Matter, infectious and corrupting: And then reflect whether it be possible for any mortal Ink and Paper of this Generation to make a suitable Resistance. Oh, that *Your Highness* would one day resolve to disarm this Usurping *Maire de Palais,*[24] of his furious Engines, and bring Your Empire *hors de Page.*[25]

It were endless to recount the several Methods of Tyranny and Destruction, which Your *Governor* is pleased to practice upon this Occasion. His inveterate Malice is such to the Writings of our Age, that of several Thousands produced yearly from this renowned City, before the next Revolution of the Sun, there is not one to be heard of: Unhappy Infants, many of them barbarously destroyed, before they have so much as learnt their *Mother-Tongue* to beg for Pity. Some he stifles in their Cradles; others he frights into Convulsions, whereof they suddenly die; Some he flays alive; others he tears Limb from Limb. Great Numbers are offered to *Moloch,*[26] and the rest tainted by his Breath, die of a languishing Consumption.

But the Concern I have most at Heart, is for our Corporation[27] of *Poets*, from whom I am preparing a Petition to *Your Highness*, to be subscribed with the Names of one hundred thirty six of the first Rate, but whose immortal Productions are never likely to reach your Eyes, though each of them is now an humble and an earnest Appellant for the Laurel,[28] and has large comely Volumes ready to show for a Support to his Pretensions. The *never-dying* Works of these illustrious Persons, *Your Governor*, sir, has devoted to unavoidable Death, and *Your Highness* is to be made believe, that our Age has never arrived at the Honour to produce one single Poet.

We confess *Immortality* to be a great and powerful Goddess, but in vain we offer up to her our Devotions and our Sacrifices, if *Your Highness's Governor*, who has usurped the *Priesthood*, must by an unparalleled Ambition and Avarice, wholly intercept and devour them.

To affirm that our Age is altogether Unlearned, and devoid of Writers in any kind, seems to be an Assertion so bold and so false, that I have been some time thinking, the contrary may almost be proved by uncontrollable Demonstration.[29] 'Tis true indeed, that although their

---

[23] *Purges . . . Pipes* unsold copies of books, especially if, as was common, they were unbound, could be used for toilet paper or wadding in pipes or pistols.

[24] *Maire de Palais* chamberlain or master of the king's palace.

[25] *hors de Page* out of its childhood.

[26] *Moloch* a false god in the Old Testament, to whom sacrifices of burning children were made.

[27] *Corporation* society or fellowship.

[28] *Laurel* crown of bay leaves symbolic of literary achievement.

[29] *uncontrollable Demonstration* irrefutable proof.

Numbers be vast, and their Productions numerous in proportion, yet are they hurried so hastily off the Scene, that they escape our Memory, and delude our Sight. When I first thought of this Address, I had prepared a copious List of *Titles* to present *Your Highness* as an undisputed Argument for what I affirm. The Originals were posted fresh upon all Gates and Corners of Streets; but returning in a very few Hours to take a Review, they were all torn down, and fresh ones in their Places: I inquired after them among Readers and Booksellers, but I inquired in vain, 'the Memorial of them was lost among Men, their Place was no more to be found';[30] and I was laughed to scorn, for a *Clown* and a *Pedant*, devoid of all Taste and Refinement, little versed in the Course of *present* Affairs, and that knew nothing of what had passed in the best Companies of Court and Town. So that I can only avow in general to *Your Highness*, that we *do* abound in Learning and Wit; but to fix upon Particulars, is a Task too slippery for my slender Abilities. If I should venture in a windy Day, to affirm to *Your Highness* that there is a huge Cloud near the *Horizon* in the Form of a *Bear*, another in the *Zenith* with the Head of an *Ass*, a third to the Westward with Claws like a *Dragon*, and *Your Highness* should in a few Minutes think fit to examine the Truth; 'tis certain, they would be all changed in Figure and Position, new ones would arise, and all we could agree upon would be, that Clouds there were, but that I was grossly mistaken in the *Zoography*[31] and *Topography* of them.

But Your *Governor,* perhaps, may still insist, and put the Question: 'What is then become of those immense Bales of Paper, which must needs have been employed in such Numbers of Books? Can these also be wholly annihilate, and so of a sudden as I pretend?' What shall I say in return of so invidious an Objection? It ill befits the Distance between *Your Highness* and Me, to send You for ocular Conviction to a *Jakes*[32] or an *Oven*; to the Windows of a *Bawdy-House,* or to a sordid *Lantern.*[33] Books like Men their Authors have no more than one Way of coming into the World, but there are ten Thousand to go out of it and return no more.

I profess to *Your Highness,* in the Integrity of my Heart, that what I am going to say is literally true this Minute I am writing; What Revolutions may happen before it shall be ready for Your Perusal, I can by no means warrant; However, I beg You to accept it as a Specimen of our Learning, our Politeness and our Wit. I do therefore affirm upon the Word of a sincere Man, that there is now actually in being, a certain Poet called *John Dryden,* whose Translation of *Virgil* was lately[34] printed in a large Folio, well bound, and if diligent search were made, for ought I know, is yet to be seen. There is another called *Nahum Tate,*[35] who is ready to make Oath that he has caused many Reams of Verse to be published, whereof both himself and his Bookseller (if lawfully required) can still produce authentic Copies, and therefore wonders why the World is pleased to make such a Secret of it. There is a Third, known by the Name of *Tom Durfey,*[36] a Poet of a vast Comprehension, an universal Genius, and most profound Learning. There are also one Mr. *Rymer,*[37] and one Mr. *Dennis,*[38] most profound Critics. There is a person styled Dr. *B—tl—y,*[39] who has written near a thousand Pages

---

[30] *Memorial . . . found*   an echo of Revelation 12.8 and other biblical passages.

[31] *Zoography*   animal outlines.

[32] *Jakes*   "A house of office" (Johnson); lavatory.

[33] *Lantern*   lighthouse.

[34] *lately*   1697.

[35] *Nahum Tate* (1652–1715) much maligned poet and dramatist, famous for revising Shakespeare's *King Lear* in a more optimistic version that held the stage for an age.

[36] *Tom Durfey*   D'Urfey (1653–1723), frequently lampooned poet and dramatist.

[37] *Rymer*   Thomas Rymer (1641–1713) dramatic critic.

[38] *Dennis*   John Dennis (1657–1734), dramatist and critic of contemporary poetry, satirized by Pope.

[39] *B—tl—y*   Richard Bentley (1662–1742), important classical scholar; supported William Wotton and the moderns in a famous debate about the relative merit of the ancient and modern writers, in which Swift fought for the ancients alongside his patron William Temple.

of immense Eruditon, *giving a full and true Account* of a certain *Squabble*, of wonderful importance between himself and a Bookseller: He is a Writer of infinite Wit and Humour; no Man rallies with a better Grace, and in more sprightly Turns. Further, I avow to *Your Highness,* that with these Eyes I have beheld the Person of *William W—tt—n*, BD,[40] who has written a good sizeable Volume against a *Friend of Your Governor* (from whom, alas! he must therefore look for little Favour) in a most gentlemanly Style, adorned with utmost Politeness and Civility: replete with Discoveries equally valuable for their Novelty and Use; and embellished with *Traits* of Wit so poignant and so apposite, that he is a worthy Yokemate to his fore-mentioned *Friend.*

Why should I go upon further Particulars, which might fill a Volume with the just Elogies[41] of my contemporary Brethren? I shall bequeath this Piece of Justice to a larger Work; wherein I intend to write a Character of the present Set of *Wits* in our Nation: Their persons I shall describe particularly and at Length, their Genius and Understandings in *Miniature.*

In the mean time, I do here make bold to present *Your Highness* with a faithful Abstract drawn from the Universal Body of all Arts and Sciences, intended wholly for Your Service and Instruction: Nor do I doubt in the least, but *Your Highness* will peruse it as carefully, and make as considerable Improvements, as *other* young *Princes* have already done by the many Volumes of late Years written for a Help to their Studies.

That *Your Highness* may advance in Wisdom and Virtue, as well as Years, and at last out-shine all Your Royal Ancestors, shall be the daily Prayer of,

SIR,

Your Highness's
Most devoted, &c.

Decemb. 1697.

THE PREFACE

The Wits of the present Age being so very numerous and penetrating, it seems, the Grandees of *Church* and *State* begin to fall under horrible Apprehensions, lest these Gentle-men during the Intervals of a long Peace, should find leisure to pick Holes in the weak sides of Religion and Government. To prevent which, there has been much Thought employed of late upon certain Projects for taking off the Force and Edge of those formidable Enquirers, from canvasing and reasoning upon such delicate Points. They have at length fixed upon one which will require some Time as well as cost to perfect. Mean while, the Danger hourly increasing, by new Levies[42] of Wits all appointed (as there is Reason to fear) with Pen, Ink, and Paper, which may at an hour's Warning be drawn out into Pamphlets, and other Offensive Weapons, ready for immediate Execution: It was judged of absolute necessity, that some present Expedient be thought on, till the main Design can be brought to Maturity. To this End, at a Grand Committee, some Days ago, this important Discovery was made by a certain curious and refined Observer; That Sea-men have a Custom when they meet a *Whale*, to fling him out an empty *Tub* by way of Amusement, to divert him from laying violent Hands upon the Ship. This Parable was immediately mythologized; The *Whale* was inter-preted to be *Hobbes's Leviathan*,[43] which tosses and plays with all Schemes of Religion and

---

[40] *William W—tt—n BD*   Wotton (1666–1727), like Bentley, an accomplished classicist who supported the claims of the moderns against the excesses of Temple's preference for the ancients in *Reflections upon Ancient and Modern Learning* (1694).

[41] *Elogies*   praises.

[42] *Levies*   conscription.

[43] *Hobbes's Leviathan*   see above p. 9.

Government, whereof a great many are hollow, and dry, and empty, and noisy, and wooden, and given to Rotation.[44] This is the *Leviathan* from whence the terrible Wits of our Age are said to borrow their Weapons. The *Ship* in danger, is easily understood to be its old Antitype the *Commonwealth*. But, how to analyse the *Tub*, was a Matter of Difficulty; when, after long Enquiry and Debate, the literal Meaning was preserved: And it was decreed, that in order to prevent these *Leviathans* from tossing and sporting with the *Commonwealth* (which it self is too apt to *fluctuate*) they should be diverted from that Game by *a Tale of a Tub*. And my Genius being conceived to lie not unhappily that way, I had the Honour done me to be engaged in the Performance.

This is the sole Design in publishing the following Treatise, which I hope will serve for an *Interim* of some Months to employ those unquiet Spirits, till the perfecting of that great Work; into the Secret of which, it is reasonable the courteous Reader should have some little Light.

It is intended that a large Academy be erected, capable of containing nine thousand seven hundred forty and three Persons, which by modest Computation is reckoned to be pretty near the current Number of *Wits* in this Island. These are to be disposed into the several Schools of this Academy, and there pursue those Studies to which their Genius most inclines them. The Undertaker himself will publish his Proposals with all convenient speed, to which I shall refer the curious Reader for a more particular Account, mentioning at present only a few of the principal Schools. There is, first, a large *Pederastic* School, with French and Italian masters. There is also, the *Spelling* School, *a very spacious Building*: The School of *Looking-Glasses*: The School of *Swearing*: The School of *Critics*: The School of *Salivation*: The School of *Hobby-horses*: The School of *Poetry*: The School of *Tops*: The School of *Spleen*: The School of *Gaming*: with many others too tedious to recount. No Person to be admitted Member into any of these Schools, without an Attestation under two sufficient Persons' Hands, certifying him to be a *Wit*.

But, to return. I am sufficiently instructed in the principal Duty of a Preface, if my Genius were capable of arriving at it. Thrice have I forced my Imagination to make the *Tour* of my Invention, and thrice it has returned empty; the latter having been wholly drained by the following Treatise. Not so, my more successful Brethren the *Moderns*, who will by no means let slip a Preface or Dedication, without some notable distinguishing Stroke, to surprise the Reader at the Entry, and kindle a wonderful Expectation of what is to ensue. Such was that of a most ingenious Poet, who soliciting his Brain for something new, compared himself to the *Hangman*, and his Patron to the *Patient*: This was *Insigne, recens, indictum ore alio*.[45] When I went through that necessary and noble course of Study, I had the happiness to observe many such egregious Touches, which I shall not injure the Authors by transplanting: Because I have remarked, that nothing is so very tender as a *Modern* Piece of Wit, and which is apt to suffer so much in the Carriage. Some things are extremely witty *to day*, or *fasting*, or *in this Place*, or *at eight a Clock*, or *over a Bottle*, or *spoken by Mr.* Whatdicall'um, or *in a Summer's Morning*: Any of which, by the smallest Transposal or Misapplication, is utterly annihilate. Thus, *Wit* has its Walks and Purlieus, out of which it may not stray the breadth of a Hair, upon peril of being lost. The *Moderns* have artfully fixed this *Mercury*,[46] and reduced it to the Circumstances of Time, Place, and Person. Such a Jest there is, that will not pass out of *Convent-Garden*, and such a one, that is no where intelligible but at *Hyde-Park Corner*.[47] Now, though it sometimes

---

[44] *Rotation* a reference to the Rota Club, and in particular, to James Harrington, author of *The Commonwealth of Oceana* (1656), a republican utopia.
[45] *Insigne . . . alio* "extraordinary, recent, untold by another author" (Horace, *Odes* 3.25.7–8).

[46] *Mercury* "Sprightly qualities" (Johnson), from the properties of the element, as chemists described them.
[47] *Convent-Garden . . . Hyde-Park Corner* neighborhoods in London.

tenderly affects me to consider, that all the towardly Passages I shall deliver in the following Treatise, will grow quite out of date and relish with the first shifting of the present Scene; yet I must need subscribe to the Justice of this Proceeding: because, I cannot imagine why we should be at Expense to furnish Wit for succeeding Ages, when the former have made no sort of Provision for ours; wherein I speak the Sentiment of the very newest, and consequently the most Orthodox Refiners, as well as my own. However, being extremely solicitous that every accomplished Person who has got into the Taste of Wit calculated for this present Month of *August* 1697, should descend to the very *bottom* of all the *Sublime*[48] throughout this Treatise; I hold fit to lay down this general Maxim. Whatever Reader desires to have a thorough Comprehension of an Author's Thoughts, cannot take a better Method, than by putting himself into the Circumstances and Posture of Life, that the Writer was in, upon every important Passage as it flowed from his Pen; For this will introduce a Parity and strict Correspondence of Ideas between the Reader and the Author. Now, to assist the diligent Reader in so delicate an Affair, as far as brevity will permit, I have recollected, that the shrewdest Pieces of this Treatise, were conceived in Bed, in a Garret: at other times (for a Reason best known to my self) I thought fit to sharpen my Invention with Hunger; and in general, the whole Work was begun, continued, and ended, under a long course of Physic,[49] and a great want of Money. Now, I do affirm, it will be absolutely impossible for the candid Peruser to go along with me in a great many bright Passages, unless upon the several Difficulties emergent, he will please to capacitate and prepare himself by these Directions. And this I lay down as my principal *Postulatum*.

Because I have professed to be a most devoted Servant of all *Modern* Forms; I apprehend some curious *Wit* may object a-me for proceeding thus far in a Preface, without declaiming according to the Custom, against the Multitude of Writers, whereof the whole Multitude of Writers most reasonably complains. I am just come from perusing some hundreds of Prefaces, wherein the Authors do at the very beginning address the gentle Reader concerning this enormous Grievance. Of these I have preserved a few Examples, and shall set them down as near as my Memory has been able to retain them.

One begins thus;

'For a Man to set up for a Writer, when the Press swarms with, &c.'

Another;

'The Tax upon Paper does not lessen the Number of Scribblers, who daily pester, &c.'

Another;

'When every little Would-be wit takes Pen in hand, 'tis in vain to enter the Lists, &c.'

Another;

'To observe what Trash the Press swarms with, &c.'

Another;

'SIR. It is merely in Obedience to your Commands that I venture into the Public; for who upon a less Consideration would be of a Party with such a Rabble of Scribblers, &c.'

Now, I have two Words in my own Defence against this Objection. First: I am far from granting the Number of Writers, a Nuisance to our Nation, having strenuously maintained the contrary in several Parts of the following Discourse. Secondly: I do not well understand the Justice of this Proceeding, because I observe many of these polite Prefaces to be not only from the same Hand, but from those who are most voluminous in their several Productions: Upon which I shall tell the Reader a short Tale.

---

[48] *the Sublime* "The grand or lofty style. The sublime is a Gallicism but now naturalised" (Johnson). [49] *Physic* medication, especially purgatives.

'A Mountebank in *Leicester-Fields*[50] had drawn a huge Assembly about him. Among the rest, a fat unwieldy Fellow, half stifled in the Press, would be every fit[51] crying out, "Lord! what a filthy Crowd is here; Pray, good People, give way a little; Bless me! what a Devil has raked this Rabble together: Z——ds,[52] what squeezing is this! Honest Friend, remove your Elbow". At last a Weaver that stood next him could hold no longer. "A plague confound you", said he, "for an overgrown Sloven; and who (in the Devil's Name) I wonder, helps to make up the Crowd half so much as your self? Don't you consider (with a Pox[53]) that you take up more room with that Carcase than any five here? Is not the Place as free for us as for you? Bring your own Guts to a reasonable Compass (and be d——n'd) and then I'll engage we shall have room enough for us all."'

There are certain common Privileges of a Writer, the Benefit whereof, I hope there will be no Reason to doubt; particularly, that where I am not understood, it shall be concluded, that something very useful and profound is couched underneath: And again, that whatever Word or Sentence is printed in a different Character, shall be judged to contain something extraordinary either of *Wit* or *Sublime*.

As for the Liberty I have thought fit to take of praising my self, upon some Occasions or none; I am sure it will need no Excuse, if a Multitude of great Examples be allowed sufficient Authority: For, it is here to be noted, that *Praise* was originally a Pension paid by the World; but the *Moderns* finding the trouble and charge too great in collecting it, have lately brought out the *Fee-Simple*;[54] since which time, the Right of Presentation is wholly in our selves. For this Reason it is, that when an Author makes his own Elogy, he uses a certain Form to declare and insist upon his Title, which is commonly in these or the like Words, 'I speak without vanity'; which I think plainly shows it to be a Matter of Right and Justice. Now, I do here once for all declare, that in every Encounter of this Nature, through the following Treatise, the Form aforesaid is implied; which I mention, to save the Trouble of repeating it on so many Occasions.

'Tis a great Ease to my Conscience that I have writ so elaborate and useful a Discourse without one grain of Satire intermixed; which is the sole Point wherein I have taken Leave to dissent from the famous Originals of our Age and Country. I have observed some Satirists to use the Public much at the rate that Pedants do a naughty Boy ready horsed[55] for Discipline; First expostulate the Case, then plead the Necessity of the Rod, from great Provocations, and conclude every Period[56] with a Lash. Now, if I know anything of Mankind, these Gentlemen might very well spare their Reproof and Correction: For, there is not through all Nature another so callous and insensible a Member as *the World's Posteriors*, whether you apply to it with the *Toe* or the *Birch*.[57] Besides, most of our late Satirists seem to lie under a sort of Mistake, that because *Nettles* have the Prerogative to Sting, therefore all *other Weeds* must do so too. I make not this Comparison out of the least Design to detract from these worthy Writers: For it is well known among *Mythologists,* that *Weeds* have the Preeminence over all other Vegetables; and therefore the first *Monarch* of this Island,[58] whose Taste and Judgement were so acute and refined, did very wisely root out the *Roses* from the Collar of *the Order*, and plant the *Thistles*[59] in their stead, as the nobler Flower of the two. For which Reason it is

---

50 *Leicester-Fields*   now Leicester Square, London.
51 *fit*   short interval of time.
52 *Z{oun}ds*   "God's wounds," a mild curse.
53 *Pox*   venereal disease, a curse.
54 *Fee-Simple*   an unconditional gift or grant.
55 *horsed*   raised up, on a man's back, for flogging.
56 *Period*   sentence.

57 *Birch*   a bundle of sticks used for flogging.
58 James I, because he was King of England, Scotland, and Wales.
59 *Thistles*   a Scottish order of knights, revived or begun by James II; it co-existed with the Order of the Garter, which has roses in its ceremonial collar, but the House of Stuart was seen to favor it.

conjectured by profounder Antiquaries, that the Satirical Itch, so prevalent in this Part of our Island, was first brought among us from beyond the *Tweed*.[60] Here may it long flourish and abound: May it survive and neglect the Scorn of the World, with as much Ease and Contempt, as the World is insensible to the Lashes of it. May their own Dullness, or that of their Party, be no Discouragement for the Authors to proceed; but let them remember, it is with *Wits* as with *Razors*, which are never so apt to *cut* those they are employed on, as when they have *lost their Edge*: Besides, those whose Teeth are too rotten to bite, are best of all others qualified to revenge that Defect with their Breath.

I am not like other Men, to envy or undervalue the Talents I cannot reach; for which Reason I must needs bear a true Honour to this large eminent Sect of our *British* Writers. And I hope this, little panegyric will not be offensive to their Ears, since it has the Advantage of being only designed for themselves. Indeed, Nature her self has taken Order, that Fame and Honour should be purchased at a better Penyworth by Satire, than by any other Productions of the Brain; the World being soonest provoked to *Praise* by *Lashes,* as Men are to *Love.* There is a Problem in an ancient Author, why Dedications, and other Bundles of Flattery run all upon stale, musty Topics, without the smallest Tincture of any thing New; not only to the torment and nauseating of the *Christian* Reader, but (if not suddenly prevented) to the universal spreading of that pestilent Disease, the Lethargy, in this Island: Whereas there is very little Satire which has not something in it untouched before. The Defects of the former are usually imputed to the want of Invention among those who are Dealers in that kind: But, I think, with a great deal of Injustice; the Solution being easy and natural. For, the Materials of Panegyric being very few in Number, have been long since exhausted: For, as Health is but one Thing and has been always the same, whereas Diseases are by thousands, besides new and daily Additions: So, all the Virtues that have been ever in Mankind, are to be counted upon a few Fingers; but his Follies and Vices are innumerable, and Time adds hourly to the Heap. Now, the utmost a poor poet can do, is to get by heart a List of the Cardinal Virtues, and deal them with his utmost Liberality to his Hero or his Patron: He may ring the Changes as far as it will go, and vary his Phrase till he has talked round; but the Reader quickly finds, it is all *Pork,* with a little variety of Sauce. For there is no inventing Terms of Art beyond our Ideas; and when Ideas are exhausted, Terms of Art must be so too.

But, though the matter for Panegyric were as fruitful as the Topics of Satire, yet would it not be hard to find out a sufficient Reason, why the latter will be always better received than the first. For, this being bestowed only upon one or a few Persons at a time, is sure to raise Envy, and consequently ill Words from the rest, who have no share in the Blessing: But Satire being levelled at all, is never resented for an Offence by any, since every individual Person makes bold to understand it of others, and very wisely removes his particular Part of the Burden upon the Shoulders of the World, which are broad enough, and able to bear it. To this purpose, I have sometimes reflected upon the Difference between *Athens* and *England*, with respect to the Point before us. In the *Attic* Commonwealth,[61] it was the Privilege and Birth-right of every Citizen and Poet, to rail aloud and in public, or to expose upon the Stage by Name, any Person they pleased, though of the greatest Figure, whether a *Creon*, an *Hyperbolus*, an *Alcibiades*, or a *Demosthenes*:[62] But, on the other side, the least reflecting Word let fall against the *People* in general, was immediately caught up, and revenged upon the Authors, however considerable for their Quality or their Merits. Whereas, in *England* it is just the Reverse of all

---

[60]   *Tweed*   river dividing England from Scotland.
[61]   *Attic Commonwealth*   vid. Xenoph. [Swift's marginal note; "see Xenophon," meaning *On the Polity of the Athenians*, a work then but not now attributed to Xenophon].

[62]   *Creon*   [a mistake for Cleon]; *Hyperbolus*; *Alcibiades*; *Demosthenes*: all Athenian generals and politicians in the late fifth century BCE, all critically discussed by Thucydides.

this. Here, you may securely display your utmost *Rhetoric* against Mankind, in the Face of the World; tell them, 'That all are gone astray; That there is none that doth good, no not one;[63] That we live in the very Dregs of Time; That Knavery and Atheism are Epidemic as the Pox; That Honesty is fled with Astræa';[64] with any other Common Places *equally* new and eloquent, which are furnished by the *Splendida bilis*.[65] And when you have done, the whole Audience, far from being offended, shall return you Thanks, as a Deliverer of precious and useful Truths. Nay further; it is but to venture your Lungs, and you may Preach in *Covent-Garden*[66] against Foppery and Fornication, and *something else*: Against Pride, and Dissimulation, and Bribery, at *White-Hall*:[67] You may expose Rapine and Injustice in the *Inns of Court*[68] Chapel: And in a *City*[69] Pulpit be as fierce as you please against Avarice, Hypocrisy, and Extortion. 'Tis but a *Ball* bandied to and fro, and every man carries a *Racket* about Him to strike it from himself among the rest of the Company. But on the other side, whoever should mistake the Nature of things so far, as to drop but a single Hint in public, How *such a one* starved half the Fleet, and half poisoned the rest: How *such a one*, from a true principle of *Love* and *Honour*, pays no Debts but for *Wenches* and *Play*: How *such a one* has got a Clap,[70] and runs out of his Estate: How *Paris* bribed by *Juno* and *Venus*, loath to offend either Party, slept out the whole Cause on the Bench: Or, how *such an Orator* makes long Speeches in the Senate, with much Thought, little Sense, and to no Purpose. Whoever, I say, should venture to be thus particular, must expect to be imprisoned for *Scandalum Magnatum*;[71] to have *Challenges* sent him; to be sued for *Defamation*, and to be *brought before the Bar of the House*.[72]

But, I forget that I am expatiating on a Subject, wherein I have no Concern, having neither a Talent nor an Inclination for Satire; On the other side, I am so entirely satisfied with the whole present Procedure of human Things, that I have been for some Years preparing Materials towards *A Panegyric upon the World*; to which I intended to add a Second Part entitled, *A Modest Defence of the Proceedings of the Rabble in all Ages*. Both these I had Thoughts to publish by way of Appendix to the following Treatise; but finding my Common-Place Book fill much slower than I had reason to expect, I have chosen to defer them to another Occasion. Besides, I have been unhappily prevented in that Design, by a certain Domestic Misfortune, in the Particulars whereof, though it would be very seasonable and much in the *Modern* way, to inform the *gentle Reader*, and would also be of great Assistance towards extending this Preface into the Size now in Vogue, which by Rule ought to be *large* in Proportion as the subsequent Volume is *small*; Yet I shall now dismiss our impatient Reader from any further Attendance at the *Porch*, and having duly prepared his Mind by a preliminary Discourse, shall gladly introduce Him to the sublime Mysteries that ensue.

A TALE OF A TUB, &C.

SECT. I

THE INTRODUCTION

Whoever hath an Ambition to be heard in a Crowd, must press, and squeeze, and thrust, and climb, with indefatigable Pains, till he has exalted himself to a certain Degree of Altitude

---

[63] *all are gone astray . . . not one* Psalm 14.3 [note in edition of 1720].

[64] *Astræa* goddess of justice who left the world in disgust.

[65] *Splendida bilis* "gleaming (black) bile, or anger" (Horace, *Satires* 2.3.141).

[66] *Covent-Garden* a district then known for prostitution.

[67] *White-Hall:* the seat of government.

[68] *Inns of Court* center of London's legal system.

[69] *City* the commercial centre.

[70] *Clap* venereal disease.

[71] *Scandalum Magnatum* libel against a high personage of the land.

[72] *Bar of the House* House of Commons constituted as a court of judgement.

above them. Now, in all Assemblies, though you wedge them ever so close, we may observe this peculiar Property: that, over their Heads there is Room enough; but how to reach it, is the difficult Point; It being as hard to get quit of *Number* as of *Hell*;

> ———*Evadere ad auras,*
> *Hoc opus, hic labor est.*———[73]

To this End, the Philosopher's Way in all Ages, has been by erecting certain *Edifices in the Air*; But, whatever Practice and Reputation these kind of Structures have formerly possessed, or may still continue in; not excepting even that of *Socrates,* when he [was] suspended in a Basket to help Contemplation;[74] I think, with due Submission, they seem to labour under two Inconveniences. First, that the Foundations being laid too high, they have been often out of *Sight*, and ever out of *Hearing*. Secondly, that the Materials being very transitory, have suffered much from Inclemencies of Air, especially in these North-West Regions.

Therefore, towards the just Performance of this great Work, there remain but three Methods that I can think on; Whereof the Wisdom of our Ancestors being highly sensible, has, to encourage all aspiring Adventurers, thought fit to erect three wooden Machines, for the Use of those Orators who desire to talk much without Interruption. These are, the *Pulpit*, the *Ladder*, and the *Stage-Itinerant*. For, as to the *Bar*, though it be compounded of the same Matter, and designed for the same Use, it cannot however be well allowed the Honour of a fourth, by reason of its level or inferior Situation, exposing it to perpetual Interruption from Collaterals. Neither can the *Bench* it self, though raised to a proper Eminency, put in a better Claim, whatever its Advocates insist on. For if they please to look into the original Design of its Erection, and the Circumstances or Adjuncts subservient to that Design, they will soon acknowledge the present Practice exactly correspondent to the Primitive Institution, and both to answer the Etymology of the Name, which in the *Phœnician* Tongue is a Word of great Signification, importing, if literally interpreted, 'The Place of Sleep'; but in common Acceptation, 'a Seat well bolstered and cushioned, for the Repose of old and gouty Limbs': *Senes ut in otia tuta recedant.*[75] Fortune being indebted to them this Part of Retaliation, that, as formerly they have long *Talked,* whilst others *Slept,* so now they may *Sleep* as long whilst others *Talk*.

But if no other Argument could occur to exclude the *Bench* and the *Bar* from the List of Oratorial Machines, it were sufficient that the Admission of them would overthrow a Number which I was resolved to establish whatever Argument it might cost me: In imitation of that prudent Method observed by many other Philosophers and great Clerks, whose chief Art in Division has been, to grow fond of some proper mystical Number, which their Imaginations have rendered Sacred, to a Degree, that they force common Reason to find room for it in every part of Nature; reducing, including, and adjusting, every *Genus* and *Species* within that Compass, by coupling some against their Wills, and banishing others at any Rate. Now, among all the rest, the profound Number THREE is that which hath most employed my sublimest Speculations, nor ever without wonderful Delight. There is now in the Press (and will be published next Term) a Panegyrical Essay of mine upon this Number, wherein I have by most convincing Proofs, not only reduced the *Senses* and the *Elements* under its Banner, but brought over several Deserters from its two great Rivals SEVEN and NINE.

---

[73] *Evadere . . . est* "But to return, and view the cheerful Skies;/In this the Task and mighty Labour lies" [note in fifth edition, citing Dryden's translation of *Aeneid* 6.128–9].

[74] *Socrates . . . Contemplation* he arrives on stage in this manner in Aristophanes' comedy *Clouds*, l. 218.

[75] *Senes . . . recedant* "so that when they are old they may retire to a life of ease" (Horace, *Satires* 1.1.31).

Now, the first of these Oratorial Machines in Place as well as Dignity, is the *Pulpit*. Of *Pulpits* there are in this Island several sorts; but I esteem only That made of Timber from the *Sylva Caledonia*,[76] which agrees very well with our Climate. If it be upon its Decay, 'tis the better, both for Conveyance of Sound and for other Reasons to be mentioned by and by. The Degree of Perfection in Shape and Size, I take to consist, in being extremely narrow, with little Ornament, and, best of all, without a Cover (for by ancient Rule it ought to be the only uncovered *Vessel* in every Assembly where it is rightfully used) by which means, from its near Resemblance to a Pillory, it will ever have a mighty Influence on human Ears.

Of *Ladders* I need say nothing: 'Tis observed by Foreigners themselves, to the Honour of our Country, that we excel all Nations in our Practice and Understanding of this Machine. The ascending Orators do not only oblige their Audience in the agreeable Delivery, but the whole World in their *early* Publication of their Speeches; which I look upon as the choicest Treasury of our British Eloquence, and whereof I am informed, that worthy Citizen and Bookseller, Mr. *John Dunton*,[77] hath made a faithful and a painful Collection which he shortly designs to publish in Twelve Volumes in Folio, illustrated with Copper-Plates. A Work highly useful and curious, and altogether worthy of such a Hand.

The last Engine of Orators, is the *stage itinerant*,[78] erected with much Sagacity, *sub Jove pluvio, in triviis & quadriviis*.[79] It is the great Seminary of the two former, and its Orators are sometimes preferred to the One, and sometimes to the Other, in proportion to their Deservings, there being a strict and perpetual Intercourse between all three.

From this accurate Deduction it is manifest that for obtaining Attention in Public, there is of necessity required *a superior Position of Place*. But, although this Point be generally granted, yet the Cause is little agreed in; and it seems to me, that very few Philosophers have fallen into a true, natural Solution of this *Phenomenon*. The deepest Account, and the most fairly digested of any I have yet met with, is this, That Air being a heavy Body, and therefore (according to the System of *Epicurus*[80]) continually descending, must needs be more so, when loaden and pressed down by Words, which are also Bodies of much Weight and Gravity, as it is manifest from those deep *Impressions* they make and leave upon us; and therefore must be delivered from a due Altitude, or else they will neither carry a good Aim, nor fall down with a sufficient Force.

> *Corpoream quoque enim vocem constare fatendum est,*
> *Et sonitum, quoniam possunt impellere Sensus.*
> LUCR. Lib. 4.[81]

And I am the readier to favour this Conjecture, from a common Observation; that in the several Assemblies of these Orators, Nature itself has instructed the Hearers to stand with their Mouths open, and erected parallel to the Horizon, so as they may be intersected by a perpendicular Line from the Zenith to the Center of the Earth. In which Position, if the Audience be well compact, every one carries home a Share, and little or nothing is lost.

---

76 *Sylva Caledonia* "Scottish forest"; Scotland was already notoriously deforested.

77 *John Dunton* (1659–1733), published over 600 books, plagued by poverty and growing insanity by 1704.

78 *stage itinerant* Is the Mountebank's Stage [note in fifth edition].

79 *sub Jove . . . quadriviis* In the open Air, and in Streets where the greatest Resort is [note in fifth edition].

80 *Epicurus* Lucret. [*De Rerum Natura*] Lib. 2 [Swift's marginal note].

81 *Corpoream . . . Lib. 4* "Tis certain then, that Voice that thus can wound / Is all Material; Body every Sound" [note in fifth edition from Creech's Lucretius (1683), 4.526–7].

I confess there is something yet more refined in the Contrivance and Structure of our Modern Theatres. For, First; the Pit is sunk below the Stage with due Regard to the Institution above deduced; that whatever *weighty* Matter shall be delivered thence (whether it be *Lead* or *Gold*) may fall plum into the Jaws of certain *Critics* (as I think they are called) which stand ready open to devour them. Then, the Boxes are built round, and raised to a Level with the Scene, in deference to the Ladies, because, That large Portion of Wit laid out in raising Pruriences[82] and Protuberances, is observed to run much upon a Line, and ever in a Circle. The whining Passions, and little starved Conceits, are gently wafted up by their own extreme Levity, to the middle Region, and there fix and are frozen by the frigid Understandings of the Inhabitants. Bombast and Buffoonery, by nature lofty and light, soar highest of all, and would be lost in the Roof, if the prudent Architect had not with much Foresight contrived for them a fourth Place, called the *Twelve-Penny Gallery*, and there planted a suitable Colony, who greedily intercept them in their Passage.

Now this Physico-logical Scheme of Oratorial Receptacles or Machines, contains a great Mystery, being a Type, a Sign, an Emblem, a Shadow, a Symbol, bearing Analogy to the spatious Commonwealth of Writers, and to those Methods by which they must exalt themselves to a certain Eminency above the inferior World. By the *Pulpit* are adumbrated the Writings of our *Modern Saints* in *Great Britain*, as they have spiritualized and refined them from the Dross and Grossness of *Sense* and *Human Reason*. The Matter, as we have said, is of rotten Wood, and that upon two Considerations; Because it is the Quality of rotten Wood to give *Light* in the Dark: And secondly, Because its Cavities are full of Worms: Which is a Type with a Pair of Handles, having a Respect to the two principal Qualifications of the Orator, and the two different Fates attending upon his Works.[83]

The *Ladder* is an adequate Symbol of *Faction*[84] pand of *Poetry*, to both of which so noble a Number of Authors are indebted for their Fame. Of *Faction* because   *   *   *   *   *   *   *   *   *   *

*   *   *   *   *   *   *   *   *   *   *

[Hiatus in MS]   *   *   *   *   *   *   *   *

*   *   *   *   *   *   * Of *poetry*, because its Orators do *perorare*[85] with a Song; and because climbing up by slow Degrees, Fate is sure to turn them off before they can reach within many Steps of the Top: And because it is a Preferment attained by transferring of Propriety, and a confounding of *Meum* and *Tuum*.[86]

Under the *Stage-itinerant* are couched those Productions designed for the Pleasure and Delight of Mortal Man, such as, *Six-penny-worth of Wit*, Westminster *Drolleries, Delightful Tales, Complete Jesters*,[87] and the like, by which the Writers of and for *GRUB-STREET,* have in these later Ages so nobly triumphed over *Time*; have clipped his Wings, pared his Nails, filed his Teeth, turned back his Hour-Glass, blunted his Scythe, and drawn the Hob-Nails out of his Shoes. It is under this *Classis*, I have presumed to list my present Treatise, being just come from having the Honour conferred upon me to be adopted a Member of that illustrious Fraternity.

Now, I am not unaware, how the Productions of the *Grub-Street* Brotherhood, have of late years fallen under many Prejudices; nor how it has been the perpetual Employment of two

---

[82]   *Prurience*   "An itching or a great desire or appetite to any thing" (Johnson, quoting Swift).

[83]   *Type . . . Works*   The Two Principal Qualifications of a fanatic Preacher are his Inward Light, and his Head full of Maggots, and the Two different Fates of his Writings are to be burnt or Worm eaten [note in fifth edition].

[84]   *Faction*   political partisanship; dissension; tumult.

[85]   *perorare*   deliver the final part of a speech.

[86]   *Meum and Tuum*   mine and yours.

[87]   *Six-penny-worth of Wit . . . Complete Jesters*   real and typical titles of cheap publications or chapbooks.

Junior start-up Societies to ridicule them and their Authors, as unworthy their established Post in the Commonwealth of Wit and Learning. Their own Consciences will easily inform them, whom I mean; Nor has the World been so negligent a Looker on, as not to observe the continual Efforts made by the Societies of *Gresham*[88] and of *Will's*[89] to edify a Name and Reputation upon the Ruin of OURS. And this is yet a more feeling Grief to Us upon the Regards of Tenderness as well as of Justice, when we reflect on their Proceedings, not only as unjust, but as ungrateful, undutiful, and unnatural. For, how can it be forgot by the World or themselves (to say nothing of our own Records, which are full and clear in the Point) that they both are Seminaries not only of our *Planting*, but our *Watering* too? I am informed, Our two *Rivals* have lately made an Offer to enter into the Lists with united Forces, and challenge Us to a Comparison of Books, both as to *Weight* and *Number*. In Return to which (with Licence from our *President*) I humbly offer two Answers: First, We say, the Proposal is like that which *Archimedes*[90] made upon a *smaller* Affair, including an Impossibility in the Practice; For, where can they find Scales of *Capacity* enough for the first, or an Arithmetician of *Capacity* enough for the second. Secondly, We are ready to accept the Challenge, but with this Condition, that a third indifferent Person be assigned, to whose impartial Judgement it shall be left to decide, which Society each Book, Treatise or Pamphlet do most properly belong to. This Point, God knows, is very far from being fixed at present; For, We are ready to produce a Catalogue of some Thousands, which in all common Justice ought to be entitled to Our Fraternity, but by the revolted and newfangled Writers most perfidiously ascribed to the others. Upon all which, we think it very unbecoming our Prudence, that the Determination should be remitted to the Authors themselves; when our Adversaries by Briguing and Caballing,[91] have caused so universal a Defection from us, that the greatest Part of our Society hath already deserted to them, and our nearest Friends begin to stand aloof, as if they were half ashamed to own Us.

This is the utmost I am authorized to say upon so ungrateful and melancholy a Subject; because We are extreme unwilling to inflame a Controversy, whose Continuance may be so fatal to the Interests of Us All, desiring much rather that Things be amicably composed. And We shall so far advance on our Side, as to be ready to receive the two *Prodigals*[92] with open Arms, whenever they shall think fit to return from their *Husks*[93] and their *Harlots;* which I think from the present Course of their Studies they most properly may be said to be engaged in; and like an indulgent Parent, continue to them our Affection and our Blessing.

But the greatest Maim given to that general Reception, which the Writings of our Society have formerly received, next to the transitory State of all sublunary Things, hath been a superficial Vein among many Readers of the present Age, who will by no means be persuaded to inspect beyond the Surface and the Rind of Things; whereas, *Wisdom* is a *Fox,* who after long hunting, will at last cost you the Pains to dig out: 'Tis a *Cheese,* which by how much the richer, has the thicker, the homelier, and the courser Coat; and whereof, to a judicious Palate, the *Maggots* are the best. 'Tis a *Sack-Posset,*[94] wherein the deeper you go, you will find it the sweeter. *Wisdom* is a *Hen,* whose *Cackling* we must value and consider, because it is attended

---

88 *Gresham* the Royal Society, which met at Gresham College until 1710.

89 *Will's* a coffee-house made a famous center for writers and wits by Dryden's patronage.

90 *Archimedes* Syracusan mathematician and philosopher of the third century BCE; Swift probably refers to one of his works *The Sand-reckoner*, which demonstrates how the number of grains of sand in the universe could be calculated.

91 *Briguing and Caballing* intriguing.

92 *Prodigals* recalling the parable of the prodigal son (Luke 15.11–32).

93 *Husks* corn husks in the biblical story, the only food left for the prodigal son before he returns home, but here, the Royal Society's meaningless objects of inquiry, as Swift saw it.

94 *Sack-Posset* a kind of alcoholic egg-nog.

with an *Egg*; But then, lastly, 'tis a *Nut*, which unless you chose with Judgement, may cost you a Tooth, and pay you with nothing but a *Worm*. In consequence of these momentous Truths, the *Grubæan* Sages have always chosen to convey their Precepts and their Arts, shut up within the Vehicles of Types and Fables, which having been perhaps more careful and curious in adorning, than was altogether necessary, it has fared with these Vehicles after the usual Fate of Coaches over-finely painted and gilt; that the transitory Gazers have so dazzled their Eyes, and filled their Imaginations with the outward Lustre, as neither to regard nor consider the Person or the Parts of the Owner within. A Misfortune we undergo with somewhat less Reluctancy, because it has been common to us with *Pythagoras*,[95] *Æsop, Socrates*, and other of our Predecessors.

However, that neither the World nor ourselves may any longer suffer by such Misunderstandings, I have been prevailed on, after much importunity from my Friends, to travail in a complete and laborious Dissertation upon the prime Productions of our Society, which besides their beautiful Externals for the Gratification of superficial Readers, have darkly and deeply couched under them, the most finished and refined Systems of all Sciences and Arts; as I do not doubt to lay open by Untwisting or Unwinding, and either to draw up by Exantlation,[96] or display by Incision.

This great Work was entered upon some Years ago, by one of our most eminent Members: He began with the History of *Reynard* the *Fox* but neither lived to publish his Essay, nor to proceed further in so useful an Attempt, which is very much to be lamented, because the Discovery he made, and communicated with his Friends, is now universally received; Nor, do I think, any of the Learned will dispute, that famous Treatise to be a complete Body of Civil Knowledge, and the *Revelation*, or rather the *Apocalypse*, of all State *Arcana*. But the Progress I have made is much greater, having already finished my Annotations upon several Dozens: From some of which, I shall impart a few Hints to the candid Reader, as far as will be necessary to the Conclusion at which I aim.

The first Piece I have handled is that of *Tom Thumb*, whose Author was a *Pythagorean* Philosopher. This dark Treatise contains the whole Scheme of the *Metempsychosis*,[97] deducing the Progress of the Soul through all her Stages.

The next is *Doctor Faustus*, penned by *Artephius*,[98] an Author *bonæ notæ* and an *Adeptus*. He published it in the nine hundred eighty fourth Year of his Age; this Writer proceeds wholly by *Reincrudation*, or in the *via humida*: And the marriage between *Faustus* and *Helen*, does most conspicuously dilucidate the fermenting of the *Male* and *Female Dragon*.

Whitington and his Cat, is the Work of that Mysterious *Rabbi, Jehuda Hannasi*; containing a Defence of the *Gemara* of the *Jerusalem Misna*, and its just preference to that of *Babylon*, contrary to the vulgar Opinion.

The Hind and Panther. This is the Masterpiece of a famous Writer now living,[99] intended for a complete Abstract of sixteen thousand Schoolmen from *Scotus* to *Bellarmine*.[100]

Tommy Pots.[101] Another Piece supposed by the same Hand, by way of Supplement to the former.

[95] *Pythagoras* his precepts were collected in the form of pithy sayings requiring interpretation.
[96] *Exantlation* "The act of drawing out; exhaustion" (Johnson).
[97] *Metempsychosis* transmigration of the soul in rebirth, a Pythagorean belief.
[98] *Artephius* an alchemist; the paragraph is full of alchemical terms.

[99] *Writer now living* Viz. in the Year 1697 [Swift's marginal note; the writer is John Dryden (d. 1700)].
[100] *Scotus* Duns Scotus, thirteenth-century Scottish theologian; *Bellarmine* Cardinal Robert Bellarmine, sixteenth-century Roman Catholic theologian.
[101] *Tommy Pots* a romantic ballad, formally entitled *The Lovers' Quarrel*.

The Wise Men of Gotham,[102] *cum Appendice*. This is a Treatise of immense Erudition, being the great Original and Fountain of those Arguments, bandied about both in *France* and *England*, for a just Defence of the *Modern* Learning and Wit, against the Presumption, the Pride, and the Ignorance of the *Ancients*. This unknown Author hath so exhausted the Subject that a penetrating Reader will easily discover, whatever hath been written since upon that Dispute, to be little more than Repetition. An Abstract of this Treatise[103] hath been lately published by a *worthy Member* of our Society.

These Notices may serve to give the Learned Reader an Idea, as well as a Taste, of what the whole Work is likely to produce: wherein I have now altogether circumscribed my Thoughts and my Studies; and if I can bring it to a Perfection before I die, shall reckon I have well employed the poor Remains of an unfortunate Life.[104] This indeed is more than I can justly expect from a Quill worn to the Pith in the Service of the State, in *Pro's* and *Con's* upon *Popish Plots*, and *Meal Tubs*, and *Exclusion Bills*, and *Passive Obedience*, and *Addresses of Lives and Fortunes*; and *Prerogative*, and *Property*, and *Liberty of Conscience*, and *Letters to a Friend*:[105] From an Understanding and a Conscience, thread-bare and ragged with perpetual turning; From a Head broken in a hundred places, by the Malignants of the opposite Factions; and from a Body spent with Poxes ill cured, by trusting to Bawds and Surgeons, who (as it afterwards appeared) were professed Enemies to Me and the Government, and revenged their Party's Quarrel upon my Nose and Shins. Fourscore and eleven Pamphlets have I writ under three Reigns, and for the service of six and thirty Factions. But finding the State has no further Occasion for Me and my Ink, I retire willingly to draw it out into Speculations more becoming a Philosopher, having to my unspeakable Comfort, passed a long Life, with a *Conscience void of Offence towards God and towards Men*.

But to return. I am assured from the Reader's Candour that the brief Specimen I have given, will easily clear all the rest of our Society's Productions, from an Aspersion grown, as it is manifest, out of Envy and Ignorance: That they are of little further Use or Value to Mankind, beyond the common Entertainments of their Wit and their Style: For, these I am sure have never yet been disputed by our keenest Adversaries: In both which, as well as the more profound and mystical Part, I have throughout this Treatise closely followed the most applauded Originals. And to render all complete, I have with much Thought and Application of Mind, so ordered that the chief Title prefixed to it (I mean, That under which I design it shall pass in the common Conversations of Court and Town) is modelled exactly after the Manner peculiar to *Our* Society.

I confess to have been somewhat liberal in the Business of Titles,[106] having observed the Humour of multiplying them, to bear great Vogue among certain Writers, whom I exceedingly Reverence. And indeed, it seems not unreasonable, that Books, the Children of the Brain, should have the Honour to be Christened with a variety of Names, as well as other Infants of Quality. Our famous *Dryden* has ventured to proceed a Point further, endeavouring to introduce also a Multiplicity of *God-fathers*;[107] which is an Improvement of much more

---

102 *Wise Men of Gotham*   another chapbook romance.
103 *An Abstract of this Treatise*   This I suppose to be understood of Mr. W[o]tt[o]n's *Discourse of Ancient and Modern Learning* [note in fifth edition].
104 *An unfortunate Life*   Here the Author seems to [im]personate [Roger]L'Estrange [1616–1704], Dryden, and some others, who after having passed their Lives in Vice, Faction and Falsehood, have the Impudence to talk of Merit and Innocence and Sufferings [note in fifth edition].

105 *Pro's* and *Con's . . . Letters to a Friend*:   polemical publications and issues addressed by Dryden and L'Estrange.
106 *Titles*   The Title Page in the Original was so torn, that it was not possible to recover several Titles which the Author here speaks of [Swift's marginal note].
107 *Multiplicity of God-fathers*   Dryden dedicated his *Aeneas* to three patrons.

Advantage, upon a very obvious Account. 'Tis a Pity this admirable invention has not been better cultivated, so as to grow by this time into general Imitation, when such an Authority serves it for a Precedent. Nor have my Endeavours been wanting to second so useful an Example: But it seems, there is an unhappy Expence usually annexed to the Calling of a God-father, which was clearly out of my Head, as it is very reasonable to believe. Where the Pinch lay, I cannot certainly affirm; but having employed a World of Thoughts and Pains, to split my Treatise into forty Sections, and having entreated forty Lords of my Acquaintance, that they would do me the Honour to stand, they all made it a Matter of Conscience and sent me their Excuses.

SECT. II

Once upon a Time, there was a Man who had three Sons[108] by one Wife, and all at a Birth, neither could the Mid-wife tell certainly which was the Eldest. Their Father died while they were young, and upon his Death-Bed, calling the Lads to him, spoke thus.

'Sons; Because I have purchased no Estate, nor was born to any, I have long considered of some good Legacies to bequeath You; And at last, with much Care as well as Expence, have provided each of you (here they are) a new Coat.[109] Now, you are to understand, that these Coats have two Virtues contained in them: One is, that with good wearing, they will last you fresh and sound as long as you live: The other is, that they will grow in the same Proportion with your Bodies, lengthening and widening of themselves, so as to be always fit. Here, let me see them on you before I die. So, very well, Pray Children, wear them clean, and brush them often. You will find in my Will[110] (here it is) full Instructions in every Particular concerning the Wearing and Management of your Coats; wherein you must be very exact, to avoid the Penalties I have appointed for every Transgression or Neglect, upon which your future Fortunes will entirely depend. I have also commanded in my Will, that you should live together in one House like Brethren and Friends, for then you will be sure to thrive, and not otherwise'.

Here the story says, this good Father died, and the three Sons went all together to seek their Fortunes.

I shall not trouble you with recounting, what Adventures they met for the first seven Years, any further than by taking notice, that they carefully observed their Father's Will, and kept their Coats in very good Order; That they travelled through several Countries, encountered a reasonable Quantity of Giants, and slew certain Dragons.

Being now arrived at the proper Age for producing themselves, they came up to Town, and fell in love with the Ladies, but especially three, who about that time were in chief Reputation: The Duchess *d'Argent, Madame de Grands Titres*, and the Countess *d'Orgeuil*.[111] On their first Appearance, our three Adventurers met with a very bad Reception; and soon with great Sagacity guessing out the Reason, they quickly began to improve in the good Qualities of the Town: They Writ, and Rallied, and Rhymed, and Sung, and Said, and said Nothing; They Drank, and Fought, and Whored, and Slept, and Swore, and took Snuff; They went to new Plays on the first Night, haunted the *Chocolate*-Houses, beat the Watch, lay on Bulks,[112] and got Claps: They bilked[113] Hackney-Coachmen, ran in Debt with Shop-keepers, and lay

---

108   *three Sons*   By these three Sons, Peter, Martin and Jask, Popery, the Church of England, and our Protestant Dissenters are designed. W. Wotton [note in fifth edition].
109   *Coat*   the Doctrine and Faith of Christianity [note in fifth edition].
110   *Will*   The New Testament [note in fifth edition].
111   *d'Argent, Grands Titres, d'Orgeuil*   Covetousness, Ambition and Pride [note in fifth edition].
112   *Bulks*   stalls outside of shops.
113   *bilked*   cheated (of fares or other profits).

with their Wives: They killed Bailiffs, kicked Fiddlers down Stairs, eat at *Lockets*,[114] loitered at *Will*'s: They talked of the Drawing-Room and never came there; Dined with Lords they never saw; Whispered a Duchess, and spoke never a Word; exposed the Scrawls of their Laundress for Billets-doux[115] of Quality; came ever just from Court, and were never seen in it; attended the Levee *sub dio*;[116] Got a List of the Peers by heart in one Company, and with great Familiarity retailed them in another. Above all, they constantly attended those Committees of Senators who are silent in the *House*, and loud in the *Coffee-House*, where they nightly adjourn to chew the Cud of Politics, and are encompassed with a Ring of Disciples, who lie in wait to catch up their Droppings. The three Brothers had acquired forty other Qualifications of the like Stamp, too tedious to recount, and by consequence, were justly reckoned the most accomplished Persons in Town: But all would not suffice, and the Ladies aforesaid continued still inflexible: To clear up which Difficulty, I must with the Reader's good Leave and Patience, have recourse to some Points of Weight which the Authors of that Age have not sufficiently illustrated.

For, about this Time it happened, a Sect arose, whose Tenets obtained and spread very far, especially in the *Grand monde,* and among every Body of good Fashion. They worshipped a sort of *Idol*,[117] who as their Doctrine delivered, did daily create Men, by a kind of Manufactory Operation. This *Idol* they placed in the highest Parts of the House, on an Altar erected about three Foot: He was shown in the Posture of a *Persian* Emperor, sitting on a *Superficies,* with his Legs interwoven under him. This God had a *Goose*[118] for his Ensign; whence it is, that some Learned Men pretend to deduce his Original from *Jupiter Capitolinus*.[119] At his left Hand, beneath the Altar, *Hell* seemed to open, and catch at the Animals the *Idol* was creating; to prevent which, certain of his Priests hourly flung in Pieces of the uninformed Mass, or Substance, and sometimes whole Limbs already enlivened, which that horrid Gulf insatiably swallowed, terrible to behold. The *Goose* was also held a Subaltern Divinity, or *Deus minorum gentium*,[120] before whose Shrine was sacrificed that Creature, whose hourly Food is Human Gore, and who is in so great Renown abroad, for being the Delight and Favourite of the *Ægyptian Cercopithecus*.[121] Millions of these Animals were cruelly slaughtered every Day, to appease the Hunger of that consuming Deity. The chief *Idol* was also worshipped as the Inventor of the *Yard*[122] and *Needle*,[123] whether as the God of Seamen, or on Account of certain other mystical Attributes, hath not been sufficiently cleared.

The Worshippers of this Deity had also a System of their Belief, which seemed to turn upon the following Fundamentals. They held the Universe to be a large *Suit of Clothes*, which *invests* every Thing: That the Earth is *invested* by the Air; The Air is *invested* by the Stars; and the Stars are *invested* by the *Primum Mobile*.[124] Look on this Globe of Earth, you will find it to be a very complete and fashionable *Dress*. What is that which some call *Land*, but a fine Coat faced with Green? or the Sea, but a Waistcoat of Water-Tabby?[125] Proceed to the particular Works of the Creation, you will find how curious *Journey-man* Nature hath been, to trim up the *vegetable* Beaux: Observe how sparkish a Periwig adorns the Head of a *Beech*, and what a

---

[114] *Lockets*   a fashionable restaurant in Charing Cross.

[115] *Billets-doux*   love letters.

[116] *Levee sub dio*   sunrise (or morning entertainment of a nobleman) in the open air.

[117] *Idol*   By this idol is meant a Tailor [note in fifth edition].

[118] *Goose*   after the goose-neck of the tailor's iron.

[119] *Jupiter Capitolinus*   Jupiter's temple, the Roman capitol, was said to have been saved by geese.

[120] *Deus minorum gentium*   "God of lesser people."

[121] *Ægyptian Cercopithecus*   The Ægyptians worshipped a Monkey, which Animal is very fond of eating Lice, styled here Creatures that feed on Human Gore [note in fifth edition].

[122] *Yard*   the support of a sail on a ship.

[123] *Needle*   compass.

[124] *Primum Mobile*   the first mover or outermost sphere in the Ptolemaic system of the universe.

[125] *Tabby*   "A kind of waved silk" (Johnson).

fine Doublet of white Satin is worn by the *Birch*. To conclude from all, What is Man himself but a *Micro-Coat*,[126] or rather a complete Suit of Clothes with all its Trimmings. As to his Body, there can be no Dispute; but examine even the Acquirements of his Mind, you will find them all contribute in their Order, towards furnishing out an exact Dress: To instance no more; Is not Religion a *Cloak*, Honesty a *Pair of Shoes*, worn out in the Dirt, Self-love a *surtout*,[127] Vanity a *Shirt*, and Conscience a *Pair of Breeches*, which though a Cover for Lewdness as well as Nastiness, is easily slipped down for the Service of both?

These *Postulata* being admitted, it will follow in due course of Reasoning, that those Beings which the World calls improperly *Suits of Clothes*, are in Reality the most refined Species of Animals, or to proceed higher, that they are Rational Creatures, or Men. For, is it not manifest, that They live, and move, and talk, and perform all other Offices of Human Life? Are not Beauty, and Wit, and Mien, and Breeding, their inseparable Proprieties? In short, we see nothing but them, hear nothing but them. Is it not They who walk the Streets, fill up *Parliament-, Coffee-, Play-, Bawdy-houses*. 'Tis true indeed, that these Animals, which are vulgarly called *Suits of Clothes*, or *Dresses*, do according to certain Compositions receive different Appellations. If one of them be trimmed up with a Gold Chain, and a red Gown, and a white Rod, and a great Horse, it is called a *Lord Mayor*; If certain Ermines and Furs be placed in a certain Position, we style them a *Judge*; and so, an apt conjunction of Lawn and black Satin, we entitle a *Bishop*.

Others of these Professors, though agreeing in the main System, were yet more refined upon certain Branches of it; and held that Man was an Animal compounded of two *Dresses*, the *Natural* and the *Celestial Suit*, which were the Body and the Soul: That the Soul was the outward, and the Body the inward Clothing; that the latter was *ex traduce*;[128] but the former, of daily Creation and Circumfusion. This last they proved by *Scripture*, because, 'in Them we Live, and Move, and have our Being';[129] As likewise by Philosophy, because they are 'All in All, and All in every Part'.[130] 'Besides', said they, 'Separate these two, and you will find the Body to be only a senseless unsavoury Carcass. By all which it is manifest, that the outward Dress must needs be the Soul'.

To this System of Religion were tagged several subaltern Doctrines, which were entertained with great Vogue; as particularly, the Faculties of the Mind were deduced by the Learned among them in this manner: *Embroidery*, was *Sheer Wit*; *Gold Fringe* was *agreeable Conversation*; *Gold Lace* was *Repartee*; a huge long *Periwig* was *Humour*; and a *Coat full of Powder* was very good *Raillery*: All which required abundance of *Finesse* and *Delicatesse* to manage with Advantage, as well as a strict Observance after Times and Fashions.

I have with much Pains and Reading, collected out of ancient Authors, this short Summary of a Body of Philosophy and Divinity, which seems to have been composed by a Vein and Race of Thinking, very different from any other Systems, either *Ancient* or *Modern*. And it was not merely to entertain or satisfy the Reader's Curiosity, but rather to give him Light into several Circumstances of the following Story: that knowing the State of Dispositions and Opinions in an Age so remote, he may better comprehend those great Events which were the Issue of them. I advise therefore the courteous Reader, to peruse with a world of

---

[126] *Micro-Coat* Alluding to the Word *Microcosm*, or a little World, as Man hath been called by Philosophers [note in fifth edition].

[127] *surtout* "A large coat worn over all the rest" (Johnson).

[128] *ex traduce* "by traduction" (see Dryden's "Ode to Anne Killigrew," l. 23, p. 379 above).

[129] *"in Them . . . Being"* see Acts 17.28, where it says. "in him," meaning God.

[130] *All in All . . . Part* I Corinthians 15.28, where God is meant.

Application, again and again, whatever I have written upon this Matter. And so leaving these broken Ends, I carefully gather up the chief Thread of my Story, and proceed.

These Opinions therefore were so universal, as well as the Practices of them, among the refined Part of Court and Town, that our three Brother Adventurers, as their Circumstances then stood, were strangely at a loss. For, on the one side, the three Ladies they addressed themselves to (whom we have named already) were ever at the very Top of the Fashion, and abhorred all that were below it, but the breadth of a Hair. On the other side, their Father's Will was very precise, and it was the main Precept in it, with the greatest Penalties annexed, not to add to, or diminish from their Coats, one Thread, without a positive Command in the Will. Now, the Coats their Father had left them, were, 'tis true, of very good Cloth, and besides, so neatly sewn, you would swear they were all of a Piece, but at the same time, very plain, and with little or no Ornament; And it happened, that before they were a Month in Town, great *Shoulder-knots*[131] came up: Straight, all the World was *Shoulder-knots*; no approaching the Ladies' *Ruelles*[132] without the *Quota* of *Shoulder-knots*: *That Fellow*, cries one, *has no Soul; where is his Shoulder-knot?* Our three Brethren soon discovered their Want by sad Experience, meeting in their Walks, with forty Mortifications and Indignities. If they went to the *Play-house*, the Door-keeper showed them into the Twelve-penny Gallery. If they called a Boat, says a Water-man, 'I am first Sculler'[133]: If they stepped to the *Rose* to take a Bottle, the Drawer would cry, 'Friend we sell no ale'. If they went to visit a Lady, a Footman met him at the Door with, 'Pray send up your message'. In this unhappy Case, they went immediately to consult their Father's Will, read it over and over, but not a Word of the *Shoulder-knots*. What should they do? What Temper should they find? Obedience was absolutely necessary, and yet *Shoulder-knots* appeared extremely requisite. After much Thought, one of the Brothers who happened to be more *Book-learned* than the other two, said, he had found an Expedient. ''Tis true, said he, there is nothing here in this Will, *totidem verbis,*[134] making mention of *Shoulder-knots,* but I dare conjecture, we may find them *inclusivè,*[135] or *totidem syllabis.*[136] This Distinction was immediately approved by all; and so they fell again to examine the Will. But their evil Star had so directed the Matter, that the first Syllable was not to be found in the whole Writing. Upon which Disappointment, he who found the former Evasion, took heart, and said, 'Brothers, there is yet Hopes; for though we cannot find them *totidem verbis,* nor *totidem syllabis,* I dare engage we shall make them out *tertio modo,* or *totidem literis.*'[137] This Discovery was also highly commended, upon which they fell once more to the Scrutiny, and soon picked out *S,H,O,U,L,D,E,R*; when the same Planet,[138] Enemy to their Repose, had wonderfully contrived, that a *K* was not to be found. Here was a weighty Difficulty! But the distinguishing Brother (for whom we shall hereafter find a Name) now his Hand was in, proved by a very good Argument that *K* was a modern illegitimate Letter, unknown to the Learned Ages nor any where to be found in ancient Manuscripts. ''Tis true', said he, 'the Word *Calendæ* hath in *Q.V.C.*[139] been sometimes writ with a *K*, but erroneously, for in the best Copies it is ever spelt with a *C*. And by consequence it was a gross Mistake in our Language to spell *Knot* with a *K*, but that from henceforward, he would take care it should be

---

[131] *Shoulder-knots* By this is understood the first introducing of Pageantry, and unnecessary Ornaments in the Church . . . [note in fifth edition; another note indicates that the Roman Catholic Church is represented in this section on Peter].

[132] *Ruelles* "circle" or "assembly at a private house" (Johnson).

[133] *Sculler* a one-man scull or small boat.

[134] *totidem verbis* "in so many words."

[135] *inclusivè* medieval Latin "included" or "by inclusion."

[136] *totidem syllabis* "in so many syllables".

[137] *totidem literis* "in so many letters".

[138] *Planet* astrological influence, fortune.

[139] *Q.V.C. Quibusdam Veteribus Codicibus* [Swift's marginal note; "certain old books"].

writ with a *C*. Upon this, all further Difficulty vanished; *Shoulder-knots* were made clearly out, to be *Jure Paterno*,[140] and our three Gentlemen swaggered with as large and as flaunting ones as the best.

But, as Human Happiness is of a very short Duration, so in those Days were Human Fashions, upon which it entirely depends. *Shoulder-knots* had their Time, and we must now imagine them in their Decline; for a certain Lord came just from *Paris* with fifty Yards of *Gold Lace* upon his Coat, exactly trimmed after the Court Fashion of *that Month*. In two Days all Mankind appeared closed up in Bars of *Gold Lace*: Whoever durst peep abroad without his Compliment of *Gold Lace*, was as scandalous as a———, and as ill received among the Women. What should our three Knights do in this momentous Affair; They had sufficiently strained a Point already, in the Affair of *Shoulder-knots*: Upon recourse to the Will, nothing appeared there but *altum silentium*.[141] That of the *Shoulder-knots* was a loose, flying, circumstantial Point; but this of *Gold Lace,* seemed too considerable an Alteration without better Warrant; it did *aliquo modo essentiæ adhærere*,[142] and therefore required a positive Precept. But about this Time it fell out, that the learned Brother aforesaid, had read *Aristotelis Dialectica*, and especially that wonderful Piece *de Interpretatione,* which has the Faculty of teaching its Readers to find out a Meaning in every Thing but it self, like Commentators on the *Revelations,* who proceed Prophets without understanding a Syllable of the Text. 'Brothers', said he, 'you are to be informed, that, of Wills, *duo sunt genera*,[143] Nuncupatory[144] and Scriptory; that in the Scriptory Will here before us, there is no Precept or Mention about Gold Lace, *conceditur*; But, *si idem affirmetur de nuncupatorio, negatur.*[145] 'For, Brothers, if you remember, we heard a Fellow say when we were Boys, that he heard my Father's Man say, that he heard my Father say, that he would advise his Sons to get *Gold Lace* on their Coats, as soon as ever they could Procure Money to buy it'. 'By G———that is very true', cries the other. 'I remember it perfectly well', said the third. And so without more ado they got the largest *Gold Lace* in the Parish, and walked about as fine as Lords.

A while after, there came up *all in Fashion,* a pretty sort of *flame-coloured Satin* for Linings, and the *Mercer* brought a Pattern of it immediately to our three Gentlemen. 'An please your worships', said he, 'my Lord C[utts] and Sir J[ohn] W[alters] had Linings out of this very Piece last Night, it takes wonderfully, and I shall not have a Remnant left, enough to make my Wife a Pin-cushion by tomorrow Morning at ten a Clock'. Upon this they fell again to rummage the Will, because the present Case also required a positive Precept, the Lining being held by Orthodox Writers to be of the Essence of the Coat. After long search, they could fix upon nothing to the Matter in hand, except a short Advice of their Father's in the Will, to take Care of *Fire,* and put out their *Candles* before they went to Sleep. This, though a good deal for the Purpose, and helping very far towards Self-Conviction, yet not seeming wholly of Force to establish a Command; and being resolved to avoid further Scruple,[146] as well as future Occasion for Scandal, says He that was the Scholar, 'I remember to have read in Wills, of a Codicil annexed, which is indeed a Part of the Will, and what it contains hath equal Authority with the rest. Now, I have been considering of this same Will here before us, and I cannot reckon it to be complete, for want of such a Codicil. I will therefore fasten one in its proper Place very dexterously; I have had it by me some Time, it was written by a Dog-

---

[140]   *Jure Paterno* "by the father's law," in imitation of *iure divino*.

[141]   *altum silentium* "deep silence."

[142]   *aliquo modo . . . adhærere* "belonged to another category."

[143]   *duo sunt genera* "there are two kinds."

[144]   *Nuncupatory* "verbally pronounced" (Johnson).

[145]   *conceditur . . . negatur* "it is conceded, but if it is affirmed concerning the nuncupatory kind, it is denied."

[146]   *Scruple* doubt.

keeper of my Grand-father's, and talks a great deal (as good Luck would have it) of this very flame-coloured Satin'. The Project was immediately approved by the other two; an old Parchment Scroll was tagged on according to Art, in the Form of a *Codicil annexed*, and the *Satin* bought and worn.

Next Winter, a *Player*, hired for the Purpose by the Corporation of *Fringe-makers*, acted his Part in a new Comedy, all covered with *Silver-Fringe*, and according to the laudable Custom gave Rise to that Fashion. Upon which, the Brothers consulting their Father's Will, to their great Astonishment found these Words, '*Item*, I charge and command my said three sons to wear no sort of *Silver Fringe* upon, or about their said coats', &c., with a Penalty in case of Disobedience, too long here to insert. However, after some Pause, the Brother so often mentioned for his Erudition, who was well skilled in Criticisms, had found in a certain Author which he said should be nameless, that the same Word which in the Will is called *Fringe*, does also signify a *Broom-stick*, and doubtless ought to have the same Interpretation in this Paragraph. This, another of the Brothers disliked, because of that Epithet, *Silver*, which could not, he humbly conceived, in Propriety of Speech be reasonably applied to a *Broom-stick*: But it was replied upon him, that this Epithet was understood in a *Mythological,* and *Allegorical* Sense. However, he objected again, why their Father should forbid them to wear a *Broom-stick* on their Coats, a Caution that seemed unnatural and impertinent: Upon which he was taken up short, as one that spoke irreverently of a *Mystery,* which doubtless was very useful and significant, but ought not to be over-curiously pried into, or nicely reasoned upon. And in short, their Father's Authority being now considerably sunk, this Expedient was allowed to serve as a lawful Dispensation, for wearing their full Proportion of *Silver Fringe.*

A while after, was revived an old Fashion, long antiquated, of *Embroidery* with *Indian Figures* of Men, Women, and Children. Here they had no Occasion to examine the Will. They remembered but too well, how their Father had always abhorred this Fashion; that he made several Paragraphs on purpose, importing his utter Detestation of it, and bestowing his everlasting Curse to his Sons, whenever they should wear it. For all this, in a few Days, they appeared higher in the Fashion than any body else in Town. But they solved the Matter by saying, that these Figures were not at all the *same* with those that were formerly worn, and were meant in the Will: Besides, they did not wear them in that Sense, as forbidden by their Father, but as they were a commendable Custom, and of great use to the Public. That these rigorous Clauses in the Will did therefore require some *Allowance*, and a favourable Interpretation, and ought to be understood *cum grano Salis*.[147]

But, Fashions perpetually altering in that Age, the Scholastic Brother grew weary of searching further Evasions, and solving everlasting Contradictions. Resolved therefore at all Hazards to comply with the Modes of the World, they concerted Matters together, and agreed unanimously, to lock up their Father's Will in a *Strong-Box*, brought out of *Greece* or *Italy*[148] (I have forgot which) and trouble themselves no further to examine it, but only refer to its Authority whenever they thought fit. In consequence whereof, a while after, it grew a general Mode to wear an infinite Number of *Points*,[149] most of them *tagged with Silver*: Upon which the Scholar pronounced *ex Cathedra,* that *Points* were absolutely *Jure Paterno,* as they might very well remember. 'Tis true indeed, the Fashion prescribed somewhat more than

---

[147]   *cum grano Salis* "with a grain of salt," i.e. loosely.
[148]   *Greece or Italy* Greek or Latin, the languages of scripture in the Roman Catholic Church, as a note in the fifth edition explains.

[149]   *Point* "A string with a tag" (Johnson) for lacing.

were directly named in the Will; However, that they, as Heirs general of their Father, had Power to make and add certain Clauses for public Emolument, though not deduceable *totidem verbis* from the Letter of the Will, or else, *Multa absurda sequerentur*.[150] This was understood for *Canonical*, and therefore on the following *Sunday* they came to Church all covered with *Points*.

The Learned Brother so often mentioned, was reckoned the best Scholar in all that, or the next Street to it; insomuch, as having run something behind-hand with the World, he obtained the Favour from a *certain Lord*, to receive him into his House and to teach his Children. A while after, the *Lord* died, and He by long practice upon his Father's Will, found the Way of contriving a *Deed of Conveyance* [151] of that House to Himself and his Heirs: Upon which he took Possession, turned the young Squires out, and received his Brothers in their stead.

SECT. III
A DIGRESSION CONCERNING CRITICS

Though I have been hitherto as cautious as I could, upon all Occasions, most nicely to follow the Rules and Methods of Writing, laid down by the Example of our illustrious *Moderns*; yet has the unhappy shortness of my Memory led me into an Error, from which I must immediately extricate my self, before I can decently pursue my principal Subject. I confess with Shame, it was an unpardonable Omission to proceed so far as I have already done, before I had performed the due Discourses, Expostulatory, Supplicatory, or Deprecatory, with my *good Lords* the *Critics*. Towards some Atonement for this grievous Neglect, I do here make humbly bold to present them with a short Account of Themselves and their *Art*, by looking into the Original and Pedigree of the Word, as it is generally understood among us, and very briefly considering the ancient and present State thereof.

By the Word, *Critic*, at this Day so frequent in all Conversations, there have sometime been distinguished three very different Species of Mortal Men, according as I have read in *Ancient Books and Pamphlets*. For first, by this Term was understood such Persons as invented or drew up Rules for Themselves and the World, by observing which, a careful Reader might be able to pronounce upon the Productions of the *Learned*, form his Taste to a true Relish of the *Sublime* and the *Admirable*, and divide every Beauty of Matter or of Style from the Corruption that Apes it: In their common Perusal of Books, singling out the Errors and Defects, the Nauseous, the Fulsome, the Dull, and the Impertinent, with the Caution of a Man that walks through *Edinburgh* Streets in a Morning, who is indeed as careful as he can, to watch diligently, and spy out the Filth in his Way; not that he is curious to observe the Colour and Complexion of the Ordure, or take its Dimensions, much less to be paddling in, or tasting it: but only with a Design to come out as cleanly as he may. These Men seem, though very erroneously, to have understood the Appellation of *Critic* in a literal Sense; That, one principal Part of his Office was, to Praise and Acquit; and, that a *Critic* who sets up to Read only for an Occasion of Censure and Reproof, is a Creature as barbarous, as a *Judge*, who should take up a Resolution to *hang* all Men that came before Him upon a Trial.

Again; by the Word, *Critic,* have been meant, the Restorers of Ancient Learning from the Worms, and Graves, and Dust of Manuscripts.

---

[150] *Multa absurda sequerentur*   "much absurdity would follow."

[151] *Deed of Conveyance*   allegorical reference to the Donation of Constantine, a document that discusses the supposed grant of spiritual and temporal authority by the emperor Constantine to Pope Sylvester I (314–335) and his successors; the validity of this forgery was still being debated in Swift's time.

Now, the Races of those two have been for some Ages utterly extinct; and besides, to Discourse any further of them would not be at all to my Purpose.

The Third, and noblest Sort, is that of the *TRUE CRITIC*, whose Original is the most Ancient of all. Every *True Critic* is a Hero born, descending in a direct Line from a Celestial Stem, by *Momus* and *Hybris*, who begat *Zoilus*, who begat *Tigellius*,[152] who begat *Etcætera* the Elder, who begat *B—t—ly*, and *Rym—r*, and *W—tt—n*, and *Perrault*,[153] and *Dennis*, who begat *Etcætera* the Younger.

And these are the *Critics*, from whom the Commonwealth of Learning has in all Ages received such immense Benefits, that the Gratitude of their Admirers placed their Origin in Heaven, among those of *Hercules, Theseus, Perseus,* and other great Deservers of Mankind. But Heroic Virtue it self hath not been exempt from the Obloquy of evil Tongues. For it hath been objected, that those Ancient Heroes, famous for their Combating so many Giants, and Dragons, and Robbers, were in their own Persons a greater Nuisance to Mankind, than any of those Monsters they subdued; And therefore, to render their Obligations more Complete, when all *other* Vermin were destroyed, should in Conscience have concluded with the same Justice upon themselves: as *Hercules* most generously did,[154] and hath upon that Score, procured to himself more Temples and Votaries than the best of his Fellows. For these Reasons, I suppose it is, why some have conceived, it would be very expedient for the Public Good of Learning, that every *True Critic*, as soon as he had finished his Task assigned, should immediately deliver himself up to Ratsbane or Hemp, or from some convenient *Altitude*; and that no Man's Pretensions to so Illustrious a Character, should by any means be received, before That Operation were performed.

Now, from this Heavenly Descent of *Criticism*, and the close Analogy it bears to *Heroic Virtue*, 'tis easy to assign the proper Employment of a *True, Ancient, Genuine Critic*; which is, to travel through this vast World of Writings: to pursue and hunt those Monstrous Faults bred within them: to drag out the lurking Errors, like *Cacus* from his Den; to multiply them like *Hydra*'s Heads; and rake them together like *Augeas*'s Dung.[155] Or else to drive away a sort of *dangerous Fowl*, who have a perverse inclination to plunder the best Branches of the *Tree of Knowledge*, like those *Stymphalian* Birds that eat up the Fruit.[156]

These Reasonings will furnish us with an adequate Definition of a *True Critic*: that, he is a *Discoverer and Collector of Writers' Faults*. Which may be further put beyond Dispute by the following Demonstration: That whoever will examine the Writings in all kinds, wherewith this ancient Sect has honoured the World, shall immediately find from the whole Thread and Tenor of them, that the Ideas of the Authors have been altogether conversant, and taken up with the Faults, and Blemishes, and Oversights, and Mistakes of other Writers; and let the Subject treated on be whatever it will, their imaginations are so entirely possessed and replete with the defects of other pens that the very quintessence of what is bad, does of necessity distill into their own; by which means the whole appears to be nothing else but an *abstract* of the *criticisms* themselves have made.

---

[152] *Momus, Hybris Zoilus, Tigellius* the first is mythological, the second allegorical (overweening pride) and the last two are real critics, of Homer and Horace respectively.

[153] *Perrault* Charles Perrault (1628–1703), French champion of the moderns in the debate in which Swift is always for the ancients.

[154] *Hercules . . . did* he immolated himself on Mount Oeta to end his suffering from the poisonous shirt of Nessus.

[155] *Cacus* (a fire-breathing giant) and *Hydra* (a nine-headed monster) were slain by Hercules; *Augeas* was a king whose huge, filthy stables Hercules had to cleanse.

[156] *Stymphalian Birds* Hercules killed them or at least expelled them from Arcadia.

Having thus briefly considered the Original and Office of a *Critic*, as the Word is understood in its most noble and universal Acceptation, I proceed to refute the Objections of those who argue from the Silence and Pretermission[157] of Authors; by which they pretend to prove, that the very Art of *Criticism,* as now exercised, and by me explained, is wholly *Modern*; and consequently, that the *Critics* of *Great Britain* and *France* have no Title to an Original so Ancient and Illustrious as I have deduced. Now, if I can clearly make out on the contrary, that the most ancient Writers have particularly described, both the Person and the Office of a *True Critic*, agreeable to the Definition laid down by me; their grand Objection from the Silence of Authors will fall to the Ground.

I confess to have for a long time born a Part in this general Error; From which I should never have acquitted my self, but through the Assistance of our Noble *Moderns* whose most edifying Volumes I turn indefatigably over Night and Day, for the Improvement of my Mind, and the Good of my Country: These have with unwearied Pains made many useful Searches into the weak Sides of the *Ancients*, and given us a comprehensive List of them. Besides, they have proved[158] beyond Contradiction, that the very finest Things delivered of old, have been long since invented, and brought to Light by much later Pens, and that the noblest Discoveries those *Ancients* ever made of Art or of Nature, have all been produced by the transcending Genius of the present Age. Which clearly shows, how little Merit those *Ancients* can justly pretend to; and takes off that blind Admiration paid them by Men in a Corner, who have the Unhappiness of conversing too little with *present Things*. Reflecting maturely upon all this, and taking in the whole Compass of Human Nature, I easily concluded, that these *Ancients*, highly sensible of their many Imperfections, must needs have endeavoured from some Passages in their Works, to obviate, soften, or divert the Censorious Reader, by *Satire*, or *Panegyric* upon the *True Critics*, in Imitation of their *Masters* the *Moderns*. Now, in the *Common-Places* of both these, I was plentifully instructed, by a long Course of useful Study in *Prefaces* and *Prologues*; and therefore immediately resolved to try what I could discover of either, by a diligent Perusal of the most Ancient Writers, and especially those who treated of the earliest Times. Here I found to my great Surprise, that although they all entered, upon Occasion, into particular Descriptions of the *True Critic*, according as they were governed by their Fears or their Hopes: yet whatever they touched of that kind, was with abundance of Caution, adventuring no further than *Mythology* and *Hieroglyphic*. This, I suppose, gave ground to superficial Readers, for urging the Silence of Authors, against the Antiquity of the *True Critic*, though the *Types* are so apposite, and the Applications so necessary and natural, that it is not easy to conceive, how any Reader of a *Modern Eye* and *Taste* could over-look them. I shall venture from a great Number to produce a few, which I am very confident, will put this Question beyond Dispute.

It well deserves considering, that these *Ancient Writers* in treating Enigmatically upon this Subject, have generally fixed upon the very *same Hieroglyph*, varying only the Story according to their Affections or their Wit. For first; *Pausanias*[159] is of Opinion, that the Perfection of Writing correct, was entirely owing to the Institution of *Critics*; and, that he can possibly mean no other than the *True Critic*, is, I think, manifest enough from the following Description. He says, 'They were a Race of Men, who delighted to nibble at the Superfluities, and Excrescencies of Books; which the Learned at length observing, took Warning of their own Accord, to lop the Luxurient, the Rotten, the Dead, the Sapless, and the Overgrown Branches

---

[157]   *Pretermission*   "The act of omitting" (Johnson).
[158]   *they have proved*   See Wotton *Of Ancient and Modern Learning* [Swift's marginal note].

[159]   *Pausanias*   Greek traveller and geographer of the second century CE.

from their Works'. But now, all this he cunningly shades under the following Allegory; that the *Nauplians* in *Argia*, learned the Art of pruning their Vines, by observing, that when an *ASS* had browsed upon one of them, it thrived the better, and bore fairer Fruit.[160] But *Herodotus*, holding the very same Hieroglyph, speaks much plainer, and almost *in terminis*. He hath been so bold to tax the *True Critics* of Ignorance and Malice; telling us openly, for I think nothing can be plainer, that in the Western Part of *Libya,* there were *ASSES* with *HORNS*:[161] Upon which Relation *Ctesias* yet refines, mentioning the very same animal about *India*, adding, That 'whereas all other *ASSES* wanted a *Gall*, these horned ones were so redundant in that Part that their Flesh was not to be eaten, because of its extreme *Bitterness*'.

Now, the Reason why those Ancient Writers treated this Subject only by Types and Figures, was, because they durst not make open Attacks against a Party so Potent and Terrible, as the *Critics* of those Ages were: whose very Voice was so Dreadful, that a Legion of Authors would tremble, and drop their Pens at the Sound; For so *Herodotus* tells us expressly in another Place, how a vast Army of *Scythians* was put to flight in a Panic Terror, by the Braying of an *ASS*.[162] From hence it is conjectured by certain profound *Philologers*, that the great Awe and Reverence paid to a *True Critic* by the Writers of *Britain,* have been derived to Us, from those our *Scythian* Ancestors. In short, this Dread was so universal, that in process of Time, those Authors who had a mind to publish their Sentiments more freely, in describing the *True Critics* of their several Ages, were forced to leave off the use of the former Hieroglyph, as too nearly approaching the *Prototype*, and invented other Terms instead thereof, that were more cautious and mystical; so *Diodorus* speaking to the same purpose, ventures no futher than to say, that 'in the Mountains of *Helicon* there grows a certain *Weed*, which bears a Flower of so damned a Scent, as to poison those who offer to smell it'. *Lucretius* gives exactly the same Relation:

> Est etiam in magnis Heliconis montibus arbos,
> Floris odore hominem retro consueta necare.
> Lib. 6.[163]

But *Ctesias*, whom we lately quoted, hath been a great deal bolder; He had been used with much severity by the *True Critics* of his own Age, and therefore could not forbear to leave behind him, at least one deep Mark of his Vengeance, against the whole Tribe. His Meaning is so near the Surface, that I wonder how it possibly came to be overlooked by those who deny the Antiquity of the *True Critics*. For pretending to make a Description of many strange Animals about *India*, he hath set down these remarkable Words. 'Among the rest,' says he, 'there is a *Serpent* that wants *Teeth,* and consequently cannot bite, but if its *Vomit* (to which it is much addicted) happens to fall upon any Thing, a certain Rottenness or Corruption ensues: These Serpents are generally found among the Mountains where *Jewels* grow, and they frequently emit a *poisonous juice,* whereof, whoever drinks, that Person's *Brains* flies out of his Nostrils'.[164]

There was also among the *Ancients* a sort of *Critic,* not distinguished in *Specie* from the Former, but in Growth or Degree, who seem to have been only the *Tyros* or *junior Scholars*; yet

---

160 *Ass . . . Fruit* Pausanias 2.38.
161 *HORNS* Herodotus 4.191.
162 *Braying of an Ass* Herodotus 4.129.
163 *Lib. 6* "Near Helicon, and round the Learned Hill, Grow Trees, whose Blossoms with their Odour

kill" [note in fifth edition, citing Creech's Lucretius, 6.786–7].
164 This and the other citations from Ctesias (fourth-century BCE Greek physician and historian of Persia and India) are genuine.

because of their differing Employments, they are frequently mentioned as a Sect by themselves. The usual exercise of these younger Students, was to attend constantly at Theatres, and learn to spy out the *worst Parts* of the Play, whereof they were obliged carefully to take Note and render a rational Account, to their tutors. Fleshed at these smaller Sports, like young Wolves, they grew up in Time, to be nimble and strong enough for hunting down large Game. For it hath been observed both among Ancients and Moderns, that a *True Critic* hath one Quality in common with a *Whore* and an *Alderman*, never to change his Title or his Nature; that a *Grey Critic* has been certainly a *green* one, the Perfections and Acquirements of his Age being only the improved Talents of his Youth; like *Hemp*, which some Naturalists inform us, is bad for *Suffocations*, though taken but in the *Seed.* I esteem the invention, or at least the Refinement of *Prologues*, to have been owing to these younger Proficients, of whom *Terence*[165] makes frequent and honourable mention, under the Name of *Malevoli.*

Now, 'tis certain, the Institution of the *True Critics,* was of absolute Necessity to the Commonwealth of Learning. For all Human Actions seem to be divided like *Themistocles* and his Company; One Man can *Fiddle*, and another can make *a Small Town a great City*;[166] and he that cannot do either one or the other, deserves to be kicked out of the Creation. The avoiding of which Penalty, has doubtless given the first Birth to the Nation of *Critics*, and withal, an Occasion for their secret Detractors to report that a *True Critic* is a sort of Mechanic,[167] set up with a Stock and Tools for his Trade, at as little Expense as a *Tailor*; and that there is much Analogy between the Utensils and Abilities of both: That the *Tailor's Hell*[168] is the Type of a Critic's *Commonplace-Book*, and his Wit and Learning held forth by the *Goose*:[169] That it requires at least as many of these, to the making up of one Scholar, as of the other to the Composition of a Man:[170] That the Valour of both is equal, and their *Weapons* near of a Size. Much may be said in answer to those invidious Reflections; and I can positively affirm the first to be a Falsehood. For, on the contrary, nothing is more certain, than that it requires greater Layings out, to be free of the *Critic*'s Company, than of any other you can name. For, as to be a *true Beggar,* it will cost the richest Candidate every Groat he is worth; so, before one can commence a *True Critic* it will cost a Man all the good Qualities of his Mind; which, perhaps, for a less Purchase, would be thought but an indifferent Bargain.

Having thus amply proved the Antiquity of *Criticism* and described the Primitive State of it; I shall now examine the present Condition of this Empire, and show how well it agrees with its ancient self. A certain Author whose Works have many Ages since been entirely lost, does in his fifth Book and eighth Chapter, say of *Critics*, that 'their Writings are the Mirrors of Learning'.[171] This I understand in a literal Sense, and suppose our Author must mean, that whoever designs to be a perfect Writer, must inspect into the Books of *Critics*, and correct his Invention there as in a Mirror. Now, whoever considers, that the *Mirrors* of the Ancients were made of Brass, and *sine Mercurio*,[172] may presently apply the two principal Qualifications of a *True Modern Critic*, and consequently, must needs conclude, that these have always been and must be for ever the same. For, *Brass* is an Emblem of Duration, and when it is

[165] *Terence* Roman comic dramatist of the second century BCE.
[166] *Themistocles . . . City* the Greek general's boyhood claim for himself, in contrast to his schoolmates, according to Plutarch, *Life of Themistocles*, 2.
[167] *Mechanic* "A manufacturer; a low workman" (Johnson).
[168] *Tailor's Hell* "The place into which the tailor throws his shreds" (Johnson).
[169] *Goose* "A tailor's smoothing iron" (Johnson).
[170] *as many . . . of a Man* "Nine tailors make a man" (*Oxford Dictionary of English Proverbs*).
[171] *A certain Author . . . Learning* A Quotation after the manner of a great Author. *Vide* Bentley's Dissertation &c. [Swift's marginal note].
[172] *sine Mercurio* "without Mercury," or without talent, since Mercury is associated with wit.

skilfully burnished, will cast *Reflections* from its own *Superficies*, without any Assistance of *Mercury* from behind. All the other Talents of a *Critic* will not require a particular Mention, being included, or easily deduceable to these. However, I shall conclude with three Maxims, which may serve both as Characteristics to distinguish a *True Modern Critic* from a Pretender, and will be also of admirable Use to those worthy Spirits, who engage in so useful and honourable an Art.

The first is, That *Criticism*, contrary to all other Faculties of the Intellect, is ever held the truest and best, when it is the very *first* Result of the *Critic's* Mind: As Fowlers reckon the first Aim for the surest, and seldom fail of missing the Mark if they stay for a Second.

Secondly, the *True Critics* are known by their Talent of swarming about the noblest Writers, to which they are carried merely by Instinct, as a Rat to the best Cheese, or a wasp to the fairest Fruit. So, when the *King* is a Horse-back, he is sure to be the *dirtiest* Person of the Company, and they that make their Court best, are such as *bespatter* him most.

Lastly, a *True Critic,* in the Perusal of a Book, is like a *Dog* at a Feast, whose Thoughts and Stomach are wholly set upon what the Guests *fling away*, and consequently, is apt to *Snarl* most, when there are the fewest *Bones*.

Thus much, I think, is sufficient to serve by way of Address to my Patrons, the *True Modern Critics*, and may very well atone for my past Silence, as well as That which I am like to observe for the future. I hope, I have deserved so well of their whole *Body,* as to meet with generous and tender Usage at their *Hands*. Supported by which Expectation, I go on boldly to pursue those Adventures already so happily begun.

SECT. IV
A TALE OF A TUB

I have now, with much Pains and Study, conducted the Reader to a Period, where he must expect to hear of great Revolutions. For no sooner had Our *Learned Brother*, so often mentioned, got a warm House of his own over his Head, than he began to look big, and to take mightily upon him; insomuch, that unless the Gentle Reader, out of his great Candour, will please a little to exalt his Idea, I am afraid he will henceforth hardly know the *Hero* of the Play, when he happens to meet Him; his Part, his Dress, and his Mien being so much altered.

He told his Brothers, he would have them to know, that he was their Elder, and consequently his Father's sole Heir; Nay, a while after, he would not allow them to call Him *Brother*, but Mr. PETER; and then he must be styled, *Father PETER*; and sometimes, *My Lord PETER*. To support this Grandeur, which he soon began to consider, could not be maintained without a Better *Fonde*[173] than what he was born to; after much Thought, he cast about at last, to turn *Projector* and *Virtuoso*; wherein he so well succeeded, that many famous Discoveries, Projects, and Machines, which bear great Vogue and Practice at present in the World, are owing entirely to *Lord Peter's* Invention. I will deduce the best Account I have been able to collect of the Chief amongst them, without considering much the Order they came out in; because I think Authors are not well agreed as to that Point.

I hope, when this Treatise of mine shall be translated into Foreign Languages (as I may without Vanity affirm, That the Labour of collecting, the Faithfulness in recounting, and the great Usefulness of the Matter to the Public, will amply deserve that Justice) that the worthy Members of the several *Academies* abroad, especially those of *France* and *Italy*, will favourably

---

[173] *Fonde* foundation.

accept these humble Offers, for the advancement of Universal Knowledge. I do also advertise the most Reverend Fathers, the *Eastern* Missionaries, that I have purely for their sakes, made use of such Words and Phrases, as will best admit an easy Turn into any of the *Oriental* Languages, especially the *Chinese*. And so I proceed with great Content of Mind, upon reflecting, how much Emolument this whole Globe of the Earth is like to reap by my Labours.

The first Undertaking of *Lord Peter* was to purchase a large Continent,[174] lately said to have been discovered in *Terra Australis incognita*.[175] This Tract of Land he bought at a very great Penny-worth from the Discoverers themselves, (though some pretended to doubt whether they had ever been there) and then retailed it into several Cantons to certain Dealers, who carried over Colonies but were all Shipwrecked in the Voyage. Upon which, *Lord Peter* sold the said Continent to other Customers *again*, and *again*, and *again*, with the same Success.

The second Project I shall mention, was his Sovereign Remedy for the *Worms*, especially those in the *Spleen*.[176] The Patient was to eat nothing after Supper for three Nights: As soon as he went to Bed, he was carefully to lie on one Side, and when he grew weary, to turn upon the other: He must also duly confine his two Eyes to the same Object; and by no means break Wind at both Ends together, without manifest Occasion. These Prescriptions diligently observed, the *Worms* would void insensibly by Perspiration, ascending through the Brain.

A third Invention, was the erecting of a *Whispering-Office*,[177] for the Public Good and Ease of all such as were Hypochondriacal, or troubled with the Cholic; likewise of all Eaves-droppers, Physicians, Midwives, small Politicians, Friends fallen out, Repeating Poets, Lovers Happy or in Despair, Bawds, Privy-Counsellors, Pages, Parasites, and Buffoons; In short, of all such as are in Danger of bursting with too much *Wind*. An *Ass*'s Head was placed so conveniently, that the Party affected might easily with his Mouth accost either of the Animal's Ears; which he was to apply close for a certain Space, and by a fugitive Faculty, peculiar to the Ears of that Animal, receive immediate Benefit either by Eructation, or Expiration, or Evomition.

Another very beneficial Project of *Lord Peter*'s, was an *Office of Insurance*[178] for Tobacco-Pipes, Martyrs of the Modern Zeal, Volumes of Poetry, Shadows, ———and Rivers: That these, nor any of these shall receive Damage by *Fire*. From whence our *Friendly Societies* may plainly find themselves, to be only Transcribers from this Original; though the one and the other have been of *great* Benefit to the Undertakers, as well as of *equal* to the Public.

Lord Peter was also held the Original Author of *Puppets* and *Raree-Shows*;[179] the great Usefulness whereof being so generally known, I shall not enlarge further upon this Particular.

But, another Discovery for which he was much renowned, was his famous universal *Pickle*.[180] For, having remarked how your common *Pickle* in use among House-wives, was of no further Benefit than to preserve dead Flesh, and certain kinds of Vegetables; *Peter*, with great Cost as well as Art, had contrived a *Pickle* proper for Houses, Gardens, Towns, Men,

---

[174] *a large Continent*   Purgatory [note in fifth edition].

[175] *Terra Australis incognita*   "unexplored southern land," the West Indies.

[176] *Sovereign Remedy . . . Spleen*   Here the Author ridicules the Penances of the Church of Rome, which may be made as easy to the Sinner as he pleases, provided he will pay for them accordingly [note in fifth edition].

[177] *Whispering-Office*   confession.

[178] *Office of Insurance*   insurance policies; indulgences, according to later notes, which could subtract time from one's future stay in Purgatory.

[179] *Puppets* and *Raree-Shows*   ceremonies.

[180] *Pickle*   holy water.

Women, Children, and Cattle; wherein he could preserve them as Sound as Insects in Amber. Now, this *Pickle* to the Taste, the Smell, and the Sight, appeared exactly the same, with what is in common Service for Beef, and Butter, and Herrings (and has been often that way applied with great Success) but for its many Sovereign Virtues, was quite a different Thing. For *Peter* would put in a certain Quantity of his *Powder Pimperlin-pimp*, after which it never failed of Success. The Operation was performed by *Spargefaction*[181] in a proper Time of the Moon. The Patient who was to be *pickled*, if it were a House, would infallibly be preserved from all Spiders, Rats, and Weasels; If the Party affected were a Dog, he should be exempt from Mange, and Madness, and Hunger. It also infallibly took away all Scabs and Lice, and scalled Heads[182] from Children never hindring the Patient from any Duty, either at Bed or Board.

But of all *Peter's* Rarities, he most valued a certain Set of *Bulls*,[183] whose Race was by great Fortune preserved in a lineal Descent from those that guarded the *Golden-Fleece*. Though some who pretended to observe them curiously, doubted the Breed had not been kept entirely chaste; because they had degenerated from their Ancestors in some Qualities, and had acquired others very extraordinary, but a Foreign Mixture. The *Bulls of Colchos* are recorded to have *brazen Feet*; But whether it happened by ill Pasture and Running, by an Allay[184] from Intervention of other Parents, from stolen Intrigues; Whether a Weakness in their Progenitors had impaired the seminal Virtue; Or by a Decline necessary through a long Course of Time, the Originals of Nature being depraved in these latter sinful Ages of the World; Whatever was the Cause, 'tis certain that *Lord Peter's Bulls* were extremely vitiated by the Rust of Time in the Metal of their Feet, which was now sunk into common *Lead*. However, the terrible *roaring* peculiar to their Lineage, was preserved; as likewise that Faculty of breathing out *Fire* from their Nostrils; which notwithstanding, many of their Detractors took to be a Feat of Art, and to be nothing so terrible as it appeared; proceeding only from their usual Course of Diet, which was of *Squibs*[185] and *Crackers*. However, they had two peculiar Marks which extremely distinguished them from the *Bulls* of *Jason*, and which I have not met together in the Description of any other Monster, beside that in Horace;

Varias inducere plumas;
and
Atrum desinit in piscem.[186]

For, these had *Fishes' Tails*, yet upon Occasion could *out-fly* any Bird in the Air. *Peter* put these *Bulls* upon several Employs. Sometimes he would set them a *roaring* to fright *Naughty Boys,* and make them quiet. Sometimes he would send them out upon Errands of great Importance; where it is wonderful to recount, and perhaps the cautious Reader may think much to believe it; an *Appetitus Sensibilis,*[187] deriving it self through the whole Family, from their Noble Ancestors, Guardians of the *Golden Fleece*; they continued so extremely fond of *Gold*, that if *Peter* sent them abroad, though it were only upon a Compliment; they would *Roar*, and *Spit*, and *Belch*, and *Piss*, and *Fart*, and *Snivel* out *Fire*, and keep a perpetual Coil, till you flung

---

181 *Spargefaction* "The act of sprinkling" (Johnson).
182 *scalled Heads* or "scall," "Leprosy; morbid baldness" (Johnson).
183 *Bulls* The Papal *Bulls* [pronouncements] are ridiculed by Name, So that here we are at no loss for the Author's Meaning. W. Wotton [note in fifth edition].
184 *Allay* repression, check (*OED*, 9).

185 *Squib* a fire-cracker.
186 *Varias . . . piscem* "to put in parti-coloured feathers" and "[a woman above] who ends as an ugly fish"; parts of the description of a ridiculous monster in the opening of Horace's "Ars Poetica."
187 *Appetitus Sensibilis* fleshly or carnal desire, as opposed to an intellectual interest.

them a Bit of *Gold*; but then *Pulveris exigui jactu*,[188] they would grow calm and quiet as Lambs. In short, whether by secret Connivance or Encouragement from their Master, or out of their own liquorish[189] Affection to Gold, or both; it is certain they were no better than a sort of sturdy, swaggering Beggars; and where they could not prevail to get an Alms, would make Women miscarry, and Children fall into Fits, who to this day usually call Sprites and Hobgoblins by the Name of *Bull-Beggars*.[190] They grew at last so very troublesome to the Neighbourhood, that some Gentlemen of the *North-West* got a Parcel of right *English Bull-Dogs*, and baited them so terribly, that they felt it ever after.[191]

I must needs mention one more of *Lord Peter*'s Projects, which was very extraordinary and discovered him to be a Master of a high Reach, and profound Invention. Whenever it happened that any Rogue of *Newgate* was condemned to be hanged, *Peter* would offer him a Pardon for a certain Sum of Money, which when the poor Caitiff had made all Shifts to scrape up and send, *His Lordship* would return a Piece of Paper in this Form:

To all Mayors, Sheriffs, Jailors, Constables, Bailiffs, Hangmen, &c. Whereas we are informed that *A. B.* remains in the Hands of you, or any of you, under the Sentence of Death. We will and command you upon Sight hereof, to let the said Prisoner depart to his own Habitation, whether he stands condemned for Murder, Sodomy, Rape, Sacrilege, Incest, Treason, Blasphemy, &c. for which this shall be your Sufficient Warrant. And if you fail hereof, G— d—mn You and Yours to all Eternity. And so we bid you heartily Farewell.

Your most Humble
Man's Man,
EMPEROR PETER.

The Wretches trusting to this, lost their Lives and Money too.

I desire of those whom the *Learned* among Posterity will appoint for Commentators upon this elaborate Treatise; that they will proceed with great Caution upon certain dark Points, wherein all who are not *Verè adepti*,[192] may be in Danger to form rash and hasty Conclusions, especially in some mysterious Paragraphs where certain *Arcana* are joined for Brevity sake, which in the Operation must be divided. And, I am certain, that future Sons of Art, will return large Thanks to my Memory, for so grateful, so useful an *Innuendo*.

It will be no difficult Part to persuade the Reader, that so many worthy Discoveries met with Great success in the World, though I may justly assure him, that I have related much the smallest Number; My Design having been only to single out such, as will be of most Benefit for Public Imitation, or which best served to give some Idea of the Reach and Wit of the Inventor. And therefore it need not be wondered, if by this Time, *Lord Peter* was become exceeding Rich. But alas, he had kept his Brain so long, and so violently upon the Rack, that at last it *shook* it self and began to *turn round* for a little Ease. In short, what with Pride, Projects, and Knavery, poor *Peter* was grown distracted, and conceived the strangest Imagi-

[188] *Pulveris exigui jactu* "after a little dusting" (Virgil, *Georgics* 4.87), a method of controlling bees.

[189] *liquorish* lickerish, lustful.

[190] *Bull-Beggars* "This word probably came from the insolence of those who begged, or raised money by the pope's bull. Something terrible; something to fright children with" (Johnson).

[191] *baited them . . . ever after* in the formation of the Church of England under Henry VIII.

[192] *Verè adepti* Latin: truly in possession (of the requisite knowledge); in its anglicized form "adept" was a name for accomplished alchemists and practitioners of other arts.

nations in the World. In the Height of his Fits (as it is usual with those who run Mad out of Pride) he would call Himself *God Almighty*, and sometimes, *Monarch of the Universe*. 'I have seen him', says my Author,[193] 'take three old *high-crowned Hats*, and clap them all on his Head, three Story high, with a huge Bunch of *Keys* at his Girdle, and an *Angling-Rod* in his Hand. In which Guise, whoever went to take him by the Hand in the Way of Salutation, *Peter* with much Grace, like a well educated Spaniel, would present them with his *Foot*; and if they refused his Civility, then he would raise it as high as their Chops, and give them a damned Kick on the Mouth, which hath ever since been called a *Salute*. Whoever walked by without paying him their Compliments, having a wonderful strong Breath, he would blow their Hats off into the Dirt'. Mean time, his Affairs at home went upside down; and his two Brothers had a wretched Time; where his first *Boutade*[194] was to kick both their *Wives* one Morning out of Doors, and his own too, and in their stead, gave Orders to pick up the first three Strollers could be met with in the Streets. A while after, he nailed up the Cellar Door, and would not allow his Brothers a Drop of *Drink* to their Victuals. Dining one Day at an Alderman's in the City, *Peter* observed him expatiating after the manner of his Brethren, in the Praises of his Sirloin of Beef. 'Beef', said the Sage Magistrate, 'is the King of Meat; Beef comprehends in it the Quintessence of Partridge, and Quail, and Venison, and Pheasant, and Plum-pudding, and Custard'. When *Peter* came home, he would needs take the Fancy of cooking up this Doctrine into use, and apply the Precept in default of a Sirloin, to his brown Loaf. 'Bread', says he, 'Dear Brothers, is the Staff of Life; in which Bread is contained, *inclusivè*, 'the Quintessence of Beef, Mutton, Veal, Venison, Partridge, Plum-pudding, and Custard: And to render all complete, there is intermingled a due Quantity of Water, whose Crudities are also corrected by Yeast or Barm, through which means it becomes a wholesome fermented Liquor, diffused through the Mass of the Bread'. Upon the Strength of these Conclusions, next Day at Dinner[195] was the brown Loaf served up in all the Formality of a City Feast. 'Come, Brothers', said Peter, 'fall to, and spare not; here is excellent good Mutton; or hold, now my Hand is in, I'll help you'. At which word, in much Ceremony, with Fork and Knife, he carves out two good Slices of the Loaf, and presents each on a Plate to his Brothers. The Elder of the two, not suddenly entering into *Lord Peter*'s Conceit, began with very civil Language to examine the Mystery. 'My Lord', said he, 'I doubt, with great Submission, there may be some Mistake'. 'What', says Peter, 'you are pleasant; Come then, let us hear this Jest, your Head is so big with'. 'None in the World, my Lord; but unless I am very much deceived, your Lordship was pleased a while ago, to let fall a word about Mutton, and I would be glad to see it with all my Heart'. 'How', said *Peter*, appearing in great Surprise, 'I do not comprehend this at all'. Upon which, the younger interposing to set the Business right, 'My Lord', said he, 'My Brother, I suppose, is hungry, and longs for the Mutton, your Lordship hath promised us to Dinner'. 'Pray', said Peter, 'take me along with you; either you are both Mad, or disposed to be merrier than I approve of: If *You* there, do not like your Piece I will carve you another, though I should take that to be the choice Bit of the whole Shoulder'.

'What then, my Lord', replied the first, 'it seems this is a Shoulder of Mutton all this while'.

'Pray, Sir', says Peter, 'eat your Vitals and leave off your Impertinence, if you please, for I am not disposed to relish it at present'. But the other could not forbear, being over provoked at the affected Seriousness of *Peter*'s Countenance. 'By G——, My Lord', said he, 'I can only say, that to my Eyes, and Fingers, and Teeth, and Nose, it seems to be nothing but a Crust of

---

193 *Author* authority, whom the speaker quotes. 195 *Dinner* holy communion.
194 *Boutade* sudden motion.

Bread'. Upon which the second put in his Word: 'I never saw a piece of Mutton in my Life, so nearly resembling a Slice from a Twelve-penny Loaf'.

'Look ye, Gentlemen', cries Peter in a Rage, 'to convince you what a couple of blind, positive, ignorant, wilful Puppies you are, I will use but this plain Argument: By G—, it is true, good, natural Mutton as any in Leaden-Hall Market; and G— confound you both eternally, if you offer to believe otherwise'. Such a thundering Proof as this, left no further Room for Objection: The two Unbelievers began to gather and pocket up their Mistake as hastily as they could. 'Why, truly', said the first, 'upon more mature Consideration' – 'Ay',says the other, interrupting him, 'now I have thought better on the Thing, your Lordship seems to have a great deal of Reason'.

'Very well', said Peter, 'Here Boy, fill me a Beer-Glass of Claret. Here's to you both with all my Heart'. The two Brethren much delighted to see him so readily appeased, returned their most humble Thanks and said they would be glad to pledge His Lordship. 'That you shall', said Peter, 'I am not a Person to refuse you any Thing that is reasonable; Wine moderately taken, is a Cordial; Here is a Glass a piece for you; 'Tis true natural Juice from the Grape; none of your damned *Vintners'* Brewings'. Having spoke thus, he presented to each of them another large dry Crust, bidding them drink it off, and not be bashful, for it would do them no Hurt. The two Brothers, after having performed the usual Office in such delicate Conjectures, of staring a sufficient Period at *Lord Peter*, and each other; and finding how Matters were like to go, resolved not to enter on a new Dispute, but let him carry the Point as he pleased; for he was now got into one of his mad Fits, and to Argue or Expostulate further, would only serve to render him a hundred times more untractable.

I have chosen to relate this worthy Matter in all its Circumstances, because it gave a principal Occasion to that great and famous *Rupture*,[196] which happened about the same time among these Brethren, and was never afterwards made up. But of that, I shall treat at large in another Section.

However, it is certain that *Lord Peter*, even in his lucid Intervals, was very lewdly given in his common Conversation, extreme wilful and positive, and would at any time rather argue to the Death, than allow himself once to be in an Error. Besides, he had an abominable Faculty of telling huge palpable *Lies* upon all Occasions; and swearing, not only to the Truth, but cursing the whole Company to Hell, if they pretended to make the least Scruple of believing Him. One time, he swore, he had a *Cow*[197] at home, which gave as much Milk at a Meal as would fill three thousand Churches; and what was yet more extraordinary, would never turn Sour. Another time, he was telling of an old *Sign-Post*[198] that belonged to his *Father*, with Nails and Timber enough on it, to build sixteen large Men of War. Talking one Day of *Chinese* Wagons, which were made so light as to sail over Mountains: 'Z—ds', said Peter, 'where's the Wonder of that? By G—, I saw a Large House[199] of Lime and Stone travel over Sea and Land (granting that it stopped sometimes to bait) above two thousand German Leagues'. And that which was the good of it, he would swear desperately all the while that he never told a Lie in his Life; And at every Word, 'By G—, Gentlemen, I tell you nothing but the Truth, and the D—l broil them eternally that will not believe me'.

---

[196] *Rupture* By this *Rupture* is meant the *Reformation* [note in fifth edition].
[197] *Cow* The ridiculous Multiplying of the Virgin *Mary's Milk* among the Papists, under the Allegory of a *Cow*, which gave as much Milk at a Meal, as would fill three thousand Churches. W. Wotton [note in fifth edition].
[198] *Sign-Post* the Cross of our Blessed Saviour [note in fifth edition].
[199] *Large House* The Chapel of Loreto [note in fifth edition; the shrine is supposed to be the house of the Virgin Mary, converted to a church, and later carried by angels in increments to Italy].

In short, *Peter* grew so scandalous, that all the Neighbourhood began in plain Words to say, he was no better than a Knave. And his two Brothers long weary of his ill Usage, resolved at last to leave him; but first, they humbly desired a Copy of their Father's *Will*, which had now lain by neglected, time out of Mind. Instead of granting this Request he called them 'damned Sons of Whores, Rogues, Traitors', and the rest of the vile Names he could muster up. However, while he was abroad one Day upon his Projects, the two Youngsters watched their Opportunity, made a Shift to come at the *Will*, and took a *Copia vera*,[200] by which they presently saw how grossly they had been abused: Their Father having left them equal Heirs, and strictly commanded, that whatever they got, should lie in common among them all. Pursuant to which, their next Enterprise was to break open the Cellar-Door, and get a little good *Drink* to spirit and comfort their Hearts. In copying the *Will*, they had met another Precept against Whoring, Divorce, and separate Maintenance; Upon which their next Work was to discard their Concubines, and send for their Wives. Whilst all this was in agitation, there enters a Solicitor from *Newgate*, desiring *Lord Peter* would please procure a *Pardon* for a *Thief* that was to be *hanged* to morrow. But the two Brothers told him, he was a Coxcomb to seek Pardons from a Fellow, who deserved to be hanged much better than his Client; and discovered all the Method of that Imposture, in the same Form I delivered it a while ago, advising the Solicitor to put his Friend upon obtaining *a Pardon from the King.*[201] In the midst of all this Clutter and Revolution, in comes *Peter* with a File of Dragoons at his Heels, and gathering from all Hands what was in the Wind, he and his Gang, after several Millions of Scurrilities and Curses, not very important here to repeat, by main Force, very fairly kicks them both out of Doors, and would never let them come under his Roof from that Day to this.

SECT. V
A DIGRESSION IN THE MODERN KIND

We whom the World is pleased to honour with the Title of *Modern Authors,* should never have been able to compass our great Design of an everlasting Remembrance, and never-dying Fame, if our Endeavours had not been so highly serviceable to the general Good of Mankind. This, *O Universe*, is the adventurous Attempt of me thy Secretary;

> —*Quemvis perferre laborem*
> *Suadet, et inducit noctes vigilare serenas.*[202]

To this End, I have some time since, with a World of Pains and Art, dissected the Carcass of *Human Nature,* and read many useful Lectures upon the several Parts, both *Containing* and *Contained*, till at last it *smelt* so strong, I could preserve it no longer. Upon which, I have been at a great Expense to fit up all the Bones with exact Contexture and in due Symmetry; so that I am ready to show a complete Anatomy thereof to all curious *Gentlemen and others*. But not to Digress further in the midst of a Digression, as I have known some Authors enclose Digressions in one another, like a Nest of Boxes, I do affirm, that having carefully cut up *Human Nature*, I have found a very strange, new, and important Discovery; that the Public Good of Mankind is performed by two Ways, *Instruction,* and *Diversion.* And I have further

---

[200] *took a Copia vera* Translated the Scriptures into the vulgar Tongues [note in fifth edition].

[201] *Pardon from the King* to implore the Mercy of God [note in fifth edition].

[202] *Quemvis . . . serenas* "it urges me to shoulder the burden and induces me to study through the calm nights" (Lucretius *De Rerum Natura* 1.141–2).

proved in my said several Readings (which, perhaps, the World may one day see, if I can prevail on any Friend to steal a Copy, or on certain Gentlemen of my Admirers, to be very Importunate) that, as Mankind is now disposed, he receives much greater Advantage by being *Diverted* than *Instructed*; His Epidemical Diseases being *Fastidiosity, Amorphy*, and *Oscitation*;[203] whereas in the present universal Empire of Wit and Learning, there seems but little Matter left for *Instruction*. However, in Compliance with a Lesson of great Age and Authority, I have attempted carrying the Point in all its Heights; and accordingly, throughout this Divine Treatise, have skilfully kneaded up both together with a *Layer* of *Utile*, and a *Layer* of *Dulce*.[204]

When I consider how exceedingly our Illustrious *Moderns* have eclipsed the weak glimmering lights of the *Ancients,* and turned them out of the Road of all fashionable Commerce, to a degree, that our choice Town Wits of most refined Accomplishments, are in grave Dispute whether there have been ever any *Ancients* or no: In which Point we are like to receive wonderful Satisfaction from the most useful Labours and Lucubrations of that Worthy *Modern*, Dr. B—*tly*. I say, when I consider all this, I cannot but bewail, that no famous *Modern* hath ever yet attempted an universal System in a small portable Volume, of all Things that are to be Known, or Believed, or Imagined, or Practised in Life. I am, however, forced to acknowledge that such an Enterprise was thought on some Time ago by a great Philosopher of *O. Brazile*.[205] The Method he proposed, was by a certain curious *Receipt*, a *Nostrum*,[206] which after his untimely Death, I found among his Papers; and do here out of my great Affection to the *Modern Learned*, present them with it, not doubting, it may one Day encourage some worthy Undertaker:

You take fair correct Copies, well bound in Calf's Skin, and Lettered at the Back, of all Modern Bodies of Arts and Sciences whatsoever, and in what Language you please. These you distil *in balneo Mariæ*, infusing *Quintessence of Poppy Q.S.*, together with three Pints of *Lethe,* to be had from the Apothecaries. You cleanse away carefully the *Sordes* and *Caput mortuum*, letting all that is volatile evaporate. You preserve only the first Running, which is again to be distilled seventeen times, till what remains will amount to about two Drams. This you keep in a Glass Vial, *Hermetically* sealed, for one and twenty Days. Then you begin your Catholic Treatise, taking every Morning fasting (first shaking the Vial) three Drops of this *Elixir*, snuffing it strongly up your Nose. It will dilate itself about the Brain (where there is any) in fourteen Minutes, and you immediately perceive in your Head an infinite Number of *Abstracts, Summaries, Compendiums, Extracts, Collections, Medullas, Excerpta quædams, Florilega*s, and the like, all disposed into great Order, and reduceable upon Paper.

I must needs own, it was by the Assistance of this *Arcanum*, that I, though otherwise *impar*, have adventured upon so daring an Attempt; never achieved or undertaken before, but by a certain Author called *Homer*, in whom, though otherwise a Person, not without some Abilities, and *for an Ancient*, of a tolerable Genius; I have discovered many gross Errors, which are not to be forgiven his very Ashes, if by chance any of them are left. For whereas, we are assured, he designed his Work for a complete Body of all Knowledge, Human, Divine,

[203]   *Oscitation*   "The act of yawning" (Johnson).
[204]   *Utile . . . Dulce*   usefulness and pleasure, age-old categories.
[205]   *O. Brazile*   an imaginary island . . . [note in fifth edition].
[206]   *Receipt, a Nostrum*   prescription; it follows, full of alchemical jargon.

JONATHAN SWIFT *A TALE OF A TUB* 615

Political, and Mechanic; it is manifest he hath wholly neglected some, and been very imperfect in the rest. For, first of all, as eminent a *Cabalist*[207] as his Disciples would represent Him, his account of the *Opus magnum* is extremely poor and deficient; he seems to have read but very superficially, either *Sendivogius, Behmen*, or *Anthroposophia Theomagica*. He is also quite mistaken about the *Sphæra Pyroplastica*, a neglect not to be atoned for; and (if the Reader will admit so severe a Censure) *Vix crederem Autorem hunc, unquam audivisse ignis vocem.*[208] His Failings are not less prominent in several Parts of the *Mechanics*. For, having read his Writings with the utmost Application usual among *Modern Wits*, I could never yet discover the least Direction about the Structure of that useful Instrument, a *Save-all*.[209] For want of which, if the *Moderns* had not lent their Assistance, we might yet have wandered *in the Dark*. But I have still behind, a Fault far more notorious to tax this Author with; I mean, his gross Ignorance in the *Common Laws of this Realm*, and in the Doctrine as well as Discipline of the Church of England. A Defect indeed, for which both he and all the Ancients stand most justly censured by my worthy and ingenious Friend Mr. W——tt—n, Batchelor of Divinity, in his incomparable Treatise of *Ancient and Modern Learning*; A Book never to be sufficiently valued, whether we consider the happy Turns and Flowings of the Author's Wit, the great Usefulness of his sublime Discoveries upon the Subject of *Flies* and *Spittle*, or the laborious Eloquence of his Style. And I cannot forbear doing that Author the Justice of my public Acknowledgments, for the great *Helps* and *Liftings* I had out of his incomparable Piece, while I was penning this Treatise.

But, besides these Omissions in *Homer* already mentioned, the curious Reader will also observe several Defects in that Author's Writings, for which he is not altogether so account- able. For whereas every Branch of Knowledge has received such wonderful Acquirements since his Age, especially within these last three Years, or thereabouts; it is almost impossible, he could be so very perfect in Modern Discoveries, as his Advocates pretend. We freely acknowledge him to be the Inventor of the *Compass*, of *Gun-powder*, and the *Circulation of the Blood*: But, I challenge any of his Admirers to show me in all his Writings, a complete Account of the *Spleen*; Does he not also leave us wholly to seek in the Art of *Political Wagering*? What can be more defective and unsatisfactory than his long Dissertation upon *Tea*? and as to his Method of *Salivation without Mercury*, so much celebrated of late, it is to my own Knowledge and Experience, a Thing very little to be relied on.

It was to supply such momentous Defects, that I have been prevailed on after long Solicitation, to take Pen in Hand; and I dare venture to Promise, the Judicious Reader shall find nothing neglected here, that can be of Use upon any Emergency of Life. I am confident to have included and exhausted all that Human Imagination can *Rise* or *Fall* to. Particularly, I recommend to the Perusal of the Learned, certain Discoveries that are wholly untouched by others; whereof I shall only mention among a great many more; *My New Help of Smatterers*, or the *Art of being Deep learned, and Shallow read*; A curious Invention about *Mouse-Traps*; An *Universal Rule of Reason, or every Man his own Carver*; Together with a most useful Engine for *catching of Owls*. All which the judicious Reader will find largely treated on, in the several Parts of this Discourse.

I hold my self obliged to give as much Light as is possible, into the Beauties and Excellencies of what I am writing, because it is become the Fashion and Humour most

---

[207] *Cabalist* mystic philosopher, therefore familiar with the occult works and writers whose names follow.
[208] *Vix . . . vocem* "I can hardly believe that this au- thor ever heard the voice of fire."

[209] *Save-all* "A small pan inserted into a candlestick to save the ends of candles" (Johnson).

applauded among the first Authors of this Polite and Learned Age, when they would correct the ill Nature of Critical, or inform the Ignorance of Courteous Readers. Besides, there have been several famous Pieces lately published both in Verse and Prose; wherein, if the Writers had not been pleased, out of their great Humanity and Affection to the Public, to give us a nice Detail of the *Sublime*, and the *Admirable* they contain; it is a thousand to one, whether we should ever have discovered one Grain of either. For my own particular, I cannot deny, that whatever I have said upon this Occasion had been more proper in a Preface, and more agreeable to the Mode, which usually directs it there. But I here think fit to lay hold on that great and honourable Privilege of being the *Last Writer*; I claim an absolute Authority in Right, as the *freshest Modern*, which gives me a Despotic Power over all Authors before me. In the Strength of which Title, I do utterly disapprove and declare against that pernicious Custom, of making the Preface a Bill of Fare to the Book. For I have always looked upon it as a high Point of Indiscretion in *Monster-mongers* and other *Retailers of strange Sights*; to hang out a fair large Picture over the door, drawn after the Life, with a most eloquent description underneath: This hath saved me many a Threepence, for my Curiosity was fully satisfied, and I never offered to go in, though often invited by the urging and attending Orator, with his last *moving* and *standing* Piece of Rhetoric, 'Sir, Upon my Word, we are just going to begin'. Such is exactly the Fate, at this time of *Prefaces, Epistles, Advertisements, Introductions, Prolegomenas, Apparatuses, To-the-Reader's.* This Expedient was admirable at first; Our Great *Dryden* has long carried it as far as it would go, and with incredible Success. He has often said to me in Confidence, that the world would have never suspected him to be so great a Poet, if he had not assured them so frequently in his Prefaces, that it was impossible they could either doubt or forget it. Perhaps it may be so; However, I much fear his Instructions have edified out of their Place, and taught Men to grow wiser in certain Points, where he never intended they should: For it is lamentable to behold, with what a lazy Scorn, many of the yawning Readers in our Age, do now a days twirl over forty or fifty Pages of *Preface* and *Dedication* (which is the usual *Modern* Stint) as if it were so much *Latin.* Though it must be also allowed on the other Hand, that a very considerable Number is known to proceed[210] *Critics* and *Wits,* by reading nothing else. Into which two Factions, I think, all present Readers may justly be divided. Now, for my self, I profess to be of the former Sort; and therefore having the *Modern* Inclination to expatiate upon the Beauty of my own Productions, and display the bright Parts of my Discourse; I thought best to do it in the Body of the Work, where, as it now lies, it makes a very considerable Addition to the Bulk of the Volume, *a Circumstance by no means to be neglected by a skilful Writer.*

Having thus paid my due Deference and Acknowledgment to an established Custom of our newest Authors, by *a long Digression unsought for*, and *an universal Censure unprovoked*; By forcing into the Light, with much Pains and Dexterity, my own Excellencies and other Men's Defaults, with great Justice to my self and Candour to them; I now happily resume my Subject, to the infinite Satisfaction both of the Reader and the Author.

SECT. VI

A TALE OF A TUB

We left *Lord Peter* in open Rupture with his two Brethren; both for ever discarded from his House, and resigned to the wide World, with little or nothing to trust to. Which are Circumstances that render them proper Subjects for the Charity of a Writer's Pen to work on;

---

[210]   *proceed*   to advance beyond the BA to a higher academic degree or position.

Scenes of Misery ever affording the fairest Harvest for great Adventures. And in this, the World may perceive the Difference between the Integrity of a generous Author and that of a common Friend. The latter is observed to adhere close in Prosperity, but on the Decline of Fortune, to drop suddenly off. Whereas, the generous Author, just on the contrary, finds his Hero on the Dunghill, from thence by gradual Steps, raises Him to a Throne, and then immediately withdraws, expecting not so much as Thanks for his Pains: In imitation of which Example, I have placed *Lord Peter* in a Noble House, given him a Title to wear, and Money to spend. There I shall leave Him for some Time, returning where common Charity directs me, to the Assistance of his two Brothers, at their lowest Ebb. However, I shall by no means forget my Character of an Historian, to follow the Truth step by step, whatever happens or wherever it may lead me.

The two Exiles so nearly united in Fortune and Interest, took a Lodging together; Where, at their first Leisure, they began to reflect on the numberless Misfortunes and Vexations of their Life past, and could not tell, of the sudden, to what Failure in their Conduct they ought to impute them; When, after some Recollection, they called to Mind the Copy of their Father's *Will*, which they had so happily recovered. This was immediately produced, and a firm Resolution taken between them, to alter whatever was already amiss, and reduce all their future Measures to the strictest Obedience prescribed therein. The main Body of the *Will* (as the Reader cannot easily have forgot) consisted in certain admirable Rules about the wearing of their Coats; in the Perusal whereof, the two Brothers at every Period duly comparing the Doctrine with the Practice, there was never seen a wider Difference between two Things; horrible down-right Transgressions of every Point. Upon which, they both resolved without further Delay, to fall immediately upon reducing the Whole, exactly after their Father's Model.

But, here it is good to stop the hasty Reader, ever impatient to see the End of an Adventure, before We Writers can duly prepare him for it. I am to record, that these two Brothers began to be distinguished at this Time, by certain Names. One of them desired to be called *MARTIN*,[211] and the other took the Appellation of *JACK*.[212] These two had lived in much Friendship and Agreement under the Tyranny of their Brother *Peter*, as it is the Talent of Fellow-Sufferers to do; Men in Misfortune, being like Men in the Dark, to whom all Colours are the same: But when they came forward into the World, and began to display themselves to each other, and to the Light, their Complexions appeared extremely different, which the present Posture of their Affairs gave them sudden Opportunity to discover.

But, here the severe Reader may justly tax me as a Writer of short Memory, a Deficiency to which a true *Modern* cannot but of Necessity be a little subject. Because, *Memory* being an Employment of the Mind upon things past, is a Faculty for which the Learned, in our Illustrious Age, have no manner of Occasion, who deal entirely with *Invention*, and strike all Things out of themselves, or at least, by Collision, from each other: Upon which Account, we think it highly reasonable to produce our great Forgetfulness, as an Argument unanswerable for our great Wit. I ought in Method, to have informed the Reader about fifty Pages ago, of a Fancy *Lord Peter* took, and infused into his Brothers, to wear on their Coats whatever Trimmings came up in Fashion; never pulling off any, as they went out of the Mode, but keeping on all together; which amounted in time to a Medley the most Antic[213] you can possibly conceive; and this to a Degree, that upon the Time of their Falling out, there was hardly a Thread of the Original Coat to be seen, but an infinite Quantity of *Lace*, and

---

211 *MARTIN* Martin Luther [note in fifth edition].
212 *JACK* John Calvin [note in fifth edition; with Luther, Calvin was a principal theologian of the Protes-

tant Reformation; Swift sees him as much more radical than Luther].
213 *Antic* absurd.

Ribbands, and *Fringe*, and *Embroidery*, and *Points;* (I mean only those *tagged with Silver*, for the rest fell off). Now, this material Circumstance, having been forgot in due Place, as good Fortune hath ordered, comes in very properly here, when the two Brothers are just going to reform their Vestures into the Primitive State, prescribed by their Father's *Will*.

They both unanimously entered upon this great Work, looking sometimes on their Coats, and sometimes on the *Will*. Martin laid the first Hand; at one Twitch brought off a large Handful of *Points*; and with a second Pull, stripped away ten dozen Yards of *Fringe*. But when He had gone thus far, he demurred a while. He knew very well, there yet remained a great deal to be done; however, the first Heat being over, his Violence began to cool, and he resolved to proceed more moderately in the rest of the Work; having already narrowly scaped a swinging Rent in pulling off the *Points*, which being *tagged with Silver* (as we have observed before) the judicious Workman had with much Sagacity, double-sewn to preserve them from *falling*. Resolving therefore to rid his Coat of a huge Quantity of *Gold Lace*; he picked up the Stitches with much Caution, and diligently gleaned out all the loose Threads as he went, which proved to be a Work of Time. Then he fell about the embroidered *Indian* Figures of Men, Women, and Children; against which, as you have heard in its due Place, their Father's Testament was extremely exact and severe: These, with much Dexterity and Application, were after a while, quite eradicated, or utterly defaced. For the rest, where he observed the Embroidery to be worked so close, as not to be got away without damaging the Cloth, or where it served to hide or strengthened any Flaw in the Body of the Coat, contracted by the perpetual tampering of Workmen upon it, he concluded the wisest Course was to let it remain, resolving in no Case whatsoever that the Substance of the Stuff should suffer Injury; which he thought the best Method for serving the true Intent and Meaning of his Father's *Will*. And this is the nearest Account I have been able to collect, of *Martin*'s Proceedings upon this great Revolution.

But, his Brother *Jack*, whose Adventures will be so extraordinary, as to furnish a great Part in the Remainder of this Discourse; entered upon the Matter with other Thoughts, and a quite different Spirit. For, the Memory of *Lord Peter*'s Injuries, produced a Degree of Hatred and Spite, which had a much greater Share of inciting Him, than any Regards after his Father's Commands, since these appeared at best, only Secondary and Subservient to the other. However, for this Medley of Humour, he made a Shift to find a very plausible Name, honouring it with the Title of *Zeal*; which is, perhaps, the most significant Word that hath been ever yet produced in any Language: As, I think, I have fully proved in my excellent *Analytical* Discourse upon that Subject; wherein I have deduced a *Histori-theo-physi-logical* Account of *Zeal*, showing how it first proceeded from a *Notion* into a *Word*, and from thence in a hot Summer, ripened into a *tangible Substance*. This Work containing three large Volumes in Folio, I design very shortly to publish by the *Modern* way of *Subscription*,[214] not doubting but the Nobility and Gentry of the Land will give me all possible Encouragement, having already had such a Taste of what I am able to perform.

I record therefore, that Brother *Jack*, brim-full of this miraculous Compound, reflecting with Indignation upon *PETER*'s Tyranny, and further provoked by the Despondency of *Martin*; prefaced his Resolutions to this purpose: 'What?' said he, 'A Rogue that locked up his Drink, turned away our Wives, cheated us of our Fortunes; palmed his damned Crusts upon us for Mutton; and at last kicked us out of Doors; must we be in his Fashions with a Pox? a Rascal, besides, that all the Street cries out against'. Having thus kindled and inflamed

[214] *Subscription* a way of financing publication by soliciting advance purchases from subscribers, whose names are then listed in the preliminary matter of the book.

himself as high as possible, and by Consequence, in a delicate Temper for beginning a Reformation, he set about the Work immediately, and in three Minutes, made more Dispatch than *Martin* had done in as many Hours. For, Courteous Reader, you are given to understand, that *Zeal* is never so highly obliged, as when you set it a *Tearing*; and *Jack*, who doted on that Quality in himself, allowed it at this Time its full Swing.[215] Thus it happened, that stripping down a Parcel of *Gold Lace*, a little too hastily, he rent the *main Body* of his *Coat* from Top to Bottom;[216] and whereas his Talent was not of the happiest in *taking up a Stitch*, he knew no better way, than to darn it again with *Packthread* and a *Skewer*. But the Matter was yet infinitely worse (I record it with Tears) when he proceeded to the *Embroidery*: For being clumsy by Nature, and of Temper, Impatient; withal, beholding Millions of Stitches that required the nicest Hand, and sedatest Constitution, to extricate; in a great Rage, he tore off the whole Piece, Cloth and all, and flung them into the Kennel,[217] and furiously thus continuing his Career: 'Ah, good brother *Martin*', said he, 'do as I do, for the Love of God; Strip, Tear, Pull, Rent, Flay off all, that we may as unlike that Rogue *Peter*, as it is possible: I would not for a hundred Pounds carry the least Mark about me, that might give Occasion to the Neighbours, of suspecting I was related to such a Rascal'. But *Martin*, who at this Time happened to be extremely phlegmatic and sedate, begged his Brother, of all Love, not to damage his Coat by any Means; for he never would get such another: Desired him to consider, that it was not their Business to form their Actions by any Reflection upon *Peter*'s, but by observing the Rules prescribed in their Father's *Will*. That he should remember, *Peter* was still their Brother, whatever Faults or Injuries he had committed; and therefore they should by all means avoid such a Thought, as that of taking Measures for Good and Evil, from no other Rule, than of Opposition to Him. That it was true, the Testament of their good Father was very exact in what related to the wearing of their *Coats;* yet it was no less penal and strict in prescribing Agreement, and Friendship, and Affection between them. And therefore, if straining a Point were at all dispensable, it would certainly be so, rather to the Advance of Unity, than Increase of Contradiction.

Martin had still proceeded as gravely as he began; and doubtless would have delivered an admirable Lecture of Morality, which might have exceedingly contributed to my Reader's *Repose, both of Body and Mind*: (the true ultimate End of *Ethics*); But *Jack* was already gone a Flight-shot[218] beyond his Patience. And as in Scholastic Disputes, nothing serves to rouse the Spleen of him that *Opposes*, so much as a kind of Pedantic affected Calmness in the *Respondent*; Disputants being for the most part like unequal Scales, where the *Gravity* of one Side advances the *Lightness* of the Other, and causes it to fly up and kick the Beam; So it happened here that the *Weight* of *Martin*'s Argument exalted *Jack*'s *Levity*, and made him fly out and spurn against his Brother's Moderation. In short, *Martin*'s *Patience* put *Jack* in a *Rage*; but that which most afflicted him was to observe his Brother's Coat so well reduced into the State of Innocence; while his own was either wholly rent to his Shirt; or those Places which had scaped his cruel Clutches, were still in *Peter*'s Livery. So that he looked like a drunken *Beau*, half rifled by *Bullies*; Or like a Fresh Tenant of *Newgate*,[219] when he has refused the Payment of *Garnish*;[220] Or like a discovered *Shoplifter*, left to the mercy of *Exchange-Women*;[221] Or like a

---

[215] *Swinge* "Sway; a sweep of any thing in motion. Not in use" (Johnson).

[216] *he rent the main Body of his Coat from Top to Bottom* removing Episcopacy and setting up Presbyterian church government.

[217] *Kennel* gutter.

[218] *Flight-shot* bow-shot, distance an arrow can travel in the air.

[219] *Newgate* a prison in London.

[220] *Garnish* the fee paid by prisoners to the jailer for food and other necessaries.

[221] *Exchange-Women* shop-women running stores in the galleries of a center for merchants.

Bawd in her old Velvet Petticoat, resigned into the secular Hands of the *Mobile*.[222] Like any, or like all of these, a Medley of *Rags*, and *Lace*, and *Rents*, and *Fringes*, unfortunate *Jack* did now appear: He would have been extremely glad to see his Coat in the Condition of *Martin*'s, but infinitely gladder to find that of *Martin*'s in the same Predicament with his. However, since neither of these was likely to come to pass, he thought fit to lend the whole Business another Turn, and to dress up Necessity as a Virtue. Therefore, after as many of the *Fox*'s Arguments[223] as he could muster up, for bringing Martin to *Reason*, as he called it; or, as he meant it, into his own ragged, bobtailed Condition; and observing he said all to little purpose; what, alas, was left for the forlorn *Jack* to do, but after a Million of Scurrilities against his Brother, to run mad with Spleen, and Spite, and Contradiction. To be short, here began a mortal Breach between these two. *Jack* went immediately to *New Lodgings*, and in a few Days it was for certain reported, that he had run out of his Wits. In a short time after, he appeared abroad, and confirmed the Report, by falling into the oddest Whimsies that ever a sick Brain conceived.

And now the little Boys in the Streets began to salute him with several Names. Sometimes they would call Him, *Jack the Bald*;[224] sometimes, *Jack with a Lantern*;[225] sometimes, *Dutch Jack*;[226] sometimes, *French Hugh*;[227] sometimes, *Tom the Beggar*;[228] and sometimes, *Knocking Jack of the North*.[229] And it was under one, or some, or all of these Appellations (which I leave the Learned Reader to determine) that he hath given Rise to the most Illustrious and Epidemic Sect of *Æolists*,[230] who, with honourable Commemoration, do still acknowledge the Renowned *JACK* for their Author and Founder. Of whose Originals, as well as Principles, I am now advancing to gratify the World with a very particular Account.

—*Mellæo contingens cuncta Lepore.*[231]

SECT. VII
A *Digression in Praise of Digressions*

I have sometimes *heard* of an *Iliad* in a *Nut-shell*; but it hath been my Fortune to have much oftener *seen* a *Nut-shell* in an *Iliad*. There is no doubt, that Human Life has received most wonderful Advantages from both; but to which of the two the World is chiefly indebted, I shall leave among the Curious, as a Problem worthy of their utmost Enquiry. For the Invention of the latter, I think the Commonwealth of Learning is chiefly obliged to the great *Modern* Improvement of *Digressions*: The late Refinements in Knowledge, running parallel to those of Diet in our Nation, which among Men of a judicious Taste are dressed up in various Compounds, consisting in *Soups* and *Olios*,[232] *Fricassees* and *Ragouts*.

---

[222] *Mobile* the mob.
[223] *the Fox's Arguments* having lost his tail in a trap, he tries to persuade the other foxes to cut off their tails (Aesop).
[224] *Jack the Bald* from Calvus [Latin], Bald [note in fifth edition].
[225] *Jack with a Lantern* All those who pretend to Inward Light [note in fifth edition].
[226] *Dutch Jack* Jack of Leyden who gave rise to the Anabaptists [note in fifth edition].
[227] *French Hugh* The Huguenots [note in fifth edition].

[228] *Tom the Beggar* The Gueuses [French, beggars] by which Name some Protestants in Flanders were called [note in fifth edition].
[229] *Knocking Jack of the North* John Knox, the Reformer of *Scotland* [note in fifth edition].
[230] *Æolists* after Æolus, a Greek god of winds; spiritualists but also those who are in any sense windy.
[231] *Mellæo contingens cuncta Lepore* "Touching all with sweet grace" (Lucretius *De Rerum Natura* 1.934, inaccurately).
[232] *Olios* stews.

'Tis true, there is a sort of morose, detracting, ill-bred People, who pretend utterly to disrelish these polite Innovations; And as to the Similitude from Diet, they allow the Parallel, but are so bold to pronounce the Example itself a Corruption and Degeneracy of Taste. They tell us, that the Fashion of jumbling fifty Things together in a Dish, was at first introduced in Compliance to a depraved and *debauched Appetite*, as well as to a *crazy Constitution*; And to see a Man hunting through an *Olio* after the *Head* and *Brains* of a *Goose*, a *Wigeon*, or a *Woodcock*, is a Sign he wants a Stomach and Digestion for more substantial Victuals. Further, they affirm, that *Digressions* in a Book, are like *Foreign Troops* in a *State*, which argue the Nation to want a *Heart* and *Hands* of its own, and often, either *subdue* the *Natives*, or drive them into the most *unfruitful Corners*.

But, after all that can be objected by these supercilious Censors, 'tis manifest, the Society of Writers would quickly be reduced to a very inconsiderable Number, if Men were put upon making Books, with the fatal Confinement of delivering nothing beyond what is to the Purpose. 'Tis acknowledged, that were the Case the same among Us as with the *Greeks* and *Romans*, when Learning was in its *Cradle*, to be reared and fed, and clothed by *Invention*, it would be an easy Task to fill up Volumes upon particular Occasions, without further expatiating from the Subject than by moderate Excursions, helping to advance or clear the main Design. But with *Knowledge*, it has fared as with a numerous Army, encamped in a fruitful Country; which for a few Days maintains it self by the Product of the Soil it is on; till Provisions being spent, they send to forage many a Mile, among Friends or Enemies it matters not. Mean while the neighbouring Fields trampled and beaten down, become barren and dry, affording no Sustenance but Clouds of Dust.

The whole Course of Things being thus entirely changed between *Us* and the *Ancients*; and the *Moderns* wisely sensible of it, we of this Age have discovered a shorter, and more prudent Method, to become *Scholars* and *Wits*, without the fatigue of *Reading* or of *Thinking*. The most accomplished Way of using Books at present, is twofold: Either first, to serve them as some Men do *Lords*, learn their *Titles* exactly, and then brag of their Acquaintance. Or Secondly, which is indeed the choicer, the profounder, and politer Method, to get a thorough Insight into the *Index*, by which the whole Book is governed and turned, like *Fishes* by the *Tail*. For, to enter the Palace of Learning at the *great Gate*, requires an Expense of Time and Forms; therefore Men of much Haste and little Ceremony, are content to get in by the *Back-Door*. For, the Arts are all in a *flying* March, and therefore more easily subdued by attacking them in the *Rear*. Thus Physicians discover the State of the whole Body, by consulting only what comes from *Behind*. Thus Men catch Knowledge by throwing their *Wit* on the Posteriors of a Book, as Boys do Sparrows with flinging *Salt* upon their *Tails*. Thus Human Life is best understood by the wise man's Rule of *Regarding the End*. Thus are the Sciences found like *Hercules*'s Oxen, by *tracing them backwards*. Thus are *old Sciences* unravelled like *old Stockings*, by beginning at the *Foot*.

Besides all this, the Army of Sciences hath been of late with a World of Martial Discipline, drawn into its *close Order*, so that a View, or a Muster may be taken of it with abundance of Expedition. For this great Blessing we are wholly indebted to *Systems* and *Abstracts*, in which the *Modern* Fathers of Learning, like prudent Usurers, spent their Sweat for the Ease of Us their Children. For *Labour* is the Seed of *Idleness*, and it is the peculiar Happiness of our Noble Age to gather the *Fruit*.

Now the Method of growing Wise, Learned, and *Sublime*, having become so regular an Affair, and so established in all its Forms, the Number of Writers must needs have increased accordingly, and to a Pitch that has made it of absolute Necessity for them to interfere continually with each other. Besides, it is reckoned that there is not at this present, a sufficient Quantity of new Matter left in Nature, to furnish and adorn any one particular Subject to the Extent of a Volume. This I am told by a very skilful *Computer*, who hath given a full Demonstration of it from Rules of *Arithmetic*.

This, perhaps, may be objected against by those, who maintain the Infinity of Matter, and therefore will not allow that any *Species* of it can be exhausted. For Answer to which, let us examine the noblest Branch of *Modern* Wit or Invention, planted and cultivated by the present Age, and, which of all others, hath borne the most and the fairest Fruit. For though some Remains of it were left us by the *Ancients*, yet have not any of those, as I remember, been translated or compiled into Systems for *Modern* Use. Therefore we may affirm, to our own Honour, that it has in some sort, been both invented, and brought to a Perfection by the same Hands. What I mean, is that highly celebrated Talent among the *Modern* Wits, of deducing Similitudes, Allusions, and Applications, very Surprising, Agreeable, and Apposite, from the *Genitals* of either Sex, together with *their proper Uses*. And truly, having observed how little Invention bears any Vogue, besides what is derived into these *Channels*, I have sometimes had a Thought, That the happy Genius of our Age and Country, was prophetically held forth by that ancient typical Description of the *Indian* Pygmies; 'whose Stature did not exceed above two Foot; sed quorum pudenda crassa, & ad talos usque pertingentia'.[233] Now, I have been very curious to inspect the late Productions, wherein the Beauties of this kind have most prominently appeared. And although this *Vein* hath bled so freely, and all Endeavours have been used in the Power of Human Breath to dilate, extend, and keep it open: Like the Scythians, 'who had a Custom, and an Instrument, to blow up the Privities of their Mares, that they might yield the more Milk';[234] Yet I am under an Apprehension, it is near growing dry, and past all Recovery; And that either some new *Fonde* of Wit should, if possible, be provided, or else that we must e'en be content with Repetition here, as well as upon all other Occasions.

This will stand as an uncontestable Argument, that our *Modern* Wits are not to reckon upon the Infinity of Matter, for a constant Supply. What remains therefore but that our last Recourse must be had to large *Indexes*, and little *Compendiums*; *Quotations* must be plentifully gathered, and booked in Alphabet; To this End, though Authors need be little consulted, yet *Critics*, and *Commentators*, and *Lexicons* carefully must. But above all, those judicious Collectors of *Bright Parts*, and *Flowers*, and *Observandas*, are to be nicely dwelt on; by some called the *Sieves* and *Bolters*[235] of Learning; though it is left undetermined, whether they dealt in *Pearls* or *Meal*, and consequently, whether we are more to value that which *passed through*, or what *stayed behind*.

By these Methods, in a few Weeks, there starts up many a Writer capable of managing the profoundest and most universal Subjects. For, what though his *Head* be empty, provided his *Commonplace Book* be full; And if you will bate him but the Circumstances of *Method*, and *Style*, and *Grammar*, and *Invention*; allow him but the common Privileges, of transcribing from others, and digressing from himself, as often as he shall see Occasion; He will desire no more Ingredients towards fitting up a Treatise, that shall make a very comely Figure on a Bookseller's Shelf; there to be preserved neat and clean, for a long Eternity, adorned with the Heraldry of its Title, fairly inscribed on a Label; never to be thumbed or greased by Students, nor bound to everlasting Chains of Darkness in a Library:[236] But when the Fullness of Time is come, shall haply undergo the Trial of Purgatory in order *to ascend the Sky*.

---

[233] *sed quorum pudenda crassa, & ad talos usque pertingentia* [but whose genitals are thick, hanging down even to their ankles] Ctesiae fragm. apud Photium [Swift's marginal note; a correct citation].

[234] *"who had a Custom . . . Milk"* Herodotus 4.2.1.

[235] *Bolter* "A sieve to separate meal from bran or husks" (Johnson).

[236] *Chains in a Library* libraries still had many chained books in Swift's time.

Without these Allowances, how is it possible we *Modern* Wits should ever have an Opportunity to introduce our Collections, listed under so many thousand Heads of a different Nature? for want of which, the Learned World would be deprived of infinite Delight, as well as Instruction, and we our selves buried beyond Redress in an inglorious and undistinguished Oblivion.

From such Elements as these, I am alive to behold the Day, wherein the Corporation of Authors can out-vie all its Brethren in the *Yield*. A Happiness derived to us with a great many others, from our *Scythian* Ancestors, among whom, the Number of *Pens* was so infinite, that the *Grecian* Eloquence had no other way of expressing it, than by saying, That 'in the Regions, far to the North, it was hardly possible for a Man to travel, the very Air was so replete with *Feathers*'.[237]

The Necessity of this Digression, will easily excuse the Length, and I have chosen for it as proper a Place as I could readily find. If the judicious Reader can assign a fitter, I do here empower him to remove it into any other Corner he please. And so I return with great Alacrity to pursue a more important Concern.

SECT. VIII
A TALE OF A TUB

The Learned *Æolists*,[238] maintain the Original Cause of all Things to be *Wind*, from which Principle this whole Universe was at first produced, and into which it must at last be resolved; that the same Breath which had kindled and blew *up* the Flame of Nature, should one Day blow it *out*.

Quod procul à nobis flectat Fortuna gubernans.[239]

This is what the *Adepti* understand by their *Anima Mundi*; that is to say, the *Spirit*, or *Breath*, or *Wind* of the World: Or Examine the whole System by the Particulars of Nature, and you will find it not to be disputed. For, whether you please to call the *Forma informans*[240] of a Man by the name of *Spiritus, Animus, Afflatus,* or *Anima*; what are all these, but several Appellations for *Wind*? which is the ruling *Element* in every Compound, and into which they all resolve upon their Corruption. Farther, what is Life it self, but as it is commonly called, the *Breath* of our Nostrils? Whence it is very justly observed by Naturalists, that *Wind* still continues of great Emolument in *certain Mysteries* not to be named, giving Occasion for those happy Epithets of *Turgidus,* and *Inflatus,* applied either to the *Emittent,* or *Recipient* Organs.

By what I have gathered out of ancient Records, I find, the *Compass* of their Doctrine took in two and thirty Points; wherein it would be tedious to be very particular. However, a few of their most important Precepts, deduceable from it, are by no means to be omitted; among which, the following Maxim was of much Weight; That since *Wind* had the Master Share, as well as Operation in every Compound, by Consequence, those Beings must be of chief Excellence wherein that *Primordium* appears most prominently to abound; and therefore, *Man* is in the highest Perfection of all created Things, as having by the great Bounty of

---

[237] *"in the Regions ... Feathers"* Herodotus 4 [7 and 13; Swift's marginal gloss].
[238] *Æolists* All Pretenders to Inspiration whatever [note in fifth edition].
[239] *Quod procul à nobis flectat Fortuna gubernans* "Which [earthquakes and other evidence of his prediction that

the earth will someday dissolve] may governing Fortune steer far from us" (Lucretius 5.107).
[240] *Forma informans* a scholastic category, the material form or idea, which sounds like a contradiction in terms.

Philosophers,[241] been endued with three distinct *Animas* or *Winds*, to which the sage *Æolists,* with much Liberality, have added a fourth, of equal Necessity, as well as Ornament with the other three; by this *quartum Principium,* taking in the four Corners of the World. Which gave Occasion to that Renowned *Cabalist, Bumbastus,*[242] of placing the Body of Man, in due position to the four *Cardinal* Points.

In Consequence of this, their next Principle was, that *Man* brings with Him into the World a peculiar Portion, or Grain of *Wind,* which may be called a *Quinta essentia,* extracted from the other four. This *Quintessence* is of a Catholic Use upon all Emergencies of Life, is improveable into all Arts and Sciences, and may be wonderfully refined, as well as enlarged by certain Methods in Education. This, when *blown* up to its Perfection, ought not to be covetously hoarded up, stifled, or hid under a Bushel, but freely communicated to Mankind. Upon these Reasons, and others of equal Weight, the Wise *Æolists,* affirm the Gift of *BELCHING* to be the noblest Act of a Rational Creature. To cultivate which Art and render it more serviceable to Mankind, they made Use of several Methods. At certain Seasons of the Year, you might behold the Priests amongst them in vast Numbers, with their *Mouths gaping wide against a Storm.* At other Times were to be seen, several Hundreds linked together in a circular Chain, with every Man a Pair of Bellows applied to his Neighbour's Breech, by which they blew up each other to the Shape and Size of a *Tun;*[243] and for that Reason, with great Propriety of Speech, did usually call their Bodies, their *Vessels.* When, by these and the like Performances, they were grown sufficiently replete, they would immediately depart, and disembogue for the Public Good a plentiful Share of their Acquirements into their Disciples' Chaps.[244] For we must here observe, that all Learning was esteemed among them, to be compounded from the same Principle. Because, First, it is generally affirmed, or confessed, that Learning *puffeth Men up:*[245] And Secondly, they proved it by the following Syllogism: 'Words are but Wind; and Learning is nothing but Words'; *Ergo,* 'Learning is nothing but Wind'. For this Reason, the Philosphers among them, did in their Schools, deliver to their Pupils, all their Doctrines and Opinions by *Eructation,* wherein they had acquired a wonderful Eloquence, and of incredible Variety. But the great Characteristic by which their chief Sages were best distinguished, was a certain Position of Countenance, which gave undoubted Intelligence to what Degree or Proportion, the Spirit agitated the inward Mass. For, after certain Gripings,[246] the *Wind* and Vapours issuing forth, having first by their Turbulence and Convulsions within caused an Earthquake in Man's little World; distorted the Mouth, bloated the Cheeks, and gave the Eyes a terrible kind of *Relievo.* At which Junctures all their *Belches* were received for Sacred, the Sourer the better, and swallowed with infinite Consolation by their meager Devotees. And to render these yet more complete, because the Breath of Man's Life is in his Nostrils, therefore, the choicest, most edifying, and most enlivening *Belches,* were very wisely conveyed through that Vehicle, to give them a Tincture as they passed.

Their Gods were the four *Winds,* whom they worshipped, as the Spirits that pervade and enliven the Universe, and as those from whom alone all *Inspiration* can properly be said to proceed. However, the Chief of these, to whom they performed the Adoration of *Latria,*[247] was

---

[241]   *Philosophers* scholastic philosophers do attribute three functional kinds of anima, or spirit, to man: vegetative, animal, and rational; the "Æolists" add spirit, or wind, as a fourth dimension of the soul's activity.

[242]   *Bumbastus* part of the name of Paracelsus, a sixteenth-century alchemist.

[243]   *Tun* barrel.

[244]   *Chaps* jaws, mouths.

[245]   *Learning puffeth Men up* "Knowledge puffeth up but Charity edifieth" (1 Corinthians 8.1).

[246]   *Gripings* colic.

[247]   *Latria* "The highest kind of worship; distinguished by the papists from dulia, or inferior worship" (Johnson).

the *Almighty North*. An Ancient Deity whom the Inhabitants of *Megalopolis* in *Greece*, had likewise in highest Reverence. *Omnium deorum Boream maxime celebrant.*[248] This God, though endued with Ubiquity, was yet supposed by the profounder *Æolists*, to possess one peculiar Habitation, or, to speak in Form, a *Cælum Empyræum*,[249] wherein he was more intimately present. This was situated in a certain Region, well known to the Ancient *Greeks*, by them called, Σκοτία,[250] or the *Land of Darkness*. And although many Controversies have arisen upon that Matter, yet so much is undisputed that from a Region of the *like Denomination*, the most refined *Æolists* have borrowed their Original, from whence in every Age, the zealous among their Priesthood, have brought over their choicest *Inspiration*, fetching it with their own Hands, from the Fountain Head, in certain *Bladders*, and disploding it among the Sectaries in all Nations, who did, and do, and ever will, daily Gasp and Pant after it.

Now, their Mysteries and Rites were performed in this Manner. 'Tis well known among the Learned, that the Virtuosos[251] of former Ages, had a Contrivance for carrying and preserving *Winds* in Casks or Barrels, which was of great Assistance upon long Sea Voyages; And the loss of so useful an Art at present, is very much to be lamented, though, I know not how, with great Negligence omitted by *Pancirolius*.[252] It was an Invention ascribed to *Æolus* himself, from whom this Sect is denominated, and who in Honour of their Founder's Memory, have to this Day preserved great Numbers of those *Barrels*, whereof they fix one in each of their Temples, first beating out the Top. Into this *Barrel*, upon solemn Days, the Priest enters; where, having before duly prepared himself by the Methods already described, a secret Funnel is also conveyed from his Posteriors, to the Bottom of the Barrel, which admits new Supplies of Inspiration, from a *Northern* Chink or Cranny. Whereupon, You behold him swell immediately to the Shape and Size of his *Vessel*. In this Posture he disembogues whole Tempests upon his Auditory, as the Spirit from beneath gives him Utterance; which issuing *ex adytis* and *penetralibus*,[253] is not performed without much Pain and Gripings. And the Wind in breaking forth deals with his Face,[254] as it does with that of the Sea; first *blackening*, then *wrinkling*, and at last *bursting it into a Foam*. It is in this Guise, the Sacred *Æolist* delivers his oracular *Belches* to his panting Disciples; Of whom, some are greedily gaping after the sanctified Breath, others are all the while hymning out the Praises of the *Winds*, and gently wafted to and fro by their own Humming, do thus represent the soft Breezes of their Deities appeased.

It is from this Custom of the Priests that some Authors maintain these *Æolists* to have been very ancient in the World. Because the Delivery of their Mysteries, which I have just now mentioned, appears exactly the same with that of other Ancient Oracles, whose Inspirations were owing to certain subterraneous *Effluviums* of *Wind*, delivered with the *same* Pain to the Priest, and much about the *same* Influence on the People. It is true indeed, that these were frequently managed and directed by *Female* Officers, whose Organs were understood to be better disposed for the Admission of those Oracular *Gusts*, as entering, and passing up through a Receptacle of greater Capacity, and causing also a Pruriency by the Way, such as

---

248 *Omnium deorum Boream maxime celebrant* "They worshipped Boreas (the north wind) the most of all the gods" (Pausanias 8.36.6).

249 *Cælum Empyræum* the highest part of the heavens.

250 Σκοτία Scotia, which does mean "darkness" as well as Scotland.

251 *Virtuoso* "A man skilled in antique or natural curiosities" (Johnson), but Swift uses it of inventors.

252 *Pancirolius* Guido Panciroli (1523–99), author of a treatise on the inventions of the ancients and the moderns.

253 *ex adytis and penetralibus* "out of the inmost part of the temple or sanctuary [where the household gods are kept]" (Virgil, *Aeneid* 2.297).

254 *Face* This is an exact Description of the Changes made in the Face by Enthusiastic Preachers [note in fifth edition].

with due Management, hath been refined from Carnal, into a Spiritual Ecstasy. And to strengthen this profound Conjecture, it is further insisted, that this Custom of *Female Priests*[255] is kept up still in certain refined Colleges of our *modern Æolists*, who are agreed to receive their Inspiration, derived through the Receptacle aforesaid, like their Ancestors, the *Sibyls*.[256]

And whereas the Mind of Man, when he gives the Spur and Bridle to his Thoughts, doth never stop, but naturally sallies out into both extremes of High and Low, of Good and Evil; his first Flight of Fancy commonly transports him to Ideas of what is most Perfect, finished, and exalted; till having soared out of his own Reach and Sight, not well perceiving how near the Frontiers of Height and Depth border upon each other; With the same Course and Wing, he falls down plum into the lowest Bottom of Things; like one who travels the *East* into the *West*; or like a straight Line drawn by its own Length into a Circle. Whether a Tincture of Malice in our Natures, makes us fond of furnishing every bright Idea with its Reverse; Or, whether Reason reflecting upon the Sum of Things, can like the Sun serve only to enlighten one half of the Globe, leaving the other half, by Necessity, under Shade and Darkness; Or, whether Fancy, flying up to the Imagination of what is Highest and Best, becomes over-shot, and spent, and weary, and suddenly falls like a dead Bird of Paradise, to the Ground. Or, whether after all these *Metaphysical* Conjectures, I have not entirely missed the true Reason; The Proposition, however, which hath stood me in so much Circumstance, is altogether true; That, as the most uncivilized Parts of Mankind have in some way or other, climbed up into the Conception of a *God*, or Supreme Power, so they have seldom forgot to provide their Fears with certain ghastly Notions, which instead of better, have served them pretty tolerably for a *Devil*. And this Proceeding seems to be natural enough; for it is with Men, whose Imaginations are lifted up very high, after the same Rate, as with those whose Bodies are so; that, as they are delighted with the Advantage of a nearer Contemplation upwards, so they are equally terrified with the dismal Prospect of the Precipice below. Thus, in the Choice of a *Devil*, it hath been the usual Method of Mankind to single out some Being, either in Act or in Vision, which was in most Antipathy to the God they had framed. Thus, also, the Sect of *Æolists,* possessed themselves with a Dread, and Horror, and Hatred of two malignant Natures, betwixt whom, and the Deities they adored, perpetual Enmity was established. The first of these, was the *Chamelion*,[257] sworn Foe to *Inspiration*, who in Scorn, devoured large Influences of their God, without refunding the smallest Blast by *Eructation*. The other was a huge terrible Monster, called *Moulinavent*,[258] who with four strong Arms, waged eternal Battle with all their Divinities, dexterously turning to avoid their Blows, and repay them with Interest.

Thus furnished, and set out with *Gods*, as well as *Devils*, was the renowned Sect of *Æolists*; which makes at this Day so illustrious a Figure in the World, and whereof, that polite Nation of *Laplanders*, are beyond all Doubt, a most Authentic Branch; Of whom I therefore cannot, without Injustice, here omit to make honourable Mention, since they appear to be so closely allied in Point of Interest as well as Inclinations with their Brother *Æolists* among Us, as not only to buy their *Winds* by wholesale from the *same* Merchants, but also to retail them the *same* Rate and Method, and to Customers much alike.

[255] *Female Priests* Quakers who suffer their Women to preach and pray [note in fifth edition].
[256] *Sibyls* prophetesses of the classical world, the most famous of whom was the Cumaean Sibyl, consulted by Aeneas before he visited Hades.
[257] *Chamelion* because this animal was popularly believed to feed on air (Browne, *Pseudodoxia Epidemica* 3.21).
[258] *Moulinavent* French, "windmill."

Now, whether the System here delivered, was wholly compiled by *Jack*, or, as some Writers believe, rather copied from the Original at *Delphos*, with certain Additions and Emendation suited to Times and Circumstances, I shall not absolutely determine. This I may affirm, that *Jack* gave it at least a new Turn, and formed it into the same Dress and Model as it lies deduced by me.

I have long sought after this Opportunity of doing Justice to a Society of Men, for whom I have a peculiar Honour, and whose Opinions, as well as Practices, have been extremely misrepresented, and traduced by the Malice or Ignorance of their Adversaries. For, I think it one of the greatest, and best of human Actions to remove Prejudices, and place Things in their truest and fairest Light; which I therefore boldly undertake without any Regards of my own, besides the Conscience, the Honour, and the Thanks.

SECT. IX

A DIGRESSION CONCERNING THE ORIGINAL, THE USE, AND IMPROVEMENT OF MADNESS IN A COMMONWEALTH

Nor shall it any ways detract from the just Reputation of this famous Sect, that its Rise and Institution are owing to such an Author as I have described *Jack* to be; A Person whose Intellectuals were overturned, and his Brain shaken out of its natural Position; which we commonly suppose to be a Distemper, and call by the name of *Madness* or *Frenzy*. For, if we take a Survey of the greatest Actions that have been performed in the World, under the Influence of Single Men, which are, *the Establishment of New Empires by Conquest; The Advance and Progress of New Schemes in Philosophy; and the contriving, as well as the propagating of New Religions*; we shall find the Authors of them all, to have been Persons, whose natural Reason hath admitted great Revolutions from their Diet, their Education, the Prevalency of some certain Temper, together with the particular Influence of Air and Climate. Besides, there is something Individual in human Minds, that easily kindles at the accidental Approach and Collision of certain Circumstances, which though of paltry and mean Appearance, do often flame out into the greatest Emergencies of Life. For, great Turns are not always given by strong Hands, but by lucky Adaptation, and at proper Seasons; and it is of no Import, where the Fire was kindled, if the Vapour has once got up into the Brain. For, the *upper Region* of Man, is furnished like the *middle Region* of the Air; The Materials are formed from Causes of the widest Difference, yet produce at last the same Substance and Effect. Mists arise from the Earth, Steams from Dunghills, Exhalations from the Sea, and Smoke from Fire; yet all Clouds are the same in Composition as well as Consequences: And the Fumes issuing from a Jakes,[259] will furnish as comely and useful a Vapour as Incense from an Altar. Thus far, I suppose, will be easily granted me: And then it will follow; that as the Face of Nature never produces Rain, but when it is overcast and disturbed; so Human Understanding, seated in the Brain, must be troubled and over-spread by Vapours, ascending from the lower Faculties to water the Invention, and render it fruitful. Now, although these Vapours (as it hath been already said) are of as various Original as those of the Skies, yet the Crop they produce, differs both in Kind and Degree, merely according to the Soil. I will produce two Instances to prove and Explain what I am now advancing.

A certain Great Prince[260] raised a mighty Army, filled his Coffers with infinite Treasures, provided an invincible Fleet; and all this without giving the least Part of his Design to his

---

[259] *Jakes* privy, toilet.

[260] *Great Prince* This was *Harry* the Great of France [Henry IV, assassinated in 1610, by a fanatical Roman Catholic; note in fifth edition].

greatest Ministers, or his nearest Favourites. Immediately the whole World was alarmed; the neighbouring Crowns, in trembling Expectation, towards what Point the Storm would burst; the small Politicians everywhere forming profound Conjectures. Some believed he had laid a Scheme for Universal Monarchy: Others, after much Insight, determined the Matter to be a Project for pulling down the *Pope*, and setting up the *Reformed* Religion, which had once been his own. Some, again, of a deeper Sagacity, sent him into *Asia* to subdue the *Turk,* and recover *Palestine*. In the midst of all these Projects and Preparations; a certain *State-Surgeon,* gathering the Nature of the Disease by these Symptoms, attempted the Cure, at one Blow performed the Operation, broke the Bag, and out flew the *Vapour*; nor did any thing want to render it a complete Remedy, only, that the Prince unfortunately happened to Die in the Performance. Now, is the Reader exceeding curious to learn from whence this *Vapour* took its Rise, which had so long set the Nations at a Gaze? What secret Wheel, what hidden Spring could put into Motion so wonderful an Engine? It was afterwards discovered, that the Movement of this whole Machine had been directed by an absent *Female,* whose Eyes had raised a Protuberancy, and before Emission, she was removed into an Enemy's Country. What should an unhappy Prince do in such ticklish Circumstances as these? He tried in vain the Poet's never-failing Receipt of *Corpora quæque*;[261] For,

> *Idque petit corpus mens unde est saucia amore;*
> *Unde feritur, eo tendit, gestitque coire.*   Lucr.[262]

Having to no purpose used all peaceable Endeavours, the collected Part of the *Semen*, raised and inflamed, became adust,[263] converted to Choler, turned head upon the spinal Duct, and ascended to the Brain. The very same Principle that influences a *Bully* to break the Windows of a Whore, who has jilted him, naturally stirs up a Great Prince to raise Mighty Armies, and dream of nothing, but Sieges, Battles, and Victories.

> —*Cunnus teterrima belli*
> *Causa*—˙[264]

The other Instance[265] is, what I have read somewhere, in a very ancient Author, of a Mighty King, who for the space of above thirty Years, amused himself to take and lose Towns; beat Armies, and be beaten; drive Princes out of their Dominions; fright Children from their Bread and Butter; burn, lay waste, plunder, dragoon, massacre, Subject and Stranger, Friend and Foe, Male and Female. 'Tis recorded, that the Philosophers of each Country were in grave Dispute, upon Causes Natural, Moral, and Political, to find out where they should assign an original Solution of this *Phenomenon*. At last the *Vapour* or *Spirit,* which animated the Hero's Brain, being in perpetual Circulation, seized upon that Region of the Human Body so renowned for furnishing the *Zibeta Occidentalis*,[266] and gathering there into

---

[261] *Corpora quæque* "any body," part of a prescription of promiscuity to avoid love (Lucretius 4.1065).

[262] *idque . . . Lucr.* "The body seeks the source of the mind's love-wound; it goes for the source and is eager for coition with it" (Lucretius 4.1048 and 1055).

[263] *adust* hot, burnt up; a description of bodily "humours" or psychological qualities, such as anger or melancholy, at one extreme.

[264] *Cunnus teterrima belli /Causa* "Cunt [was, long before Helen of Troy] the most hideous cause of war"

(Horace, *Satires* 1.3.107; "cunnus" was deleted in the fifth edition.

[265] *other Instance* This is meant of the Present *French* King [Louis XIV; note in fifth edition].

[266] *Zibeta Occidentalis* Paracelsus . . . tried an Experiment upon human Excrement, to make a Perfume of it, which when he had brought to Perfection, he called *Zibeta Occidentalis,* or Western-Civet, the back Parts of Man (according to his Division mentioned by the Author, page [624]) being West [note in fifth edition].

a Tumor, left the rest of the World for that Time in Peace. Of such mighty Consequence it is, where those Exhalations fix, and of so little, from whence they proceed. The same Spirits which in their superior Progress, would conquer a Kingdom, descending upon the *Anus*, conclude in a *Fistula*.[267]

Let us next examine the great Introducers of new Schemes in Philosophy, and search till we can find from what Faculty of the Soul, the Disposition arises in mortal Man, of taking it into his Head, to advance new Systems with such an eager Zeal in Things agreed on all Hands impossible to be known: From what Seeds this Disposition springs, and to what Quality of human Nature these Grand Innovators have been indebted for their Number of Disciples. Because, it is plain, that several of the Chief among them, both *Ancient* and *Modern*, were usually mistaken by their Adversaries, and indeed by all except their own Followers, to have been Persons crazed, or out of their Wits, having generally proceeded in the common Course of their Words and Actions, by a Method very different from the vulgar Dictates of *unrefined* Reason, agreeing for the most Part in their several Models, with their present undoubted Successors in the *Academy* of *Modern Bedlam*[268] (whose Merits and Principles I shall further examine in due Place.) Of this Kind were *Epicurus*,[269] *Diogenes*,[270] *Apollonius*,[271] *Lucretius*, *Paracelsus*,[272] *Descartes*, and others; who, if they were now in the World, tied fast, and separate from their Followers, would in this our undistinguishing Age, incur manifest Danger of *Phlebotomy*,[273] and *Whips*, and *Chains*, and *dark Chambers*, and *Straw*. For, what Man in the natural State, or Course of Thinking, did ever conceive it in his Power, to reduce the Notions of all Mankind, exactly to the same Length, and Breadth, and Height of his own? Yet this is the first humble and civil Design of all Innovators in the Empire of Reason. *Epicurus*, modestly hoped, that one Time or other, a certain Fortuitous Concourse of all Men's Opinions, after perpetual Justlings, the Sharp with the Smooth, the Light and the Heavy, the Round and the Square, would by certain *Clinamina*,[274] unite in the Notions of *Atoms* and *Void*, as these did in the Originals of all things. *Cartesius* reckoned to see before he died, the Sentiments of all Philosophers, like so many lesser Stars in his *Romantic*[275] System, rapt and drawn within his own *Vortex*.[276] Now, I would gladly be informed, how it is possible to account for such Imaginations as these in particular Men, without recourse to my *Phenomenon* of *Vapours*, ascending from the lower Faculties to over-shadow the Brain, and thence distilling into Conceptions for which the Narrowness of our Mother-Tongue has not yet assigned any other Name, beside that of *Madness* or *Frenzy*. Let us therefore now conjecture how it comes to pass, that none of these great Prescribers, do ever fail providing themselves and their Notions, with a number of implicit Disciples. And, I think, the Reason is easy to be assigned: For, there is a peculiar *String* in the Harmony of Human Understanding which in several Individuals, is exactly of the same Tuning. This, if you can dexterously screw up to its right Key, and then strike gently upon it; Whenever you have the good Fortune to light among those of the same Pitch, they will, by a secret necessary Sympathy, strike exactly at the same

[267] *Fistula* "A sinuous ulcer, callous within" (Johnson).

[268] *Bedlam* London asylum for the insane.

[269] *Epicurus* founded a radical third school in Athens, opposed to Plato's Academy and Aristotle's Lyceum, but his materialism or atomism, like *Lucretius'* and *Descartes'*, is what singles him out for ridicule here.

[270] *Diogenes* the Cynic, famous for taking up residence in a barrel and carrying a lighted candle symbolic of his search for an honest man.

[271] *Apollonius* of Tyana, a neo-Pythagorean of the first century CE, said to have performed miracles.

[272] *Paracelsus* Bombast von Hohenheim, Philippus Aureolus Theophrastus (1493–1541), alchemist and physician, known as Paracelsus after the ancient medical writer Celsus.

[273] *Phlebotomy* blood-letting.

[274] *Clinamina* the principle of swerving that explains the concourse of atoms in Lucretius' cosmology.

[275] *Romantic* "Improbable; false" (Johnson).

[276] *Vortex* a feature of Descartes' materialist cosmology.

Time. And in this one Circumstance, lies all the Skill or Luck of the Matter; for if you chance to jar the String amon2g those who are either above or below your own Height, instead of subscribing to your Doctrine, they will tie you fast, call you Mad, and feed you with Bread and Water. It is therefore a Point of the nicest Conduct to distinguish and adapt this noble Talent, with respect to the Differences of Persons and Times. *Cicero* understood this very well, when writing to a Friend in *England*, with a Caution, among other Matters, to beware of being cheated by our *Hackney-Coachmen* (who, it seems, in those Days were as arrant Rascals, as they are now) has these remarkable Words, *Est quod gaudeas te in ista loca venisse, ubi aliquid sapere viderere.*[277] For, to speak a bold Truth, it is a fatal Miscarriage, so ill to order Affairs, as to pass for a *Fool* in one Company, when in another, you might be treated as a *Philosopher.* Which I desire *some certain Gentlemen of my Acquaintance,* to lay up in their Hearts, as a very seasonable *Innuendo.*

This, indeed, was the Fatal Mistake of that worthy Gentleman, my most ingenious Friend, Mr. *W—tt—n:* A Person, in Appearance, ordained for great Designs, as well as Performances; whether you will consider his *Notions* or his *Looks.* Surely, no Man ever advanced into the Public with fitter Qualifications of Body and Mind for the Propagation of a new Religion. Oh, had those happy Talents, misapplied to vain Philosophy, been turned into their proper Channels of Dr*eams* and *Visions,* where *Distortion* of Mind and Countenance are of such Sovereign Use; the base detracting World would not then have dared to report, that something is amiss, that his Brain hath undergone an unlucky Shake, which even his Brother *Modernists* themselves, like Ungrates, do whisper so loud, that it reaches up to the very *Garret* I am now writing in.

Lastly, whoever pleases to look into the Fountains of *Enthusiasm,* from whence in all Ages, have eternally proceeded such fattening Streams, will find the Spring Head to have been as *Troubled* and *Muddy* as the Current; Of such great Emolument, is a Tincture of this *Vapour,* which the World calls *Madness,* that without its Help, the World would not only be deprived of those two great Blessings, *Conquests* and *Systems,* but even all Mankind would unhappily be reduced to the same Belief in Things Invisible. Now, the former *Postulatum* being held, that it is of no Import, from what Originals this *Vapour* proceeds, but either in what *Angles* it strikes and spreads over the Understanding, or upon what *Species* of Brain it ascends; It will be a very delicate Point, to cut the Feather, and divide the several Reasons to a nice and curious Reader, how this numerical Difference in the Brain can produce Effects of so vast a Difference from the same *Vapour,* as to be the sole Point of Individuation between *Alexander the Great, Jack* of *Leyden,* and *Monsieur Des Cartes.* The present Argument, is the most abstracted that I ever engaged in; it strains my Faculties to their highest Stretch; and I desire the Reader to attend with the utmost Perpensity; For, I now proceed to unravel this knotty Point.

There is in mankind a certain[278]   *   *   *   *   *   *
          *

*   *   *   *   *   *   *   *   *   *   *   *

Hic multa   *   *   *   *   *   *   *   *   *   *

---

[277]   *Est quod . . . viderere*   "You may well congratulate yourself on having reached those regions where you pass for a man who knows something [of the law]" (Cicero, *Letters to his Friends* 7.10; Loeb 216.33).

[278]   *a certain* . . . Here is another Defect in the Manuscript, but I think the Author did wisely, and that the Matter which thus strained his Faculties, was not worth a Solution; and it were well if all Metaphysical Cobweb Problems were no otherwise answered [note in fifth edition].

desiderantur.[279]   *   *   *   *   *   *   *   *   *
                  *

*   *   *   *   *   *   *   *   *   *   *
*   *   *   *   *   *   And this I take to be a clear Solution of
the Matter.

Having therefore so narrowly past through this intricate Difficulty, the Reader will, I am sure, agree with me in the Conclusion; that if the *Moderns* mean by *Madness*, only a Disturbance or Transportation of the Brain, by Force or certain *Vapours* issuing up from the lower Faculties; then has this *Madness* been the Parent of all those mighty Revolutions, that have happened in *Empire*, in *Philosophy*, and in *Religion*. For, the Brain, in its natural Position and State of Serenity, disposeth its Owner to pass his Life in the common Forms, without any Thought of subduing Multitudes to his own *Power*, his *Reasons*, or his *Visions*; And the more he shapes his Understanding by the Pattern of Human Learning, the less he is inclined to form Parties after his particular Notions; Because that instructs him in his private Infirmities, as well as in the stubborn Ignorance of the People. But when a Man's Fancy gets *astride* on his Reason, when Imagination is at Cuffs with the Senses, and common Understanding as well as common Sense, is kicked out of Doors; the first Proselyte he makes is Himself, and when that is once compassed, the Difficulty is not so great in bringing over others; A strong Delusion always operating from *without*, as vigorously as from *within*. For Cant and Vision are to the Ear and the Eye, the same that Tickling is to the Touch. Those Entertainments and Pleasures we most value in Life are such as *Dupe* and play the Wag with the Senses. For, if we take an Examination of what is generally understood by *Happiness*, as it has Respect either to the Understanding or the Senses; We shall find all its Properties and Adjuncts will herd under this short Definition; That, *it is a perpetual Possession of being well Deceived*. And first, with Relation to the Mind or Understanding; 'tis manifest, what mighty Advantages Fiction has over Truth; and the Reason is just at our Elbow; because Imagination can build nobler Scenes and produce more wonderful Revolution than Fortune or Nature will be at Expense to furnish. Nor is Mankind so much to blame in his Choice, thus determining him, if we consider that the Debate merely lies between *Things past*, and *Things conceived*; And so the Question is only this; Whether Things that have Place in the *Imagination*, may not as properly be said to *Exist*, as those that are seated in the *Memory*; which may be justly held in the Affirmative, and very much to the Advantage of the former, since this is acknowledged to be the *Womb* of Things, and the Other allowed to be no more than the *Grave*. Again, if we take this Definition of Happiness, and examine it with Reference to the Senses, it will be acknowledged wonderfully adapt. How fade and insipid do all Objects accost us, that are not conveyed in the Vehicle of *Delusion*? How shrunk is every Thing, as it appears in the Glass of Nature! So, that if it were not for the Assistance of artificial *Mediums*, false Lights, refracted Angles, Varnish, and Tinsel; there would be a mighty Level in the Felicity and Enjoyments of Mortal Men. If this were seriously considered by the World, as I have a certain Reason to Suspect it hardly will; Men would no longer reckon among their high Points of Wisdom the Art of exposing weak Sides, and publishing Infirmities; an Employment, in my Opinion, neither better nor worse than that of *Unmasking*, which, I think has never been allowed fair Usage, either in the *World* or the *Play-house*.

In the Proportion that Credulity is a more peaceful Possession of the Mind than Curiosity, so far preferable is that Wisdom, which converses about the Surface, to that pretended Philosophy which enters into the Depth of Things, and then comes gravely back with

---

[279] *Hic multa desiderantur* "Here much is lacking."

632 JONATHAN SWIFT A TALE OF A TUB

Informations and Discoveries, that in the Inside they are good for nothing. The two Senses, to which all Objects first Address themselves, are the Sight and the Touch; These never examine further than the Colour, the Shape, the Size, and whatever other Qualities dwell, or are drawn by Art upon the Outward of Bodies; and then comes Reason, officiously, with Tools for cutting, and opening, and mangling, and piercing, offering to demonstrate that they are not of the same consistence quite through. Now, I take all this to be the last Degree of perverting Nature; one of whose eternal Laws it is, to put her best Furniture[280] forward. And therefore, in order to save the Charges of all such expensive Anatomy for the Time to come; I do here think fit to inform the Reader, that in such Conclusions as these, Reason is certainly in the Right; And that in most Corporeal Beings which have fallen under my Cognisance, the Outside hath been infinitely preferable to the *In*: Whereof I have been further convinced from some late Experiments. Last Week I saw a Woman *flayed*, and you will hardly believe, how much it altered her Person for the worse. Yesterday I ordered the Carcass of *Beau* to be stripped in my Presence; when we were all amazed to find so many unsuspected Faults under one Suit of Clothes: Then I laid open his *Brain*, his *Heart*, and his *Spleen*; But, I plainly perceived at every Operation, that the further we proceeded, we found the Defects increase upon us in Number and Bulk: From all which, I justly formed this Conclusion to my self. That whatever Philosopher or Projector can find out an Art to solder and patch up the Flaws and Imperfections of Nature, will deserve much better of Mankind, and teach us a more useful Science, than that so much in present Esteem, of widening and exposing them (like him who held *Anatomy* to be the ultimate End of *Physic.*) And he, whose Fortunes and Dispositions have placed him in a convenient Station to enjoy the Fruits of this noble Art; He that can with *Epicurus* content his Ideas with the *Films* and *Images* that fly off upon his Senses from the *Superficies* of Things; Such a Man truly Wise, creams off Nature, leaving the Sour and the Dregs for Philosophy and Reason to lap up. This is the sublime and refined Point of Felicity, called, *the Possession of being well deceived*; The Serene peaceful State of being a Fool among Knaves.

But to return to *Madness*. It is certain, that according to the System I have above deduced; every *Species* thereof proceeds from a Redundancy of *Vapour*; therefore, as some Kinds of *Frenzy* give a double Strength to the Sinews, so there are of other *Species* which add Vigour, and Life, and Spirit to the Brain: Now, it usually happens, that these active Spirits, getting Possession of the Brain, resemble those that haunt other Waste and Empty Dwellings, which for want of Business, either vanish, and carry away a piece of the House, or else stay at home, and fling it all out of the Windows. By which are mystically displayed the two principal Branches of *Madness*; and which some Philosophers not considering so well as I, have mistook to be different in their Causes, over-hastily assigning the first to Deficiency, and the other to Redundance.

I think it therefore manifest, from what I have here advanced, that the main Point of Skill and Address is to furnish Employment for this Redundancy of *Vapour*, and prudently to adjust the Seasons of it; by which Means it may certainly become of cardinal and catholic Emolument in a Commonwealth. Thus, one Man chosing a proper Juncture, leaps into a Gulf, from thence proceeds a Hero, and is called the Saver of his Country; Another achieves the same Enterprise, but unluckily timing it, has left the Brand of *Madness* fixed as a Reproach upon his Memory; Upon so nice a Distinction are we taught to repeat the Name of *Curtius*[281] with Reverence and Love; that of *Empedocles*,[282] with Hatred and Contempt. Thus, also it is

---

[280] *Furniture* "Equipage; embellishments; decorations" (Johnson).

[281] *Curtius* Marcus Curtius sacrificed himself for Rome in 352 BCE.

[282] *Empedocles* jumped into flaming Mount Aetna in an attempt to gain immortal fame.

usually conceived, that the elder *Brutus*[283] only personated the *Fool* and *Madman*, for the good of the Public: but this was nothing else, than a Redundancy of the same *Vapour*, long misapplied, called by the *Latins, Ingenium par negotiis*:[284] Or, (to translate it as nearly as I can) a sort of *Frenzy*, never in its right Element, till you take it up in Business of the State.

Upon all which, and many other Reasons of equal Weight, though not equally curious; I do here gladly Embrace an Opportunity I have long sought for, of Recommending it as a very noble Undertaking, to Sir E——d S——r, Sir C——r M——ve, Sir J—n B—ls, J—n H——, Esq;[285] and other Patriots[286] concerned, that they would move for Leave to bring in a Bill, for appointing Commissioners to Inspect into *Bedlam*, and the Parts adjacent; who shall be empowered to *send for Persons, Papers, and Records*, to examine into the Merits and Qualifications of every Student and Professor; to observe with utmost Exactness their several Dispositions and Behaviour; by which means, duly distinguishing and adapting their Talents, they might produce admirable Instruments for the several Offices in a State, * * * * *,[287] *Civil*, and *Military*, proceeding in such Methods, as I shall here humbly propose. And, I hope, the Gentle Reader will give some Allowance to my great Solicitudes in this important Affair, upon Account of the high Esteem I have ever borne that honourable Society, whereof I had some time the Happiness to be an unworthy Member.

Is any Student[288] tearing his Straw in piece-meal, Swearing and Blaspheming, biting his Grate, foaming at the Mouth, and emptying his Pisspot in the Spectators' Faces? Let the Right Worshipful, the *Commissioners of Inspection*, give him a Regiment of Dragoons, and send him into Flanders among the *rest*. Is another eternally talking, sputtering, gaping, bawling, in a Sound without Period or Article? What wonderful Talents are here mislaid! Let him be furnished immediately with a green Bag and Papers and *three Pence*[289] in his Pocket, and away with Him to *Westminster-Hall*. You will find a Third, gravely taking the Dimensions of his Kennel, a Person of Foresight and Insight, though kept quite in the Dark; for why, like *Moses, Ecce cornuta erat ejus facies*.[290] He walks duly in one Pace, entreats your Penny with due Gravity and Ceremony, talks much of hard Times, and Taxes, and the *Whore of Babylon*;[291] Bars up the wooden Window of his Cell constantly at eight a Clock, Dreams of *Fire*, and *Shoplifters*, and *Court-Customers*, and *Privileged Places*. Now, what a Figure would all these Acquirements amount to, if the Owner were sent into the *City* among his Brethren! Behold a Fourth, in much and deep Conversation with himself, biting his Thumbs at proper Junctures; his Countenance chequered with Business and Design; sometimes walking very fast, with his Eyes nailed to a Paper that he holds in his Hands, a great Saver of Time, somewhat thick of Hearing, very short of Sight, but more of Memory. A Man ever in Haste, a great Hatcher and Breeder of Business, and excellent at the Famous Art of *whispering Nothing*. A huge Idolator

---

[283] *Brutus* Lucius Junius Brutus, consul of Rome (509 BCE), feigned madness to escape murder by Tarquin, the last Roman king.

[284] *Ingenium par negotiis* ability equal to the tasks at hand.

[285] *Sir E{dwar}d S{eymou}r, Sir C{hristophe}r M{usgra}ve, Sir J{oh}n B{ow}les, J{oh}n H{o}we Esq* leading Tory politicians of the time.

[286] *Patriots* a name adopted by anti-government Tories.

[287] * * . . . * Ecclesiastical.

[288] *Student* inmate of Bedlam, the London asylum for the insane; for another description, see the selection from Mackenzie, below, p. 1131.

[289] *three Pence* A Lawyer's Coach-hire [Swift's marginal note].

[290] *Ecce cornuta erat ejus facies* "Lo, his face was horned," a well-known mistranslation in the Latin or Vulgate Bible for a Hebrew word meaning "shining," like the surface of polished horn; a note in the fifth edition suggests this.

[291] *Whore of Babylon* a figure in the Book of Revelation taken by some Protestants to represent the Roman Catholic Church.

of Monosyllables and Procrastination: so ready to *Give* his Word to every Body that he never *keeps* it. One that has forgot the common *Meaning* of Words, but an admirable Retainer of the *Sound*. Extremely subject to the *Looseness*, for his *Occasions* are perpetually *calling him away*. If you approach his Grate in his familiar Intervals; 'Sir', says he, 'Give me a Penny, and I'll sing you a Song: But give me the Penny first'. (Hence comes the common Saying, and commoner Practice of parting with Money for a *Song*.) What a complete System of *Court-Skill* is here described in every Branch of it, and all utterly lost with wrong Application? Accost the Hole of another Kennel, first stopping your Nose, you will behold a surley, gloomy, nasty, slovenly Mortal, raking in his own Dung, and dabbling in his Urine. The best Part of his Diet, is the Reversion of his own Ordure, which expiring into Steams, whirls perpetually about, and at last reinfunds. His Complexion is of a dirty Yellow, with a thin scattered Beard, exactly agreeable to that of his Diet upon its first Declination; like other Insects, who having their Birth and Education in an Excrement, from thence borrow their Colour and their Smell. The Student of this Apartment is very sparing of his Words, but somewhat over-liberal of his Breath; He holds his Hand out ready to receive your Penny, and immediately upon Receipt, withdraws to his former Occupations. Now, is it not amazing to think, the society of *Warwick-Lane*,[292] should have no more Concern for the Recovery of so useful a Member, who, if one may judge from these Appearances, would become the greatest Ornament to that Illustrious Body? Another Student struts up fiercely to your Teeth, puffing with his Lips, half squeezing out his Eyes, and very graciously holds you out his Hand to kiss. The *Keeper* desires you not to be afraid of this Professor, for he will do you no Hurt: To him alone is allowed the Liberty of the Anti-chamber, and the *Orator* of that Place gives you to understand, that this solemn Person is a *Tailor* run mad with Pride. This considerable Student is adorned with many other Qualities, upon which, at present, I shall not further enlarge — —*Hark in your Ear* — — — —[293] I am strangely mistaken, if all his Address, his Motions, and his Airs, would not then be very natural, and in their proper Element.

I shall not descend so minutely, as to insist upon the vast Number of *Beaux, Fiddlers, Poets*, and *Politicians*, that the World might recover by such a Reformation: But what is more material, beside the clear Gain redounding to the Commonwealth, by so large an Acquisition of Persons to employ, whose Talents and Acquirements, if I may be so bold to affirm it, are now buried, or at least misapplied: It would be a mighty Advantage accruing to the Public from this Enquiry, that all these would very much excel, and arrive at great Perfection in their several Kinds; which, I think, is manifest from what I have already shown; and shall enforce by this one plain Instance; That even I my self, the Author of these momentuous Truths, am a Person, whose Imaginations are hard-mouthed,[294] and exceedingly disposed to run away with his *Reason*, which I have observed from long Experience, to be a very light Rider, and easily shook off; upon which Account, my Friends will never trust me alone, without a solemn Promise, to vent my Speculations in this, or the like manner, for the universal Benefit of Human kind; which, perhaps, the gentle, courteous, and candid Reader, brimful of that *Modern* Charity and Tenderness, usually annexed to his *Office*, will be very hardly persuaded to believe.

---

292   *society of Warwick-Lane* the Royal College of Physicians.
293   — —*Hark in your Ear* — — — — I cannot conjecture what the Author means here, or how this Chasm could be filled, though it is capable of more than one Interpretation [note in fifth edition].
294   *hard-mouthed* like a disobedient horse that does not feel the bit.

SECT. X
A TALE OF A TUB

It is an unanswerable Argument of a very refined Age, the wonderful Civilities that have passed of late Years, between the Nation of *Authors,* and that of *Readers.* There can hardly pop out a *Play,* a *Pamphlet,* or a *Poem,* without a Preface full of Acknowledgements to the World, for the general Reception and Applause they have given it, which the Lord knows where, or when, or how, or from whom it received. In due Deference to so laudable a Custom, I do here return my humble Thanks to *His Majesty,* and both Houses of *Parliament;* To the *Lords* of the King's most honourable Privy-Council; To the Reverend the *Judges;* To the *Clergy,* and *Gentry,* and *Yeomanry* of this Land: But in a more especial manner to my worthy Brethren and Friends at *Will's Coffee-house,* and *Gresham-College,* and *Warwick-Lane,* and *Moor-Fields,*[295] and *Scotland-Yard,* and *Westminister-Hall,* and *Guild-hall;*[296] In short, to all Inhabitants and Retainers whatsoever, either in Court, or Church, or Camp, or City, or Country, for their generous and universal Acceptance of this Divine Treatise. I accept their Approbation, and good Opinion with extreme Gratitude, and to the utmost of my poor Capacity, shall take hold of all Opportunities to return the Obligation.

I am also happy that Fate has flung me into so blessed an Age for the mutual Felicity of *Booksellers* and *Authors,* whom I may safely affirm to be at this Day the two only satisfied Parties in *England.* Ask an *Author* how his last Piece hath succeeded; 'Why, truly he thanks his Stars, the World has been very favourable, and he has not the least Reason to complain: And yet, By G—, He writ it in a Week, at Bits and Starts, when he could steal an Hour from his urgent Affairs'; as, it is a hundred to one, you may see further in the Preface; to which he refers you, and for the rest, to the Bookseller. There you go as a Customer, and make the same Question: He blesses his God the *Thing* takes wonderfully, he is just printing a Second Edition, and has but three left in his Shop. You beat down the Price: 'Sir, we shall not differ'; and in hopes of your Custom another Time, lets you have it as reasonable as you please; 'And, pray send as many of your Acquaintance as you will, I shall, upon your Account furnish them all at the same Rate'.

Now, it is not well enough considered, to what Accidents and Occasions the World is indebted for the greatest Part of these noble Writings, which hourly start up to entertain it. If it were not for a *rainy Day, a drunken Vigil, a Fit of the Spleen, a Course of Physic, a sleepy Sunday, an ill Run at Dice, a long Tailor's Bill, a Beggar's Purse, a factious Head, a hot Sun, costive Diet, Want of Books, and a just Contempt of Learning.* But for these Events, I say, and some Others too long to recite (especially *a prudent Neglect of taking Brimstone inwardly*) I doubt the Number of *Authors* and of *Writings* would dwindle away to a Degree most woeful to behold. To confirm this Opinion, hear the Words of the famous *Troglodyte* Philosopher: ' 'Tis certain', said he, 'some Grains of Folly are of course annexed, as Part in the Composition of Human Nature, only the Choice is left us, whether we please to wear them *Inlaid* or *Embossed*: And we need not go very far to seek how That is usually determined, when we remember, it is with Human Faculties as with Liquors, the lightest will be ever at the Top'.

There is in this famous Island of *Britain* a certain paltry *Scribbler,* very voluminous, whose Character the Reader cannot wholly be Stranger to. He deals in a pernicious Kind of Writings called *Second Parts,* and usually passes under the Name of *The Author of the First.* I easily foresee, that as soon as I lay down my Pen, this nimble *Operator* will have stole it, and treat

---

[295] *Moor-Fields* the location of Bedlam.   [296] *Guild-hall* a London courthouse.

me as inhumanly as he hath already done Dr. B———re,[297] L———ge,[298] and many others who shall here be nameless. I therefore fly for Justice and Relief, into the Hands of that great *Rectifier of Saddles*, and *Lover of Mankind*, Dr. B———tly, begging he will take this enormous Grievance into his most *Modern* Consideration: And if it should so happen that the *Furniture*[299] *of an Ass*, in the Shape of a *Second Part*, must for my Sins, be clapped by a Mistake, upon my Back, that he will immediately please, in the Presence of the World, to lighten me of the Burthen, and take it Home to *his own House,* till the *true Beast* thinks fit to call for it.

In the mean time I do here give this public Notice, that my Resolutions are to circumscribe within this Discourse the whole Stock of Matter I have been so many Years providing. Since my V*ein* is once opened, I am content to exhaust it all at a Running, for the peculiar Advantage of my dear Country, and for the universal Benefit of Mankind. Therefore, hospitably considering the Number of my Guests, they shall have my whole Entertainment at a Meal; And I scorn to set up the *Leavings* in the Cupboard. What the *Guests* cannot eat may be given to the *Poor*, and the *Dogs* under the Table may gnaw the *Bones*; This I understand for a more generous Proceeding, than to turn the Company's Stomachs, by inviting them again to morrow to a scurvy Meal of *Scraps*.

If the Reader fairly considers the Strength of what I have advanced in the foregoing Section, I am convinced it will produce a wonderful Revolution in his Notions and Opinions; And he will be abundantly better prepared to receive and to relish the concluding Part of this miraculous Treatise. Readers may be divided into three Classes – the *Superficial*, the *Ignorant*, and the *Learned*: and I have with much Felicity fitted my Pen to the Genius and Advantage of each. The *Superficial* Reader will be strangely provoked to *Laughter*; which clears the Breast and the Lungs, is Sovereign against the *Spleen*, and the most innocent of all *Diuretics*. The *Ignorant* Reader (between whom and the former, the Distinction is extremely nice) will find himself disposed to *Stare*; which is an admirable Remedy for ill Eyes, serves to raise and enliven the Spirits, and wonderfully helps *Perspiration*. But the Reader truly *Learned*, chiefly for whose Benefit, I wake when others sleep, and sleep when others wake, will here find sufficient Matter to employ his Speculations for the rest of his Life. It were much to be wished, and I do here humbly propose for an Experiment, that every Prince in *Christendom* will take seven of the *deepest Scholars* in his Dominions, and shut them up close for *seven* Years in *seven* Chambers, with a Command to write *seven* ample Commentaries on this comprehensive Discourse. I shall venture to affirm, that whatever Difference may be found in their several Conjectures, they will be all without the least Distortion, manifestly deduceable from the Text. Mean time, it is my earnest Request, that so useful an Undertaking may be entered upon (if their Majesties please) with all convenient Speed; because, I have a strong Inclination, before I leave the World, to taste a Blessing which we *Mysterious* Writers can seldom reach, till we have got into our Graves. Whether it is that F*ame,* being a Fruit grafted on the Body, can hardly grow, and much less ripen, till the *Stock*[300] is in the Earth: Or, whether she be a Bird of Prey, and is lured among the rest, to pursue after the Scent of a *Carcass*: Or, whether she conceives her Trumpet sounds best and farthest, when she stands on a *Tomb*, by the Advantage of a rising Ground, and the Echo of a hollow Vault.

'Tis true, indeed, the Republic of *dark* Authors, after they once found out this excellent Expedient of *Dying*, have been peculiarly happy in the Variety as well as extent of their

---

[297]   *B———re*   Richard Blackmore (1655–1729), physician and author of two epic poems.
[298]   *L———ge*   Roger L'Estrange (1616–1704) Tory journalist, prolific writer and translator.
[299]   *Furniture*   saddle, stirrups, etc.
[300]   *Stock*   "The trunk into which a graft is inserted" (Johnson).

Reputation. For, *Night* being the universal Mother of things, wise Philosophers hold all Writings to be *fruitful*, in the Proportion they are *dark;* And therefore, the *true Illuminated* (that is to say, the *Darkest* of all) have met with such numberless Commentators, whose *Scholiastic*[301] Midwifery hath delivered them of Meanings that the Authors themselves perhaps never conceived, and yet may very justly be allowed the Lawful Parents of them: the Words of such Writers being like Seed, which, however scattered at random, when they light upon a fruitful Ground, will multiply far beyond either the Hopes or Imagination of the Sower.

And therefore in order to promote so useful a Work, I will here take Leave to glance a few *Innuendoes*, that may be of great Assistance to those sublime Spirits, who shall be appointed to labour in a universal Comment upon this wonderful Discourse. And First, I have couched a very profound Mystery in the Number of O's multiplied by *Seven*, and divided by *Nine*. Also, if a devout Brother of the *Rosy-cross*[302] will pray fervently for sixty three Mornings, with a lively Faith, and then transpose certain Letters and Syllables according to Prescription in the second and fifth Section; they will certainly reveal into a full Receipt of the *Opus Magnum*. Lastly, Whoever will be at the Pains to calculate the whole Number of each Letter in this Treatise, and sum up the Difference exactly between the several Numbers, assigning the true natural Cause for every such Difference, the Discoveries in the Product, will plentifully Reward his Labour. But then he must beware of *Bythus* and *Sigè*,[303] and be sure not to forget the Qualities of *Acamoth*; *A cujus lacrymis humecta prodit Substantia, à risu lucida, à tristitia solida, et à timore mobilis*; wherein *Eugenius Philalethes*[304] hath committed an unpardonable Mistake.[305]

SECT. XI

A TALE OF A TUB

After so wide a Compass as I have wandered, I do now gladly overtake and close in with my Subject, and shall henceforth hold on with it an even Pace to the End of my Journey, except some beautiful Prospect appears within sight of my Way; whereof, though at present I have neither Warning nor Expectation, yet upon such an Accident, come when it will, I shall beg my Reader's Favour and Company, allowing me to conduct him through it along with my self. For in *Writing,* it is as in *Travelling*: If a Man is in haste to be at home (which

---

[301] *Scholiastic* having to do with commentary, or the practice of adding scholia (notes).

[302] *Rosy-cross* Rosicrucian Society, a christian brotherhood with mystical beliefs.

[303] *Bythus* and *Sigè* I was told by an Eminent Divine, whom I consulted on this Point, that these two Barbarous Words, with that of *Acamoth* [Hebrew, "wisdom"] and its Qualities, as here set down, are quoted from *Irenaeus*. This he discoverd by searching that Ancient Writer for another Quotation of our Author, which he has placed in the Title Page, and refers to the Book and Chapter; the Curious were very Inquisitive, whether those Barbarous Words, *Basima Eacabasa*, &c. are really in *Irenaeus* [*Against Heresies* 1.4.2] , and upon enquiry 'twas found they were a sort of Cant or Jargon of certain Heretics, and therefore very properly prefixed to such a Book as this is of our Author [note in fifth edition].

[304] *Eugenius Philalethes* To the abovementioned [in Swift's marginal note] Treatise, called *Anthroposophia Theomagica*, there is another annexed, called *Anima Magica Abscondita*, written by the same Author [Thomas] Vaughan, under the Name of Eugenius Philalethes, but in neither of those Treatises is there any mention of Acamoth or its Qualities, so that this is nothing but Amusement, and a Ridicule of dark, unintelligible Writers; only the Words, A cujus lacrymis, &c. are as we have said, transcribed from Irenaeus, though I know not from what part. I believe one of the Author's Designs was to set curious Men a hunting through Indexes, and enquiring for Books out of the common Road [note in fifth edition].

[305] *A cujus lacrymis . . . mobilis* "from the tears of which come damp essences, from the laughter light ones, from the sadness solid ones, and from the fear moving essences."

I acknowledge to be none of my Case, having never so little Business, as when I am there), if his *Horse* be tired with long Riding and ill Ways or be naturally a Jade, I advise him clearly to make the straightest and the commonest Road, be it ever so dirty; But then surely we must own such a Man to be a scurvy Companion at best; He *spatters* himself and his Fellow-Travellers at every Step: All their Thoughts, and Wishes, and Conversation turn entirely upon the Subject of their Journey's End; and at every Splash, and Plunge, and Stumble, they heartily wish one another at the Devil.

On the other side, when a Traveller and his *Horse* are in Heart and Plight, when his Purse is full and the Day before him; he takes the Road only where it is clean or convenient; entertains his Company there as agreeably as he can; but upon the first Occasion, carries them along with him to every delightful Scene in View, whether of Art, of Nature, or of both; and if they chance to refuse out of Stupidity or Weariness; let them jog on by themselves, and be d—n'd; He'll overtake them at the next Town; at which arriving, he Rides furiously through, the Men, Women, and Children run out to gaze, a hundred *noisy Curs*[306] run *barking* after him, of which, if he honours the boldest with a *Lash of his Whip*, it is rather out of Sport than Revenge: But should some *sourer Mongrel* dare too near an Approach, he receives a *Salute* on the Chaps by an accidental Stroke from the Courser's Heels (nor is any Ground lost by the Blow) which sends him yelping and limping home.

I now proceed to sum up the singular Adventures of my renowned *Jack*; the State of whose Dispositions and Fortunes, the careful Reader does, no doubt, most exactly remember, as I last parted with them in the Conclusion of a former Section. Therefore, his next Care must be from two of the foregoing, to extract a Scheme of Notions, that may best fit his Understanding for a true Relish of what is to ensue.

Jack had not only calculated the first Revolution of his Brain so prudently, as to give Rise to that Epidemic Sect of *Æolists,* but succeeding also into a new and strange Variety of Conceptions, the Fruitfulness of his Imagination led him into certain Notions, which, although in Appearance very unaccountable, were not without their Mysteries and their Meanings, nor wanted Followers to countenance and improve them. I shall therefore be extremely careful and exact in recounting such material Passages of this Nature, as I have been able to collect, either from undoubted Tradition, or indefatigable Reading; and shall describe them as graphically as it is possible, and as far as Notions of that Height and Latitude can be brought within the Compass of a Pen. Nor do I at all question, but they will furnish Plenty of noble Matter for such, whose converting Imaginations dispose them to reduce all Things into *Types*; who can make *Shadows*, no thanks to the Sun; and then mould them into Substances, no thanks to Philosophy; whose peculiar Talent lies in fixing Tropes and Allegories to the *Letter*, and refining what is Literal into Figure and Mystery.

Jack had provided a fair Copy of his Father's *Will* engrossed in Form upon a large Skin of Parchment; and resolving to act the Part of a most dutiful Son, he became the fondest Creature of it imaginable. For, although, as I have often told the Reader, it consisted wholly in certain plain, easy Directions about the management and wearing of their Coats, with Legacies and Penalties in case of Obedience or Neglect; yet He began to entertain a Fancy, that the matter was *deeper* and *darker*, and therefore must needs have a great deal more of Mystery at the Bottom. 'Gentlemen', said he, 'I will prove this very Skin of Parchment to be Meat, Drink, and Cloth, to be the Philosopher's Stone,[307] and the Universal Medicine'. In

---

[306] *noisy Curs* By these are meant what the Author calls, The *True Critics* [note in fifth edition].

[307] *Philosopher's Stone* "A stone dreamed of by alchemists, which, by its touch, converts base metals into gold" (Johnson).

consequence of which Raptures, he resolved to make use of it in the most necessary, as well as the most paltry Occasions of Life. He had a Way of working it into any Shape he pleased; so that it served him for a Night-cap when he went to Bed, and for an Umbrella in rainy Weather. He would lap a Piece of it about a sore Toe, or when he had Fits, burn two Inches under his Nose; or if any Thing lay heavy on his Stomach, scrape off and swallow as much of the Powder as would lie on a silver Penny, they were all infallible Remedies. With Analogy to these Refinements, his common Talk and Conversation, ran wholly in the Phrase of his Will, and he circumscribed the utmost of his Eloquence within that Compass, not daring to let slip a Syllable without Authority from thence. Once at a strange House he was suddenly taken short, upon an urgent Juncture, whereon it may not be allowed too particularly to dilate; and being not able to call to mind, with that Suddenness, the Occasion required, an Authentic Phrase for demanding the Way to the Backside;[308] he chose rather as the more prudent Course, to incur the Penalty in such Cases usually annexed. Neither was it possible for the united Rhetoric of Mankind to prevail with him to make himself clean again: Because having consulted the Will upon this Emergency, he met with a Passage near the Bottom[309] (whether foisted in by the Transcriber, is not known) which seemed to forbid it.

He made it a Part of his Religion, never to say Grace to his Meat, nor could all the World persuade him, as the common Phrase is, to eat his Victuals *like a Christian*.

He bore a strange kind of Appetite to *Snap-Dragon*,[310] and to the livid Snuffs of a burning Candle, which he would catch and swallow with an Agility, wonderful to conceive; and by this Procedure, maintained a perpetual Flame in his Belly, which issuing in a glowing Stream from both his Eyes as well as his Nostrils, and his Mouth; made his Head appear in a dark Night, like the Skull of an Ass, wherein a roguish Boy hath conveyed a Farthing Candle, *to the Terror of his Majesty's Liege Subjects*. Therefore, he made use of no other Expedient to light himself home, but was wont to say, That 'a Wise Man was his own Lantern'.

He would shut his Eyes as he walked along the Streets, and if he happened to bounce his Head against a Post, or fall into the Kennel (as he seldom missed either to do one or both) he would tell the gibing Prentices, who looked on, that he submitted with entire Resignation, as to a Trip, or a Blow of Fate, with whom he found by long Experience, how vain it was either to wrestle or to cuff; and whoever durst undertake to do either, would be sure to come off with a swinging Fall, or a bloody Nose. 'It was ordained', said he, 'some few Days before the Creation, that my Nose and this very Post should have a Recounter, and therefore Nature thought fit to send us both into the World in the same Age, and to make us Country-men and Fellow-Citizens. Now, had my Eyes been open it is very likely, the Business might have been a great deal worse: For how many a confounded Slip is daily got by Man, with all his Foresight about him? Besides, the Eyes of the Understanding see best, when those of the Senses are out of the way; and therefore, blind Men are observed to tread their Steps with much more Caution, and Conduct, and Judgement, than those why rely with too much Confidence, upon the Virtue of the visual Nerve which every little Accident shakes out of Order, and a Drop, or a Film, can wholly disconcert; like a Lantern among a Pack of roaring Bullies, when they scour the Streets; exposing its Owner and itself to outward Kicks and Buffets, which both might have escaped if the Vanity of Appearing would have suffered them

---

[308] *Backside* backyard.

[309] I cannot guess the Author's meaning here, which I would be very glad to know, because it seems to be of Importance [note in fifth edition; an industrious editor has identified the passage as Revelation 22.11, "he which is filthy, let him be filthy still"].

[310] *Snap-Dragon* "A kind of play, in which brandy is set on fire, and raisins thrown into it, which those who are unused to the sport are afraid to take out; but which may be safely snatched by a quick motion, and put blazing into the mouth, which being closed, the fire is at once extinguished" (Johnson).

to walk in the Dark. But further, if we examine the *Conduct* of these boasted Lights, it will prove yet a great deal worse than their *Fortune*: 'Tis true, I have broke my Nose against this Post because Providence either forgot, or did not think it convenient, to twitch me by the Elbow, and give me notice to avoid it. But let not this encourage either the present Age or Posterity, to trust their *Noses* into the keeping of their Eyes, which may prove the fairest Way of losing them for good and all. For, O ye Eyes, Ye blind Guides; miserable Guardians are Ye of our frail Noses; Ye, I say, who fasten upon the first Precipice in view, and then tow our wretched willing Bodies after You, to the very Brink of Destruction: But, alas, that Brink is rotten, our Feet slip, and we tumble down prone into a Gulf, without one hospitable Shrub in the Way to break the Fall; a Fall, to which not any Nose of mortal Make is equal, except that of the Giant *Lauralco*,[311] who was Lord of the *Silver Bridge*. Most properly therefore, O Eyes, and with great Justice, may You be compared to those foolish Lights, which conduct Men through Dirt and Darkness, till they fall into a deep Pit, or a noisome Bog'.

This I have produced as a Scantling of *Jack*'s great Eloquence and the Force of his Reasoning upon such abstruse Matters.

He was, besides, a Person of great Design and Improvement in Affairs of *Devotion,* having introduced a new Deity, who hath since met with a vast Number of Worshippers; by some called *Babel,* by others, *Chaos;* who had an ancient temple of *Gothic* Structure upon *Salisbury* Plain;[312] famous for its Shrine and Celebration by Pilgrims.

When he had some Roguish Trick to play, he would down with his Knees, up with his Eyes, and fall to Prayers, though in the midst of the Kennel. Then it was that those who understood his Pranks, would be sure to get far enough out of his Way; And whenever Curiosity attracted Strangers to Laugh, or to Listen; he would of a sudden, with one Hand, out with his *Gear,* and piss full in their Eyes, and with the other, all to-bespatter them with Mud.

In Winter he went always loose and unbuttoned, and clad as thin as possible, to let *in* the ambient Heat; and in Summer, lapped himself close and thick to keep it *out.*

In all Revolutions of Government, he would make his Court for the Office of *Hangman* General; and in the Exercise of that Dignity, wherein he was very dexterous, would make use of no other *Vizard*[313] than a *long Prayer.*

He had a Tongue so Musculous and Subtle, that he could twist it up into his Nose, and deliver a strange Kind of Speech from thence. He was also the first in these Kingdoms, who began to improve the *Spanish* Accomplishment of *Braying*;[314] and having large Ears, perpetually exposed and erect, he carried his Art to such a Perfection, that it was a Point of great Difficulty to distinguish either, by the View or the Sound, between the *Original* and the *Copy.*

He was troubled with a Disease, reverse to that called the Stinging of the *Tarantula*; and would run Dog-mad at the Noise of *Music*,[315] especially a *Pair of Bag-Pipes.* But he would cure himself again, by taking two or three Turns in *Westminster-Hall,* or *Billingsgate,*[316] or in a *Boarding-School,* or the *Royal-Exchange,* or a *State Coffee-House.*

He was a Person that *feared* no *Colours* but mortally *hated* all, and upon that Account, bore a cruel Aversion to *Painters*; insomuch, that in his Paroxysms, as he walked the Streets, he would have his Pockets loaden with Stone, to pelt at the *Signs.*

Gothic Structure upon Salisbury Plain Stonehenge.
Vizard mask.
Braying an allusion to *Don Quixote,* chapters 25 and 27.

Music the poison of the tarantula was supposed to be counteracted by the effects of music.
Billingsgate the fish market.

Having from this manner of Living, frequent Occasions to *wash* himself, he would often leap over Head and Ears into the Water, though it were in the midst of the Winter, but was always observed to come out again much *dirtier*, if possible, than he went in.

He was the first that ever found out the Secret of contriving a *Soporiferous* Medicine to be conveyed in at the *Ears*; It was a Compound of *Sulphur* and *Balm of Gilead*,[317] with a little *Pilgrim's Salve*.

He wore a large Plaster of artificial *Caustics* on his Stomach, with the Fervour of which, he could set himself a *groaning*, like the famous *Board*[318] upon Application of a red hot Iron.

He would stand in the Turning of a Street, and calling to those who passed by, would cry to One; 'Worthy Sir, do me the Honour of a good Slap in the Chaps'. To another, 'Honest Friend, pray, favour me with a handsome Kick on the Arse'. 'Madam, shall I entreat a small Box in the Ear from your Ladyship's fair Hands?' 'Noble Captain, Lend a reasonable Thwack, for the Love of God, with that Cane of yours, over these poor Shoulders'. And when he had by such earnest Solicitations, made a shift to procure a Basting sufficient to swell up his Fancy and his Sides; He would return home extremely comforted, and full of terrible Accounts of what he had undergone for the *Public Good.* 'Observe this Stroke', said he, showing his bare Shoulders, 'a plaguey *Janisary* gave it me this very Morning at seven a Clock, as, with much ado, I was driving off the *Great Turk*. Neighbours mine, this broken Head deserves a Plaster; had poor *Jack* been tender of his Noddle you would have seen the *Pope*, and the *French* King, long before this time of Day, among your Wives and your Ware-houses. Dear *Christians*, the *Great Mogul was come as far as White-Chapel*, and you may thank these poor Sides that he hath not (God bless us) already swallowed up Man, Woman, and Child'.

It was highly worth observing the singular Effects of that Aversion, or Antipathy, which *Jack* and his Brother *Peter* seemed, even to an Affectation, to bear towards each other. *Peter* had lately done *some Rogueries,* that forced him to abscond; and he seldom ventured to stir out before Night, for fear of Bailiffs. Their Lodgings were at the two most distant Parts of the Town, from each other; and whenever their Occasions, or Humours called them abroad, they would make Choice of the oddest unlikely Times, and most uncouth Rounds they could invent, that they might be sure to avoid one another: Yet after all this, it was their perpetual Fortune to meet. The Reason of which, is easy enough to apprehend: For, the Frenzy and the Spleen of both, having the same Foundation, we may look upon them as two Pair of Compasses, equally extended, and the fixed Foot of each, remaining in the same Centre; which, though moving contrary Ways at first, will be sure to encounter somewhere or other in the Circumference. Besides, it was among the great Misfortunes of *Jack,* to bear a huge Personal Resemblance with his Brother *Peter*. Their Humour and Dispositions were not only the same, but there was a close Analogy in their Shape, their Size, and their Mien. Insomuch, as nothing was more frequent than for a Bailiff to seize *Jack* by the Shoulders, and cry: 'Mr. *Peter*, You are the king's Prisoner'. Or, at other Times, for one of *Peter*'s nearest Friends, to accost *Jack* with open Arms, 'Dear *Peter*, I am glad to see thee, pray send me one of your best Medicines for the Worms'. This we may suppose, was a mortifying Return of those Pains and Proceedings, *Jack* had laboured in so long; And finding, how directly opposite all his Endeavours had answered to the sole End and Intention, which he had proposed to himself; How could it avoid having terrible Effects upon a Head and Heart so furnished as his? However, the poor Remainders of his *Coat* bore all the Punishment; The orient Sun never entered upon his diurnal Progress, without missing a Piece of it. He hired a Tailor to stitch

317 *Balm of Gilead* "juice drawn from the balsam tree" (Johnson translating Calmet's dictionary of the Bible).   318 *famous Board* the "groaning board" was a kind of hoax displayed in London for a time.

up the Collar so close, that it was ready to choke him, and squeezed out his Eyes at such a Rate, as one could see nothing but the White. What little was left of the main Substance of the Coat, he rubbed every Day for two hours, against a rough-cast Wall, in order to grind away the Remnants of *Lace* and *Embroidery*; but at the same time went on with so much Violence, that he proceeded a *Heathen Philosopher*. Yet after all he could do of this kind, the Success continued still to disappoint his Expectation. For, as it is the Nature of Rags, to bear a kind of mock Resemblance to Finery; there being a sort of fluttering Appearance in both, which is not to be distinguished at a Distance, in the Dark, or by short-sighted Eyes; So, in those Junctures, it fared with *Jack* and his Tatters, that they offered to the first View, a ridiculous Flaunting, which, assisting the Resemblance in Person and Air, thwarted all his Projects of Separation, and left so near a Similitude between them, as frequently deceived the very Disciples and followers of both.

* * * * * * * * * * * *
* * * * * * * * * * * *
Desunt non- * * * * * * * *
nulla[319] * * * * * * * * *
  *
* * * * * * * * * * * *
* * * * * * * * * * * *

The old *Sclavonian* Proverb said well, That 'it is with *Men* as with Asses; whoever would keep them fast, may find a very good Hold at their *Ears*'. Yet, I think, we may affirm, and it hath been verified by repeated Experience, that,

Effugiet tamen hæc sceleratus vincula Proteus.[320]

It is good, therefore, to read the Maxims of our Ancestors, with great Allowances to Times and Persons: For, if we look into Primitive Records, we shall find, that no Revolutions have been so great, or so frequent, as those of human *Ears*. In former Days, there was a curious Invention to catch and keep them; which, I think, we may justly reckon among the *Artes perditæ*:[321] And how can it be otherwise, when in these latter Centuries, the very Species is not only diminished to a very lamentable Degree, but the poor Remainder is also degenerated so far, as to mock our skilfullest *Tenure?* For, if the only slitting of one *Ear* in a Stag, hath been found sufficient to propagate the Defect through a whole Forest; Why should we wonder at the greatest Consequences, from so many Loppings and Mutilations, to which the *Ears* of our Fathers and our own, have been of late so much exposed? 'Tis true, indeed, that while this *Island* of ours, was under the *Dominion of Grace*, many Endeavours were made to improve the Growth of *Ears* once more among us. The Proportion of Largeness was not only looked upon as an Ornament of the *Outward* Man, but as a Type of Grace in the *Inward*.[322] Besides, it is held by Naturalists, that if there be a Protuberancy of Parts in the *Superior* Region of the Body, as in the *Ears* and *Nose*, there must be a Parity also in the *Inferior*: And therefore in that truly pious Age, the *Males* in every Assembly, according as they were gifted, appeared very forward in exposing their *Ears* to view, and the Regions about them; because *Hippocrates*[323]

---

[319] *Desunt non-nulla* "Much is missing."
[320] *Effugiet tamen hæc sceleratus vincula Proteus* "Nevertheless, that rascal Proteus escapes all these chains" (Horace, *Satires* 2.3.71, where Proteus is a debtor from whom it is impossible to collect).
[321] *Artes perditæ* lost arts.

[322] *Grace in the Inward* Protestants who look for signs of inner grace, or Roundheads in the Civil War, who wore short hair and thus exposed their ears.
[323] *Hippocrates* Lib. de aëre locis & aquis [Swift's marginal note, which gives true citations of the early Greek physician and aphorist].

tells us, 'that when the Vein behind the *Ear* happens to be cut, a Man becomes a Eunuch'. And the *Females* were nothing backwarder in beholding and edifying by them: Whereof those who had already *used the Means*, looked about them with great Concern, in hopes of conceiving a suitable Offspring by such a Prospect: Others, who stood Candidates for *Benevolence*, found there a plentiful Choice, and were sure to fix upon such as discovered the largest *Ears*, that the Breed might not dwindle between them. Lastly, the devouter Sisters, who looked upon all extraordinary Dilatations of that Member, as Protrusions of Zeal, or spiritual Excrescencies, were sure to honour every Head they sat upon, as if they had been *cloven Tongues*;[324] but, especially, that of the Preacher, whose *Ears* were usually of the prime Magnitude: which upon that Account, he was very frequent and exact in exposing with all Advantages to the people: in his Rhetorical *Paroxysms,* turning sometimes to *hold forth* the one, and sometimes to *hold forth* the other: From which Custom, the whole Operation of Preaching is to this very Day among their Professors, styled by the Phrase of *Holding forth.*

Such was the Progress of the *Saints,* for advancing the Size of that Member. And it is thought, the Success would have been every way answerable, if in process of time, a cruel King[325] had not arose, who raised a bloody Persecution against all *Ears,* above a certain Standard: Upon which, some were glad to hide their flourishing Sprouts in a black Border, others crept wholly under a Periwig: some were slit, others cropped, and a great Number sliced off to the Stumps. But of this, more hereafter, in my *general History of Ears*; which I design very speedily to bestow upon the Public.

From this brief Survey of the falling State of E*ars,* in the last Age, and the small Care had to advance their ancient Growth in the present, it is manifest, how little Reason we can have to rely upon a Hold so short, so weak, and so slippery; and that, whoever desires to catch Mankind fast, must have Recourse to some other Methods. Now, he that will examine Human Nature with Circumspection enough, may discover several *Handles*, whereof the *Six* Senses afford one apiece, beside a great Number that are screwed to the Passions, and some few riveted to the Intellect. Among these last, *Curiosity* is one, and of all others, affords the firmest Grasp; *Curiosity*, that Spur in the side, that Bridle in the Mouth, that Ring in the Nose, of a lazy, an impatient, and a grunting Reader. By this *Handle* it is, that an Author should seize upon his Readers; which as soon as he hath once compassed, all Resistance and struggling are in vain; and they become his Prisoners as close as he pleases, till Weariness or Dullness force him to let go his Grip.

And therefore, I the Author of this miraculous Treatise, having hitherto, beyond Expectation, maintained by the aforesaid *Handle*, a firm Hold upon my gentle Readers; it is with great Reluctance, that I am at length compelled to remit my Grasp; leaving them in the Perusal of what remains, to that natural *Oscitancy* inherent in the Tribe. I can only assure thee, Courteous Reader, for both our Comforts, that my Concern is altogether equal to thine, for my Unhappiness in losing, or mislaying among my Papers the remaining Part of these Memoirs; which consisted of Accidents, Turns, and Adventures, both New, Agreeable, and Surprising; and therefore, calculated in all due Points, to the delicate Taste of this our noble Age. But, alas, with my utmost Endeavours, I have been able only to retain a few of the Heads. Under which, there was a full Account, how *Peter* got a *Protection* out of the *King's-Bench*; And of a Reconcilement between *Jack* and Him, upon a Design they had in a certain

---

[324] *cloven Tongues* part of the pentecostal vision described in Acts 2.3.

[325] *cruel King* This was King *Charles* the Second, who at his Restoration turned out all the Dissenting Teachers that would not conform [note in fifth edition].

rainy Night to trepan[326] Brother *Martin* into a *Spunging-house*,[327] and there strip him to the Skin. How *Martin*, with much ado, showed them both a fair pair of Heels. How a *new Warrant* came out against *Peter;* upon which, how *Jack* left him in the lurch, *stole his Protection, and made use of it himself.* How *Jack*'s Tatters came into Fashion in *Court* and *City*; How *he got upon a great Horse, and eat Custard.*[328] But the Particulars of all these, with several others, which have now slid out of my Memory, are lost beyond all Hopes of Recovery. For, which Misfortune, leaving my Readers to condole with each other, as far as they shall find it to agree with their several Constitutions; but conjuring them by all the Friendship that hath passed between Us, from the Title-Page to this, not to proceed so far as to injure their Healths, for an Accident past Remedy; I now go on to the Ceremonial Part of an accomplished Writer and therefore, by a Courtly *Modern*, least of all others to be omitted.

THE CONCLUSION

Going too long is a Cause of Abortion as effectual, though not so frequent, as *Going too short*; and holds true especially in the *Labours* of the Brain. Well fare the Heart of that Noble *Jesuit*,[329] who first adventured to confess in Print, that Books must be suited to their several Seasons, like Dress, and Diet, and Diversions: And better fare our noble Nation, for refining upon this, among other *French* Modes. I am living fast, to see the Time, when a *Book* that misses its Tide shall be neglected, as the *Moon* by Day, or like *Mackerel* a Week after the Season. No Man hath more nicely observed our Climate, than the Bookseller who bought the Copy of this Work; He knows to a Tittle,[330] what Subjects will best go off in a *dry Year*, and which it is proper to expose foremost, when the Weather-glass is fallen to *much Rain*. When he had seen this Treatise, and consulted his *Almanac* upon it; he gave me to understand, that he had maturely considered the two Principal Things, which were the *Bulk* and the *Subject*; and found, it would never *take*, but after a long Vacation, and then only, in case it should happen to be a hard Year for Turnips. Upon which I desired to know, *considering my urgent Necessities*, what he thought might be acceptable this Month. He looked *Westward*, and said, I doubt we shall have a fit of bad Weather; However, if you could prepare some pretty little *Banter* (*but not in Verse*) or a small Treatise upon the——, it would run like Wild Fire. But, *if it hold up*, I have already hired an Author to write something against Dr. B—tl—y, which, I am sure will turn to Account.

At length we agreed upon this Expedient; That when a Customer comes for one of these, and desires in Confidence to know the Author; he will tell him very privately, as a Friend, naming whichever of the Wits shall happen to be that Week in the Vogue; and if *D'Urfey*'s last Play should be in Course, I had as lieve he may be[331] the Person as *Congreve*. This I mention, because I am wonderfully well acquainted with the present Relish of Courteous Readers; and have often observed, with singular Pleasure, that a *Fly* driven from a *Honey-pot*, will immediately, with very good Appetite alight, and finish his Meal on an *Excrement*.

I have one Word to say upon the Subject of *Profound Writers*, who are grown very numerous of late; And, I know very well, the judicious World is resolved to list me in that

---

[326] *trepan* trick, ensnare.

[327] *Spunging-house* "A house to which debtors are taken before commitment to prison, where the bailiffs spunge upon them, or riot at their cost" (Johnson).

[328] *Custard* Custard is a famous Dish at a Lord-Mayor's Feast [note in fifth edition suggests the passage is about a particular Protestant mayor, Sir Humphrey Edwin].

[329] *Jesuit* Pere d' Orleans [Swift's accurate marginal note].

[330] *Tittle* small part of a piece of writing, a dot or whit.

[331] *I had as lieve he may be* it is all the same to me if he is.

Number. I conceive therefore, as to the Business of being *Profound*, that it is with *Writers* as with *Wells*; A Person with good Eyes may see to the Bottom of the deepest, provided any *Water* be there; and, that often, when there is nothing in the world at the Bottom, besides *Dryness* and *Dirt*, though it be but a Yard and half under Ground, it shall pass, however, for wondrous *Deep*, upon no wiser a Reason than because it is wondrous *Dark*.

I am now trying an Experiment very frequent among Modern Authors; which is *to write upon Nothing*: When the Subject is utterly exhausted, to let the Pen still move on; by some called the Ghost of Wit, delighting to walk after the Death of its Body. And to say the Truth, there seems to be no Part of Knowledge in fewer Hands, than That of Discerning *when to have Done*. By the Time that an Author has writ out a Book, he and his Readers are become old Acquaintance, and grow very loath to part: So that I have sometimes known it to be in Writing, as in Visiting, where the Ceremony of taking Leave, has employed more Time than the whole Conversation before. The Conclusion of a Treatise, resembles the Conclusion of Human Life, which hath sometimes been compared to the End of a Feast, where few are satisfied to depart, *ut plenus vitæ conviva:*[332] For men will sit down after the fullest Meal, though it be only to *doze,* or to *sleep* out the rest of the Day. But, in this latter, I differ extremely from other Writers; and shall be too proud, if by all my Labours, I can have any ways contributed to the *Repose* of Mankind, in Times so turbulent and unquiet as these. Neither, do I think such an Employment so very alien from the Office of a *Wit*, as some would suppose. For among a very polite Nation in *Greece*, there were the *same* Temples built and consecrated to *Sleep* and the *Muses*, between which two Deities they believed the strictest Friendship was established.

I have one concluding Favour, to request of my Reader; that he will not expect to be equally diverted and informed by every Line, or every Page of this Discourse; but give some Allowance to the Author's Spleen, and short Fits or Intervals of Dullness, as well as his own; And lay it seriously to his Conscience, whether, if he were walking the Streets in dirty Weather, or a rainy Day, he would allow it fair dealing in Folks at their Ease from a Window, to critic his Gait, and ridicule his Dress at such a Juncture.

In my Disposure of Employments of the Brain, I have thought fit to make *Invention* the *Master*, and to give *Method* and *Reason*, the Office of its *Lackeys*. The Cause of this Distribution was, from observing it my peculiar Case, to be often under a Temptation of being *Witty* upon Occasions, where I could be neither *Wise* nor *Sound*, nor any thing to the Matter in hand. And, I am too much a Servant of the *Modern* Way, to neglect any such Opportunities, what ever Pains or Improprieties I may be at, to introduce them. For, I have observed, that from a laborious Collection of Seven Hundred Thirty Eight *Flowers*, and *shining Hints* of the best *Modern* Authors, digested with great Reading, into my Book of *Common-Places*; I have not been able after five Years to draw, hook, or force, into common Conversation, any more than a Dozen. Of which Dozen, the one Moiety failed of Success, by being dropped among unsuitable Company; and the other cost me so many Strains, and Traps, and *Ambages* to introduce, that I at length resolved to give it over. Now, this Disappointment (to discover a Secret) I must own gave me the first Hint of setting up for an *Author*, and I have since found, among some particular Friends, that it is become a very general Complaint and has produced the same Effects upon many others. For, I have remarked many a *towardly Word*, to be wholly neglected or despised in *Discourse*, which has passed very smoothly, with some Consideration

---

[332] *ut plenus vitæ conviva* "[why not withdraw calmly into death] like a banqueter fed full of life" (Lucretius 3.938).

and Esteem, after its Preferment and Sanction in *Print*. But, now, since by the Liberty and Encouragement of the Press, I am grown absolute Master of the Occasions and Opportunities, to expose the Talents I have acquired; I already discover that the *Issues* of my *Observanda* begin to grow too large for the *Receipts*. Therefore, I shall here pause awhile, till I find, by feeling the World's Pulse, and my own, that it will be of absolute Necessity for us both, to resume my Pen.

FINIS

A Modest Proposal
for Preventing the Children of Poor People from Being a Burden to Their Parents or the Country, and for Making Them Beneficial to the Public (1729)

It is a melancholy Object to those who walk through this great town,[1] or travel in the Country, when they see the *Streets*, the *Roads*, and *Cabin-Doors* crowded with Beggars of the Female Sex, followed by three, four, or six Children, *all in Rags*, and importuning every Passenger for an Alms. These *Mothers* instead of being able to work for their honest Livelihood, are forced to employ all their Time in strolling[2] to beg Sustenance for their *helpless Infants* who, as they grow up, either turn *Thieves* for want of Work or leave their *dear native Country to fight for the Pretender*[3] *in Spain*, or sell themselves to the *Barbadoes*.[4]

I think it is agreed by all Parties that this prodigious Number of Children, in the Arms, or on the Backs, or at the *Heels* of their *Mothers*, and frequently of their *Fathers*, is *in the present deplorable State of the Kingdom*,[5] a very great additional Grievance; and therefore whoever could find out a Fair, Cheap and Easy Method of making these Children Sound and Useful Members of the Common-wealth would deserve so well of the Public, as to have his Statue set up for a Preserver of the Nation.

But my Intention is very far from being confined to provide only for the Children of *professed Beggars*; it is of a much greater Extent, and shall take in the whole Number of Infants at a certain Age, who are born of Parents in effect as little able to support them as those who demand our Charity in the Streets.

As to my own Part, having turned my Thoughts for many Years upon this important Subject, and maturely weighed the several *Schemes of other Projectors*,[6] I have always found them grossly mistaken in their *Computation*. 'Tis true, a Child *just dropped from its Dam* may be supported by her Milk for a Solar Year with little other Nourishment, at most not above the Value of two Shillings,[7] which the mother may certainly get, or the Value in *Scraps*, by her *lawful Occupation of Begging*; and it is exactly at one Year old that I propose to provide for them, in such a manner, as, instead of being a *Charge* upon their *Parents*, or the *Parish*, or

A MODEST PROPOSAL
[1] *this great town*   Dublin.
[2] *strolling*   from "stroll," "To wander; to ramble; to rove; to be a vagrant" (Johnson).
[3] *Pretender*   James Francis Edward (1688–1766), son of James II, recognized as James III in some Catholic countries.
[4] *Barbadoes*   where the sugar mills attracted slave and indentured labor.
[5] *Kingdom*   Ireland.
[6] *Projector*   "1. One who forms schemes or designs; 2. One who forms wild impracticable schemes" (Johnson).
[7] *two shillings*   ten pence, perhaps £25 or $40 in present value.

wanting Food and Raiment for the rest of their Lives, they shall, on the contrary, contribute to the *Feeding* and partly to the *Clothing* of many Thousands.

There is likewise another great Advantage in my Scheme, that it will prevent those *voluntary Abortions*, and that horrid practice of *Women murdering their Bastard Children*, alas! too frequent among us; Sacrificing the poor innocent Babes, I doubt,[8] more to avoid the Expense than the Shame, which would move Tears and Pity in the most savage and inhuman Breast.

The Number of Souls in this Kingdom being usually reckoned One million and a half; of these I calculate there may be about Two hundred Thousand Couple whose Wives are Breeders, from which Number I subtract Thirty thousand Couples who are able to maintain their own Children; although I apprehend there cannot be as many under *the present Distresses of the Kingdom*: but this being granted, there will remain One hundred and seventy thousand Breeders.

I again subtract Fifty thousand for those Women who miscarry, or whose Children die by Accident, or Disease within the Year; there only remain One hundred and twenty thousand Children of poor Parents annually born: the Question therefore is, How this Number shall be reared and provided for; which, as I have already said, under the present Situation of Affairs is utterly impossible, by all the Methods hitherto proposed: for we can neither employ them in Handicraft, or Agriculture; we neither build Houses (I mean in the country) nor cultivate land.[9] They can very seldom pick up a Livelihood by Stealing till they arrive at six Years old, except where they are of Towardly Parts, although I confess they learn the Rudiments much earlier, during which time they can however be properly looked upon only as Probationers, as I have been informed by a principal gentleman in the County of Cavan, who protested to me that he never knew above one or two Instances under the Age of Six, even in a part of the Kingdom *so renowned for the quickest Proficiency in that Art*.

I am assured by our Merchants, that a Boy or a Girl, *before twelve Years old*, is no saleable Commodity; and even when they come to this Age, they will not yield above three Pounds, or three Pounds and half a Crown[10] at most on the Exchange: which cannot turn to Account either to the *Parents* or the *Kingdom*, the Charge of Nutriment and Rags having been at least four times that Value.

I shall now therefore humbly propose my own Thoughts, which I hope will not be liable to the least Objection.

I have been assured by a very knowing *American* of my acquaintance in *London*, that a young healthy child, well nursed, is at a Year old a most *delicious, nourishing*, and *wholesome* Food, whether *stewed, roasted, baked*, or *boiled*; and I make no doubt that it will equally serve in a *Fricassee*, or a *Ragout*.

I do therefore humbly offer it to *public Consideration*, that of the Hundred and twenty thousand Children already computed, Twenty thousand may be reserved for *Breed*, whereof only one Fourth part to be Males, which is more than we allow to *Sheep, black Cattle*,[11] or *Swine*, and my Reason is that these Children are seldom the Fruits of Marriage, *a Circumstance not much regarded by our Savages*; therefore *one Male* will be sufficient to serve *four Females*. That the remaining Hundred thousand may, at a Year old, be offered *in Sale* to the *Persons of Quality*

---

[8] *doubt* believe, think.

[9] *we neither build Houses . . . land* absentee landlords and British restrictions on Irish agricultural trade contributed to the impoverishment of Ireland.

[10] *Crown* five shillings or twenty-five pence.

[11] *black Cattle* "Oxen; bull; and cows. 'The other part of the grazier's business is what we call *black-cattle*, producing hides, tallow, and beef, for exportation' Swift" (Johnson).

and *Fortune* through the Kingdom, always advising the Mother to let them suck plentifully of the last Month, so as to *render them plump and fat for a good Table*. A Child will make two Dishes at an Entertainment for Friends, and when the Family dines alone, the fore or hind *Quarter* will make a reasonable Dish, and seasoned with a little *Pepper* or *Salt* will be very good boiled on the fourth Day, especially in *Winter*.

I have reckoned upon a Medium, that a Child just born will weigh twelve Pounds, and, in a solar Year, if tolerably nursed, increaseth to Twenty-eight Pounds.

I grant this Food will be somewhat dear, and therefore *very proper for Landlords*, who, as they have already devoured most of the *Parents*, seem to have the best Title to the *Children*.

Infants' Flesh will be in Season throughout the Year, but more plentiful in *March*, and a little *before* and *after*, for we are told by a grave Author,[12] an eminent *French* physician, that *Fish being a prolific Diet*,[13] there are more children born in *Roman Catholic Countries* about nine Months after *Lent*, than at any other Season: therefore, reckoning a Year after *Lent*, the Markets will be more glutted than usual, because the Number of *Popish Infants* is at least three to one in this Kingdom, and therefore it will have one other collateral Advantage by lessening the Number of Papists among us.

I have already computed the Charge of Nursing a Beggar's Child (in which list I reckon all *Cottagers*,[14] *Labourers*, and Four Fifths of the *Farmers*) to be about two Shillings *per Annum*, Rags included; and I believe no Gentleman would repine to give Ten Shillings for the *Carcass of a good fat Child*, which, as I have said, will make four Dishes of excellent Nutritive Meat, when he hath only some particular Friend, or his own Family to dine with him. Thus the Esquire[15] will learn to be a good Landlord, and grow popular among his Tenants, the Mother will have Eight Shillings net Profit, and be fit for Work till she produces another Child.

Those who are more thrifty (*as I must confess the Times require*) may flay the Carcass; the Skin of which, artificially[16] dressed, will make admirable *Gloves for Ladies*, and *Summer Boots for fine Gentlemen*.

As to our City of *Dublin*, shambles[17] may be appointed for this Purpose in the most convenient Parts of it, and Butchers we may be assured will not be wanting; although I rather recommend buying the Children alive, and dressing them hot from the Knife, as we do *Roasting Pigs*.

A very worthy Person, *a true Lover of his Country*, and whose virtues I highly esteem, was lately pleased in discoursing on this Matter, to offer a Refinement upon my Scheme. He said that many Gentlemen of this Kingdom, having of late destroyed their Deer, he conceived that the want of Venison might be well supplied by the Bodies of young Lads and Maidens, not exceeding fourteen Years of Age, nor under twelve; so great a Number of both Sexes in every County being now ready to starve for want of Work and Service:[18] And these to be disposed of by their Parents, if alive, or otherwise by their nearest Relations. But with due deference to so excellent a Friend, and so deserving a Patriot,[19] I cannot be altogether in his Sentiments: for as to the Males, my *American* Acquaintance assured me from frequent Experience that their Flesh was generally Tough and Lean, like that of our School-Boys, by continual Exercise,

---

[12] *a grave Author*   the sixteenth-century physician and satirist François Rabelais.

[13] *prolific Diet*   one that promotes productive sexual activity.

[14] *Cottagers*   tenant farmers.

[15] *Esquire*   "A title of dignity and next in degree below a knight" (Johnson).

[16] *artificially*   skilfully.

[17] *shambles*   "The place where butchers kill or sell their meat" (Johnson).

[18] *Service*   position as a servant.

[19] *Patriot*   a name taken by some Tories at this time.

and their Taste disagreeable; and to Fatten them would not answer the Charge. Then as to the Females, it would, I think, with humble Submission, *be a Loss to the Public*, because they soon would become Breeders themselves: And besides, it is not improbable that some scrupulous People might be apt to censure such a Practice (although indeed very unjustly) as a little bordering upon Cruelty; which, I confess, hath always been with me the strongest Objection against any Project, however well intended.

But in order to justify my Friend, he confessed that this Expedient was put into his head by the famous *Psalmanaazar*,[20] a native of the island of Formosa, who came from thence to *London* above twenty Years ago; and in Conversation told my Friend that in his Country when any young Person happened to be put to death, the Executioner sold the Carcass to *Persons of Quality*, as a prime Dainty, and that, in his Time, the Body of a plump Girl of fifteen, who was crucified for an Attempt to poison the Emperor, was sold to his *Imperial Majesty's Prime Mininster of State*, and other great *Mandarins* of the Court, *in Joints from the Gibbet*, at four hundred Crowns. Neither indeed can I deny, that if the same Use were made of several plump young Girls in this Town, who, without one single Groat[21] to their Fortunes, cannot stir abroad without a Chair,[22] and appear at the *Play-House* and *Assemblies* in foreign Fineries, which they never will pay for, the Kingdom would not be the worse.

Some Persons of a desponding Spirit are in great concern about that vast Number of poor People who are aged, diseased, or maimed; and I have been desired to employ my Thoughts what Course may be taken to ease the Nation of so grievous an Encumbrance. But I am not in the least Pain upon that Matter, because it is very well known that they are every Day *dying*, and *rotting*, by *Cold* and *Famine*, and *Filth*, and *Vermin*, as fast as can be reasonably expected. And as to the younger Labourers, they are now in almost as hopeful a Condition. They cannot get Work, and consequently pine away for want of Nourishment, to a Degree that if at any time they are accidentally hired to common Labour, they have not Strength to perform it: and thus the Country and themselves are happily delivered from the Evils to come.

I have too long digressed, and therefore shall return to my Subject. I think the Advantages by the Proposal which I have made are obvious and many, as well as of the highest Importance.

For first, as I have already observed, it would greatly lessen *the Number of Papists*, with whom we are yearly over-run, being the principal Breeders of the Nation, as well as our most dangerous Enemies; and who stay at Home on purpose with a design *to deliver the Kingdom to the Pretender*; hoping to take their Advantage by the Absence *of so many good Protestants*, who have chosen rather to leave their Country, than stay at home and pay Tithes[23] against their Conscience to an Episcopal Curate.

2dly, the poorer Tenants will have something valuable of their own, which by Law may be made liable to Distress,[24] and help to pay their Landlord's Rent; their Corn and Cattle being already seized, and *Money a thing unknown*.

---

[20] *Psalmanaazar* George Psalmanaazar (*c.* 1679–1763) although he had never been out of Europe, he pretended to be from Formosa (modern Taiwan) and wrote a book about the island's customs; he even invented an alphabet and language that he called theirs; the hoax was successful for many years, but it was discovered and Psalmanaazar repented and pursued a legitimate career in publishing.

[21] *Groat* a very small amount of money.
[22] *Chair* "A vehicle borne by men; a sedan" (Johnson).
[23] *Tithes* taxes to support the ministry of the Church of Ireland; non-conformists or lower-church Christians (*Protestants*) become absentee landlords in order to avoid the tax, Swift suggests.
[24] *Distress* "The act of making a legal seizure" (Johnson).

3dly, Whereas the Maintenance of an hundred thousand Children, from two Years old and upwards, cannot be computed at less than ten Shillings a-piece *per Annum,* the Nation's Stock will be thereby increased fifty thousand Pounds *per Annum,* besides the Profit of a new Dish introduced to the Tables of all *Gentlemen of Fortune* in the Kingdom who have any refinement in Taste; and the Money will circulate among our selves, the Goods being entirely of our own Growth and Manufacture.

4ly, the constant Breeders, besides the Gain of eight Shillings sterling *per Annum* by the Sale of their Children, will be rid of the Charge of maintaining them after the first Year.

5ly, this Food would likewise bring great *Customs to Taverns,* where the Vintners will certainly be so prudent as to procure the best Receipts[25] for dressing it to Perfection, and consequently have their Houses frequented by all the *fine Gentlemen,* who justly value themselves upon their Knowledge in good Eating; and a skilful Cook, who understands how to oblige his Guests, will contrive to make it as expensive as they please.

6ly, This would be a great Inducement to Marriage, which all wise Nations have either encouraged by Rewards, or enforced by Laws and Penalties. It would increase the Care and Tenderness of Mothers toward their Children, when they were sure of a Settlement for Life to the poor Babes, provided in some Sort by the Public to their annual Profit instead of Expense; we should soon see an honest Emulation among the married Women, *which of them could bring the fattest Child to Market;* Men would become as fond of their *Wives,* during the Time of their Pregnancy, as they are now of their *Mares* in Foal, their *Cows* in Calf, or *Sows* when they are ready to farrow; nor offer[26] to beat or kick them (as it is too frequent a Practice) for fear of a Miscarriage.

Many other Advantages might be enumerated: For Instance, the Addition of some thousand Carcasses in our Exportation of barrelled Beef: The Propagation of *Swine's Flesh* and Improvement in the Art of making good *Bacon,* so much wanted among us by the great Destruction of *Pigs,* too frequent at our Tables, which are no way comparable in Taste, or Magnificence to a well-grown, fat Yearling Child, which roasted whole will make a considerable Figure at a *Lord Mayor's Feast,* or any other public Entertainment. But this and many others I omit, being studious of Brevity.

Supposing that One thousand Families in this City, would be constant Customers for Infants' Flesh, besides others who might have it at Merry-meetings, particularly *Weddings* and *Christenings,* I compute that *Dublin* would take off annually about Twenty thousand Carcasses, and the rest of the Kingdom (where probably they will be sold somewhat cheaper) the remaining Eighty thousand.

I can think of no one Objection that will possibly be raised against this Proposal, unless it should be urged that the number of People will be thereby much lessened in the Kingdom. This I freely own, and it was indeed one principal Design in offering it to the World. I desire the Reader will observe, that I calculate my Remedy *for this one individual Kingdom of* Ireland, *and for no other that ever was, is, or, I think, ever can be upon Earth.* Therefore let no Man talk to me of other Expedients: *Of taxing our Absentees at five Shillings a Pound: Of using neither Clothes, nor Household Furniture, except what is of our own Growth and Manufacture: Of utterly rejecting the* materials *and* instruments *that promote Foreign Luxury: Of curing the Expensiveness of Pride, Vanity, Idleness, and Gaming in our Women: Of introducing a Vein of Parsimony, Prudence and Temperance: Of learning to love our Country, wherein we differ even from* Laplanders, *and the inhabitants of* Topinanmou:[27] *Of quitting our Animosities and Factions, nor act any longer like the*

---

[25] *Receipts* recipes.
[26] *offer* attempt; begin.

[27] *Topinanmou* part of modern Brazil.

Jews, who were murdering one another at the very moment their City was taken:[28] *Of being a little cautious not to sell our Country and Consciences for nothing: Of teaching Landlords to have at least one Degree of Mercy toward their Tenants: Lastly, Of putting a Spirit of Honesty, Industry and Skill into our Shop Keepers, who, if a Resolution could now be taken to buy only our Native Goods, would immediately unite to cheat and exact upon us in the Price, the Measure, and the Goodness, nor could ever yet be brought to make one fair Proposal of just Dealing, though often in earnest invited to it.*

Therefore I repeat, let no Man talk to me of these and the like Expedients, till he hath at least some Glimpse of Hope that there will ever be some hearty and sincere Attempt to put them in practice.

But as to myself, having been wearied out for many Years with offering vain, idle, visionary Thoughts, and at length utterly despairing of Success, I fortunately fell upon this Proposal; which, as it is wholly new, so it hath something solid and real, of no Expense and little Trouble, full in our own Power, and whereby we can incur no Danger in disobliging *England.* For this kind of Commodity will not bear exportation, the Flesh being of too tender a Consistence to admit a long Continuance in Salt, although perhaps I could name a Country which would be glad to eat up our whole Nation without it.

After all, I am not so violently bent upon my own Opinion as to reject any Offer proposed by wise Men, which shall be found equally innocent, cheap, easy and effectual. But before something of that kind shall be advanced in contradiction to my Scheme, and offering a better, I desire the Author, or Authors, will be pleased maturely to consider two Points.

1st, As things now stand, how they will be able to find Food and Raiment for One hundred thousand useless Mouths and Backs.

And *2dly,* There being a round Million of Creatures in human Figure throughout this Kingdom, whose whole Subsistence put into a common Stock would leave them in Debt Two million of Pounds *Sterling,* adding those who are Beggars by Profession, to the Bulk of Farmers, Cottagers and Labourers, with their Wives and Children, who are Beggars in effect.

I desire those *Politicians* who dislike my Overture and may perhaps be so bold to attempt an Answer, that they will first ask the Parents of these Mortals, whether they would not at this Day think it a great Happiness to have been sold for Food at a Year old, in the manner I prescribe, and thereby have avoided such a perpetual Scene of Misfortunes as they have since gone through, by *the Oppression of Landlords,* the Impossibility of paying Rent without Money or Trade, the want of common Sustenance, with neither House nor Clothes to cover them from the Inclemencies of the Weather, and the most inevitable Prospect of entailing the like, or greater Miseries upon their *Breed* for ever.

I profess in the Sincerity of my Heart, that I have not the least Personal Interest in endeavouring to promote this necessary Work, having no other Motive than the *Public Good of my Country,* by *advancing our Trade, providing for Infants, relieving the Poor, and giving some Pleasure to the Rich.* I have no Children by which I can propose to get a single Penny, the youngest being nine Years old, and my Wife past Child-bearing.

A Description of the Morning (1709)

Now hardly here and there a Hackney-coach[1]
Appearing, showed the ruddy Morn's approach.

---

[28] *Jews . . . their City was taken*   Titus destroyed Jerusalem and the Temple in 70 CE; Flavius Josephus, who was with Titus during the siege, wrote the history that Swift knew.

A DESCRIPTION OF THE MORNING
[1]   hardly "Unwelcomely; harshly" (Johnson); *Hackney-coach* coach and horses for hire, a version of Apollo's chariot.

Now *Betty* from her Master's Bed had flown,[2]
And softly stole to discompose her own.
The Slip-shod 'Prentice from his master's door 5
Had pared the street, and sprinkled round the floor[3]
Now *Moll* had whirled her Mop with dext'rous Airs,
Prepared to scrub the Entry and the Stairs.
The youth with broomy stumps began to trace
The kennel edge, where wheels had worn the place.[4] 10
The Small-coal Man was heard with Cadence deep,[5]
Till drowned in shriller Notes of *Chimney Sweep*.
Duns at his lordship's gate began to meet;[6]
And brickdust-*Moll* had screamed through half a Street.[7]
The Turnkey now his flock Returning sees, 15
Duly let out a-Nights to steal for Fees.[8]
The watchful Bailiffs take their silent Stands;
And School-boys lag with Satchels in their Hands.

A Beautiful Young Nymph Going to Bed
Written for the Honour of the Fair Sex (1734)

Corinna, Pride of *Drury Lane*,[1]
For whom no Shepherd sighs in vain;
Never did *Covent Garden* boast
So bright a battered, strolling Toast;
No drunken Rake to pick her up, 5
No Cellar where on Tick to sup;[2]
Returning at the Midnight Hour;
Four Stories climbing to her Bow'r;
Then, seated on a three-legg'd Chair,
Takes off her artificial Hair: 10
Now, picking out a Crystal Eye,
She wipes it clean, and lays it by.
Her Eye-brows from a Mouse's Hide,
Stuck on with Art on either Side,
Pulls off with Care, and first displays 'em, 15
Then in a Play-book smoothly lays 'em.
Now dext'rously her Plumpers draws,[3]
That serve to fill her hollow Jaws.

---

2   *Betty*. typical name for a maid.
3   *pared* trimmed, or cleaned; *sprinkled . . . floor* with fresh sawdust to absorb dirt.
4   *The Youth . . . place* To find old Nails [note in Faulkner's edition, probably by Swift]; *kennel* gutter.
5   *Small-coal* bits of wood coal used to light fires.
6   *Dun* "A clamorous, importunate, troublesome creditor" (Johnson).
7   *brickdust* used for sharpening knives.

8   *Fees* the "garnish" paid by prisoners to the *Bailiff* or *Turnkey* for food and other things in jail.
A BEAUTIFUL YOUNG NYMPH GOING TO BED
1   *Drury Lane* street in *Covent Garden*, a theater and red-light district.
2   *Tick* credit.
3   *Plumper* "Something worn in the mouth to swell out the cheeks" (Johnson).

Untwists a Wire; and from her Gums
A Set of Teeth completely comes.   20
Pulls out the Rags contrived to prop
Her flabby Dugs, and down they drop.
Proceeding on, the lovely Goddess
Unlaces next her Steel-ribbed Bodice;
Which, by the Operator's Skill,   25
Press down the Lumps, the Hollows fill.
Up goes her Hand, and off she slips
The Bolsters that supply her Hips
With gentlest Touch, she next explores
Her Shankers, Issues, running Sores;[4]   30
Effects of many a sad Disaster,
And then to each applies a Plaster.
But must, before she goes to Bed,
Rub off the Daubs of White and Red.[5]
And smooth the Furrows in her Front,[6]   35
With greasy Paper stuck upon't.
She takes a *Bolus* ere she sleeps;[7]
And then between two Blankets creeps.
With Pains of Love tormented lies;
Or, if she chance to close her Eyes,   40
Of *Bridewell* and the *Compter* dreams,[8]
And feels the Lash, and faintly screams.
Or, by a faithless Bully drawn,
At some Hedge-Tavern lies in Pawn.[9]
Or to Jamaica seems transported,[10]   45
Alone, and by no Planter courted;[11]
Or, near *Fleet-Ditch*'s oozy Brinks,[12]
Surrounded with a Hundred Stinks,
Belated, seems on Watch to lie,
And snap some Cully passing by;[13]   50
Or, struck with Fear, her Fancy runs[14]
On Watchmen, Constables and Duns,[15]
From whom she meets with frequent Rubs;[16]

[4] *Shankers* canker sores; *Issues* medical incisions made to drain boils or other infections.

[5] *Daubs of White and Red* facial make-up.

[6] *Front* forehead.

[7] *Bolus* "A form of medicine in which the ingredients are made up into a soft mass, larger than pills, to be swallowed at once" (Johnson).

[8] *Bridewell and the Compter* correctional facilities in London.

[9] *Hedge-Tavern* a low, rough tavern.

[10] *transported* a common punishment of convicted prostitutes and thieves.

[11] *Et longam incomitata videtur/Ire viam* [Swift's note: "She seemed to be going on a long journey alone"; this is the feverish dream of Dido that precedes her determination to commit suicide (*Aeneid* 4.467–8)].

[12] *Fleet-Ditch* a creek carrying filth south-east through the City and emptying into the Thames.

[13] *Cully* dupe or victim.

[14] *Fancy* imagination.

[15] *Dun* "A clamorous, importunate, troublesome creditor" (Johnson).

[16] *Rub* "Collision; hindrance; obstruction" (Johnson).

But, never from religious Clubs;[17]
Whose Favour she is sure to find,   55
Because she pays them all in Kind.
    Corinna wakes. A dreadful Sight!
Behold the Ruins of the Night!
A wicked Rat her Plaister stole,
Half eat, and dragged it to his Hole.[18]   60
The Crystal Eye, alas, was missed;
And Puss had on her plumpers p——sed;
A Pigeon picked her Issue-peas;[19]
And *Shock* her *Tresses* filled with fleas.[20]
    The Nymph, though in this mangled Plight,   65
Must every Morn her Limbs unite;
But, how shall I describe her Arts
To recollect her scattered Parts?
Or show the Anguish, Toil, and Pain,
Of gathering up herself again?   70
The bashful Muse will never bear
In such a Scene to interfere.
Corinna in the Morning dizened,[21]
Who sees will spew; who smells be poisoned.

A Description of a City Shower (1710)

Careful Observers may foretell the Hour
By sure Prognostics when to dread a Show'r:
While Rain depends, the pensive Cat gives o'er
Her Frolics, and pursues her Tail no more.
Returning Home at Night, you find the Sink[1]   5
Strike your offended Sense with double Stink.
If you be wise, then go not far to dine:
You spend in Coach-hire more than save in Wine.
A coming Show'r your shooting Corns presage;
Old Aches throb, your hollow Tooth will rage:[2]   10
A Saunt'ring in Coffee-house is *Dulman* seen;
He damns the Climate, and complains of Spleen.[3]
Mean while the South, rising with dabbled Wings,[4]
A sable Cloud athwart the Welkin flings[5]
That swilled more Liquor than it could contain,   15

---

[17] *religious Clubs* dissenting Protestant societies, which Swift derides for their pretensions to visionary understanding.
[18] *eat* an old form of the past tense.
[19] *Issue-peas* rolled-up bits of ivy-root inserted in an issue to keep it running.
[20] *Shock* stock name for a lap dog.
[21] *dizen* "To dress; to deck; to rig out. A low word" (Johnson).

A DESCRIPTION OF A CITY SHOWER
[1] *Sink* "A drain; a jakes [outhouse]" (Johnson); a lavatory.
[2] *Aches* a disyllable (as if "aitch-es").
[3] *Spleen* "Melancholy; hypochondriacal vapours" (Johnson); the name of a variety of ills, like today's "depression."
[4] *dabbled* muddy.
[5] *Welkin* sky (consciously archaic).

And, like a Drunkard, gives it up again.
Brisk *Susan* whips her Linen from the Rope,[6]
While the first drizzling Show'r is borne aslope:[7]
Such is that Sprinkling, which some careless Quean[8]
Flirts on you from her Mop; but not so clean:[9]   20
You fly, invoke the Gods; then turning, stop
To rail; she singing still whirls on her Mop.
Nor yet the Dust had shunned th' unequal Strife,
But, aided by the Wind, fought still for Life;
And wafted with its Foe by violent Gust,   25
'Twas doubtful which was Rain, and which was Dust.
Ah! where must needy Poet seek for Aid,
When Dust and Rain at once his Coat invade?
Sole Coat, where Dust cemented by the Rain,
Erects the Nap, and leaves a cloudy Stain.   30
   Now, in contiguous Drops the Flood comes down,
Threat'ning with Deluge this *devoted* Town.
To Shops in Crowds the daggled Females fly,[10]
Pretend to cheapen Goods, but nothing buy.[11]
The Templer spruce, while every Spout's abroach,[12]   35
Stays till 'tis fair, yet *seems* to call a Coach.
The tucked-up Sempstress walks with hasty Strides,
While Streams run down her oil'd Umbrella's Sides.[13]
Here various Kinds, by various Fortunes led,
Commence Acquaintance underneath a Shed: 40
Triumphant Tories, and desponding Whigs,[14]
Forget their Feuds, and join to save their Wigs.
Boxed in a Chair the Beau impatient sits,[15]
While Spouts run clatt'ring o'er the Roof by Fits,
And ever and anon with frightful Din   45
The Leather sounds; he trembles from within.
So when *Troy* Chairmen bore the wooden Steed,[16]
Pregnant with *Greeks* impatient to be freed;
(Those Bully *Greeks*, who, as the Moderns do,
Instead of paying Chair-men, run them through)   50
Laocoon struck the Out-side with his Spear,
And each imprisoned Hero quaked for Fear.
   Now from all Parts the swelling Kennels flow,

---

[6] *Susan* a typical maid's name.
[7] *aslope* on a slant; obliquely (a word used to describe the way a lance or sword might strike a knight's shield).
[8] *Quean* "A worthless woman; generally a strumpet" (Johnson).
[9] *Flirt* "To throw anything with a quick, elastic motion" (Johnson).
[10] *daggled* muddied.
[11] *cheapen* "Attempt to purchase" (Johnson); shop for.
[12] *Templer* law student; *abroach* overflowing.
[13] *oil'd* so as to be waterproof.

[14] *Triumphant Tories, and desponding Whigs* the poem was written in 1710, the first year of the Tory ministry under Queen Anne.
[15] *Chair* "A vehicle borne by men; a sedan" (Johnson); this one is covered.
[16] *Troy Chairmen . . . quaked with fear* tricked into believing the Greeks had given up the siege, the Trojans carried a wooden horse (supposedly an offering to the gods) concealing lethal soldiers into their city; the priest Laocoon advised against this, struck the horse, and frightened the Greeks (Virgil, *Aeneid* 2.50–2).

And bear their Trophies with them, as they go:
Filths of all Hues and Odours seem to tell
What Street they sailed from, by the Sight and Smell.   55
They, as each Torrent drives with rapid Force,
From *Smithfield*, or *St. Pulchre*'s shape their course,[17]
And in huge Confluent joined at *Snow-hill* Ridge,
Fall from the *Conduit* prone to *Holborn-Bridge*.   60
Sweepings from Butchers' Stalls, Dung, Guts, and Blood,
Drowned Puppies, stinking Sprats, all drenched in Mud,
Dead Cats, and Turnip-Tops come tumbling down the Flood.[18]

Stella's Birth-Day[1] (13 March 1719)

Stella this Day is Thirty-four
(We shan't dispute a Year or more).
However, *Stella*, be not troubled,
Although thy Size and Years be doubled,
Since first I saw thee at Sixteen,[2]   5
The brightest Virgin on the Green;
So little is thy Form declined,
Made up so largely in thy Mind.
    Oh! would it please the Gods to *split*
Thy Beauty, Size, and Years, and Wit,   10
No Age could furnish out a Pair
Of Nymphs so graceful, wise, and fair;
With half the Lustre of your Eyes,
With half your Wit, your Years, and Size,
And then, before it grew too late,   15
How should I beg of gentle Fate,
(That either Nymph might have her Swain)
To split my Worship too in twain.

---

[17] *Smithfield*   an open area just north-west of the City, used as a cattle market and sometimes for hangings; *St. Pulchre's*   a suburban parish just west of the Newgate prison; the water would flow south-east past the other places mentioned on its way into the Fleet and through the City to the Thames.

[18] These three last lines were intended against that licentious Manner of modern Poets, in making three Rhymes together, which they call *Triplets*; and the last of the three, was two or sometimes more Syllables longer, called an *Alexandrine*. These *Triplets* and *Alexandrines* were brought in by Dryden, and other Poets in the Reign of Charles II. They were the mere Effect of Haste, Idle-ness, and want of Money; and have been wholly avoided by the best Poets, since these Verses were written [Note in Faulkner's edition, probably by Swift].

STELLA'S BIRTH-DAY

[1] *Stella*   Esther Johnson (1681–1728), whom Swift loved and supported almost from the time he met her in 1689 until her death; written in 1719, when Stella turned thirty-eight, this is the first in a series of annual birthday poems that concluded with her last birthday in 1727.

[2] *sixteen*   she was eight, but perhaps Swift first looked on her as a woman at sixteen or perhaps this is part of his gentlemanly looseness about her age.

Sarah Fyge Egerton (1670?–1722)

At the age of about sixteen Sarah Fyge published The Female Advocate *(1686), a poem in answer to a misogynistic verse satire by Robert Gould called* Love Given O'er *(1682). Her parents disapproved, and she was soon unwillingly married off. When her husband died, she married the much older Egerton, although she evidently loved another. Many of her poems are about the difficulty of this situation. But Egerton did not only express her dissatisfaction with marriage and her wish for freedom in poetry, she also sued for divorce (unsuccessfully), and was public enough in repudiation of her husband to earn a place in Delarivière Manley's* New Atalantis. *Mr Egerton is described as "an old, thin, raw-boned priest" who pulls his wife's hair, but she fares even worse, being described as "a she-devil incarnate" with a violent temper who is open in her professions of love for another, a man she calls Alexis in her poetry. The two poems by Egerton offered here come from* Poems on Several Occasions *(1703).*

from *Poems on Several Occasions* (1703)

THE POWER OF LOVE

In this soft Amrous Age now Love is grown,
The modish Entertainment of the Town,[1]
And the fond Beau loves his half score a-day,
The Ladies too almost as Vain as they;
Spare me, ye cruel Powers, let me not prove,   5
The only Victim of a lasting Love.
I had my share three tedious Years a Slave,
And knew no Joys but what *Phylaster* gave,
When spite of Vows he proved unjust at last,
In distant Shades contending Months I passed,[2]   10
Thought I could see the Youth at my return,
With gay Indifference and Unconcern.
I longed to know the Temper of my Heart,
And see if Passion could outlive desert;
But this my Curiosity has won,   15
To know alas! I am again undone:
I thought my self with Resolution blessed,
But the soft Gods came crowding to my Breast.[3]
The sporting Boys delight in Amorous Pain,
And flocked in haste to Revel here again;   20
With downy Wings they Fan the couchant Fire,[4]
And every Spark revives with fresh desire:
I Gaze and Sigh, and wish I'm just the same,
As the first Transports of my blooming Flame.
Almighty Love thy Power to me is known,   25

THE POWER OF LOVE
[1] *modish* fashionable.
[2] *contending* proceeding with difficulty.

[3] *the soft Gods* gods of love, cupids.
[4] *couchant* resting, lying down (usually descriptive of animals, especially in heraldry).

Without new Tortures I'll thy Godhead own;[5]
But if I'm doomed to Love may my Fate be,
(Rather than him) to love each Face I see.
Tis Sin against the custom of the Nation,
To love but one and all this while with Passion,   30
I'd rather be the shifting Fool in Fashion.
Then if I'm tortured with Variety,
I shan't be blamed for Nonconformity.[6]

THE EMULATION[1]

Say Tyrant Custom, why must we obey,
The impositions of thy haughty Sway;
From the first dawn of Life, unto the Grave,
Poor Womankind's in every State, a Slave.
The Nurse, the Mistress, Parent and the Swain,   5
For Love she must, there's none escape that Pain;
Then comes the last, the fatal Slavery,
The Husband with insulting Tyranny
Can have ill Manners justified by Law;
For Men all join to keep the Wife in awe.   10
Moses who first our Freedom did rebuke,
Was Married when he writ the Pentateuch;[2]
They're Wise to keep us Slaves, for well they know,
If we were loose, we soon should make them so.
We yield like vanquished Kings whom Fetters bind,   15
When chance of War is to Usurpers kind;
Submit in Form; but they'd our Thoughts control,
And lay restraints on the impassive Soul:
They fear we should excel their sluggish Parts,[3]
Should we attempt the Sciences and Arts.   20
Pretend they were designed for them alone,
So keep us Fools to raise their own Renown;
Thus Priests of old their Grandeur to maintain,
Cried vulgar Eyes would sacred Laws Profane.
So kept the Mysteries behind a Screen,   25
Their Homage and the Name were lost had they been seen:
But in this blessèd Age, such Freedom's given,
That every Man explains the Will of Heaven;
And shall we Women now sit tamely by,
Make no excursions in Philosophy,   30
Or grace our Thoughts in tuneful Poetry?
We will our Rights in Learning's World maintain,

---

5   *own*   acknowledge.
6   *Nonconformity*   in contemporary politics, the state of
those who could not attest their belief in all thirty-nine
articles of faith presented by the Church of England;
"refusal to join the established religion" (Johnson).

THE EMULATION
1   *Emulation*   "Rivalry; desire of superiority"
(Johnson).
2   *Pentateuch*   the first five books of the Bible.
3   *Parts*   intellectual ability.

Wits Empire, now, shall know a Female Reign;
Come all ye Fair, the great Attempt improve,
Divinely imitate the Realms above: 35
There's ten celestial Females govern Wit,[4]
And but two Gods that dare pretend to it;[5]
And shall these finite Males reverse their Rules,
No, we'll be Wits, and then Men must be Fools.

George Cheyne (1671–1743)

In 1733, beset with nervous disorders, a twenty-four year-old college drop-out still uncertain of his direction in life, Samuel Johnson purchased a copy of Dr George Cheyne's new book of popular medicine The English Malady. *There is evidence that he followed Cheyne's prescriptions for treating melancholy, or depression, including his vegetarian, milk diet and extensive doses of exercise. As a a learned medical writer, and as Bath physician tending to the ills of the upper class, Cheyne was already famous. Unfortunately, he had fallen prey to the diseases of his patients, especially gout and corpulence. He recounts his own case in* The English Malady: *he had reached a weight of thirty-two stone (450 pounds), and he had become immobile as well as, understandably, depressed. He proved the efficacy of his vegetarian diet on himself, recovered his health, and enjoyed enormous popularity.*

from The English Malady: or, a Treatise of Nervous Diseases of all Kinds, as Spleen, Vapours, Lowness of Spirits, Hypochondriacal Distempers &c. (1733)

CHAPTER 6
OF THE FREQUENCY OF NERVOUS DISORDERS IN LATER YEARS,[1] BEYOND WHAT THEY HAVE BEEN OBSERVED IN FORMER TIMES

§1. If what I have advanced in the former *Chapter* have any Truth or *Verisimilitude*, it will be no hard Matter to account for the Frequency of Nervous Distempers observed of late Years, beyond what they have been in former Times. There is nothing more common, than to hear Men (even those, who, on other Subjects, reason justly and solidly) ascribe their Distempers, *acute* or *chronical*, to a wet Room, damp Sheets, catching Cold, ill or under-dressed Food, or Eating too plentifully of this or the other Dish at a certain Time, and to such like trivial Circumstances, being unwilling to own the true Cause, to wit, their continued Luxury and Laziness, because they would gladly continue this Course, and yet be well, if possible. And there have not wanted learned Physicians, who have ascribed the Frequency of these Nervous Distempers of late, especially among the fair Sex, to *Coffee, Tea, Chocolate,* and *Snuff*: I would not affirm that there could be no Abuses of these otherwise innocent Foods or Amusements,

---

4 *ten celestial Females* Mnemosyne (Memory) and her nine daughters, the muses governing all the arts and sciences.

5 *two Gods* Apollo and Hermes.
THE ENGLISH MALADY
1 *later Years* recent times.

or that these mentioned Circumstance and Accidents may have no Effects, but they are so Weak, Insensible, and Transitory, if they meet with Constitutions tolerably Clean and Healthy, that whoever would attribute any considerable Disorder to them, argues with as much Reason and true Philosophy, as he who ascribes his good Liquor entirely to the Yeast or other Helps of its Fermentation, or the Death of a Man killed by a Gun-shot to the Paper or Tow that held down the Bullet: Health and Life, however Frail and Brittle, are too strong Forts to be taken or destroyed by such puny and insufficient Pop-gun Artillery. The Matter, as I take it, stands thus:

§2. Since our Wealth has increased, and our Navigation has been extended, we have ransacked all the Parts of the *Globe* to bring together its whole Stock of Materials for *Riot, Luxury,* and to provoke *Excess.* The Tables of the Rich and Great (and indeed of all Ranks who can afford it) are furnished with Provision of Delicacy, Number, and Plenty, sufficient to provoke, and even gorge, the most large and voluptuous Appetite. The whole *Controversy* among us, seems to lie in out-doing one another in such Kinds of Profusion. *Invention* is racked, to furnish the Materials of our Food the most Delicate and Savoury possible: Instead of the plain *Simplicity* of leaving the Animals to range and feed in their proper *Element,* with their natural Nourishment, they are physicked[2] almost out of their Lives, and made as great *Epicures,* as those that feed on them; and by *Stalling, Cramming, Bleeding, Laming, Sweating, Purging,* and *Thrusting* down such unnatural and high-seasoned Foods into them, these Nervous Diseases are produced in the *Animals* themselves, who complain of such Disorders. Add to all this, the *torturing* and *lingering* Way of taking away the Lives of some of them, to make them more delicious: and the Dressing of them, by culinary Torments while alive, for their Purchaser's Table: All which must necessarily sharpen, impoison, corrupt, and putrify their natural Juices and Substances. The *Liquors* [3] also that are used for *Vehicles* to such Food, are the highest and most spirituous, the most scorched by the *Solar* Beams, or inflamed by repeated Distillations, to carry of the present Load, and leave a Disposition and Craving for a new one in the shortest Time possible. Any one who has but a tolerable Knowledge in *Philosophy,* or is acquainted with the Animal *Economy,*[4] can easily tell what the necessary Consequences of such a Diet must be in naturally weak Habits.[5]

§3. Not only the Materials of *Luxury* are such as I have described, but the Manner of Dressing or Cooking them, is carried on to an exalted Height. The ingenious mixing and compounding of *Sauces* with foreign *Spices* and Provocatives, are contrived, not only to rouse a sickly Appetite to receive the unnatural Load, but to render a natural good one incapable of knowing when it has enough. Since *French Cookery* has been in such Repute in *England,* and has been improved from *Spain, Italy, Turkey,* and every other Country that has any thing remarkably delicious, high, or savoury in Food; since *Eastern* Pickles and Sauces have been brought to embellish our continual Feasts; dressing, which was designed to assist the Labour of Digestion, as it is now managed, not only counteracts that Design, but is become the most *difficult, curious, ingenious,* and at the same Time, one of the most profitable Trades.

§4. Such a Course of Life must necessarily beget an Inaptitude for Exercise, and accordingly *Assemblies, Music-Meetings, Plays, Cards,* and *Dice,* are the only Amusements, or perhaps Business followed by such Persons as live in the Manner mentioned, and are most subject to such Complaints, on which all their Thoughts and Attention, nay, their Zeal and Spirits are spent. And to convey them with the least Pain and Uneasiness possible from Motion, or slavish Labour, to these still and bewitching Employments: *Coaches* are improved with

---

[2]   *physicked*   medicated.
[3]   *Liquors*   "Any thing liquid" (Johnson).

[4]   *Economy*   disposition.
[5]   *Habits*   constitutions.

Springs, *Horses* are taught to pace and amble, *Chairmen*[6] to wriggle and swim along, to render the Obstructions more firm and fixed in the small Vessels,[7] and to prevent all the Secretions that would any ways lighten the Burthen. Is it any Wonder then, that the Diseases which proceed from *Idleness* and *Fullness* of Bread, should increase in Proportion, and keep equal Pace with those Improvements of the Matter and Cause of Diseases?

§5. It is a common Observation (and, I think, has great Probability on its Side) that *Fools, weak* or *stupid* Persons, *heavy* and *dull Souls*, are seldom much troubled with Vapours or Lowness of Spirits. The intellectual Faculty, without all manner of Doubt, has material and animal Organs, by which it mediately works, as well as the animal Functions. What they are, and how they operate, as, I believe, very few know, so it is very little necessary to know them for my present Purpose. As a philosophical Musician may understand Proportions and Harmony, and yet never be in a Condition to gratify a Company with a fine Piece of Music, without the Benefit of Sounds from proper Organs, so the intellectual Operations (as long as the present Union between the Soul and Body[8] lasts) can never be performed in the best Manner without proper Instruments. The Works of *Imagination* and *Memory*, of *Study, Thinking,* and *Reflecting*, from whatever Source the Principle on which they depend springs, must necessarily require bodily Organs. Some have these Organs finer, quicker, more agile, and sensible,[9] and perhaps more numerous than others; *Brute* Animals have few or none, at least none that belong to *Reflection*; Vegetables certainly none at all. There is no Account to be given how a *Disease*, a *Fall*, a *Blow*, a *Debauch*, *Poisons*, *violent Passions*, *astral* and *aerial* Influences, much Application, and the like, should possibly alter or destroy these intellectual Operations without this Supposition. It is evident, that in *nervous* Distempers, and a great many other bodily Diseases, these Faculties, and their Operations, are impaired, nay totally ruined and extinguished to all Appearance; and yet, by proper Remedies, and after Recovery of Health, they are restored and brought to their former State. Now since this present Age has made Efforts to go beyond former Times, in all the Arts of *Ingenuity, Invention, Study, Learning,* and all the contemplative and sedentary Professions (I speak only here of our own Nation, our own Times, and of the better Sort, whose chief Employments and Studies these are), the Organs of these Faculties being thereby worn and spoiled, must affect and deaden the whole *System*, and lay a Foundation for the Diseases of Lowness and Weakness. Add to this, that those who are likeliest to excel and apply in this Manner, are most capable, and most in hazard of following that Way of Life which I have mentioned, as the likeliest to produce these Diseases. *Great Wits* are generally great *Epicures*, at least Men of *Taste*. And the Bodies and Constitutions of one Generation, are still more corrupt, infirm, and diseased, than those of the former, as they advance in Time, and the Use of the Causes assigned.

§6. To all these Considerations, if we add the present Custom of Living, so much in great, populous, and over-grown Cities; *London* (where nervous Distempers are most frequent, outrageous, and unnatural) is, for ought I know, the greatest, most capacious, close, and populous City of the *Globe*, the infinite Number of Fires, Sulphureous and Bituminous, the vast Expense of Tallow and fœtid Oil in Candles in Lamps, under and above Ground, the Clouds of stinking Breaths, and Perspiration, not to mention the Ordure of so many diseased, both intelligent and unintelligent Animals, the crowded Churches, Church-yards and Burying Places, with putrifying Bodies, the *Sinks, Butcher-Houses, Stables, Dunghills,* &c. and the necessary Stagnation, Fermentation, and Mixture of such Variety of all Kinds of Atoms, are

---

6 *Chairmen* those who bear sedan chairs through the streets for their masters or customers.
7 *Vessels* blood vessels.

8 *the present Union between the Soul and Body* life on earth.
9 *sensible* sensitive.

more than sufficient to putrify, poison and infect the Air for twenty Miles round it, and which, in Time, must alter, weaken, and destroy the healthiest Constitutions of Animals of All Kinds; and accordingly it is in such like Cities, that these Distempers are to be found in their highest and most astonishing Symptoms, and seldom any lasting or solid Cure is performed till the Diseased be *rusticated* and purified from the infectious Air and Damps transubstantiated into their Habits by a great City, and till they have sucked in and incorporated the sweet, balmy, clear Air of the Country, and driven the other out of their Habit. For by innumerable Experiments it is certain, that the Nitre or Acid of fresh, new Air, is as necessary towards Life and Health as fresh balmy[10] Food.

§7. All these together will, I think, be sufficient to account for the Frequency of *Nervous Distempers* of late. And, in fact, the same Causes, pretty near, have been assigned by all Observers, Physicians, and Philosophers, in all Ages and Countries, to have produced similar Effects. The *Egyptians*, as they seem to have been the first who cultivated the Arts of Ingenuity and Politeness, so they seem likewise to have been the first who brought *Physic* to any tolerable Degree of Perfection. The ancient *Greeks*, while they lived in their Simplicity and Virtue, were healthy, strong, and valiant: But afterwards, in Proportion as they advanced in Learning, and the Knowledge of the Sciences, and distinguished themselves from other Nations by their Politeness and Refinement, they sunk into *Effeminacy, Luxury,* and *Diseases*, and began to study *Physic*, to remedy those Evils which their Luxury and Laziness had brought upon them. In like manner, the *Romans* fell from their former Bravery, Courage, and *heroic Virtue*, which had gained them the Empire of the World. As *Celsus*[11] observes, where he is giving some Account of the Rise and Improvement of Physic, according to the Prevalency of these two general Causes of Diseases, *Idleness* and *Intemperance*; That 'these two had first spoil'd the Constitutions of the *Greeks,* and afterwards those of his own Countrymen the *Romans*, when become Masters of the Luxury as well as the Country of those polite People.'

§8. It were easy to show, from the best Philosophy, confirmed by the most solid Experience, that Distempers of all Kinds owe their more remote Origin, Cause, and Rise to the same Principles: And that the Pains and Trouble some have taken to search and discover from *History*, the Occasions and Times of the Appearance of such and such Distempers, ends only in gathering and collecting some new Names, which Mankind have arbitrarily bestowed upon some particular Symptoms, Degrees, or Paroxysms of universally known Diseases; and that these Enquiries, though they may divert and amuse the Enquirer and the Reader, like any other Pieces of History, are of no further Use or Advantage to the World, than in so far as they at the same Time discover the Means and Medicines by which such Symptoms or Degrees of Distempers were remedied or overcome. For, I think, it is plain to a Demonstration, that all Diseases whatsoever, by whatever Names or Titles dignified or distinguished, so far as they are natural and internal Distempers, and not caused by Accident, must in the main proceed (if we suppose, as we must, that Mankind at first were healthy and sound) from Intemperance, or some Error in the Quantity or Quality of their Food, and Laziness or Neglect of due Exercise: by which as the Solids and Juices of the Parents have been spoiled, so their Posterity by continuing the same Courses, have gradually suffered higher and more extreme Disorders or Symptoms, arising from the same general Causes: which upon their first Appearance receiving new Names by their Observers, as new and particular Distempers, have increased to such a Number, as to exhibit that numerous Train of Miseries with which our

---

10   *balmy* soothing.

11   *Celsus* Aurelius Cornelius Celsus, first-century CE Roman medical writer.

Books of Physic and *Bills of Mortality*[12] are filled: And as the Age grew worse, and the same Causes have been continued, and consequently the Constitutions more depraved, not only more numerous, but higher and more terrible Symptoms have arisen, till they have come at last to such a Degree of Malignity, as to infect and contaminate by mere Touch or Contact; nay, even by the Smoke or Steam emitted from such diseased Habits. Not that I would deny that *Seasons*, *Climates*, *astral* and *aerial* Influences, and many other Circumstances, had any Effect or Influence in begetting or propagating these Distempers, but that these are slight, partial, and occasional Causes only, in respect of those others mentioned. And he that will consult History, will find sufficient Arguments to draw the same Conclusions.

§9. All Diseases have in some Degree or other, or in Embryo, been extant at all Times, at least, might have been, if the efficient Causes, *Idleness* and *Luxury*, had been sufficiently set to *work*, which were chiefly in the Power of Men themselves. What we call Nervous Distempers, were certainly, in some small Degree, known and observed by the *Greek*, *Roman*, and *Arabian* Physicians, though not such a Number of them as now, not with so high Symptoms, so as to be so particularly taken notice of, except those called *Hysteric*,[13] which seem to have been known in *Greece*, from whence they have derived their Name: But as they were probably a stronger People, and lived in a warmer Climate, the slow, cold, and nervous Diseases were less known and observed; the Distempers of all the *Eastern* and *Southern* Countries being mostly *acute*.

§10. When these general Causes I have mentioned, came to exist in some more considerable Degree, and operate in the more *Northern* Climates, then these Nervous Diseases began to show themselves more eminently, and appear with higher and more numerous, and atrocious Symptoms. *Sydenham*,[14] our Countryman, was the Physician of Note who made the most particular and full Observations on them, and established them into a particular Class and Tribe, with a proper, though different, Method of Cure from other chronical and humorous[15] Distempers, though their true Nature, Cause, and Cure has been less universally laboured and known, than that of most other Diseases, so that those who could give no tolerable Account of them have called them *Vapours*, *Spleen*, *Flatus*, *Nervous*, *Hysterical*, and *Hypochondriacal* Distempers.

Joseph Addison (1672–1719) and Richard Steele (1672–1729)

The names of Addison and Steele are permanently linked in literary history because of their collaboration on the most important, broadly influential and popular journal published in the eighteenth century. The Spectator *began appearing on March 1, 1711, just about two months after the last issue of Steele's immensely popular* Tatler, *a series of thrice-weekly papers he wrote under the name of Isaac Bickerstaff. Steele was a well-known man about town with several successful plays to his credit and a conspicuous record of service as a writer under the Whig*

---

12 *Bills of Mortality*   records of deaths.
13 *Hysteric*   "Troubled with fits; disordered in the region of the womb" [Gk ὑστηρικός] (Johnson).
14 *Sydenham*   Thomas (1624–89), one of the most famous physicians of his day.

15 *humorous*   having to do with "the different kind of moisture in man's body, reckoned by the old physicians to be phlegm, blood, choler, and melancholy, which, as they predominated, were supposed to determine the temper of mind" (Johnson).

government of Queen Anne. The public immediately recognized The Spectator *as his, although, as was usual, the essays were signed in code only. Since the papers appeared every day, it was clear there must be a collaborator. The wit and learning of the papers made Swift a candidate, but it soon became clear that he was defecting from Steele's political party to join the newly formed Tory administration. Because of the change in government, Addison was unemployed and available to bring his considerable accomplishments as a classicist to the task of writing a daily paper. He was soon identified by the public as a principal in the new paper.*

There were several other contributors to The Spectator, *but Addison and Steele divided the vast majority of the 555 numbers that appeared continuously into December of 1712. There was a brief revival in 1714, but the real longevity of the paper came from the numerous collected editions, which were considered essential reading across a broad spectrum of the reading public, and, in fact, were influential in shaping that public. The papers employ a set of dramatis personae, led by Mr. Spectator, who visit places, mostly in London, and supply information and opinion from an urbane yet learned and witty point of view. As a kind of extension and apotheosis of coffee-house chat,* The Spectator *helped create the public sphere of private individuals, which recent sociologists have seen as so important in the formation of modern society.*

When the Whigs returned to power after 1714, Addison rose high, probably too high for his abilities, in the state department. Steele became the commissioner for forfeited Scottish estates and went on to become embroiled in further controversies in politics and literature. But it was their collaboration, during only two of the scant four years that their party was out of office, that has given them their lasting fame. Here are one number by Steele and two of Addison's pieces on Milton. They are characteristic of the respective collaborators in that Addison was always the arbiter of taste and style, as well as the classicist, whereas Steele was the large-souled observer of the human condition. The text is based on the collected edition of 1712, in which both authors, but especially the more deliberate Addison, made numerous small changes. The standard edition of The Spectator *is by Donald Bond (Clarendon Press, 1965). I am indebted to Bond's notes, his introduction, and his textual apparatus.*

from *The Spectator*

NUMBER 11 *TUESDAY, MARCH* 13, 1711
[INKLE AND YARICO]

Dat veniam corvis, vexat censura columbas. Juv.[1]

Arietta is visited by all Persons of both Sexes, who have any Pretence to Wit and Gallantry. She is in that time of Life which is neither affected with the Follies of Youth, or Infirmities of Age; and her Conversation is so mixed with Gaiety and Prudence, that she is agreeable both to the Young and the Old. Her Behaviour is very frank, without being in the least blameable; and she is out of the Tract[2] of any amorous or ambitious Pursuits of her own, her Visitants entertain her with Accounts of themselves very freely, whether they concern their Passions or their Interests. I made her a Visit this Afternoon, having been formerly

---

NUMBER 11 *TUESDAY*
[1]   *Dat veniam . . . Juv.* "He pardons the ravens and crucifies the doves" (Juvenal 2.63), a proverbial sentence, given by the female speaker of the poem, when she has

shown the folly of criticizing women when men are so much worse.
[2]   *Tract* period or duration.

introduced to the Honour of her Acquaintance, by my Friend WILL HONEYCOMB,[3] who has prevailed upon her to admit me sometimes into her Assembly, as a civil inoffensive Man. I found her accompanied with one Person only, a Common-Place Talker,[4] who, upon my Entrance, rose, and after a very slight Civility sat down again; then turning to *Arietta*, pursued his Discourse, which I found was upon the old Topic, of Constancy in Love. He went on with great Facility in repeating what he talks every Day of his Life; and, with the Ornaments of insignificant Laughs and Gestures, enforced his Arguments by Quotations out of Plays and Songs, which allude to the Perjuries of the Fair, and the general Levity of Women. Methought he strove to shine more than ordinarily in his Talkative Way, that he might insult my Silence, and distinguish himself before a Woman of *Arietta*'s Taste and Understanding. She had often an Inclination to interrupt him, but could find no Opportunity, 'till the Larum[5] ceased on its self; which it did not 'till he had repeated and murdered the celebrated Story of the *Ephesian* Matron[6].

Arietta seemed to regard this Piece of Raillery as an Outrage done to her Sex; as indeed I have always observed that Women, whether out of a nicer Regard to their Honour, or what other Reason, I cannot tell, are more sensibly touched with those general Aspersions, which are cast upon their Sex, than Men are by what is said of theirs.

When she had a little recovered her self from the serious Anger she was in, she replied in the following manner.

'Sir, When I consider, how perfectly new all you have said on this Subject is, and that the Story you have given us is not quite Two thousand Years Old, I cannot but think it a Piece of Presumption to dispute with you: But your Quotations put me in Mind of the Fable of the Lion and the Man. The Man walking with that noble Animal, showed him, in the Ostentation of Human Superiority, a Sign of a Man killing a Lion. Upon which the Lion said very justly, "We Lions are none of us Painters, else we could show a hundred Men killed by Lions, for one Lion killed by a Man". You Men are Writers, and can represent us Women as Unbecoming as you please in your Works, while we are unable to return the Injury. You have twice or thrice observed in your Discourse, that Hypocrisy is the very Foundation of our Education; and that an Ability to dissemble our Affections, is a professed Part of our Breeding. These, and such other Reflections, are sprinkled up and down the Writings of all Ages, by Authors, who leave behind them Memorials of their Resentment against the Scorn of particular Women, in Invectives against the whole Sex. Such a Writer, I doubt not, was the celebrated *Petronius*, who invented the pleasant Aggravations of the Frailty of the *Ephesian* Lady; but when we consider this Question between the Sexes, which has been either a Point of Dispute or Raillery ever since there were Men and Women, let us take Facts from plain People, and from such as have not either Ambition or Capacity to embellish their Narrations with any Beauties of Imagination. I was the other Day amusing my self with *Ligon*'s Account of *Barbadoes*;[7] and, in Answer to your well-wrought Tale, I will give you (as it dwells upon my Memory) out of that honest Traveller, in his Fifty-fifth Page, the History of *Inkle* and *Yarico*.

---

[3] *WILL HONEYCOMB* one of the characters who appears repeatedly in the essays; he is a friend of Mr. Spectator whose opinions about women are valued.
[4] *Common-Place Talker* one who rehashes well known subjects, or commonplaces.
[5] *Larum* alarm.
[6] *the Ephesian Matron Petronius* (d. 65 CE) tells this story in the *Satyricon* about a woman from Ephesus who

is courted by a soldier, as she weeps by the tomb of her recently killed husband; in the end, she gives in to the soldier and saves his life by offering to let him put her husband's body on the cross he has left unguarded in his ardor (Loeb edition, pp. 268–76).
[7] *Ligon's . . . Barbadoes* Richard Ligon, *A True and Exact History of the Island of Barbadoes* (1657).

Mr. *Thomas Inkle*, of *London*, aged twenty Years, embarked in the *Downs* on the good Ship called the *Achilles*, bound for the *West-Indies*, on the 16th of *June* 1647, in order to improve his Fortune by Trade and Merchandise. Our Adventurer was the third Son of an eminent Citizen, who had taken particular Care to instill into his Mind an early Love of Gain, by making him a perfect Master of Numbers, and consequently giving him a quick View of Loss and Advantage, and preventing the natural Impulses of his Passions, by Prepossession towards his Interests. With a Mind thus turned, young *Inkle* had a Person every way agreeable, a ruddy Vigour in his Countenance, Strength in his Limbs, with Ringlets of fair Hair loosely flowing on his Shoulders. It happened, in the Course of the Voyage, that the *Achilles*, in some Distress, put into a Creek on the Main of *America*, in Search of Provisions: The Youth, who is the Hero of my Story, among others, went ashore on this Occasion. From their first Landing they were observed by a Party of *Indians*, who hid themselves in the Woods for that Purpose. The *English* unadvisedly marched a great distance from the Shore into the Country, and were intercepted by the Natives, who slew the greatest Number of them. Our Adventurer escaped among others, by flying into a Forest. Upon his coming into a remote and pathless Part of the Wood, he threw himself, tired and breathless, on a little Hillock, when an *Indian* Maid rushed from a Thicket behind him: After the first Surprise, they appeared mutually agreeable to each other. If the *European* was highly Charmed with the Limbs, Features, and wild Graces of the Naked *American*; the *American* was no less taken with the Dress, Complexion and Shape of an *European,* covered from Head to Foot. The *Indian* grew immediately enamoured of him, and consequently solicitous for his Preservation: She therefore conveyed him to a Cave, where she gave him a Delicious Repast of Fruits, and led him to a Stream to slake his Thirst. In the midst of these good Offices, she would sometimes play with his Hair, and delight in the Opposition of its Colour, to that of her Fingers: Then open his Bosom, then laugh at him for covering it. She was, it seems, a Person of Distinction, for she every day came to him in a different Dress, of the most beautiful Shells, Bugles and Bredes.[8] She likewise brought him a great many Spoils, which her other Lovers had presented to her; so that his Cave was richly adorned with all the spotted Skins of Beasts, and most Party-coloured Feathers of Fowls, which that World afforded. To make his Confinement more tolerable, she would carry him in the Dusk of the Evening, or by the favour of Moon-light, to unfrequented Groves and Solitudes, and show him where to lie down in Safety, and sleep amidst the Falls of Waters, and Melody of Nightingales. Her Part was to watch and hold him in her Arms, for fear of her Country-men, and wake him on Occasions to consult his Safety. In this manner did the Lovers pass away their Time, till they had learned a Language of their own, in which the Voyager communicated to his Mistress, how happy he should be to have her in his Country, where she should be Clothed in such Silks as his Waistcoat was made of, and be carried in Houses drawn by Horses, without being exposed to Wind or Weather. All this he promised her the Enjoyment of, without such Fears and Alarms as they were there Tormented with. In this tender Correspondence these Lovers lived for several Months, when *Yarico*, instructed by her Lover, discovered a Vessel on the Coast, to which she made the Signals; and in the Night, with the utmost Joy and Satisfaction accompanied him to a Ship's-Crew of his Country-men, bound for *Barbadoes*. When a Vessel from the Main arrives in that Island, it seems the Planters come down to the Shore, where there is an immediate Market of the *Indians* and other Slaves, as with us of Horses and Oxen.

To be short, Mr. *Thomas Inkle*, now coming into *English* Territories, began seriously to reflect upon his loss of Time, and to weigh with himself how many Days Interest of his Money

---

[8]   *Bugles*   "Shining beads of black glass" (Johnson);
Bredes   braids.

he had lost during his stay with *Yarico*. This Thought made the Young Man very pensive, and careful what Account he should be able to give his Friends of his Voyage. Upon which Considerations, the prudent and frugal young Man sold *Yarico* to a *Barbadian* Merchant; notwithstanding that the poor Girl, to incline him to commiserate her Condition, told him that she was with Child by him: But he only made use of that Information to rise in his Demands upon the Purchaser.

I was so touched with this Story (which I think should be always a Counterpart to the *Ephesian* Matron) that I left the Room with Tears in my Eyes; which a Woman of *Arietta*'s good Sense, did, I am sure, take for greater Applause, than any Compliments I could make her.

R[9]

NUMBER 267 *Saturday, January* 5, 1712
[The Plot of *Paradise Lost*]

Cedite Romani Scriptores, cedite Graii. Propert.[1]

There is nothing in Nature so irksome than general Discourses, especially when they turn chiefly upon Words. For this Reason I shall waive the Discussion of that Point which was started some Years since, Whether *Milton*'s *Paradise Lost* may be called an Heroic Poem?[2] Those who will not give it that Title, may call it (if they please) a *Divine Poem*. It will be sufficient to its Perfection, if it has in it all the Beauties of the highest kind of Poetry; and as for those who allege it is not an Heroic Poem, they advance no more to the Diminution of it, than if they should say *Adam* is not *Æneas*, nor *Eve Helen*.

I shall therefore examine it by the Rules of Epic Poetry, and see whether it falls short of the *Iliad* or *Æneid*, in the Beauties which are essential to that Kind of Writing. The first Thing to be considered in an Epic Poem, is the Fable,[3] which is perfect or imperfect, according as the Action which it relates is more or less so. This Action should have three Qualifications in it. First, It should be but one Action. Secondly, It should be an entire Action; and Thirdly, it should be a great Action.[4] To consider the Action of the *Iliad*, *Æneid*, and *Paradise Lost*, in these three several Lights. *Homer* to preserve the Unity of his Action hastens into the midst of things, as *Horace* has observed:[5] Had he gone up to *Leda*'s Egg, or begun much later, even at the Rape of *Helen*, or the Investing of *Troy*, it is manifest that the Story of the Poem would have been a Series of several Actions. He therefore opens his Poem with the Discord of his Princes, and with great art interweaves in the several succeeding Parts of it, an account of every Thing material which relates to them, and has passed before this fatal Dissention. After the same Manner *Æneas* makes his first appearance in the *Tyrrhene* Seas, and within Sight of *Italy*, because the Action proposed to be celebrated was that of his Settling himself in *Latium*. But because it was necessary for the Reader to know what had happened to him in the taking of *Troy*, and in the preceding parts of his Voyage, *Virgil* makes his Hero relate it by Way of Episode in the second and third Books of the *Æneid*. The Contents of both which Books come before those of the first Book in the Thread of the Story,

---

[9] *R* the code signature of Richard Steele.
Number 267 *Saturday*
[1] *Cedite . . . Propert*[ius] "Make way, Roman writers! Make way, Greeks" (*Elegies* 2.34.65; applied to Virgil by Propertius and transferred to Milton in one of the laudatory poems at the beginning of the second edition of *Paradise Lost* (1674).

[2] *Heroic Poem* an Epic.
[3] *Fable* the story, or plot.
[4] *Action* Addison's criteria follow Aristotle's requirements for the action of a tragedy, stated in his *Poetics*.
[5] *as Horace has observed* in *Ars Poetica*, ll. 147–8.

though for preserving of this Unity of Action, they follow it in the Disposition of the Poem. *Milton,* in Imitation of these two great Poets, opens his *Paradise Lost* with an infernal Council plotting the Fall of Man, which is the Action he proposed to celebrate; and as for those great Actions which preceded, in Point of Time, the Battle of the Angels, and the Creation of the World (which would have entirely destroyed the Unity of his principal Action, had he related them in the same Order that they happened), he cast them into the fifth, sixth and seventh Books, by way of Episode to this noble Poem.

Artistotle himself allows, that *Homer* has nothing to boast of as to the Unity of his Fable, though at the same time that great Critic and Philosopher endeavours to palliate this Imperfection in the *Greek* Poet, by imputing it in some Measure to the very Nature of an Epic Poem. Some have been of Opinion, that the *Æneid* also labours in this Particular, and has Episodes which may be looked upon as Excrescencies rather than as Parts of the Action. On the contrary, the Poem which we have now under our Consideration hath no other Episodes than such as naturally arise from the Subject, and yet is filled with such a Multitude of astonishing Incidents, that it gives us at the same Time a Pleasure of the greatest Variety, and of the greatest Simplicity.

I must observe also, that as *Virgil* in the Poem which was designed to celebrate the Original of the *Roman* Empire, has described the Birth of its great Rival, the *Carthaginian* Commonwealth: *Milton* with the like Art in his Poem on the Fall of Man, has related the Fall of those Angels who are his professed Enemies. Besides the many other Beauties in such an Episode, its running Parallel with the great Action of the Poem hinders it from breaking the Unity so much as another Episode had done, that had not so great an Affinity with the principal Subject. In short, this is the same kind of Beauty which the Critics admire in the *Spanish Fryar*, or the *Double Discovery*,[6] where the two different Plots look like Counterparts and Copies of one another.

The second Qualification required in the Action of an Epic Poem is, that it should be an *entire* Action: An Action is entire when it is complete in all its Parts; or as *Artistotle* describes it, when it consists of a Beginning, a Middle, and an End. Nothing should go before it, be intermixed with it, or follow after it, that is not related to it. As on the contrary, no single Step should be omitted in that just and regular Progress which it must be supposed to take from its Original to its Consummation. Thus we see the Anger of *Achilles* in its Birth, its Continuance and Effects; and *Æneas*'s Settlement in *Italy*, carried on through all the Oppositions in his Way to it both by Sea and Land. The Action in *Milton* excels (I think) both the former in this Particular; we see it contrived in Hell, executed upon Earth, and punished by Heaven. The Parts of it are told in the most distinct Manner, and grow out of one another in the most natural Method.

The third Qualification of an Epic Poem is its *Greatness*. The Anger of *Achilles* was of such Consequence, that it embroiled the Kings of *Greece*, destroyed the Heroes of *Asia*, and engaged all the Gods in Factions. *Æneas*'s Settlement in *Italy* produced the *Cæsars*, and gave Birth to the *Roman* Empire. *Milton*'s Subject was still greater than either of the former; it does not determine the Fate of single Persons or Nations, but of a whole Species. The united Powers of Hell are joined together for the Destruction of Mankind, which they effected in Part, and would have completed, had not Omnipotence it self interposed. The principal Actors are Man in his greatest Perfection, and Woman in her highest Beauty. Their Enemies

---

[6]   *Spanish Fryar, or the Double Discovery*   a play by John
Dryden (1681).

are the fallen Angels: The Messiah their Friend, and the Almighty their Protector. In short, every Thing that is great in the whole Circle of Being, whether within the Verge of Nature, or out of it, has a proper Part assigned it in this noble Poem.

In Poetry, as in Architecture, not only the Whole, but the principal Members, and every Part of them, should be Great. I will not presume to say, that the Book of Games in the *Æneid*, or that in the *Iliad*,[7] as liable to any Censure in this Particular; but I think we may say, without derogating from those wonderful Performances, that there is an unquestionable Magnificence in every Part of *Paradise Lost*, and indeed a much greater than could have been formed upon any Pagan System.

But *Aristotle*, by the Greatness of the Action, does not only mean that it should be great in its Nature, but also in its Duration, or in other Words, that it should have a due Length in it, as well as what we properly call Greatness. The just Measure of this Kind of Magnitude, he explains by the following Similitude. An Animal, no bigger than a Mite, cannot appear perfect to the Eye, because the Sight takes it in at once, and has only a confused Idea of the Whole, and not a distinct Idea of all its Parts; If on the contrary you should suppose an Animal of ten thousand Furlongs in Length, the Eye would be so filled with a single Part of it, that it could not give the Mind an Idea of the Whole. What these Animals are to the Eye, a very short or a very long Action would be to the Memory. The first would be, as it were, lost and swallowed up by it, and the other difficult to be contained in it. *Homer* and *Virgil* have shown their principal Art in this Particular; the Action of the *Iliad*, and that of the *Æneid*, were in themselves exceeding short, but are so beautifully extended and diversified by the Invention of *Episodes*, and the Machinery of the Gods,[8] with the like poetical Ornaments, that they make up an agreeable Story sufficient to employ the Memory without overchanging it. *Milton*'s Action is enriched with such a variety of Circumstances, that I have taken as much Pleasure in reading the Contents[9] of his Books, as in the best invented Story I ever met with. It is possible, that the Traditions on which the *Iliad* and *Æneid* were built had more Circumstances in them than the History of *the Fall of Man*, as it is related in the Scripture. Besides it was easier for *Homer* and *Virgil* to dash the Truth with Fiction, as they were in no danger of offending the Religion of their Country by it. But as for *Milton*, he had not only a very few Circumstances upon which to raise his Poem, but was also obliged to proceed with the greatest Caution in every Thing that he added out of his own Invention. And, indeed, notwithstanding all the Restraints he was under, he has filled his Story with so many surprising Incidents, which bear so close Analogy with what is delivered in Holy Writ, that it is capable of pleasing the most delicate Reader, without giving Offence to the most scrupulous.

The modern Critics have collected from several Hints in the *Iliad* and the *Æneid* the Space of Time, which is taken up by the Action of each of those Poems; but as a great Part of *Milton*'s Story was transacted in Regions that lie out of the reach of the Sun and the Sphere of Day, it is impossible to gratify the Reader with such a Calculation, which indeed would be more curious than instructive; none of the Critics, either Ancient or Modern, having laid down Rules to circumscribe the Action of an Epic Poem with any determined number of Years, Days or Hours.

---

[7] *Book of Games Æneid* Book 5, which tells of the games held in honour of the first anniversary of Anchises' death and *Iliad* 23, about the games in honour of Patroclus.

[8] *Machinery of the Gods* "that part which the deities, angels, or demons act in a poem" (Johnson, citing Pope).

[9] *Contents* the "Arguments" at the beginning of each book.

This Piece of Criticism on Milton's Paradise Lost *shall be carried on in the following* Saturday's *Papers.*

L[10]

NUMBER 279 SATURDAY, JANUARY 19, 1712
[THE SENTIMENTS AND LANGUAGE OF *PARADISE LOST*]

Reddere personæ scit convenientia cuique. Hor.[1]

We have already taken a general Survey of the Fable and Characters in *Milton's Paradise Lost*: The Parts which remain to be considered, according to *Aristotle's* Method,[2] are the *Sentiments* and the Language. Before I enter upon the first of these, I must advertise[3] my Reader, that it is my Design as soon as I have finished my general Reflections on these four several Heads, to give particular Instances out of the Poem now before us of Beauties and Imperfections which may be observed under each of them, as also of such other Particulars as may not properly fall under any of them. This I thought fit to premise, that the Reader may not judge too hastily of this Piece of Criticism, or look upon it as Imperfect, before he has seen the whole Extent of it.

The Sentiments in an Epic Poem are the Thoughts and Behaviour which the Author ascribes to the Persons whom he introduces, and are *just* when they are conformable to the Characters of the several Persons. The Sentiments have likewise a Relation to *Things* as well as *Persons*, and are then perfect when they are such as are adapted to the Subject. If in either of these Cases the Poet argues, or explains, magnifies or diminishes, raises Love or Hatred, Pity or Terror, or any other Passion, we ought to consider whether the Sentiments he makes Use of are proper for those Ends. *Homer* is censured by the Critics for his Defect as to this Particular in several Parts of the *Iliad* and *Odyssey*, though at the same Time those who have treated this great Poet with Candour,[4] have attributed this Defect to the Times in which he lived. It was the Fault of the Age, and not of *Homer*, if there wants that Delicacy in some of his Sentiments, which appears in the Works of Men of a much inferior Genius. Besides, if there are Blemishes in any particular Thoughts, there is an infinite Beauty in the greatest Part of them. In short, if there are many Poets who would not have fallen into the Meanness of some of his Sentiments, there are none who could have risen up to the Greatness of others. *Virgil* has excelled all others in the Propriety of his Sentiments. *Milton* shines likewise very much in this Particular: Nor must we omit one Consideration which adds to his Honour and Reputation. *Homer* and *Virgil* introduced Persons whose Characters are commonly known among Men, and such as are to be met with either in History, or in ordinary Conversation. *Milton's* Characters, most of them, lie out of Nature, and were to be formed purely by his own Invention. It shows a greater Genius in *Shakespeare* to have drawn his *Caliban*, than his *Hotspur* or *Julius Cæsar*: The one was to be supplied out of his own Imagination, whereas the other might have been formed upon Tradition, History and Observation. It was much easier

---

[10]   *L* one of Addison's signature letters, C-L-I-O, which spells the name of the muse of history; Addison continued his remarks on *Paradise Lost* over the course of eighteen *Spectator* papers.

NUMBER 279

[1]   *Reddere . . . Hor{ace}*   "[the wise man or poet] understands what is appropriate for each person [or character]" "Ars Poetica" 316.

[2]   *Aristotle's Method*   in the *Poetics*, which also includes a discussion of spectacle, a part of tragedy which appears in production and so does not pertain to epic poetry.

[3]   *advertise*   inform.

[4]   *Candour*   kindness.

therefore for *Homer* to find proper Sentiments for an Assembly of *Grecian* Generals, than for *Milton* to diversify his infernal Council with proper Characters, and inspire them with a Variety of Sentiments. The Loves of *Dido* and *Æneas* are only Copies of what has passed between other Persons. *Adam* and *Eve*, before the Fall, are a different Species from that of Mankind, who are descended from them; and none but a Poet of the most unbounded Invention, and the most exquisite Judgement, could have filled their Conversation and Behaviour with such beautiful Circumstances during their State of Innocence.

Nor is it sufficient for an Epic Poem to be filled with such Thoughts as are *natural*, unless it also abound with such as are *sublime*. *Virgil* in this Particular falls short of *Homer*. He has not indeed so many Thoughts that are low and vulgar; but at the same Time has not so many Thoughts that are sublime and noble. The Truth of it is, *Virgil* seldom rises into very astonishing Sentiments, where he is not fired by the *Iliad*. He every where charms and pleases us by the Force of his own Genius; but seldom elevates and transports us where he does not fetch his Hints from *Homer*.

Milton's chief Talent, and indeed his distinguishing Excellence, lies in the Sublimity of his Thoughts. There are other of the Moderns who rival him in every other Part of Poetry; but in the Greatness of his Sentiments he triumphs over all the Poets both Modern and Ancient, *Homer* only excepted. It is impossible for the Imagination of Man to distend it self with greater Ideas, than those which he has laid together in his first, second and tenth Books. The Seventh, which describes the Creation of the World, is likewise wonderfully sublime, though not so apt to stir up Emotion in the Mind of the Reader, nor consequently so perfect in the Epic Way of Writing, because it is filled with less Action. Let the Reader compare what *Longinus*[5] has observed on several Passages in *Homer*, and he will find Parallels for most of them in the *Paradise Lost*.

From what has been said we may infer, that as there are two Kinds of Sentiments, the Natural and the Sublime, which are always to be pursued in an heroic Poem, there are also two Kinds of Thoughts which are carefully to be avoided. The first are such as are affected and unnatural; the second such as are mean and vulgar. As for the first Kind of Thoughts we meet with little or Nothing that is like them in *Virgil*: He has none of those trifling Points and Puerilities that are so often to be met with in *Ovid*, none of the Epigrammatic Turns of *Lucan*, none of those swelling Sentiments which are so frequent in *Statius* and *Claudian*, none of those mixed Embellishments of *Tasso*.[6] Every Thing is just and natural. His Sentiments show that he had perfect Insight into human Nature, and that he knew every Thing which was the most proper to affect it.

Mr. *Dryden* has in some Places, which I may hereafter take Notice of, misrepresented *Virgil*'s way of Thinking as to this Particular, in the Translation he has given us of the *Æneid*. I do not remember that *Homer* any where falls into the Faults above mentioned, which were indeed the false Refinements of later Ages. *Milton*, it must be confessed, has sometimes erred in this Respect, as I shall show more at large in another Paper;[7] though considering all the Poets of the Age in which he writ were infected with this Wrong way of Thinking, he is rather to be admired[8] that he did not give more into it, than that he did sometimes comply with the vicious Taste which prevails so much among Modern Writers.

But since several Thoughts may be natural which are low and grovelling, an Epic Poet

---

5   *Longinus*   supposed author of a treatise on the sublime in poetry (περὶ ὕψους; lit. "on elevation").
6   *Lucan, Statius, Claudian, Tasso*   three Roman epic
poets and one Italian, chronologically arranged.

7   *another Paper*   no. 297.
8   *admired*   wondered at; found surprising.

should not only avoid such Sentiments as are unnatural or affected, but also such as are low and vulgar. *Homer* has opened a great Field of Raillery to Men of more Delicacy than Greatness of Genius by the Homeliness of some of his Sentiments. But, as I have before said, these are rather to be imputed to the Simplicity of the Age in which he lived, to which I may also add, of that which he described, than to any Imperfection in that Divine Poet. *Zoilus*,[9] among the Ancients, and Monsieur *Perrault*,[10] among the Moderns, pushed their Ridicule very far upon him, on Account of some such Sentiments. There is no Blemish to be observed in *Virgil*, under this Head, and but a very few in *Milton*.

I shall give but one Instance of this Impropriety of Sentiments in *Homer*, and at the same Time compare it with an Instance of the same Nature, both in *Virgil* and *Milton*. Sentiments which raise Laughter, can very seldom be admitted with any Decency into an heroic Poem, whose Business is to excite Passions of a much nobler Nature. *Homer*, however, in his Characters of *Vulcan* and *Thersites*,[11] in his Story of *Mars* and *Venus*,[12] in his Behaviour of *Irus*,[13] and in other Passages, has been observed to have lapsed into the Burlesque Character, and to have departed from that serious Air which seems essential to the Magnificence of an Epic Poem. I remember but one Laugh in the whole *Æneid*, which rises in the fifth Book upon *Monœtes*, where he is represented as thrown overboard, and drying himself upon a Rock.[14] But this Piece of Mirth is so well timed, that the severest Critic can have nothing to say against it, for it is in the Book of Games and Diversions, where the Reader's Mind may be supposed to be sufficiently relaxed for such an Entertainment. The only Piece of Pleasantry in *Paradise Lost* is where the evil Spirits are described as rallying the Angels upon the Success of their new invented Artillery. This Passage I look upon to be the most exceptionable in the whole Poem, as being nothing else but a String of Puns, and those too very indifferent ones.

> ——Satan beheld their Plight,
> And to his Mates thus in derision called.
> 'O Friends, why come not on these Victors proud!
> Ere while they fierce were coming, and when we,
> To entertain them fair with *open Front*,   5
> And Breast, (what could we more) propounded Terms
> Of *Composition*; straight they changed their Minds,
> Flew off, and into strange Vagaries fell,
> As they would dance, yet for a Dance they seemed
> Somewhat extravagant and wild, perhaps   10
> For Joy of offered Peace; but I suppose
> If our Proposals once again were *heard*,
> We should compel them to a quick *Result*.'
> To whom thus *Belial* in like gamesome Mood.
> 'Leader, the Terms we sent, were Terms of *Weight*,   15
> Of *hard Contents*, and full of Force urged home,
> Such as we might perceive amused them all,

---

[9] *Zoilus* Cynic philosopher and critic of the fourth century BCE.
[10] *Perrault* Charles Perrault (1628–1703) French critic and defender of the moderns in the long debate concerning their inferiority or superiority to the ancients.
[11] *Vulcan* and *Thersites* physically unattractive charac-

ters (*Iliad* 1.595–600 and 2.211–77, respectively).
[12] *Mars* and *Venus* Vulcan traps them in his net while they are in the act (*Odyssey* 8.266–366).
[13] *Irus* the vulgar beggar beaten by Odysseus on his return to Ithaka (*Odyssey* 18.1–107).
[14] *Monœtes . . . upon a Rock* Aeneid 5.158–82.

And *stumbled* many; who received them right,
Had need, from Head to Foot, well *understand*;
Not *understood*, this Gift they have besides,   20
They show us when our Foes *walk not upright.*
    Thus they among themselves in pleasant vein
Stood scoffing———[15]

L

Isaac Watts (1674–1748)

Watts was one of the five poets whom Samuel Johnson personally recommended that the publishers include in their enormous collection of British Poets, *for which he wrote his famous biographical prefaces known as* The Lives of the Poets. *Watts was a dissenting minister who wrote against the established church, but his simplicity, his piety, his evident sincerity, and his determination to write for the purpose of improving his readers were irresistible to Johnson. Watts was also a skillful versifier, and a great number of his songs have found their way into all sorts of Christian hymnals. He wrote a great deal of verse and prose for children and students, and he gave generously of his own meagre property to assist educational projects, such as a fledgling American college called Yale that so badly needed books.*

The texts presented here come from Divine Songs Attempted in Easy Language for the Use of Children *(1715).*

from *Divine Songs Attempted in Easy Language for the Use of Children* (1715)

AGAINST QUARRELLING AND FIGHTING

Let Dogs delight to bark and bite,
    For GOD hath made them so;
Let Bears and Lions growl and fight,
    For 'tis their Nature too.

But, Children, you should never let   5
    Such angry Passions rise;
Your little Hands were never made
    To tear each other's Eyes.

Let Love through all your Actions run,
    And all your Words be mild;   10
Live like the blessèd Virgin's Son,
    That sweet and lovely Child.

His Soul was gentle as a Lamb;
    And as his Stature grew,

---

[15] *... Stood scoffing Paradise Lost* 6.607–29, with Addison's italics added for emphasis; "Thus they" for "So they" in l. 628; and some minor deviations from the punctuation in the standard texts.

He grew in Favour both with Man   15
    And God his Father too.

Now, Lord of all, he reigns above,
    And from his heav'nly Throne,
He sees what Children dwell in Love,
    And marks them for his own.   20

THE SLUGGARD[1]

'Tis the Voice of the Sluggard. I hear him complain
'You have waked me too soon, I must slumber again.'
As the Door on it Hinges, so he on his Bed,
Turns his Sides, and his Shoulders, and his heavy Head.

'A little more Sleep, and a little more Slumber';   5
Thus he wastes half his Days, and his Hours without number:
And when he gets up, he sits folding his Hands
Or walks about saunt'ring, or trifling he stands.

I passed by his Garden, and saw the wild Briar
The Thorn and the Thistle grow broader and higher: 10
The Clothes that hang on him are turning to Rags;
And his Money still wastes, still he starves, or he begs.

I made him a Visit, still hoping to find
He had took better care for improving his Mind:
He told me his Dreams, talked of eating and drinking,   15
But he scarce reads his Bible, and never loves thinking.

Said I then to my Heart, 'Here's a Lesson for me',
That Man's but the Picture of what I might be:
But thanks to my Friends for their care in my Breeding:
Who taught me betimes to love Working and Reading.[2]   20

Elizabeth Singer Rowe (1674–1737)

In the last ten years of her life Rowe was influenced by mystical religious ideas and produced her best known work Friendship in Death, or Letters from the Dead to the Living *(1728). The spiritual world is even closer in* Devout Exercises *(1738), which Rowe consigned to her friend and fellow dissenter Isaac Watts for posthumous publication. Earlier, however, Rowe wrote boldly about earthly love in poems that she later repudiated. But both early and late in her career Rowe's poetry makes unusual combinations of romantic and religious imagery. The poems that follow come from her earliest volume,* Poems on Several Occasions *(1696).*

THE SLUGGARD
[1] *The Sluggard* he is one kind of "fool" mentioned frequently in the Book of Proverbs, which supplies the background of Watts's poem.

[2] *betimes* early.

from *Poems on Several Occasions* (1696)

A FAREWELL TO LOVE

When, since in spite of all that Love can do,
The dangerous steps of Honour thoul't pursue,
I'll just grow Wise and Philosophic too:
I'll bid these tender silly things Farewell;
And Love, with thy great Antidote, expel: 5
I'll tread the same Ambitious Paths with thee,
And Glory too shall be my Deity.
And now I'll once release my Train of Fools,
In *Sheer good* Nature to the Loving Souls;
For Pity's-sake at last I'll set at rights   10
The vain conceits of the presumptuous Wights:
For though I shake off *Theron's* Chains, yet he[1]
Is all that e'er deserved a Smile from me.
But he's unjust, and false; and I a part
Would not accept, though of *a MONARCH's* heart.   15
And therefore flattering hopes, and wishes too,
With all Love's soft Concomitants, adieu:
No more to its Imperious Yoke I'll bow;
Pride and Resentment fortify me now.
My Inclinations are reversed; nor can   20
I but abhor the Slavery of Man,
How e'er the *empty Lords of Nature* boast
O'er me, their Fond Prerogative is lost:
For, Uncontrolled, I thus resolve to rove,
And hear no more of *Hymen,* or of *Love:*[2]   25
No more such Wild Fantastic things shall Charm:
My Breast; nor these Serener Thoughts Alarm.
No more for Farce, I'll make a Lover Creep,
And look as Scurvy as if he had bit a Sheep.[3]
Nor with Dissembled Smiles indulge the Fops,[4]   30
In pure Revenge to their Audacious hopes;
Though at my Feet a thousand Victims lay,
I'd proudly spurn the Whining Slaves away.
Deaf, as the Winds, or *Theron,* would I prove,
And hear no more of Hymen, *or of* Love.   35
Like bright *Diana* now I'll range the Woods,[5]
And haunt the silent Shades and silver Floods.

A FAREWELL TO LOVE
[1] *Theron* name of the tyrant of Acragas, Sicily, to whom Pindar (b. 518 BCE) wrote many of his odes.
[2] *Hymen* god of marriage.
[3] *Scurvy . . . Sheep* poorly dressed meat was considered a cause of scurvy (as well as melancholy and other inexplicable diseases) until mid-century when James Lind discovered it was a lack of vitamin C.
[4] *Fop* "a man fond of show, dress, and flutter" (Johnson).
[5] *Diana* the chaste huntress of the gods.

I'll find out the Remotest Paths I can,
To shun th' Offensive, Hated Face of Man.
Where I'll Indulge my Liberty and Bliss,   40
And no *Endymion* shall obtain a Kiss.[6]
Now, *Cupid, Mourn;* the enlargement of my fate.

THE RAPTURE

1

Lord! if one distant glimpse *of thee*
  Thus elevate *the* Soul,
In what a heighth of Ecstasy
  Do those bless'd Spirits *roll,*

2

Who by a fixed eternal View   5
  Drink in immortal Rays;
To whom unveiled *thou dost show*
  Thy Smiles *without* Allays?[1]

3

An Object which if mortal Eyes
  Could make approaches *to,*   10
They'd soon esteem their best-loved Toys
  Not worth one scornful View.

4

How then, beneath its load *of* Flesh
  Would the vexed Soul *complain!*
And how the Friendly Hand *she'd bless*   15
  Would break her hated Chain![2]

Mary Molesworth Monck (1677?–1715)

Even upper-class women of the eighteenth century, like Monck, were usually denied the advantages of learning. There were, of course, some enlightened parents, but most often it took sheer determination for a woman to learn classical languages and accumulate other literary capital. Monck must have been determined because her translations show that she was adept at Latin, Spanish, and Italian. In her poem "To a Romantic Lady," she looks askance at the kind of romance reading that

---

[6]   *Endymion*   a beautiful youth loved by Selene, goddess of the Moon.
THE RAPTURE
[1]   *Allay*   "Any thing, being added, which abates the

predominant quality of that with which it is mingled" (Johnson).
[2]   *Chain*   a common name in poetry for the link between body and soul.

was considered ladies' fare, but she probably knew it as well. Some of her writing is about reading and other literary matters, and much is devoted to translation. However, the long poem Moccoli *shows that she could render her direct perceptions of landscape into verse, and her final poem to her husband is both formal and emotional. The shorter poems offered here come from* Marinda, Poems and Translations upon Several Occasions *(1716), except for the last poem, which comes from the important collection of women's verse* Poems by Eminent Ladies *(1755).* Moccoli *seems to have been published with* Marinda, *though it has its own title page.*

from *Marinda, Poems and Translations upon Several Occasions* (1716)

ON THE INVENTION OF LETTERS

from Brébeuf[1]

The Noble Art from Cadmus took its rise[2]
Of painting Words, and speaking to the Eyes:
He first in wondrous Magic Fetters bound
The Airy Voice, and stopped the flying Sound:
The various Figures by his Pencil wrought,   5
Gave Colour, and a Body to the Thought.

ON A *ROMANTIC* LADY

This poring over your grand *Cyrus*[1]
Must ruin you, and will tire us:
It makes you think, that an Affront 'tis,
Unless your Lover's an *Orontes*,[2]
And courts you with a Passion frantic,   5
In Manner and in Style Romantic.
Now though I count myself no *Zero*,
I don't pretend to be a *Hero*.
Or a By-blow of him that thunders,
Nor are you one of the sev'n Wonders,   10
But a young Damsel very pretty,
And your true Name is Mistress *Betty*.

ON *MARINDA*'S TOILETTE

Hence vulgar Beauties take their pow'rful Arms,
And from their Toilette borrow all their Charms:

ON THE INVENTION OF LETTERS
[1] *Brébeuf* St Jean de Brébeuf (1593–1649), Jesuit priest and patron saint of Canada, author of a book on the language of the Huron Indians and of the French poem from which Monck translates.
[2] *Cadmus* legendary founder of Thebes, said to have taught the Boetians of central Greece to write with Phonecian letters.

ON A *ROMANTIC* LADY
[1] *grand Cyrus* a romance, *Artamène, ou le Grand Cyrus*, 10 vols (1649–53) by Madeleine de Scudéry.
[2] *Orontes* perhaps Oroondates, a character in *Cassandra*, a romance by La Calprenède, 10 vols (1642–5).

678   MARY MOLESWORTH MONCK

But bright Marinda with a kinder Care
Rebares her sharper-pointed Glances here.
With our weak Sight in pity she complies,   5
And with our Fashions veils the Glories of her Eyes.
The Angels thus descending from above
To visit Men with Messages of Love,
Such Shape assumed our Blessing to complete,
And make the Favour kind as it was great.   10
Through mortal Vestments shone th' Angelic Air,
And though in human Form they seemed most heav'nly Fair.

from *Moccoli*[1]

ADDRESSED TO COLONEL RICHARD MOLESWORTH[2]

The Hilly *Apennine*, hence all around   84
With long indented Ridge our View does bound,
The scattered *Villas* to his Shoulders cling,
And his steep Sides a plenteous Harvest bring,
The craggy Glebe vexed with continued Toil[3]
His Lord enriches with a noble Spoil,
Chequers with various Fruits the wanton Board,   90
Whilst his deep Vaults with Wine and Oil are stored,
And from the Silk-worm's Loom, the gaudy Bride
Goes forth attired, in more than Eastern Pride:
Hills heaped on Hills, *here*, scarce their Load sustain,
There pointed Rocks hang threat'ning o'er the Plain,   95
And from behind the jutting Heights you spy
The stately Fabric's start, and fill the Eye.[4]
As when Armida, by the force of Charms[5]
Allures the Hero to her longing Arms,
The Pond'rous Scene shakes at the Magic Noise,   100
Shifts unperceived, obedient to her Voice,
And th' Airy Pile on well ranged Columns placed,
Gilds the rude horror of the dreary Waste.
    Here the bold Eye, the dark Recess invades
Of *Valombrosa*, which our Landscape shades[6]   105
With bord'ring Gloom: But how dare I rehearse
Those awful Beauties sung in *Milton*'s Verse?
Thrice happy Vale! by his Immortal Wit

FROM *MOCCOLI*
[1] *Moccoli* A villa near Florence where His Majesty's
Envoy lived [Monck's note].
[2] *Richard Molesworth* her brother and a military hero
(1680–1758).

[3] *Glebe* soil, earth.
[4] *Fabric* building.
[5] *Armida* an Amazonian heroine in *Rinaldo*, an opera
by Handel (1711) based on an episode in Tasso.
[6] *Valombrosa* see *Paradise Lost* 1.303.

You'll flourish, when your agèd Trees submit
To Avarice, or Fate – A numerous Fry,[7]   110
The Lumber of the World, are here thrown by,[8]
Who've yet thought good enough their God to please,
And here devoutly dull in reverend Ease
Doze away Life, and in a Mystic Round
Of senseless Rites their Days and Nights confound.   115
Strange Charms this Place enchant with Holy Art,
They enter Fools, live Drones, and Saints depart.
As if by a Caprice of Power were giv'n
To the most Worthless the best Posts in Heav'n;
Or God, like Eastern Monarchs, thought it State[9]   120
That Mutes and Eunuchs should about him wait;
As if his Courts were filled, like those below,
With useless Numbers to make up the Show.
But let them rest in Peace, nor shall my Muse
Their Claim to all the Rights o' th' Dead refuse.   125

from *Poems by Eminent Ladies* (1755)

VERSES WRITTEN ON HER DEATH-BED AT BATH TO HER HUSBAND IN LONDON

Thou who dost all my worldly thoughts employ,
Thou pleasing source of all my earthly joy,
Thou tenderest husband and thou dearest friend,
To thee this first, this last adieu I send!
At length the conqueror Death asserts his right,   5
And will for ever veil me from thy sight;
He woos me to him with a cheerful grace,
And not one terror clouds his meagre face;
He promises a lasting rest from pain,
And shows that all life's fleeting joys are vain;   10
Th' eternal scenes of Heaven he sets in view,
And tells me that no other joys are true.
But love, fond love, would yet resist his power,
Would fain awhile defer the parting hour;
He brings thy mourning image to my eyes,   15
And would obstruct my journey to the skies.
But say, thou dearest, thou unwearied friend!

---

[7] *A numerous Fry* In *Valombrosa* there is a Famous Rich Monastery of Benedictines [Monck's note].

[8] *Lumber* "anything useless or cumbersome" (Johnson).

[9] *State* "Dignity; grandeur" (Johnson).

Say, shouldst thou grieve to see my sorrows end?
Thou know'st a painful pilgrimage I've passed;
And shouldst thou grieve that rest is come at last?   20
Rather rejoice to see me shake off life,
And die as I have lived, thy faithful wife.

John Gay (1685–1732)

At age seventy Johnson recognized in Gay a quality that he knew himself to lack, at least as a younger man: "Gay is represented as a man easily incited to hope and deeply depressed when his hopes were disappointed. This is not the character of a hero; but it may naturally imply something more generally welcome, a soft and civil companion. Whoever is apt to hope good from others is diligent to please them; but he that believes his powers strong enough to force their own way, commonly tries only to please himself." Gay's attempts to please brought him from Devon to London, where he was an apprentice to a silk mercer and learned things about the world of fashion that show up consistently in his poetry. To increase his available time for writing, however, he became a steward in the house of the Duchess of Monmouth, the first of his many noble patrons. About the same time he established what would be a life-long friendship with Alexander Pope and became acquainted with Swift, Arbuthnot, and other important writers. Gay's success at pleasing the public was more variable than his happiness in his friendships with writers and patrons. His drinking songs, burlesque plays, and farces about modern life had some popularity. But Trivia, *a poem about life in London was both a great success and a work of enduring merit. In its use of classical literature as a lens through which to see modern life,* Trivia *can be seen as a forerunner of James Joyce's* Ulysses. *Part three, presented here, especially deserves comparison to Joyce's description of Bloom in Night-town. Although it is neither as pathetic or as psychological in its approach to character, Gay's work, like Joyce's, presents experience as a fusion of personal sensations and impersonal, literary categories of perception.*

Characteristically, Gay could not manage his money. Like many other Englishmen he lost a small fortune in the South Seas Company investment scheme, when the so-called "Bubble" burst in 1720, and he was forever falling back on the help of patrons, despite bouts of tremendous success. The Beggar's Opera *is Gay's most famous work; it established the genre of musical comedy, and its popularity has continued into the present; it made Gay somewhat wealthy, but it ruined his hopes for political preferment because of its satire of Walpole. Equally popular and even more frequently reprinted are Gay's* Fables. *More than 350 editions have appeared since they first came out in 1727. When he died at forty-seven, Gay was living in the household of the Duke and Duchess of Queensbury. He had savings of over £3000 and could finance his own publications, but he never married, never had his own house, and never achieved the sort of independence that Pope enjoyed or that Johnson so highly valued.*

The texts of Trivia *and* The Toilette *are based on the versions Gay included in the second edition of his* Poems on Several Occasions *(1720); the excerpts from* Fables *are based on the first edition (1727). I have consulted the collations in the standard edition of Gay's poetry, edited by Vinton A. Dearing and Charles E. Beckwith (Clarendon Press, 1974), and my notes are indebted to the work of these editors. There is a sound and entertaining critical biography by David Noakes,* John Gay: A Profession of Friendship *(Oxford University Press, 1995).*

from *Poems on Several Occasions* (1720)

FROM *TRIVIA: OR, THE ART OF WALKING THE STREETS OF LONDON*
BOOK III
OF WALKING THE STREETS BY NIGHT

O *Trivia*, Goddess, leave these low Abodes,
And traverse o'er the wide Ethereal Roads,
Celestial Queen, put on thy Robes of Light,
Now *Cynthia* named, fair Regent of the Night.[1]
At Sight of thee, the Villain sheaths his Sword,   5
Nor scales the Wall, to steal the wealthy Hoard.
Oh! may thy Silver Lamp in Heav'n's high Bow'r
Direct my Footsteps in the Midnight Hour!
   When Night first bids the twinkling Stars appear,
Or with her cloudy Vest inwraps the Air,   10
Then swarms the busy Street; with Caution tread,
Where the Shop-Windows falling threat thy Head;[2]
Now Lab'rers home return, and join their Strength
To bear the tott'ring Plank, or Ladder's Length;
Still fix thy Eyes intent upon the Throng,   15
And as the Passes open, wind along.
   Where the fair Columns of Saint *Clement* stand,[3]
Whose straitened Bounds encroach upon the *Strand*;
Where the low Penthouse bows the Walker's Head,[4]
And the rough Pavement wounds the yielding Tread;   20
Where not a Post protects the narrow Space;
And strung in Twines, Combs dangle in thy Face,
Summon at once thy Courage, rouse thy Care,
Stand firm, look back, be resolute, beware.
Forth issuing from steep Lanes, the *Collier*'s Steeds   25
Drag the black Load; another Cart succeeds,
Team follows Team, Crowds heaped on Crowds appear,
And wait impatient, 'till the Road grow clear.
Now all the Pavement sounds with trampling Feet,
And the mixed Hurry barricades the Street,   30
Entangled here, the Wagon's lengthened Team
Cracks the tough Harness: here a pond'rous Beam
Lies overturned athwart; For Slaughter fed
Here lowing Bullocks raise their hornèd Head.
Now Oaths grow loud, with Coaches Coaches jar,   35
And the smart Blow provokes the sturdy War;

OF WALKING THE STREETS
[1] *Cynthia* Diana, the chaste huntress of the gods, associated with the Moon.
[2] *Shop-Windows* display windows, hinged at the top.

[3] *Saint Clement* a church in the Strand, the main thor-
oughfare in the City of London.
[4] *Penthouse* "A shed hanging out aslope from the main
wall" (Johnson).

From the high Box they whirl the Thong around,[5]
And with the twining Lash their Shins resound:
Their Rage ferments, more dang'rous Wounds they try,
And the Blood gushes down their painful Eye,   40
And now on Foot the frowning Warriors light
And with their pond'rous Fists renew the Fight;
Blow answers Blow, their cheeks are smeared with Blood,
'Till down they fall, and grappling roll in Mud.
So when two Boars, in wild *Ytene* bred,[6]   45
Or on *Westphalia*'s fatt'ning Chestnuts fed,[7]
Gnash their sharp Tusks, and roused with equal Fire,
Dispute the Reign of some luxurious Mire;
In the black Flood they wallow o'er and o'er,
'Till their armed Jaws distil with Foam and Gore.[8]   50
　　Where the Mob gathers, swiftly shoot along,
Nor idly mingle in the noisy Throng.
Lured by the Silver Hilt, amid the Swarm,[9]
The subtle Artist will thy Side disarm.
Nor is thy Flaxen Wig with Safety worn;[10]   55
High on the Shoulder in a Basket borne
Lurks the sly Boy; whose Hand to Rapine bred,
Plucks off the curling Honours of thy Head.
Here dives the skulking Thief, with practised Sleight,
And unfelt Fingers make thy Pocket light.   60
Where's now thy Watch, with all its Trinkets, flown?
And thy late Snuff-Box is no more thy own.
But lo! his bolder Thefts some Tradesman spies,
Swift from his Prey the scudding Lurcher flies;
Dext'rous he scapes the Coach with nimble Bounds.   65
Whilst ev'ry honest Tongue 'Stop Thief' resounds.
So speeds the wily Fox, alarm'd by Fear,
Who lately filch'd the Turkey's callow care;[11]
Hounds following Hounds, grow louder as he flies,
And injured Tenants join the Hunter's cries.   70
Breathless he stumbling falls: Ill-fated Boy!
Why did not honest Work thy Youth employ?
Seized by rough Hands, he's dragged amid the Rout,
And stretched beneath the Pump's incessant Spout:
Or plunged in miry Ponds, he gasping lies,   75
Mud chokes his Mouth, and plasters o'er his Eyes.
　　Let not the Ballad-Singer's shrilling strain
Amid the Swarm thy list'ning Ear detain:

---

[5] *high Box* the coach driver's seat; *Thong* "A strap or string of leather" (Johnson).
[6] *Ytene* New Forest in Hampshire, anciently so called [Gay's note].
[7] *Westphalia* a region in north-west Germany famous for pork production.

[8] *distil* drip.
[9] *Silver hilt* of a gentleman's dress sword.
[10] *Flaxen Wig* wigs of several colours were worn by gentlemen at this time, but blond ones were the most expensive.
[11] *callow care* its young.

Guard well thy Pocket; for these *Sirens* stand,[12]
To aid the Labours of the diving Hand;   80
Confed'rate in the Cheat, they draw the Throng,
And *Cambric* Handkerchiefs reward the Song.
But soon as Coach or Cart drives rattling on,
The Rabble part, in Shoals they backward run.
So *Jove's* loud Bolts the mingled War divide,   85
And *Greece* and *Troy* retreat on either side.[13]
    If the rude Throng pour on with furious Pace,
And hap to break thee from a Friend's Embrace,
Stop short; nor struggle through the Crowd in vain,
But watch with careful Eye the passing Train.   90
Yet I (perhaps too fond) if chance the Tide
Tumultous, bears my Partner from my Side,
Impatient venture back; despising Harm,
I force my Passsage where the thickest swarm.
Thus his lost bride the *Trojan* sought in vain[14]   95
Through night, and arms, and flames, and hills of slain.
Thus *Nisus* wander'd o'er the pathless grove,
To find the brave companion of his love,
The pathless grove in vain he wanders o'er;
Euryalus, alas! is now no more.[15]   100
    That walker, who regardless of his Pace,[16]
Turns oft to pore upon the Damsel's Face,
From Side to Side by thrusting Elbows tossed,
Shall strike his aching Breast against the Post;
Or water, dashed from fishy Stall, shall stain   105
His hapless Coat with Spurts of scaly Rain.
But if unwarily he chance to stray,
Where twirling Turnstiles intercept the Way,[17]
The thwarting passenger shall force them round,[18]
And beat the wretch half breathless to the ground.   110
    Let constant Vigilance thy Footsteps guide,
And wary Circumspection guard thy Side;
Then shalt thou walk unharmed the dang'rous Night,
Nor need th' officious Link-Boy's smoky Light.[19]
Thou never wilt attempt to cross the Road,   115
Where Alehouse Benches rest the Porter's Load,
Grievous to heedless Shins; No Barrow's Wheel,
That bruises oft the Truant School-Boy's Heel,

---

[12] *Sirens* sea-nymphs in Greek mythology with the power of charming sailors and luring them to destruction on their rocks (*Odyssey* 13.142–200).
[13] *Jove's loud Bolts . . . side* recalls *Iliad* 8.133–6.
[14] *the Trojan* Aeneas searching for Creusa, whose ghost tells him to flee Troy (*Aeneid* 2.749–95).
[15] *Nisus . . . no more* Nisus goes back, finds Euryalus dead and is himself killed (*Aeneid* 9.390–445).

[16] *regardless* not mindful.
[17] *Turnstile* "A cross of two bars armed with pikes at the end, and turning on a pin" (Johnson); the *wretch* is stationed there to collect a toll or regulate traffic.
[18] *passenger* traveller.
[19] *Link-Boy* "A boy that carries a torch to accommodate passengers with light" (Johnson); he would expect payment.

Behind thee rolling, with insidious Pace,
Shall mark thy Stocking with a miry Trace.   120
Let not thy vent'rous Steps approach too nigh,
Where gaping wide, low steepy Cellars lie;[20]
If thy Shoe wrench aside, down, down you fall,
And overturn the scolding Huckster's stall,
The scolding Huckster shall not o'er thee moan,   125
But Pence exact for Nuts and Pears o'erthrown.
    Though you through cleanlier Allies wind by Day,
To shun the Hurries of the public Way,
Yet ne'er to those dark Paths by Night retire;
Mind only Safety and contemn the Mire,   130
Then no impervious Courts thy Haste detain,[21]
Nor sneering Ale-wives bid thee turn again.[22]
    Where *Lincoln's-Inn*, wide space is railed around,[23]
Cross not with vent'rous Step, there oft is found
The lurking Thief, who while the Day-light shone,   135
Made the Walls echo with his begging Tone:
That Crutch which late Compassion moved, shall wound
Thy bleeding Head, and fell thee to the Ground.
Though thou art tempted by the Link-man's Call,
Yet trust him not along the lonely Wall;   140
In the mid-way he'll quench the flaming brand,[24]
And share the Booty with the pilf'ring Band.
Still keep the public streets, where oily Rays
Shot from the Crystal Lamp, o'erspread the Ways.[25]
Happy *Augusta*! Law-defended town![26]   145
Here no dark Lanthorns shade the Villain's Frown;
No *Spanish* Jealousies thy Lanes infest,
Nor *Roman* vengeance stabs th' unwary Breast;
Here *Tyranny* ne'er lifts her purple Hand,
But Liberty and Justice guard the Land;   150
No *Bravos* here profess the bloody trade,[27]
Nor is the Church the Murd'rer's Refuge made.
    Let not the Chairman, with assuming Stride,[28]
Press near the Wall, and rudely thrust thy Side:
The Laws have set him Bounds; his servile Feet   155
Should ne'er encroach where Posts defend the Street.
Yet who the Footman's Arrogance can quell,
Whose Flambeau gilds the sashes of *Pell-mell*,[29]

---

[20] *steepy* "Having a precipitous declivity; a poetical word for *steep*" (Johnson).
[21] *impervious Courts* dead-ends, closed courtyards.
[22] *sneer* "To show awkward mirth" (Johnson).
[23] *Lincoln's-Inn* Lincoln's Inn Fields, public walks and gardens enclosed by fashionable houses and a rail fence; named for the nearby society devoted to the study of law.
[24] *flaming brand* the torch used for a light.
[25] *Crystal Lamps* bright oil lamps.
[26] *Augusta* Augusta Trinobantes ("capital of the Trinobantes") was an old Roman name for London.
[27] *Bravo* "A man who murders for hire" (Johnson).
[28] *Chairman* one carrying a sedan chair for his master or for hire.
[29] *Flambeau* a superior kind of torch; *Pell-mell* now Pall Mall, a fashionable street in London.

When in long Rank a Train of Torches flame,
To light the Midnight visits of the Dame?   160
Others, perhaps, by happier Guidance led,
May where the Chairman rests, with Safety tread;
Whene'er I pass, their Poles unseen Below,
Make my Knee tremble with the jarring Blow.

    If Wheels bar up the Road where Streets are crossed,   165
With gentle Words the Coachman's Ear accost:
He ne'er the Threat, or harsh Command obeys,
But with Contempt the spatter'd Shoe surveys.
Now Man with utmost Fortitude thy Soul,
To cross the Way where Carts and Coaches roll;   170
Yet do not in thy hardy Skill confide,
Nor rashly risk the Kennel's spacious stride;[30]
Stay till afar the distant Wheel you hear,
Like dying Thunder in the breaking Air;
Thy Foot will slide upon the miry Stone,   175
And passing Coaches crush thy tortured Bone,
Or Wheels enclose the Road; on either Hand
Pent round with Perils, in the Midst you stand,
And call for Aid in vain; the Coachman swears,
And Carmen drive, unmindful of thy Prayers.   180
Where wilt thou turn? ah! whither wilt thou fly?
On every side the pressing Spokes are nigh.
So Sailors, while *Charybdis'* gulph they shun,
Amazed, on *Scylla's* craggy dangers run.[31]

    Be sure observe where brown Ostrea stands,[32]   185
Who boasts her shelly ware from Wallfleet sands;[33]
There may'st thou pass, with safe unmiry Feet,
Where the raised Pavement leads athwart the Street.
If where *Fleet-Ditch* with muddy Current flows,[34]
You chance to roam; where Oyster-Tubs in Rows   190
Are ranged beside the Posts; there stay thy haste,
And with the sav'ry Fish indulge thy Taste:
The Damsel's Knife the gaping Shell commands,
While the salt Liquor streams between her Hands.

    The Man had sure a Palate covered o'er   195
With Brass or Steel, that on the rocky Shore
First broke the oozy Oyster's pearly Coat,
And risked the living Morsel down his Throat.
What will not Lux'ry taste? Earth, Sea, and Air
Are daily ransacked for the Bill of Fare.   200
Blood stuffed in Skins is *British* Christians' Food,[35]

---

[30] *Kennel* gutter.
[31] *Charybdis . . . Scylla . . . run* the whirlpool and the man-eating monster on either side of the Straits of Messina (*Odyssey* 12).
[32] *Ostrea* an oyster-girl.

[33] *Wallfleet* a place in Essex county, famous for oysters.
[34] *Fleet-Ditch* a stream running into the Thames from north-west of the City.
[35] *Blood stuffed in Skins* blood sausage.

And *France* robs Marshes of the croaking Brood;
Spongy *Morels* in strong *Ragousts* are found,[36]
And in the Soup the slimy Snail is drowned.
    When from high Spouts the dashing Torrents fall,   205
Ever be watchful to Maintain the wall;[37]
For shouldst thou quit thy Ground, the rushing Throng
Will with impetuous Fury drive along;
All press to gain those Honours thou hast lost,
And rudely shove thee far without the Post.[38]   210
Then to retrieve the Shed you strive in vain,[39]
Draggled all o'er, and soaked in Floods of Rain.
Yet rather bear the Show'r, and Toils of Mud,[40]
Than in the doubtful Quarrel risk thy Blood.
O think on *Oedipus'* detested State,   215
And by his Woes be warned to shun thy Fate.
    Where three Roads joined, he met his Sire unknown;
(Unhappy Sire, but more unhappy Son!)
Each claimed the Way, their Swords the Strife decide,
The hoary Monarch fell, he groaned and died![41]   220
Hence sprung the fatal Plague that thinned thy Reign,
Thy cursed Incest! and thy Children slain!
Hence wert thou doomed in endless Night to stray
Through *Theban* streets, and cheerless grope thy Way.
    Contemplate, Mortal, on thy fleeting Years;   225
See, with black Train the Funeral Pomp appears!
Whether some Heir attends in sable State,
And mourns with outward Grief a parent's Fate;
Or the fair Virgin, nipped in Beauty's Bloom,
A Crowd of Lovers follow to her Tomb.   230
Why is the Hearse with 'scutcheons blazoned round,[42]
And with the nodding Plume of Ostrich crowned?
No: the Dead know it not, nor Profit gain;
It only serves to prove the Living vain.
How short is Life! how frail is human Trust!   235
Is all this Pomp for laying Dust to Dust?
    Where the nailed Hoop defends the painted Stall,[43]
Brush not thy sweeping Skirt too near the Wall;
Thy heedless Sleeve will drink the coloured Oil,
And Spot indelible thy Pocket soil.   240
Has not wise Nature strung the Legs and Feet
With firmest Nerves, designed to walk the Street?

---

[36] *Morel* edible fungus; *Ragoust* stew.
[37] *Maintain the wall* keep away from the street side of the path; Johnson told Boswell that when he first came to London "there were two sets of people, those who gave the wall, and those who took it: the peaceable and the quarrelsome" (*Life* 1.110).
[38] *without* beyond.
[39] *Shed* the overhanging portion of a building, the penthouse.
[40] *toils* nets, traps.
[41] *hoary* grey.
[42] *'scutcheons* armorial badges.
[43] *painted* freshly painted, that is.

Has she not given us Hands to grope aright,
Amidst the frequent Dangers of the Night?
And think'st thou not the double Nostril meant,   245
To warn from oily Woes by previous Scent?
    Who can the various City Frauds recite,
With all the petty Rapines of the night?
Who now the Guinea-Dropper's Bait regards,[44]
Tricked by the Sharper's Dice, or Juggler's cards?   250
Why should I warn thee ne'er to join the Fray,
Where the Sham-Quarrel interrupts the Way?
Lives there in these our Days so soft a Clown,
Braved by the Bully's Oaths, or threat'ning Frown?[45]
I need not strict enjoin the Pocket's Care,   255
When from the crowded *Play* thou lead'st the Fair;
Who has not here or Watch or Snuff-Box lost,[46]
Or Handkerchiefs that *India's* Shuttle boast?[47]
    O! may thy Virtue guard thee through the Roads
Of *Drury's* mazy Courts, and dark Abodes,[48]   260
The Harlot's guileful Paths, who nightly stand,
Where *Katherine-street* descends into the *Strand*.
Say, vagrant Muse, their wiles and subtle Arts,
To lure the Stranger's unsuspecting Hearts;
So shall our Youth on healthful Sinews tread,   265
And City Cheeks grow warm with rural Red.
    'Tis she who nightly strolls with saunt'ring Pace,
No stubborn Stays her yielding Shape embrace;
Beneath the Lamp her tawdry Ribbons glare,
The new-scoured Manteau, and the slattern Air;[49]   270
High-draggled Petticoats her Travels show,[50]
And hollow Cheeks with artful Blushes glow;
With flatt'ring Sounds she soothes the cred'lous Ear,
My noble Captain! Charmer! Love! my Dear!
In riding Hood near Tavern-Doors she plies,   275
Or muffled Pinners hide her livid Eyes.[51]
With empty Bandbox she delights to range,[52]
And feigns a distant Errand from the Change:[53]
Nay, she will oft the Quaker's Hood profane,
And trudge demure the Rounds of *Drury-Lane*.   280
She darts from Sarsnet Ambush wily Leers,[54]
Twitches thy Sleeve, or with familiar Airs

---

44 *Guinea-Dropper* a con-man who lures victims by pretending to find money on the street and sharing it with them to gain their confidence.
45 *Braved* defied.
46 *or . . . or* either . . . or.
47 *India's Shuttle boast* made on Indian looms.
48 *Drury* Drury Lane and Little Drury Lane, a street famous for its theatre and prostitutes.

49 *new-scoured* freshly bleached.
50 *High-draggled* muddied above the hem line.
51 *Pinners* the loose parts of a headdress, here entangled with a muffler.
52 *Bandbox* a small, light box.
53 *Change* one of several commercial centers or gallerias in the City.
54 *Sarsnet* a very fine silk.

Her Fan will pat thy Cheek; these Snares disdain.
Nor gaze behind thee, when she turns again.
   I knew a Yeoman, who for thirst of Gain,   285
To the great City drove from *Devon*'s Plain
His num'rous lowing Herd; his Herds he sold,
And his deep leathern Pocket bagged with Gold;
Drawn by a fraudful Nymph, he gazed, he sighed;
Unmindful of his Home, and distant Bride,   290
She leads the willing Victim to his Doom,
Through winding Alleys to her cobweb Room.
Thence through the Street he reels, from Post to Post,
Valiant with Wine, nor knows his Treasure lost.
The vagrant Wretch the assembled Watchmen spies,   295
He waves his Hanger, and their Poles defies;
Deep in the *Round-House* pent, all Night he snores,[55]
And the next Morn in vain his Fate deplores.
   Ah hapless Swain, unused to Pains and Ills!
Canst thou forgo Roast-Beef for nauseous Pills?   300
How wilt thou lift to Heav'n thy Eyes and Hands,
When the long Scroll the surgeon's Fees demands!
Or else (ye Gods avert that worst Disgrace)
Thy ruined Nose falls level with thy Face,[56]
Then shall thy Wife thy loathsome Kiss disdain,   305
And wholesome Neighbours from thy Mug refrain.
   Yet there are Watchmen who with friendly Light
Will teach thy reeling Steps to tread aright;
For *Sixpence* will support thy helpless Arm,
And Home conduct thee, safe from nightly Harm,   310
But if they shake their Lanthorns, from afar,
To call their Brethren to confed'rate War
When Rakes resist their Pow'r; if hapless you
Should chance to wander with the scouring Crew;[57]
Though Fortune yield thee Captive, ne'er despair,   315
But seek the Constable's consid'rate Ear;
He will reverse the Watchman's harsh Decree,
Moved by the Rhet'ric of a silver Fee.
Thus would you gain some favourite Courtier's Word;
Fee not the petty Clerks, but bribe my Lord.   320
   Now is the time that Rakes their Revels keep;
Kindlers of Riot, Enemies of Sleep.
His scattered Pence the flying *Nicker* flings,[58]
And with the Copper Show'r the Casement rings.

---

[55] *Round-House* "The constable's prison in which disorderly persons found in the street are detained" (Johnson).

[56] *Nose . . . Face* a result of syphilis frequently mentioned in eighteenth-century poetry.

[57] *Scouring* "To range in order to catch or drive away something" (Johnson).

[58] *Nicker* Gentlemen, who delighted to break Windows with Half-pence [Gay's note].

Who has not heard the *Scowrer*'s midnight fame?[59]   325
Who has not trembled at the *Mohock*'s Name?[60]
Was there a Watchman took his hourly Rounds,
Safe from their Blows, or new-invented Wounds!
I pass their desperate Deeds, and Mischiefs done,
Where from *Snow-hill* black steepy Torrents run;[61]   330
How Matrons, hooped within the Hogshead's Womb,[62]
Were tumbled furious thence, the rolling Tomb
O'er the Stones thunders, bounds from Side to Side:
So *Regulus* to save his Country died.[63]
Where a dim Gleam the paly Lanthorn throws   335
O'er the mid-Pavement, heapy Rubbish grows,
Or archèd Vaults their gaping Jaws extend,
Or the dark Caves to common Sewers descend.
Oft by the Winds, extinct the Signal lies,
Or smothered in the glimm'ring Socket dies,[64]   340
Ere Night has half rolled round her Ebon Throne;
In the wide Gulf the shattered Coach o'erthrown
Sinks with the snorting Steeds; the Reins are broke,
And from the crackling Axle flies the Spoke,
So when famed Eddystone's far shooting Ray,[65]   345
That led the Sailor through the stormy Way,
Was from its rocky Roots by Billows torn,
And the high Turret in the Whirlwind borne,
Fleets bulged their Sides against the craggy Land,
And pitchy Ruins blackened all the Strand.[66]   350
Who then through Night would hire the harnessed Steed,
And who would choose the rattling Wheel for Speed:
But hark! Distress with screaming Voice draws nigh'r,
And wakes the slumb'ring Street with cries of Fire.
At first a glowing Red enwraps the Skies,   355
And borne by Winds the scatt'ring Sparks arise;
From Beam to Beam the fierce Contagion spreads:
The spiry Flames now lift aloft their Heads,
Through the burst Sash a blazing Deluge pours,
And splitting Tiles descend in rattling Show'rs.   360
Now with thick Crowds th' enlightened Pavement swarms,
The Fire-man sweats beneath his crooked Arms,
A leathern Casque his vent'rous Head defends,[67]

---

[59] *Scowrer* a street tough, after Thomas Shadwell's play of the same name.
[60] *Mohock* a gang of toughs, elaborately described in *Spectator* Number 324.
[61] *Snow-hill* a place just north-west of the City, from which the Fleet runs into the Thames.
[62] *Hogshead* a large barrel.

[63] *Regulus* Roman Consul in 256 and 267 BCE, supposedly tortured to death by the Carthaginians in a steel-studed chest, glorified by Horace (*Odes* 3.5).
[64] *Signal . . . Socket* signal, light or lantern; socket, hollow tube in which the light is inserted.
[65] *Eddystone* the first lighthouse, built in 1700, wrecked in 1703.
[66] *Strand* beach.
[67] *Casque* helmet.

Boldly he climbs where thickest Smoke ascends,
Moved by the Mother's streaming Eyes and Prayers,   365
The helpless Infant through the Flame he bears,
With no less Virtue, than through hostile Fire
The Dardan Hero bore his aged sire.[68]
See forceful Engines spout their levelled Streams,[69]
To quench the Blaze that runs along the Beams;   370
The grappling Hook plucks Rafters from the Walls,
And Heaps on Heaps the smoky Ruin falls.
Blown by strong Winds the fiery Tempest roars,
Bears down new Walls, and pours along the Floors;
The Heav'ns are all a-blaze, the Face of Night   375
Is cover'd with a sanguine dreadful Light;[70]
'Twas such a Light involved thy Tow'rs, O *Rome*,
The dire Presage of mighty *Caesar*'s Doom,
When the Sun veiled in Rust his mourning Head,
And frightful Prodigies the Skies o'erspread.[71]   380
Hark! the Drum thunders! far, ye Crowds, retire:
Behold! the ready Match is tipped with Fire,
The nitrous Store is laid, the smutty train[72]
With running Blaze awakes the barelled Grain;
Flames sudden wrap the Walls; with sullen Sound   385
The shattered Pile sinks on the smoky Ground.
So when the Years shall have revolved the Date,
Th' inevitable Hour of *Naples*' Fate,[73]
Her sapped Foundations shall with Thunders shake,
And heave and toss upon the sulph'rous Lake;   390
Earth's Womb at once the fiery Flood shall rend,
And in th' Abyss her plunging Tow'rs descend.
  Consider, Reader, what Fatigues I've known,
The Toils, the Perils of the wintry Town;
What Riots seen, what bustling Crowds I bored,   395
How oft I crossed where Carts and Coaches roared;
Yet shall I bless my Labours, if Mankind
Their Future Safety from my Dangers find.
Thus the bold Traveller (inured to Toil,
Whose Steps have printed *Asia*'s desert Soil,   400
The barb'rous *Arabs* haunt; or shiv'ring crossed
Dark *Greenland*'s Mountains of eternal Frost;
Whom Providence in length of Years restores
To the wished Harbour of his native Shores)
Sets forth his Journals to the public View,   405
To caution, by his Woes, the wand'ring Crew.

---

[68] *Dardan Hero* Aeneas (*Aeneid* 2).
[69] *levelled* correctly aimed.
[70] *sanguine* ruddy, blood-red.
[71] *Prodigies the Skies o'erspread* elaborated in Virgil's *Georgics* 1.461ff.

[72] *nitrous Store* kegs of gun powder; *smutty train* black powder used as a fuse; firemen sometimes blew up houses to isolate a blaze.
[73] *Naples' Fate* to be destroyed by an inevitable eruption of Mount Vesuvius.

And now complete my gen'rous Labours lie,
Finished, and ripe for Immortality.
Death shall entomb in Dust this mould'ring Frame,
But never reach th' eternal Part, my Fame.
When W* and G*, mighty names, are dead;[74]
Or but at *Chelsea* under Custards read;[75]
When Critics crazy Bandboxes repair,[76]
And Tragedies, turned Rockets, bounce in Air;[77]
High-raised on *Fleetstreet* Posts, consigned to Fame,[78]
This Work shall shine, and Walkers bless my Name.

410

415

THE *TOILETTE*
A *TOWN* ECLOGUE[1]
LYDIA

Now twenty springs had clothed the Park with green,[2]
Since *Lydia* knew the blossom of fifteen;
No lovers now her morning hours molest,
And catch her at her toilette half undressed;[3]
The thund'ring knocker wakes the street no more,
No chairs, no coaches crowd her silent door;
Her midnights once at cards and *Hazard* fled,[4]
Which now, alas! she dreams away in bed.
Around her wait Shocks, monkeys, and macaws,[5]
To fill the place of fops, and perjured beaus;[6]
In these she views the mimicry of man,
And smiles when grinning *Pug* gallants her fan;[7]
When *Poll* repeats, the sounds deceive her ear,
For sounds, like his, once told her *Damon*'s care.
With these alone her tedious mornings pass;
Or at the dumb devotion of her glass,[8]
She smooths her brow, and frizzles forth her hairs,
And fancies youthful dress gives youthful airs;
With crimson wool she fixes every grace,

5

10

15

---

74   *W* and *G*   Ned Ward (1667–1731) and Charles Gildon (1665–1724), Grubstreet writers and unsuccessful competitors with Gay and Pope for fame.

75   *under Custards read*   their unsold pages having been used to wrap baked goods in the London district of Chelsea.

76   *crazy*   broken.

77   *Tragedies, turned Rockets*   unsold works could also be used to make fire crackers.

78   *Fleetstreet Posts*   door posts of shops in the printing district, where new books were advertised.

THE *TOILETTE*

1   *Eclogue*   a brief poem on a subject of relatively minor importance; the name was often given to pastoral poems in antiquity and so became associated with rural subjects; this poem was originally pirated by the publisher Edmund Curl and printed in a volume called *Court Poems* (1716), which also includes pieces by Pope and Lady Mary Wortley Montagu.

2   *the Park*   St James's Park, the most fashionable park in London.

3   *toilette*   dressing table, or the process of dressing.

4   *Hazard*   dice, craps.

5   *Shock*   "A rough dog" (Johnson), but often the ironic name of a lap dog.

6   *fop*   "a man fond of show, dress, and flutter; an impertinent" (Johnson); *perjured*   falsely sworn.

7   *Pug*   her monkey; *gallants*   toys with or breaks on purpose, as a gallant might do for the pleasure of buying the lady a new one.

8   *glass*   mirror.

That not a blush can discompose her face.   20
Reclined upon her arm she pensive sate,
And cursed th' inconstancy of youth too late.
    'O youth! O spring of life! for ever lost!
No more my name shall reign the favourite Toast,
On glass no more the diamond grave my name,   25
And rhymes misspelled record a lover's flame:
Nor shall side-boxes watch my restless eyes,
And as they catch the glance in rows arise
With humble bows; nor white-gloved Beaus encroach
In crowds behind, to guard me to my coach.   30
Ah, hapless nymph! such conquests are no more,
For *Chloe*'s now what *Lydia* was before!
    ''Tis true, this *Chloe* boasts the peach's bloom,
But does her nearer whisper breathe perfume?
I own her taper shape is formed to please –   35
Yet if you saw her unconfined by stays!
She doubly to fifteen may make pretence,
Alike we read it in her face and sense.
Her reputation! but that never yet
Could check the freedoms of a young coquette.   40
Why will ye then, vain fops, her eyes believe?
Her eyes can, like your perjured tongues, deceive.
    'What shall I do? how spend the hateful day?
At chapel shall I wear the morn away?
Who there frequents at these unmodish hours,   45
But ancient matrons with their frizzled towers,⁹
And grey religious maids? my presence there
Amid that sober train would own despair;
Nor am I yet so old; nor is my glance
As yet fixed wholly to devotion's trance.   50
    'Straight then I'll dress, and take my wonted range
Through every Indian shop, through all the Change;¹⁰
Where the tall jar erects his costly pride,
With antic shapes in china's azure dyed;¹¹
There careless lies the rich brocade unrolled,   55
Here shines a cabinet with burnished gold;
But then remembrance will my grief renew,
'Twas there the raffling dice false *Damon* threw;¹²
The raffling dice to him decide the prize.
'Twas there he first conversed with *Chloe*'s eyes;   60
Hence sprung th' ill-fated cause of all my smart,
To me the toy he gave, to her his heart.
But soon thy perj'ry in the gift was found,

---

⁹   *towers* high headdresses.
¹⁰ *Change* one of several commercial complexes with
galleries, such as the New Exchange.

¹¹ *antic* antique.
¹² *raffling dice* three of them for the dice game raffle.

The shivered china dropped upon the ground;
Sure omen that thy vows would faithless prove;   65
Frail was thy present, frailer is thy love.
   'O happy *Poll*, in wiry prison pent;
Thou ne'er hast known what love or rivals meant;
And *Pug* with pleasure can his fetters bear,
Who ne'er believed the vows that lovers swear!   70
How am I cursed! (unhappy and forlorn)
With perjury, with love, and rival's scorn!
False are the loose coquet's inveigling airs,
False is the pompous grief of youthful heirs,
False is the cringing courtier's plighted word,   75
False are the dice when gamesters stamp the board:[13]
False is the sprightly widow's public tear;
Yet these to *Damon*'s oaths are all sincere.
   'Fly from perfidious man, the sex disdain;
Let servile *Chloe* wear the nuptial chain.   80
Damon is practised in the modish life,
Can hate, and yet be civil to a wife.
He games; he swears; he drinks; he fights; he roves;
Yet *Chloe* can believe he fondly loves.
Mistress and wife can well supply his need,   85
A miss for pleasure, and a wife for breed.
But *Chloe*'s air is unconfined and gay,
And can perhaps an injured bed repay;
Perhaps her patient temper can behold
The rival of her love adorned with gold,   90
Powdered with diamonds; free from thought and care,
A husband's sullen humours she can bear.
   'Why are these sobs? and why these streaming eyes?
Is love the cause? no, I the sex despise;
I hate, I loathe his base perfidious name.   95
Yet if he should but feign a rival flame?
But *Chloe* boasts and triumphs in my pains,
To her he's faithful, 'tis to me he feigns'.
    Thus love-sick *Lydia* raved. Her maid appears;
A band-box in her steady hand she bears.[14]   100
'How well this ribband's gloss becomes your face!'
She cries, in raptures; then, 'so sweet a lace!
How charmingly you look! so bright! so fair!
'Tis to your eyes the head-dress owes its air'.
Straight *Lydia* smiled; the comb adjusts her locks,   105
And at the playhouse *Harry* keeps her box.[15]

---

13 *stamp the board* with the inverted dice-box, in making the throw.
14 *band-box* a small, light box.

15 *Harry* a servant's name; he is holding a seat for Lydia at the playhouse.

from *Fables* (1727)

THE TURKEY AND THE ANT

In other men we faults can spy,
And blame the mote that dims their eye,
Each little speck and blemish find,
To our own stronger errors blind.
A Turkey, tired of common food,   5
Forsook the barn and sought the wood,
Behind her ran her infant train,
Collecting here and there a grain.
'Draw near, my birds', the mother cries,
'This hill delicious fare supplies;   10
Behold, the busy *Negro* race,
See, millions blacken all the place!
Fear not. Like me with freedom eat;
An ant is most delightful meat.
How blest, how envied were our life,   15
Could we but 'scape the poult'rer's knife!
But man, cursed man on turkey preys,
And *Christmas* shortens all our days;
Sometimes with oysters we combine,
Sometimes assist the sav'ry chine.[1]   20
From the low peasant to the lord,
The turkey smokes on every board.
Sure men for gluttony are cursed,
Of the sev'n deadly sins the worst'.
An Ant, who climbed beyond his reach,   25
Thus answered from the neighb'ring beech.
'Ere you remark another's sin,
Bid thy own conscience look within.
Control thy more voracious bill,
Nor for a breakfast nations kill'.   30

THE MAN AND THE FLEA

Whether on earth, in air, or main,[1]
Sure every thing alive is vain!
Does not the hawk all fowls survey,
As destined only for his prey?
And do not tyrants, prouder things,   5

THE TURKEY AND THE ANT
[1] *chine* a piece of pork, the backbone.

THE MAN AND THE FLEA
[1] *main* the sea.

Think men were born for slaves to kings?
    When the crab views the pearly strands,
Or *Tagus*, bright with golden sands,[2]
Or crawls beside the coral grove,
And hears the ocean roll above;   10
'Nature is too profuse', says he,
'Who gave all these to pleasure me!'
    When bord'ring pinks and roses bloom,
And every garden breathes perfume,
When peaches glow with sunny dyes,   15
Like *Laura*'s cheek, when blushes rise;
When with huge figs the branches bend;
When clusters from the vine depend:[3]
The snail looks round on flow'r and tree,
And cries, 'All these were made for me!'   20
    'What dignity's in human nature',
Says Man, the most conceited creature,
As from a cliff he cast his eye,
And viewed the sea and archèd sky!
The sun was sunk beneath the main,   25
The moon, and all the starry train
Hung the vast vault of heav'n. The Man
His contemplation thus began.
    'When I behold this glorious show,
And the wide watry world below,   30
The scaly people of the main,[4]
The beasts that range the wood or plain,
The winged inhabitants of air,
The day, the night, the various year,
And know all these by heav'n designed   35
As gifts to pleasure human kind,
I cannot raise my worth too high;
Of what vast consequence am I!'
    'Not of th' importance you suppose',
Replies a Flea upon his nose: 40
'Be humble, learn thyself to scan;
Know, pride was never made for man.
'Tis vanity that swells thy mind.
What, heav'n and earth for thee designed!
For thee! made only for our need;   45
That more important Fleas might feed'.

---

[2] *Tagus*   longest river on the Iberian peninsula, famed
for alluvial deposits of gold.

[3] *depend*   hang down.

[4] *scaly people*   fish.

Allan Ramsay (1686–1758)

It was under the auspices of The Easy Club, *which Ramsay helped found in Edinburgh, that the poet began to make a name for himself. He read his poems to the other young men, and under the poetical name of Gawin Douglas (a sixteenth-century Scots translator of Virgil) became poet laureate to the group. His first hit was a satiric elegy on a country woman who brewed and sold beer to the local lads. Filled with Scottish words, it begins:*

> Auld Reeky, mourn in sable hue,[1]
> Let fouth of tears dreep like May dew;[2]
> To braw tippony bid adieu,[3]
>   Which we with greed
> Bended as fast as she could brew:
>   But ah! she's dead.

Ramsay went on to publish volumes of his own poetry, collections of songs and ballads, a play, a mock epic, and loosely edited versions of old Scots poetry. His songs remain his most famous works, but he also produced a good deal of interesting satire, mingling, like Gay, classic forms and modern, often rural, imagery. He was an admirer of Pope, whom he celebrated as "Sandy" in several tributes to his favorite British writers.

For convenience's sake, I have used The Poems of Allan Ramsay *(London, 1800) as my copytext. Like the collections that began coming out in 1721, this edition includes a glossary of Scottish words, and I have used it in my notes.*

from *The Poems of Allan Ramsay* (1800)

POLWART ON THE GREEN (1721)

> At Polwart on the green,
> If you'll meet me the morn,
> Where lasses do convene
> To dance about the thorn;
> A kindly welcome ye shall meet   5
>   Frae her wha likes to view
> A lover and a lad complete,
>   The lad and lover you.
>
> Let dorty dames say na,[1]
> As lang as e'er they please,   10
> Seem caulder than the sna',
> While inwardly they bleeze;

ALLAN RAMSAY
[1] *Auld Reeky* "old smokey," Edinburgh.
[2] *fouth* "plenty."

[3] *braw tippony* ["brave twopenny"] She sold the Scots pint, which is near two quarts English for two pence [Ramsay's note].
POLWART ON THE GREEN
[1] *dorty* proud, not to be spoken to.

But I will frankly shaw my mind,
    And yield my heart to thee;
Be ever to the captive kind,   15
    That langs na to be free.

At Polwart on the Green,
    Among the new-mawn hay,
With sangs and dancing keen
    We'll pass the heartsome day,   20
At night if beds be o'er thrang laid,²
    And thou be twined of thine,³
Thou shalt be welcome, my dear lad,
    To take a part of mine.

GIVE ME A LASS WITH A LUMP OF LAND (1721)

Gi'e me a lass with a lump of land,
    And we for life shall gang the gither;¹
Though daft or wise I'll never demand,
    Or black or fair it maks na whether.
I'm aff with wit, and beauty will fade,²   5
    And blood alane is no worth a shilling;
But she that's rich, her market's made,
    For ilka charm about her is killing.³

Gi'e me a lass with a lump of land,
    And in my bosom I'll hug my treasure;   10
Gin I had anes her gear in my hand,⁴
    Should love turn dowf, it will find pleasure.⁵
Laugh on what likes, but there's my hand,
    I hate with poortith, though bonny, to meddle;⁶
Unless they bring cash, or a lump of land,   15
    They'se never get me to dance to their fiddle.

There's meikle good love in bands and bags,⁷
    And siller and gowd's a sweet complexion;⁸
But beauty, and wit, and virtue in rags,
    Have tint the art of gaining affection.⁹   20
Love tips his arrows with woods and parks,
    And castles, and riggs, and moors, and meadows;¹⁰
And nathing can catch our modern sparks,¹¹
    But well tochered lasses, or jointured widows.¹²

---

² *thrang* crowded.
³ *twined of* separated from.
GIVE ME A LASS WITH A LUMP OF LAND
¹ *gang the gither* go together.
² *aff with* off, finished with.
³ *ilka* every.
⁴ *Gin* if; *anes* once; *gear* stuff.
⁵ *dowf* mournful, wanting variety.

⁶ *poortith* poverty.
⁷ *meikle* mighty.
⁸ *siller and gowd* silver and gold.
⁹ *tint* lost.
¹⁰ *rigg* measure of land.
¹¹ *sparks* beaux, men about town.
¹² *tocher* dowry; *jointure* "Estate settled on a wife to be enjoyed after her husband's decease" (Johnson).

Ephraim Chambers (c. 1680–1740)

It is remarkable how little is known about Chambers in view of the great importance of his Cyclopaedia. *First published in 1728 in two volumes folio, this encyclopedia was not only the most comprehensive reference book for eighteenth-century English readers, it also became the basis of the larger and even more influential French* Encyclopédie. *Chambers was a "free-thinker," which means that he rejected established religion in favour of more rational beliefs about divinity and the natural world. He is supposed to have been irritable but kind to the poor. He had an influence on the life of Samuel Johnson. Not only did he publish the first review of Johnson's first book, in a journal called the* Literary Magazine, *he also wrote one of the two works on which Johnson said he formed his literary style. I present excerpts from that work, a proposal for a new edition of his* Cyclopaedia, *which I take from a rare copy in the John Johnson Collection at the Bodleian Library. The piece is less interesting for its influence on Johnson, which is hard to perceive, than for its important information on how the field of knowledge was unfolding and expanding in the eighteenth-century public sphere.*

from
Some
CONSIDERATIONS
Offered to the PUBLIC,
preparatory to a second Edition of
CYCLOPÆDIA:
or, an
UNIVERSAL DICTIONARY
of
ARTS and SCIENCES (c. 1738)

A Redaction of the Body of Learning is growing every Day more and more necessary; as the Objects of our Knowledge are increasing, Books becoming more numerous, and new Points of Dispute and Enquiry turning up. For want of this, the Sciences remain in great Measure at a Stand, or can advance only imperceptibly; since the whole Life of those who should make Discoveries is spent in learning what is already found out. Hence such Improvements as are made rarely arrive at any maturity, but terminate in Hints and imperfect Openings, or in Queries and Proposals for further Enquiry. Most of the late Discoveries in the Sciences remain thus crude and imperfect; the whole vast Systems of Microscopical Plants and Animals; and Telescopic Worlds, of Attractions, Magnetism, Electricity, and the like, remain as it were in Embryo . . .

'Tis true, we do not want for Auxiliary Books. *Dictionaries, Bibliothecas, Journals, Apparatuses, Introductions*, and *Methods of Study*, are already Extant and that in such Number, as has in great Measure defeated the Intention of them, and given Occasion to frequent Complaints, that they retard rather than promote, and bewilder instead of guiding us. The very evil they were intended to remove has seized them; I mean, Multitude and Voluminousness; so that it has been found necessary to frame a secondary Kind of Auxiliaries to facilitate the Study of the first . . . The *Text* would afford a View of *General* Knowledge; the *Notes* would give a further Detail of the more curious *Particulars*; and both together afford a proper Introduction to the Study of any Science: At the same Time the *literary* part by directing to the Fountain Heads, would put us in a Way to arrive at a thorough Knowledge in any One. There would be *Extracts* of Books as in a Journal; *Catalogues* of authors as in *Bibliotheca*; and the Whole ranged alphabetically, like a *Dictionary*.

It were easy to enumerate many other Advantages to accrue from such a Work; particularly to *Inventors*, as this would serve as a Kind of Register to secure their Property, and prevent all After-Claims of second and third Inventors. To *Authors*, by the Detail it would present of Books, to be consulted for Materials and to prevent the growing Evil of endless repetitions. To *Readers*, by the Characters it would exhibit of Writers and Editions, and indicating, in the larger Articles, the Order and Method of Reading them; To *Philosophers*, by removing in some measure the Ambiguities of Language, that Source of endless Misunderstandings and Disputes; to the *English Language*, by fixing the Use and Acceptation of an infinite Number of words; and thus supplying in some Measure the Want of an *English Academy* . . .

But the Misfortune is, the great Difficulty of producing a Work capable of answering so many good Purposes, which, to most Readers, will rather form a Thing to be desired, than to be reasonably expected; the Materials of the former Book[1] will not go a great Way towards rebuilding it on a Plan so much Richer as well as more expensive. A vast Stock of new ones will be wanted, as well as infinite Labour to employ them. What Fund so Rich to supply the one? What Author indefatigable enough for the other? The Qualifications requisite to enable him to achieve such a Work are very extraordinary, and hardly to be expected in any one Person. He must have a Compass of Learning more universal than was ever found in the most celebrated Polyhistors[2] . . . more Reading than a Leibniz or LeClerc; more Reflections than a Hobbes, Malebranche, or Locke; more Acquaintance with the Ancients than a Grævius; with the Middle Age Writers than a DuCange; with the Moderns than a Boyle . . .

If a Person thus qualified can not be found, yet it does not follow that the Work is utterly impracticable; since what one Person cannot do, may be done by several. There are not wanting Hands enough in the World to do the Work in Perfection; the great Difficulty is, how to excite and apply them to it. Various kinds of Communities have heretofore been formed on the like Occasions; as that of Justinian for making a Digest of the Roman Laws . . . the French Academy for composing a Dictionary, Grammar, and Rhetoric . . . to say nothing of Monastic Congregations . . . who have published divers Works by joint Labour.

But none of these Methods seem adapted to the present State of Things, at least in our Nation: Monastic Communities we have none, since Henry VIII, and for Royal Academies, and Institutions on purpose, I know not whether any are to be expected. Besides, the Ceremony and Form which reign in such Assemblies with the Jealousies and Disputes which arise in them from different Systems and ways of Thinking, have been found to defeat, in great measure, the Intention of them; so that their Works go heavily on, and with great interruption and after all commonly baulk the public Expectation. How many Years were the French Academists, to the Number of Forty, the choicest Wits in France, in composing their Dictionary? How often did they alter the Plan of it; and yet when finished how many faults did Furetière find in a single Sheet published as a Specimen? . . .

---

[1] *former Book*   the first edition of *Cyclopaedia* (1728).   [2] *Polyhistor*   a universal scholar.

In effect, none of these Methods seem adapted to the English Taste and manner, who love to pursue their Speculations more at Liberty, as well as with less Show and Parade – One yet remains which is almost peculiar to themselves; and in which they have produced Works beyond what any neighbouring nation can boast of: I mean, the way of Voluntary, or Occasional *Communications*, where public-spirited Persons at their Leisure and Liberty, furnish Materials and Intelligences to the Undertakers of useful Designs. Thus it was the *Spectators, Tatlers*, and many other Papers were carried on with surprising Spirit and Success; and to this Day most of our *Journals* and other periodical Works are in great measure supported this way.

This method seems no where practicable to better Advantage than in the Work before us. A great Part of the Copies of the former Edition have fallen into the Hands of persons intelligent, some in one Branch of Knowledge, some in another; many of whom have Opportunities of noting certain Defects in it which they may be prevailed on to communicate. Many others having the Book at hand may be pleased to cast an Eye over it with the same view; and as any thing offers worthy Notice, to impart it as above. Lastly, All other Persons are desired, as any thing occurs in the Course either of their Reading or Speculation that appears new or uncommon, any Point set in a better Light than usual, or brought into a shorter Compass, or reduced to a juster Principle, or disposed in a more convenient Method, or pursued to a greater Length, to communicate the same by this means to the Public; whether it be in Real or Verbal matters, Philosophic or Literary ones, Civil or Ecclesiastical, Manual or Intellectual, Secret or Vulgar, Written or Unwritten ones. Any uncommon phenomenon, Experiment, Problem, Solution, Calculation, Instrument, Process, Trade, or Business; any new Term lately adopted, or old one lost or revived; any genealogy of a Word not commonly known, or Variation in the Use of it, or Acceptation not sufficiently authorized or Orthography that has escaped common Notice: In fine, any Rule, Custom, Explication, Correction, Judgement of Book, or Edition, Detection of Anonymous or Pseudonymous Author; Censure, or Defence of Opinion, Principle, or the like.

In this Invitation are included Persons of every Rank, Profession, and Degree of Knowledge; Men of Letters, of Business, and of Pleasure, the Universities, the Court, Country, Army, and Navy. Not a College, a Chapter, a mercantile Company, a Ship, scarce an House or even a man but may contribute his Quota to the public instruction. It will be no Disparagement to the most Learned to throw a few Materials into this general Magazine; the less Learned may here lay aside their Apprehensions of appearing in a Work of Literature; being Masters of the Subject, they need not be solicitous as to the style and manner; many even among the illiterate may here find Place and be of Use to men of the profoundest Learning; they will find an Amanuensis, in me, who shall even think it an honour to be dictated to by some who can neither Write nor Read.

Numerous Things are wanted from this last Quarter; and the more so, as they are not extant in Books, Libraries, and Cabinets of Virtuosi; but hid in Shops, Garrets, Cellars, Mines, and other obscure Places, where Men of Learning rarely penetrate: Rich Fields of Science lie thus neglected under Ground. Trades, Crafts, Mysteries, Practices, short Ways, with the whole vast apparatus of unwritten Philosophy . . .

I know not how far this Proposal will be complied with; but if only a Moiety of what be expected from it take Effect, it may furnish the best Book in the Universe; and abundantly indemnify us in the Want of what other Countries are so fond of, Royal, Imperial, Caesarian, and Ducal Academies, Palatine Societies, and the like: Splendid Names, pompous Titles, but rarely productive of fruits answerable thereto!

Alexander Pope (1688–1744)

Pope was the most important, popular, and influential poet of his time. He excelled at versification, and set a standard in manipulation of the heroic couplet that every young poet emulated but none could match. He also went a long way towards defining poetic diction, the sort of language that is proper for and to poetry, for his age. No poet has ever been more adept at putting lines of verse together, and few poets have worked over their lines with more care and attention. Pope was the consummate literary craftsman, but there is disagreement about the importance and penetration of the thoughts he put into such memorable and excellently wrought poetry.

His first important work, published when he was twenty-three, was An Essay on Criticism. *Like Horace's "Ars Poetica," most of the sentiments expressed in* An Essay *were already commonplaces of literary theory. But Pope exemplifies them so well, and embodies them in his own composition so nicely that he redefines the standards he adopts. Pope is the master of "true wit" (insight as well as mere repartee), as he himself defines it: "What oft was thought but ne'er so well expressed." The work that made him famous and financially independent was, appropriately, a translation. Pope's Homer began appearing in* 1715. *It is not the work of a Hellenistic scholar, but it represents a transmission of poetry from one great poetic talent to another. The work now seems somewhat anachronistically marked by the trappings of its own age; it makes Homer's heroes live to an extent in Queen Anne's age. But it is a triumph of versification and diction. Later in his career Pope wrote numerous looser translations, called imitations, in which he consciously substitutes contemporary names and manners for those described in Horace and some other important classical writers. These somewhat learned, elegant, yet sometimes gossipy works are also emblematic of the literary era that Pope did so much to create.*

Despite the fact that all his poetry is written in heroic couplets, Pope was a terrifically versatile writer, and he is particularly difficult to anthologize for that reason. However, The Rape of the Lock (1714) *is too attractive to leave out, and* The Dunciad *seems essential both to Pope and his age. Both works are mock epics that readers of* Paradise Lost *must appreciate for their ironic application of the heroic mode to modern life.* The Dunciad, *first published in* 1728, *is a much sharper satire than* The Rape, *and in its final version and expansion (1743) becomes the most philosophical and universal of Pope's satires, despite its deep involvement with now obscure, real people. For inclusion here I have selected Book I of* The Dunciad Variorum (1729), *including much of the preliminary matter and many of the notes that Pope (with a little help from his friends) added to the first edition. In addition, I include the full text and some of the notes of* The New Dunciad (1742), *the fourth book, which Pope added when he revamped the original three books and composed the final form of the poem,* The Dunciad, In Four Books (1743). *I incorporate Pope's final revisions in my presentation of* The New Dunciad, *so that, except for the prefatory remarks "To the Reader", my text is very close to that of Book IV of the* The Dunciad, In Four Books.

Because of his Roman Catholic background Pope was excluded from the sort of university education his talents deserved. Early in life, Pope's aspirations to elite society were also blocked by his creed. Later, when fame might have brought him into any company and conferred any honor on him, Pope was understandably somewhat bitter. The final book of The Dunciad *is in many ways a rejection of the Oxford honors that were offered too late to be acceptable. Pope's private life was restricted by poor health and congenital scholiosis which made him small and stooped. He had some kind of infatuation with Lady Mary Wortley Montagu (as the following letter to her suggests),*

*although her marriage made anything like consummation unthinkable. He had a deeper attachment
to Martha Blount, who was his life-long friend and endured public obloquy to live as his mistress.
Both of these important women in Pope's life suffered permanent disfigurement from small-pox. In
his comprehensive biography (Norton, 1985) Maynard Mack suggests that Pope's consciousness of
his own infirmities may have led him to a kind of fellow-feeling with these women, who were also
highly intelligent and physically marred.*

 Pope is blessed with a sumptuous standard edition of his poetry, The Twickenham Edition
of the Poems of Alexander Pope, *edited by John Butt and others, 11 vols (Methuen, 1938–
68). Although I take my texts of the poems from the first editions specified here, I rely on the
Twickenham Pope for those of Pope's corrections to later editions which I incorporate; he was a
relentless corrector and reviser. I am also indebted to the Twickenham editors for much help with
my footnotes. For the letter from Pope I draw on* The Correspondence of Alexander Pope, *edited
by George Sherburn, 5 vols (Clarendon Press, 1956).*

The *RAPE* of the *LOCK.*
AN
HEROI-COMICAL
POEM (1714)

In Five Canto's
—*A tonso est hoc nomen adepta capillo.*
Ovid.[1]

TO
MRS. *ARABELLA FERMOR*[2]

MADAM,

It will be in vain to deny that I have some Value for this Piece, since I Dedicate it to You.
Yet You may bear me Witness, it was intended only to divert a few young Ladies, who have
good Sense and good Humour enough, to laugh not only at their Sex's little unguarded
Follies, but at their own. But as it was communicated with the Air of a Secret, it soon found
its Way into the World. An imperfect Copy having been offered to a Bookseller, You had the
Good-Nature for my Sake to consent to the Publication of one more correct:[3] This I was
forced to before I had executed half my Design, for the *Machinery* was entirely wanting to
complete it.

 The *Machinery*, Madam, is a Term invented by the Critics, to signify that Part which the
Deities, Angels, or Dæmons, are made to act in a Poem: For the ancient Poets are in one

---

THE *RAPE* OF THE *LOCK*

[1] *A tonso . . . Ovid* "the name taken from a shorn lock
of hair" (*Metamorphoses* 8.151), from the story of Scylla,
who is turned into a bird and renamed Ciris (Latin,
"lock," "curl") after she betrays her father by cutting off
a special lock of his hair and presenting it to his handsome enemy. In later editions, Pope replaced the motto
with a quotation from Martial, "Nolueram, [Belinda],
tuos violare capillos/ Sed juvat hoc precibus me tribuisse
tuis" (*Epigrams* 12.84.1–2; "I did not wish, [Belinda], to

violate your locks, but I rejoice to have yielded this to
your wishes").
[2] *Arabella Fermor* (1690?–1738), Belinda in the
poem, who really was the victim of the prank that Pope
describes with such grandeur; "Mrs," as usual in the
eighteenth century, is a title of respect rather than one
that indicates marriage; Fermor married in 1714 or early
1715, shortly after this expanded version of the poem
was first published.
[3] *Publication of one more correct* this was the version in
two cantos, published in 1712.

respect like many modern Ladies; Let an Action be never so trivial in it self, they always make it appear of the utmost Importance. These Machines I determined to raise on a very new and odd Foundation, the *Rosicrucian* Doctrine of Spirits.

I know how disagreeable it is to make use of hard Words before a Lady; but 'tis so much the Concern of a Poet to have his Works understood, and particularly by your Sex, that You must give me leave to explain two or three difficult Terms.

The *Rosicrucians* are a People I must bring You acquainted with. The best Account I know of them is in a French Book called *Le Comte de Gabalis*,[4] which both in its Title and Size is so like a *Novel*, that many of the Fair Sex have read it for one by Mistake. According to these Gentlemen, the four Elements are inhabited by Spirits, which they call *Sylphs*, *Gnomes*, *Nymphs*, and *Salamanders*. The *Gnomes*, or Dæmons of Earth, delight in Mischief; but the *Sylphs*, whose Habitation is in the Air, are the best-conditioned Creatures imaginable. For they say, any Mortals may enjoy the most intimate Familiarities with these gentle Spirits, upon a Condition very easy to all true *Adepts*, an inviolate Preservation of Chastity.

As to the following Cantos, all the Passages of them are as Fabulous, as the Vision at the Beginning, or the Transformation at the End (except the Loss of your Hair, which I always mention with Reverence). The Human Persons are as Fictitious as the Airy ones; and the Character of *Belinda*, as it is now managed, resembles You in nothing but in Beauty.

If this Poem had as many Graces as there are in Your Person, or in Your Mind, yet I could never hope it should pass through the World half so Uncensured as You have done. But let its Fortune be what it will, mine is happy enough, to have given me this Occasion of assuring You that I am, with the truest Esteem,

Madam,
Your Most Obedient
Humble Servant.
A. Pope

THE
RAPE *of the* Lock

CANTO I

What dire Offence from am'rous Causes springs,
What mighty Quarrels rise from trivial Things,
I sing – This Verse to C—*l*, Muse! is due;[6]
This, ev'n *Belinda* may vouchsafe to view:
Slight is the Subject, but not so the Praise,   5
If she inspire, and He approve my Lays.
    Say what strange Motive, Goddess! could compel
A well-bred *Lord* t'assault a gentle *Belle*?

---

[4] *Le Comte de Gabalis* by Abbé de Montfaucon de Villars (1670).
[5] *Salamanders* elemental, fire-inhabiting beings.
[6] *C—l* John Caryll (1666?–1736), a wealthy land-owner, friend, and correspondent of Pope; he was related both to Robert, Lord Petre (the Baron of the poem) and to Arabella Fermor (Belinda), and wished for continued good relations among the three well-to-do Catholic families.

Oh say what stranger Cause, yet unexplored
Could make a gentle *Belle* reject a *Lord*?   10
And dwells such Rage in softest Bosoms then?
And lodge such daring Souls in Little Men?
  Sol through white Curtains shot a tim'rous Ray,[7]
And op'd those Eyes that must eclipse the Day;
Now Lapdogs give themselves the rousing Shake,   15
And sleepless Lovers, just at Twelve, awake:
Thrice rung the Bell, the Slipper knocked the Ground,[8]
And the pressed Watch returned a silver Sound.[9]
Belinda still her downy Pillow pressed,
Her Guardian *Sylph* prolonged the balmy Rest.   20
'Twas he had summoned to her silent Bed
The Morning Dream that hovered o'er her Head.
A Youth more glitt'ring than a *Birth-night Beau*,[10]
(That ev'n in Slumber caused her Cheek to glow)
Seemed to her Ear his winning Lips to lay,   25
And thus in Whispers said, or seemed to say,
  'Fairest of Mortals, thou distinguished Care
Of thousand bright Inhabitants of Air!
If e'er one Vision touched thy infant Thought,
Of all the Nurse and all the Priest have taught,   30
Of airy Elves by Moonlight Shadows seen,
The silver Token, and the circled Green,[11]
Or Virgins visited by Angel-Powers,[12]
With Golden Crowns and Wreaths of heav'nly Flowers,
Hear and believe! thy own Importance know,   35
Nor bound thy narrow Views to Things below.
Some secret Truths from Learned Pride concealed,
To Maids alone and Children are revealed:
What though no Credit doubting Wits may give?
The Fair and Innocent shall still believe.   40
Know then, unnumbered Spirits round thee fly,
The light *Militia* of the lower Sky;
These, though unseen, are ever on the Wing,
Hang o'er the *Box*, and hover round the *Ring*.[13]
Think what an Equipáge thou hast in Air,[14]   45
And view with scorn *Two Pages* and a *Chair*.[15]

---

[7] *Sol*   Latin for "Sun."
[8] *Slipper knocked*   to call the maid from her station downstairs.
[9] *pressed Watches* or "repeaters," sounded when pressed open.
[10] *Birth-night Beau*   a fashionable suitor, dressed up for the celebration of a royal birthday.
[11] *circled Green*   a fairy-ring, a circle of grass with a different color than the rest, supposed to be left, like silver coins, by fairies (but actually caused by fungus).

[12] *Virgins*   particularly, the Virgin Mary at the Annunciation, which is depicted with similar images.
[13] *the Ring*   a track cruised by fashionable coaches on the north side of Hyde Park.
[14] *Equipáge*   "Attendance; retinue" (Johnson).
[15] *Chair*   a sedan chair borne by two pages.

As now your own, our Beings were of old,
And once enclosed in a Woman's beauteous Mould;
Thence, by a soft Transition, we repair
From earthly Vehicles to these of Air.   50
Think not, when Woman's transient Breath is fled,
That all her Vanities at once are dead:
Succeeding Vanities she still regards,
And though she plays no more, o'erlooks the Cards.
Her Joy in gilded Chariots, when alive,   55
And Love of *Ombre*, after Death survive.[16]
For when the Fair in all their Pride expire,
To their first Elements their Souls retire:[17]
The Sprites of fiery Termagants in Flame[18]
Mount up, and take a *Salamander's* Name.[19]   60
Soft yielding Minds to Water glide away,
And sip with *Nymphs*, their Elemental Tea.
The graver Prude sinks downward to a *Gnome*,
In search of Mischief still on Earth to roam.
The light Coquettes in *Sylphs* aloft repair,   65
And sport and flutter in the Fields of Air.
     'Know farther yet; Whoever fair and chaste
Rejects Mankind, is by some *Sylphs* embraced:
For Spirits, freed from mortal Laws, with ease
Assume what Sexes and what Shapes they please.   70
What guards the Purity of melting Maids,
In Courtly Balls, and Midnight Masquerades,
Safe from the treach'rous Friend, the daring Spark,[20]
The Glance by Day, the Whisper in the Dark;
When kind Occasion prompts their warm Desires,   75
When Music softens, and when Dancing fires?
'Tis but their *Sylph*, the wise Celestials know,
Though *Honour* is the Word with Men below.
     'Some Nymphs there are, too conscious of their Face,
For Life predestined to the *Gnomes'* Embrace.   80
These swell their Prospects and exalt their Pride,
When Offers are disdained, and Love denied.
Then gay Ideas crowd the vacant Brain;
While Peers and Dukes, and all their sweeping Train,
And Garters, Stars and Coronets appear,[21]   85
And in soft Sounds, "Your Grace" salutes their Ear.

---

[16] *Ombre* a card game in which one player (the ombre), depending on the deal, declares which cards are trumps and competes for tricks with the other two players.
[17] *first elements* predominant of the four "elements" of fire, water, earth, and air, supposed to comprise all things and, by their proportions in the soul, to determine personality.

[18] *Termagant* "A scold; a brawling, turbulent woman" (Johnson).
[19] *Salamander's Name* because salamanders were popularly believed to live in fire (Browne, *Pseudodoxia Epidemica*, chapter 14).
[20] *Spark* dashing, bold man about town.
[21] *Garters, Stars and Coronets* badges of nobility.

'Tis these that early taint the Female Soul,
Instruct the Eyes of young *Coquettes* to roll,
Teach Infant Cheeks a bidden Blush to know,
And little Hearts to flutter at a *Beau*.   90
   'Oft when the World imagine Women stray,
The *Sylphs* through mystic Mazes guide their Way,
Through all the giddy Circle they pursue,
And old Impertinence expel by new.
What tender Maid but must a Victim fall   95
To one Man's Treat, but for another's Ball?[22]
When *Florio* speaks, what Virgin could withstand,
If gentle *Damon* did not squeeze her Hand?
With varying Vanities, from every Part,
They shift the moving Toyshop of their Heart;   100
Where Wigs with Wigs, with Sword-knots Sword-knots strive,[23]
Beaus banish Beaus, and Coaches Coaches drive.
This erring Mortals Levity may call,
Oh blind to Truth! the *Sylphs* contrive it all.
   'Of these am I, who thy Protection claim,   105
A watchful Sprite, and *Ariel* is my Name.
Late, as I ranged the Crystal Wilds of Air,
In the clear Mirror of thy ruling *Star*
I saw, alas! some dread Event impend,
Ere to the Main this Morning's Sun descend.[24]   110
But Heav'n reveals not what, or how, or where:
Warned by thy *Sylph*, oh Pious Maid beware!
This to disclose is all thy Guardian can.
Beware of all, but most beware of Man!'
   He said; when *Shock*, who thought she slept too long,[25] 115
Leapt up, and waked his Mistress with his Tongue.
'Twas then *Belinda*! if Report say true,
Thy Eyes first opened on a *Billet-doux*;[26]
Wounds, *Charms*, and *Ardours*, were no sooner read,
But all the Vision vanished from thy Head.   120
   And now, unveiled, the *Toilet* stands displayed,[27]
Each Silver Vase in mystic Order laid.
First, robed in White, the Nymph intent adores
With Head uncovered, the *Cosmetic* Powers.
A heav'nly Image in the Glass appears,   125
To that she bends, to that her Eyes she rears;
Th' inferior Priestess, at her Altar's side,
Trembling, begins the sacred Rites of Pride.
Unnumbered Treasures ope at once, and here

---

[22] *Treat* "An entertainment given" (Johnson).
[23] *Sword-knot* "Ribband tied to the hilt of the sword"
(Johnson), worn in fancy dress.
[24] *Main* ocean.

[25] *Shock* stock name for a lap dog, as well as a breed
from Iceland.
[26] *Billet-doux* love letter.
[27] *Toilet* dressing table.

The various Off'rings of the World appear;   130
From each she nicely culls with curious Toil,
And decks the Goddess with the glitt'ring Spoil.
This Casket *India*'s glowing Gems unlocks,
And all *Arabia* breathes from yonder Box.
The Tortoise here and Elephant unite,   135
Transformed to *Combs*, the speckled and the white.
Here Files of Pins extend their shining Rows,
Puffs, Powders, Patches, Bibles, Billet-doux.²⁸
Now awful Beauty puts on all its Arms;
The Fair each moment rises in her Charms,   140
Repairs her Smiles, awakens every Grace,
And calls forth all the Wonders of her Face;
Sees by Degrees a purer Blush arise,
And keener Lightnings quicken in her Eyes.
The busy *Sylphs* surround their darling Care;   145
These set the Head, and those divide the Hair,
Some fold the Sleeve, whilst others plait the Gown;
And *Betty*'s praised for Labours not her own.

CANTO II

Not with more Glories, in th' Ethereal Plain,
The Sun first rises o'er the purpled Main,
Than issuing forth, the Rival of his Beams
Launched on the Bosom of the Silver *Thames*.
Fair Nymphs, and well-dressed Youths around her shone,   5
But every Eye was fixed on her alone.
On her white Breast a sparkling *Cross* she wore,
Which *Jews* might kiss, and Infidels adore.
Her lively Looks a sprightly Mind disclose,
Quick as her Eyes, and as unfixed as those: 10
Favours to none, to all she Smiles extends,
Oft she rejects, but never once offends.
Bright as the Sun, her Eyes the Gazers strike,
And, like the Sun, they shine on all alike.
Yet graceful Ease, and Sweetness void of Pride,   15
Might hide her Faults, if *Belles* had Faults to hide:
If to her share some Female Errors fall,
Look on her Face, and you'll forget 'em all.
    This Nymph, to the Destruction of Mankind,
Nourished two Locks, which graceful hung behind   20
In equal Curls, and well conspired to deck
With shining Ringlets the smooth Iv'ry Neck.
Love in these Labyrinths his Slaves detains,
And mighty Hearts are held in slender Chains.

---

²⁸ *Patch*   "A small spot of black silk put on the face."

With hairy Springès we the Birds betray,[29]   25
Slight Lines of Hair surprise the Finny Prey,
Fair Tresses Man's Imperial Race ensnare,
And Beauty draws us with a single Hair.
      Th' Adventrous *Baron* the bright Locks admired,[30]
He saw, he wished, and to the Prize aspired: 30
Resolved to win, he meditates the way,
By Force to ravish, or by Fraud betray;
For when Success a Lover's Toil attends,
Few ask, if Fraud or Force attained his Ends.
      For this, ere *Phœbus* rose, he had implored,   35
Propitious Heav'n, and every Power adored,
But chiefly *Love* – to *Love* an Altar built,
Of twelve vast *French* Romances, neatly gilt.
There lay three Garters, half a Pair of Gloves;
And all the Trophies of his former Loves.   40
With tender *Billet-doux* he lights the Pyre,
And breathes three am'rous Sighs to raise the Fire.
Then prostrate falls, and begs with ardent Eyes
Soon to obtain, and long possess the Prize:
The Pow'rs gave Ear, and granted half his Prayer,   45
The rest, the Winds dispersed in empty Air.
      But now secure the painted Vessel glides,
The Sun-beams trembling on the floating Tides,
While melting Music steals upon the Sky,
And softened Sounds along the Waters die.   50
Smooth flow the Waves, the Zephyrs gently play,
Belinda smiled, and all the World was gay.
All but the *Sylph* – With careful Thought oppressed,
Th'impending Woe sate heavy on his Breast.
He summons straight his Denizens of Air;   55
The lucid Squadrons round the Sails repair:
Soft o'er the Shrouds Aërial Whispers breathe,
That seemed but *Zephyrs* to the Train beneath.
Some to the Sun their Insect-Wings unfold,
Waft on the Breeze, or sink in Clouds of Gold.   60
Transparent Forms, too fine for mortal Sight,
Their fluid Bodies half dissolved in Light.
Loose to the Wind their airy Garments flew,
Thin glitt'ring Textures of the filmy Dew;
Dipped in the richest Tincture of the Skies,   65
Where Light disports in ever-mingling Dyes,
While every Beam new transient Colours flings,

---

[29] *Springes* "A gin; noose which fastened to any elastic body catches by a spring or jerk" (Johnson).

[30] *Baron* Robert, Lord Petre (1690–1713); on 1 March 1712, just before the publication of the short version of *The Rape*, Lord Petre married Catherine Warmsley, a younger, richer belle than Arabella Fermor.

Colours that change whene'er they wave their Wings.
Amid the Circle, on the gilded Mast,
Superior by the Head, was *Ariel* placed;   70
His Purple Pinions opening to the Sun,
He raised his Azure Wand, and thus begun.
   'Ye *Sylphs* and *Sylphids*, to your Chief give Ear,
Fays, Fairies, Genii, Elves and *Dæmons* hear![31]
Ye know the Spheres and various Tasks assigned,   75
By Laws Eternal, to th' Aerial Kind.
Some in the Fields of purest *Æther* play,[32]
And bask and whiten in the Blaze of Day.
Some guide the Course of wand'ring Orbs on high,
Or roll the Planets through the boundless Sky.   80
Some less refined, beneath the Moon's pale Light
Pursue the Stars that shoot athwart the Night,
Or suck the Mists in grosser Air below,
Or dip their Pinions in the painted Bow,
Or brew fierce Tempests on the wintry Main,   85
Or o'er the Glebe distill the kindly Rain.
Others on Earth o'er human Race preside,
Watch all their Ways, and all their Actions guide:
Of these the Chief the Care of Nations own,
And guard with Arms Divine the *British Throne*.   90
   'Our humbler Providence is to tend the Fair,
Not a less pleasing, though less glorious Care.
To save the Powder from too rude a Gale,[33]
Nor let th' imprisoned Essences exhale,
To draw fresh Colours from the vernal Flow'rs,   95
To steal from Rainbows ere they drop in Show'rs
A brighter Wash; to curl their waving Hairs,[34]
Assist their Blushes, and inspire their Airs;
Nay oft, in Dreams, Invention we bestow,
To change a *Flounce*, or add a *Furbelo*.[35]   100
   'This Day, black Omens threat the brightest Fair
That e'er deserved a watchful Spirit's Care;
Some dire Disaster, or by Force, or Slight,[36]
But what, or where, the Fates have wrapped in Night.
Whether the Nymph shall break *Diana*'s Law,[37]   105
Or some frail *China* Jar receive a Flaw,
Or stain her Honour, or her new Brocade,
Forget her Prayers, or miss a Masquerade,
Or lose her Heart, or Necklace at a Ball;

---

[31] *Fays, Fairies, Genii, Elves and Dæmons hear!* in imitation of *Paradise Lost* 5.601.
[32] *Æther* "An element more fine and subtle than air" (Johnson).
[33] *Gale* "A wind not tempestuous, yet stronger than a breeze" (Johnson).
[34] *Wash* "A medical or cosmetic lotion" (Johnson).
[35] *Furbelo* "Fur sewed on the lower part of the garment; an ornament of dress" (Johnson).
[36] *or . . . or* either . . . or.
[37] *Diana* goddess of chastity.

Or whether Heav'n has doomed that *Shock* must fall. 110
Haste then ye Spirits! to your Charge repair;
The flutt'ring Fan be *Zephyretta*'s Care;
The Drops to thee, *Brillantè*, we consign;[38]
And, *Momentilla*, let the Watch be thine;
Do thou, *Crispissa*, tend her favourite Lock; 115
Ariel himself shall be the Guard of *Shock*.
   'To Fifty chosen *Sylphs*, of special Note,
We trust th' important Charge, the *Petticoat*:
Oft have we known that sev'nfold Fence to fail,[39]
Though stiff with Hoops, and armed with Ribs of Whale. 120
Form a strong Line about the Silver Bound,
And guard the wide Circumference around.
   'Whatever Spirit, careless of his Charge,
His Post neglects, or leaves the Fair at large,
Shall feel sharp Vengeance soon o'ertake his Sins, 125
Be stop't in *Vials*, or transfixed with *Pins*;
Or plunged in Lakes of bitter *Washes* lie,
Or wedged whole Ages in a *Bodkin*'s Eye:[40]
Gums and *Pomatums* shall his Flight restrain,[41]
While clogged he beats his silken Wings in vain; 130
Or Alum-*Styptics* with contracting Power[42]
Shrink his thin Essence like a rivelled Flower.[43]
Or as *Ixion* fixed, the Wretch shall feel[44]
The giddy Motion of the whirling Mill,
In Fumes of burning Chocolate shall glow, 135
And tremble at the Sea that froths below!'
   He spoke; the Spirits from the Sails descend;
Some, Orb in Orb, around the Nymph extend,
Some thrid the mazy Ringlets of her Hair,[45]
Some hang upon the Pendants of her Ear; 140
With beating Hearts the dire Event they wait,
Anxious, and trembling for the Birth of Fate.

CANTO III

Close by those Meads for ever crowned with Flow'rs,
Where *Thames* with Pride surveys his rising Tow'rs,
There stands a Structure of Majestic Frame,[46]
Which from the neighb'ring *Hampton* takes its Name.

---

[38] *Drop* "Diamond hanging in the ear" (Johnson).
[39] *sev'nfold Fence* with its seven layers and silver band, the petticoat is a version of an epic hero's shield (see *Iliad* 18 or *Aeneid* 8).
[40] *Bodkin* "An instrument to draw a thread or ribband through a loop" (Johnson).
[41] *Gums and Pomatums* medicinal ointments.
[42] *Alum-Styptics* an astringent used to close small cuts and blemishes.

[43] *rivel* "To contract into wrinkles and corrugations" (Johnson).
[44] *Ixion* the first Greek to murder a kinsman; for this crime Zeus had him bound to a perpetually revolving wheel of fire.
[45] *thrid* "To slide through a narrow passage" (Johnson).
[46] *Structure of Majestic Frame* Hampton Court, a palace built by Cardinal Wolsey in the sixteenth century, renovated and enlarged by William III.

Here *Britain*'s Statesmen oft the Fall foredoom 5
Of Foreign Tyrants, and of Nymphs at home;
Here Thou, Great *Anna*! whom three Realms obey,[47]
Dost sometimes Counsel take – and sometimes *Tea*.
　　Hither the Heroes and the Nymphs resort,
To taste awhile the Pleasures of a Court; 10
In various Talk th' instructive hours they passed,
Who gave the *Ball*, or paid the *Visit* last:
One speaks the Glory of the *British Queen*,
And one describes a charming *Indian Screen*;
A third interprets Motions, Looks, and Eyes; 15
At every Word a Reputation dies.
Snuff, or the *Fan*, supply each Pause of Chat,
With singing, laughing, ogling, and all that.[48]
　　Mean while declining from the Noon of Day,
The Sun obliquely shoots his burning Ray; 20
The hungry Judges soon the Sentence sign,
And Wretches hang that Jury-men may Dine;
The Merchant from th' *Exchange* returns in Peace,[49]
And the long Labours of the *Toilette* cease –
Belinda now, whom Thirst of Fame invites, 25
Burns to encounter two adventrous Knights,
At *Ombre* singly to decide their Doom;
And swells her Breast with Conquest yet to come.
Straight the three Bands prepare in Arms to join,
Each Band the number of the Sacred Nine.[50] 30
Soon as she spreads her Hand, th' Aerial Guard
Descend, and sit on each important Card:
First *Ariel* perched upon a *Matadore*,[51]
Then each, according to the Rank they bore;
For *Sylphs*, yet mindful of their ancient Race, 35
Are, as when Women, wondrous fond of Place.
　　Behold, four *Kings* in Majesty revered,
With hoary Whiskers and a forky Beard;
And four fair *Queens* whose hands sustain a Flower,
Th' expressive Emblem of their softer Power; 40
Four *Knaves* in Garbs succinct, a trusty Band,
Caps on their heads, and Halberds in their hand;
And Particoloured Troops, a shining Train,
Draw forth to Combat on the Velvet Plain.
　　The skilful Nymph reviews her Force with Care; 45
'Let Spades be Trumps!', she said, and Trumps they were.[52]
　　Now move to War her Sable *Matadores*,
In Show like Leaders of the swarthy *Moors*.

---

[47] *three Realms* England, Ireland, and Scotland.
[48] *ogle* "To view with side glances, as in fondness" (Johnson).
[49] *Exchange* one of several merchants' centers, such as New Exchange.

[50] *Sacred Nine* the muses.
[51] *Matadore* the three best cards in the game: the black aces, plus the 2 or 7 of the trumps suit.
[52] *'Let Spades be Trumps'* in imitation of "Let there be light . . ." (Genesis 1.3).

Spadillio first, unconquerable Lord!⁵³
Led off two captive Trumps, and swept the Board.   50
As many more *Manillio* forced to yield,⁵⁴
And marched a Victor from the verdant Field.
Him *Basto* followed, but his Fate more hard⁵⁵
Gained but one Trump and one *Plebeian* Card.
With his broad Sabre next, a Chief in Years,   55
The hoary Majesty of *Spades* appears;
Puts forth one manly Leg, to sight revealed;
The rest his many-coloured Robe concealed.
The Rebel-*Knave*, who dares his Prince engage,
Proves the just Victim of his Royal Rage.   60
Ev'n mighty *Pam* that Kings and Queens o'erthrew,⁵⁶
And mowed down Armies in the Fights of *Lu*,
Sad Chance of War! now, destitute of Aid,
Falls undistinguished by the Victor *Spade*!
    Thus far both Armies to *Belinda* yield;   65
Now to the *Baron* Fate inclines the Field.
His warlike *Amazon* her Host invades,
Th' Imperial Consort of the Crown of *Spades*.
The *Club*'s black Tyrant first her Victim died,
Spite of his haughty Mien, and barb'rous Pride: 70
What boots the Regal Circle on his Head,
His Giant Limbs in State unwieldy spread?
That long behind he trails his pompous Robe,
And of all the Monarchs only grasps the Globe?
    The *Baron* now his *Diamonds* pours apace;   75
Th' embroidered *King* who shows but half his Face,
And his refulgent *Queen*, with Pow'rs combined,
Of broken Troops an easy Conquest find.
Clubs, Diamonds, Hearts, in wild Disorder seen,
With Throngs promiscuous strow the level Green.   80
Thus when dispersed a routed Army runs,
Of *Asia*'s Troops, and *Afric*'s Sable Sons,
With like Confusion different Nations fly,
Of various Habit and of various Dye,
The pierced Battalions dis-united fall,   85
In Heaps on Heaps; one Fate o'erwhelms them all.
    The *Knave of Diamonds* tries his wily Arts,
And wins (oh shameful Chance!) the *Queen of Hearts*.⁵⁷
At this, the Blood the Virgin's Cheek forsook,
A livid Paleness spreads o'er all her Look;   90
She sees, and trembles at th' approaching Ill,

⁵³ *Spadillio* the ace of spades.
⁵⁴ *Manillio* 2 of spades, second highest card when spades are trumps.
⁵⁵ *Basto* ace of clubs, the third best card.

⁵⁶ *Pam* jack, or knave, of clubs, the best card in the equally popular game of *Lu*.
⁵⁷ *Knave of Diamonds ... Hearts* because diamonds was led, even the higher heart loses.

Just in the Jaws of Ruin, and *Codille*.[58]
And now (as oft in some distempered State),
On one nice *Trick* depends the gen'ral Fate,
An *Ace* of Hearts steps forth: The *King* unseen   95
Lurked in her Hand, and mourned his captive *Queen*.
He springs to Vegeance with an eager pace,
And falls like Thunder on the prostrate *Ace*.[59]
The Nymph exulting fills with *Shouts* the Sky,[60]
The Walls, the Woods, and long Canals reply.   100
　　Oh thoughtless Mortals! ever blind to Fate,
Too soon dejected, and too soon elate!
Sudden these Honours shall be snatched away,
And cursed for ever this Victorious Day.
　　For lo! the Board with Cups and Spoons is crowned,   105
The Berries crackle, and the Mill turns round.[61]
On shining Altars of *Japan* they raise[62]
The silver Lamp, the fiery Spirits blaze.
From silver Spouts the grateful Liquors glide,
While *China*'s Earth receives the smoking Tide.   110
At once they gratify their Scent and Taste,
And frequent Cups prolong the rich Repast.
Straight hover round the Fair her Airy Band;
Some, as she sipped, the fuming Liquor fanned,
Some o'er her Lap their careful Plumes displayed,   115
Trembling, and conscious of the rich Brocade.
Coffee (which makes the Politician wise,
And see through all things with his half-shut Eyes)
Sent up in Vapours to the *Baron*'s Brain[63]
New Stratagems, the radiant Lock to gain.   120
Ah cease rash Youth! desist ere 'tis too late,
Fear the just Gods, and think of *Scylla*'s Fate![64]
Changed to a Bird, and sent to flit in Air,
She dearly pays for *Nisus*' injured Hair!
　　But when to Mischief Mortals bend their Mind,   125
How soon fit Instruments of Ill they find!
Just then, *Clarissa* drew with tempting Grace
A two-edged Weapon from her shining Case;
So Ladies in Romance assist their Knight,
Present the Spear, and arm him for the Fight.   130
He takes the Gift with rev'rence, and extends
The little Engine on his Finger's Ends,[65]
This just behind *Belinda*'s Neck he spread,

---

[58] *Codille* to give *codille* to the *ombre* means to defeat
her.
[59] *Ace* with spades as trumps, the ace of hearts has no
value, unless Belinda fails to follow suit.
[60] *Shouts* like those issued by a conquering Homeric
warrior (Gk. ἀλαλάζω).

[61] *Berries* coffee beans.
[62] *Altars of Japan* japanned (heavily lacquered) tables.
[63] *Vapours* "Mental fume; vain imagination" as well
as "steam" (Johnson).
[64] *Scylla* see epigraph; p. 702, footnote 1 above.
[65] *Engine* "Any instrument" (Johnson).

As o'er the fragrant Steams she bends her Head:
Swift to the Lock a thousand Sprites repair,   135
A thousand Wings, by turns, blow back the Hair,
And thrice they twitched the Diamond in her Ear,
Thrice she looked back, and thrice the Foe drew near.
Just in that instant, anxious *Ariel* sought
The close Recesses of the Virgin's Thought;   140
As on the Nosegay in her Breast reclined,
He watched th' Ideas rising in her Mind,[66]
Sudden he viewed, in spite of all her Art,
An Earthly Lover lurking at her Heart.
Amazed, confused, he found his Pow'r expired,   145
Resigned to Fate, and with a Sigh retired.
      The Peer now spreads the glitt'ring *Forfex* wide,[67]
T' enclose the Lock; now joins it, to divide.
Ev'n then, before the fatal Engine closed,
A wretched *Sylph* too fondly interposed;   150
Fate urged the Sheers, and cut the *Sylph* in twain,
(But Airy Substance soon unites again)[68]
The meeting Points the sacred Hair dissever
From the fair Head, for ever and for ever!
      Then flashed the living Lightning from her Eyes,   155
And Screams of Horror rend th' affrighted Skies.
Not louder Shrieks by Dames to Heav'n are cast,
When Husbands or when Monkeys breathe their last,
Or when rich *China* Vessels, fall'n from high,
In glitt'ring Dust and painted Fragments lie!   160
      'Let Wreaths of Triumph now my Temples twine',
The Victor cried, 'the glorious Prize is mine!
While Fish in Streams, or Birds delight in Air,
Or in a Coach and Six the *British* Fair,
As long as *Atalantis* shall be read,[69]   165
Or the small Pillow grace a Lady's Bed,
While *Visits* shall be paid on solemn Days,
When numerous Wax-lights in bright Order blaze,[70]
While Nymphs take Treats, or Assignations give,
So long my Honour, Name, and Praise shall live!'   170
      What Time would spare, from Steel receives its date,
And Monuments, like Men, submit to Fate!
Steel did the Labour of the Gods destroy,[71]
And strike to Dust th' Imperial Tow'rs of *Troy*;

---

[66] *Idea* "Mental imagination. 'Whatsoever the mind perceives in itself, or is the immediate object of perception, thought, or understanding, that I call *idea*.' Locke" (Johnson).
[67] *Forfex* Latin for scissors.
[68] *Airy Substance . . . again* See *Milton* lib. 6 [Pope's note; *Paradise Lost* 6.344].

[69] *Atalantis Secret Memoirs and Manners of Several Persons of Quality* (1709), Delarivière Manley (see selection above, pp. 550–62).
[70] *Wax-lights* candles made of wax, rather than the cheaper, greasy tallow.
[71] *Labour of the Gods* Apollo and Poseidon were the legendary builders of the city of Troy.

Steel could the Works of mortal Pride confound,   175
And hew Triumphal Arches to the Ground.
What Wonder then, fair Nymph! thy Hairs should feel
The conqu'ring Force of unresisted Steel?

CANTO IV

But anxious Cares the pensive Nymph oppressed,
And secret Passions laboured in her Breast.
Not youthful Kings in Battle seized alive,
Not scornful Virgins who their Charms survive,
Not ardent Lovers robbed of all their Bliss,   5
Not ancient Ladies when refused a Kiss,
Not Tyrants fierce that unrepenting die,
Not *Cynthia* when her *Manteau*'s pinned awry,[72]
E'er felt such Rage, Resentment and Despair,
As Thou, sad Virgin! for thy ravished Hair.   10
     For, that sad moment, when the *Sylphs* withdrew,
And *Ariel* weeping from *Belinda* flew,
Umbriel, a dusky melancholy Sprite,
As ever sullied the fair face of Light,
Down to the Central Earth, his proper Scene,   15
Repaired to search the gloomy Cave of *Spleen*.[73]
     Swift on his sooty Pinions flits the *Gnome*,
And in a Vapour reached the dismal Dome.
No cheerful Breeze this sullen Region knows,
The dreaded *East* is all the Wind that blows.[74]   20
Here, in a Grotto, sheltered close from Air,[75]
And screened in Shades from Day's detested Glare,
She sighs for ever on her pensive Bed,
Pain at her Side, and *Megrim* at her Head.[76]
     Two Handmaids wait the Throne: Alike in Place,   25
But diff'ring far in Figure and in Face.
Here stood *Ill-nature* like an *ancient Maid*,
Her wrinkled Form in *Black* and *White* arrayed;
With store of Prayers, for Mornings, Nights, and Noons,
Her Hand is filled; her Bosom with Lampoons.   30
     There *Affectation* with a sickly Mien
Shows in her Cheek the Roses of Eighteen,
Practised to Lisp, and hang the Head aside,
Faints into Airs, and languishes with Pride;
On the rich Quilt sinks with becoming Woe,   35

---

[72] *Manteau* or "mantua," a loose-fitting gown.
[73] *Spleen* "The milt; one of the viscera, of which the use is scarcely known. It is supposed to be the seat of anger and melancholy [meaning all sorts of psychological ills]" (Johnson); also the name of an ill-defined constellation of ailments, like modern "depression" or eighteenth-century "vapours."

[74] *East* the east wind was supposed to bring on spleen.
[75] *Grotto* "A cavern or cave made for coolness. It is not used properly of a dark, horrid cavern" (Johnson); Pope had a grotto on his estate in Twickenham.
[76] *Megrim* or "migraine," severe headache.

Wrapped in a Gown, for Sickness, and for Show.
The Fair ones feel such Maladies as these,
When each new Night-Dress gives a new Disease.
    A constant *Vapour* o'er the Palace flies;
Strange Phantoms rising as the Mists arise;⁣ 40
Dreadful, as Hermit's Dreams in haunted Shades,
Or bright as Visions of expiring Maids.⁷⁷
Now glaring Fiends, and Snakes on rolling Spires,
Pale Spectres, gaping Tombs, and Purple Fires:
Now Lakes of liquid Gold, *Elysian* Scenes,⁷⁸ 45
And Crystal Domes, and Angels in Machines.
    Unnumbered Throngs on every side are seen
Of Bodies changed to various Forms by Sp*leen*.
Here living *Teapots* stand, one Arm held out,⁷⁹
One bent; the Handle this, and that the Spout: 50
A Pipkin there like *Homer*'s *Tripod* walks;⁸⁰
Here sighs a Jar, and there a Goose-pie talks;⁸¹
Men prove with Child, as powerful Fancy works,
And Maids turned Bottles, call aloud for Corks.
    Safe past the *Gnome* through this fantastic Band, 55
A Branch of healing *Spleenwort* in his hand.⁸²
Then thus addressed the Power – 'Hail wayward Queen!
Who rule the Sex to Fifty from Fifteen,
Parent of Vapours and of Female Wit,
Who give th' *Hysteric* or *Poetic* Fit, 60
On various Tempers act by various ways,
Make some take Physic, others scribble Plays;⁸³
Who cause the Proud their Visits to delay,
And send the Godly in a Pet, to pray.
A Nymph there is, that all thy Pow'r disdains, 65
And thousands more in equal Mirth maintains.
But oh! if e'er thy *Gnome* could spoil a Grace,
Or raise a Pimple on a beauteous Face,
Like Citron-Waters Matrons' Cheeks inflame,⁸⁴
Or change Complexions at a losing Game; 70
If e'er with airy Horns I planted Heads,⁸⁵
Or rumpled Petticoats, or tumbled Beds,
Or caused Suspicion when no Soul was rude,

---

⁷⁷ *Hermit's Dreams . . . Visions of . . . Maids*   these are religious hallucinations of hell and heaven.
⁷⁸ *Elysian*   the best part of the classical underworld.
⁷⁹ *living Teapots*   Robert Burton records two instances of insane persons who think they are pitchers (*Anatomy of Melancholy* 1.3.1.3).
⁸⁰ *Pipkin*   "A small earthen boiler" (Johnson, 1773); *Tripod*   See *Hom*. Iliad 18 [373–7], of *Vulcan*'s Walking tripods [Pope's note; they have wheels and move at his command].

⁸¹ *Goose-pie*   Alludes to a real fact, a Lady of distinction imagined herself in this condition [Pope's note].
⁸² *Spleenwort*   an herb said to be good for the spleen; this is a version of the golden bough that Aeneas used to pass safely through the Cave of Avernus into Hades (*Aeneid* 6).
⁸³ *Physic*   any medicine, but also, specifically, a purgative.
⁸⁴ *Citron-Waters*   a flavored liquor.
⁸⁵ *airy Horns*   imagined signs that the wearer has been cuckolded.

Or discomposed the Head-dress of a Prude,
Or e'er to costive Lap-Dog gave Disease, 75
Which not the Tears of brightest Eyes could ease:
Hear me, and touch *Belinda* with Chagrin;
That single Act gives half the World the Spleen'.
    The Goddess with a discontented Air
Seems to reject him, though she grants his Prayer. 80
A wondrous Bag with both her Hands she binds,
Like that where once *Ulysses* held the Winds;[86]
There she collects the Force of Female Lungs,
Sighs, Sobs, and Passions, and the War of the Tongues.
A Vial next she fills with fainting Fears, 85
Soft Sorrows, melting Griefs, and flowing Tears.
The *Gnome* rejoicing bears her Gifts away,
Spreads his black Wings, and slowly mounts to Day.
    Sunk in *Thalestris'* Arms the Nymph he found,[87]
Her Eyes dejected and her Hair unbound. 90
Full o'er their Heads the swelling Bag he rent,
And all the Furies issued at the Vent.
Belinda burns with more than mortal Ire,
And fierce *Thalestris* fans the rising Fire.
'O wretched Maid!' she spread her Hands, and cried, 95
(While *Hampton*'s Echoes, 'wretched Maid', replied),
'Was it for this you took such constant Care
The *Bodkin, Comb,* and *Essence* to prepare;
For this your Locks in Paper-Durance bound,
For this with tort'ring Irons wreathed around? 100
For this with Fillets strained your tender Head,[88]
And bravely bore the double Loads of Leads?[89]
Gods! shall the Ravisher display your Hair,
While the Fops envy, and the Ladies stare!
Honour forbid! at whose unrivalled Shrine 105
Ease, Pleasure, Virtue, All, our Sex resign.
Methinks already I your tears survey,
Already hear the horrid things they say,
Already see you a degraded Toast,
And all your Honour in a Whisper lost! 110
How shall I, then, your helpless Fame defend?
'Twill then be Infamy to seem your Friend!
And shall this Prize, th' inestimable Prize,
Exposed through Crystal to the gazing Eyes,
And heightened by the Diamond's circling Rays, 115
On that Rapacious Hand for ever blaze?

---

[86] *Ulysses held the Winds* in the bag given him by
Aeolus at the beginning of *Odyssey* Book 10.
[87] *Thalestris* name of a queen of the Amazons; here,
Mrs Morley, Arabella's second cousin by her marriage to
Sir George Browne (Sir Plume).
[88] *Fillet* "A band tied around the head" (Johnson).
[89] *Leads* soft wire ties.

Sooner shall Grass in *Hyde*-Park *Circus* grow,[90]
And Wits take Lodgings in the Sound of *Bow*;[91]
Sooner let Earth, Air, Sea to *Chaos* fall,
Men, Monkies, Lap-dogs, Parrots, perish all!'   120
  She said; then raging to *Sir Plume* repairs,[92]
And bids her *Beau* demand the precious Hairs:
(*Sir Plume*, of *Amber Snuff-box* justly vain,
And the nice Conduct of a *clouded Cane*)[93]
With earnest Eyes, and round unthinking Face,   125
He first the Snuff-box opened, then the Case,
And thus broke out – 'My Lord, why, what the Devil?
Z—ds! damn the Lock! 'fore Gad, you must be civil![94]
Plague on't! 'tis past a Jest – nay prithee, Pox!
Give her the Hair' – he spoke, and rapped his Box.   130
  'It grieves me much', replied the Peer again,
'Who speaks so well should ever speak in vain.
But by this Lock, this sacred Lock I swear.
(Which never more shall join its parted Hair,
Which never more its Honours shall renew,   135
Clipped from the lovely Head where late it grew)
That while my Nostrils draw the vital Air,
This Hand, which won it, shall for ever wear'.
He spoke, and speaking, in proud Triumph spread
The long-contended Honours of her Head.   140
  But *Umbriel*, hateful *Gnome*! forbears not so;
He breaks the Vial whence the Sorrows flow.
Then see! the *Nymph* in beauteous Grief appears,
Her eyes half-languishing, half-drowned in Tears;
On her heaved Bosom hung her drooping Head,   145
Which, with a Sigh, she raised; and thus she said.
  'For ever cursed be this detested Day,
Which snatched my best, my fav'rite Curl away!
Happy! ah ten times happy, had I been,
If *Hampton-Court* these Eyes had never seen!   150
Yet am not I the first mistaken Maid,
By Love of *Courts* to num'rous Ills betrayed.
Oh had I rather un-admired remained
In some lone Isle, or distant *Northern* Land;
Where the gilt *Chariot* never marked the way,   155
Where none learn *Ombre*, none e'er taste *Bohea*![95]
There kept my Charms concealed from mortal Eye,
Like Roses that in Deserts bloom and die.
What moved my Mind with youthful Lords to roam?

---

[90] *Hyde-Park Circus* the Ring (cf. canto 1, l. 44 above).
[91] *Sound of Bow* the bells of the church of St Mary-le-bow in Cheapside, which had become expensive and commercial.
[92] *Sir Plume* Arabella's second cousin, Sir George Browne.
[93] *clouded Cane* one with a head of polished stone, variegated with dark veins.
[94] *Z—ds!* "God's wounds," a mild curse.
[95] *Bohea* a fancy tea.

O had I stayed, and said my Prayers at home!   160
'Twas this, the Morning *Omens* did foretell;
Thrice from my trembling hand the *Patch-box* fell;
The tott'ring *China* shook without a Wind,
Nay, *Poll* sate mute, and *Shock* was most Unkind!
A *Sylph* too warned me of the Threats of Fate,   165
In mystic Visions, now believed too late!
See the poor Remnants of these slighted Hairs!
My hands shall rend what ev'n thy own did spare:
These, in two sable Ringlets taught to break,
Once gave new Beauties to the snowy Neck.   170
The Sister-Lock now sits uncouth, alone,
And in its Fellow's Fate foresees its own;
Uncurled it hangs, the fatal Sheers demands;
And tempts once more thy sacrilegious Hands.
Oh hadst thou, Cruel! been content to sieze   175
Hairs less in sight, or any Hairs but these!'

CANTO V

She said: the pitying Audience melt in Tears,
But *Fate* and *Jove* had stopped the *Baron*'s Ears.
In vain *Thalestris* with Reproach assails,
For who can move when fair *Belinda* fails?
Not half so fixed the *Trojan* could remain,[96]   5
While *Anna* begged and *Dido* raged in vain.
Then grave Clarissa graceful waved her Fan;[97]
Silence ensued, and thus the Nymph began.
    'Say, why are Beauties praised and honoured most,
The wise Man's Passion, and the vain Man's Toast?   10
Why decked with all that Land and Sea afford,
Why Angels called, and Angel-like adored?
Why round our Coaches crowd the white-gloved Beaus,
Why bows the Side-box from its inmost Rows?
How vain are all these Glories, all our Pains,   15
Unless good Sense preserve what Beauty gains:
That Men may say, when we the Front-box grace,
Behold the first in Virtue, as in Face!
Oh! if to dance all Night, and dress all Day,
Charmed the Small-pox, or chased old Age away;   20
Who would learn one earthly Thing of Use?
To patch, nay ogle, might become a Saint,
Nor could it sure be such a Sin to paint.
But since, alas! frail Beauty must decay,

---

[96] *Trojan* Aeneas beseeched to stay in Carthage by Dido and her sister Anna (*Aeneid* 4).

[97] *Clarissa* A new Character introduced in the subsequent Editions, to open more clearly the Moral of the Poem, in a parody of the speech of Sarpedon to Glaucus in Homer [*Iliad* 12; Pope's note; lines 7–36 were added in 1717; Clarissa is new in that she now has a speaking part; she appeared in the earlier edition of the poem, as here in canto 3, line 127, as the silent supplier of the forfex for the Baron's wicked deed].

Curled or uncurled, since Locks will turn to grey,   25
Since painted, or not painted, all shall fade,
And she who scorns a Man, must die a Maid;
What then remains, but well our Pow'r to use,
And keep good Humour still whate'er we lose?
And trust me, Dear! good Humour can prevail,   30
When Airs, and Flights, and Screams, and Scolding fail.
Beauties in vain their pretty Eyes may roll;
Charms strike the Sight, but Merit wins the Soul'.
    So spoke the Dame, but no Applause ensued;
Belinda frowned, *Thalestris* called her Prude.   35
'To Arms, to Arms!' the fierce Virago cries,[98]
And swift as Lightning to the Combat flies.
All side in Parties, and begin th' Attack;
Fans clap, Silks russle, and tough Whalebones crack;
Heroes' and Heroines' Shouts confusedly rise,   40
And bass, and treble Voices strike the Skies.
No common Weapons in their Hands are found,
Like Gods they fight, nor dread a mortal Wound.
    So when bold *Homer* makes the Gods engage,
And heav'nly Breasts with human Passions rage;   45
'Gainst *Pallas*, *Mars*; *Latona*, *Hermes* Arms;[99]
And all *Olympus* rings with loud Alarms.
Jove's Thunder roars, Heav'n trembles all around;
Blue *Neptune* storms, the bellowing Deeps resound;
Earth shakes her nodding Towers, the Ground gives way;   50
And the pale Ghosts start at the Flash of Day!
    Triumphant *Umbriel* on a Sconce's Height[100]
Clapped his glad Wings, and sate to view the Fight,
Propped on their Bodkin Spears, the Sprites survey
The growing Combat, or assist the Fray.   55
    While through the Press enraged *Thalestris* flies,
And scatters Deaths around from both her Eyes,
A *Beau* and *Witling* perished in the Throng,
One died in *Metaphor*, and one in *Song*.
'O cruel Nymph! a living Death I bear',   60
Cried *Dapperwit*, and sunk beside his Chair.
A mournful Glance Sir *Fopling* upwards cast,
'Those Eyes are made so killing' – was his last:[101]
Thus on *Meander*'s flow'ry Margin lies
Th' expiring Swan, and as he sings he dies.[102]   65
    When bold Sir *Plume* had drawn *Clarissa* down,
Chloe stepped in, and killed him with a Frown;

---

[98]   *Virago* "A female warrior; a woman with the qualities of a man" (Johnson).
[99]   *Latona* mother of Artemis and Apollo.
[100] *Sconce* a flat candlestick with a handle for hanging.

[101]   "*Those Eyes are made so killing*" A song in the opera of *Camilla* [Pope's note].
[102]   *Th' expiring Swan* as Pope noted in later editions, this is a reference to the opening of Ovid's *Heroides* 7, a lament from Dido to Aeneas.

She smiled to see the doughty Hero slain,
But at her Smile, the Beau revived again.

Now *Jove* suspends his golden Scales in Air,[103]   70
Weighs the Men's Wits against the Lady's Hair;
The doubtful Beam long nods from side to side;
At length the Wits mount up, the Hairs subside.

See fierce *Belinda* on the *Baron* flies
With more than usual Lightning in her Eyes;   75
Nor feared the Chief th' unequal Fight to try,
Who sought no more than on his Foe to die.
But this bold Lord, with manly Strength endued,
She with one Finger and a Thumb subdued:
Just where the Breath of Life his Nostrils drew,   80
A Charge of *Snuff* the wily Virgin threw;
The *Gnomes* direct, to ev'ry Atom just,
The pungent Grains of titillating Dust.
Sudden, with starting Tears each Eye o'erflows,
And the high Dome re-echoes to his Nose.   85

'Now meet thy Fate', th' incensed *Virago* cried,
And drew a deadly *Bodkin* from her Side.
(The same, his ancient Personage to deck,
Her great great Grandsire wore about his Neck
In three *Seal-Rings*; which after, melted down,   90
Formed a vast *Buckle* for his Widow's Gown:
Her infant Grandame's *Whistle* next it grew,
The *Bells* she jingled, and the *Whistle* blew;
Then in a *Bodkin* graced her Mother's Hairs,
Which long she wore, and now *Belinda* wears.)   100

'Boast not my Fall', he cried, 'insulting Foe!
Thou by some other shalt be laid as low.
Nor think, to die dejects my lofty Mind;
All that I dread, is leaving you behind!
Rather than so, ah let me still survive,   105
And burn in *Cupid*'s Flames, – but burn alive'.

'Restore the Lock!' she cries; and all around
'Restore the Lock!' the vaulted Roofs rebound.
Not fierce *Othello* in so loud a Strain
Roared for the Handkerchief that caused his Pain.   110
But see how oft Ambitious Aims are crossed,
And Chiefs contend 'till all the Prize is lost!
In every place is sought, but sought in vain:
With such a Prize no Mortal must be blest,
So Heav'n decrees! with Heav'n who can contest?   115

Some thought it mounted to the Lunar Sphere,[104]
Since all things lost on Earth, are treasured there.

---

[103] *golden Scales* Vid. *Homer* II. 22 & *Virg. Æn.* 12   [104] *the Lunar Sphere* Pope refers this vision to Ariosto's
[Pope's note; see *Paradise Lost* 4.996–8].   *Orlando Furioso*, but see also *Paradise Lost* 3.444ff.

There Heroes' Wits are kept in pond'rous Vases,
And Beau's in *Snuff-boxes* and *Tweezer-Cases*.
There broken Vows, and Death-bed Alms are found,   120
And Lovers' Hearts with Ends of Ribband bound;
The Courtier's Promises, and Sick Man's Prayers,
The Smiles of Harlots, and the Tears of Heirs,
Cages for Gnats, and Chains to Yoke a Flea;
Dried Butterflies, and Tomes of Casuistry.[105]   125
      But trust the Muse – she saw it upward rise,
Though marked by none but quick Poetic Eyes:
(So *Rome*'s great Founder to the Heav'ns withdrew,
To *Proculus* alone confessed in view.)[106]
A sudden Star, it shot through liquid Air,   130
And drew behind a radiant *Trail of Hair*.
Not *Berenice*'s Locks first rose so bright,[107]
The Skies bespangling with dishevelled Light.
The *Sylphs* behold it kindling as it flies,
And pleased pursue its Progress through the Skies.   135
      This the *Beau-monde* shall from the *Mall* survey,[108]
And hail with Music its propitious Ray.
This, the blessed Lover shall for *Venus* take,
And send up Vows from *Rosamonda*'s Lake.[109]
This *Partridge* soon shall view in cloudless Skies,[110]   140
When next he looks through *Galileo*'s Eyes;
And hence th' Egregious Wizard shall foredoom
The Fate of *Louis*, and the Fall of *Rome*.
      Then cease, bright Nymph! to mourn thy ravished Hair
Which adds new Glory to the shining Sphere!   145
Not all the Tresses that fair Head can boast
Shall draw such Envy as the Lock you lost.
For, after all the Murders of your Eye,
When after Millions slain, your self shall die;
When those fairs Suns shall set, as set they must,   150
And all those Tresses shall be laid in Dust;
This Lock, the Muse shall consecrate to Fame,
And mid'st the Stars inscribe *Belinda*'s Name!

FINIS

[105] *Casuistry* "the doctrine of cases of conscience" (Johnson).

[106] *Rome's great Founder ... in view* Romulus was killed in a storm (or by angry senators), and Proculus, to calm the bereaved populace supported the explanation that he had been swept up into heaven with a story about seeing him descend to give a prophecy of Rome's greatness (Livy 1.16).

[107] *Berenice's Locks* the votive offering of hair from a queen of Egypt for the safe return of her husband; when it was lost, the court astronomer claimed to find it in a hitherto unnamed constellation; Callimachus and Catullus used the myth in poetry before Pope.

[108] *Mall* a walk in St James's Park, as fashionable for cruising as the Ring.

[109] *Rosamonda's Lake* a pond in St James's Park famous as a meeting place for lovers.

[110] *Partridge* John Partridge [1644–1715] was a ridiculous Star-gazer, who in his Almanacs every year, never failed to predict the downfall of the Pope, and the King of *France*, then at war with the *English* [Pope's note].

from *The Dunciad Variorum* (1729)

MARTINUS SCRIBLERUS,
OF THE
POEM

This Poem, as it celebrateth the most grave and ancient of things, Chaos, Night and Dullness, so is it of the most grave and ancient kind. *Homer*, saith *Aristotle*, was the first who gave the *Form*, and, saith *Horace*, who adapted the *Measure*, to heroic poetry. But even before this, [as] may be rationally presumed from what the ancients have left written, was a piece by *Homer* composed, of like nature and matter with this of our Poet. For of Epic sort it appeareth to have been, yet of matter surely not unpleasant, witness what is reported of it by the learned Archbishop *Eustathius*,[1] in Odyss. K. And accordingly *Aristotle* in his poetic, chap. 4. doth further set forth, that as the Iliad and Odyssey gave example to Tragedy, so did this poem to Comedy its first Idæa.

From these authors also it should seem, that the Hero or chief personage of it was no less *obscure*, and his *understanding* and *sentiments* no less quaint and strange (if indeed not more so) than any of the actors in our poem. MARGITES was the name of this personage, whom Antiquity recordeth to have been *Dunce the First;* and surely from what he hear of him, not unworthy to be the root of so spreading a tree, and so numerous a posterity. The poem therefore celebrating him, was properly and absolutely a *Dunciad*; which though now unhappily lost, yet is its nature sufficiently known by the infallible tokens aforesaid. And thus it doth appear, that the first Dunciad was the first Epic poem, written by *Homer* himself, and anterior even to the Iliad or Odyssey.

Now forasmuch as our Poet had translated those two famous works of *Homer* which are yet left; he did conceive it in some sort his duty to imitate that also which was lost: And was therefore induced to bestow on it the same Form which *Homer*'s is reported to have had, namely that of Epic poem, with a title also framed after the ancient *Greek* manner, to wit, that of *Dunciad*.

Wonderful it is, that so few of the moderns have been stimulated to attempt some Dunciad! Since in the opinion of the multitude, it might cost less pain and oil, than an imitation of the greater Epic. But possible it is also that on due reflection, the maker might find it easier to paint a *Charlemagne*, a *Brute*[2] or a *Godfry*,[3] with just pomp and dignity heroic, than a *Margites*,[4] a *Codrus*,[5] a *Flecknoe*,[6] or *Tibbald*.[7]

We shall next declare the occasion and the cause which moved our Poet to this particular work. He lived in those days, when (after providence had permitted the Invention of Printing as a scourge for the Sins of the learned) Paper also became so cheap, and printers so numerous, that a deluge of authors covered the land: Whereby not only the peace of the honest unwriting subject was daily molested, but unmerciful demands were made of his applause,

[1] *Archbishop Eustathius* of Thessalonica, twelfth-century commentator on Homer.

[2] *Brute* the grandson of Aeneas, founder of Britain in fables.

[3] *Godfry* Godfrey of Bouillon, eleventh-century crusader, the perfect knight.

[4] *Margites* hero and title of a lost mock heroic poem attributed to Homer.

[5] *Codrus* a poor garret-dweller (hence, prototypical Grubstreet hack) in Juvenal, *Satire* 3.203–11.

[6] *Flecknoe* Richard (d. 1678), a poet ridiculed by Marvell and Dryden (see "Mac Flecknoe," p. 372 above).

[7] *Tibbald* Lewis Theobald (1688–1744), author of *Shakespeare Restored* (1726), a critique of Pope's edition of Shakespeare.

yea of his money, by such as would neither earn the one, or deserve the other: At the same time, the Liberty of the Press was so unlimited, that it grew dangerous to refuse them either: For they would forthwith publish slanders unpunished, the authors being anonymous; nay the immediate publishers thereof lay skulking under the wings of an Act of Parliament,[8] assuredly intended for better purposes.

Now our author living in those times, did conceive it an endeavour well worthy an honest satirist, to dissuade the dull and punish the malicious, *the only way that was left*. In that public-spirited view he laid the plan of this Poem, as the greatest service he was capable (without much hurt or being slain) to render his dear country. First, taking things from their original, he considereth the Causes creative of such authors, namely *Dullness* and *Poverty*; the one born with them, the other contracted, by neglect of their proper talent through self conceit of great abilities. This truth he wrapped in an *Allegory* (as the constitution of Epic poesy requires) and feigns, that one of these Goddesses had taken up her abode with the other, and that they jointly inspired all such writers and such works. He proceedeth to show the *qualities* they bestow on these authors, and the *effects* they produce: Then the *materials* or *stock* with which they furnish them, and (above all) that *self-opinion* which causeth it to seem to themselves vastly greater than it is, and is the prime motive of their setting up in this sad and sorry merchandise. The great power of these Goddesses acting in alliance (whereof as the one is the mother of industry, so is the other of plodding) was to be exemplified in some *one, great* and *remarkable action*. And none could be more so than that which our poet hath chosen, the introduction of the lowest diversions of the rabble in *Smithfield* to be the entertainment of the court and town; or in other words, the Action of the Dunciad is the Removal of the Imperial seat of Dullness from the City to the polite world; as that of the Æneid is the Removal of the Empire of *Troy* to *Latium*. But as *Homer*, singing only the *Wrath* of *Achilles*, yet includes in his poem the whole history of the *Trojan* war, in like manner our author hath drawn into this single action the whole history of Dullness and her children. To this end she is represented at the very opening of the poem, taking a view of her forces, which are distinguished into these three kinds, Party writers, dull poets, and wild critics.

A *Person* must be fixed upon to support this action, who (to agree with the said design) must be such an one as is capable of being all three. This *phantom* in the poet's mind, must have a *name*: He seeks for one who hath been concerned in the *Journals*, written bad *Plays* or *Poems*, and published low *Criticisms*: He finds his name to be *Tibbald*, and he becomes of course the Hero of the poem.

The *Fable* being thus according to best example one and entire, as contained in the proposition; the *Machinery* is a continued chain of Allegories, setting forth the whole power, ministry, and empire of Dullness, extended through her subordinate instruments, in all her various operations.

This is branched into *Episodes*, each of which hath its Moral apart, tho' all conducive to the main end. The crowd assembled in the second book demonstrates the design to be more extensive than to bad poets only, and that we may expect other Episodes, of the Patrons, Encouragers, or Paymasters of such authors, as occasion shall bring them forth. And the third book, if well considered, seemeth to embrace the whole world. Each of the Games relateth to some or other vile class of writers. The first concerneth the Plagiary, to whom he giveth the name of *More*; the second the libellous Novelist, whom he styleth *Eliza*; the third the

---

[8]   *an Act of Parliament*   10 Anne, C. 19.113 required that the publisher's real name appear on all publications; it was frequently ignored.

flattering Dedicator; the fourth the bawling Critic or noisy Poet; the fifth the dark and dirty Party-writer; and so of the rest, assigning to each some *proper name* or other, such as he could find.

As for the *Characters*, the public hath already acknowledged how justly they are drawn: The manners are so depicted, and the sentiments so peculiar to those to whom applied, that surely to transfer them to any other, or wiser, personages, would be exceeding difficult. And certain it is, that every person concerned, being consulted apart, will readily own the resemblance of every portrait, his own excepted.

The Descriptions are singular; the Comparisons very quaint; the Narrations various, yet of one colour. The purity and chastity of Diction is so preserved, that in the places most suspicious not the *words* but only the *images* have been censured, and yet are those images no other than have been sanctified by ancient and classical authority (though as was the manner of those good times, not so curiously wrapped up) yea and commented upon by most grave doctors, and approved critics.

As it beareth the name of Epic, it is thereby subjected to such severe indispensable rules as are laid on all Neotericks,[9] a strict imitation of the ancient; insomuch that any deviation accompanied with whatever poetic beauties, hath always been censured by the sound critic. How exact that Imitation hath been in this piece, appeareth not only by its general structure, but by particular allusions infinite, many whereof have escaped both the commentator and poet himself; yea divers by his exceeding diligence are so altered and interwoven with the rest, that several have already been, and more will be, by the ignorant abused, as altogether and originally his own.

In a word, the whole poem proveth itself to be the work of our Author when his faculties were in full vigour and perfection: at that exact time of life when years have ripened the judgement, without diminishing the imagination; which by good critics is held to be punctually at *forty*. For, at that season it was that *Virgil* finished his *Georgics*; and Sir *Richard Blackmore*[10] at the like age composing his Epic poesy: though since he hath altered it to *sixty*, the year in which he published his *Alfred*. True it is, that the talents for Criticism, namely smartness, quick censure, vivacity of remark, certainty of asseveration, indeed all but acerbity, seem rather the gifts of Youth than of riper age: But it is far otherwise in *Poetry*; witness the works of Mr. *Rymer* and Mr. *Dennis*,[11] who beginning with criticism, became afterwards such Poets as no age hath paralleled. With good reason therefore did our author choose to write his *Essay* on that subject at twenty, and reserve for his maturer years, this great and wonderful work of the *Dunciad*.

DUNCIADOS PERIOCHA:
OR,
ARGUMENTS TO THE BOOKS
Book the First

The Proposition of the subject. The Invocation, and the Inscription. Then the Original of the great empire of *Dullness*, and cause of the continuance thereof. The beloved seat of the Goddess is described, with her chief attendants and officers, her functions, operations, and

---

9 *Neotericks* moderns.
10 *Richard Blackmore* (1655–1729), physician and epic poet.

11 *Rymer and Dennis* Thomas Rymer (1641–1713) and John Dennis (1657–1734), two of the best known critics of their time, not much valued for their poetry.

effects. Then the poem hastes into the midst of things, presenting her on the evening of a Lord Mayor's day, revolving the long succession of her sons, and the glories past, and to come. She fixes her eye on *Tibbald* to be the instrument of that great event which is the subject of the poem. He is described pensive in his study, giving up the cause, and apprehending the period of her empire from the old age of the present monarch *Settle*. Wherefore debating whether to betake himself to law or politics, he raises an altar of proper books, and (making first his solemn prayer and declaration) purposes thereon to sacrifice all his unsuccessful writings. As the pile is kindled, the Goddess beholding the flame from her seat, flies in person and puts it out, by casting upon it the poem of *Thule*. She forthwith reveals her self to him, transports him to her Temple, unfolds all her arts, and initiates him into her mysteries; then announcing the death of *Settle* that night, anoints, and proclaims him Successor.

Book the Second

The King being proclaimed, the solemnity is graced with public Games and sports of various kinds (not instituted by the Hero, as by *Æneas* in *Virgil*, but for greater honour by the Goddess in person; in like manner as the games *Pythia, Isthmia, &c.* were anciently said to be by the Gods, and as *Thetis* herself appearing according to *Homer* Odyss. 24. proposed the prizes in honour of her son *Achilles*. Hither flock the Poets and Critics, attended (as is but just) with their Patrons and Book-sellers. The Goddess is first pleased for her disport to propose games to the latter, and setteth up the phantom of a poet which the booksellers contend to overtake. The races described, with their divers accidents: Next, the game for a Poetess: Afterwards the exercises for the *Poets*, of Tickling, Vociferating, Diving: the first holds forth the arts and practices of Dedicators, the second of Disputants and fustian[12] poets, the third of profound, dark, and dirty authors. Lastly, for the *Critics*, the Goddess proposes (with great Propriety) an exercise not of their parts but their patience; in hearing the works of two voluminous authors, one in verse and the other in prose, deliberately read, without sleeping: The various effects of which, with the several degrees and manners of their operation, are here most lively set forth: Till the whole number, not of critics only, but of spectators, actors, and all present fall fast asleep, which naturally and necessarily ends the games.

Book the Third

After the other persons are disposed in their proper places of rest, the Goddess transports the King to her Temple, and there lays him to slumber with his head on her lap; a position of marvellous virtue, which causes all the visions of wild enthusiasts, projectors,[13] politicians, inamorato's, castle-builders, chemists[14] and poets. He is immediately carried on the wings of fancy to the *Elizian* shade, where on the banks of *Lethe* the souls of the dull are dipped by *Bavius*, before their entrance into this world. There he is met by the ghost of *Settle*, and by him made acquainted with the wonders of the place, and with those which he is himself destined to perform. He takes him to a *Mount of Vision*, from whence he shews him the past triumphs of the empire of Dullness, then the present, and lastly the future. How small a part of the world was ever conquered by *Science*, how soon those conquests were stopped, and those very

---

[12] *fustian* "Swelling; unnaturally pompous" (Johnson).

[13] *projectors* "One who forms wild, impracticable schemes" (Johnson).

[14] *chemists* alchemists.

nations again reduced to her dominion. Then distinguishing the Island of *Great Britain*, shows by what aids, and by what persons, it shall be forthwith brought to her empire. These he causes to pass in review before his eyes, describing each by his proper figure, character, and qualifications. On a sudden the Scene shifts, and a vast number of miracles and prodigies appear, utterly surprising and unknown to the King himself, till they are explained to be the wonders of his own reign now commencing. On this subject *Settle* breaks into a congratulation, yet not unmixed with concern, that his own times were but the types of these; He prophecies how first the nation shall be overrun with farces, operas, shows: Then how her sons shall preside in the seats of arts and sciences, till in conclusion all shall return to their original Chaos: A scene, of which the present Action of the Dunciad is but a Type or Foretaste, giving a Glimpse or *Pisgah-sight*[15] of the promised Fullness of her Glory; the Accomplishment whereof will, in all probability, hereafter be the Theme of many other and greater Dunciads.

THE DUNCIAD*

*The *Dunciad, Sic* M.S. It may be well disputed whether this be a right Reading. Ought it not rather to be spelled *Dunceiad*, as the Etymology evidently demands? *Dunce* with an *e*, therefore *Dunceiad* with an *e*. That accurate and punctual Man of Letters, the Restorer of *Shakespeare*, constantly observes the preservation of this very Letter *e*, in spelling the Name of his beloved Author, and not like his common careless Editors, with the omission of one, nay sometimes of two *ee*'s (as *Shak'spear*) which is utterly unpardonable. Nor is the neglect of a *Single Letter* so trivial as to some it may appear; the alteration whereof in a learned language is an *Achievement that brings honour* to the Critic who advances it; and Dr. *{Richard}B{entley}*. will be remembered to posterity for his performances of *this sort*, as long as the world shall have any Esteem for the Remains of [the Greek comic playwrights] *Menander* and *Philemon*. THEOBALD [Pope's note].

I have a just value for the Letter E, and the same affection for the Name of this Poem, as the forecited Critic for that of his Author; yet cannot it induce me to agree with those who would add yet another *e* to it, and call it the *Dunceiade*, which being a French and foreign Termination, is no way proper to a word entirely English, and Vernacular. One E therefore in this case is right, and two E's wrong; yet upon the whole I shall follow the Manuscript, and print it without any E at all; moved thereto by Authority, at all times with Critics equal if not superior to Reason. In which method of proceeding, I can never enough praise my very good Friend, the exact Mr. *Tho. Hearne* [Wormius in the poem; scholar; antiquary; Bodleian librarian], who, if any word occur which to him and all mankind is evidently wrong, yet keeps he it in the Text with due reverence, and only remarks in the Margin, *sic* M.S. In like manner we shall not amend this error in the Title itself, but only note it *obiter* [incidentally], to evince to the learned that it was not our fault, nor any effect of our own Ignorance or Inattention. SCRIBLERUS [Pope's note].

---

[15] *Pisgah-sight* an anticipation or view from afar, after the mountain from which Moses glimpsed the promised land that he was never to enter.

BOOK THE FIRST

Books and the Man I sing, the first who brings[16]
The Smithfield Muses to the Ear of Kings.[17]
Say great Patricians! (since your selves inspire
These wond'rous works; so Jove and Fate require
Say from what cause, in vain decried and cursed,   5
Still Dunce the second reigns like Dunce the first?

In eldest time, ere mortals writ or read,
Ere Pallas issued from the Thund'rer's head,[18]
Dullness o'er all possessed her ancient right,
Daughter of Chaos and eternal Night:[19]   10
Fate in their dotage this fair idiot gave,
Gross as her sire, and as her mother grave,
Laborious, heavy, busy, bold, and blind,
She ruled, in native Anarchy, the mind.

Still her old empire to confirm, she tries,   15
For born a Goddess, Dullness never dies.

O thou! whatever Title please thine ear,
Dean, Drapier, Bickerstaff, or Gulliver![20]
Whether thou choose Cervantes' serious air,
Or laugh and shake in Rab'lais' easy Chair,   20
Or praise the Court, or magnify Mankind,
Or thy grieved Country's copper chains unbind;[21]
From thy Bæotia though Her Pow'r retires[22]
Grieve not at aught our sister realms acquire:
Here pleased behold her mighty wings out-spread,   25
To hatch a new Saturnian age of Lead.[23]
Where wave the tattered ensigns of Rag-Fair,[24]

[16] *Books and the Man I sing* ... Wonderful is the stupidity of all the former Critics and Commentators on this Poem! It breaks forth at the very first line. The Author of the Critique prefixed to *Sawney*, a Poem [by James Ralph, 1728], *p. 5*. hath been so dull as to explain *The Man who brings*, &c. not of the Hero of the Piece, but of our Poet himself, as if he vaunted that *Kings* were to be his Readers (an Honour which though this Poem hath had, yet knoweth he how to receive it with more Modesty.)

We remit this Ignorant to the first lines of the *Æneid*; assuring him, that *Virgil* there speaketh not of himself, but of *Æneas*, *Arma virumq; cano* ... *Vexatus.*, SCRIBLERUS [Pope's note].

[17] *The Smithfield-Muses* Smithfield is the place where Bartholomew Fair was kept, whose Shows, Machines, and Dramatical Entertainments, formerly agreeable only to the Taste of the Rabble, were, by the Hero of this Poem and others of equal Genius, brought to the Theatres of Covent-Garden, Lincolns-Inn-Fields, and the Hay-Market, to be the reigning Pleasures of the Court and Town. This happened in the Year 1725, and contin-

ued to the Year 1728. See Book 3. Vers. 191, &c. [Pope's note].

[18] Athena, goddess of wisdom, born from the head of Zeus.

[19] *Daughter of Chaos, &c.*] The beauty of this whole Allegory being purely of the Poetical kind, we think it not our proper business as a Scholiast, to meddle with it; but leave it (as we shall in general all such) to the Reader: remarking only, that Chaos (according to *Hesiod*, Θεογονία) was the Progenitor of all the Gods. SCRIBL. [see *Paradise Lost* 2.894–6; DeMaria].

[20] *Dean* ... *Gulliver* all names used by Jonathan Swift in his satires.

[21] *copper chains* an allusion to Swift's successful combat against a form of currency imposed on Ireland by England.

[22] *Bæotia* a large Greek island.

[23] *A new Saturnian Age of Lead* The ancient Golden Age is by Poets stiled *Saturnian*; but in the Chemical language, *Saturn* is Lead. [Pope's note].

[24] *Rag-fair* a place near the *Tower* of *London*, where old clothes and frippery are sold. [Pope's note].

A yawning ruin hangs and nods in air;
Keen, hollow winds howl through the bleak recess,
Emblem of Music caused by Emptiness: 30
Here in one bed two shiv'ring sisters lie,
The cave of Poverty and Poetry.
This, the Great Mother dearer held than all[25]
The clubs of Quidnunc's, or her own Guild-hall.
Here stood her Opium, here she nursed her Owls, 35
And destined here th' imperial seat of Fools.
Hence springs each weekly Muse, the living boast
Of Curl's chaste press, and Lintot's rubric post,[26]
Hence hymning Tyburn's elegiac lay,[27]
Hence the soft sing-song on Cecilia's day, 40
Sepulchral lies our holy walls to grace,
And New-year Odes, and all the Grubstreet race.[28]
        'Twas here in clouded majesty she shone;
Four guardian Virtues, round, support her Throne;
Fierce champion Fortitude, that knows no fears 45
Of hisses, blows, or want, or loss of ears:
Calm Temperance, whose blessings those partake
Who hunger, and who thirst, for scribbling sake:
Prudence, whose glass presents th' approaching jail:[29]
Poetic Justice, with her lifted scale; 50
Where in nice balance, truth with gold she weighs,
And solid pudding against empty praise.
        Here she beholds the Chaos dark and deep,
Where nameless somethings in their causes sleep,
'Till genial Jacob, or a warm Third-day[30] 55

---

[25] *Great Mother Magna mater*, here applied to *Dullness*. The *Quidnunc's* was a name given to the ancient Members of certain political Clubs, who were constantly enquiring, *Quid nunc?* what news? [Pope's note].

[26] [Edmund] *Curl* . . . [Bernard] *Lintot* Two Booksellers, of whom see Book 2 [49 ff]. The former was fined by the Court of King's-Bench for publishing obscene books; the latter usually adorned his shop with Titles in red letters [Pope's note; *rubric post* a show board or marquee outside the shop on which title pages with their rubrics (titles or headings in red letters) were displayed].

[27] *Tyburn's elegiac lay* It is an ancient English custom for the Malefactors to sing a Psalm at their Execution at *Tyburn*; and no less customary to print Elegies on their deaths, at the same time, or before. [Pope's note].

[28] *Cecilia's day* . . . *New-year Odes* Allude to the annual Songs composed to Music on St. *Cecilia's* Feast, and those made by the Poet-Laureat for the time being to be sung at Court, on every New-Years-Day, the words of which are happily drowned in the voices and Instruments. [*Sepulchral lies*] is a just Satire on the Flatteries and Falsehoods admitted to be inscribed on the Walls of Churches in Epitaphs. [Pope's notes].

I must not here omit a Reflection, which will occur perpetually through this Poem, and cannot but greatly endear the Author to every attentive Observer of it: I mean that *Candour* and *Humanity* which every where appears in him, to those unhappy Objects of the Ridicule of all mankind, the bad Poets. He here imputes all scandalous rhymes, scurrilous weekly papers, lying news, base flatteries, wretched elegies, songs, and verses (even from those sung at Court, to ballads in the streets) not so much to Malice or Servility as to Dullness; and not so much to Dullness, as to Necessity; And thus at the very commencement of his Satire, makes an Apology for all that are to be satirized. [Pope's note].

[29] *glass* spyglass or small telescope, with which Prudence was usually represented in allegorical pictures.

[30] *genial Jacob* Jacob Tonson, a very important publisher until 1720 (when his nephew Jacob II took over the business); also secretary and sometime host of the Kit Cat Club, which included Addison, Steele and other prominent Whigs; *a warm Third-day* a prosperous author's night (the profits of every third night of a dramatic production went to the author).

Call forth each mass, a poem or a play.
How Hints, like spawn, scarce quick in embryo lie,
How new-born Nonsense first is taught to cry,
Maggots half-formed, in rhyme exactly meet,
And learn to crawl upon poetic feet.   60
Here one poor Word a hundred clenches makes,[31]
And ductile dullness new meanders takes;
There motley Images her fancy strike,
Figures ill-paired, and Similes unlike.
She sees a Mob of Metaphors advance,   65
Pleased with the Madness of the mazy dance:
How Tragedy and Comedy embrace;
How Farce and Epic get a jumbled race;
How Time himself stands still at her command,
Realms shift their place, and Ocean turns to land.   70
Here gay Description Ægypt glads with showers;[32]
Or gives to Zembla fruits, to Barca flowers;[33]
Glitt'ring with ice here hoary hills are seen,
There painted vallies of eternal green,
On cold December fragrant chaplets blow,[34]   75
And heavy harvests nod beneath the snow.
    All these and more, the cloud-compelling Queen[35]
Beholds through fogs that magnify the scene:
She, tinselled o'er in robes of varying hues,
With self-applause her wild creation views,   80
Sees momentary monsters rise and fall,
And with her own fool's colours gilds them all.
    'Twas on the day, when Thorold, rich and grave,[36]
Like Cimon triumphed, both on land and wave:
(Pomps without guilt, of bloodless swords and maces,   85
Glad chains, warm furs, broad banners, and broad faces)[37]
Now Night descending, the proud scene was o'er,

---

[31] *one poor Word . . . clenches* [puns] It may not be amiss
to give an instance or two of these operations of *Dullness*
out of the Authors celebrated in the Poem. A great Critic
[Dennis] formerly held these Clenches in such abhorrence, that he declared, "He that would Pun, would pick
a Pocket". Yet Mr. *Dennis*'s Works afford us notable
Examples in this kind. "*Alexander* Pope hath sent abroad
into the world as many *Bulls* as his Namesake Pope
Alexander". – "Let us take the initial and final letters of
his Surname, viz., A. P—E, and they give you the idea of
an *Ape*. – *Pope* comes from the Latin word *Popa*, which
signifies a little Wart; or from *Poppysma*, because he
was continually *popping* out squibs of wit, or rather
Popysmata, or *Po-pisms*". DENNIS. *Daily-Journal* June
11.1728. [Pope's note; the source, a letter in the *Daily
Journal*, is signed Philoscriblerus, a lover of Martinus
Scriblerus].

[32] *Ægypt glads with showers* In the lower *Ægypt* rain is
of no use, the overflowing of the *Nile* being sufficient to
impregnate the soil [Pope's note].
[33] *Zembla* an arctic island; *Barca* a place in the
Libyan desert.
[34] *chaplets* garlands
[35] *cloud-compelling* Homer's epithet for Zeus.
[36] *Thorold* Sir *George Thorold* Lord Mayor of *London*, in
the Year 1720. The Procession of a Lord Mayor is made
partly by land, and partly by water. – *Cimon* the famous
Athenian General obtained a Victory by sea, and another
by land, on the same day, over the *Persians* and *Barbarians*. [Pope's note].
[37] *Glad Chains* The Ignorance of these Moderns! This
was altered in one Edition to *Gold Chains* . . . [Pope's
note].

But lived, in Settle's numbers, one day more.[38]
Now May'rs and Shrieves all hushed and satiate lay,[39]
Yet eat in dreams the custard of the day;   90
While pensive Poets painful vigils keep,
Sleepless themselves to give their readers sleep.
Much to the mindful Queen the feast recalls,
What City-Swans, once sung within the walls;
Much she resolves their arts, their ancient praise,   95
And sure succession down from Heywood's days.[40]
She saw with joy the line immortal run,
Each sire impressed and glaring in his son;[41]
So watchful Bruin forms with plastic care
Each growing lump, and brings it to a Bear.[42]   100
She saw old Pryn in restless Daniel shine,[43]
And Eusden eke out Blackmore's endless line;[44]
She saw slow Philips creep like Tate's poor page,[45]
And all the Mighty Mad in Dennis rage.[46]
    In each she marks her image full expressed,   105
But chief, in Tibbald's monster-breeding breast;
Sees Gods with Dæmons in strange league engage,

---

[38] {Elkanah} Settle [1648–1724] was alive at this time, and Poet to the City of London. His office was to compose yearly panegyrics upon the Lord Mayors, and Verses to be spoken in the Pageants: But that part of the shows being by the frugality of some Lord Mayors at length abolished, the employment of City Poet ceased; so that upon Settle's demise, there was no successor to that place. This important point of time our Poet has chosen, as the Crisis of the Kingdom of Dullness, who thereupon decrees to remove her imperial seat from the City, and over-spread the other parts of the Town: To which great Enterprise all things being now ripe, she calls the Hero of this Poem. [Pope's note].

[39] Shrieves   sheriffs.

[40] Heywood   probably Thomas, a dramatist, like Settle, ridiculed by Dryden (see "Mac Flecknoe," l. 29), though Pope's note points to John, a Tudor poet.

[41] impressed   as on the face of a medal or coin.

[42] Bruin . . . Bear   "Bruin" was a name for a bear; it was popularly believed that bears licked their cubs into shape.

[43] Prynn . . . Daniel   William Prynn [1600–69] and Daniel de Foe were writers of Verses, as well as of Politics . . . Both these Authors had a resemblance in their fates as well as writings, having been a-like sentenced to the Pillory. [Pope's note; the Protestant Prynne had his ears cut off for writing Histrio-Mastix (1633) and DeFoe was pilloried and jailed for The Shortest Way with the Dissenters].

[44] Eusden   Lawrence (1688–1730), poet laureate; Blackmore   Richard (c. 1655–1729) physician and epic poet.

[45] Philips   Ambrose (1674–1749), author of pastorals and Whig journalist; Tate   Nahum (1652–1715), another poet laureate, famous for revising Shakespeare's King Lear so that it ends more happily.

[46] And all the mighty Mad   This is by no means to be understood literally, as if Mr. D. were really mad . . . No – it is spoken of that Excellent and Divine Madness, so often mentioned by Plato, that poetical rage and enthusiasm, with which no doubt Mr. D. hath, in his time, been highly possessed SCRIBL. . . .

It would be unjust not to add his Reasons for this Fury, they are so strong and so coercive. "I regard him", saith he, "as an Enemy, not so much to me, as to my King, to my Country, to my Religion, and to that Liberty which has been the sole felicity of my life. A vagary of fortune, who is sometimes pleased to be frolicksome, and the epidemic Madness of the times, have given him Reputation, and Reputation (as Hobbs says) is Power, and that has made him dangerous. Therefore I look on it as my duty to King George, whose faithful subject I am, to my Country, of which I have appeared a constant lover; to the Laws, under whose protection I have so long lived; and to the Liberty of my Country, more dear than life to me, of which I have now for forty years been a constant asserter, &c. I look upon it as my duty, I say, to do – you shall see what – to pull the Lion's skin from this little Ass, which popular errors has thrown round him; and to show, that this Author who has been lately so much in vogue, has neither sense in his thoughts, nor English in his expressions". DENNIS, Rem. on Hom. Pref. p. 2 and p. 91, &c. . . . [Pope's note, which goes on for several pages].

And earth, and heav'n, and hell her battles wage.
   She eyed the Bard, where supperless he sate,[47]
And pined, unconscious of his rising fate;   110
Studious he sate, with all his books around,
Sinking from thought to thought, a vast profound!
Plunged for his sense, but found no bottom there;
Then writ, and floundered on, in mere dispair.
He rolled his eyes that witnessed huge dismay,[48]   115
Where yet unpawned, much learned lumber lay,
Volumes, whose size the space exactly filled;
Or which fond authors were so good to gild;
Or where, by sculpture made for ever known,
The page admires new beauties, not its own.   120
Here swells the shelf with Ogilby the great:[49]
There, stamped with arms, Newcastle shines compleat,[50]
Here all his suff'ring brotherhood retire,
And 'scape the martyrdom of jakes and fire;[51]
A Gothic Vatican! of Greece and Rome   125
Well-purged, and worthy Withers, Quarles, and Blome.[52]
   But high above, more solid Learning shone,
The Classics of an Age that heard of none;
There Caxton slept, with Wynkyn at his side,[53]
One clasped in wood, and one in strong cow-hide.   130
There saved by spice, like mummies, many a year,
Old Bodies of Philosophy appear.

---

[47] *supperless he sate*   It is amazing how the sense of this line hath been mistaken by all the former Commentators, who most idly suppose it to imply, that the Hero of the Poem wanted a supper. In truth a great absurdity! Not that we are ignorant that the Hero of *Homer*'s *Odyssey* is frequently in that circumstance, and therefore it can no way derogate from the grandeur of the Epic Poem to represent such Hero under a Calamity, to which the greatest not only of Critics and Poets, but of Kings and Warriors, have been subject. But much more refined, I will venture to say, is the meaning of our author: It was to give us obliquely a curious precept, or what *Bossu* calls a *dignified sentence,* that "Temperance is the life of Study". The language of Poesy brings all into Action; and to represent a Critic encompassed with books, but without a supper, is a picture which lively expresseth how much the true Critic prefers the diet of the mind to that of the body, one of which he always castigates and often totally neglects, for the greater improvement of the other. SCRIBLERUS [Pope's note].

[48] *He rolled his eyes*   [*Paradise Lost* 1.56-7, incorrect] The progress of a bad Poet in his thoughts being (like the progress of the Devil in *Milton*) through a Chaos, might probably suggest this imitation [Pope's note].

[49] *Ogilby the great*   John Ogilby [1600-76] was one, who from a late initiation into literature, made such a progress as might well style him the *Prodigy* of his time!

sending into the world so many *large Volumes!* . . . [Pope's note].

[50] *Newcastle*   The *Dutchess of Newcastle* [Margaret Cavendish] was one who busied herself in the ravishing delights of Poetry; leaving to posterity in print three *ample Volumes* of her studious endeavours . . . [Pope's note].

[51] *jakes*   "A house of office" (Johnson), a toilet.

[52] *Withers, Quarles, and Blome*   George Withers (1588-1667); Francis Quarles, author of *Emblemes* (1635); Richard Blome (d. 1705); all three used illustrations and were considered authors of children's or coffeetable books.

   George Withers was a great pretender to poetical zeal against the vices of the times, and abused the greatest Personages in power, which brought upon him *frequent correction.* The *Marshalsea* and *Newgate* were no strangers to him. WINSTANLY. *Quarles* was as dull a writer, but an honester man. *Blome*'s books are remarkable for their cuts [Pope's note].

[53] *Caxton*   William Caxton (1422-91), first English printer; *Wynkyn* de Worde (d. 1534) another important early printer; Theobald used Caxton's prose *Aeneid* to correct one of Pope's errors in his edition of Shakespeare; Pope actually included the work in one of the appendices of the *Dunciad* in 1729.

De Lyra here a dreadful front extends,[54]
And there, the groaning shelves Philemon bends.[55]
    Of these twelve volumes, twelve of amplest size,   135
Redeemed from tapers and defrauded pies,
Inspired he seizes: These an altar raise:
An hecatomb of pure, unsullied lays
That altar crowns: A folio Common-place[56]
Founds the whole pile, of all his works the base;   140
Quartos, Octavos, shape the less'ning pyre,
And last, a little Ajax tips the spire.[57]
    Then he. Great Tamer of all human art!
First in my care, and nearest at my heart:
Dullness! whose good old cause I yet defend,[58]   145
With whom my Muse began, with whom shall end!
O thou, of business the directing soul,
To human heads like bias to the bowl,[59]
Which as more pond'rous makes their aim more true,
Obliquely waddling to the mark in view.   150
O ever gracious to perplexed mankind!
Who spread a healing mist before the mind,
And, lest we err by Wit's wild, dancing light,
Secure us kindly in our native night.
Ah! still o'er Britain stretch that peaceful wand,   155
Which lulls th' Helvetian and Batavian land.[60]
Where rebel to thy throne if Science rise,
She does but show her coward face and dies:
There, thy good Scholiasts with unwearied pains
Make Horace flat, and humble Maro's strains;[61]   160
Here studious I unlucky moderns save,
Nor sleeps one error in its father's grave,
Old puns restore, lost blunders nicely seek,
And crucify poor Shakespeare once a week.[62]
For thee I dim these eyes, and stuff this head,   165
With all such reading as was never read;[63]
For thee supplying, in the worst of days,
Notes to dull books, and prologues to dull plays;
For thee explain a thing till all men doubt it,

---

[54] *De Lyra* Nicholas of Lyra (*c.* 1270–1349), French scholar, author of a biblical commentary in fifty volumes.
[55] *Philemon* Holland, [1552–1637] Dr. in Physic. He translated *so many books*, that a man would think he had done *nothing else*, insomuch that he might be called *Translator General of his age* . . . [Pope's note].
[56] *folio Common-place* a large notebook full of quotations.
[57] *a little Ajax* In *duodecimo*, translated from *Sophocles* by *Tibbald* [Pope's note].
[58] *good old cause* the cause of the Protestants and republicans in the Civil War.

[59] *bowl* a ball in lawn bowling, which was weighted or biased.
[60] *Helvetian and Batavian* Swiss and Netherlandish.
[61] *Maro* Virgil's surname.
[62] *once a week* For some time, once a week or fortnight, he printed in *Mist's Journal* a single remark or poor conjecture on some *word* or *pointing* of *Shakespeare* [Pope's note].
[63] *such reading as was never read* Such as *Caxton* above-mentioned; the three destructions of *Troy* by *Wynkyn*, and other like classics [Pope's note].

And write about it, Goddess, and about it;   170
So spins the silkworm small its slender store,
And labours, 'till it clouds itself all o'er.
Not that my quill to Critiques was confined,
My Verse gave ampler lessons to mankind;
So gravest precepts may successless prove,   175
But sad examples never fail to move.
As forced from wind-guns, lead itself can fly,
And pond'rous slugs cut swiftly through the sky;
As clocks to weight their nimble motion owe,
The wheels above urged by the load below;   180
Me, Emptiness and Dullness could inspire,
And were my Elasticity and Fire.
Had heav'n decreed such works a longer date,
Heav'n had decreed to spare the Grubstreet-state.
But see great Settle to the dust descend,   185
And all thy cause and empire at an end!
Could Troy be saved by any single hand,
His grey-goose-weapon must have made her stand.
But what can I? my Flaccus cast aside,[64]
Take up th' *Attorney's* (once my better) *Guide*?[65]   190
Or rob the Roman geese of all their glories,[66]
And save the state by cackling to the Tories?
Yes, to my Country I my pen consign,
Yes, from this moment, mighty Mist! am thine,[67]
And rival, Curtius! of thy fame and zeal,[68]   195
O'er head and ears plunge for the public weal.
'Adieu my children! better thus expire[69]
Un-stalled, unsold; thus glorious mount in fire
Fair without spot; than greased by grocer's hands,
Or shipped with Ward to ape and monkey lands,[70]   200
Or wafting ginger, round the streets to go,
And visit alehouse where ye first did grow'.
With that, he lifted thrice the sparkling brand,

---

[64] *My Flaccus* [Roman epic poet] A familiar manner of speaking used by modern Critics of a favourite Author. Mr. *T.* might as justly speak thus of *Horace*, as a French wit did of *Tully* seeing his works in a library, *Ah! mon cher Ciceron! Je le connois bien: c'est le même que Marc Tulle.* [Pope's note].

[65] *Attorney* In allusion to his first profession [Pope's note].

[66] *Roman geese* Relates to the well-known story of the geese that saved the Capitol of which Virgil, Æn. 8 [655–6; Pope's note; the geese awakened the Romans to a night attack of Gauls (Livy 5.47)].

[67] *Mighty Mist!* Nathaniel Mist [d. 1737] was a publisher of a famous Tory Paper . . . [Pope's note].

[68] *Curtius* the Roman who sacrificed himself for the Republic by riding in full armor into a huge chasm in the Forum (Livy 7.6).

[69] *Adieu my children* This is a tender and passionate Apostrophe to his own Works which he is going to sacrifice, agreeable to the nature of a man in great affliction, and reflecting like a parent, on the many miserable fates to which they would otherwise be subject.

> ——*Felix Priameïa virgo!*
> *Jussa mori: quæ sortitus non pertulit ullos,*
> *Nec victoris heri tetigit captiva cubile!*
> *Nos patriâ incensâ, diversa per æquora vectæ,* &c.
>   Virg. Æn. 3. [321–4] [Pope's note].

[70] *Ward Edward Ward* [1667–1731] a very voluminous Poet . . . best known by the *London Spy* . . . Great numbers of his works are yearly sold into the Plantations. [Pope's note].

And thrice he dropped it from his quiv'ring hand:
Then lights the structure, with averted eyes;   205
The rolling smokes involve the sacrifice.
The opening clouds disclose each work by turns,
Now flames old Memnon, now Rodrigo burns,[71]
In one quick flash see Proserpine expire,[72]
And last, his own cold Æschylus took fire.[73]   210
Then gushed the tears, as from the Trojan's eyes
When the last blaze sent Ilion to the skies.
Roused by the light, old Dullness heaved the head,
Then snatched a sheet of Thulè from her bed;[74]
Sudden she flies, and whelms it o'er the pyre: 215
Down sink the flames, and with a hiss expire.
        Her ample presence fills up all the place;
A veil of fogs dilates her awful face;
Great in her charms! as when on Shrieves and May'rs
She looks, and breathes her self into their airs.   220
She bids him wait her to the sacred Dome;[75]
Well-pleased he entered, and confessed his Home:
So spirits ending their terrestrial race,
Ascend, and recognize their native place:
Raptured, he gazes round the dear retreat,   225
And in sweet numbers celebrates the seat.[76]
        Here to her Chosen all her works she shows;
Prose swelled to verse, Verse loit'ring into prose;
How random Thoughts now meaning chance to find,
Now leave all memory of sense behind: 230
How Prologues into Prefaces decay,

---

[71] *old Memnon* a Hero in *The Persian Princess* [by Theobald] very apt to take fire, as appears by these lines with which he begins the Play:

  By heav'n it fires my frozen blood with rage,
  And makes it *scald* my aged Trunk——

Rodrigo, the chief personage of *The Perfidious Brother*, a play written between *T.* and a Watchmaker. [Pope's notes].
[72] *Proserpine* The *Rape* of *Proserpine*, one of the Farces of this Author, in which *Ceres* sets fire to a Corn-field, which endangered the burning of the Play-house. [Pope's note].
[73] *his own cold Æschylus* He had been (to use an expression of our Poet) "about Æschylus" for ten years, and had received Subscriptions for the same, but then went "about" other Books. The character of this tragic Poet is Fire and Boldness in a high degree; but our Author supposes it to be very much cooled by the translation; Upon sight of a specimen of it, was made this Epigram,

  Alas! poor Æschylus! unlucky Dog!
  Whom once a *Lobster* kill'd, and now a *Log*.

But this is a grievous error, for Æschylus was not slain by the fall of a Lobster on his head, but of a Tortoise . . . SCRIBL. [Pope's note; Theobald never finished his proposed translation of Aeschylus].
[74] *Thulè* [1718] An unfinished Poem of that name, of which one sheet was printed fifteen Years ago; by A{mbrose} Ph{ilips} a Northern Author. It is an usual method of putting out a fire, to cast wet sheets upon it. Some Critics have been of opinion, that this sheet was of the nature of the *Asbestos*, which cannot be consumed by fire; but I rather think it only an allegorical allusion to the coldness and heaviness of the writing. [Pope's note].
[75] *sacred Dome* The *Cave of Poverty* above-mentioned; where he no sooner enters, but he Reconnoitres the place of his original . . . [Pope's note].
[76] *sweet numbers* He writ a Poem called the *Cave of Poverty*, which concludes with a very extraordinary Wish, "That some great Genius, or man of distinguished merit may be *starved*, in order to celebrate her power, and describe her Cave". It was printed in octavo, 1715. [Pope's note; Pope is misquoting].

And these to Notes are frittered quite away.
How Index-learning turns no student pale,
Yet holds the Eel of science by the Tail.
How, with less reading than makes felons 'scape,[77]   235
Less human genius than God gives an ape,
Small thanks to France and none to Rome or Greece,
A past, vamped, future, old, revived, new piece,[78]
'Twixt Plautus, Fletcher, Congreve, and Corneille,
Can make a Cibber, Johnson, or Ozell.[79]   240
    The Goddess then o'er his anointed head,
With mystic words, the sacred Opium shed;
And lo! her Bird (a monster of a fowl!
Something betwixt a H***r and Owl)[80]
Perched on his crown. All hail! and hail again,   245
My son! the promised land expects thy reign.
Know, Settle, cloyed with custard and with praise,
Is gathered to the Dull of ancient days,
Safe, where no critics damn, no duns molest,
Where Gildon, Banks, and high-born Howard rest.[81]   250
I see a King! who leads my chosen sons
To lands, that flow with clenches and with puns:
'Till each famed Theatre my empire own,
'Till Albion, as Hibernia, bless my throne!
I see! I see! – Then rapt, she spoke no more.   255
God save King Tibbald! Grubstreet alleys roar.
    So when Jove's block descended from on high,
(As sings thy great fore-father, Ogilby,)[82]

---

77   *reading*   proving that one could read at this time still gave some accused criminals "benefit of clergy" and pardon.
78   *vamp*   "To piece an old thing with some new part" (Johnson).
79   *Cibber*   Colly (1671–1757) actor and playwright; his elevation to poet laureate in 1730 helped earn him an equivalent depression as hero of Pope's *New Dunciad* (1742); *Johnson* Charles (1679–1748), dramatist and Whig; *Ozell* John (d. 1743), a voluminous translator.
80   *a H***r* A strange Bird from *Switzerland*. [Pope's note; John James Heidegger (d. 1749), famous for promoting masquerades and other entertainments].
81   *Gildon* Charles (1665–1724), critic and dramatist; he called Pope "a little diminutive Creature, who had got a sort of Knack in smooth Versification"; *Banks* John (fl. 1677–96); *Howard* Edward, author of an epic poem; known as "foolish Ned."
82   *As sings thy great fore-father, Ogilby* See his *Æsop Fab.* where this excellent hemistich [half-line] is to be found [see next note]. Our author shows here and elsewhere, a prodigious Tenderness for a *bad writer*. We see he selects the only good passage perhaps in all that ever *Ogilby* writ; which shows how candid and patient a reader

he must have been. What can be more kind and affectionate than these words in the preface to his Poems, quarto, 1717, where he labours to call up all our humanity and forgiveness toward them, by the most moderate representation of their case that has ever been given by any Author? "Much may be said to extenuate the fault of bad Poets: What we call a *Genius* is hard to be distinguished, by a man himself, from a prevalent inclination: And if it be never so great, he can at first discover it no other way, than by that strong propensity, which renders him the more liable to be mistaken. He has no other method but to make the experiment by writing, and so appealing to the judgement of others: And if he happens to write ill (which is certainly no sin in itself) he is immediately made the Object of Ridicule! I wish we had the humanity to reflect, that even the worst Authors might endeavour to please us, and in that endeavour, deserve something at our hands. We have no cause to quarrel with them, but for their obstinacy in persisting, and even that may admit of alleviating circumstances: For their particular friends may be either ignorant, or unsincere; and the rest of the world too well-bred, to shock them with a truth, which generally their Booksellers are the first that inform them of" [Pope's note].

Loud thunder to its bottom shook the bog,
And the hoarse nation croaked, God save King Log![83]   260

Of the Characters of Women: An Epistle to a Lady (1735)

Advertisement[1]
The Author being very sensible how particular a Tenderness is due to the FEMALE SEX,
and at the same time how little they generally show to each other; declares, upon his Honour,
that no one Character is drawn from the Life, in this Epistle. It would otherwise be most
improperly inscribed to a Lady,[2] *who, of all the Women he knows, is the last that would be*
entertained at the Expense of Another.

Nothing so true as what you once let fall,
'Most Women have no Characters at all'.
Matter too soft a lasting mark to bear,
And best distinguished by black, brown, or fair.
How many pictures of one Nymph we view,   5
All how unlike each other, all how true!
Arcadia's Countess, here, in ermined pride,[3]
Is there, *Pastorella* by a Fountain side:
Here *Fannia*, leering on her own good man,[4]
Is there, a naked *Leda* with a Swan.[5]   10
Let then the Fair-one beautifully cry,
In *Magdalen*'s loose hair and lifted eye,[6]
Or dressed in smiles of sweet *Cecilia* shine,[7]
With simp'ring Angels, Palms, and Harps divine;
Whether the Charmer sinner it, or saint it,   15
If Folly grows romantic, we must paint it.[8]
Come then, the Colours and the ground prepare!
Dip in the Rainbow, trick her off in Air,
Choose a firm Cloud, before it fall, and in it
Catch, ere she change, the *Cynthia* of this minute.[9]   20
Rufa, whose eye quick-glancing o'er the *Park*,
Attracts each light gay Meteor of a Spark,[10]

---

[83] *King Log* in Ogilby's translation of Aesop (1651) the frogs "cry *Jove* save King Log" when Zeus answers their prayers by sending a wooden god; when they are dissatisfied with the stump, he sends them a stork who eats them up.

OF THE CHARACTERS OF WOMEN

[1] *Advertisement* this appears in the first edition of the poem (1735), which I use as a basis for the text, while inserting all the additions and most of the corrections that Pope made in his so-called "death-bed" edition of *Epistles to Several Persons* [*Moral Essays*] (1744).

[2] *Lady* Martha Blount (1690–1763), Pope's mistress and legatee.

[3] *Arcadia's Countess* the Countess of Pembroke wearing formal, state dress.

[4] *Fannia* an important Roman family, one of whose well-known members was a lady who was said to have committed adultery to save the life of the Roman general Marius.

[5] *Leda* impregnated by Zeus in the form of a swan, a favorite subject of painting.

[6] *Magdalen* Mary Magdalen, often pictured in crucifixion paintings.

[7] *Cecilia* St Cecilia, patron saint of music.

[8] *romantic* "fanciful" (Johnson).

[9] *Cynthia* goddess of the moon, and therefore changeful.

[10] *Spark* a man about town.

Agrees as well with *Rufa* studying *Locke*,
As *Sappho's* diamonds with her dirty smock,[11]
Or *Sappho* at her toilet's greasy task,[12]   25
With *Sappho* fragrant at an evening Mask:[13]
So morning Insects that in Muck begun,
Shine, buzz, and fly-blow in the setting-sun.
  How soft is *Silia*! fearful to offend,
The Frail one's Advocate, and weak one's Friend: 30
To her, *Calista* proved her Conduct nice,[14]
And good *Simplicius* asks of her Advice.
Sudden, she storms! she raves! You tip the wink,[15]
But spare your censure; *Silia* does not drink.
All eyes may see from what the change arose,   35
All eyes may see – a Pimple on her nose.
  Papillia, wedded to her am'rous Spark,[16]
Sighs for the Shades – 'How charming is a *Park*!'
A *Park* is purchased, but the Fair he sees
All bathed in tears – 'Oh odious, odious *Trees*!'   40
  Ladies, like variegated Tulips, show,
'Tis to their Changes half their Charms we owe;
Such happy Spots the nice Admirer take,
Fine by defect, and delicately weak.
'Twas thus *Calypso* once each heart alarmed,[17]   45
Awed without Virtue, without Beauty charmed;
Her Tongue bewitched as oddly as her Eyes,
Less Wit than Mimic, more a Wit than wise:
Strange Graces still, and stranger Flights she had,
Was just not ugly, and was just not mad;   50
Yet ne'er so sure our passion to create,
As when she touched the brink of all we hate.
  Narcissa's nature, tolerably mild,
To make a wash, would hardly stew a child;[18]
Has ev'n been proved to grant a Lover's prayer,   55
And paid a Tradesman once to make him stare;
Gave alms at *Easter*, in a christian trim,
And made a Widow happy, for a whim.
Why then declare Good-nature is her scorn,
When 'tis by that alone she can be born?   60
Why pique all mortals, yet affect a name?[19]
A Fool to Pleasure, and a Slave to Fame!

---

[11] *Sappho*   here and elsewhere in his poetry Pope uses
the name of the Greek lyric poet to represent Lady Mary
Wortley Montagu; in 1735 he wrote "Flavia" instead and
meant only a general type of learned lady, who were
always satirized for dirtiness.
[12] *toilet*   dressing table.
[13] *Mask*   a masquerade.

[14] *Calista*   a nymph who tried to hide her pregnancy
by Zeus, and the name of a guilty heroine in the popular
play *The Fair Penitent*.
[15] *tip the wink*   wink knowingly.
[16] *Papillia*   derived from the Latin word for butterfly.
[17] *Calypso*   a temptress in the *Odyssey*.
[18] *wash*   cosmetic lotion; *hardly*   well, completely.
[19] *pique*   "To offend; to irritate" (Johnson).

Now deep in *Taylor*[20] and the Book of *Martyrs*,[21]
Now drinking Citron with his Grace and Ch**:[22]
Now Conscience chills her, and now Passion burns;   65
And Atheism and Religion take their turns;
A very Heathen in the carnal part,
Yet still a sad, good Christian at her heart.
   See Sin in State, majestically drunk,[23]
Proud as a Peeress, prouder as a Punk;[24]   70
Chaste to her Husband, frank to all beside,
A teeming Mistress, but a barren Bride.
What then? let Blood and Body bear the fault,
Her Head's untouched, that noble Seat of Thought:
Such this day's doctrine – in another fit   75
She sins with Poets through pure Love of Wit.
What has not fired her bosom or her brain?
Caesar and Tall-boy, Charles and Charlema'ne.[25]
As Helluo, late Dictator of the Feast,[26]
The Nose of Hautgout, and the Tip of Taste,[27]   80
Criticked your wine, and analysed your meat,
Yet on plain Pudding deigned at-home to eat;
So Philomedé, lect'ring all mankind[28]
On the soft Passion, and the Taste refined,
Th' Address, the Delicacy – stoops at once,[29]   85
And makes her hearty meal upon a Dunce.
   Flavia's a Wit, has too much sense to *pray*,
To toast our wants and wishes, is her way;
Nor asks of *God*, but of her *Stars* to give
The mighty blessing, 'while we live, to live'.   90
Then all for Death, that Opiate of the soul!
Lucretia's Dagger, *Rosamonda*'s Bowl.[30]
Say, what can cause such impotence of mind?
A Spark too fickle, or a Spouse too kind.
Wise Wretch! of Pleasures too refined to please,   95
With too much Spirit to be e'er at Ease,
With too much Quickness ever to be taught,
With too much Thinking to have common Thought:
You purchase Pain with all that Joy can give,

---

[20] *Taylor*   Jeremy (1613–67), author of *Holy Living, Holy Dying*, and other works of stringent and lugubrious morality.
[21] *Book of Martyrs Actes and Monuments* by John Foxe (1516–87) was known by this title.
[22] *Citron*   flavoured brandy; *Ch*** Francis Charteris (1675–1732), a notorious rake and cheat.
[23] This verse paragraph was absent in 1735.
[24] *Punk*   whore.
[25] *Tall-boy*   a stupid young lover in a play by Richard Brome; *Charles*   a generic name for a footman; both are meant as opposites to Caesar and Charlemagne.

[26] *Helluo*   Latin, "glutton."
[27] *Hautgout*   the height of taste, full ripeness.
[28] *Philomedé*   laughter-loving, the epithet of Aphrodite in Homer and Hesiod.
[29] *Address*   "Manner of addressing another" or "Courtship" (Johnson).
[30] *Lucretia*   a Roman who committed suicide after being raped by Tarquin; *Rosamonda*   mistress of Henry II (1133–89) who poisoned herself.

And die of nothing but a Rage to live.   100
    Turn then from Wits; and look on *Simo's* Mate,[31]
No Ass so meek, no Ass so obstinate:
Or her, that owns her Faults, but never mends
Because she's honest, and the best of Friends:
Or her, whose life the Church and Scandal share,   105
For ever in a Passion, or a Prayer:
Or her, who laughs at Hell, but (like her Grace)
Cries, 'Ah! how charming if there's no such place!'
Or who in sweet Vicissitude appears
Of Mirth and Opium, Ratafie and Tears,[32]   110
The daily Anodyne, and nightly Draught,
To kill those foes to Fair ones, Time and Thought.
Woman and Fool are *two* hard things to hit,
For true No-meaning puzzles more than Wit.
    But what are these to great Atossa's mind?[33]   115
Scarce once herself, by turns all Womankind!
Who, with herself, or others, from her birth
Finds all her life one warfare upon earth:
Shines, in exposing Knaves, and painting Fools,
Yet is, whate'er she hates and ridicules.   120
No Thought advances, but her Eddy Brain
Whisks it about, and down it goes again.
Full sixty years the World has been her Trade,
The wisest Fool much Time has ever made.
From loveless youth to unrespected age,   125
No Passion gratified except her Rage.
So much the Fury still out-ran the Wit,
The Pleasure missed her, and the Scandal hit.
Who breaks with her, provokes Revenge from Hell,
But he's a bolder man who dares be well: 130
Her every turn with Violence pursued,
Nor more a storm her Hate than Gratitude.
To that each Passion turns, or soon or late;[34]
Love, if it makes her yield, must make her hate:
Superiors? death! and Equals? what a curse!   135
But an Inferior not dependant? worse.
Offend her, and she knows not to forgive;
Oblige her, and she'll hate you while you live:
But die, and she'll adore you – Then the Bust
And Temple rise – then fall again to dust.   140
Last night, her Lord was all that's good and great,
A Knave this morning, and his Will a Cheat.

---

[31] *Simo's Mate* shrewish wife of a typical sour old man in Roman comedy.
[32] *Ratafie* cherry brandy.
[33] This verse paragraph was absent in 1735 and probably suppressed because it would be taken as a lampoon on a living member of nobility, now identified as Katherine Darnley, Duchess of Buckinghamshire (1682?–1743); *Atossa* was the name of the very noble daughter of Cyrus, King of Persia.
[34] *or . . . or* either . . . or.

Strange! by the Means defeated of the Ends,
By Spirit robbed of Pow'r, by Warmth of Friends,
By Wealth of Follow'rs! without one distress   145
Sick of herself through very selfishness!
Atossa, cursed with every granted prayer,
Childless with all her Children, wants an Heir.
To Heirs unknown descends th' unguarded store
Or wanders, Heav'n-directed, to the Poor.   150
    Pictures like these (dear Madam) to design,
Asks no firm hand, and no unerring line;
Some wand'ring Touches, some reflected Light,
Some flying Stroke alone can hit them right:
For how should equal Colours do the knack?   155
Chameleons who can paint in White and Black?
    'Yet Cloe sure was formed without a spot —'[35]
Nature in her then erred not, but forgot.
'With every pleasing, every prudent part,
Say, what can Cloe want?' — she wants a Heart.   160
She speaks, behaves, and acts just as she ought;
But never, never, reached one gen'rous Thought.
Virtue she finds too painful an endeavour,
Content to dwell in Decencies for ever.
So very reasonable, so unmoved,   165
As never yet to love, or to be loved.
She, while her Lover pants upon her breast,
Can mark the figures on an Indian chest;
And when she sees her Friend in deep despair,
Observes how much a Chintz exceeds Mohair.   170
Forbid it Heav'n, a Favour or a Debt
She e'er should cancel — but she may forget.
Safe is your Secret still in Cloe's ear;
But none of Cloe's shall you ever hear.
Of all her Dears she never slandered one,   175
But cares not if a thousand are undone.
Would Cloe know if you're alive or dead?
She bids her footman put it in her head.
Cloe is prudent — would you too be wise?
Then never break your heart when Cloe dies.   180
    One certain Portrait may (I grant) be seen,
Which Heav'n has varnished out, and a made a *Queen*:[36]
The same for ever! and described by all
With Truth and Goodness, as with Crown and Ball:

---

[35] This verse paragraph was absent in 1735; it was printed separately in 1738 and first added to this poem in 1744. If she represents a particular person, it may be Henrietta Hobart, later Mrs Howard, later Countess of Suffolk, a mistress of George II (1681–1767).

[36] *Queen* Queen Caroline, wife of George II (1683–1737).

Poets heap Virtues, Painters Gems at will,   185
And show their zeal, and hide their want of skill.
'Tis well – but, Artists! who can paint or write,
To draw the Naked is your true delight;
That Robe of Quality so struts and swells,
None see what Parts of Nature it conceals.   190
Th' exactest traits of Body or of Mind,
We owe to models of an humble kind.
If Queensberry to strip there's no compelling,[37]
'Tis from a Handmaid we must take a Helen.
From Peer or Bishop 'tis no easy thing   195
To draw the man who loves his God, or King:
Alas! I copy (or my draught would fail)
From honest Mah'met, or plain Parson Hale.[38]
    In public Stations Men sometimes are shown,
A Woman's seen in Private life alone: 200
Our bolder Talents in full light displayed,
Your Virtues open fairest in the Shade.
Bred to disguise, in Public 'tis you hide;
Where none distinguish 'twixt your *Shame* and *Pride*,
Weakness or *Delicacy*; all so nice,   205
Each is a sort of *Virtue*, and of *Vice*.
    In several Men, we several Passions find,
In Women, two almost divide the Kind;
Those only fixed, they first or last obey,
The Love of Pleasure, and the Love of Sway.   210
    That, Nature gives; and where the lesson taught
Is but to please, Can Pleasure seem a fault?
Experience, This; by Man's Oppression cursed,
They seek the second not to lose the first.
    Men, some to Business, some to Pleasure take,   215
But every Woman is, at heart, a Rake:
Men, some to Quiet, some to public Strife;
But every Lady would be Queen for life.
    Yet mark the fate of a whole Sex of Queens!
Pow'r all their end, but Beauty all the means.   220
In Youth they conquer, with so wild a rage,
As leaves them scarce a Subject in their Age:
For foreign Glory, foreign Joy, they roam;
No thought of Peace or Happiness at home.
But Wisdom's Triumph is well-timed Retreat,   225
As hard a Science to the Fair as Great!
Beauties, like Tyrants, old and friendless grown,

---

[37] *Queensberry* Catherine Hyde, Duchess of
Queensbury (1700–77), a famous beauty.
[38] *honest Mah'met* Servant to the late king, said to be
the son of a Turkish Bassa, whom he took at the siege of
Buda, and constantly kept about his person. [Pope's
note]; *Parson Hale* Pope's neighbor and friend, the
physiologist Stephen Hales (1677–1761).

Yet hate Repose, and dread to be Alone,
Worn out in public, weary every eye,
Nor leave one sigh behind them when they die.   230
    Pleasures the Sex, as Children Birds, pursue,
Still out of reach, yet never out of view,
Sure, if they catch, to spoil the Toy at most,
To covet flying, and regret when lost:
At last, to Follies Youth could scarce defend,   235
It grows their Age's prudence to pretend;
Ashamed to own they gave delight before,
Reduced to feign it, when they give no more:
As Hags hold *Sabbaths*, less for joy than spite,[39]
So these their merry, miserable Night;   240
Still round and round the Ghosts of Beauty glide,
And haunt the places where their Honour died.
    See how the World its Veterans rewards!
A Youth of Frolics, an old Age of Cards,
Fair to no purpose, artful to no end,   245
Young without Lovers, old without a Friend,
A Fop their Passion, but their Prize a Sot,
Alive, ridiculous, and dead, forgot!
    Ah Friend! to dazzle let the Vain design,
To raise the Thought and touch the Heart, be thine!   250
That Charm shall grow, while what fatigues the Ring[40]
Flaunts and goes down, an unregarded thing.
So when the Sun's broad beam has tired the sight,
All mild ascends the Moon's more sober light,
Serene in Virgin Modesty she shines,   255
And unobserved the glaring Orb declines.
    Oh! blessed with *Temper*, whose unclouded ray
Can make to morrow cheerful as to day;
That pleased can see a younger charm, or hear
Sighs for a Sister with unwounded ear;   260
That ne'er shall answer till a Husband cool,
Or, if you rule him, never shows you rule;
Please by receiving, by submitting sway,
Yet have your humour most, when you obey;
Lets Fops or Fortune fly which way they will;   265
Despise all loss of Tickets, or Codille;[41]
Spleen, Vapours, or Small-pox, above them all,[42]
And Mistress of yourself, though China fall.
    And yet believe me, good as well as ill,
Woman's at best a Contradiction still.   270

---

[39] *Sabbaths* midnight meetings of witches.
[40] *Ring* a fashionable drive on the north side of Hyde Park.
[41] *Tickets* lottery tickets; *Codille* the term applied to the loser in the card game ombre.

[42] *Spleen . . . Small-pox* the first two were vaguely defined ailments, like modern depression; the third often left its victims scarred (see the selection from Dorothy Osborne Temple, p. 352 above).

Heav'n, when it strives to polish all it can
Its last best work, but forms a *softer Man*;
Picks from each Sex, to make its Favourite blessed,
Your love of Pleasure, our desire of Rest,
Blends, in exception to all general rules,   275
Your Taste of Follies, with our Scorn of Fools,
Reserve with Frankness, Art with Truth allied,
Courage with Softness, Modesty with Pride,
Fixed Principles, with Fancy ever new;
Shakes all together, and produces – *You*.   280
    Be this a Woman's Fame: With this un-blessed,
Toasts live a scorn, and Queens may die a jest.
This *Phoebus* promised, I forget the Year,
When those blue eyes first opened on the Sphere;
Ascendant *Phoebus* watched that hour with care,   285
Averted half your Parents' simple Prayer,
And gave you *Beauty*, but denied the *Pelf*[43]
That buys your Sex a Tyrant o'er itself:
The gen'rous God, who Wit and Gold refines,
And ripens Spirits as he ripens Mines,   290
Kept Dross for Duchesses, the world shall know it,
To you gave Sense, Good-humour, and a Poet.

from *The New Dunciad: as it was Found in the Year* 1741

TO THE READER

We apprehend it can be deemed no Injury to the Author of the *Three first Books* of the *Dunciad*, that we publish this *Fourth*. It was found merely by Accident, in taking a Survey of the *Library* of a late eminent Nobleman; but in so blotted a condition, and in so many detached pieces, as plainly showed it to be not only *incorrect* but *unfinished*: That the Author of the three first Books had a design to extend and complete his Poem in this manner, appears from the Dissertation prefixed to it, where it is said, that 'the Design is more extensive, and that we may expect other Episodes to complete it': And from the Declaration in the Argument to the third Book, that 'the Accomplishment of the Prophecies therein would be the Theme hereafter of a Greater Dunciad'. But whether or no he be the Author of this, we declare ourselves ignorant. If he be, we are no more to be blamed for the Publication of it than Tucca and Varius[1] for that of the last six books of the *Æneid*, though perhaps inferior to the former.

If any person be possessed of a more perfect Copy of this Work, or of any other Fragments of it, and will communicate them to the Publisher, we shall make the next Edition more complete: In which, we also promise to insert any *Criticisms* that shall be published, if at all to the purpose, with the *Names* of the *Authors*; or any Letters sent us (though not to the

---

[43] *Pelf* spoils belonging to a victor.

THE NEW DUNCIAD
[1] *Tucca and Varius* Virgil's literary executors, said to have published the *Aeneid*, which was left slightly unfinished, against the author's wishes.

purpose) shall yet be printed under the Title of *Epistulae Obscurorum Virorum*[2]; which together with some others of the same kind (formerly laid by for that purpose) may make no unpleasant Addition to the future Impressions of this Poem.

THE ARGUMENT
BOOK THE FOURTH

The poet being, in this Book, to declare the *Completion* of the *Prophecies* mentioned at the end of the former, makes a new *Invocation* (as the greater Poets are wont, when some high and worthy matter is to be sung). He shows the Goddess coming in her Majesty, to destroy *Order* and *Science*, and to substitute the *Kingdom of the Dull* upon earth. How she leads captive the *Sciences*, and silenceth the *Muses*; and *what* they be who succeed in their stead. All her Children, by a wonderful attraction, are drawn about her; and bear along with them also divers others, who promote her Empire by connivance, weak resistance, or discouragement of Arts; such as Half wits, tasteless Admirers, vain Pretenders, the Flatterers of dunces, or the Patrons of them. All these crowd round her; one of them offering to approach her, is driven back by a Rival, but she commends and encourages both. The first who speak in form are the *Geniuses* of the *Schools*, who assure her of their care to advance her Cause, by confining Youth to *words*, and keeping them out of the way of real Knowledge. Their Address, and her gracious Answer; with her Charge to them and the Universities. The *Universities* appear by their proper Deputies, and assure her that the same method is observed in the progress of *Education*; The speech of *Aristarchus* on this subject. They are driven off by a band of young Gentlemen returned from *Travel* with their *Tutors*; one of whom delivers to the Goddess, in a polite oration, an account of the whole Conduct and Fruits of their *Travels*: presenting to her at the same time a young Nobleman perfectly accomplished. She receives him graciously, and endues him with the happy quality of *Want of Shame*. She sees loitering about her a number of *Indolent Persons* abandoning all business and duty, and dying with laziness: to whom approaches the Antiquary *Annius*, entreating her to make them *Virtuosos*,[3] and assign them over to him: But *Mummius*, another Antiquary, complaining of his fraudulent proceeding, she finds a method to reconcile their difference. Then enter a troop of people fantastically adorned, offering her strange and exotic presents: Amongst them, one stands forth and demands justice on another, who had deprived him of one of the greatest Curiosities in nature: but he justifies himself so well, that the Goddess gives them both her approbation. She recommends to them to find proper employment for the *Indolents* before-mentioned, in the study of Butterflies, Shells, Birds-nests, Moss, & cetera but with particular caution, not to proceed beyond *Trifles*, to any useful or extensive views of Nature, or of the Author of Nature. Against the last of these apprehensions, she is secured by a hearty Address from the *Minute Philosophers* and *Free-thinkers*,[4] one of whom speaks in the name of the rest. The Youth thus instructed and principled,[5] are delivered to her in a body, by the hands of *Silenus*; and then admitted to taste the Cup of the *Magus* her *High Priest*, which causes a total oblivion of all Obligations, divine, civil, moral or rational. To these her Adepts she sends *Priests*, *Attendants*, and *Comforters*, of various kinds; confers on them *Orders* and *Degrees*; and then dismissing them with a speech, confirming to each his *Privileges*, and telling what she expects

[2] *Epistulae Obscurorum Virorum* "Letters of Obscure Men," the title of a satire (1516) on the scholasticism of some contemporary scholars, often amplified and reissued even into the second half of the eighteenth century.

[3] *Virtuoso* "A man skilled in antique or natural curiosities" (Johnson).
[4] *Free-thinker* "A libertine; a contemner of religion" (Johnson).
[5] *principled* given principles or basic instruction.

from each,[6] concludes with a *Yawn* of extraordinary virtue:[7] The Progress and Effects whereof on all Orders of men, and the Consummation of all, in the Restoration of *Night* and *Chaos*, conclude the Poem.

> Yet, yet a moment, one dim Ray of Light
> Indulge, dread Chaos, and eternal Night!
> Of darkness visible so much be lent,[8]
> As half to show, half veil the deep Intent.
> Ye Pow'rs! whose Mysteries restored I sing,   5
> To whom Time bears me on his rapid wing,
> Suspend a while your Force inertly strong,
> Then take at once the Poet and the Song.
>   Now flamed the Dog-star's unpropitious ray,[9]
> Smote every Brain, and withered every Bay;[10]   10
> Sick was the Sun, the Owl forsook his bow'r,
> The moon-struck Prophet felt the madding hour:
> Then rose the Seed of Chaos, and of Night,
> To blot out Order, and extinguish Light,
> Of dull and venal a new World to mould,   15
> And bring Saturnian days of Lead and Gold.[11]
>   She mounts the Throne: her head a Cloud concealed,
> In broad Effulgence all below revealed,[12]
> ('Tis thus aspiring Dullness ever shines)
> Soft on her lap her Laureat son reclines.   20
> Beneath her foot-stool, *Science* groans in Chains,
> And *Wit* dreads Exile, Penalties and Pains.
> There foamed rebellious *Logic*, gagged and bound,
> There, stripped, fair *Rhet'ric* languished on the ground;
> His blunted Arms by *Sophistry* are born,   25
> And shameless *Billinsgate* her Robes adorn.[13]
> *Morality*, by her false Guardians drawn,
> *Chicane* in Furs, and *Casuistry* in Lawn,[14]
> Gasps, as they straighten at each end the cord,
> And dies, when Dullness gives her Page the word.   30

---

[6] *telling what she expects from each* this clause and the rest of the sentence are from the version of the Argument published in 1743 and reflect the new ending composed for that edition and included herewith.

[7] *virtue* power.

[8] *darkness visible* see *Paradise Lost* 1.63.

[9] *Dog-star* Sirius, which shines brightly in the late summer before the harvest, a dry time, a time of famine in Roman times and also of poetry recitals.

[10] *Bay* bay laurel, the leaves of which were symbolic of poetic achievement.

[11] *Saturnian days* the Roman festival of Saturn was the day of misrule or saturnalia; Saturn was also associated with the harvest, and his temple served as a treasury.

[12] *all below revealed* It was the opinion of the Ancients that the Divinities revealed themselves to Men by their

Back-parts . . . But this passage may admit of a more modern Exposition by the Adage "The higher you climb, the more you show your A—. Verified in no instance more than in Dullness aspiring. Emblematized also by an Ape climbing and exposing his posteriors. Scribl[erus] [Pope's note].

[13] *Billinsgate* "A cant word [jargon], borrowed from Billingsgate in London, a place where there is always a crowd of low people, and frequent brawls and foul language. Ribaldry; foul language" (Johnson).

[14] *Chicane in Furs* corrupt, sophistical legal pleading in the ermine robes of a judge; *Casuistry in Lawn* corrupt moral pleading in the fine linen of a bishop's robes.

Mad *Mathesis* alone was unconfined,[15]
Too mad for mere material chains to bind,
Now to pure Space lifts her ecstatic stare,
Now running round the Circle, finds it square.
But held in ten-fold bonds the Muses lie,   35
Watched both by Envy's and by Flatt'ry's eye:
There to her heart sad Tragedy addressed
The dagger wont to pierce the Tyrant's breast;
But sober History restrained her rage,
And promised Vengeance on a barb'rous age.   40
There sunk Thalia, nerveless, cold, and dead,[16]
Had not her Sister Satire held her head:
Nor could'st thou, CHESTERFIELD! a tear refuse,[17]
Thou wept'st, and with thee wept each gentle Muse!

    When lo! a Harlot form soft sliding by,[18]   45
With mincing step, small voice, and languid eye;
Foreign her air, her robe's discordant pride
In patch-work flutt'ring, and her head aside.
By singing Peers up-held on either hand,
She tripped and laughed, too pretty much to stand;   50
Cast on the prostrate Nine a scornful look,
Then thus in quaint Recitativo spoke.
    'O *Cara! Cara!* silence all that train:
Joy to great Chaos! let Division reign:[19]
Chromatic tortures soon shall drive them hence,   55
Break all their nerves, and fritter all their sense:
One Trill shall harmonize joy, grief, and rage,
Wake the dull Church, and lull the ranting Stage;
To the same notes thy sons shall hum, or snore,
And all thy yawning daughters cry, *encore.*   60
Another Phoebus, thy own Phoebus, reigns,[20]
Joys in my jigs, and dances in my chains.
But soon, ah soon Rebellion will commence,
If Music meanly borrows aid from Sense:
Strong in new Arms, lo! Giant Handel stands,[21]   65

---

[15] *Mad Mathesis* Alluding to the strange Conclusions some Mathematicians have deduced from their principles concerning the real Quantity of Matter, the Reality of Space, &c. [Pope's note].

[16] *Thalia* the muse of comedy.

[17] *CHESTERFIELD* Philip Stanhope, fourth Earl of Chesterfield (1694–1773), statesman, author, and sometime patron of the arts.

[18] *Harlot form* The Attitude given to this Phantom represents the nature and genius of the Italian Opera; its affected airs, its luxurious and effeminating sounds, and the practice of patching up these Operas with favourite Songs, incoherently put together. These things were supported by the subscriptions of the Nobility. [Pope's note].

[19] *Division* in music, a run or variation, in which several notes are interpolated between those of the main melody in the musical composition.

[20] *Phoebus* a French term for a figure of speech in which nonsense is presented with a glimmer of sense.

[21] *Handel* produced large-scale, spectacular orchestral works, such as the *Firework Music*, opera, oratorios and overtures with every kind of sound, including that of cannons; he did go to Ireland when he became temporarily unpopular in London.

Like bold Briareus, with a hundred hands;[22]
To stir, to rouse, to shake the Soul he comes,
And Jove's own Thunders follow Mars's Drums.
Arrest him, Empress; or you sleep no more' —
She heard, and drove him to th' Hibernian shore.   70

    And now had Fame's posterior Trumpet blown,[23]
And all the Nations summoned to the Throne.
The young, the old, who feel her inward sway,
One instinct seizes, and transports away.
None need a guide, by sure Attraction led,   75
And strong impulsive gravity of head:
None want a place, for all their Centre found,
Hung to the Goddess, and cohered around.
Not closer, orb in orb, conglobed are seen
The buzzing Bees about their dusky Queen.   80

    The gath'ring number, as it moves along,
Involves a vast involuntary throng,
Who gently drawn, and struggling less and less,
Roll in her Vortex, and her pow'r confess.
Not those alone who passive own her laws,   85
But who, weak rebels, more advance her cause.
Whate'er of dunce in College or in Town
Sneers at another, in toupee or gown;[24]
Whate'er of mongrel no one class admits,
A wit with dunces, and a dunce with wits.   90

    Nor absent they, no members of her state,
Who pay her homage in her sons, the Great;
Who false to Phoebus, bow the knee to Baal;[25]
Or impious, preach his Word without a call.
Patrons, who sneak from living worth to dead,   95
With-hold the pension, and set up the head;[26]
Or vest dull Flatt'ry in the sacred Gown;[27]
Or give from fool to fool the Laurel crown.
And (last and worst) with all the cant of wit,
Without the soul, the Muse's Hypocrite.   100

    There marched the bard and blockhead, side by side,
Who rhymed for hire, and patronized for pride.
Narcissus, praised with all a Parson's pow'r,[28]
Looked a white lilly sunk beneath a show'r.

---

[22] *Briareus* a hundred-armed giant in Greek mythology (cf. Paradise Lost 1.199).
[23] *Posterior viz.* her second or more certain Report: unless we imagine this word *posterior* to relate to the position of one of her Trumpets . . . [Pope's note].
[24] *toupee* curl crowning a fashionable periwig.
[25] *Phoebus* Spoken of the ancient and true *Phoebus*, not the *French Phoebus*, who hath no chosen Priests or Poets, but equally inspires any man that pleaseth to sing or preach. Scribl. [Pope's note]; *Baal* a false god in the Bible.
[26] *the head* memorial bust for the deceased author.
[27] *sacred Gown* of a cleric or bishop, given in this case for flattery.
[28] *Narcissus* John, Baron Hervey (1696–1743), to whom Dr Conyers Middleton dedicated his edition of Cicero.

There moved Montalto with superior air;[29]   105
His stretched-out arm displayed a Volume fair;
Courtiers and Patriots in two ranks divide,
Through both he passed, and bowed from side to side:
But as in graceful act, with awful eye
Composed he stood, bold Benson thrust him by:[30]   110
On two unequal crutches propped he came,
Milton's on this, on that one Johnston's name.[31]
The decent Knight retired with sober rage,
Withdrew his hand, and closed the pompous page.
       When Dullness, smiling – 'Thus revive the Wits!   115
But murder first, and mince them all to bits;
As erst Medea (cruel, so to save!)[32]
A new Edition of old Æson gave,
Let standard-Authors, thus, like trophies born,
Appear more glorious as more hacked and torn,   120
And you, my Critics! in the chequered shade,
Admire new light through holes yourselves have made.
       'Leave not a foot of verse, a foot of stone,
A Page, a Grave, that they can call their own;
But spread, my sons, your glory thin or thick,   125
On passive paper, or on solid brick.
So by each Bard an Alderman shall sit,[33]
A heavy Lord shall hang at every Wit,
And while on Fame's triumphal Car they ride,
Some Slave of mine be pinioned to their side'.[34]   130
       Now crowds on crowds around the Goddess press,
Each eager to present the first Address.
Dunce scorning Dunce beholds the next advance,
But Fop shows Fop superior complaisance.
When lo! a Spectre rose, whose index-hand[35]   135
Held forth the Virtue of the dreadful wand;[36]
His beavered brow a birchen garland wears,[37]
Dropping with Infant's blood, and Mother's tears.
O'er every vein a shudd'ring horror runs;

---

[29] *Montalto* An eminent person of Quality [Sir Thomas Hanmer] who was about to publish a very pompous Edition of a great Author [Shakespeare, 1744], very much at his own expense indeed [Pope's note].

[30] *Benson* [William (1682–1754)] This man endeavoured to raise himself to Fame by erecting monuments, striking coins, setting up heads, and procuring translations, of *Milton*; and afterwards by a great passion for *Arthur Johnston* [neo-Latin poet, 1587–1641], a Scots physician's Version of the Psalms, of which he printed many fine Editions . . . [Pope's note].

[31] *Johnston* Arthur (1587–1641), Scots physician and author of Latin verse, including a paraphrase of the Psalms.

[32] *Medea* she gave Æson a new form by boiling him in a cauldron with magic herbs.

[33] *by each Bard an Alderman* among the monuments to the dead in Westminster Abbey.

[34] *Slave* alludes to the Roman custom of chaining a slave to the chariot of a victorious general riding in triumph.

[35] *Spectre* the ghost of Richard Busby, famous head of Westminster School; teacher, and beater, of Dryden, Locke and many other luminaries of the period.

[36] *Virtue* power.

[37] *beavered* covered with "a hat of the best kind, so called from being made of the fur of beaver" (Johnson).

Eton and Winton shake throught all their Sons.[38]   140
All Flesh is humbled, Westminster's bold race
Shrink, and confess the Genius of the place:
The pale Boy-Senator yet tingling stands,[39]
And holds his breeches close with both his hands.
   Then thus: 'Since Man from beast by Words is known,   145
Words are Man's province, Words we teach alone.
When Reason doubtful, like the Samian letter,[40]
Points him two ways, the narrower is the better.
Placed at the door of Learning, youth to guide,
We never suffer it to stand too wide.   150
To ask, to guess, to know, as they commence,
As Fancy opens the quick springs of Sense,
We ply the Memory, we load the brain,
Bind rebel Wit, and double chain on chain,
Confine the thought, to exercise the breath;[41]   155
And keep them in the pale of Words till death.
Whate'er the talents, or howe'er designed,
We hang one jingling padlock on the mind:
A Poet the first day, he dips his quill;
And what the last? a very Poet still.   160
Pity! the charm works only in our wall,
Lost, lost too soon in yonder House or Hall.[42]
There truant WYNDHAM every Muse gave o'er,[43]
There TALBOT sunk, and was a Wit no more![44]
How sweet an Ovid, MURRAY was our boast![45]   165
How many Martials were in PULT'NEY lost![46]
Else sure some Bard, to our eternal praise,
In twice ten thousand rhyming nights and days,
Had reached the Work, the All that mortal can;
And South beheld that Master-piece of Man'.[47]   170
   'Oh', cried the Goddess, 'for some pedant Reign!
Some gentle JAMES, to bless the land again;[48]
To stick the Doctor's Chair into the Throne,

---

[38] *Eton and Winton* [Winchester] prestigious British schools.

[39] *Senator* member of Parliament.

[40] *the Samian letter* the letter Y, used by Pythagoras [who was born in Samos] as an emblem of the different roads of Virtue and Vice [Pope's note].

[41] *to exercise the breath* By obliging them to get the classic poets by heart, which furnishes them with endless matter for Conversation, and Verbal amusement for their whole lives [Pope's note].

[42] *House or Hall* Westminster-hall and the House of Commons [Pope's note].

[43] *WYNDHAM* Sir William (1687–1740), a Tory leader, whose untimely death helped preserve Robert Walpole, the Whig leader of Parliament, from removal.

[44] *TALBOT* Charles, Baron Talbot (1685–1737), a fine and witty orator.

[45] *MURRAY* William, first Earl of Mansfield (1705–93), prize-winning student latinist.

[46] *PULT'NEY* William Pulteney, Earl of Bath (1684–1764), Walpole's most powerful opponent and a political writer, whom Pope compares to the brilliant first-century CE Roman epigrammatist, Martial.

[47] *Master-piece of Man viz.* an Epigram. The famous Dr. [Robert] *South* [1634–1716] declared a perfect Epigram to be as difficult a performance as an Epic Poem. And the Critics say, "an Epic Poem is the greatest work human nature is capable of" [Pope's note].

[48] *JAMES* James the first took upon himself to teach the Latin tongue to Car, Earl of Somerset; and that Gondomar the Spanish Ambassador would speak false Latin to him, on purpose to give him the pleasure of correcting it, whereby he wrought himself into his good graces [Pope's note].

Give law to Words, or war with Words alone,
Senates and Courts with Greek and Latin rule,   175
And turn the Council to a Grammar School!
For sure, if Dullness sees a grateful Day,
'Tis in the shade of Arbitrary Sway.
O! if my sons may learn one earthly thing,
Teach but that one, sufficient for a King;   180
That which my Priests, and mine alone, maintain,
Which as it dies, or lives, we fall, or reign:
May you, may Cam, and Isis preach it long![49]
"The RIGHT DIVINE of Kings to govern wrong"'
    Prompt at the call, around the Goddess roll   185
Broad hats, and hoods, and caps, a sable shoal:[50]
Thick and more thick the black blockade extends,
A hundred head of Aristotle's friends.
Nor wert thou, Isis! wanting to the day,
    [Though Christ-church long kept prudishly away.][51]   190
Each staunch Polemic, stubborn as a rock,
Each fierce Logician, still expelling Locke,[52]
Came whip and spur, and dashed through thin and thick
On German Crouzaz, and Dutch Burgersdyck.[53]
As many quit the streams that murm'ring fall[54]   195
To lull the sons of Margaret and Clare-hall,
Where Bentley late tempestuous wont to sport
In troubled waters, but now sleeps in Port.[55]
Before them marched that awful Aristarch;[56]
Ploughed was his front with many a deep Remark: 200
His Hat, which never veiled to human pride,
Walker with reverence took, and laid aside.[57]
Low bowed the rest: He, kingly, did but nod;
So upright Quakers please both Man and God.
'Mistress! dismiss that rabble from your throne: 205
Avaunt – is Aristarchus yet unknown?[58]
Thy mighty Scholiast, whose unwearied pains

[49] *Cam, and Isis* Cambridge and Oxford, after their respective rivers.
[50] *Broad hats, and hoods, and caps* pieces of academic dress; *shoal* school (of fish).
[51] *Christ-church* [an Oxford college that housed some of Bentley's adversaries] This line is doubtless spurious, and foisted in by the impertinence of the Editor; and accordingly we have put it between Hooks. For I affirm this College came as early as any other, by its *proper Deputies*; nor did any College pay homage to Dullness in its *whole body*. Bentl. [Richard Bentley (1662–1742), important classical scholar and critic, often satirized by Pope, Swift, and others; Pope's note].
[52] *Locke* In the year 1703 there was a meeting of the heads of the University of Oxford to censure Mr. Locke's Essay on Human Understanding, and to forbid the reading it [Pope's note].
[53] *Crouzaz* Jean Pierre de Crousaz (1663–1748) Swiss scholar who criticized Pope's long philosophical poem *An Essay on Man; Burgersdyck* (1590–1629), Dutch logician.
[54] *the streams* The River Cam, running by the walls of these Colleges, which are particularly famous for the skill in Disputation [Pope's note].
[55] *Port* Bentley's favorite beverage.
[56] *Aristarch* see note 58 below.
[57] *Walker* Dr Richard, Vice-Master of Trinity College, Cambridge, Bentley's college.
[58] *Aristarchus* A famous Commentator, and Corrector of Homer [and librarian at Alexandria], whose name has been frequently used to signify a severe Critic [Pope's note; he means Bentley, as indicated in his preface to the 1742 edition by *Ricardus Aristarchus*].

Made Horace dull, and humbled Milton's strains.
Turn what they will to Verse, their toil is vain,
Critics like me shall make it Prose again.   210
Roman and Greek Grammarians! know your Better:
Author of something yet more great than Letter;
While tow'ring o'er your Alphabet, like Saul,[59]
Stands our Digamma, and o'er-tops them all.[60]
'Tis true, on Words is still our whole debate,   215
Disputes of *Me* or *Te*, of *aut* or *at*,
To sound or sink in *cano*, O or A,
Or give up Cicero to C or K.
Let Freind affect to speak as Terence spoke,
And Alsop never but like Horace joke:[61]   220
For me, what Virgil, Pliny may deny,
Manilius or Solinus shall supply:[62]
For Attic Phrase in Plato let them seek,
I poach in Suidas for unlicensed Greek.
In ancient Sense if any needs will deal,   225
Be sure I give them Fragments, not a Meal;
What Gellius or Stobæus hashed before,[63]
Or chewed by blind old Scholiasts o'er and o'er.
The critic Eye, that microscope of Wit,
Sees hairs and pores, examines bit by bit: 230
How parts relate to parts, or they to whole,
The body's harmony, the beaming soul,
Are things which Kuster, Burman, Wasse shall see,[64]
When Man's whole frame is obvious to a *Flea*.
    'Ah, think not, Mistress! more true Dullness lies   235
In Folly's Cap, than Wisdom's grave disguise.
Like buoys, that never sink into the flood,
On Learning's surface we but lie and nod.
Thine is the genuine head of many a house,
And much Divinity without a Νοῦς.[65]   240

---

[59] *Saul*   he is head and shoulders taller than his brethren (1 Samuel 9.2).
[60] *Digamma*   a Greek letter (*F*), made of two gammas and so, tall; discovered by Bentley in a brilliant insight that revolutionized knowledge of Homeric prosody and pronunciation.
[61] *Freind, – Alsop*   Dr. Robert Freind [1667–1751], master of Westminster-school, and canon of Christchurch – Dr. Anthony Alsop [d. 1726], a happy imitator of the Horatian style [Pope's note].
[62] *Manilius or Solinus*   Some Critics having had it in their choice to comment either on Virgil or Manilius, Pliny or Solinus, have chosen the worse author, the more freely to display their critical capacity [Pope's note; Bentley edited Manilius, as A. E. Housman later did; Solinus based his work on Pliny's encyclopedia].

[63] *Suidas, Gellius, Stobæus*   The first a Dictionary-writer, a collector of impertinent fact and barbarous words; the second a minute Critic; the third an author, who gave his Common-place book to the public, where we happen to find much Mince-meat of old books [Pope's note; all three collected classical fragments in compilations that are, in some cases, the only records of what they preserved].
[64] *Kuster, Burman, Wasse*   important classical scholars associated with Bentley.
[65] Νοῦς   the Platonic term for *Mind*, or the *first Cause*, and that system of Divinity is here hinted at which terminates in blind nature without a Νοῦς [Pope's note].

Nor could a BARROW work on every block,
Nor has one ATTERBURY spoil'd the flock.[66]
See! still thy own, the heavy Canon roll,
And Metaphysic smokes involve the Pole.[67]
For thee we dim the eyes, and stuff the head   245
With all such reading as was never read:
For thee explain a thing till all men doubt it,
And write about it, Goddess, and about it:
So spins the silk-worm small its slender store,
And labours till it clouds itself all o'er.   250
      'What though we let some better sort of fool
Thrid every science, run through every school?
Never by tumbler through the hoops was shown
Such skill in passing all, and touching none.
He may indeed (if sober all this time)   255
Plague with Dispute, or persecute with Rhyme.
We only furnish what he cannot use,
Or wed to what he must divorce, a Muse:
Full in the midst of Euclid dip at once,
And petrify a Genius to a Dunce: 260
Or set on Metaphysic ground to prance,
Show all his paces, not a step advance.
With the same Cement, ever sure to bind,
We bring to one dead level every mind.
Then take him to develop, if you can,   265
And hew the Block off, and get out the Man.[68]
But wherefore waste I words? I see advance
Whore, Pupil, and laced Governor from France.[69]
Walker! our hat' — nor more he deigned to say,
But, stern as Ajax' spectre, strode away.[70]   270
      In flowed at once a gay embroidered race,
And titt'ring pushed the Pedants off the place:
Some would have spoken, but the voice was drowned
By the French horn, or by the op'ning hound.
The first came forward, with as easy mien,   275

[66] *BARROW, ATTERBURY* Isaac Barrow [1630–77] Master of Trinity [College, Cambridge], Francis Atterbury Dean of Christ-church, both great Geniuses and eloquent Preachers [Pope's note; Atterbury was Pope's friend and collaborator].

[67] *Pole* sky, as in Milton, for example *Paradise Lost* 4.724.

[68] *hew the Block off* A notion of Aristotle, that there was originally in every block of marble, a Statue, which would appear on the removal of the superfluous parts. [Pope's note].

[69] *Whore, Pupil, and laced Governor* Some Critics have objected to the order here, being of opinion that the Governor [the pupil's tutor and chaperone] should have the precedence before the Whore, if not before the Pupil. But were he so placed, he might be supposed to lead the Governor to her. But our impartial Poet as he is drawing their picture, represents them in the order in which they are generally seen; namely the Pupil between the Whore and the Governor; but placeth the Whore first, as she usually governs both the other. [Pope's note].

[70] *Ajax' spectre* Odysseus sees the sullen shade of Ajax Telamon on his visit to Hades in Book 11 of the *Odyssey*; the story behind this scene is that Bentley was supposed to have walked out peremptorily on a dinner at Trinity College when he felt importuned by a learned question.

As if he saw St. James's and the Queen.[71]
When thus th'attendant Orator begun.[72]
'Receive, great Empress! thy accomplished Son:
Thine from the birth, and sacred from the rod,
A dauntless infant! never scared with God.   280
The Sire saw, one by one, his Virtues wake:
The Mother begged the blessing of a Rake.[73]
Thou gav'st that Ripeness, which so soon began,
And ceased so soon, he ne'er was Boy, nor Man.
Through School and College, thy kind cloud o'ercast,   285
Safe and unseen the young Æneas passed:[74]
Thence bursting glorious, all at once let down,
Stunned with his giddy Larum half the town.[75]
Intrepid then, o'er seas and lands he flew:
Europe he saw, and Europe saw him too.   290
There all thy gifts and graces we display,
Thou, only thou, directing all our way!
To where the Seine, obsequious as she runs,
Pours at great Bourbon's feet her silken sons;
Or Tiber, now no longer Roman, rolls,   295
Vain of Italian Arts, Italian Souls:
To happy Convents, bosomed deep in vines,
Where slumber Abbots, purple as their wines:
To Isles of fragrance, lilly-silvered vales,
Diffusing languor in the panting gales:[76]   300
To lands of singing, or of dancing slaves,
Love-whisp'ring woods, and lute-resounding waves.
But chief her shrine where naked Venus keeps,
And Cupids ride the Lion of the Deeps;[77]
Where, eased of Fleets, the Adriatic main   305
Wafts the smooth Eunuch and enamoured swain.
Led by my hand, he sauntered Europe round,
And gathered every Vice on Christian ground;
Saw every Court, heard every King declare
His royal Sense, of Operas or the Fair;   310
The Stews and Palace equally explored,
Intrigued with glory, and with spirit whored;
Tried all *hors-d'oeuvres*, all *liqueurs* defined,
Judicious drank, and greatly-daring dined;

---

[71] *St. James's* the palace.
[72] *th'attendant Orator* The Governor abovesaid. The Poet gives him no particular name, being unwilling, I presume, to offend or do injustice to any, by celebrating one only with whom this character agrees, in preference to so many who equally deserve it. Scribl. [Pope's note].
[73] *Mother begged the blessing of a Rake* she hoped he would become one.

[74] *young Æneas passed* in imitation of *Aeneid* 1.411–14.
[75] *Larum* alarm, commotion.
[76] *gales* gentle winds.
[77] *Lion of the Deeps* The winged Lion, the arms of Venice. This Republic heretofore the most considerable in Europe, for her Naval Force and the extent of her Commerce; now illustrious for her Carnivals. [Pope's note].

Dropped the dull lumber of the Latin store,   315
Spoil'd his own language, and acquired no more;
All Classic learning lost on Classic ground;
And last turned *Air*, the Echo of a Sound![78]
See now, half-cured, and perfectly well-bred,
With nothing but a Solo in his head;   320
As much Estate, and Principle, and Wit,
As Jansen, Fleetwood, Cibber shall think fit;[79]
Stol'n from a Duel, followed by a Nun,
And, if a Borough choose him, not undone;[80]
See, to my country happy I restore   325
This glorious Youth, and add one Venus more.
Her too receive (for her my soul adores)
So may the sons of sons of sons of whores,
Prop thine, O Empress! like each neighbour Throne,
And make a long Posterity thy own'.   330
     Pleased, she accepts the Hero, and the Dame,
Wraps in her Veil, and frees from sense of Shame.
     Then looked, and saw a lazy, lolling sort,
Unseen at Church, at Senate, or at Court,
Of ever-listless Loit'rers, that attend   335
No cause, no Trust, no Duty, and no Friend.
Thee too, my Paridel! she marked thee there,[81]
Stretched on the rack of a too easy chair,
And heard thy everlasting yawn confess
The Pains and Penalties of Idleness.   340
She pitied! but her Pity only shed
Benigner influence on thy nodding head.
     But Annius, crafty Seer, with ebon wand,[82]
And well dissembled emerald on his hand,
False as his Gems, and cankered as his Coins,   345
Came, crammed with capon, from where Pollio dines.[83]
Soft, as the wily Fox is seen to creep,
Where bask on sunny banks the simple sheep,
Walk round and round, now prying here, now there;
So he; but pious, whispered first his prayer.   350

---

[78] *Air* Yet less a Body than Echo itself; for Echo reflects *Sense* or *Words* at least, this Gentleman only *Airs* and *Tunes* [Pope's note].

[79] *Jansen, Fleetwood, Cibber* Three very eminent persons, all Managers of Plays . . . [the first a gambler, the last two, Charles and Colly, theater managers].

[80] *Borough* a voting district entitled to elect a member of Parliament, who would then enjoy the "privilege" of freedom from prosecution for debts.

[81] *Paridel* The name is taken from Spenser, who gives it to a *wandering Courtly Squire* [Pope's note; said to be Henry Hyde, Viscount Cornbury (1710–53), MP for Oxford].

[82] *Annius* The name taken from Annius the Monk of Viterbo, famous for many Impositions and Forgeries of ancient manuscripts and inscriptions, which he was prompted to by mere Vanity, but our Annius had a more substantial motive. [Pope's note; he is supposed to represent Sir Andrew Fountaine (1676–1753), an antiquarian who did research in Italy, perhaps in Viterbo, in central Italy].

[83] *Pollio* a Roman statesman turned poet, critic, and patron of the first century BCE, said to represent Henry Herbert, Earl of Pembroke.

'Grant, gracious Goddess! grant me still to cheat,
O may thy cloud still cover the deceit!
Thy choicer mists on this assembly shed,
But pour them thickest on the noble head.
So shall each youth, assisted by our eyes,   355
See other Cæsars, other Homers rise;
Through twilight ages hunt th' Athenian fowl,[84]
Which Chalcis Gods, and mortals call an Owl,[85]
Now see an Attys, now a Cecrops clear,[86]
Nay, Mahomet! the Pigeon at thine ear;[87]   360
Be rich in ancient brass, though not in gold,
And keep his Lares, though his house be sold;[88]
To headless Phoebe his fair bride postpone,
Honour a Syrian Prince above his own;
Lord of an Otho, if I vouch it true;[89]   365
Blest in one Niger, till he knows of two.'

   Mummius o'erheard him; Mummius, Fool-renowned,[90]
Who like his Cheops stinks above the ground,
Fierce as a startled Adder, swelled, and said,
Rattling an ancient Sistrum at his head.[91]   370

   'Speak'st thou of Syrian Princes? Traitor base!
Mine, Goddess! mine is all the hornèd race.[92]
True, he had wit, to make their value rise;
From foolish Greeks to steal them, was as wise;
More glorious yet, from barb'rous hands to keep,   375
When Sallee Rovers chased him on the deep.[93]
Then taught by Hermes, and divinely bold,
Down his own throat he risked the Grecian gold;
Received each Demi-God, with pious care,
Deep in his Entrails – I revered them there,   380
I bought them, shrouded in that living shrine,
And, at their second birth, they issue mine.'

   'Witness great Ammon! by whose horns I swore',
Replied soft Annius, 'this our paunch before
Still bears them, faithful; and that thus I eat,   385

---

[84] *Athenian fowl*   the owl, which appears on Athenian coins.
[85] *Chalcis*   transliteration of a Greek word meaning some kind of bird, unhelpfully written by Hobbes in his translation of Homer, according to Pope's note.
[86] *Attys . . . Cecrops*   The first Kings of Athens, of whom it is hard to suppose any Coins extant; but not so improbable as what follows, that there should be any of Mahomet, who forbade all Images. Nevertheless one of these Anniuses made a counterfeit one, now in the collection of a learned Nobleman [Pope's note].
[87] *Mahomet*   supposed to have had a pigeon whom he claimed was the Angel Gabriel whispering at his ear.
[88] *Lares*   household gods.

[89] *Otho*   a coin bearing the head of this short-lived Roman emperor; *Niger*   was a second century CE emperor; the coin is also meant here.
[90] *Mummius*   This name is not merely an allusion to the Mummies he was so fond of, but probably referred to the Roman General of that name, who burned Corinth [Pope's note; Mummius has been identified as the physician Richard Mead (1673–1754), a friend of Bentley's].
[91] *Sistrum*   a metal rattle used in ancient Egyptian religious ceremonies.
[92] *the hornèd race*   after Ammon, a god depicted as Zeus with ram's horns, originating in Egypt but worshipped in Libya, Syria, and elsewhere.
[93] *Sallee Rovers*   pirates.

Is to refund the Medals with the meat.
To prove me, Goddess! clear of all design,
Bid me with Pollio sup, as well as dine:
There all the Learn'd shall at the labour stand,
And Douglas lend his soft, obstetric hand'.[94]   390
    The Goddess smiling seemed to give consent;
So back to Pollio, hand in hand, they went.
    Then thick as Locusts black'ning all the ground,
A tribe, with weeds and shells fantastic crowned,
Each with some wond'rous gift approached the Pow'r,   395
A Nest, a Toad, a Fungus, or a Flow'r.
But far the foremost, two, with earnest zeal,
And aspect ardent to the Throne appeal.
    The first thus opened: 'Hear thy suppliant's call,
Great Queen, and common Mother of us all!   400
Fair from its humble bed I reared this Flow'r,
Suckled, and cheered, with air, and sun, and show'r,
Soft on the paper ruff its leaves I spread,
Bright with the gilded button tipp't its head,
Then throned in glass, and named it CAROLINE:[95]   405
Each Maid cried, "charming!" and each Youth, "divine!"
And lo the wretch! whose vile, whose insect lust
Laid this gay daughter of the Spring in dust.
Oh punish him, or to th' Elysian shades
Dismiss my soul, where no Carnation fades'.   410
    He ceased, and wept. With innocence of mien,
Th' Accused stood forth, and thus addressed the Queen.
    'Of all th' enamelled race, whose silv'ry wing
Waves to the tepid Zephyrs of the spring,
Or swims along the fluid atmosphere,   415
Once brightest shined this child of Heat and Air.
I saw, and started from its vernal bow'r
The rising game, and chased from flow'r to flow'r.
It fled, I followed; now in hope, now pain;
It stopped, I stopped; it moved, I moved again.   420
At last it fixed, 'twas on what plant it pleased,
And where it fixed, the beauteous bird I seized:
Rose or Carnation was below my care;
I meddle, Goddess! only in my sphere.
I tell the naked fact without disguise,   425
And, to excuse it, need but show the prize;
Whose spoils this paper offers to your eye,
Fair ev'n in death! this peerlees *Butterfly*'.
    'My sons!' she answered, 'both have done your parts:
Live happy both, and long promote our arts.   430

---

[94] *Douglas* James Douglas (1675–1742), a famous obstetrician and collector.

[95] *CAROLINE* queen of George II (1678–1737), a supporter of Walpole and patron of the arts.

But hear a Mother, when she recommends
To your fraternal care, our sleeping friends.
Of Souls the greater part, of Heav'n's more frugal make,[96]
Serve but to keep fools pert, and knaves awake:
A drowsy Watchman, that just gives a knock,   435
And breaks our rest, to tell us what's a clock.
Yet by some object every brain is stirred;
The dull may waken to a Humming-bird;
The most recluse, discreetly opened, find
Congenial matter in the Cockle-kind;   440
The mind, in Metaphysics at a loss,
May wander in a wilderness of Moss;
The head that turns at super-lunar things,
Poised with a tail, may steer on Wilkins' wings.[97]

      'O! would the Sons of Men once think their Eyes   445
And Reason giv'n them but to study *Flies!*
See Nature in some partial narrow shape,
And let the Author of the Whole escape:
Learn but to trifle; or, who most observe,
To wonder at their Maker, not to serve'.   450
      'Be that my task', replies a gloomy Clerk,[98]
Sworn foe to Mystery, yet divinely dark;
Whose pious hope aspires to see the day
When Moral Evidence shall quite decay,[99]
And damns implicit faith, and holy lies,   455
Prompt to impose, and fond to dogmatize:
'Let others creep by timid steps, and slow,
On plain Experience lay foundations low,
By common sense to common knowledge bred,
And last, to Nature's Cause through Nature led.[100]   460
All-seeing in thy mists, we want no guide,
Mother of Arrogance, and Source of Pride!
We nobly take the high Priori Road,[101]
And reason downward, till we doubt of God:
Make Nature still encroach upon his plan;   465
And shove him off as far as e'er we can:
Thrust some Mechanic Cause into his place;
Or bind in Matter, or diffuse in Space.

---

[96]   *Souls*   minds.
[97]   *Wilkins' wings*   One of the first Projectors of the Royal Society, who, among many enlarged and useful notions, entertained the extravagant hope of a possibility to fly to the Moon; which has put some volatile Geniuses upon making wings for that purpose. [Pope's note; see John Wilkins, *The Discovery of a World in the Moon* (1638)].
[98]   *Clerk*   perhaps a pun on the name of Samuel Clarke (1675–1729), whom Pope sees as an exponent of a stripped-down, rational theology.

[99]   *Moral*   "Popular; such as is known or admitted in the general business of life" (Johnson).
[100]   *Cause*   first cause, or maker (an Aristotelian term).
[101]   *high Priori*   a pun on "a priori"; in Pope's view, theologians ought to reason up from natural fact to God, their cause; his gloomy theologians reason down from a priori conception of God that, in the end, is not supported by the facts of the natural world.

Or, at one bound o'er-leaping all his laws,
Make God Man's Image, Man the final Cause,[102]   470
Find Virtue local, all Relation scorn,
See all in *Self*, and but for self be born:
Of nought so certain as our *Reason* still,
Of nought so doubtful as of *Soul* and *Will*.
Oh hide the God still more! and make us see   475
Such as Lucretius drew, a God like Thee:[103]
Wrapped up in Self, a God without a Thought,
Regardless of our merit or default.
Or that bright Image to our fancy draw,[104]
Which Theocles in raptured vision saw,[105]   480
While through Poetic scenes the Genius roves,
Or wanders wild in Academic Groves;
That NATURE our Society adores,
Where Tindal dictates, and Silenus snores'.[106]

Roused at his name, up rose the bowzy Sire,[107]   485
And shook from out his Pipe the seeds of fire;
Then snapped his box, and stroked his belly down:
Rosy and reverend, though without a Gown.
Bland and familiar to the throne he came,
Led up the Youth, and called the Goddess *Dame*.   490
Then thus: 'From Priest-craft happily set free,
Lo! every finished Son returns to thee:
First slave to Words, then vassal to a Name,[108]
Then dupe to Party; child and man the same;
Bounded by Nature, narrowed still by Art,   495
A trifling head, and a contracted heart.
Thus bred, thus taught, how many have I seen,
Smiling on all, and smiled on by a Queen.
Marked out for Honours, honoured for their Birth,
To thee the most rebellious things on earth: 500
Now to thy gentle shadow all are shrunk,
All melted down, in Pension, or in Punk![109]

---

[102] *final Cause* an Aristotelian term meaning the purpose for which anything is done.
[103] *Lucretius* first-century BCE Roman philosopher who expounded a materialist cosmology in his didactic poem *De Rerum Natura*.
[104] *bright Image* the Title given by the later Platonists to that Idea of Nature, which they had formed in their fancy, so bright, that they called it αὐτοπου ἄγαλμα or the *Self-seen Image* [Pope's note].
[105] *Theocles* the name of a philosopher in the neo-Platonistic writings of Anthony Ashley Cooper, third Earl of Shaftesbury.
[106] *Tindal* Matthew (d. 1733), a famous deist, a theologian who reduced religion to the barest, most rational essentials; *Silenus* half-man, half-beast, a drinker but a wise creature in mythology (said to represent Thomas

Gordon, a classicist, a supporter of Walpole, and a political reporter for the *London Magazine*.
[107] *bowzy* drunken.
[108] *First slave to Words, &c.* A recapitulation of the whole Course of Modern Education described in this book, which confines Youth to the study of *Words* only in Schools, subjects them to the authority of *Systems* in the Universities, and deludes them with the names of *Party-distinctions*. All equally concurring to narrow the Understanding, and establish Slavery and Error in Literature, Philosophy, and Politics. The whole finished in modern Free-thinking; the completion of whatever is vain, wrong, and destructive to the happiness of mankind, as it establishes Self-love for the sole Principle of Action. [Pope's note].
[109] *Punk* a whore.

So * so ** sneaked into the grave,
A Monarch's half, and half a Harlot's slave.
Poor W ** nipt in Folly's broadest bloom,[110]   505
Who praises now? his Chaplain on his Tomb.
Then take them all, oh take them to thy breast!
Thy *Magus*, Goddess! shall perform the rest.'
  With that, a WIZARD OLD his *Cup* extends;[111]
Which whoso tastes, forgets his former friends,   510
Sire, Ancestors, Himself. One casts his eyes
Up to a *Star*, and like Endymion dies:[112]
A *Feather* shooting from another's head,
Extracts his brain, and Principle is fled,
Lost is his God, his Country, every thing;   515
And nothing left but Homage to a King!
The vulgar herd turn off to roll with Hogs,
To run with Horses, or to hunt with Dogs;
But, sad example! never to escape
Their Infamy, still keep the human shape.   520
  But she, good Goddess, sent to every child
Firm Impudence, or Stupefaction mild;
And straight succeeded, leaving shame no room,
Cibberian forehead, or Cimmerian gloom.[113]
  Kind Self-conceit to some her glass applies,   525
Which no one looks in with another's eyes:
But as the Flatt'rer or Dependent paint,
Beholds himself a Patriot, Chief, or Saint.
  On others Interest her gay livery flings,
Interest, that waves on Party-coloured wings: 530
Turned to the Sun, she casts a thousand dyes,
And, as she turns, the colours fall or rise.
  Others the Siren Sisters warble round,
And empty heads console with empty sound.
No more, alas! the voice of Fame they hear,   535
The balm of Dullness trickling in their ear.
Great Shades of **, **, **, **, *,[114]
Why all your Toils? your Sons have learned to sing.
How quick Ambition hastes to ridicule!
The Sire is made a Peer, the Son a Fool.   540
  On some, a Priest succinct in amice white[115]

---

[110] *W ** * the identification remains uncertain, as does those of the vaguer ones above (though Pope added some letters in later editions).
[111] *WIZARD* suggesting Circe who turns men into animals (*Odyssey* 10); said to be Robert Walpole.
[112] *Endymion* the beautiful youth beloved of the moon (a star) and doomed to eternal sleep; but the star, like the feather, are insignia of royal orders conferred by the King; Walpole was a member of the Most Noble Order of the Garter.
[113] *Cimmerian* proper to Hades, from the far-western land where Odysseus gains entrance into the underworld.
[114] ** Pope added initials in his revision, but the identifications remain uncertain, and part of the joke is that their names have disappeared.
[115] *succinct* "having the clothes drawn up to disengage the legs" (Johnson); *amice* "The first or undermost part of a priest's habit" (Johnson).

Attends; all flesh is nothing in his sight!
Beeves, at his touch, at once to jelly turn,[116]
And the huge Boar is shrunk into an Urn:
The board with specious miracles he loads,   545
Turns Hares to Larks, and Pigeons into Toads.
Another (for in all what one can shine?)
Explains the *Seve* and *Verdeur* of the Vine.[117]
What cannot copious Sacrifice atone?
Thy Truffles, Perigord! thy Hams, Bayonne![118]   550
With French Libation, and Italian Strain,
Wash Bladen white, and expiate Hay's stain.
Knight lifts the head, for what are crowds undone[119]
To three essential Partridges in one?[120]
Gone every blush, and silent all reproach,   555
Contending Princes mount them in their Coach.
   Next bidding all draw near on bended knees,
The Queen confers her *Titles* and *Degrees*.
Her children first of more distinguished sort,
Who study Shakespeare at the Inns of Court,[121]   560
Impale a Glow-worm, or Vertù profess,[122]
Shine in the dignity of F. R. S.[123]
Some, deep Free-Masons, join the silent race
Worthy to fill Pythagoras's place:
Some Botanists, or Florists at the least,   565
Or issue Members of an Annual feast.
Nor passed the meanest unregarded, one
Rose a Gregorian, one a Gormogon.[124]
The last, not least in honour or applause,
Isis and Cam made Doctors of her Laws.   570
   Then blessing all, 'Go Children of my care!
To Practice now from Theory repair.
All my commands are easy, short, and full:
My Sons! be proud, be selfish, and be dull.
Guard my Prerogative, assert my Throne: 575
This Nod confirms each Privilege your own.
The Cap and Switch be sacred to his Grace;
With Staff and Pumps the Marquis lead the Race;[125]

---

[116] *Beeves* oxen.

[117] *Seve and Verdeur* special qualities of wine.

[118] *Perigord, Bayonne* places in France.

[119] *Bladen, Hay, White* Names of Gamesters. Bladen is a black man. Robert Knight Cashier of the South-sea Company, who fled from England in 1720 [when the South-sea "bubble" of over-investment collapsed and many stock-holders were "undone"] – These lived with the utmost magnificence at Paris, and kept open Tables, frequented by persons of the first Quality of England, and even by Princes of the Blood of France.

The Note of "Bladen is a black man" is very absurd. The Manuscript here is partly obliterated, and doubtless could only have been, "Wash Blackmoors white", alluding to a known Proverb. Scrib. [Pope's note].

[120] *three essential Partridges in one* i.e. two dissolved into Quintessence to make a sauce for the third [Pope's note].

[121] *Inns of Court* law schools.

[122] *Vertù* "A love of, or taste for, works of art, or curios" (*OED*).

[123] *F. R. S.* Fellow of the Royal Society.

[124] *Gregorian, Gormogon* secret societies like the *Free-Masons*.

[125] *Cap and Switch* accoutrements of a jockey; *Staff and Pumps* also suggests the gear of professional horse-drivers, who were usually servants.

From Stage to Stage the licensed Earl may run,
Paired with his Fellow-Charioteer the Sun;   580
The learnèd Baron Butterflies design,
Or draw to silk Arachne's subtle line;[126]
The Judge to dance his brother Sergeant call;
The Senator at Cricket urge the Ball;
The Bishop stow (Pontific Luxury!)   585
An hundred Souls of Turkeys in a pie;
The sturdy Squire to Gallic masters stoop,
And drown his Lands and Manors in a Soup.
Others import yet nobler arts from France,
Teach Kings to fiddle, and make Senates dance.   590
Perhaps more high some daring son may soar,
Proud to my list to add one Monarch more;
And nobly conscious, Princes are but things
Born for First Ministers, as Slaves for Kings,[127]
Tyrant supreme! shall three Estates command,   595
And MAKE ONE MIGHTY DUNCIAD OF THE LAND!'
    More she had spoke, but yawned – All Nature nods:
What Mortal can resist the Yawn of the Gods?
Churches and Chapels instantly it reached;
(St. James's first, for leaden Gilbert preached)[128]   600
Then catched the Schools; the Hall scarce kept awake;[129]
The Convocation gaped, but could not speak:[130]
Lost was the Nation's Sense, nor could be found,
While the long solemn Unison went round:
Wide, and more wide, it spread o'er all the realm;   605
Ev'n Palinurus nodded at the Helm:[131]
The Vapour mild o'er each Committee crept;
Unfinished Treaties in each Office slept;
And Chiefless Armies dozed out the Campaign;
And Navies yawned for Orders on the Main.   610
    O Muse! relate (for you can tell alone,
Wits have short Memories, and Dunces none)
Relate, who first, who last resigned to rest;
Whose Heads she partly, whose completely blessed;
What Charms could Faction, what Ambition lull,   615
The Venal quiet, and entrance the Dull;
'Till drowned was Sense, and Shame, and Right, and Wrong –
O sing, and hush the Nations with thy Song!
While the Great Mother bids Britannia Sleep,

---

[126] *Arachne* she wove a tapestry depicting the amours of the gods and was turned into a spider by jealous Athena (Ovid, *Metamorphoses* 6.1–145).
[127] *First Ministers* roughly equivalent to prime ministers; Robert Walpole at the time.
[128] *Gilbert* John (1693–1761), preached a moving sermon on the death of Queen Caroline.
[129] *Hall* Parliament.
[130] *Convocation* national assembly of clerics.
[131] *Palinurus* helmsman of Aeneas, here Walpole.

And pours her Spirit o'er the Land and Deep.[132]   620

* * * * * * *

    In vain, in vain, – the all-composing Hour
Resistless falls: The Muse obeys the Pow'r.
She comes! she comes! the sable Throne behold
Of *Night* Primæval, and of *Chaos* old!   625
Before her, *Fancy's* gilded clouds decay,
And all its varying Rainbows die away.
Wit shoots in vain its momentary fires,
The meteor drops, and in a flash expires.
As one by one, at dread Medea's strain,[133]   630
The sick'ning stars fade off th'ethereal plain;
As Argus' eyes by Hermes' wand oppressed,[134]
Closed one by one to everlasting rest;
Thus at her felt approach, and secret might,
Art after *Art* goes out, and all is Night.   635
See skulking *Truth* to her old Cavern fled,[135]
Mountains of Casuistry heaped o'er her head!
Philosophy, that leaned on Heav'n before,
Shrinks to her second cause, and is no more.[136]
Physic of *Metaphysic* begs defence,   640
And *Metaphysic* calls for aid on *Sense*!
See *Mystery* to *Mathematics* fly!
In vain! they gaze, turn giddy, rave, and die.
Religion blushing veils her sacred fires,
And unawares *Morality* expires.   645
Nor *public* Flame, nor *private,* dares to shine;
Nor *human* Spark is left, nor Glimpse *divine*!
Lo! thy dread Empire, CHAOS! is restored;
Light dies before thy uncreating word:
Thy hand, great Anarch! lets the curtain fall;   650
And Universal Darkness buries All.

FINIS

from *Letters*

TO LADY MARY WORTLEY MONTAGU (1 SEPTEMBER 1718)

Madam, – I have been (what I never was till now) in debt to you for a letter some weeks. I
was informed you were at Sea, & that 'twas to no purpose to write, till some news had been

[132] *While . . . Deep* the poem ended here in 1742 with
a mock footnote lamenting the loss of the rest, but in
1743 Pope omitted the last couplet and went on as
follows.
[133] *Medea* the scorned wife of Jason, whose magical
incantations caused the stars to fall.
[134] *Argus* the herdsman given a hundred eyes by Hera
in order to watch over beautiful Io; *Hermes* god of po-

ets, thieves, and sleep, has the epithet Argus-killer in
Homer.
[135] *Cavern* Alluding to the saying of Democritus,
That Truth lay at the bottom of a deep well [Pope's
note].
[136] *second cause* in Aristotelian cosmology, the immediate agent of creation or change.

heard of your arriving somewhere or other. Besides, I have had a second dangerous Illness, from which I was more diligent to be recovered than from the first, having now some hopes of seeing you again. If you make any Tour in Italy, I shall not easily forgive you for not acquainting me soon enough to have met you there: I am very certain I can never be Polite, unless I travel with you. And it is never to be repaired, the loss that Homer has sustained, for my want of translating him in Asia.[1] You will come hither full of criticisms against a man, who wanted nothing to be in the right but to have kept your company. You have no way of making me amends, but by continuing an Asiatic when you return, to me, whatever English Airs you may put on to other people. I prodigiously long for your Sonnets, your remarks, your oriental learning; but I long for nothing so much as your Oriental Self. You must of necessity be *advanced* so far *Back* into true nature & simplicity of manners, by these 3 years residence in the East, that I shall look upon you as so many years Younger than you was, so much nearer Innocence (that is, Truth) & Infancy (that is Openness.) I expect to see your Soul as much thinner dressed as your Body; and that you have left off, as wieldly & cumbersome, a great many damned European Habits. Without offence to your modesty be it spoken, I have a burning desire to see your Soul stark naked, for I am confident 'tis the prettiest kind of white Soul, in the universe – But I forget whom I am talking to: you may possibly by this time Believe according to the Prophet, that you have none.[2] If so, show me That which comes next to a Soul; you may easily put it upon a poor ignorant Christian for a Soul, & please him as well with it: I mean your Heart: Mahomet I think allows you Hearts: which (together with fine eyes & other agreeable equivalents) are worth all the Souls on this side of the world. But if I must be content with seeing your body only, God send it to come quickly: I honour it more than the Diamond-Casket that held Homer's *Iliads*. For in the very twinkle of one eye of it, there is more Wit; and in the very dimple of one cheek of it, there is more Meaning, than in all the Souls that ever were casually put into Women since Men had the making them.

I have a mind to fill the rest of this paper with an accident that happened just under my eyes, and has made a great Impression upon me. I have passed part of this Summer at an old romantic Seat of my Lord Harcourt's which he lent me; It overlooks a Common-field, where under the Shade of a Hay cock sate two Lovers, as constant as ever were found in Romance, beneath a spreading Beech. The name of one (let it sound as it will) was John Hewet, of the other Sarah Drew. John was a wellset man about five and twenty, Sarah a brown woman of about eighteen. John had for several months borne the labour of the day in the same field with Sarah; When she milked, it was his morning & evening charge to bring the Cows to her pail: Their Love was the Talk, but not the Scandal, of the whole neighbourhood, for all they aimed at was the blameless possession of each other in marriage. It was but this very morning that he had obtained her Parents' consent, and it was but till next week that they were to wait to be happy. Perhaps, this very day in the intervals of their work, they were talking of their wedding clothes, and John was matching several kinds of poppies and field-flowers to her Complexion, to make her a Present of Knots for the day. While they were thus employed (it was on the last of July) a terrible Storm of Thunder and Lightning arose, that drove the Labourers to what Shelter the Trees or hedges afforded. Sarah frighted, and out of breath, sunk down on a Haycock, & John (who never separated from her) sat by her side, having raked two or three heaps together to secure her. Immediately there was heard so loud a Crack as if

To Lady Mary Wortley Montagu
[1] *Homer . . . Asia* Lady Mary praised Pope's translation of the *Iliad* (vol. 2 came out in 1716) in a letter to him dated 1 April 1717 and told him that it helped

explain many customs that she was witnessing on her Turkish travels.
[2] *Prophet* Muhammad.

Heaven had burst assunder: the Labourers, all solicitous for each other's safety, called to one another: those that were nearest our Lovers, hearing no answer, stepped to the place where they lay; they first saw a little Smoke, & after, this faithful Pair. John with one arm about his Sarah's neck, and the other held over her face as if to screen her from the Lightning. They were struck dead, & already grown stiff and cold in this tender posture. There was no mark or discolouring on their bodies, only that Sarah's eyebrow was a little singed, and a small Spot appeared between her breasts. They were buried the next day in one grave, in the Parish of Stanton-Harcourt in Oxfordshire, where my Lord Harcourt, at my request, has erected a monument over them. Of the following Epitaphs which I made, the Critics have chosen the godly one: I like neither, but wish you had been in England to have done this office better; I think 'twas what you could not have refused me on so moving an occasion.

> When Eastern Lovers feed the fun'ral fire,
> On the same Pile their faithful Fair expire;
> Here pitying Heav'n that virtue mutual found,
> And blasted both, that it might neither wound.
> Hearts so sincere, th' Almighty saw well-pleased,
> Sent his own Lightning, & the Victims seized.

1

> Think not, by rig'rous Judgement seized,
>   A Pair so faithful could expire;
> Victims so pure Heav'n saw well-pleased,
>   And snatched them in celestial fire.

2

> Live well, & fear no sudden fate:
>   When God calls Virtue to the grave,
> Alike 'tis Justice, soon, or late,
>   Mercy alike, to kill, or save.
> Virtue unmoved, can hear the Call,
> And face the Flash that melts the Ball.

Upon the whole, I can't think these people unhappy: The greatest happiness, next to living as they would have done, was to die as they did. The greatest honour people of this low degree could have was to be remembered on a little monument; unless you will give them another, that of being honoured with a Tear from the finest eyes in the world. I know you have Tenderness; you must have it: It is the very Emanation of Good Sense & virtue: The finest minds like the finest metals, dissolve the easiest.

But when you are reflecting upon Objects of pity, pray do not forget one, who had no sooner found out an Object of the highest Esteem, than he was separated from it: And who is so very unhappy as not to be susceptible of Consolation from others, by being so miserably in the right as to think other women what they really are. Such an one can't but be desperately fond of any creature that is quite different from these. If the Circassian[3] be utterly void of such Honour as these have, and such virtue as these boast of, I am content. I have detested the

<hr>

[3] *Circassian* in an earlier letter Pope jested about Lady Mary procuring him a female slave from that place near southern Russia; Lady Mary had suggested in another letter that such slaves were notoriously dishonorable.

Sound of *honest Woman*, & *loving Spouse* ever since I heard the pretty name of Odaliche. Dear Madam I am for ever Yours, and your Slave's Slave, & Servant.

> My most humble Services to Mr Wortley.
> Pray let me hear from you soon:
> Though I shall very soon write again.
> I am confident half our letters have been lost.

Samuel Richardson (1689–1761)

Richardson's novels are an extension of his first literary achievement, which was letter writing. As a child he wrote love letters for illiterate servants, and by the time he was fifty he had enough acknowledged skill in the art to put together a collection of model letters. At the same time, Richardson began writing his first novel, Pamela *(1740–4), in which the action is related in a series of letters. The book was a tremendous success. He followed it with two greater and much longer epistolary novels,* Clarissa *(1747–8) and* Sir Charles Grandison *(1753–4). Long before he started writing novels, Richardson had established himself as an important printer. With his fame as a writer, he expanded his publishing activities and became a central figure, especially among women writers of the period. His was a literary circle to which they were invited and which they could decently frequent. Moreover, his work promoted a growing literary interest in representations of sensibility and sentimentality that were more attractive to many women writers than the often scatological satire of some of the age's other great writers.*

The selection is from the matrix of Richardson's work as a novelist, Letters Written to and for Particular Friends, on the Most Important Occasions, Directing not only the Requisite Style and Forms to be Observed in Writing Familiar Letters; but How to Think and Act Justly and Prudently, in the Common Concerns of Human Life *(London, 1741).*

from *Letters Written to and for Particular Friends, on the Most Important Occasions, Directing not only the Requisite Style and Forms to be Observed in Writing Familiar Letters; but How to Think and Act Justly and Prudently, in the Common Concerns of Human Life* (1741)

LETTER 58
TO A FRIEND, ON OCCASION OF HIS NOT ANSWERING HIS LETTERS

Dear Sir,

It is so long since I had the Favour of a Line from you, that I am under great Apprehensions in relation to your Health and Welfare. I beg you, Sir, to renew to me the Pleasure you used to give me in your Correspondence; for I have writen three Letters to you before this, to which I have had no Answer, and am not conscious of having any way disobliged you. If I have, I will most willingly ask your Pardon; for nobody can be more than I am,

> Your affectionate and faithful Friend and Servant.

LETTER 59
IN ANSWER TO THE PRECEDING

Dear Sir,

You have not, cannot disoblige me; but I have greatly disobliged myself, in my own faulty Remissness. I cannot account for it as I ought. To say I had Business one time, Company another, was distant from home a third, will be but poor Excuses, for not answering one of your kind Letters in four long Months. I therefore ingenuously take Shame to myself, and promise future Amendment. And that nothing shall ever, while I am able to hold a Pen, make me guilty of the like Neglect to a Friend I love so well, and have so much Reason so to do. Forgive me then, my good, my kind, my generous Friend; and believe me ever,

Your highly obliged humble Servant

LETTER 153

FROM A YOUNG LADY IN TOWN TO HER AUNT IN THE COUNTRY
DESCRIBING *BETHLEHEM* HOSPITAL[1]

Honoured Madam,

YOU tell me, in your last, that my Descriptions and Observations are very superficial, and that both my Uncle and yourself expect from me much better Accounts than I have yet given you: For I must deliver my *Opinion*, it seems, on what I see, as well as tell you what I have been shown. 'Tis well I left my bettermost Subjects to the last; such, I mean, as will best bear Reflection; and I must try what I can do, to regain that Reputation which your Indulgence, rather than my Merit, had formed for me in your kind Thoughts – Yet, I doubt[2] I shan't please you, after all. But 'tis my Duty to try for it, and it will be yours, I had almost said, to forgive Imperfections which I should have concealed, but for your undeserved good Opinions of me, which draw them into Light.

I have this Afternoon been with my Cousins to gratify the odd Curiosity most People have to see *Bethlehem* or *Bedlam* Hospital.

A more affecting Scene my Eyes never beheld; and surely, Madam, any one inclined to be proud of human Nature, and to value themselves above others, cannot go to a Place that will more effectually convince them of their Folly: For there we see men destitute of every Mark of Reason and Wisdom, and levelled to the Brute Creation, if not beneath it; and all the Remains of good Sense or Education serve only to make the unhappy Person appear more deplorable.

I had the Shock of seeing the late polite, and ingenious Mr.——in one of these woeful Chambers. We had heard, you know, of his being somewhat disordered; but I did not expect to find him here: No sooner did I put my Face to the Grate, but he leaped from his Bed, and called me, with frightful Fervency, to come into his Room. The Surprise affected me pretty much; and my Confusion being observed by a Crowd of Strangers, I heard it presently whispered, That I was his Sweetheart, and the Cause of his Misfortune. My Cousin assured

---

LETTER 153
[1] This is the fifth in a series of letters "From a young Lady in Town to her Aunt in the Country"; there were eleven in this series and 123 in the whole volume.

Bethlehem or Bedlam, long a hospital or asylum for the insane, was rebuilt in 1675 in Moorfields, where it remained until the nineteenth century.
[2] *doubt* expect.

me, such Fancies were frequent upon these Occasions: But this Accident drew so many Eyes upon me, as obliged me soon to quit the Place.

I was much at a Loss to account for the Behaviour of the Generality of People, who were looking at these melancholy Objects. Instead of the Concern I think unavoidable at such a Sight, a sort of Mirth appeared on their Countenances; and the distempered Fancies of the miserable Patients most unaccountably provoked Mirth, and loud Laughter, in the unthinking Auditors; and the many hideous Rantings, and wild Motions of others, seemed equally entertaining to them. Nay, so shamefully inhuman were some, among whom (I am sorry to say it) were several of my own Sex, as to endeavour to provoke the Patients into Rage to make them Sport.

I have been told, this dreadful Place is often used for the Resort of lewd Persons to meet and make Assignments: But that I cannot credit; since the Heart must be abandoned indeed, that could be vicious amidst so many Examples of Misery, and of such Misery, as, being wholly involuntary, may overtake the most secure.

I am no great Admirer of public Charities, as they are too often managed; but if we consider the Impossibility of poor Peoples bearing this Misfortune, or providing suitably for the Distempered at their own Beings,[3] no Praise can, surely, be too great for the Founders and Supporters of an Hospital, which none can visit, without receiving the most melancholy *Proof* of its being needful. I am, with Respects where due, honoured Madam, *Your most dutiful Niece.*

Lady Mary Wortley Montagu (1689–1762)

A noblewoman by birth, Lady Mary Pierrepont eloped with Edward Wortley Montagu at the age of twenty-three. An accomplished, largely self-taught scholar, she accompanied her husband on his embassy to Turkey in 1716 and sent back to friends and family some of the most remarkable letters of the eighteenth century. Not only was she the first European woman to travel in many of the places she visited, she was the first European person to witness the private lives of Islamic women, because they were utterly closed to males. The letters, which are the basis of her literary fame, were not published until after Lady Mary's death. On her return from her two years of travel, however, she enjoyed London literary society, patronized some poets, and wrote a play and some poetry, much of which she did not intend to publish. She also brought back to England knowledge about small pox inoculation which helped establish the practice there. Her learning and elegance fascinated Alexander Pope and some other great writers of the day, though she was not equally smitten. Her youthful marriage turned cold in the early stages, and some of her poetry reflects a pessimism about the possibility of successful relations between the sexes. However, she enjoyed her daughter, who was born on her journey and married a Prime Minister, and she suffered through the vicissitudes of a strange and wayward son's life. She became a single emigrée and lived nearly the last twenty years of her life on the Continent, not returning to London once until the death of her estranged husband.

Most of the modern scholarly work on Montagu was done by the late Robert Halsband, who based his editorial work on the manuscripts, many of which are in private hands. I rely on the notes

---

[3] *at their own Beings* out of their own funds.

to his edition of the letters (3 vols, Clarendon Press, 1965), and I use his edition of the poems (edited with Isobel Grundy, Clarendon Press, 1977). As a copytext for the letters I include here, I have used the second edition (1763), but substituted a few readings from Halsband's superior edition. The standard biography is also by Halsband (Clarendon Press, 1956). Montagu's romance writings have very recently been edited by Isobel Grundy (Oxford University Press, 1996).

from LETTERS Of the Right Honourable Lady M——y W———y M————u: Written, during her Travels in EUROPE, ASIA and AFRICA, TO Persons of Distinction, Men of Letters, &c. in different Parts of Europe. WHICH CONTAIN, Among other CURIOUS Relations, Accounts of the POLICY and MANNERS of the TURKS; Drawn from Sources that have been inaccessible to other Travellers

TO THE LADY X——

Vienna, Oct. I, O.S. 1716[1]

You desire me, Madam, to send you some accounts of the customs here, and at the same time a description of Vienna. I am always willing to obey your Commands, but you must upon this occasion, take the Will for the deed. If I should undertake to tell you all the particulars, in which the manners here differ from ours, I must write a whole quire[2] of the dullest stuff that was ever read, or printed without being read. Their dress agrees with the French or English in no one article, but wearing petticoats. They have many fashions peculiar to themselves; they think it indecent for a widow ever to wear green or rose colour, but all the other gayest colours at her own discretion. The assemblies here are the only regular diversion, the operas being always at court, and commonly on some particular occasion. Madam *Rabutin* has the assembly constantly every night at her house; and the other ladies whenever they have a mind to display the magnificence of their apartments, or oblige a friend by complimenting them on the day of their Saint, they declare, that on such a day the assembly shall be at their house in honour of the feast of the Count or Countess——*such a one*. These days are called days of *Gala*, and all the friends or relations of the lady, whose Saint it is, are obliged to appear in their best clothes and all their jewels. The mistress of the house takes no particular notice of any body, nor returns any body's visit; and, whoever pleases, may go without the formality of being presented. The company are entertained with ice in several forms, winter and summer; afterwards they divide into parties of ombre, piquett[3] or conversation, all games of hazard being forbid.

I saw t'other day the *Gala* for Count *Altheim*, the Emperor's favourite, and never in my life saw so many fine clothes ill fancied. They embroider the richest gold stuffs, and provided they can make their clothes expensive enough, that is all the taste they show in them. On other days the general dress is a scarf, and what you please under it.

But now I am speaking of Vienna, I am sure you expect I should say something of the

---

TO THE LADY X——
[1] *O.S.* old style, meaning the Julian calendar, which was eleven days behind the reformed Gregorian method and counted March 25 as the first day of the new year.

[2] *quire* "A bundle of paper consisting of twenty-four sheets" (Johnson).
[3] *ombre, piquett* card games.

convents; they are of all sorts and sizes, but I am best pleased with that of *St. Lawrence*, where the ease and neatness they seem to live with, appears to me much more edifying than those stricter orders, where perpetual penance and nastinesses must breed discontent and wretch- edness. The nuns are all of quality.[4] I think there are to the number of fifty. They have each of them, a little cell perfectly clean, and all the walls covered with pictures, more or less fine, according to their quality. A long white stone gallery runs by all of them, furnished with the pictures of exemplary sisters; the chapel is extremely neat and richly adorned. But I could not forbear laughing at their showing me a wooden head of our Saviour, which they assured me, spoke during the siege of Vienna;[5] and, as a proof of it, bid me remark his mouth, which had been open ever since. Nothing can be more becoming than the dress of these nuns. It is a fine white camlet,[6] the sleeves turned up with fine white callico, and their head dress the same, excepting a small veil of black crepe that falls behind. They have a lower sort of serving nuns, that wait on them as their chamber-maids. They receive all visits of women, and play at ombre in their chambers with permission of the Abbess, which is very easy to be obtained. I never saw an older woman so good-natured; she is near fourscore, and yet shows very little sign of decay, being still lively and cheerful. She caressed me as if I had been her daughter, giving me some pretty things of her own work, and sweetness in abundance. The grate[7] is not one of the most rigid; it is not very hard to put a head through; and I don't doubt but a man, a little more slender than ordinary, might squeeze in his whole person. The young Count of *Salmis* came to the grate, while I was there, and the Abbess gave him her hand to kiss. But I was surprised to find here, the only beautiful young woman I have seen at Vienna, and not only beautiful but genteel, witty and agreeable, of a great family, and who had been the admiration of the town. I could not forbear showing my surprise at seeing a nun like her. She made me a thousand obliging compliments, and desired me to come often. 'It will be an infinite pleasure to me', said she, sighing, 'but I avoid, with the greatest care, seeing any of my former acquaintance, and whenever they come to our convent, I lock my self in my cell'. I observed tears come into her eyes, which touched me extremely, and I began to talk to her in that strain of tender pity she inspired me with; but she would not own to me, that she is not perfectly happy. I have since endeavoured to learn the real cause of her retirement, without being able to get any account, but that every body was surprised at it, and nobody guessed the reason. I have been several times to see her; but it gives me too much melancholy to see so agreeable a young creature buried alive. I am not surprised that Nuns have so often inspired violent passions; the pity one naturally feels for them, when they seem worthy of another destiny, making an easy way for yet more tender sentiments. I never in my life had so little charity for the Roman Catholic religion, as since I see the misery it occasions; so many poor unhappy women! and then the gross superstition of the common people, who are some or other of them, day or night, offering bits of candle to the wooden figures, that are set up almost in every street. The processions I see very often are a pageantry, as offensive and apparently contradictory to common sense, as the pagods[8] of China. God knows whether it be the *womanly* spirit of contradiction that works in me, but there never, before, was so much zeal against popery in the heart of,

Dear Madam, &c. &c.

---

[4] *of quality* upper-class, ladies.
[5] *the siege of Vienna* in 1683 by the Turks.
[6] *camlet* "A kind of stuff originally made by a mixture of silk and camel's hair; it is now made with wool and silk" (Johnson).

[7] *grate* "A partition made with bars placed near to one another, or crossing each other: such as are in clois- ters or prisons" (Johnson).
[8] *pagod* Buddhist monastery.

To the Lady——
Adrianople, April I, O.S. 1717.

I am now got into a new world, where every thing I see, appears to me a change of scene; and I write to your ladyship with some content of mind, hoping, at least that you will find the charm of novelty in my letters, and no longer reproach me, that I tell you nothing extraordinary. I won't trouble you with a relation of our tedious journey; but I must not omit what I saw remarkable at *Sophia*, one of the most beautiful towns in the Turkish Empire, and famous for its hot baths, that are resorted to both for diversions and for health. I stopped here one day, on purpose to see them; and designing to go *incognito*, I hired a Turkish coach. These *voitures*[9] are not at all like ours, but much more convenient for the country, the heat being so great that glasses would be very troublesome. They are made a good deal in the manner of Dutch stage coaches, having wooden lattices painted and gilded; the inside being also painted with baskets and nosegays of flowers, intermixed commonly with little poetical mottoes. They are covered all over with scarlet cloth, lined with silk and very often richly embroidered and fringed. This covering entirely hides the persons in them, but may be thrown back at pleasure, and thus permit the ladies to peep through the lattices. They hold four people very conveniently, seated on cushions, but not raised.

In one of these covered waggons, I went to the *Bagnio*[10] about ten a clock. It was already full of women. It is built of stone, in the shape of a dome, with no windows but in the roof, which gives light enough. There was five of these domes joined together, the outmost being less than the rest, and serving only as a hall, where the *Portress* stood at the door. Ladies of quality generally give this woman a crown or ten shillings, and I did not forget that ceremony. The next room is a very large one, paved with marble, and all round it are two raised Sofas of marble, one above another. There were four fountains of cold water in this room, falling first into marble basins, and then running on the floor in little channels made for that purpose, which carried the streams into the next room, something less than this, with the same sort of marble Sofas, but so hot with streams of sulphur proceeding from the baths joining to it, 'twas impossible to stay there with one's clothes on. The two other domes were the hot baths, one of which had cocks of cold water turning into it, to temper it to what degree of warmth the bathers have a mind to.

I was in my travelling habit, which is a riding dress, and certainly appeared very extraordinary to them. Yet there was not one of them that showed the least surprise or impertinent curiosity, but received me with all the obliging civility possible. I know no European court, where the ladies would have behaved themselves in so polite a manner to a stranger.

I believe, in the whole, there were 200 women, and yet none of those disdainful smiles, and satiric whispers, that never fail in our assemblies, when any body appears that is not dressed exactly in fashion. They repeated over and over to me: 'Uzelle, pek, Uzelle,' which is nothing but, 'Charming, very Charming.' – The first Sofas were covered with cushions and rich carpets, on which sat the ladies; and on the second, their slaves behind them, but without any distinction of rank by their dress, all being in the state of nature, that is, in plain English, stark naked, without any Beauty or defect concealed. Yet there was not the least wanton smile or immodest gesture amongst them. They walked and moved with the same majestic grace, which Milton describes of our General Mother.[11] There were many amongst them, as exactly

---

[9]   *voitures*   French, carriages.
[10]   *Bagnio*   bath or spa.

[11]   *General Mother*   *Paradise Lost* 4.304–18.

proportioned as ever any goddess was drawn by the pencil of Guido or Titian,[12] – and most of their skins shiningly white, only adorned by their beautiful hair, divided into many tresses, hanging on their shoulders, braided either with pearl or ribbon, perfectly representing the figures of the graces.

I was here convinced of the truth of a reflection that I had often made, *that if it were the fashion to go naked, the face would be hardly observed.* I perceived that the Ladies of the most delicate skins and finest shapes, had the greatest share of my admiration, though their faces were sometimes less beautiful than those of their companions. To tell you the truth, I had wickedness enough, to wish secretly, that Mr. *Jervas*[13] could have been there invisible. I fancy it would have very much improved his art, to see so many fine women naked, in different postures, some in conversation, some working, others drinking coffee or sherbet, and many negligently lying on their cushions, while their slaves (generally pretty girls of 17 or 18) were employed in braiding their hair in several pretty fancies. In short, 'tis the women's coffee-house, where all the news of the town is told, scandal invented, &c. – They generally take this diversion once a week, and stay there at least four or five hours, without getting cold, or immediately coming out of the hot-bath into the cool room, which was very surprising to me. The lady, that seemed the most considerable amongst them, entreated me to sit by her, and would fain have undressed me for the bath. I excused myself with some difficulty. They being all so earnest in persuading me, I was at last forced to open my skirt, and show them my stays, which satisfied them very well; for, I saw, they believed I was locked up in that machine, that it was not in my own power to open it, which contrivance they attributed to my husband. – I was charmed with their civility and beauty, and should have been very glad to pass more time with them; but Mr. Wortley resolving to pursue his journey the next morning early, I was in haste to see the ruins of Justinian's church, which did not afford me so agreeable a prospect as I had left, being little more than a heap of stones.

Adieu, Madam. I am sure I have now entertained you, with an account of such a sight as you have never saw in your life, and what no book of travels could inform you of, as 'tis no less than death for a man to be found in one of these places.

[To Lady Mar]

Adrianople, April 18, O.S.

I wrote to you, dear sister, and to all my other English correspondents, by the last ship, and only Heaven can tell, when I shall have another opportunity of sending to you; but I cannot forbear to write again, though perhaps my letter may lie upon my hands this two months. To confess the truth, my head is so full of my entertainment yesterday, that 'tis absolutely necessary, for my own repose, to give it some vent. Without farther preface I will then begin my story.

I was invited to dine with the Grand *Vizier*'s lady,[14] and it was with a great deal of pleasure I prepared myself for an entertainment, which was never given before to any Christian. I thought, I should very little satisfy her curiosity (which I did not doubt was a considerable motive to the invitation) by going in a dress she was used to see, and therefore dressed myself

---

[12] *Guido or Titian* the Italian artists Guido di Pietro, Fra Angelico (c. 1400–55) and Tiziano Vecelli (1490?–1576).

[13] *Mr. Jervas* Charles (1675?–1739), a fashionable portrait artist who had painted Lady Mary as a shepherdess in 1710.

[14] *Grand Vizier* the principal minister of the Sultan; Arnand Khalil Pasha (c. 1655–1733) at this time.

in the court habit of *Vienna*, which is much more magnificent than ours. However, I chose to go *incognito*, to avoid any disputes about ceremony, and went in a Turkish coach, only attended by my woman that held up my train, and the Greek lady, who was my interpretress. I was met, at the court-door by her black Eunuch, who helped me out of the coach with great respect, and conducted me through several rooms, where her she-slaves, finely dressed, were ranged on each side. In the innermost, I found the lady sitting on her sofa, in a sable vest. She advanced to meet me, and presented me half a dozen of her friends, with great civility. She seemed a very good woman, near fifty years old. I was surprised to observe so little magnificence in her house, the furniture being all very moderate; and except the habits and number of her slaves, nothing about her appeared expensive. She guessed at my thoughts, and told me, that she was no longer of an age to spend either her time or money in superfluities; that her whole expense was in charity, and her employment praying to God. There was no affectation in this speech; both she and her husband are entirely given up to devotion. He never looks upon any other woman; and what is much more extraordinary, touches no bribes, notwithstanding the example of all his predecessors. He is so scrupulous in this point, he would not accept Mr. Wortley's present till he had been assured over and over, that it was a settled perquisite of his place, at the entrance of every Ambassador. She entertained me with all kind of civility, till Dinner came in, which was served, one dish at a time, to a vast number, all finely dressed after their manner, which I do not think so bad as you have perhaps heard it represented. I am a very good judge of their eating, having lived three weeks in the house of an *Effendi*[15] at Belgrade, who gave us very magnificent dinners, dressed by his own cooks. The first week pleased me extremely; but, I own, I then begun to grow weary of their table, and desired our own cook might add a dish or two after our manner. But I attribute this to custom, and am very much inclined to believe that an Indian, who had never tasted of either, would prefer their cookery to ours. Their sauces are very high, all the roast very much done. They use a great deal of very rich spice. The soup is served for the last dish; and they have, at least, as great variety of ragouts, as we have. I was very sorry I could not eat of as many as the good lady would have had me, who was very earnest in serving me of every thing. The treat concluded with coffee and perfumes, which is a high mark of respect; two slaves kneeling *censed* my hair, clothes, and handkerchief. After this ceremony, she commanded her slaves to play and dance, which they did with their guitars in their hands, and she excused to me their want of skill, saying she took no care to accomplish them in that art. I returned her thanks, and soon after took my leave.

I was conducted back in the same manner I entered, and would have gone straight to my own house, but the Greek lady, with me, earnestly solicited me to visit the *Kahya*'s lady,[16] saying he was the second officer in the Empire, and ought indeed to be looked upon as the first, the Grand Visier having only the name, while he exercised the authority. I had found so little diversion in the Vizier's *Harem*, that I had no mind to go to another. But her importunity prevailed with me, and I am extreme glad, I was so complaisant. All things here were with quite another air than at the Grand Vizier's; and the very house confessed the difference between an old devotee, and a young beauty. It was nicely clean and magnificent. I was met at the door by two black Eunuchs, who led me through a long gallery between two ranks of beautiful young girls with their hair finely plaited almost hanging to their feet, all dressed in fine light damasks, brocaded with silver. I was sorry that decency did not permit me to stop to consider them nearer. But that thought was lost upon my entrance into a large room, or rather pavilion, built round with gilded sashes, which were most of them thrown up,

---

[15] *Effendi*   scholar.   [16] *Kahya*   steward.

and the trees planted near them gave an agreeable shade, which hindered the Sun from being troublesome. The jessamines and honeysuckles that twisted round their trunks, shed a soft perfume, increased by a white marble fountain playing sweet water in the lower part of the room, which fell into three or four basins, with a pleasing sound. The roof was painted with all sort of flowers, falling out of gilded baskets, that seemed tumbling down. On a Sofa, raised three steps, and covered with fine Persian carpets, sat the Kahya's lady, leaning on cushions of white satin embroidered; and at her feet, sat two young girls about twelve years old, lovely as angels, dressed perfectly rich, and almost covered with jewels. But they were hardly seen near the fair *Fatima* (for that is her name) so much her beauty effaced every thing I have seen, nay, all that has been called lovely either in England or Germany. I must own, that I never saw any thing so gloriously beautiful, nor can I recollect a face that would have been taken notice of near hers. She stood up to receive me, saluting me, after their fashion, putting her hand upon her heart with a sweetness full of majesty, that no court breeding could ever give. She ordered cushions to be given me, and took care to place me in the corner, which is the place of honour. I confess, though the Greek lady had before me given me a great opinion of her beauty, I was so struck with admiration, that I could not, for some time, speak to her, being wholly taken up in gazing. That surprising harmony of features! That charming result of the whole! That exact proportion of body! That lovely bloom of complexion unsullied by art! The unutterable enchantment of her smile! – But her eyes! – Large and black, with all the soft languishment of the blue! every turn of her face discovering some new charm.

After my first surprise was over, I endeavoured, by nicely examining her face, to find out some imperfection, without any fruit of my search, but being clearly convinced of the error of that vulgar notion, that a face perfectly regular would not be agreeable; nature having done for her, with more success, what *Apelles*[17] is said to have essayed by a collection of the most exact features to form a perfect face. Add to all this, a behaviour so full of grace and sweetness, such easy motions with an air so majestic, yet free from stiffness or affectation, that I am persuaded, could she be transported upon the most polite throne of Europe, no body would think her other than born and bred to be a Queen, though educated in a country we call barbarous. To say all in a word, our most celebrated English Beauties would vanish near her.

She was dressed in a *Caftan* of gold brocade, flowered with silver, very well fitted to her shape, and showing to advantage the beauty of her bosom, only shaded by the thin gauze of her shift. Her drawers were pale pink, her waistcoat green and silver, her slippers white satin finely embroidered; her lovely arms adorned with bracelets of diamonds, and her broad girdle set round with diamonds; upon her head a rich Turkish handkerchief of pink and silver, her own fine black hair hanging a great length, in various tresses, and on one side of her head some bodkins of jewels.[18] I am afraid you will accuse me of extravagance in this description. I think I have read some where, that women always speak in rapture, when they speak of beauty, and I cannot imagine why they should not be allowed to do so. I rather think it a virtue to be able to admire without any mixture of desire or envy. The gravest writers have spoke with great warmth of some celebrated pictures and statues. The workmanship of Heaven, certainly excels all our weak imitations, and I think, has a much better claim to our praise. For me, I am not ashamed to own, I took more pleasure in looking on the beauteous *Fatima*, than the finest piece of sculpture could give me. She told me the two girls at her feet were her daughters, though she appeared too young to be their mother. Her fair maids were

---

[17]   *Apelles*   fourth-century BCE Greek painter.   [18]   *bodkins*   ornamented hair-pins or combs.

ranged below the Sofa to the number of twenty, and put me in mind of the pictures of the ancient nymphs. I did not think all nature could have furnished such a scene of beauty. She made them a sign to play and dance. Four of them immediately begun to play some soft airs on instruments, between a lute and a guitar, which they accompanied with their voices, while the others danced by turns. This dance was very different from what I had seen before. Nothing could be more artful, or more proper to raise *certain ideas*. The tunes so soft! – The motions so languishing! – Accompanied with pauses and dying eyes! half-falling back, and then recovering themselves in so artful a manner, that I am very positive, the coldest and most rigid prude upon earth, could not have looked upon them without thinking of *something not to be spoke of*. – I suppose you may have read that the Turks have no music, but what is shocking to the ears; but this account is from those who never heard any but what is played in the streets, and is just as reasonable as if a foreigner should take his ideas of the English music from the *bladder* and *string*, and *marrow bones* and *cleavers*. I can assure you, that the music is extremely pathetic;[19] 'tis true, I am inclined to prefer the Italian, but perhaps I am partial. I am acquainted with a Greek Lady, who sings better than Mrs. *Robinson*,[20] and is very well skilled in both, who gives the preference to the Turkish. 'Tis certain they have very fine natural voices, these were very agreeable. When the dance was over, four fair slaves came into the room, with silver censers in their hands, and perfumed the air with amber, aloes-wood and other scents. After this, they served me coffee upon their knees, in the finest japan china, with *soucoups*[21] of silver gilt. The lovely *Fatima* entertained me, all this while, in the most polite agreeable manner, calling me often 'Uzelle Sultanam', or the Beautiful Sultana, and desiring my friendship with the best grace in the world, lamenting that she could not entertain me in my own language.

When I took my leave, two maids brought in a fine silver basket of embroidered handkerchiefs; she begged I would wear the richest for her sake, and gave the others to my woman and interpretress. – I retired through the same ceremonies as before, and could not help thinking, I had been some time in Mahomet's paradise, so much I was charmed with what I had seen. I know not how the relation of it appears to you. I wish it may give you part of my pleasure; for I would have my dear sister share in all the diversions of,

Yours, &c. &c.

To Mr. [Alexander] Pope
Belgrade-Village, June 17, O.S.

I hope, before this time, you have received two or three of my letters. I had yours but yesterday, though dated the third of February, in which you suppose me to be dead and buried. I have already let you know that I am still alive; but to say truth, I look upon my present circumstances to be exactly the same with those of departed spirits. The heats of Constantinople have driven me to this place, which perfectly answers the description of the Elysian fields.[22] I am in the middle of a wood, consisting chiefly of fruit trees, watered by a vast number of fountains, famous for the excellency of their water, and divided into many shady walks, upon short grass, that seems to me artificial; but I am assured, is the pure work of nature – within view of the Black Sea, from whence we perpetually enjoy the refreshments

---

[19] *pathetic* capable of producing feelings in the hearer.
[20] *Mrs. Robinson* Anastasia Robinson (d. 1755).
[21] *soucoups* saucers.

[22] *Elysian fields* the best part of the classical underworld.

of cool breezes, that makes us insensible of the heat of the summer. The village is only inhabited by the richest among the Christians, who meet every night at a fountain, forty paces from my house, to sing and dance. The beauty and dress of the women, exactly resemble the ideas of the ancient nymphs, as they are given us by the representations of the poets and painters. But what persuades me more fully of my decease, is the situation of my own mind, the profound ignorance I am in, of what passes among the living (which only comes to me by chance) and the great calmness with which I receive it. Yet I have still a hankering after my friends and acquaintance left in the world, according to the authority of that admirable author,

> That spirits departed are wonderous kind
> To friends and Relations left behind,
> Which no body can deny.

Of which Solemn Truth I am a *dead* Instance. I think *Virgil* is of the same opinion, that in human souls there will still be some remains of human passions:

> —*Curæ non ipsa in morte relinquunt.*[23]

And 'tis very necessary to make a perfect Elysium, that there should be a river *Lethe*,[24] which I am not so happy to find. To say truth, I am sometimes very weary of the singing and dancing and sunshine, and wish for the smoke and impertinencies in which you toil; though I endeavour to persuade myself that I live in a more agreeable Variety than you do; and that *Monday*, setting of partridges; *Tuesday*, reading English; *Wednesday*, studying in the Turkish language (in which, by the way, I am already very learned) *Thursday*, classical authors; *Friday*, spent in writing; *Saturday*, at my needle, and *Sunday*, admitting of visits and hearing of music, is a better way of disposing the week, than, *Monday* at the drawing room; *Tuesday*, Lady Mohun's; *Wednesday*, at the opera; *Thursday*, the play; *Friday*, Mrs. Chetwynd's, &c. a perpetual round of hearing the same scandal and seeing the same follies acted over and over, which here affect me more than they do other dead people. I can now hear of displeasing things with pity and without indignation. The reflection on the great gulf between you and me, cools all news that come hither. I can neither be sensibly touched with joy or grief, when I consider that, possibly, the cause of either is removed, before the letter comes to my hands. But (as I said before) this indolence does not extend to my few friendships; I am still warmly sensible of yours and Mr. *Congreve's*[25] and desire to live in your remembrance, though dead to all the world beside.

I am, &c. &c.

TO MR. [ALEXANDER] P[OPE]
Dover, Nov. I, O.S. 1718.

I have this minute received a letter of yours sent me from Paris. I believe and hope I shall very soon see both you and Mr. *Congreve*; but as I am here in an inn where we stay to regulate

---

[23] *Curæ non ... relinquunt* "not in death itself do the cares leave them" (*Aeneid* 6.444).
[24] *Lethe* the river of forgetfulness, beyond which is Elysium.

[25] *Mr. Congreve* William (1670–1729), greatest English dramatist of his time.

our march to London, bag and baggage, I shall employ some of my leisure time in answering that part of yours that seems to require an answer.

I must applaud your good nature in supposing that your pastoral lovers (vulgarly called Haymakers) would have lived in everlasting joy and harmony if the lightning had not interrupted their scheme of happiness. I see no reason to imagine that *John Hughes* and *Sarah Drew*[26] were either wiser or more virtuous than their neighbours. That a well set man of twenty-five should have a fancy to marry a brown woman of eighteen is nothing marvellous; and I cannot help thinking that had they married, their lives would have passed in the common tract with their fellow-parishioners. His endeavouring to shield her from the storm was a natural action and what he would have certainly done for his horse, if he had been in the same situation. Neither am I of opinion that their sudden death was a reward of their mutual virtue. You know the Jews were reproved for thinking a village destroyed by fire, more wicked than those that had escaped the thunder. Time and chance happen to all men. Since you desire me to try my skill in an *epitaph*, I think the following lines perhaps more just, though not so poetical as yours.

> Here lies John Hughes and Sarah Drew;
> Perhaps you'll say, what's that to you?
> Believe me, friend, much may be said
> On this poor couple that are dead.
> On Sunday next they should have married;
> *But see how oddly things are carried!*
> On Thursday last it rained and lighten'd,
> These tender lovers sadly frightened,
> Sheltered beneath the cocking hay
> In hopes to pass the time away.
> But the BOLD THUNDER found them out
> (Commissioned for that end no doubt)
> And seizing on their trembling breath,
> Consigned them to the shades of death.
> Who knows if 'twas not kindly done?
> For had they seen the next year's sun,
> A beaten wife and cuckold swain
> Had jointly cursed the marriage chain;
> Now they are happy in their doom,
> *FOR POPE HAS WROTE UPON THEIR*
> *TOMB.*

I confess these sentiments are not altogether so heroic as yours; but I hope you will forgive them in favour of the two last lines. You see how much I esteem the honour you have done them; though I am not very impatient to have the same, and had rather continue to be your stupid, *living*, humble servant than be *celebrated* by all the pens in Europe.

I would write to Mr. C[ongreve]; but suppose you will read this to him if he enquires after me.

---

[26]   *John Hughes* and *Sarah Drew*   see the letter from
Pope to Lady Mary (above, p. 763).

The Lover (1721–5)
A Ballad

1

At length by so much Importunity pressed,
Take, Molly, at once the Inside of my Breast:
This stupid Indifference so often you blame
Is not owing to Nature, to fear, or to Shame,
I am not as cold as a Virgin in Lead[1]   5
Nor is Sunday's Sermon so strong in my Head,
I know but too well how Time flies along,
That we live but few Years and yet fewer are young.

2

But I hate to be cheated, and never will buy
Long years of Repentance for moments of Joy;   10
Oh was there a Man (but where shall I find
Good sense, and good Nature so equally joined?)
Would value his pleasure, contribute to mine,
Not meanly would boast, nor lewdly design,
Not over severe, yet not stupidly vain,   15
For I would have the power though not give the pain.

3

No Pedant yet learned, not rakehelly Gay
Or laughing because he has nothing to say,
To all my whole sex, obliging and Free,
Yet never be fond of any but me.   20
In public preserve the Decorums are just
And show in his Eyes he is true to his Trust,
Then rarely approach, and respectfully Bow,
Yet not fulsomely pert, nor yet foppishly low.

4

But when the long hours of Public are past   25
And we meet with Champagne and a Chicken at last,
May every fond Pleasure that hour endear,
Be banished afar both Discretion and Fear,
Forgetting or scorning the Airs of the Crowd
He may cease to be formal, and I to be proud,   30
Till lost in the Joy we confess that we live
And he may be rude, and yet I may forgive.

THE LOVER
[1] *a Virgin in Lead*   the decoration of a funeral casket.

5

And that my Delight may be solidly fixed
Let the Friend, and the Lover be handsomely mixed,
In whose tender Bosom my Soul might confide,   35
Whose kindness can soothe me, whose Counsel could guide,
From such a dear Lover as here I describe
No danger should fright me, no Millions should bribe,
But till this astonishing creature I know
As I long have lived Chaste I will keep my self so.   40

6

I never will share with the wanton Coquette
Or be caught by a vain affectation of Wit.
The Toasters, and Songsters may try all their Art
But never shall enter the pass of my Heart;
I loath the Lewd Rake, the dressed Fopling despise,   45
Before such pursuers the nice Virgin flies,
And as Ovid has sweetly in Parables told
We harden like Trees, and like Rivers are cold.[2]

The Reasons that Induced Dr S[wift] to Write a Poem Called the Lady's Dressing Room[1] (1732–4)

The Doctor in a clean starched band,
His Golden Snuff box in his hand,
With care his Diamond Ring displays
And Artful shows its various Rays,
While Grave he stalks down —————— Street   5
His dearest Betty ——— to meet.
      Long had he waited for this Hour,
Nor gained Admittance to the Bower,
Had joked and punned, and swore and writ,
Tried all his Gallantry and Wit,[2]   10
Had told her oft what part he bore
In Oxford's Schemes in days of yore,[3]
But Bawdy, Politics nor Satire
Could move this dull hard hearted Creature.
Jenny her Maid could taste a Rhyme   15

---

[2] *harden like Trees, and like Rivers are cold* Daphne
turned into a laurel to escape Apollo and Arethusa into a
stream to escape Alpheus.
THE REASONS
[1] *the Lady's Dressing Room* Swift published this poem
in 1734; it has much in common with "A Beautiful
Young Nymph Going to Bed" (above, p. 652).

[2] *Had joked . . . and Wit* this couplet is an imitation
of one Swift wrote about himself in his long poem
Cadenus and Vanessa (ll. 542–3).
[3] *Oxford* Robert Harley, first Earl of Oxford (1661–
1724) formed the Tory administration which ruled
from 1710–14 and for which Swift worked; subsequently
impeached and imprisoned for two years for his
"schemes."

And grieved to see him lose his Time,
Had kindly whispered in his Ear,
For twice two pound you enter here,
My Lady vows without that Sum
It is in vain you write or come.   20
    The Destined Offering now he brought
And in a paradise of thought
With a low Bow approached the Dame
Who smiling heard him preach his Flame.
His Gold she takes (such proofs as these   25
Convince most unbelieving shees)
And in her trunk rose up to lock it
(Too wise to trust it in her pocket)
And then returned with Blushing Grace
Expects the Doctor's warm Embrace.   30
    But now this is the proper place
Where mortals Stare me in the Face
And for the sake of fine Expression
I'm forced to make a small digression.
Alas for wretched Humankind,   35
With Learning Mad, with wisdom blind!
The Ox thinks he's for Saddle fit
(As long ago Friend Horace writ)[4]
And Men their Talents still mistaking,
The stutterer fancies his is speaking.   40
With Admiration oft we see
Hard Features heightened by Toupée,[5]
The Beau affects the Politician,
Wit is the citizen's Ambition,
Poor Pope Philosophy displays on   45
With so much Rhyme and little reason,
And though he argues ne'er so long
That, all is right, his Head is wrong.[6]
    None strive to know their proper merit
But strain for Wisdom, Beauty, Spirit   50
And lose the Praise that is their due
While they've th' impossible in view.
So have I seen the Injudicious Heir
To add one Window the whole House impair.
    Instinct the Hound does better teach   55
Who never undertook to preach,
The frighted Hare from Dogs does run
But not attempts to bear a Gun.

---

[4] Horace *Epistles* 1.14.43 ". . . and the horse, when
lazy, longs to plough."
[5] *Toupée* the top curl on a fashionable wig.

[6] *all is right* a reference to Pope's philosophical poem
An Essay on Man, which expounds a kind of theodicy in
which all things human and divine are in a harmony, the
cosmic benevolence of which is hidden from mere
mortals.

Here many Noble thoughts occur
But I prolixity abhor,   60
And will pursue th'instructive Tale
To show the Wise in some things fail.
    The Reverend Lover with surprise
Peeps in her Bubbies, and her Eyes,
And kisses both, and tries – and tries.   65
The Evening in this Hellish Play,
Beside his Guineas thrown away,
Provoked the Priest to that degree[7]
He swore, 'the Fault is not in me.
Your damned Close stool so near my Nose,   70
Your Dirty Smock, and Stinking Toes
Would make a Hercules as tame
As any Beau that you can name'.
    The nymph grown Furious roared by God
'The blame lies all in Sixty odd',   75
And scornful pointing to the door
Cried, 'Fumbler see my Face no more'.
'With all my Heart I'll go away
But nothing done, I'll nothing pay.
Give back the Money' – 'How', cried she,   80
'Would you palm such a cheat on me!
For poor 4 pound to roar and bellow,
Why sure you want some new Prunella?'[8]
'I'll be revenged you saucy Quean'
Replies the disappointed Dean,   85
'I'll so describe your dressing room
The very Irish shall not come'.
She answered short, 'I'm glad you'll write,
You'll furnish paper when I shite'.

To the Memory of Mr Congreve[1] (1729?)

Farewell the best and loveliest of Mankind
Where Nature with a happy hand had joined
The softest temper with the strongest mind,
In pain could counsel and could charm when blind.

In this Lewd age when Honour is a Jest   5
He found a refuge in his Congreve's breast,
Superior there, unsullied, and entire;
And only could with the last breath expire.

---

[7] *Priest* Swift was an ordained priest and Dean of St
Paul's Cathedral, Dublin.
[8] *Prunella* a material used in clerical gowns and the
name of a heroine in a popular play of the time.

TO THE MEMORY OF MR CONGREVE
[1] *Mr Congreve* William (1670–1729), pre-eminent
dramatist of his time.

His wit was never by his Malice stained,
No rival writer of his Verse complained,   10
For neither party drew a venal pen
To praise bad measures or to blast good men.

A Queen indeed he mourned, but such a Queen[2]
Where Virtue mixed with royal Blood was seen,
With equal merit graced each Scene of Life   15
An Humble Regent and Obedient Wife.

If in a Distant State blest Spirits know
The Scenes of Sorrow of a World below,
This little Tribute to thy Fame approve,
A Trifling Instance of a boundless Love.   20

[A Summary of Lord Lyttelton's advice to a Lady[1]] (1731–3)

Be plain in Dress, and sober in your Diet,
In short, my Dearee, kiss me, and be quiet.

Mary Barber (1690–1757)

Barber's only publication is Poems on Several Occasions *(1734). Like many books of poetry by women, this was published by subscription, which means the money for production was raised by advance sales to "patrons" who then had the honour of seeing their names in print in the preliminary pages of the volume. To help promote the book, Jonathan Swift wrote a letter to the Earl of Orrery, which also became part of the book:*

> *I have read most of her Poems; and believe your Lordship will observe, that they generally contain something new and useful, tending to the Reproof of some Vice or Folly, or recommending some Virtue. She never writes on a Subject with general unconnected Topics, but always with a Scheme and Method driving to some particular End; wherein many Writers in Verse, and of some Distinction, are so often known to fail. In short, she seemeth to have a true poetical Genius, better cultivated than could well be expected, either from her Sex, or the Scene she hath acted in as the Wife of a Citizen. Yet I am assured that no Woman was ever more useful to her Husband in the way of his Business. Poetry hath only been her favourite Amusement; for which she hath one Qualification, that I wish all good Poets possessed a Share of; I mean, that she is ready to take Advice, and submit to have her Verses corrected, by those who are generally allowed to be the best Judges.*

---

[2] *Queen* Mary, Queen of William III.
A SUMMARY OF LORD LYTTELTON'S ADVICE TO A LADY
[1] *Summary* Lady Mary wrote this couplet on a scribal copy of Lord Lyttelton's poem "Advice to a Lady" (1733); the title was added by the editor who first printed it in 1803.

Swift's attitude towards women apart, this is high praise. Barber's sense of point, or "driving to some particular End," is unfailing, but she is neither blunt nor tendentious. Her concern with some of the details of daily life and the experience of parenting seems strikingly contemporary. The poems offered here are based on the second edition of her only book (1735).

from *Poems on Several Occasions* (1734)

THE CONCLUSION OF A LETTER TO THE REV. MR. C——

'Tis Time to conclude; for I make it a Rule,
To leave off all Writing, when *Con* comes from School.
He dislikes what I've written, and says, I had better
To send what he calls a 'poetical' Letter.
    To this I replied, 'You are out of your Wits;   5
A Letter in Verse would put him in Fits:
He thinks it a Crime in a Woman to read –
Then, what would he say, should your Counsel succeed?
    "I Pity poor *Barber*, his Wife's so romantic:
A Letter in Rhyme! – Why, the Woman is frantic!   10
This Reading the Poets has quite turned her Head!
On my Life, she should have a dark Room, and Straw Bed.
I often heard say, that St. *Patrick* took care,
No poisonous Creature should live in this Air:
He only regarded the Body, I find;   15
But *Plato* considered who poisoned the Mind.
Would they'd follow his Precepts, who sit at the Helm,
And drive Poetasters from out of the Realm!
    "Her Husband has surely a terrible Life;
There's nothing I dread, like a verse-writing Wife: 20
Defend me, ye Powers, from that fatal Curse;
Which must heighten the Plagues of 'for better for worse'!
    "May I have a Wife, that will dust her own Floor;
And not the fine Minx, recommended by *More*.[1]
(That he was a Dotard, is granted, I hope,   25
Who died for asserting the Rights of the *Pope*.)[2]
If ever I marry, I'll choose me a Spouse,
That shall *serve* and *obey*, as she's bound by her Vows;
That shall, when I'm dressing, attend like a Valet;
Then go to the Kitchen, and study my Palate.   30
She has Wisdom enough, that keeps out of the Dirt,
And can make a good *Pudding*, and cut out a *Shirt*.
What Good's in a Dame, that will pore on a Book?
No! – Give me the Wife, that shall save me a Cook"'.

THE CONCLUSION OF A LETTER
[1] *More* See Sir Thomas More's *Advice to his Son* [Barber's note].

[2] *a Dotard . . . Pope* More was executed in 1535 because he opposed Henry VIII's renunciation of papal authority.

Thus far I had written – Then turned to my Son,   35
To give him Advice, ere my Letter was done.
'My Son, should you marry, look out for a Wife,
That's fitted to lighten the Labours of Life.
Be sure, wed a Woman you thoroughly know,
And shun, above all Things, a *housewifely Shrew*;   40
That would fly to your Study, with Fire in her Looks,
And ask what you got by your poring on Books;
Think Dressing of Dinner the Height of all Science,
And to Peace, and good Humour bid open Defiance.
'Avoid the fine Lady, whose Beauty's her Care;   45
Who sets a high Price on her Shape, and her Air;
Who in Dress, and in Visits, employs the whole Day;
And longs for the Evening, to sit down to play.
'Choose a Woman of Wisdom, as well as good Breeding,
With a Turn, at least no Aversion, to Reading: 50
In the Care of her Person, exact and refined;
Yet still, let her principal Care be her Mind:
Who can, when her Family Cares give her Leisure,
Without the dear Cards, pass an Evening with Pleasure;
In forming her Children to Virtue and Knowledge,   55
Nor trust, for that Care, to a School, or a College:
By Learning made humble, not thence taking Airs,
To despise, or neglect, her domestic Affairs:
Nor think her less fitted for doing her Duty,
By knowing its Reasons, its Use, and its Beauty.   60
'When you gain her Affection, take care to preserve it,
Lest others persuade her, you do not deserve it.
Still study to heighten the Joys of her Life;
Nor treat her the worse, for her being your Wife.
If in Judgement she errs, set her right, without Pride: 65
'Tis the Province of insolent Fools, to deride.
A Husband's first Praise, is a *Friend* and *Protector*:
Then change not these Titles, for *Tyrant* and *Hector*.
Let your Person be neat, unaffectedly clean,
Though alone with your Wife the whole Day you remain.   70
Choose Books, for her Study, to fashion her Mind,
To emulate those who excelled of her Kind.
Be Religion the principal Care of your Life,
As you hope to be blest in your Children and Wife:
So you, in your Marriage, shall gain its true End;   75
And find, in your Wife, a *Companion* and *Friend*.'

A LETTER FOR MY SON TO ONE OF HIS SCHOOL-FELLOWS, SON TO *HENRY ROSE*, ESQ.

Dear *Rose*, as I lately was writing some Verse,
Which I next Day intended in School to rehearse,

My Mother came in, and I thought she'd run wild:
'This Mr. *Macmullen* has ruined my Child:
He uses me ill, and the World shall know it;   5
I sent you to *Latin*, he makes you a Poet:
A fine Way of training a Shop-keeper's Son!
'Twould better become him to teach you to dun:[1]
Let him teach both his Wit, and his Rhyming, to *Rose*;
And give you some Lessons, to help to sell Clothes: 10
He'll have an Estate, and 'twill do very well,
That he, like his Father, in Arts should excel;
But for *you*, if your Father will take my Advice,
He'll send you no more, till he lowers his Price:
A Guinea a Quarter! 'tis monstrously dear! —[2]   15
You might learn to *dance* for four Guineas a Year:
Then, Sir, tell your Master, That these are hard Times;
And Paper's too dear to be wasted in Rhymes:
I'll teach you a Way of employing it better;
As, "*July* the fifteenth, Lord *Levington* Debtor":   20
You may rhyme till you're blind, what arises from thence?
But *Debtor* and *Creditor* brings in the Pence:
Those beggarly Muses but come for a Curse;
But give me the Wit, that puts Gold in the Purse'.
    From what she then told me, I plainly discern,   25
What different Lessons we Scholars must learn.[3]
You're happy, dear Rose; for, as far as I find,
You've nothing to do, but embellish your Mind.
What different Tasks are assigned us by Fate!
'Tis yours to *become*, mine to *get* an Estate.   30
Then, Rose, mind your Learning, whatever you do;
For I have the easier Task of the two.

Eliza Fowler Haywood (1693–1756)

When she about twenty-eight years old, Eliza Haywood left her husband of ten years, a Norfolk minister, and struck out on her own for the city. She supported herself in London as a writer, and occasionally as an actress, producing at least sixty separate publications. She wrote plays, translations, both edited and, for the most part, wrote a successful magazine, The Female Spectator *(1744–6). But the bulk of her work and the most innovative part of it was prose fiction. She produced numerous romances and many other works that combined contemporary gossip and fiction; in both forms she contributed to the development of the novel. In 1724 Haywood had ten new*

A LETTER FOR MY SON
[1] *dun* "To claim a debt with vehemence and importunity" (Johnson).

[2] *Guinea* a little over a pound sterling, around £300 or $500 in modern money.
[3] *Scholars* students.

publications, and in that year her first hit, Love in Excess *(1719–20), reached a fifth edition. Her works are romances in which women are usually the central figures. Haywood's heroines are often intriguers who find ways over, around and through the web of social conventions that restrict their freedom. The darker side of her work, however, is its recognition that the barriers to women's freedom have their foundations in nature or in the deepest and oldest social assumptions: men are naturally unfaithful; unwanted pregnancy is often the result of pursuing sexual desires; and the most superficial qualities of women are those that count for the most in the world created by males and for males. In some of her works Haywood explores the possibility of more lasting relations between women and of other kinds of sexual freedom. She also wrote some sharp political satire of Walpole's administration, but what really made her a threat to the establishment in London was her successful appeal to female readers. Pope satirizes her nastily in* The Dunciad *not because of her politics but rather because she led a shift in the nature of reading and readership that would displace classically based, relatively highbrow poetry, and then poetry in general, from its central position. In the end, Pope was more successful at defeating the scholarly and antiquarian threats to his kind of literature than he was at staving off the encroachments of popular literature.*

Numerous volumes of Haywood's writings have been reprinted in various forms in recent years, though only The Female Spectator *and* Love in Excess *(Broadview Press, 1995) have achieved scholarly editions. Despite prominence in several studies of women writers and in others devoted to prose fiction, Haywood has not yet been the sole subject of major biographical or critical study. The text presented here is based on the edition of* Fantomina *included, with separate title page in* Secret Histories, Novels and Poems, *4 vols, second edition (1725).*

FANTOMINA:
OR,
LOVE in a MAZE (1724)

A Masquerade Novel by
Eliza Haywood

A Young Lady of distinguished Birth, Beauty, Wit, and Spirit, happened to be in a Box one Night at the Playhouse; where, though there were a great Number of celebrated Toasts, she perceived several Gentlemen extremely pleased themselves with entertaining a Woman who sat in a Corner of the Pit, and, by her Air and Manner of receiving them, might easily be known to be one of those who come there for no other Purpose, than to create Acquaintance with as many as seem desirous of it. She could not help testifying her Contempt of Men, who, regardless either of the Play, or Circle, threw away their Time in such a Manner, to some Ladies that sat by her: But they, either less surprised by being more accustomed to such Sights, than she who had been bred for the most Part in the Country, or not of a Disposition to consider any Thing very deeply, took but little Notice of it. She still thought of it, however; and the longer she reflected on it, the greater was her Wonder, that Men, some of whom she knew were accounted to have Wit, should have Tastes so very depraved. – This excited a Curiosity in her to know in what Manner these Creatures were addressed: – She was young, a Stranger to the World, and consequently to the Dangers of it; and having no Body in Town, at that Time, to whom she was obliged to be accountable for her Actions, did in every Thing as her Inclinations or Humours[1] rendered most agreeable to her: Therefore thought it not in the least a Fault to put in practice a little Whim which came immediately into her Head, to dress herself as near as she could in the Fashion of those Women who make sale of their Favours, and set herself in the Way of being accosted as such a one, having at that Time no other Aim, than the Gratification of an innocent Curiosity. – She no sooner designed this Frolic, than she put it in Execution; and muffling her Hoods over her Face, went the next Night into the Gallery-Box,[2] and practising as much as she had observed, at that Distance, the Behaviour of that Woman, was not long before she found her Disguise had answered the Ends she wore it for: – A Crowd of Purchasers of all Degrees and Capacities were in a Moment gathered about her, each endeavouring to out-bid the other, in offering her a Price for her Embraces. – She listened to 'em all, and was not a little diverted in her Mind at the Disappointment she should give to so many, each of which thought himself secure of gaining her. – She was told by 'em all, that she was the most lovely Woman in the World; and some cried, 'Gad, she is mighty like my fine Lady Such-a-one', – naming her own Name. She was naturally vain, and received no small Pleasure in hearing herself praised, though in the Person of another, and a supposed Prostitute; but she dispatched as soon as she could all that had hitherto attacked her, when she saw the accomplished *Beauplaisir* was making his Way through the Crowd as fast as he was able, to reach the Bench she sat on. She had often seen him in the Drawing-Room, had talked with him; but then her Quality[3] and reputed Virtue kept him from using her with that Freedom she now expected he would do, and had discovered something in him, which had made her often think she should not be displeased, if he would abate some Part of his Reserve. – Now was the Time to have her Wishes answered: – He looked in her Face, and fancied, as many others had done, that she very much resembled that Lady whom she really was; but the vast Disparity there appeared between their Characters, prevented him from entertaining even the most distant Thought that they could be the same. – He addressed her at first with the usual Salutations of her pretended Profession, as, 'Are you engaged, Madam? – Will you permit me to wait on you home after the Play? – By Heaven, you are a fine Girl! – How long have you used this House?' – And such like Questions; but perceiving she had a Turn of Wit, and a genteel Manner in her Raillery, beyond what is frequently to be found among those Wretches, who are for the most part Gentlewomen but by Necessity, few of 'em having had an Education suitable to what they affect to appear, he changed the Form of his Conversation, and showed her it was not because he understood no better, that he had made use of Expressions so little polite. – In fine,[4] they were infinitely charmed with each other: He was transported to find so much Beauty and Wit in a Woman, who he doubted not but on very easy Terms he might enjoy; and she found a vast deal of Pleasure in conversing with him in this free and unrestrained Manner. They passed their Time all the Play with an equal Satisfaction; but when it was over, she found herself involved in a Difficulty, which before never entered into her Head, but which she knew not well how to get over. – The Passion he professed for her, was not of that humble Nature which can be content with distant Adorations: – He resolved not to part from her without the Gratifications of those Desires she had inspired; and presuming on the Liberties which her supposed Function allowed of, told her she must either go with him to some

FANTOMINA
[1] *Humour* "Present disposition" (Johnson).
[2] *Gallery-Box* a place for ladies among the highest and cheapest seats in a theatre.
[3] *Quality* nobility.
[4] *In fine* in conclusion.

convenient House of his procuring, or permit him to wait on her to her own Lodgings. –
Never had she been in such a *Dilemma*: Three or four Times did she open her Mouth to confess
her real Quality; but the Influence of her ill Stars prevented it, by putting an Excuse into her
Head, which did the Business as well, and at the same Time did not take from her the Power
of seeing and entertaining him a second Time with the same Freedom she had done this. –
She told him, she was under Obligations to a Man who maintained her, and whom she durst
not disappoint, having promised to meet him that Night at a House hard by. – This Story
so like what those Ladies sometimes tell, was not at all suspected by *Beauplaisir*; and assuring
her he would be far from doing her a Prejudice,[5] desired that in return for the Pain he should
suffer in being deprived of her Company that Night, that she would order her Affairs, so as
not to render him unhappy the next. She gave a solemn Promise to be in the same Box on the
Morrow Evening; and they took Leave of each other; he to the Tavern to drown the
Remembrance of his Disappointment; she in a Hackney-Chair[6] hurried home to indulge
Contemplation on the Frolic she had taken, designing nothing less on her first Reflections,
than to keep the Promise she had made him, and hugging herself with Joy, that she had the
good Luck to come off undiscovered.

But these Cogitations were but of a short Continuance, they vanished with the Hurry of
her Spirits, and were succeeded by others vastly different and ruinous: – All the Charms of
Beauplaisir came fresh into her Mind; she languished, she almost died for another Opportunity of conversing with him; and not all the Admonitions of her Discretion were effectual to
oblige her to deny laying hold of that which offered itself the next Night. – She depended on
the Strength of her Virtue, to bear her fate through Trials more dangerous than she apprehended this to be, and never having been addressed by him as Lady, – was resolved to receive
his Devoirs[7] as a Town-Mistress, imagining a world of Satisfaction to herself in engaging him
in the Character of such a one, and in observing the Surprise he would be in to find himself
refused by a Woman, who he supposed granted her Favours without Exception. – Strange
and unaccountable were the Whimsies she was possessed of, – wild and incoherent her
Desires, – unfixed and undetermined her Resolutions, but in that of seeing *Beauplaisir* in
the Manner she had lately done. As for her Proceedings with him, or how a second Time to
escape him, without discovering who she was, she could neither assure herself, nor whither or
not in the last Extremity she would do so. – Bent, however, on meeting him, whatever should
be the Consequence, she went out some Hours before the Time of going to the Playhouse, and
took Lodgings in a House not very far from it, intending, that if he should insist on passing
some Part of the Night with her, to carry him there, thinking she might with more Security
to her Honour entertain him at a Place where she was Mistress, than at any of his own
choosing.

The appointed Hour being arrived, she had the Satisfaction to find his Love in his
Assiduity: He was there before her; and nothing could be more tender than the Manner in
which he accosted her: But from the first Moment she came in, to that of the Play being done,
he continued to assure her that no Consideration should prevail with him to part from her
again, as she had done the Night before; and she rejoiced to think she had taken that
Precaution of providing herself with a Lodging, to which she thought she might invite him,
without running any Risk, either of her Virtue or Reputation. Having told him she would

---

[5] *Prejudice* "Mischief; detriment; hurt; injury"
(Johnson).
[6] *Hackney-Chair* a hired sedan chair, an enclosed seat
carried by two men.

[7] *Devoir* "Act of civility or obsequiousness"
(Johnson).

admit of his accompanying her home, he seemed perfectly satisfied; and leading her to the Place, which was not above twenty Houses distant, would have ordered a Collation[8] to be brought after them. But she would not permit it, telling him she was not one of those who suffered themselves to be treated at their own Lodgings; and as soon she was come in, sent a Servant, belonging to the House, to provide a very handsome Supper, and Wine, and every Thing was served to Table in a Manner which showed the Director neither wanted Money, nor was ignorant how it should be laid out.

This Proceeding, though it did not take from him the Opinion that she was what she appeared to be, yet it gave him Thoughts of her, which he had not before. – He believed her a *Mistress*, but believed her to be one of a superior Rank, and began to imagine the Possession of her would be much more Expensive than at first he had expected: But not being of a Humour to grudge any Thing for his Pleasures, he gave himself no further Trouble, than what were occasioned by Fears of not having Money enough to reach her Price, about him.

Supper being over, which was intermixed with a vast deal of amorous Conversation, he began to explain himself more than he had done; and both by his Words and Behaviour let her know, he would not be denied that Happiness the Freedoms she allowed had made him hope. – It was in vain; she would have retracted the Encouragement she had given: – In vain she endeavoured to delay, till the next Meeting, the fulfilling of his Wishes: – She had now gone too far to retreat: – *He* was bold; – he was resolute: *She* fearful, – confused, altogether unprepared to resist in such Encounters, and rendered more so, by the extreme Liking she had to him. – Shocked, however, at the Apprenhension of really losing her Honour, she struggled all she could, and was just going to reveal the whole Secret of her Name and Quality, when the Thoughts of the Liberty he had taken with her, and those he still continued to prosecute, prevented her, with representing the Danger of being exposed, and the whole Affair made a Theme for public Ridicule. – Thus much, indeed, she told him, that she was a Virgin, and had assumed this Manner of Behaviour only to engage him. But that he little regarded, or if he had, would have been far from obliging him to desist; – nay, in the present burning Eagerness of Desire, 'tis probable, that had he been acquainted both with who and what she really was, the Knowledge of her Birth would not have influenced him with Respect sufficient to have curbed the wild Exuberance of his luxurious Wishes, or made him in that longing, that impatient Moment, change the Form of his Addresses. In fine, she was undone; and he gained a Victory, so highly rapturous, that had he known over whom, scarce could he have triumphed more. Her Tears, however, and the Destraction she appeared in, after the ruinous Ecstasy was past, as it heightened his Wonder, so it abated his Satisfaction: – He could not imagine for what Reason a Woman, who, if she intended not to be a *Mistress*, had counterfeited the Part of one, and taken so much Pains to engage him, should lament a Consequence which she could not but expect, and till the last Test, seemed inclinable to grant; and was both surprised and troubled at the Mystery. – He omitted nothing that he thought might make her easy; and still retaining an Opinion that the Hope of Interest had been the chief Motive which had led her to act in the Manner she had done, and believing that she might know so little of him, as to suppose, now that she had nothing left to give, he might not make that Recompence she expected for her Favours: To put her out of that Pain, he pulled out of his Pocket a Purse of Gold, entreating her to accept of that as an Earnest of what he intended to do for her; assuring her, with ten thousand Protestations, that he would spare nothing, which his whole Estate could purchase, to procure her Content and Happiness. This Treat-

---

[8] *Collation* a light meal.

ment made her quite forget the Part she had assumed, and throwing it from her with an Air of Disdain, 'Is this a Reward', said she, 'for Condescensions,[9] such as I have yielded to? – Can all the Wealth you are possessed of, make a Reparation for my Loss of Honour? – Oh! no, I am undone beyond the Power of Heaven itself to help me!' – She uttered many more such Exclamations; which the amazed *Beauplaisir* heard without being able to reply to, till by Degrees sinking from that Rage of Temper, her Eyes resumed their softening Glances, and guessing at the Consternation he was in, 'No, my dear *Beauplaisir*', added she, 'your Love alone can compensate for the Shame you have involved me in; be you sincere and constant, and I hereafter shall, perhaps, be satisfied with my Fate, and forgive myself the Folly that betrayed me to you'.

Beauplaisir thought he could not have a better Opportunity than these Words gave him of enquiring who she was, and wherefore she had feigned herself to be of a Profession which he was now convinced she was not; and after he had made her thousand Vows of an Affection, as inviolable and ardent as she could wish to find in him, entreated she would inform him by what Means his Happiness has been brought about, and also to whom he was indebted for the Bliss he had enjoyed. – Some remains of yet unextinguished Modesty, and Sense of Shame, made her Blush exceedingly at this Demand; but recollecting herself in a little Time, she told him so much of the Truth, as to what related to the Frolic she had taken of satisfying her Curiosity in what Manner *Mistresses*, of the sort she appeared to be, were treated by those who addressed them; but forbore discovering her true Name and Quality, for the Reasons she had done before, resolving, if he boasted of this Affair, he should not have it in his Power to touch her Character: She therefore said she was the Daughter of a Country Gentleman, who was come to Town to buy Clothes, and that she was called *Fantomina*. He had no Reason to distrust the Truth of this Story, and was therefore satisfied with it; but did not doubt by the Beginning of her Conduct, but that in the End she would be in Reality, the Thing she so artfully had counterfeited; and had good Nature enough to pity the Misfortunes he imagined would be her Lot: But to tell her so, or offer his Advice in that Point, was not his Business, at least, as yet.

They parted not till towards Morning; and she obliged him to a willing Vow of visiting her the next Day at Three in the Afternoon. It was too late for her to go home that Night; [she] therefore contented herself with lying there. In the Morning she sent for the Woman of the House to come up to her; and easily perceiving, by her Manner, that she was a Woman who might be influenced by Gifts, made her a Present of a Couple of Broad Pieces,[10] and desired her, that if the Gentleman, who had been there the Night before, should ask any Questions concerning her, that he should be told, she was lately come out of the Country, had lodged there about a Fortnight, and that her Name was *Fantomina*. I shall (also added she) lie but seldom here; nor, indeed, ever come but in those Times when I expected to meet him: I would, therefore, have you order it so, that he may think I am but just gone out, if he should happen by any Accident to call when I am not here; for I would not, for the World, have him imagine I do not constantly lodge here. The Landlady assured her she would do every Thing as she desired, and gave her to understand she wanted not the Gift of Secrecy.

Every Thing being ordered at this Home for the Security of her Reputation, she repaired to the other, where she easily excused to an unsuspecting Aunt, with whom she boarded, her having been abroad all Night, saying, she went with a Gentleman and his Lady in a Barge, to a little Country Seat of theirs up the River, all of them designing to return the same

---

9   *Condescension* "Voluntary humiliation" (Johnson).   10   *Broad Piece* seventeenth-century gold coin roughly equivalent to the later guinea or modern pound.

Evening; but that one of the Bargemen happening to be taken ill on the sudden, and no other Waterman to be got that Night, they were obliged to tarry till Morning. Thus did this Lady's Wit and Vivacity assist her in all, but where it was most needful. – She had Discernment to forsee, and avoid all those Ills which might attend the loss of her *Reputation*, but was wholly blind to those of the Ruin of her *Virtue*; and having managed her Affairs so as to secure the *one*, grew perfectly easy with the Remembrance, she had forfeited the *other*. – The more she reflected on the Merits of *Beauplaisir*, the more she excused herself for what she had done; and the Prospect of that continued Bliss she expected to share with him, took from her all Remorse for having engaged in an Affair which promised her so much Satisfaction, and in which she found not the least Danger of Misfortune. – 'If he is really', said she, to herself, 'the faithful, the constant Lover he has sworn to be, how charming will be our Amour? – And if he should be false, grow satiated, like other Men, I shall but, at the worst, have the private Vexation of knowing I lost him; – the Intrigue being a Secret, my Disgrace will be so too: – I shall hear no Whispers as I pass, – "She is Forsaken": – The odious Word *Forsaken* will never wound my Ears; nor will my Wrongs excite either Mirth or Pity of the talking World: – It will not be even in the Power of my Undoer Himself to triumph over me; and while he laughs at, and perhaps despises the fond, the yielding *Fantomina*, he will revere and esteem the virtuous, the reserved Lady'. – In this Manner did she applaud her own Conduct, and exult with the Imagination that she had more Prudence than all her Sex beside. And it must be confessed, indeed, that she preserved an Economy in the management of this Intrigue, beyond what almost any Woman but herself ever did: In the first Place, by making no Person in the World a Confidant in it; and in the next, in concealing from *Beauplaisir* himself the Knowledge who she was; for though she met him three or four Days in a Week, at the Lodging she had taken for that Purpose, yet as much as he employed her Time and Thoughts, she was never missed from any Assembly she had been accustomed to frequent. – The Business of her Love has engrossed her till Six in the Evening, and before Seven she has been dressed in a different Habit, and in another Place. – Slippers, and a Nightgown loosely flowing, has been the Garb in which he has left the languishing *Fantomina*; – Laced, and adorned with all the Blaze of Jewels, has he, in less than an Hour after, beheld at the Royal Chapel, the Palace Gardens, Drawing-Room, Opera, or Play, the Haughty Awe-inspiring Lady – A thousand Times has he stood amazed at the prodigious Likeness between his little Mistress, and this Court Beauty; but was still as far from imagining they were the same, as he was the first Hour he accosted her in the Playhouse, though it is not impossible, but that her Resemblance to this celebrated Lady, might keep his Inclinations alive something longer than otherwise they would have been; and that it was to the Thoughts of this (as he supposed) unenjoyed Charmer, she owed in great measure the Vigour of his latter Caresses.

But he varied not so much from his Sex as to be able to prolong Desire, to any great Length after Possession: The rifled Charms of *Fantomina* soon lost their Poignancy, and grew tasteless and insipid; and when the Season of the Year inviting the Company to the *Bath*, she offered to accompany him, he made an Excuse to go without her. She easily perceived his Coldness, and the Reason why he pretended her going would be inconvenient, and endured as much from the Discovery as any of her Sex could do: She dissembled it, however, before him, and took her Leave of him with the Show of no other Concern than his Absence occasioned: But this she did to take from him all Suspicion of her following him, as she intended, and had already laid a Scheme for. – From her first finding out that he designed to leave her behind, she plainly saw it was for no other Reason, than being tired of her Conversation, he was willing to be at liberty to pursue new Conquests; and wisely considering that Complaints,

Tears, Swooning, and all the Extravagancies which Women make use of in such Cases, have little Prevalence over a Heart inclined to rove, and only serve to render those who practice them more contemptible, by robbing them of that Beauty which alone can bring back the fugitive Lover, she resolved to take another Course; and remembering the Height of Transport she enjoyed when the agreeable *Beauplaisir* kneeled at her Feet, imploring her first Favours, she longed to prove the same again. Not but a Woman of her Beauty and Accomplishments might have beheld a Thousand in that Condition *Beauplaisir* had been; but with her Sex's Modesty, she had not also thrown off another Virtue equally valuable, though generally unfortunate, *Constancy*: She loved *Beauplaisir*; it was only he whose Solicitations could give her Pleasure; and had she seen the whole Species despairing, dying for her sake, it might, perhaps, have been a Satisfaction to her Pride, but none to her more tender Inclination. – Her Design was once more to engage him, to hear him sigh, to see him languish, to feel the strenuous Pressures of his eager Arms, to be compelled, to be sweetly forced to what she wished with equal Ardour, was what she wanted, and what she had formed a Stratagem to obtain, in which she promised herself Success.

She no sooner heard he had left the Town, than making a Pretence to her Aunt, that she was going to visit a Relation in the Country, went towards *Bath*, attended but by two Servants, who she found Reasons to quarrel with on the Road and discharged: Clothing herself in a Habit she had brought with her, she forsook the Coach, and went into a Wagon, in which Equipage she arrived at *Bath*. The Dress she was in, was a round-eared Cap, a short Red Petticoat, and a little Jacket of Grey Stuff; all the rest of her Accoutrements were answerable to these, and joined with a broad Country Dialect, a rude unpolished Air, which she, having been bred in these Parts, knew very well how to imitate, with her Hair and Eyebrows blacked, made it impossible for her to be known, or taken for any other than what she seemed. Thus disguised did she offer herself to Service in the House where *Beauplaisir* lodged, having made it her Business to find out immediately where he was. Notwithstanding this Metamorphosis she was still extremely pretty; and the Mistress of the House happening at that Time to want a Maid, was very glad of the Opportunity of taking her. She was presently received into the Family; and had a Post in it (such as she would have chose, had she been left at her Liberty), that of making the Gentlemen's Beds, getting them their Breakfasts, and waiting on them in their Chambers. Fortune in this Exploit was extremely on her side; there were no others of the Male-Sex in the House, than an old Gentleman, who had lost the Use of his Limbs with the Rheumatism, and had come thither for the Benefit of the Waters, and her beloved *Beauplaisir*; so that she was in no Apprehensions of any Amorous Violence, but where she wished to find it. Nor were her Designs disappointed: He was fired with the first Sight of her; and though he did not presently take any further Notice of her, than giving her two or three hearty Kisses, yet she, who now understood that Language but too well, easily saw they were the Prelude to more substantial Joys. – Coming the next Morning to bring his Chocolate, as he ordered, he catched her by the pretty Leg, which the Shortness of her Petticoat did not in the least oppose; then pulling her gently to him, asked her, how long she had been at Service? – How many Sweethearts she had? If she had ever been in Love? and many other such Questions, befitting one of the Degree she appeared to be: All which she answered with such seeming Innocence, as more inflamed the amorous Heart of him who talked to her. He compelled her to sit in his Lap; and gazing on her blushing Beauties, which, if possible, received Addition from her plain and rural Dress, he soon lost the Power of containing himself. – His wild Desires burst out in all his Words and Actions: he called her little Angel, Cherubim, swore he must enjoy her, though Death were to be the Consequence, devoured her Lips, her Breasts with greedy Kisses, held to his burning Bosom her half-yielding, half-reluctant Body, nor suffered her to get loose, till he had ravaged all, and glutted each rapacious Scene with the sweet Beauties of the pretty *Celia*, for that was the name she bore in this second Expedition.   Generous as Liberality itself to all who gave him Joy this way, he gave her a handsome Sum of Gold, which she durst not now refuse, for fear of creating some Mistrust, and losing the Heart she so lately had regained; therefore taking it with an humble Curtesy, and a well counterfeited Show of Surprise and Joy, cried, 'O Law, Sir! what must I do for all this?' He laughed at her Simplicity, and kissing her again, though less fervently than he had done before, bade her not be out of the Way when he came home at Night. She promised she would not, and very obediently kept her Word.

His Stay at *Bath* exceeded not a Month; but in that Time his supposed Country Lass had persecuted him so much with her Fondness, that in spite of the Eagerness with which he first enjoyed her, he was at last grown more weary of her, than he had been of *Fantomina*; which she perceiving, would not be troublesome, but quitting her Service, remained privately in the Town till she heard he was on his Return; and in that Time provided herself of another Disguise to carry on a third Plot, which her inventing Brain had furnished her with, once more to renew his twice-decayed Ardours. The Dress she had ordered to be made, was such as Widows wear in their first Mourning, which, together with the most afflicted and penitential Countenance that ever was seen, was no small Alteration to her who used to seem all Gaiety. – To add to this, her Hair, which she was accustomed to wear very loose, both when *Fantomina* and *Celia*, was now tied back so straight, and her Pinners[11] coming so very forward, that there was none of it to be seen. In fine, her Habit and her Air were so much changed, that she was not more difficult to be known in the rude Country *Girl*, than she was now in the sorrowful *Widow*.

She knew that *Beauplaisir* came alone in his Chariot to the *Bath*, and in the Time of her being Servant in the House where he lodged, heard nothing of any Body that was to accompany him to *London*, and hoped he would return in the same Manner he had gone: She therefore hired Horses and a Man to attend her to an Inn about ten Miles on this side *Bath*, where having discharged them, she waited till the Chariot should come by; which when it did, and she saw that he was alone in it, she called to him that drove it to stop a Moment, and going to the Door saluted the Master with these Words: 'The Distressed and Wretched, Sir', said she, 'never fail to excite Compassion in a generous Mind; and I hope I am not deceived in my Opinion that yours is such: – You have the Appearance of a Gentleman, and cannot, when you hear my Story, refuse that Assistance which is in your Power to give to an unhappy Woman, who without it, may be rendered the most miserable of all created Beings'.

It would not be very easy to represent the Surprise, so odd an Address created in the Mind of him to whom it was made. – She had not the Appearance of one who wanted Charity; and what other Favour she required he could not conceive: But telling her, she might command any Thing in his Power, gave her Encouragement to declare herself in this Manner: 'You may judge', resumed she, 'by the melancholy Garb I am in, that I have lately lost all that ought to be valuable to Womankind; but it is impossible for you to guess the Greatness of my Misfortune, unless you had known my Husband, who was Master of every Perfection to endear him to a Wife's Affections. – But, notwithstanding, I look on myself as the most unhappy of my Sex in out-living him, I must so far obey the Dictates of my Discretion, as to take care of the little Fortune he left behind him, which being in the hands of a Brother of his in *London*, will be all carried off to *Holland*, where he is going to settle; if I reach not the

---

[11]   *Pinners*   the long flaps of a coif or head dress worn by women of rank.

Town before he leaves it, I am undone for ever. – To which End I left *Bristol*, the Place where we lived, hoping to get a Place in the Stage at *Bath*, but they were all taken up before I came; and being, by a Hurt I got in a Fall, rendered incapable of travelling any long Journey on Horseback, I have no Way to go to *London*, and must be inevitably ruined in the Loss of all I have on Earth, without you have good Nature enough to admit me to take Part of your Chariot'.

Here the feigned Widow ended her sorrowful Tale, which had been several Times interrupted by a Parenthesis of Sighs and Groans; and *Beauplaisir*, with a complaisant and tender Air, assured her of his Readiness to serve her in Things of much greater Consequence than what she desired of him; and told her, it would be an Impossibility of denying a Place in his Chariot to a Lady, who he could not behold without yielding one in his Heart. She answered the Compliments he made her but with Tears, which seemed to stream in such abundance from her Eyes, that she could not keep her handkerchief from her Face one Moment. Being come into the Chariot, *Beauplaisir* said a thousand handsome Things to persuade her from giving way to so violent a Grief, which, he told her, would not only be destructive to her Beauty, but likewise her Health. But all his Endeavours for Consolement appeared ineffectual, and he began to think he should have but a dull Journey in the Company of one who seemed so obstinately devoted to the Memory of her dead Husband, that there was no getting a Word from her on any other Theme: – But bethinking himself of the celebrated Story of the *Ephesian* Matron,[12] it came into his Head to make Trial, she who seemed equally suspectible of *Sorrow*, might not also be so too of *Love*; and having begun a Discourse on almost every other Topic, and finding her still incapable of answering, resolved to put it to the Proof, if this would have no more Effect to rouse her sleeping Spirits: – With a gay Air, therefore, though accompanied with the greatest Modesty and Respect, he turned the Conversation, as though without Design, on that Joy-giving Passion, and soon discovered that was indeed the Subject she was best pleased to be entertained with; for on his giving her a Hint to begin upon, never any Tongue run more voluble than hers, on the prodigious Power it had to influence the Souls of those possessed of it, to Actions even the most distant from their Intentions, Principles, or Humours.[13] – From that she passed to a Description of the Happiness of mutual Affection; – the unspeakable Ecstasy of those who meet with equal Ardency; and represented it in Colours so lively, and disclosed by the Gestures with which her Words were accompanied, and the Accent of her Voice so true a Feeling of what she said, that *Beauplaisir*, without being as stupid, as he was really the contrary, could not avoid perceiving there were Seeds of Fire, not yet extinguished, in this fair Widow's Soul, which wanted but the kindling Breath of tender Sighs to light into a Blaze. – He now thought himself as fortunate, as some Moments before he had the Reverse; and doubted not, but, that before they parted, he should find a Way to dry the Tears of this lovely Mourner, to the Satisfaction of them both. He did not, however, offer, as he had done to *Fantomina* and *Celia*, to urge his Passion directly to her, but by a thousand little softening Artifices, which he well knew how to use, gave her leave to guess he was enamoured. When they came to the Inn where they were to lie, he declared himself somewhat more freely, and perceiving she did not

---

12   *Ephesian Matron*   Petronius (*Satyricon* 111–12) tells the story of a chaste wife who weeps for days at her husband's grave but is seduced by a soldier who courts her and weds her in the tomb; in the end she gives her husband's body to save him from punishment for the theft of the crucified criminal's body that he was sup-

posed to be guarding; the story, which Petronius tells at the expense of women, became a commonplace in the literature of sensibility and she a kind of heroine.
13   *Humour*   "General turn or temper of mind" (Johnson).

resent it past Forgiveness, grew more encroaching still: – He now took the Liberty of kissing away her Tears, and catching the Sighs as they issued from her Lips; telling her if Grief was infectious, he was resolved to have his Share; protesting he would gladly exchange Passions with her, and be content to bear her Load of *Sorrow*, if she would as willingly ease the Burden of his *Love*. – She said little in answer to the strenuous Pressures with which at last he ventured to enfold her, but not thinking it Decent, for the Character she had assumed, to yield so suddenly, and unable to deny both his and her own Inclinations, she counterfeited a fainting, and fell motionless upon his Breast. – He had no great Notion that she was in a real Fit, and the Room they supped in happening to have a Bed in it, he took her in his Arms and laid her on it, believing, that whatever her Distemper was, that was the most proper Place to convey her to. – He laid himself down by her, and endeavoured to bring her to herself; and she was too grateful to her kind Physician at her returning Sense, to remove from the Posture he had put her in, without his Leave.

It may, perhaps, seem strange that *Beauplaisir* should in such near Intimacies continue still deceived: I know there are Men who will swear it is an Impossibility, and that no Disguise could hinder them from knowing a Woman they had once enjoyed. In answer to these Scruples, I can only say, that besides the Alteration which the Change of Dress made in her, she was so admirably skilled in the Art of feigning, that she had the Power of putting on almost what Face she pleased, and knew so exactly how to form her Behaviour to the Character she represented, that all the Comedians at both Playhouses[14] are infinitely short of her Performances: She could vary her very Glances, tune her Voice to Accents the most different imaginable from those in which she spoke when she appeared herself. – These Aids from Nature, joined to the Wiles of Art, and the Distance between the Places where the imagined *Fantomina* and *Celia* were, might very well prevent his having any Thought that they were the same, or that the fair *Widow* was either of them: It never so much as entered his Head, and though he did fancy he observed in the Face of the latter, Features which were not altogether unknown to him, yet he could not recollect when or where he had known them; – and being told by her, that from her Birth, she had never removed from *Bristol*, a Place where he never was, he rejected the Belief of having seen her, and supposed his Mind had been deluded by an Idea of some other, whom she might have a Resemblance of.

They passed the Time of their Journey in as much Happiness as the most luxurious Gratification of wild Desires could make them; and when they came to the End of it, parted not without a mutual Promise of seeing each other often. – He told her to what Place she should direct a Letter to him; and she assured him she would send to let him know where to come to her, as soon as she was fixed in Lodgings.

She kept her Promise; and charmed with the Continuance of his eager Fondness, went not home, but into private Lodgings, whence she wrote to him to visit her the first Opportunity, and enquire for the Widow *Bloomer*. – She had no sooner dispatched this Billet, than she repaired to the House where she had lodged as *Fantomina*, charging the People if *Beauplaisir* should come there, not to let him know she had been out of Town. From thence she wrote to him, in a different Hand, a long Letter of Complaint, that he had been so cruel in not sending one Letter to her all the Time he had been absent, entreated to see him, and concluded with subscribing herself his unalterably Affectionate *Fantomina*. She received in one Day Answers to both these. The first contained these Lines:

---

14   *both Playhouses*   Covent Garden and Drury Lane, the King's Theatre in Haymarket being used for opera.

To the Charming Mrs. Bloomer,

It would be impossible, my Angel! for me to express the thousandth Part of that Infinity of Transport, the Sight of your dear Letter gave me. – Never was Woman formed to charm like you: Never did any look like you, – write like you, – bless like you; – nor did ever Man adore as I do. – Since Yesterday we parted, I have seemed a Body without a Soul; and had you not by this inspiring Billet, given me new Life, I know not what by To-morrow I should have been. – I will be with you this Evening about Five: – O, 'tis an Age till then! – But the cursed formalities of Duty oblige me to Dine with my Lord – who never rises from Table till that Hour; – therefore Adieu till then sweet lovely Mistress of the Soul and all the Faculties of

Your most faithful,
BEAUPLAISIR

The other was in this Manner:

To the Lovely Fantomina

If you were half so sensible as you ought of your own Power of charming, you would be assured, that to be unfaithful or unkind to you, would be among the Things that are in their very Natures Impossibilities. – It was my Misfortune, not my Fault, that you were not persecuted every Post with a Declaration of my unchanging Passion; but I had unluckily forgot the Name of the Woman at whose House you are, and knew not how to form a Direction that it might come safe to your Hands. – And, indeed, the Reflection how you might misconstrue my Silence, brought me to Town some Weeks sooner than I intended – If you knew how I have languished to renew those Blessings I am permitted to enjoy in your Society, you would rather pity than condemn

Your ever faithful,
BEAUPLAISIR

P.S. I fear I cannot see you till To-morrow; some Business has unluckily fallen out that will engross my Hours till then. – Once more, my Dear, *Adieu*.

'TRAITOR!' cried she, as soon as she had read them, ''tis thus our silly, fond, believing Sex are served when they put Faith in Man: So had I been deceived and cheated, had I like the rest believed, and sat down mourning in Absence, and vainly waiting recovered Tenderness. – How do some Women', continued she 'make their Life a Hell, burning in fruitless Expectations, and dreaming out their Days in Hopes and Fears, then wake at last to all the Horror of Despair? – But I have outwitted even the most Subtle of the deceiving Kind, and while he thinks to fool me, is himself the only beguiled Person'.

She made herself, most certainly, extremely happy in the Reflection on the Success of her Stratagems; and while the Knowledge of his Inconstancy and Levity of Nature kept her from having that real Tenderness for him she would have else have had, she found the Means of gratifying the Inclination she had for his agreeable Person, in as full a Manner as she could wish. She had all the Sweets of Love, but as yet had tasted none of the Gall, and was in a State of Contentment, which might be envied by the more Delicate.

When the expected Hour arrived, she found that her Lover had lost no part of the Fervency with which he had parted from her; but when the next Day she received him as *Fantomina*, she perceived a prodigious Difference; which led her again into Reflections on the Unaccountableness of Men's Fancies, who still prefer the last Conquest, only because it is the last. – Here was an evident Proof of it; for there could not be a Difference in Merit, because they were the same Person; but the Widow *Bloomer* was a more new Acquaintance than *Fantomina*, and therefore esteemed more valuable. This, indeed, must be said of *Beauplaisir*, that he had a greater Share of good Nature than most of his Sex, who, for the most part, when they are weary of an Intrigue, break it entirely off, without any Regard to the Despair of the abandoned Nymph. Though he retained no more than a bare Pity and Complaisance for *Fantomina*, yet believing she loved him to an Excess, would not entirely forsake her, though the Continuance of his Visits was now become rather a Penance than a Pleasure.

The Widow *Bloomer* triumphed some Time longer over the Heart of this Inconstant, but at length her Sway was at an End, and she sunk in this Character, to the same Degree of Tastelessness, as she had done before in that of *Fantomina* and *Celia*. – She presently perceived it, but bore it as she had always done; it being but what she expected, she had prepared herself for it, and had another Project in *embryo*, which she soon ripened into Action. She did not, indeed, complete it altogether so suddenly as she had done the others, by reason there must be Persons employed in it; and the Aversion she had to any *Confidants* in her Affairs, and the Caution with which she had hitherto acted, and which she was still determined to continue, made it very difficult for her to find a Way without breaking through that Resolution to compass what she wished. – She got over the Difficulty at last, however, by proceeding in a Manner, if possible, more extraordinary than all her former Behaviour: – Muffling herself up in her Hood one Day, she went into the Park about the Hour when there are a great many necessitous Gentlemen, who think themselves above what they call little Things for a Maintenance, walking in the *Mall*,[15] to take a *Chamelion* Treat,[16] and fill their Stomachs with Air instead of Meat. Two of those, who by their Physiognomy she thought most proper for her Purpose, she beckoned to come to her; and taking them into a Walk more remote from Company, began to communicate the Business she had with them in these Words: 'I am sensible, Gentlemen', said she, 'that, through the Blindness of Fortune, and Partiality of the World, Merit frequently goes unrewarded, and that those of the best Pretensions meet with the least Encouragement: – I ask your Pardon', continued she, perceiving they seemed surprised, 'if I am mistaken in the Notion, that you two may, perhaps, be of the Number of those who have Reason to complain of the Injustice of Fate; but if you are such as I take you for, have a Proposal to make you, which may be of some little Advantage to you'. Neither of them made any immediate Answer, but appeared buried in Consideration for some Moments. At length, 'We should, doubtless, Madam', said one of them, 'willingly come into any Measure to oblige you, provided they are such as may bring us into no Danger, either as to our Persons or Reputations'.

'That which I require of you', resumed she, 'has nothing in it criminal: All that I desire is *Secrecy* in what you are entrusted, and to disguise yourselves in such a Manner as you cannot be known, if hereafter seen by the Person on whom you are to impose. – In fine, the Business is only an innocent Frolic, but if blazed abroad, might be taken for too great a Freedom in me: – Therefore, if you resolve to assist me, here are five Pieces to Drink my Health, and assure you, that I have not discoursed you on an Affair, I design not to proceed in; and when it is

---

15   *Mall*   a fashionable walk in St James's Park.   16   *Chamelion Treat*   it was once popularly believed that chamelions subsist on air.

accomplished fifty more lie ready for your Acceptance'. These Words, and, above all, the Money, which was a Sum which, 'tis probable, they had not seen of a long Time, made them immediately assent to all she desired, and press for the Beginning of their Employment: But things were not yet ripe for Execution; and she told them, that the next Day they should be let into the Secret, charging them to meet her in the same Place at an hour she appointed. 'Tis hard to say, which of these Parties went away best pleased; *they*, that Fortune had sent them so unexpected a Windfall; or *she*, that she had found Persons, who appeared so well qualified to serve her.

Indefatigable in the Pursuit of whatsoever her Humour was bent upon, she had no sooner left her new-engaged Emissaries, than she went in search of a House for the completing her Project. – She pitched on one very large, and magnificently furnished, which she hired by the Week, giving them the Money before-hand, to prevent any Inquiries. The next Day she repaired to the Park, where she met the punctual Squires of low Degree; and ordering them to follow her to the House she had taken, told them they must condescend to appear like Servants, and gave each of them a very rich Livery. Then writing a Letter to *Beauplaisir*, in a Character vastly different from either of those she had made use of, as *Fantomina*, or the fair Widow *Bloomer*, ordered one of them to deliver it into his own Hands, to bring back an Answer, and to be careful that he sifted out nothing of the Truth. – 'I do not fear', said she, 'that you should discover to him who I am, because that is a Secret, of which you yourselves are ignorant; but I would have you be so careful in your Replies, that he may not think the Concealment springs from any other Reasons than your great Integrity to your Trust. – Seem therefore to know my whole Affairs; and let your refusing to make him Partaker in the Secret, appear to be only the Effect of your Zeal for my Interest and Reputation'. Promises of entire Fidelity on the one side, and Reward on the other, being passed, the Messenger made what haste he could to the House of *Beauplaisir*; and being there told where he might find him, performed exactly the Injunction that had been given him. But never Astonishment exceeding that which *Beauplaisir* felt at the reading this Billet, in which he found these Lines:

To the All-conquering Beauplaisir.

I Imagine not that 'tis a new Thing to you, to be told, you are the greatest Charm in Nature to our Sex: I shall therefore, not to fill up my Letter with any impertinent Praises on your Wit or Person, only tell you, that I am infinite in Love with both, and if you have a Heart not too deeply engaged, should think myself the happiest of my Sex in being capable of inspiring it with some Tenderness. – There is but one Thing in my Power to refuse you, which is the Knowledge of my Name, which believing the Sight of my Face will render no Secret, you must not take it ill that I conceal from you. – The Bearer of this is a Person I can trust; send by him your Answer; but endeavour not to dive into the Meaning of this Mystery, which will be impossible to unravel, and at the same Time very much disoblige me: – But that you may be in no Apprehensions of being imposed on by a Woman unworthy of your Regard, I will venture to assure you, the first and greatest Men in the Kingdom, would think themselves blest to have that Influence over me you have, though unknown to yourself acquired. – But I need not go about to raise your Curiosity, by giving you any Idea of what my Person is; if you think fit to be satisfied, resolve to visit me To-morrow about Three in the afternoon; and though my Face is hid, you shall not want sufficient Demonstration, that she who takes these unusual Measures to commence a Friendship with you, is neither Old, nor Deformed. Till then I am,

Yours,
INCOGNITA

He had scarce come to the Conclusion, before he asked the Person who brought it, from what Place he came; – the Name of the Lady he served; – if she were a Wife, or Widow, and several other Questions directly opposite to the Directions of the Letter; but Silence would have availed him as much as did all those Testimonies of Curiosity: No *Italian Bravo*,[17] employed in a Business of the like Nature, performed his Office with more Artifice; and the impatient Enquirer was convinced that nothing but doing as he was desired, could give him any Light into the Character of the Woman who declared so violent a Passion for him; and little fearing any Consequence which could ensue from such an Encounter, resolved to rest satisfied till he was informed of every Thing from herself, not imagining this *Incognita* varied so much from the Generality of her Sex, as to be able to refuse the Knowledge of any Thing to the Man she loved with that Transcendency of Passion she professed, and which his many Successes with the Ladies gave him Encouragement enough to believe. He therefore took Pen and Paper, and answered her Letter in terms tender enough for a Man who had never seen the Person to whom he wrote. The Words were as follows:

To the Obliging and Witty
INCOGNITA.

Though to tell me I am happy enough to be liked by a Woman, such, as by your Manner of Writing, I imagine you to be, is an Honour which I can never sufficiently acknowledge, yet I know not how I am able to content myself with admiring the Wonders of your Wit alone: I am certain, a Soul like yours must shine in your Eyes with a Vivacity, which must bless all they look on. – I shall, however, endeavour to restrain myself in those Bounds you are pleased to set me, till by the Knowledge of my inviolable Fidelity, I may be thought worthy of gazing on that Heaven I am now but to enjoy in Contemplation. – You need not doubt my glad Compliance with your obliging Summons: There is a Charm in your Lines, which gives too sweet an Idea of their lovely Author to be resisted. – I am all impatient for the blissful Moment, which is to throw me at your Feet, and give me an Opportunity of convincing you that I am,

Your everlasting Slave,
BEAUPLAISIR

Nothing could be more pleased than she, to whom it was directed, at the Receipt of this Letter; but when she was told how inquisitive he had been concerning her Character and Circumstances, she could not forbear laughing heartily to think of the Tricks she had played him, and applauding her own Strength of Genius, and Force of Resolution, which by such unthought-of Ways could triumph over her Lover's Inconstancy, and render that very Temper, which to other Women is the greatest Curse, a Means to make herself more blessed. – 'Had he been faithful to me', said she, to herself, 'either as *Fantomina*, or *Celia*, or the Widow *Bloomer*, the most violent Passion, if it does not change its Object, in Time will wither: Possession naturally abates the Vigour of Desire, and I should have had, at best, but a cold, insipid, husband-like Lover in my Arms; but by these Arts of passing on him as a new Mistress whenever the Ardour, which alone makes Love a Blessing, begins to diminish, for the former one, I have him always raving, wild, impatient, longing, dying. – O that all neglected Wives, and fond abandoned Nymphs would take this Method! – Men would be caught in their own Snare, and have no Cause to scorn our easy, weeping, wailing Sex!' Thus did she pride herself as if secure she never should have any Reason to repent the present

---

[17]   *Bravo*   "A man who murders for hire" (Johnson).

Gaiety of her Humour. The Hour drawing near in which he was to come, she dressed herself in as magnificent a Manner, as if she were to be that Night at a Ball at Court, endeavouring to repair the want of those Beauties which the Vizard[18] should conceal, by setting forth the others with the greatest Care and Exactness. Her fine Shape, and Air, and Neck, appeared to great Advantage; and by that which was to be seen of her, one might believe the rest to be perfectly agreeable. *Beauplaisir* was prodigiously charmed, as well with her Appearance, as with the Manner she entertained him: But though he was wild with Impatience for the Sight of a Face which belonged to so exquisite a Body, yet he would not immediately press for it, believing before he left her he should easily obtain that Satisfaction. – A noble Collation being over, he began to sue for the Performance of her Promise of granting every Thing he could ask, excepting the Sight of her Face, and knowledge of her Name. It would have been a ridiculous Piece of Affection in her to have seemed coy in complying with what she herself had been the first in desiring: She yielded without even a Show of Reluctance: And if there be any true Felicity in an Amour such as theirs, both here enjoyed it to the full. But not in the Height of all their mutual Raptures, could he prevail on her to satisfy his Curiosity with the Sight of her Face: She told him that she hoped he knew so much of her, as might serve to convince him, she was not unworthy of his tenderest Regard; and if he could not content himself with that which she was willing to reveal, and which was the Conditions of their meeting, dear as he was to her, she would rather part with him for ever, than consent to gratify an Inquisitiveness, which, in her Opinion, had no Business with his Love. It was in vain that he endeavoured to make her sensible of her Mistake; and that this Restraint was the greatest Enemy imaginable to the Happiness of them both: She was not to be persuaded, and he was obliged to desist his Solicitations, though determined in his Mind to compass what he so ardently desired, before he left the House. He then turned the Discourse wholly on the Violence of the Passion he had for her; and expressed the greatest Discontent in the World at the Apprehensions of being separated; – swore he could dwell for ever in her Arms, and with such an undeniable Earnestness pressed to be permitted to tarry with her the whole Night, that had she been less charmed with his renewed Eagerness of Desire, she scarce would have had the Power of refusing him; but in granting this Request, she was not without a Thought that he had another Reason for making it besides the Extremity of his Passion, and had it immediately in her Head how to disappoint him.

The Hours of Repose being arrived, he begged she would retire to her Chamber; to which she consented, but obliged him to go to Bed first; which he did not much oppose, because he supposed she would not lie in her Mask, and doubted not but the Morning's Dawn would bring the wished Discovery. – The two imagined Servants ushered him to his new Lodging; where he lay some Moments in all the Perplexity imaginable at the Oddness of this Adventure. But she suffered not these Cogitations to be of any long Continuance: She came, but came in the Dark; which being no more than he expected by the former Part of her Proceedings, he said nothing of; but as much Satisfaction as he found in her Embraces, nothing ever longed for the Approach of Day with more Impatience than he did. At last it came; but how great was his Disappointment, when by the Noises he heard in the Street, the Hurry of the Coaches, and the Cries of Penny-Merchants, he was convinced it was Night no where but with him? He was still in the same Darkness as before; for she had taken care to blind the Windows in such a manner, that not the least Chink was left to let in Day. – He complained of her Behaviour in Terms that she would not have been able to resist yielding to, if she had not been certain it would have been the Ruin of her Passion: – She, therefore,

---

answered him only as she had done before; and getting out of the Bed from him, flew out of the Room with too much Swiftness for him to have overtaken her, if he had attempted it. The Moment she left him, the two Attendants entered the Chamber, and plucking down the Implements which had screened him from the Knowledge of that which he so much desired to find out, restored his Eyes once more to Day: – They attended to assist him in Dressing, brought him Tea, and by their Obsequiousness, let him see there was but one Thing which the Mistress of them would not gladly oblige him in. – He was so much out of Humour, however, at the Disappointment of his Curiosity, that he resolved never to make a second Visit. – Finding her in an outer Room, he made no Scruples of expressing the Sense he had of the little Trust she reposed in him, and at last plainly told her, he could not submit to receive Obligations from a Lady, who thought him incapable of keeping a Secret, which she made no Difficulty of letting her Servants into. – He resented, – he once more entreated, – he said all that Man could do, to prevail on her to unfold the Mystery; but all his Adjurations were fruitless; and he went out of the House determined never to re-enter it, till she should pay the Price of his Company with the Discovery of her Face and Circumstances. – She suffered him to go with this Resolution, and doubted not but he would recede from it, when he reflected on the happy Moments they had passed together; but if he did not, she comforted herself with the Design of forming some other Stratagem, with which to impose on him a fourth Time.

She kept the House, and her Gentlemen-Equipage[19] for about a Fortnight, in which Time she continued to write to him as *Fantomina* and the Widow *Bloomer*, and received the Visits he sometimes made to each; but his Behaviour to both was grown so cold, that she began to grow as weary of receiving his now insipid Caresses as he was of offering them: She was beginning to think in what Manner she should drop these two Characters, when the sudden Arrival of her Mother, who had been some Time in a foreign Country, obliged her to put an immediate Stop to the Course of her whimsical Adventures. – That Lady, who was severely virtuous, did not approve of many Things she had been told of the Conduct of her Daughter; and though it was not in the Power of any Person in the World to inform her of the Truth of what she had been guilty of, yet she heard enough to make her keep her afterwards in a Restraint, little agreeable to her Humour, and the Liberties to which she had been accustomed.

But this Confinement was not the greatest Part of the Trouble of this now afflicted Lady: She found the Consequences of her amorous Follies would be, without almost a Miracle, impossible to be concealed: – She was with Child; and though she would easily have found Means to have screened even this from the Knowledge of the World, had she been at liberty to have acted with the same unquestionable Authority over herself, as she did before the coming of her Mother, yet now all her Invention was at a Loss for a Stratagem to impose on a Woman of her Penetration: – By eating little, lacing prodigious straight, and the Advantage of a great Hoop-Petticoat, however, her Bigness was not taken notice of, and, perhaps, she would not have been suspected till the Time of her going into the Country, where her Mother designed to send her, and from whence she intended to make her escape to some Place where she might be delivered with Secrecy, if the Time of it had not happened much sooner than she expected. – A Ball being at Court, the good Old Lady was willing she should partake of the Diversion of it as a Farewell to the Town. – It was there she was seized with those Pangs, which none in her Condition are exempt from: – She could not conceal the sudden Rack which all at once invaded her; or had her Tongue been mute, her wildly rolling Eyes,

---

[19] *Equipage* "Attendance, retinue" (Johnson).

the Distortion of her Features, and the Convulsions which shook her whole Frame, in spite of her, would have revealed she laboured under some terrible Shock of Nature. – Every Body was surprised, every Body was concerned, but few guessed at the Occasion. – Her Mother grieved beyond Expression, doubted not but she was struck with the Hand of Death; and ordered her to be carried Home in a Chair, while herself followed in another. – A Physician was immediately sent for: But he presently perceiving what was her Distemper, called the old Lady aside, and told her, it was not a Doctor of his Sex, but one of her own, her Daughter stood in need of. – Never was Astonishment and Horror greater than that which seized the Soul of this afflicted Parent at these Words: She could not for a Time believe the Truth of what she heard; but he insisting on it, and conjuring her to send for a Midwife, she was at length convinced of it. – All the Pity and Tenderness she had been for some Moment before possessed of, now vanished, and were succeeded by an adequate Shame and Indignation: – She flew to the Bed where her Daughter was lying, and telling her what she had been informed of, and which she was now far from doubting, commanded her to reveal the Name of the Person whose Insinuations had drawn her to this Dishonour. – It was a great while before she could be brought to confess any Thing, and much longer before she could be prevailed on to name the Man whom she so fatally had loved; but the Rack of Nature growing more fierce, and the enraged old Lady protesting no Help should be afforded her while she persisted in her Obstinancy, she, with great Difficulty and Hesitation in her Speech, at last pronounced the Name of *Beauplaisir*. She had no sooner satisfied her weeping Mother, than that sorrowful Lady Sent Messengers at the same Time, for a Midwife, and for that Gentleman who had occasioned the other's being wanted. – He happened by Accident to be at home, and immediately obeyed the Summons, though prodigiously surprised what Business a Lady so much a Stranger to him could have to impart. – But how much greater was his Amazement, when taking him into her Closet, she there acquainted him with her Daughter's Misfortune, of the Discovery she had made, and how far he was concerned in it? – All the Idea one can form of wild Astonishment, was mean to what he felt: – He assured her, that the young Lady her Daughter was a Person whom he had never, more than at a Distance, admired: – That he had indeed, spoke to her in public Company, but that he never had a Thought which tended to her Dishonour. – His Denials, if possible, added to the Indignation she was before inflamed with: – She had no longer Patience; and carrying him into the Chamber, where she was just delivered of a fine Girl, cried out, I will not be imposed on: The Truth by one of you shall be revealed. ———*Beauplaisir* being brought to the Bed side, was beginning to address himself to the Lady in it, to beg she would clear the Mistake her Mother was involved in; when she, covering herself with the Clothes, and ready to die a second Time with the inward Agitations of her Soul, shrieked out, 'Oh, I am undone! – I cannot live, and bear this Shame!' – But the old Lady believing that now or never was the Time to dive into the Bottom of this Mystery, forcing her to rear her Head, told her, she should not hope to Escape the Scrutiny of a Parent she had dishonoured in such a Manner, and pointing to *Beauplaisir*, 'Is this the Gentleman', said she, 'to whom you owe your Ruin? or have you deceived me by a fictitious Tale?'

'Oh! no', resumed the trembling Creature, 'he is, indeed, the innocent Cause of my Undoing: – Promise me your Pardon', continued she, 'and I will relate the Means'. Here she ceased, expecting what she would reply, which, on hearing *Beauplaisir* cry you out, 'What mean you Madam? I your Undoing, who never harboured the least Design on you in my Life', she did in these Words, 'Though the Injury you have done your Family', said she, 'is of a Nature which cannot justly hope Forgiveness, yet be assured, I shall much sooner excuse you when satisfied of the Truth, than while I am kept in a Suspense, if possible, as vexatious as the Crime itself is to me'. Encouraged by this she related the whole Truth. And 'tis difficult to determine, if *Beauplaisir*, or the Lady, were most surprised at what they heard; he, that he should have been blinded so often by her Artifice; or she, that so young a Creature should have the Skill to make use of them. Both sat for some Time in a profound Revery; till at length she broke it first in these Words: 'Pardon, Sir', said she, 'the Trouble I have given you: I must confess it was with a Design to oblige you to repair the supposed Injury you had done this unfortunate Girl, by marrying her, but now I know not what to say; – The Blame is wholly hers, and I have nothing to request further of you, than that you will not divulge the distracted Folly she has been guilty of'. – He answered her in Terms perfectly polite; but made no Offer of that which, perhaps, she expected, though could not, now informed of her Daughter's Proceedings, demand. He assured her, however, that if she would commit the new-born Lady to his Care, he would discharge it faithfully. But neither of them would consent to that; and he took his Leave, full of Cogitations, more confused than ever he had known in his whole Life. He continued to visit there, to enquire after her Health every Day; but the old Lady perceiving there was nothing likely to ensue from these Civilities, but, perhaps, a Renewing of the Crime, she entreated him to refrain; and as soon as her Daughter was in a Condition, sent her to a Monastery in *France*, the Abbess of which had been her particular Friend. And thus ended an Intrigue, which, considering the Time it lasted, was as full of Variety as any, perhaps, that many Ages has produced.

FINIS

Trials at the Old Bailey (1722–1727)

Unlike the proceedings of Parliament, the sessions held in the Central Criminal Court of London (the Old Bailey) were not legally closed to journalists. Court sessions thus provided an early form of eye-witness reporting and news. As in journalism of all times, there was a sensational element in the reports, which tended to focus on trials that excited the most interest – those involving violence and sex. In making the following selection, I have followed the same time-honoured principles. I take my texts from the first edition of Select Trials at the Sessions House in the Old Bailey *(1742). In several of my notes I have taken advantage of information in the landmark study by J. M. Beattie,* Crime and the Courts in England 1660–1800 *(Princeton University Press, 1986).*

from *Select TRIALS at the Sessions House in the Old Bailey* (1742)

H——— J ———, FOR A RAPE,

1722

H——— J———, of *Alhallows*, *Lombard Street*, was indicted for assaulting, ravishing, and, against her Will, carnally knowing *Mary Hicks*, Spinster,[1] *April 29*.

H——— J———, FOR A RAPE
[1] *Spinster* "In law, the general term for a girl or maiden woman" (Johnson).

Mary Hicks. The Prisoner was Journeyman to my Master, Mr. *Allen*, a Confectioner, in *Grace-church-street*. He came hither the 29th of last Month, between 9 and 10 at Night. He went into the Kitchen, where he fell asleep. Between eleven and twelve the Family were going to Bed, and another Journeyman waked him, and said, he should lie with him;[2] but the Prisoner refused, and pretended to fall asleep again, and so he sat till the Journeyman and Boy were a-bed. A young Woman that lodged in the House was going to Bed too; but, upon my desiring her to bear me Company, because I was not willing to be left alone with the Prisoner, she came down, and stayed with me: But it was not long before the Prisoner went up into the Garret, in order, as I supposed, to go to Bed to the Apprentice. Then I and the young Woman both went up, but were greatly surprised to find that the Keys of both our Chamber Doors were taken out; and, as we had no other fastening, and suspected some Design, we were afraid to go to Bed; but, at last, as we thought it was the Prisoner who had taken the Keys out, we went up into the Garret, and asked him for them. He said, he had left them in the young Woman's Room, and would go down and show us the Place where they lay: So down we came, and all three went into the Room, and presently the Prisoner took the Key out of his Pocket, locked the Door, put the Key into his Pocket again, seized upon me, threw me down on upon the Bed, and used me in a violent Manner.

Court. What did he do to ye?

Mary Hicks. He threw up my Coats. I strove to save myself as much as I was able for half an Hour, but then I was quite spent, and could resist no longer.

Court. But did not the other Woman help you?

M. H. Yes, as far as she could; but he was so violent, that, notwithstanding all that she and I could do, he overpowered us both.

Court. He did not ravish ye both, I hope?

M. H. No; he did not offer the Thing to her.

Court. You say there was another Man and a Boy in the House.

M. H. Yes.

Court. And could not they have heard you if you had cried out?

M. H. Lord! I was quite spent and out of Breath with struggling, so that I could not call loud enough to be heard.

Court. But sure you might have called loud enough when he had begun to be rude with ye – or at least the other Woman might.

M. H. We did make what Noise we could; but the Door was locked, and the Window-shutters were nailed up, and I suppose the other Man and the Boy were fast asleep.

Court. In what Manner did he use ye?

M. H. He forced my Body with what he had.

Court. You must explain yourself.[3]

M. H. ———

Court. What followed? Did you perceive——

M. H. Yes; —— And the next Day I was so very bad that I could hardly turn myself in my Bed.

Mrs. —— I was present at the same Time. She called out for Help, and I did what I could to prevent his Rudeness with her; but I could do her no good, though I knocked as hard as I could, and would have broke open the Door, if I had been able.

---

[2] *lie with him*   beds were still scarce in the eighteenth century, and it was common for people to share them when they were guests in private homes or inns.

[3] *You must explain yourself*   conviction for rape depended upon proof that the rape had been accomplished, including full penetration.

Mr. *Allen.* I was in the Country when this Affair happened. At my coming Home I found my Maid – or House-keeper in some Disorder, and when she saw me, she cried. I inquired what was the Matter, and she gave me an Account how she had been abused.

Prisoner. Whatever I did, I did not force her, nor did she next Morning show any Resentment of the Usage that she met with over Night; for she drank Coffee with me at Breakfast.

Court to the Prosecutrix.[4] What do you say to that?

M. H. I drank Coffee next Morning with the rest of the Family, but we had half breakfasted before he came up, and then it was above half an Hour before I would let him have any.

Another Evidence[5] for the Prisoner deposed, that after he had heard of this Prosecution, he went to *Mary Hicks*, and asked her if she intended to hang the Prisoner, and that she answered, 'No, I had rather marry him than hang him'.[6]

The Jury acquitted him.

GABRIEL LAWRENCE, FOR SODOMY,
APRIL, 1726

GABRIEL LAWRENCE was indicted for committing, with *Thomas Newton*, aged thirty Years, the heinous and detestable Sin of Sodomy,[1] not to be named among Christians, *July* 20, 1725.

Thomas Newton. About the End of *June*, or the Beginning of July, one *Peter Bavidge*, who is not yet taken, and —— *Eccleston*, who died last Week in *Newgate*,[2] carried me to the House of *Margaret Clap*, who is now at the *Compter*,[3] and there I first became acquainted with the Prisoner. Mother *Clap*'s House bore the public Character of a Place of Rendezvous for Sodomites. ——For the more convenient Entertainment of her Customers, she had provided Beds in every Room in the House. She had commonly thirty or forty of such Kind of Chaps every Night, but more especially on *Sunday* Nights. I was conducted to a Bed up one Pair of Stairs, where, by the Persuasion of *Bavidge*, who was present all the while, I suffered the Prisoner to ——. He, and one *Daniel*, having attempted the same since that Time, but I refused, though they bussed[4] me, and stroked me over the Face, and said I was a very pretty fellow. —— When Mother *Clap* was taken up in *February* last, I went to put in Bail for her; at which Time Mr. *Williams* and Mr. *Willis* told me they believed I could give Information; which I promised to do: but at the End of the same Month I was taken up myself.

—— *Willis.* In *March, Newton* was set at Liberty, but he came the next Day, and made a voluntary Information.[5]

—— *Williams.* He informed against several of the Sodomites at that Time, but did not discover the Prisoner till the 2d of this Month, and then I took his Information at Sir *John Fryer*'s.

[4] *Prosecutrix* feminine form of "prosecutor," "one who pursues another by law in a criminal case."
[5] *Evidence* witness.
[6] *rather marry him than hang him* such settlements could be negotiated in or out of court and were not uncommon; conviction for rape was difficult but did occur and was punished with hanging.
GABRIEL LAWRENCE
[1] *Sin of Sodomy* "An unnatural form of sexual intercourse, esp. that of one male with another" (*OED*); it is not "named" in Johnson's *Dictionary*.

[2] *Newgate* the main prison in the City of London.
[3] *Compter* the counter or sheriff's prison, used for holding those arrested, especially on civil charges, such as debt.
[4] *bussed* kissed.
[5] *Information* "Charge or accusation exhibited" (Johnson).

Samuel Stevens. Mother *Clap*'s House was in *Field lane*, in *Hilburn*, it was next to the *Bunch of Grapes*[6] on one Side, and joined to an Arch on the other Side. It was notorious for being a *Molly-house*.[7] I have been there several Times, in order to detect those who frequented it: I have seen 20 or 30 of them together, kissing and hugging, and making Love (as they called it) in a very indecent Manner. Then they used to go out by Couples into another Room, and, when they came back, they would tell what they had been doing, which, in their Dialect, they called *Marrying*.

Joseph Sellers. I have been twice at that House, and seen the same Practices.

The Prisoner's Defence

Prisoner. I own I have been several Times at Mrs. *Clap*'s House to drink, as any other Person might do; but I never knew that it was a Resort for People that followed such Sort of Practices.

Henry Yoxan. I am a Cow-keeper, and the Prisoner is a Milk-man. I have kept him Company, and served him with Milk these eighteen Years. I have been with him at the *Oxfordshire-Feast*, where we have both got drunk, and then come Home together in a Coach, and yet he never offered any such Indecencies to me.

Samuel Pullen. I am a Cow-keeper too, and have served him with Milk several Years, but never heard any such Thing of him before.

Margaret Chapman. I have known him seven Years. He has often been at my House, and, if I had suspected any such Stories of him, he should never have darkened my Doors, I'll assure ye.

William Preston. I know him to be a very *sober* Man, and have often been in his Company when he was *drunk*, but never found any ill by him.

Thomas Fuller. Nor I either. He married my Daughter eighteen Years ago: She has been dead seven Years. He had a Child by her, which is now living, and thirteen Years old.

Charles Bell. He married my Wife's Sister. I never heard the like before of the Prisoner; but, as for the Evidence,[8] *Newton*, I know that he bears a vile Character.

The Jury found him guilty. *Death.*

He was a second Time indicted for committing Sodomy with P——, *November* 10. But, being convicted of the former, he was not tried for this.

The Ordinary's[9] Account of Gabriel Lawrence

Gabriel Lawrence, aged 43 Years, was a Papist, and did not make any particular Confessions to me. He kept the Chapel with the rest for the most part; was always very grave, and made frequent Responses with the rest, and said the Lord's Prayer and Creed after me. He owned himself of the *Romish* Communion; but said, that he had *a great liking to the Church of* England, *and could communicate with them*; but this I would not allow, unless he renounced his Error. He said *Newton* had perjured himself, and that in all his Life he had never been guilty of that detestable Sin; but that he had lived many Years with a Wife who had borne several Children, and kept a good sober House.——

---

[6] *Bunch of Grapes* a tavern with that name and, no doubt, a suitable banner, which served as an address before numbers were introduced on buildings later in the century.

[7] *Molly* "an effeminate fellow, a sodomite" (Grose's *Dictionary of the Vulgar Tongue*, 1785).

[8] *Evidence* witness.

[9] *Ordinary* the chaplain of Newgate prison, who would prepare prisoners for execution.

At the Place of Execution he said, that a certain Person had injured him when he took him before a Justice of the Peace, who committed him, in swearing or affirming, that fifteen Years ago he had been taken up for that unnatural Sin, and, that it cost him Twenty Pounds, to get himself free, which, he said, was utterly false; for, 'till this Time, he was never suspected.

He was hanged at *Tyburn*, on *Monday, May* 9, 1726.

MARY PICART, *ALIAS* GANDON, *FOR* BIGAMY, *JUNE*, 1725

MARY PICART, alias *GANDON*, was indicted for marrying *Philip Bouchain* on the 24th of *June* last, her former Husband being then living.

Paul Gandon. Mine Broder,[1] *Jean Gandon*, and dis Voman, de Preesonar, vas marie togader at de *Stapaney-Shursh*, and I vas den prasant – It is vary long time ago, – me no remamber ow long – 'tis more as twanty Year. – Dare vas de Ministar *Anglois*, dare vas de putting de Ring upon de Feengar, dare vas de putting de Hands togader, and de oder tings dat be made use of in de Marriage. Den after dis vas done da bote leeve a togader so as de Man and de Vife: and mine broder *Jean* make von, two, tree Shile upon her: But now mine Broder be grown von old Man: he no make more Shile, and so she marie vid dis oder Man *Philip Bouchain*.

Philip Bouchain. Me vas marie to dis Voman; dat is de trute, upon the twenty-four of dis Mont, a sis heures after de noon, a l'Engseigne de *Hand* and de *Pen* in de *Fleet Lane*, and my give tree Shilling and tree quartern of *Sheneva*[2] to de Parsoong. But me vas vary mush elevate vid de Liquor, and dis and dat and t'oder, so dat me no cou'd tell vat I do ven de ting vas done. But me no go to de bed vid mine Vife at all, for in tree, four heures atter de Saremonee vas over, dare come in some Relationg of mine Spouse, and dey make de grand Noise and de Uproar, dat me no could tink vat a diable vas de maiter vid 'em. But, in a leetel time da tell me dat I must no do vid mine Vife, for she vas belong to anoder Man: and so da take her avay, and me vas force to go to bed vid mine own salf.

Prisoner. Me ave but von Husband, and dat is *Jean Gandon*; for dis oder Man, *Philip Bouchain*, be none Husband for me. Vat signify de Parsoong and de Ring, all de Saremonee? Vy dat no make a de Husband ——Dare be no Husband no Vife, till da go to bed togader. But Monsieur *Bouchain* he do no vid me in bed; he do noting in de Varld.——Noting but de Saremonee.——Vy dat be no Husband.

There being no Proof that the second Marriage was consummated, the Jury acquitted the Prisoner.

RICHARD SAVAGE, JAMES GREGORY, *AND* WILLIAM MERCHANT, *FOR* MURDER, *THURSDAY, DEC.* 7, 1727[1]

Richard Savage, James Gregory, and *William Merchant* were indicted for the Murder of *James Sinclair: Savage* by giving him with a drawn Sword, one mortal Wound in the lower Part of

---

MARY PICART
[1] *Mine Broder* the report is trying to represent a foreign accent with a combination of Dutch, French, and, occasionally, Italian imitations.
[2] *Sheneva* gin.

RICHARD SAVAGE
[1] *Richard Savage* a poet and playwright who claimed to be the unacknowledged, illegitimate child of two members of the nobility; he pursued this claim in public and private attacks on his putative mother, Lady Macclesfield; after his death in 1743 Savage's memory was blessed with a powerful apologist in the famous biography by Samuel Johnson (see below, p. 838).

the Belly, of the Length of half an Inch, and the Depth of nine Inches, on the 20th of *Nov.* last, of which mortal Wound he languished till the next Day, and then died: And *Gregory* and *Merchant* by being present, aiding, abetting, comforting, and maintaining the said *Savage*, in committing the said Murder.

At the Request of the Prisoners, the Witnesses against them were examined a-part.

Mr. *Nuttal.* On *Monday* the 20th of *Nov.* about 11 at Night, the Deceased, and Mr. *Lemery*, and his Brother, and I, went to *Robinson's* Coffee-house, near *Charing Cross*, where we stayed till one or two in the Morning. We had drank two Three-Shilling Bowls of Punch, and were just concluding to go, when the Prisoners came into the Room. *Merchant* entered first, and, turning his Back to the Fire, he kicked down our Table without any Provocation. 'What do ye mean?' says I. And 'what do *you* mean?' says *Gregory*. Presently *Savage* drew his Sword, and we retreated to the farther End of the Room. *Gregory* drawing too, I desired them to put up their Swords, but they refused. I did not see the Deceased draw, but *Gregory*, turning to him, said, 'Villain, deliver your Sword': And, soon after, he took the Sword from the Deceased. *Gregory's* Sword was broke in the Scuffle; but, with the Deceased's Sword, and Part of his own, he came and demanded mine; and, I refusing to deliver it, he made a Thrust at me. I defended myself. He endeavoured to get my Sword from me; but he either fell of himself, or I threw him, and took the (Deceased's) Sword from him; and three Soldiers coming into the Room, they rescued him.——I did not see *Savage* push at the Deceased, but I heard the Deceased say, 'I am a dead Man!' And soon after the Candles were put out. I afterwards went up to the Deceased, and saw something hang out at his Belly which I took to be his Caul.[2] The Maid of the House came in, and kneeled to suck the Wound, and it was after this, that the Soldiers came in: And I and *Gregory* were carried to the Watch-house.

Gregory. Did not I say, 'Put up your Swords'.

Nuttal. There might be such an Expression, but I can't call to mind when it was spoke.

Mr. *Lemery.* I was with the Deceased, and Mr. *Nuttal*, and my Brother, at *Robinson's* Coffee-house, and we were ready to go Home, when somebody knocked at the (Street) Door. The Landlady opened it, and let in the Prisoners, and lighted them into another Room. They would not stay there, but rudely came into ours. *Merchant* kicked down the Table. Our Company all retreated. *Gregory* came up to the Deceased, and said, 'G-d damn ye, you Rascal, deliver your Sword!' Swords were drawn. *Savage* made a Thrust at the Deceased, who stooped, and cried, 'Oh!' At which *Savage* turned pale, stood for some Time astonished, and then endeavoured to get away: but I held him. The Lights were then put out. We struggled together. The Maid came to my Assistance, pullected[3] off his Hat and Wig, and clung about him. He, in striving to force himself from her, struck at her, cut her in the Head with his Sword, and at last got away. I went to a Night-cellar,[4] and called two or three Soldiers, who took him and *Merchant* in a back Court.——When *Savage* gave the Wound, the Deceased had his Sword drawn, but held it with the Point down towards the Ground, on the Left Side. As to *Merchant*, I did not see that he had any Sword.

Mr. *Nuttal* again. Nor I: Nor did I see him in the Room after the Fray began. But after the Candles were put out, he was taken with *Savage* in a back Court.

Jane Leader. I was in the Room, and saw *Savage* draw first. Then *Gregory* went up to the Deceased, and *Savage* stabbed him; and, turning back, he looked pale. The Deceased cried, 'I am dead! I am dead!'——I opened his Coat, and bid the Maid-Servant suck the Wound. She

---

[2] *Caul*   part of the membrane encasing the stomach and intestines.

[3] *pullected*   plucked, tore off.

[4] *Night-cellar*   "a tavern or other place serving as a resort at night for persons of the lowest class" (*OED*).

did, but no Blood came.——I went to see the Deceased upon his Death bed, and desired him to tell me how he was wounded. He said, that the Wound was given him by the least Man in Black.——*That* was *Savage*, for *Merchant* was in coloured Clothes, and had no Sword,——and that the tallest of them,——which was *Gregory*,——passed, or struck his Sword, while *Savage* stabbed him.——I did not see the Deceased's Sword at all, nor did he open his Lips, or speak one Word to the Prisoners.

Mrs. *Endersby*. I keep *Robinson's* Coffee house. When I let the Prisoners in, I perceived they were in Drink. I showed them a Room. They were very rude to me. I told them, if they wanted any Liquor, they should have it; but, if they did not, I desired their Absence. Upon which one of them took up a Chair, and offered to strike me with it——They went into the next Room, which is a public Coffee-Room in the Day-time. *Merchant* kicked down the Table.——Whether the other Company were sitting or standing at that Table I cannot be positive; but it is a folding Table with two Leaves, and there were two other Tables in the same Room.——Swords were drawn,——the Deceased was wounded,——and *Savage* struggled with the Maid-Servant, and cut her over the Head with his Sword.

Mary Rock, the Maid. My Mistress and I let the Prisoners into the House. My Mistress showed them a Room. *Merchant* pulled her about very rudely, and she making Resistance, he took up a Chair, and offered to strike her with it. Then asking, who was in the next Room? I answered, 'Some Company that have paid their Reckoning, and are just a going, and you have the Room to yourselves if you'll have but a little Patience': But they would not, and so they ran in. I went in not long after, and saw *Gregory* and *Savage* with their Swords drawn, and the Deceased with his Sword in his Hand, and the Point from him.——Soon after, I heard *Jane Leader* say, 'Poor Dear *Sinclair* is killed! I sucked the Wound, but it would not bleed. *Savage* endeavoured to get away, but I stopped him'.——I did not see the Wound given to the Deceased, but I afterwards saw the Encounter between Mr. *Nuttal* and Mr. *Gregory*.

Mr. *Taylor*, a Clergyman. On the 21st of *November*, I was sent for to pray by the Deceased, and, after I had recommended him to the Mercy of Almighty God, Mr. *Nuttal* desired me to ask him a few Questions; but, as I thought it not belonging to my Province, I declined it. Mr. *Nuttal* however, willing to have a Witness to the Words of a dying Man, persuaded me to stay while he himself asked a Question. And then, turning to the Deceased, he said, 'Do you know from which of the Gentlemen you received the Wound?' The Deceased answered, 'From the shortest in Black', which was Mr. *Savage*, 'the tallest commanded my Sword, and the other stabbed me'.

Rowland Holderness, Watchman. I came to the Room just after the Wound was given, and then I heard the Deceased say, 'I was stabbed barbarously before my Sword was drawn'.

'*John Wilcox*, another Watchman. I saw the Deceased leaning his Head upon his Hand, and heard him then say, 'I am a dead Man, and was stabbed cowardly'.

Mr. *Wilkey*, the Surgeon. I searched the Wound, it was on the left Side of the Belly, as high as the Navel. The Sword had grazed on the Kidney, and I believe that Wound was the Cause of his Death.

Court. Do you think this Deceased could receive that Wound in a Posture of Defence?

Mr. *Wilkey*. I believe he could not, except he was Left-handed.

The Defence of the Prisoners

Mr. *Gregory* said, That the Reason of their going into that Room, was for the Benefit of the Fire: That the Table was thrown down accidentally. That the House bore an infamous Character, and some of the Witnesses lay under the Imputation of being Persons who had no Regard to Justice and Morality.

Mr. *Savage*, having given the Court an Account of his meeting with *Gregory* and *Merchant*, and going with them to *Robinson*'s Coffee-house, made some Remarks on what had been sworn by the Witnesses, and declared, that his endeavouring to escape, was only to avoid the Inclemency, of a Jail.

And then the Prisoners called their Witnesses.

Henry Huggins, Thomas Huggins, and *Robert Fish* deposed, That they were present at the latter Part of the Quarrel, and saw Mr. *Nuttal* engaged with Mr. *Gregory*, and struggling with a Sword.——This only confirmed Part of *Nuttal's* Evidence.——They added, that the Coffee-house was a House of ill Fame.

Mary Stanly deposed, That she had seen the Deceased in a Quarrel, before *that* in which he was killed: That Mr. *Nuttal* and he were very well acquainted, and that she had seen Mrs. *Nuttal* and Mr. *Leader* in Bed together.

John Pearse deposed, That *Jane Leader* told him, that when the Swords were drawn, she went out of the Room, and did not see the Wound given: That she was a Woman of ill Reputation, and that the Coffee-house had a bad Character.

Daniel Boyle deposed, That the Deceased bore the Character of an idle Person, who had no settled Place of Residence.

John Eaton deposed, That he had known the Deceased about two Months, and had heard that his Character was but indifferent.

Mr. *Rainby* deposed, That, the Morning after the Accident, he went to the Coffee-House to enquire for Mr. *Merchant*, and then heard Mr. *Nuttal* say, that, if he had any of the Prisoners in a convenient Place, he would cut their Throats, provided he could be sure of escaping the Law.

Mr. *Cheesborough* deposed to the same Effect.

Mr. *Nuttal*. Being moved with the barbarous Treatment my Friend had met with, I believe I might say, That if I had them in an open Field, I would not have Recourse to the Law, but do them Justice myself.

Then Mr. *Nuttal* called some Gentlemen who deposed, that he was a Man of Reputation, Civility, and good Manners.

Several Persons of Distinction appeared in behalf of the Prisoners, and gave them the Characters of good-natured, quiet, peaceable Men, and by no means inclinable to be quarrelling

And the Prisoners then said, they hoped the good Characters which had been given them, the Suddenness of the unfortunate Accident, and their having no premeditated Malice, would entitle them to some Favour.

The Court, having summed up the Evidence, observed to the Jury, That as the Deceased and his Company were in Possession of the Room, if the Prisoners were the Aggressors by coming into that Room, kicking down the Table, and immediately thereupon drawing their Swords without Provocation, and the Deceased retreated, was pursued, attacked, and killed in the Manner as had been sworn by the Witnesses, it was Murder, not only in him who gave the Wound, but in the others, who aided and abetted him. That as to the Characters of the Prisoners, good Character is of Weight where the Proof is doubtful, but flies up,[5] when put in the Scale against plain and positive Evidence: And, as to the Suddenness of the Action; where there is a sudden Quarrel, and a Provocation is given by him who is killed, or where suddenly and mutually Persons attack each other and fight, and one of them is killed in the

---

[5] *flies up* does not count for much; the metaphor is that of a balance with opposing scales holding weights on either end of a balance.

Heat of Blood, it is Manslaughter. But, where one is the Aggressor, pursues the Insult, and kills the Person attacked, without any Provocation, though on a sudden, the Law implies Malice, and it is Murder.

The Trial lasted about eight Hours. The Jury found *Richard Savage* and *James Gregory* guilty of Murder, and *William Merchant* guilty of Manslaughter.

On *Monday, December* 11, being the last Day of the Sessions, *Richard Savage*, and *James Gregory*, with four other capitally convicted Prisoners, were brought again to the bar, to receive Sentence of Death. And being severally asked (as is usual on such Occasions) what they had to say, why Judgement should not be passed upon them, Mr. *Savage* addressed himself to the Court in the following Terms:

> It is now, my Lord, too late to offer any Thing by Way of Defence, or Vindication; nor can we expect ought from your Lordships, in this Court, but the Sentence which the Law requires you as Judges to pronounce against Men of our calamitous Condition.——But we are also persuaded, that as mere Men, and out of this Seat of rigorous Justice, you are susceptive of the tender Passions, and too humane, not to commiserate the unhappy Situation of those, whom the Law – sometimes perhaps – exacts from you to pronounce upon. No doubt you distinguish between Offences, which arise out of Premeditation, and a Disposition habitual to Vice or Immorality, and Transgressions, which are the unhappy and unforeseen Effects of a casual Absence of Reason, and sudden Impulse of Passion: We, therefore, hope you will contribute all you can to an Extension of that Mercy, which the Gentlemen of the Jury have been pleased to show Mr. *Merchant*, who (allowing Facts as sworn against us by the Evidence) has led us into this our Calamity. I hope, this will not be construed as if we meant to reflect upon[6] that Gentleman, or remove any Thing from us upon him, or, that we repine the more at our Fate, because he has no Participation of it: No, my Lord! For my Part, I declare nothing could more soften my Grief, than to be without any Companion in so great a Misfortune.

Mr. *Merchant* was burnt in the Hand.

At the End of the next Sessions, which was on *Saturday* the 20th of *January, Richard Savage*, and *James Gregory* were admitted to Bail, in order to their pleading the King's Pardon.[7] And, on the last Day of the following Sessions, being the 5th of *March*, 1727–8, they accordingly pleaded his Majesty's Pardon, and their bail were discharged.[8]

James Thomson (1700–1748)

Like many other poets in the eighteenth century, Thomson left home to seek fame and fortune in London. He arrived from Edinburgh, as Samuel Johnson reports in his biography, in need of a pair of shoes and with no capital except the manuscript of his poem Winter. *He finally found a publisher willing to take the manuscript for £3, and he published it in 1726 with a dedication to a prospective patron. Through the help of friends, the patron was alerted that his help had been*

---

6   *to reflect upon*   criticize.
7   *the King's Pardon*   this process would have been initiated by the judge, and he probably did so under pressure of popular sentiment stirred up by a pamphlet biography of Savage, published while the prisoner was under sentence; the report goes on to quote the pamphlet at some length.
8   *their bail were discharged*   they were released from any obligation to present themselves to the court; their sentences were dismissed.

solicited, and Thomson received a "present" of £20. On the heels of this windfall, came widespread popular excitement over Thomson's poem. He produced poems on the other seasons, and all four poems together became The Seasons, *one of the most successful publications of the century, and one of the few that suffered no loss of reputation after the "Romantic revolution" that ushered in the new aesthetic of the nineteenth century. In fact, Thomson has often been seen as a precursor of that revolution in taste.*

Thomson wrote several plays, a long historical poem called Liberty *(1735) and two cantos of a verse romance in the manner of Edmund Spenser called* The Castle of Indolence *(1748), but his reputation rests on* The Seasons. *I have chosen the first part of that poem to be printed and its first edition. It is considerably shorter than Thomson's final revision of the poem, perhaps less carefully connected, and certainly less correct. However, as Johnson said, adopting a metaphor from wine-tasting, the "race" of Thomson's verse, its own unique quality, is most clear in the original version. In choosing blank verse over heroic couplets and in representing the effects on the mind of grand natural events, Thomson sought to ally himself with epic poets, especially "the British Muse," Milton.*

The standard edition of The Seasons *is edited by James Sambrook (Clarendon Press, 1981).*

Winter. A Poem (1726)

See! Winter comes, to rule the varied Year,
Sullen, and sad; with all his rising Train,[1]
Vapours, and *Clouds*, and *Storms*: Be these my Theme,
These, that exalt the Soul to solemn Thought,
And heavenly musing. Welcome kindred Glooms!   5
Wished, wintry, Horrors, hail! – With frequent Foot,
Pleased, have I, in my cheerful Morn of Life,
When, nursed by careless *Solitude*, I lived,
And sung of Nature with unceasing Joy,
Pleased, have I wandered through your rough Domains;   10
Trod the pure, virgin, Snows, my self as pure:
Heard the Winds roar, and the big Torrent burst:
Or seen the deep, fermenting, Tempest brewed,
In the red, evening, Sky. – Thus passed the Time,
Till, through the opening Chambers of the South,   15
Looked out the joyous *Spring*, looked out, and smiled.
      Thee too, Inspirer of the toiling Swain!
Fair AUTUMN, yellow robed! I'll sing of thee,
Of thy last, tempered, Days, and sunny Calms;
When all the golden *Hours* are on the Wing,[2]   20
Attending thy Retreat, and round thy Wain,[3]
Slow-rolling, onward to the Southern Sky.
      Behold! the well-poised *Hornet*, hovering, hangs,

WINTER. A POEM
[1] *sad* serious.

[2] *the golden Hours* the horae, goddesses of the seasons.
[3] *Wain* wagon.

With quivering Pinions, in the genial Blaze;[4]
Flies off, in airy Circles: then returns,   25
And hums, and dances to the beating Ray.
Nor shall the Man, that, musing, walks alone,
And, heedless, strays within his radiant Lists,[5]
Go unchastised away. – Sometimes, a Fleece
Of Clouds, wide-scattering, with a lucid Veil,[6]   30
Soft, shadow o'er th' unruffled Face of Heaven;
And, through their dewy Sluices, shed the Sun,
With tempered Influence down. Then is the Time,
For those, whom *Wisdom*, and whom *Nature* charm,
To steal themselves from the degenerate Crowd,   35
And soar above this *little* Scene of Things:
To tread low-thoughted *Vice* beneath their Feet:
To lay their Passions in a gentle Calm,
And woo lone *Quiet*, in her silent *Walks*.
    Now, solitary, and in pensive Guise,   40
Oft, let me wander o'er the russet Mead,[7]
Or through the pining Grove; where scarce is heard
One dying Strain, to cheer the *Woodman*'s Toil:
Sad *Philomel*,[8] perchance, pours forth her Plaint,
Far, through the withering Copse. Mean while, the Leaves,   45
That, late, the Forest clad with lively Green,
Nipped by the drizzly Night, and Sallow hued,
Fall, wavering, through the Air; or shower amain,[9]
Urged by the Breeze, that sobs amid the Boughs.
Then list'ning *Hares* forsake the rustling Woods,   50
And, starting at the frequent Noise, escape
To the rough Stubble, and the rushy Fen.
The *Woodcocks*, o'er the fluctuating Main,
That glimmers to the Glimpses of the Moon,
Stretch their long Voyage to the woodland Glade:[10]   55
Where, wheeling with uncertain Flight, they mock
The nimble *Fowler*'s Aim. – Now *Nature* droops;
Languish the living Herbs, with pale Decay:
And all the *various Family* of Flowers
Their sunny Robes resign. The falling Fruits,   60
Through the still Night, forsake the Parent-Bough,
That, in the first, grey, Glances of the Dawn,
Looks wild, and wonders at the wintry Waste.
    The *Year*, yet pleasing, but declining fast,

---

[4] *genial* "That gives cheerfulness or supports life" (Johnson).
[5] *Lists* borders, but also the enclosed ground on which knights jousted.
[6] *lucid* made of light.
[7] *Mead* meadow.

[8] *Philomel* the nightingale, the bird into which Philomela is transformed when she flees from Tereus, who raped her and cut out her tongue (see Ovid, *Metamorphoses* 6.412–721).
[9] *amain* in full force.
[10] *Stretch* direct, steer.

Soft, o'er the secret Soul, in gentle Gales,[11]   65
A philosophic Melancholy breathes,
And bears the swelling Thought aloft to Heaven.
The forming *Fancy* rouses to conceive,
What never mingled with the Vulgar's Dream:[12]
Then wake the tender *Pang*, the pitying *Tear*,   70
The *Sigh* for suffering Worth, the *Wish* preferred[13]
For Humankind, the *Joy* to see them blessed,
And all the *Social Off-spring* of the Heart!
      Oh! bear me then to high, embowering, Shades;
To twilight Groves, and visionary Vales;   75
To weeping Grottos, and to hoary Caves;
Where Angel-Forms are seen, and Voices heard,
Sighed in low Whispers, that abstract the Soul,
From outward Sense, far into Worlds remote.
      Now, when the Western Sun withdraws the Day,   80
And humid *Evening*, gliding o'er the Sky,
In her chill Progress, checks the straggling Beams,
And robs them of their gathered, vapoury, Prey,
Where Marshes stagnate, and where Rivers wind,
Cluster the rolling *Fogs*, and swim along   85
The dusky-mantled Lawn: then slow descend,
Once more to mingle with their *Wat'ry Friends*.
The vivid Stars shine out, in radiant Files;
And boundless *Ether* glows, till the fair Moon[14]
Shows her broad Visage, in the crimsoned East;   90
Now, stooping, seems to kiss the passing Cloud:
Now, o'er the pure *Cerulean*, rides sublime.[15]
Wide the pale Deluge floats, with silver Waves,
O'er the sky'd Mountain, to the low-laid Vale;[16]
From the white Rocks, with dim Reflection, gleams,   95
And faintly glitters through the waving Shades.
      All Night, abundant Dews, unnoted, fall,
And, at Return of Morning, silver o'er
The Face of Mother-Earth; from every Branch
Depending, tremble the translucent Gems,[17]   100
And, quivering, seem to fall away, yet cling,
And sparkle in the Sun, whose rising Eye,
With Fogs bedimmed, portends a beauteous Day.
      Now, giddy Youth, whom headlong Passions fire,
Rouse the wild Game, and stain the guiltless Grove,   105

---

[11] *Gale*   "A wind not tempestuous, yet stronger than a breeze" (Johnson).
[12] *Vulgar*   common folk.
[13] *prefer*   "To offer solemnly" (Johnson), as a prayer.
[14] *Ether*   "The matter of the highest regions above" (Johnson).

[15] *Cerulean*   the blue of the sky.
[16] *sky'd*   "Enveloped by the skies. This is unusual and unauthorized" (Johnson, citing this passage).
[17] *Depending*   hanging.

With Violence, and Death; yet call it Sport,
To scatter Ruin through the Realms of *Love*,
And *Peace*, that thinks no Ill: But These, the *Muse*,
Whose Charity, unlimited, extends
As wide as *Nature* works, disdains to sing,   110
Returning to her nobler Theme in view –
   For, see! where *Winter* comes, himself, confessed,[18]
Striding the gloomy Blast. First Rains obscure
Drive through the mingling Skies, with Tempest foul;
Beat on the Mountain's Brow, and shake the Woods,   115
That, sounding, wave below. The dreary Plain
Lies overwhelmed, and lost. The bellying Clouds
Combine, and deepening into Night, shut up
The Day's fair Face. The Wanderers of Heaven,[19]
Each to his Home, retire; save those that love   120
To take their Pastime in the troubled Air,
And, skimming, flutter round the dimply Flood.
The Cattle, from th' untasted Fields, return,
And ask, with Meaning low, their wonted Stalls;[20]
Or ruminate in the contiguous Shade:[21]   125
Thither, the household, feathery, People crowd,[22]
The crested Cock, with all his female Train,
Pensive, and wet. Mean while, the Cottage-Swain
Hangs o'er th' enlivening Blaze, and taleful, there,
Recounts his simple Frolic: Much he talks,   130
And much he laughs, nor recks the Storm that blows[23]
Without, and rattles on his humble Roof.
   At last, the muddy Deluge pours along,
Resistless, roaring; dreadful down it comes
From the chapped Mountain, and the mossy Wild,[24]   135
Tumbling through Rocks abrupt, and sounding far:[25]
Then o'er the sanded Valley, floating, spread,[26]
Calm, sluggish, silent; till again constrained,
Betwixt two meeting Hills, it bursts a Way,
Where Rocks, and Woods o'erhang the turbid Stream.   140
There gathering triple Force, rapid, and deep,
It boils, and wheels, and foams, and thunders through.
   Nature! great Parent! whose directing Hand
Rolls round the Seasons of the changeful Year,
How mighty! how majestic are thy Works!   145
With what a pleasing Dread they swell the Soul,
That sees, astonished! and, astonished sings!

---

[18] *confessed* openly appearing.
[19] *Wanderers of Heaven* birds.
[20] *low* bellow of a cow.
[21] *ruminate* chew the cud.
[22] *People* "those who compose a community" (Johnson).
[23] *recks* minds.
[24] *chapped* cleft.
[25] *abrupt* "Broken; craggy" (Johnson).
[26] *sanded* covered with sand or silt.

You too, ye *Winds*! that now begin to blow,
With boisterous Sweep, I raise my Voice to you.
Where are your Stores, ye viewless *Beings*! say?   150
Where your aerial Magazines reserved,
Against the Day of Tempest perilous?
In what untravelled Country of the Air, –
Hushed in still Silence, sleep you, when 'tis calm?
    Late, in the louring Sky, red, fiery, Streaks[27]   155
Begin to flush about; the reeling Clouds[28]
Stagger with dizzy Aim, as doubting yet
Which Master to obey: while rising, slow,
Sad, in the Leaden-coloured East, the Moon
Wears a bleak Circle round her sullied Orb.   160
Then issues forth the Storm, with loud Control,[29]
And the thin Fabric of the pillared Air[30]
O'erturns, at once. Prone, on th' uncertain Main,
Descends th' Etherial Force, and ploughs its Waves,
With dreadful Rift: from the mid-Deep, appears,   165
Surge after Surge, the rising, wat'ry, War.
Whitening, the angry Billows roll immense,
And roar their Terrors, through the shuddering Soul
Of feeble Man, amidst their Fury caught,
And, dashed upon his Fate: Then, o'er the Cliff,   170
Where dwells the *Sea-Mew*, unconfined, they fly,[31]
And, hurrying, swallow up the sterile Shore.
    The Mountain growls; and all its sturdy *Sons*[32]
Stoop to the Bottom of the Rocks they shade:
Lone, on its Midnight-Side, and all aghast,   175
The dark, way-faring, *Stranger*, breathless, toils,
And climbs against the Blast –
Low, waves the rooted Forest, vexed, and sheds
What of its leafy Honours yet remains.
Thus, struggling through the dissipated Grove,   180
The whirling Tempest raves along the Plain;
And, on the Cottage thatched, or lordly Dome,[33]
Keen-fastening, shakes 'em to the solid Base.
Sleep, frighted, flies; the hollow Chimney howls,
The Windows rattle, and the Hinges creak.   185
    Then, too, they say, through all the burthened Air,
Long Groans are heard, shrill Sounds, and distant Sighs
That, murmured by the *Demon* of the Night,
Warn the devoted *Wretch* of Woe, and Death![34]
Wild Uproar lords it wide: the Clouds commix't,   190

---

[27] *louring* "dark, stormy, and gloomy" (Johnson).
[28] *flush* "To glow in the skin; to produce a colour in the face" (Johnson).
[29] *Control* power.
[30] *Fabric* building.

[31] *Sea-Mew* "A fowl that frequents the sea" (Johnson).
[32] *sturdy Sons* trees.
[33] *Dome* "A building; a house; a fabric" (Johnson).
[34] *devoted* cursed, doomed to destruction.

With Stars, swift-gliding, sweep along the Sky.
All Nature reels. – But hark! the *Almighty* speaks:
Instant, the chidden Storm begins to pant,
And dies, at once, into a noiseless Calm.
As yet, 'tis Midnight's Reign; the weary Clouds   195
Slow-meeting, mingle into solid Gloom:
Now, while the drowsy World lies lost in Sleep,
Let me associate with the low-browed *Night*,³⁵
And *Contemplation*, her sedate Compeer;
Let me shake off th' intrusive Cares of Day,   200
And lay the medling Senses all aside.
    And now, ye lying *Vanities* of Life!
You ever-tempting, ever-cheating Train!
Where are you now? and what is your Amount?
Vexation, Disappointment, and Remorse.   205
Sad, sickening, Thought! and yet, deluded Man,
A Scene of wild, disjointed, Visions past,
And broken Slumbers, rises, still resolved,
With new-flushed Hopes, to run your giddy Round.
    Father of Light, and Life! Thou *Good Supreme*!   210
O! teach me what is Good! teach me thy self!
Save me from Folly, Vanity and Vice,
From every low Pursuit! and feed my Soul,
With Knowledge, conscious Peace, and Virtue pure,
Sacred, substantial, never-fading Bliss!³⁶   215
    Lo! from the livid East, or piercing North,
Thick Clouds ascend, in whose capacious Womb,
A vapoury Deluge lies, to Snow congealed:
Heavy, they roll their fleecy World along;
And the Sky saddens with th' impending Storm.   220
Through the hushed Air, the whitening Shower descends,
At first, thin-wavering; till, at last, the Flakes
Fall broad, and wide, and fast, dimming the Day,
With a continual Flow. See! sudden, hoared,
The Woods beneath the stainless Burden bow,   225
Black'ning, along the mazy Stream it melts;
Earth's universal Face, deep-hid, and chill,
Is all one, dazzling, Waste. The Labourer-Ox
Stands covered o'er with Snow, and then demands
The Fruit of all his Toil. The Fowls of Heaven,   230
Tamed by the cruel Season, crowd around
The winnowing Store, and claim the little Boon,³⁷
That *Providence* allows. The foodless Wilds
Pour forth their brown *Inhabitants*; the Hare,
Though timorous of Heart, and hard beset   235

---

³⁵ *low-browed* louring, gloomy.
³⁶ *substantial* "Real; actually existing" (Johnson).

³⁷ *winnowing Store* the stored grain being winnowed
by the wind.

By death, in various Forms, dark Snares, and Dogs,
And more unpitying Men, the Garden seeks,
Urged on by *fearless* Want. The bleating Kind
Eye the bleak Heavens, and next, the glistening Earth,
With Looks of dumb Despair; then sad, dispersed,   240
Dig, for the withered Herb, through Heaps of Snow.
    Now, *Shepherds*, to your helpless Charge be kind;
Baffle the raging Year, and fill their Pens
With Food, at will: lodge them below the Blast,
And watch them strict; for from the bellowing East,   245
In this dire Season, oft the Whirlwind's Wing
Sweeps up the Burthen of whole wintry Plains,
In one fierce Blast, and o'er th' unhappy Flocks,
Lodged in the Hollow of two neighbouring Hills,
The billowy Tempest whelms; till, upwards urged,   250
The Valley to a shining Mountain swells,
That curls its Wreaths amid the freezing Sky.[38]
    Now, all amid the Rigours of the Year,
In the wild Depth of Winter, while without
The ceaseless Winds blow keen, be my Retreat   255
A rural, sheltered, solitary, Scene;
Where ruddy Fire, and beaming Tapers join
To chase the cheerless Gloom: there let me sit,
And hold high Converse with the mighty Dead.[39]
Sages of ancient Time, as Gods revered,   260
As Gods beneficent, who blessed Mankind,
With Arts, and Arms, and humanized a World.
Roused at th' inspiring Thought – I throw aside
The long-lived Volume, and, deep-musing, hail[40]
The sacred *Shades*, that, slowly-rising, pass   265
Before my wondering Eyes – First, *Socrates*,
Truth's early Champion, Martyr for his God:[41]
Solon, the next, who built his Commonweal,[42]
On Equity's firm Base: *Lycurgus*, then,[43]
Severely good, and him of rugged *Rome*,   270
Numa, who softened *her* rapacious *Sons*.[44]
Cimon sweet-soul'd, and *Aristides* just.[45]
Unconquered *Cato*, virtuous in Extreme;[46]

---

[38] *Wreaths* snowdrifts, Scottish.
[39] *Converse with the mighty Dead* a conventional description of reading.
[40] *long-lived Volume* Plutarch's *Parallel Lives* of Greeks and Romans; Plutarch wrote about all the heroes whom Thomson praises.
[41] *Martyr for his God* perhaps Platonic dialogues like *Parmenides* and Socrates' *Apology* were read as showing that Socrates was a monotheist and a prototype of Moses; he is important in Plutarch's life of Alcibiades.

[42] *Solon* (639–559 BCE), great Athenian law maker.
[43] *Lycurgus* Spartan law-giver of the ninth century BCE.
[44] *Numa* Numa Pompilius legendary second king of Rome.
[45] *Cimon* Athenian general and statesman of the fifth century BCE; *Aristides* great Athenian general of the early fifth century BCE.
[46] *Cato* Cato Uticensis, first-century BCE Roman general and statesman who killed himself rather than submit to the conquering Julius Caesar.

With that attempered Hero, mild, and firm,[47]
Who wept the Brother, while the Tyrant bled.   275
Scipio, the humane Warrior, gently brave,[48]
Fair Learning's Friend; who early sought the Shade,
To dwell, with *Innocence*, and *Truth*, retired.
And, equal to the best, the *Theban*, *He*[49]
Who, *single*, raised his Country into Fame.   280
Thousands behind, the Boast of *Greece* and *Rome*,
Whom *Virtue* owns, the Tribute of a Verse
Demand, but who can count the Stars of Heaven?
Who sing their Influence on this lower World?
But see who yonder comes! nor comes alone,   285
With *sober* State, and of *majestic* Mien,
The Sister-Muses in his Train — 'Tis He!
Maro! the best of Poets, and of Men![50]
Great *Homer* too appears, of *daring* Wing!
Parent of Song! and, *equal*, by his Side,   290
The *British Muse*, joined Hand in Hand, they walk,[51]
Darkling, nor miss their Way to Fame's Ascent.[52]
      Society divine! Immortal Minds!
Still visit thus my Nights, for *you* reserved,
And mount my soaring Soul to Deeds like yours.   295
Silence! thou lonely *Power*! the Door be thine:
See, on the hallow'd Hour, that none intrude,
Save *Lycidas*, the Friend, with Sense refined,[53]
Learning digested well, exalted Faith,
Unstudied Wit, and Humour ever gay.   300
      Clear Frost succeeds, and through the blue Serene,
For Sight too fine, th' Etherial Nitre flies,[54]
To bake the Glebe, and bind the slip'ry Flood.[55]
This of the wintry Season is the Prime;
Pure are the Days, and lustrous are the Nights,   305
Brightened with starry Worlds, till then unseen.
Mean while, the Orient, darkly red, breathes forth
An Icy Gale, that, in its mid Career,
Arrests the bickering Stream. The nightly Sky,
And all her glowing Constellations pour   310

[47] *that attempered Hero*   Timoleon [d. 337 BCE] killed his brother when he tried to usurp the government of Corinth; expelled Roman tyrants from the Greek cities of Sicily and ruled well in their stead [Thomson's note].
[48] *Scipio*   Scipio Africanus, third-century BCE Roman general who defeated Hannibal; popular support defeated an attempt by political enemies to prosecute him seventeen years later to the day; but after that he retired to his country estate.
[49] *Theban*   Pelopidas or Epaminondas fourth-century BCE friends who expelled the Spartans from Thebes [Thomson changed "Theban" to "Theban pair" in later versions of the poem and indicated whom he meant in a footnote].
[50] *Maro*   Virgil.
[51] *British Muse*   Milton.
[52] *Darkling*   because they were blind.
[53] *Lycidas*   the title of Milton's famous elegy (1638), the friend from whom the poet takes inspiration.
[54] *Nitre*   a salt thought to be borne by the North wind and impressing coldness on what it touched.
[55] *Glebe*   soil.

Their rigid Influence down: It freezes on[56]
Till Morn, late-rising, o'er the drooping World
Lifts her pale Eye, unjoyous: then appears
The various Labour of the silent Night,
The pendant Icicle, the Frost-Work fair,   315
Where thousand Figures rise, the crusted Snow,
Tho' white, made whiter, by the fining North.[57]
On blithesome Frolics bent, the youthful Swains,
While every Work of Man is laid at Rest,
Rush o'er the watry Plains, and, shuddering, view   320
The fearful Deeps below: or with the Gun,
And faithful Spaniel, range the ravaged Fields,
And, adding to the Ruins of the Year,
Distress the Feathery, or the Footed *Game*.
But hark! the nightly Winds, with hollow Voice,   325
Blow, blustering, from the South – the Frost subdued,
Gradual, resolves into a weeping Thaw.[58]
Spotted, the Mountains shine: loose Sleet descends,
And floods the Country round: the Rivers swell,
Impatient for the Day. – Those sullen Seas,   330
That wash th' ungenial Pole, will rest no more,[59]
Beneath the Shackles of the mighty North;
But, rousing all their Waves, resistless heave, –
And hark! – the length'ning Roar, continuous, runs
Athwart the rifted Main; at once, it bursts,   335
And piles a thousand Mountains to the Clouds!
Ill fares the Bark, the Wretches' last Resort,[60]
That, lost amid the floating Fragments, moors
Beneath the Shelter of an Icy Isle;
While Night o'erwhelms the Sea, and Horror looks   340
More horrible. Can human Hearts endure
Th' assembled *Mischiefs*, that besiege them round:
Unlist'ning *Hunger*, fainting *Weariness*,
The *Roar* of Winds, and Waves, the *Crush* of Ice,
Now, ceasing, now, renewed, with louder Rage,   345
And bellowing round the Main: Nations remote,
Shook from their Midnight-Slumbers, deem they hear
Portentous Thunder, in the troubled Sky.
More to embroil the Deep, Leviathan,[61]
And his unwieldy Train, in horrid Sport,   350
Tempest the loosened Brine; while, through the Gloom,
Far, from the dire, unhospitable Shore,
The Lion's Rage, the Wolf's sad Howl is heard,

---

[56] *Influence* "Power of celestial aspects operating upon terrestrial bodies and affairs" (Johnson).
[57] *fining* refining.
[58] *resolves* melts.

[59] *ungenial* "Not kind or favourable to nature" (Johnson).
[60] *Bark* a poetic name for a boat; the passage recalls *Paradise Lost* 1.203–8.
[61] *Leviathan* biblical sea-monster, the whale.

And all the fell Society of Night.[62]
Yet, *Providence*, that ever-waking *Eye*   355
Looks down, with Pity, on the fruitless Toil
Of Mortals, lost to Hope, and *lights* them safe,
Through all this dreary Labyrinth of Fate.
    'Tis done! – Dread WINTER has subdued the Year,
And reigns, tremendous, o'er the desert Plains!   360
How dead the Vegetable Kingdom lies!
How dumb the Tuneful! *Horror* wide extends
His solitary Empire. – Now, fond *Man*!
Behold thy pictured Life: pass some few Years,
Thy flow'ring SPRING, thy short-lived SUMMER's Strength,   365
Thy sober AUTUMN, fading into Age,
And pale, concluding, WINTER shuts thy Scene,
And shrouds *Thee* in the Grave – where now, are fled
Those Dreams of Greatness? those unsolid Hopes
Of Happiness? those Longings after Fame?   370
Those restless Cares? those busy, bustling Days?
Those Nights of secret Guilt? those veering Thoughts,
Flutt'ring 'twixt Good, and Ill, that shared thy Life?
All, now, are vanished! *Virtue*, sole, survives,
Immortal, Mankind's never-failing Friend,   375
His Guide to Happiness on high – and see!
'Tis come, the Glorious *Morn*! the second Birth
Of Heaven, and Earth! – awakening *Nature* hears
Th' Almighty Trumpet's Voice, and starts to Life,
Renewed, unfading. Now, th' Eternal *Scheme*,   380
That Dark Perplexity, that Mystic Maze,
Which Sight could never trace, nor Heart conceive,
To *Reason*'s Eye, refined, clears up apace.
Angels, and Men, astonished, pause – and dread
To travel through the Depths of Providence,   385
Untried, unbounded. Ye vain *Learned*! see,
And, prostrate in the Dust, adore that *Power*,
And *Goodness*, oft arraigned. See now the Cause,
Why conscious *Worth*, oppressed, in secret long
Mourned, unregarded: Why the *Good Man*'s Share   390
In Life, was Gall, and Bitterness of Soul:
Why the lone *Widow*, and her *Orphans*, pined,
In starving Solitude; while *Luxury*,
In Palaces, lay prompting her low Thought,
To form unreal Wants: why Heaven-born *Faith*,   395
And *Charity*, prime Grace! wore the *red* Marks
Of *Persecution*'s Scourge: why licensed *Pain*,
That cruel *Spoiler*, that embosomed *Foe*,
Embittered all our Bliss. Ye Good *Distressed*!

---

[62] *fell* cruel.

Ye Noble *Few*! that, here, unbending, stand   400
Beneath Life's Pressures – yet a little while,
And all your Woes are past. *Time* swiftly fleets,
And wished *Eternity*, approaching, brings
Life undecaying, Love without Allay,[63]
Pure flowing Joy, and Happiness sincere.   405

Stephen Duck (1705–1756)

*By the age of fourteen Duck was a full-time agricultural laborer earning the equivalent in
modern money of about £65 or $100 per week. By the age of twenty-five he was supporting a
wife and three children. Around this time he began to teach himself how to read and write poetry.
He got hold of Milton, Addison, Shakespeare, and Dryden, and soon he began writing verse
himself. His fame spread from his native Wiltshire to Oxford, and then to Queen Caroline, who
gave him a salary of about four times what he was making as a laborer. He became the keeper of
her library in Richmond, and later was ordained a priest and appointed to a rectory in Surrey.
Unfortunately, however, Duck became a victim of depression and drowned himself in a trout stream.
He was known to his contemporaries as "the thresher poet" after his most famous poem "The
Thresher's Labour." It was the main piece in* Poems on Several Subjects, *which ran to ten
editions in a single year, 1730. My text is based on the sixth of these and represents a little over
a third of the poem.*

from *Poems on Several Subjects* (1730)

FROM THE THRESHER'S LABOUR

But now the Field we must no longer range,   206
And yet, hard Fate! still Work for Work we change.
Back to the Barns again in haste we're sent,
Where lately so much Time we pensive spent:
Not pensive now; we bless the friendly Shade,   210
And to avoid the parching Sun are glad.
But few Days here we're destined to remain,
Before our Master calls us forth again:
'For Harvest now', says he, 'yourselves prepare,
The ripened Harvest now demands your Care.   215
Early next Morn I shall disturb your Rest,
Get all things ready, and be quickly dressed'.
Strict to his Word, scarce the next Dawn appears,
Before his hasty Summons fills our Ears.
Obedient to his Call, straight up we get,   220
And finding soon our Company complete;
With him, our Guide, we to the Wheat-Field go;

---

[63]   *without Allay*   undiminished; unstinting.

He, to appoint, and we, the Work to do.
Ye Reapers, cast your Eyes around the Field,
And view the Scene its different Beauties yield: 225
Then look again with a more tender Eye,
To think how soon it must in Ruin lie.
For once set in, where-e'er our Blows we deal,
There's no resisting of the well-whet Steel:
But here or there, where-e'er our Course we bend,   230
Sure Desolation does our Steps attend.
Thus, when *Arabia*'s Sons, in hopes of Prey,
To some more fertile Country take their way;
How beauteous all things in the Morn appear,
There Villages, and pleasing Cots are here;[1]   235
So many pleasing Objects meet the Sight,
The ravished Eye could willing gaze 'till Night:
But long e'er then, where-e'er their Troops have passed,
Those pleasant Prospects lie a gloomy Waste.

    The Morning passed, we sweat beneath the Sun,   240
And but uneasily our Work goes on.
Before us we perplexing Thistles find,
And Corn blown adverse with the ruffling Wind:[2]
Behind our Backs the Female Gleaners wait,
Who sometimes stoop, and sometimes hold a Chat.   245
Each Morn we early rise, go late to Bed,
And lab'ring hard, a painful Life we lead:
For Toils, scarce ever ceasing, press us now,
Rest never does, but on the Sabbath show,
And barely that, our Master will allow.   250
Nor, when asleep, are we secure from Pain,
We then perform our Labours o'er again:
Our mimic Fancy always restless seems,
And what we act awake, she acts in Dreams.
Hard Fate! Our Labours ev'n in Sleep don't cease,   255
Scarce *Hercules* e'er felt such Toils as these.
At length in Rows stands up the well-dried Corn,
A grateful Scene, and ready for the Barn.
Our well-pleased Master views the Sight with joy,
And we for carrying all our Force employ.   260
Confusion soon o'er all the Field appears,
And stunning Clamours fill the Workmen's Ears;
The Bells, and clashing Whips, alternate sound,
And rattling Waggons thunder o'er the Ground.
The Wheat got in, the Peas, and other Grain,   265
Share the same Fate, and soon leave bare the Plain:
In noisy Triumph the last Load moves on,

FROM THE THRESHER'S LABOUR   [2] *Corn* unreaped or unthreshed grain in general.
[1] *Cots* cottages.

The loud Huzzas proclaim the Harvest done.
Our Master joyful at the welcome Sight,
Invites us all to feast with him at Night.   270
A Table plentifully spread we find,
And Jugs of humming Beer to cheer the Mind;
Which he, too generous, pushes on so fast,
We think no Toils to come, nor mind the past.
But the next Morning soon reveals the Cheat,   275
When the same Toils we must again repeat:
To the same Barns again must back return,
To labour there for room for next Year's Corn.
        Thus, as the Year's revolving Course goes round,
No respite from our Labour can be found: 280
Like *Sisyphus,* our Work is never done,[3]
Continually rolls back the restless Stone:
Now growing Labours still succeed the past,
And growing always new, must always last.

Henry Fielding (1707–1754)

Fielding and Richardson were the two greatest novelists of their time, and it has always been a happy accident for literary critics that they are so different from each other. Fielding's best-loved novels, Joseph Andrews *(1742) and* Tom Jones *(1749), are comic and exuberant works which celebrate impulsiveness and courage, as long as a spirit of magnanimity presides over all. Richardson's world is more confined and more dangerous; civility and good-heartedness are hard won, and impulsiveness is usually evil or leads to no good. Johnson preferred Richardson (he even preferred Sarah Fielding to Henry); most modern readers have preferred Fielding, although in very recent times Richardson's stock has been on the rise. His greatest novel,* Clarissa, *did not, like* Tom Jones, *become a Hollywood blockbuster, but it did achieve a BBC television production.*

Early in his career Fielding produced numerous comedies and farces, the most famous of which is the mock heroic tragedy Tom Thumb *(1730); a bit later, he wrote a mock novel, a parody of Richardson's* Pamela *called* Shamela *(1741), complete with Swiftian preliminary matter. Then came the larger more profoundly comic novels. In between there was political journalism and numerous stories based on popular criminal cases that Fielding knew well because of his other career as a barrister and Justice of the Peace.* The Female Husband *(1746), for example, tells the sensational and severely cautionary tale of a lesbian who disguised herself as a man and married a woman. The most famous of Fielding's criminal documentaries, however, is* Jonathan Wild, *which is about the most famous criminal of the day. This work first appeared in a three-volume set called* Miscellanies *(1743). In the first volume Fielding published several essays in which he expresses some of what might loosely be called his "philosophy." I present part of one of these essays as it appeared in 1743. "An Essay on Conversation" does something to flesh out the values implicit in Fielding's great comedies, and in the darker comedy* Amelia *(1752). Fielding's*

---

[3] *Sisyphus* doomed forever to roll a rock unsuccessfully up a steep incline in Hades.

growing sobriety and his concern with disease in Amelia *may reflect his own prematurely weakening health. He went south in an attempt to cure himself and died an invalid in Lisbon at the age of forty-seven.*

from *Miscellanies* (1743)

FROM *An Essay on Conversation*

Man is generally represented as an Animal formed for and delighting in Society: In this State alone, it is said, his various Talents can be exerted, his numberless Necessities relieved, the Dangers he is exposed to can be avoided, and many of the Pleasures he eagerly affects, enjoyed. If these Assertions be as I think they are, undoubtedly and obviously certain, those few who have denied Man to be a social Animal,[1] have left us these two Solutions of their Conduct: either that there are Men as bold in Denial as can be found in Assertion; and as *Cicero* says, there is no Absurdity which some Philosopher or other hath not asserted;[2] so we may say, there is no Truth so glaring, that some have not denied it. Or else; that these Rejectors of Society borrow all their Information from their own savage Dispositions, and are indeed themselves, the only Exceptions to the above general Rule.

But to leave such Persons to those who have thought them more worthy of an Answer; there are others who are so seemingly fond of this social State, that they are understood absolutely to confine it to their own Species; and, entirely excluding the tamer and gentler, the herding and flocking Parts of the Creation, from all Benefits of it, to set up this as one grand general Distinction, between the Human and the Brute Species.

Shall we conclude this *Denial* of all Society to the Nature of Brutes, which seems to be in Defiance of every Day's Observation, to be as bold, as the Denial of it to the Nature of Men? Or, may we not more justly derive the Error from an improper understanding of this Word *Society* in too confined and special a Sense? In a Word: Do those who utterly deny it to the Brutal Nature, mean any other by Society than Conversation?

Now if we comprehend them in this Sense, as I think we very reasonably may, the Distinction appears to me to be truly just; for though other Animals are not without all Use of Society, yet this noble Branch of it seems, of all the Inhabitants of this Globe, confined to Man only, the narrow Power of communicating some few Ideas of Lust, or Fear, or Anger, which may be observable in Brutes, falling infinitely short of what is commonly meant by Conversation, as may be deduced from the Origination of the Word itself, the only accurate Guide to Knowledge. The primitive and literal Sense of this Word is, I apprehend, to turn round together;[3] and in its more copious Usage we intend by it, that reciprocal Interchange of Ideas, by which Truth is examined, Things are, in a manner, *turned round*, and sifted, and all our Knowledge communicated to each other.

In this Respect Man stands, I conceive, distinguished from and superior to all other Earthly Creatures: it is this Privilege which, while he is inferior in Strength to some, in Swiftness to others; without Horns, or Claws, or Tusks to attack them, or even to defend himself against them, hath made him Master of them all. Indeed, in other Views, however

---

FROM *An Essay on Conversation*
[1] *few who have denied Man to be a social Animal* Hobbes, among them (see the selection from Hobbes p. 9 above).

[2] *Cicero says . . . asserted* De Divinatione 2.58.
[3] *turn round together* Latin *versare*, to turn round, and *con*, together.

vain Men may be of their Abilities, they are greatly inferior to their animal Neighbours. With what Envy must a Swine, or a much less voracious Animal, be surveyed by a Glutton; and how contemptible must the Talents of other Sensualists appear, when opposed, perhaps, to some of the lowest and meanest of Brutes: but in Conversation Man stands alone, at least in this Part of the Creation;[4] he leaves all others behind him at his first Start, and the greater Progress he makes, the greater Distance is between them.

Conversation is of three Sorts. Men are said to converse with God, with themselves, and with one another. The two first of these have been so liberally and excellently spoken to by others, that I shall at present, pass them by, and confine myself, in this Essay to the third only: Since it seems to me amazing, that this grand Business of our Lives, the Foundation of every Thing, either useful or pleasant, should have been so slightly treated of; that while there is scarce a Profession or Handicraft in Life, however mean and contemptible, which is not abundantly furnished with proper Rules to the attaining its Perfection, Men should be left almost totally in the Dark, and without the least Light to direct, or any Guide to conduct them in the proper exerting of those Talents, which are the noblest Privilege of human Nature, and productive of all rational Happiness; and the rather as this Power is by no means self-instructed, and in the Possession of the artless and ignorant, is of so mean Use, that it raises them very little above those Animals who are void of it.

As Conversation is a Branch of Society, it follows, that it can be proper to none who is not in his Nature social. Now Society is agreeable to no Creatures who are not inoffensive to each other; and we therefore observe in Animals who are entirely guided by Nature, that it is cultivated by such only, while those of more noxious Disposition addict themselves to Solitude, and, unless when prompted by Lust, or that necessary Instinct implanted in them by Nature, for the Nurture of their Young, shun as much as possible the Society of their own Species. If therefore there should be found some human Individuals of so savage a Habit,[5] it would seem they were not adapted to Society, and consequently, not to Conversation: nor would any Inconvenience ensue the Admittance of such Exceptions, since it would by no means impeach the general Rule of Man's being a social Animal; especially when it appears (as is sufficiently and admirably proved by my Friend, the author of *An Enquiry into Happiness*)[6] that these Men live in a constant opposition to their own Nature, and are no less Monsters than the most wanton Abortions, or extravagant[7] Births.

Again; if Society requires that its Members should be inoffensive, so the more useful and beneficial they are to each other, the more suitable are they to the social Nature, and more perfectly adapted to its Institution: for all Creatures seek their own Happiness, and Society is therefore natural to any, because it is naturally productive of this Happiness. To render therefore any Animal social is to render it inoffensive; an Instance of which is to be seen in those the Ferocity of whose Nature can be tamed by Man. And here the Reader may observe a double Distinction of Man from the more savage Animals by Society, and from the social by Conversation.

But if Men were merely inoffensive to each other, it seems as if Society and Conversation would be merely indifferent; and that in order to make it desirable by a sensible Being,[8] it is necessary we should go further, and propose some positive Good to ourselves from it; and this presupposes not only negatively, our not receiving any Hurt; but positively, our receiving some Good, some Pleasure or Advantage from each other in it, something which we could not

---

4   *this Part of Creation*   the known universe.
5   *Habit*   nature, frame of mind.
6   *Friend . . . Happiness*   James Harris (1709–80).

7   *extravagant*   "Irregular; wild" (Johnson).
8   *a sensible Being*   one with feelings.

find in an unsocial and solitary State: otherwise we might cry out with the right honourable poet;

> Give us our Wildness and our Woods,
> Our Huts and Caves again.[9]

The Art of pleasing or doing Good to one another is therefore the Art of Conversation. It is this Habit which gives it all its Value. And as Man's being a social Animal . . . presupposes a natural Desire or Tendency this Way, it will follow, that we can fail in attaining this truly desirable End from Ignorance only in the Means; and how general this Ignorance is, may be, with some Probability, inferred from our want of even a Word to express this Art by: that which comes the nearest to it, and by which, perhaps, we would sometimes intend it, being so horribly and barbarously corrupted, that it contains at present scarce a simple Ingredient of what it seem originally to have been designed to express.

The Word I mean is *Good Breeding*; a Word, I apprehend, not at first confined to Externals, much less to any particular Dress or Attitude of the Body: nor were the Qualifications expressed by it to be furnished by a Milliner, a Tailor, or a Periwig-maker; no, nor even by a Dancing-Master himself. According to the Idea I myself conceive from this Word, I should not have scrupled to call Socrates a well-bred Man, though I believe he was very little instructed by any of the Persons I have above enumerated. In short, by *Good Breeding* (notwithstanding the corrupt Use of the Word in a very different Sense) I mean the Art of pleasing, or contributing as much as possible to the Ease and Happiness of those with whom you converse. I shall contend therefore no longer on this Head: for whilst my Reader clearly conceives the Sense in which I use this Word, it will not be very material whether I am right or wrong in its original Application.

Good Breeding then, or the *Art of pleasing in Conversation*, is expressed two different Ways, viz. in our Actions and our Words, and our Conduct in both may be reduced to that concise, comprehensive Rule in Scripture; 'Do unto all Men as you would they should do unto you'.[10] Indeed, concise as this Rule is, and plain as it appears, what are all Treatises on Ethics, but Comments upon it? And whoever is well-read in the Book of Nature, and hath made much Observation on the Actions of Men, will perceive so few capable of judging, or rightly pursuing their own Happiness, that he will be apt to conclude that some Attention is necessary (and more than is commonly used) to enable Men to know truly, 'what they would have done unto them', or at least, what it would be their interest 'to have done'.

If therefore Men, through Weakness or Inattention, often err in their Conceptions of what would produce their own Happiness, no wonder they should miss in the Application of what will contribute to that of others; and thus we may, without too severe a Censure on their Inclinations, account for that frequent Failure in true *Good Breeding*, which daily Experience gives us Instances of.

Besides, the Commentators have well paraphrased on the abovementioned divine rule, that it is, to 'do unto Men what you would they', IF THEY WERE IN YOUR SITUATION AND CIRCUMSTANCES, AND YOU IN THEIRS, 'should do unto you': and as this Comment is necessary to be observed in Ethics, so it is particularly useful in this our Art, where the Degree[11] of the Person is always to be considered, as we shall explain more at large hereafter.

---

9 *Give . . . again* The Duke of Buckingham [from his play *Julius Caesar*; Fielding's note].

10 *Do unto all Men as you would they should do unto you* Matthew 7.12

11 *Degree* place in society.

We see then a possibility for a Man well disposed to this Golden Rule, without some Precautions, to err in the Practice; nay, even Good-Nature itself, the very Habit of Mind most essential to furnish us with true *Good Breeding*, the latter so nearly resembling the former, that it hath been called, and with the appearance at least of Propriety, artificial *Good Nature*. The excellent Quality itself sometimes shoots us beyond the Mark, and shows the Truth of those lines in *Horace*:

> Insani sapiens nomen ferat, aequus iniqui,
> Ultra quam satis est, Virtutem si petat ipsam.[12]

Instances of this will be naturally produced where we show the Deviations from those Rules, which we shall now attempt to lay down.

As this *Good Breeding* is the Art of pleasing, it will be first necessary, with the utmost Caution, to avoid hurting or giving any Offence to those with whom we converse. And here we are surely to shun any kind of actual Disrespect, or Affront to their Persons, by Insolence, which is the severest Attack that can be made on the Pride of Man, and of which *Florus*[13] seems to have had no inadequate Opinion, when speaking of the second *Tarquin*,[14] he says; 'In omnes superbia (quae Crudelitate gravior est Bonis) grassatus'; 'He trod on all with INSO-LENCE, which sits heavier on Men of great Minds than Cruelty itself'. If there is any Temper in Man which more than all others disqualifies him for Society, it is this Insolence or Haughtiness, which, blinding a Man to his own Imperfections, and giving him a Hawk's Quick-sightedness to those of others, raises in him that Contempt for his Species, which inflates the Cheeks, erects the Head, and stiffens the Gait of those strutting Animals who sometimes stalk in Assemblies, for no other Reason, but to show in their Gesture and Behaviour the Disregard they have for the Company. Though to a truly great and philosophi-cal Mind, it is not easy to conceive a more ridiculous Exhibition than this Puppet; yet to others he is little less than a Nuisance; for Contempt is a murderous Weapon, and there is this Difference only between the greatest and weakest Men, when attacked by it; that, in order to wound the former, it must be just; whereas without the Shields of Wisdom and Philosophy, which God knows are in the possession of very few, it wants no Justice to point it; but is certain to penetrate, from whatever Corner it comes. It is this Disposition which inspires the empty *Cacus* to deny his Acquaintance, and overlook Men of Merit in Distress; and the little, silly, pretty *Phillida*, or *Foolida*, to stare at the strange Creatures round her. It is this Temper which constitutes the supercilious Eye, the reserved Look, the distant Bow, the scornful Leer, the affected Astonishment, the loud Whisper, ending in a Laugh directed full in the Teeth of another. Hence spring, in short, those numberless Offences given too frequently, in public and private Assemblies, by Persons of weak Understandings, indelicate Habits, and so hungry and foul-feeding a Vanity, that it wants to devour whatever comes in its way. Now, if *Good Breeding* be what we have endeavoured to prove it, how foreign, and indeed how opposite to it, must such a Behaviour be? And can any Man call a Duke or a Duchess who wears it, well-bred? or are they not more justly entitled to those inhuman Names which they themselves allot to the lowest Vulgar?[15] But behold a more pleasing Picture on the reverse. See the Earl

---

[12] *Insani . . . ipsam*   "Let the wise man bear the name of madman, the just of unjust, should he pursue Virtue herself beyond due bounds" (*Epistles* 1.6.15–16; Loeb translation).

[13] *Florus*   Roman historian of the second century CE (his *Epitomae* are cited here).
[14] *Tarquin*   Tarquin the Proud, seventh king of Rome (sixth century BCE).
[15] *Vulgar*   common people.

of C[hesterfield][16] noble in his Birth, splendid in his Fortune, and embellished with every Endowment of Mind; how affable, how condescending![17] himself the only one who seems ignorant that he is in every way the greatest Person in the Room.

But it is not sufficient to be inoffensive, we must be profitable Servants to each other; we are, in the second Place, to proceed to the utmost Verge in paying the Respect due to others. We had better go a little too far than stop short in this Particular . . .

It would be tedious, and perhaps impossible, to specify every Instance, or to lay down exact Rules for our Conduct in every minute Particular. However, I shall mention some of the chief which most ordinarily occur, after premising, that the Business of the whole is no more than to convey to others an Idea of your Esteem of them, which is indeed the Substance of all the Compliments, Ceremonies, Presents, and whatever passes between well-bred People. And here I shall lay down these Positions.

First, that all mere Ceremonies exist in *Form* only, and have in them no Substance at all; but being imposed by the laws of Custom, become essential to Good Breeding, from those high-flown Compliments paid to the Eastern Monarchs, and which pass between *Chinese* Mandarins, to those coarser Ceremonials in use between *English* Farmers and *Dutch* Boors.

Secondly, that these Ceremonies, poor as they are, are of more Consequence than they at first appear, and, in Reality, constitute the only external Difference between Man and Man. Thus, His Grace, Right Honourable, My Lord, Right Reverend, Reverend, Honourable, Sir, Esquire, Mr. &c. have in a philosophical Sense, no meaning, yet are, perhaps, politically essential, and must be preserved by *Good Breeding*; because,

Thirdly, They raise an Expectation in the Person by Law and Custom entitled to them, and who will consequently be displeased with the Disappointment.

Now, in order to descend minutely into any rules for Good Breeding, it will be necessary to lay some Scene, or to throw our Disciple into some particular Circumstance. We will begin then with a Visit in the Country; and as the principal Actor on this Occasion is the Person who receives it, we will, as briefly as possible, lay down some general Rules for his Conduct; marking, at the same time, the principal Deviations we have observed on these Occasions.

When an expected Guest arrives to Dinner at your House, if your Equal, or indeed not greatly your Inferior, he should be sure to find your Family in some Order, and yourself dressed and ready to receive him at your Gate with a smiling Countenance. This infuses an immediate Cheerfulness into your Guest, and persuades him of your Esteem and desire of his Company. Not so is the Behaviour of *Polysperchon*, at whose Gate you are obliged to knock a considerable Time before you gain Admittance. At length, the Door being opened to you by a Maid, or some improper Servant, who wonders where the Devil all the Men[18] are; and being asked if the Gentleman is at Home, answers, She believes so; you are conducted into a Hall, or back Parlour, where you stay some Time, before the Gentleman, in dishabile from his Study or his Garden, waits upon you, asks Pardon, and assures you he did not expect you so soon.

Your Guest, being introduced into a Drawing-Room, is after the first Ceremonies, to be asked whether he will refresh himself after his Journey, before Dinner (for which he is never to stay[19] longer than the usual or fixed hour). But this request is never to be repeated oftener

---

[16] *C[hesterfield]*   Philip Stanhope, fourth Earl of Chesterfield (1694–1773).

[17] *condescending* from "to condescend," "To depart from the privileges of superiority by a voluntary submission; to sink willingly to equal terms with inferiors; to soothe with familiarity" (Johnson).

[18] *Men* male servants, who were responsible for answering the door.

[19] *stay* wait.

than twice, in imitation of *Chalepus*, who, as if hired by a Physician, crams Wine in a Morning down the Throats of his most temperate Friends, their Constitutions being not so dear to them as their present Quiet.

When Dinner is on the Table, and the Ladies have taken their Places, the Gentlemen are to be introduced into the Eating-Room, where they are to be seated with as much seeming Indifference as possible, unless there be any present whose Degrees claim an undoubted Precedence. As to the rest, the general Rules of Precedence are by Marriage, Age, and Profession. Lastly in placing your Guests, Regard is rather to be had to Birth than Fortune; for though Purse-Pride is forward enough to exalt itself, it bears a Degradation with more secret Comfort and Ease than the former, as being more inwardly satisfied with itself, and less apprehensive of Neglect or Contempt . . .

When Dinner is ended, and the Ladies retired, though I do not hold the Master of the Feast obliged to Fuddle[20] himself through Complacence;[21] and indeed it is his own Fault generally, if his Company be such as would desire it, yet he is to see that the Bottle circulate sufficiently to afford every Person present a moderate Quantity of Wine, if he chooses it; at the same time permitting those who desire it, either to pass the Bottle, or to fill their Glass as they please. Indeed, the beastly Custom of besotting, and ostentatious Contention for Pre-eminence in their Cups, seems at present pretty well abolished among the better sort of people. Yet *Methus* still remains, who measures the Honesty and Under-standing of Mankind by the Capaciousness of their Swallow; who sings forth the Praises of a Bumper, and complains of the Light in your Glass; and at whose Table it is as difficult to preserve your Senses, as to preserve your Purse at a gaming Table or your Health at a B[audy] House . . .

Let us now consider a little the Part which the Visitor himself is to act. And first, he is to avoid the two Extremes of being too early, or too late, so as neither to surprise his Friend unawares or unprovided, nor detain him too long in Expectation. *Orthrius*, who hath nothing to do, disturbs your Rest in a Morning; and the frugal *Chronophidus*, lest he should waste some Minutes of his precious Time, is sure to spoil your Dinner . . .

Never refuse any Thing offered you out of Civility, unless in preference of a Lady, and that no oftener than once; for nothing is more truly Good Breeding, than to avoid being troublesome. Though the Taste and Humour of the Visitor is to be chiefly considered, yet is some Regard likewise to be had to that of the Master of the House; for otherwise your company will be rather a Penance than a Pleasure. *Methus* plainly discovers his Visit to be paid to his sober Friend's Bottle; nor will *Philopasus* abstain from Cards, though he is certain they are agreeable only to himself; whilst the slender *Leptines* gives his fat Entertainer a Sweat, and makes him run the Hazard of breaking his Wind[22] up his own Mounts.

If Conveniency allows your staying longer than the Time proposed, it may be civil to offer to depart, lest your Stay may be incommodious to your Friend: but if you perceive the contrary, by his Solicitations, they should be readily accepted; without tempting him to break these Rules we have above laid down for him; causing a Confusion in his Family, and among his Servants, by Preparations for your Departure. Lastly, when you are resolved to go, the same Method is to be observed which I have prescribed at your Arrival. No tedious Ceremonies of taking leave: not like *Hyperphylus*, who bows and kisses and squeezes by the Hand as heartily, and wishes you as much Health and Happiness, when he is going a Journey home of ten Miles, from a common Acquaintance, as if he was leaving his nearest Friend or Relation on a Voyage to the East-Indies . . .

---

[20]   *Fuddle*   "To make drunk" (Johnson).
[21]   *Complacence*   civility.

[22]   *breaking his Wind*   hurting his respiratory organs; a casualty of horses.

{Here Fielding begins his section on proper behavior in public assemblies.}

But as there are are many who will not in the least Instance mortify their own Humour to purchase the Satisfaction of all Mankind, so there are some who make no Scruple of satisfying their own Pride and Vanity, at the Expense of the most cruel Mortification of others. Of this kind is *Agroicus*, who seldom goes to an Assembly, but he affronts half his Acquaintance, by overlooking or disregarding them.

As this is a very common Offence, and indeed much more criminal, both in its Cause and Effect than is generally imagined, I shall examine it very minutely; and I doubt not but to make it appear, that there is no Behaviour (to speak like a Philosopher) more contemptible, not, in a civil sense, more detestable than this.

The first Ingredient in this Composition is PRIDE, which, according to the doctrine of some,[23] is the universal Passion. There are others who consider it as the Foible of great Minds; and others again, who will have it to be the very Foundation of Greatness; and perhaps it may be of that Greatness which we have endeavoured to expose in many parts of these Works: but to real Greatness, which is the Union of a good Heart with a good Head, it is almost diametrically opposite as it generally proceeds from the Depravity of both, and almost certainly from the Badness of the latter. Indeed, a little Observation will show us, that Fools are the most addicted to this Vice; and a little Reflection will teach us, that it is incompatible with true understanding. Accordingly we see, that while the wisest of Men have constantly lamented the Imbecility and Imperfection of their own Nature, the meanest and weakest have been trumpeting forth their own Excellencies, and triumphing in their own Sufficiency.

PRIDE may, I think, be properly defined, 'the Pleasure we feel in contemplating our own superior Merit, on *comparing* it with that of others. That it arises from this supposed superiority is evident: for however great you admit a Man's Merit to be, if all Men were equal to him, there would be no Room for Pride: now if it stop here, perhaps there is no enormous Harm in it, or at least, no more than is common to all other Folly, every Species of which is always liable to produce every Species of Mischief: Folly I fear it is; for should the Man estimate rightly on this Occasion, and the Balance should fairly turn on his Side in this particular Instance; should he be indeed a greater Orator, Poet, General; should he be more wise, witty, learned, young, rich, healthy, or in whatever Instance he may excel one, or many, or all; yet, if he examine himself thoroughly, will he find no Reason to abate his Pride? Is the Quality, in which he is so eminent, so generally or justly esteemed; is it so entirely his own? Doth he not rather owe his Superiority to the Defects of others, than to his own Perfection? Or, lastly, can he find in no part of his Character, a weakness which may counterpoise this Merit, and which as justly, at least, threatens him with Shame, as this entices him to Pride? I fancy, if such a Scrutiny was made (and nothing so ready as good Sense to make it), a proud Man would be as rare as in Reality he is a ridiculous Monster. But suppose a Man, on this Comparison, is (as may sometimes happen) a little partial to himself, the Harm is to himself, and he becomes only ridiculous from it. If I prefer my Excellence in poetry to Pope or Young:[24] if an inferior Actor should, in his opinion, exceed Quin or Garrick;[25] or a sign-post painter set himself above the inimitable Hogarth;[26] we become only ridiculous by our Vanity; and the Persons themselves, who are thus humbled in the Comparison, would laugh with more Reason than any other. PRIDE therefore, hitherto, seems an inoffensive Weakness only,

[23] *some* Hobbes, among others.
[24] *Young* Edward Young (1683–1765), a highly esteemed poet of the age.
[25] *Quin or Garrick* James Quin (1693–1766), preceded David Garrick (1717–79) as England's preeminent actor.
[26] *Hogarth* William Hogarth (1697–1764), most famous for his satirical drawings.

and entitles a man to no worse an Appellation than that of a FOOL: but it will not stop here; though FOOL be perhaps no desirable term, the proud Man will deserve worse: he is not contented with the Admiration he pays himself; he now becomes ARROGANT, and requires the same Respect and Preference from the World; for Pride, though the greatest of Flatterers, is by no means a profitable Servant to itself; it resembles the Parson of the Parish more than the Squire, and lives rather on the Tithes, oblations and contributions it collects from others, than on its own Demesne. As Pride therefore is seldom without Arrogance, so is this never to be found without Insolence. The Arrogant Man must be Insolent, in order to attain his own Ends: and to convince and remind Men of the Superiority he affects, will naturally, by ill Words, Actions, and Gestures, endeavour to throw the despised Person at as much Distance as possible from him. Hence proceeds that supercilious Look, and all those visible Indignities with which Men behave in Public, to those whom they fancy their Inferiors. Hence the very notable custom of deriding and often denying the nearest Relations, Friends, and Acquaintance, in Poverty and Distress; lest we should anywise be levelled with the Wretches we despise either in their own Imagination, or in the Conceit of any who should behold Familiarities pass between us.

But besides Pride, Folly, Arrogance, and Insolence, there is another simple[27] (which Vice never willingly leaves out of any Composition) and that is Ill-Nature. A good-natured Man may indeed (provided he is a Fool) be Proud, but Arrogant and Insolent he cannot be; unless we will allow to such a still greater Degree of Folly, and Ignorance of human Nature; which may indeed entitle them to Forgiveness, in the benign Language of Scripture, because 'they know not what they do'.[28]

For when we come to consider the Effect of this Behaviour on the Person who suffers it, we may perhaps have Reason to conclude, that Murder is not a much more cruel Injury. What is the Consequence of this Contempt? or indeed, What is the Design of it, but to expose the Object of it to Shame? a Sensation as uneasy, and almost as intolerable, as those which arise from the severest Pains inflicted on the Body: a convulsion of the Mind (if I may so call it) which immediately produces Symptoms of universal Disorder in the whole Man; which hath sometimes been attended with Death itself, and to which Death hath, by great Multitudes, been with much Alacrity preferred. Now, what less than the highest Degree of Ill-Nature can permit a Man to pamper his own Vanity at the Price of another's Shame? Is the Glutton, who, to raise the Flavour of his Dish, puts some Bird or Beast to exquisite Torment, more cruel to the Animal, than this our proud Man to his own Species?

This Character then is a Composition made up of those odious comtemptible Qualities, Pride, Folly, Arrogance, Insolence, and Ill-Nature. I shall dismiss it with some general Observations, which will place it in so ridiculous a Light, that a Man must hereafter be possessed of a very considerable Portion, either of Folly or Impudence, to assume it.

First, it proceeds on one grand Fallacy: for whereas this Wretch is endeavouring, by a supercilious Conduct, to lead the Beholder into an Opinion of his Superiority to the despised Person, he inwardly flatters his own Vanity with a deceitful Presumption, that this his Conduct is founded on a general pre-conceived Opinion of this Superiority.

Secondly, this Caution to preserve it, plainly indicates a Doubt,[29] that the Superiority of our own Character is very slightly established; for which Reason we see it chiefly practised by Men who have the weakest Pretensions to the Reputation they aim at: and indeed, none was

---

[27] *simple* element.
[28] *"they know not what they do"*   Jesus's words at Luke 23: 24.

[29] *Doubt* suspicion.

ever freer from it than that noble Person whom we have already mentioned in this essay, and who can never be mentioned but with Honour, by those who know him.[30]

Thirdly, this Opinion of our Superiority is commonly very erroneous. Who hath not seen a General behaving in this supercilious Manner to an Officer of lower Rank, who hath been greatly his Superior in that very Art, to his Excellence in which the General ascribes all his Merit. Parallel Instances occur in every other Art, Science, or Profession.

Fourthly, Men who excel others in trifling Instances, frequently cast a supercilious Eye on their Superiors in the highest. Thus the least Pretensious to Pre-eminence in Title, Birth, Riches, Equipage, Dress, &c. constantly overlook the most noble Endowments of Virtue, Honour, Wisdom, Sense, Wit, and every other Quality which can truly dignify and adorn a Man.

Lastly, the lowest and meanest of our Species are the most strongly addicted to this Vice. Men who are a scandal to their Sex, and Women who disgrace Human Nature: for the basest Mechanic[31] is so far from being exempt, that he is generally the most Guilty of it. It visits Ale-Houses and Gin-Shops, and whistles in the empty Heads of Fiddlers, Mountebanks, and Dancing-Masters.

To conclude a Character, on which we have already dwelt longer than is consistent with the intended Measure of this Essay: this Contempt of others is the truest Symptom of a base and a bad Heart. While it suggests itself to the Mean and the Vile, and tickles their little Fancy on every Occasion, it never enters the great and good Mind, but on the strongest Motives, nor is it then a welcome Guest, affording only an uneasy Sensation, and brings always with it a Mixture of Concern and Compassion.

We will now proceed to inferior Criminals in Society . . . {after these, Fielding goes on to discuss the rules for speech in conversation, including those for conducting the proper sort of good-natured raillery}

I shall conclude this Essay with these two Observations, which I think may be clearly deduced from what hath been said.

First, that every Person who indulges his Ill-Nature or Vanity, at the Expense of others; and in introducing Uneasiness, Vexation, and Confusion into Society, however exalted or high-titled he may be, is thoroughly Ill-Bred.

Secondly, that whoever, from the Goodness of his Disposition or Understanding, endeavours to his utmost to cultivate the Good-Humour and Happiness of others, and to contribute to the Ease and Comfort of all his Acquaintance, however low in Rank Fortune may have placed him, or however clumsy he may be in his Figure or Demeanour, hath, in the truest Sense of the Word, a claim to Good-Breeding.

Mary Jones (d. 1778)

Jones lived all her life in Oxford with her brother River Jones, who was the Chanter at Christ Church College. She had very little money or social standing. Her poverty is a subject in her poetry, but it fuels mostly comic rather than pathetic expressions of her lot in life. She associated with the Oxford professor Thomas Warton, and through him became friends with Samuel Johnson. She published one book, Miscellanies in Prose and Verse *(1750), the first forty-six pages of which*

---

[30] *him* Lord Chesterfield.   [31] *Mechanic* manual labourer.

are devoted to listing the names of the subscribers. The following selections come from that lone volume.

from *Miscellanies in Prose and Verse* (1750)

SOLILOQUY, ON AN EMPTY PURSE

Alas! my Purse! how lean and low!
My silken Purse! what art thou now!
Once I beheld – but stocks will fall –
When *both* thy ends had *wherewithal*.
When I within thy slender fence   5
My fortune placed, and confidence;
A poet's fortune! – not immense:
Yet, mixed with keys, and coins among,
Chinked to the melody of song.

    Canst thou forget, when, high in air,   10
I saw thee flutt'ring at a fair?
And took thee, destined to be sold,
My lawful Purse, to *have* and *hold*?
Yet used so oft to disembogue,[1]
No prudence could thy fate prorogue.[2]   15
Like wax thy silver melted down,
Touch but the brass, and lo! 'twas gone:
And gold would never with thee stay,
For gold had wings, and flew away.

    Alas! my Purse! yet still be proud,   20
For see the *Virtues* round thee crowd!
See, in the room of paltry wealth,[3]
Calm Temp'rance rise, the nurse of Health;
And Self-denial, slim and spare,
And Fortitude, with look severe;   25
And Abstinence, to leanness prone,
And Patience, worn to skin and bone:
Prudence and Foresight on thee wait,
And Poverty lies here in state!
Hopeless her spirits to recruit,[4]   30
For every Virtue is a mute.

    Well then, my Purse, thy sabbaths keep;
Now thou art empty, I shall sleep.
No silver sounds shall thee molest,
Nor golden dreams disturb my breast.   35
Safe shall I walk the streets along,
Amidst temptations thick and strong;

SOLILOQUY, ON AN EMPTY PURSE
[1] *disembogue* to pour out; to flow.
[2] *prorogue* delay or protract.

[3] *room* place.
[4] *recruit* "To repair any thing wasted by new supplies" (Johnson).

Catched by the eye, no more shall stop
At *Wildey*'s toys, or *Pinchbeck*'s shop;[5]
Nor cheap'ning *Payne*'s ungodly books,[6]   40
Be drawn aside by pastry cooks:
But fearless now we both may go
Where *Ludgate*'s Mercers bow so low;[7]
Beholding all with equal eye,
Nor moved at – 'Madam, what d'ye buy?'   45

   Away, far hence each worldly care!
Nor dun nor pick-purse shalt Thou fear,[8]
Nor flatt'rer base annoy My ear.
Snug shalt thou travel through the mob,
For who a Poet's purse will rob?   50
And softly sweet in garret high[9]
Will I thy virtues magnify;
Out-soaring flatt'rers' stinking breath,
And gently rhyming rats to death.

AFTER THE SMALL POX

When skilful traders first set up,
To draw the people to their shop,
They straight hang out some gaudy sign,
Expressive of the goods within.
The Vintner has his boy and grapes,   5
The Haberdasher thread and tapes,
The Shoemaker exposes boots,
And Monmouth Street old tattered suits,

   So fares it with the nymph divine;
For what is Beauty but a Sign?   10
A face hung out, through which is seen
The nature of the goods within.
   Thus the coquette her beau ensnares
With studied smiles, and forward airs:
The graver prude hangs out a frown   15
To strike th' audacious gazer down;
But she alone, whose temperate wit
Each nicer medium can hit,
Is still adorned with every grace,
And wears a sample in her face.   20

---

[5] *toy* "A petty commodity" (Johnson), including make-up, fans, and other trifles for ladies; *Pinchbeck's shop* where clocks designed by Christopher Pinchbeck (1670?–1732) were sold.
[6] *cheap'ning* bargaining for; attempting to buy; *Payne* probably Thomas (1719–99), who succeeded his brother Oliver in 1740; the Paynes were among the first booksellers to issue catalogues and sell books at advertised prices, so "cheap'ning" has special emphasis here.
[7] *Ludgate's Mercers* tradesmen in an area just west of the City where there was a minimum security debtors' prison.
[8] *dun* "To claim a debt with vehemence and importunity" (Johnson).
[9] *garret* "A room on the highest floor of a house" (Johnson), the cheapest room to rent.

What though some envious folks have said,
That *Stella* now must hide her head,[1]
That all her stock of beauty's gone,
And ev'n the very sign took down;
Yet grieve not at the fatal blow;   25
For if you break a while, we know,[2]
'Tis bankrupt like, more rich to grow,
A fairer sign you'll soon hang up,
And with fresh credit open shop:
For nature's pencil soon shall trace,   30.
And once more finish off your face,
Which all your neighbours shall out-shine,
And of your Mind remain the Sign.

HER EPITAPH

(Which the Author hopes will live as long as she does)

Here rests poor *Stella*'s restless part:
A riddle! but I loved her heart.
Through life she rushed a headlong wave,
And never slept, but in her grave.
Some wit, I think, and worth she had: 5
No saint indeed, nor yet quite mad;
But laughed, built castles, rhymed and sung,
'Was everything, but nothing long.'[1]
Some honest truths she would let fall;
But much too wise to tell you all.   10

From thought to thought incessant hurled,
Her scheme was – but to rule the world.
At morn she won it with her eyes,
At night, when beauty sick'ning sighs,
Like the mad *Macedonian* cried,[2]   15
'What, no more worlds, ye Gods!' – and died.

Samuel Johnson (1709–1784)

*Although he was disfigured by scrofula (a form of tuberculosis), the wounds made in treating it,
by small pox, and by nervous disorders that resembled Tourette's syndrome, Johnson was gifted
with extraordinary mental powers. Through intellectual achievement he hoped to vault himself
out of the confines of his middle-class home and the family business of bookselling in
provincial Lichfield. He went to Oxford in 1728, but his financial and emotional resources*

AFTER THE SMALL POX
[1]   *Stella*   Jones's poetic name for herself.
[2]   *break*   "To become bankrupt" (Johnson, sense 7).

HER EPITAPH
[1]   *"Was everything . . . long"* a general reference to
Pope's "Of the Characters of Women" (above, p. 737).
[2]   *mad Macedonian*   Alexander the Great.

lasted only thirteen months. After the death of his father in 1731 he realized he would have to make a living on his own. He nevertheless clung for some years to his adolescent dream of becoming a Latin poet–scholar and joining the European community of the learned that knew few boundaries of time or place. He was all his life an admirer of great humanists like Joseph Scaliger, and he hoped to perform in their league. But it was impossible to unite such dreams with the requirement that he earn a living. His failed attempt to publish by subscription an edition of Politian's Latin poetry gave Johnson an early indication of this fact. He turned to teaching, but his personal appearance was against him as much as his own inclination. In 1732 he went to Birmingham and began producing articles for the publisher of a newspaper who then commissioned him to write his first book, a translation of a Jesuit priest's narrative of his travels in Abyssinia.

Johnson's first book came out in 1735, the same year he married and attempted to establish his own boarding school. The academy at Edial was a failure, and Johnson went to London with David Garrick, one of his few pupils, to earn his living as a writer. He carried with him Irene, *a learned tragedy, but he was unable to produce or publish this work until 1749. Instead, he sought the offices of Edward Cave, publisher of* The Gentleman's Magazine. *First publishing Latin verse in the monthly journal, Johnson went on to be its greatest contributor and virtual editor in the late 1730s. Among other things, he wrote book reviews and imaginative accounts of the debates in Parliament, which were not allowed to be reported at that time. Johnson and his publisher protected themselves from prosecution partly by printing the debates well after they occurred and by thinly disguising them as* Debates in the Senate of Lilliput. *Meanwhile, Johnson also published* London (1738), *an imitation or adaptation of Juvenal's third satire, and began to make a name for himself as a learned writer.*

Although he had written numerous short biographies and a longer Life of Richard Savage (1744), *various translations, political pamphlets, a huge catalogue of the Harleian Library, and the specimen of an edition of Shakespeare, Johnson was still struggling in 1746 when he signed a contract with a syndicate of London booksellers to produce* A Dictionary of the English Language. *His advance allowed him to lease a couple of years later a large house in Gough Square. In this location beside Fleet Street Johnson produced the* Dictionary (1755) *as well as the periodical* Rambler (1750–52). *He also published his most famous and greatest poem at this time,* The Vanity of Human Wishes (1749), *which was the first work to bear his name on the title page. But the* Dictionary *was the turning point in Johnson's career, and in some ways its climax: it made him famous, though only temporarily well-heeled, and it represented an ingenious and satisfying compromise between his wish for traditional scholarly achievement and his need to earn money. The* Dictionary *is a work on a par with the great achievements of continental academies of learning and aspires to the greatness of the Latin and Greek dictionaries produced by Johnson's humanist heroes.*

Johnson's wife Elizabeth died in 1752, and Johnson lived the rest of his life without an intimate companion. He formed close friendships, however, with many people: the most famous of these is his friendship with James Boswell, which led to the Life of Samuel Johnson LLD (1791); *the closest was his friendship with Hester Thrale, which ended sadly in 1783 when, a few years after the death her husband, she remarried. About 1755 Johnson courted a woman named Hill Boothby, but her life changed tragically and marriage became impossible. From 1755 to 1762 Johnson was again writing journalism and doing odd literary jobs to make ends meet. He was incensed by the Seven Years War (called the French and Indian War in America), and spoke out against it in* The Literary Magazine (1756). *He wrote* The Idler (1758–61); *an easier series of essays than* The Rambler, *and in 1759 he quickly contracted for and wrote* Rasselas, *to defray the costs of his mother's death.*

In 1762, to the amazement and disgust of those who knew his anti-Hanoverian talk and journalism, Johnson received and accepted a pension from King George III. He was now secure with a living of £300 per year. It was a fixed income, however, and especially later in life, he had to augment it by writing for money. Partly from a sense of obligation to his government patrons, Johnson wrote four political pamphlets. His response to the American discontent in 1776, Taxation no Tyranny, *is the source, along with Boswell's partial accounts, of Johnson being generally and incorrectly seen as a kind of arch-conservative. His politics contain elements of that at times, but politically, and every other way, Johnson is complex. In 1765 Johnson produced his long-promised edition of* The Plays of William Shakespeare, *which includes both his own commentary and selections from that of earlier editors. Again Johnson brought to the more popular and financially viable project his proclivity for classical scholarship. He revised this work, as well as his* Dictionary *for re-publication in 1773, whereupon he took his famous journey to the Western Isles of Scotland with Boswell. Johnson published an account of his journey in 1775. His last major work was a series of introductions to a huge collection put together by the London publishers called Johnson's* Prefaces Biographical and Critical, to The Works of the English Poets *(1779–81) were collected and published separately as* The Lives of the Most Eminent English Poets, 4 vols (1781).*

The Yale Edition of the Works of Samuel Johnson (1958–) is the standard, but it is only about half finished, and when all twenty-two volumes are completed, much that Johnson wrote, including the body of his Dictionary, *or may have written will still have to be sought elsewhere. The standard bibliography, the work of a lifetime for the late David Fleeman, is now in press. My texts here are based on first editions, but I have benefited from the Yale volumes of the* Poems, *ed. E. L. MacAdam, Jr. (1964),* The Rambler, *ed. W. J. Bate and Albrecht Strauss (1969),* Johnson on Shakespeare, *ed. Arthur Sherbo (1968),* Rasselas, *ed. Gwin Kolb, and the unpublished volume* Johnson on Language., *ed. Gwin Kolb and myself. I have also reveled in the notes to G. B. Hill's edition of* The Lives of the Poets *(Clarendon Press, 1905), which includes the* Life of Richard Savage. *There are many fine biographies of Johnson. W. J. Bate's* Samuel Johnson *(1977) is indispensable; despite its flaws, however, and the sometimes obnoxiously invasive personality of its author, Boswell's biography will probably always be the best. In the edition edited by G. B. Hill, revised by L. F. Powell, 6 vols (Clarendon Press, 1934–64), there is no more essential reading for students of the eighteenth century.*

from *The Life of Mr. Richard Savage, Son of the Earl of Rivers* (1744)[1]

It has been observed in all Ages, that the Advantages of Nature or of Fortune have contributed very little to the Promotion of Happiness; and that those whom the Splendour of their Rank or the Extent of their Capacity, have placed upon the Summits of human Life,

FROM *THE LIFE OF MR. RICHARD SAVAGE*
[1] *Richard Savage* (d. 1743), a poet and playwright who claimed he was the illegitimate son of Richard Savage, fourth Earl of Rivers and Lady Macclesfield; there is no evidence that his claim was just, but Johnson and many others believed him; see the official account of his trial (p. 807 above).

have not often given any just Occasion to Envy in those who look up to them from a lower Station. Whether it be that apparent Superiority incites great Designs, and great Designs are naturally liable to fatal Miscarriages; or that the general Lot of Mankind is Misery, and the Misfortunes of those whose Eminence drew upon them an universal Attention have been more carefully recorded, because they were more generally observed, and have in reality been only more conspicuous than those of others, not more frequent, or more severe.

That Affluence and Power, Advantages extrinsic and adventitious, and therefore easily separable from those by whom they are possessed, should very often flatter the Mind with Expectation of Felicity which they cannot give, raises no Astonishment; but it seems rational to hope, that intellectual Greatness should produce better Effects, that Minds qualified for great Attainments should first endeavour their own Benefit; and that they who are most able to teach others the Way to Happiness should with most Certainty follow it themselves.

But this Expectation, however plausible, has been very frequently disappointed. The Heroes of literary as well as civil History have been very often no less remarkable for what they have suffered than for what they have achieved; and Volumes have been written only to enumerate the Miseries of the Learned, and relate their unhappy Lives and untimely Deaths.

To these mournful Narratives I am about to add the Life of *Richard Savage*, a Man whose Writings entitle him to an eminent Rank in the Classes of Learning, and whose Misfortunes claim a Degree of Compassion, not always due to the Unhappy, as they were often the Consequences of the Crimes of others rather than his own . . .

He was now advancing in Reputation, and, though frequently involved in very distressful Perplexities, appeared however to be gaining upon Mankind, when both his Fame and his Life were endangered by an event, of which it is not yet determined, whether it ought to be mentioned as a Crime or a Calamity.

On the 20th of November 1727. Mr. *Savage* came from *Richmond*, where he then lodged, that he might pursue his Studies with less Interruption, with an Intent to discharge another Lodging which he had in *Westminster*, and accidentally meeting two Gentlemen, his Acquaintances, whose Names were *Merchant* and *Gregory*, he went in with them to a neighbouring Coffee-house, and sat drinking till it was late, it being in no Time of Mr. *Savage*'s Life any Part of his Character to be the first of the Company that desired to separate. He would willingly have gone to Bed in the same House; but there was not Room for the whole Company, and therefore they agreed to ramble about the Streets, and divert themselves with such Amusements as should offer themselves till Morning.

In their Walk they happened unluckily to discover Light in *Robinson*'s Coffee-house, near *Charing-Cross*, and therefore went in. *Merchant*, with some Rudeness, demanded a Room, and was told that there was a good Fire in the next Parlour, which the Company were about to leave, being then paying their Reckoning. *Merchant*, not satisfied with this Answer, rushed into the Room, and was followed by his Companions. He then petulantly placed himself between the Company and the Fire, and soon after kicked down the Table. This produced a Quarrel, Swords were drawn on both Sides, and one Mr. *James Sinclair* was killed. *Savage* having wounded likewise a Maid that held him, forced his Way with *Merchant* out of the House; but being intimidated and confused, without Resolution either to fly or stay, they were taken in a back Court by one of the Company and some Soldiers, whom he had called to his Assistance.

Being secured and guarded that Night, they were in the Morning carried before three Justices, who committed them to the *Gate-house*, from whence, upon the Death of Mr. *Sinclair*, which happened the same Day, they were removed in the Night to *Newgate*, where they were however treated with some Distinction, exempted from the Ignominy of Chains, and confined, not among the common Criminals, but in the *Press-yard*.[2]

When the Day of Trial came, the Court was crowded in a very unusual Manner, and the Public appeared to interest itself as in a Cause of general Concern. The Witnesses against Mr. *Savage* and his Friends were, the Woman who kept the House, which was a House of ill Fame, and her Maid, the Men who were in the Room with Mr. *Sinclair*, and a Woman of the Town, who had been drinking with them, and with whom one of them had been seen in Bed. They swore in general, that *Merchant* gave the Provocation, which *Savage* and *Gregory* drew their Swords to justify; that *Savage* drew first, and that he stabbed *Sinclair* when he was not in a Posture of Defence, or while *Gregory* commanded his Sword; that after he had given the Thrust he turned pale, and would have retired, but that the Maid clung round him, and one of the Company endeavoured to detain him, from whom he broke, by cutting the Maid on the Head, but was afterwards taken in a Court.

There was some Difference in their Depositions; one did not see *Savage* give the Wound, another saw it given when *Sinclair* held his Point towards the Ground; and the Woman of the Town asserted, that she did not see *Sinclair*'s Sword at all: This Difference, however, was very far from amounting to Inconsistency, but it was sufficient to show, that the Hurry of the Quarrel was such, that it was not easy to discover the Truth with relation to particular Circumstances, and that therefore some Deductions were to be made from the Credibility of the Testimonies.

Sinclair had declared several times before his Death, that he received his Wound from *Savage*; nor did *Savage* at his Trial deny the Fact, but endeavoured partly to extenuate it by urging the Suddenness of the whole Action, and the Impossibility of any ill Design, or premeditated Malice, and partly to justify it by the Necessity of Self-Defence, and the Hazard of his own Life, if he had lost that Opportunity of giving the Thrust: He observed that neither Reason nor Law obliged a Man to wait for the Blow which was threatened, and which, if he should suffer it, he might never be able to return; that it was always allowable to prevent an Assault, and to preserve Life by taking away that of the Adversary, by whom it was endangered.

With regard to the Violence with which he endeavoured to Escape, he declared, that it was not his Design to fly from Justice, or decline a Trial, but to avoid the Expenses and Severities of a Prison,[3] and that he intended to have appeared at the Bar without Compulsion.

This Defence, which took up more than an Hour, was heard by the Multitude that thronged the Court with the most attentive and respectful Silence: Those who thought he ought not to be acquitted owned that Applause could not be refused him; and those who before pitied his Misfortunes, now reverenced his Abilities.

The Witnesses which appeared against him were proved to be Persons of Characters which did not entitle them to much Credit: a common Strumpet, a Woman by whom Strumpets were entertained, and a Man by whom they were supported; and the Character of *Savage* was by several Persons of Distinction asserted to be that of a modest inoffensive Man, not inclined to Broils,[4] or to Insolence, and who had, to that Time, been only known for his Misfortunes and his Wit.

Had his Audience been his Judges, he had undoubtedly been acquitted; but Mr. *Page*, who was then upon the Bench, treated him with his usual Insolence and Severity, and when he had

---

[2] *Press-yard* a place of confinement outside Newgate prison, where punishments were inflicted.

[3] *Expenses . . . of a Prison* prisoners were expected to pay fees (called a garnish) to their jailers.

[4] *Broils* fights.

summed up the Evidence, endeavoured to exasperate the Jury, as Mr. *Savage* used to relate it, with this eloquent Harangue:

'Gentlemen of the Jury, you are to consider that Mr. *Savage* is a very great Man, a much greater Man than you or I, Gentlemen of the Jury; that he wears very fine Clothes, much finer Clothes than you or I, Gentlemen of the Jury; that he has Abundance of Money in his Pocket, much more Money than you or I, Gentlemen of the Jury; but, Gentlemen of the Jury, is it not a very hard Case, Gentlemen of the Jury, that Mr. *Savage* should therefore kill you or me, Gentlemen of the Jury?'

Mr. *Savage* hearing his defence thus misrepresented, and the Men who were to decide his Fate incited against him by invidious Comparisons, resolutely asserted that his Cause was not candidly explained, and began to recapitulate what he had before said with regard to his Condition, and the Necessity of endeavouring to escape the Expenses of Imprisonment; but the Judge, having ordered him to be silent, and repeated his Orders without Effect, commanded that he should be taken from the Bar by Force.

The Jury then heard the Opinion of the Judge, that good Characters were of no Weight against positive Evidence, though they might turn the Scale, where it was doubtful; and that though when two Men attack each other, the Death of either is only Manslaughter; but where one is the Aggressor, as in the Case before them, and, in Pursuance of his first Attack, kills the other, the Law supposes the Action, however sudden, to be malicious. They then deliberated upon their Verdict, and determined that Mr. *Savage* and Mr. *Gregory* were guilty of Murder, and Mr. *Merchant*, who had no Sword, only of Manslaughter . . .

Mr. Savage had now no Hopes of Life, but from the Mercy of the Crown, which was very earnestly solicited by his Friends, and which, with whatever Difficulty the Story may obtain Belief, was obstructed only by his Mother.

To prejudice the Queen against him, she made use of an Incident, which was omitted in the order of Time, that it might be mentioned together with the purpose which it was made to serve. Mr. *Savage*, when he had discovered his Birth, had an incessant Desire to speak to his Mother, who always avoided him in public, and refused him Admission into her House. One Evening walking, as it was his Custom, in the Street that she inhabited, he saw the Door of her House by Accident open; he entered it, and, finding none in the Passage, to hinder him, went up Stairs to salute[5] her. She discovered him before he could enter her Chamber, alarmed the Family with the most distressful Outcries, and when she had by her Screams gathered them about her, ordered them to drive out of the House that Villain, who had forced himself in upon her, and endeavoured to murder her. *Savage*, who had attempted with the most submissive Tenderness to soften her Rage, hearing her utter so detestable an Accusation, thought it prudent to retire, and, I believe, never attempted afterwards to speak to her.

But, shocked as he was with her Falsehood and her Cruelty, he imagined that she intended no other Use of her Lie, than to set herself free from his Embraces and Solicitations, and was very far from suspecting that she would treasure it in her Memory, as an Instrument of future Wickednesss, or that she would endeavour for this fictitious Assault to deprive him of his Life.

But when the Queen was solicited for his Pardon, and informed of the severe Treatments which he had suffered from his Judge, she answered, that however unjustifiable might be the Manner of his Trial, or whatever Extenuation the Action for which he was condemned might admit, she could not think that Man a proper Object of the King's Mercy, who

---

[5] *salute* greet.

had been capable of entering his Mother's House in the Night, with an Intent to murder her.

By whom this atrocious Calumny had been transmitted to the Queen, whether she that invented, had the Front to relate it; whether she found any one weak enough to credit it, or corrupt enough to concur with her in her hateful Design, I know not; but Methods had been taken to persuade the Queen so strongly of the Truth of it, that she for a long Time refused to hear any of those who petitioned for his Life.

Thus had *Savage* perished by the evidence of a Bawd, a Strumpet, and his Mother, had not Justice and Compassion procured him an Advocate of Rank too great to be rejected unheard, and of Virtue too eminent to be heard without being believed. His Merit and his Calamities happened to reach the ear of the Countess of *Hertford*, who engaged in his Support with all the Tenderness that is excited by Pity, and all the Zeal which is kindled by Generosity, and demanding an Audience of the Queen, laid before her the whole Series of his Mother's Cruelty, exposed the Improbability of an Accusation by which he was charged with an Intent to commit a Murder that could produce no Advantage, and soon convinced her how little his former Conduct could deserve to be mentioned as a Reason for extraordinary Severity.

The Interposition of this Lady was so successful, that he was soon after admitted to Bail, and, on the 9th of *March*, 1728, pleaded the King's Pardon.

It is natural to enquire upon what Motives his Mother could persecute him in a Manner so outrageous and implacable; for what Reason she could employ all the Acts of Malice, and all the Snares of Calumny, to take away the Life of her own Son, of a Son who never injured her, who was never supported by her Expense, nor obstructed any Prospect of Pleasure or Advantage; why she should endeavour to destroy him by a Lie – a Lie which could not gain Credit, but must vanish of itself at the first Moment of Examination, and of which only this can be said to make it probable, that it may be observed from her Conduct, that the most execrable Crimes are sometimes committed without apparent Temptation.

This Mother is still alive, and may perhaps even yet, though her Malice was so often defeated, enjoy the Pleasure of reflecting that the Life, which she often endeavoured to destroy, was at least shortened by her maternal Offices; that though she could not transport her Son to the Plantations,[6] bury him in the Shop of a Mechanic,[7] or hasten the Hand of the public Executioner, she has yet had the Satisfaction of embittering all his Hours, and forcing him into Exigencies, that hurried on his Death.

It is by no Means necessary to aggravate the Enormity of this Woman's Conduct, by placing it in Opposition to that of the Countess of *Hertford*; no one can fail to observe how much more amiable it is to relieve, than to oppress, and to rescue Innocence from Destruction than to destroy without an Injury.

Mr. *Savage*, during his Imprisonment, his Trial, and the Time in which he lay under Sentence of Death, behaved with great Firmness and Equality of Mind, and confirmed by his Fortitude the Esteem of those, who before admired him for his Abilities. The peculiar Circumstances of his Life were made more generally known by a short Account, which was then published, and of which several thousands were in a few Weeks dispersed over the Nation; and the Compassion of Mankind operated so powerfully in his Favour, that he was enabled by frequent Presents, not only to support himself, but to assist Mr. *Gregory* in Prison; and when he was pardoned and released, he found the Number of his Friends not lessened.

---

[6] *transport her Son to the Plantations* transportation to the colonies was a common substitute for execution in capital offenses.   [7] *Mechanic* manual laborer.

   The Nature of the Act for which he had been tried was in itself doubtful; of the Evidences which appeared against him, the Character of the Man was not unexceptionable, that of the Women notoriously infamous; she whose Testimony chiefly influenced the Jury to condemn him, afterwards retracted her Assertions. He always himself denied that he was drunk, as had been generally reported. Mr. *Gregory*, who is now Collector[8] of *Antigua*, is said to declare him far less criminal than he was imagined, even by some who favoured him: And *Page* himself afterwards confessed that he had treated him with uncommon Rigour. When all these Particulars are rated together, perhaps the Memory of Savage may not be much sullied by his Trial.

   Some Time after he had obtained his Liberty he met in the Street the Woman who had sworn with so much malignity against him. She informed him, that she was in Distress, and, with a Degree of Confidence not easily attainable, desired him to relieve her. He, instead of insulting her Misery, and taking Pleasure in the Calamities of one who had brought his Life into Danger, reproved her gently for her Perjury, and changing the only Guinea that he had, divided it equally between her and himself.

   This is an Action which in some Ages would have made a Saint, and perhaps in others a Hero, and which, without any hyperbolical Encomiums, must be allowed to be an Instance of uncommon Generosity, an Act of complicated Virtue; by which he at once relieved the Poor, corrected the Vicious, and forgave an Enemy; by which he at once remitted the strongest Provocations, and exercised the most ardent Charity . . .

The Vanity of Human Wishes (1749)

The Tenth Satire of *Juvenal*, Imitated

Let Observation with extensive View,
Survey Mankind, from *China* to *Peru*;
Remark each anxious Toil, each eager Strife,
And watch the busy Scenes of crowded Life;
Then say how Hope and Fear, Desire and Hate,   5
O'erspread with Snares the clouded Maze of Fate,
Where wav'ring Man, betrayed by vent'rous Pride,
To tread the dreary Paths without a Guide;
As treach'rous Phantoms in the Mist delude,
Shuns fancied Ills, or chases airy Good.   10
How rarely Reason guides the stubborn Choice,
Rules the bold Hand, or prompts the suppliant Voice,
How Nations sink, by darling Schemes oppressed,
When Vengeance listens to the Fool's Request.
Fate wings with every Wish th' afflictive Dart,[1]   15
Each Gift of Nature, and each Grace of Art,
With fatal Heat impetuous Courage glows,
With fatal Sweetness Elocution flows,
Impeachment stops the Speaker's pow'rful Breath,

---

8   *Collector* tax collector.

THE VANITY OF HUMAN WISHES
1   *wing* "To furnish with wings; to enable to fly" (Johnson).

And restless Fire precipitates on Death.[2]   20
    But scarce observed the Knowing and the Bold,
Fall in the gen'ral Massacre of Gold;
Wide-wasting Pest! that rages unconfined,
And crowds with Crimes the Records of Mankind,
For Gold his Sword the Hireling Ruffian draws,   25
For Gold the hireling Judge distorts the Laws;
Wealth heaped on wealth, nor Truth nor Safety buys,[3]
The Dangers gather as the Treasures rise.
    Let Hist'ry tell where rival Kings command,
And dubious Title shakes the madded Land,[4]   30
When Statutes glean the Refuse of the Sword,[5]
How much more safe the Vassal than the Lord,
Low skulks the Hind beneath the Rage of Pow'r,
And leaves the *bonny Traitor* in the *Tow'r*,[6]   35
Untouched his Cottage, and his Slumbers sound,
Though Confiscation's Vultures clang around.
    The needy Traveller, serene and gay,
Walks the wild Heath, and sings his Toil away.
Does Envy seize thee? crush th' upbraiding Joy,   40
Increase his Riches and his Peace destroy;
Now Fears in dire Vicissitude invade,
The rustling Brake alarms, and quiv'ring Shade,
Nor Light nor Darkness bring his Pain Relief,
One shows the Plunder, and one hides the Thief.   45
    Yet still one gen'ral Cry the Skies assails,
And Gain and Grandeur load the tainted Gales;[7]
Few know the toiling Statesman's Fear or Care,
Th' insidious Rival and the gaping Heir.
    Once more, Democritus, arise on Earth,[8]   50
With cheerful Wisdom and instructive Mirth,
See motley Life in modern Trappings dressed,[9]
And feed with varied Fools th' eternal Jest:
Thou who couldst laugh where Want enchained Caprice,
Toil crushed Conceit, and Man was of a Piece;   55
Where Wealth unloved without a Mourner died,
And scarce a Sycophant was fed by pride;
Where ne'er was known the Form of mock Debate,
Or seen a new-made Mayor's unwieldy State;

[2] *precipitates on* "To hasten without just preparation" (Johnson).
[3] *nor . . . nor* neither . . . nor.
[4] *madded* driven mad.
[5] *When Statutes glean the Refuse of the Sword* taxes take what direct assault leaves behind.
[6] *bonny Traitor* four Scottish lords imprisoned and executed after the Jacobite rebellion of 1745; Johnson dropped the allusion in the revision of 1755.
[7] *Gale* "A wind not tempestuous, yet stronger than a breeze" (Johnson).
[8] *Democritus* (*fl.* fifth century BCE), known as the "laughing philosopher" because of his ideal of cheerfulness, despite recognition of severe human limitation; Robert Burton styled himself Democritus Junior in his *Anatomy of Melancholy* (1628), one of Johnson's favorite books.
[9] *motley* the dress of court jesters or fools.

Where change of Fav'rites made no Change of Laws,[10]   60
And Senates heard before they judged a Cause;
How wouldst thou shake at *Britain*'s modish Tribe,
Dart the quick Taunt, and edge the piercing Gibe?
Attentive Truth and Nature to descry,
And pierce each Scene with Philosophic Eye.   65
To thee were solemn Toys or empty Show,
The Robes of Pleasure and the Veils of Woe:
All aid the Farce, and all thy Mirth maintain,
Whose Joys are causeless, or whose Griefs are vain.

    Such was the Scorn that filled the Sage's Mind,   70
Renewed at every Glance on Humankind;
How just that Scorn ere yet thy Voice declare,
Search every State, and canvass every Prayer.

    Unnumbered Suppliants crowd Preferment's Gate,
Athirst for Wealth, and burning to be great;   75
Delusive Fortune hears th' incessant Call,
They mount, they shine, evaporate, and fall.[11]
On every Stage the Foes of Peace attend,[12]
Hate dogs their Flight, and Insult mocks their End.
Love ends with Hope, the sinking Statesman's Door   80
Pours in the Morning Worshipper no more;
For growing Names the weekly Scribbler lies,[13]
To growing Wealth the Dedicator flies,[14]
From every Room descends the painted Face,
That hung the bright *Palladium* of the Place,[15]   85
And smoked in Kitchens, or in Auctions sold,
To better Features yields the Frame of Gold;
For now no more we trace in every Line
Heroic Worth, Benevolence Divine:
The Form distorted justifies the Fall,   90
And Detestation rids th' indignant Wall.

    But will not *Britain* hear the last Appeal,
Sign her Foes' Doom, or guard her Favourites' Zeal?
Through Freedom's Sons no more Remonstrance rings,[16]
Degrading Nobles and controlling Kings;   95
Our supple Tribes repress their Patriot Throats,
And ask no Questions but the Price of Votes;
With Weekly Libels and Septennial Ale,[17]

[10] *Change of Laws* in 1746 the Act of 19 George II, *c*. 8 changed the administrative structure of London, giving more power to the Common Council and less to the Aldermen as a separate group.
[11] *evaporate* "To fly away in vapours or fumes; to waste insensibly as a volatile spirit" (Johnson); the image is of a meteor.
[12] *Stage* "Any place where any thing public is transacted or performed" (Johnson).
[13] *weekly Scribbler* journalist.

[14] *Dedicator* an author writing a dedication of his book or poem to someone important.
[15] *Palladium* the sacred image of Pallas Athena sent by Zeus as symbol of protection to the city of Troy.
[16] *Remonstrance* recalling the Grand Remonstrance, a catalog of grievances against the king narrowly passed by the House of Commons in 1641.
[17] *Libels* pamphlets for railing (Latin, *libellus*); *Septennial Ale* free booze for rioting on election day; parliaments were made seven years long under George I.

Their Wish is full to riot and to rail.

In full-blown dignity, see *Wolsey* stand,[18]   100
Law in his Voice, and Fortune in his Hand:
To him the Church, the Realm, their Pow'rs consign,
Through him the Rays of regal Bounty shine,
Turned by his Nod the Stream of Honour flows,
His Smile alone Security bestows: 105
Still to new Heights his restless Wishes tow'r,
Claim leads to Claim, and Pow'r advances Pow'r;
Till Conquest unresisted ceased to please,
And Rights submitted, left him none to seize.
At length his Sovereign frowns – the Train of State   110
Mark the keen Glance, and watch the Sign to hate.
Where-e'er he turns he meets a Stranger's Eye,
His Suppliants scorn him, and his Followers fly;
Now drops at once the Pride of awful State,
The golden Canopy, the glitt'ring Plate,   115
The regal Palace, the luxurious Board,
The liv'ried Army, and the menial Lord.[19]
With Age, with Cares, with Maladies oppressed,
He seeks the Refuge of Monastic Rest.
Grief aids Disease, remembered Folly stings,   120
And his last Sighs reproach the Faith of Kings.

Speak thou, whose Thoughts at humble Peace repine,
Shall *Wolsey*'s Wealth, with *Wolsey*'s End be thine?
Or liv'st thou now, with safer Pride content,
The richest Landlord on the Banks of *Trent*?[20]   125
For why did *Wolsey* by the Steps of Fate,
On weak Foundations raise th' enormous Weight?
Why but to sink beneath Misfortune's Blow,
With louder Ruin to the Gulfs below?

What gave great *Villiers* to th' Assassin's Knife,[21]   130
And fixed Disease on *Harley*'s closing Life?[22]
What murdered *Wentworth*, and what exiled *Hyde*,[23]
By Kings protected and to Kings allied?
What but their Wish indulged in Courts to shine,
And Pow'r too great to keep or to resign?   135

---

[18] *Wolsey*   Thomas (1475?–1530), Cardinal and Lord
Chancellor under Henry VIII, until he lost favour, was
indicted in the King's Bench (1529), forfeited his estate,
was falsely accused of treason, and soon died.
[19] *menial*   "Belonging to the retinue or train of servants" (Johnson).
[20] *Trent*   the river goes no further south than the environs of Lichfield, Johnson's home town about 85 miles
north of London, the center of wealth and fame; in 1755
Johnson changed "richest landlord" to "wisest justice."
[21] *Villiers*   George, first Duke of Buckingham (1592–
1628), court favorite whom the Commons tried to force

Charles I to remove; his assassin, a naval lieutenant,
believed he was acting on the will of the people.
[22] *Harley*   Robert (1661–1724), first Earl of Oxford,
leader of the Tory ministry in 1710, dismissed in 1714,
imprisoned in 1715, and impeached after the fact in
1717.
[23] *Wentworth*   Thomas, first Earl of Strafford (1593–
1641), Charles I's chief advisor, impeached by the House
of Commons and executed in a flurry of rumors and
fears of mob violence; *Hyde*   Edward, Earl of Clarendon
(1609–74), Lord Chancellor in 1660, impeached by the
Commons and banished in 1668, died in exile.

When first the College Rolls receive his Name,
The young Enthusiast quits his Ease for Fame;[24]
Through all his Veins the Fever of Renown,
Burns from the strong Contagion of the Gown;[25]
O'er *Bodley*'s Dome his future Labours spread,[26]   140
And *Bacon*'s Mansion trembles o'er his Head;[27]
Are these thy Views? proceed, illustrious Youth,
And virtue guard thee to the Throne of Truth!
Yet should thy Soul indulge the gen'rous Heat,
Till captive Science yields her last Retreat;[28]   145
Should Reason guide thee with her brightest Ray,
And pour on misty Doubt resistless Day;
Should no false Kindness lure to loose Delight,
Nor Praise relax, nor Difficulty fright;
Should tempting Novelty thy Cell refrain,   150
And Sloth effuse her Opiate Fumes in vain;
Should Beauty blunt on Fops her fatal Dart,
Nor claim the Triumph of a lettered Heart;
Should no Disease thy torpid Veins invade,
Nor Melancholy's Phantoms haunt thy Shade;   155
Yet hope not Life from Grief or Danger free,
Nor think the Doom of Man reversed for thee:
Deign on the passing World to turn thine Eyes,
And pause awhile from Learning, to be wise;
There mark what Ills the Scholar's Life assail,   160
Toil, Envy, Want, the Patron, and the Jail.[29]
See Nations slowly wise, and meanly just,
To buried Merit raise the tardy Bust.[30]
If Dreams yet flatter, once again attend,
Hear *Lydiat*'s life, and *Galileo*'s end.[31]   165
　　Nor deem, when Learning her lost Prize bestows
The glitt'ring Eminence exempt from Foes;
See when the Vulgar 'scaped, despised or awed,[32]
Rebellion's vengeful Talons seize on *Laud*.[33]

---

[24] *Enthusiast* "One of a hot imagination, or violent passions" (Johnson).
[25] *Gown* "The long habit of a man dedicated to acts of peace, as divinity, medicine, law" (Johnson).
[26] *Dome* building; Sir Thomas Bodley (1545–1613) formed, endowed and gave his name to the Oxford University library.
[27] *Bacon's Mansion* the study used by the philosopher Roger Bacon (1214?–94), a gatehouse on Folly Bridge in Oxford; an Oxford tradition said that the study would fall if someone more learned than Bacon walked under the bridge.
[28] *Science* knowledge.
[29] *Patron* "Commonly a wretch who supports with insolence, and is paid with flattery" (Johnson); it was "Garret" in the first edition; the change is connected

with Johnson's formal repudiation of Chesterfield's tardy patronage of the *Dictionary*, which he effected with a famous letter written about the same time that he revised his poem in 1755.
[30] *tardy Bust* the burial monument; see Pope: "Patrons, who sneak from living worth to dead, / With-hold the pension, and set up the head" (*Dunciad* 4.95–6).
[31] *Lydiat* Thomas (1572–1646), a famous astronomer in his time, died in poverty and was forgotten; *Galileo* (1564–1642), the great astronomer, forced by the church to deny his Copernican views, lived the last eight years of his life under house arrest.
[32] *Vulgar* common, unlearned persons.
[33] *Laud* William (1573–1645), Archbishop of Canterbury under Charles I, accused of high treason by Parliament and executed in 1645.

From meaner Minds, though smaller Fines content   170
The plundered Palace or sequestered Rent;
Marked out by dangerous Parts he meets the Shock,
And fatal Learning leads him to the Block:
Around his Tomb let Art and Genius weep,
But hear his Death, ye Blockheads, hear and sleep.   175
    The festal Blazes, the triumphal Show,
The ravished Standard, and the captive Foe,
The Senate's Thanks, the Gázette's pompous Tale,[34]
With Force resistless o'er the Brave prevail.
Such Bribes the rapid *Greek* o'er *Asia* whirled[35]   180
For such the steady *Romans* shook the World;
For such in distant Lands the *Britons* shine,[36]
And stain with Blood the *Danube* or the *Rhine*;
This Pow'r has Praise, that Virtue scarce can warm,
Till Fame supplies the universal Charm.   185
Yet Reason frowns on War's unequal Game,
Where wasted Nations raise a single Name,
And mortgaged States their Grandsires Wreaths regret,[37]
From Age to Age in everlasting Debt;
Wreaths which at last the dear-bought Right convey   190
To rust on Medals, or on Stones decay.
    On what Foundation stands the Warrior's Pride?
How just his Hopes let *Swedish Charles* decide;[38]
A Frame of Adamant, a Soul of Fire,
No Dangers fright him, and no Labours tire;   195
O'er Love, o'er Force, extends his wide Domain,
Unconquered Lord of Pleasure and of Pain;
No Joys to him pacific Sceptres yield,
War sounds the Trump, he rushes to the Field;
Behold surrounding Kings their Pow'r combine,   200
And One capitulate, and One resign;
Peace courts his Hand, but spread her Charms in vain.
'Think Nothing gained', he cries, 'till nought remain,
On *Moscow*'s Walls till *Gothic* Standards fly,
And all is Mine beneath the Polar Sky'.   205
The March begins in Military State,
And Nations on his Eye suspended wait;
Stern Famine guards the solitary Coast,
And Winter barricades the Realms of Frost;

---

[34] *Gazette* the government-run newspaper.
[35] *the rapid Greek* Alexander the Great.
[36] *the Britons* an allusion to the surprising and ambitious military victory over the French at Blenheim by the brilliant and ambitious John Churchill (1650–1722), first Duke of Marlborough.
[37] *Wreaths* victory garlands.

[38] *Swedish Charles* Charles XII of Sweden (1682–1718), a very active general and statesman; pursued the Russian army towards Moscow in 1707; defeated at *Pultowa* (Ukraine) in 1709; sought allies in Turkey, where he was involved in intrigues; sympathized with English Jacobites as a threat to George I and Hanover; began a new military campaign in 1718 but was killed in battle before it was well under way.

He comes, nor Want nor Cold his Course delay; — 210
Hide, blushing Glory, hide *Pultowa*'s Day:
The vanquished Hero leaves his broken Bands,
And shows his Miseries in distant Lands;
Condemned a needy Supplicant to wait,
While Ladies interpose, and Slaves debate. 215
But did not Chance at length her Error mend?
Did no subverted Empire mark his End?
Did rival Monarchs give the fatal Wound?
Or hostile Millions press him to the Ground?
His Fall was destined to a barren Strand, 220
A petty Fortress, and a dubious Hand;[39]
He left the Name, at which the World grew pale,
To point a Moral, or adorn a Tale.

    All Times their Scenes of pompous Woes afford,
From *Persia*'s Tyrant to *Bavaria*'s Lord.[40] 225
In gay Hostility, and barb'rous Pride,
With half Mankind embattled at his Side,
Great *Xerxes* comes to seize the certain Prey,
And starves exhausted Regions in his Way;
Attendant Flatt'ry counts his Myriads o'er, 230
Till counted Myriads soothe his Pride no more;
Fresh Praise is tried till Madness fires his Mind,
The Waves he lashes, and enchains the Wind;[41]
New Pow'rs are claimed, new Pow'rs are still bestowed,
Till rude Resistance lops the spreading God; 235
The daring *Greeks* deride the Martial Show,
And heap their Vallies with the gaudy Foe;[42]
Th' insulted Sea with humbler Thoughts he gains,
A single kiff to spead his light remains;
Th' incumbered Car scarce leaves the dreaded Coast 240
Through purple Billows and a floating Host.

    The bold *Bavarian*, in a luckless Hour,
Tries the dread Summits of *Cesarean* Pow'r,
With unexpected Legions bursts away,
And sees defenceless Realms receive his Sway; 245
Short Sway! fair *Austria* spreads her mournful Charms,[43]
The Queen, the Beauty, sets the World in Arms;

---

[39] *a dubious hand* some say Charles was killed by one of his own soldiers at the siege of Frederikshald (Halden, Norway).

[40] *Persia's Tyrant* Xerxes the Great (519–465 BCE), whose massive invasions of Greece failed; *Bavaria's Lord* Charles Albert (1697–1745), Elector of Bavaria, became Holy Roman Emperor in 1742.

[41] *Waves ... Wind* when bad weather hindered his assault, he ordered his men to punish the sea and air (Herodotus 7.35, 54).

[42] *Vallies* especially Thermopylae, where Xerxes won a costly victory, before he was defeated at sea near Salamis and had to retreat.

[43] *fair Austria* Maria Theresa of Austria, ruler of the Hapsburg dominions; led the attack on Bavaria even as Charles was being crowned Emperor.

From Hill to Hill the Beacons rousing Blaze
Spreads wide the Hope of Plunder and of Praise;
The fierce *Croatian*, and the wild *Hussar*,[44]   250
And all the Sons of Ravage crowd the War;
The baffled Prince in Honour's flatt'ring Bloom
Of hasty Greatness finds the fatal Doom,
His Foes' Derision, and his Subjects' Blame,
And steals to Death from Anguish and from Shame.   255
    Enlarge my Life with Multitude of Days,
In Health, in Sickness, thus the Suppliant prays;
Hides from himself his State, and shuns to know,
That Life protracted is protracted Woe.
Time hovers o'er, impatient to destroy,   260
And shuts up all the Passages of Joy:
In vain their Gifts the bounteous Seasons pour,
The Fruit Autumnal, and the Vernal Flow'r,
With listless Eyes the Dotard views the Store,
He views, and wonders that they please no more;   265
Now pall the tastless Meats, and joyless Wines,
And Luxury with Sighs her Slave resigns.
Approach, ye Minstrels, try the soothing Strain,
And yield the tuneful Lenitives of Pain:
No Sounds alas would touch th' impervious Ear,   270
Though dancing Mountains witnessed *Orpheus* near;[45]
Nor Lute nor Lyre his feeble Pow'rs attend,
Nor sweeter Music of a virtuous Friend,
But everlasting Dictates crowd his Tongue,
Perversely grave, or positively wrong.   275
The still returning Tale, and ling'ring Jest,
Perplex the fawning Niece and pampered Guest,
While growing Hopes scarce awe the gath'ring Sneer,
And scarce a Legacy can bribe to hear;
The watchful Guests still hint the last Offence,   280
The Daughter's Petulance, the Son's Expense,
Improve his heady Rage with treach'rous Skill,
And mould his Passions till they make his Will.
    Unnumbered Maladies each Joint invade,
Lay Siege to Life and press the dire Blockade;   285
But unextinguished Av'rice still remains,
And dreaded Losses aggravate his Pains;
He turns, with anxious Heart and crippled Hands,
His Bonds of Debt, and Mortgages of Lands;
Or views his Coffers with suspicious Eyes,   290
Unlocks his Gold, and counts it till he dies.

---

[44] *Hussar*   Hungarian cavalryman.

[45] *Orpheus*   legendary pre-Homeric poet whose music
could charm beasts and animate rocks.

But grant, the Virtues of a temp'rate Prime
Bless with an Age exempt from Scorn or Crime;
An Age that melts in unperceived Decay,
And glides in modest Innocence away;   295
Whose peaceful Day Benevolence endears,
Whose Night congratulating Conscience cheers;
The gen'ral Fav'rite as the gen'ral Friend:
Such Age there is, and who could wish its End?

Yet ev'n on this her Load Misfortune flings,   300
To press the weary Minutes' flagging Wings:
New Sorrow rises as the Day returns,
A Sister sickens, or a Daughter mourns.
Now Kindred Merit fills the sable Bier,
Now lacerated Friendship claims a Tear.   305
Year chases Year, Decay pursues Decay,
Still drops some Joy from with'ring Life away;
New Forms arise, and diff'rent Views engage,
Superfluous lags the Vet'ran on the Stage
Till pitying Nature signs the last Release,   310
And bids afflicted Worth retire to Peace.

But few there are whom Hours like these await,
Who set unclouded in the Gulfs of Fate.
From *Lydia*'s Monarch should the Search descend,[46]
By *Solon* cautioned to regard his End,[47]   315
In Life's last Scene what Prodigies surprise,
Fears of the Brave, and Follies of the Wise?
From *Marlborough*'s Eyes the Streams of Dotage flow,
And *Swift* expires a Driv'ler and a Show.[48]

The teeming Mother, anxious for her Race,[49]   320
Begs for each Birth the Fortune of a Face:
Yet *Vane* could tell what Ills from Beauty spring;[50]
And *Sedley* cursed the Form that pleased a King.[51]
Ye Nymphs of rosy Lips and radiant Eyes,
Whom Pleasure keeps too busy to be wise,   325
By Day the Frolic, and the Dance by Night,
Who frown with Vanity, who smile with Art,
And ask the latest Fashion of the Heart,
What Care, what Rules your heedless Charms shall save,
Each Nymph your Rival, and each Youth your Slave?   330
Against your Fame with Fondness Hate combines,

---

[46] *Lydia's Monarch* Croesus, the wealthy sixth-century BCE king defeated by Cyrus of Persia.
[47] *Solon* the Athenian lawgiver was to have advised Croesus that fortune, not wealth, determined happiness; Johnson has him repeat a version of the Latin motto to that effect: *respice finem*.

[48] *Swift* at the age of seventy-three, four years before his death, Swift was declared legally incompetent.
[49] *teeming* pregnant.
[50] *Vane* Anne (1705–36), mistress of Frederick, Prince of Wales.
[51] *Sedley* Catherine (1657–1717), mistress of the Duke of York (later James II).

The Rival batters, and the Lover mines.
With distant Voice neglected Virtue calls,
Less heard, and less the faint Remonstrance falls;
Tir'd with Contempt, she quits the slipp'ry Reign,   335
And Pride and Prudence take her Seat in vain.
In crowd at once, where none the Pass defend,
The harmless Freedom, and the private Friend.
The Guardians yield, by Force superior plied;
By Int'rest, Prudence; and by Flatt'ry, Pride.   340
Here Beauty falls betrayed, despised, distressed,
And hissing Infamy proclaims the rest.
      Where then shall Hope and Fear their Objects find?
Must dull Suspense corrupt the stagnant Mind?
Must helpless Man, in Ignorance sedate,   345
Roll darkling down the Current of his Fate?
Must no Dislike alarm, no Wishes rise,
No Cries attempt the Mercies of the Skies?
Enquirer, cease, Petitions yet remain,
Which Heav'n may hear, nor deem Religion vain.   350
Still raise for Good the supplicating Voice,
But leave to Heav'n the Measure and the Choice.
Safe in his Pow'r, whose Eyes discern afar
The secret Ambush of a specious Pray'r.
Implore his Aid, in his Decisions rest,   355
Secure whate'er he gives, he gives the best.
Yet when the Sense of sacred Presence fires,
And strong Devotion to the skies aspires,
Pour forth thy Fervours for a healthful Mind,
Obedient Passions, and a Will resigned;   360
For Love, which scarce collective Man can fill;
For Patience sovereign o'er transmuted Ill;
For Faith, that panting for a happier Seat,
Counts Death kind Nature's Signal of Retreat:
These Goods for Man the Laws of Heav'n ordain,   365
These Goods he grants, who grants the Pow'r to gain;
With these celestial Wisdom calms the Mind,
And makes the Happiness she does not find.

from THE RAMBLER

NUMBER 2
SATURDAY, 24 MARCH 1750

Stare Loco nescit, pereunt Vestigia mille
Ante Fugam, absentemque ferit gravis Ungula Campum.
                              Statius, *Thebaid* 6.400–01

Th' impatient courser pants in every vein,
And pawing seems to beat the distant plain;
Hills, vales, and floods, appear already cross't,
And, ere he starts, a thousand steps are lost.

Pope [*Windsor Forest*, 151–4]

That the Mind of Man is never satisfied with the Objects immediately before it, but is always breaking away from the present Moment, and losing itself in Schemes of future Felicity – that we forget the proper Use of the Time now in our Power, to provide for the Enjoyment of that which, perhaps, may never be granted us – has been frequently remarked; and as this Practice is a commodious Subject of Raillery to the Gay, and of Declamation to the Serious, it has been ridiculed with all the Pleasantry of Wit, and exaggerated with all the Amplifications of Rhetoric. Every Instance, by which its Absurdity might appear most flagrant, has been studiously collected; it has been marked with every Epithet of Contempt, and all the Tropes and Figures have been called forth against it.

Censure is willingly indulged, because it always implies some Superiority. Men please themselves with imagining that they have made a deeper Search, or wider Survey, than others, and detected Faults and Follies, which escaped vulgar Observation; and the Pleasure of wantoning in common Topics is so tempting to a Writer, that he cannot easily resign it. A Train of Sentiments generally received enables him to shine without Labour, and to conquer without a Contest. It is so easy to laugh at the Folly of him who lives only in Idea, refuses immediate Ease for distant Pleasures, and, instead of enjoying the Blessings of Life, lets Life glide away in Preparations to enjoy them; it affords such Opportunities of triumphant Exultations, to exemplify the Uncertainty of the human State, to rouse Mortals from their Dream, and inform them of the silent Celerity of Time, that we may reasonably believe most Authors willing rather to transmit than examine so advantageous a Principle, and more inclined to pursue a Track so smooth and so flowery, than attentively to consider whether it leads to Truth.

This Quality of looking forward into Futurity seems the unavoidable Condition of a Being, whose Motions are gradual, and whose Life is progressive: As his Powers are limited, he must use Means for the Attainment of his Ends, and must intend first what he performs last; as, by continual Advances from his first Stage of Existence, he is perpetually varying the Horizon of his Prospects, he must always discover new Motives of Action, new Excitements of Fear, and Allurements of Desire.

The End, therefore, which, at present, calls forth our Efforts will be found, when it is once gained, to be only one of the Means to some remoter End. The natural Flights of the human Mind are not from Pleasure to Pleasure, but from Hope to Hope.

He that directs his Steps to a certain Point, must frequently turn his Eyes to that Place which he strives to reach; he that undergoes the Fatigue of Labour, must solace his Weariness with the Contemplation of its Reward. In Agriculture, one of the most simple and necessary Employments, no Man turns up the Ground, but because he thinks of the Harvest, that Harvest which Blights may intercept, which Inundations may sweep away, or which Death, or Calamity, may hinder him from reaping.

Yet as few Maxims are widely received, or long retained, but for some Conformity with Truth and Nature, it must be confessed, that this Caution against keeping our View too intent upon remote Advantages is not without its Propriety or Usefulness, though it may have been recited with too much Levity, or enforced with too little Distinction: for, not to speak of that Vehemence of Desire which presses through right and wrong to its Gratification, or that anxious Inquietude which is justly chargeable with Distrust of Heaven, Subjects too solemn for my present Purpose; it frequently happens that, by indulging too early the Raptures of Success, we forget the Measures necessary to secure it; and suffer the Imagination to riot in the Fruition of some possible Good, till the Time of obtaining it has slipped away.

There would however be few Enterprises of great Labour or Hazard, undertaken, if we had not the Power of magnifying the Advantages, which we persuade ourselves to expect from them. When the Knight of *La Mancha*[1] gravely recounts to his Companion the Adventures by which he is to signalize himself in such a manner that he shall be summoned to the Support of Empires, solicited to accept the Heiress of the Crown he has preserved, have Honours and Riches to scatter about him, and an Island to bestow on his worthy Squire, very few Readers, amidst their Mirth or Pity, can deny that they have admitted Visions of the same Kind; though they have not, perhaps, expected Events equally strange, or by Means equally inadequate. When we pity him, we reflect our own Disappointments, and when we laugh, our Hearts inform us that he is not more ridiculous than ourselves, except that he tells what we have only thought.

The Understanding of a Man, naturally sanguine, may, indeed, be easily vitiated by too luxurious an Indulgence of the Pleasures of Hope, however necessary to the Production of every Thing great or excellent, as some Plants are destroyed by a too open Exposure to that Sun which gives Life and Beauty to the vegetable World.

Perhaps no Class of the Human Species requires more to be cautioned against this Anticipation of Happiness, than those that aspire to the Name of Authors. A Man of lively Fancy no sooner finds a Hint moving in his Mind, than he makes momentaneous Excursions to the Press, and to the World; and, with a little Encouragement from Flattery, pushes forward into future Ages, and prognosticates the Honours to be paid him, when Envy is extinct, and Faction forgotten; and those, whom the Partiality of the present Generation suffers to obscure him, shall give way to other Triflers of as short Duration as themselves.

Those, who have proceeded so far as to appeal to the Tribunal of succeeding Times, are not likely to be cured of their Infatuation; but all Endeavours ought to be used for the Prevention of a Disease, for which, when it has attained its Height, perhaps, no Remedy will be found in the Gardens of Philosophy; however she may boast her Physic[2] of the Mind, her Cathartics of Vice, or Lenitives[3] of Passion.

I shall, therefore, while I am yet but lightly touched with the Symptoms of the Writer's Malady,[4] endeavour to fortify myself against the Infection, not without some weak Hope, that my Preservatives may extend their Virtue to others, whose Employment exposes them to the same Danger:

> *Laudis Amore tumes? Sunt certa Piacula, quæ te*
> *Ter pure lecto poterunt recreare Libello.*
>
> Horace, *Epistles* 1.1.36–7

> Is fame your passion? Wisdom's pow'rful charm,
> If thrice read over, shall its force disarm.
>
> [Philip] Francis [1708–73]

---

[1] *the Knight of La Mancha* the hero of Cervantes' *Don Quixote*.
[2] *Physic* medical treatment, especially purges.
[3] *Lenitive* emolient, soothing agent.
[4] *lightly touched ... Malady* Johnson is speaking in the character of Mr Rambler, who has just begun his career as a writer.

It is the sage Advice of *Epictetus*,[5] that a Man should accustom himself often to think of what is most shocking and terrible, that by such Reflections he may be preserved from too ardent Wishes for seeming Good, and from too much Dejection in real Evil.

There is nothing more dreadful to an Author than Neglect; compared with which Reproach, Hatred, and Opposition, are Names of Happiness: yet this worst, this meanest Fate every Man who dares to write has Reason to fear.

I nunc, et Versus tecum meditare canoros.
Horace, *Epistles* 2.2.76

Go now, and meditate thy tuneful lays.
[James] Elphinstone [1721–1809]

It may not be unfit for him who makes a new Entrance into the lettered World, so far to suspect his own Powers as to believe that he possibly may deserve Neglect; that Nature may not have qualified him much to enlarge or embellish Knowledge, nor sent him forth entitled by indisputable Superiority to regulate the Conduct of the Rest of Mankind; that, though the World must be granted to be yet in Ignorance, he is not destined to dispel the Cloud, nor to shine out as one of the Luminaries of Life: For this Suspicion, every Catalogue of a Library will furnish sufficient Reason; as he will find it crowded with Names of Men, who, though now forgotten, were once no less enterprising or confident than himself, equally pleased with their own Productions, equally caressed by their Patrons, and flattered by their Friends.

But, though it should happen that an Author is capable of excelling, yet his Merit may pass without Notice, huddled in the Variety of things, and thrown into the general Miscellany of Life. He that endeavours after Fame, by writing, solicits the Regard of a Multitude fluctuating in Pleasures, or immersed in Business, without Time for intellectual Amusements; he appeals to Judges prepossessed by Passions, or corrupted by Prejudices, which preclude their Approbation of any new Performance. Some are too indolent to read any Thing, till its Reputation is established; others too envious to promote that Fame, which gives them Pain by its Increase. What is new is opposed, because most are unwilling to be taught; and what is known is rejected, because it is not sufficiently considered, that Men more frequently require to be reminded than informed. The Learned are afraid to declare their Opinion early, lest they should put their Reputation in Hazard; the Ignorant always imagine themselves giving some Proof of Delicacy, when they refuse to be pleased: and he that finds his Way to Reputation, through all these Obstructions, must acknowledge that he is indebted to other Causes besides his Industry, his Learning, or his Wit.

from the Preface to A *Dictionary of the English Language* (1755)

It is the fate of those who toil at the lower employments of life, to be rather driven by the fear of evil, than attracted by the prospect of good; to be exposed to censure, without hope of praise; to be disgraced by miscarriage, or punished for neglect, where success would have been without applause, and diligence without reward.

---

[5] *Epictetus* Stoic philosopher of the first century CE whose teachings are collected in a manual, *Enchiridion*.

Among these unhappy mortals is the writer of dictionaries; whom mankind have considered, not as the pupil, but the slave of science, the pioneer[1] of literature, doomed only to remove rubbish and clear obstructions from the paths through which Learning and Genius press forward to conquest and glory, without bestowing a smile on the humble drudge that facilitates their progress.[2] Every other author may aspire to praise; the lexicographer can only hope to escape reproach, and even this negative recompense has been yet granted to very few.

I have, notwithstanding this discouragement, attempted a dictionary of the *English* language, which, while it was employed in the cultivation of every species of literature, has itself been hitherto neglected, suffered to spread, under the direction of chance, into wild exuberance, resigned to the tyranny of time and fashion, and exposed to the corruptions of ignorance, and caprices of innovation.

When I took the first survey of my undertaking, I found our speech copious without order, and energetic without rules: wherever I turned my view, there was perplexity to be disentangled, and confusion to be regulated; choice was to be made out of boundless variety, without any established principle of selection; adulterations were to be detected, without a settled test of purity, and modes of expression to be rejected or received, without the suffrages of any writers of classical reputation or acknowledged authority.

Having therefore no assistance but from general grammar, I applied myself to the perusal of our writers; and noting whatever might be of use to ascertain or illustrate any word or phrase, accumulated in time the materials of a dictionary, which, by degrees, I reduced to method, establishing to myself, in the progress of the work, such rules as experience and analogy suggested to me; experience, which practice and observation were continually increasing; and analogy, which, though in some words obscure, was evident in others.

In adjusting the ORTHOGRAPHY, which has been to this time unsettled and fortuitous, I found it necessary to distinguish those irregularities that are inherent in our tongue, and perhaps coeval with it, from others which the ignorance or negligence of later writers has produced. Every language has its anomalies, which, though inconvenient, and in themselves once unnecessary, must be tolerated among the imperfections of human things, and which require only to be registered, that they may not be increased, and ascertained, that they may not be confounded: but every language has likewise its improprieties and absurdities, which it is the duty of the lexicographer to correct or proscribe.

As language was at its beginning merely oral, all words of necessary or common use were spoken before they were written; and while they were unfixed by any visible signs, must have been spoken with great diversity, as we now observe those who cannot read to catch sounds imperfectly, and utter them negligently. When this wild and barbarous jargon was first reduced to an alphabet, every penman endeavoured to express, as he could, the sounds which he was accustomed to pronounce or to receive, and vitiated in writing such words as were already vitiated in speech. The powers of the letters, when they were applied to a new language, must have been vague and unsettled, and therefore different hands would exhibit the same sound by different combinations.

From this uncertain pronunciation arise in a great part the various dialects of the same country, which will always be observed to grow fewer, and less different, as books are

---

[1] *pioneer* "One whose business is to level the road, throw up the works, or sink the mines in military operations" (Johnson).

[2] *humble drudge* Johnson defines "lexicographer" in the *Dictionary* as "A harmless drudge, that busies himself in tracing the original, and detailing the signification of words."

multiplied; and from this arbitrary representation of sounds by letters, proceeds that diversity of spelling observable in the *Saxon* remains, and I suppose in the first books of every nation, which perplexes or destroys analogy, and produces anomalous formations, that, being once incorporated, can never be afterward dismissed or reformed . . .

In this part of the work, where caprice has long wantoned without control, and vanity sought praise by petty reformation, I have endeavoured to proceed with a scholar's reverence for antiquity, and a grammarian's regard to the genius of our tongue. I have attempted few alterations, and among those few, perhaps the greater part is from the modern to the ancient practice, and I hope I may be allowed to recommend to those, whose thoughts have been, perhaps, employed too anxiously on verbal singularities, not to disturb, upon narrow views, or for minute propriety, the orthography of their fathers. It has been asserted, that for the law to be *known*, is of more importance than to be *right*.[3] Change, says *Hooker*, is not made without inconvenience, even from worse to better.[4] There is in constancy and stability a general and lasting advantage, which will always overbalance the slow improvements of gradual correction. Much less ought our written language to comply with the corruptions of oral utterance, or copy that which every variation of time or place makes different from itself, and imitate those changes, which will again be changed, while imitation is employed in observing them.

This recommendation of steadiness and uniformity does not proceed from an opinion, that particular combinations of letters have much influence on human happiness; or that truth may not be successfully taught by modes of spelling fanciful and erroneous: I am not yet so lost in lexicography, as to forget that *words are the daughters of earth, and that things are the sons of heaven*.[5] Language is only the instrument of science, and words are but the signs of ideas: I wish, however, that the instrument might be less apt to decay, and that signs might be permanent, like the things which they denote . . .

That part of my work on which I expect malignity most frequently to fasten, is the *Explanation*; in which I cannot hope to satisfy those, who are perhaps not inclined to be pleased, since I have not always been able to satisfy myself. To interpret a language by itself is very difficult; many words cannot be explained by synonyms, because the idea signified by them has not more than one appellation; nor by paraphrase, because simple ideas cannot be described. When the nature of things is unknown, or the notion unsettled and indefinite, and various in various minds, the words by which such notions are conveyed, or such things denoted, will be ambiguous and perplexed. And such is the fate of hapless lexicography, that not only darkness, but light, impedes and distresses it; things may be not only too little, but too much known, to be happily illustrated. To explain, requires the use of terms less abstruse than that which is to be explained, and such terms cannot always be found; for as nothing can be proved but by supposing something intuitively known, and evident without proof, so nothing can be defined but by the use of words too plain to admit a definition.

Other words there are, of which the sense is too subtle and evanescent to be fixed in a paraphrase; such are all those which are by the grammarians termed *expletives*, and, in dead languages, are suffered to pass for empty sounds, of no other use than to fill a verse, or to modulate a period, but which are easily perceived in living tongues to have power and emphasis, though it be sometimes such as no other form of expression can convey.

---

[3] *It has been asserted . . . right* see, e.g., Michel   [5] *words . . . heaven* a paraphrase of an ancient thought.
Montaigne, *Essais* 3.13, "Of Experience."
[4] *Change . . . better* Richard Hooker (1554?–1600) *Of the Laws of Ecclesiastical Polity*, 4.14.

My labour has likewise been much increased by a class of verbs too frequent in the *English* language, of which the signification is so loose and general, the use so vague and indeterminate, and the senses detorted so widely from the first idea, that it is hard to trace them through the maze of variation, to catch them on the brink of utter inanity, to circumscribe them by any limitations, or interpret them by any words of distinct and settled meaning: such are *bear, break, come, cast, fall, get, give, do, put, set, go, run, make, take, turn, throw.* If of these the whole power is not accurately delivered, it must be remembered, that while our language is yet living, and variable by the caprice of every tongue that speaks it, these words are hourly shifting their relations, and can no more be ascertained in a dictionary, than a grove, in the agitation of a storm, can be accurately delineated from its picture in the water . . .

In every word of extensive use, it was requisite to mark the progress of its meaning, and show by what gradations of intermediate sense it has passed from its primitive to its remote and accidental signification; so that every foregoing explanation should tend to that which follows, and the series be regularly concatenated from the first notion to the last.

This is specious, but not always practicable; kindred senses may be so interwoven, that the perplexity cannot be disentangled, nor any reason be assigned why one should be ranged before the other. When the radical idea branches out into parallel ramifications, how can a consecutive series be formed of senses in their nature collateral? The shades of meaning sometimes pass imperceptibly into each other; so that though on one side they apparently differ, yet it is impossible to mark the point of contact. Ideas of the same race, though not exactly alike, are sometimes so little different, that no words can express the dissimilitude, though the mind easily perceives it, when they are exhibited together; and sometimes there is such a confusion of acceptations, that discernment is wearied, and distinction puzzled, and perseverance herself hurries to an end, by crowding together what she cannot separate.

These complaints of difficulty will, by those that have never considered words beyond their popular use, be thought only the jargon of a man willing to magnify his labours, and procure veneration to his studies by involution and obscurity. But every art is obscure to those that have not learned it: this uncertainty of terms, and commixture of ideas, is well known to those who have joined philosophy with grammar; and if I have not expressed them very clearly, it must be remembered that I am speaking of that which words are insufficient to explain . . .

All the interpretations of words are not written with the same skill, or the same happiness: things equally easy in themselves, are not all equally easy to any single mind. Every writer of a long work commits errors, where there appears neither ambiguity to mislead, nor obscurity to confound him; and in a search like this, many felicities of expression will be casually overlooked, many convenient parallels will be forgotten, and many particulars will admit improvement from a mind utterly unequal to the whole performance.

The solution of all difficulties, and the supply of all defects, must be sought in the examples, subjoined to the various senses of each word, and ranged according to the time of their authors.

When first I collected these authorities, I was desirous that every quotation should be useful to some other end than the illustration of a word; I therefore extracted from philosophers principles of science; from historians remarkable facts; from chemists complete processes; from divines striking exhortations; and from poets beautiful descriptions. Such is design, while it is yet at a distance from execution. When the time called upon me to range this accumulation of elegance and wisdom into an alphabetical series, I soon discovered that the bulk of my volumes would fright away the student, and was forced to depart from my scheme of including all that was pleasing or useful in *English* literature, and reduce my transcripts very often to clusters of words, in which scarcely any meaning is retained; thus to the weariness of copying, I was condemned to add the vexation of expunging. Some passages I have yet spared, which may relieve the labour of verbal searches, and intersperse with verdure and flowers the dusty deserts of barren philology.

The examples, thus mutilated, are no longer to be considered as conveying the sentiments or doctrine of their authors; the word for the sake of which they are inserted, with all its appendant clauses, has been carefully preserved; but it may sometimes happen, by hasty detruncation, that the general tendency of the sentence may be changed: the divine may desert his tenets, or the philosopher his system.[6]

Some of the examples have been taken from writers who were never mentioned as masters of elegance or models of style; but words must be sought where they are used; and in what pages, eminent for purity, can terms of manufacture or agriculture be found? Many quotations serve no other purpose, than that of proving the bare existence of words, and are therefore selected with less scrupulousness than those which are to teach their structures and relations.

My purpose was to admit no testimony of living authors, that I might not be misled by partiality, and that none of my contemporaries might have reason to complain; nor have I departed from this resolution, but when some performance of uncommon excellence excited my veneration, when my memory supplied me, from late books, with an example that was wanting, or when my heart, in the tenderness of friendship, solicited admission for a favourite name.[7]

So far have I been from any care to grace my pages with modern decorations, that I have studiously endeavoured to collect examples and authorities from the writers before the restoration, whose works I regard as *the wells of English undefiled*, as the pure sources of genuine diction. Our language, for almost a century, has, by the concurrence of many causes, been gradually departing from its original *Teutonic* character, and deviating towards a *Gallic* structure and phraseology, from which it ought to be our endeavour to recall it, by making our ancient volumes the ground-work of style, admitting among the additions of later times, only such as may supply real deficiencies, such as are readily adopted by the genius of our tongue, and incorporate easily with our native idioms.

But as every language has a time of rudeness antecedent to perfection, as well as of false refinement and declension, I have been cautious lest my zeal for antiquity might drive me into times too remote, and crowd my book with words now no longer understood. I have fixed *Sidney*'s work[8] for the boundary, beyond which I make few excursions. From the authors which rose in the time of *Elizabeth*, a speech might be formed adequate to all the purposes of use and elegance. If the language of theology were extracted from *Hooker* and the translation of the Bible;[9] the terms of natural knowledge from Bacon; the phrases of policy, war, and navigation from *Raleigh*; the dialect of poetry and fiction from *Spenser* and *Sidney*; and the diction of common life from *Shakespeare*, few ideas would be lost to mankind, for want of *English* words, in which they might be expressed . . .

There is more danger of censure from the multiplicity than paucity of examples; authorities will sometimes seem to have been accumulated without necessity or use, and perhaps

---

[6] *divine . . . system* in fact, this rarely happens.
[7] *a favourite name* among the living authors whom Johnson cited were David Garrick, Charlotte Lennox, Samuel Richardson, and himself.

[8] *Sidney's work* Sir Philip Sidney (1554–86).
[9] *Bible* the King James Version (1611).

some will be found, which might, without loss, have been omitted. But a work of this kind is not hastily to be charged with superfluities: those quotations which to careless or unskilful perusers appear only to repeat the same sense, will often exhibit, to a more accurate examiner, diversities of signification, or, at least, afford different shades of the same meaning: one will show the word applied to persons, another to things; one will express an ill, another a good, and a third a neutral sense; one will prove the expression genuine from an ancient author; another will show it elegant from a modern: a doubtful authority is corroborated by another of more credit; an ambiguous sentence is ascertained by a passage clear and determinate; the word, how often soever repeated, appears with new associates and in different combinations, and every quotation contributes something to the stability or enlargement of the language . . .

I have sometimes, though rarely, yielded to the temptation of exhibiting a genealogy of sentiments, by showing how one author copied the thoughts and diction of another: such quotations are indeed little more than repetitions, which might justly be censured, did they not gratify the mind, by affording a kind of intellectual history . . .

When first I engaged in this work, I resolved to leave neither words nor things unexamined, and pleased myself with a prospect of the hours which I should revel away in feasts of literature, the obscure recesses of northern learning, which I should enter and ransack, the treasures with which I expected every search into those neglected mines to reward my labour, and the triumph with which I should display my acquisitions to mankind. When I had thus enquired into the original of words, I resolved to show likewise my attention to things; to pierce deep into every science, to enquire the nature of every substance of which I inserted the name, to limit every idea by a definition strictly logical, and exhibit every production of art or nature in an accurate description, that my book might be in place of all other dictionaries whether appellative or technical. But these were the dreams of a poet doomed at last to wake a lexicographer. I soon found that it is too late to look for instruments, when the work calls for execution, and that whatever abilities I had brought to my task, with those I must finally perform it. To deliberate whenever I doubted, to enquire whenever I was ignorant, would have protracted the undertaking without end, and, perhaps, without much improvement; for I did not find by my first experiments, that what I had not of my own was easily to be obtained: I saw that one enquiry only gave occasion to another, that book referred to book, that to search was not always to find, and to find was not always to be informed; and that thus to pursue perfection, was, like the first inhabitants of Arcadia, to chase the sun, which, when they had reached the hill where he seemed to rest, was still beheld at the same distance from them . . .

A large work is difficult because it is large, even though all its parts might singly be performed with facility; where there are many things to be done, each must be allowed its share of time and labour, in the proportion only which it bears to the whole; nor can it be expected, that the stones which form the dome of a temple, should be squared and polished like the diamond of a ring.

Of the event[10] of this work, for which, having laboured it with so much application, I cannot but have some degree of parental fondness, it is natural to form conjectures. Those who have been persuaded to think well of my design, will require that it should fix our language, and put a stop to those alterations which time and chance have hitherto been suffered to make in it without opposition. With this consequence I will confess that I flattered myself for a while; but now begin to fear that I have indulged expectation which

---

[10] *event* the outcome, the result.

neither reason nor experience can justify. When we see men grow old and die at a certain time one after another, from century to century, we laugh at the elixir that promises to prolong life to a thousand years; and with equal justice may the lexicographer be derided, who being able to produce no example of a nation that has preserved their words and phrases from mutability, shall imagine that his dictionary can embalm his language, and secure it from corruption and decay, that it is in his power to change sublunary nature, and clear the world at once from folly, vanity, and affectation.

With this hope, however, academies have been instituted, to guard the avenues of their languages, to retain fugitives, and repulse intruders; but their vigilance and activity have hitherto been vain; sounds are too volatile and subtle for legal restraints; to enchain syllables, and to lash the wind,[11] are equally the undertakings of pride, unwilling to measure its desires by its strength . . .

Total and sudden transformations of a language seldom happen; conquests and migrations are now very rare: but there are other causes of change, which, though slow in their operation, and invisible in their progress, are perhaps as much superior to human resistance, as the revolutions of the sky, or intumescence of the tide. Commerce, however necessary, however lucrative, as it depraves the manners, corrupts the language; they that have frequent intercourse with strangers, to whom they endeavour to accommodate themselves, must in time learn a mingled dialect, like the jargon which serves the traffickers on the *Mediterranean* and *Indian* coasts. This will not always be confined to the exchange, the warehouse, or the port, but will be communicated by degrees to other ranks of the people, and be at last incorporated with the current speech.

There are likewise internal causes equally forcible. The language most likely to continue long without alteration, would be that of a nation raised a little, and but a little, above barbarity, secluded from strangers, and totally employed in procuring the conveniencies of life; either without books, or, like some of the *Mahometan* countries, with very few: men thus busied and unlearned, having only such words as common use requires, would perhaps long continue to express the same notions by the same signs. But no such constancy can be expected in a people polished by arts, and classed by subordination, where one part of the community is sustained and accommodated by the labour of the other. Those who have much leisure to think, will always be enlarging the stock of ideas, and every increase of knowledge, whether real or fancied, will produce new words, or combinations of words. When the mind is unchained from necessity, it will range after convenience; when it is left at large in the fields of speculation, it will shift opinions; as any custom is disused, the words that expressed it must perish with it; as any opinion grows popular, it will innovate speech in the same proportion as it alters practice.

As by the cultivation of various sciences, a language is amplified, it will be more furnished with words deflected from their original sense; the geometrician will talk of a courtier's *zenith*, or the *eccentric* virtue of a wild hero, and the physician of sanguine expectations and phlegmatic delays. Copiousness of speech will give opportunities to capricious choice, by which some words will be preferred, and others degraded; vicissitudes of fashion will enforce the use of new, or extend the signification of known terms. The tropes of poetry will make hourly encroachments, and the metaphorical will become the current sense: pronunciation will be varied by levity or ignorance, and the pen must at length comply with the tongue; illiterate writers[12] will at one time or other, by public infatuation, rise into renown, who, not knowing

---

[11] *to lash the wind* Xerxes' mad attempt (see *The Vanity of Human Wishes*, l. 232 above, p. 849).

[12] *illiterate writers* who do not know Latin or the history of English.

the original import of words, will use them with colloquial licentiousness, confound distinction, and forget propriety. As politeness increases, some expressions will be considered as too gross and vulgar for the delicate, others as too formal and ceremonious for the gay and airy; new phrases are therefore adopted, which must, for the same reasons, be in time dismissed . . .

If the changes that we fear be thus irresistible, what remains but to acquiesce with silence, as in the other insurmountable distresses of humanity? It remains that we retard what we cannot repel, that we palliate what we cannot cure. Life may be lengthened by care, though death cannot be ultimately defeated: tongues, like governments, have a natural tendency to degeneration; we have long preserved our constitution, let us make some struggles for our language.

In hope of giving longevity to that which its own nature forbids to be immortal, I have devoted this book, the labour of years, to the honour of my country, that we may no longer yield the palm of philology, without a contest, to the nations of the continent.[13] The chief glory of every people arises from its authors: whether I shall add any thing by my own writings to the reputation of *English* literature, must be left to time: much of my life has been lost under the pressures of disease; much has been trifled away; and much has always been spent in provision for the day that was passing over me; but I shall not think my employment useless or ignoble, if by my assistance foreign nations, and distant ages, gain access to the propagators of knowledge, and understand the teachers of truth; if my labours afford light to the repositories of science, and add celebrity to *Bacon*, to *Hooker*, to *Milton*, and to *Boyle*.[14]

When I am animated by this wish, I look with pleasure on my book, however defective, and deliver it to the world with the spirit of a man that has endeavoured well. That it will immediately become popular I have not promised to myself: a few wild blunders, and risible absurdities, from which no work of such multiplicity was ever free, may for a time furnish folly with laughter, and harden ignorance in contempt; but useful diligence will at last prevail, and there never can be wanting some who distinguish desert; who will consider that no dictionary of a living tongue ever can be perfect, since while it is hastening to publication, some words are budding, and some falling away; that a whole life cannot be spent upon syntax and etymology, and that even a whole life would not be sufficient; that he, whose design includes whatever language can express, must often speak of what he does not understand; that a writer will sometimes be hurried by eagerness to the end, and sometimes faint with weariness under a task, which *Scaliger* compares to the labours of the anvil and the mine;[15] that what is obvious is not always known, and what is known is not always present; that sudden fits of inadvertency will surprise vigilance, slight avocations will seduce attention, and casual eclipses of the mind will darken learning; and that the writer shall often in vain trace his memory at the moment of need, for that which yesterday he knew with intuitive readiness, and which will come uncalled into his thoughts to-morrow.

In this work, when it shall be found that much is omitted, let it not be forgotten that much likewise is performed; and though no book was ever spared out of tenderness to the

---

[13] *the nations of the continent* Italy and France had both produced national dictionaries through the work of academies formed for the purpose.

[14] *Boyle* Robert (1627–91), chemist and, like the other three, an author whose works are frequently cited in the *Dictionary*.

[15] *Scaliger . . . mine* Joseph Scaliger (1540–1609), one of Johnson's heroes, author of an Arabic-Latin dictionary, so described lexicography in a Latin poem.

author, and the world is little solicitous to know whence proceeded the faults of that which it condemns; yet it may gratify curiosity to inform it, that the *English Dictionary* was written with little assistance of the learned, and without any patronage of the great; not in the soft obscurities of retirement, or under the shelter of academic bowers, but amidst inconvenience and distraction, in sickness and in sorrow. It may repress the triumph of malignant criticism to observe, that if our language is not here fully displayed, I have only failed in an attempt which no human powers have hitherto completed. If the lexicons of ancient tongues, now immutably fixed, and comprised in a few volumes, are yet, after the toil of successive ages, inadequate and delusive; if the aggregated knowledge, and co-operating diligence of the *Italian* academicians, did not secure them from the censure of *Beni*;[16] if the embodied critics of *France*, when fifty years had been spent upon their work, were obliged to change its economy, and give their second edition another form,[17] I may surely be contented without the praise of perfection, which, if I could obtain, in this gloom of solitude, what would it avail me? I have protracted my work till most of those whom I wished to please, have sunk into the grave,[18] and success and miscarriage are empty sounds: I therefore dismiss it with frigid tranquillity, having little to fear or hope from censure or from praise.

The History of Rasselas, Prince of Abyssinia (1759)

CHAPTER 1
DESCRIPTION OF A PALACE IN A VALLEY

Ye who listen with credulity to the whispers of fancy, and pursue with eagerness the phantoms of hope; who expect that age will perform the promises of youth, and that the deficiencies of the present day will be supplied by the morrow; attend to the history of Rasselas prince of Abyssinia.

Rasselas was the fourth son of the mighty emperor, in whose dominions the Father of waters begins his course; whose bounty pours down the streams of plenty, and scatters over half the world the harvests of Egypt.

According to the custom which has descended from age to age among the monarchs of the torrid zone, he was confined in a private palace, with the other sons and daughters of Abyssinian royalty, till the order of succession should call him to the throne.

The place, which the wisdom or policy of antiquity had destined for the residence of the Abyssinian princes, was a spacious valley in the kingdom of Amhara, surrounded on every side by mountains, of which the summits overhang the middle part. The only passage, by which it could be entered, was a cavern that passed under a rock, of which it has long been disputed whether it was the work of nature or of human industry. The outlet of the cavern was concealed by a thick wood, and the mouth which opened into the valley was closed with gates of iron, forged by the artificers of ancient days, so massy that no man could, without the help of engines, open or shut them.

From the mountains on every side, rivulets descended that filled all the valley with verdure and fertility, and formed a lake in the middle inhabited by fish of every species, and frequented by every fowl whom nature has taught to dip the wing in water. This lake

---

[16] *Beni* Paolo Beni attacked the first edition of the *Vocabolario della Crusca* (1612).

[17] *another form* for the second edition (1718) the editors strengthened the alphabetical ordering of the book by listing many words separately that had first appeared under their root forms.

[18] *sunk into the grave* Johnson was thinking especially of his wife Elizabeth, who died in 1752.

discharged its superfluities by a stream which entered a dark cleft of the mountain on the northern side, and fell with dreadful noise from precipice to precipice till it was heard no more.

The sides of the mountains were covered with trees, the banks of the brooks were diversified with flowers; every blast shook spices from the rocks, and every month dropped fruits upon the ground. All animals that bite the grass, or browse the shrub, whether wild or tame, wandered in this extensive circuit, secured from beasts of prey by the mountains which confined them. On one part were flocks and herds feeding in the pastures, on another all the beasts of chase frisking in the lawns;[1] the spritely kid was bounding on the rocks, the subtle monkey frolicking in the trees, and the solemn elephant reposing in the shade. All the diversities of the world were brought together, the blessings of nature were collected, and its evils extracted and excluded.

The valley, wide and fruitful, supplied its inhabitants with the necessaries of life, and all delights and superfluities were added at the annual visit which the emperor paid his children, when the iron gate was opened to the sound of music; and during eight days every one that resided in the valley was required to propose whatever might contribute to make seclusion pleasant, to fill up the vacancies of attention, and lessen the tediousness of time. Every desire was immediately granted. All the artificers of pleasure were called to gladden the festivity; the musicians exerted the power of harmony, and the dancers showed their activity before the princes, in hope that they should pass their lives in this blissful captivity, to which those only were admitted whose performance was thought able to add novelty to luxury. Such was the appearance of security and delight which this retirement afforded, that they to whom it was new always desired that it might be perpetual; and as those, on whom the iron gate had once closed, were never suffered to return, the effect of longer experience could not be known. Thus every year produced new schemes of delight, and new competitors for imprisonment.

The palace stood on an eminence raised about thirty paces above the surface of the lake. It was divided into many squares or courts, built with greater or less magnificence according to the rank of those for whom they were designed. The roofs were turned into arches of massy stone joined with a cement that grew harder by time, and the building stood from century to century, deriding the solstitial rains and equinoctial hurricanes, without need of reparation.

This house, which was so large as to be fully known to none but some ancient officers who successively inherited the secrets of the place, was built as if suspicion herself had dictated the plan. To every room there was an open and secret passage, every square had a communication with the rest, either from the upper stories by private galleries, or by subterranean passages from the lower apartments. Many of the columns had unsuspected cavities, in which successive monarchs reposited their treasures. They then closed up the opening with marble, which was never to be removed but in the utmost exigencies of the kingdom; and recorded their accumulations in a book which was itself concealed in a tower not entered but by the emperor, attended by the prince who stood next in succession.

CHAPTER 2
THE DISCONTENT OF RASSELAS IN THE HAPPY VALLEY

Here the sons and daughters of Abyssinia lived only to know the soft vicissitudes of pleasure and repose, attended by all that were skilful to delight, and gratified with whatever

---

The History of Rasselas, Prince of Abyssinia
[1]   *lawn*   "An open space between woods" (Johnson).

the senses can enjoy. They wandered in gardens of fragrance, and slept in the fortresses of security. Every art was practised to make them pleased with their own condition. The sages who instructed them, told them of nothing but the miseries of public life, and described all beyond the mountains as regions of calamity, where discord was always raging, and where man preyed upon man.

To heighten their opinion of their own felicity, they were daily entertained with songs, the subject of which was the *happy valley*. Their appetites were excited by frequent enumerations of different enjoyments, and revelry and merriment was the business of every hour from the dawn of morning to the close of even.

These methods were generally successful; few of the princes had ever wished to enlarge their bounds, but passed their lives in full conviction that they had all within their reach that art or nature could bestow, and pitied those whom fate had excluded from this seat of tranquillity, as the sport of chance, and the slaves of misery.

Thus they rose in the morning, and lay down at night, pleased with each other and with themselves, all but Rasselas, who, in the twenty-sixth year of his age, began to withdraw himself from their pastimes and assemblies, and to delight in solitary walks and silent meditation. He often sat before tables covered with luxury, and forgot to taste the dainties that were placed before him: he rose abruptly in the midst of the song, and hastily retired beyond the sound of music. His attendants observed the change and endeavoured to renew his love of pleasure: he neglected their endeavours, repulsed their invitations, and spent day after day on the banks of rivulets sheltered with trees, where he sometimes listened to the birds in the branches, sometimes observed the fish playing in the stream, and anon cast his eyes upon the pastures and mountains filled with animals, of which some were biting the herbage, and some sleeping among the bushes.

This singularity of his humour made him much observed. One of the Sages, in whose conversation he had formerly delighted, followed him secretly, in hope of discovering the cause of his disquiet. Rasselas, who knew not that any one was near him, having for some time fixed his eyes upon the goats that were browsing among the rocks, began to compare their condition with his own.

'What', said he, 'makes the difference between man and all the rest of the animal creation? Every beast that strays beside me has the same corporal necessities with myself; he is hungry and crops the grass, he is thirsty and drinks the stream, his thirst and hunger are appeased, he is satisfied and sleeps; he rises again and is hungry, he is again fed and is at rest. I am hungry and thirsty like him, but when thirst and hunger cease I am not at rest; I am, like him, pained with want, but am not, like him, satisfied with fullness. The intermediate hours are tedious and gloomy; I long again to be hungry that I may again quicken my attention. The birds peck the berries or the corn, and fly away to the groves where they sit in seeming happiness on the branches, and waste their lives in tuning one unvaried series of sounds. I likewise can call the lutanist and the singer, but the sounds that pleased me yesterday weary me to day, and will grow yet more wearisome tomorrow. I can discover within me no power of perception which is not glutted with its proper pleasure, yet I do not feel myself delighted. Man has surely some latent sense for which this place affords no gratification, or he has some desires distinct from sense which must be satisfied before he can be happy'.[2]

After this he lifted up his head, and seeing the moon rising, walked towards the palace. As he passed through the fields, and saw the animals around him, 'Ye', said he, 'are happy, and need not envy me that walk thus among you, burthened with myself; nor do I, ye gentle

---

[2]   *Man . . . happy*   among many theologians this was a standard argument for the existence of an immortal soul.

beings, envy your felicity; for it is not the felicity of man. I have many distresses from which ye are free; I fear pain when I do not feel it; I sometimes shrink at evils recollected, and sometimes start at evils anticipated: surely the equity of providence has balanced peculiar sufferings with peculiar enjoyments'.

With observations like these the prince amused himself as he returned, uttering them with a plaintive voice, yet with a look that discovered him to feel some complacence in his own perspicacity, and to receive some solace of the miseries of life, from consciousness of the delicacy with which he felt, and the eloquence with which he bewailed them. He mingled cheerfully in the diversions of the evening, and all rejoiced to find that his heart was lightened.

CHAPTER 3
THE WANTS OF HIM THAT WANTS NOTHING

On the next day his old instructor, imagining that he had now made himself acquainted with his disease of mind, was in hope of curing it by counsel, and officiously sought an opportunity of conference, which the prince, having long considered him as one whose intellects were exhausted, was not very willing to afford: 'Why', said he, 'does this man thus intrude upon me; shall I be never suffered to forget those lectures which pleased only while they were new, and to become new again must be forgotten?' He then walked into the wood, and composed himself to his usual meditations; when, before his thoughts had taken any settled form, he perceived his pursuer at his side, and was at first prompted by his impatience to go hastily away; but, being unwilling to offend a man whom he had once reverenced and still loved, he invited him to sit down with him on the bank.

The old man, thus encouraged, began to lament the change which had been lately observed in the prince, and to enquire why he so often retired from the pleasures of the palace, to loneliness and silence. 'I fly from pleasure', said the prince, 'because pleasure has ceased to please; I am lonely because I am miserable, and am unwilling to cloud with my presence the happiness of others'. 'You, Sir', said the sage, 'are the first who has complained of misery in the *happy valley*. I hope to convince you that your complaints have no real cause. You are here in full possession of all that the emperor of Abyssinia can bestow; here is neither labour to be endured nor danger to be dreaded, yet here is all that labour or danger can procure. Look round and tell me which of your wants is without supply: if you want nothing, how are you unhappy?'

'That I want nothing', said the prince, 'or that I know not what I want, is the cause of my complaint; if I had any known want, I should have a certain wish; that wish would excite endeavour, and I should not then repine to see the sun move so slowly towards the western mountain, or lament when the day breaks and sleep will no longer hide me from myself. When I see the kids and the lambs chasing one another, I fancy that I should be happy if I had something to pursue. But, possessing all that I can want, I find one day and one hour exactly like another, except that the latter is still more tedious than the former. Let your experience inform me how the day may now seem as short as in my childhood, while nature was yet fresh, and every moment showed me what I never had observed before. I have already enjoyed too much; give me something to desire'.

The old man was surprised at this new species of affliction, and knew not what to reply, yet was unwilling to be silent. 'Sir', said he, 'if you had seen the miseries of the world, you would know how to value your present state'. 'Now', said the prince, 'you have given me something to desire; I shall long to see the miseries of the world, since the sight of them is necessary to happiness'.

CHAPTER 4
THE PRINCE CONTINUES TO GRIEVE AND MUSE

At this time the sound of music proclaimed the hour of repast, and the conversation was concluded. The old man went away sufficiently discontented to find that his reasonings had produced the only conclusion which they were intended to prevent. But in the decline of life shame and grief are of short duration; whether it be that we bear easily what we have borne long, or that, finding ourselves in age less regarded, we less regard others; or, that we look with slight regard upon afflictions, to which we know that the hand of death is about to put an end.

The prince, whose views were extended to a wider space, could not speedily quiet his emotions. He had been before terrified at the length of life which nature promised him, because he considered that in a long time much must be endured; he now rejoiced in his youth, because in many years much might be done.

This first beam of hope, that had been ever darted into his mind, rekindled youth in his cheeks, and doubled the lustre of his eyes. He was fired with the desire of doing something, though he knew not yet with distinctness, either end or means.

He was now no longer gloomy and unsocial; but, considering himself as master of a secret stock of happiness, which he could enjoy only by concealing it, he affected to be busy in all schemes of diversion, and endeavoured to make others pleased with the state of which he himself was weary. But pleasures never can be so multiplied or continued, as not to leave much of life unemployed; there were many hours, both of the night and day, which he could spend without suspicion in solitary thought. The load of life was much lightened: he went eagerly into the assemblies, because he supposed the frequency of his presence necessary to the success of his purposes; he retired gladly to privacy, because he had now a subject of thought.

His chief amusement was to picture to himself that world which he had never seen; to place himself in various conditions; to be entangled in imaginary difficulties, and to be engaged in wild adventures: but his benevolence always terminated his projects in the relief of distress, the detection of fraud, the defeat of oppression, and the diffusion of happiness.

Thus passed twenty months of the life of Rasselas. He busied himself so intensely in visionary bustle, that he forgot his real solitude; and, amidst hourly preparations for the various incidents of human affairs, neglected to consider by what means he should mingle with mankind.

One day, as he was sitting on a bank, he feigned to himself an orphan virgin robbed of her little portion[3] by a treacherous lover, and crying after him for restitution and redress. So strongly was the image impressed upon his mind, that he started up in the maid's defence, and ran forward to seize the plunderer with all the eagerness of real pursuit. Fear naturally quickens the flight of guilt. Rasselas could not catch the fugitive with his utmost efforts; but, resolving to weary, by perseverance, him whom he could not surpass in speed, he pressed on till the foot of the mountain stopped his course.

Here he recollected himself, and smiled at his own useless impetuosity. Then raising his eyes to the mountain, 'This', said he, 'is the fatal obstacle that hinders at once the enjoyment of pleasure, and the exercise of virtue. How long is it that my hopes and wishes have flown beyond this boundary of my life, which yet I never have attempted to surmount!'

---

[3] *portion* inheritance.

Struck with this reflection, he sat down to muse, and remembered, that since he first resolved to escape from his confinement, the sun had passed twice over him in his annual course. He now felt a degree of regret with which he had never been before acquainted. He considered how much might have been done in the time which had passed, and left nothing real behind it. He compared twenty months with the life of man. 'In life', said he, 'is not to be counted the ignorance of infancy, or imbecility of age. We are long before we are able to think, and we soon cease from the power of acting. The true period of human existence may be reasonably estimated as forty years, of which I have mused away the four and twentieth part. What I have lost was certain, for I have certainly possessed it; but of twenty months to come who can assure me?'

The consciousness of his own folly pierced him deeply, and he was long before he could be reconciled to himself. 'The rest of my time', said he, 'has been lost by the crime or folly of my ancestors, and the absurd institutions of my country; I remember it with disgust, but without remorse: but the months that have passed since new light darted into my soul, since I formed a scheme of reasonable felicity, have been squandered by my own fault. I have lost that which can never be restored: I have seen the sun rise and set for twenty months, an idle gazer on the light of heaven: In this time the birds have left the nest of their mother, and committed themselves to the woods and to the skies: the kid has forsaken the teat, and learned by degrees to climb the rocks in quest of independent sustenance. I only have made no advances, but am still helpless and ignorant. The moon, by more than twenty changes, admonished me of the flux of life; the stream that rolled before my feet upbraided my inactivity. I sat feasting on intellectual luxury, regardless alike of the examples of the earth, and the instructions of the planets. Twenty months are past, who shall restore them!'

These sorrowful meditations fastened upon his mind; he passed four months in resolving to lose no more time in idle resolves, and was awakened to more vigorous exertion by hearing a maid, who had broken a porcelain cup, remark, that what cannot be repaired is not to be regretted.

This was obvious; and Rasselas reproached himself that he had not discovered it, having not known, or not considered, how many useful hints are obtained by chance, and how often the mind, hurried by her own ardour to distant views, neglects the truths that lie open before her. He, for a few hours, regretted his regret, and from that time bent his whole mind upon the means of escaping from the valley of happiness.

CHAPTER 5
THE PRINCE MEDITATES HIS ESCAPE

He now found that it would be very difficult to effect that which it was very easy to suppose effected. When he looked round about him, he saw himself confined by the bars of nature which had never yet been broken, and by the gate, through which none that once had passed it were ever able to return. He was now impatient as an eagle in a grate.[4] He passed week after week in clambering the mountains, to see if there was any aperture which the bushes might conceal, but found all the summits inaccessible by their prominence. The iron gate he despaired to open; for it was not only secured with all the power of art, but was always watched by successive sentinels, and was by its position exposed to the perpetual observation of all the inhabitants.

---

[4]   *grate*   prison cell with bars or a cage.

He then examined the cavern through which the waters of the lake were discharged; and, looking down at a time when the sun shone strongly upon its mouth, he discovered it to be full of broken rocks, which, though they permitted the stream to flow through many narrow passages, would stop any body of solid bulk. He returned discouraged and dejected; but, having now known the blessing of hope, resolved never to despair.

In these fruitless searches he spent ten months. The time, however, passed cheerfully away: in the morning he rose with new hope, in the evening applauded his own diligence, and in the night slept sound after his fatigue. He met a thousand amusements which beguiled his labour, and diversified his thoughts. He discerned the various instincts of animals, and properties of plants, and found the place replete with wonders, of which he purposed to solace himself with the contemplation, if he should never be able to accomplish his flight; rejoicing that his endeavours, though yet unsuccessful, had supplied him with a source of inexhaustible enquiry.

But his original curiosity was not yet abated; he resolved to obtain some knowledge of the ways of men. His wish still continued, but his hope grew less. He ceased to survey any longer the walls of his prison, and spared to search by new toils for interstices which he knew could not be found, yet determined to keep his design always in view, and lay hold on any expedient that time should offer.

CHAPTER 6
A DISSERTATION ON THE ART OF FLYING

Among the artists that had been allured into the happy valley, to labour for the accommodation and pleasure of its inhabitants, was a man eminent for his knowledge of the mechanic powers, who had contrived many engines both of use and recreation. By a wheel, which the stream turned, he forced the water into a tower, whence it was distributed to all the apartments of the palace. He erected a pavilion in the garden, around which he kept the air always cool by artificial showers. One of the groves, appropriated to the ladies, was ventilated by fans, to which the rivulet that ran through it gave a constant motion; and instruments of soft music were placed at proper distances, of which some played by the impulse of the wind, and some by the power of the stream.

This artist was sometimes visited by Rasselas, who was pleased with every kind of knowledge, imagining that the time would come when all his acquisitions should be of use to him in the open world. He came one day to amuse himself in his usual manner, and found the master busy in building a sailing chariot: he saw that the design was practicable upon a level surface, and with expressions of great esteem solicited its completion. The workman was pleased to find himself so much regarded by the prince, and resolved to gain yet higher honours. 'Sir', said he, 'you have seen but a small part of what the mechanic[5] sciences can perform. I have been long of opinion, that, instead of the tardy conveyance of ships and chariots, man might use the swifter migration of wings; that the fields of air are open to knowledge, and that only ignorance and idleness need crawl upon the ground'.

This hint rekindled the prince's desire of passing the mountains; and having seen what the mechanist had already performed, he was willing to fancy that he could do more; yet resolved to enquire further before he suffered hope to afflict him by disappointment. 'I am afraid', said he to the artist, 'that your imagination prevails over your skill, and that you now tell me rather what you wish than what you know. Every animal has his element assigned him; the

---

[5] *mechanic*   practical or applied.

birds have the air, and man and beasts the earth'. 'So', replied the mechanist, 'fishes have the water, in which yet beasts can swim by nature, and men by art. He that can swim needs not despair to fly: to swim is to fly in a grosser fluid, and to fly is to swim in a subtler.[6] We are only to proportion our power of resistance to the different density of the matter through which we are to pass. You will be necessarily upborne by the air, if you can renew any impulse upon it, faster than the air can recede from the pressure'.

'But the exercise of swimming, said the prince, is very laborious; the strongest limbs are soon wearied; I am afraid the act of flying will be yet more violent, and wings will be of no great use, unless we can fly further than we can swim'.

'The labour of rising from the ground', said the artist, 'will be great, as we see it in the heavier domestic fowls; but, as we mount higher, the earth's attraction, and the body's gravity, will be gradually diminished, till we shall arrive at a region where the man will float in the air without any tendency to fall: no care will then be necessary, but to move forwards, which the gentlest impulse will effect. You, Sir, whose curiosity is so extensive, will easily conceive with what pleasure a philosopher, furnished with wings, and hovering in the sky, would see the earth, and all its inhabitants, rolling beneath him, and presenting to him successively, by its diurnal motion, all the countries within the same parallel. How must it amuse the pendent[7] spectator to see the moving scene of land and ocean, cities and deserts! To survey with equal security the marts of trade, and the fields of battle; mountains infested by barbarians, and fruitful regions gladdened by plenty, and lulled by peace! How easily shall we then trace the Nile through all his passage; pass over to distant regions, and examine the face of nature from one extremity of the earth to the other!'

'All this', said the prince, 'is much to be desired, but I am afraid that no man will be able to breathe in these regions of speculation and tranquillity. I have been told, that respiration is difficult upon lofty mountains, yet from these precipices, though so high as to produce great tenuity[8] of the air, it is very easy to fall: therefore I suspect, that from any height, where life can be supported, there may be danger of too quick descent'.

'Nothing', replied the artist, 'will ever be attempted, if all possible objections must be first overcome. If you will favour my project I will try the first flight at my own hazard. I have considered the structure of all volant[9] animals, and find the folding continuity of the bat's wings most easily accommodated to the human form. Upon this model I shall begin my task tomorrow, and in a year expect to tower into the air beyond the malice or pursuit of man. But I will work only on this condition, that the art shall not be divulged, and that you shall not require me to make wings for any but ourselves'.

'Why', said Rasselas, 'should you envy others so great an advantage? All skill ought to be exerted for universal good; every man has owed much to others, and ought to repay the kindness that he has received'.

'If men were all virtuous', returned the artist, 'I should with great alacrity teach them all to fly. But what would be the security of the good, if the bad could at pleasure invade them from the sky? Against an army sailing through the cloud neither walls, nor mountains, nor seas, could afford any security. A flight of northern savages might hover in the wind, and light at once with irresistible violence upon the capital of a fruitful region that was rolling under them. Even this valley, the retreat of princes, the abode of happiness, might be violated by the sudden descent of some of the naked nations that swarm on the coast of the southern sea'.

---

6   *subtle*   "Thin; not dense; not gross" (Johnson).
7   *pendent*   suspended, in air.
8   *tenuity*   thinness.

9   *volant*   flying (latinate words, like "tenuity" and "volant" comprised the technical vocabulary of contemporary researchers and inventors).

The prince promised secrecy, and waited for the performance, not wholly hopeless of success. He visited the work from time to time, observed its progress, and remarked many ingenious contrivances to facilitate motion, and unite levity with strength. The artist was every day more certain that he should leave vultures and eagles behind him, and the contagion of his confidence seized upon the prince.

In a year the wings were finished, and, on a morning appointed, the maker appeared furnished for flight on a little promontory: he waved his pinions a while to gather air, then leaped from his stand, and in an instant dropped into the lake. His wings, which were of no use in the air, sustained him in the water, and the prince drew him to land, half dead with terror and vexation.

CHAPTER 7
THE PRINCE FINDS A MAN OF LEARNING

The prince was not much afflicted by this disaster, having suffered himself to hope for a happier event, only because he had no other means of escape in view. He still persisted in his design to leave the happy valley by the first opportunity.

His imagination was now at a stand; he had no prospect of entering into the world; and, notwithstanding all his endeavours to support himself, discontent by degrees preyed upon him, and he began again to lose his thoughts in sadness, when the rainy season, which in these countries is periodical, made it inconvenient to wander in the woods.

The rain continued longer and with more violence than had been ever known: the clouds broke on the surrounding mountains, and the torrents streamed into the plain on every side, till the cavern was too narrow to discharge the water. The lake overflowed its banks, and all the level of the valley was covered with the inundation. The eminence, on which the palace was built, and some other spots of rising ground, were all that the eye could now discover. The herds and flocks left the pastures, and both the wild beasts and the tame retreated to the mountains.

This inundation confined all the princes to domestic amusements, and the attention of Rasselas was particularly seized by a poem, which Imlac recited, upon the various conditions of humanity. He commanded the poet to attend him in his apartment, and recite his verses a second time; then entering into familiar talk, he thought himself happy in having found a man who knew the world so well, and could so skilfully paint the scenes of life. He asked a thousand questions about things, to which, though common to all other mortals, his confinement from childhood had kept him a stranger. The poet pitied his ignorance, and loved his curiosity, and entertained him from day to day with novelty and instruction, so that the prince regretted the necessity of sleep, and longed till the morning should renew his pleasure.

As they were sitting together, the prince commanded Imlac to relate his history, and to tell by what accident he was forced, or by what motive induced, to close his life in the happy valley. As he was going to begin his narrative, Rasselas was called to a concert, and obliged to restrain his curiosity till the evening.

CHAPTER 8
THE HISTORY OF IMLAC

The close of the day is, in the regions of the torrid zone, the only season of diversion and entertainment, and it was therefore mid-night before the music ceased, and the princesses retired. Rasselas then called for his companion and required him to begin the story of his life.

'Sir', said Imlac, 'my history will not be long: the life that is devoted to knowledge passes silently away, and is very little diversified by events. To talk in public, to think in solitude, to read and to hear, to enquire, and answer enquiries, is the business of a scholar. He wanders about the world without pomp or terror, and is neither known nor valued but by men like himself.

'I was born in the kingdom of Goiama, at no great distance from the fountain of the Nile. My father was a wealthy merchant, who traded between the inland countries of Africka and the ports of the Red Sea. He was honest, frugal and diligent, but of mean sentiments, and narrow comprehension: he desired only to be rich, and to conceal his riches, lest he should be spoiled by the governors of the province'.

'Surely', said the prince, 'my father must be negligent of his charge, if any man in his dominions dares take that which belongs to another. Does he not know that kings are accountable for injustice permitted as well as done? If I were emperor, not the meanest of my subjects should be oppressed with impunity. My blood boils when I am told that a merchant durst not enjoy his honest gains for fear of losing them by the rapacity of power. Name the governor who robbed the people, that I may declare his crimes to the emperor'.

'Sir', said Imlac, 'your ardour is the natural effect of virtue animated by youth: the time will come when you will acquit your father, and perhaps hear with less impatience of the governor. Oppression is, in the Abyssinian dominions, neither frequent nor tolerated; but no form of government has been yet discovered, by which cruelty can be wholly prevented. Subordination supposes power on one part and subjection on the other; and if power be in the hands of men, it will sometimes be abused. The vigilance of the supreme magistrate may do much, but much will still remain undone. He can never know all the crimes that are committed, and can seldom punish all that he knows'.

'This', said the prince, 'I do not understand, but I had rather hear thee than dispute. Continue thy narration'.

'My father', proceeded Imlac, 'originally intended that I should have no other education, than such as might qualify me for commerce; and discovering in me great strength of memory, and quickness of apprehension, often declared his hope that I should be some time the richest man in Abyssinia'.

'Why', said the prince, 'did thy father desire the increase of his wealth, when it was already greater than he durst discover or enjoy? I am unwilling to doubt thy veracity, yet inconsistencies cannot both be true'.

'Inconsistencies', answered Imlac, 'cannot both be right, but, imputed to man, they may both be true. Yet diversity is not inconsistency. My father might expect a time of greater security. However, some desire is necessary to keep life in motion, and he, whose real wants are supplied, must admit those of fancy'.

'This', said the prince, 'I can in some measure conceive. I repent that I interrupted thee'.

'With this hope', proceeded Imlac, 'he sent me to school; but when I had once found the delight of knowledge, and felt the pleasure of intelligence and the pride of invention, I began silently to despise riches, and determined to disappoint the purpose of my father, whose grossness of conception raised my pity. I was twenty years old before his tenderness would expose me to the fatigue of travel, in which time I had been instructed, by successive masters, in all the literature of my native country. As every hour taught me something new, I lived in a continual course of gratifications; but, as I advanced towards manhood, I lost much of the reverence with which I had been used to look on my instructors; because, when the lesson was ended, I did not find them wiser or better than common men.

'At length my father resolved to initiate me in commerce, and, opening one of his subterranean treasuries, counted out ten thousand pieces of gold. "This, young man", said he, "is the stock with which you must negotiate. I began with less than the fifth part, and you see how diligence and parsimony have increased it. This is your own to waste or to improve. If you squander it by negligence or caprice, you must wait for my death before you will be rich: if, in four years, you double your stock, we will thenceforward let subordination cease, and live together as friends and partners; for he shall always be equal with me, who is equally skilled in the art of growing rich" '.

'We laid our money upon camels, concealed in bales of cheap goods, and travelled to the shore of the Red Sea. When I cast my eye on the expanse of waters my heart bounded like that of a prisoner escaped. I felt an unextinguishable curiosity kindle in my mind, and resolved to snatch this opportunity of seeing the manners of other nations, and of learning sciences unknown in Abyssinia.

'I remembered that my father had obliged me to the improvement of my stock, not by a promise which I ought not to violate, but by a penalty which I was at liberty to incur; and therefore determined to gratify my predominant desire, and by drinking at the fountains of knowledge, to quench the thirst of curiosity.

'As I was supposed to trade without connection with my father, it was easy for me to become acquainted with the master of a ship, and procure a passage to some other country. I had no motives of choice to regulate my voyage; it was sufficient for me that, wherever I wandered, I should see a country which I had not seen before. I therefore entered a ship bound for Surat,[10] having left a letter for my father declaring my intention.

CHAPTER 9
THE HISTORY OF IMLAC CONTINUED

'When I first entered upon the world of waters, and lost sight of land, I looked round about me with pleasing terror, and thinking my soul enlarged by the boundless prospect, imagined that I could gaze round for ever without satiety; but, in a short time, I grew weary of looking on barren uniformity, where I could only see again what I had already seen. I then descended into the ship, and doubted for a while whether all my future pleasures would not end like this in disgust and disappointment. Yet, surely, said I, the ocean and the land are very different; the only variety of water is rest and motion, but the earth has mountains and valleys, deserts and cities: it is inhabited by men of different customs and contrary opinions; and I may hope to find variety in life, though I should miss it in nature.

'With this hope I quieted my mind; and amused myself during the voyage; sometimes by learning from the sailors the art of navigation, which I have never practised, and sometimes by forming schemes for my conduct in different situations, in not one of which I have been ever placed.

'I was almost weary of my naval amusements when we landed safely at Surat. I secured my money, and purchasing some commodities for show, joined myself to a caravan that was passing into the inland country. My companions, for some reason or other, conjecturing that I was rich, and, by my enquiries and admiration, finding that I was ignorant, considered me as a novice whom they had a right to cheat, and who was to learn at the usual expense the art of fraud. They exposed me to the theft of servants, and the exaction of officers, and saw me

---

[10]   *Surat*   a city in India famous for trade.

plundered upon false pretences, without any advantage to themselves, but that of rejoicing in the superiority of their own knowledge'.

'Stop a moment', said the prince. 'Is there such depravity in man, as that he should injure another without benefit to himself? I can easily conceive that all are pleased with superiority; but your ignorance was merely accidental, which, being neither your crime nor your folly, could afford them no reason to applaud themselves; and the knowledge which they had, and which you wanted, they might as effectually have shown by warning, as betraying you'.

'Pride, said Imlac, 'is seldom delicate, it will please itself with very mean advantages; and envy feels not its own happiness, but when it may be compared with the misery of others. They were my enemies because they thought me rich, and my oppressors because they delighted to find me weak'.

'Proceed', said the prince: 'I doubt not of the facts which you relate, but imagine that you impute them to mistaken motives'.

'In this company', said Imlac, 'I arrived at Agra,[11] the capital of Indostan, the city in which the great Mogul commonly resides. I applied myself to the language of the country, and in a few months was able to converse with the learned men; some of whom I found morose and reserved, and others easy and communicative; some were unwilling to teach another what they had with difficulty learned themselves; and some showed that the end of their studies was to gain the dignity of instructing.

'To the tutor of the young princes I recommended myself so much, that I was presented to the emperor as a man of uncommon knowledge. The emperor asked me many questions concerning my country and my travels; and though I cannot now recollect any thing that he uttered above the power of a common man, he dismissed me astonished at his wisdom, and enamoured of his goodness.

'My credit was now so high, that the merchants, with whom I had travelled, applied to me for recommendations to the ladies of the court. I was surprised at their confidence of solicitation, and gently reproached them with their practices on the road. They heard me with cold indifference, and showed no tokens of shame or sorrow.

'They then urged their request with the offer of a bribe; but what I would not do for kindness I would not do for money; and refused them, not because they had injured me, but because I would not enable them to injure others; for I knew they would have made use of my credit to cheat those who should buy their wares.

'Having resided at Agra till there was no more to be learned, I travelled into Persia, where I saw many remains of ancient magnificence, and observed many new accommodations of life. The Persians are a nation eminently social, and their assemblies afforded me daily opportunities of remarking characters and manners, and of tracing human nature through all its variations.

'From Persia I passed into Arabia, where I saw a nation at once pastoral and warlike; who live without any settled habitation; whose only wealth is their flocks and herds; and who have yet carried on, through all ages, an hereditary war with all mankind, though they neither covet nor envy their possessions'.

---

[11] *Agra* city in north central India, the capital of the Islamic Mughal Empire, which controlled the subcontinent from the early sixteenth century until 1761.

Chapter 10

Imlac's history continued: A dissertation upon poetry

'Wherever I went, I found that Poetry was considered as the highest learning, and regarded with a veneration somewhat approaching to that which man would pay to the Angelic Nature. And it yet fills me with wonder, that, in almost all countries, the most ancient poets are considered as the best: whether it be that every other kind of knowledge is an acquisition gradually attained, and poetry is a gift conferred at once; or that the first poetry of every nation surprised them as a novelty, and retained the credit by consent which it received by accident at first: or whether the province of poetry is to describe Nature and passion, which are always the same, the first writers took possession of the most striking objects for description, and the most probable occurrences for fiction, and left nothing to those that followed them, but transcription of the same events, and new combinations of the same images. Whatever be the reason, it is commonly observed that the early writers are in possession of nature, and their followers of art: that the first excel in strength and invention, and the latter in elegance and refinement.

'I was desirous to add my name to this illustrious fraternity. I read all the poets of Persia and Arabia, and was able to repeat by memory the volumes that are suspended in the mosque of Mecca. But I soon found that no man was ever great by imitation. My desire of excellence impelled me to transfer my attention to nature and to life. Nature was to be my subject, and men to be my auditors: I could never describe what I had not seen: I could not hope to move those with delight or terror, whose interests and opinions I did not understand.

'Being now resolved to be a poet, I saw every thing with a new purpose; my sphere of attention was suddenly magnified: no kind of knowledge was to be overlooked. I ranged mountains and deserts for images and resemblances, and pictured upon my mind every tree of the forest and flower of the valley. I observed with equal care the crags of the rock and the pinnacles of the palace. Sometimes I wandered along the mazes of the rivulet, and sometimes watched the changes of the summer clouds. To a poet nothing can be useless. Whatever is beautiful, and whatever is dreadful, must be familiar to his imagination: he must be conversant with all that is awfully vast or elegantly little. The plants of the garden, the animals of the wood, the minerals of the earth, and meteors of the sky, must all concur to store his mind with inexhaustible variety: for every idea is useful for the enforcement or decoration of moral or religious truth; and he, who knows most, will have most power of diversifying his scenes, and of gratifying his reader with remote allusions and unexpected instruction.

'All the appearances of nature I was therefore careful to study, and every country which I have surveyed has contributed something to my poetical powers'.

'In so wide a survey', said the prince, 'you must surely have left much unobserved. I have lived, till now, within the circuit of these mountains, and yet cannot walk abroad without the sight of something which I had never beheld before, or never heeded'.

'The business of a poet', said Imlac, 'is to examine, not the individual, but the species; to remark general properties and large appearances: he does not number the streaks of the tulip, or describe the different shades in the verdure of the forest. He is to exhibit in his portraits of nature such prominent and striking features, as recall the original to every mind; and must neglect the minuter discriminations, which one may have remarked, and another have neglected, for those characteristics which are alike obvious to vigilance and carelessness.

'But the knowledge of nature is only half the task of a poet; he must be acquainted likewise with all the modes of life. His character requires that he estimate the happiness and misery of every condition; observe the power of all the passions in all their combinations, and trace the changes of the human mind as they are modified by various institutions and accidental influences of climate or custom, from the spriteliness of infancy to the despondence of decrepitude. He must divest himself of the prejudices of his age or country; he must consider right and wrong in their abstracted and invariable state; he must disregard present laws and opinions, and rise to general and transcendental truths, which will always be the same: he must therefore content himself with the slow progress of his name; contemn the applause of his own time, and commit his claims to the justice of posterity. He must write as the interpreter of nature, and the legislator of mankind, and consider himself as presiding over the thoughts and manners of successive generations; as a being superior to time and place. His labour is not yet at an end: he must know many languages and many sciences; and, that his style may be worthy of his thoughts, must, by incessant practice, familiarize to himself every delicacy of speech and grace of harmony'.

CHAPTER 11
IMLAC'S NARRATIVE CONTINUED: A HINT ON PILGRIMAGE

Imlac now felt the enthusiastic fit, and was proceeding to aggrandize his own profession, when the prince cried out, 'Enough! Thou hast convinced me, that no human being can ever be a poet. Proceed with thy narration'.

'To be a poet', said Imlac, 'is indeed very difficult'. 'So difficult', returned the prince, 'that I will at present hear no more of his labours. Tell me whither you went when you had seen Persia'.

'From Persia', said the poet, 'I travelled through Syria, and for three years resided in Palestine, where I conversed with great numbers of the northern and western nations of Europe; the nations which are now in possession of all power and all knowledge; whose armies are irresistible, and whose fleets command the remotest parts of the globe. When I compared these men with the natives of our own kingdom, and those that surround us, they appeared almost another order of beings. In their countries it is difficult to wish for any thing that may not be obtained: a thousand arts, of which we never heard, are continually labouring for their convenience and pleasure; and whatever their own climate has denied them is supplied by their commerce'.

'By what means', said the prince, 'are the Europeans thus powerful? or why, since they can so easily visit Asia and Africa for trade or conquest, cannot the Asiatics and Africans invade their coasts, plant colonies in their ports, and give laws to their natural princes? The same wind that carries them back would bring us thither'.

'They are more powerful, Sir, than we', answered Imlac, 'because they are wiser; knowledge will always predominate over ignorance, as man governs the other animals. But why their knowledge is more than ours, I know not what reason can be given, but the unsearchable will of the Supreme Being'.

'When', said the prince with a sigh, 'shall I be able to visit Palestine, and mingle with this mighty confluence of nations? Till that happy moment shall arrive, let me fill up the time with such representations as thou canst give me. I am not ignorant of the motive that assembles such numbers in that place, and cannot but consider it as the centre of wisdom and piety, to which the best and wisest men of every land must be continually resorting'.

'There are some nations', said Imlac, 'that send few visitants to Palestine; for many numerous and learned sects in Europe concur to censure pilgrimage as superstitious, or deride it as ridiculous'.

'You know', said the prince, 'how little my life has made me acquainted with diversity of opinions: it will be too long to hear the arguments on both sides; you, that have considered them, tell me the result'.

'Pilgrimage', said Imlac, 'like many other acts of piety, may be reasonable or superstitious, according to the principles upon which it is performed. Long journeys in search of truth are not commanded. Truth, such as is necessary to the regulation of life, is always found where it is honestly sought. Change of place is no natural cause of the increase of piety, for it inevitably produces dissipation of mind. Yet, since men go every day to view the fields where great actions have been performed, and return with stronger impressions of the event, curiosity of the same kind may naturally dispose us to view that country whence our religion had its beginning; and I believe no man surveys those awful scenes without some confirmation of holy resolutions. That the Supreme Being may be more easily propitiated in one place than in another, is the dream of idle superstition; but that some places may operate upon our own minds in an uncommon manner, is an opinion which hourly experience will justify. He who supposes that his vices may be more successfully combatted in Palestine, will, perhaps, find himself mistaken, yet he may go thither without folly: he who thinks they will be more freely pardoned, dishonours at once his reason and religion'.

'These', said the prince, 'are European distinctions. I will consider them another time. What have you found to be the effect of knowledge? Are those nations happier than we?'

'There is so much infelicity', said the poet, 'in the world, that scarce any man has leisure from his own distresses to estimate the comparative happiness of others. Knowledge is certainly one of the means of pleasure, as is confessed by the natural desire which every mind feels of increasing its ideas. Ignorance is mere privation, by which nothing can be produced: it is a vacuity in which the soul sits motionless and torpid for want of attraction; and, without knowing why, we always rejoice when we learn, and grieve when we forget. I am therefore inclined to conclude, that, if nothing counteracts the natural consequence of learning, we grow more happy as our minds take a wider range.

'In enumerating the particular comforts of life we shall find many advantages on the side of the Europeans. They cure wounds and diseases with which we languish and perish. We suffer inclemencies of weather which they can obviate. They have engines for the dispatch of many laborious works, which we must perform by manual industry. There is such communication between distant places, that one friend can hardly be said to be absent from another. Their policy removes all public inconveniencies: they have roads cut through their mountains, and bridges laid upon their rivers. And, if we descend to the privacies of life, their habitations are more commodious, and their possessions are more secure'.

'They are surely happy', said the prince, 'who have all these conveniencies, of which I envy none so much as the facility with which separated friends interchange their thoughts'.

'The Europeans', answered Imlac, 'are less unhappy than we, but they are not happy. Human life is every where a state in which much is to be endured, and little to be enjoyed'.

CHAPTER 12
THE STORY OF IMLAC CONTINUED

'I am not yet willing', said the prince, 'to suppose that happiness is so parsimoniously distributed to mortals; nor can believe but that, if I had the choice of life, I should be able to

878 SAMUEL JOHNSON *THE HISTORY OF RASSELAS, PRINCE OF ABYSSINIA*

fill every day with pleasure. I would injure no man, and should provoke no resentment: I would relieve every distress, and should enjoy the benedictions of gratitude. I would choose my friends among the wise, and my wife among the virtuous; and therefore should be in no danger from treachery, or unkindness. My children should, by my care, be learned and pious, and would repay to my age what their childhood had received. What would dare to molest him who might call on every side to thousands enriched by his bounty, or assisted by his power? And why should not life glide quietly away in the soft reciprocation of protection and reverence? All this may be done without the help of European refinements, which appear by their effects to be rather specious than useful. Let us leave them and pursue our journey'.

'From Palestine', said Imlac, 'I passed through many regions of Asia; in the more civilized kingdoms as a trader, and among the Barbarians of the mountains as a pilgrim. At last I began to long for my native country, that I might repose after my travels, and fatigues, in the places where I had spent my earliest years, and gladden my old companions with the recital of my adventures. Often did I figure to myself those, with whom I had sported away the gay hours of dawning life, sitting round me in its evening, wondering at my tales, and listening to my counsels.

'When this thought had taken possession of my mind, I considered every moment as wasted which did not bring me nearer to Abyssinia. I hastened into Egypt, and, notwithstanding my impatience, was detained ten months in the contemplation of its ancient magnificence, and in enquiries after the remains of its ancient learning. I found in Cairo a mixture of all nations; some brought thither by the love of knowledge, some by the hope of gain, and many by the desire of living after their own manner without observation, and of lying hid in the obscurity of multitudes: for, in a city, populous as Cairo, it is possible to obtain at the same time the gratifications of society, and the secrecy of solitude.

'From Cairo I travelled to Suez, and embarked on the Red Sea, passing along the coast till I arrived at the port from which I had departed twenty years before. Here I joined myself to a caravan and re-entered my native country.

'I now expected the caresses of my kinsmen, and the congratulations of my friends, and was not without hope that my father, whatever value he had set upon riches, would own with gladness and pride a son who was able to add to the felicity and honour of the nation. But I was soon convinced that my thoughts were vain. My father had been dead fourteen years, having divided his wealth among my brothers, who were removed to some other provinces. Of my companions the greater part was in the grave; of the rest some could with difficulty remember me, and some considered me as one corrupted by foreign manners.

'A man used to vicissitudes is not easily dejected. I forgot, after a time, my disappointment, and endeavoured to recommend myself to the nobles of the kingdom: they admitted me to their tables, heard my story, and dismissed me. I opened a school, and was prohibited to teach. I then resolved to sit down in the quiet of domestic life, and addressed a lady that was fond of my conversation, but rejected my suit, because my father was a merchant.

'Wearied at last with solicitation and repulses, I resolved to hide myself for ever from the world, and depend no longer on the opinion or caprice of others. I waited for the time when the gate of the *happy valley* should open, that I might bid farewell to hope and fear: the day came; my performance was distinguished with favour, and I resigned myself with joy to perpetual confinement'.

'Hast thou here found happiness at last?' said Rasselas. 'Tell me without reserve; art thou content with thy condition? or, dost thou wish to be again wandering and enquiring? All the inhabitants of this valley celebrate their lot, and, at the annual visit of the emperor, invite others to partake of their felicity'.

'Great prince', said Imlac, 'I shall speak the truth: I know not one of all your attendants who does not lament the hour when he entered this retreat. I am less unhappy than the rest, because I have a mind replete with images, which I can vary and combine at pleasure. I can amuse my solitude by the renovation of the knowledge which begins to fade from my memory, and by recollection of the accidents of my past life. Yet all this ends in the sorrowful consideration, that my acquirements are now useless, and that none of my pleasures can be again enjoyed. The rest, whose minds have no impression but of the present moment, are either corroded by malignant passions, or sit stupid in the gloom of perpetual vacancy'.

'What passions can infest those', said the prince, 'who have no rivals? We are in a place where impotence precludes malice, and where all envy is repressed by community of enjoyments'.

'There may be community', said Imlac, 'of material possessions, but there can never be community of love or of esteem. It must happen that one will please more than another; he that knows himself despised will always be envious; and still more envious and malevolent, if he is condemned to live in the presence of those who despise him. The invitations, by which they allure others to a state which they feel to be wretched, proceed from the natural malignity of hopeless misery. They are weary of themselves, and of each other, and expect to find relief in new companions. They envy the liberty which their folly has forfeited, and would gladly see all mankind imprisoned like themselves.

'From this crime, however, I am wholly free. No man can say that he is wretched by my persuasion. I look with pity on the crowds who are annually soliciting admission to captivity, and wish that it were lawful for me to warn them of their danger'.

'My dear Imlac', said the prince, 'I will open to thee my whole heart. I have long meditated an escape from the happy valley. I have examined the mountains on every side, but find myself insuperably barred: teach me the way to break my prison; thou shalt be the companion of my flight, the guide of my rambles, the partner of my fortune, and my sole director in the choice of life'.

'Sir', answered the poet, 'your escape will be difficult, and, perhaps, you may soon repent your curiosity. The world, which you figure to yourself smooth and quiet as the lake in the valley, you will find a sea foaming with tempests, and boiling with whirlpools: you will be sometimes overwhelmed by the waves of violence, and sometimes dashed against the rocks of treachery. Amidst wrongs and frauds, competitions and anxieties, you will wish a thousand times for these seats of quiet, and willingly quit hope to be free from fear'.

'Do not seek to deter me from my purpose', said the prince: 'I am impatient to see what thou hast seen; and, since thou art thyself weary of the valley, it is evident, that thy former state was better than this. Whatever be the consequence of my experiment, I am resolved to judge with my own eyes of the various conditions of men, and then to make deliberately my *choice of life*'.

'I am afraid', said Imlac, 'you are hindered by stronger restraints than my persuasions; yet, if your determination is fixed, I do not counsel you to despair. Few things are impossible to diligence and skill'.

CHAPTER 13
RASSELAS DISCOVERS THE MEANS OF ESCAPE

The prince now dismissed his favourite to rest, but the narrative of wonders and novelties filled his mind with perturbation. He revolved all that he had heard, and prepared innumerable questions for the morning.

Much of his uneasiness was now removed. He had a friend to whom he could impart his thoughts, and whose experience could assist him in his designs. His heart was no longer condemned to swell with silent vexation. He thought that even the *happy valley* might be endured with such a companion, and that, if they could range the world together, he should have nothing further to desire.

In a few days the water was discharged, and the ground dried. The prince and Imlac then walked out together to converse without the notice of the rest. The prince, whose thoughts were always on the wing, as he passed by the gate, said, with a countenance of sorrow, 'Why art thou so strong, and why is man so weak?'

'Man is not weak', answered his companion; 'knowledge is more than equivalent to force. The master of mechanics laughs at strength. I can burst the gate, but cannot do it secretly. Some other expedient must be tried'.

As they were walking on the side of the mountain, they observed that the conies,[12] which the rain had driven from their burrows, had taken shelter among the bushes, and formed holes behind them, tending upwards in an oblique line. 'It has been the opinion of antiquity', said Imlac, 'that human reason borrowed many arts from the instinct of animals; let us, therefore, not think ourselves degraded by learning from the coney. We may escape by piercing the mountain in the same direction. We will begin where the summit hangs over the middle part, and labour upward till we shall issue out beyond the prominence'.

The eyes of the prince, when he heard this proposal, sparkled with joy. The execution was easy, and the success certain.

No time was now lost. They hastened early in the morning to choose a place proper for their mine. They clambered with great fatigue among crags and brambles, and returned without having discovered any part that favoured their design. The second and the third day were spent in the same manner, and with the same frustration. But, on the fourth, they found a small cavern, concealed by a thicket, where they resolved to make their experiment.

Imlac procured instruments proper to hew stone and remove earth, and they fell to their work on the next day with more eagerness than vigour. They were presently exhausted by their efforts, and sat down to pant upon the grass. The prince, for the moment, appeared to be discouraged. 'Sir', said his companion, 'practice will enable us to continue our labour for a longer time; mark, however, how far we have advanced, and you will find that our toil will some time have an end. Great works are performed, not by strength but perseverance: yonder palace was raised by single stones, yet you see its height and spaciousness. He that shall walk with vigour three hours a day will pass in seven years a space equal to the circumference of the globe'.

They returned to their work day after day, and, in a short time, found a fissure in the rock, which enabled them to pass far with very little obstruction. This Rasselas considered as a good omen. 'Do not disturb your mind', said Imlac, 'with other hopes or fears than reason may suggest: if you are pleased with prognostics of good, you will be terrified likewise with tokens of evil, and your whole life will be a prey to superstition. Whatever facilitates our work is more than an omen, it is a cause of success. This is one of those pleasing surprises which often happen to active resolution. Many things difficult to design prove easy in performance'.

---

[12] *conies* rabbits.

CHAPTER 14
RASSELAS AND IMLAC RECEIVE AN UNEXPECTED VISIT

They had now wrought their way to the middle, and solaced their labour with the approach of liberty, when the prince, coming down to refresh himself with air, found his sister Nekayah standing before the mouth of the cavity. He started and stood confused, afraid to tell his design, and yet hopeless to conceal it. A few moments determined him to repose on her fidelity, and secure her secrecy by a declaration without reserve.

'Do not imagine', said the princess, 'that I came hither as a spy: I had often observed from my window, that you and Imlac directed your walk every day towards the same point, but I did not suppose you had any better reason for the preference than a cooler shade, or more fragrant bank; nor followed you with any other design than to partake of your conversation. Since then not suspicion but fondness has detected you, let me not lose the advantage of my discovery. I am equally weary of confinement with yourself, and not less desirous of knowing what is done or suffered in the world. Permit me to fly with you from this tasteless tranquillity, which will yet grow more loathsome when you have left me. You may deny me to accompany you, but cannot hinder me from following'.

The prince, who loved Nekayah above his other sisters, had no inclination to refuse her request, and grieved that he had lost an opportunity of showing his confidence by a voluntary communication. It was therefore agreed that she should leave the valley with them; and that, in the mean time, she should watch, lest any other straggler should, by chance or curiosity, follow them to the mountain.

At length their labour was at an end; they saw light beyond the prominence, and, issuing to the top of the mountain, beheld the Nile, yet a narrow current, wandering beneath them.

The prince looked round with rapture, anticipated all the pleasures of travel, and in thought was already transported beyond his father's dominions. Imlac, though very joyful at his escape, had less expectation of pleasure in the world, which he had before tried, and of which he had been weary.

Rasselas was so much delighted with a wider horizon, that he could not soon be persuaded to return into the valley. He informed his sister that the way was open, and that nothing now remained but to prepare for their departure.

CHAPTER 15
THE PRINCE AND PRINCESS LEAVE THE VALLEY, AND SEE MANY WONDERS

The prince and princess had jewels sufficient to make them rich whenever they came into a place of commerce, which, by Imlac's direction, they hid in their clothes, and, on the night of the next full moon, all left the valley. The princess was followed only by a single favourite, who did not know whither she was going.

They clambered through the cavity, and began to go down on the other side. The princess and her maid turned their eyes towards every part, and, seeing nothing to bound their prospect, considered themselves as in danger of being lost in a dreary vacuity. They stopped and trembled. 'I am almost afraid', said the princess, 'to begin a journey of which I cannot perceive an end, and to venture into this immense plain where I may be approached on every side by men whom I never saw'. The prince felt nearly the same emotions, though he thought it more manly to conceal them.

Imlac smiled at their terrors, and encouraged them to proceed; but the princess continued irresolute till she had been imperceptibly drawn forward too far to return.

In the morning they found some shepherds in the field, who set milk and fruits before them. The princess wondered that she did not see a palace ready for her reception, and a table spread with delicacies; but, being faint and hungry, she drank the milk and eat[13] the fruits, and thought them of a higher flavour than the products of the valley.

They travelled forward by easy journeys, being all unaccustomed to toil or difficulty, and knowing, that though they might be missed, they could not be pursued. In a few days they came into a more populous region, where Imlac was diverted with the admiration which his companions expressed at the diversity of manners, stations and employments.

Their dress was such as might not bring upon them the suspicion of having any thing to conceal, yet the prince, wherever he came, expected to be obeyed, and the princess was frighted, because those that came into her presence did not prostrate themselves before her. Imlac was forced to observe them with great vigilance, lest they should betray their rank by their unusual behaviour, and detained them several weeks in the first village to accustom them to the sight of common mortals.

By degrees the royal wanderers were taught to understand that they had for a time laid aside their dignity, and were to expect only such regard as liberality and courtesy could procure. And Imlac, having, by many admonitions, prepared them to endure the tumults of a port, and the ruggedness of the commercial race, brought them down to the seacoast.

The prince and his sister, to whom every thing was new, were gratified equally at all places, and therefore remained for some months at the port without any inclination to pass further. Imlac was content with their stay, because he did not think it safe to expose them, unpractised in the world, to the hazards of a foreign country.

At last he began to fear lest they should be discovered, and proposed to fix a day for their departure. They had no pretensions to judge for themselves, and referred the whole scheme to his direction. He therefore took passage in a ship to Suez; and, when the time came, with great difficulty prevailed on the princess to enter the vessel. They had a quick and prosperous voyage, and from Suez travelled by land to Cairo.

CHAPTER 16
THEY ENTER CAIRO, AND FIND EVERY MAN HAPPY

As they approached the city, which filled the strangers with astonishment, 'This', said Imlac to the prince, 'is the place where travellers and merchants assemble from all the corners of the earth. You will here find men of every character, and every occupation. Commerce is here honourable: I will act as a merchant, and you shall live as strangers, who have no other end of travel than curiosity; it will soon be observed that we are rich; our reputation will procure us access to all whom we shall desire to know; you will see all the conditions of humanity, and enable yourself at leisure to make your *choice of life*'.

They now entered the town, stunned by the noise, and offended by the crowds. Instruction had not yet so prevailed over habit but that they wondered to see themselves pass undistinguished along the street, and met by the lowest of the people without reverence or notice. The

---

[13] *eat*   an acceptable form of the past tense at this time.

princess could not at first bear the thought of being levelled with the vulgar, and, for some days, continued in her chamber, where she was served by her favourite as in the palace of the valley.

Imlac, who understood traffic,[14] sold part of the jewels the next day, and hired a house, which he adorned with such magnificence, that he was immediately considered as a merchant of great wealth. His politeness attracted many acquaintances, and his generosity made him courted by many dependents. His table was crowded by men of every nation, who all admired his knowledge, and solicited his favour. His companions, not being able to mix in the conversation, could make no discovery of their ignorance or surprise, and were gradually initiated in the world as they gained knowledge of the language.

The prince had, by frequent lectures, been taught the use and nature of money; but the ladies could not, for a long time, comprehend what the merchants did with small pieces of gold and silver, or why things of so little use should be received as equivalent to the necessaries of life.

They studied the language two years, while Imlac was preparing to set before them the various ranks and conditions of mankind. He grew acquainted with all who had any thing uncommon in their fortune or conduct. He frequented the voluptuous and the frugal, the idle and the busy, the merchants and the men of learning.

The prince, being now able to converse with fluency, and having learned the caution necessary to be observed in his intercourse with strangers, began to accompany Imlac to places of resort, and to enter into all assemblies, that he might make his *choice of life*.

For some time he thought choice needless, because all appeared to him equally happy. Wherever he went he met gaiety and kindness, and heard the song of joy, or the laugh of carelessness. He began to believe that the world overflowed with universal plenty, and that nothing was withheld either from want or merit; that every hand showered liberality, and every heart melted with benevolence: 'and who then', says he, 'will be suffered to be wretched?'

Imlac permitted the pleasing delusion, and was unwilling to crush the hope of inexperience; till one day, having sat a while silent, 'I know not', said the prince, 'what can be the reason that I am more unhappy than any of our friends. I see them perpetually and unalterably cheerful, but feel my own mind restless and uneasy. I am unsatisfied with those pleasures which I seem most to court; I live in the crowds of jollity, not so much to enjoy company as to shun myself, and am only loud and merry to conceal my sadness'.

'Every man', said Imlac, 'may, by examining his own mind, guess what passes in the minds of others: when you feel that your own gaiety is counterfeit, it may justly lead you to suspect that of your companions not to be sincere. Envy is commonly reciprocal. We are long before we are convinced that happiness is never to be found, and each believes it possessed by others, to keep alive the hope of obtaining it for himself. In the assembly, where you passed the last night, there appeared such spriteliness of air, and volatility of fancy as might have suited beings of an higher order, formed to inhabit serener regions inaccessible to care or sorrow: yet, believe me, prince, there was not one who did not dread the moment when solitude should deliver him to the tyranny of reflection'.

'This', said the prince, 'may be true of others, since it is true of me; yet, whatever be the general infelicity of man, one condition is more happy than another, and wisdom surely directs us to take the least evil in the *choice of life*'.

---

[14]   *traffic*   commerce.

'The causes of good and evil', answered Imlac, 'are so various and uncertain, so often entangled with each other, so diversified by various relations, and so much subject to accidents which cannot be foreseen, that he who would fix his condition upon incontestable reasons of preference, must live and die enquiring and deliberating'.

'But surely', said Rasselas, 'the wise men, to whom we listen with reverence and wonder, chose that mode of life for themselves which they thought most likely to make them happy'.

'Very few', said the poet, 'live by choice. Every man is placed in his present condition by causes which acted without his foresight, and with which he did not always willingly co-operate; and therefore you will rarely meet one who does not think the lot of his neighbour better than his own'.

'I am pleased to think', said the prince, 'that my birth has given me at least one advantage over others, by enabling me to determine for myself. I have here the world before me; I will review it at leisure: surely happiness is somewhere to be found'.

CHAPTER 17
THE PRINCE ASSOCIATES WITH YOUNG MEN OF SPIRIT AND GAIETY

Rasselas rose next day, and resolved to begin his experiments upon life. 'Youth', cried he, 'is the time of gladness: I will join myself to the young men, whose only business is to gratify their desires, and whose time is all spent in a succession of enjoyments'.

To such societies he was readily admitted, but a few days brought him back weary and disgusted. Their mirth was without images, their laughter without motive; their pleasures were gross and sensual, in which the mind had no part; their conduct was at once wild and mean; they laughed at order and at law, but the frown of power dejected, and the eye of wisdom abashed them.

The prince soon concluded, that he should never be happy in a course of life of which he was ashamed. He thought it unsuitable to a reasonable being to act without a plan, and to be sad or cheerful only by chance. 'Happiness', said he, 'must be something solid and permanent, without fear and without uncertainty'.

But his young companions had gained so much of his regard by their frankness and courtesy, that he could not leave them without warning and remonstrance. 'My friends', said he, 'I have seriously considered our manners and our prospects, and find that we have mistaken our own interest. The first years of man must make provision for the last. He that never thinks never can be wise. Perpetual levity must end in ignorance; and intemperance, though it may fire the spirits for an hour, will make life short or miserable. Let us consider that youth is of no long duration, and that in maturer age, when the enchantments of fancy shall cease, and phantoms of delight dance no more about us, we shall have no comforts but the esteem of wise men, and the means of doing good. Let us, therefore, stop, while to stop is in our power: let us live as men who are sometime to grow old, and to whom it will be the most dreadful of all evils not to count their past years but by follies, and to be reminded of their former luxuriance of health only by the maladies which riot has produced'. They stared a while in silence one upon another, and, at last, drove him away by a general chorus of continued laughter.

The consciousness that his sentiments were just, and his intentions kind, was scarcely sufficient to support him against the horror of derision. But he recovered his tranquillity, and pursued his search.

CHAPTER 18
THE PRINCE FINDS A WISE AND HAPPY MAN

As he was one day walking in the street, he saw a spacious building which all were, by the open doors, invited to enter: he followed the stream of people, and found it a hall or school of declamation, in which professors read lectures to their auditory.[15] He fixed his eye upon a sage raised above the rest, who discoursed with great energy on the government of the passions. His look was venerable, his action graceful, his pronunciation clear, and his diction elegant. He showed, with great strength of sentiment, and variety of illustration, that human nature is degraded and debased, when the lower faculties predominate over the higher; that when fancy, the parent of passion, usurps the dominion of the mind, nothing ensues but the natural effect of unlawful government, perturbation and confusion; that she betrays the fortresses of the intellect to rebels, and excites her children to sedition against reason, their lawful sovereign.[16] He compared reason to the sun, of which the light is constant, uniform, and lasting; and fancy to a meteor, of bright but transitory lustre, irregular in its motion, and delusive in its direction.

He then communicated the various precepts given from time to time for the conquest of passion, and displayed the happiness of those who had obtained the important victory, after which man is no longer the slave of fear, nor the fool of hope; is no more emaciated by envy, inflamed by anger, emasculated by tenderness, or depressed by grief; but walks on calmly through the tumults or the privacies of life, as the sun pursues alike his course through the calm or the stormy sky.

He enumerated many examples of heroes immovable by pain or pleasure, who looked with indifference on those modes or accidents to which the vulgar give the names of good and evil. He exhorted his hearers to lay aside their prejudices, and arm themselves against the shafts of malice or misfortune, by invulnerable patience; concluding, that this state only was happiness, and that this happiness was in every one's power.

Rasselas listened to him with the veneration due to the instructions of a superior being, and, waiting for him at the door, humbly implored the liberty of visiting so great a master of true wisdom. The lecturer hesitated a moment, when Rasselas put a purse of gold into his hand, which he received with a mixture of joy and wonder.

'I have found', said the prince, at his return to Imlac, 'a man who can teach all that is necessary to be known, who, from the unshaken throne of rational fortitude, looks down on the scenes of life changing beneath him.[17] He speaks, and attention watches his lips. He reasons, and conviction closes his periods. This man shall be my future guide: I will learn his doctrines, and imitate his life'.

'Be not too hasty', said Imlac, 'to trust, or to admire, the teachers of morality: they discourse like angels, but they live like men'.

Rasselas, who could not conceive how any man could reason so forcibly without feeling the cogency of his own arguments, paid his visit in a few days, and was denied admission. He had now learned the power of money, and made his way by a piece of gold to the inner apartment, where he found the philosopher in a room half darkened, with his eyes misty, and

---

15 *auditory* audience.

16 *He showed ... sovereign* as Johnson's readers would readily have recognized, the "wise and happy man" propounds a version of Stoicism.

17 *from the unshaken throne ... beneath him* one of the most traditional images of Stoicism (e.g. Lucretius *De Rerum Natura* 2.7–10).

his face pale. 'Sir', said he, 'you are come at a time when all human friendship is useless; what I suffer cannot be remedied, what I have lost cannot be supplied. My daughter, my only daughter, from whose tenderness I expected all the comforts of my age, died last night of a fever. My views, my purposes, my hopes are at an end: I am now a lonely being disunited from society'.

'Sir', said the prince, 'mortality is an event by which a wise man can never be surprised: we know that death is always near, and it should therefore always be expected'. 'Young man', answered the philosopher, 'you speak like one that has never felt the pangs of separation'. 'Have you then forgot the precepts', said Rasselas, 'which you so powerfully enforced? Has wisdom no strength to arm the heart against calamity? Consider, that external things are naturally variable, but truth and reason are always the same'. 'What comfort', said the mourner, 'can truth and reason afford me? of what effect are they now, but to tell me, that my daughter will not be restored?'

The prince, whose humanity would not suffer him to insult misery with reproof, went away convinced of the emptiness of rhetorical sound, and the inefficacy of polished periods and studied sentences.

CHAPTER 19
A GLIMPSE OF PASTORAL LIFE

He was still eager upon the same enquiry; and, having heard of a hermit, that lived near the lowest cataract of the Nile, and filled the whole country with the fame of his sanctity, resolved to visit his retreat, and enquire whether that felicity, which public life could not afford, was to be found in solitude; and whether a man, whose age and virtue made him venerable, could teach any peculiar art of shunning evils, or enduring them.

Imlac and the princess agreed to accompany him, and, after the necessary preparations, they began their journey. Their way lay through fields, where shepherds tended their flocks, and the lambs were playing upon the pasture. 'This', said the poet, 'is the life which has been often celebrated for its innocence and quiet: let us pass the heat of the day among the shepherds' tents, and know whether all our searches are not to terminate in pastoral simplicity'.

The proposal pleased them, and they induced the sheperds, by small presents and famil-iar[18] questions, to tell their opinion of their own state: they were so rude and ignorant, so little able to compare the good with the evil of the occupation, and so indistinct in their narratives and descriptions, that very little could be learned from them. But it was evident that their hearts were cankered with discontent; that they considered themselves as con-demned to labour for the luxury of the rich, and looked up with stupid malevolence toward those that were placed above them.

The princess pronounced with vehemence, that she would never suffer these envious savages to be her companions, and that she should not soon be desirous of seeing any more specimens of rustic happiness; but could not believe that all the accounts of primeval pleasures were fabulous, and was yet in doubt whether life had any thing that could be justly preferred to the placid gratifications of fields and woods. She hoped that the time would come, when with a few virtuous and elegant companions, she should gather flowers planted by her own hand, fondle the lambs of her own ewe, and listen, without care, among brooks and breezes, to one of her maidens reading in the shade.

---

[18] *familiar* "Affable; not formal; easy in conversation" (Johnson).

Chapter 20
The danger of prosperity

On the next day they continued their journey, till the heat compelled them to look round for shelter. At a small distance they saw a thick wood, which they no sooner entered than they perceived that they were approaching the habitations of men. The shrubs were diligently cut away to open walks where the shades were darkest; the boughs of opposite trees were artificially interwoven; seats of flowery turf were raised in vacant spaces, and a rivulet, that wantoned along the side of a winding path, had its banks sometimes opened into small basins, and its stream sometimes obstructed by little mounds of stone heaped together to increase its murmurs.

They passed slowly through the wood, delighted with such unexpected accommodations, and entertained each other with conjecturing what, or who, he could be, that, in those rude and unfrequented regions, had leisure and art for such harmless luxury.

As they advanced, they heard the sound of music, and saw youths and virgins dancing in the grove; and, going still further, beheld a stately palace built upon a hill surrounded with woods. The laws of eastern hospitality allowed them to enter, and the master welcomed them like a man liberal and wealthy.

He was skilful enough in appearances soon to discern that they were no common guests, and spread his table with magnificence. The eloquence of Imlac caught his attention, and the lofty courtesy of the princess excited his respect. When they offered to depart he entreated their stay, and was the next day still more unwilling to dismiss them than before. They were easily persuaded to stop, and civility grew up in time to freedom and confidence.

The prince now saw all the domestics cheerful, and all the face of nature smiling round the place, and could not forbear to hope that he should find here what he was seeking; but when he was congratulating the master upon his possessions, he answered with a sigh, 'My condition has indeed the appearance of happiness, but appearances are delusive. My prosperity puts my life in danger; the Bassa[19] of Egypt is my enemy, incensed only by my wealth and popularity. I have been hitherto protected against him by the princes of the country; but, as the favour of the great is uncertain, I know not how soon my defenders may be persuaded to share the plunder with the Bassa. I have sent my treasures into a distant country, and, upon the first alarm, am prepared to follow them. Then will my enemies riot in my mansion, and enjoy the gardens which I have planted'.

They all joined in lamenting his danger, and deprecating his exile; and the princess was so much disturbed with the tumult of grief and indignation, that she retired to her apartment. They continued with their kind inviter a few days longer, and then went forward to find the hermit.

Chapter 21
The happiness of solitude: The hermit's history

They came on the third day, by the direction of the peasants, to the Hermit's cell: it was a cavern in the side of a mountain, over-shadowed with palm-trees; at such a distance from the cataract, that nothing more was heard than a gentle uniform murmur, such as composed

---

[19] *Bassa* or "bashaw," "A title of honour and command among the Turks, the viceroy of a province; the general of an army" (Johnson).

the mind to pensive meditation, especially when it was assisted by the wind whistling among the branches. The first rude essay of nature had been so much improved by human labour, that the cave contained several apartments, appropriated to different uses, and often afforded lodging to travellers, whom darkness or tempests happened to overtake.

The hermit sat on a bench at the door, to enjoy the coolness of the evening. On one side lay a book with pens and papers, on the other mechanical instruments of various kinds. As they approached him unregarded, the princess observed that he had not the countenance of a man that had found, or could teach, the way to happiness.

They saluted him with great respect, which he repaid like a man not unaccustomed to the forms of courts, 'My children', said he, 'if you have lost your way, you shall be willingly supplied with such conveniences for the night as this cavern will afford. I have all that nature requires, and you will not expect delicacies in a hermit's cell'.

They thanked him, and entering, were pleased with the neatness and regularity of the place. The hermit set flesh and wine before them, though he fed only upon fruits and water. His discourse was cheerful without levity, and pious without enthusiasm.[20] He soon gained the esteem of his guests, and the princess repented of her hasty censure.

At last Imlac began thus: 'I do not now wonder that your reputation is so far extended; we have heard at Cairo of your wisdom, and came hither to implore your direction for this young man and maiden in the *choice of life*'.

'To him that lives well', answered the hermit, 'every form of life is good; nor can I give any other rule for choice, than to remove from all apparent evil'.

'He will remove most certainly from evil', said the prince, 'who shall devote himself to that solitude which you have recommended by your example'.

'I have indeed lived fifteen years in solitude', said the hermit, 'but have no desire that my example should gain any imitators. In my youth I professed arms, and was raised by degrees to the highest military rank. I have traversed wide countries at the head of my troops, and seen many battles and sieges. At last, being disgusted by the preferment of a younger officer, and finding my vigour was beginning to decay, I resolved to close my life in peace, having found the world full of snares, discord, and misery. I had once escaped from the pursuit of the enemy by the shelter of this cavern, and therefore chose it for my final residence. I employed artificers to form it into chambers, and stored it with all that I was likely to want.

'For some time after my retreat, I rejoiced like a tempest-beaten sailor at his entrance into the harbour, being delighted with the sudden change of the noise and hurry of war, to stillness and repose. When the pleasure of novelty went away, I employed my hours in examining the plants which grow in the valley, and the minerals which I collected from the rocks. But that enquiry is now grown tasteless and irksome. I have been for some time unsettled and distracted: my mind is disturbed with a thousand perplexities of doubt, and vanities of imagination, which hourly prevail upon me, because I have no opportunities of relaxation or diversion. I am sometimes ashamed to think that I could not secure myself from vice, but by retiring from the exercise of virtue, and begin to suspect that I was rather impelled by resentment, than led by devotion, into solitude. My fancy riots in scenes of folly, and I lament that I have lost so much, and have gained so little. In solitude, if I escape the example of bad men, I want likewise the counsel and conversation of the good. I have been long comparing the evils with the advantages of society, and resolve to return into

---

[20]   *enthusiasm*   "A vain belief of private revelation; a vain confidence of divine favour or communication" (Johnson).

the world tomorrow. The life of a solitary man will be certainly miserable, but not certainly devout'.

They heard his resolution with surprise, but, after a short pause, offered to conduct him to Cairo. He dug up a considerable treasure which he had hid among the rocks, and accompanied them to the city, on which, as he approached it, he gazed with rapture.

CHAPTER 22
THE HAPPINESS OF A LIFE LED ACCORDING TO NATURE

Rasselas went often to an assembly of learned men, who met at stated times to unbend their minds, and compare their opinions. Their manners were somewhat coarse, but their conversation was instructive, and their disputations acute, though sometimes too violent, and often continued till neither controvertist[21] remembered upon what question they began. Some faults were almost general among them: every one was desirous to dictate to the rest, and every one was pleased to hear the genius or knowledge of another depreciated.

In this assembly Rasselas was relating his interview with the hermit, and the wonder with which he heard him censure a course of life which he had so deliberately chosen, and so laudably followed. The sentiments of the hearers were various. Some were of opinion, that the folly of his choice had been justly punished by condemnation to perpetual perseverance. One of the youngest among them, with great vehemence, pronounced him an hypocrite. Some talked of the right of society to the labour of individuals, and considered retirement as a desertion of duty. Others readily allowed, that there was a time when the claims of the public were satisfied, and when a man might properly sequester himself, to review his life, and purify his heart.

One, who appeared more affected with the narrative than the rest, thought it likely, that the hermit would, in a few years, go back to his retreat, and, perhaps, if shame did not restrain, or death intercept him, return once more from his retreat into the world: 'For the hope of happiness', says he, 'is so strongly impressed, that the longest experience is not able to efface it. Of the present state, whatever it be, we feel, and are forced to confess, the misery, yet, when the same state is again at a distance, imagination paints it as desirable. But the time will surely come, when desire will be no longer our torment, and no man shall be wretched but by his own fault'.

'This', said a philosopher, who had heard him with tokens of great impatience, 'is the present condition of a wise man. The time is already come, when none are wretched but by their own fault. Nothing is more idle, than to enquire after happiness, which nature has kindly placed within our reach. The way to be happy is to live according to nature,[22] in obedience to that universal and unalterable law with which every heart is originally impressed; which is not written on it by precept, but engraven by destiny, not instilled by education but infused at our nativity. He that lives according to nature will suffer nothing from the delusions of hope, or importunities of desire: he will receive and reject with equability of temper; and act or suffer as the reason of things shall alternately prescribe. Other men may amuse themselves with subtle definitions, or intricate ratiocination. Let them learn to be wise by easier means: let them observe the hind of the forest, and the linnet of the grove: let them consider the life of animals, whose motions are regulated by instinct; they obey their

---

21 *controvertist* disputant.

22 *to live according to nature* Johnson is parodying the tenets of Deism or Natural Religion, which were contro- versial contemporary movements, although they have classical backgrounds.

guide and are happy. Let us therefore, at length, cease to dispute, and learn to live; throw away the encumbrance of precepts, which they who utter them with so much pride and pomp do not understand, and carry with us this simple and intelligible maxim, That deviation from nature is deviation from happiness'.

When he had spoken, he looked round him with a placid air, and enjoyed the consciousness of his own beneficence. 'Sir', said the prince, with great modesty, 'as I, like all the rest of mankind, am desirous of felicity, my closest attention has been fixed upon your discourse: I doubt not the truth of a position which a man so learned has so confidently advanced. Let me only know what it is to live according to nature'.

'When I find young men so humble and so docile', said the philosopher, 'I can deny them no information which my studies have enabled me to afford. To live according to nature, is to act always with due regard to the fitness arising from the relations and qualities of causes and effects; to concur with the great and unchangeable scheme of universal felicity; to co-operate with the general disposition and tendency of the present system of things'.

The prince soon found that this was one of the sages whom he should understand less as he heard him longer. He therefore bowed and was silent, and the philosopher, supposing him satisfied, and the rest vanquished, rose up and departed with the air of a man that had co-operated with the present system

CHAPTER 23
THE PRINCE AND HIS SISTER DIVIDE BETWEEN THEM THE
WORK OF OBSERVATION

Rasselas returned home full of reflections, doubtful how to direct his future steps. Of the way to happiness he found the learned and simple equally ignorant; but, as he was yet young, he flattered himself that he had time remaining for more experiments, and further enquiries. He communicated to Imlac his observations and his doubts, but was answered by him with new doubts, and remarks that gave him no comfort. He therefore discoursed more frequently and freely with his sister, who had yet the same hope with himself, and always assisted him to give some reason why, though he had been hitherto frustrated, he might succeed at last.

'We have hitherto', said she, 'known but little of the world: we have never yet been either great or mean. In our own country, though we had royalty, we had no power, and in this we have not yet seen the private recesses of domestic peace. Imlac favours not our search, lest we should in time find him mistaken. We will divide the task between us: you shall try what is to be found in the splendour of courts, and I will range the shades of humbler life. Perhaps command and authority may be the supreme blessings, as they afford most opportunities of doing good: or, perhaps, what this world can give may be found in the modest habitations of middle fortune; too low for great designs, and too high for penury and distress'.

CHAPTER 24
THE PRINCE EXAMINES THE HAPPINESS OF HIGH STATIONS

Rasselas applauded the design, and appeared next day with a splendid retinue at the court of the Bassa. He was soon distinguished for his magnificence, and admitted, as a prince whose curiosity had brought him from distant countries, to an intimacy with the great officers, and frequent conversation with the Bassa himself.

He was at first inclined to believe, that the man must be pleased with his own condition, whom all approached with reverence, and heard with obedience, and who had the power to extend his edicts to a whole kingdom. 'There can be no pleasure', said he, 'equal to that of feeling at once the joy of thousands all made happy by wise administration. Yet, since, by the law of subordination, this sublime delight can be in one nation but the lot of one, it is surely reasonable to think that there is some satisfaction more popular and accessible, and that millions can hardly be subjected to the will of a single man, only to fill his particular breast with incommunicable content'.

These thoughts were often in his mind, and he found no solution of the difficulty. But as presents and civilities gained him more familiarity, he found that almost every man who stood high in employment hated all the rest, and was hated by them, and that their lives were a continual succession of plots and detections, stratagems and escapes, faction and treachery. Many of those, who surrounded the Bassa, were sent only to watch and report his conduct; every tongue was muttering censure, and every eye was searching for a fault.

At last the letters of revocation arrived, the Bassa was carried in chains to Constantinople, and his name was mentioned no more.

'What are we now to think of the prerogatives of power', said Rasselas to his sister; 'is it without any efficacy to good? or, is the subordinate degree only dangerous, and the supreme safe and glorious? Is the Sultan the only happy man in his dominions? or, is the Sultan himself subject to the torments of suspicion, and the dread of enemies?'

In a short time the second Bassa was deposed. The Sultan, that had advanced him, was murdered by the Janisaries,[23] and his successor had other views and different favourites.

CHAPTER 25
THE PRINCESS PURSUES HER ENQUIRY WITH MORE DILIGENCE
THAN SUCCESS

The princess, in the mean time, insinuated herself into many families; for there are few doors, through which liberality, joined with good humour, cannot find its way. The daughters of many houses were airy and cheerful, but Nekayah had been too long accustomed to the conversation of Imlac and her brother to be much pleased with childish levity and prattle which had no meaning. She found their thoughts narrow, their wishes low, and their merriment often artificial. Their pleasures, poor as they were, could not be preserved pure, but were embittered by petty competitions and worthless emulation. They were always jealous of the beauty of each other; of a quality to which solicitude can add nothing, and from which detraction can take nothing away. Many were in love with triflers like themselves, and many fancied that they were in love when in truth they were only idle. Their affection was seldom fixed on sense or virtue, and therefore seldom ended but in vexation. Their grief, however, like their joy, was transient; every thing floated in their mind unconnected with the past or future, so that one desire easily gave way to another, as a second stone cast into the water effaces and confounds the circles of the first.

With these girls she played as with inoffensive animals, and found them proud of her countenance, and weary of her company.

---

[23] *Janisary* "One of the guards of the Turkish king [sultan]" (Johnson).

But her purpose was to examine more deeply, and her affability easily persuaded the hearts that were swelling with sorrow to discharge their secrets in her ear: and those whom hope flattered, or prosperity delighted, often courted her to partake their pleasures.

The princess and her brother commonly met in the evening in a private summer-house on the bank of the Nile, and related to each other the occurrences of the day. As they were sitting together, the princess cast her eyes upon the river that flowed before her. 'Answer', said she, 'great father of waters, thou that rollest thy floods through eighty nations, to the invocations of the daughter of thy native king. Tell me if thou waterest, through all thy course, a single habitation from which thou dost not hear the murmurs of complaint?'

'You are then', said Rasselas, 'not more successful in private houses than I have been in courts'. 'I have, since the last partition of our provinces', said the princess, 'enabled myself to enter familiarly into many families, where there was the fairest show of prosperity and peace, and know not one house that is not haunted by some fiend that destroys its quiet.

'I did not seek ease among the poor, because I concluded that there it could not be found. But I saw many poor whom I had supposed to live in affluence. Poverty has, in large cities, very different appearances: it is often concealed in splendour, and often in extravagance. It is the care of a very great part of mankind to conceal their indigence from the rest: they support themselves by temporary expedients, and every day is lost in contriving for the morrow.

'This, however, was an evil, which, though frequent, I saw with less pain, because I could relieve it. Yet some have refused my bounties; more offended with my quickness to detect their wants, than pleased with my readiness to succour them: and others, whose exigencies compelled them to admit my kindness, have never been able to forgive their benefactress. Many, however, have been sincerely grateful without the ostentation of gratitude, or the hope of other favours'.

CHAPTER 26[24]
THE PRINCESS CONTINUES HER REMARKS UPON PRIVATE LIFE

Nekayah perceiving her brother's attention fixed, proceeded in her narrative.

'In families, where there is or is not poverty, there is commonly discord: if a kingdom be, as Imlac tells us, a great family, a family likewise is a little kingdom, torn with factions and exposed to revolutions. An unpractised observer expects the love of parents and children to be constant and equal; but this kindness seldom continues beyond the years of infancy: in a short time the children become rivals to their parents. Benefits are allayed by reproaches, and gratitude debased by envy.

'Parents and children seldom act in concert: each child endeavours to appropriate the esteem or fondness of the parents, and the parents, with yet less temptation, betray each other to their children; thus some place their confidence in the father, and some in the mother, and, by degrees, the house is filled with artifices and feuds.

'The opinions of children and parents, of the young and the old, are naturally opposite, by the contrary effects of hope and despondence, of expectation and experience, without crime or folly on either side. The colours of life in youth and age appear different, as the face of nature in spring and winter. And how can children credit the assertions of parents, which their own eyes show them to be false?

'Few parents act in such a manner as much to enforce their maxims by the credit of their lives. The old man trusts wholly to slow contrivance and gradual progression: the youth

---

[24]   *Chapter* 26   this is the beginning of volume 2 in the original edition.

expects to force his way by genius, vigour, and precipitance. The old man pays regard to riches, and the youth reverences virtue. The old man deifies prudence: the youth commits himself to magnanimity and chance. The young man, who intends no ill, believes that none is intended, and therefore acts with openness and candour: but his father, having suffered the injuries of fraud, is impelled to suspect, and too often allured to practise it. Age looks with anger on the temerity of youth, and youth with contempt on the scrupulosity of age. Thus parents and children, for the greatest part, live on to love less and less: and, if those whom nature has thus closely united are the torments of each other, where shall we look for tenderness and consolation?'

'Surely', said the prince, 'you must have been unfortunate in your choice of acquaintance: I am unwilling to believe, that the most tender of all relations is thus impeded in its effects by natural necessity'.

'Domestic discord', answered she, 'is not inevitably and fatally necessary; but yet is not easily avoided. We seldom see that a whole family is virtuous: the good and evil cannot well agree; and the evil can yet less agree with one another: even the virtuous fall sometimes to variance, when their virtues are of different kinds and tending to extremes. In general, those parents have most reverence who most deserve it: for he that lives well cannot be despised.

'Many other evils infest private life. Some are the slaves of servants whom they have trusted with their affairs. Some are kept in continual anxiety to the caprice of rich relations, whom they cannot please, and dare not offend. Some husbands are imperious, and some wives perverse: and, as it is always more easy to do evil than good, though the wisdom or virtue of one can very rarely make many happy, the folly or vice of one may often make many miserable'.

'If such be the general effect of marriage', said the prince, 'I shall, for the future, think it dangerous to connect my interest with that of another, lest I should be unhappy by my partner's fault'.

'I have met', said the princess, 'with many who live single for that reason; but I never found that their prudence ought to raise envy. They dream away their time without friendship, without fondness, and are driven to rid themselves of the day, for which they have no use, by childish amusements, or vicious delights. They act as beings under the constant sense of some known inferiority, that fills their minds with rancour, and their tongues with censure. They are peevish at home, and malevolent abroad; and, as the outlaws of human nature, make it their business and their pleasure to disturb that society which debars them from its privileges. To live without feeling or exciting sympathy, to be fortunate without adding to the felicity of others, or afflicted without tasting the balm of pity, is a state more gloomy than solitude: it is not retreat but exclusion from mankind. Marriage has many pains, but celibacy has no pleasures'.

'What then is to be done?' said Rasselas; 'the more we enquire, the less we can resolve. Surely he is most likely to please himself that has no other inclination to regard'.

CHAPTER 27
DISQUISITION UPON GREATNESS

The conversation had a short pause. The prince having considered his sister's observations, told her, that she had surveyed life with prejudice, and supposed misery where she did not find it. 'Your narrative', says he, 'throws yet a darker gloom upon the prospects of futurity: the predictions of Imlac were but faint sketches of the evils painted by Nekayah. I have been lately convinced that quiet is not the daughter of grandeur, or of power: that her presence is not to be bought by wealth, nor enforced by conquest. It is evident, that as any man acts in a wider compass, he must be more exposed to opposition from enmity or miscarriage from chance; whoever has many to please or to govern, must use the ministry of many agents, some of whom will be wicked, and some ignorant; by some he will be misled, and by others betrayed. If he gratifies one he will offend another: those that are not favoured will think themselves injured; and, since favours can be conferred but upon few, the greater number will be always discontented'.

'The discontent', said the princess, 'which is thus unreasonable, I hope that I shall always have spirit to despise, and you, power to repress'.

'Discontent', answered Rasselas, 'will not always be without reason under the most just or vigilant administration of public affairs. None however attentive, can always discover that merit which indigence or faction may happen to obscure; and none, however powerful, can always reward it. Yet, he that sees inferior desert advanced above him, will naturally impute that preference to partiality or caprice; and, indeed, it can scarcely be hoped that any man, however magnanimous by nature, or exalted by condition, will be able to persist for ever in fixed and inexorable justice of distribution: he will sometimes indulge his own affections, and sometimes those of his favourites; he will permit some to please him who can never serve him; he will discover in those whom he loves qualities which in reality they do not possess; and to those, from whom he receives pleasure, he will in his turn endeavour to give it. Thus will recommendations sometimes prevail which were purchased by money, or by the more destructive bribery of flattery and servility.

'He that has much to do will do something wrong, and of that wrong must suffer the consequences; and, if it were possible that he should always act rightly, yet when such numbers are to judge of his conduct, the bad will censure and obstruct him by malevolence, and the good sometimes by mistake.

'The highest stations cannot therefore hope to be the abodes of happiness, which I would willingly believe to have fled from thrones and palaces to seats of humble privacy and placid obscurity. For what can hinder the satisfaction, or intercept the expectations, of him whose abilities are adequate to his employments, who sees with his own eyes the whole circuit of his influence, who chooses by his own knowledge all whom he trusts, and whom none are tempted to deceive by hope or fear? Surely he has nothing to do but to love and to be loved, to be virtuous and to be happy'.

'Whether perfect happiness would be procured by perfect goodness', said Nekayah, 'this world will never afford an opportunity of deciding. But this, at least, may be maintained, that we do not always find visible happiness in proportion to visible virtue. All natural and almost all political evils, are incident alike to the bad and good: they are confounded in the misery of a famine, and not much distinguished in the fury of a faction; they sink together in a tempest, and are driven together from their country by invaders. All that virtue can afford is quietness of conscience, a steady prospect of a happier state; this may enable us to endure calamity with patience; but remember that patience must suppose pain'.

CHAPTER 28
RASSELAS AND NEKAYAH CONTINUE THEIR CONVERSATION

'Dear princess', said Rasselas, 'you fall into the common errors of exaggeratory declamation, by producing, in a familiar disquisition, examples of national calamities, and scenes of extensive misery, which are found in books rather than in the world, and which, as they are horrid, are ordained to be rare. Let us not imagine evils which we do not feel, nor injure life by misrepresentations. I cannot bear that querulous eloquence which threatens every city with a siege like that of Jerusalem,[25] that makes famine attend on every flight of locusts, and suspends pestilence on the wing of every blast that issues from the south.

'On necessary and inevitable evils, which overwhelm kingdoms at once, all disputation is vain: when they happen they must be endured. But it is evident, that these bursts of universal distress are more dreaded than felt: thousands and ten thousands flourish in youth, and wither in age, without the knowledge of any other than domestic evils, and share the same pleasures and vexations whether their kings are mild or cruel, whether the armies of their country pursue their enemies, or retreat before them. While courts are disturbed with intestine competitions, and ambassadors are negotiating in foreign countries, the smith still plies his anvil, and the husbandman drives his plough forward; the necessaries of life are required and obtained, and the successive business of the seasons continues to make its wonted[26] revolutions.

'Let us cease to consider what, perhaps, may never happen, and what, when it shall happen, will laugh at human speculation. We will not endeavour to modify the motions of the elements, or to fix the destiny of kingdoms. It is our business to consider what beings like us may perform; each labouring for his own happiness, by promoting within his circle, however narrow, the happiness of others.

'Marriage is evidently the dictate of nature; men and women were made to be companions of each other, and therefore I cannot be persuaded but that marriage is one of the means of happiness'.

'I know not', said the princess, 'whether marriage be more than one of the innumerable modes of human misery. When I see and reckon the various forms of connubial infelicity, the unexpected causes of lasting discord, the diversities of temper, the oppositions of opinion, the rude collisions of contrary desire where both are urged by violent impulses, the obstinate contests of disagreeing virtues, where both are supported by consciousness of good intention, I am sometimes disposed to think with the severer casuists[27] of most nations, that marriage is rather permitted than approved, and that none, but by the instigation of a passion too much indulged, entangle themselves with indissoluble compacts'.

'You seem to forget', replied Rasselas, 'that you have, even now, represented celibacy as less happy than marriage. Both conditions may be bad, but they cannot both be worst. Thus it happens when wrong opinions are entertained, that they mutually destroy each other, and leave the mind open to truth'.

'I did not expect', answered the princess, 'to hear that imputed to falsehood which is the consequence only of frailty. To the mind, as to the eye, it is difficult to compare with exactness objects vast in their extent, and various in their parts. Where we see or conceive the whole at once we readily note the discriminations and decide the preference: but of two systems, of which neither can be surveyed by any human being in its full compass of magnitude and multiplicity of complication, where is the wonder, that judging of the whole by parts, I am alternately affected by one and the other as either presses on my memory or fancy? We differ from ourselves just as we differ from each other, when we see only part of the question, as in the multifarious relations of politics and morality: but when we perceive the whole at once, as in numerical computations, all agree in one judgement, and none ever varies his opinion'.

---

[25] *Jerusalem* the city was brutally besieged by the Emperor Titus in 70 CE and by the Christian crusaders in 1099, among others.

[26] *wonted* usual, customary.
[27] *casuists* moralists.

'Let us not add', said the prince, 'to the other evils of life, the bitterness of controversy, nor endeavour to vie with each other in subtleties of argument. We are employed in a search, of which both are equally to enjoy the success, or suffer by the miscarriage. It is therefore fit that we assist each other. You surely conclude too hastily from the infelicity of marriage against its institution. Will not the misery of life prove equally that life cannot be the gift of heaven? The world must be peopled by marriage, or peopled without it'.

'How the world is to be peopled', returned Nekayah, 'is not my care, and needs not be yours. I see no danger that the present generation should omit to leave successors behind them: we are not now enquiring for the world, but for ourselves'.

CHAPTER 29
THE DEBATE ON MARRIAGE CONTINUED

'The good of the whole', says Rasselas, 'is the same with the good of all its parts. If marriage be best for mankind it must be evidently best for individuals, or a permanent and necessary duty must be the cause of evil, and some must be inevitably sacrificed to the convenience of others. In the estimate which you have made of the two states, it appears that the incommodities of a single life are, in a great measure, necessary and certain, but those of the conjugal state accidental and avoidable.

'I cannot forbear to flatter myself that prudence and benevolence will make marriage happy. The general folly of mankind is the cause of general complaint. What can be expected but disappointment and repentance from a choice made in the immaturity of youth, in the ardour of desire, without judgement, without foresight, without an enquiry after conformity of opinions, similarity of manners, rectitude of judgement, or purity of sentiment.

'Such is the common process of marriage. A youth and maiden meeting by chance, or brought together by artifice, exchange glances, reciprocate civilities, go home, and dream of one another. Having little to divert attention, or diversify thought, they find themselves uneasy when they are apart, and therefore conclude that they shall be happy together. They marry, and discover what nothing but voluntary blindness had before concealed; they wear out life in altercations, and charge nature with cruelty.

'From those early marriages proceeds likewise the rivalry of parents and children: the son is eager to enjoy the world before the father is willing to forsake it, and there is hardly room at once for two generations. The daughter begins to bloom before the mother can be content to fade, and neither can forbear to wish for the absence of the other.

'Surely all these evils may be avoided by that deliberation and delay which prudence prescribes to irrevocable choice. In the variety and jollity of youthful pleasures life may be well enough supported without the help of a partner. Longer time will increase experience, and wider views will allow better opportunities of enquiry and selection: one advantage, at least, will be certain; the parents will be visibly older than their children'.

'What reason cannot collect', said Nekayah, 'and what experiment has not yet taught, can be known only from the report of others. I have been told that late marriages are not eminently happy. This is a question too important to be neglected, and I have often proposed it to those, whose accuracy of remark, and comprehensiveness of knowledge, made their suffrages worthy of regard. They have generally determined, that it is dangerous for a man and woman to suspend their fate upon each other, at a time when opinions are fixed, and habits are established; when friendships have been contracted on both sides, when life has been planned into method, and the mind has long enjoyed the contemplation of its own prospects.

'It is scarcely possible that two travelling through the world under the conduct of chance, should have been both directed to the same path, and it will not often happen that either will quit the track which custom has made pleasing. When the desultory levity of youth has settled into regularity, it is soon succeeded by pride ashamed to yield, or obstinacy delighting to contend. And even though mutual esteem produces mutual desire to please, time itself, as it modifies unchangeably the external mien, determines likewise the direction of the passions, and gives an inflexible rigidity to the manners. Long customs are not easily broken: he that attempts to change the course of his own life, very often labours in vain; and how shall we do that for others which we are seldom able to do for ourselves?'

'But surely', interposed the prince, 'you suppose the chief motive of choice forgotten or neglected. Whenever I shall seek a wife, it shall be my first question, whether she be willing to be led by reason?'

'Thus it is', said Nekayah, 'that philosophers are deceived. There are a thousand familiar disputes which reason never can decide; questions that elude investigation, and make logic ridiculous; cases where something must be done, and where little can be said. Consider the state of mankind, and enquire how few can be supposed to act upon any occasions, whether small or great, with all the reasons of action present to their minds. Wretched would be the pair above all names of wretchedness, who should be doomed to adjust by reason every morning all the minute detail of a domestic day.

'Those who marry at an advanced age, will probably escape the encroachments of their children; but, in diminution of this advantage, they will be likely to leave them, ignorant and helpless, to a guardian's mercy: or, if that should not happen, they must at least go out of the world before they see those whom they love best either wise or great.

'From their children, if they have less to fear, they have less also to hope, and they lose, without equivalent, the joys of early love and the convenience of uniting with manners pliant, and minds susceptible of new impressions, which might wear away their dissimilitudes by long cohabitation, as soft bodies, by continual attrition, conform their surfaces to each other.

'I believe it will be found that those who marry late are best pleased with their children, and those who marry early with their partners'.

'The union of these two affections', said Rasselas, 'would produce all that could be wished. Perhaps there is a time when marriage might unite them, a time neither too early for the father, nor too late for the husband'.

'Every hour', answered the princess, 'confirms my prejudice in favour of the position so often uttered by the mouth of Imlac, "That nature sets her gifts on the right hand and on the left". Those conditions, which flatter hope and attract desire, are so constituted, that, as we approach one, we recede from another. There are goods so opposed that we cannot seize both, but, by too much prudence, may pass between them at too great a distance to reach either. This is often the fate of long consideration; he does nothing who endeavours to do more than is allowed to humanity. Flatter not yourself with contrarieties of pleasure. Of the blessings set before you make your choice, and be content. No man can taste the fruits of autumn while he is delighting his scent with the flowers of the spring: no man can, at the same time, fill his cup from the source and from the mouth of the Nile'.

CHAPTER 30
IMLAC ENTERS, AND CHANGES THE CONVERSATION

Here Imlac entered, and interrupted them. His look was clouded with thought. 'Imlac', said Rasselas, 'I have been taking from the princess the dismal history of private life, and am almost discouraged from further search'.

'It seems to me', said Imlac, 'that while you are making the choice of life, you neglect to live. You wander about a single city, which, however large and diversified, can now afford few novelties, and forget that you are in a country, famous among the earliest monarchies for the power and wisdom of its inhabitants; a country where the sciences first dawned that illuminate the world, and beyond which the arts cannot be traced of civil society or domestic life.

'The old Egyptians have left behind them monuments of industry and power before which all European magnificence is confessed to fade away. The ruins of their architecture are the schools of modern builders, and from the wonders which time has spared we may conjecture, though uncertainly, what it has destroyed'.

'My curiosity', said Rasselas, 'does not very strongly lead me to survey piles of stone, or mounds of earth; my business is with man. I came hither not to measure fragments of temples, or trace choked aqueducts, but to look upon the various scenes of the present world'.

'The things that are now before us', said the princess, 'require attention, and deserve it. What have I to do with the heroes or the monuments of ancient times? with times which never can return, and heroes, whose form of life was different from all that the present condition of mankind requires or allows'.

'To know any thing', returned the poet, 'we must know its effects; to see men we must see their works, that we may learn what reason has dictated, or passion has incited, and find what are the most powerful motives of action. To judge rightly of the present we must oppose it to the past; for all judgement is comparative, and of the future nothing can be known. The truth is, that no mind is much employed upon the present: recollection and anticipation fill up almost all our moments. Our passions are joy and grief, love and hatred, hope and fear. Of joy and grief the past is the object, and the future of hope and fear; even love and hatred respect the past, for the cause must have been before the effect.

'The present state of things is the consequence of the former, and it is natural to enquire what were the sources of the good that we enjoy, or of the evil that we suffer. If we act only for ourselves, to neglect the study of history is not prudent: if we are entrusted with the care of others, it is not just. Ignorance, when it is voluntary, is criminal; and he may properly be charged with evil who refused to learn how he might prevent it.

'There is no part of history so generally useful as that which relates the progress of the human mind, the gradual improvement of reason, the successive advances of science, the vicissitudes of learning and ignorance, which are the light and darkness of thinking beings, the extinction and resuscitation of arts, and all the revolutions of the intellectual world. If accounts of battles and invasions are peculiarly the business of princes, the useful or elegant arts are not to be neglected; those who have kingdoms to govern, have understandings to cultivate.

'Example is always more efficacious than precept. A soldier is formed in war, and a painter must copy pictures. In this, contemplative life has the advantage: great actions are seldom seen, but the labours of art are always at hand for those who desire to know what art has been able to perform.

'When the eye or the imagination is struck with any uncommon work the next transition of an active mind is to the means by which it was performed. Here begins the true use of such contemplation; we enlarge our comprehension by new ideas, and perhaps recover some art lost to mankind, or learn what is less perfectly known in our own country. At least we compare our own with former times, and either rejoice at our improvements, or, what is the first motion towards good, discover our defects'.

'I am willing', said the prince, 'to see all that can deserve my search'. 'And I', said the princess, 'shall rejoice to learn something of the manners of antiquity'.

'The most pompous monument of Egyptian greatness, and one of the most bulky works of manual industry', said Imlac, 'are the pyramids; fabrics[28] raised before the time of history, and of which the earliest narratives afford us only uncertain traditions. Of these the greatest is still standing, very little injured by time'.

'Let us visit them to morrow', said Nekayah. 'I have often heard of the Pyramids, and shall not rest, till I have seen them within and without with my own eyes'.

CHAPTER 31
THEY VISIT THE PYRAMIDS

The resolution being thus taken, they set out the next day. They laid tents upon their camels, being resolved to stay among the pyramids till their curiosity was fully satisfied. They travelled gently, turned aside to every thing remarkable, stopped from time to time and conversed with the inhabitants, and observed the various appearances of towns ruined and inhabited, of wild and cultivated nature.

When they came to the Great Pyramid they were astonished at the extent of the base, and the height of the top. Imlac explained to them the principles upon which the pyramidal form was chosen for a fabric intended to co-extend its duration with that of the world: he showed that its gradual diminution gave it such stability, as defeated all the common attacks of the elements, and could scarcely be overthrown by earthquakes themselves, the least resistible of natural violence. A concussion that should shatter the pyramid would threaten the dissolution of the continent.

They measured all its dimensions, and pitched their tents at its foot. Next day they prepared to enter its interior apartments, and having hired the common guides climbed up to the first passage, when the favourite of the princess, looking into the cavity, stepped back and trembled. 'Pekuah', said the princess, 'of what art thou afraid?' 'Of the narrow entrance', answered the lady, 'and of the dreadful gloom. I dare not enter a place which must surely be inhabited by unquiet souls. The original possessors of these dreadful vaults will start up before us, and, perhaps, shut us in for ever'. She spoke, and threw her arms round the neck of her mistress.

'If all your fear be of apparitions', said the prince, 'I will promise you safety: there is no danger from the dead; he that is once buried will be seen no more'.

'That the dead are seen no more', said Imlac, 'I will not undertake to maintain against the concurrent and unvaried testimony of all ages, and of all nations. There is no people, rude or learned, among whom apparitions of the dead are not related and believed. This opinion, which, perhaps, prevails as far as human nature is diffused, could become universal only by its truth: those, that never heard of one another, would not have agreed in a tale which nothing but experience can make credible. That it is doubted by single cavillers can very little weaken the general evidence, and some who deny it with their tongues confess it by their fears.

'Yet I do not mean to add new terrors to those which have already seized upon Pekuah. There can be no reason why spectres should haunt the pyramid more than other places, or why they should have power or will to hurt innocence and purity. Our entrance is no violation of their privileges; we can take nothing from them, how then can we offend them?'

'My dear Pekuah', said the princess, 'I will always go before you, and Imlac shall follow you. Remember that you are the companion of the princess of Abyssinia'.

---

[28] *fabrics* buildings.

'If the princess is pleased that her servant should die', returned the lady, 'let her command some death less dreadful than enclosure in this horrid cavern. You know I dare not disobey you: I must go if you command me; but, if I once enter, I never shall come back'.

The princess saw that her fear was too strong for expostulation or reproof, and embracing her, told her that she should stay in the tent till their return. Pekuah was yet not satisfied, but entreated the princess not to pursue so dreadful a purpose, as that of entering the recesses of the pyramid. 'Though I cannot teach courage', said Nekayah, 'I must not learn cowardice; nor leave at last undone what I came hither only to do'.

CHAPTER 32
THEY ENTER THE PYRAMID

Pekuah descended to the tents and the rest entered the pyramid: they passed through the galleries, surveyed the vaults of marble, and examined the chest in which the body of the founder is supposed to have been reposited. They then sat down in one of the most spacious chambers to rest a while before they attempted to return.

'We have now', said Imlac, 'gratified our minds with an exact view of the greatest work of man, except the wall of China.

'Of the wall it is very easy to assign the motives. It secured a wealthy and timorous nation from the incursions of Barbarians, whose unskilfulness in arts made it easier for them to supply their wants by rapine than by industry, and who from time to time poured in upon the habitations of peaceful commerce, as vultures descend upon domestic fowl. Their celerity and fierceness made the wall necessary, and their ignorance made it efficacious.

'But for the pyramids no reason has ever been given adequate to the cost and labour of the work. The narrowness of the chambers proves that it could afford no retreat from enemies, and treasures might have been reposited at far less expense with equal security. It seems to have been erected only in compliance with that hunger of imagination which preys incessantly upon life, and must be always appeased by some employment. Those who have already all that they can enjoy, must enlarge their desires. He that has built for use, till use is supplied, must begin to build for vanity, and extend his plan to the utmost power of human performance, that he may not be soon reduced to form another wish.

'I consider this mighty structure as a monument of the insufficiency of human enjoyments. A king, whose power is unlimited, and whose treasures surmount all real and imaginary wants, is compelled to solace, by the erection of a pyramid, the satiety of dominion and tastelessness of pleasures, and to amuse the tediousness of declining life, by seeing thousands labouring without end, and one stone, for no purpose, laid upon another. Whoever thou art, that, not content with a moderate condition, imaginest happiness in royal magnificence, and dreamest that command or riches can feed the appetite of novelty with perpetual gratifications, survey the pyramids, and confess thy folly!'

CHAPTER 33
THE PRINCESS MEETS WITH AN UNEXPECTED MISFORTUNE

They rose up, and returned through the cavity at which they had entered, and the princess prepared for her favourite a long narrative of dark labyrinths, and costly rooms, and of the different impressions which the varieties of the way had made upon her. But, when they came to their train, they found every one silent and dejected: the men discovered shame and fear in their countenances, and the women were weeping in the tents.

What had happened they did not try to conjecture, but immediately enquired. 'You had scarcely entered into the pyramid', said one of the attendants, 'when a troop of Arabs rushed upon us: we were too few to resist them, and too slow to escape. They were about to search the tents, set us on our camels, and drive us along before them, when the approach of some Turkish horsemen put them to flight; but they seized the lady Pekuah with her two maids, and carried them away: the Turks are now pursuing them by our instigation, but I fear they will not be able to overtake them'.

The princess was overpowered with surprise and grief. Rasselas, in the first heat of his resentment, ordered his servants to follow him, and prepared to pursue the robbers with his sabre in his hand. 'Sir', said Imlac, 'what can you hope from violence or valour? the Arabs are mounted on horses trained to battle and retreat; we have only beasts of burthen. By leaving our present station we may lose the princess, but cannot hope to regain Pekuah'.

In a short time the Turks returned, having not been able to reach the enemy. The princess burst out into new lamentations, and Rasselas could scarcely forbear to reproach them with cowardice; but Imlac was of opinion, that the escape of the Arabs was no addition to their misfortune, for, perhaps, they would have killed their captives rather than have resigned them.

CHAPTER 34
THEY RETURN TO CAIRO WITHOUT PEKUAH

There was nothing to be hoped from longer stay. They returned to Cairo repenting of their curiosity, censuring the negligence of the government, lamenting their own rashness which had neglected to procure a guard, imagining many expedients by which the loss of Pekuah might have been prevented, and resolving to do something for her recovery, though none could find any thing proper to be done.

Nekayah retired to her chamber, where her women attempted to comfort her, by telling her that all had their troubles, and that lady Pekuah had enjoyed much happiness in the world for a long time, and might reasonably expect a change of fortune. They hoped that some good would befall her wheresoever she was, and that their mistress would find another friend who might supply her place.

The princess made them no answer, and they continued the form of condolence, not much grieved in their hearts that the favourite was lost.

Next day the prince presented to the Bassa a memorial of the wrong which he had suffered, and a petition for redress. The Bassa threatened to punish the robbers, but did not attempt to catch them, nor, indeed, could any account or description be given by which he might direct the pursuit.

It soon appeared that nothing would be done by authority. Governors, being accustomed to hear of more crimes than they can punish, and more wrongs than they can redress, set themselves at ease by indiscriminate negligence, and presently forget the request when they lose sight of the petitioner.

Imlac then endeavoured to gain some intelligence by private agents. He found many who pretended to an exact knowledge of all the haunts of the Arabs, and to regular correspondence with their chiefs, and who readily undertook the recovery of Pekuah. Of these, some were furnished with money for their journey, and came back no more; some were liberally paid for accounts which a few days discovered to be false. But the princess would not suffer any means, however improbable, to be left untried. While she was doing something she kept her hope alive. As one expedient failed, another was suggested; when one messenger returned unsuccessful, another was dispatched to a different quarter.

Two months had now passed, and of Pekuah nothing had been heard; the hopes which they had endeavoured to raise in each other grew more languid, and the princess, when she saw nothing more to be tried, sunk down inconsolable in hopeless dejection. A thousand times she reproached herself with the easy compliance by which she permitted her favourite to stay behind her. 'Had not my fondness', said she, 'lessened my authority, Pekuah had not dared to talk of her terrors. She ought to have feared me more than spectres. A severe look would have overpowered her; a peremptory command would have compelled obedience. Why did foolish indulgence prevail upon me? Why did I not speak and refuse to hear?'

'Great princess', said Imlac, 'do not reproach yourself for your virtue, or consider that as blameable by which evil has accidentally been caused. Your tenderness for the timidity of Pekuah was generous and kind. When we act according to our duty, we commit the event to him by whose laws our actions are governed, and who will suffer none to be finally punished for obedience. When, in prospect of some good, whether natural or moral, we break the rules prescribed us, we withdraw from the direction of superior wisdom, and take all consequences upon ourselves. Man cannot so far know the connection of causes and events, as that he may venture to do wrong in order to do right. When we pursue our end by lawful means, we may always console our miscarriage by the hope of future recompense. When we consult only our own policy, and attempt to find a nearer way to good, by overleaping the settled boundaries of right and wrong, we cannot be happy even by success, because we cannot escape the consciousness of our fault; but, if we miscarry, the disappointment is irremediably embittered. How comfortless is the sorrow of him; who feels at once the pangs of guilt, and the vexation of calamity which guilt has brought upon him?

'Consider, princess, what would have been your condition, if the lady Pekuah had entreated to accompany you, and, being compelled to stay in the tents, had been carried away; or how would you have born the thought, if you had forced her into the pyramid, and she had died before you in agonies of terror'.

'Had either happened', said Nekayah, 'I could not have endured life till now: I should have been tortured to madness by the remembrance of such cruelty, or must have pined away in abhorrence of myself'.

'This at least', said Imlac, 'is the present reward of virtuous conduct, that no unlucky consequence can oblige us to repent it'.

CHAPTER 35
THE PRINCESS CONTINUES TO LAMENT PEKUAH

Nekayah, being thus reconciled to herself, found that no evil is insupportable but that which is accompanied with consciousness of wrong. She was, from that time, delivered from the violence of tempestuous sorrow, and sunk into silent pensiveness and gloomy tranquillity. She sat from morning to evening recollecting all that had been done or said by her Pekuah, treasured up with care every trifle on which Pekuah had set an accidental value, and which might recall to mind any little incident or careless conversation. The sentiments of her, whom she now expected to see no more, were treasured in her memory as rules of life, and she deliberated to no other end than to conjecture on any occasion what would have been the opinion and counsel of Pekuah.

The women, by whom she was attended, knew nothing of her real condition, and therefore she could not talk to them but with caution and reserve. She began to remit her curiosity, having no great care to collect notions which she had no convenience of uttering. Rasselas endeavoured first to comfort and afterwards to divert her; he hired musicians, to whom she seemed to listen, but did not hear them, and procured masters to instruct her in various arts, whose lectures, when they visited her again, were again to be repeated. She had lost her taste of pleasure and her ambition of excellence. And her mind, though forced into short excursions, always recurred to the image of her friend.

Imlac was every morning earnestly enjoined to renew his enquiries, and was asked every night whether he had yet heard of Pekuah, till not being able to return the princess the answer that she desired, he was less and less willing to come into her presence. She observed his backwardness, and commanded him to attend her. 'You are not', said she, 'to confound impatience with resentment, or to suppose that I charge you with negligence, because I repine at your unsuccessfulness. I do not much wonder at your absence; I know that the unhappy are never pleasing, and that all naturally avoid the contagion of misery. To hear complaints is wearisome alike to the wretched and the happy; for who would cloud by adventitious grief the short gleams of gaiety which life allows us? or who, that is struggling under his own evils, will add to them the miseries of another?

'The time is at hand, when none shall be disturbed any longer by the sighs of Nekayah: my search after happiness is now at an end. I am resolved to retire from the world with all its flatteries and deceits, and will hide myself in solitude, without any other care than to compose my thoughts, and regulate my hours by a constant succession of innocent occupations, till, with a mind purified from all earthly desires, I shall enter into that state, to which all are hastening, and in which I hope again to enjoy the friendship of Pekuah'.

'Do not entangle your mind', said Imlac, 'by irrevocable determinations, nor increase the burden of life by a voluntary accumulation of misery: the weariness of retirement will continue or increase when the loss of Pekuah is forgotten. That you have been deprived of one pleasure is no very good reason for rejection of the rest'.

'Since Pekuah was taken from me', said the princess, 'I have no pleasure to reject or to retain. She that has no one to love or trust has little to hope. She wants the radical principle of happiness. We may, perhaps, allow that what satisfaction this world can afford, must arise from the conjunction of wealth, knowledge and goodness: wealth is nothing but as it is bestowed, and knowledge nothing but as it is communicated: they must therefore be imparted to others, and to whom could I now delight to impart them? Goodness affords the only comfort which can be enjoyed without a partner, and goodness may be practised in retirement'.

'How far solitude may admit goodness, or advance it, I shall not', replied Imlac, 'dispute at present. Remember the confession of the pious hermit. You will wish to return into the world, when the image of your companion has left your thoughts'. 'That time', said Nekayah, 'will never come. The generous frankness, the modest obsequiousness,[29] and the faithful secrecy of my dear Pekuah, will always be more missed, as I shall live longer to see vice and folly'.

'The state of a mind oppressed with a sudden calamity', said Imlac, 'is like that of the fabulous inhabitants of the new created earth, who, when the first night came upon them, supposed that day never would return. When the clouds of sorrow gather over us, we see nothing beyond them, nor can imagine how they will be dispelled: yet a new day succeeded to the night, and sorrow is never long without a dawn of ease. But they who restrain themselves from receiving comfort, do as the savages would have done, had they put out their

---

[29] *obsequiousness* "Obedience; compliance" (Johnson).

eyes when it was dark. Our minds, like our bodies, are in continual flux; something is hourly lost, and something acquired. To lose much at once is inconvenient to either, but while the vital powers remain uninjured, nature will find the means of reparation. Distance has the same effect on the mind as on the eye, and while we glide along the stream of time, whatever we leave behind us is always lessening, and that which we approach increasing in magnitude. Do not suffer life to stagnate; it will grow muddy for want of motion: commit yourself again to the current of the world; Pekuah will vanish by degrees; you will meet in your way some other favourite, or learn to diffuse yourself in general conversation'.

'At least', said the prince, 'do not despair before all remedies have been tried: the enquiry after the unfortunate lady is still continued, and shall be carried on with yet greater diligence, on condition that you will promise to wait a year for the event, without any unalterable resolution'.

Nekayah thought this a reasonable demand, and made the promise to her brother, who had been advised by Imlac to require it. Imlac had, indeed, no great hope of regaining Pekuah, but he supposed, that if he could secure the interval of a year, the princess would be then in no danger of a cloister.

CHAPTER 36
PEKUAH IS STILL REMEMBERED BY THE PRINCESS

Nekayah, seeing that nothing was omitted for the recovery of her favourite, and having, by her promise, set her intention of retirement at a distance, began imperceptibly to return to common cares and common pleasures. She rejoiced without her own consent at the suspension of her sorrows, and sometimes caught herself with indignation in the act of turning away her mind from the remembrance of her, whom yet she resolved never to forget.

She then appointed a certain hour of the day for meditation on the merits and fondness of Pekuah, and for some weeks retired constantly at the time fixed, and returned with her eyes swollen and her countenance clouded. By degrees she grew less scrupulous, and suffered any important and pressing avocation to delay the tribute of daily tears. She then yielded to less occasions; sometimes forgot what she was indeed afraid to remember, and, at last, wholly released herself from the duty of periodical affliction.

Her real love of Pekuah was yet not diminished. A thousand occurrences brought her back to memory, and a thousand wants, which nothing but the confidence of friendship can supply, made her frequently regretted. She, therefore, solicited Imlac never to desist from enquiry, and to leave no art of intelligence untried, that, at least, she might have the comfort of knowing that she did not suffer by negligence or sluggishness. 'Yet what', said she, 'is to be expected from our pursuit of happiness, when we find the state of life to be such, that happiness itself is the cause of misery? Why should we endeavour to attain that, of which the possession cannot be secured? I shall henceforward fear to yield my heart to excellence, however bright, or to fondness, however tender, lest I should lose again what I have lost in Pekuah'.

CHAPTER 37
THE PRINCESS HEARS NEWS OF PEKUAH

In seven months, one of the messengers, who had been sent away upon the day when the promise was drawn from the princess, returned, after many unsuccessful rambles, from the borders of Nubia,[30] with an account that Pekuah was in the hands of an Arab chief, who possessed a castle or fortress on the extremity of Egypt. The Arab, whose revenue was plunder, was willing to restore her, with her two attendants, for two hundred ounces of gold.

The price was no subject of debate. The princess was in ecstasies when she heard that her favourite was alive, and might so cheaply be ransomed. She could not think of delaying for a moment Pekuah's happiness or her own, but entreated her brother to send back the messenger with the sum required. Imlac, being consulted, was not very confident of the veracity of the relator, and was still more doubtful of the Arab's faith, who might, if he were too liberally trusted, detain at once the money and the captives. He thought it dangerous to put themselves in the power of the Arab, by going into his district, and could not expect that the Rover would so much expose himself as to come into the lower country, where he might be seized by the forces of the Bassa.

It is difficult to negotiate where neither will trust. But Imlac, after some deliberation, directed the messenger to propose that Pekuah should be conducted by ten horsemen to the monastery of St. Antony, which is situated in the deserts of Upper-Egypt,[31] where she should be met by the same number, and her ransom should be paid.

That no time might be lost, as they expected that the proposal would not be refused, they immediately began their journey to the monastery; and, when they arrived, Imlac went forward with the former messenger to the Arab's fortress. Rasselas was desirous to go with them, but neither his sister nor Imlac would consent. The Arab, according to the custom of his nation, observed the laws of hospitality with great exactness to those who put themselves into his power, and, in a few days, brought Pekuah with her maids, by easy journeys, to their place appointed, where receiving the stipulated price, he restored her with great respect to liberty and her friends, and undertook to conduct them back towards Cairo beyond all danger of robbery or violence.

The princess and her favourite embraced each other with transport too violent to be expressed, and went out together to pour the tears of tenderness in secret, and exchange professions of kindness and gratitude. After a few hours they returned into the refectory of the convent, where, in the presence of the prior and his brethren, the prince required of Pekuah the history of her adventures.

CHAPTER 38
THE ADVENTURES OF THE LADY PEKUAH

'At what time, and in what manner, I was forced away', said Pekuah, 'your servants have told you. The suddenness of the event struck me with surprise, and I was at first rather stupefied than agitated with any passion of either fear or sorrow. My confusion was increased by the speed and tumult of our flight while we were followed by the Turks, who, as it seemed, soon despaired to overtake us, or were afraid of those whom they made a show of menacing.

'When the Arabs saw themselves out of danger they slackened their course, and, as I was less harassed by external violence, I began to feel more uneasiness in my mind. After some time we stopped near a spring shaded with trees in a pleasant meadow, where we were set upon the ground, and offered such refreshments as our masters were partaking. I was suffered to sit with my maids apart from the rest, and none attempted to comfort or insult us. Here

---

[30]   *Nubia*   an ancient region in north-eastern Africa, south of Egypt, north of Abyssinia.   [31]   *Upper-Egypt*   southern, higher Egypt; the monastery was mentioned in books that Johnson knew.

I first began to feel the full weight of my misery. The girls sat weeping in silence, and from time to time looked on me for succour. I knew not to what condition we were doomed, nor could conjecture where would be the place of our captivity, or whence to draw any hope of deliverance. I was in the hands of robbers and savages, and had no reason to suppose that their pity was more than their justice, or that they would forbear the gratification of any ardour of desire, or caprice of cruelty. I, however, kissed my maids, and endeavoured to pacify them by remarking, that we were yet treated with decency, and that, since we were now carried beyond pursuit, there was no danger of violence to our lives.

'When we were to be set again on horseback, my maids clung round me, and refused to be parted, but I commanded them not to irritate those who had us in their power. We travelled the remaining part of the day through an unfrequented and pathless country, and came by moonlight to the side of a hill, where the rest of the troop was stationed. Their tents were pitched, and their fires kindled, and our chief was welcomed as a man much beloved by his dependents.

'We were received into a large tent, where we found women who had attended their husbands in the expedition. They set before us the supper which they had provided, and I eat it rather to encourage my maids than to comply with any appetite of my own. When the meat was taken away they spread the carpets for repose. I was weary, and hoped to find in sleep that remission of distress which nature seldom denies. Ordering myself therefore to be undressed, I observed that the women looked very earnestly upon me, not expecting, I suppose, to see me so submissively attended. When my upper vest was taken off, they were apparently struck with the splendour of my clothes, and one of them timorously laid her hand upon the embroidery. She then went out, and, in a short time, came back with another woman, who seemed to be of higher rank, and greater authority. She did, at her entrance, the usual act of reverence, and, taking me by the hand, placed me in a smaller tent, spread with finer carpets, where I spent the night quietly with my maids.

'In the morning, as I was sitting on the grass, the chief of the troop came towards me. I rose up to receive him, and he bowed with great respect. "Illustrious lady", said he, "my fortune is better than I had presumed to hope; I am told by my women, that I have a princess in my camp". "Sir", answered I, "your women have deceived themselves and you; I am not a princess, but an unhappy stranger who intended soon to have left this country, in which I am now to be imprisoned for ever".

"Whoever, or whencesoever, you are", returned the Arab, "your dress, and that of your servants, show your rank to be high, and your wealth to be great. Why should you, who can so easily procure your ransom, think yourself in danger of perpetual captivity? The purpose of my incursions is to increase my riches, or more properly to gather tribute. The sons of Ishmael are the natural and hereditary lords of this part of the continent, which is usurped by late invaders, and low-born tyrants, from whom we are compelled to take by the sword what is denied to justice. The violence of war admits no distinction; the lance that is lifted at guilt and power will sometimes fall on innocence and gentleness".

"How little", said I, "did I expect that yesterday it should have fallen upon me".

"Misfortunes", answered the Arab, "should always be expected. If the eye of hostility could learn reverence or pity, excellence like yours had been exempt from injury. But the angels of affliction spread their toils[32] alike for the virtuous and the wicked, for the mighty and the mean. Do not be disconsolate; I am not one of the lawless and cruel rovers of the desert; I know the rules of civil life: I will fix your ransom, give a passport to your messenger, and perform my stipulation with nice punctuality".

---

[32] *toils* traps.

'You will easily believe that I was pleased with his courtesy; and finding that his predominant passion was desire of money, I began now to think my danger less, for I knew that no sum would be thought too great for the release of Pekuah. I told him that he should have no reason to charge me with ingratitude, if I was used with kindness, and that any ransom, which could be expected for a maid of common rank, would be paid, but that he must not persist to rate me as a princess. He said, he would consider what he should demand, and then, smiling, bowed and retired.

'Soon after the women came about me, each contending to be more officious[33] than the other, and my maids themselves were served with reverence. We travelled onward by short journeys. On the fourth day the chief told me, that my ransom must be two hundred ounces of gold, which I not only promised him, but told him, that I would add fifty more, if I and my maids were honourably treated.

'I never knew the power of gold before. From that time I was the leader of the troop. The march of every day was longer or shorter as I commanded, and the tents were pitched where I chose to rest. We now had camels and other conveniencies for travel, my own women were always at my side, and I amused myself with observing the manners of the vagrant nations, and with viewing remains of ancient edifices with which these deserted countries appear to have been, in some distant age, lavishly embellished.

'The chief of the band was a man far from illiterate: he was able to travel by the stars or the compass, and had marked in his erratic expeditions such places as are most worthy the notice of a passenger.[34] He observed to me, that buildings are always best preserved in places little frequented, and difficult of access: for, when once a country declines from its primitive splendour, the more inhabitants are left, the quicker ruin will be made. Walls supply stones more easily than quarries, and palaces and temples will be demolished to make stables of granite, and cottages of porphyry'.

CHAPTER 39
THE ADVENTURES OF PEKUAH CONTINUED

'We wandered about in this manner for some weeks, whether, as our chief pretended, for my gratification, or, as I rather suspected, for some convenience of his own. I endeavoured to appear contented where sullenness and resentment would have been of no use, and that endeavour conduced much to the calmness of my mind; but my heart was always with Nekayah, and the troubles of the night much overbalanced the amusements of the day. My women, who threw all their cares upon their mistress, set their minds at ease from the time when they saw me treated with respect, and gave themselves up to the incidental alleviations of our fatigue without solicitude or sorrow. I was pleased with their pleasure, and animated with their confidence. My condition had lost much of its terror, since I found that the Arab ranged the country merely to get riches. Avarice is an uniform and tractable vice: other intellectual distempers are different in different constitutions of mind; that which soothes the pride of one will offend the pride of another; but to the favour of the covetous there is a ready way, bring money and nothing is denied.

'At last we came to the dwelling of our chief, a strong and spacious house built with stone in an island of the Nile, which lies, as I was told, under the tropic.[35] "Lady", said the Arab, "you shall rest after your journey a few weeks in this place, where you are to consider yourself as sovereign. My occupation is war: I have therefore chosen this obscure residence, from which

---

[33] *officious* kind.
[34] *passenger* traveller.

[35] *the tropic* latitude 23.5 degrees north.

I can issue unexpected, and to which I can retire unpursued. You may now repose in security: here are few pleasures, but here is no danger". He then led me into the inner apartments, and seating me on the richest couch, bowed to the ground. His women, who considered me as a rival, looked on me with malignity; but being soon informed that I was a great lady detained only for my ransom, they began to vie with each other in obsequiousness and reverence.

'Being again comforted with new assurances of speedy liberty, I was for some days diverted from impatience by the novelty of the place. The turrets overlooked the country to a great distance, and afforded a view of many windings of the stream. In the day I wandered from one place to another as the course of the sun varied the splendour of the prospect, and saw many things which I had never seen before. The crocodiles and river-horses[36] are common in this unpeopled region, and I often looked upon them with terror, though I knew that they could not hurt me. For some time I expected to see mermaids and tritons,[37] which, as Imlac has told me, the European travellers have stationed in the Nile, but no such beings ever appeared, and the Arab, when I enquired after them, laughed at my credulity.

'At night the Arab always attended me to a tower set apart for celestial observations, where he endeavoured to teach me the names and courses of the stars. I had no great inclination to this study, but an appearance of attention was necessary to please my instructor, who valued himself for his skill, and, in a little while, I found some employment requisite to beguile the tediousness of time, which was to be passed always amidst the same objects. I was weary of looking in the morning on things from which I had turned away weary in the evening: I therefore was at last willing to observe the stars rather than do nothing, but could not always compose my thoughts, and was very often thinking on Nekayah when others imagined me contemplating the sky. Soon after the Arab went upon another expedition, and then my only pleasure was to talk with my maids about the accident by which we were carried away, and the happiness that we should all enjoy at the end of our captivity'.

'There were women in your Arab's fortress', said the princess, 'why did you not make them your companions, enjoy their conversation, and partake their diversions? In a place where they found business or amusement, why should you alone sit corroded with idle melancholy? or why should not you bear for a few months that condition to which they were condemned for life?'

'The diversions of the women', answered Pekuah, 'were only childish play, by which the mind accustomed to stronger operations could not be kept busy. I could do all which they delighted in doing by powers merely sensitive,[38] while my intellectual faculties were flown to Cairo. They ran from room to room as a bird hops from wire to wire in his cage. They danced for the sake of motion, as lambs frisk in a meadow. One sometimes pretended to be hurt that the rest might be alarmed, or hid herself that another might seek her. Part of their time passed in watching the progress of light bodies that floated on the river, and part in marking the various forms into which clouds broke in the sky.

'Their business was only needlework, in which I and my maids sometimes helped them; but you know that the mind will easily straggle from the fingers, nor will you suspect that captivity and absence from Nekayah could receive solace from silken flowers.

'Nor was much satisfaction to be hoped from their conversation: for of what could they be expected to talk? They had seen nothing; for they had lived from early youth in that narrow spot: of what they had not seen they could have no knowledge, for they could not read. They

---

[36]   *river-horse*   hippopotamus.
[37]   *tritons*   minor sea or river gods.

[38]   *sensitive*   "Having sense or perception, but not reason" (Johnson).

had no ideas but of the few things that were within their view, and had hardly names for any thing but their clothes and their food. As I bore a superior character, I was often called to terminate their quarrels, which I decided as equitably as I could. If it could have amused me to hear the complaints of each against the rest, I might have been often detained by long stories, but the motives of their animosity were so small that I could not listen without intercepting[39] the tale'.

'How', said Rasselas, 'can the Arab, whom you represented as a man of more than common accomplishments, take any pleasure in his seraglio, when it is filled only with women like these. Are they exquisitely beautiful?'

'They do not', said Pekuah, 'want that unaffecting and ignoble beauty which may subsist without spriteliness or sublimity, without energy of thought or dignity of virtue. But to a man like the Arab such beauty was only a flower casually plucked and carelessly thrown away. Whatever pleasures he might find among them, they were not those of friendship or society. When they were playing about him he looked on them with inattentive superiority: when they vied for his regard he sometimes turned away disgusted. As they had no knowledge, their talk could take nothing from the tediousness of life: as they had no choice, their fondness, or appearance of fondness, excited in him neither pride nor gratitude; he was not exalted in his own esteem by the smiles of a woman who saw no other man, nor was much obliged by that regard, of which he could never know the sincerity, and which he might often perceive to be exerted not so much to delight him as to pain a rival. That which he gave, and they received, as love, was only a careless distribution of superfluous time, such love as man can bestow upon that which he despises, such as has neither hope nor fear, neither joy nor sorrow'.

'You have reason, lady, to think yourself happy', said Imlac, 'that you have been thus easily dismissed. How could a mind, hungry for knowledge, be willing, in an intellectual famine, to lose such a banquet as Pekuah's conversation?'

'I am inclined to believe', answered Pekuah, 'that he was for some time in suspense; notwithstanding his promise, whenever I proposed to dispatch a messenger to Cairo, he found some excuse for delay. While I was detained in his house he made many incursions into the neighbouring countries, and, perhaps, he would have refused to discharge me, had his plunder been equal to his wishes. He returned always courteous, related his adventures, delighted to hear my observations, and endeavoured to advance my acquaintance with the stars. When I importuned him to send away my letters, he soothed me with professions of honour and sincerity; and, when I could be no longer decently denied, put his troop again in motion, and left me to govern in his absence. I was much afflicted by this studied procrastination, and was sometimes afraid that I should be forgotten; that you would leave Cairo, and I must end my days in an island of the Nile.

'I grew at last hopeless and dejected, and cared so little to entertain him, that he for a while more frequently talked with my maids. That he should fall in love with them, or with me, might have been equally fatal, and I was not much pleased with the growing friendship. My anxiety was not long; for, as I recovered some degree of cheerfulness, he returned to me, and I could not forbear to despise my former uneasiness.

'He still delayed to send for my ransom, and would, perhaps, never have determined, had not your agent found his way to him. The gold, which he would not fetch, he could not reject when it was offered. He hastened to prepare for our journey hither, like a man delivered from

---

[39] *intercept* "To stop; to cut off; to stop from being communicated" (Johnson).

the pain of an intestine conflict. I took leave of my companions in the house, who dismissed me with cold indifference'.

Nekayah, having heard her favourite's relation, rose and embraced her, and Rasselas gave her an hundred ounces of gold, which she presented to the Arab for the fifty that were promised.

CHAPTER 40
THE HISTORY OF A MAN OF LEARNING

They returned to Cairo, and were so well pleased at finding themselves together, that none of them went much abroad. The prince began to love learning, and one day declared to Imlac, that he intended to devote himself to science, and pass the rest of his days in literary solitude.

'Before you make your final choice', answered Imlac, 'you ought to examine its hazards, and converse with some of those who are grown old in the company of themselves. I have just left the observatory of one of the most learned astronomers in the world, who has spent forty years in unwearied attention to the motions and appearances of the celestial bodies, and has drawn out his soul in endless calculations. He admits a few friends once a month to hear his deductions and enjoy his discoveries. I was introduced as a man of knowledge worthy of his notice. Men of various ideas and fluent conversation are commonly welcome to those whose thoughts have been long fixed upon a single point, and who find the images of other things stealing away. I delighted him with my remarks, he smiled at the narrative of my travels, and was glad to forget the constellations, and descend for a moment into the lower world.

'On the next day of vacation I renewed my visit, and was so fortunate as to please him again. He relaxed from that time the severity of his rule, and permitted me to enter at my own choice. I found him always busy, and always glad to be relieved. As each knew much which the other was desirous of learning, we exchanged our notions with great delight. I perceived that I had every day more of his confidence, and always found new cause of admiration in the profundity of his mind. His comprehension is vast, his memory capacious and retentive, his discourse is methodical, and his expression clear.

'His integrity and benevolence are equal to his learning. His deepest researches and most favourite studies are willingly interrupted for any opportunity of doing good by his counsel or his riches. To his closest retreat at his most busy moments, all are admitted that want his assistance: "For though I exclude idleness and pleasure I will never", says he, "bar my doors against charity. To man is permitted the contemplation of the skies, but the practice of virtue is commanded".

'Surely', said the princess, 'this man is happy'.

'I visited him', said Imlac, 'with more and more frequency and was every time more enamoured of his conversation: he was sublime without haughtiness, courteous without formality, and communicative without ostentation. I was at first, Madam, of your opinion, thought him the happiest of mankind, and often congratulated him on the blessing that he enjoyed. He seemed to hear nothing with indifference but the praises of his condition, to which he always returned a general answer, and diverted the conversation to some other topic.

'Amidst this willingness to be pleased, and labour to please, I had always reason to imagine that some painful sentiment pressed upon his mind. He often looked up earnestly towards the sun, and let his voice fall in the midst of his discourse. He would sometimes, when we were alone, gaze upon me in silence with the air of a man who longed to speak what he was yet resolved to suppress. He would often send for me with vehement injunctions of haste, though, when I came to him, he had nothing extraordinary to say. And sometimes, when I was leaving him, would call me back, pause a few moments and then dismiss me'.

CHAPTER 41
THE ASTRONOMER DISCOVERS[40] THE CAUSE OF HIS UNEASINESS

'At last the time came when the secret burst his reserve. We were sitting together last night in the turret of his house, watching the emersion[41] of a satellite of Jupiter. A sudden tempest clouded the sky, and disappointed our observation. We sat a while silent in the dark, and then he addressed himself to me in these words: "Imlac, I have long considered thy friendship as the greatest blessing of my life. Integrity without knowledge is weak and useless, and knowledge without integrity is dangerous and dreadful. I have found in thee all the qualities requisite for trust, benevolence, experience, and fortitude. I have long discharged an office which I must soon quit at the call of nature, and shall rejoice in the hour of imbecility and pain to devolve it upon thee".

'I thought myself honoured by this testimony, and protested that whatever could conduce to his happiness would add likewise to mine.

'"Hear, Imlac, what thou wilt not without difficulty credit. I have possessed for five years the regulation of weather, and the distribution of the seasons: the sun has listened to my dictates, and passed from tropic to tropic by my direction; the clouds, at my call, have poured their waters, and the Nile has overflowed at my command; I have restrained the rage of the dog-star,[42] and mitigated the fervours of the crab.[43] The winds alone, of all the elemental powers, have hitherto refused my authority, and multitudes have perished by equinoctial tempests which I found myself unable to prohibit or restrain. I have administered this great office with exact justice, and made to the different nations of the earth an impartial dividend of rain and sunshine. What must have been the misery of half the globe, if I had limited the clouds to particular regions, or confined the sun to either side of the equator?"

CHAPTER 42
THE ASTRONOMER JUSTIFIES HIS ACCOUNT OF HIMSELF

'I suppose he discovered in me, through the obscurity of the room, some tokens of amazement and doubt, for, after a short pause, he proceeded thus:

'"Not to be easily credited will neither surprise nor offend me; for I am, probably, the first of human beings to whom this trust has been imparted. Nor do I know whether to deem this distinction as reward or punishment; since I have possessed it I have been far less happy than before, and nothing but the consciousness of good intention could have enabled me to support the weariness of unremitted vigilance".

'"How long, Sir", said I, "has this great office been in your hands?"

'"About ten years ago", said he, "my daily observations of the changes of the sky led me to consider, whether, if I had the power of the seasons, I could confer greater plenty upon the

---

[40] *discovers* reveals.
[41] *emersion* "The time when a star, having been obscured by its too near approach to the sun, appears again" (Johnson).

[42] *dog-star* Sirius, which rises with the Sun in late summer and is blamed for scorching heat and famine.
[43] *crab* a constellation in the zodiac also known as cancer, in which the Sun is at its strongest.

inhabitants of the earth. This contemplation fastened on my mind, and I sat days and nights in imaginary dominion, pouring upon this country and that the showers of fertility, and seconding every fall of rain with a due proportion of sunshine. I had yet only the will to do good, and did not imagine that I should ever have the power.

'"One day as I was looking on the fields withering with heat, I felt in my mind a sudden wish that I could send rain on the southern mountains, and raise the Nile to an inundation. In the hurry of my imagination I commanded rain to fall, and, by comparing the time of my command, with that of the inundation, I found that the clouds had listened to my lips".

'"Might not some other cause", said I, "produce this concurrence? the Nile does not always rise on the same day".

'"Do not believe", said he with impatience, "that such objections could escape me: I reasoned long against my own conviction, and laboured against truth with the utmost obstinacy. I sometimes suspected myself of madness, and should not have dared to impart this secret but to a man like you, capable of distinguishing the wonderful from the impossible, and the incredible from the false".

'"Why, Sir", said I, "do you call that incredible, which you know, or think you know, to be true?"

'"Because", said he, "I cannot prove it by any external evidence; and I know too well the laws of demonstration to think that my conviction ought to influence another, who cannot, like me, be conscious of its force. I, therefore, shall not attempt to gain credit by disputation. It is sufficient that I feel this power, that I have long possessed, and every day exerted it. But the life of man is short, the infirmities of age increase upon me, and the time will soon come when the regulator of the year must mingle with the dust. The care of appointing a successor has long disturbed me; the night and the day have been spent in comparisons of all the characters which have come to my knowledge, and I have yet found none so worthy as thyself"'.

CHAPTER 43
THE ASTRONOMER LEAVES IMLAC HIS DIRECTIONS

'"Hear therefore, what I shall impart, with attention, such as the welfare of a world requires. If the task of a king be considered as difficult, who has the care only of a few millions, to whom he cannot do much good or harm, what must be the anxiety of him, on whom depend the action of the elements, and the great gifts of light and heat! – Hear me therefore with attention.

'"I have diligently considered the position of the earth and sun, and formed innumerable schemes in which I changed their situation. I have sometimes turned aside the axis of the earth, and sometimes varied the ecliptic of the sun: but I have found it impossible to make a disposition by which the world may be advantaged; what one region gains, another loses by any imaginable alteration, even without considering the distant parts of the solar system with which we are unacquainted. Do not, therefore, in thy administration of the year, indulge thy pride by innovation; do not please thyself with thinking that thou canst make thyself renowned to all future ages, by disordering the seasons. The memory of mischief is no desirable fame. Much less will it become thee to let kindness or interest prevail. Never rob other countries of rain to pour it on thine own. For us the Nile is sufficient".

'I promised that when I possessed the power, I would use it with inflexible integrity, and he dismissed me, pressing my hand. "My heart", said he, "will be now at rest, and my benevolence will no more destroy my quiet: I have found a man of wisdom and virtue, to whom I can cheerfully bequeath the inheritance of the sun"'.

The prince heard this narration with very serious regard, but the princess smiled, and Pekuah convulsed herself with laughter. 'Ladies', said Imlac, 'to mock the heaviest of human afflictions is neither charitable nor wise. Few can attain this man's knowledge, and few practise his virtues; but all may suffer his calamity. Of the uncertainties of our present state, the most dreadful and alarming is the uncertain continuance of reason'.

The princess was recollected, and the favourite was abashed. Rasselas, more deeply affected, enquired of Imlac, whether he thought such maladies of the mind frequent, and how they were contracted.

CHAPTER 44
THE DANGEROUS PREVALENCE OF IMAGINATION

'Disorders of intellect', answered Imlac, 'happen much more often than superficial observers will easily believe. Perhaps, if we speak with rigorous exactness, no human mind is in its right state. There is no man whose imagination does not sometimes predominate over his reason, who can regulate his attention wholly by his will, and whose ideas will come and go at his command. No man will be found in whose mind airy notions do not sometimes tyrannise, and force him to hope or fear beyond the limits of sober probability. All power of fancy over reason is a degree of insanity; but while this power is such as we can control and repress, it is not visible to others, nor considered as any depravation of the mental faculties: it is not pronounced madness but when it comes ungovernable, and apparently influences speech or action.

'To indulge the power of fiction, and send imagination out upon the wing, is often the sport of those who delight too much in silent speculation. When we are alone we are not always busy; the labour of excogitation is too violent to last long; the ardour of enquiry will sometimes give way to idleness or satiety. He who has nothing external that can divert him, must find pleasure in his own thoughts, and must conceive himself what he is not; for who is pleased with what he is? He then expatiates in boundless futurity, and culls from all imaginable conditions that which for the present moment he should most desire, amuses his desires with impossible enjoyments, and confers upon his pride unattainable dominion. The mind dances from scene to scene, unites all pleasures in all combinations, and riots in delights which nature and fortune, with all their bounty, cannot bestow.

'In time some particular train of ideas fixes the attention, all other intellectual gratifications are rejected, the mind, in weariness or leisure, recurs constantly to the favourite conception, and feasts on the luscious falsehood whenever she is offended with the bitterness of truth. By degrees the reign of fancy is confirmed; she grows first imperious, and in time despotic. Then fictions begin to operate as realities, false opinions fasten upon the mind, and life passes in dreams of rapture or of anguish.

'This, Sir, is one of the dangers of solitude, which the hermit has confessed not always to promote goodness, and the astronomer's misery has proved to be not always propitious to wisdom'.

'I will no more', said the favourite, 'imagine myself the queen of Abyssinia. I have often spent the hours, which the princess gave to my own disposal, in adjusting ceremonies and regulating the court; I have repressed the pride of the powerful, and granted the petitions of the poor; I have built new palaces in more happy situations, planted groves upon the tops of mountains, and have exulted in the beneficence of royalty, till, when the princess entered, I had almost forgotten to bow down before her'.

'And I', said the princess, 'will not allow myself any more to play the shepherdess in my waking dreams. I have often soothed my thoughts with the quiet and innocence of pastoral employments, till I have in my chamber heard the winds whistle, and the sheep bleat; sometimes freed the lamb entangled in the thicket, and sometimes with my crook encountered the wolf. I have a dress like that of the village maids, which I put on to help my imagination, and a pipe on which I play softly, and suppose myself followed by my flocks'.

'I will confess', said the prince, 'an indulgence of fantastic delight more dangerous than yours. I have frequently endeavoured to image the possibility of a perfect government, by which all wrong should be restrained, all vice reformed, and all the subjects preserved in tranquillity and innocence. This thought produced innumerable schemes of reformation, and dictated many useful regulations and salutary edicts. This has been the sport and sometimes the labour of my solitude; and I start, when I think with how little anguish I once supposed the death of my father and my brothers'.

'Such', says Imlac, 'are the effects of visionary schemes: when we first form them we know them to be absurd, but familiarise them by degrees, and in time lose sight of their folly'.

CHAPTER 45
THEY DISCOURSE WITH AN OLD MAN

The evening was now far past, and they rose to return home. As they walked along the bank of the Nile, delighted with the beams of the moon quivering on the water, they saw at a small distance an old man, whom the prince had often heard in the assembly of the sages. 'Yonder', said he, 'is one whose years have calmed his passions, but not clouded his reason: let us close the disquisitions of the night, by enquiring what are his sentiments of his own state, that we may know whether youth alone is to struggle with vexation, and whether any better hope remains for the latter part of life'.

Here the sage approached and saluted them. They invited him to join their walk, and prattled a while as acquaintance that had unexpectedly met one another. The old man was cheerful and talkative, and the way seemed short in his company. He was pleased to find himself not disregarded, accompanied them to their house, and, at the prince's request, entered with them. They placed him in the seat of honour, and set wine and conserves[44] before him.

'Sir', said the princess, 'an evening walk must give to a man of learning, like you, pleasures which ignorance and youth can hardly conceive. You know the qualities and the causes of all that you behold, the laws by which the river flows, the periods in which the planets perform their revolutions. Every thing must supply you with contemplation, and renew the consciousness of your own dignity'.

'Lady', answered he, 'let the gay and the vigorous expect pleasure in their excursions; it is enough that age can obtain ease. To me the world has lost its novelty: I look round, and see what I remember to have seen in happier days. I rest against a tree, and consider, that in the same shade I once disputed upon the annual overflow of the Nile[45] with a friend who is now

---

[44]   *conserve* "A sweetmeat made of the inspissated juices of fruit, boiled with sugar till they will harden and candy" (Johnson).

[45]   *the annual overflow of the Nile*   like the source of the Nile, an age-old subject of debate, which was still not fully understood in Johnson's time.

silent in the grave. I cast my eyes upwards, fix them on the changing moon, and think with pain on the vicissitudes of life. I have ceased to take much delight in physical truth; for what have I to do with those things which I am soon to leave?'

'You may at least recreate yourself', said Imlac, 'with the recollection of an honourable and useful life, and enjoy the praise which all agree to give you'.

'Praise', said the sage, with a sigh, 'is to an old man an empty sound. I have neither mother to be delighted with the reputation of her son, nor wife to partake the honours of her husband. I have outlived my friends and my rivals. Nothing is now of much importance; for I cannot extend my interest beyond myself. Youth is delighted with applause, because it is considered as the earnest of some future good, and because the prospect of life is far extended: but to me, who am now declining to decrepitude, there is little to be feared from the malevolence of men, and yet less to be hoped from their affection or esteem. Something they may yet take away, but they can give me nothing. Riches would now be useless, and high employment would be pain. My retrospect of life recalls to my view many opportunities of good neglected, much time squandered upon trifles, and more lost in idleness and vacancy. I leave many great designs unattempted, and many great attempts unfinished. My mind is burthened with no heavy crime, and therefore I compose myself to tranquillity; endeavour to abstract my thoughts from hopes and cares, which, though reason knows them to be vain, still try to keep their old possession of the heart; expect, with serene humility, that hour which nature cannot long delay; and hope to possess in a better state that happiness which here I could not find, and that virtue which here I have not attained'.

He rose and went away, leaving his audience not much elated with the hope of long life. The prince consoled himself with remarking, that it was not reasonable to be disappointed by this account; for age had never been considered as the season of felicity, and, if it was possible to be easy in decline and weakness, it was likely that the days of vigour and alacrity might be happy: that the moon of life might be bright, if the evening could be calm.

The princess suspected that age was querulous and malignant, and delighted to repress the expectations of those who had newly entered the world. She had seen the possessors of estates look with envy on their heirs, and known many who enjoy pleasure no longer than they can confine it to themselves.

Pekuah conjectured, that the man was older than he appeared, and was willing to impute his complaints to delirious dejection; or else supposed that he had been unfortunate, and was therefore discontented: 'For nothing', said she, 'is more common than to call our own condition, the condition of life'.

Imlac, who had no desire to see them depressed, smiled at the comforts which they could so readily procure to themselves, and remembered, that at the same age, he was equally confident of unmingled prosperity, and equally fertile of consolatory expedients. He forbore to force upon them unwelcome knowledge, which time itself would too soon impress. The princess and her lady retired; the madness of the astronomer hung upon their minds, and they desired Imlac to enter upon his office, and delay next morning the rising of the sun.

CHAPTER 46
THE PRINCESS AND PEKUAH VISIT THE ASTRONOMER

The princess and Pekuah having talked in private of Imlac's astronomer, thought his character at once so amiable and so strange, that they could not be satisfied without a nearer knowledge, and Imlac was requested to find the means of bringing them together.

This was somewhat difficult; the philosopher had never received any visits from women, though he lived in a city that had in it many Europeans who followed the manners of their own countries, and many from other parts of the world that lived there with European liberty. The ladies would not be refused, and several schemes were proposed for the accomplishment of their design. It was proposed to introduce them as strangers in distress, to whom the sage was always accessible; but, after some deliberation, it appeared, that by this artifice, no acquaintance could be formed, for their conversation would be short, and they could not decently importune him often. 'This', said Rasselas, 'is true; but I have yet a stronger objection against the misrepresentation of your state. I have always considered it as treason against the great republic of human nature, to make any man's virtues the means of deceiving him, whether on great or little occasions. All imposture weakens confidence and chills benevolence. When the sage finds that you are not what you seemed, he will feel the resentment natural to a man who, conscious of great abilities, discovers that he has been tricked by understandings meaner than his own, and, perhaps, the distrust, which he can never afterwards wholly lay aside, may stop the voice of counsel, and close the hand of charity; and where will you find the power of restoring his benefactions to mankind, or his peace to himself?'

To this no reply was attempted, and Imlac began to hope that their curiosity would subside; but, next day, Pekuah told him, she had now found an honest pretence for a visit to the astronomer, for she would solicit permission to continue under him the studies in which she had been initiated by the Arab, and the princess might go with her either as a fellow-student, or because a woman could not decently come alone. 'I am afraid', said Imlac, 'that he will be soon weary of your company: men advanced far in knowledge do not love to repeat the elements of their art, and I am not certain that even of the elements, as he will deliver them connected with inferences, and mingled with reflections, you are a very capable auditress'. 'That', said Pekuah, 'must be my care: I ask of you only to take me thither. My knowledge is, perhaps, more than you imagine it, and by concurring always with his opinions I shall make him think it greater than it is'.

The astronomer, in pursuance of this resolution, was told, that a foreign lady, travelling in search of knowledge, had heard of his reputation, and was desirous to become his scholar.[46] The uncommonness of the proposal raised at once his surprise and curiosity, and when, after a short deliberation, he consented to admit her, he could not stay without impatience till the next day.

The ladies dressed themselves magnificently, and were attended by Imlac to the astronomer, who was pleased to see himself approached with respect by persons of so splendid an appearance. In the exchange of the first civilities he was timorous and bashful; but when the talk became regular, he recollected his powers, and justified the character which Imlac had given. Enquiring of Pekuah what could have turned her inclination towards astronomy, he received from her a history of her adventure at the pyramid, and of the time passed in the Arab's island. She told her tale with ease and elegance, and her conversation took possession of his heart. The discourse was then turned to astronomy: Pekuah displayed what she knew: he looked upon her as a prodigy of genius, and entreated her not to desist from a study which she had so happily begun.

They came again and again, and were every time more welcome than before. The sage endeavoured to amuse them, that they might prolong their visits, for he found his thoughts grow brighter in their company; the clouds of solicitude vanished by degrees, as he forced

---

[46] *scholar* student.

himself to entertain them, and he grieved when he was left at their departure to his old employment of regulating the seasons.

The princess and her favourite had now watched his lips for several months, and could not catch a single word from which they could judge whether he continued, or not, in the opinion of his preternatural commission. They often contrived to bring him to an open declaration, but he easily eluded all their attacks, and on which side soever they pressed him escaped from them to some other topic.

As their familiarity increased they invited him often to the house of Imlac, where they distinguished him by extraordinary respect. He began gradually to delight in sublunary pleasures. He came early and departed late; laboured to recommend himself by assiduity and compliance; excited their curiosity after new arts, that they might still want his assistance; and when they made any excursion of pleasure or enquiry, entreated to attend them.

By long experience of his integrity and wisdom, the prince and his sister were convinced that he might be trusted without danger; and lest he should draw any false hopes from the civilities which he received, discovered to him their condition with the motives of their journey, and required his opinion on the choice of life.

'Of the various conditions which the world spreads before you, which you shall prefer', said the sage, 'I am not able to instruct you. I can only tell that I have chosen wrong. I have passed my time in study without experience; in the attainment of sciences which can, for the most part, be but remotely useful to mankind. I have purchased knowledge at the expense of all the common comforts of life: I have missed the endearing elegance of female friendship, and the happy commerce of domestic tenderness. If I have obtained any prerogatives above other students, they have been accompanied with fear, disquiet, and scrupulosity; but even of these prerogatives, whatever they were, I have, since my thoughts have been diversified by more intercourse with the world, begun to question the reality. When I have been for a few days lost in pleasing dissipation, I am always tempted to think that my enquiries have ended in error, and that I have suffered much, and suffered it in vain'.

Imlac was delighted to find that the sage's understanding was breaking through its mists, and resolved to detain him from the planets till he should forget his task of ruling them, and reason should recover its original influence.

From this time the astronomer was received into familiar friendship, and partook of all their projects and pleasures: his respect kept him attentive, and the activity of Rasselas did not leave much time unengaged. Something was always to be done; the day was spent in making observations which furnished talk for the evening, and the evening was closed with a scheme for the morrow.

The sage confessed to Imlac, that since he had mingled in the gay tumults of life, and divided his hours by a succession of amusements, he found the conviction of his authority over the skies fade gradually from his mind, and began to trust less to an opinion which he never could prove to others, and which he now found subject to variation from causes in which reason had no part. 'If I am accidentally left alone for a few hours', said he, 'my inveterate persuasion rushes upon my soul, and my thoughts are chained down by some irresistible violence, but they are soon disentangled by the prince's conversation, and instantaneously released at the entrance of Pekuah. I am like a man habitually afraid of spectres, who is set at ease by a lamp, and wonders at the dread which harassed him in the dark, yet, if his lamp be extinguished, feels again the terrors which he knows that when it is light he shall feel no more. But I am sometimes afraid lest I indulge my quiet by criminal negligence, and voluntarily forget the great charge with which I am entrusted. If I favour myself in a known error, or am determined by my own ease in a doubtful question of this importance, how dreadful is my crime!'

'No disease of the imagination', answered Imlac, 'is so difficult of cure, as that which is complicated with the dread of guilt: fancy and conscience then act interchangeably upon us, and so often shift their places, that the illusions of one are not distinguished from the dictates of the other. If fancy presents images not moral or religious, the mind drives them away when they give it pain, but when melancholic notions take the form of duty, they lay hold on the faculties without opposition, because we are afraid to exclude or banish them. For this reason the superstitious are often melancholy, and the melancholy almost always superstitious.

'But do not let the suggestions of timidity overpower your better reason: the danger of neglect can be but as the probability of the obligation, which when you consider it with freedom, you find very little, and that little growing every day less. Open your heart to the influence of the light which, from time to time, breaks in upon you: when scruples importune you, which you in your lucid moments know to be vain, do not stand to parley, but fly to business or to Pekuah, and keep this thought always prevalent, that you are only one atom of the mass of humanity, and have neither such virtue nor vice, as that you should be singled out for supernatural favours or afflictions'.

CHAPTER 47
THE PRINCE ENTERS AND BRINGS A NEW TOPIC

'All this', said the astronomer, 'I have often thought, but my reason has been so long subjugated by an uncontrollable and overwhelming idea, that it durst not confide in its own decisions. I now see how fatally I betrayed my quiet, by suffering chimeras to prey upon me in secret; but melancholy shrinks from communication, and I never found a man before, to whom I could impart my troubles, though I had been certain of relief. I rejoice to find my own sentiments confirmed by yours, who are not easily deceived, and can have no motive or purpose to deceive. I hope that time and variety will dissipate the gloom that has so long surrounded me, and the latter part of my days will be spent in peace'.

'Your learning and virtue', said Imlac, 'may justly give you hopes'.

Rasselas then entered with the princess and Pekuah, and enquired whether they had contrived any new diversion for the next day. 'Such', said Nekayah, 'is the state of life, that none are happy but by the anticipation of change: the change itself is nothing; when we have made it, the next wish is to change again. The world is not yet exhausted; let me see something tomorrow which I never saw before'.

'Variety', said Rasselas, 'is so necessary to content, that even the happy valley disgusted me by the recurrence of its luxuries; yet I could not forbear to reproach myself with impatience, when I saw the monks of St. Anthony support without complaint, a life, not of uniform delight, but uniform hardship'.

'Those men', answered Imlac, 'are less wretched in their silent convent than the Abyssinian princes in their prison of pleasure. Whatever is done by the monks is incited by an adequate and reasonable motive. Their labour supplies them with necessaries; it therefore cannot be omitted, and is certainly rewarded. Their devotion prepares them for another state, and reminds them of its approach, while it fits them for it. Their time is regularly distributed; one duty succeeds another, so that they are not left open to the distraction of unguided choice, nor lost in the shades of listless inactivity. There is a certain task to be performed at an appropriated hour; and their toils are cheerful, because they consider them as acts of piety, by which they are always advancing towards endless felicity'.

'Do you think', said Nekayah, 'that the monastic rule is a more holy and less imperfect state than any other? May not he equally hope for future happiness who converses openly with mankind, who succours the distressed by his charity, instructs the ignorant by his learning, and contributes by his industry to the general system of life; even though he should omit some of the mortifications which are practised in the cloister, and allow himself such harmless delights as his condition may place within his reach?'

'This', said Imlac, 'is a question which has long divided the wise, and perplexed the good. I am afraid to decide on either part. He that lives well in the world is better than he that lives well in a monastery. But, perhaps, every one is not able to stem the temptations of public life; and, if he cannot conquer, he may properly retreat. Some have little power to do good, and have likewise little strength to resist evil. Many are weary of their conflicts with adversity, and are willing to eject those passions which have long busied them in vain. And many are dismissed by age and diseases from the more laborious duties of society. In monasteries the weak and timorous may be happily sheltered, the weary may repose, and the penitent may meditate. Those retreats of prayer and contemplation have something so congenial to the mind of man that, perhaps, there is scarcely one that does not purpose to close his life in pious abstraction with a few associates serious as himself'.

'Such', said Pekuah, 'has often been my wish, and I have heard the princess declare, that she should not willingly die in a crowd'.

'The liberty of using harmless pleasures', proceeded Imlac, 'will not be disputed; but it is still to be examined what pleasures are harmless. The evil of any pleasure that Nekayah can image is not in the act itself, but in its consequences. Pleasure, in itself harmless, may become mischievous, by endearing to us a state which we know to be transient and probatory, and withdrawing our thoughts from that, of which every hour brings us nearer to the beginning, and of which no length of time will bring us to the end. Mortification is not virtuous in itself, nor has any other use, but that it disengages us from the allurements of sense. In the state of future perfection, to which we all aspire, there will be pleasure without danger, and security without restraint'.

The princess was silent, and Rasselas, turning to the astronomer, asked him, whether he could not delay her retreat, by showing her something which she had not seen before.

'Your curiosity', said the sage, 'has been so general, and your pursuit of knowledge so vigorous, that novelties are not now very easily to be found: but what you can no longer procure from the living may be given by the dead. Among the wonders of this country are the catacombs, or the ancient repositories, in which the bodies of the earliest generations were lodged, and where, by the virtue of the gums which embalmed them, they yet remain without corruption'.

'I know not', said Rasselas, 'what pleasure the sight of the catacombs can afford; but, since nothing else is offered, I am resolved to view them, and shall place this with many other things which I have done, because I would do something'.

They hired a guard of horsemen, and the next day visited the catacombs. When they were about to descend into the sepulchral caves, 'Pekuah', said the princess, 'we are now again invading the habitations of the dead; I know that you will stay behind; let me find you safe when I return'. 'No, I will not be left', answered Pekuah; 'I will go down between you and the prince'.

They then all descended, and roved with wonder through the labyrinth of subterraneous passages, where the bodies were laid in rows on either side.

CHAPTER 48
IMLAC DISCOURSES ON THE NATURE OF THE SOUL

'What reason', said the prince, 'can be given, why the Egyptians should thus expensively preserve those carcasses which some nations consume with fire, others lay to mingle with the earth, and all agree to remove from their sight, as soon as decent rites can be performed?'

'The original of ancient customs', said Imlac, 'is commonly unknown; for the practice often continues when the cause has ceased; and concerning superstitious ceremonies it is vain to conjecture; for what reason did not dictate reason cannot explain. I have long believed that the practice of embalming arose only from tenderness to the remains of relations or friends, and to this opinion I am more inclined, because it seems impossible that this care should have been general: had all the dead been embalmed, their repositories must in time have been more spacious than the dwellings of the living. I suppose only the rich or honourable were secured from corruption, and the rest left to the course of nature.

'But it is commonly supposed that the Egyptians believed the soul to live as long as the body continued undissolved and therefore tried this method of eluding death'.

'Could the wise Egyptians', said Nekayah, 'think so grossly of the soul? If the soul could once survive its separation, what could it afterwards receive or suffer from the body?'

'The Egyptians would doubtless think erroneously', said the astronomer, 'in the darkness of heathenism,[47] and the first dawn of philosophy.[48] The nature of the soul is still disputed amidst all our opportunities of clearer knowledge: some yet say that it may be material, who, nevertheless, believe it to be immortal'.

'Some', answered Imlac, 'have indeed said that the soul is material, but I can scarcely believe that any man has thought it, who knew how to think; for all the conclusions of reason enforce the immateriality of mind, and all the notices of sense and investigations of science concur to prove the unconsciousness of matter.

'It was never supposed that cogitation is inherent in matter, or that every particle is a thinking being. Yet, if any part of matter be devoid of thought, what part can we suppose to think? Matter can differ from matter only in form, density, bulk, motion, and direction of motion: to which of these, however varied or combined, can consciousness be annexed? To be round or square, to be solid or fluid, to be great or little, to be moved slowly or swiftly one way or another, are modes of material existence, all equally alien from the nature of cogitation. If matter be once without thought, it can only be made to think by some new modification, but all the modifications which it can admit are equally unconnected with cogitative powers'.

'But the materialists', said the astronomer, 'urge that matter may have qualities with which we are unacquainted'.

'He who will determine', returned Imlac, 'against that which he knows, because there may be something which he knows not; he that can set hypothetical possibility against acknowledged certainty, is not to be admitted among reasonable beings. All that we know of matter

---

[47] *heathenism*   the religion of those who did not know of or acknowledge the Judeo-Christian God.

[48] *philosophy*   particularly Socratic thought, which was regarded as proto-Judeo-Christian.

is, that matter is inert, senseless and lifeless; and if this conviction cannot be opposed but by referring us to something that we know not, we have all the evidence that human intellect can admit. If that which is known may be over-ruled by that which is unknown, no being, not omniscient, can arrive at certainty'.

'Yet let us not', said the astronomer, 'too arrogantly limit the Creator's power'.

'It is no limitation of omnipotence', replied the poet, 'to suppose that one thing is not consistent with another, that the same proposition cannot be at once true and false, that the same number cannot be even and odd, that cogitation cannot be conferred on that which is created incapable of cogitation'.

'I know not', said Nekayah, 'any great use of this question. Does that immateriality, which, in my opinion, you have sufficiently proved, necessarily include eternal duration?'

'Of immateriality', said Imlac, 'our ideas are negative, and therefore obscure. Immaterial-ity seems to imply a natural power of perpetual duration as a consequence of exemption from all causes of decay: whatever perishes, is destroyed by the solution of its contexture, and separation of its parts; nor can we conceive how that which has no parts, and therefore admits no solution,[49] can be naturally corrupted or impaired'.

'I know not', said Rasselas, 'how to conceive any thing without extension: what is extended must have parts, and you allow, that whatever has parts may be destroyed'.

'Consider your own conceptions', replied Imlac, 'and the difficulty will be less. You will find substance without extension. An ideal form is no less real than material bulk: yet an ideal form has no extension. It is no less certain, when you think on a pyramid, that your mind possesses the idea of a pyramid, than that the pyramid itself is standing. What space does the idea of a pyramid occupy more than the idea of a grain of corn? or how can either idea suffer laceration? As is the effect such is the cause; as thought is, such is the power that thinks; a power impassive and indiscerptible'.[50]

'But the Being', said Nekayah, 'whom I fear to name, the Being which made the soul, can destroy it'.

'He, surely, can destroy it', answered Imlac, 'since, however unperishable, it receives from a superior nature its power of duration. That it will not perish by any inherent cause of decay, or principle of corruption, may be shown by philosophy; but philosophy can tell no more. That it will not be annihilated by him that made it, we must humbly learn from higher authority'.

The whole assembly stood a while silent and collected.[51] 'Let us return', said Rasselas, 'from this scene of mortality. How gloomy would be these mansions of the dead to him who did not know that he shall never die; that what now acts shall continue its agency, and what now thinks shall think on for ever. Those that lie here stretched before us, the wise and the powerful of ancient times, warn us to remember the shortness of our present state; they were, perhaps, snatched away while they were busy, like us, in the choice of life'.

'To me', said the princess, 'the choice of life is become less important; I hope hereafter to think only on the choice of eternity'.

They then hastened out of the caverns, and, under the protection of their guard, returned to Cairo.

---

[49] *solution* dissolution.
[50] *indiscerptible* "not to be broken or destroyed by dis-solution of parts" (Johnson).

[51] *collected* gained command over their thoughts (see Johnson, sense 5).

CHAPTER 49
THE CONCLUSION, IN WHICH NOTHING IS CONCLUDED

It was now the time of the inundation of the Nile: a few days after their visit to the catacombs, the river began to rise.

They were confined to their house. The whole region being underwater gave them no invitation to any excursions, and, being well supplied with materials for talk, they diverted themselves with comparisons of the different forms of life which they had observed, and with various schemes of happiness which each of them had formed.

Pekuah was never so much charmed with any place as the convent of St. Anthony, where the Arab restored her to the princess, and wished only to fill it with pious maidens, and to be made prioress of the order: she was weary of expectation and disgust, and would gladly be fixed in some unvariable state.

The princess thought, that of all sublunary things, knowledge was the best: She desired first to learn all sciences,[52] and then purposed to found a college of learned women, in which she would preside, that, by conversing with the old, and educating the young, she might divide her time between the acquisition and communication of wisdom, and raise up for the next age models of prudence, and patterns of piety.

The prince desired a little kingdom, in which he might administer justice in his own person, and see all the parts of government with his own eyes; but he could never fix the limits of his dominion, and was always adding to the number of his subjects.

Imlac and the astronomer were contented to be driven along the stream of life without directing their course to any particular port.

Of these wishes that they had formed they well knew that none could be obtained. They deliberated a while what was to be done, and resolved, when the inundation should cease, to return to Abyssinia.

FINIS

from the Preface to *The Plays of William Shakespeare* (1765)

That praises are without reason lavished on the dead, and that the honours due only to excellence are paid to antiquity is a complaint likely to be always continued by those, who, being able to add nothing to truth, hope for eminence from the heresies of paradox; or those, who, being forced by disappointment upon consolatory expedients, are willing to hope from posterity what the present age refuses, and flatter themselves that the regard which is yet denied by envy, will be at last bestowed by time.

Antiquity, like every other quality that attracts the notice of mankind, has undoubtedly votaries that reverence it, not from reason, but from prejudice. Some seem to admire indiscriminately whatever has been long preserved, without considering that time has sometimes co-operated with chance; and perhaps are more willing to honour past than present excellence; and the mind contemplates genius through the shades of age, as the eye surveys the sun through artificial opacity. The great contention of criticism is to find the faults of the moderns, and the beauties of the ancients. While an author is yet living

---

[52]   *sciences*   all fields of knowledge.

we estimate his powers by his worst performance, and when he is dead we rate them by his best.

To works, however, of which the excellence is not absolute and definite, but gradual and comparative; to works not raised upon principles demonstrative and scientific, but appealing wholly to observation and experience, no other test can be applied than length of duration and continuance of esteem. What mankind have long possessed they have often examined and compared, and if they persist to value the possession, it is because frequent comparisons have confirmed opinion in its favour. As among the works of nature no man can properly call a river deep or mountain high, without the knowledge of many mountains and many rivers; so in the productions of genius, nothing can be styled excellent till it has been compared with other works of the same kind. Demonstration immediately displays its power, and has nothing to hope or fear from the flux of years; but works tentative and experimental must be estimated by their proportion to the general and collective ability of man, as it is discovered in a long succession of endeavours. Of the first building that was raised, it might be with certainty determined that it was round or square, but whether it was spacious or lofty must have been referred to time. The Pythagorean scale of numbers[1] was at once discovered to be perfect; but the poems of Homer we yet know not to transcend the common limits of human intelligence, but by remarking, that nation after nation, and century after century, has been able to do little more than transpose his incidents, new name his characters, and paraphrase his sentiments.

The reverence due to writings that have long subsisted arises therefore not from any credulous confidence in the superior wisdom of past ages, or gloomy persuasion of the degeneracy of mankind, but is the consequence of acknowledged and indubitable positions, that what has been longest known has been most considered, and what is most considered is best understood.

The poet, of whose works I have undertaken the revision, may now begin to assume the dignity of an ancient, and claim the privilege of established fame and prescriptive veneration.[2] He has long outlived his century, the term commonly fixed as the test of literary merit. Whatever advantages he might once derive from personal allusions, local customs, or temporary opinions, have for many years been lost; and every topic of merriment or motive of sorrow, which the modes of artificial life afforded him, now only obscure the scenes which they once illuminated. The effects of favour and competition are at an end; the tradition of his friendships and his enmities has perished; his works support no opinion with arguments, nor supply any faction with invectives; they can neither indulge vanity nor gratify malignity, but are read without any other reason than the desire for pleasure, and are therefore praised only as pleasure is obtained; yet, thus unassisted by interest or passion, they have passed through variations of taste and changes of manners, and, as they developed from one generation to another, have received new honours at every transmission.

But because human judgement, though it be gradually gaining upon certainty, never becomes infallible; and approbation, though long continued, may yet be only the approbation of prejudice and fashion; it is proper to enquire, by what peculiarities of excellence Shakespeare has gained and kept the favour of his countrymen.

FROM THE PREFACE
[1] *Pythagorean scale of numbers*   the system of ratios in math and music established by the sixth-century BCE philosopher.

[2] *century . . . merit*   "We cannot say that this or that is a custom, except we can justify that it hath continued so one hundred years" (Johnson citing John Cowell under *custom*, sense 6).

Nothing can please many, and please long, but just representations of general nature. Particular manners can be known to few, and therefore few only can judge how nearly they are copied. The irregular combinations of fanciful invention may delight a-while, by that novelty of which the common satiety of life sends us all in quest; but the pleasures of sudden wonder are soon exhausted, and the mind can only repose on the stability of truth.

Shakespeare is above all writers, at least above all modern writers, the poet of nature; the poet that holds up to his readers a faithful mirror of manners and of life. His characters are not modified by the customs of particular places, unpractised by the rest of the world; by the peculiarities of studies or professions, which can operate but upon small numbers; or by the accidents of transient fashions or temporary opinions: they are the genuine progeny of common humanity, such as the world will always supply, and observation will always find. His persons act and speak by the influence of those general persons and principles by which all minds are agitated, and the whole system of life is continued in motion. In the writings of other poets a character is too often an individual; in those of Shakespeare it is commonly a species.

It is from this wide extension of design that so much instruction is derived. It is this which fills the plays of Shakespeare with practical axioms and domestic wisdom. It was said of Euripides, that every verse was a precept; and it may be said of Shakespeare, that from his works may be collected a system of civil and economical[3] prudence. Yet his real power is not shown in the splendour of particular passages, but by the progress of his fable,[4] and the tenor of his dialogue; and that he that tries to recommend him by select quotations, will succeed like the pedant in Hierocles, who, when he offered his house to sale, carried a brick in his pocket as a specimen.[5]

It will not easily be imagined how much Shakespeare excels in accommodating his sentiments to real life, but by comparing him with other authors. It was observed of the ancient schools of declamation, that the more diligently they were frequented, the more was the student disqualified for the world, because he found nothing there which he should ever meet in any other place. The same remark may be applied to every stage but that of Shakespeare. The theatre, when it is under any other direction, is peopled by such characters as were never seen, conversing in a language which was never heard, upon topics which will never arise in the commerce of mankind. But the dialogue of this author is often so evidently determined by the incident which produces it, and is pursued with so much ease and simplicity, that it seems scarcely to claim the merit of fiction, but to have been gleaned by diligent selection out of common conversation, and common occurrences.

Upon every other stage the universal agent is love, by whose power all good and evil is distributed, and every action quickened or retarded. To bring a lover, a lady and a rival into the fable; to entangle them in contradictory obligations, perplex them with oppositions of interest, and harass them with violence of desires inconsistent with each other; to make them meet in rapture and part in agony; to fill their mouths with hyperbolical joy and outrageous sorrow; to distress them as nothing human ever was distressed; to deliver them as nothing human ever was delivered, is the business of a modern dramatist. For this, probability is violated, life is misrepresented, and language is depraved. But love is only one of many passions, and as it has no great influence upon the sum of life, it has little operation in the

---

3 *economical* "Pertaining to the regulation of household" (Johnson).
4 *fable* story or plot.

5 *the pedant in Hierocles ... specimen* in one of the Ἀστεῖα (urbanities or jests) attributed to this neoplatonic, fifth-century philosopher and included in a commentary on Pythagoras.

dramas of a poet, who caught his ideas from the living world, and exhibited only what he saw before him. He knew, that any other passion, as it was regular or exorbitant, was a cause of happiness or calamity.

Characters thus ample and general were not easily discriminated or preserved, yet perhaps no poet ever kept his personages more distinct from each other. I will not say with Pope, that every speech may be assigned to the proper speaker,[6] because many speeches there are which have nothing characteristical; but perhaps, though some may be equally adapted to every person, it will be difficult to find any that can be properly transferred from the present possessor to another claimant. The choice is right, when there is reason for choice.

Other dramatists can only gain attention by hyperbolical or aggravated characters, by fabulous and unexampled excellence or depravity, as the writers of barbarous romances invigorated the reader by a giant and a dwarf; and he that should form his expectations of human affairs from the play, or from the tale, would be equally deceived. Shakespeare has no heroes; his scenes are occupied only by men, who act and speak as the reader thinks that he should himself have spoken or acted on the same occasion: Even where the agency is supernatural the dialogue is level with life. Other writers disguise the most natural passions and most frequent incidents; so that he who contemplates them in the book will not know them in the world: Shakespeare approximates the remote, and familiarises the wonderful; the event which he represents will not happen, but if it were possible, its effects would probably be such as he assigned; and it may be said, that he has not only shown human nature as it acts in real exigences, but as it would be found in trials, to which it cannot be exposed.

This therefore is the praise of Shakespeare, that his drama is the mirror of life; that he who has mazed his imagination, in following the phantoms which other writers raise up before him, may here be cured of his delirious ecstasies, by reading human sentiments in human language; by scenes from which a hermit may estimate the transactions of the world, and a confessor[7] predict the progress of the passions.

His adherence to general nature has exposed him to the censure of critics, who form their judgements upon narrower principles. Dennis and Rhymer[8] think his Romans not sufficiently Roman; and Voltaire censures his kings as not completely royal.[9] Dennis is offended, that Menenius, a senator of Rome, should play the buffoon; and Voltaire perhaps thinks decency violated when the Danish usurper[10] is represented as a drunkard. But Shakespeare always makes nature predominate over accident; and if he preserves the essential character, is not very careful of distinctions superinduced and adventitious. His story requires Romans or kings, but he thinks only on men. He knew that Rome, like every other city, had men of all dispositions; and wanting a buffoon, he went into the senate-house for that which the senate-house would certainly have afforded him. He was inclined to show an usurper and a murderer not only odious but despicable; he therefore added drunkenness to his other qualities, knowing that kings love wine like other men, and that wine exerts its natural power upon kings. These are the petty cavils of petty minds; a poet overlooks the casual distinction of country and condition, as a painter, satisfied with the figure, neglects the drapery.

The censure which he has incurred by mixing comic and tragic scenes, as it extends to all his works, deserves more consideration. Let the fact be first stated, and then examined.

---

6 *Pope . . . proper speaker* he made this remark in the Preface to his edition of Shakespeare (1725).
7 *confessor* "He that hears confessions, and prescribes rules and measures of penitence" (Johnson).

8 *Dennis and Rhymer* John (1657–1734) and Thomas (1643–1713), leading critics of their day.
9 *Voltaire* see *Appel à toutes les nations de l'Europe* (1761).
10 *Danish usurper* Claudius in *Hamlet*.

Shakespeare's plays are not in the rigorous and critical sense either tragedies or comedies, but compositions of a distinct kind; exhibiting the real state of sublunary nature, which partakes of good and evil, joy and sorrow, mingled with endless variety of proportion and innumerable modes of communication; and expressing the course of the world, in which the loss of one is the gain of another; in which, at the same time, the reveller is hasting to his wine, and the mourner burying his friend; in which the malignity of one is sometimes defeated by the frolic of another; and many mischiefs and many benefits are done and hindered without design.

Out of this chaos of mingled purposes and casualities the ancient poets, according to the laws which custom had prescribed, selected some the crimes of men, and some their absurdities; some the momentous vicissitudes of life, and some the lighter occurrences; some the terrors of distress, and some the gaieties of prosperity. Thus rose the two modes of imitation, known by the names of tragedy and comedy, compositions intended to promote different ends by contrary means, and considered as so little allied, that I do not recollect among the Greeks or Romans a single writer who attempted both.

Shakespeare has united the powers of exciting laughter and sorrow not only in one mind but in one composition. Almost all his plays are divided between serious and ludicrous characters, and, in the successive evolutions of the design, sometimes produce seriousness and sorrow, and sometimes levity and laughter.

That this is a practice contrary to the rules of criticism will be readily allowed; but there is always an appeal open from criticism to nature. The end of writing is to instruct; the end of poetry is to instruct by pleasing. That the mingled drama may convey all the instruction of tragedy or comedy cannot be denied, because it includes both in its alterations of exhibition, and approaches nearer than either to the appearance of life, by showing how great machinations and slender designs may promote or obviate one another, and the high and the low co-operate in the general system by unavoidable concatenation.

It is objected, that by this change of scenes the passions are interrupted in their progression, and that the principal event, being not advanced by a due graduation of preparatory incidents, wants at last the power to move, which constitutes the perfection of dramatic poetry. This reasoning is so specious, that it is received as true even by those who in daily experience feel it to be false. The interchanges of mingled scenes seldom fail to produce the intended vicissitudes of passion. Fiction cannot move so much, but that the attention may be easily transferred; and though it must be allowed that pleasing melancholy be sometimes interrupted by unwelcome levity, yet let it be considered likewise, that melancholy is often not pleasing, and that the disturbance of one man may be the relief of another; that different auditors have different habitudes; and that, upon the whole, all pleasure consists in variety.

The players, who in their edition[11] divided our author's works into comedies, histories, and tragedies, seem not to have distinguished the three kinds, by any very exact or definite ideas.

An action which ended happily to the principal persons, however serious or distressful through its intermediate incidents, in their opinion constituted a comedy. This idea of a comedy continued long amongst us, and plays were written, which, by changing the catastrophe, were tragedies to-day and comedies to-morrow.

Tragedy was not in those times a poem of more general dignity or elevation than comedy; it required only a calamitous conclusion, with which the common criticism of that age was satisfied, whatever lighter pleasure it afforded in its progress.

---

[11]　*their edition*　the First Folio, edited by John Heming and Henry Condell (1623).

History was a series of actions, with no other than chronological succession, independent on each other, and without any tendency to introduce or regulate the conclusion. It is not always very nicely distinguished from tragedy. There is not much nearer approach to unity of action[12] in the tragedy of *Antony and Cleopatra*, than in the history of *Richard the Second*. But a history might be continued through many plays; as it had no plan, it had no limits.

Through all these denominations of the drama, Shakespeare's mode of composition is the same; an interchange of seriousness and merriment, by which the mind is softened at one time, and exhilarated at another. But whatever be his purpose, whether to gladden or depress, or to conduct the story, without vehemence or emotion, through tracts of easy and familiar dialogue, he never fails to attain his purpose; as he commands us, we laugh or mourn, or sit silent with quiet expectation, in tranquillity without indifference.

When Shakespeare's plan is understood, most of the criticisms of Rhymer and Voltaire vanish away. The play of *Hamlet* is opened, without impropriety, by two sentinels; Iago bellows at Brabantio's window,[13] without injury to the scheme of the play, though in terms which a modern audience would not easily endure; the character of Polonius is seasonable and useful; and the Grave-diggers themselves may be heard with applause.[14]

Shakespeare engaged in dramatic poetry with the world open before him; the rules of the ancients were yet known to few; the public judgement was uninformed; he had no example of such fame as might force him upon imitation, nor critics of such authority as might restrain his extravagance: He therefore indulged his natural disposition, and his disposition, as Rhymer has remarked, led him to comedy. In tragedy he often writes with great appearance of toil and study, what is written at last with little felicity; but in his comic scenes, he seems to produce without labour, what no labour can improve. In tragedy he is always struggling after some occasion to be comic, but in comedy he seems to repose, or to luxuriate, as in a mode of thinking congenial to his nature. In his tragic scenes there is always something wanting, but his comedy often surpasses expectation or desire. His comedy pleases by the thoughts and the language, and his tragedy for the greater part by incident and action. His tragedy seems to be skill, his comedy to be instinct.

The force of his comic scenes has suffered little diminution from the changes made by a century and a half, in manners or in words. As his personages act upon principles arising from genuine passion, very little modified by particular forms, their pleasures and vexations are communicable to all times and to all places; they are natural, and therefore durable; the adventitious peculiarities of personal habits, are only superficial dies, bright and pleasing for a little while, yet soon fading to a dim tinct, without any remains of former lustre; but the discriminations of true passion are the colours of nature; they pervade the whole mass, and can only perish with the body that exhibits them. The accidental compositions of heterogeneous modes are dissolved by the chance which combined them; but the uniform simplicity of primitive qualities neither admits increase, nor suffers decay. The sand heaped by one flood is scattered by another, but the rock always continues in its place. The stream of time, which is continually washing the dissoluble fabrics of other poets, passes without injury by the adamant of Shakespeare.

If there be, what I believe there is, in every nation, a style which never becomes obsolete, a certain mode of phraseology so consonant and congenial to the analogy and principles of its respective language as to remain settled and unaltered; this style is to be sought in the common intercourse of life, among those who speak only to be understood, without ambition of elegance. The polite are always catching modish innovations, and the learned depart from

---

[12] *unity of action* a neo-classical standard of dramatic criticism derived from Aristotle's *Poetics*.

[13] *Iago bellows at Brabantio's window* *Othello* 1.1.

[14] *Grave-diggers . . . applause* *Hamlet* 5.1.

established forms of speech, in hope of finding or making better; those who wish for distinction forsake the vulgar, when the vulgar is right; but there is a conversation above grossness and below refinement, where propriety resides, and where this poet seems to have gathered his comic dialogue. He is therefore more agreeable to the ears of the present age than any other author equally remote, and among his other excellencies deserves to be studied as one of the original masters of our language.

These observations are to be considered not as unexceptionably constant, but as containing general and predominant truth. Shakespeare's familiar dialogue is affirmed to be smooth and clear, yet not wholly without ruggedness or difficulty; as a country may be eminently fruitful, though it has spots unfit for cultivation: His characters are praised as natural, though their sentiments are sometimes forced, and their actions improbable; as the earth upon the whole is spherical, though its surface is varied with protuberances and cavities.

Shakespeare with his excellencies has likewise faults, and faults sufficient to obscure and overwhelm any other merit. I shall show them in the proportion in which they appear to me, without envious malignity or superstitious veneration. No question can be more innocently discussed than a dead poet's pretensions to renown; and little regard is due to that bigotry which sets candour[15] higher than truth.

His first defect is that to which may be imputed most of the evil in books or in men. He sacrifices virtue to convenience, and is so much more careful to please than to instruct, that he seems to write without any moral purpose. From his writings indeed a system of social duty may be selected, for he that thinks reasonably must think morally; but his precepts and axioms drop casually from him; he makes no just distribution of good or evil, nor is always careful to show in the virtuous a disapprobation of the wicked; he carries his persons indifferently through right and wrong, and at the close dismisses them without further care, and leaves their examples to operate by chance. This fault the barbarity of his age cannot extenuate; for it is always a writer's duty to make the world better, and justice is a virtue independant on time or place.

The plots are often so loosely formed, that a very slight consideration may improve them, and so carelessly pursued, that he seems not always fully to comprehend his own design. He omits opportunities of instructing or delighting which the train of his story seems to force upon him, and apparently rejects those exhibitions which would be more affecting, for the sake of those which are more easy.

It may be observed, that in many of his plays the latter part is evidently neglected. When he found himself near the end of his work, and in view of his reward, he shortened the labour, to snatch the profit. He therefore remits his efforts where he should most vigorously exert them, and his catastrophe is improbably produced or imperfectly represented.

He had no regard to distinction of time or place, but gives to one age or nation, without scruple, the customs, institutions, and opinions of another, at the expense not only of likelihood, but of possibility. These faults Pope has endeavoured, with more zeal than judgement, to transfer to his imagined interpolators.[16] We need not wonder to find Hector quoting Aristotle,[17] when we see the loves of Theseus and Hippolyta combined with the Gothic mythology of fairies.[18] Shakespeare, indeed, was not the only violator of chronology, for in the same age Sidney,[19] who wanted not the advantage of learning, has, in his *Arcadia*,

---

[15] *candour* mildness, gentleness.
[16] *interpolators* editors who may have added passages to the plays.

[17] *Hector quoting Aristotle* *Troilus and Cressida* 2.2.166–7.
[18] *mythology of fairies* in *A Midsummer Night's Dream*.
[19] *Sidney* Sir Philip (1554–86).

confounded the pastoral with the feudal times, the days of innocence, quiet and security, with those of turbulence, violence and adventure.

In his comic scenes he is seldom very successful, when he engages his characters in reciprocations of smartness and contests of sarcasm; their jests are commonly gross, and their pleasantry licentious; neither his gentlemen nor his ladies have much delicacy, nor are sufficiently distinguished from his clowns by any appearance of refined manners. Whether he represented the real conversation of his time is not easy to determine; the reign of Elizabeth is commonly supposed to have been a time of stateliness, formality and reserve, yet perhaps the relaxations of that severity were not very elegant. There must, however, have always been some modes of gaiety preferable to others, and a writer ought to choose best.

In tragedy his performance seems constantly to be worse, as his labour is more. The effusions of passion which exigence forces out are for the most part striking and energetic; but whenever he solicits his invention, or strains his faculties, the offspring of his throws is tumour, meanness, tediousness, and obscurity.

In narration he affects a disproportionate pomp of diction and a wearisome train of circumlocution, and tells the incident imperfectly in many words, which might have been more plainly delivered in few. Narration in dramatic poetry is naturally tedious, as it is unanimated and inactive, and obstructs the progress of the action; it should therefore always be rapid, and enlivened by frequent interruption. Shakespeare found it an encumbrance, and instead of lightening it by brevity, endeavoured to recommend it by dignity and splendour.

His declamations or set speeches are commonly cold and weak, for his power was the power of nature; when he endeavoured, like other tragic writers, to catch opportunities of amplification, and instead of enquiring what the occasion demanded, to show how much his stores of knowledge could supply, he seldom escapes without the pity or resentment of his reader.

It is incident to him to be now and then entangled with an unwieldy sentiment, which he cannot well express, and will not reject; he struggles with it a while, and if it continues stubborn, comprises it in words such as occur, and leaves it to be disentangled and evolved by those who have more leisure to bestow upon it.

Not that always where the language is intricate the thought is subtle, or the image always great where the line is bulky; the equality of words to things is very often neglected, and trivial sentiments and vulgar ideas disappoint the attention, to which they are recommended by sonorous epithets and swelling figures.[20]

But the admirers of this great poet have most reason to complain when he approaches nearest to his highest excellence, and seems fully resolved to sink them in dejection, and mollify them with tender emotions by the fall of greatness, the danger of innocence, or the crosses of love. What he does best, he soon ceases to do. He is not long soft and pathetic without some idle conceit, or contemptible equivocation. He no sooner begins to move, than he counteracts himself; and terror and pity, as they are rising in the mind, are checked and blasted by sudden frigidity.

A quibble is to Shakespeare, what luminous vapours[21] are to the traveller; he follows it at all adventures, it is sure to lead him out of the way, and sure to engulf him in the mire. It has some malignant power over his mind, and its fascinations are irresistible. Whatever be the dignity or profundity of his disquisition, whether he be enlarging knowledge or exalting

---

20   *figures*   figures of speech, like metaphor.
21   *luminous vapours*   "*ignis fatuus*, will-o'-the-wisp, or Jack with a lanthorn, marsh gas that travellers take for   beacons and, following them, lose their way (see Johnson *will*, sense 11).

affection, whether he be amusing attention with incidents, or enchaining it in suspense, let but a quibble spring up before him, and he leaves his work unfinished. A quibble is the golden apple for which he will always turn aside from his career, or stoop from his elevation.[22] A quibble, poor and barren as it is, gave him such delight, that he was content to purchase it, by the sacrifice of reason, propriety and truth. A quibble was to him the fatal Cleopatra for which he lost the world, and was content to lose it . . .

from *The Lives of the Most Eminent English Poets* (1781)

FROM *MILTON*

He now hired a lodging at the house of one Russel, a tailor in St. Bride's Churchyard,[1] and undertook the education of John and Edward Phillips, his sister's sons. Finding his rooms too little, he took a house and garden in Aldersgate-street,[2] which was not then so much out of the world as it is now; and chose his dwelling at the upper end of a passage, that he might avoid the noise of the street. Here he received more boys, to be boarded and instructed.

Let not our veneration for Milton forbid us to look with some degree of merriment on great promises and small performance, on the man who hastens home,[3] because his country-men are contending for their liberty, and, when he reaches the scene of action, vapours away his patriotism in a private boarding-school. This is the period of his life from which all his biographers seem inclined to shrink. They are unwilling that Milton should be degraded to a school-master; but, since it cannot be denied that he taught boys, one finds out that he taught for nothing, and another that his motive was only zeal for the propagation of learning and virtue; and all tell what they do not know to be true, only to exuse an act which no wise man will consider as in itself disgraceful. His father was alive; his allowance was not ample, and he supplied his deficiencies by an honest and useful employment.

It is told that in the art of education he performed wonders; and a formidable list is given of the authors, Greek and Latin, that were read in Aldersgate-street, by youth between ten and fifteen or sixteen years of age. Those who tell or receive these stories should consider that nobody can be taught faster than he can learn. The speed of the horseman must be limited by the power of his horse. Every man, that has ever undertaken to instruct others, can tell what slow advances he has been able to make, and how much patience it requires to recall vagrant inattention, to stimulate sluggish indifference, and to rectify absurd misapprehension.

The purpose of Milton, as it seems, was to teach something more solid than the common literature of Schools, by reading those authors that treat of physical subjects; such as the Georgic,[4] and astronomical treatises of the ancients. This was a scheme of improvement which seems to have busied many literary projectors of that age. Cowley,[5] who had more means than Milton of knowing what was wanting to the embellishments of life, formed the same plan of education in his imaginary College.

---

[22] *golden apple . . . elevation* an allusion to the story of Atalanta who paused in her race to pick up the golden apples dropped by her opponent and suitor.
FROM *MILTON*
[1] *St. Bride's Churchyard* on the east end of Fleet Street in the City of London.
[2] *Aldersgate-street* in the easternmost part of the city, north of the Tower.

[3] *hastens home* Milton was touring Italy; hearing of the growing political unrest, he returned to England in 1639.
[4] *Georgic* agricultural.
[5] *Cowley* Abraham (1618–67) in his long poem *Davideis*.

But the truth is, that the knowledge of external nature, and of the sciences which that knowledge requires or includes is, not the great or the frequent business of the human mind. Whether we provide for action or conversation, whether we wish to be useful or pleasing, the first requisite is the religious and moral knowledge of right and wrong; the next is an acquaintance with the history of mankind, and with those examples which may be said to embody truth, and prove by events the reasonableness of opinions. Prudence and Justice are virtues, and excellencies, of all times and of all places; we are perpetually moralists, but we are geometricians only by chance. Our intercourse with intellectual nature is necessary; our speculations upon matter are voluntary, and at leisure. Physical knowledge[6] is of such rare emergence, that one man may know another half his life without being able to estimate his skill in hydrostatics or astronomy; but his moral and prudential[7] character immediately appears.

Those authors, therefore, are to be read at schools that supply most axioms of prudence, most principles of moral truth, and most materials for conversation; and these purposes are best served by poets, orators, and historians.

Let me not be censured for this digression as pedantic or paradoxical; for if I have Milton against me, I have Socrates on my side. It was his labour to turn philosophy from the study of nature to speculations upon life; but the innovators whom I oppose are turning off attention from life to nature. They seem to think, that we are placed here to watch the growth of plants, or the motions of the stars. Socrates was rather of opinion, that what we had to learn was, how to do good, and avoid evil:

$$\text{ὅττι τοι ἐν μεγάροισι κακόν τ' ἀγαθόν τε τέτυκται}^8$$

Of institutions we may judge by their effects. From this wonder-working academy, I do not know that there ever proceeded any man very eminent for knowledge: its only genuine product, I believe, is a small History of Poetry, written in Latin by his nephew,[9] of which perhaps none of my readers has ever heard.

That in his school, as in every thing else which he undertook, he laboured with great diligence, there is no reason for doubting. One part of his method deserves general imitation. He was careful to instruct his scholars in religion. Every Sunday was spent upon theology; in which he dictated a short system, gathered from the writers that were then fashionable in the Dutch universities.

He set his pupils an example of hard study and spare diet; only now and then he allowed himself to pass a day of festivity and indulgence with some gay gentlemen of Gray's Inn[10] . . .

Those little pieces[11] may be despatched without much anxiety; a greater work calls for greater care. I am now to examine *Paradise Lost*; a poem, which, considered with respect to design, may claim the first place, and with respect to performance the second, among the productions of the human mind.

By the general consent of critics, the first praise of genius is due to the writer of an epic poem, as it requires an assemblage of all the powers which are singly sufficient for other compositions. Poetry is the art of uniting pleasure with truth, by calling imagination to the

---

6 *Physical knowledge* knowledge of the natural sciences.
7 *prudential* Johnson defines "prudence" as "Wisdom applied to practice."
8 "what good or bad has happened at home" (*Odyssey* 4.392).

9 *his nephew* Edward Phillips (1630–96?).
10 *Gray's Inn* one of the Inns of Court, the institutions responsible for training students in law.
11 *little pieces* Milton's sonnets.

help of reason. Epic poetry undertakes to teach the most important truths by the most pleasing precepts, and therefore relates some great event in the most affecting manner. History must supply the writer with the rudiments of narration, which he must improve and exalt by a nobler art, animate by dramatic energy, and diversify by retrospection and anticipation; morality must teach him the exact bounds, and different shades, of vice and virtue; from policy, and the practice of life, he has to learn the discriminations of character, and the tendency of the passions, either single or combined; and physiology[12] must supply him with illustrations and images. To put these materials to poetical use, is required an imagination capable of painting nature, and realizing fiction. Nor is he yet a poet till he has attained the whole extension of his language, distinguished all the delicacies of phrase, and all the colours of words, and learned to adjust their different sounds to all the varieties of metrical modulation.

Bossu[13] is of opinion that the poet's first work is to find a *moral*, which his fable is afterwards to illustrate and establish. This seems to have been the process only of Milton; the moral of other poems is incidental and consequent; in Milton's only it is essential and intrinsic. His purpose was the most useful and the most arduous; 'to vindicate the ways of God to man';[14] to show the reasonableness of religion, and the necessity of obedience to the Divine Law.

To convey this moral, there must be a *fable*, a narration artfully constructed, so as to excite curiosity, and surprise expectation. In this part of his work, Milton must be confessed to have equalled every other poet. He has involved in his account of the Fall of Man the events which preceded, and those that were to follow it: he has interwoven the whole system of theology with such propriety, that every part appears to be necessary; and scarcely any recital is wished shorter for the sake of quickening the progress of the main action.

The subject of an epic poem is naturally an event of great importance. That of Milton is not the destruction of a city, the conduct of a colony, or the foundation of an empire. His subject is the fate of worlds, the revolutions of heaven and of earth; rebellion against the Supreme King, raised by the highest order of created beings; the overthrow of their host, and the punishment of their crime; the creation of a new race of reasonable creatures; their original happiness and innocence, their forfeiture of immortality, and their restoration to hope and peace.

Great events can be hastened or retarded only by persons of elevated dignity. Before the greatness displayed in Milton's poem, all other greatness shrinks away. The weakest of his agents are the highest and noblest of human beings, the original parents of mankind; with whose actions the elements consented; on whose rectitude or deviation of will depended the state of terrestrial nature and the condition of all the future inhabitants of the globe.

Of the other agents in the poem, the chief are such as it is irreverence to name on slight occasions. The rest were lower powers,

> of which the least could wield
> Those elements, and arm him with the force
> Of all their regions [*Paradise Lost* 6.221–3],

---

[12] *physiology* "The doctrine of the constitution of the works of nature" (Johnson).
[13] *Bossu* René le Bossu, seventeenth-century French critic, in *Traité du Poeme Epique*.

[14] *"to vindicate the ways of God to man"* recalls *Paradise Lost* 1.26, but actually quotes Pope's *Essay on Man* 1.16.

powers, which only the control of Omnipotence restrains from laying creation waste, and filling the vast expanse of space with ruin and confusion. To display the motives and actions of beings thus superior, so far as human reason can examine them, or human imagination represent them, is the task which this mighty poet has undertaken and performed.

In the examination of epic poems much speculation is commonly employed upon the *characters*. The characters in the *Paradise Lost,* which admit of examination, are those of angels and of man; of angels good and evil, of man in his innocent and sinful state.

Among the angels, the virtue of Raphael is mild and placid, of easy condescension and free communication; that of Michael is regal and lofty, and, as may seem, attentive to the dignity of his own nature. Abdiel and Gabriel appear occasionally, and act as every incident requires; the solitary fidelity of Abdiel is very amiably painted.

Of the evil angels the characters are more diversified. To Satan, as Addison observes, such sentiments are given as suit 'the most exalted and most depraved being'.[15] Milton has been censured, by Clarke,[16] for the impiety which sometimes breaks from Satan's mouth. For there are thoughts, as he justly remarks, which no observation of character can justify, because no good man would willingly permit them to pass, however transiently, through his own mind. To make Satan speak as a rebel, without any such expressions as might taint the reader's imagination, was indeed one of the great difficulties in Milton's undertaking, and I cannot but think that he has extricated himself with great happiness. There is in Satan's speeches little that can give pain to a pious ear. The language of rebellion cannot be the same with that of obedience. The malignity of Satan foams in haughtiness and obstinacy; but his expressions are commonly general, and no otherwise offensive than as they are wicked.

The other chiefs of the celestial rebellion are very judiciously discriminated in the first and second books; and the ferocious character of Moloch appears, both in the battle and the council, with exact consistency.

To Adam and to Eve are given, during their innocence, such sentiments as innocence can generate and utter. Their love is pure benevolence and mutual veneration; their repasts are without luxury, and their diligence without toil. Their addresses to their Maker have little more than the voice of admiration and gratitude. Fruition left them nothing to ask, and Innocence left them nothing to fear.

But with guilt enter distrust and discord, mutual accusation, and stubborn self-defence; they regard each other with alienated minds, and dread their Creator as the avenger of their transgression. At last they seek shelter in his mercy, soften to repentance, and melt in supplication. Both before and after the Fall, the superiority of Adam is diligently sustained.

Of the *probable* and the *marvellous*, two parts of a vulgar[17] epic poem, which immerge[18] the critic in deep consideration, the *Paradise Lost* requires little to be said. It contains the history of a miracle, of Creation and Redemption; it displays the power and the mercy of the Supreme Being; the probable therefore is marvellous, and the marvellous is probable. The substance of the narrative is truth; and as truth allows no choice, it is, like necessity, superior to rule. To the accidental or adventitious parts, as to every thing human, some slight exceptions may be made. But the main fabric[19] is immovably supported.

It is justly remarked by Addison, that this poem has, by the nature of its subject, the advantage above all others, that it is universally and perpetually interesting.[20] All mankind

[15] *Addison observes . . . being* Spectator 303.
[16] *Clarke* John, Master of Hull Grammar School, in his *Essay upon Study* (1731).
[17] *vulgar* written in a spoken, rather than a classical, language.
[18] *immerge* "To put under water" (Johnson).
[19] *fabric* building, structure.
[20] *perpetually interesting* Addison, *Spectator* 273.

will, through all ages, bear the same relation to Adam and to Eve, and must partake of that good and evil which extend to themselves.

Of the *machinery*, so called from, θεὸς ἀπὸ μηχανῆς[21] by which is meant the occasional interposition of supernatural power, another fertile topic of critical remarks, here is no room to speak, because every thing is done under the immediate and visible direction of Heaven; but the rule is so far observed, that no part of the action could have been accomplished by any other means.

Of *episodes*,[22] I think there are only two, contained in Raphael's relation of the war in heaven,[23] and Michael's prophetic account of the changes to happen in this world.[24] Both are closely connected with the great action; one was necessary to Adam as a warning, the other as a consolation.

To the completeness or *integrity* of the design nothing can be objected; it has distinctly and clearly what Aristotle requires, a beginning, a middle, and an end. There is perhaps no poem, of the same length, from which so little can be taken without apparent mutilation. Here are no funeral games, nor is there any long description of a shield.[25] The short digressions at the beginning of the third, seventh, and ninth books might doubtless be spared; but superfluities so beautiful, who would take away? or who does not wish that the author of the *Iliad* had gratified succeeding ages with a little knowledge of himself? Perhaps no passages are more frequently or more attentively read than those extrinsic paragraphs; and, since the end of poetry is pleasure, that cannot be unpoetical with which all are pleased.

The questions, whether the action of the poem be strictly *one*, whether the poem can be properly termed *heroic*, and who is the hero, are raised by such readers as draw their principles of judgement rather from books than from reason. Milton, though he entitled *Paradise Lost* only a *poem*; yet he calls it himself 'heroic song'. Dryden, petulantly and indecently, denies the heroism of Adam, because he was overcome; but there is no reason why the hero should not be unfortunate, except established practice, since success and virtue do not go necessarily together. Cato is the hero of Lucan;[26] but Lucan's authority will not be suffered by Quintilian[27] to decide. However, if success be necessary, Adam's deceiver was at last crushed; Adam was restored to his Maker's favour, and therefore may securely resume his human rank.

After the scheme and fabric of the poem must be considered its component parts, the sentiments, and the diction.

The *sentiments*, as expressive of manners, or appropriated to character, are, for the greater part, unexceptionably just.

Splendid passages, containing lessons of morality, or precepts of prudence, occur seldom. Such is the original formation of this poem, that as it admits no human manners till the Fall, it can give little assistance to human conduct. Its end is to raise the thoughts above sublunary cares or pleasures. Yet the praise of that fortitude, with which Abdiel maintained his singularity of virtue against the scorn of multitudes,[28] may be accommodated to all times; and Raphael's reproof of Adam's curiosity after the planetary motions, with the

---

[21] θεὸς ἀπὸ μηχανῆς *deus ex machina*, contrived stage appearance of gods.
[22] *episode* "An incidental narrative or digression in a poem, separable from the main subject, yet rising naturally from it" (Johnson).
[23] *war in heaven Paradise Lost* 5.577 through Book 6.
[24] *Michael's prophetic ... world Paradise Lost* 11.334 through Book 12.

[25] *funeral games ... long description of a shield* features of the *Iliad* and *Aeneid*.
[26] *Lucan* first-century CE Latin poet, author of an epic on the Roman civil war, *Pharsalia*.
[27] *Quintilian* critic and rhetorician contemporary with Lucan.
[28] *praise of that fortitude ... multitudes Paradise Lost* 5.896–903.

answer returned by Adam, may be confidently opposed to any rule of life which any poet has delivered.[29]

The thoughts which are occasionally called forth in the progress, are such as could only be produced by an imagination in the highest degree fervid and active, to which materials were supplied by incessant study and unlimited curiosity. The heat of Milton's mind might be said to sublimate his learning, to throw off into his work the spirit of science,[30] unmingled with its grosser parts.

He had considered creation in its whole extent, and his descriptions are therefore learned. He had accustomed his imagination to unrestrained indulgence, and his conceptions therefore were extensive. The characteristic quality of his poem is sublimity. He sometimes descends to the elegant, but his element is the great. He can occasionally invest himself with grace; but his natural port is gigantic loftiness. He can please when pleasure is required; but it is his peculiar power to astonish.

He seems to have been well acquainted with his own genius, and to know what it was that Nature had bestowed upon him more bountifully than upon others; the power of displaying the vast, illuminating the splendid, enforcing the awful,[31] darkening the gloomy, and aggravating the dreadful: he therefore chose a subject on which too much could not be said, on which he might tire his fancy without the censure of extravagance.

The appearances of nature, and the occurrences of life, did not satiate his appetite of greatness. To paint things as they are, requires a minute attention, and employs the memory rather than the fancy. Milton's delight was to sport in the wide regions of possibility; reality was a scene too narrow for his mind. He sent his faculties out upon discovery, into worlds where only imagination can travel, and delighted to form new modes of existence, and furnish sentiment and action to superior beings, to trace the counsels of hell, or accompany the choirs of heaven.

But he could not be always in other worlds: he must sometimes revisit earth, and tell of things visible and known. When he cannot raise wonder by the sublimity of his mind, he gives delight by its fertility.

Whatever be his subject, he never fails to fill the imagination. But his images and descriptions of the scenes or operations of Nature do not seem to be always copied from original form, nor to have the freshness, raciness, and energy of immediate observation. He saw Nature, as Dryden expresses it, 'through the spectacles of books';[32] and on most occasions calls learning to his assistance. The garden of Eden brings to his mind the vale of *Enna*, where Proserpine was gathering flowers. Satan makes his way through fighting elements, like *Argo* between the *Cyanean* rocks, or Ulysses between the two *Sicilian* whirlpools, when he shunned *Charybdis* on the *larboard*. The mythological allusions have been justly censured, as not being always used with notice of their vanity; but they contribute variety to the narration, and produce an alternate exercise of the memory and the fancy.

His similes are less numerous, and more various, than those of his predecessors. But he does not confine himself within the limits of rigorous comparison: his great excellence is amplitude, and he expands the adventitious image beyond the dimensions which the occasion required. Thus, comparing the shield of Satan to the orb of the Moon, he crowds the imagination with the discovery of the telescope, and all the wonders which the telescope discovers.

[29] *Raphael's reproof of Adam's curiosity . . . delivered Paradise Lost* 8.66–197.
[30] *science* knowledge.
[31] *awful* causing awe, astonishing.
[32] *spectacles of books* Dryden says Shakepeare saw nature without them in *Of Dramatic Poesy: An Essay* (1668).

Of his moral sentiments it is hardly praise to affirm that they excel those of all other poets; for this superiority he was indebted to his acquaintance with the sacred writings. The ancient epic poets, wanting the light of Revelation, were very unskilful teachers of virtue: their principal characters may be great, but they are not amiable. The reader may rise from their works with a greater degree of active or passive fortitude, and sometimes of prudence; but he will be able to carry away few precepts of justice, and none of mercy.

From the Italian writers it appears, that the advantages of even Christian knowledge may be possessed in vain. Ariosto's[33] pravity is generally known; and though the *Deliverance of Jerusalem*[34] may be considered as a sacred subject, the poet has been very sparing of moral instruction.

In Milton every line breathes sanctity of thought, and purity of manners, except when the train of the narration requires the introduction of the rebellious spirits; and even they are compelled to acknowledge their subjection to God, in such a manner as excites reverence, and confirms piety.

Of human beings there are but two; but those two are the parents of mankind, venerable before their fall for dignity and innocence, and amiable after it for repentance and submission. In their first state their affection is tender without weakness, and their piety sublime without presumption. When they have sinned, they show how discord begins in mutual frailty, and how it ought to cease in mutual forbearance; how confidence of the divine favour is forfeited by sin, and how hope of pardon may be obtained by penitence and prayer. A state of innocence we can only conceive, if indeed, in our present misery, it be possible to conceive it; but the sentiments and worship proper to a fallen and offending being, we have all to learn, as we have all to practice.

The poet, whatever be done, is always great. Our progenitors, in their first state, conversed with angels; even when folly and sin had degraded them, they had not in their humiliation the 'port of mean suitors';[35] and they rise again to reverential regard, when we find that their prayers were heard.

As human passions did not enter the world before the Fall, there is in the *Paradise Lost* little opportunity for the pathetic; but what little there is has not been lost. That passion which is peculiar to rational nature, the anguish arising from the consciousness of transgression, and the horrors attending the sense of the Divine Displeasure, are very justly described and forcibly impressed. But the passions are moved only on one occasion; sublimity is the general and prevailing quality in this poem; sublimity variously modified, sometimes descriptive, sometimes argumentative.

The defects and faults of *Paradise Lost*, for faults and defects every work of man must have, it is the business of impartial criticism to discover. As, in displaying the excellence of Milton, I have not made long quotations, because of selecting beauties there had been no end, I shall in the same general manner mention that which seems to deserve censure; for what Englishman can take delight in transcribing passages, which, if they lessen the reputation of Milton, diminish in some degree the honour of our country?

The generality of my scheme does not admit the frequent notice of verbal inaccuracies; which Bentley,[36] perhaps better skilled in grammar than in poetry, has often found, though he sometimes made them, and which he imputed to the obtrusions of a reviser whom the

---

[33] *Ariosto* Ludovico (1473–1533), author of the epic poem *Orlando Furioso*.

[34] *Deliverance of Jerusalem* *Gerusalemme liberata* (1575) by Torquato Tasso.

[35] *port of mean suitors* *Paradise Lost* 11.8–9.

[36] *Bentley* Richard (1662–1742), an important classical scholar, edited *Paradise Lost* (1732) on the assumption that the text was corrupt, but he confined his speculative emendations to the footnotes.

author's blindness obliged him to employ. A supposition rash and groundless, if he thought it true; and vile and pernicious, if, as is said, he in private allowed it to be false.

The plan of *Paradise Lost* has this inconvenience, that it comprises neither human actions nor human manners. The man and woman who act and suffer, are in a state which no other man or woman can ever know. The reader finds no transaction in which he can be engaged; beholds no condition in which he can by any effort of imagination place himself; he has, therefore, little natural curiosity or sympathy.

We all, indeed, feel the effects of Adam's disobedience; we all sin like Adam, and like him must all bewail our offences; we have restless and insidious enemies in the fallen angels, and in the blessed spirits we have guardians and friends; in the Redemption of mankind we hope to be included: and in the description of heaven and hell we are surely interested, as we are all to reside hereafter either in the regions of horror or of bliss.

But these truths are too important to be new; they have been taught to our infancy; they have mingled with our solitary thoughts and familiar conversation, and are habitually interwoven with the whole texture of life. Being therefore not new, they raise no unaccustomed emotion in the mind; what we knew before, we cannot learn; what is not unexpected, cannot surprise.

Of the ideas suggested by these awful scenes, from some we recede with reverence, except when stated hours require their association; and from others we shrink with horror, or admit them only as salutary inflictions, as counterpoises to our interests and passions. Such images rather obstruct the career of fancy than incite it.

Pleasure and terror are indeed the genuine sources of poetry; but poetical pleasures must be such as human imagination can at least conceive, and poetical terror such as human strength and fortitude may combat. The good and evil of Eternity are too ponderous for the wings of wit; the mind sinks under them in passive helplessness, content with calm belief and humble adoration.

Known truths, however, may take a different appearance, and be conveyed to the mind by a new train of intermediate images. This Milton has undertaken, and performed with pregnancy and vigour of mind peculiar to himself. Whoever considers the few radical positions[37] which the Scriptures afforded him, will wonder by what energetic operations he expanded them to such extent, and ramified them to so much variety, restrained as he was by religious reverence from licentiousness of fiction.

Here is a full display of the united force of study and genius; of a great accumulation of materials, with judgement to digest and fancy to combine them: Milton was able to select from nature, or from story, from ancient fable, or from modern science, whatever could illustrate or adorn his thoughts. An accumulation of knowledge impregnated his mind, fermented by study, and exalted by imagination.

It has been therefore said, without an indecent hyperbole, by one of his encomiasts, that in reading *Paradise Lost* we read a book of universal knowledge.

But original deficience cannot be supplied. The want of human interest is always felt. *Paradise Lost* is one of the books which the reader admires and lays down, and forgets to take up again.[38] Its perusal is a duty rather than a pleasure. We read Milton for instruction, retire harassed and overburdened, and look elsewhere for recreation; we desert our master, and seek for companions.

Another inconvenience of Milton's design is that it requires the description of what cannot be described, the agency of spirits. He saw that immateriality supplied no images, and that

---

[37] *radical positions* basic tenets.

[38] *forgets to take up again* in later editions Johnson added here, "None ever wished it longer than it is."

he could not show angels acting but by instruments of action; he therefore invested them with form and matter. This, being necessary, was therefore defensible; and he should have secured the consistency of his system, by keeping immateriality out of sight, and enticing his reader to drop it from his thoughts. But he has unhappily perplexed his poetry with his philosophy. His infernal and celestial powers are sometimes pure spirit, and sometimes animated body. When Satan walks with his lance upon the 'burning marle',[39] he has a body; when, in his passage between hell and the new world, he is in danger of sinking in the vacuity, and is supported by a gust of rising vapours,[40] he has a body; when he animates the toad, he seems to be mere spirit, that can penetrate matter at pleasure; when he 'starts up in his own shape', he has at least a determined form; and when he is brought before Gabriel, he has a 'spear and a shield',[41] which he had the power of hiding in the toad, though the arms of the contending angels are evidently material.

The vulgar inhabitants of Pandæmonium, being 'incorporeal spirits', are 'at large, though without number', in a limited space;[42] yet in the battle, when they were overwhelmed by mountains, their armour hurt them, 'crushed in upon their substance, now grown gross by sinning'.[43] This likewise happened to the uncorrupted angels, who were overthrown 'the sooner for their arms, for unarmed they might easily as spirits have evaded by contraction or remove'.[44] Even as spirits they are hardly spiritual; for 'contraction' and 'remove' are images of matter; but if they could have escaped without their armour, they might have escaped from it, and left only the empty cover to be battered. Uriel, when he rides on a sun-beam, is material;[45] Satan is material when he is afraid of the prowess of Adam.[46]

The confusion of spirit and matter which pervades the whole narration of the war of heaven fills it with incongruity; and the book, in which it is related, is, I believe, the favourite of children, and gradually neglected as knowledge is increased.

After the operation of immaterial agents, which cannot be explained, may be considered that of allegorical persons, which have no real existence. To exalt causes into agents, to invest abstract ideas with form, and animate them with activity, has always been the right of poetry. But such airy beings are, for the most part, suffered only to do their natural office, and retire. Thus Fame tells a tale, and Victory hovers over a general, or perches on a standard; but Fame and Victory can do no more. To give them any real employment, or ascribe to them any material agency, is to make them allegorical no longer, but to shock the mind by ascribing effects to non-entity. In the *Prometheus* of Æschylus, we see *Violence* and *Strength*, and in the *Alcestis* of Euripides, we see *Death*, brought upon the stage, all as active persons of the drama; but no precedents can justify absurdity.

Milton's allegory of Sin and Death is undoubtedly faulty. Sin is indeed the mother of Death, and may be allowed to be the portress of hell; but when they stop the journey of Satan, a journey described as real, and when Death offers him battle, the allegory is broken. That Sin and Death should have shown the way to hell, might have been allowed; but they cannot facilitate the passage by building a bridge, because the difficulty of Satan's passage is described as real and sensible, and the bridge ought to be only figurative.[47] The hell assigned to the rebellious spirits is described as not less local[48] than the residence of man. It is placed in some distant part of space, separated from the regions of harmony and order by a chaotic

---

[39] *burning marle* Paradise Lost 1.296.
[40] *... vapours* ibid. 2.931–8.
[41] *toad ... spear and shield* ibid. 4.799–990.
[42] *incorporeal ... space* ibid. 1.789–91.
[43] *crushed ... sinning* ibid. 6.656–61.

[44] *the sooner ... remove* ibid. 6.595–7.
[45] *Uriel ... material* ibid. 4.555–9.
[46] *Satan ... Adam* ibid 9.484–6.
[47] *the bridge ... figurative* ibid. 2.1024–33.
[48] *local* "Having the properties of place" (Johnson).

waste and an unoccupied vacuity; but *Sin* and *Death* worked up a 'mole' of 'aggregated soil', cemented with 'asphaltus'; a work too bulky for ideal architects.[49]

This unskilful allegory appears to me one of the greatest faults of the poem; and to this there was no temptation, but the author's opinion of its beauty.

To the conduct of the narrative some objections may be made. Satan is with great expectation brought before Gabriel in Paradise, and is suffered to go away unmolested.[50] The creation of man is represented as the consequence of the vacuity left in heaven by the expulsion of the rebels; yet Satan mentions it as a report 'rife in heaven'[51] before his departure.

To find sentiments for the state of innocence, was very difficult; and something of anticipation perhaps is now and then discovered. Adam's discourse of dreams[52] seems not to be the speculation of a new-created being. I know not whether his answer to the angel's reproof for curiosity[53] does not want something of propriety: it is the speech of a man acquainted with many other men. Some philosophical notions, especially when the philosophy is false, might have been better omitted. The angel in a comparison speaks of 'timorous deer';[54] before deer were yet timorous, and before Adam could understand the comparison.

Dryden remarks, that Milton has some flats among his elevations. This is only to say, that all the parts are not equal. In every work, one part must be for the sake of others; a palace must have passages; a poem must have transitions. It is no more to be required that wit should always be blazing, than that the sun should always stand at noon. In a great work there is a vicissitude of luminous and opaque parts, as there is in the world a succession of day and night. Milton, when he has expatiated in the sky, may be allowed sometimes to revisit earth; for what other author ever soared so high, or sustained his flight so long?

Milton, being well versed in the Italian poets, appears to have borrowed often from them; and, as every man catches something from his companions, his desire of imitating Ariosto's levity has disgraced his work with the *Paradise of Fools*;[55] a fiction not in itself ill-imagined, but too ludicrous for its place.

His play on words, in which he delights too often; his equivocations, which Bentley endeavours to defend by the example of the ancients; his unnecessary and ungraceful use of terms of art; it is not necessary to mention, because they are easily remarked, and generally censured, and at last bear so little proportion to the whole, that they scarcely deserve the attention of a critic.

Such are the faults of that wonderful performance *Paradise Lost*; which he who can put in balance with its beauties must be considered not as nice but as dull, as less to be censured for want of candour, than pitied for want of sensibility . . .

Through all his greater works there prevails an uniform peculiarity of *diction*, a mode and cast of expression which bears little resemblance to that of any former writer, and which is so far removed from common use, that an unlearned reader, when he first opens his book, finds himself surprised by a new language.

This novelty has been, by those who can find nothing wrong in Milton, imputed to his laborious endeavours after words suitable to the grandeur of his ideas. 'Our language', says

---

[49] *mole . . . architects* Paradise Lost 10.293–8.
[50] *Satan . . . unmolested* ibid. 4.874–1015.
[51] *rife in heaven* ibid. 1.650 1.
[52] *Adam's discourse of dreams* ibid. 5.100–13.

[53] *his answer to the angel's reproof for curiosity* ibid. 8.179–97.
[54] *timorous deer* ibid. 6.857.
[55] *Paradise of Fools* ibid. 3.440–97.

Addison, 'sunk under him'.[56] But the truth is, that both in prose and verse, he had formed his style by a perverse and pedantic principle. He was desirous to use English words with a foreign idiom. This in all his prose is discovered and condemned; for there judgement operates freely, neither softened by the beauty, nor awed by the dignity of his thoughts; but such is the power of his poetry, that his call is obeyed without resistance, the reader feels himself in captivity to a higher and a nobler mind, and criticism sinks in admiration.

Milton's style was not modified by his subject: what is shown with greater extent in *Paradise Lost*, may be found in *Comus*. One source of his peculiarity was his familiarity with the Tuscan poets: the disposition of his words is, I think, frequently Italian; perhaps sometimes combined with other tongues. Of him, at last, may be said what [Ben] Jonson says of Spenser, that he 'wrote no language', but has formed what *Butler* calls a 'Babylonish Dialect',[57] in itself harsh and barbarous, but made by exalted genius, and extensive learning, the vehicle of so much instruction and so much pleasure, that, like other lovers, we find grace in its deformity.

Whatever be the faults of his diction, he cannot want the praise of copiousness and variety: he was master of his language in its full extent; and has selected the melodious words with such diligence, that from his book alone the Art of English Poetry might be learned.

After his diction, something must be said of his versification. 'The measure', he says, 'is the English heroic verse without rhyme'.[58] Of this mode he had many examples among the Italians, and some in his own country. The Earl of Surrey is said to have translated one of Virgil's books without rhyme;[59] and besides our tragedies, a few short poems had appeared in blank verse; particularly one tending to reconcile the nation to Raleigh's wild attempt upon Guiana, and probably written by Raleigh himself. These petty performances cannot be supposed to have much influenced Milton, who more probably took his hint from Trisino's *Italia Liberata*;[60] and, finding blank verse easier than rhyme, was desirous of persuading himself that it is better.

'Rhyme', he says, and says truly, 'is no necessary adjunct of true poetry'. But perhaps, of poetry as a mental operation, metre or music is no necessary adjunct: it is however by the music of metre that poetry has been discriminated in all languages; and in languages melodiously constructed, by a due proportion of long and short syllables, metre is sufficient. But one language cannot communicate its rules to another: where metre is scanty and imperfect, some help is necessary. The music of the English heroic line strikes the ear so faintly that it is easily lost, unless all the syllables of every line co-operate together: this co-operation can be only obtained by the preservation of every verse unmingled with another, as a distinct system of sounds; and this distinctness is obtained and preserved by the artifice of rhyme. The variety of pauses, so much boasted by the lovers of blank verse, changes the measures of an English poet to the periods of a declaimer; and there are only a few skilful and happy readers of Milton, who enable their audience to perceive where the lines end or begin. 'Blank verse', said an ingenious critic, 'seems to be verse only to the eye'.[61]

Poetry may subsist without rhyme, but English poetry will not often please; nor can rhyme ever be safely spared but where the subject is able to support itself. Blank verse makes some approach to that which is called the 'lapidary style'; has neither the easiness of prose, nor

---

[56] *Our Language . . . him* *Spectator* 297.

[57] *Butler . . . Dialect* Samuel Butler (1612–80), *Hudibras* 1.1.93.

[58] *The measure . . . rhyme* *Paradise Lost*, preface.

[59] *Earl of Surrey . . . without rhyme* Henry Howard (1517?–47) translated Books 2 and 4 into blank verse.

[60] *Trisino's Italia Liberata* *L'Italia liberata dai Goti* (1547–8) by Gian Giorgio Trissino.

[61] *Blank verse . . . eye* William Locke (1732–1810) told Johnson this in conversation.

the melody of numbers, and therefore tires by long continuance. Of the Italian writers without rhyme, whom Milton alleges as precedents, not one is popular; what reason could urge in its defence, has been confuted by the ear.

But, whatever be the advantage of rhyme, I cannot prevail on myself to wish that Milton had been a rhymer, for I cannot wish his work to be other than it is; yet, like other heroes, he is to be admired rather than imitated. He that thinks himself capable of astonishing, may write blank verse; but those that hope only to please, must condescend to rhyme.

The highest praise of genius is original invention. Milton cannot be said to have contrived the structure of an epic poem, and therefore must yield to that vigour and amplitude of mind to which all generations must be indebted for the art of poetical narration, for the texture of the fable, the variation of incidents, the interposition of dialogue, and all the stratagems that surprise and enchain attention. But, of all the borrowers from Homer, Milton is perhaps the least indebted. He was naturally a thinker for himself, confident of his own abilities and disdainful of help or hindrance: he did not refuse admission to the thoughts or images of his predecessors, but he did not seek them. From his contemporaries he neither courted nor received support; there is in his writings nothing by which the pride of other authors might be gratified, or favour gained, no exchange of praise, nor solicitation of support. His great works were performed under discountenance, and in blindness, but difficulties vanished at his touch; he was born for whatever is arduous; and his work is not the greatest of heroic poems, only because it is not the first.

John Armstrong, MD (1709–1779)

Armstrong wanted to be a poet before he began studying medicine. At the age of sixteen he sent manuscripts of his poetry to fellow Scots who had became famous British poets. By 1735 he was practicing medicine in London and publishing papers in his field. He was highly critical of his profession, however, and continued to write poetry. In 1744 he had his greatest success with The Art of Preserving Health, *which combines his two avocations. The poem remained in print well into the nineteenth century. The small excerpt here must have had particular poignance as London became more populous, and the air grew worse and worse. It is ironic that Armstrong thought the burning of coal mitigated the corrosive effects of the air. But it is interesting that this combination of blank verse and practical advice on health enjoyed such popularity. Many of Armstrong's other works and some of his behavior earned him ridicule from other writers of his time, but the success of* Health *outlived them all.*

from *The Art of Preserving Health: A Poem* (1744)

> Ye who amid this feverish world would wear
> A body free of pain, of cares a mind;
> Fly the rank city, shun its turbid air;
> Breathe not the chaos of eternal smoke
> And volatile corruption, from the dead,   5
> The dying, sick'ning, and the living world
> Exhaled, to sully heaven's transparent dome

With dim mortality. It is not air
That from a thousand lungs reeks back to thine,
Sated with exhalations rank and fell,   10
The spoil of dunghills, and the putrid thaw
Of Nature; when from shape and texture she
Relapses into fighting elements:
It is not air, but floats a nauseous mass
Of all obscene, corrupt, offensive things.   15
Much moisture hurts; but here a sordid bath,
With oily rancour fraught, relaxes more
The solid frame than simple moisture can.
Besides, immured in many a sullen bay
That never felt the freshness of the breeze,   20
This slumbering deep remains, and ranker grows
With slickly rest: and (though the lungs abhor
To drink the dun fuliginous abyss)[1]
Did not the acid vigour of the mine,
Rolled from so many thundering chimneys, tame   25
The putrid steams that overswarm the sky;
This caustic venom would perhaps corrode
Those tender cells that draw the vital air,
In vain with all their unctuous rills bedewed;
Or, by the drunken venous tubes, that yawn[2]   30
In countless pores o'er all the pervious skin,
Imbibed, would poison the balsamic blood,[3]
And rouse the heart to every fever's rage.
While yet you breathe, away! the rural wilds
Invite; the mountains call you, and the vales;   35
The woods, the streams, and each ambrosial breeze
That fans the ever undulating sky;
A kindly sky! whose fostering power regales
Man, beast, and all the vegetable reign.
Find then some woodland scene where Nature smiles   40
Benign, where all her honest children thrive.

Mary Collier (*fl.* 1740–1760)

Almost all that is known of Mary Collier is contained in the following "advertisement" to The
Woman's Labour, *which was written by the unknown M. B.*

FROM *THE ART OF PRESERVING HEALTH*
[1] *fuliginous* "Sooty; smoky" (Johnson).
[2] *venous* vein-like, or having veins.
[3] *balsamic* "Having the qualities of balsam; unctuous;
mitigating; soft; mild; oily" (Johnson).

THE Woman's Labour: (1739)
AN EPISTLE TO Mr. STEPHEN DUCK;[1] In ANSWER to his late Poem, called
THE THRESHER'S LABOUR . . .
By Mary Collier, Now a *Washer-Woman*, at Petersfield in Hampshire

ADVERTISEMENT

It is thought proper to assure the Reader, that the following Verses are the real Productions of the Person to whom the Title-Page ascribes them.

Though She pretends not to the Genius of Mr. Duck, nor hopes to be taken Notice of by the Great, yet her Friends are of Opinion that the Novelty of a *Washer-Woman*'s turning Poetess, will procure her some Readers.

If all that follow the same Employment would amuse themselves, and one another, during the tedious Hours of their Labour, in this, or some other Ways as innocent, instead of tossing Scandal to and fro, many Reputations would remain unwounded, and the Peace of Families be less disturbed.

I think it no Reproach to the Author, whose Life is toilsome, and her Wages inconsiderable, to confess honestly, that the View of her putting a small Sum of Money in her Pocket, as well as the Reader's Entertainment, had its Share of Influences upon this Publication. And she humbly hopes she shall not be absolutely disappointed; since, though she is ready to own that her Performance could by no Means stand a critical Examination, yet she flatters herself that, with all its Faults and Imperfections, the candid Reader will judge it to be something considerably beyond the common Capacity of those of her own Rank and Occupation.

M. B.

Immortal Bard! thou Favourite of the Nine!
Enriched by Peers, advanced by Caroline!
Deign to look down on One that's poor and low,
Remembering you yourself was lately so;
Accept these Lines: Alas! what can you have   5
From her, who ever was, and's still a Slave?
No Learning ever was bestowed on me;
My Life was always spent in Drudgery:
And not alone; alas! with Grief I find,
It is the Portion of poor Woman-kind.   10
Oft have I thought as on my Bed I lay,
Eased from the tiresome Labours of the Day,
Our first Extraction from a Mass refined,
Could never be for Slavery designed;

THE WOMAN'S LABOUR
[1] *Mr. Duck*   Stephen Duck (1705–56), see above p. 822, who was given an income by Queen Caroline.

Till Time and Custom by degrees destroyed   15
That happy State our sex at first enjoyed.
When Men had used their utmost Care and Toil,
Their Recompense was but a Female Smile;
When they by Arts or Arms were rendered Great,
They laid their Trophies at a Woman's Feet;   20
They, in those Days, unto our Sex did bring
Their Hearts, their All, a Free-will Offering;
And as from us their Being they derive,
They back again should all due Homage give.
    Jove once descending from the Clouds, did drop   25
In Show'rs of Gold on lovely Danae's Lap;[2]
The sweet-tongued Poets, in those generous Days,
Unto our Shrine still offered up their Lays:
But now, alas! that Golden Age is past,
We are the Objects of your Scorn at last.   30
And you, great Duck, upon whose happy Brow
The Muses seem to fix the Garland now,
In your late Poem boldly did declare[3]
Alcides' Labours can't with yours compare;[4]
And of your annual Task have much to say,   35
Of threshing, Reaping, Mowing Corn and Hay;
Boasting your daily Toil, and nightly Dream,
But can't conclude your never-dying Theme,
And let our hapless Sex in Silence lie
Forgotten, and in dark Oblivion die;   40
But on our abject State you throw your Scorn,
And Women wrong, your Verses to adorn.
You of Hay-making speak a Word or two,
As if our Sex but little Work could do:
This makes the honest Farmer smiling say,   45
He'll seek for Women still to make his Hay;
For if his Back be turned, their Work they mind
As well as men, as far as he can find.
For my own Part, I many a Summer's Day
Have spent in throwing, turning, making Hay;   50
But ne'er could see, what you have lately found,
Our Wages paid for sitting on the Ground.
'Tis true, that when our Morning's Work is done,
And all our Grass exposed unto the Sun,
While that his scorching Beams do on it shine,   55
As well as you, we have a Time to dine:
I hope, that since we freely toil and sweat
To earn our Bread, you'll give us Time to eat.

---

[2] Show'rs of Gold Jove took this form to penetrate the defenses erected by Danae's father and with her conceived Perseus.

[3] Poem "The Thresher's Labour" (1730); see above, p. 822.

[4] Alcides Heracles or Hercules, as Duck calls him.

That over, soon we must get up again,
And nimbly turn our Hay upon the Plain;   60
Nay, rake and prow it in, the Case is clear;⁵
Or how should Cocks in equal Rows appear?⁶
But if you'd have what you have wrote believed.
I find, that you to hear us talk are grieved:
In this, I hope, you do not speak your Mind,   65
For none but *Turks*, that ever could I find,
Have Mutes to serve them, or did e'er deny
Their Slaves, at Work, to chat it merrily.
Since you have Liberty to speak your Mind,
And are to talk, as well as we, inclined,   70
Why should you thus repine, because that we,
Like you, enjoy that pleasing Liberty?
What! would you lord it quite, and take away
The only Privilege our Sex enjoy?

    When Evening does approach, we homeward hie,   75
And our domestic Toils incessant ply:
Against your coming Home prepare to get
Our Work all done, our House in order set;
'Bacon' and 'Dumpling' in the Pot we boil,⁷
Our Beds we make, our Swine we feed the while;   80
Then wait at Door to see you coming Home,
And set the Table out against you come:
Early next Morning we on you attend;
Our Children dress and feed, their Clothes we mend;
And in the Field our daily Task renew,   85
Soon as the rising Sun has dried the Dew.

    When Harvest comes, into the Field we go,
And help to reap the Wheat as well as you;
Or else we go the Ears of Corn to glean;
No Labour scorning, be it e'er so mean;   90
But in the Work we freely bear a Part,
And what we can, perform with all our Heart.
To get a Living we so willing are,
Out tender Babes into the Field we bear,
And wrap them in our Clothes to keep them warm,   95
While round about we gather up the Corn;
And often unto them our Course do bend,
To keep them safe, that nothing them offend:
Our children that are able, bear a Share
In gleaning Corn, such is our frugal care.   100

---

⁵ *prow* (not in *OED*) "plough" or "drow" (a dialectical
from of "draw") if the *p* is actually an upside-down *d*.
⁶ *Cocks* haycocks, haystacks; the line, like many
others in the poem, alludes to one just like it in
Duck's poem.

⁷ *"Bacon" and "Dumpling"* allusions to Duck's poem.

When Night comes on, unto our Home we go,
Our Corn we carry, and our Infant too;
Weary, alas! but 'tis not worth our while
Once to complain, or 'rest at every Stile';[8]
We must make haste, for when we Home are come,   105
Alas! we find our Work but just begun;
So many Things for our Attendance call,
Had we ten Hands, we could employ them all.
Our Children put to Bed, with greatest Care
We all Things for your coming Home prepare: 110
You sup, and go to Bed without delay,
And rest yourselves till the ensuing Day;
While we, alas! but little Sleep can have,
Because our froward Children cry and rave;[9]
Yet, without fail, soon as Day-light doth spring,   115
We in the Field again our Work begin,
And there, with all our Strength, our Toil renew,
Till *Titan's* golden Rays have dried the Dew;
Then home we go unto our Children dear,
Dress, feed, and bring them to the Field with care.   120
Were this your Case, you justly might complain
That Day nor Night you are secure from Pain;
Those mighty Troubles which perplex your Mind,
(*Thistles* before, and *Females* come behind)
Would vanish soon, and quickly disappear,   125
Were you, like us, encumbered thus with Care.
What you would have of us we do not know:
We oft' take up the Corn that you do mow;
We cut the Pease, and always ready are
In every Work to take our Proper Share;   130
And from the Time that Harvest doth begin,
Until the Corn be cut and carried in,
Our Toil and Labour's daily so extreme,
That we have hardly ever *Time to dream*.

   The Harvest ended, Respite none we find;   135
The hardest of our Toil is still behind:
Hard labour we most cheerfully pursue,
And out, abroad, a Charing often go:[10]
Of which I now will briefly tell in part,
What fully to declare is past my Art;   140
So many Hardships daily we go through,
I boldly say, the like *you* never knew.
   When bright *Orion* glitters in the Skies

---

8 *"rest at every Stile"* the men do this on their way
home in Duck's poem.
9 *froward* "Peevish; ungovernable; angry; perverse"
(Johnson).

10 *a Charing* from "to char," "To work at others
houses by the day, without being hired as a servant"
(Johnson).

In *Winter* Nights, then early we must rise;
The Weather ne'er so bad, Wind, Rain, or Snow.   145
Our Work appointed, we must rise and go;
While you on easy Beds may lie and sleep,
Till Light does through your Chamber-windows peep.
When to the House we come where we should go,
How to get in, alas! we do not know: 150
The Maid quite tir'd with Work the Day before,
O'ercome with Sleep; we standing at the Door
Oppressed with Cold, and often call in vain,
Ere to our Work we can Admittance gain:
But when from Wind and Weather we get in,   155
Briskly with Courage we our Work begin;
Heaps of fine Linen we before us view,
Whereon to lay our Strength and Patience too;
Cambrics and Muslins, which our ladies wear,[11]
Laces and Edgings, costly, fine, and rare,   160
Which must be washed with utmost Skill and care;
With Holland Shirts, Ruffles and Fringes too,[12]
Fashions which our Fore-fathers never knew.
For several Hours here we work and slave,
Before we can one Glimpse of Day-light have;   165
We labour hard before the Morning's past,
Because we fear the Time runs on too fast.
    At length bright *Sol* illuminates the Skies,
And summons drowsy Mortals to arise;
Then comes our Mistress to us without fail,   170
And in her Hand, *perhaps*, a Mug of Ale
To cheer our Hearts, and also to inform
Herself, what Work is done that very Morn;
Lays her Command upon us, that we mind
Her Linen well, nor 'leave the Dirt behind':   175
Not this alone, but also to take care
We don't her Cambrics nor her Ruffles tear;
And *these* most strictly does of us require,
'To save her Soap, and sparing be of Fire';
Tells us her Charge is great, nay furthermore,   180
Her Clothes are fewer than the Time before.
Now we drive on, resolved our Strength to try,
And what we can, we do most willingly;
Until with Heat and Work, 'tis often known
Not only Sweat, but Blood runs trickling down   185
Our Wrists and Fingers; still our Work demands
The constant Action of our lab'ring Hands.
    Now Night comes on, from whence you have Relief,
But that, alas! does but increase our Grief;

---

[11] *Cambrics* fine linens from Flanders.   [12] *Holland* "Fine linen made in Holland" (Johnson).

With heavy Hearts we often view the Sun,   190
Fearing he'll set before our Work is done;
For either in the Morning, or at Night,
We piece the *Summer*'s Day with Candle-light.[13]
Though we all Day with Care our Work attend,
Such is our Fate, we know not when 'twill end: 195
When Evening's come, you Homeward take your Way,
We, till our Work is done, are forced to stay;
And after all our Toil and Labour past,
Six-pence or Eight-pence pays us off at last;
For all our Pains, no Prospect can we see   200
Attend us, but *Old Age* and *Poverty*.
    The *Washing* is not all we have to do:
We oft change Work for Work as well as you.
Our Mistress of her Pewter doth complain,
And 'tis our Part to make it clean again.   205
This Work, though very hard and tiresome too,
Is not the worst we hapless Females do:
When Night comes on, and we quite weary are,
We scarce can count what falls unto our Share;
Pots, Kettles, Sauce-pans, Skillets, we may see,   210
Skimmers and Ladles, and such Trumpery,
Brought in to make complete our Slavery,
Though early in the Morning 'tis begun,
'Tis often very late before we've done;
Alas! our Labours never know an End;   215
On Brass and Iron we our Strength must spend;
Our tender Hands and Fingers scratch and tear:
All this, and more, with Patience we must bear.
Coloured with Dirt and Filth we now appear;
Your threshing 'sooty Peas' will not come near.   220
All the Perfections Woman once could boast,
Are quite obscured, and altogether lost.
    Once more our Mistress sends to let us know
She wants our Help, because the Beer runs low:
Then in much haste for Brewing we prepare,   225
The Vessels clean, and scald with greatest care;
Often at Midnight, from our Bed we rise
At other Times, ev'n *that* will not suffice;
Our Work at Evening oft we do begin,
And ere we've done, the Night comes on again.   230
Water we pump, the Copper we must fill,
Or tend the Fire; for if we e'er stand still,
Like you, when threshing, we a Watch must keep,
Our Wort boils over if we dare to sleep.[14]

---

[13] *piece* eke out; stretch.

[14] *Wort* "A plant of the cabbage kind" perhaps with a pun on another meaning, fermenting beer, which the threshers drink.

But to rehearse all Labour is in vain,   235
Of which we very justly might complain:
For us, you see, but little Rest is found;
Our Toil increases as the Year runs round.
While you to *Sisyphus* yourselves compare,[15]
With *Danaus' Daughters* we may claim a Share;[16]   240
For while *he* labours against the Hill,
Bottomless Tubs of Water *they* must fill.
So the industrious Bees do hourly strive
To bring their Loads of Honey to the Hive;
Their sordid Owners always reap the Gains,[17]   245
And poorly recompense their Toil and Pains.

Jane Collier (d. 1755)

Jane Collier was the daughter of Arthur Collier of Wiltshire, an Anglican priest devoted to Berkeleyan metaphysics, which he expounded in Clavis Universalis, or a New Inquiry after Truth, being a demonstration of the non-existence or impossibility of an external world *(1713). Although it is not kind to the memory of Arthur, it is possible to imagine that his daughter's realistic, satirical bent is a response to her father's idealist philosophical position. After their father's death Jane and her sister Margaret lived in London and enjoyed the literary society of both the Fielding family and Samuel Richardson. Jane collaborated with Sarah Fielding (Henry's sister) on a three-volume didactic romance called* The Cry *(1754) at about the same time that she wrote the* Art of Tormenting *(1753). Collier's collaborative novel adopts and projects the view that marriage should solemnize a relationship between candid, consenting, and spiritually equal adults. She must have provided much of the support for her little household because her sister, who had accompanied the Fieldings on their famous trip to Lisbon, was afterward forced by poverty to retreat to the Isle of Wight, then a very cheap place to live. There are extant a few letters exchanged between Richardson and both sisters. Those from Jane show that she was a skilfull critic whose comments were valued. Those from her sister show that she was sorely missed after her death.*

There were several editions of the Art of Tormenting, *including some with aquatints in the early nineteenth century. The following is a series of excerpts from the second edition, revised, 1757.*

from *An Essay on the Art of Ingeniously Tormenting; with Proper Rules for the Exercise of that Pleasant Art* (1753)

. . . England has ever been allowed to excel most other nations in her improvements of arts and sciences, although she seldom claims to herself the merit of invention: to her improvements also are many of her neighbours indebted, for the exercise of some of their most useful arts.

---

[15] *Sisyphus* condemned to push a stone unsuccessfully up an incline in Hades.

[16] *Danaus' Daughters* these Egyptians suffered the specified fate for murdering their husbands at their father's behest.

[17] *sordid* "Covetous; niggardly" (Johnson, sense 3).

'Tis not the benefit that may arise to the few from any invention, but its general utility, which ought to make such invention of universal estimation. Had the art of navigation gone no higher than to direct the course of a small boat by oars, the Low Countries only could have been the better for it. Again, should the inhabitants of Lapland invent the most convenient method for warming their houses by stoves, bringing them, by their improvements, to the utmost perfection; yet could not those who live within the Tropics receive the least benefits from such their improvements; any more than the Laplanders could, from the invention of fans, umbrellas, and cooling grottoes.

But as the science recommended in this short essay will be liable to no such exceptions; being, we presume, adapted to the circumstances, genius, and capacity, of every nation under heaven, why should I doubt of that deserved fame, generally given to those

Inventas aut qui vitam excoluere per artes,
Quique sui memores alios fecere merendo?[1]
Virg. 6. v. 663.

Unless, indeed, I should be told, that mankind are already too great adepts in this art, to need any further instructions.

May I hope that my dear countrymen will pardon me for presuming (by the very publication of these rules) that they are not already absolutely perfect in this our science? Or at least, that they may not always have an ingenious Torment ready at hand to inflict?

By the common run of Servants, it might have been presumed, that Dean Swift's instructions[2] to them were unnecessary: but I dare believe no one ever read over that ingenious work, without finding there some inventions for idleness, carelessness, and ill-behaviour, which had never happened within his own experience.

Although I do not suppose mankind in general to be thorough proficients in this our art; yet wrong not my judgement so much, gentle reader, as to imagine, that I would write *institutes*[3] of any science, to those who are unqualified for its practice, or do not show some genius in themselves towards it. Should you observe in one child a delight of drawing, in another a turn towards music, would you not do your utmost to assist their genius, and to further their attempts? 'Tis the great progress that I have observed to be already made in this our pleasant art, and the various attempts that I daily see towards bringing it to perfection, that encouraged me to offer this my poor assistance.

One requisite for approbation I confess, is wanting in this work; for, alas! I fear it will contain nothing new. But what is wanting in novelty, shall be made up in utility; for, although I may not be able to show one new and untried method of plaguing, teasing, or tormenting; yet will it not be a very great help to any one, to have all the best and most approved methods collected together, in one small pocket volume? Did I promise a new set of rules, then, whatever was not mine, might be claimed by its proper owner; and, like the jay in the fable, I should justly be stripped of my borrowed plumes:[4] but, as I declare myself only an humble collector, I doubt not, but every one, who has practised, or who in writing

---

FROM *AN ESSAY ON THE ART OF INGENIOUSLY TORMENTING*
[1] *Inventas . . . merendo* "who improved life by means of ingenious arts and made others mindful of them through their own merit."
[2] *Dean Swift's instructions Directions to Servants*, an ironic essay by Swift, posthumously published in 1745.

[3] *institute* "Precept; maxim; principle" (Johnson).
[4] *jay in the fable . . . plumes* in Aesop's fable the jay, or jackdaw, dresses himself in the feathers of his competitors in the beauty contest held by Zeus; he is embarrassed when they take their own back again.

has described, an ingenious Torment, will thank me for putting it into this my curious collection.

The following instructions are divided into Two Parts. This First Part is addressed to those, who may be said to have an exterior power from visible authority, such as if vested, by law or custom, in matters over their servants; parents over their children; husbands over their wives; and many others. The Second Part will be addressed to those, who have an interior power, arising from the affection of the person on whom they are to work; as in the case of the wife, the friend, &c.

It would be tiresome, and almost endless, to enumerate every connexion under the two foregoing Heads: I have therefore taken only a few of the principal ones in each division; and shall begin with masters and mistresses, as in the following Chapter.

CHAPTER 2
TO THE PATRONESSES OF AN HUMBLE COMPANION

I have often wondered, considering the great number of families there are, whose fortunes are so large, that the addition of one, or even two, would hardly be felt, that they should not more frequently take into their houses, and under their protection, young women who have been well-educated; and who, by the misfortune or death of their friends, have been left destitute of all means of subsistence. There are many methods for young men, in the like circumstances, to acquire a genteel maintenance; but for a girl, I know not of one way of support, that does not by the custom of the world, throw her below the rank of a gentlewoman.

There are two motives for taking such young women under protection.

One is, the pleasure which ('tis said) kind and benevolent hearts must take in relieving from distress one of their fellow-creatures; and, for their repeated kindness and indulgence to an unforunate deserving person, receiving the daily tribute of grateful assiduity, and cheerful looks. For I have been informed, by a friend well versed in human nature, that, however loud the outcry is against ingratitude for real kindness, yet that true and real kindness seldom or never did excite ingratitude: and moreover, that when those violent outcries came to be examined into, the obliged person had, in fact, been guilty of no ingratitude, or the patron had bestowed no real kindness. Nay, further, that, should it be proved, that ungrateful returns are sometimes made for real favours, it would commonly be found, upon inquiry, that the persons conferring such favours had a blind fate open to flattery, or some other passion; by which means they had shut their eyes, and plucked a poisonous weed to place in their bosoms, instead of using their power of sight and distinction, in order to gather one of those many grateful flowers, which nature has scattered over the face of the earth: the intoxicating quality of which weed has still kept their eyes closed, till they are roused by some racking pain, which it instils into the inmost recesses of the heart.

But, notwithstanding the before-mentioned outcry against ingratitude, there are some, I must confess, who, from compassion and generosity, have taken the distressed into their protection, and have treated them with the highest kindness and indulgence. Nay, I have known a set of tasteless, silly, people, who are so void of any relish for this our pleasant game, that they would never wish to see a face in sorrow or tears, unless 'twas in their power to dry those tears, and turn that sorrow into cheerful smiles. But to such insipid folks I write not; as I know my rules, to them, would be of little service. I address myself, therefore, in this chapter, only to those who take young women into their houses, as new subjects of their power . . .

In the first place, let me advise you to be very careful in the choice of an humble companion; for be it always remembered, that, in every connexion where this art of Teasing and Tormenting is exercised, much depends upon the subject of your power.

In a servant, you have little to look for but diligence and good-nature; but in a dependent there are many more requisites.

Let her be well born, and well educated. The more acquirements she has, the greater field will you have for insolence, and the pleasure of mortifying her. Out of the numberless families in the church and army, that outlive themselves, and come to decay, great will be your choice. Pick out, if possible, one that has lived a happy life, under tender and indulgent parents. Beauty, or deformity; good sense, or the want of it; may any of them, with proper management, so well answer your purpose, that you need not be very curious as to that matter: but on no account take into your house one that has not a tender heart, with a meek and gentle disposition; for if she has spirit enough to despise your insults, and has not tender affections enough to be soothed and melted by your kindness (which must be sparingly bestowed), all your sport is lost; and you might as well shoot your venom at a marble statue in your garden.

Although I have supposed, that beauty or deformity, good sense or folly, in your dependent, are in some measure indifferent, yet I would have you, if possible, mix them thus: take good sense, with plainness or deformity; and beauty, with a very weak capacity.

If your humble companion be handsome, with no great share of understanding, observe the following directions, towards Miss Kitty:

Take care seldom to call her anything but *Beauty, Pretty Idiot, Puppet, Baby-face*; with as many more of such sarcastical epithets as you can invent.

If you can provoke her enough to show any resentment in her countenance, looking at her with a mixture of anger and contempt, you may say, 'I *beseech* you Child to spare your frowns for those who will fear them; and keep your disdainful looks for the footmen, when they make love to you; which, by your flirting airs, I make no doubt they are encouraged to do'.

If by your discourse, you move her tears, you may call her *Weeping beauty*; and ask her, out of what play, or idle romance, she had learnt, that tears were becoming. Then drive her out of the room with these words, 'Begone out of my sight, you blubbering fool – *Handsome indeed*! If I had a dog that looked so frightful, I would hang him'.

Although you may, generally, insult her with her beauty, yet be sure, at times, to say so many mortifying things, as shall make her believe you don't think her in the least handsome. If her complexion is fair, call her *Whey-face*; if she is really an olive beauty, you may tell her, she is as brown as Mahogany: if she is inclinable to pale, tell her she always looks as white as a cloth: and you may add, 'That whatever people may fancy of their own sweet persons, yet, in your opinion, there could be no beauty in a whited wall'. In this case, sometimes, insultingly, the name of *Lily-face*! will come in. If she has a fine bloom, tell her she looks as red-faced, as if she drank brandy; and you have no notion, you may say, of cook-maid beauty. Thus, by right management, every personal perfection may be turned to her reproach. Fine large eyes may be accused of goggling;[5] small ones may be termed unmeaning, and insignificant; and so of every feature besides. But if she has fine, white, even, teeth, you have no resource, but to tell her, whenever you catch her smiling, that she is mighty fond of grinning, to show her white teeth. Then add, 'Pray remember, child, that you can't show your teeth, without showing your folly'. You may likewise declare, that if you had a girl of your own, who showed such a silly vanity, you would flay her alive.

---

[5] *goggling* squinting.

One thing be sure not to omit, altho' it is ever so false; which is, to tell her, and in the plainest and grossest terms, that she has (oh shocking accusation to a fine girl!) sweaty feet, and a nauseous breath.

To a young creature of beauty, and any degree of delicacy, nothing can be more teasing and grating to hear, than this. From the extreme mortification she must feel, 'tis ten to one but she will deny it, with some resentment, or will shed tears of vexation for the charge: these will both equally serve your purpose. If the first, you have many ways to deal with her. Furious scolding and abuse is no bad method, if not too lately practised; but insulting taunts, I think, will do rather better. Such as follows:

'Oh to be sure! you are too delicate a creature to have any human failings? you are all sweetness and perfection! well, heaven defend me from such *sweet* creatures!' Then changing your tone and looks into fierceness, you may proceed: 'I tell you, Madam Impertinence, whatever you may think, and how impudently soever you may dare to contradict me in this manner, that all your nasty odious imperfections have been often taken notice of by many people besides myself, though nobody has enough regard for you, to tell you of such things. – You may toss your head, and look with as much indignation as you please; but these airs, child, will not do long with me. – If you don't like to be told of your faults, you must find some other person to support you. So pray, for the present, walk off to your own apartment; and consider whether you choose to lay aside that pretty, becoming resentment of yours; or be thrown friendless, as I found you, on the wide world again. – You must not be told of your failings, truly, must you! Oh I would not have such a proud heart as thine is in my breast, for the world! Though let me tell you, Mistress minx, 'twould much better become my station, than yours'.

For fear this kind and gentle speech of yours should have wounded too deeply; and Miss Kitty should really, on consideration, prefer wandering, beggary, or the most menial service, to such life of dependence, and you should thereby lose your game, be sure not to let it be above half an hour before you send your woman up-stairs to her, with some sweet-meats, fruit, or any thing you know she is fond of. Order your woman, if she finds her in a rage, to soften her mind, till she brings her to tears; then to comfort her; and tell her how kindly you had been just then talking of her; and to leave no means untried to coax her down. You must then receive her with the highest good humour; and tell her, you intend for her some new clothes, a pleasant jaunt or any indulgence that you know would please her: continue this good humour so strongly, that she shall not have the least opportunity of telling you, what undoubtedly, she must have resolved above-stairs; namely that she could live with you no longer. And if this fit of kindness be carried into a proper excess, the poor girl will, at last, begin to think herself to blame; and that you are the kindest, best creature to her in the world. Then is she properly prepared for the next Torment you shall think fit to inflict.

Should Miss Kitty, on the mortifying accusation before-mentioned, burst into tears, you must proceed in a contrary method: and, in a soft and gentle accent, you may say to her, 'I cannot imagine, my dear, what should make you cry, when I am only kindly telling you, as a friend, of some misfortunes you cannot possibly help. I am very far from blaming you, my love; for although, I thank heaven, I am myself free from all such shocking and disagreeable things, yet nobody pities people with such imperfections more than I do'. You might here, also, aggravate the misfortune it was, to so young and so pretty a girl, to have such personal defects: for (you may add) that you had often heard the men declare (and you thought 'em very much in the right), that they should prefer the ugliest girl that was ever born, who was sweet in her person, to the greatest beauty upon the earth, with such nauseous, disgustful imperfections . . .

So far for a handsome girl. But, if plainness, with a good share of natural parts, should be the lot of this your dependent, whom we will call Miss Fanny, great scope will you have in a different way, for Tormenting, Teasing, and Plaguing her.

You must begin with all sorts of mortifying observations on her person; and frequently declare, that you hate any thing about you that is not agreeable to look at. This, in the beginning, will vex the girl; first, as 'tis not very pleasant to have a mirror perpetually held to our view, where the reflection is so mortifying: and next, as she will be sorry to find herself disagreeable to a person she would wish to please. But in time she will find you out: she will perceive the malice of such reflections; and, if she has good sense, will get above any concern about what you can say of her person. As soon as you perceive this, change your method; and level most of your darts against her understanding. Never let a day pass, without calling her, in that day, a Wit, at least a hundred times. Begin most requests, or rather commands, with these sort of phrases, 'Will your *Wisdom* please to do so or so, &c. Can a lady of your *fine parts* condescend to darn this apron? Would it not be too great a condescension for a Wit, to submit to look over my housekeeper's accounts?' Whatever answer she makes to these things; whether it be showing a little resentment for such insolent treatment; or saying, with mildness, that she is ready to do any thing you command her; let your reply be – 'I don't hear, child, what you say – However, I presume it was something mighty smart and witty. – But let me give you one piece of advice; which is, to be more sparing of your tongue, and less sparing of your labour, if you expect a continuance of my favour to you –'.

Although your chief mark is her understanding; yet I would not have you quite drop your reflections on the plainness of her person: for, by continual teasing, you may possibly bring her to say something to the following effect: – That she could not help the plainness of her person: – That she endeavoured to be as contented as she could; but, in short, she did not much concern herself about the matter. – Then have you a double road for Teasing her still more on that head.

If she is clean and well dressed, you may put on a malicious sneer; and, looking her over from top to toe, you may noddle your head; and say, 'So Miss, considering you are a Wit, and a lady who despises all personal advantages, I must needs say you have tricked yourself out pretty handsomely to-day'. Then may you add, that you would hold a good wager, she was every day longer prinking[6] in the glass than you was. – But it was always so. – You had ever observed, that the ugliest women were much fonder of their persons, than the most beautiful.

If she fails, in the least particular, of nicety in dress, than have you the old beaten path before you: load her with the names of trollop, slattern, slut, dirty beast, &c. omit not any of those trite observations; that all Wits are slatterns; – that no girl ever delighted in reading, that was not a slut; – that well might the men say they would not for the world marry a Wit; that they had rather have a woman who could make a pudden, than one who could make a poem; – and that it was the ruin of all girls who had not independent fortunes, to have learnt either to read or write. You may tell her also, that she may thank God, that her ugliness will preserve her from being a whore. – Then conclude all these pious reflexions with thanking heaven, that, for your part, you are no Wit; and that you will take care your children shall not be of that stamp.

---

[6] *prink* "To prank; to deck for show" (Johnson, citing this passage).

PART THE SECOND
CHAPTER 2
TO THE WIFE

The common disposition with which a married couple generally come together (except for mere lucrative motives) is this.

The man, for some qualification, either personal or mental, which he sees, or dreams he sees, in some woman, fixes his affections on that woman: then, instead of endeavouring to fix her affections on himself, he directs all her thoughts, and her enjoyment, on settlements, equipage, fine clothes, and every other gratification of vanity within his power and fortune to give her. He pays so thorough an adoration and submission to her in all respects, that he soon perfects a work before half finished to his hands; namely, the making her completely and immoveably in love with – herself. – This puts her, for the present, into such good spirits, and good humour, that the poor man, from the pleasure he finds in her company, believes her to be in love with him. This thought, joined to his first inclination to her person, creates in him a pretty strong affection towards her, and gives her that power over him, which I would willingly assist her in exerting. This affection, when he becomes her husband, generally shows itself in real kindness. But as soon as all the joy arising from courtship is gone, the wife generally grows uneasy; her husband, being no longer her lover, grows disgustful to her; and, if she be a woman of violent passions, she turns fractious and sour; and a breach soon ensues. The husband may bluster, and rave, and talk of his authority and power, as much as he pleases; but it is very easy to grow into such a perfect disregard of such storms, that, by wrapping one's self up in a proper degree of contempt, they will blow as vainly over our heads, as the wind over our houses. Besides, if there are not emoluments enough in the husband's house, to make it worth while to bear the ill-humours raised by our own forward-ness, separation is the word; to which if a husband will not consent, a cause of cruelty against him, in Doctors Commons,[7] I will soon bring him to; for (as I have heard) the husband there, by paying the expenses of both sides, will be obliged, in a manner, to supply his wife with the means of carrying her own point, and will be glad therefore to make any conditions with her. But a woman of prudence will know when she is well; will take no such precipitate steps; but will rejoice in the discovery of her husband's great affection towards her, as a means for pursuing the course of Teasing and Tormenting, which I here recommend.

Oh the joy it is to have a good servant, cried Sophronia, who had not goodness of heart enough to be kind to any human creature, and whose joy must therefore arise from having a proper subject to torment! But with what ecstasy then, might the artful Livia cry out – Oh the joy it is to have a good husband! . . .

Besides nourishing in your mind an inveterate hatred against all your husband's relations and acquaintance, you may show the highest dislike to every place he was fond of before he married: but express the highest joy and raptures on the very mention of any place, that you used to live in yourself before your union with him; and be as lavish as possible of your praises of a single life. You may also, if your husband be not of a very jealous temper, hoard up a parcel of your favourite trinkets, as rings, snuffboxes, &c. which were given you before marriage; and let it appear, from your immoderate fondness for those baubles, that the givers of them are still nearest to your heart.

Carefully study your husband's temper, and find out what he likes, in order never to do any one thing that will please him.

---

7 *Doctors Commons*   a court of law near St Paul's.

If he expresses his approbation of the domestic qualities of a wife; such as family economy, and that old-fashioned female employment, the needle; neglect your family as much as ever his temper will bear; and always have your white gloves on your hand. Tell him, that every woman of spirit ought to hate and despise a man who could insist on his wife's being a family drudge; and declare, that you will not submit to be a cook and seamstress to any man. But if he loves company, and cheerful parties of pleasure, and would willingly have you always with him, insult him with your great love of needle-work and housewifery. Or should he be a man of genius, and should employ his leisure hours in writing, be sure to show a tasteless indifference to everything he shows you of his own. The same indifference, also, may you put on, if he should be a man who loves reading, and is of so communicative a disposition, as to take delight in reading to you any of our best and most entertaining authors. If, for instance, he desires you to hear one of Shakespeare's plays, you may give him perpetual interruptions, by sometimes going out of the room, sometimes ringing the bell to give orders for what cannot be wanted till the next day; at other times taking notice (if your children are in the room), that Molly's cap is awry, or that Jackey looks pale; and then begin questioning the child, whether he has done any thing to make himself sick. If you have needle-work in your hands, you may be so busy in cutting out, and measuring one part with another, that it will plainly appear to your husband, that you mind not one word he reads. If all this teases him enough to make him call on you for your attention, you may say, that indeed you have other things to mind besides poetry; and if he was uneasy at your taking care of your family and children, and mending *his* shirts, you wished he had a learned wife; and then he would soon see himself in a jail, and his family in rags. Fail not to be as eloquent as possible on this subject, for I could bring you numberless precedents of silly and illiterate wives, who have half talked their husbands to death, in exclaiming against the loquacity of ALL WOMEN, who have any share of understanding or knowledge . . .

If your husband, on observing you particularly fond of something at a friend's table, should desire you to get it for yourself at home, you may say, that you are so little selfish, that you cannot bear to provide any thing for your own eating; and this you may boldly declare, although it should be your common practice to provide some delicacy for yourself every day. It is most likely, that your husband will let this pass, but should he not, you may, on detection, fly to tears, and complaints of his cruelty and barbarity, in upbraiding you with so small an indulgence as that of a chicken, or a tart sometimes, for your own eating, when he knows, that your weak stomach will not give you leave to make the horse-like meals that he does.

If you manage this scene rightly, and sufficiently reiterate in your husband's ears the words *cruel, unkind, barbarous,* &c. he will, it is most likely, forget the true occasion of all this uproar; will begin to think he had been a little hard upon you in taking notice of a daily indulgence, which he himself had not only allowed, but requested you to accept; he will ask your pardon, and confess himself in fault, doubling his diligence for the future, in providing all sorts of rarities to gratify your palate.

Be it observed, that this knack of turning the tables, and forcing the offended person to ask pardon of the first aggressor, is one of the most ingenious strokes of our art, and may be practised in every connexion, where the power is founded in love.

CONCLUSION OF THE ESSAY

. . . I know that many learned and good men have taken great pains to undermine this our noble art, by laying down rules, and giving exemplars, in order to teach mankind to give no offence to any one, and instead of being a torment, to be as great a help and comfort to their friends, as it is in their power to be. But with infinite pleasure do I perceive, either that they are not much read, or, at least, that they have not the power of rooting from the human breast, that growing sprig of mischief there implanted with our birth; and generally, as we come to years of discretion, flourishing like a green palm-tree: yet, to show my great candour[8] and generosity to these my mortal (or rather moral) foes, I will endeavour, as far as my poor recommendation will go, to forward the sale of their books, even among my own pupils. For if, my good scholars, you will guard your minds against the doctrines they intend to teach; if you will consider them as mere amusements; you have my leave to peruse them. Or rather, if you will only remember to observe my orders, in acting in direct opposition to all that a Swift, an Addison, a Richardson, a Fielding, or any other good ethical writer intended to teach, you may (by referring sometimes to these my rules, as helps to your memory) become as profound adepts in this Art, as any of the readers of Mr. Hoyle are in the science of whist.[9]

Great are the disputes amongst the learned, whether man, as an animal, be a savage and ferocious, or a gentle and social beast. Swift's picture, in his Yahoos,[10] gives us not a very favourable view of the natural disposition of the animal man; yet I remember not, that he supposes him naturally to delight in tormenting; nor does he make him guilty of any vices, but following his brutish appetites. Must not this love of Tormenting therefore be cultivated and cherished? There are many tastes, as that of the olive, the oyster, with several high sauces, cooked up with assa foetida and the like, which are at first disgustful to the palate, but when once a man has so far depraved his natural taste, as to get a relish for those dainties, there is nothing he is half so fond of.

I can recollect but one kind of brute, that seems to have any notion of this pleasant practice of Tormenting; and that is the cat, when she has got a mouse – She delays the gratification of her hunger, which prompted her to seek for food, and triumphs in her power over her wretched captive – She not only sticks her claws into it, making it feel the sharpness of her teeth (without touching the vitals enough to render it insensible to her tricks), but she tosses it over her head in sport, seems in the highest joy imaginable, and is also, to all appearance, at that very time, the sweetest, best-humoured animal in the world. Yet should anything approach her, that she fears will rob her of her play-thing (holding her prey fast in her teeth), she swears, she growls, and shows all the savage motions of her heart. As soon as her fears are over, she again resumes her sport; and is, in this one instance only, kinder to her victim, than her imitators men, that by death she at lasts puts a final end to the poor wretch's torments.

Was I to rack my invention and memory for ever, I could not find a more adequate picture of the true lovers of Tormenting than this sportive cat: nor will I tire my reader's patience longer, than to add this further precept:

REMEMBER ALWAYS TO DO UNTO EVERY ONE, WHAT YOU WOULD LEAST WISH TO HAVE DONE UNTO YOURSELF; for in this is contained the whole of our excellent SCIENCE.

---

[8]   *candour* kindness, mildness.
[9]   *Hoyle ... whist* Edmund Hoyle (1672–1769) author of treatises on whist and other card games.

[10] *Swift's picture, in his Yahoos* *Gulliver's Travels*, Book 4.

Madam Johnson

Although her portrait appears on the frontispiece of her book, I have been unable to identify Madam Johnson. Whoever she was, she produced a handbook for women of the mid-eighteenth century that says a great deal about how they were encouraged to see themselves, especially as they made the transition from girls to married women. The following excerpt is one of many mnemonics in the book for inculcating proper behaviour, but the title says as much as any other part of the book about its tone and contents.

from *Madam JOHNSON's Present:*
Or, the best
INSTRUCTIONS
FOR
YOUNG WOMEN,
IN
Useful and Universal KNOWLEDGE.
WITH A
Summary of the late Marriage Act,
and Instructions how to marry pursuant thereto (1754)

Select PRUDENTIAL MAXIMS, *in Prose and Verse; alphabetically disposed for the Ease of* Young Women's *Memories, and their further Improvement in the Art of* WRITING *First Set, in single Lines.*

A	Art polishes and improves Nature.
B	Beauty is a fair, but fading Flower.
C	Content alone is true Happiness.
D	Delays often ruin the best Designs.
E	Encouragement is the Life of Action.
F	Fortune is a fair but fickle Mistress.
G	Grandeur is no true Happiness.
H	Health is Life's choicest Blessing.
I	Indolence is the Inlet to every Vice.
K	Knowledge is a godlike Attribute.
L	Liberty is an invaluable Blessing.
M	Modest Merit finds but few Admirers.
N	Necessity is the Mother of Invention.
O	One bad Sheep infects the whole Flock.
P	Pride is a Passion not made for Man.
Q	Quick Resentments prove often fatal.
R	Riches are precarious Blessings.
S	Self-Love is the Bane of Society.
T	The Hope of Reward sweetens Labour.
V	Variety is the Beauty of the World.

W	Wisdom is more valuable than Riches.
X	'Xcess kills more than the Sword.
Y	Yesterday mispent can never be recalled.
Z	Zeal misapplied is pious Frenzy.

David Hume (1711–1776)

Hume's short autobiographical sketch, "My Own Life," makes up the bulk of my minor offering from this major philosopher and supplies sufficient biographical information. The piece was considered offensive by many people at the time because it stresses Hume's composure in the face of death despite his lack of belief in the Christian dispensation. Hume's atheism was a matter more of personal conviction than public exposition. His works are philosophical, what we would call psychological, historical, and social. They do not talk about theology; they just exclude it. The work for which he is now best known was his first and least successful, A Treatise of Human Nature: Being an Attempt to Introduce the Experimental Method of Reasoning into Moral Subjects *(1739). Book 1 treats the understanding and establishes an empirical epistemology that is even more thoroughgoing than Locke's. Book 3 is about morals and largely focuses on the concept of justice. Best of all, however, is the centerpiece of the central book on the passions, the discussion of pride. Pride and humility are simple, unanalyzable passions, for Hume, the causes of which, being constant and uniform through the ages, provide an unmoving Sun for his moral Copernican revolution. Here, surely, is a landmark in the emergence of everything, good and ill, that we call modern.*

The pieces presented here are from Hume's far more successful and very variously republished essays. "Of the Liberty of the Press" was one of Hume's first essays; it suggests how very much his career and his approach to the world was that of writer working in an environment that permitted and even fostered the profession of writing. The text is based on that in Essays Moral and Political *(1742); The autobiographical essay speaks for itself. The text is based on its first publication in* Essays and Treatises on Several Subjects *(1777).*

from *Essays Moral and Political* (1742)

OF THE LIBERTY OF THE PRESS

Nothing is more apt to surprise a foreigner, than the extreme liberty, which we enjoy in this country, of communicating whatever we please to the public, and of openly censuring every measure, entered into by the king or his ministers. If the administration resolve upon war, it is affirmed, that, either wilfully or ignorantly, they mistake the interests of the nation, and that peace, in the present situation of affairs, is infinitely preferable. If the passion of the ministers lie towards peace, our political writers breathe nothing but war and devastation, and represent the pacific conduct of the government as mean and pusillanimous. As this liberty is not indulged in any other government, either republican or monarchical; in HOLLAND and VENICE, more than in FRANCE or SPAIN; it may very naturally give occasion to a question, 'How it happens that GREAT BRITAIN alone enjoys this peculiar privilege? And whether the unlimited exercise of this liberty be advantageous or prejudicial to the public?'

The reason, why the laws indulge us in such a liberty seems to be derived from our mixed form of government, which is neither wholly monarchical, nor wholly republican. It will be found, if I mistake not, a true observation in politics, that the two extremes in government, liberty and slavery, commonly approach nearest to each other; and that, as you depart from the extremes, and mix a little of monarchy with liberty, the government becomes always the more free; and on the other hand, when you mix a little of liberty with monarchy, the yoke becomes always the more grievous and intolerable. In a government, such as that of FRANCE, which is absolute, and where law, custom, and religion concur, all of them, to make people fully satisfied with their condition, the monarch cannot entertain any *jealousy*[1] against his subjects, and therefore is apt to indulge them in great *liberties* both of speech and action. In a government altogether republican, such as that of HOLLAND, where there is no magistrate so eminent as to give *jealousy* to the state, there is no danger in entrusting the magistrates with large discretionary powers; and though many advantages result from such powers, in preserving peace and order, yet they lay a considerable restraint on men's actions, and make every private citizen pay a great respect to the government. Thus it seems evident, that the two extremes of absolute monarchy and of a republic, approach near to each other in some material circumstances. In the *first,* the magistrate has no jealousy of the people: in the *second*, the people have none of the magistrate: Which want of jealousy begets a mutual confidence and trust in both cases, and produces a species of liberty in monarchies, and of arbitrary power in republics.

To justify the other part of the foregoing observation, that, in every government, the means are most wide of each other, and that the mixtures of monarchy and liberty render the yoke more easy or more grievous; I must take notice of a remark in TACITUS with regard to the ROMANS under the emperors, that they neither could bear total slavery not total liberty, *Nec totam servitutem, nec totam libertatem pati possunt*. This remark a celebrated poet has translated and applied to the ENGLISH, in his lively description of queen ELIZABETH's policy and government,

> Et fit aimer son joug a l'Anglois indompté,
> Qui ne peut ni servir, ni vivre en liberté.
> > HENRIADE, *liv.* 1.[2]

According to these remarks, we are to consider the ROMAN government under the emperors as a mixture of despotism and liberty, where the despotism prevailed; and the ENGLISH government as a mixture of the same kind, where the liberty predominates. The consequences are conformable to the foregoing observation; and such as may be expected from those mixed forms of government, which beget a mutual watchfulness and jealousy. The ROMAN emperors were, many of them, the most frightful tyrants that ever disgraced human nature; and it is evident, that their cruelty was chiefly excited by their *jealousy,* and by their observing that all the great men of ROME bore with impatience the dominion of a family, which, but a little before, was no wise superior to their own. On the other hand, as the republican part of the government prevails in ENGLAND, though with a great mixture of monarchy, it is obliged, for its own preservation, to maintain a watchful *jealousy* over the

---

OF THE LIBERTY OF THE PRESS
[1] *Jealousy* "suspicious fear" (Johnson).

[2] *Henriade Book 1* Voltaire's epic, first published in England (1729) and dedicated to Queen Caroline: "She made her reign agreeable to the untamed English, who could neither serve nor live free."

magistrates, to remove all discretionary powers, and to secure every one's life and fortune by general and inflexible laws. No action must be deemed a crime but what the law has plainly determined to be such: No crime must be imputed to a man but from a legal proof before his judges; and even these judges must be his fellow-subjects, who are obliged, by their own interest, to have a watchful eye over the encroachments and violence of the ministers. From these causes it proceeds, that there is as much liberty, and, even, perhaps, licentiousness in GREAT BRITAIN, as there were formerly slavery and tyranny in ROME.

These principles account for the great liberty of the press in these kingdoms, beyond what is indulged in any other government. 'Tis sufficiently known that arbitrary power would steal in upon us, were we not careful to prevent its progress, and were there not an easy method of conveying the alarm from one end of the kingdom to the other. The spirit of the people must frequently be roused, in order to curb the ambition of the court; and the dread of rousing this spirit must be employed to prevent that ambition. Nothing so effectual to this purpose as the liberty of the press, by which all the learning, wit, and genius of the nation may be employed on the side of freedom, and every one be animated to its defence. As long, therefore, as the republican part of our government can maintain itself against the monarchical, it will naturally be careful to keep the press open, as of importance to its own preservation.

Since[3] therefore that liberty is so essential to the support of our mixed government; this sufficiently decides the second question, 'Whether such a liberty be advantageous or prejudicial'; there being nothing of greater importance in every state than the preservation of the ancient government, especially if it be a free one. But I would fain go a step further, and assert, that this liberty is attended with so few inconveniencies, that it may be claimed as the common right of mankind, and ought to be indulged them almost in every government: except the ecclesiastical, to which indeed it would prove fatal. We need not dread from this liberty any such ill consequences as followed from the harangues of the popular demagogues of ATHENS and tribunes of ROME. A man reads a book or pamphlet alone and coolly. There is none present from whom he can catch the passion by contagion. He is not hurried away by the force and energy of action. And should he be wrought up to ever so seditious a humour, there is no violent resolution presented to him, by which he can immediately vent his passion. The liberty of the press, therefore, however abused, can scarce ever excite popular tumults or rebellion. And as to those murmurs or secret discontents it may occasion, 'tis better they should get vent in words, that they may come to the knowledge of the magistrate before it be too late, in order to his providing a remedy against them. Mankind, it is true, have always a greater propension to believe what is said to the disadvantage of their governors, than the contrary; but this inclination is inseparable from them, whether they have liberty or not. A whisper may fly as quick, and be as pernicious as a pamphlet. Nay, it will be more pernicious, where men are not accustomed to think freely, or distinguish between truth and falsehood.

It has also been found, as the experience of mankind increases, that the *people* are no such dangerous monster as they have been represented, and that it is in every respect better to guide them, like rational creatures, than to lead or drive them, like brute beasts. Before the United Provinces set the example, toleration was deemed incompatible with good government; and it was thought impossible, that a number of religious sects could live together in harmony and peace, and have all of them an equal affection to their common country, and to each other. ENGLAND has set a like example of civil liberty; and though this liberty seems

---

[3] *Since* . . . Hume omitted the following two paragraphs in his revision of 1770.

to occasion some small ferment at present, it has not as yet produced any pernicious effects; and it is to be hoped, that men, being every day more accustomed to the free discussion of public affairs, will improve in the judgement of them, and be with greater difficulty seduced by every idle rumour and popular clamour.

It is a very comfortable reflection to the lovers of liberty, that this peculiar privilege of BRITAIN is of a kind that cannot easily by wrested from us, but must last as long as our government remains, in any degree, free and independent. It is seldom, that liberty of any kind is lost all at once. Slavery has so frightful an aspect to men accustomed to freedom, that it must steal upon them by degrees, and must disguise itself in a thousand shapes, in order to be received. But, if the liberty of the press ever be lost, it must be lost at once. The general laws against sedition and libelling are at present as strong as they possibly can be made. Nothing can impose a further restraint, but either the clapping an IMPRIMATUR[4] upon the press, or the giving to the court very large discretionary powers to punish whatever displeases them. But these concessions would be such a bare-faced violation of liberty, that they will probably be the last efforts of a despotic government. We may conclude, that the liberty of *Britain* is gone for ever when these attempts shall succeed.

from *Essays and Treatises on Several Subjects* (1777)

MY OWN LIFE

It is difficult for a man to speak long of himself without vanity; therefore, I shall be short. It may be thought an instance of vanity that I pretend at all to write my life; but this Narrative shall contain little more than the History of my Writings; as, indeed, almost all my life has been spent in literary pursuits and occupations. The first success of most of my writings was not such as to be an object of vanity.

I was born the 26th of April 1711, old style,[1] at Edinburgh. I was of a good family, both by father and mother: my father's family is a branch of the Earl of Home's, or Hume's; and my ancestors had been proprietors of the estate, which my brother possesses, for several generations. My mother was daughter of Sir David Falconer, President of the College of Justice: the title of Lord Halkerton came by succession to her brother.

My family, however, was not rich, and being myself a younger brother, my patrimony, according to the mode of my country, was of course very slender. My father, who passed for a man of parts,[2] died when I was an infant, leaving me, with an elder brother and a sister, under the care of our mother, a woman of singular merit, who, though young and handsome, devoted herself entirely to the rearing and educating of her children. I passed through the ordinary course of education with success, and was seized very early with a passion for literature, which has been the ruling passion of my life, and the great source of my enjoyments. My studious disposition, my sobriety, and my industry, gave my family a notion that the law was a proper profession for me; but I found an insurmountable aversion to every thing but the pursuits of philosophy and general learning; and while they fancied I was

---

[4]   *IMPRIMATUR* "let it be printed," the indication of papal permission to print, applied to other forms of licensing.

MY OWN LIFE
[1]   *old style* according to the old Julian calendar, which was eleven days short of the reformed Gregorian calendar.
[2]   *a man of parts* a talented, resourceful man.

poring upon Voet and Vinnius,[3] Cicero and Virgil were the authors which I was secretly devouring.

My very slender fortune, however, being unsuitable to this plan of life, and my health being a little broken by my ardent application, I was tempted, or rather forced, to make a very feeble trial for entering into a more active scene of life. In 1734, I went to Bristol, with some recommendations to eminent merchants, but in a few months found that scene totally unsuitable to me. I went over to France, with a view of prosecuting my studies in a country retreat; and I there laid that plan of life, which I have steadily and successfully pursued. I resolved to make a very rigid frugality supply my deficiency of fortune, to maintain unimpaired my independency, and to regard every object as contemptible, except the improvement of my talents in literature.

During my retreat in France, first at Reims, but chiefly at La Fleche, in Anjou, I composed my *Treatise of Human Nature*. After passing three years very agreeably in that country, I came over to London in 1737. In the end of 1738, I published my Treatise, and immediately went down to my mother and my brother, who lived at his country house, and was employing himself very judiciously and successfully in the improvement of his fortune.

Never literary attempt was more unfortunate than my Treatise of Human Nature. It fell *dead-born from the press*, without reaching such distinction, as even to excite a murmur among the zealots. But being naturally of a cheerful and sanguine temper, I very soon recovered the blow, and prosecuted with great ardour my studies to the contrary. In 1742 I printed at Edinburgh the first part of my Essays: the work was favourably received, and soon made me entirely forget my former disappointment. I continued with my mother and brother in the country, and in that time recovered the knowledge of the Greek language, which I had too much neglected in my early youth.

In 1745, I received a letter from the Marquis of Annandale, inviting me to come and live with him in England; I found also, that the friends and family of that young nobleman were desirous of putting him under my care and direction, for the state of his mind and health required it. I lived with him a twelvemonth. My appointments during that time made a considerable accession to my small fortune. I then received an invitation from General St. Clair to attend him as a secretary to his expedition, which was at first meant against Canada, but ended in an incursion on the coast of France. Next year, to wit, 1747, I received an invitation from the General to attend him in the same station in his military embassy to the courts of Vienna and Turin. I then wore the uniform of an officer, and was introduced at these courts as aide-de-camp to the general, along with Sir Harry Erskine and Captain Grant, now General Grant. These two years were almost the only interruptions which my studies have received during the course of my life: I passed them agreeably and in good company; and my appointments, with my frugality, had made me reach a fortune, which I called independent, though most of my friends were inclined to smile when I said so; in short, I was now master of near a thousand pounds.

I had always entertained a notion, that my want of success in publishing the Treatise of Human Nature, had proceeded more from the manner than the matter, and that I had been guilty of a very usual indiscretion, in going to the press too early. I, therefore, cast the first part of that work anew in the Enquiry concerning Human Understanding, which was

---

[3] *Voet and Vinnius* the legal writers Voetius
Gysbertus (1588–1676) and Arnold Vinnen (Vinnius)
(1588–1657).

published while I was at Turin. But this piece was at first little more successful than the Treatise of Human Nature. On my return from Italy, I had the mortification to find all England in a ferment, on account of Dr. Middleton's Free Enquiry,[4] while my performance was entirely overlooked and neglected. A new edition, which had been published at London, of my Essays, moral and political, met not with a much better reception.

Such is the force of natural temper, that these disappointments made little or no impression on me. I went down in 1749, and lived two years with my brother at his country house, for my mother was now dead. I there composed the second part of my Essays, which I called Political Discourses, and also my Enquiry concerning the Principles of Morals, which is another part of my treatise that I cast anew. Meanwhile, my bookseller, A. Millar, informed me, that my former publications (all but the unfortunate Treatise) were beginning to be the subject of conversation; that the sale of them was gradually increasing, and that new editions were demanded. Answers by Reverends, and Right Reverends, came out two or three in a year; and I found, by Dr. Warburton's railing,[5] that the books were beginning to be esteemed in good company. However, I had fixed a resolution, which I inflexibly maintained, never to reply to anybody; and not being very irascible in my temper, I have easily kept myself clear of all literary squabbles. These symptoms of a rising reputation gave me encouragement, as I was ever more disposed to see the favourable than unfavourable side of things; a turn of mind which it is more happy to possess, than to be born to an estate of ten thousand a year.

In 1751, I removed from the country to the town, the true scene for a man of letters. In 1752, were published at Edinburgh, where I then lived, my Political Discourses, the only work of mine that was succesful on the first publication. It was well received abroad and at home. In the same year was published at London, my Enquiry concerning the Principles of Morals; which, in my own opinion (who ought not to judge on that subject), is of all my writings, historical, philosophical, or literary, incomparably the best. It came unnoticed and unobserved into the world.

In 1752, the Faculty of Advocates chose me their Librarian, an office from which I received little or no emolument, but which gave me the command of a large library. I then formed the plan of writing the History of England; but being frightened with the notion of continuing a narrative through a period of 1700 years, I commenced with the accession of the House of Stuart, an epoch when, I thought, the misrepresentations of faction began chiefly to take place. I was, I own, sanguine in my expectation of the success of this work. I thought that I was the only historian, that had at once neglected present power, interest, and authority, and the cry of popular prejudices; and as the subject was suited to every capacity, I expected proportional applause. But miserable was my disappointment: I was assailed by one cry of reproach, disapprobation, and even detestation; English, Scotch, and Irish, Whig and Tory, churchman and sectary,[6] free-thinker[7] and religionist, patriot[8] and courtier, united in their rage against the man, who had presumed to shed a generous tear for the fate of Charles I and the Earl of Strafford;[9] and after the first ebullitions of their fury were over, what was still more mortifying, the book seemed to sink into oblivion. Mr. Millar told me, that in a twelvemonth

---

[4] *Dr. Middleton's Free Enquiry* Conyers Middleton (1683–1750), author of *A Free Inquiry into Miracles* (1748).

[5] *Dr. Warburton* William (1698–1779), later Bishop of Gloucester, editor of Shakespeare and Pope as well as a theological writer.

[6] *sectary* one who belongs to a sect, a different church than the Church of England.

[7] *free-thinker* one who stresses reason in theology over faith.

[8] *patriot* an opponent of the (Hanoverian) court, its government and its proponents or courtiers.

[9] *Earl of Strafford* Thomas Wentworth, executed by Parliament in 1641.

he sold only forty-five copies of it. I scarcely, indeed, heard of one man in the three kingdoms,[10] considerable for rank of letters, that could endure the book. I must only except the primate of England, Dr. Herring, and the primate of Ireland, Dr. Stone, which seem two odd exceptions. These dignified prelates separately sent me messages not to be discouraged.

I was, however, I confess, discouraged; and had not the war been at that time breaking out between France and England,[11] I had certainly retired to some provincial town of the former kingdom, have changed my name, and never more have returned to my native country. But as this scheme was not now practicable, and the subsequent volume was considerably advanced, I resolved to pick up courage and to persevere.

In this interval, I published at London my Natural History of Religion, along with some other small pieces: its public entry was rather obscure, except only that Dr. Hurd[12] wrote a pamphlet against it, with all the illiberal petulance, arrogance, and scurrility which distinguish the Warburtonian school. This pamphlet gave me some consolation for the otherwise indifferent reception of my performance.

In 1756, two years after the fall of the first volume, was published the second volume of my History, containing the period from the death of Charles I till the Revolution. This performance happened to give less displeasure to the Whigs, and was better received. It not only rose itself, but helped to buoy up its unfortunate brother.

But though I had been taught by experience, that the Whig party were in possession of bestowing all places, both in the state and in literature, I was so little inclined to yield to their senseless clamour, that in about a hundred alterations, which further study, reading, or reflection engaged me to make in the reigns of the first two Stuarts, I have made all of them invariably to the Tory side. It is ridiculous to consider the English constitution before that period as a regular plan of liberty.

In 1759, I published my History of the House of Tudor. The clamour against this performance was almost equal to that against the History of the two first Stuarts. The reign of Elizabeth was particularly obnoxious. But I was now callous against the impressions of public folly, and continued very peaceably and contentedly in my retreat at Edinburgh, to finish, in two volumes, the more early part of the English History, which I gave to the public in 1761, with tolerable, and but tolerable success.

But, notwithstanding this variety of winds and seasons, to which my writings had been exposed, they had still been making such advances, that the copy-money[13] given me by the booksellers, much exceeded any thing formerly known in England; I was become not only independent, but opulent. I retired to my native country of Scotland, determined never more to set my foot out of it; and retaining the satisfaction of never having preferred[14] a request to one great man, or even making advances of friendship to any of them. As I was now turned of fifty, I thought of passing all the rest of my life in this philosophical manner, when I received, in 1763, an invitation from the Earl of Hertford, with whom I was not in the least acquainted, to attend him on his embassy to Paris, with a near prospect of being appointed secretary to the embassy; and, in the meanwhile of performing the functions of that office. This offer, however inviting, I at first declined, both because I was reluctant to begin

---

[10] *the three kingdoms* England, Scotland, and Ireland.
[11] *war . . . France and England* the Seven Years War, known in America as the French and Indian War.
[12] *Dr. Hurd* Richard Hurd (1720–1808), editor of Horace, colleague of Warburton and author of

theological, literary, and political essays; later Bishop of Worcester.
[13] *copy-money* payment by a publisher to an author for his manuscript or for the copyright.
[14] *prefer* "To offer solemnly; to propose publicly; to exhibit" (Johnson).

connections with the great, and because I was afraid that the civilities and gay company of Paris, would prove disagreeable to a person of my age and humour: but on his lordship's repeating the invitation, I accepted of it. I have every reason, both of pleasure and interest, to think myself happy in my connections with that nobleman, as well as afterwards with his brother, General Conway.

Those who have not seen the strange effects of modes,[15] will never imagine the reception I met with at Paris, from men and women of all ranks and stations. The more I resiled[16] from their excessive civilities, the more I was loaded with them. There is, however, a real satisfaction in living at Paris, from the great number of sensible, knowing, and polite company with which that city abounds above all places in the universe. I thought once of settling there for life.

I was appointed secretary to the embassy; and in summer 1765, Lord Hertford left me, being appointed Lord Lieutenant of Ireland. I was *chargé d'affaires* till the arrival of the Duke of Richmond, towards the end of the year. In the beginning of 1766, I left Paris, and next summer went to Edinburgh, with the same view as formerly, of burying myself in a philosophical retreat. I returned to that place, not richer, but with much more money, and a much larger income, by means of Lord Hertford's friendship, than I left it; and I was desirous of trying what superfluity could produce, as I had formerly made an experiment of a competency.[17] But in 1767, I received from Mr. Conway an invitation to be Under-secretary; and this invitation, both the character of the person, and my connections with Lord Hertford, prevented me from declining. I returned to Edinburgh in 1769, very opulent (for I possessed a revenue of £1,000 a year), healthy, and though somewhat stricken in years, with the prospect of enjoying long my ease, and of seeing the increase of my reputation.

In spring 1775, I was struck with a disorder in my bowels, which at first gave me no alarm, but has since, as I apprehend it, become mortal and incurable. I now reckon upon a speedy dissolution.[18] I have suffered very little pain from my disorder; and what is more strange, have, notwithstanding the great decline of my person, never suffered a moment's abatement of my spirits; insomuch, that were I to name the period of my life, which I should most choose to pass over again, I might be tempted to point to this latter period. I possess the same ardour as ever in study, and the same gaiety in company. I consider, besides, that a man of sixty-five, by dying, cuts off only a few years of infirmities; and though I see many symptoms of my literary reputation's breaking out at last with additional lustre, I know that I could have but few years to enjoy it. It is difficult to be more detached from life than I am at present.

To conclude historically with my own character. I am, or rather was (for that is the style I must now use in speaking of myself, which emboldens me the more to speak my senti-ments); I was, I say, a man of mild dispositions, of command of temper, of an open, social, and cheerful humour, capable of attachment, but little susceptible of enmity, and of great moderation in all my passions. Even my love of literary fame, my ruling passion, never soured my temper, notwithstanding my frequent disappointments. My company was not unaccept-able to the young and careless, as well as to the studious and literary; and as I took a particular pleasure in the company of modest women, I had no reason to be displeased with the reception I met with from them. In a word, though most men anywise eminent, have found

---

[15]   *mode*   "Fashion; custom" (Johnson).
[16]   *resiled*   drew back (a Scottish usage).
[17]   *competency*   "Such a fortune as, without exuberance, is equal to the necessities of life" (Johnson).

[18]   *dissolution*   "Death; the resolution of the body into its constituent elements" (Johnson).

reason to complain of calumny, I never was touched, or even attacked by her baleful tooth: and though, I wantonly exposed myself to the rage of both civil and religious factions, they seemed to be disarmed in my behalf of their wonted[19] fury. My friends never had occasion to vindicate any one circumstance of my character and conduct: not but that the zealots, we may well suppose, would have been glad to invent and propagate any story to my disadvantage, but they could never find any which they thought would wear the face of probability. I cannot say there is no vanity in making this funeral oration of myself, but I hope it is not a misplaced one; and this is a matter of fact which is easily cleared and ascertained.

APRIL 18, 1776.[20]

Thomas Gray (1716–1771)

Gray was the only one of his mother's twelve children to survive infancy, and he himself was somewhat weak and sickly throughout his life. His father was a brutal, abusive husband against whom his mother unsuccessfully sought legal redress. At the age of eleven Gray went to Eton College, where his mother's brother was a master. He formed important relationships there with classmates Richard West and Horace Walpole, who were also interested in cultivating their minds and avoiding physical education. Gray went to Cambridge, toured Europe with Walpole, and returned to Cambridge, where he spent most of his life in quiet retirement and scholarship. He had a circle of friends, but he never married and perhaps never formed an intimate attachment after the death of West in 1742 (though late in life he was briefly infatuated with a young Swiss scholar named Bonstetten). He was evidently shy and somewhat fussy; he was frightened of fire and kept a rope ladder in his rooms at Peterhouse College, Cambridge. The young men of the college once tormented him by pretending there was a fire and had the pleasure of seeing him descend his rope ladder into a tub of cold water, which they had strategically positioned under his window.

The death of West evidently galvanized Gray and got him writing poetry. But his real inclination was for study rather than production, and he only published thirteen poems in his lifetime. One of these, however, was An Elegy Wrote in a Country Church Yard *(1751). Gray published the poem reluctantly when it was about to be pirated, and he said little about it the rest of his life. However, the work was an immediate critical and popular success: there were twelve editions in the next twelve years, and it was stolen by numerous magazines all over England. Memorization of the poem was required in many British schools literally for centuries, and it is one of the best known English poems in the world. It is certainly a large part of the reason that Gray was offered the post of poet laureate, which he immediately rejected, even though the government was willing to excuse him from the duty of writing birthday odes for the King. Gray preferred retirement and study. In 1757 he published two poems about which he really cared, a pair of Pindaric odes, "The Progress of Poetry" and "The Bard." These works are even more learned and more highly allusive than Gray's other works, and they did not achieve popularity. From 1759, Gray spent three years doing research at the newly opened British Library, but sent most of his notes on a prospective history of English literature to Thomas Warton, who was a much more productive scholar. Gray left behind many other unfinished projects, and when Samuel Johnson wrote the*

---

[19] *wonted* usual, customary.   [20] APRIL 18, 1776 Hume died on 25 August 1776.

preface to his works about 1781, ten years after Gray's death, the professional writer was somewhat contemptuous of the fussy and pampered academic: "As a writer," says Johnson, Gray "had this peculiarity, that he did not write his pieces first rudely, and then correct them, but laboured every line as it arose in the train of his composition; and he had a notion not very peculiar, that he could not write but at certain times, or at happy moments; a fantastic foppery, to which my kindness for a man of learning and virtue wishes him to have been superior." Johnson was not a great admirer of Gray's poetry, much of which he considered inaccessible to the "common reader," but he closed his life of Gray by saying, "The Church-yard abounds with images which find a mirror in every mind, and with sentiments to which every bosom returns an echo. The four stanzas beginning 'Yet even these bones' are to me original: I have never seen the notions in any other place; yet he that reads them here, persuades himself that he has always felt them. Had Gray written often thus, it had been vain to blame, and useless to praise him."

As the bases of the following texts I have used first editions supplemented by versions in the collection of his works assembled under Gray's direction in 1768. I have benefited from the collations in the edition by H. W. Starr and J. R. Hendrickson (Clarendon Press, 1966). I have also learned a great deal and borrowed some from the extensive commentary by Roger Lonsdale in The Poems of Gray, Collins, and Goldsmith *(Longman, 1969). The text of Gray's letter to Richard West is based on* The Correspondence of Thomas Gray, *ed. Paget Toynbee and Leonard Whibley, 3 vols, Clarendon Press, 1933.*

Letter to Richard West[1]
Florence, 21 April 1741

I know not what degree of satisfaction it will give you to be told that we shall set out from hence the 24th of this month, and not stop above a fortnight at any place in our way. This I feel, that you are the principal pleasure I have to hope for in my own country. Try at least to make me imagine myself not indifferent to you; for I must own I have the vanity of desiring somebody should be one whom I esteem as much as I do you. As I am recommending myself to your love, methinks I ought to send you my picture (for I am no more what I was, some circumstances excepted, which I hope I need not particularize to you); you must add then, to your former idea, two years of age, reasonable quantity of dullness, a great deal of silence, and something that rather resembles, than is, thinking; a confused notion of many strange and fine things that have swum before my eyes for some time, a want of love for general society, indeed an inability to it. On the good side you may add a sensibility for what others feel, and indulgence for their faults or weaknesses, a love of truth, and detestation of every thing else. Then you are to deduct a little impertinence, a little laughter, a great deal of pride, and some spirits. These are all the alteration I know of, you perhaps may find more. Think not that I have been obliged for this reformation of manners to reason or reflection, but to a severer school-mistress, Experience. One has little merit in learning her lessons, for one cannot well help it; but they are more useful than others, and imprint themselves in the very heart. I find I have been haranguing in the style of the Son of Sirach,[2] so shall finish here, and

LETTER TO RICHARD WEST
[1] *Richard West* Gray's classmate at Eton and close friend; he died 1 June 1742 at the age of twenty-five; Gray wrote frequently to West during the two years he spent touring the Continent as the guest of another Eton classmate, Horace Walpole; by the time Gray wrote this letter, the two had separated because of irreconcilable differences of style in traveling.
[2] *Son of Sirach* the author of Ecclesiasticus, a book of wisdom in the Apocrypha.

tell you that our route is settled as follows: First to Bologna for a few days, to hear the Viscontina[3] sing; next to Reggio, where is a Fair. Now, you must know, a Fair here is not a place where one eats gingerbread or rides upon hobby-horses; here are no musical clocks, nor tall Leicestershire women; one has nothing but masking, gaming, and singing. If you love operas, there will be the most splendid in Italy, four tip-top voices, a new theatre, the Duke and Duchess in all their pomps and vanities. Does not this sound magnificent? Yet is the city of Reggio[4] but one step above Old Brentford.[5] Well; next to Venice by the 11th of May, there to see the old Doge[6] wed the Adriatic Whore. Then to Verona, so to Milan, so to Marseilles, so to Lyons, so to Paris, so to West, &c. in sæcula sæculorum.[7] Amen.

Sonnet [on the Death of Mr Richard West][1] (1742)

In vain to me the smiling Mornings shine,
And red'ning Phoebus lifts his golden Fire:
The Birds in vain their amorous descant join;[2]
Or cheerful Fields resume their green attire:
These ears, alas! for other notes repine,   5
A different object do these eyes require.
My lonely anguish melts no heart, but mine;
And in my Breast the imperfect joys expire.
Yet Morning smiles the busy race to cheer,
And new-born Pleasure brings to happier Men: 10
The Fields to all their wonted tribute bear:[3]
To warm their little loves the birds complain:
I fruitless mourn to him, that cannot hear,
And weep the more, because I weep in vain.

Ode on the Death of a Favourite Cat[1] (1748)

I

'Twas on a lofty vase's side,
Where China's gayest art had dyed
The azure flowers, that blow;
Demurest of the Tabby kind,
The pensive Selima reclined,   5
Gazed on the lake below.

---

[3] *Viscontina* Caterina Visconti.
[4] *Reggio* the city where Walpole and Gray quarreled and parted ways.
[5] *Brentford* a proverbially ugly town about ten miles west of London.
[6] *Doge* Luigi Pisani, Doge (ruler) of Venice 1735–41.
[7] *in sæcula sæculorum* forever and forever.
SONNET [ON THE DEATH OF MR RICHARD WEST]
[1] Gray wrote this poem in August 1742 about two months after the death of his close friend; the sonnet was

not published in Gray's lifetime, and he evidently did not think highly of it. The text is that of the first printing, in William Mason's edition of Gray's poems (1775).
[2] *amorous descant* see *Paradise Lost* 4.603.
[3] *wonted* customary.
ODE ON THE DEATH OF A FAVOURITE CAT
[1] The text is based on that in *A Collection of Poems by Several Hands*, ed. Robert Dodsley, 3 vols (1748) with a few widely accepted changes from later editions.

2

Her conscious tail her joy declared;
The fair round face, the snowy beard,
   The velvet of her paws,
The coat that with the tortoise vies,   10
Her ears of jet, and emerald eyes,
   She saw; and purred applause.

3

Still had she gazed: but 'midst the tide
Two angel forms were seen to glide,
   The Genii of the stream:[2]   15
Their scaly armour's Tyrian hue[3]
Through richest purple to the view
   Betrayed a golden gleam.

4

The hapless nymph with wonder saw:
A whisker first and then a claw,   20
   With many an ardent wish,
She stretched in vain to reach the prize.
What female heart can gold despise?
   What cat's averse to fish?

5

Presumptuous maid! with looks intent   25
Again she stretched, again she bent,
   Nor knew the gulf between;
(Malignant fate sat by and smiled)
The slipp'ry verge her feet beguiled.
   She tumbled headlong in.   30

6

Eight times emerging from the flood
She mewed to every watry God,
   Some speedy aid to send.
No Dolphin came, no Nereid stirred:
Nor cruel Tom, nor Harry heard.[4]   35
A favourite has no friend![5]

---

[2] *Genii* plural of *genius*, "The protecting or ruling power of men, places, or things" (Johnson).
[3] *Tyrian* purple, a color produced from shellfish near the eastern Mediterranean city of Tyre.

[4] *Harry* other editions read "Susan"; all three are stereotypical servants' names.
[5] *favourite* the meaning includes "One chosen as a companion by his superior; a mean wretch whose whole business is by any means to please" (Johnson, sense 2).

7

From hence, ye beauties, undeceived,
Know, one false step is ne'er retrieved,
  And be with caution bold.
Not all that tempts your wand'ring eyes   40
And heedless hearts, is lawful prize;
  Nor all, that glisters, gold.

AN
ELEGY
WROTE IN A
COUNTRY CHURCH YARD (1751)

The *Curfew*[1] tolls the Knell of parting Day,
The lowing Herd wind slowly o'er the Lea,
The Plow-man homeward plods his weary Way,
And leaves the World to Darkness, and to me.

  Now fades the glimmering Landscape on the Sight,   5
And all the Air a solemn Stillness holds;
Save where the Beetle wheels his droning Flight,
And drowsy Tinklings lull the distant Folds.[2]

  Save that from yonder Ivy-mantled Tow'r
The moping Owl does to the Moon complain   10
Of such, as wand'ring near her sacred Bower,
Molest her ancient solitary Reign.

  Beneath those rugged Elms, that Yew-Tree's Shade,
Where heaves the Turf in many a mould'ring Heap,
Each in his narrow Cell for ever laid,   15
The rude Forefathers of the Hamlet sleep.

  The breezy Call of Incense-breathing Morn,
The Swallow twitt'ring from the Straw-built Shed,
The Cock's shrill Clarion, or the echoing Horn,
No more shall rouse them from their lowly Bed.   20

  For them no more the blazing Hearth shall burn,
Or busy Houswife ply her Evening Care:
No Children run to lisp their Sire's Return,
Or climb his Knees the envied Kiss to share.

  Oft did the Harvest to their Sickle yield,   25
Their Furrow oft the stubborn Glebe has broke;[3]
How jocund did they drive their Team afield!

AN ELEGY WROTE
[1] *Curfew* "An evening peal, by which [William] the conqueror willed that every man should rake up his fire, and put out his light; so that in many places at this today where a bell is customarily rung towards bed time, it is said to ring curfew" (Johnson citing John Cowell, *The Interpreter*, who cites John Stowe).
[2] *Fold* "The ground in which sheep are confined" (Johnson).
[3] *Glebe* soil.

How bowed the Woods beneath their sturdy Stroke!
 Let not Ambition mock their useful Toil,
Their homely Joys and Destiny obscure;   30
Nor Grandeur hear with a disdainful Smile,
The short and simple Annals of the Poor.

 The boast of Heraldry, the Pomp of Power,
And all that Beauty, all that Wealth e'er gave,
Awaits alike th' inevitable Hour.   35
The Paths of Glory lead but to the Grave.

 Nor you, ye Proud, impute to these the Fault,
If Mem'ry o'er their Tomb no Trophies raise,
Where through the long-drawn Aisle and fretted Vault[4]
The pealing Anthem swells the Note of Praise.[5]   40

 Can storied Urn or animated Bust
Back to its Mansion call the fleeting Breath?
Can Honour's Voice provoke the silent Dust,
Or Flatt'ry soothe the dull cold Ear of Death!

 Perhaps in this neglected Spot is laid   45
Some Heart once pregnant with celestial Fire,
Hands that the Rod of Empire might have swayed,
Or waked to Ecstasy the living Lyre.

 But Knowledge to their Eyes her ample Page
Rich with the Spoils of Time did ne'er unroll;   50
Chill Penury repressed their noble Rage,
And froze the genial Current of the Soul.

 Full many a Gem of purest Ray serene,[6]
The dark unfathomed Caves of Ocean bear:
Full many a Flower is born to blush unseen,[7]   55
And waste its Sweetness on the desert Air.

 Some village-*Hampden* that with dauntless Breast[8]
The little Tyrant of his Fields withstood;
Some mute inglorious *Milton* here may rest,
Some *Cromwell* guiltless of his Country's Blood.   60

 Th' Applause of list'ning Senates to command,
The Threats of Pain and Ruin to despise,
To scatter Plenty o'er a smiling Land,
And read their Hist'ry in a Nation's Eyes,

 Their Lot forbade: nor circumscribed alone   65
Their growing Virtues, but their Crimes confined;
Forbade to wade through Slaughter to a Throne,
And Shut the Gates of Mercy on Mankind,

 The struggling Pangs of conscious Truth to hide,
To quench the Blushes of ingenuous Shame,   70
Or heap the Shrine of Luxury and Pride

---

[4] *fretted* ornamented.
[5] *Anthem* "A holy song" (Johnson).
[6] *serene* clear, bright.
[7] *Full many a Flower* two verse feet only.

[8] *Hampden* John (1594–1643) like Milton and Cromwell, he opposed the "Tyrant" Charles I and urged civil war, in which he died fighting; in one manuscript version of the poem, Gray had Cato, Cicero, and Caesar in place of these English figures.

With Incense, kindled at the Muse's Flame.[9]
    Far from the madding Crowd's ignoble Strife,
Their sober Wishes never learned to stray;
Along the cool sequestered Vale of Life   75
They kept the noiseless Tenor of their Way.[10]

    Yet ev'n these Bones from Insult to protect
Some frail Memorial still erected nigh,
With uncouth Rhymes and shapeless Sculpture decked,[11]
Implores the passing Tribute of a Sigh.   80

    Their Name, their Years, spelt by th' unlettered Muse,[12]
The Place of Fame and Elegy supply:
And many a holy Text around she strews,
That teach the rustic Moralist to die.

    For who to dumb Forgetfulness a Prey,   85
This pleasing anxious Being e'er resigned,
Left the warm Precints of the cheerful Day,
Nor cast one longing ling'ring Look behind![13]

    On some fond Breast the parting Soul relies,
Some pious Drops the closing Eye requires;   90
Ev'n from the Tomb the Voice of Nature cries
Awake, and faithful to her wonted Fires.[14]

    For thee, who mindful of th' unhonoured Dead
Dost in these Lines their artless Tale relate;
If chance, by lonely Contemplation led,   95
Some kindred Spirit shall inquire thy Fate,[15]

    Haply some hoary-headed Swain may say,
'Oft have we seen him at the Peep of Dawn
Brushing with hasty Steps the Dews away
To meet the Sun upon the upland Lawn.[16]   100
    'There at the Foot of yonder nodding Beech
That wreathes its old fantastic Roots so high,

---

[9] At one stage in its composition the poem may have concluded after line 72 with the following four stanzas in the Eton College manuscript:

The thoughtless World to Majesty may bow
Exalt the brave, & idolise Success
But more to Innocence their Safety owe
Than Power & Genius e'er conspired to bless
And thou, who mindful of the unhonoured Dead
Dost in these Notes their artless Tale relate
By Night & lonely Contemplation led
To linger in the gloomy Walks of Fate
Hark how the sacred Calm, that broods around
Bids every fierce tumultuous Passion cease
In still small Accents whispering from the Ground
A grateful Earnest of eternal Peace
No more with Reason & thyself at Strife;
Give anxious Cares & endless Wishes room
But through the cool sequestered Vale of Life
Pursue the silent Tenor of thy Doom.

[10] *Tenor* "Continuity of state" (Johnson).
[11] *uncouth* "Odd; strange; unusual" (Johnson).
[12] *unlettered* "Unlearned; untaught" (Johnson).
[13] *For who . . . Look behind* compare *Paradise Lost* 2.146–51.
[14] *wonted* customary.
[15] In the Eton College manuscript this stanza is replaced by the following:

If chance that e'er some pensive Spirit more
By sympathetic Musings here delayed,
With vain, though kind, Inquiry shall explore
Thy once-loved Haunt, this long-deserted Shade.

[16] After this line the Eton manuscript has,

Him have we seen the Green-wood Side along,
While o'er the Heath we hied, our Labours done,
Oft as the Woodlark piped her farewell Song
With wistful eyes pursue the setting Sun.

His listless Length at Noontide would he stretch,
And pore upon the Brook that babbles by.
    'Hard by yon Wood, now frowning as in Scorn,   105
Mutt'ring his wayward Fancies he would rove,
Now drooping, woeful wan, like one forlorn,
Or crazed with Care, or crossed in hopeless Love.
    'One Morn I missed him on the customed Hill,
Along the Heath, and near his favourite Tree;   110
Another came; nor yet beside the Rill,
Nor up the Lawn, nor at the Wood was he.
    'The next with Dirges due in sad Array
Slow through the Church-way Path we saw him borne.
Approach and read (for thou can'st read) the Lay,   115
Graved on the Stone beneath yon aged Thorn.'

The EPITAPH

Here rests his Head upon the Lap of Earth
A Youth to Fortune and to Fame unknown:
Fair Science frowned not on his humble Birth,[17]
And Melancholy marked him for her own.[18]   120
    Large was his Bounty, and his Soul sincere,
Heav'n did a Recompense as largely send:
He gave to Misery all he had, a Tear:
He gained from Heav'n ('twas all he wished) a Friend.
    No further seek his Merits to disclose,   125
Or draw his Frailties from their dread Abode,
(There they alike in trembling Hope repose)
The Bosom of his Father and his God.

The Progress of Poesy: A Pindaric Ode[1] (1768)

I.1[2]

AWAKE, Æolian lyre, awake,[3]
And give to rapture all thy trembling strings.

---

17 *Science* knowledge.
18 *Melancholy* one of the characteristics of those favoured by "Science"; a positive attribute, like sensibility, Lonsdale suggests.
THE PROGRESS OF POESY
1 Gray originally published this poem and "The Bard" in *Odes by Mr. Gray* (1757); the text follows the edition in *Poems by Mr. Gray* (1768), to which Gray added the present title and footnotes. The original title was "Ode in the Greek manner." Referring the style to Pindar, the fifth-century BCE praise poet, signaled that the work would be irregular, rapid, and highly allusive, but Gray correctly understood Pindar's prosody as various and complex rather than wild. His divisions indicate three rounds of strophe, antistrophe, and epode, the regular parts of Pindar's odes.
2 *I.1* The subject and the simile, as usual with Pindar, are united. The various sources of poetry, which gives life and lustre to all it touches, are here described; its quiet majestic progress enriching every subject (otherwise dry and barren) with a pomp of diction and luxuriant harmony of numbers; and its more rapid and irresistible course, when swollen and hurried away by the conflict of tumultuous passions [Gray's note].
3 *Æolian lyre* by citing Pindar in a footnote Gray suggests the phrase means lyric poetry of the kind written by Pindar, which originated in the Aeolian islands, especially Lesbos.

From Helicon's harmonious springs[4]
A thousand rills their mazy progress take:
The laughing flowers, that round them blow,[5]   5
Drink life and fragrance as they flow.
Now the rich stream of music winds along
Deep, majestic, smooth, and strong,
Through verdant vales, and Ceres' golden reign:[6]
Now rolling down the steep amain,   10
Headlong, impetuous, see it pour:
The rocks and nodding groves rebellow to the roar.

I.2[7]

Oh! Sovereign of the willing soul,
Parent of sweet and solemn-breathing airs,
Enchanting shell! the sullen Cares[8]   15
And frantic Passions hear thy soft control.
On Thracia's hills the Lord of War,[9]
Has curbed the fury of his car,
And dropped his thirsty lance at thy command.
Perching on the sceptred hand   20
Of Jove, thy magic lulls the feathered king[10]
With ruffled plumes and flagging wing:
Quenched in dark clouds of slumber lie
The terror of his beak, and lightnings of his eye.

I.3[11]

Thee the voice, the dance, obey,   25
Tempered to thy warbled lay.
O'er Idalia's velvet-green[12]
The rosy-crownèd Loves are seen
On Cytherea's day[13]
With antic Sports and blue-eyed Pleasures,[14]   30
Frisking light in frolic measures;
Now pursuing, now retreating,
Now in circling troops they meet:

---

[4] *Helicon* a mountain inhabited by the muses; its springs inspire those who drink from them.

[5] *blow* blossom.

[6] *Ceres* an Italian goddess of vegetable regeneration associated with Greek Demeter.

[7] *I.2* Power of harmony to calm the turbulent sallies of the soul. The thoughts are borrowed from the first Pythian of Pindar [especially the first strophe; Gray's note].

[8] *shell* lyre, because the first such instruments are said to have been strung on tortoise shells.

[9] *Thracia* Thrace, the northernmost part of Greece, considered a rough place with rough gods; *Lord of War* Mars.

[10] *feathered king* the eagle ("ruler of birds" in Pythian 1).

[11] *I.3* Power of harmony to produce all the graces of motion in the body [Gray's note].

[12] *Idalia* Aphrodite, after a town on Cyprus, which was sacred to her.

[13] *Cytherea* another name for Aphrodite derived from an island sacred to her.

[14] *antic* "Odd; ridiculously wild" (Johnson).

To brisk notes in cadence beating
Glance their many-twinkling feet.[15]
Slow melting strains their Queen's approach declare: 35
Where'er she turns the Graces homage pay.[16]
With arms sublime, that float upon the air,
In gliding state she wins her easy way:
O'er her warm cheek and rising bosom move   40
The bloom of young Desire and purple light of Love.

II.1[17]

Man's feeble race what ills await,
Labour, and Penury, the racks of Pain,
Disease, and Sorrow's weeping train,
And Death, sad refuge from the storms of Fate!   45
The fond complaint, my song, disprove,
And justify the laws of Jove.[18]
Say, has he giv'n in vain the heav'nly Muse?
Night, and all her sickly dews,
Her spectres wan, and birds of boding cry,   50
He gives to range the dreary sky:
Till down the eastern cliffs afar
Hyperion's march they spy, and glitt'ring shafts of war.[19]

II.2[20]

In climes beyond the solar road,
Where shaggy forms o'er ice-built mountains roam,   55
The Muse has broke the twilight-gloom
To cheer the shiv'ring native's dull abode.
And oft, beneath the od'rous shade
Of Chili's boundless forests laid,
She deigns to hear the savage youth repeat   60
In loose numbers wildly sweet
Their feather-cinctured chiefs, and dusky loves.
Her track, where'er the goddess roves,
Glory pursue, and generous Shame,
Th' unconquerable Mind, and Freedom's holy flame.   65

---

[15] *Glance* "To move nimbly" (Johnson); "twinkling" is a translation of a word Homer used to describe the nimble feet of dancers (*Odyssey* 8.265), as Gray noted.
[16] *Graces* the Charites, three goddesses personifying grace and beauty, associated with Aphrodite.
[17] *II.1* To compensate the real and imaginary ills of life, the Muse was given to Mankind by the same Providence that sends the Day by its cheerful presence to dispel the gloom and terrors of the Night. [Gray's note].

[18] *And justify the laws of Jove* compare *Paradise Lost* 1.26.
[19] *Hyperion* a Titan identified with the Sun.
[20] *II.2* Extensive influence of poetic Genius over the remotest and most uncivilised nations: its connection with liberty, and the virtues that naturally attend on it. (See the Erse, Norwegian, and Welsh Fragments, the Lapland and American songs.) [Gray's note].

II.3[21]

Woods, that wave o'er Delphi's steep,[22]
Isles, that crown th' Ægean deep,
Fields, that cool Ilissus laves,[23]
Or where Mæander's amber waves[24]
In lingering Lab'rinths creep,   70
How do your tuneful Echoes languish,
Mute, but to the voice of Anguish?
Where each old poetic Mountain
Inspiration breathed around:
Every shade and hallowed Fountain   75
Murmured deep a solemn sound:
Till the sad Nine in Greece's evil hour[25]
Left their Parnassus for the Latian plains.[26]
Alike they scorn the pomp of tyrant Power,
And coward Vice, that revels in her chains.   80
When Latium had her lofty spirit lost,
They sought, O Albion! next thy sea-encircled coast.[27]

III.1

Far from the sun and summer-gale,[28]
In thy green lap was Nature's Darling laid,[29]
What time, where lucid Avon strayed,[30]   85
To Him the mighty Mother did unveil
Her awful face: the dauntless Child
Stretched forth his little arms, and smiled.
'This pencil take', she said 'whose colours clear
Richly paint the vernal year: 90
Thine too these golden keys, immortal Boy!
This can unlock the gates of Joy;
Of Horror that, and thrilling Fears,
Or ope the sacred source of sympathetic Tears'.

III.2

Nor second he, that rode sublime[31]   95
Upon the seraph-wings of Ecstasy,

---

[21] *II.3* Progress of Poetry from Greece to Italy, and from Italy to England. Chaucer was not unacquainted with the writings of Dante or of Petrarch. The Earl of Surrey and Sir Thomas Wyatt had travelled in Italy, and formed their taste there; Spenser imitated the Italian writers; Milton improved on them: but this School expired soon after the Restoration, and a new one arose on the French model, which has subsisted ever since. [Gray's note].

[22] *Delphi* site of the oracle of Apollo, the god of poetry.

[23] *Ilissus* a stream running past Athens.

[24] *Mæander* a winding river in Asia Minor.

[25] *the sad Nine* the Muses; *Greece's evil hour* when it was conquered by Alexander.

[26] *Parnassus* the mountain above Delphi sacred to the Muses; *Latian* Italian.

[27] *Albion* England, after its white (Latin, *albus*) cliffs.

[28] *gale* "A wind not tempestuous, yet stronger than a breeze" (Johnson).

[29] *Nature's Darling* Shakespeare [Gray's note].

[30] *Avon* the river that flows through Stratford, where Shakespeare was born.

[31] *He* Milton [Gray's note].

The secrets of th' Abyss to spy.
He passed the flaming bounds of Place and Time:
The living Throne, the sapphire-blaze,
Where Angels tremble, while they gaze,   100
He saw; but blasted with excess of light,
Closed his eyes in endless night.[32]
Behold, where Dryden's less presumptuous car,[33]
Wide o'er the fields of Glory bear
Two Coursers of ethereal race,[34]   105
With necks in thunder clothed, and long-resounding pace.

III.3

Hark, his hands the lyre explore![35]
Bright-eyed Fancy hovering o'er
Scatters from her pictured urn
Thoughts that breathe, and words, that burn.   110
But ah! 'tis heard no more —[36]
O lyre divine, what daring Spirit
Wakes thee now? though he inherit[37]
Nor the pride, nor ample pinion,[38]
That the Theban Eagle bear,[39]   115
Sailing with supreme dominion
Through the azure deep of air:
Yet oft before his infant eyes would run
Such forms, as glitter in the Muse's ray
With orient hues, unborrowed of the Sun: 120
Yet shall he mount, and keep his distant way
Beyond the limits of a vulgar fate,
Beneath the Good how far — but far above the Great.

Horace Walpole (1717–1797)

Like his schoolmate Thomas Gray, Walpole was fastidious, shy, and physically slight. He also led a life devoted to scholarship, and never married. As the son of Robert Walpole, the most important politician of his day, however, Horace was forced into public life. While Gray returned from their tour of the Continent to begin lifelong seclusion in Cambridge University, Walpole returned to find

---

[32] *endless night*   Milton became totally blind in the winter of 1650–51, well before he began work in earnest on *Paradise Lost*.

[33] *car* chariot.

[34] *Two Coursers of ethereal race*   Meant to express the stately march and sounding energy of Dryden's rhymes [i.e. heroic couplets; Gray's note].

[35] *the lyre*   lyric poetry, particularly his odes (see the selections from Dryden above).

[36] *'tis heard no more*   We have had in our language no other odes of the sublime kind, than that of Dryden on

St. Cecilia's day: for Cowley (who had his merit) yet wanted judgement, style, and harmony, for such a task. That of Pope is not worthy of so great a man . . . [Gray's note].

[37] *he*   Gray.

[38] *nor . . . nor*   neither . . . nor.

[39] *Theban Eagle*   Pindar compares himself to that bird, and his enemies to ravens that croak and clamour in vain below, while it pursues its flight regardless of their noise [Gray's note, citing *Olympian* 2.8].

himself elected to Parliament, where he represented various constituencies for the next twenty-five years. In 1768 he retired to give all his time to his collections of books, manuscripts, prints, and paintings at Strawberry Hill. He had begun his own press there in 1757, and he produced catalogues of his collections as well as other works by himself, by friends, or by writers whom he admired. Some of Walpole's bibliographical work is still very valuable, and the quality of his publications is consistently high. He reached a broader audience in 1764–5 when he published The Castle of Otranto, *a gothic novel that started a literary fashion which was very significant in the development and deepening of the novel as an important literary genre. In 1791 Walpole succeeded to the family fortune, and he spent much of his later life attending to that responsibility. Through it all, Walpole wrote letters, and produced the most interesting collection of correspondence of the century. It was published many times, but with the help of scores of scholars W. S. Lewis gradually completed a grand edition in forty-eight volumes (Yale University Press, 1937–83), which stands as one of the great resources for the study of eighteenth-century British culture. It is not inappropriate for Walpole to be at the center of such a resource. Volumes 13 (1948) and 31 (1961) supply the text and much of the supporting notation for the following brief selections.*

Letter to Richard West[1]
Florence, 4 December 1740

Child, I am going to let you see your shocking proceedings with us. On my conscience, I believe 'tis three months since you wrote to either Gray or me. If you had been ill, Ashton would have said so; and if you had been dead, the gazettes would have said it. If you had been angry, – but that's impossible; how can one quarrel with folks three thousand miles off? We are neither divines nor commentators, and consequently have not hated you on paper. 'Tis to show that my charity for you cannot be interrupted at this distance that I write to you, though I have nothing to say, for 'tis a bad time for small news; and when emperors and czarinas are dying all up and down Europe, one can't pretend to tell you of any thing that happens within our sphere. Not but that we have our accidents too. If you have had a great wind in England, we have had a great water at Florence. We have been trying to set out every day, and pop upon you *****[2] It is fortunate that we stayed, for I don't know what had become of us! Yesterday, with violent rains, there came flouncing down from the mountains such a flood that it floated the whole city. The jewellers on the Old Bridge[3] removed their commodities, and in two hours after the bridge was cracked. The torrent broke down the quays and drowned several coach-horses, which are kept here in stables under ground. We were moated into our house all day, which is near the Arno, and had the miserable spectacles of the ruins that were washed along with the hurricane. There was a cart with two oxen not quite dead, and four men in it drowned: but what was ridiculous, there came tiding along a fat hay-cock, with a hen and her eggs, and a cat. The torrent is considerably abated; but we expect terrible news from the country, especially from Pisa, which stands so much lower, and nearer the sea. There is a stone here, which, when the water overflows, Pisa is entirely flooded. The water rose two ells[4] yesterday above that stone. Judge!

LETTER TO RICHARD WEST
[1] *Richard West* a classmate and close friend from Eton who died of tuberculosis in 1742 at the age of twenty-five; West, Wapole, Thomas Gray, and Thomas Ashton called themselves the "quadruple alliance"; see Gray's

letter to West and his sonnet on the death of West, above, pp. 968–9.
[2] **** part of the manuscript is torn away here.
[3] *Old Bridge* the Ponte Vecchio over the Arno river in Florence is famous for its shops.
[4] *two ells* two and a half yards.

For this last month we have passed our time but dully; all diversions silenced on the emperor's death,[5] and every body out of town. I have seen nothing but cards and dull pairs of cicisbeos.[6] I have literally seen so much love and pharaoh[7] since being here, that I believe I shall never love either again as long as I live. Then I am got into a horrid lazy way of a morning. I don't believe I should know seven o'clock in the morning again if I was to see it. But I am returning to England, and shall grow very solemn and wise! Are you wise? Dear West, have pity on one who have [sic] done nothing of gravity for these two years, and do laugh sometimes. We do nothing else, and have contracted such formidable ideas of the good people of England that we are already nourishing great black eyebrows and great black beards, and teasing our countenances into wrinkles. Then for the common talk of the times we are quite at a loss, and for the dress. You would oblige us extremely by forwarding to us the votes of the Houses, the King's speech,[8] and the magazines; or if you had any such thing as a little book called the Foreigner's Guide through the city of London and the Liberties[9] of Westminster; or a Letter to a Freeholder; or the Political Companion:[10] then 'twould be an infinite obligation if you would neatly band-box up a baby dressed after the newest Temple fashion now in use at both play-houses.[11] Alack-a-day! We shall just arrive in the tempest of elections!

As our departure depends entirely upon the weather, we cannot tell you to a day when we shall say, 'Dear West, how glad I am to see you!' and all the many questions and answers that we shall give and take. Would the day were come! Do but figure to yourself the journey we are to pass through first! But you can't conceive Alps, Apennines, Italian inns and postchaises. I tremble at the thoughts. They were just sufferable while new and unknown, and as we met them by the way in coming to Florence, Rome, and Naples; but they are passed, and the mountains remain! Well, write to one in the interim; direct to me addressed to Monsieur Selwyn, *chez Monsieur Alexandre, rue St. Apolline, à Paris*. If Mr. Alexandre is not there, the street is, and I believe that will be sufficient. Adieu, my dear child!

Yours ever,

Hor. Walpole

Letter to Hannah More[1]
Strawberry Hill,[2] 4 November 1789

I am not surprised, my dear Madam, that the notice of my illness should have stimulated your predominant quality, your sensibility. I cannot do less in return than relieve it immediately, by assuring you that I am in a manner recovered; and should have gone out before this

---

[5] *the emperor's death* Charles VI, Emperor of Germany, died on October 20.

[6] *cicisbeos* lovers of married women.

[7] *pharaoh* a card game.

[8] *King's speech* on the opening of Parliament, November 29.

[9] *Liberties* "the district, extending beyond the bounds of the city, which is subject to the control of the municipal authority."

[10] *Letter to a Freeholder; or the Political Companion* typical titles of election-year pamphlets; only men with

property in freehold, not subject to a landlord's seizure in their lifetime, could vote.

[11] *baby dressed . . . both play-houses* a doll dressed like a young law student going out to Covent Garden or Drury Lane Theatre.

LETTER TO HANNAH MORE

[1] *Hannah More* (1745–1833), playwright, novelist, political writer, moralist, and important member of the circle of literary women known as the Bluestockings or *Bas Bleu*; see the selections from More, below.

[2] *Strawberry Hill* Walpole's estate near Twickenham, about ten miles west of central London.

time, if my mind were as much at ease as my poor limbs. I have passed five months most uncomfortably; the two last most unhappily. In June and September I had two bad falls by my own lameness and weakness, and was much bruised; while I was witness to the danger, and then to the death, of my invaluable niece, Lady Dysart.[3] She was angelic, and has left no children. The unexpected death of Lord Waldegrave,[4] one of the most amiable of men, has not only deprived me of him, but has opened a dreadful scene of calamities! He and my niece were the happiest and most domestic of couples.

Your kind inquiries after me have drawn these details from me, for which I make no excuse: good-nature never grudges its pity. I, who love to force your gravity to smile, am seriously better pleased to indulge your benevolence with a subject of esteem, which, though moving your compassion, will be accompanied by no compunction. I will now answer your letter. Your pleas, that not composition, but business, has occasioned your silence, is no satisfaction to *me*. In my present anxious solitude I have again read *Bonner* and *Florio*, and the *Bas Bleu*;[5] and do you think I am pleased to learn that you have not been writing? Who is it says something like this line? –

Hannah will *not* write, and Lactilla *will*.[6]

They who think her *Earl Goodwin* will outgo Shakspeare, might be in the right, if they specified in what way. I believe she may write worse than he sometimes did, though that is not easy; but to excel him – oh! I have not words adequate to my contempt for those who can suppose such a possibility!

I am sorry, very sorry, for what you tell me of poor Barrett's[7] fate. Though he did write worse than Shakespeare, it is great pity he was told so, as it killed him; and I rejoice that I did not publish a word in contradiction of the letters which he said Chatterton[8] sent to me, as I was advised to do. I might have laughed at the poor man's folly, and then I should have been miserable to have added a grain to the poor man's mortification.

You rejoice *me*, not my vanity, by telling me my idea of a mechanic succedaneum[9] to the labour of negroes is not visionary, but thought practicable. Oh! how I wish I understood sugar and ploughs, and could marry them! Alas! I understand nothing useful. My head is as un-mechanic as it is un-arithmetic, un-geometric, un-metaphysic, un-commercial: but will not some one of those superior heads to whom you have talked on my indigested hint reduce it to practicability? How a feasible scheme would stun those who call humanity romantic, and show, from the books of the Custom-house, that murder is a great improvement of the revenue! Even the present situation of France is favourable. Could not Mr. Wilberforce[10] obtain to have the enfranchisement of the negroes started there?

---

[3] *Lady Dysart* Charlotte (1738–89).

[4] *Lord Waldegrave* George Waldegrave (1751–89), married to one of Walpole's grand-nieces.

[5] *Bonner and Florio, and the Bas Bleu* Bishop Bonner's *Ghost*; *Florio, a Tale for Fine Gentlemen and Fine Ladies*; *Bas Bleu, or Conversation*, all works by More.

[6] *Lactilla* the poetic name used by Ann Yearsley, "the Milk-maid of Bristol" (see selection below), author of the play *Earl Goodwin*.

[7] *Barrett* William (1733–89), a surgeon and amateur antiquarian, who defended the authenticity of Thomas Chatterton's supposedly medieval Rowley poems.

[8] *Chatterton* Thomas (1752–70) a precocious poet, author of poems he claimed were written by a medieval monk named Rowley (see selection below); Barrett and others accused Walpole of hastening him to his early suicide by cruelly challenging his claims.

[9] *succedaneum* "That which is put to serve for something else" (Johnson).

[10] *Wilberforce* William (1759–1833) an important advocate for the abolition of slavery, which was finally achieved in 1833.

The Jews are claiming their natural rights there;[11] and blacks are certainly not so great defaulters[12] as the Hebrews, though they too have undergone ample persecutions. Methinks, as Lord George Gordon[13] is in correspondence with the *États*,[14] he has been a little remiss in not signing the petition of those of his new communion.

The *États* are detestable and despicable; and, in fact, guilty of the outrages of the Parisian and provincial mobs. The mob of twelve hundred, not legislators, but dissolvers of all laws, unchained the mastiffs that had been tied up, and were sure to worry all who fell in their way. To annihilate all laws, however bad, and to have none ready to replace them, was proclaiming anarchy. What should one think of a mad-doctor, who should let loose a lunatic, suffer him to burn Bedlam,[15] chop off the heads of the keepers, and then consult with some students in physic[16] on the gentlest mode of treating delirium? By a late vote I see that the twelve hundred praters are reduced to five hundred:[17] *vive la reine Billingsgate!*[18] the Thalestris[19] who has succeeded Louis Quatorze! A committee of those Amazons stopped the Duke of Orleans,[20] who, to use their style, I believe is not *a barrel the better herring.*[21]

Your reflections on Vertot's[22] passion for revolutions are admirable, and yet it is natural for an historian to like to describe times of action. Halcyon days do not furnish matter for talents; they are like the virtuous couple in a comedy, a little insipid. Mr. Manly and Lady Grace,[23] Mellefont and Cynthia,[24] do not interest one much. Indeed, in a tragedy where they are unhappy, they give the audience full satisfaction, and no envy. The newspapers, no doubt, thought Dr. ——[25] could not do better than to espouse you. He certainly would be very judicious, could he obtain your consent; but, alas! you would soon squabble about Socinian*ism*,[26] or some of those *isms*. To tell you the truth, I hate all those Constantinopolitan jargons, that set people together by the ears about pedantic terms. When you apply scholastic phrases as happily and genteely as you do in your *Bas Bleu*, they are delightful; but don't muddify your charming simplicity with controversial distinctions, that will sour your sweet piety. Sects are the bane of charity, and have deluged the world with blood.

---

[11] *Jews are claiming their natural rights there* Jews living in the provinces of Alsace and Lorraine petitioned the French Assembly for protection in 1789 and gradually achieved civil rights throughout the country in the next couple of years.

[12] *defaulter* one who does not appear in court on the assigned day.

[13] *Lord George Gordon* (1751–93) instigator of the anti-Catholic assault on government known as the Gordon Riots in 1780, in which state buildings were burned and 450 people killed or wounded; arrested for treason but acquitted; later imprisoned in Newgate, where he spent the last five years of his life; he converted to Judaism, his "new communion" towards the end of his life.

[14] *États* the French revolutionary government.

[15] *Bedlam* the asylum for the insane in London.

[16] *physic* medicine.

[17] *twelve hundred praters are reduced to five hundred* London newspapers reported that only 553 of 1200 members cast votes in the election of a new President of the French Revolutionary Assembly.

[18] *vive la reine Billingsgate* "Hooray for Queen Billingsgate" (a fish market renowned for foul language and synonymous with it).

[19] *Thalestris* queen of the Amazons.

[20] *A committee . . . stopped the Duke of Orleans* a noble sympathizer with the revolution, the Duke was nevertheless detained on route to England on state business by what the English papers described as a band of "fish-women."

[21] *a barrel the better herring* "never one better than another, nothing to choose between them" (*OED*).

[22] *Vertot* René Aubert de Vertot (1655–1735), author of a book on revolutions in the Roman republic (1719).

[23] *Mr. Manly and Lady Grace* characters in *The Provoked Husband* by Cibber and Vanbrugh (1728).

[24] *Mellefont and Cynthia* characters in Congreve's *The Double Dealer* (1694).

[25] *{Priestly}* Joseph (1733–1804), social theorist, psychologist, and scientist; celebrated the fall of the Bastille, which led to a riot that wrecked his house.

[26] *Socinianism* a doctrine begun by Lelio Sozzini in the sixteenth century that rejected the divinity of Christ.

I do not mean, by what I am going to say, to extort another letter from you before I have the pleasure of seeing you at Hampton; but I really shall be much obliged to you for a single line soon, only to tell me if Miss Williams is at Stoke with the Duchess of Beaufort. To a short note, cannot you add a short P.S. on the fate of Earl Goodwin?

Lac mihi – novum non frigore desit.[27]

Adieu! my amiable friend!

Yours most sincerely,
Hor. Walpole

Elizabeth Carter (1717–1806)

When Samuel Johnson tried to make his way on to the literary scene in London in 1737 he found Elizabeth Carter already busily at work. Johnson made his way into the stable of writers kept by Edward Cave, editor of The Gentleman's Magazine *partly by addressing Latin poems to the owner and to those already in service. But to Carter he wrote and received an answer in Greek. Carter was unusually learned, although she had to make her acquisitions almost entirely on her own. Her Greek was good enough to enable her to engage in scholarly disputes and eventually to make the first complete translation of the philosopher Epictetus (1758), on which she made the remarkable sum of £1,000. She translated many other languages, and even outdid Johnson by learning Arabic. Carter published her first volume of poems in 1738, the same year that Johnson published* London. *She also wrote essays, and participated very actively in the intellectual life of her times. Walpole admired her more for her humanity than her literature. Her company was so desired at all the great houses where the Bluestockings (a society of intellectual women) met that Mrs. Vesey and others of her patrons would send carriages to her house in Clarges Street.*

The selections here come from a collection of her works called Memoirs of the Life of Mrs. Elizabeth Carter, *fourth edition (1825); like many accomplished women in the eighteenth century, Carter enjoyed the title "Mrs" as an indication of respect rather than of marital status. She was always single but always social.*

On the Death of Mrs. Rowe (1739)[1]

Oft' did Intrigue its guilty arts unite,
To blacken the records of female wit:
The tuneful song lost every modest grace,
And lawless freedoms triumphed in their place:
The Muse, for vices not her own accused,   5
With blushes viewed her sacred gifts abused;
Those gifts for nobler purposes assigned,
To raise the thoughts, and moralize the mind;

---

[27] *Lac . . . desit* "new milk does not fail me in winter" a deliberate misquotation of Virgil, *Eclogues* 2.22, which adds "or summer."

ON THE DEATH OF MRS. ROWE
[1] *Mrs. Rowe* Elizabeth Singer Rowe (1674–1737); called Philomela; see selection above.

The chaste delights of virtue to inspire,
And warm the bosom with seraphic fire;   10
Sublime the passions, lend devotion wings,
And celebrate the first great CAUSE of things.[2]
   Those glorious tasks were Philomela's part,
Who charms the fancy, and who mends the heart.
In her was every bright distinction joined,   15
Whate'er adorns, or dignifies the mind:
Hers every happy elegance of thought,
Refined by virtue, as by genius wrought.
Each low-born care her pow'rful strains control,
And wake the nobler motions of the soul.   20
When to the vocal wood or winding stream,
She hymned the Almighty AUTHOR of its frame,
Transported echoes bore the sounds along,
And all creation listened to the song:
Full, as when raptured seraphs strike the lyre;   25
Chaste, as the vestal's consecrated fire:
Soft as the balmy airs that gently play
In the calm sun-set of a vernal day;
Sublime as Virtue; elegant as Wit;
As Fancy various; and as Beauty sweet.   30
Applauding Angels with attention hung,
To learn the heav'nly accents from her tongue;
They, in the midnight hour, beheld her rise
Beyond the verge of sublunary skies;
Where, rapt in joys to mortal sense unknown,   35
She felt a flame ecstatic as their own.
   O while distinguished in the realms above,
The blest abode of harmony and love,
Thy happy spirit joins the heav'nly throng,
Glows with their transports, and partakes their song;   40
Fixed on my soul shall thy example grow,
And be my genius and my guide below;
To this I'll point my first, my noblest views,
Thy spotless verse shall regulate my Muse.
And O forgive, though faint the transcript be,   45
That copies an original like thee:
My justest pride, my best attempt for fame,
That joins my own to Philomela's name.

Ode to Melancholy (1739)

Alas! shades of night, my day,
O darkness, light to me,

---

[2] *CAUSE* God, in philosophical language.

Take, oh take me away to dwell with you,
Take me away[1]

Come Melancholy! silent Pow'r,
Companion of my lonely hour,
   To sober thought confined:
Thou sweetly-sad ideal guest,[2]
In all thy soothing charms confessed,   5
   Indulge my pensive mind.

No longer wildly hurried through
The tides of Mirth, that ebb and flow,
   In Folly's noisy stream:
I from the busy crowd retire,   10
To court the objects that inspire
   Thy philosophic dream.

Through yon dark grove of mournful yews
With solitary steps I muse,
   By thy direction led: 15
Here, cold to Pleasure's tempting forms,
Consociate with my sister-worms,[3]
   And mingle with the dead.

Ye midnight horrors! awful gloom!
Ye silent regions of the tomb,   20
   My future peaceful bed:
Here shall my weary eyes be closed,
And every sorrow lie reposed
   In Death's refreshing shade.

Ye pale inhabitants of night,   25
Before my intellectual sight
   In solemn pomp ascend:
O tell how trifling now appears
The train of idle hopes and fears
   That varying life attend.   30

Ye faithless idols of our sense,
Here own how vain your fond pretence,
   Ye empty names of joy!
Your transient forms like shadows pass,
Frail offspring of the magic glass,   35
   Before the mental eye.

The dazzling colours, falsely bright,
Attract the gazing vulgar sight

ODE TO MELANCHOLY
[1] *Alas . . . me away* Sophocles, *Ajax* 394–7; Carter put the Greek above; this translation appears in a note.

[2] *ideal* not real.
[3] *sister-worms* Job 17.14 [Carter's or her editor's note].

With superficial state:[4]
Through Reason's clearer optics viewed,
How stripped of all its pomp, how rude
    Appears the painted cheat.   40

Can wild ambition's tyrant pow'r,
Or ill-got Wealth's superfluous store,
    The dread of death control?   45
Can Pleasure's more bewitching charms
Avert, or soothe the dire alarms
    That shake the parting soul?

Religion! ere the hand of Fate
Shall make Reflection plead too late,   50
    My erring senses teach,
Amidst the flatt'ring hopes of youth,
To meditate the solemn truth,
    These awful relics preach.

Thy penetrating beams disperse   55
The mist of error, whence our fears
    Derive their fatal spring:
'Tis thine the trembling heart to warm,
And soften to an angel form
    The pale terrific King.[5]   60

When sunk by guilt in sad despair,
Repentance breathes her humble prayer,
    And owns thy threat'nings just:
Thy voice the shudd'ring suppliant cheers,
With Mercy calms her tort'ring fears,   65
    And lifts her from the dust.

Sublimed by thee, the soul aspires
Beyond the range of low desires,
    In nobler views elate:
Unmoved her destined change surveys,   70
And, armed by Faith, intrepid pays
    The universal debt.

In Death's soft slumber lulled to rest,
She sleeps, by smiling visions blest,
    That gently whisper peace: 75
'Till the last morn's fair op'ning ray
Unfolds the bright eternal day
    Of active life and bliss.

---

[4] *state* pomp.   [5] *terrific King* terrifying king, death.

To Miss Lynch (1744)

Occasioned by an Ode Written by Mrs. Philips[1]

Narcissa! still through every varying name
My constant care and bright enliv'ning theme.
In what soft language shall the Muse declare
The fond extravagance of love sincere?
How all those pleasing sentiments convey,   5
That charms my fancy, when I think on thee?
A theme like this Orinda's thoughts inspired,
Nor less by Friendship than by Genius fired.
Then let her happier, more persuasive art
Explain th' agreeing dictates of my heart: 10
Sweet may her fame to late remembrance bloom,
And everlasting laurels shade her tomb,
Where spotless verse with genuine force expressed
The brightest passion of the human breast.
        In what blest clime, beneath what fav'ring skies,   15
Did thy fair form, propitious Friendship rise?
With mystic sense, the poet's tuneful tongue[2]
Urania's birth in glitt'ring fiction sung.[3]
That Paphos first her smiling presence owned,[4]
Which wide diffused its happy influence round.   20
With hands united, and with looks serene,
Th' attending Graces hailed their new-born Queen;[5]
The Zephyrs round her waved their purple wing,[6]
And shed the fragrance of the breathing Spring:
The rosy Hours, advanced in silent flight,[7]   25
Led sparkling Youth, and ever new Delight.
Soft sigh the winds, the waters gently roll,
A purer azure vests the lucid Pole,[8]
All Nature welcomed in the beauteous train,
And Heav'n and Earth smiled conscious of the scene.   30
But long ere Paphos rose, or Poet sung,
In heav'nly breasts the sacred passion sprung:
The same bright flames in raptured Seraphs glow,
And warm consenting tempers here below:

To MISS LYNCH
[1] *Mrs. Philips* Katherine Philips (1631–64); called
herself Orinda (see selection above); Carter may be referring to the poem "Friendship" beginning "Let the dull
brutish World that know not Love / Continue Heretics."
[2] *the poet* Hesiod (he describes the birth of Aphrodite
in *Theogony* 188–206, but Carter's description recalls his
two Homeric hymns to Aphrodite, numbers 5 and 6).
[3] *Urania* [a name for Aphrodite] "There were two
Venuses among the Ancients; one called Pandemus, to
whom they attributed the love of wild disorderly pleas-

ures; the other named Urania, the patroness and inspirer
of Friendship, Knowledge, and Virtue" [Carter's or her
editor's note].
[4] *Paphos* Greek isle, birthplace of Aphrodite, here
called Urania.
[5] *Graces* the three Charites, personifications of grace
and beauty, closely associated with Aphrodite.
[6] *Zephyrs* gentle west winds.
[7] *Hours* goddesses of the seasons and natural order.
[8] *Pole* sky, as in Milton, *Paradise Lost* 4.724, for
example.

While one attraction mortal, Angel, binds,   35
Virtue, which forms the unison of minds:
Friendship her soft harmonious touch affords,
And gently strikes the sympathetic chords,
Th' agreeing notes in social measures roll,
And the sweet concert flows from soul to soul.   40
   By Heav'n's enthusiastic impulse taught
What shining visions rose on Plato's thought!
While by the Muses' gently winding flood[9]
His searching fancy traced the sovereign good!
The laurelled Sisters touched the vocal lyre,[10]   45
And Wisdom's goddess led their tuneful choir.[11]
Beneath the genial Plantane's spreading shade,
How sweet the philosophic music played!
Through all the gore, along the flow'ry shore[12]
The charming sounds responsive echoes bore.   50
Here, from the cares of vulgar life refined,
Immortal pleasures opened on his mind:
In gay succession to his ravished eyes
The animating pow'rs of beauty rise;
On every object round, above, below,   55
Quick to the sight her vivid colours glow:
Yet, not to Matter's shadowy forms confined,
The *Fair* and *Good* he sought remained behind:
'Till gradual rising through the boundless whole,
He viewed the blooming graces of the soul;   60
Where, to the beam of intellectual day,
The genuine charms of *moral Beauty* play:
With pleasing force the strong attractions move
Each finer sense, and tune it into love.

To———[1] (1753)

Say, dear Emilia, what untried delight
   Has Earth, or Air, or Ocean to bestow,
That checks thy active spirit's nobler flight,
   And bounds its narrow view to scenes below?

Is Life thy passion? Let it not depend   5
   On flutt'ring pulses, and a fleeting breath:
In sad Despair the fruitless wish must end,
   That seeks it in the gloomy range of Death.

---

[9] *flood* "Ilyssus, a river near Athens, dedicated to the Muses. On the banks of this river, under a plantane, Plato lays the scene of some of his Dialogues on Love and Beauty" [Carter's or her editor's note].
[10] *laurelled Sisters* the Muses, crowned with laurel, symbolic of artistic achievement.
[11] *Wisdom's goddess* Athena.

[12] *gore* low-lying land.
To———
[1] *To———* Of this beautiful Poem Mrs. Carter never chose to say to whom it was addressed, as some degree of censure seems to be implied by it [original editor's note].

This world, deceitful idol of thy soul,
　　Is all devoted to his tyrant pow'r: 10
To form his prey the genial planets roll,
　　To speed his conquests flies the rapid hour.

This verdant Earth, these fair surrounding skies,
　　Are all the triumphs of his wasteful reign:
'Tis but to set, the brightest suns arise;   15
　　'Tis but to wither, blooms the flow'ry plain.

'Tis but to die, Mortality was born;
　　Nor struggling Folly breaks the dread decree:
Then cease the common destiny to mourn,   20
　　Nor wish thy Nature's laws reversed for thee.

The sun that sets, again shall gild the skies;
　　The faded plain reviving flow'rs shall grace:
But hopeless fall, no more on earth to rise,
　　The transitory forms of human race.   25

No more on Earth: but see, beyond the gloom,
　　Where the short reign of Time and Death expires,
Victorious o'er the ravage of the tomb,
　　Smiles the fair object of thy fond desires.

The seed of Life, below, imperfect lies,   30
　　To Virtue's hand its cultivation giv'n:
Formed by her care, the beauteous plant shall rise,
　　And flourish with unfading bloom in heav'n.

On the Indulgence of Fancy (1770)

To Mrs. Vesey[1]

Such are the chances of this 'worky-day world', and thus passes life in an alteration of
private and of social suffering; and yet so wonderful and so merciful is the composition of our
existence, that innumerable pleasures find a place amidst the evils of mortality; and, upon the
whole, we suffer only just enough to reconcile us to the limits of our present duration, and
to extend our views to futurity.

You are now at leisure to amuse yourself with those enchanting scenes which your
imagination is always ready to present to you whenever you bid it wave its magic wand. I am
inexpressibly delighted with your Gothic retirement, which I shall certainly visit every
moonlight; and I hope you will advance to meet me with the first ray, which you discover
gleaming through your cathedral window. I am indeed a little apprehensive that you will
make some scruple of admitting my vacant round face to so solemn an entertainment; but if
you can once get over this mere prejudice of appearance, you will find me a very tractable

---

ON THE INDULGENCE OF FANCY
[1] *Mrs. Vesey* Elizabeth (*c.* 1715–91), a blue-stocking
patron and host, friend of Carter, Hannah More, and
Horace Walpole; she lived in Clarges Street near Carter,

though Carter here refers to her country estate; this
"essay" was actually a letter to Vesey, published among
many others to her in 1809.

companion, and ready to follow your imagination wherever it will lead me 'through the dark postern of time long elapsed'.[2]

When the twilight aids the visions of contemplation, and the owl begins his melancholy serenade, we will conjure up the Lady Abbess, and fix her in her niche in the wall. We will summon together a long series of the successive restraints of this venerable fabric,[3] and we will make them recount to us the adventures of former days. And in what will this information end, but in bringing us back to our own, in dissolving the spell of fancy, and annihilating all our reverence for antiquity?

Vexed and fatigued by the faults and follies of others, and mortified by our own, we are fond of retiring back to the transactions of remote generations, in which we suppose that human creatures were wiser and better than ourselves, and their pursuits of more importance than our own. The telescope through which we survey the actors on the theatre of past ages, can give us only a general view; while the distance conceals from us the whole play of those little interests and passions, which, though too insignificant to make any figure in the revolutions of states and empires, form most of the business and bustle of general and private life.

The imagination, however, is so agreeably deluded by our prejudices in favour of antiquity, that one cannot much regret there should be so many histories in the world, and so few biographers. Biography by entering into minute details of personal and private transaction, forms such a connection and similitude between past and present ages, that all idea of difference is lost, and we are affected in just the same manner by the one as by the other. I have lately felt this very strongly in reading Plutarch's lives, which have been one of my studies this summer. I find very little difference between what passed among the inhabitants of Athens and Rome, and the news of the day in London; and when I read of Cicero's and Pompey's[4] appointment to sup with Lucullus,[5] it is no more than hearing that my Lord Lyttelton[6] and Mr. Pitt[7] had engaged themselves to dine with Sir Laurence Dundas,[8] on condition that he would not set all his six men cooks to work for their entertainment. Do pray tell me, for it is past my comprehension, how the subject with which I set out could possibly lead me to Sir Laurence Dundas and his six men cooks.

To return to it, however, I am highly obliged to you for wishing me to share your solemn retreat when the moon-light gleams through the Gothic window. I hope you will transport yourself on one of the beams to return my visit on the seashore,[9] where the moon forms a scene equally solemn, though in a different style; and I believe you would find the soft murmurs of the ebbing waves as musically soothing as the whispers of your trees.

I do not at all wonder that your fine philosophical harrangue on the thunder had so disgraceful a conclusion. It would often be our wisest choice to adhere to the principles we received in the nursery. No one, I believe, ever yet acquired fortitude by being told that any object of terror proceeded from natural causes: thousands have acquired it by a reliance on *superior power*. *Superior power* is an intelligible expression; *natural causes* is not: this is by no

---

[2]   *through the dark postern of time long elapsed*   Edward Young, *Night Thoughts* 1.224; a postern is a back door or secret entrance.

[3]   *fabric*   building.

[4]   *Pompey*   important first-century BCE Roman general and political leader, succeeded *Lucullus* as commander of the Roman army.

[5]   *Lucullus*   Roman general, conqueror of Mithridates, lived in great luxury after Pompey succeeded him; the story of "Cicero's and Pompey's appointment" is told in Plutarch's life of Lucullus; the two agreed to dine, if

Lucullus would not make any special preparations, telling only one servant of their coming.

[6]   *Lord Lyttelton*   George Lyttelton (1709–73), politician, poet, and patron of the arts.

[7]   *Mr. Pitt*   William Pitt, the elder (1708–78), Whig statesman and orator.

[8]   *Sir Laurence Dundas*   Carter may mean Henry Dundas, first Viscount Melville (1742–1811), a wealthy member of Parliament, considered coarse.

[9]   *the seashore*   Carter spent summers at in the seaside town of Deal, Kent, where she was born.

means the only instance in which the nursery teaches common sense, and Philosophy talks jargon.

William Collins (1721–1759)

A brilliant student at Winchester school and highly regarded at Oxford, Collins seemed bound for literary success when he graduated with his BA in 1743. He arrived in London in 1744 and began making ambitious plans to write a History of the Revival of Learning, 1300–1521. Later he planned a translation of Aristotle's Poetics with a commentary. He evidently made progress on these projects, or spoke very plausibly about them, because both were publicly described by others as "in press." Nothing appeared, however, and there are reports that Collins spent a good deal of time going to assemblies or masqnes at Ranelagh and frequenting the playhouses. Collins was not altogether idle: in 1746 he wrote a series of odes published in that year as Odes on Several Descriptive and Allegoric Subjects (dated 1747). In the succeeding years he wrote a few more odes. Collins published few other poems, but his odes make a major contribution to English lyric poetry. They are a little less learned but more daring than Gray's odes; they link the poetry of the middle of the eighteenth century with the line of imaginative poetry established by Spenser and Milton, and they pave the way for the odes of John Keats. As small a body of work as Collins produced, British literature would be very different without him.

The facts are unclear, but Collins evidently became both physically and mentally ill around 1751. He traveled to Bath and to France for his health, but ended up confined in a madhouse for a while in England in 1754. Johnson visited him in Islington, London around this time, but evidence of his whereabouts and mental state are spotty. There were evidently periods of remission in the course of his disease, but after eight years of suffering what Johnson called "misery and degradation" Collins died at the age of thirty-seven.

The following texts are based on those in Odes on Several Descriptive and Allegoric Subjects *(1747). The "Ode to Evening," however was reprinted by Robert Dodsley in the second edition of his* A Collection of Poems by Several Hands *(1748), and I incorporate the changes introduced there. In doing so, I follow Richard Wendorf and Charles Ryskamp, editors of* The Works of William Collins *(Clarendon Press, 1979). I take advantage also of their commentary and that of Roger Lonsdale in his edition of Collins (Longman, 1969).*

from *Odes on Several Descriptive and Allegoric Subjects* (1747)

ODE TO FEAR

Thou, to whom the World unknown
With all its shadowy Shapes is shown;
Who see'st appalled th' unreal Scene
While Fancy lifts the Veil between:
    Ah *Fear*! Ah frantic *Fear*!   5
    I see, I see Thee near.
I know thy hurried Step, thy haggard Eye!
Like Thee I start, like Thee disordered fly,
For lo what *Monsters* in thy Train appear!
Danger, whose Limbs of Giant Mould   10
What mortal Eye can fixed behold?
Who stalks his Round, an hideous Form,

Howling amidst the Midnight Storm,
Or throws him on the ridgy Steep
Of some loose hanging Rock to sleep: 15
And with him thousand Phantoms joined,
Who prompt to Deeds accursed the Mind:
And those, the Fiends, who near allied,
O'er Nature's Wounds, and Wrecks preside;
Whilst *Vengeance*, in the lurid Air,   20
Lifts her red Arm, exposed and bare:
On whom that rav'ning Brood of Fate,[1]
Who lap the Blood of Sorrow, wait;
Who, *Fear*, this ghastly Train can see,
And look not madly wild, like Thee?   25

EPODE

In earliest *Greece* to Thee with partial Choice,
    The Grief-ful Muse addressed her infant Tongue;
The Maids and Matrons, on her awful Voice,
    Silent and pale in wild Amazement hung.

Yet He the Bard[2] who first invoked thy Name,   30
    Disdained in *Marathon* its Pow'r to feel:
For not alone he nursed the Poet's flame,
    But reached from Virtue's Hand the Patriot's Steel.

But who is He[3] whom later Garlands grace,
    Who left a-while o'er *Hybla*'s Dews to rove,[4]   35
With trembling Eyes thy dreary Steps to trace,
    Where Thou and *Furies* shared the baleful Grove?[5]

Wrapped in thy cloudy Veil th' *Incestuous Queen*[6]
    Sighed the sad Call her Son and Husband heared,[7]
When once alone it broke the silent Scene,   40
    And He the Wretch of *Thebes* no more appeared.

O *Fear*, I know Thee by my throbbing Heart,
    Thy with'ring Pow'r inspired each mournful Line,
Though gentle *Pity* claim her mingled Part,[8]
    Yet all the Thunders of the Scene are thine!   45

ODE TO FEAR
[1] *that rav'ning Brood of Fate*   Alluding to the Κυνας
ἀφυκτους [hounds which none can escape – the Furies]
of Sophocles. See the *Electra* [l. 1388 where the case and
order of words are different; Collins' note].
[2] *the Bard*   Aeschylus [Greek tragic poet who fought
the Persians at the battle of Marathon; Collins' note].
[3] *He*   Sophocles, Greek tragic poet thirty years
younger than Aeschylus.
[4] *Hybla*   a place in Sicily famous for honey; Sophocles
was, like Xenophon, praised as a bee because of his fine
style.

[5] *Furies*   the Eumenides, avenging deities, to whom
"the baleful Grove" in Sophocles' *Oedipus at Colonus* is
dedicated.
[6] *Incestuous Queen*   Jocasta [wife and mother of Oedipus, King of Thebes; Collins' note].
[7] *the sad Call*   Collins quotes *Oedipus at Colonus* ll.
1622–5, although the "call" comes from the heavens, not
Jocasta.
[8] *Pity*   in his *Poetics* Aristotle says tragedy must raise
the emotions of fear and pity in the audience.

ANTISTROPHE

Thou who such weary Lengths hast past,
Where wilt thou rest, mad Nymph, at last?
Say, wilt thou shroud in haunted Cell,[9]
Where gloomy *Rape* and *Murder* dwell?
Or in some hollowed Seat,   50
'Gainst which the big Waves beat,
Hear drowning Sea-men's Cries in Tempests brought!
Dark Pow'r, with shudd'ring meek submitted Thought
Be mine, to read the Visions old,
Which thy awak'ning Bards have told:[10]   55
And lest thou meet my blasted View,[11]
Hold each strange tale devoutly true;
Ne'er be I found, by Thee o'erawed,
In that thrice-hallowed Eve abroad,[12]
When Ghosts, as Cottage-Maids believe,   60
Their pebbled Beds permitted leave,
And *Goblins* haunt from Fire, or Fen,
Or Mine, or Flood, the Walks of Men!
     O Thou whose Spirit most possessed
The sacred Seat of *Shakespeare*'s Breast!   65
But all that from thy Prophet broke,
In thy Divine Emotions spoke:
Hither again thy Fury deal,
Teach me but once like Him to feel:
His *Cypress Wreath* my Meed decree,[13]   70
And I, O *Fear*, will dwell with *Thee!*

ODE ON THE POETICAL CHARACTER

As once, if not with light Regard,[1]
I read aright that gifted Bard[2]
(Him whose School above the rest[3]
His Loveliest *Elfin* Queen has blest),[4]
One, only One, unrivalled Fair,[5]   5
Might hope the magic Girdle wear,
At solemn Tourney hung on high,

---

[9] *shroud* "To harbour; to take shelter" (Johnson).
[10] *awak'ning* exciting.
[11] *blasted* confounded, struck with terror (Johnson, "blast"), as though Fear were a Gorgon, blasting or killing those who look on her.
[12] *thrice-hallowed Eve* Hallowe'en, 31 October.
[13] *Cypress Wreath* a triumphal crown for a tragic poet because cypress is a funereal plant; *Meed* "Reward; recompense. Now rarely used" (Johnson).
ODE ON THE POETICAL CHARACTER
[1] *Regard* attention.
[2] *Bard* Edmund Spenser, author of *The Faerie Queene.*

[3] *School* numerous writers followed in Spenser's school, including Milton (see ll. 55–76).
[4] *Elfin Queen* Spenser's Land of Faerie is a place of the imagination, so its Queen is a center of poetic inspiration, a muse (although the allegory also has a political dimension, in which the Queen is Elizabeth I).
[5] *unrivalled Fair* Florimel [Collins' note, with a reference to *The Faerie Queene*, which editors have improved to 4. 5.1–20; a pretend Florimel wins the beauty contest described there, but she cannot don the girdle for the reasons Collins states; the true Florimel gets the girdle back at 5.3.27–8].

The Wish of each love-darting Eye;
Lo! to each other Nymph in turn applied,
   As if, in Air unseen, some hov'ring Hand,   10
Some chaste and Angel-Friend to Virgin-Fame,
   With whispered Spell had burst the starting Band,
It left unblest her loathed dishonoured Side;
     Happier hopeless Fair, if never
     Her baffled Hand with vain Endeavour   15
Had touched that fatal Zone to her denied![6]
Young *Fancy* thus, to me Divinest Name,
To whom, prepared and bathed in Heav'n,
The Cest[7] of amplest Pow'r is giv'n:
To few the God-like Gift assigns,   20
To gird their blest prophetic Loins,
And gaze her Vision wild, and feel unmixed her Flame!

2

The Band, as Fairy Legends say,
Was wove on that creating Day,[8]
When He, who called with Thought to Birth   25
Yon tented Sky, this laughing Earth,
And dressed with Springs, and Forest tall,
And poured the Main engirting all,
Long by the loved *Enthusiast* wooed,[9]
Himself in some Diviner Mood,   30
Retiring, sate with her alone,
And placed her on his Sapphire Throne,
The whiles, the vaulted Shrine around,
Seraphic Wires were heard to sound,[10]
Now sublimest Triumph swelling,   35
Now on Love and Mercy dwelling;
And she, from out the veiling Cloud,
Breathed her magic Notes aloud:
And Thou, Thou rich-haired Youth of Morn,[11]
And all thy subject Life was born!   40
The dang'rous Passions kept aloof,
Far from the sainted growing Woof:[12]
But near it sate Ecstatic *Wonder*,
List'ning the deep applauding Thunder:
And *Truth*, in sunny Vest arrayed,   45
By whose the Tarsel's[13]
Eyes were made;

---

[6] *Zone* the girdle or belt.
[7] *Cest* belt or girdle, particularly the one belonging to Aphrodite.
[8] *that creating Day* the fourth day of creation; see *Paradise Lost* 7.339–56.
[9] *by* beside; *Enthusiast* "Young *Fancy*," l. 17.

[10] *Wires* strings of a harp or other instrument.
[11] *rich-haired Youth of Morn* the Sun and Apollo, god of the Sun, and of poetry.
[12] *sainted* "Holy; sacred" (Johnson); *Woof* woven cloth, tapestry.
[13] *By whose* on the model of whose (eyes); *Tarsel* Tercel or male hawk.

All the shad'wy Tribes of *Mind*,
In braided Dance their Murmurs joined,
And all the bright uncounted *Pow'rs*,   50
Who feed on Heav'n's ambrosial Flow'rs.[14]
Where is the Bard, whose Soul can now
Its high presuming Hopes avow?
Where He who thinks, with Rapture blind,
This hallowed Work for Him designed?[15]   55

3

High on some Cliff, to Heav'n up-piled
Of rude Accéss, of Prospect wild,[16]
Where, tangled round the jealous Steep,
Strange Shades o'erbore the Valleys deep,
And holy Genii guard the Rock,[17]   60
Its Glooms embrown, its Springs unlock,
While on its rich ambitious Head,
An Eden, like his own, lies spread:
I view that Oak, the fancied Glades among,[18]
    By which as Milton lay, His Evening Ear,   65
From many a Cloud that dropped Ethereal Dew,
    Nigh sphered in Heav'n its native Strains could hear:
On which that ancient Trump he reached was hung;
    Thither oft his Glory greeting,
    From *Waller*'s Myrtle Shades retreating,[19]   70
With many a Vow from Hope's aspiring Tongue,
My trembling Feet his guiding Steps pursue;
In vain – Such Bliss to One alone,
Of all the Sons of Soul was known,
And Heav'n, and Fancy, *kindred* Pow'rs,   75
Have now o'erturned th' inspiring Bow'rs,
Or curtained close such Scene from every future View.

from *A Collection of Poems by Several Hands* (1748)

ODE TO EVENING

If aught of Oaten Stop, or Pastoral Song,[1]
May hope, chaste *Eve*, to soothe thy modest Ear,

---

[14]   *ambrosial Flow'rs*   see *Paradise Lost* 2.245.
[15]   *This hallowed Work*   the girdle.
[16]   *Of rude Accéss*   this phrase and the whole description of Mount Parnassus (sacred to Apollo and poetry) recall Milton's descriptions of Eden as it appeared to those, like Satan, who sought entrance from without (*Paradise Lost* 4.132–8; 172–7; 543–50).
[17]   *Genii*   more than one genius, "The protecting or ruling power of men, places, or things" (Johnson).

[18]   *that Oak*   a reference to the place where Milton receives poetic inspiration in *Il Penseroso* (l. 60).
[19]   *Waller*   Edmund (1606–87), a poet whom Dryden (Preface to the *Fables*, 1700) identified as belonging to a different poetic school than Spenser and Milton; *Myrtle* "A fragrant tree sacred to Venus" (Johnson).
ODE TO EVENING
[1]   *Oaten Stop*   a fingerhole on and hence a rustic flute, which, with the lyre, accompanied the performance of classical odes.

Like thy own solemn Springs,
Thy Springs and dying Gales,²
O *Nymph* reserved, while now the bright-haired Sun   5
Sits in yon western Tent, whose cloudy Skirts,
With Brede ethereal wove,³
O'erhang his wavy Bed:
Now Air is hushed, save where the weak-eyed Bat,
With short shrill Shriek, flits by on leathern Wing,   10
Or where the Beetle winds
His small but sullen Horn,
As oft he rises 'midst the twilight Path,
Against the Pilgrim borne in heedless Hum:⁴
Now teach me, *Maid* composed,   15
To breathe some softened Strain,
Whose Numbers stealing through thy dark'ning Vale⁵
May not unseemly with its Stillness suit,
As musing slow, I hail
Thy genial loved Return!   20
For when thy folding Star arising shows⁶
His paly Circlet, at his warning Lamp
The fragrant *Hours*, and *Elves*⁷
Who slept in Flow'rs the Day,
And many a *Nymph* who wreathes her Brows with Sedge,   25
And sheds the fresh'ning Dew, and, lovelier still,
The *Pensive Pleasures* sweet,
Prepare thy shadowy Car.⁸
Then lead, calm *Vot'ress*, where some sheety Lake⁹
Cheers the lone Heath, or some time-hallowed Pile,¹⁰   30
Or up-land Fallows grey
Reflect its last cool Gleam.
But when chill blust'ring Winds, or driving Rain,
Forbid my willing Feet, be mine the Hut
That from the Mountain's Side   35
Views Wilds, and swelling Floods,
And Hamlets brown, and dim-discovered Spires,
And hears their simple Bell, and marks o'er all
Thy Dewy Fingers draw
The gradual dusky Veil.   40
While *Spring* shall pour his Show'rs, as oft he wont,¹¹

---

² *Gale* "A wind not tempestuous, yet stronger than a breeze" (Johnson).
³ *Brede* braid, "Applied by the poets to things that show or suggest interweaving of colours, or embroidery" (*OED*).
⁴ *Pilgrim* "A traveller; a wanderer" (Johnson).
⁵ *Numbers* "Harmony" (Johnson).
⁶ *folding Star* an evening star signaling the time for shepherds to fold or pen their sheep.

⁷ *Hours* the Horae, minor goddesses of natural order.
⁸ *Car* chariot.
⁹ *Vot'ress* "A woman devoted to any worship or state" (Johnson).
¹⁰ *Pile* building.
¹¹ *wont* is accustomed to do.

And bathe thy breathing Tresses, meekest *Eve*!
While *Summer* loves to sport
Beneath thy ling'ring Light;
While sallow *Autumn* fills thy Lap with Leaves;   45
Or *Winter*, yelling through the troublous Air,
Affrights thy shrinking Train,
And rudely rends thy Robes;
So long, sure-found beneath the Sylvan Shed,
Shall *Fancy, Friendship, Science*, rose-lip'd *Health*,[12]   50
Thy gentlest Influence own,
And hymn thy favourite Name!

Catherine Talbot (1721–1770)

The Rambler Number 30 is the only literary work of Talbot's to be published in her lifetime. It is one of only four Ramblers written by someone other than Johnson; two of the total of 208 were written by Elizabeth Carter, who was Talbot's best friend. She was widely admired for her learning, and her correspondence with Carter was published in 1809 after both women had died. It is interesting to see how an outsider, especially a woman, steps into Johnson's shoes. Of course no one was Johnson, and even Johnson was seldom as elevated as he is in Rambler 2 (see selection above), but the contrast between the two numbers is nevertheless striking.

from THE RAMBLER

NUMBER 30
SATURDAY, 30 *June* 1750

————*Vultus ubi tuus*
Affulsit Populo, gratior it Dies,
Et Soles melius nitent.

Horace *Odes* 4.5.6–8

Whene'er thy countenance divine
    Th' attendant people cheers,
The genial suns more radiant shine,
    The day more glad appears.

[James] Elphinstone [1721–1809]

MR RAMBLER,

There are a few Tasks more ungrateful, than for Persons of Modesty to speak their own Praises. In some Cases, however, this must be done for the general Good, and a generous spirit will on such Occasions assert its Merit, and vindicate itself with becoming Warmth.

---

[12] *Science* knowledge.

My Circumstances, Sir, are very hard and peculiar. Could the World be brought to treat me as I deserve, it would be a public Benefit. This makes me apply to you, that my Case being fairly stated in a Paper so generally esteemed, I may suffer no longer from ignorant and childish Prejudices.

My elder Brother was a Jew. A very respectable Person, but somewhat austere in his Manner: Highly and deservedly valued by his near Relations and Intimates, but utterly unfit for mixing in a larger Society, or gaining a general Acquaintance among Mankind. In a venerable old Age he retired from the World, and I in the Bloom of Youth came into it, succeeding him in all his Dignities, and formed, as I might reasonably flatter myself, to be the Object of universal Love and Esteem. Joy and Gladness were born with me; cheerfulness Good Humour and Benevolence always attended and endeared my Infancy. That Time is long past. So long, that idle Imaginations are apt to fancy me wrinkled, old, and disagreeable; but, unless my Looking-glass deceives me, I have not yet lost one Charm, one Beauty of my earliest Years. However, thus far is too certain, I am to every Body just what they choose to think me; so that to very few I appear in my right Shape; and though naturally I am the Friend of Human-kind, to few, very few comparatively, am I useful or agreeable.

This is the more grievous, as it is utterly impossible for me to avoid being in all Sorts of Places and Companies; and I am therefore liable to meet with perpetual Affronts and Injuries. Though I have as natural an Antipathy to Cards and Dice, as some People have to a Cat, many and many an Assembly am I forced to endure; and though Rest and Composure are my peculiar Joy, am worn out, and harassed to Death with Journeys by Men and Women of Quality, who never take one, but when I can be of the Party. Some, on a contrary Extreme, will never receive me but in Bed, where they spend at least half of the Time I have to stay with them; and others are so monstrously ill bred as to take Physic[1] on purpose when they have reason to expect me. Those who keep upon Terms of more Politeness with me, are generally so cold and constrained in their Behaviour, that I cannot but perceive myself an unwelcome Guest; and even among Persons deserving of Esteem, and who certainly have a Value for me, it is too evident that generally whenever I come I throw a Dullness over the whole Company, that I am entertained with a formal stiff Civility, and that they are glad when I am fairly gone.

How bitter must this kind of Reception be to one formed to inspire Delight, Admiration and Love! To one capable of answering and rewarding the greatest Warmth and Delicacy of Sentiments!

I was bred up among a Set of excellent People, who affectionately loved me, and treated me with the utmost Honour and Respect. It would be tedious to relate the Variety of my Adventures, and strange Vicissitudes of my Fortune in many different Countries. Here in *England* there was a Time when I lived according to my Heart's Desire. Whenever I appeared, Public Assemblies appointed for my Reception were crowded with Persons of Quality and Fashion, early dressed as for a Court, to pay me their Devoirs.[2] Cheerful Hospitality every where crowned my Board, and I was looked upon in every Country Parish as a kind of social Bond between the Squire, the Parson, and the Tenants. The laborious Poor every where blessed my Appearance: They do so still, and keep their best Clothes to do me Honour; though as much as I delight in the honest Country Folks, they do now and then throw a Pot of Ale at my Head, and sometimes an unlucky Boy will drive his Cricket-Ball full in my Face.

NUMBER 30   SATURDAY
[1] *Physic*   a purge.

[2] *Devoir*   "Act of civility or obsequiousness" (Johnson).

Even in those my best Days there were Persons who thought me too demure and grave. I must forsooth by all means be instructed by foreign Masters, and taught to dance and play. This Method of Education was so contrary to my Genius, formed for much nobler Entertainments, that it did not succeed at all.

I fell next into the Hands of a very different Set. They were so excessively scandalized at the Gaiety of my Appearance, as not only to despoil me of the foreign Fopperies, the Paint and the Patches[3] that I had been tricked out with by my last misjudging Tutors, but they robbed me of every innocent Ornament I had from my Infancy been used to gather in the Fields and Gardens; nay they blacked my Face, and covered me all over with a Habit of Mourning, and that too very coarse and awkward. I was now obliged to spend my whole Life in hearing Sermons; nor permitted so much as to smile upon any Occasion.

In this melancholy Disguise I became a perfect Bugbear to all Children and young Folks. Wherever I came there was a general Hush, an immediate Stop to all Pleasantness of Look or Discourse; and not being permitted to talk with them in my own Language at that Time, they took such a Disgust to me in those tedious Hours of Yawning, that having transmitted it to their Children, I cannot now be heard, though 'tis long since I have recovered my natural Form, and pleasing Tone of Voice. Would they but receive my Visits kindly, and listen to what I could tell them – let me say it without Vanity – how charming a Companion should I be! to every one could I talk on the Subjects most interesting and most pleasing. With the Great and Ambitious, I would discourse of Honours and Advancements, of Distinctions to which the whole World should be Witness, of unenvied Dignities and durable Preferments. To the Rich I would tell of inexhaustible Treasures, and the sure Method to attain them. I would teach them to put out their Money on the best Interest, and instruct the Lovers of Pleasure how to secure and improve it to the highest Degree. The Beauty should learn of me how to preserve an everlasting Bloom. To the Afflicted I would administer Comfort; and Relaxation to the Busy.

As I dare promise myself you will attest the Truth of all I have advanced, there is no doubt but many will be desirous of improving their Acquaintance with me; and that I may not be thought too difficult, I will tell you, in short, how I wish to be received.

You must know I equally hate lazy Idleness and Hurry. I would every where be welcomed at a tolerably early Hour with decent Good-humour and Gratitude. I must be attended in the Great Halls peculiarly appropriated to me with Respect; but I do not insist upon Finery: Propriety of Appearance and perfect Neatness is all I require. I must at Dinner be treated with a temperate, but a cheerful social Meal; both the Neighbours, and the Poor should be the better for me. Some Time I must have Tête à Tête with my kind Entertainers, and the rest of my Visit should be spent in pleasant Walks and Airings among Sets of agreeable People, in such Discourse as I shall naturally dictate, or in reading some few selected out of those numberless Books that are dedicated to me, and go by my Name. A name that, alas! as the World stands at present, makes them oftener thrown aside than taken up. As those Conversations and Books should be both well chosen, to give some Advice on that Head may possibly furnish you with a future Paper, and any Thing you shall offer on my Behalf will be of great Service to,

> Good Mr Rambler,
> *Your Faithful Friend and Servant,*
> SUNDAY

---

[3] *Patch* "A small spot of black silk put on the face" (Johnson).

Tobias Smollett (1721–1771)

At the age of eighteen Smollett shipped out on the HMS Chichester *as a second surgeon's mate. He sailed to the West Indies at the outbreak of the War of Jenkins Ear with Spain and was in Admiral Vernon's fleet at the bloody, unsuccessful siege of Cartagena on the north-east coast of South America. The British fleet retreated to Jamaica, and Smollett was discharged from the navy in the West Indies. He married there and returned to England expecting to resume the medical career he had begun at the age of fifteen as the apprentice to a Glasgow surgeon. He was too choleric and irritable, however, to support the bedside manner required of a successful doctor, so he turned naturally to literature, which had always been his first love. He wrote about the siege of Cartagena and other exploits in his satirical novel* Roderick Random *(1748), and his career was successfully launched.* Peregrine Pickle, *another satire, followed in 1751, and Smollett played his part in the Grubstreet wars as editor of* The Critical Review.

By 1763 Smollett had worked himself sick, and was suffering from consumption, the eighteenth-century name for a number of pulmonary disorders. Distressed too by the loss of his only child, he and his wife set out for the warmer weather and worlds elsewhere of France and Italy. Smollett described his travels in a series of letters, some of which may have actually been sent, but maybe not: the letter had long been a conventional way of reporting news, especially foreign news, and of piecing together other narratives, including travel books and novels. Travels through France and Italy *was published in 1766. There were five editions of the work in Smollett's lifetime, but it was overshadowed by Laurence Sterne's* Sentimental Journey *(1768), which was written partly in response to Smollett's work. Sterne rode the current of contemporary fashion in preferring the sentimental and genial approach to the somewhat outdated, irascible, cranky, but also realistic attitude to travel displayed in Smollett. The one chapter here, based on the first edition, shows some of the virtues of Smollett's realism and was widely taken later as a remarkable prediction of the French Revolution over twenty years before it occurred.*

I am indebted to the notes and introduction to Smollett's Travels *in the edition by Frank Felsenstein (Oxford University Press, 1979). The complete works of Smollett are being edited with commentary and textual apparatus by the University of Georgia Press.*

from *Travels through France and Italy* (1766)

LETTER 36

Nice, March 23, 1765

Dear Sir,

You ask whether I think the French people are more taxed than the English; but I apprehend, the question would more apropos if you asked whether the French taxes are more insupportable than the English; for, in comparing burthens we ought always to consider the strength of the shoulders that bear them. I know no better way of estimating the strength, than by examining the face of the country, and observing the appearance of the common people, who constitute the bulk of every nation. When I, therefore see the country of England smiling with cultivation; the grounds exhibiting all the perfection of agriculture, parcelled out into beautiful enclosures, cornfields, hay and pasture, woodland and common; when I see her meadows well stocked with black cattle; her downs covered with sheep; when I view her teams of horses and oxen, large and strong, fat and sleek; when I see her farm-houses the habitations of plenty, cleanliness, and convenience; and her peasants well fed, well lodged, well clothed, tall and stout, and hale and jolly; I cannot help concluding that the people are well able to bear those impositions which the public necessities have rendered necessary. On the other hand, when I perceive such signs of poverty, misery, and dirt, among the commonalty of France, their unfenced fields dug up in despair, without the interventions of meadow or fallow ground, without cattle to furnish manure, without horses to execute the plans of agriculture; their farm-houses mean, their furniture wretched, their apparel beggarly; themselves and their beasts the images of famine; I cannot help thinking they groan under oppression, either from their land-lords, or their government; probably from both.

The principal impositions of the French government are these: first, the taille, paid by all the commons, except those that are privileged: secondly, the capitation, from which no persons (not even the nobles) are excepted: thirdly, the tenths and twentieths, called Dixiêmes and Vingtiêmes, which every body pays. This tax was originally levied as an occasional aid in times of war, and other emergencies; but by degrees is become a standing revenue even in time of peace. All the money arising from these impositions goes directly to the king's treasure; and must undoubtedly amount to a very great sum. Besides these, he has the revenue of the farms,[1] consisting of the droit d'aides, or excise on wine, brandy, &c; of the custom-house duties; of the gabelle, comprehending that most oppressive obligation on individuals to take a certain quantity of salt at the price which the farmers shall please to fix; of the exclusive privilege to sell tobacco; of the droits de contrôle,[2] insinuation,[3] centiême denier,[4] franc-fiefs,[5] aubaine,[6] échange et contre-échange arising from the acts of voluntary jurisdiction, as well as certain law-suits. These farms are said to bring into the king's coffers above one hundred and twenty millions of livres yearly, amounting to near five millions sterling: but the poor people are said to pay about a third more than this sum, which the farmers retain to enrich themselves, and bribe the great for their protection; which protections of the great is the true reason why this most iniquitous, oppressive, and absurd method of levying money is not laid aside. Over and above those articles I have mentioned, the French king draws considerable sums from his clergy, under the denomination of dons gratuits, or free gifts; as well as from the subsidies given by the pays d'états, such as Provence, Languedoc, and Bretagne, which are exempted from the taille. The whole revenue of the French king amounts to between twelve and thirteen millions sterling. These are great resources for the king: but they will always keep the people miserable, and effectually prevent them from making such improvements as might turn their lands to the best advantage. But besides being eased in the article of taxes, there is something else required to make them exert themselves for the benefit of their country. They must be free in their persons, secure in their property, indulged with reasonable leases, and effectually protected by law from the insolence and oppression of their superiors.

Great as the French king's resources may appear, they are hardly sufficient to defray the enormous expense of his government. About two millions sterling per annum of his revenue are said to be anticipated for paying the interest of the public debts; and the rest is found inadequate to the charge of a prodigious standing army, a double frontier[7] of fortified towns,

LETTER 36

[1] *farms* fermiers généraux – financial companies that purchased from the state concessions for collecting taxes.
[2] *droits de contrôle* a kind of stamp tax.
[3] *insinuation* a tax applied to donations and loans.
[4] *centiême denier* a sort of inheritance tax.

[5] *franc-fiefs* a tax on non-nobles who held noble lands.
[6] *aubaine* droit d'aubaine, explained by Smollett in Letter 2 as allowing the seizure of the estates of foreigners who die in France.
[7] *frontier* border.

and the extravagant appointments of ambassadors, generals, governors, intendants, commandants, and other officers of the crown, all of whom affect a pomp, which is equally ridiculous and prodigal. A French general in the field is always attended by thirty or forty cooks; and thinks it is incumbent upon him, for the glory of France, to give a hundred dishes every day at his table. When don Philip, and the marechal duke de Belleisle, had their quarters at Nice, there were fifty scullions constantly employed in the great square in plucking poultry. This absurd luxury infects their whole army. Even the commissaries keep open table; and nothing is seen but prodigality and profusion. The king of Sardinia proceeds upon another plan. His troops are better clothed, better paid, and better fed than those of France. The commandant of Nice[8] has about four hundred a year of appointments, which enable him to live decently, and even to entertain strangers. On the other hand, the commandant of Antibes, which is in all respects more inconsiderable than Nice, has from the French king above five times the sum to support the glory of his monarch, which all the sensible part of mankind treat with ridicule and contempt. But the finances of France are so ill managed, that many of their commandants, and other officers, have not been able to draw their appointments these two years. In vain they complain and remonstrate. When they grow troublesome they are removed. How then must they support the glory of France? how, but by oppressing the poor people. The treasurer makes use of their money for his own benefit. The king knows it; he knows his officers, thus defrauded, fleece and oppress his people: he thinks [it] proper to wink at these abuses. That government may be said to be weak and tottering which finds itself obliged to connive[9] at such proceedings. The king of France, in order to give strength and stability to his administration, ought to have sense to adopt a sage plan of economy, and vigour of mind sufficient to execute it in all its parts, with the most rigorous exactness. He ought to have courage enough to find fault, and even to punish the delinquents, of what quality soever they may be: and the first act of reformation ought to be a total abolition of all the farms. There are, undoubtedly, many marks of relaxation in the reins of the French government, and, in all probability, the subjects of France will be the first to take advantage of it. There is at present a violent fermentation of different principles among them, which under the reign of a very weak prince, or during a long minority,[10] may produce a great change in the constitution. In proportion to the progress of reason and philosophy, which have made great advances in this kingdom, superstition loses ground; ancient prejudices give way; a spirit of freedom takes the ascendant. All the learned laity of France detest the hierarchy as a plan of despotism, founded on imposture and usurpation. The protestants, who are very numerous in the southern parts, abhor it with all the rancour of religious fanaticism. Many of the commons, enriched by commerce and manufacture, grow impatient of those odious distinctions, which exclude them from the honours and privileges due to their importance in the commonwealth; and all the parliaments, or tribunals of justice in the kingdom, seem bent upon asserting their rights and independence in the face of the king's prerogative, and even at the expense of his power and authority. Should any prince therefore be seduced by evil counsellors, or misled by his own bigotry to take some arbitrary step, that may be extremely disagreeable to all those comunities, without having spirit to exert the violence of his power for the support of his measures, he will become equally detested and despised; and the influence of the commons will insensibly encroach upon the pretensions of the crown. But if in the time of a minority,

---

8   *commandant of Nice*   at this time Nice was part of the Kingdom of Sardinia, the title of the lands ruled by the House of Savoy; the French attacked and occupied it after the Revolution, in which Savoy backed the monarchy.

9   *connive*   wink.
10   *minority*   when the kingdom is ruled by a regency, the rightful heir being under age.

the power of the government should be divided among different competitors for the regency, the parliaments and people will find it still more easy to acquire and ascertain the liberty at which they aspire, because they will have the balance of power in their hands, and be able to make either scale preponderate. I could say a great deal more upon this subject; and I have some remarks to make relating to the methods which might be taken in case of a fresh rupture with France, for making a vigorous impression on that kingdom. But these I must defer till another occasion, having neither room nor leisure at present to add any thing, but that I am, with great truth,

Dear Sir
Your very humble servant

Christopher Smart (1722–1771)

Sometime late in 1758 or early 1759, Smart entered a private asylum for the insane near London and remained there for at least four years. He was troubled for a few years before that; it is hard to determine if his illness was primarily physical or psychological, but it clearly rendered him mentally infirm. When he emerged from his disease, his marriage to the stepdaughter of the successful publisher John Newberry was over, and his life was in shambles. He was arrested numerous times for debt, and, despite the efforts of friends to save him, Smart died in the debtors' prison known as the King's Bench.

Smart distinguished himself in Classics at Pembroke College, Cambridge and held a fellowship there until marriage disqualified him for it in 1753. Smart pursued serious poetry, publishing Latin versions of some of Pope's poems and winning the Seatonian prize for the best poem on God's attributes five of the first six years it was offered. In addition, Smart launched himself as a journalist, working mostly for John Newberry but contributing to numerous London periodicals. Samuel Johnson gave Smart some assistance in providing copy for the Universal Visiter, *which began publication in 1756, about the time that Smart's health began to fail.*

For all its strangeness, Jubilate Agno *is comprised of the same elements that make up the rest of Smart's works: it expresses devotional themes, and it combines biblical and historical imagery with material of a more personal nature. The "Let . . . For" structure of the poem comes from biblical hymns or canticles; the* Song of Solomon, *also known as* Canticles, *begins, "Let him kiss me with the kisses of his mouth: for thy love is better than wine." The Jubilate is a part of the Christian Mass which uses Psalm 100, but Smart indicated that his poem most resembled a similar part of the service called the Magnificat, which relies on the hymn of the Virgin Mary (Luke 1.46–55), beginning "My soul doth magnify the Lord." Considering Smart's elaborate magnification of his cat Jeoffry, many readers will feel Smart may have been chasing a quibble or a pun as well as stating his real intentions when he called his poem a magnificat.*

The autograph manuscript of Jubilate Agno *is in the Houghton Library at Harvard University. The text is clearly incomplete, with some pages missing or perhaps never written. Fragment A is on a sheet of paper numbered "1" and contains only "Let" lines; the corresponding "For" passages and the leaf that would have been numbered "2" are missing. Fragment B contains four pairs of leaves: there are more "Fors" than "Lets" in this section, but some pairs on leaves both numbered "3" clearly go together. This correspondence helped the scholar Donald Bond to recognize the pattern of the unfinished poem. The selections here follow Bond's discoveries of 1950, as*

*represented in the edition by Karina Williamson (Clarendon Press, 1980). I follow Williamson
in printing the "For" verses in italics, but only when they follow "Let" verses. Both my notes and
my introductory remarks here are deeply indebted to Williamson's work.*

from *Jubilate Agno*[1] (c. 1758–63)

FROM FRAGMENT A (c. 1758–9)

Rejoice in God, O ye Tongues; give the glory to the Lord, and the Lamb.
Nations, and languages, and every Creature, in which is the breath of Life.
Let man and beast appear before him, and magnify his name together.
Let Noah and his company approach the throne of Grace, and do homage to the
  Ark of their Salvation.
Let Abraham present a Ram, and worship the God of his Redemption.   5
Let Isaac, the Bridegroom, kneel with his Camels, and bless the hope of his
  pilgrimage.
Let Jacob, and his speckled Drove adore the good Shepherd of Israel.
Let Esau offer a scape Goat for his seed, and rejoice in the blessing of God his
  father.
Let Nimrod, the mighty hunter, bind a Leopard to the altar, and consecrate his
  spear to the Lord.
Let Ishmael dedicate a Tiger, and give praise for the liberty, in which the Lord
  has set him at large . . .[2]   10

FROM FRAGMENT B[3]

Let Elizur rejoice with the Partridge,[4] who is a prisoner of state and is proud
  of his keepers.
*For I am not without authority in my jeopardy,[5] which I derive inevitably from the
  glory of the name of the Lord.*
Let Shedeur rejoice with Pyrausta,[6] who dwelleth in a medium of fire, which
  God hath adapted for him.
*For I bless God whose name is Jealous[7] – and there is a zeal to deliver us from
  everlasting burnings.*
Let Shelumiel rejoice with Olor,[8] who is of a godly savour, and the very look
  of him harmonizes the mind.

FRAGMENT A
[1] *Jubilate Agno* "Rejoice in the Lamb"; Christ is several times referred to as the lamb of God; particularly in John (e.g. 1.29) and Revelation (e.g. 22.1); the opening lines of the poem suggest Revelation 7.9–17, where the tribes of Israel are "sealed" against destruction in the apocalypse by God (compare the selection from Anna Trapnel above); the tribes of all tongues respond by offering "salus," "health" or "salvation," to God and to the Lamb.
[2] All ellipses in the text are mine [ed.]
[3] *Fragment B* this section was begun in July 1759 during the Seven Years War (known in America as the French and Indian War); the biblical names come from Genesis and Numbers.
[4] *Partridge* see Ecclesiasticus 11.30: "As a decoy partridge in a cage, so is the heart of a proud man."
[5] *jeopardy* captivity.
[6] *Pyrausta* Latin, a fly supposed to live in fire (*pyralis* is the more common Latin word for it).
[7] *Jealous* see Exodus 20.5: "I the Lord thy God am a jealous God" and, for the protective rather than punitive implications of the appelation, see Joel 2.18.
[8] *Olor* Latin "swan"; the word resembles Latin *oleo*, to give off a smell, to savor.

*For my existimation[9] is good even amongst the slanderers and my memory shall arise for
a sweet savour unto the Lord.*

Let Jael[10] rejoice with the Plover, who whistles for his life, and foils the
marksmen and their guns.

*For I bless the PRINCE of PEACE and pray that all the guns may be nailed up, save
such are for the rejoicing days.*

Let Raguel rejoice with the Cock of Portugal[11] – God send good Angels to the
allies of England! 5

For I have abstained from the blood of the grape and that even at the Lord's table.

Let Hobab rejoice with Necydalus,[12] who is the Greek of a Grub.

*For I have glorified God in GREEK and LATIN, the consecrated languages spoken by
the Lord on earth.*

Let Zurishaddai with the Polish Cock rejoice – The Lord restore peace to Europe

For I meditate the peace of Europe amongst family bickerings and domestic jars.

Let Zuar rejoice with the Guinea Hen – The Lord add to his mercies in the
WEST![13]

For the HOST is in the WEST – The Lord make us thankful unto salvation.

Let Chesed rejoice with Strepsiceros,[14] whose weapons are the ornaments of his
peace.

*For I preach the very GOSPEL of CHRIST without comment & with this weapon
shall I slay envy . . .*

For I will consider my Cat Jeoffry. 695

For he is the servant of the Living God, duly and daily serving him.

For at the first glance of the glory of God in the East he worships in his way.

For is this done by wreathing his body seven times round with elegant
quickness.

For then he leaps up to catch the musk, which is the blessing of God upon
his prayer.

For he rolls upon prank to work it in.[15] 700

For having done duty and received blessing he begins to consider himself.

For this he performs in ten degrees.

For first he looks upon his fore-paws to see if they are clean.

For secondly he kicks up behind to clear away there.

For thirdly he works it upon stretch with the fore paws extended. 705

For fourthly he sharpens his paws by wood.

For fifthly he washes himself.

For sixthly he rolls upon wash.

For Seventhly he fleas himself,[16] that he may not be interrupted upon the beat.

---

[9] *existimation*   "Esteem" (Johnson).
[10] *Jael*   the wife of Heber, killed Sisera, leader of Jabin
the Canaanite's army, by driving a nail through his temples; this and the nails with which Christ is crucified
suggest "nailed up" in the "For" verse.
[11] *Portugal*   a long-standing ally of England.
[12] *Necydalus*   from Greek, the nymph of the silkworm;
the word is related to νέκυς, corpse.
[13] *WEST*   the West Indies, where part of the Seven
Years War was fought, and some of the enemies of Israel,

in biblical terms (e.g. Zechariah 8.7: "Behold, I will save
my people from the east country, and from the west
country").
[14] *Strepsiceros*   "A kind of animal with twisted horns"
(Lewis and Short).
[15] *prank*   "A frolic; a wild flight; a ludicrous trick"
(Johnson).
[16] *fleas himself*   rids himself of fleas.

For Eighthly he rubs himself against a post. 710

For Ninthly he looks up for his instructions.

For Tenthly he goes in quest of food.

For having considered God and himself he will consider his neighbour.

For if he meets another cat he will kiss her in kindness.

For when he takes his prey he plays with it to give it chance. 715

For one mouse in seven escapes by his dallying.

For when his day's work is done his business more properly begins.

For he keeps the Lord's watch in the night against the adversary.

For he counteracts the powers of darkness by his electrical skin & glaring eyes.

For he counteracts the Devil, who is death, by brisking about the life. 720

For in his morning orisons[17] he loves the sun and the sun loves him.

For he is of the tribe of Tiger.

For the Cherub Cat is a term of the Angel Tiger.

For he has the subtlety and hissing of a serpent, which in goodness he
    suppresses.

For he will not do destruction, if he is well-fed, neither will he spit without
    provocation. 725

For he purrs in thankfulness, when God tells him he's a good Cat.

For he is an instrument for the children to learn benevolence upon.

For every house is incomplete without him & a blessing is lacking in the
    spirit.

For the Lord commanded Moses concerning the cats at the departure of the
    Children of Israel from Egypt.[18]

For every family had one cat at least in the bag. 730

For the English Cats are the best in Europe.

For he is the cleanest in the use of his fore-paws of any quadruped.

For the dexterity of his defence is an instance of the love of God to him
    exceedingly.

For he is the quickest to his mark of any creature.

For he is tenacious of his point. 735

For he is a mixture of gravity and waggery.

For he knows that God is his Saviour.

For there is nothing sweeter than his peace when at rest.

For there is nothing brisker than his life when in motion.

For he is of the Lord's poor and so indeed is he called by benevolence
    perpetually – Poor Jeoffry! poor Jeoffry! the rat has bit thy throat. 740

For I bless the name of the Lord Jesus that Jeoffry is better.

For the divine spirit comes about his body to sustain it in complete cat.

For his tongue is exceeding pure so that it has in purity what it wants in music.

For he is docile and can learn certain things.

For he can set up with gravity which is patience upon approbation. 745

For he can fetch and carry, which is patience in employment.

For he can jump over a stick which is patience upon proof positive.

---

[17] *orisons* prayers.

[18] *Lord commanded Moses concerning the cats* the Lord
says, "Take your flocks and your herds . . ." (Exodus
12.32); there is no order concerning cats.

For he can spraggle upon waggle at the word of command.
For he can jump from an eminence into his master's bosom.
For he can catch the cork and toss it again. 750
For he is hated by the hypocrite and miser.
For the former is afraid of detection.
For the latter refuses his charge.
For he camels his back to bear the first notion of business.
For he is good to think on, if a man would express himself neatly. 755
For he made a great figure in Europe for his signal services.
For he killed the Ichneumon-rat[19] very pernicious by land.
For his ears are so acute that they sting again.
For from this proceeds the passing quickness of his attention.
For by stroking of him I have found out electricity. 760
For I perceived God's light about him both wax and fire.
For the Electrical fire is the spiritual substance, which God sends from heaven
    to sustain the bodies both of man and beast.
For God has blessed him in the variety of his movements.
For, though he cannot fly, he is an excellent clamberer.
For his motions upon the face of the earth are more than any other quadruped. 765
For he can tread to all the measures upon the music.
For he can swim for life.
For he can creep.

Mary Leapor (1722–1746)

Leapor's father was a gardener in Northamptonshire, and she worked for a time in the kitchen of an estate near Brackley. Despite discouragement from her mother and other local folk, from an early age Leapor spent her time reading and, much more unusually for a woman, writing. Her poems circulated in manuscript and came to the attention of Bridget Fremantle, daughter of the former rector of Hinton. Fremantle became Leapor's friend, patron, and, after Leapor's very early death, her literary executor. She saw two volumes of Leapor's poems through subscription publication, both called Poems on Several Occasions *(1748 and 1751). The second volume was printed by Samuel Richardson who also participated in editing it, with some members of his literary circle. Richardson described Leapor's poems as "sweetly easy." They are easy in that they are not highly allusive or learned, but many of Leapor's poems have a satiric edge as well as a country sweetness. As a versifier, she was an imitator of Alexander Pope, but her sphere is rural and domestic. Her manor poem, "Crumble Hall," is altogether different in feeling from Pope's great house poem* Windsor Forest. *Her "Epistle to a Lady" incorporates some elements of Pope's poem of the same name, but there is again a sharp contrast in feeling and, quite obviously, in point of view. Like many other women writers of the period, Leapor regularly used poetic names for herself and for friends who appear in her verse: Mira is her name for herself and Artemisia for her patron, Bridget Fremantle.*

---

[19] *Ichneumon-rat* "A small animal that breaks the eggs of the crocodile" (Johnson); it was valued by the Egyptians; Smart means to praise cats for killing rats which carried the fleas that spread bubonic plague.

The texts presented here are based on the first editions. Richard Greene is producing an edition of Leapor's poems. There is a good selection of her verse in Roger Lonsdale's Eighteenth-Century Women Poets *(Oxford University Press, 1989).*

from *Poems on Several Occasions* (1748)

THE MONTH OF AUGUST

Sylvanus, *a Courtier.* Phillis, *a Country Maid.*

SYLVANUS

Hail, *Phillis,* brighter than a Morning Sky,
Joy of my Heart, and Darling of my Eye;
See the kind Year her grateful Tribute yields,
And round-faced Plenty triumphs o'er the Fields.
But to yon Gardens let me lead thy Charms,   5
Where the curled Vine extends her willing Arms:
Whose purple Clusters lure the longing Eye,
And the ripe Cherries show their scarlet Dye.

PHILLIS

Not all the Sights your bloated Gardens yield,
Are half so lovely as my Father's Field,   10
Where large Increase has blessed the fruitful Plain,
And we with Joy behold the swelling Grain,
Whose heavy Ears towards the Earth reclined,
Wave, nod, and tremble to the whisking Wind.

SYLVANUS

But see, to emulate those Cheeks of thine,   15
On yon fair Tree the blushing Nect'rins shine:
Beneath their Leaves the ruddy Peaches glow,
And the plump Figs compose a gallant Show.
With gaudy Plums see yonder Boughs recline,
And ruddy Pears in yon *Espalier* twine.   20
There humble Dwarfs in pleasing Order stand,
Whose golden Product see till comes thy Hand.

PHILLIS

In vain you tempt me while our Orchard bears
Long-keeping Russets, lovely Cath'rine Pears,
Pearmains and Codlings, wheaten Plums enough,[1]   25
And the black Damsons load the bending Bough.
No Pruning-knives our fertile Branches tease,

THE MONTH OF AUGUST
[1] *Russets, Pearmains and Codlings*   varieties of apples.

While yours must grow but as their Masters please.
The grateful Trees our Mercy well repay,
And rain us Bushels at the rising Day.   30

SYLVANUS
Fair are my Gardens, yet you slight them all;
Then let us haste to yon majestic Hall,
Where the glad Roofs shall to thy Voice Resound,
Thy Voice more sweet than Music's melting Sound:
Now *Orion*'s Beam infests the sultry Sky,[2]   35
And scorching Fevers through the Welkin fly;
But Art shall teach us to evade his Ray,
And the forced Fountains near the Windows play;
There choice Perfumes shall give a pleasing Gale,[3]
And Orange-flow'rs their od'rous Breath exhale,   40
While on the Walls the well-wrought Paintings glow,
And dazzling Carpets deck the Floors below:
O tell me, Thou whose careless Beauties charm,
Are these not fairer than a Thresher's Barn?

PHILLIS
Believe me, I can find no Charms at all   45
In your fine Carpets and your painted Hall.
'Tis true our Parlour has an earthen Floor,
The Sides of Plaster and of Elm the Door:
Yet the rubbed Chest and Table sweetly shines,
And the spread Mint along the Window climbs: 50
An agèd Laurel keeps away the Sun,
And two cool Streams across the Garden run.

SYLVANUS
Can Feasts or Music win my lovely maid?
In both those Pleasures be her Taste obeyed.
The ransacked Earth shall all its Dainties send,   55
Till with its Load her plenteous Tables bend.
Then to the Roofs the swelling Notes shall rise,
Pierce the glad Air and gain upon the Skies,
While Ease and Rapture spreads itself around,
And distant Hills roll back the charming Sound.   60

PHILLIS
Not this will lure me, for I'd have you know
This Night to feast with *Corydon* I go:
To Night his Reapers bring the gathered Grain,
Home to his Barns, and leave the naked Plain:

---

[2] *Orion* the constellation in the ascendant at the warmest time of year. [3] *Gale* breeze.

Then Beef and Coleworts, Beans and Bacon too,[4]   65
And the Plum-pudding of delicious Hue,
Sweet-spiced Cake, and Apple-pies good Store,
Deck the brown Board; who can desire more?
His Flute and Tabor too *Amyntor* brings,[5]
And while he plays soft *Amaryllis* sings.   70
Then strive no more to win a simple maid,
From her loved Cottage and her silent Shade.
Let *Phillis* ne'er, ah never let her rove
From her first Virtue and her humble grove.
Go seek some Nymph that equals your Degree,   75
And leave Content and *Corydon* for me.

AN EPISTLE TO A LADY

In vain, dear Madam, yes, in vain you strive,
Alas! to make your luckless *Mira* thrive,[1]
For *Tycho*[2] and *Copernicus* agree,
No golden Planet bent its Rays on me.[3]

'Tis twenty Winters, if it is no more,   5
To speak the Truth it may be Twenty four:
As many Springs their 'pointed Space have run,
Since *Mira*'s eyes first opened on the Sun.
'Twas when the Flocks on slabby Hillocks lie,
And the cold Fishes rule the watry sky:[4]   10
But though these eyes the learnèd page explore,
And turn the ponderous volumes o'er and o'er,
I find no comfort from their systems flow,
But am dejected more as more I know.
Hope shines a while, but like a vapour flies   15
(The fate of all the curious and the wise),
For, ah! cold Saturn triumphed on that day,[5]
And frowning Sol denied his golden ray.[6]

You see I'm learnèd, and I show't the more,
That none may wonder when they find me poor.   20
Yet *Mira* dreams, as slumbering poets may,
And rolls in Treasures till the breaking Day,
While Books and Pictures in bright Order rise,
And painted Parlours swim before her Eyes:
Till the shrill Clock impertinently rings,   25
And the soft Visions move their shining Wings:

---

[4] *Coleworts* cabbages.
[5] *Tabor* a kind of drum.
AN EPISTLE TO A LADY
[1] *Mira* Leapor's poetic name for herself.
[2] *Tycho* Tycho Brahe (1546–1601), Danish astronomer who rejected Copernican theory.
[3] *No golden planet bent its rays on me* her astrological chart is not favourable.

[4] *Fishes* the constellation Pisces, a water sign, which "rules" in late winter.
[5] *Saturn* "The remotest planet of the Solar System, supposed by astrologers to impress melancholy, dullness, or severity of temper" (Johnson).
[6] *Sol* the Sun.

Then *Mira* wakes, – her Pictures are no more,
And through her Fingers slides the vanished Ore.
Convinced too soon, her Eye unwilling falls
On the blue Curtains and the dusty Walls: 30
She wakes, alas! to Business and to Woes,
To sweep her Kitchen, and to mend her Clothes.

But see pale Sickness with her languid Eyes,
At whose Appearance all Delusion flies:
The World recedes, its Vanities decline,   35
Clorinda's Features seem as faint as mine:
Gay Robes no more the aching Sight admires,
Wit grates the Ear, and melting Music tires.
Its wonted Pleasures with each Sense decay,[7]
Books please no more, and Paintings fade away,   40
The sliding Joys in misty Vapours end:
Yet let me still, ah! let me grasp a Friend:
And when each Joy, when each loved Object flies,
Be you the last that leaves my closing Eyes.

But how will this dismantled Soul appear,   45
When stripped of all it lately held so dear,
Forced from its Prison of expiring Clay,
Afraid and shivering at the doubtful Way?

Yet did these Eyes a dying Parent see,
Loosed from all Cares except a Thought for me,   50
Without a Tear resign her shortening Breath,
And dauntless meet the lingering Stroke of Death.
Then at th' Almighty's Sentence shall I mourn,
'Of Dust thou art, to Dust shalt thou return'?
Or shall I wish to stretch the Line of Fate,   55
That the dull Years may bear a longer Date,
To share the Follies of succeeding Times
With more Vexations and with deeper Crimes?
Ah no – though Heav'n brings near the final Day,
For such a Life I will not, dare not pray;   60
But let the Tear for future Mercy flow,
And fall resigned beneath the mighty Blow.
Nor I alone – for through the spacious Ball,
With me will Numbers of all Ages fall:
And the same Day that *Mira* yields her Breath,   65
Thousands may enter through the Gates of Death.

MIRA'S WILL

IMPRIMIS – My departed Shade I trust[1]
To Heav'n – My Body to the silent Dust;

---

[7] *wonted* customary.

MIRA'S WILL
[1] *IMPRIMIS* in the first place.

My Name to public Censure I submit,
To be disposed of as the World thinks fit;
My Vice and Folly let Oblivion close,　　　　　　　　　　5
The World already is o'erstocked with those;
My Wit I give, as Misers give their Store,
To those who think they had enough before.
Bestow my Patience to compose the Lives
Of slighted Virgins and neglected Wives;　　　　　　　10
To modish Lovers I resign my Truth,
My cool Reflection to unthinking Youth;
And some Good-nature give ('tis my Desire)
To surly Husbands, as their Needs require;
And first discharge my Funeral – and then　　　　　　15
To the small Poets I bequeath my Pen.
　　Let a small Sprig (true Emblem of my Rhyme)
Of blasted Laurel on my Hearse recline;[2]
Let some grave Wight, that struggles for renown
By chanting Dirges through a Market-Town,　　　　　20
With gentle Step precede the solemn Train;
A broken Flute upon his Arm shall lean.[3]
Six comic Poets may the Corse surround,
And All Free-holders, if they can be found:[4]
Then follow the next melancholy Throng,　　　　　　25
As shrewd Instructors, who themselves are wrong:
The Virtuoso, rich in Sun-dried Weeds,[5]
The Politician, whom no Mortal heeds,
The silent Lawyer, chambered all the day,
And the stern Soldier that receives no Pay.　　　　　30
But stay – the Mourners should be first our care:
Let the freed Prentice lead the Miser's Heir;
Let the young Relict[6] wipe her mournful Eye,
And widowed Husbands o'er their Garlic cry.

　　All this let my executors fulfil,　　　　　　　　　35
And rest assured that this is *Mira*'s will,
Who was, when she these legacies designed,
In body healthy, and composed in mind.

from *Poems on Several Occasions* (1751)

AN ESSAY ON WOMAN

Woman, a pleasing but a short-lived Flow'r,
Too soft for Business and too weak for Power:

---

[2]　*blasted Laurel*　bay laurel, symbolic of poetic achievement, withered by weather or the change of seasons.
[3]　*Flute*　symbolic of lyric poetry.

[4]　*Free-holder*　one who owns property or holds it free from seizure for his lifetime.
[5]　*Virtuoso*　natural scientist.
[6]　*relict*　widow.

A Wife in Bondage, or neglected Maid;
Despised, if ugly; if she's fair, Betrayed.
'Tis Wealth alone inspires every Grace, 5
And calls the Raptures to her plenteous Face.
What Numbers for those charming Features pine,
If blooming Acres round her Temples twine!
Her Lip the Strawberry, and her Eyes more bright
Than sparkling Venus in a frosty Night; 10
Pale Lillies fade and, when the Fair appears,
Snow turns a Negro and dissolves in Tears,
And, where the Charmer treads her magic Toe,
On *English* ground *Arabian* odours grow;[1]
Till mighty Hymen lifts his sceptred Rod,[2] 15
And sinks her Glories with a fatal Nod,
Dissolves her Triumphs, sweeps her Charms away,
And turns the Goddess to her native Clay.
  But, *Artemisia*, let your Servant sing
What small Advantage Wealth and Beauties bring. 20
Who would be Wise, that knew *Pamphilia*'s fate?
Or who be Fair, and joined to *Sylvia*'s mate?
Sylvia, whose Cheeks are fresh as early Day,
As Evening mild, and sweet as spicy May:
And yet that Face her partial Husband tires, 25
And those bright Eyes, that all the World admires.
Pamphilia's Wit who does not strive to shun,
Like Death's Infection or a Dog-day's Sun?[3]
The Damsels view her with malignant Eyes,
The Men are vexed to find a Nymph so Wise: 30
And Wisdom only serves to make her know
The keen Sensation of superior Woe.
The secret Whisper and the list'ning Ear,
The scornful Eyebrow and the hated Sneer,
The giddy Censures of her babbling Kind, 35
With thousand Ills that grate a gentle Mind,
By her are tasted in the first Degree,
Though overlooked by *Simplicius* and me.
Does thirst of Gold a Virgin's Heart inspire,
Instilled by Nature or a careful Sire? 40
Then let her quit Extravagance and Play,
The brisk Companion and expensive Tea,
To feast with *Cordia* in her filthy Sty
On stewed Potatoes or on a mouldy Pie;
Whose eager Eyes stare ghastly at the Poor, 45
And fright the Beggars from her hated Door;

AN ESSAY ON WOMAN
[1] *Arabian odours* Arabia was an old source of aromatic spices and gums.

[2] *Hymen* god of marriage.
[3] *Dog-day's* late summer, when Sirius, the dog-star, is prominent in the sky.

In greasy Clouts she wraps her smoky Chin,[4]
And holds that Pride's a never-pardoned Sin.
    If this be Wealth, no matter where it falls;
But save, ye Muses, save your *Mira*'s walls: 50
Still give me pleasing Indolence and Ease,
A Fire to warm me and a Friend to please.
    Since, whether sunk in Avarice or Pride,
A wanton Virgin or a starving Bride,
Or wond'ring Crowds attend her charming Tongue,   55
Or, deemed an Idiot, ever speaks the Wrong;
Though Nature armed us for the growing Ill
With fraudful Cunning and a headstrong Will;
Yet, with ten thousand Follies to her Charge,
Unhappy Woman's but a Slave at large.   60

CRUMBLE-HALL

When Friends or Fortune frown on *Mira*'s Lay,
Or gloomy Vapours hide the Lamp of Day;
With low'ring Forehead, and with aching Limbs,
Oppressed with Head-ache, and eternal Whims,
Sad *Mira* vows to quit the darling Crime: 5
Yet takes her Farewell, and repents, in Rhyme.

    But see (more charming than *Armida*'s Wiles)
The Sun returns, and *Artemisia* smiles:
Then in a trice the Resolutions fly;
And who so frolic as the Muse and I?   10
We sing once more, obedient to her Call;
Once more we sing; and 'tis of *Crumble-Hall*;[1]
That *Crumble-Hall*, whose hospitable Door
Has fed the Stranger, and relieved the Poor;
Whose *Gothic* Towers, and whose rusty Spires,   15
Were known of old to Knights, and hungry Squires.
There powdered Beef, and Warden-Pies, were found;[2]
And Pudden dwelt within her spacious Bound:
Pork, Peas, and Bacon (good old *English* Fare!),
With tainted Ven'son, and with hunted Hare:[3]   20
With humming Beer her Vats were wont to flow,[4]
And ruddy *Nectar* in her Vaults to glow.[5]
Here came the Wights, who battled for Renown,
The sable Friar, and the russet Clown:
The loaded Tables sent a sav'ry Gale,[6]   25

---

[4] *Clouts* rags.
CRUMBLE-HALL
[1] *Crumble-Hall* Lonsdale suggests the model for this
was Weston Hall, where Leapor was probably employed
as a cook-maid.
[2] *powdered* salted or pickled, preserved; *Warden-*
Pies the warden was a kind of baking pear.
[3] *tainted* "Imbued with the scent of an animal (usually a hunted animal)" (*OED*).
[4] *humming* strong, as well as frothing;
wont accustomed.
[5] *ruddy Nectar* cider.
[6] *gale* a breeze.

And the brown bowls were crowned with simp'ring Ale;[7]
While the Guests ravaged on the smoking Store,
Till their stretched Girdles would contain no more.

Of this rude Palace might a Poet sing
From cold *December* to returning Spring;   30
Tell how the Building spreads on either hand,
And two grim Giants o'er the Portals stand;
Whose grilléd Beards are neither combed nor shorn,[8]
But look severe, and horribly adorn.

Then step within – there stands a goodly Row   35
Of oaken Pillars – where a gallant Show
Of mimic Pears and carved Pom'granates twine,
With the plump Clusters of the spreading Vine.
Strange Forms above, present themselves to View;
Some mouths that grin, some smile, and some that spew.   40
Here a soft Maid or Infant seems to cry:
Here stares a Tyrant, with distorted Eye:
The Roof – no *Cyclops* e'er could reach so high:
Not *Polypheme*, though, formed for dreadful Harms,[9]
The Top could measure with extended Arms.   45
Here the pleased Spider plants her peaceful Loom:
Here weaves secure, nor dreads the hated Broom.
But at the Head (and furbished once a Year)
The Herald's mystic Compliments appear:
Round the fierce Dragon *Honi Soit* twines,[10]   50
And Royal *Edward* o'er the Chimney shines.

Safely the Mice through yon dark Passage run,
Where the dim Windows ne'er admit the Sun.
Along each Wall the Stranger blindly feels;
And (trembling) dreads a Spectre at his heels.   55

The sav'ry Kitchen much Attention calls:
Westphalia Hams adorn the sable Walls:
The Fires blaze; the greasy Pavements fry;
And steaming Odours from the Kettles fly.

See! yon brown Parlour on the Left appears,   60
For nothing famous, but its leathern Chairs,
Whose shining Nails like polished Armour glow,
And the dull Clock beats audible and slow.
But on the Right we spy a Room more fair:
The Form – 'tis neither long, nor round, nor square;   65
The Walls how lofty, and the Floor how wide,
We leave for learned *Quadrus* to decide.

7 *simp'ring* simmering.
8 *grilled* helmeted; grills are the bars on a knight's helmet.
9 *Polypheme* the name of the cyclops (a race of one-eyed giants) whom Odysseus outwits.
10 *Honi Soit* qui mal y pense "evil to him who thinks evil," the motto of the Most Noble Order of the Garter, founded by Edward III in 1348.

Gay *China* Bowls o'er the broad Chimney shine,
Whose long Description would be too sublime:
And much might of the Tapestry be sung: 70
But we're content to say, The Parlour's hung.

We count the Stairs, and to the Right ascend,
Where on the Walls the gorgeous Colours blend.
There doughty *George* bestrides the goodly Steed;[11]
The Dragon's slaughtered, and the Virgin freed: 75
And there (but lately rescued from their Fears)
The Nymph and serious *Ptolemy* appears:[12]
Their awkward Limbs unwieldy are displayed;
And, like a Milk-wench, glares the royal Maid.

From hence we turn to more familiar Rooms;   80
Whose Hangings ne'er were wrought in *Grecian* Looms:[13]
Yet the soft Stools, and eke the lazy Chairs,
To sleep invite the Weary, and the Fair.

Shall we proceed? – Yes, if you'll break the Wall:
If not, return, and tread once more the Hall.   85
Up ten Stone Steps now please to drag your Toes,
And a brick Passage will succeed to those.
Here the strong Doors were aptly framed to hold
Sir *Wary*'s Person, and Sir *Wary*'s Gold.
Here *Biron* sleeps, with Books encircled round;   90
And him you'd guess a Student most profound,
Not so – in Form the dusty Volumes stand:
There's few that wear the Mark of *Biron*'s Hand.

Would you go further? – Stay a little then:
Back through the Passage – down the Steps again;   95
Through yon dark Room – Be careful how you tread
Up these steep Stairs – or you may break your Head.
These Rooms are furnished amiably, and full:
Old Shoes, and Sheep-ticks bred in Stacks of Wool;
Grey *Dobbin*'s Gears, and Drenching-Horns enow;[14]   100
Wheel-spokes – the Irons of a tattered Plough.

No further – Yes, a little higher, pray:
At yon small Door you'll find the Beams of Day,
While the hot Leads return the scorching Ray.[15]
Here a gay Prospect meets the ravished Eye: 105
Meads, Fields, and Groves, in beauteous Order lie.
From hence the Muse precipitant is hurled,
And drags down *Mira* to the nether World.

---

[11] *George* St George is the patron saint of the Order of
the Garter.
[12] *Ptolemy* first-century CE astronomer, author of the
Almagest, an encyclopedic work.

[13] *Grecian Looms* synonymous with fine weaving.
[14] *Drenching-Horn* an instrument for administering
medicine to a horse.
[15] *Leads* lead roofs.

Thus far the Palace – Yet there still remain
Unsung the Gardens and the menial Train.   110
Its Groves anon – its People first we sing:
Hear, *Artemisia*, hear the Song we bring.
Sophronia first in Verse shall learn to chime,
And keep her Station, though in *Mira*'s Rhyme;
Sophronia sage! whose learned Knuckles know   115
To form round Cheese-cakes of the pliant Dough;
To bruise the Curd, and through her Fingers squeeze
Ambrosial Butter with the tempered Cheese:
Sweet Tarts and Pudden, too, her Skill declare;
And the soft Jellies, hid from baneful Air.   120

O'er the warm Kettles, and the sav'ry Steams,
Grave *Colinettus* of his Oxen dreams:
Then starting, anxious for his new-mown Hay,
Runs headlong out to view the doubtful Day:
But Dinner calls with more prevailing Charms;   125
And surly *Grusso* in his awkward Arms
Bears the tall Jug, and turns a glaring Eye,
As though he feared some Insurrection nigh
From the fierce Crew, that gaping stand a-dry.

O'er-stuffed with Beef; with Cabbage much too full,   130
And Dumpling too (fit Emblem of his Skull!)
With Mouth wide open, but with closing Eyes
Unwieldy *Roger* on the Table lies.
His able Lungs discharge a rattling Sound:
Prince barks, *Spot* howls, and the tall Roofs rebound.   135
Him *Urs'la* views; and, with dejected Eyes,
'Ah! *Roger*, Ah!' the mournful Maiden cries:
Is wretched *Ur'sla* then your Care no more,
That, while I sigh, thus you can sleep and snore?
Ingrateful *Roger*! wilt thou leave me now?   140
For you these Furrows mark my fading Brow:
For you my Pigs resign their Morning Due:
My hungry Chickens lose their Meat for you:
And, was it not, Ah! was it not for thee,
No goodly Pottage would be dressed by me.   145
For thee these Hands wind up the whirling Jack,[16]
Or place the Spit across the sloping Rack.
I baste the Mutton with a cheerful Heart,
Because I know my *Roger* will have Part'.

Thus she – But now her Dish-kettle began   150
To boil and blubber with the foaming Bran.
The greasy Apron round her Hips she ties,

---

[16] *Jack*   an instrument for turning the *Spit* in cooking
over the *Rack*, or grate, of an open fire.

And to each Plate the scalding Clout applies:[17]
The purging Bath each glowing Dish refines,
And once again the polished Pewter shines.   155

    Now to those Meads let frolic Fancy rove,[18]
Where o'er yon Waters nods a pendant Grove;[19]
In whose clear Waves the pictured Boughs are seen,
With fairer Blossoms, and a brighter Green.
Soft flow'ry Banks the spreading Lakes divide: 160
Sharp-pointed Flags adorn each tender Side.
See! the pleased Swans along the Surface play;
Where yon cool Willows meets the scorching Ray,
When fierce *Orion* gives too warm a Day.[20]

    But, hark! what Scream the wond'ring Ear invades!   165
The *Dryads* howling for their threatened Shades:[21]
Round the dear Grove each Nymph distracted flies
(Though not discovered but with Poet's Eyes):
And shall those Shades, where *Philomela*'s Strain[22]
Has oft to Slumber lulled the hapless Swain;   170
Where Turtles used to clap their silken Wings;[23]
Whose rev'rend Oaks have known a hundred Springs;
Shall these ignobly from their Roots be torn,
And perish shameful, as the abject Thorn;
While the slow Car bears off their aged Limbs,[24]   175
To clear the Way for Slopes, and modern Whims;
Where banished Nature leaves a barren Gloom,
And awkward Art Supplies the vacant Room?
Yet (or the Muse for Vengeance calls in vain)
The injured Nymphs shall haunt the ravaged Plain: 180
Strange Sounds and Forms shall tease the gloomy Green;
And Fairy-Elves by *Urs'la* shall be seen:
Their new-built Parlour shall with Echoes ring:
And in their Hall shall doleful Crickets sing.

    Then cease, *Diracto*, stay thy desp'rate Hand;   185
And let the Grove, if not the Parlour, stand.

MAN THE MONARCH

    Amazed we read of Nature's early Throes,
How the fair Heav'ns and pond'rous Earth arose;
How blooming Trees unplanted first began;
And Beasts submissive to their Tyrant, Man:
To Man, invested with despotic Sway,   5

[17] *Clout* "A cloth for any mean use" (Johnson).
[18] *Meads* meadows.
[19] *pendant* hanging, or weeping, like a willow.
[20] *Orion* a constellation in the ascension in mid-summer; Sirius, the star representing Orion's dog, brings in the dog-days of late summer.
[21] *Dryads* demi-goddesses of the forest.
[22] *Philomela* the nightingale.
[23] *Turtles* turtle-doves.
[24] *Car* wagon.

While his mute Brethren tremble and obey;
Till Heav'n beheld him insolently vain,
And checked the Limits of his haughty Reign.
Then from their Lord the rude Deserters fly,
And grinning back, his fruitless Rage defy;   10
Pards, Tigers, Wolves to gloomy Shades retire,
And Mountain-Goats in purer Gales respire.[1]
To humble Valleys, where soft Flow'rs blow,
And fatt'ning Streams in crystal mazes flow,
Full of new Life, the untamed Coursers run,   15
And roll and wanton in the cheerful Sun;
Round their gay Hearts in dancing Spirits rise,
And rouse the Lightnings in their rolling Eyes:
To craggy Rocks destructive Serpents glide,
Whose mossy Crannies hide their speckled Pride;   20
And monstrous Whales on foamy Billows ride.
Then joyful Birds ascend their native Sky:
But where! ah, where shall helpless Woman fly?

   Here smiling Nature brought her choicest Stores,
And roseate Beauty on her favourite Pours: 25
Pleased with her Labour, the officious Dame[2]
Withheld no Grace would deck the rising Frame.
Then viewed her Work, and viewed and smiled again,
And kindly whispered, 'Daughter, live and reign'.
But now the Matron mourns her latest Care,   30
And sees the Sorrows of her darling Fair;
Beholds a Wretch, whom she designed a Queen,
And weeps that e'er she formed the weak Machine.
In vain she boasts her Lip of scarlet dyes,
Cheeks like the Morning, and far-beaming Eyes;   35
Her Neck refulgent, fair and feeble Arms –
A Set of useless and neglected Charms.
She suffers Hardship with afflictive Moans:
Small tasks of Labour suit her slender Bones.
Beneath a Load her weary Shoulders yield,   40
Nor can her Fingers grasp the sounding Shield;
She sees and trembles at approaching Harms,
And Fear and Grief destroy her fading Charms.
Then her pale Lips no pearly Teeth disclose,
And Time's rude sickle cuts the yielding Rose.   45
Thus wretched woman's shortlived Merit dies:
In vain to Wisdom's sacred Help she flies,
Or sparkling Wit but lends a feeble Aid:
'Tis all Delirium from a wrinkled Maid.

MAN THE MONARCH   [2] *officious* kind.
[1] *Gales* breezes; *respire* breathe.

A tattling Dame, no matter where or who –   50
Me it concerns not, and it need not you –
Once told this Story to the list'ning Muse,
Which we, as now it serves our Turn, shall use.

When our Grandsire named the feathered Kind,
Pondering their Natures in his careful Mind,   55
'Twas then, if on our Author we rely,
He viewed his Consort with an envious Eye;
Greedy of Power, he hugged the tott'ring Throne,
Pleased with the Homage, and would reign alone;
And, better to secure his doubtful Rule,   60
Rolled his wise Eyeballs, and pronounced her *Fool*.
The regal Blood to distant Ages runs:
Sires, Brothers, Husbands, and commanding Sons,
The Sceptre claim; and every Cottage brings
A long Succession of domestic Kings.   65

Now the dull Muses took their usual Rest;
The Babes slept soundly in their tiny Chest.
Not so their Parent: Fortune still would send
Some proud Director, or ill-meaning Friend:
At least we thought their sour Meanings ill,   70
Whose Lectures strove to cross a stubborn Will.

Parthenia cries, 'Why, *Mira*, you are dull,
And ever musing, till you crack your Skull;
Still poking o'er your what-d'ye-call-your Muse:
But prithee, *Mira*, when dost clean thy Shoes?'   75

Then comes *Sophronia*, like a barbarous Turk:
'You thoughtless Baggage, when d'ye mind your Work?
Still o'er a Table leans your bending Neck:
Your Head will grow preposterous, like a Peck.
Go, ply your Needle: you might earn your Bread: 80
Or who must feed you when your Father's dead?'
She sobbing answers, 'Sure, I need not come
To you for Lectures: I have store at home.
What can I do?'
                         – 'Not scribble.'   85
                         – 'But I will'.
'Then get thee packing – and be awkward still'.

Thus wrapped in Sorrow, wretched *Mira* lay,
Till *Artemisia* swept the Gloom away:[3]
The laughing Muse, by her Example led,   90
Shakes her glad Wings, and quits the drowsy Bed.

---

[3] *Artemisia* Leapor's name for her patron, Bridget
Freemantle.

Joshua Reynolds (1723–1792)

In 1763, when he received his pension of £300 per year, Samuel Johnson accompanied Joshua Reynolds on a visit to his home in Devonshire. By that time Reynolds had been making about £6000 per year for about ten years painting portraits of the most important people in England. He began at the age of twenty as an apprentice to Thomas Hudson, spent three important years in Italy imbibing a love of the grand style of Michelangelo and Titian, and returned to become the most important English portrait painter in history. He was so busy with work that he established a kind of assembly line of portrait production in which his assistants took care of less important parts of the pictures, like the drapery and background, and he stepped in to execute the face and hands of the subject. Reynolds had as many as 156 sitters in a single year. His procedure was in stark contrast to that of Gainsborough, the second best known portraitist of the time.

Reynolds's penchant for organization and cooperation displayed itself not only in his artistic method but in his many administrative achievements. He had much to do with founding the Royal Academy and served as its first president from 1768. He instituted the Academy's schools, and from 1769–90 at the annual prize-awarding ceremony Reynolds delivered a "Discourse" to the students. For the benefit of the students he often stressed the importance of hard work, the need to learn one's craft from earlier practitioners, and the folly of relying on natural talent alone. However, Reynolds expanded his remarks to cover a great deal of painting history and, most importantly, to establish an aesthetic point of view that is applicable to any of the arts. It is not an unchanging, formulaic view, but Reynolds's Discourses represented the established view of art clearly enough that William Blake could define his revolutionary approach in diametrical opposition to them, as his thickly and fiercely annotated copy of Reynolds shows.

Blake's annotations, beginning with his declaration on the title page, "This Man was Hired to Depress Art," appear in the appendix to the fine edition of Reynolds's Discourses by Robert R. Wark (1959; rev. Yale University Press, 1975). The text of Discourse 14 is based on the first edition of 1788 but incorporates changes made by Reynolds but not appearing until the edition of 1797. I am indebted to Wark's commentary. The "Ironical Discourse" was Reynolds's reaction to the French Revolution written in terms of his life-long occupation with his art. Reynolds drafted it on the back of a fair copy of Discourse 15, his last, in the summer of 1791. The draft, which Reynolds never finished for delivery or publication, displays his own views in reverse, and it shows how great a wave the Revolution sent through the artistic and personal, as well as the political, strata of life in England. It was found among the papers in James Boswell's hoard at Malahide Castle and it is printed in Portraits by Sir Joshua Reynolds, edited by Frederick W. Hilles (Heinemann, 1952).

from Discourse 14

DELIVERED TO THE STUDENTS OF THE ROYAL ACADEMY, ON THE DISTRIBUTION OF THE PRIZES, 10 DECEMBER 1788

Gentlemen,

In the study of our Art, as in the study of all Arts, something is the result of *our own* observation of Nature; something, and that not a little, the effect of the example of those who have studied the same nature before us, and who have cultivated before us the same Art, with diligence and success. The less we confine ourselves in the choice of those examples, the more advantage we shall derive from them; and the nearer we shall bring our performances to a correspondence with nature and the great general rules of Art. When we draw our examples from remote and revered antiquity – with some advantage undoubtedly in that selection – we subject ourselves to some inconveniencies. We may suffer ourselves to be too much led away by great names, and to be too much subdued by overbearing authority. Our learning, in that case, is not so much an exercise of our judgement, as a proof of our docility. We find ourselves perhaps too much over-shadowed; and the character of our pursuits is rather distinguished by the tameness of the follower, than animated by the spirit of emulation. It is sometimes of service, that our examples should be *near* us; and such as raise a reverence, sufficient to induce us carefully to observe them, yet not so great as to prevent us from engaging with them in something like a generous contention.

We have lately lost Mr. Gainsborough,[1] one of the greatest ornaments of our Academy. It is not our business here, to make panegyrics on the living, or even on the dead who were of our body. The praise of the former might bear the appearance of adulation; and the latter of untimely justice; perhaps of envy to those whom we still have the happiness to enjoy, by an oblique suggestion of invidious comparisons. In discoursing, therefore, on the talents of the late Mr. Gainsborough, my object is, not so much to praise or to blame him, as to draw from his excellencies and defects, matter of instruction to the Students in our Academy. If ever this nation should produce genius sufficient to acquire to us the honourable distinction of an English School, the name of Gainsborough will be transmitted to posterity, in the history of the art, among the very first of that rising name. That our reputation in the Arts is now only rising, must be acknowledged; and we must expect our advances to be attended with old prejudices, as adversaries, and not as supporters; standing in this respect in a very different situation from the late artists of the Roman school, to whose reputation ancient prejudices have certainly contributed: the way was prepared for them, and they may be said rather to have lived in the reputation of their country, than to have contributed to it; whilst whatever celebrity is obtained by English Artists, can arise only from the operation of a fair and true comparison. And when they communicate to their country a share of their reputation, it is a portion of fame not borrowed from others, but solely acquired by their own labour and talents. As Italy has undoubtedly a prescriptive right to an admiration bordering on prejudice, as a soil peculiarly adapted, congenial, and, we may add, destined to the production of men of great genius in our Art, we may not unreasonably suspect that a portion of the great fame of some of their late artists has been owing to the general readiness and disposition of mankind, to acquiesce in their original prepossession in favour of the productions of the Roman School.

On this ground, however unsafe, I will venture to prophesy, that two of the last distinguished painters of that country, I mean Pompeio Batoni and Raphael Mengs,[2] however great their names may at present sound in our ears, will very soon fall into the rank of Imperiale, Sabastiano Conca, Placido Costanzi, Masucci,[3] and the rest of their immediate predecessors; whose names, though equally renowned in their lifetime, are now fallen into what is little short of total oblivion. I do not say that those painters were not superior to the artist I allude to, and whose loss we lament, in a certain routine of practice, which, to the eyes of common observers, has the air of a learned composition, and bears a sort of superficial resemblance to

DELIVERED TO THE STUDENTS OF THE ROYAL ACADEMY
[1] *Gainsborough* Thomas (1727–August 2 1788), an original member of the Royal Academy (1768), but quarreled on and off with Reynolds and the Academy and exhibited his paintings elsewhere over half of his final twenty years.

[2] *Pompeio Batoni and Raphael Mengs* very important historical and portrait painters of the eighteenth century, both recently deceased.
[3] *Imperiale [Francesco Fernandi], Sabastiano Conca, Placido Costanzi, Masucci* painters just a generation earlier than Batoni and Mengs.

the manner of the great men who went before them. I know this perfectly well; but I know likewise, that a man looking for real and lasting reputation, must unlearn much of the common-place method so observable in the works of the artists whom I have named. For my own part, I confess, I take more interest in and am more captivated with the powerful impression of nature, which Gainsborough exhibited in his portraits and in his landscapes, and the interesting simplicity and elegance of his little ordinary beggar-children, than with any of the works of that School, since the time of Andrea Sacchi,[4] or perhaps we may say Carlo Maratti;[5] two painters who may truly be said to be ULTIMI ROMANORUM.[6]

I am well aware how much I lay myself open to the censure and ridicule of the academical professors of other nations, in preferring the humble attempts of Gainsborough to the works of those regular graduates in the great historical style. But we have the sanction of all mankind in preferring genius in a lower rank of art, to feebleness and insipidity in the highest.

It would not be to the present purpose, even if I had the means and materials, which I have not, to enter into the private life of Mr. Gainsborough. The history of his gradual advancement, and the means by which he acquired such excellence in his art, would come nearer to our purposes and wishes, if it were by any means attainable; but the slow progress of advancement is in general imperceptible to the man himself who makes it; it is the consequence of an accumulation of various ideas which his mind has received, he does not perhaps know how or when. Sometimes indeed it happens, that he may be able to mark the time when from the sight of a picture, a passage in an author, or a hint in conversation, he has received, as it were, some new and guiding light, something like inspiration, by which his mind has been expanded; and is morally sure that his whole life and conduct has been affected by that accidental circumstance. Such interesting accounts, we may however sometimes obtain from a man who has acquired an uncommon habit of self-examination, and has attended to the progress of his own improvement.

It may not be improper to make mention of some of the customs and habits of this extraordinary man; points which come more within the reach of an observer; I however mean such only as are connected with his art, and indeed were, as I apprehended, the causes of his arriving to that high degree of excellence, which we see and acknowledge in his works. Of these causes we must state, as the fundamental, the love which he had to his art; to which, indeed, his whole mind appears to have been devoted, and to which every thing was referred; and this we may fairly conclude from various circumstances of his life, which were known to his intimate friends. Among others, he had a habit of continually remarking to those who happened to be about him whatever peculiarity of countenance, whatever accidental combination of figure, or happy effects of light and shadow, occurred in prospects, in the sky, in walking the streets, or in company. If, in his walks, he found a character that he liked, and whose attendance was to be obtained, he ordered him to his house: and from the fields he brought into his painting-room, stumps of trees, weeds, and animals of various kinds; and designed them not from memory, but immediately from the objects. He even framed a kind of model of landscapes on his table; composed of broken stones, dried herbs, and pieces of looking glass, which he magnified and improved into rocks, trees, and water. How far this latter practice may be useful in giving hints, the professors of landscape can best determine. Like every other technical practice, it seems to me wholly to depend on the general talent of him who uses it. Such methods may be nothing better than contemptible and mischievous

4   *Andrea Sacchi* (1599–1661), a chief Italian exponent of classicism in seventeenth-century Italian painting.
5   *Carlo Maratti* (1625–1713), master of the late Roman Baroque school of painting.

6   *ULTIMI ROMANORUM*   "the last of the Romans"; Gaius Cassius Longinus, who helped kill Caesar, was called this by someone (perhaps Brutus) sympathetic to his cause.

trifling; or they may be aids. I think, upon the whole, unless we constantly refer to real nature, that practice may be more likely to do harm than good. I mention it only, as it shows the solicitude and extreme activity which he had about everything that related to his art; that he wished to have his objects embodied as it were, and distinctly before him; that he neglected nothing which could keep his faculties in exercise, and derived hints from every sort of combination.

We must not forget, whilst we are on this subject, to make some remarks on his custom of painting by night, which confirms what I have already mentioned – his great affection to his art – since he could not amuse himself in the evening by any other means so agreeable to himself. I am indeed much inclined to believe that it is a practice very advantageous and improving to an artist: for by this means he will acquire a new and a higher perception of what is great and beautiful in nature. By candlelight, not only objects appear more beautiful, but from their being in a greater breadth and uniformity of colour, nature appears in a higher style; and even the flesh seems to take a higher and richer tone of colour. Judgement is to direct us in the use to be made of this method of study; but the method itself is, I am very sure, advantageous. I have often imagined that the two great colourists, Titian and Correggio,[7] though I do not know that they painted by night, formed their high ideas of colouring from the effects of objects by this artifical light: but I am more assured that whoever attentively studies the first and best manner of Guercino,[8] will be convinced that he either painted by this light, or formed his manner on this conception.

Another practice of Gainsborough had, which is worth mentioning, as it is certainly worthy of imitation; I mean his manner of forming all the parts of his picture together; the whole going on at the same time, in the same manner as nature creates her works. Though this method is not uncommon to those who have been regularly educated, yet probably it was suggested to him by his own natural sagacity. That this custom is not universal appears from the practice of a painter whom I have just mentioned, Pompeio Batoni, who finished his historical pictures part after part, and in his portraits completely finished one feature before he proceeded to another. The consequence was, as might be expected; the countenance was never well expressed; and, as the painters say, the whole was not well put together.

The first thing required to excel in our art, or I believe in any art, is not only a love for it, but even an enthusiastic ambition to excel in it. This never fails of success proportioned to the natural abilities with which the artist has been endowed by Providence. Of Gainsborough, we certainly know, that his passion was not the acquirement of riches, but excellence in his art; and to enjoy that honourable fame which is sure to attend it. – That *he felt this ruling passion strong in death*, I am myself a witness. A few days before he died, he wrote me a letter, to express his acknowledgments for the good opinion I entertained of his abilities, and the manner in which (he had been informed) I always spoke of him; and desired he might see me once before he died. I am aware how flattering it is to myself to be thus connected with the dying testimony which this excellent painter bore to his art. But I cannot prevail on myself to suppress that I was not connected with him, by any habits of familiarity: if any little jealousies had subsisted between us, they were forgotten, in those moments of sincerity; and he turned towards me as one, who was engrossed by the same pursuits, and who deserved his good opinion, by being sensible of his excellence. Without entering into a detail of what passed at this last interview, the impression of it upon my mind was, that his regret at losing life, was principally the regret of leaving his art; and more especially as he now began, he said,

7   *Titian and Correggio* Tiziano Vecellio and Antonio Allegri, great sixteenth-century Italian painters.

8   *Guercino* Giovanni Francesco Barbieri (1591–1666).

to see what his deficiencies were; which, he said he flattered himself in his last works were in some measure supplied.

When such a man as Gainsborough arrives to great fame, without the assistance of an academical education, without travelling to Italy, or any of those preparatory studies which have been so often recommended, he is produced as an instance, how little such studies are necessary; since so great excellence may be acquired without them. This is an inference not waranted by the success of any individual; and I trust it will not be thought that I wish to make this use of it.

It must be remembered that the style and department of art which Gainsborough chose, and in which he so much excelled, did not require that he should go out of his own country for the objects of his study; they were every where about him; he found them in the streets, and in the fields, and from the models thus accidently found, he selected with great judgement such as suited his purpose. As his studies were directed to the living world principally, he did not pay a general attention to the works of the various masters, though they are, in my opinion, always of great use, even when the character of our subject requires us to depart from some of their principles. It cannot be denied, that excellence in the department of the art which he professed may exist without them; that in such subjects, and in the manner that belongs to them, the want of them is supplied, and more than supplied, by natural sagacity, and a minute observation of particular nature. If Gainsborough did not look at nature with a poet's eye, it must be acknowledged that he saw her with the eye of a painter; and gave a faithful, if not a poetical, representation of what he had before him.

Though he did not much attend to the works of great historical painters of former ages, yet he was well aware that the language of the art – the art of imitation – must be learned somewhere; and as he knew that he could not learn it in an equal degree from his contemporaries, he very judiciously applied himself to a Flemish School, who are undoubtedly the greatest masters of one necessary branch of art; and he did not need to go out of his own country for examples of that school: from that he learnt the harmony of colouring, the management and disposition of light and shadow, and every means which the masters of it practised, to ornament and give splendour to their works. And to satisfy himself as well as others, how well he knew the mechanism and artifice which they employed to bring out that tone of colour which we so much admire in their works, he occasionally made copies from Rubens, Teniers, and Vandyck,[9] which it would be no disgrace to the most accurate connoisseur to mistake, at the first sight, for the works of those masters. What he thus learned, he applied to the originals of nature, which he saw with his own eyes; and imitated, not in the manner of those masters, but in his own.

Whether he most excelled in portraits, landscapes, and fancy-pictures,[10] it is difficult to determine: whether his portraits were most admirable for exact truth of resemblance, or his landscapes for a portrait-like representation of nature, such as we see in the works of Rubens, Ruysdael,[11] and others of those schools. In his fancy-pictures, when he had fixed on his object of imitation, whether it was the mean and vulgar form of a wood-cutter, or a child of an interesting character, as he did not not attempt to raise the one, so neither did he lose any of the natural graces and elegance, of the other; such a grace, and such an elegance, as are more frequently found in cottages than in courts. This excellence was his own, the result of his particular observation and taste; for this he was certainly not indebted to the Flemish School,

---

9   *Rubens, Teniers, and Vandyck* Flemish painters of the seventeenth century.

10   *fancy-pictures* fantasies.

11   *Ruysdael* seventeenth-century Dutch landscape artist.

nor indeed to any School; for his grace was not academical or antique, but selected by himself from the great school of nature; and there are yet a thousand modes of grace, which are neither theirs, nor his, but lie open in the multiplied scenes and figures of life, to be brought out by skilful and faithful observers.

Upon the whole, we may justly say, that whatever he attempted he carried to a high degree of excellence. It is to the credit of his good sense and judgement, that he never did attempt that style of historical painting, for which his previous studies had made no preparation.

And here it naturally occurs to oppose the sensible conduct of Gainsborough in this respect, to that of our late excellent Hogarth,[12] who, with all his extraordinary talents, was not blessed with this knowledge of his own deficiency; or of the bounds which were set to the extent of his own powers. After this admirable artist had spent the greatest part of his life in an active, busy, and we may add, successful attention to the ridicule of life; after he had invented a new species of dramatic painting, in which probably he will never be equalled, and had stored his mind with infinite materials to explain and illustrate the domestic and familiar scenes of common life, which were generally, and ought to have been always, the subject of his pencil; he very imprudently, or rather presumptuously, attempted the great historical style, for which his previous habits had by no means prepared him: he was indeed so entirely unacquainted with the principles of this style, that he was not even aware, that any artificial[13] preparation was at all necessary. It is to be regretted, that any part of the life of such a genius should be fruitlessly employed. Let his failure teach us not to indulge ourselves in the vain imagination, that by a momentary resolution we can give either dexterity to the hand, or a new habit to the mind . . .

[The Ironical Discourse] (1791)

SIR JOSHUA'S PREFACE

The following ironical discourse owes its origin to a conversation on Burke's *Reflections on the Revolution of France*,[1] of which book Sir Joshua Reynolds expressed the most enthusiastic admiration, both in regard to the doctrine which it contained, and the eloquence in which that doctrine was conveyed.

The conversation turned on the power which is lodged in majorities. It was said that the French nation having almost unanimously adopted the revolution had in its favour this greatest criterion of truth. This inference was disputed. Sir Joshua was of opinion that if matters of taste are determined as he thinks they ought to be, by weight rather than by tale,[2] much more political questions, which involved so much science,[3] ought to be determined by the few learned in that art, and not by the ignorant majority.

That the majority were ignorant was denied, and much was said of the 'present enlightened age', and on the general diffusion of knowledge amongst all ranks of people. They were therefore capable of judging for themselves. They had tasted of the tree of knowledge: they now knew good from evil, and would not take it as they done. That [they had tasted] of the tree of knowledge was granted, but they had only tasted and, it appears, as much to their own loss as 'twas to our first parents. Our poet says, 'Drink deep, or taste not'.[4]

---

[12] *Hogarth* William (1697–1764), painter, engraver, satirist.
[13] *artificial* learned.
SIR JOSHUA'S PREFACE
[1] *Reflections on the Revolution of France* see the selection from Burke, p. 1038 below.

[2] *tale* count, tally.
[3] *science* knowledge.
[4] *"Drink deep, or taste not"* "A little Learning is a dangerous thing, / . . . the *Pierian* Spring" Pope, *An Essay on Criticism*, 215–16.

This tree of knowledge, on which they pretend to say that mankind now have battened, does not grow upon a new made, slender soil, but is fastened by strong roots of ancient rocks, and is the slow growth of ages. There are but few of strength sufficient to climb the summit of this rock, from whence indeed they may look down to us and clouds below.

It was acknowledged that more people could read and write and cast accounts than in any former age, and that more people read newspapers, magazines, &c. But it was not to be inferred from thence that this smattering of knowledge capacitated them to set up for legislators, or to measure, separate, and balance exactly rational liberty against sound and necessary restraint; or, in regard to taste and skill in arts, that we were a jot the nearer to see a Michaelangelo, Raphael, Titian, or Correggio, because there were at present a greater number of middling artists than at any other period; or, because we have more dabblers in poetry, that there is a greater probablity of our seeing arise amongst us [a] Homer or a Milton.

It is now as it ever has been. Few people reach the summit from which they look down on the rest of mankind. However it may be in arithmetic, in such studies ever so many additions of units will not possess the efficacy of the compact number of twenty. A hundred thousand near-sighted men, that see only what is just before them, make no equivalent to one man whose view extends to the whole horizon round him, though we may safely acknowledge at the same time that like the real near-sighted men, they see and comprehend as distinctly what is within the focus of their sight as accurately (I will allow sometimes more accurately) than the others. Though a man may see his way in management of his own affairs, within his own little circle, with the greatest acuteness and sagacity, such habits give him no pretensions to set up for a politician. So far is this diffusion of superficial knowledge from being an argument of our superiority in the deeper recesses of science, that on the contrary we hear it continually given as a reason why there are not at present such learned men as in former ages, from this very circumstance – that every man, having a mouthful (just enough to save himself from an intellectual famine), does not take the pains necessary to get a bellyful. If this be true, the diffusion of knowledge is against them, instead of an argument in their favour. It was asked likewise whether, from a little smattering in physic,[5] a man would act wisely in discarding his physicians and prescribe to himself, whether by such quacking, sound constitutions have not been often destroyed.

Sir Joshua added, that to be a politician was, he apprehended, as much trade or profession as his own: that the science of politics, as well as a true taste in works of art, was acquired by labour and study, and by other means; and that in both cases, we are sure that half-educated minds are in a worse state than total ignorance: the worst will appear the best, as being within their narrrow comprehension. He instanced a certain painter now in England, an artist of great merit, though he paints in a different and a much inferior style to Vandyck; yet if the merit of each of them was to be determined by the majority, there would be 99 in 100 in favour of this artist.

He proceeded to observe [that] he would undertake to write a discourse on those obvious and vulgar principles, which should come home to the bosoms of the ignorant (which are always the majority) and which should be thought to contain more sound doctrine than those which he had delivered in the Academy; and such doctrine, proceeding *ex cathedra*, would probably so poison the minds of the students as might eventually keep back the harvest of arts which we expect from the nation, perhaps for fifty years. A few days after was produced the following discourse, which, though a playful trifle, he is persuaded by his friends to let it bring up the rear of his last volume, as they think it may contribute towards banishing from the world the popular and vulgar notions about genius and inspiration, as well as those

---

[5] *physic* medicine.

opinions which have been entertained both by the great vulgar and the small, of what ought to be the object of art.

THE DISCOURSE

Gentlemen:

It is with great regret that I see so many students labouring day after day in the Academy, as if they imagined that a liberal art, as ours is, was to be acquired like a mechanical trade, by dint of labour, or I may add the absurdity of supposing that it could be acquired by any means whatever. We know that if you are born with a genius, labour is unnecessary; if you have it not, labour is in vain; genius is all in all. It was wittily said by a bright genius, who observed another to labour in the composition of a discourse which he was to deliver in public, that such a painstaker was fitter to make a pulpit than to preach in it.

Genius, as it disdains all assistance, so it defies all obstacles. The student here may inform himself whether he has been favoured by heaven with this truly divine gift. If he finds it necessary to copy, to study the works of other painters, or any way to seek for help out of himself, he may be sure that he has received nothing of that inspiration. My advice is that he immediately quit the Academy, and apply to something to which his genius is adapted. Let the student consider with himself whether he is impelled forward by irresistible instinct. He himself is little more than a machine, unconscious of the power which impels him forward to the instant performance of what others learn by the slow method of rules and precepts. Who does not feel the highest disdain for all the *imitatores servum pecus*[6] as well as the most sovereign contempt for all rules, or rather receipts,[7] which dullness have prescribed for the acquisition of this great and liberal art?

What is the use of rules, but to cramp and fetter genius? The rules which dull men have introduced into liberal arts smother that flame which would otherwise blaze out in originality of invention. Shakespeare, as the great Ralph says, writ without rules. (Quote the note of the *Dunciad*.[8] He made the following wise answer.) The idea of making a work of genius by rule has been sufficiently laughed at. (Swift in his receipt to make an epic poem.)[9]

One is at a loss, says the great Bacon, to determine which was the greater trifler [Apelles[10] or Albert Dürer,[11] 'whereof the one would make a personage by geometrical proportions; the other, by taking the best parts out of divers faces to make one excellent'.][12] It is but too true that this weak observation is found in Bacon's *Essay*, as if he thought that there was no rule for beauty and proportion. Cardinal Bembo[13] had a true idea of what the highest excellence consists, and in his epitaph on Raphael has flattered him as supposing he possessed it, but alas!

---

[6] *imitatores servum pecus* imitators, a slavish herd (Horace, *Epistles* 1.19.19).
[7] *receipts* recipes.
[8] *Dunciad* (1729), 3.159: Pope's note reads, "He was wholly illiterate, and knew no Language not even *French*: Being advised to read the Rules of Dramatic Poetry before he began a Play, he smiled and replied, 'Shakespeare writ without Rules'"; James Ralph (1705?–62) is ridiculed several times in the *Dunciad*.
[9] *Swift . . . epic poem Peri Bathous: or Martinus Scriblerus, His Treatise of the Art of Sinking in Poetry*, chapter 15; this chapter and much of this humorous work is mostly by Pope, though other "Scriblerians" (Swift, Gay, Arbuthnot) were involved.
[10] *Apelles* fourth-century BCE painter, famous for portraits.
[11] *Albert Dürer* foremost German painter of the Renaissance.
[12] The material in brackets is supplied from Reynolds's third Discourse; the citation is from Bacon's essay "Of Beauty."
[13] *Cardinal Bembo* Pietro (1470–1547), important Italian critic and scholar; his epitaph appears in Vasari's life of Raphael.

Having given my idea of genius, before I proceed to explain how it shows itself and what are its operations, it is necessary that you should be aware that our art is in a corrupted state, and has been gradually departing from simple first principles ever since the time of Michelangelo, the first grand corrupter of the natural taste of man. He first introduced and substituted this style founded on imagination, of which we may truly say there is not even the least gleam of common sense. The mere stating the question discovers its absurdity. What is cultivating the imagination, but to open a school to teach systematically madness and folly, and to renounce reason and even common sense?

It is not easy to account for the tame submission of mankind, either in first adopting this new style, or for its authority continuing to this present age. We can only put it to the account of a prejudice, which perhaps originated from his being highly favoured by the popes and great men of his time and is handed down to our time. But shall we in these enlightened times tamely adopt and inherit their ignorant prejudices? No! Let us examine everything by the standard of our own reason, renounce all prejudices for the reputed wisdom of others. Let me ask any sensible artist who has seen the Cappella Sistina of Michelangelo whether he found in the works of this great teacher of the nonsense of imagination that true nature which he had been taught to expect to find and which he knows he ought to find.

It has been often remarked by many of our learned connoisseurs, that painters are the worst judges of pictures; and the reason why they are so, is from their imbibing prejudices. A man who never saw a picture is therefore the best judge. He has no rule but his taste and feeling . . . [We should remember Apelles's critic] and Molière's old woman;[14] and above all, what that excellent philosopher and connoisseur Pliny has recorded as the greatest effort of art of two of the greatest painters of antiquity, Zeuxis and Parrhasius, one painting a bunch of grapes that the birds pecked at and the other a curtain which deceived even the painter himself.[15] What a poor figure Michelangelo would have made in this noble contention of superiority! We must not forget in more modern times Giotto's Circle.[16] These great masters knew what was the real object of art, and went directly to the point. Nature herself was always at their elbow, and they wanted no other instruction.

Let the works in the Cappella Sistina – or to refer to what we have in our own nation, the vaunted cartoons[17] – let them be examined by the criterion of nature, and we shall be convinced how much the art has swerved from truth. Does any man, when he looks at those pictures, recognise his neighbour's face? Does anybody mistake the drapery, as it is called, for real stuff such as they are intended to represent? Is it silk, satin, or velvet? What a falling off from the ancient simplicity of art! Let us imitate the great Mirabeau.[18] Set fire to all the pictures, prints, and drawings of Raphael and Michelangelo; *non tali auxilio*.[19] Destroy every

---

14   *Apelles's critic and Molière's old woman*   refer to stories in which artists are criticized by common people for their inadequate representation of daily things, as the common folk see them; the material in brackets is supplied from Reynolds' thirteenth Discourse.

15   *Pliny has recorded . . . even the painter himself* Zeuxis requested the curtain be drawn to reveal Parrhasius' entry in the competition; when he realized his mistake, Zeuxis granted the victory to Parrhasius (Pliny, *Natural History* 35.36.65–6).

16   *Giotto's Circle* the most important painter of the fourteenth century is reported to have drawn a perfect

circle in his successful response to a papal request for a demonstration of his art.

17   *the vaunted cartoons*   preparatory sketches for historical paintings by Raphael, part of the British royal collection; in his thirteenth Discourse Reynolds said, "Raphael is praised for naturalness and deception, which he certainly has not accomplished, and as certainly never intended."

18   *Mirabeau*   (1749–91) leader of the National Assembly established in the French Revolution.

19   *non tali auxilio* a quotation from Virgil, *Aeneid* 2.521 meaning "[the present] requires no such assistance."

trace that remains of ancient taste. Let us pull the whole fabric[20] down at once, root it up even to its foundation. Let us begin the art again upon this solid ground of nature and of reason. The world will then see what naked art is, in its uneducated, unprejudiced, unadulterated state.

The daring to give this advice, the glory of stepping forth in this great work of reformation, and endeavouring to rescue the world from the worse than barbarous tyranny of prejudice, and restore the sovereignty of reason, will be sufficient honour for me and my poor endeavours.

I have only a few words to add respecting sculpture. As monuments are now erecting in St. Paul's,[21] I would recommend to the committee that the sculptor be obliged to dress his figures, whether one or many, in the very dress of the times – the dress which they themselves wore. If this obliges the sculptor to acquire an accurate observation of the fashions as they fluctuate, this additional trouble, will be fully compensated by [his] being saved another trouble, the disposition of the drapery, that being already done to his hands by the tailor. And, by the way, the tailor will be found a necessary person to be consulted [as to] what exact fashions were in that very year when the person died, that the monument may be correct in the 'costume' as the learned call it. We know very well what a difference every year makes in the cut of our clothes.

When it shall be determined by the committee that no monumental figure shall be suffered in St. Paul's but in the modern dress, it will be necessary to add to the committee a certain number of the most ingenious tailors, who shall have a voice in regard to fashion. After the people have been a little accustomed to this naturalness, the Academy will, upon the same principles, proceed a step further and add colour to these statues, which will complete the description [and] complete the honour of the Royal Academy. This improvement is reserved for this enlightened age, when knowledge is so generally diffused – i.e., when we think for ourselves and dare to reason without prejudices for the opinions of others. We shall soon not leave one stone upon another in the fabric of art. We then rear an edifice not founded on imagination, castles in the air, but on common sense adapted to the meanest capacity, equally comprehended by the ignorant as the learned. My last words are: follow reason, follow nature.

Edmund Burke (1729–1797)

In his Life of Johnson *Boswell reports, "once, when Johnson was ill, and unable to exert himself as much as usual without fatigue, Mr. Burke having been mentioned, he said, 'That fellow calls forth all my powers. Were I to see Burke now, it would kill me.'" Johnson's meaning is explained a little by another of his remarks about Burke: "His stream of mind is perpetual." Most of Burke's professional life was spent as a very active member of Parliament. He was a Whig allied to Lord Rockingham, and he made a famous and original defense of party politics, but in all of his opinions and all of his writing there is evidence of the quality that Johnson perceived and even occasionally feared. Political opinions or positions in Burke's work are always rooted not only in a sense of*

---

[20]   *fabric*   structure.

[21]   *monuments are now erecting in St. Paul's*   one of the first placed in the cathedral, after his death, was a statue of Reynolds.

cultural history but also in an appreciation of his participation in the ongoing, longstanding life of culture. He was critical of George III's handling of the American colonies and infuriated by the corruption of the British administration in India, yet he was horrified by the French Revolution and the sympathy it aroused in England. This constellation of opinions used to be looked upon as representative of Burke's growing conservatism, but a deeper appreciation of his thought shows broad areas of consistency throughout his apparently diverse positions. There are principles of civility and compassion, a confidence in the benefits of conversation and compromise, and a hatred of mechanistic or absolutist approaches to human problems that persist throughout his political writings.

In 1790, when Burke published his Reflections on the Revolution in France, *Mary Wollstonecraft and others in England who thought about the wretched lives of the French people under the old regime would have none of his sympathy for Marie Antoinette and the world of chivalry that seemed to die along with her. It is perhaps even harder today to worry about the loss of chivalry, but like all works with real "mind," Burke's contains a prophetic element, and seems now to have predicted the excesses and tyranny of the new French Republic and its eventual turn to imperialism under Napoleon.*

Born in Dublin, educated at Trinity College and then at Middle Temple (law school) in London, Burke did not successfully enter politics until 1765. Before that he wrote some philosophical works, including his very influential Philosophical Inquiry into the Origin of our Ideas of the Sublime and the Beautiful *(1757). This became an important text for continental writers like Lessing and in the whole movement of Romanticism. Burke also started* The Annual Register, *a review of worldwide political events, in 1758 and continued to make contributions to it throughout his lifetime.*

The following extract from Burke's Philosophical Inquiry *is based on the second edition (1759); the small selection from his* Reflections *comes from the first edition. I have benefited from the Penguin edition of* Reflections on the Revolution in France *edited by Connor Cruise O'Brien. His* Great Melody: a Biography and Commented Anthology of Edmund Burke *(University of Chicago Press, 1993) is impassioned and interesting. Volume eight of* The Writings and Speeches of Edmund Burke, *ed. L. G. Mitchell (Clarendon Press, 1989) provides standard texts of Burke's writings on the French Revolution.*

from A *Philosophical Inquiry into the Origin of our Ideas of the Sublime and the Beautiful* (1759)

PART 2, SECTION 1
OF THE PASSION CAUSED BY THE SUBLIME

The passion caused by the great and sublime in *nature*, when those causes operate most powerfully, is Astonishment; and astonishment is that state of the soul, in which all its motions are suspended, with some degree of horror. In this case the mind is so entirely filled with its object, that it cannot entertain any other, nor by consequence reason on that object which employs it. Hence arises the great power of the sublime, that far from being produced by them, it anticipates our reasonings, and hurries us on by an irresistible force. Astonishment, as I have said, is the effect of the sublime in its highest degree; the inferior effects are admiration, reverence and respect.

SECTION 2
TERROR

No passion so effectually robs the mind of all its powers of acting and reasoning as fear. For fear being an apprehension of pain or death, it operates in a manner that resembles actual pain. Whatever therefore is terrible, with regard to sight, is sublime too, whether this cause of terror, be endued with greatness of dimensions or not; for it is impossible to look on any thing as trifling, or contemptible, that may be dangerous. There are many animals, who though far from being large, are yet capable of raising ideas of the sublime, because they are considered as objects of terror. As serpents and poisonous animals of almost all kinds. And to things of great dimensions, if we annex an adventitious idea of terror, they become without comparison greater. A level plain of a vast extent on land, is certainly no mean idea; the prospect of such a plain may be as extensive as a prospect of the ocean; but can it ever fill the mind with any thing so great as the ocean itself? This is owing to several causes, but it is owing to none more than this, that the ocean is an object of no small terror. Indeed terror is in all cases whatsoever, either more openly or latently the ruling principle of the sublime. Several languages bear a strong testimony to the affinity of these ideas. They frequently use the same word, to signify indifferently the modes of astonishment or admiration and those of terror. θάμβος is in Greek, either fear or wonder; δεινός is terrible or respectable; αἰδέω to reverence or fear. *Vereor* in Latin, is what αἰδέω is in Greek. The Romans used the verb *stupeo*, a term which strongly marks the state of an astonished mind, to express the effect either of simple fear, or of astonishment; the word *attonitus* (thunderstruck) is equally expressive of the alliance of these ideas; and do not the French *étonnement*, and the English *astonishment* and *amazement*, point out as clearly the kindred emotions which attend fear and wonder? They who have a more general knowledge of languages, could produce, I make no doubt, many other and equally striking examples.

SECTION 3
OBSCURITY

To make any thing very terrible, obscurity seems in general to be necessary. When we know the full extent of any danger, when we can accustom our eyes to it, a great deal of the apprehension vanishes. Every one will be sensible of this, who considers how greatly night adds to our dread, in all cases of danger, and how much the notions of ghosts and goblins, of which none can form clear ideas, affect minds, which give credit to the popular tales concerning such sorts of beings. Those despotic governments, which are founded on the passions of men, and principally upon the passion of fear, keep their chief as much as may be from the public eye. The policy has been the same in many cases of religion. Almost all the heathen temples were dark. Even in the barbarous temples of the Americans at this day, they keep their idol in a dark part of the hut, which is consecrated to his worship. For this purpose too the Druids performed all their ceremonies in the bosom of the darkest woods, and in the shade of the oldest and most spreading oaks. No person seems better to have understood the secret of heightening, or of setting terrible things, if I may use the expression, in their strongest light by the force of a judicious obscurity, than Milton. His description of Death in the second book[1] is admirably studied; it is astonishing with what a gloomy pomp, with what

---

A PHILOSOPHICAL INQUIRY
[1]   *Paradise Lost*   2.666–73.

a significant and expressive uncertainty of strokes and colouring he has finished the portrait of the king of terrors.

> The other shape,
> If shape it might be called that shape had none
> Distinguishable, in member, joint, or limb;
> Or substance might be called that shadow seemed,
> For each seemed either; black he stood at night;
> Fierce as ten furies; terrible as hell;
> And shook a deadly dart. What seemed his head
> The likeness of a kingly crown had on.

In this description all is dark, uncertain, confused, terrible, and sublime to the last degree.

SECTION 4
OF THE DIFFERENCE BETWEEN CLEARNESS AND OBSCURITY WITH REGARD TO THE PASSIONS

It is one thing to make an idea clear, and another to make it *affecting* to the imagination. If I make a drawing of a palace, or a temple, or a landscape, I present a very clear idea of those objects; but then (allowing for the effect of imitation which is something) my picture can at most affect only as the palace temple, or landscape would have affected in the reality. On the other hand, the most lively and spirited verbal description I can give, raises a very obscure and imperfect *idea* of such objects; but then it is in my power to raise a stronger *emotion* by the description than I could do by the best painting. This experience constantly evinces. The proper manner of conveying the *affections* of the mind from one to another, is by words; there is a great insufficiency in all other methods of communication; and so far is a clearness of imagery from being absolutely necessary to an influence upon the passions, that they may be considerably operated upon without presenting any image at all, by certain sounds adapted to that purpose; of which we have sufficient proof in the acknowledged and powerful effects of instrumental music. In reality a great clearness helps but little towards affecting the passions, as it is in some sort an enemy to all enthusiasms whatsoever.

SECTION [5]
THE SAME SUBJECT CONTINUED

There are two verses in Horace's art of poetry that seem to contradict this opinion, for which reason I shall take a little more pains in clearing it all up. The verses are,

> Segnius irritant animos demissa per aures
> Quam quæ sunt oculis subjecta fidelibus[2]

On this the Abbé du Bos[3] founds a criticism, wherein he gives painting the preference to poetry in the article of moving the passions; principally on account of the greater *clearness* of the idea it represents. I believe this excellent judge was led into this mistake (if it be a

---

[2] "[actions] reported in hearing affect the mind more sluggishly than those which are exposed to the faithful eyes" (*Ars Poetica*, 180–1).

[3] *Abbé du Bos* Jean-Baptiste Dubos (1670–1742), author of *Réflexions critiques sur la poésie et sur la peinture* (1719; trans. Thomas Nuggent, 1748).

mistake) by his system, to which he found it more conformable than I imagine it will be found to experience. I know several who admire and love painting, and yet who regard the objects of their admiration in that art, with coolness enough, in comparison of that warmth with which they are animated by affecting pieces of poetry or rhetoric. Among the common sort of people, I could never perceive that painting had much influence on their passions. It is true that the best sorts of painting, as well as the best sorts of poetry, are not much understood in that sphere. But it is most certain, that their passions are very strongly roused by a fanatic preacher, or by the ballads of Chevy-chase, or the children in the wood, and by other little popular poems and tales that are current in that rank of life. I do not know of any paintings, bad or good, that produce the same effect. So that poetry with all its obscurity, has a more general as well as a more powerful dominion over the passions than the other art. And I think there are reasons in nature why the obscure idea, when properly conveyed, should be more affecting than the clear. It is our ignorance of things that causes all our admiration, and chiefly excites our passions. Knowledge and acquaintance make the most striking causes affect but little. It is thus with the vulgar, and all men are as vulgar in what they do not understand. The ideas of eternity, and infinity, are among the most affecting we have, and yet perhaps there is nothing of which we really understand so little, as of infinity and eternity. We do not any where meet a more sublime description than this justly celebrated one of Milton, wherein he gives the portrait of Satan with a dignity so suitable to the subject.

> He above the rest
> In shape and gesture proudly eminent
> Stood like a tower; his form had not yet lost
> All her original brightness, nor appeared
> Less than archangel ruined, and th' excess
> Of glory obscured: as when the sun new ris'n
> Looks through the horizontal misty air
> Shorn of his beams; or from behind the moon
> In dim eclipse disastrous twilight sheds
> On half the nations; and with fear of change
> Perplexes monarchs. [*Paradise Lost* 1.589–99]

Here is a very noble picture; and in what does this poetical picture consist? in images of a tower, an archangel, the sun rising through the mists, or in an eclipse, the ruin of monarchs, and the revolution of kingdoms. The mind is hurried out of itself, by a crowd of great and confused images; which affect because they are crowded and confused. For separate them, and you lose much of the greatness, and join them, and you infallibly lose the clearness. The images raised by poetry are always of this obscure kind; though in general the effects of poetry, are by no means to be attributed to the images it raises; which point we shall examine more at large hereafter. But painting, when we have allowed for the pleasure of imitation, can only affect simply by the images it presents; and even in painting a judicious obscurity in some things contributes to the effect of the picture; because the images in painting are exactly similar to those in nature; and in nature dark, confused, uncertain images have a greater power on the fancy[4] to form the grander passions than those have which are more clear and

---

[4] *fancy* imagination.

determinate. But where and when this observation may be applied to practice, and how far it shall be extended, will be better deduced from the nature of the subject, and from the occasion, than from any rules that can be given.

I am sensible that this idea has met with opposition, and is likely still to be rejected by several. But let it be considered that hardly any thing can strike the mind with its greatness, which does not make some sort of approach towards infinity; which nothing can do whilst we are able to perceive its bounds; but to see an object distinctly, and to perceive its bounds, is one and the same thing. A clear idea is therefore another name for a little idea. There is a passage in the book of Job amazingly sublime, and this sublimity is principally due to the terrible uncertainty of the thing described. 'In thoughts from the visions of the night, when deep sleep falleth upon men, fear came upon me and trembling, which made all my bones to shake. Then a spirit passed before my face. The hair of my flesh stood up. It stood still, but I could not discern the form thereof; an image was before mine eyes; there was silence; and I heard a voice, – Shall mortal man be more just than God?' [4. 13–17] We are first prepared with the utmost solemnity for the vision; we are first terrified, before we are let even into the obscure cause of our emotion; but when this grand cause of terror makes its appearance, what is it? is it not, wrapt up in the shades of its own incomprehensible darkness, more awful, more striking, more terrible, than the liveliest description, than the clearest painting could possibly represent it? When painters have attempted to give us a clear representation of these fanciful and terrible ideas, they have I think almost always failed; insomuch that I have been at a loss, in all the pictures I have seen of hell, whether the painter did not intend something ludicrous. Several painters have handled a subject of this kind, with a view of assembling as many horrid phantoms as their imagination could suggest; but all the designs I have chanced to meet of the temptations of St. Anthony,[5] were rather a sort of odd wild grotesques, than any thing capable of producing a serious passion. In all these subjects poetry is very happy. Its apparitions, its chimeras, its harpies, its allegorical figures, are grand and affecting; and though Virgil's Fame, and Homer's Discord, are obscure, they are magnificent figures. These figures in painting would be clear enough, but I fear they might become ridiculous . . .

SECTION 13
BEAUTIFUL OBJECTS SMALL

The most obvious point that presents itself to us in examining any object, is its extent or quantity. And what degree of extent prevails in bodies, that are held beautiful, may be gathered from the usual manner of expression concerning it. I am told that in most languages, the objects of love are spoken of under diminutive epithets. It is so in all the languages of which I have any knowledge. In Greek the ιον,[6] and other diminutive terms, are almost always the terms of affection and tenderness. These diminutives were commonly added by the Greeks to the names of persons with whom they conversed on terms of friendship and familiarity. Though the Romans were a people of less quick and delicate feelings, yet they naturally slid into the lessening termination upon the same occasions. Anciently in the English language the diminishing *ling* was added to the names of persons and things that were the objects of love. Some we retain still, as darling (or little dear) and a few others. But

---

[5] *temptations of St. Anthony* e.g. engraving by Martin Schongauer (c. 1480–90; Metropolitan Museum of Art, New York), in which demons of all sorts pull and cudgel him every which way.
[6] ιον a diminutive suffix.

to this day in ordinary conversation, it is usual to add the endearing name of *little* to every thing we love; the French and Italians make use of these affectionate diminutives even more than we. In the animal creation, out of our own species, it is the small we are inclined to be fond of; little birds, and some of the smaller kinds of beasts. A great beautiful thing, is a manner of expression scarcely ever used; but that of a great ugly thing, is very common. There is a wide difference between admiration and love. The sublime, which is the cause of the former, always dwells on great objects, and terrible; the latter on small ones, and pleasing; we submit to what we admire, but we love what submits to us; in one case we are forced, in the other we are flattered into compliance. In short, the ideas of the sublime and the beautiful stand on foundations so different, that it is hard, I had almost said impossible, to think of reconciling them in the same subject, without considerably lessening the effect of the one or the other upon the passions. So that attending to their quantity, beautiful objects are comparatively small.

SECTION 14
SMOOTHNESS

The next property constantly observable in such objects is *Smoothness*. A quality so essential to beauty, that I do not now recollect any thing beautiful that is not smooth. In trees and flowers, smooth leaves are beautiful; smooth slopes of earth in gardens; smooth streams in the landscape; smooth coats of birds and beasts in animal beauties; in fine women, smooth skins; and in several sorts of ornamental furniture, smooth and polished surfaces. A very considerable part of the effect of beauty is owing to this quality; indeed the most considerable. For take any beautiful object, and give it a broken and rugged surface, and however well formed it may be in other respects, it pleases no longer. Whereas let it want ever so many of the other constituents, if it wants not this, it becomes more pleasing than almost all the others without it. This seems to me so evident, that I am a good deal surprised, that none who have handled the subject have made any mention of the quality of smoothness in the enumeration of those that go to the forming of beauty. For indeed any ruggedness, any sudden projection, any sharp angle, is in the highest degree contrary to that idea.

SECTION 15
GRADUAL VARIATION

But as perfectly beautiful bodies are not composed of angular parts, so their parts never continue long in the same right line. They vary their direction every moment, and they change under the eye by a deviation continually carrying on, but for whose beginning or end you will find it difficult to ascertain a point. The view of a beautiful bird will illustrate this observation. Here we see the head increasing insensibly to the middle, from whence it lessens gradually until it mixes with the neck; the neck loses itself in a larger swell, which continues to the middle of the body, when the whole decreases again to the tail; the tail takes a new direction; but it soon varies its new course; it blends again with the other parts; and the line is perpetually changing, above, below, upon every side. In this description I have before me the idea of a dove; it agrees very well with most of the conditions of beauty. It is smooth and downy; its parts are (to use that expression) melted into one another; you are presented with no sudden protuberance through the whole, and yet the whole is continually changing. Observe that part of a beautiful woman where she is perhaps the most beautiful, about the neck and the breasts; the smoothness; the softness; the easy and insensible swell; the variety of the surface, which is never for the smallest space the same; the deceitful maze, through which the unsteady eye slides giddily, without knowing where to fix, or whither it is carried. Is not this a demonstration of that change of surface continual and yet hardly perceptible at any point which forms one of the great constituents of beauty? It gives me no small pleasure to find that I can strengthen my theory in this point, by the opinion of the very ingenious Mr. Hogarth; whose idea of the line of beauty[7] I take in general to be extremely just. But the idea of variation, without attending so accurately to the *manner* of the variation, has led him to consider angular figures as beautiful; these figures, it is true, vary greatly; yet they vary in a sudden and broken manner; and I do not find any natural object which is angular, and at the same time beautiful. Indeed few natural objects are entirely angular. But I think those which approach the most nearly to it, are the ugliest. I must add too, that, so far as I could observe of nature, though the varied line is that alone in which complete beauty is found, yet there is no particular line which is always found in the most completely beautiful; and which is therefore beautiful in preference to all other lines. At least I never could observe it.

SECTION 16
DELICACY

An air of robustness and strength is very prejudicial to beauty. An appearance of *delicacy*, and even of fragility, is almost essential to it. Whoever examines the vegetable or animal creation, will find this observation to be founded in nature. It is not the oak, the ash, or the elm, or any of the robust trees of the forest, which we consider as beautiful; they are awful and majestic; they inspire a sort of reverence. It is the delicate myrtle, it is the orange, it is the almond, it is the jessamine, it is the vine, which we look on as vegetable beauties. It is the flowery species, so remarkable for its weakness and momentary duration, that gives us the liveliest idea of beauty, and elegance. Among animals; the greyhound is more beautiful than the mastiff; and the delicacy of a jennet,[8] a barb,[9] or an Arabian horse, is much more amiable than the strength and stability of some horses of war or carriage. I need here say little of the fair sex, where I believe the point will be easily allowed me. The beauty of women is considerably owing to their weakness, or delicacy, and is even enhanced by their timidity, a quality of mind analogous to it. I would not here be understood to say, that weakness betraying very bad health has any share in beauty; but the ill effect of this is not because it is weakness, but because the ill state of health which produces such weakness alters the other conditions of beauty; the parts in such a case collapse; the bright colour, the *lumen purpureum juventae*[10] is gone; and the fine variation is lost in wrinkles, sudden breaks, and right lines.

---

[7] *Hogarth . . . line of beauty* William Hogarth, in his *Analysis of Beauty* (1753), proposes an essential aesthetic standard in his "line of beauty," a serpentine or winding line, combining uniformity and variety in the most pleasing proportion.

[8] *jennet* a small Spanish horse.
[9] *barb* or Barbary, a Moroccan horse noted for speed.
[10] *lumen purpureum juventae* "the beautiful light of youth" (Virgil, *Aeneid* 1.590–1).

from REFLECTIONS
ON THE
REVOLUTION IN FRANCE,
AND ON THE
PROCEEDINGS IN CERTAIN SOCIETIES
IN LONDON
RELATIVE TO THAT EVENT (1790)

IN A
LETTER
INTENDED TO HAVE BEEN SENT TO A GENTLEMAN
IN PARIS

Far am I from denying in theory; full as far is my heart from withholding in practice (if I were of power to give or to withhold) the *real* rights of men.[1] In denying their false claims of right, I do not mean to injure those which are real, and are such as their pretended rights would totally destroy. If civil society be made for the advantage of man, all the advantages for which it is made become his right. It is an institution of beneficence; and law itself is only beneficence acting by a rule. Men have a right to live by that rule; they have a right to do justice; as between their fellows, whether their fellows are in public function or in ordinary occupation. They have a right to the fruits of their industry; and to the means of making their industry fruitful. They have a right to the acquisitions of their parents; to the nourishment and improvement of their offspring; to instruction in life, and to consolation in death. Whatever each man can separately do, without trespassing upon others, he has a right to do for himself; and he has a right to a fair portion of all which society, with all its combinations of skill and force, can do in his favour. But as to the share of power, authority, and direction which each individual ought to have in the management of the state, that I must deny to be amongst the direct original rights of man in civil society; for I have in my contemplation the civil social man, and no other. It is a thing to be settled by convention.

If civil society be the offspring of convention, that convention must be its law. That convention must limit and modify all the descriptions of constitution which are formed under it. Every sort of legislative, judicial, or executory power are its creatures. They can have no being in any other state of things; and how can any man claim under the conventions of civil society, rights which do not so much as suppose its existence? Rights which are absolutely repugnant to it? One of the first motives to civil society, and which becomes one of its fundamental rules, is, *that no man should be judge in his own cause.* By this each person has at once divested himself of the first fundamental right of uncovenanted man,[2] that is, to judge for himself, and to assert his own cause. He abdicates all right to be his own governor. He inclusively, in a great measure, abandons the right of self-defence, the first law of nature. Men cannot enjoy the rights of an uncivil and of a civil state together. That he may obtain justice

FROM REFLECTIONS
[1]   *rights of men*   or the *Rights of Man,* as Thomas Paine would entitle his response to Burke (see below), was a key phrase in the rhetoric of the French Revolution, but it already had a history in seventeenth- and eighteenth- century political writings (such as John Locke's) with which most commentators in the late eighteenth century agreed.
[2]   *uncovenanted man*   human beings with no covenant or compact of society, asocial, barbarous humanity.

he gives up his right of determining what it is in points the most essential to him. That he may secure some liberty, he makes a surrender in trust of the whole of it.

Government is not made in virtue of natural rights, which may and do exist in total independence of it; and exist in much greater clearness, and in a much greater degree of abstract perfection: but their abstract perfection is their practical defect. By having a right to every thing they want[3] every thing. Government is a contrivance of human wisdom to provide for human *wants*. Men have a right that these wants should be provided for by this wisdom. Among these wants is to be reckoned the want, out of civil society, of a sufficient restraint upon their passions. Society requires not only that the passions of individuals should be subjected, but that even in the mass and body as well as in the individuals, the inclinations of men should frequently be thwarted, their will controlled, and their passions brought into subjection. This can only be done *by a power out of themselves*; and not, in the exercise of its function, subject to that will and to those passions which it is its office to bridle and subdue. In this sense the restraints on men, as well as their liberties, are to be reckoned among their rights. But as the liberties and the restrictions vary with times and circumstances, and admit of infinite modifications, they cannot be settled upon any abstract rule; and nothing is so foolish as to discuss them upon that principle.

The moment you abate anything from the full rights of men, each to govern himself, and suffer any artificial positive limitation upon those rights, from that moment the whole organization of government becomes a consideration of convenience. This it is which makes the constitution of a state, and the due distribution of its powers, a matter of the most delicate and complicated skill. It requires a deep knowledge of human nature and human necessities, and of the things which facilitate or obstruct the various ends which are to be pursued by the mechanism of civil institutions. The state is to have recruits to its strength, and remedies to its distempers. What is the use of discussing a man's abstract right to food or medicine? The question is upon the method of procuring and administering them. In that deliberation I shall always advise to call in the aid of the farmer and the physician, rather than the professor of metaphysics. The science of constructing a commonwealth, or renovating it, or reforming it, is, like every other experimental science, not to be taught *a priori*. Nor is it a short experience that can instruct us in that practical science; because the real effects of moral causes are not always immediate; but that which in the first instance is prejudicial may be excellent in its remoter operation; and its excellence may arise even from the ill effects it produces in the beginning. The reverse also happens; and very plausible schemes, with very pleasing commencements, have often shameful and lamentable conclusions. In states there are often some obscure and almost latent causes, things which appear at first view of little moment, on which a very great part of its prosperity or adversity may most essentially depend. The science of government being therefore so practical in itself, and intended for such practical purposes, a matter which requires experience, and even more experience than any person can gain in his whole life, however sagacious and observing he may be, it is with infinite caution that any man ought to venture upon pulling down an edifice which has answered in any tolerable degree for ages the common purposes of society, or on building it up again, without having models and patterns of approved utility before his eyes.

These metaphysic rights entering into common life, like rays of light which pierce into a dense medium, are, by the laws of nature refracted from their straight line. Indeed in the gross and complicated mass of human passions and concerns, the primitive rights of men undergo such a variety of refractions and reflections, that it becomes absurd to talk of them

---

3   *want*   lack, need.

as if they continued in the simplicity of their original direction. The nature of man is intricate; the objects of society are of the greatest possible complexity; and therefore no simple disposition or direction of power can be suitable either to man's nature, or to the quality of his affairs. When I hear the simplicity of contrivance aimed at and boasted of in any new political constitutions, I am at no loss to decide that the artificers are grossly ignorant of their trade, or totally negligent of their duty. The simple governments are fundamentally defective, to say no worse of them. If you were to contemplate society in but one point of view, all these simple modes of polity are infinitely captivating. In effect each would answer its single end much more perfectly than the more complex is able to attain all its complex purposes. But it is better that the whole should be imperfectly and anomalously answered than that, while some parts are provided for with great exactness, others might be totally neglected, or perhaps materially injured, by the over-care of a favourite member.

The pretended rights of these theorists are all extremes; and in proportion as they are metaphysically true, they are morally and politically false. The rights of men are in a sort of *middle*, incapable of definition, but not impossible to be discerned. The rights of men in governments are their advantages; and these are often in balances between differences of good; in compromises sometimes between good and evil, and sometimes between evil and evil. Political reason is a computing principle; adding, subtracting, multiplying, and dividing, morally and not metaphysically or mathematically, true moral denominations.

By these theorists the right of the people is almost always sophistically confounded with their power. The body of the community, whenever it can come to act, can meet with no effectual resistance; but till power and right are the same, the whole body of them has no right inconsistent with virtue, and the first of all virtues, prudence. Men have no right to what is not reasonable, and to what is not for their benefit; for though a pleasant writer said, *Liceat perire poetis* when one of them, in cold blood, is said to have leaped into the flames of a volcanic revolution, *Ardentem frigidus Ætnam insiluit*,[4] I consider such a frolic rather as an unjustifiable poetic licence, than as one of the franchises of Parnassus;[5] and whether he was a poet or divine, or politician that chose to exercise this kind of right, I think that more wise, because more charitable thoughts would urge me rather to save the man, than to preserve his brazen slippers as the monuments of his folly.

The kind of anniversary sermons,[6] to which a great part of what I write refers, if men are not shamed out of their present course, in commemorating the fact, will cheat many out of the principles, and deprive them of the benefits of the Revolution they commemorate. I confess to you, Sir, I never liked this continual talk of resistance and revolution, or the practice of making the extreme medicine of the constitution its daily bread. It renders the habit of society dangerously valetudinary: it is taking periodical doses of mercury sublimate,[7] and swallowing down repeated provocatives of cantharides[8] to our love of liberty.

This distemper of remedy, grown habitual, relaxes and wears out, by a vulgar and prostituted use, the spring of that spirit which is to be exerted on great occasions. It was in

---

[4] *Ardentem frigidus Ætnam insiluit . . . liceat perire poetis* "[Empedocles] coolly leapt into volcanic Mount Ætna . . . let poets have the right to depart from life" (Horace, *Ars Poetica*, 465–6); the poet did this in hope of convincing people that he had left the world and become a god; only his bronze sandals were found to indicate his fate.

[5] *franchises of Parnassus* rights of poets, those inhabiting the mountain sacred to Apollo and the muses.

[6] *anniversary sermons* Burke refers to a sermon by Richard Price, a dissenting minister, who celebrated the hundredth anniversary of the Glorious Revolution (1688) and expressed much sympathy for the French Revolution.

[7] *mercury sublimate* also called "corrosive sublimate," once a common but admittedly dangerous treatment for many diseases, including syphilis.

[8] *cantharides* Spanish Fly, used as a stimulant.

the most patient period of Roman servitude that themes of tyrannicide made the ordinary exercise of boys at school – *cum perimit sævos classis numerosa tyrannos.*[9] In the ordinary state of things, it produces in a country like ours the worst effects, even on the cause of that liberty which it abuses with the dissoluteness of an extravagant speculation. Almost all the high-bred republicans[10] of my time have, after a short space, become the most decided, thorough-paced courtiers; they soon left the business of a tedious, moderate, but practical resistance to those of us whom, in the pride and intoxication of their theories, they have slighted, as not much better than tories.[11] Hypocrisy, of course, delights in the most sublime speculations; for, never intending to go beyond speculation, it costs nothing to have it magnificent. But even in cases where rather levity than fraud was to be suspected in these ranting speculations, the issue has been much the same. These professors, finding their extreme principles not applicable to cases which call only for a qualified, or, as I may say, civil and legal resistance, in such cases employ no resistance at all. It is with them a war or a revolution, or it is nothing. Finding their schemes of politics not adapted to the state of the world in which they live, they often come to think lightly of all public principle; and are ready, on their part, to abandon for a very trivial interest what they find of very trivial value. Some indeed are of more steady and persevering natures; but these are eager politicians out of parliament who have little to tempt them to abandon their favourite projects. They have some change in the church or state, or both, constantly in their view. When that is the case, they are always bad citizens, and perfectly unsure connections. For, considering their speculative designs as of infinite value, and the actual arrangement of the state as of no estimation, they are at best indifferent about it. They see no merit in the good, and no fault in the vicious, management of public affairs; they rather rejoice in the latter, as more propitious to revolution. They see no merit or demerit in any man, or any action, or any political principle, any further than as they may forward or retard their design of change: they therefore take up, one day, the most violent and stretched prerogative,[12] and another time the wildest democratic ideas of freedom, and pass from one to the other without any sort of regard to cause, to person, or to party.

In France you are now in the crisis of a revolution, and in the transit from one form of government to another – you cannot see that character of men exactly in the same situation in which we see it in this country. With us it is militant; with you it is triumphant; and you know how it can act when its power is commensurate to its will. I would not be supposed to confine those observations to any description of men, or to comprehend all men of any description within them – No! far from it. I am as incapable of that injustice, as I am of keeping terms with those who profess principles of extremes; and who under the name of religion teach little else than wild and dangerous politics. The worst of these politics of revolution is this; they temper and harden the breast, in order to prepare it for the desperate strokes which are sometimes used in extreme occasions. But as these occasions may never arrive, the mind receives a gratuitous taint; and the moral sentiments suffer not a little, when no political purpose is served by the depravation. This sort of people are so taken up with their theories about the rights of man, that they have totally forgotten his nature. Without opening one new avenue to the understanding, they have succeeded in stopping up those that

---

[9] *cum perimit sævos classis numerosa tyrannos* "when a numerous class slays the wretched tyrant" to fulfil their hackneyed assignment in rhetoric (Juvenal 6.151).

[10] *republican* "One who thinks a commonwealth without monarchy the best government" (Johnson, 1773).

[11] *tory* "One who adheres to the ancient constitution of the state and the apostolical hierarchy of the church of England; opposed to a *whig*" (Johnson, 1773).

[12] *prerogative* the king's right to power.

lead to the heart. They have perverted in themselves, and in those that attend to them, all the well-placed sympathies of the human breast.

This famous sermon of the Old Jewry[13] breathes nothing but this spirit through all the political part. Plots, massacres, assassinations seem to some people a trivial price for obtaining a revolution. Cheap, bloodless reformation, a guiltless liberty appear flat and vapid to their taste. There must be a great change of scene; there must be a magnificent stage effect; there must be a grand spectacle to rouse the imagination, grown torpid with the lazy enjoyment of sixty years security, and the still unanimating repose of public prosperity. The Preacher found them all in the French revolution. This inspires a juvenile warmth through his whole frame. His enthusiasm kindles as he advances; and when he arrives at his peroration, it is in a full blaze. Then viewing, from the Pisgah[14] of his pulpit, the free, moral, happy, flourishing and glorious state of France as in a birds-eye landscape of a promised land, he breaks out into the following rapture:

What an eventful period is this! I am *thankful* that I have lived to it; I could almost say, 'Lord, now lettest thou thy servant depart in peace, for mine eyes have seen thy salvation'. I have lived to see a *diffusion* of knowledge, which has undermined superstition and error. – I have lived to see *the rights of men* better understood than ever; and nations panting for liberty which seemed to have lost the idea of it. – I have lived to see *Thirty Millions of People*, indignant and resolute, spurning at slavery, and demanding liberty with an irresistible voice. *Their King led in triumph, and an arbitrary monarch surrendering himself to his subjects.*

Before I proceed further, I have to remark, that Dr. Price seems rather to over-value the great acquisitions of light which he has obtained and diffused in this age. The last century appears to me to have been quite as much enlightened. It had, though in a different place, a triumph as memorable as that of Dr. Price; and some of the great preachers of that period partook of it as eagerly as he has done in the triumph of France. On the trial of the Rev. Hugh Peters[15] for high treason, it was deposed, that when King Charles was brought to London for his trial, the Apostle of Liberty in that day conducted the *triumph*. 'I saw', says the witness, 'his majesty in the coach with six horses, and Peters riding before the king *triumphing*'. Dr. Price, when he talks as if he had made a discovery, only follows a precedent; for after the commencement of the king's trial this precursor, the same Dr. Peters, concluding a long prayer at the royal chapel at Whitehall (he had very triumphantly chosen his place) said, 'I have prayed and preached these twenty years; and now I may say with old Simeon, 'Lord, now lettest thou thy servant depart in peace, for mine eyes have seen thy salvation'.[16] Peters had not the fruits of his prayer; for he neither departed so soon as he wished, nor in peace. He became (what I heartily hope none of his followers may be in this country) himself a sacrifice to the triumph which he led as Pontiff. They dealt at the Restoration, perhaps, too hardly with this poor good man. But we owe it to his memory and his sufferings, that he had as much illumination, and as much zeal, and had as effectually undermined all 'the superstition

---

[13] *Old Jewry* the dissenters chapel, where Price gave his sermon.

[14] *Pisgah* the mount from which Moses had a view of the Promised Land.

[15] *Hugh Peters* (1598–1660), independent minister, executed for complicity in the execution of Charles I.

[16] *old Simeon . . . salvation* the Holy Spirit revealed to Simeon that he would not die until he had seen "the Lord's Christ"; he speaks these words when he sees the baby Jesus (Luke 2.29–30).

and error' which might impede the great business he was engaged in, as any who follow and repeat after him, in this age, which would assume to itself an exclusive title to the knowledge of the rights of men, and all the glorious consequences of that knowledge.

After this sally of the preacher of the Old Jewry, which differs only in place and time, but agrees perfectly with the spirit and letter of the rapture of 1648, the Revolution Society,[17] the fabricators of governments, the heroic band of *cashierers*[18] of *monarchs*, electors of sovereigns, and leaders of kings in triumph, strutting with a proud consciousness of the diffusion of knowledge, of which every member had obtained so large a share in the donative, were in haste to make a generous diffusion of the knowledge they had thus gratuitously received. To make this bountiful communication, they adjourned from the church in the Old Jewry, to the London Tavern; where the same Dr. Price, in whom the fumes of his oracular tripod[19] were not entirely evaporated, moved and carried the resolution, or address of congratulation, transmitted by Lord Stanhope[20] to the National Assembly of France.

I find a preacher of the gospel profaning the beautiful and prophetic ejaculation, commonly called *nunc dimittis*[21] made on the first presentation of our Saviour in the Temple, and applying it with an inhuman and unnatural rapture, to the most horrid, atrocious, and afflicting spectacle, that perhaps ever was exhibited to the pity and indignation of mankind. This 'leading in triumph', a thing in its best form unmanly and irreligious, which fills our Preacher with such unhallowed transports, must shock, I believe, the moral taste of every well-born mind. Several English were the stupefied and indignant spectators of that triumph. It was (unless we have been strangely deceived) a spectacle more resembling a procession of American savages, entering into Onondaga,[22] after some of their murders called victories, and leading into hovels hung round with scalps, their captives, overpowered with the scoffs and buffets of women as ferocious as themselves, much more than it resembled the triumphal pomp of a civilized martial nation; – if a civilized nation, or any men who had a sense of generosity, were capable of a personal triumph over the fallen and afflicted.

This, my dear Sir, was not the triumph of France. I must believe that, as a nation, it overwhelmed you with shame and horror. I must believe that the National Assembly find themselves in the state of the greatest humiliation, in not being able to punish the authors of this triumph, or the actors in it; and that they are in a situation in which any inquiry they may make upon the subject, must be destitute even of the appearance of liberty or impartiality. The apology of that Assembly is found in their situation; but when we approve what they *must* bear, it is in us the degenerate choice of a vitiated mind.

With a compelled appearance of deliberation, they vote under the dominion of a stern necessity. They sit in the heart, as it were, of a foreign republic: they have their residence in a city whose constitution has emanated neither from the charter of their king nor from their legislative power. There they are surrounded by an army not raised either by the authority of their crown, or by their command; and which, if they should order to dissolve itself, would instantly dissolve them. There they sit, after a gang of assassins had driven away all the men

[17] *Revolution Society* founded in 1788 to celebrate the centenary of the Glorious Revolution.
[18] *cashierers* deposers; eliminators.
[19] *oracular tripod* the Pythia at Delphi, inspired by Apollo, sat on a tripod and made oracular pronouncements.
[20] *Lord Stanhope* Charles, third Earl Stanhope, leader of the Revolution Society, sent congratulations to the National Assembly.
[21] *nunc dimittis* the Latin version of the first words of old Simeon (above), used in evening masses since the fourth century.
[22] *Onondaga* the name of a tribe of Iroquois-speaking Indians, some of whom favored the French in the Seven Years War and migrated to Catholic settlements on the St Lawrence River called by the name of the tribe.

of moderate minds and moderating authority amongst them, and left them as a sort of dregs and refuse, under the apparent lead of those in whom they do not so much as pretend to have any confidence. There they sit, in mockery of legislation, repeating in resolutions the words of those whom they detest and despise. Captives themselves, they compel a captive king to issue as royal edicts, at third hand, the polluted nonsense of their most licentious and giddy coffee-houses. It is notorious, that all their measures are decided before they are debated. It is beyond doubt, that under the terror of the bayonet, and the lamp-post,[23] and the torch to their houses, they are obliged to adopt all the crude and desperate measures suggested by clubs composed of a monstrous medley of all conditions, tongues, and nations. Among these are found persons, in comparison of whom Catiline[24] would be thought scrupulous, and Cethegus[25] a man of sobriety and moderation. Nor is it in these clubs alone that the public measures are deformed into monsters. They undergo a previous distortion in academies, intended as so many seminaries for these clubs, which are set up in all the places of public resort. In these meetings of all sorts, every counsel, in proportion as it is daring, and violent, and perfidious, is taken for the mark of superior genius. Humanity and compassion are ridiculed as the fruits of superstition and ignorance. Tenderness to individuals is considered as treason to the public. Liberty is always to be estimated perfect as property is rendered insecure. Amidst assassination, massacre, and confiscation, perpetrated or meditated, they are forming plans for the good order of future society. Embracing in their arms the carcasses of base criminals, and promoting their relations on the title of their offences, they drive hundreds of virtuous persons to the same end, by forcing them to subsist by beggary or by crime.

The Assembly, their organ, acts before them the farce of deliberation with as little decency as liberty. They act like the comedians of a fair before a riotous audience; they act amidst the tumultuous cries of a mixed mob of ferocious men, and of women lost to shame, who, according to their insolent fancies, direct, control, applaud, explode[26] them; and sometimes mix and take their seats amongst them; domineering over them with a strange mixture of servile petulance and proud, presumptuous authority. As they have inverted order in all things, the gallery is in the place of the house. This Assembly, which overthrows kings and kingdoms, has not even the physiognomy and aspect of a grave legislative body – *nec color imperii, nec frons ulla senatus*.[27] They have a power given to them, like that of the evil principle, to subvert and destroy; but none to construct, except such machines as may be fitted for further subversion and further destruction.

Who is it that admires, and from the heart is attached to national representative assemblies, but must turn with horror and disgust from such a profane burlesque, and abominable perversion of that sacred institute? Lovers of monarchy, lovers of republics must alike abhor it. The members of your Assembly must themselves groan under the tyranny of which they have all the shame, none of the direction, and little of the profit. I am sure many of the members who compose even the majority of that body, must feel as I do, notwithstanding the applauses of the Revolution Society. – Miserable king! miserable Assembly! How must that assembly be silently scandalized with those of their members, who could call a day which

---

[23] *lamp-post* where the heads of those decapitated were displayed.
[24] *Catiline* a demagogue and conspirator, successfully prosecuted by Cicero and killed in 62 BCE.
[25] *Cethegus* a corrupt political insider in early first-century BCE Rome; like Catiline, he was active in the bloody purges following the first Roman civil war.

[26] *explode* "To drive out disgracefully with some noise of contempt" (Johnson, 1773).
[27] *nec color imperii, nec frons ulla senatus* Lucan, *Pharsalia* (9.207), an epic poem about the Roman Civil Wars; Burke translates in the previous clause.

seemed to blot the sun out of Heaven, 'un beau jour!'[28] How must they be inwardly indignant at hearing others, who thought fit to declare to them, 'that the vessel of the state would fly forward in her course toward regeneration with more speed than ever,' from the stiff gale of treason and murder which preceded our Preacher's triumph! What must they have felt, whilst with outward patience and inward indignation they heard of the slaughter of innocent gentlemen in their houses, that 'the blood spilled was not the most pure?'[29] What must they have felt, when they were besieged by complaints of disorders which shook their country to its foundations, at being compelled coolly to tell the complainants, that they were under the protection of the law, and that they would address the king (the captive king) to cause the laws to be enforced for their protection; when the enslaved ministers of that captive king had formally notified to them, that there were neither law, nor authority, nor power left to protect? What must they have felt at being obliged, as a felicitation on the present new year, to request their captive king to forget the stormy period of the last, on account of the great good which *he* was likely to produce to his people; to the complete attainment of which good they adjourned the practical demonstrations of their loyalty, assuring him of their obedience, when he should no longer possess any authority to command?

This address was made with much good-nature and affection, to be sure. But among the revolutions in France, must be reckoned a considerable revolution in their ideas of politeness. In England we are said to learn manners at second-hand from your side of the water, and that we dress our behaviour in the frippery of France. If so, we are still in the old cut; and have not so far conformed to the new Parisian mode of good breeding, as to think it quite in the most refined strain of delicate compliment (whether in condolence or congratulation) to say, to the most humiliated creature that crawls upon the earth, that great public benefits are derived from the murder of his servants, the attempted assassination of himself and of his wife, and the mortification, disgrace, and degradation that he has personally suffered. It is a topic of consolation which our ordinary of Newgate[30] would be too humane to use to a criminal at the foot of the gallows. I should have thought that the hangman of Paris, now that he is liberalized by the vote of the National Assembly, and is allowed his rank and arms in the Herald's College of the rights of men, would be too generous, too gallant a man, too full of the sense of his new dignity, to employ that cutting consolation to any of the persons whom the *lese nation*[31] might bring under the administration of his *executive powers*.

A man is fallen indeed, when he is thus flattered. The anodyne draught of oblivion, thus drugged, is well calculated to preserve a galling wakefulness, and to feed the living ulcer of a corroding memory. Thus to administer the opiate potion of amnesty, powdered with all the ingredients of scorn and contempt, is to hold to his lips, instead of 'the balm of hurt minds',[32] the cup of human misery full to the brim and to force him to drink it to the dregs.

Yielding to reasons, at least as forcible as those which were so delicately urged in the compliment on the new year, the king of France will probably endeavour to forget these events, and that compliment. But history, who keeps a durable record of all our acts, and exercises her awful censure over the proceedings of all sorts of sovereigns, will not forget either those events, or the era of this liberal refinement in the intercourse of mankind. History

---

[28] *un beau jour* October 6, 1789 ["a beautiful day"; Burke's note; the date when the King and Queen of France were taken from their palace at Versailles to Paris].
[29] *the blood spilled was not the most pure* the quotation has been attributed to Barnave, a member of the National Assembly upon hearing of further mob lynchings of unpopular beneficiaries of government corruption.

[30] *ordinary of Newgate* the priest assigned to minister to condemned criminals in Newgate prison.
[31] *lese nation* injured nation (formed after *lese-majesty*, the French name for high treason).
[32] *"the balm of hurt minds"* *Macbeth* 2.2.39 (said of sleep).

will record, that on the morning of the 6th of October, 1789, the king and queen of France, after a day of confusion, alarm, dismay, and slaughter, lay down, under the pledged security of public faith, to indulge nature in a few hours of respite, and troubled, melancholy repose. From this sleep the queen was first startled by the sentinel at her door, who cried out to her, to save herself by flight – that this was the last proof of fidelity he could give – that they were upon him, and he was dead. Instantly he was cut down. A band of cruel ruffians and assassins, reeking with his blood, rushed into the chamber of the queen, and pierced with a hundred strokes of bayonets and poniards the bed, from whence this persecuted woman had but just time to fly almost naked, and through ways unknown to the murderers, had escaped to seek refuge at the feet of a king and husband, not secure of his own life for a moment.

This king, to say no more of him, and this queen, and their infant children (who once would have been the pride and hope of a great and generous people) were then forced to abandon the sanctuary of the most splendid palace in the world, which they left swimming in blood, polluted by massacre and strewed with scattered limbs and mutilated carcasses. Thence they were conducted into the capital of their kingdom. Two had been selected from the unprovoked, unresisted, promiscuous slaughter, which was made of the gentlemen of birth and family who composed the king's body guard. These two gentlemen, with all the parade of an execution of justice, were cruelly and publicly dragged to the block, and beheaded in the great court of the palace. Their heads were stuck upon spears and led the procession; whilst the royal captives who followed in the train were slowly moved along, amidst the horrid yells, and shrilling screams, and frantic dances, and infamous contumelies, and all the unutterable abominations of the furies of hell, in the abused shape of the vilest of women. After they had been made to taste, drop by drop, more than the bitterness of death in the slow torture of a journey of twelve miles, protracted to six hours, they were, under a guard, composed of those very soldiers who had thus conducted them through this famous triumph, lodged in one of the old palaces of Paris, now converted into a Bastille for kings.

Is this a triumph to be consecrated at altars? to be commemorated with grateful thanksgiving? to be offered to the divine humanity with fervent prayer and enthusiastic ejaculation?[33] – These Theban and Thracian Orgies,[34] acted in France, and applauded only in the Old Jewry, I assure you, kindle prophetic enthusiasm in the minds but of very few people in this kingdom; although a saint and apostle, who may have revelations of his own, and who has so completely vanquished all the mean superstitions of the heart, may incline to think it pious and decorous to compare it with the entrance into the world of the Prince of Peace, proclaimed in a holy temple by a venerable sage,[35] and not long before not worse announced by the voice of angels to the quiet innocence of shepherds.

At first I was at a loss to account for this fit of unguarded transport. I knew, indeed, that the sufferings of monarchs make a delicious repast to some sort of palates. There were reflections which might serve to keep this appetite within some bounds of temperance. But when I took one circumstance into my consideration, I was obliged to confess, that much allowance ought to be made for the Society, and that the temptation was too strong for common discretion; I mean, the circumstance of the Io Pæan[36] of the triumph, the animating cry which called 'for all the BISHOPS to be hanged on the lamp-posts,'[37] might well have

---

[33] *enthusiastic ejaculation* inspired, religious utterance.
[34] *Theban and Thracian Orgies* Bacchic or Dionysian revels.
[35] *venerable sage* old Simeon (above).

[36] *Io Pæan* beginning of a Greek song of triumph, properly addressed to Apollo.
[37] *all the BISHOPS to be hanged on the lamp-posts* "Tous les Eveques à la lanterne" [Burke's note].

brought forth a burst of enthusiasm on the foreseen consequences of this happy day. I allow to so much enthusiasm some little deviation from prudence. I allow this prophet to break forth into hymns of joy and thanksgiving on an event which appears like the precursor of the Millennium, and the projected fifth monarchy,[38] in the destruction of all church establishments. There was, however (as in all human affairs there is) in the midst of this joy something to exercise the patience of these worthy gentlemen, and to try the long-suffering of their faith. The actual murder of the king and queen, and their child, was wanting to the other auspicious circumstances of this *beautiful day.* The actual murder of the bishops, though called for by so many holy ejaculations, was also wanting. A group of regicide and sacrilegious slaughter, was indeed boldly sketched, but it was only sketched. It unhappily was left unfinished in this great history-piece of the massacre of innocents.[39] What hardy pencil of a great master, from the school of the rights of man will finish it is to be seen hereafter. The age has not yet the complete benefit of that diffusion of knowledge that has undermined superstition and error; and the king of France wants another object or two, to consign to oblivion, in consideration of all the good which is to arise from his own sufferings, and the patriotic crimes of an enlightened age.

Although this work of our new light and knowledge, did not go to the length, that in all probability it was intended it should be carried; yet I must think, that such treatment of any human creatures must be shocking to any but those who are made for accomplishing Revolutions. But I cannot stop here. Influenced by the inborn feelings of my nature, and not being illuminated by a single ray of this new-sprung modern light, I confess to you, Sir, that the exalted rank of the persons suffering, and particularly the sex, the beauty, and the amiable qualities of the descendant of so many kings and emperors, with the tender age of royal infants, insensible only through infancy and innocence of the cruel outrages to which their parents were exposed, instead of being a subject of exultation, adds not a little to any sensibility on that most melancholy occasion.

I hear that the august person, who was the principal object of our preacher's triumph, though he supported himself, felt much on that shameful occasion. As a man, it became him to feel for his wife and his children, and the faithful guards of his person, that were massacred in cold blood about him; as a prince, it became him to feel for the strange and frightful transformation of his civilised subjects, and to be more grieved for them than solicitous for himself. It derogates little from his fortitude, while it adds infinitely to the honour of his humanity. I am very sorry to say it, very sorry indeed, that such personages are in a situation in which it is not unbecoming in us to praise the virtues of the great.

I hear, and I rejoice to hear, that the great lady, the other object of the triumph, has borne that day (one is interested that beings made for suffering should suffer well) and that she bears all the succeeding days, that she bears the imprisonment of her husband, and her own captivity, and the exile of her friends, and the insulting adulation of addresses, and the whole weight of her accumulated wrongs, with a serene patience, in a manner suited to her rank and race, and becoming the offspring of a sovereign distinguished for her piety and her courage; that like her she has lofty sentiments; that she feels with the dignity of a Roman matron; that in the last extremity she will save herself from the last disgrace, and that, if she must fall, she will fall by no ignoble hand.

[38] *fifth monarchy* the everlasting kingdom described in the prophetic book of Daniel (2.44) and associated with the Millennium, or thousand-year reign of Christ described in Revelation (20.1–5); there was radical sect of Protestants called Fifth-Monarchy Men during the British Civil War.
[39] *the massacre of innocents* a common topic of grand historical painting of the high Renaissance, depicting the events described in Matthew 2.16–18.

It is now sixteen or seventeen years since I saw the queen of France, then the dauphiness, at Versailles; and surely never lighted on this orb, which she hardly seemed to touch, a more delightful vision. I saw her just above the horizon, decorating and cheering the elevated sphere she just began to move in, – glittering like the morning-star, full of life, and splendour and joy. Oh! what a revolution! and what a heart must I have to contemplate without emotion that elevation and that fall! Little did I dream that, when she added titles of veneration to those of enthusiastic, distant, respectful love, that she should ever be obliged to carry the sharp antidote against disgrace concealed in that bosom; little did I dream that I should have lived to see such disasters fallen upon her in a nation of gallant men, in a nation of men of honour and of cavaliers. I thought ten thousand swords must have leaped from their scabbards to avenge even a look that threatened her with insult. – But the age of chivalry is gone. – That of sophisters, economists, and calculators, has succeeded; and the glory of Europe is extinguished for ever. Never, never more, shall we behold that generous loyalty to rank and sex, that proud submission, that dignified obedience, that subordination of the heart which kept alive, even in servitude itself, the spirit of an exalted freedom. The unbought grace of life, the cheap defence of nations, the nurse of manly sentiment and heroic enterprise, is gone! It is gone, that sensibility of principle, that chastity of honour which felt a stain like a wound, which inspired courage whilst it mitigated ferocity, which ennobled whatever it touched, and under which vice itself lost half its evil, by losing all its grossness.

This mixed system of opinion and sentiment had its origin in the ancient chivalry; and the principle, though varied in its appearance by the varying state of human affairs, subsisted and influenced through a long succession of generations even to the time we live in. If it should ever be totally extinguished, the loss I fear will be great. It is this which has given its character to modern Europe. It is this which has distinguished it under all its forms of government, and distinguished it to its advantage, from the states of Asia, and possibly from those states which flourished in the most brilliant periods of the antique world. It was this, which, without confounding ranks, had produced a noble equality, and handed it down through all the gradations of social life. It was this opinion which mitigated kings into companions, and raised private men to be fellows with kings. Without force, or opposition, it subdued the fierceness of pride and power; it obliged sovereigns to submit to the soft collar of social esteem, compelled stern authority to submit to elegance, and gave domination, a vanquisher of laws,[40] to be subdued by manners.

But now all is to be changed. All the pleasing illusions, which made power gentle, and obedience liberal, which harmonized the different shades of life, and which, by a bland assimilation, incorporated into politics the sentiments which beautify and soften private society, are to be dissolved by this new conquering empire of light and reason. All the decent drapery of life is to be rudely torn off. All the superadded ideas, furnished from the wardrobe of a moral imagination, which the heart owns, and the understanding ratifies, as necessary to cover the defects of our naked shivering nature, and to raise it to dignity in our own estimation, are to be exploded as a ridiculous, absurd, and antiquated fashion.

On this scheme of things, a king is but a man; a queen is but a woman; a woman is but an animal; and an animal not of the highest order. All homage paid to the sex in general as such, and without distinct views, is to be regarded as romance and folly. Regicide, and parricide, and sacrilege, are but fictions of superstition, corrupting jurisprudence by destroying its simplicity. The murder of a king, or a queen, or a bishop, or a father, are only

---

[40]   *domination, a vanquisher of laws*   I have emended this from "a domination vanquisher of laws."

common homicide; and if the people are by any chance, or in any way gainers by it, a sort of homicide much the most pardonable, and into which we ought not to make too severe a scrutiny.

On the scheme of this barbarous philosophy, which is the offspring of cold hearts and muddy understandings, and which is as void of solid wisdom, as it is destitute of all taste and elegance, laws are to be supported only by their own terrors, and by the concern, which each individual may find in them, from his own private speculations, or can spare to them from his own private interests. In the groves of *their* academy, at the end of every visto,[41] you see nothing but the gallows. Nothing is left which engages the affections on the part of the commonwealth. On the principles of this mechanic philosophy, our institutions can never be embodied, if I may use the expression, in persons; so as to create in us love, veneration, admiration, or attachment. But that sort of reason which banishes the affections is incapable of filling their place. These public affections, combined with manners, are required some-times as supplements, sometimes as correctives, always as aids to law. The precept given by a wise man, as well as a great critic, for the construction of poems, is equally true as to states. *Non satis est pulchra esse poemata, dulcia sunto.*[42] There ought to be a system of manners in every nation which a well-informed mind would be disposed to relish. To make us love our country, our country ought to be lovely.

But power, of some kind or other, will survive the shock in which manners and opinions perish; and it will find other and worse means for its support. The usurpation which, in order to subvert ancient institutions, has destroyed ancient principles, will hold power by arts similar to those by which it has acquired it. When the old feudal and chivalrous spirit of *Fealty*, which, by freeing kings from fear, freed both kings and subjects from the precautions of tyranny, shall be extinct in the minds of men, plots and assassinations will be anticipated by preventive murder and preventive confiscation, and that long roll of grim and bloody maxims, which form the political code of all power, not standing on its own honour, and the honour of those who are to obey it. Kings will be tyrants from policy when subjects are rebels from principle.

When ancient opinions and rules of life are taken away, the loss cannot possibly be estimated. From that moment we have no compass to govern us; nor can we know distinctly to what port we steer. Europe undoubtedly, taken in a mass, was in a flourishing condition the day on which your Revolution was completed. How much of that prosperous state was owing to the spirit of our old manners and opinions is not easy to say; but as such causes cannot be indifferent in their operation, we must presume, that, on the whole, their operation was beneficial.

We are but too apt to consider things in the state in which we find them, without sufficiently adverting to the causes by which they have been produced and possibly may be upheld. Nothing is more certain, than that our manners, our civilization, and all the good things which are connected with manners, and with civilization, have, in this European world of ours, depended for ages upon two principles; and were indeed the result of both combined; I mean the spirit of a gentleman and the spirit of religion. The nobility and the clergy, the one by profession, the other by patronage, kept learning in existence, even in the midst of arms and confusions, and whilst governments were rather in their causes[43] than formed.

---

41 *visto* vista, "View; prospect through an avenue" (Johnson, 1773).

42 *Non satis est pulchra esse poemata, dulcia sunto* "It is not enough for poems to be beautiful; they must also be pleasing" (Horace, *Ars Poetica*, 99).

43 *causes* the state or condition that gives rise to something.

Learning paid back what it received to nobility and to priesthood; and paid it with usury, by enlarging their ideas and by furnishing their minds. Happy if they had all continued to know their indissoluble union, and their proper place! Happy if learning, not debauched by ambition, had been satisfied to continue the instructor, and not aspired to be the master! Along with its natural protectors and guardians, learning will be cast into the mire and trodden down under the hoofs of a swinish multitude.

If, as I suspect, modern letters owe more than they are always willing to own to ancient manners, so do other interests which we value full as much as they are worth. Even commerce, and trade, and manufacture, the gods of our economical politicians, are themselves perhaps but creatures; are themselves but effects, which, as first causes, we choose to worship. They certainly grew under the same shade in which learning flourished. They too may decay with their natural protecting principles. With you, for the present at least, they all threaten to disappear together. Where trade and manufactures are wanting to a people, and the spirit of nobility and religion remains, sentiment supplies, and not always ill supplies their place; but if commerce and the arts should be lost in an experiment to try how well a state may stand without these old fundamental principles, what sort of a thing must be a nation of gross, stupid, ferocious, and at the same time, poor and sordid barbarians, destitute of religion, honour, or manly pride, possessing nothing at present, and hoping for nothing hereafter?

I wish you may not be going fast, and by the shortest cut, to that horrible and disgustful situation. Already there appears a poverty of conception, a coarseness and a vulgarity in all the proceedings of the assembly and of all their instructors. Their liberty is not liberal. Their science[44] is presumptuous ignorance. Their humanity is savage and brutal.

It is not clear, whether in England we learned those grand and decorous principles, and manners, of which considerable traces yet remain, from you, or whether you took them from us. But to you, I think, we trace them best. You seem to me to be – *gentis incunabula nostræ*.[45] France has always more or less influenced manners in England; and when your fountain is choked up and polluted, the stream will not run long, or not run clear with us or perhaps with any nation. This gives all Europe, in my opinion, but too close and connected a concern in what is done in France. Excuse me, therefore, if I have dwelt too long on the atrocious spectacle of the sixth of October 1789, or have given too much scope to the reflections which have arisen in my mind on occasion of the most important of all revolutions, which may be dated from that day, I mean a revolution in sentiments, manners, and moral opinions. As things now stand, with everything respectable destroyed without us, and an attempt to destroy within us every principle of respect, one is almost forced to apologise for harbouring the common feelings of men.

Why do I feel so differently from the Reverend Dr. Price, and those of his lay flock, who will choose to adopt the sentiments of his discourse? – For this plain reason – because it is *natural* I should; because we are so made as to be affected at such spectacles with melancholy sentiments upon the unstable condition of mortal prosperity, and the tremendous uncertainty of human greatness; because in those natural feelings we learn great lessons; because in events like these our passions instruct our reason; because when kings are hurled from their thrones by the Supreme Director of this great drama, and become the objects of insult to the base, and of pity to the good, we behold such disasters in the moral as we should behold a miracle in the physical order of things. We are alarmed into reflection; our minds (as it has long since been observed) are purified by terror and pity;[46] our weak, unthinking pride is humbled, under the dispensations of a mysterious wisdom. – Some tears might be drawn from me, if

---

44 *science* knowledge.

45 *gentis incunabula nostræ* "the cradle of our race."

46 *our minds . . . by terror and pity* adapted from Aristotle's *Poetics*.

such a spectacle were exhibited on the stage. I should be truly ashamed of finding in myself that superficial, theatric sense of painted distress, whilst I could exult over it in real life. With such a perverted mind, I could never venture to show my face at a tragedy. People would think the tears that Garrick[47] formerly, or that Siddons[48] not long since, have extorted from me, were the tears of hypocrisy; I should know them to be the tears of folly.

Indeed the theatre is a better school of moral sentiments than churches, where the feelings of humanity are thus outraged. Poets, who have to deal with an audience not yet graduated in the school of the rights of men, and who must apply themselves to the moral constitution of the heart, would not dare to produce such a triumph as a matter of exultation. There, where men follow their natural impulses, they would not bear the odious maxims of a Machiavellian policy, whether applied to the attainments of monarchical or democratic tyranny. They would reject them on the modern, as they once did on the ancient stage, where they could not bear even the hypothetical proposition of such wickedness in the mouth of a personated tyrant, though suitable to the character he sustained. No theatric audience in Athens would bear what has been borne, in the midst of the real tragedy of this triumphal day; a principal actor weighing, as it were in scales hung in a shop of horrors, – so much actual crime against so much contingent advantage, – and after putting in and out weights, declaring that the balance was on the side of the advantages. They would not bear to see the crimes of new democracy posted as in a ledger against the crimes of old despotism, and the book-keepers of politics finding democracy still in debt, but by no means unable or unwilling to pay the balance. In the theatre, the first intuitive glance, without any elaborate process of reasoning, would show that this method of political computation would justify every extent of crime. They would see, that on these principles, even where the very worst acts were not perpetrated, it was owing rather to the fortune of the conspirators than to their parsimony in the expenditure of treachery and blood. They would soon see, that criminal means once tolerated are soon preferred. They present a shorter cut to the object than through the highway of the moral virtues. Justifying perfidy and murder for public benefit, public benefit would soon become the pretext, and perfidy and murder the end; until rapacity, malice, revenge, and fear more dreadful than revenge could satiate their insatiable appetites. Such must be the consequences of losing in the splendour of these triumphs of the rights of men, all natural sense of wrong and right.

Oliver Goldsmith (1730?–1774)

Known sometimes as ursa minor, *little bear, to Samuel Johnson's* ursa major, *Goldsmith was as productive a writer as any in his time. Having dropped out once and even sold his books, Goldsmith achieved his BA at Trinity College Dublin in 1749. He went first to Edinburgh and then to Padua to study medicine, and, having dallied in Europe, he arrived destitute in London in 1756. He tried on and off to establish a medical practice but soon gave all of his considerable energies to writing. Between 1759 and 1774 he published an extraordinary number of works; many were poorly researched and hastily compiled, such as his histories of England, Rome, and Greece, but all display his characteristically easy or, as we might say now, his friendly style.*

The Citizen of the World; or, Letters from a Chinese Philosopher, Residing in London, to his Friends in the East *(1762) established Goldsmith's reputation, but his most*

---

[47] *Garrick* David (1717–79), greatest actor of his age.   [48] *Siddons* Sarah Kemble (1755–1831), famous Shakespearean actress.

popular work, and one of the most popular works in British literary history is The Vicar of Wakefield *(1766). Johnson sold the manuscript for Goldsmith for the sum of £63. The work went into nine editions in the next eight years, and there have been over a hundred since. Like the* Vicar, *Goldsmith's* Deserted Village *evokes sympathy and sentiment for country life. Unlike traditional pastoral poetry, Goldsmith's works do not present the country as an Arcadian paradise, but rather as a paradise lost. As he makes clear in his important essay, "The Revolution in Low Life," Goldsmith believed country life was being ruined by British interest in foreign trade and the concentration of capital and land in the hands of a small number of millionaires. He did not live long enough to witness the impact of the industrial revolution, which would finish, in some respects, the degradation he deplored.*

Goldsmith produced a couple of important plays, She Stoops to Conquer *and* The Good Natured Man. *His long poem* The Traveller *and his eight-volume* History of the Earth and Animated Nature *are are also very worthy of mention. The standard edition of Goldsmith's Collected Works, which cannot of course include everything, is edited by Arthur Friedman, 5 vols (Clarendon Press, 1966). The poems are edited with a complete commentary by Roger Lonsdale (Longman, 1969). My text of* The Deserted Village *is based on the first quarto edition (1770) with variants from the fourth quarto edition (also 1770). The text of "The Revolution in Low Life" comes from* Lloyd's Evening Post, *14–16 June 1762. I am indebted to Lonsdale's and Friedman's editions for help with my notes.*

The Revolution in Low Life (1762)

To the EDITOR *of* LLOYD'S EVENING POST (14–16 June 1762)

SIR,

I spent part of the last summer in a little village, distant about fifty miles from town, consisting of near an hundred houses. It lay entirely out of the road of commerce, and was inhabited by a race of men who followed the primeval profession of agriculture for several generations. Though strangers to opulence, they were unacquainted with distress; few of them were known either to acquire a fortune or to die in indigence. By a long intercourse and frequent intermarriages they were all become in a manner one family; and, when the work of the day was done, spent the night agreeably in visits at each other's houses. Upon those occasions the poor traveller and stranger were always welcome; and they kept up the stated days of festivity with the strictest observance. They were merry at Christmas and mournful in Lent, got drunk on St. George's-day,[1] and religiously cracked nuts on Michaelmas-eve.[2]

Upon my first arrival I felt a secret pleasure in observing this happy community. The cheerfulness of the old, and the blooming beauty of the young, was no disagreeable change to one like me, whose whole life had been spent in cities. But my satisfaction was soon repressed, when I understood that they were shortly to leave this abode of felicity, of which they and their ancestors had been in possession time immemorial, and that they had received orders to seek for a new habitation. I was informed that a Merchant of immense fortune in London, who had lately purchased the estate on which they lived, intended to lay the whole out in a seat

---

THE REVOLUTION IN LOW LIFE
[1] *St. George's-day*   23 April.

[2] *Michaelmas*   the Feast of St Michael and All Angels, 29 September.

of pleasure for himself. I stayed till the day on which they were compelled to remove, and own I never felt so sincere a concern before.

I was grieved to see a generous, virtuous race of men, who should be considered as the strength and the ornament of their country, torn from their little habitations, and driven out to meet poverty and hardship among strangers. No longer to earn and enjoy the fruits of their labour, they were now going to toil as hirelings under some rigid Master, to flatter the opulent for a precarious meal, and to leave their children the inheritance of want and slavery. The modest matron followed her husband in tears, and often looked back at the little mansion[3] where she had passed her life in innocence, and to which she was never more to return; while the beautiful daughter parted for ever from her Lover, who was now become too poor to maintain her as his wife. All the connections of kindred were now irreparably broken; their neat gardens and well cultivated fields were left to desolation.

Strata jacent passim, hominumque boumque labores.[4]

Such was their misery, and I could wish that this were the only instance of such migrations of late. But I am informed that nothing is at present more common than such revolutions. In almost every part of the kingdom the laborious husbandman has been reduced, and the lands are now either occupied by some general undertaker, or turned into enclosures destined for the purposes of amusement or luxury. Wherever the traveller turns, while he sees one part of the inhabitants of the country becoming immensely rich, he sees the other growing miserably poor, and the happy equality of condition now entirely removed.

Let others felicitate their country upon the increase of foreign commerce and the extension of our foreign conquests; but for my part, this new introduction of wealth gives me but very little satisfaction. Foreign commerce, as it can be managed only by a few, tends proportionably to enrich only a few; neither moderate fortunes nor moderate abilities can carry it on; thus it tends rather to the accumulation of immense wealth in the hands of some, than to a diffusion of it among all; it is calculated rather to make individuals rich, than to make the aggregate happy.

Wherever we turn we shall find those governments that have pursued foreign commerce with too much assiduity at length becoming Aristocratical; and the immense property, thus necessarily acquired by some, has swallowed up the liberties of all. Venice, Genoa, and Holland, are little better at present than retreats for tyrants and prisons for slaves. The Great, indeed, boast of their liberties there, and they have liberty. The poor boast of liberty too; but, alas, they groan under the most rigorous oppression.

A country, thus parcelled out among the rich alone, is of all others the most miserable. The Great, in themselves, perhaps, are not so bad as they are generally represented; but I have almost ever found the dependents and favourites of the Great, strangers to every sentiment of honour and generosity. Wretches, who, by giving up their own dignity to those above them, insolently exact the same tribute from those below. A country, therefore, where the inhabitants are thus divided into the very rich and very poor, is, indeed, of all others the most helpless; without courage and without strength; neither enjoying peace within itself, and, after a time, unable to resist foreign invasion.

---

[3] *mansion* home.

[4] *Strata . . . labores* the works of men and beasts are strewn all over (echoing Virgil, *Eclogues* 7.54).

I shall conclude this paper with a picture of Italy just before its conquest, by Theodoric the Ostrogoth.[5] 'The whole country was at that time', says the Historian, 'one garden of pleasure; the seats of the great men of Rome covered the face of the whole kingdom; and even their villas were supplied with provisions not of their own growth, but produced in distant countries, where they were more industrious. But in proportion as Italy was then beautiful, and its possessors rich, it was also weak and defenceless. The rough peasant and hardy husbandman had been long obliged to seek for liberty and subsistence in Britain or Gaul; and, by leaving their native country, brought with them all the strength of the nation. There was none now to resist an invading army, but the slaves of the nobility or the effeminate citizens of Rome, the one without motive, the other without strength to make any opposition. They were easily, therefore, overcome, by a people more savage indeed, but far more brave than they'.

THE DESERTED VILLAGE, A POEM (1770)

SWEET Auburn! loveliest village of the plain,[1]
Where health and plenty cheered the labouring swain,
Where smiling spring its earliest visit paid,
And parting summer's lingering blooms delayed:
Dear lovely bowers of innocence and ease,   5
Seats of my youth, when every sport could please,
How often have I loitered o'er thy green,
Where humble happiness endeared each scene!
How often have I paused on every charm,
The sheltered cot, the cultivated farm,   10
The never-failing brook, the busy mill,
The decent church that topped the neighbouring hill,
The hawthorn bush, with seats beneath the shade,
For talking age and whisp'ring lovers made!
How often have I blest the coming day,   15
When toil remitting lent its turn to play,
And all the village train, from labour free,
Led up their sports beneath the spreading tree;
While many a pastime circled in the shade,
The young contending as the old surveyed;   20
And many a gambol frolicked o'er the ground,
And sleights of art and feats of strength went round;
And still, as each repeated pleasure tired,
Succeeding sports the mirthful band inspired;
The dancing pair that simply sought renown   25
By holding out to tire each other down:

---

5   *Theodoric the Ostrogoth*   he became King of Italy in 493 and died in 526; among Goldsmith's many rapid productions was a Roman history (1769).
THE DESERTED VILLAGE, A POEM
1   *Auburn*   Goldsmith uses the name of one or more real villages in rural England, and there are some resem-

blances between "Auburn" and Lissoy near Kilkenny West, Ireland, where Goldsmith grew up. However, Goldsmith is mostly talking about an abstract place that exemplifies the ills of rural depopulation, which he also discusses in "The Revolution in Low Life" (above).

The swain mistrustless of his smutted face,
While secret laughter tittered round the place;
The bashful virgin's sidelong looks of love,
The matron's glance that would those looks reprove: 30
These were thy charms, sweet village! sports like these
With sweet succession, taught e'en toil to please:
These round thy bowers their cheerful influence shed,
These were thy charms – but all these charms are fled.

    Sweet smiling village, loveliest of the lawn,   35
Thy sports are fled, and all thy charms withdrawn;
Amidst thy bowers the tyrant's hand is seen,
And desolation saddens all thy green:
One only master grasps the whole domain,
And half a tillage stints thy smiling plain.[2]   40
No more thy glassy brook reflects the day,
But, choked with sedges, works its weedy way;
Along thy glades, a solitary guest,
The hollow-sounding bittern guards its nest;[3]
Amidst thy desert walks the lapwing flies,[4]   45
And tires their echoes with unvaried cries;
Sunk are thy bowers in shapeless ruin all,
And the long grass o'ertops the mould'ring wall;
And trembling, shrinking from the spoiler's hand,
Far, far away, thy children leave the land.   50

    Ill fares the land, to hastening ills a prey,
Where wealth accumulates, and men decay:
Princes and lords may flourish, or may fade;
A breath can make them, as a breath has made:
But a bold peasantry, their country's pride,   55
When once destroyed, can never be supplied.

    A time there was, ere England's griefs began,
When every rood of ground maintained its man;[5]
For him light labour spread her wholesome store,
Just gave what life required, but gave no more: 60
His best companions, innocence and health;
And his best riches, ignorance of wealth.

    But times are altered; trade's unfeeling train
Usurp the land and dispossess the swain;
Along the lawn, where scattered hamlets rose,   65
Unwieldy wealth and cumbrous pomp repose,
And every want to opulence allied,
And every pang that folly pays to pride.
Those gentle hours that plenty bade to bloom,
Those calm desires that asked but little room,   70

---

[2] *tillage* plowed land (as opposed to pasturage) which now occupies only half of what it once did.

[3] *bittern* a marsh bird known for its booming sound.

[4] *lapwing* "A clamorous bird with long wings" (Johnson); a kind of plover.

[5] *rood* a quarter of an acre.

Those healthful sports that graced the peaceful scene,
Lived in each look, and brightened all the green, –
These, far departing, seek a kinder shore,
And rural mirth and manners are no more.

   Sweet Auburn! parent of the blissful hour,   75
Thy glades forlorn confess the tyrant's power.
Here, as I take my solitary rounds,
Amidst thy tangling walks and ruined grounds,
And, many a year elapsed, return to view
Where once the cottage stood, the hawthorn grew,   80
Remembrance wakes with all her busy train,
Swells at my breast, and turns the past to pain.
   In all my wand'rings round this world of care,
In all my griefs – and God has giv'n my share –
I still had hopes, my latest hours to crown,   85
Amidst these humble bowers to lay me down;
To husband out life's taper at the close,
And keep the flame from wasting by repose:
I still had hopes, for pride attends us still,
Amidst the swains to show my booklearned skill,   90
Around my fire an evening group to draw,
And tell of all I felt and all I saw;
And as a hare whom hounds and horns pursue,
Pants to the place from whence at first she flew,
I still had hopes, my long vexations past,   95
Here to return, and die at home at last.
   O blest retirement, friend to life's decline,
Retreats from care, that never must be mine!
How happy he who crowns in shades like these
A youth of labour with an age of ease;   100
Who quits a world where strong temptations try,
And, since 'tis hard to combat, learns to fly!
For him no wretches, born to work and weep,
Explore the mine, or tempt the dangerous deep;⁶
No surly porter stands in guilty state,   105
To spurn imploring famine from the gate;
But on he moves to meet his latter end,
Angels around befriending virtue's friend;
Bends to the grave with unperceived decay,
While resignation gently slopes the way;   110
And, all his prospects bright'ning to the last,
His heav'n commences ere the world be past!
   Sweet was the sound, when oft at evening's close
Up yonder hill the village murmur rose.
There, as I passed with careless steps and slow,   115
The mingling notes came softened from below;

---

⁶ *tempt*   attempt, try; venture upon.

The swain responsive as the milk-maid sung,
The sober herd that lowed to meet their young,
The noisy geese that gabbled o'er the pool,
The playful children just let loose from school, 120
The watch-dog's voice that bayed the whisp'ring wind,
And the loud laugh that spoke the vacant mind, –
These all in sweet confusion sought the shade,
And filled each pause the nightingale had made.
But now the sounds of population fail, 125
No cheerful murmurs fluctuate in the gale,[7]
No busy steps the grass-grown foot-way tread,
For all the bloomy flush of life is fled!
All but yon widowed, solitary thing,
That feebly bends beside the plashy spring:[8] 130
She, wretched matron, forced in age for bread,
To strip the brook with mantling cresses spread,[9]
To pick her wintry faggot from the thorn,[10]
To seek her nightly shed, and weep till morn;
She only left of all the harmless train, 135
The sad historian of the pensive plain.
    Near yonder copse, where once the garden smiled,
And still where many a garden flower grows wild;
There, where a few torn shrubs the place disclose,
The village preacher's modest mansion rose.[11] 140
A man he was to all the country dear,
And passing rich with forty pounds a year;[12]
Remote from towns he ran his godly race,
Nor e'er had changed, nor wished to change, his place;
Unpractised he to fawn, or seek for power, 145
By doctrines fashioned to the varying hour;
Far other aims his heart had learned to prize,
More skilled to raise the wretched than to rise.
His house was known to all the vagrant train;
He chid their wand'rings but relieved their pain; 150
The long remembered beggar was his guest,
Whose beard descending swept his aged breast;
The ruined spendthrift, now no longer proud,
Claimed kindred there, and had his claims allowed;
The broken soldier, kindly bade to stay, 155
Sat by his fire, and talked the night away,
Wept o'er his wounds, or, tales of sorrow done,
Shouldered his crutch and showed how fields were won.
Pleased with his guests, the good man learned to glow,

---

[7] *gale* breeze.
[8] *plashy* "Watry; filled with puddles" (Johnson).
[9] *cresses* such as watercress, a green used in salads.
[10] *faggot* "A bundle of sticks bound together for the fire" (Johnson).

[11] *village preacher* said to portray Goldsmith's father, the Reverend Charles Goldsmith.
[12] *passing rich* exceedingly rich.

And quite forgot their vices in their woe;   160
Careless their merits or their faults to scan,
His pity gave ere charity began.
   Thus to relieve the wretched was his pride,
And e'en his failings leaned to virtue's side;
But in his duty prompt at every call,   165
He watched and wept, he prayed and felt for all;
And, as a bird each fond endearment tries
To tempt its new-fledged offspring to the skies,
He tried each art, reproved each dull delay,
Allured to brighter worlds, and led the way.   170
   Beside the bed where parting life was laid,
And sorrow, guilt, and pain, by turns dismayed
The rev'rend champion stood. At his control
Despair and anguish fled the struggling soul;
Comfort came down the trembling wretch to raise,   175
And his last falt'ring accents whispered praise.
   At church, with meek and unaffected grace,
His looks adorned the venerable place;
Truth from his lips prevailed with double sway,
And fools who came to scoff remained to pray.   180
The service past, around the pious man,
With steady zeal, each honest rustic ran;
E'en children followed with endearing wile,
And plucked his gown to share the good man's smile.
His ready smile a parent's warmth expressed: 185
Their welfare pleased him, and their cares distressed:
To them his heart, his love, his griefs were given,
But all his serious thoughts had rest in Heaven.
As some tall cliff that lifts its awful form,
Swells from the vale, and midway leaves the storm,   190
Though round its breast the rolling clouds are spread,
Eternal sunshine settles on its head.
   Beside yon straggling fence that skirts the way,
With blossomed furze unprofitably gay,[13]
There, in his noisy mansion, skilled to rule,   195
The village master taught his little school.
A man severe he was, and stern to view;
I knew him well, and every truant knew;
Well had the boding tremblers learned to trace[14]
The day's disasters in his morning face;   200
Full well they laughed with counterfeited glee
At all his jokes, for many a joke had he;
Full well the busy whisper circling round
Conveyed the dismal tidings when he frowned.
Yet he was kind, or, if severe in aught,   205

---

[13] *furze*   gorse, a spiny evergreen shrub.   [14] *boding*   foreboding, foretelling.

The love he bore to learning was in fault;
The village all declared how much he knew;
'Twas certain he could write, and cipher too:[15]
Lands he could measure, terms and tides presage,[16]
And ev'n the story ran that he could gauge.[17]   210
In arguing, too, the parson owned his skill,
For, ev'n though vanquished, he could argue still;
While words of learned length and thundering sound
Amazed the gazing rustics ranged around;
And still they gazed, and still the wonder grew,   215
That one small head could carry all he knew.
    But past is all his fame. The very spot
Where many a time he triumphed is forgot.
Near yonder thorn, that lifts its head on high,
Where once the sign-post caught the passing eye,   220
Low lies that house where nut-brown draughts inspired,[18]
Where grey-beard mirth and smiling toil retired,
Where village statesmen talked with looks profound,
And news much older than their ale went round.
Imagination fondly stoops to trace   225
The parlour splendours of that festive place;
The white-washed wall, the nicely-sanded floor,
The varnished clock that clicked behind the door;
The chest contrived a double debt to pay,
A bed by night, a chest of drawers by day;   230
The pictures placed for ornament and use,
The Twelve Good Rules, the Royal Game of Goose;[19]
The hearth, except when winter chilled the day,
With aspen boughs, and flowers, and fennel gay;
While broken tea-cups, wisely kept for show,   235
Ranged o'er the chimney, glistened in a row.
    Vain transitory splendours! could not all
Reprieve the tottering mansion from its fall?
Obscure it sinks, nor shall it more impart
An hour's importance to the poor man's heart.   240
Thither no more the peasant shall repair
To sweet oblivion of his daily care;
No more the farmer's news, the barber's tale,
No more the woodman's ballad shall prevail;
No more the smith his dusky brow shall clear,   245
Relax his pond'rous strength, and lean to hear;

---

[15] *cipher*   "To practise arithmetic" (Johnson).
[16] *terms and tides*   calendar dates for the payment of debts and the celebration of holidays respectively.
[17] *gauge*   "Measure with respect to the contents of a vessel" (Johnson); this involved dipping a gauge, or measuring rod, in a barrel containing some liquid and figuring its volume.

[18] *nut-brown draughts*   ale.
[19] *The Twelve Good Rules*   short bits of practical advice for living (e.g. "lay no wagers"), supposedly found in Charles I's study after his execution; *Goose*   a simple game like Chutes and Ladders (Snakes and Ladders) in which players roll dice and advance their pieces on a board with hazards.

The host himself no longer shall be found
Careful to see the mantling bliss go round;
Nor the coy maid, half willing to be pressed,
Shall kiss the cup to pass it to the rest.   250
   Yes! let the rich deride, the proud disdain,
These simple blessings of the lowly train;
To me more dear, congenial to my heart,
One native charm, than all the gloss of art;
Spontaneous joys, where nature has its play,   255
The soul adopts, and owns their first born sway;
Lightly they frolic o'er the vacant mind,
Unenvied, unmolested, unconfined.
But the long pomp, the midnight masquerade,
With all the freaks of wanton wealth arrayed –   260
In these, ere triflers half their wish obtain,
The toiling pleasure sickens into pain;
And, e'en while fashion's brightest arts decoy,
The heart distrusting asks if this be joy.
   Ye friends to truth, ye statesmen who survey   265
The rich man's joys increase, the poor's decay,
'Tis yours to judge, how wide the limits stand
Between a splendid and a happy land.
Proud swells the tide with loads of freighted ore,
And shouting Folly hails them from her shore;   270
Hoards e'en beyond the miser's wish abound,
And rich men flock from all the world around.
Yet count our gains. This wealth is but a name
That leaves our useful products still the same.
Not so the loss. The man of wealth and pride   275
Takes up a space that many poor supplied;
Space for his lake, his park's extended bounds,
Space for his horses, equipage, and hounds:
The robe that wraps his limbs in silken sloth
Has robbed the neighb'ring fields of half their growth: 280
His seat, where solitary sports are seen,
Indignant spurns the cottage from the green:
Around the world each needful product flies,
For all the luxuries the world supplies;
While thus the land adorned for pleasure all,   285
In barren splendour feebly waits the fall.
   As some fair female unadorned and plain,
Secure to please while youth confirms her reign,
Slights every borrowed charm that dress supplies,
Nor shares with art the triumph of her eyes;   290
But when those charms are past, for charms are frail,
When time advances, and when lovers fail,
She then shines forth, solicitous to bless,
In all the glaring impotence of dress.

Thus fares the land by luxury betrayed: 295
In nature's simplest charms at first arrayed,
But verging to decline, its splendours rise,
Its vistas strike, its palaces surprise;
While, scourged by famine from the smiling land,
The mournful peasant leads his humble band,   300
And while he sinks, without one arm to save,
The country blooms – a garden and a grave.
    Where then, ah! where, shall poverty reside,
To 'scape the pressure of contiguous pride?
If to some common's fenceless limits strayed[20]   305
He drives his flock to pick the scanty blade,
Those fenceless fields the sons of wealth divide,
And ev'n the bare-worn common is denied.
    If to the city sped – what waits him there?
To see profusion that he must not share;   310
To see ten thousand baneful arts combined
To pamper luxury, and thin mankind;
To see those joys the sons of pleasure know
Extorted from his fellow-creature's woe.
Here while the courtier glitters in brocade,   315
There the pale artist plies the sickly trade;
Here while the proud their long-drawn pomps display,
There the black gibbet glooms beside the way.[21]
The dome where pleasure holds her midnight reign[22]
Here, richly decked, admits the gorgeous train: 320
Tumultuous grandeur crowds the blazing square,
The rattling chariots clash, the torches glare.
Sure scenes like these no troubles e'er annoy!
Sure these denote one universal joy!
Are these thy serious thoughts? – Ah, turn thine eyes   325
Where the poor houseless shiv'ring female lies.
She once, perhaps, in village plenty blest,
Has wept at tales of innocence distressed;
Her modest looks the cottage might adorn
Sweet as the primrose peeps beneath the thorn: 330
Now lost to all – her friends, her virtue fled,
Near her betrayer's door she lays her head,
And, pinched with cold, and shrinking from the shower,
With heavy heart deplores that luckless hour,
When idly first, ambitious of the town,   335
She left her wheel and robes of country brown.[23]
    Do thine, sweet Auburn, thine, the loveliest train –
Do thy fair tribes participate her pain?

---

[20] *common* public lands for grazing, which were increasingly "enclosed" or acquired and fenced by the wealthy in the late eighteenth and nineteenth centuries.

[21] *gibbet* gallows.
[22] *dome* grand house.
[23] *wheel* spinning wheel.

Ev'n now, perhaps, by cold and hunger led,
At proud men's doors they ask a little bread!   340
    Ah, no! To distant climes, a dreary scene,
Where half the convex world intrudes between,
Through torrid tracts with fainting steps they go,
Where wild Altama murmurs to their woe.[24]
Far different there from all that charmed before,   345
The various terrors of that horrid shore:
Those blazing suns that dart a downward ray,
And fiercely shed intolerable day;
Those matted woods, where birds forget to sing,
But silent bats in drowsy clusters cling;   350
Those pois'nous fields with rank luxuriance crowned,
Where the dark scorpion gathers death around;
Where at each step the stranger fears to wake
The rattling terrors of the vengeful snake;
Where crouching tigers wait their hapless prey,[25]   355
And savage men more murd'rous still than they;
While oft in whirls the mad tornado flies,
Mingling the ravaged landscape with the skies.
Far different these from every former scene,
The cooling brook, the grassy-vested green,   360
The breezy covert of the warbling grove,
That only sheltered thefts of harmless love.
    Good Heaven! what sorrows gloomed that parting day,
That called them from their native walks away;
When the poor exiles, every pleasure past,   365
Hung round their bowers, and fondly looked their last,
And took a long farewell, and wished in vain
For seats like these beyond the western main,[26]
And shudd'ring still to face the distant deep,
Returned and wept, and still returned to weep!   370
The good old sire the first prepared to go
To new found worlds, and wept for others' woe;
But for himself, in conscious virtue brave,
He only wished for worlds beyond the grave.
His lovely daughter, lovelier in her tears,   375
The fond companion of his helpless years,
Silent went next, neglectful of her charms,
And left a lover's for a father's arms.
With louder plaints the mother spoke her woes,
And blessed the cot where every pleasure rose,[27]   380
And kissed her thoughtless babes with many a tear,

---

[24] *Altama*   the Altamaha river in south-east Georgia, then a British colony to which many bankrupt or otherwise disgraced persons fled or were sent.

[25] *tigers*   naturalists of Goldsmith's day used the name for cougars as well as for other large cats.

[26] *seats*   abodes, residences.

[27] *cot*   cottage.

And clasped them close, in sorrow doubly dear,
Whilst her fond husband strove to lend relief
In all the silent manliness of grief.
   O luxury! thou cursed by Heaven's decree, 385
How ill exchanged are things like these for thee!
How do thy potions, with insidious joy,
Diffuse their pleasures only to destroy!
Kingdoms by thee, to sickly greatness grown,
Boast of a florid vigour not their own. 390
At every draught more large and large they grow,
A bloated mass of rank unwieldy woe;
Till sapped their strength, and every part unsound,
Down, down they sink, and spread a ruin round.
   Ev'n now the devastation is begun, 395
And half the business of destruction done;
Ev'n now, methinks, as pond'ring here I stand,
I see the rural virtues leave the land.
Down where yon anchoring vessel spreads the sail,
That idly waiting flaps with every gale, 400
Downward they move, a melancholy band,
Pass from the shore, and darken all the strand.
Contented toil, and hospitable care,
And kind connubial tenderness, are there;
And piety, with wishes placed above, 405
And steady loyalty, and faithful love.
And thou, sweet Poetry, thou loveliest maid,
Still first to fly where sensual joys invade;
Unfit in these degenerate times of shame
To catch the heart, or strike for honest fame; 410
Dear charming nymph, neglected and decried,
My shame in crowds, my solitary pride;
Thou source of all my bliss, and all my woe,
That found'st me poor at first, and keep'st me so;
Thou guide by which the nobler arts excel, 415
Thou nurse of every virtue, fare thee well!
Farewell, and oh! where'er thy voice be tried,
On Torno's cliffs, or Pambamarca's side,[28]
Whether where equinoctial fervours glow,
Or winter wraps the polar world in snow, 420
Still let thy voice, prevailing over time,
Redress the rigours of th' inclement clime;
Aid slighted truth, with thy persuasive strain
Teach erring man to spurn the rage of gain;
Teach him that states of native strength possessed, 425
Though very poor, may still be very blest;

---

[28] *Torno* a river in Sweden; *Pambamarca* a mountain
in Equador.

That trade's proud empire hastes to swift decay,
As ocean sweeps the laboured mole away;[29]
While self-dependent power can time defy,
As rocks resist the billows and the sky.[30]

430

William Cowper (1731–1800)

At the age of thirty-two, Cowper was offered a government sinecure, Clerk of the Journals of the House of Lords. He had been in the legal profession as a student in Middle Temple, then at the bar and in Inner Temple, for fifteen years; he had done some writing for journals, some translations, and some poetry; he was well-read and literary; he was not particularly ambitious; he was obviously intelligent and came from a distinguished family. In short, he was just the sort of man for whom sinecures were made. However, there was a dispute about the offer, and Cowper was required to appear in court to defend his qualifications for the position. But he found he was unable to do this, and the feelings of self-reproach and self-doubt that surrounded the event plunged Cowper into a depression so severe that he attempted suicide at least three times and wound up in an asylum for the insane for a period of two years. When he emerged, he was a changed person: no longer a man about town, he embraced evangelical ideas and feelings; he retreated from the town to live in the country; he interested himself in gardening and later in pet animals.

Around 1770 poetry became Cowper's principal means of dealing with depression and his main activity. He lived in a long-term, intimate, but perhaps not fully adult relationship with Mary Unwin, the surviving member of a couple who befriended him and took him in shortly after his departure from the insane asylum. He continued to have serious bouts of depression, and his last five years, after the death of Unwin, were lived in continuous emotional pain, with a fear of personal inadequacy and of impending damnation at the hands of an angry God. But through it all, Cowper produced poetry. His collected poems came out in 1782; The Task, a long, autobiographical, immensely popular poem about country, household life, came out in 1785; he undertook and eventually finished a new translation of Homer; and many other poems of varying lengths appeared in successive editions of his collected poems that came out frequently before and after his death. The poetry reflects Cowper's painful inner life and his frightening identification of his own troubled state with the lives of caged animals and the victims of disaster or oppression. Yet, his acts of identification are not without sympathy for creatures outside of himself and not without an appreciation of other lives than his own.

Cowper's bibliography is complicated. I have indicated the bases of my texts in the footnotes to each poem. Cowper's poetry from 1748 to 1782 has been edited by John Baird and Charles Ryskamp (Clarendon Press, 1980); a second volume will perhaps follow now that the Letters and Prose Writings *(5 vols, Clarendon Press, 1979–86) have been completed by Ryskamp and James King. I have also benefited from the collations in the edition of the Poetical Works by H. S. Milford (corr. Norma Russell, Oxford, 1967).*

---

[29] *mole*   a pier or breakwater.

[30] *That trade's . . . and the sky*   these lines were written by Samuel Johnson.

ON A GOLDFINCH STARVED TO DEATH IN HIS CAGE (1782)[1]

Time was when I was as free as air,
The thistle's downy seed my fare,
   My drink the morning dew;
I perched at will on every spray,
My form genteel, my plumage gay,   5
   My strains for ever new.

But gaudy plumage, sprightly strain,
And form genteel, were all in vain,
   And of a transient date;
For, caught and caged, and starved to death,   10
In dying sighs my little breath
   Soon passed the wiry gate.

Thanks, gentle swain, for all my woes,
And thanks for this effectual close
   And cure of every ill!   15
More cruelty could none express;
And I, if you had shown me less,
   Had been your pris'ner still.

EPITAPH ON AN HARE (1784)[1]

HERE lies, whom hound did ne'er pursue,
   Nor swifter greyhound follow,
Whose foot ne'er tainted morning dew,[2]
   Nor ear heard huntsman's halloo,

Tiney, the surliest of his kind,   5
   Who, nursed with tender care,
And to domestic bounds confined,
   Was still a wild Jack-hare.

Though duly from my hand he took
   His pittance every night,   10
He did it with a jealous look,
   And, when he could, would bite.

His diet was of wheaten bread,
   And milk, and oats, and straw;
Thistles, or lettuces instead;   15
   And sand to cleanse his maw.

ON A GOLDFINCH STARVED
[1] The text is based on the first printing in *Poems by William Cowper, of the Inner Temple, Esq.* (1782).

EPITAPH ON AN HARE
[1] The text is based on the first printing (*Gentleman's Magazine*, December 1784).
[2] *tainted* gave a scent to.

On twigs of hawthorn he regaled,
    On pippins' russet peel;[3]
And, when his juicier salads failed,
    Sliced carrot pleased him well.   20

A Turkey carpet was his lawn,
    Whereon he loved to bound,
To skip and gambol like a faun,
    And swing himself around.[4]

His frisking was at evening hours,   25
    For then he lost his fear;
But most before approaching showers,
    Or when a storm drew near.

Eight years and five round rolling moons
    He thus saw steal away,   30
Dozing out all his idle noons,
    And every night at play.

I kept him for old service sake,[5]
    For he would oft beguile
My heart of thoughts that made it ache,   35
    And force me to a smile.

But now, beneath this walnut-shade
    He finds his long, last home,
And waits in snug concealment laid,
    Till gentler Puss shall come.   40

He, in his turn, must feel the shocks[6]
    From which no care can save,
And, partner once of Tiney's box,
    Be partner of his grave.[7]

TO THE IMMORTAL MEMORY OF THE HALIBUT

ON WHICH I DINED THIS DAY[1] (1784)

Where hast thou floated, in what seas pursued
Thy pastime? when wast thou an egg new-spawned,
Lost in th' immensity of ocean's waste?[2]
Roar as they might, the overbearing winds
That rocked the deep, thy cradle, thou wast safe –   5
And in thy minikin and embryo state,[3]
Attached to the firm leaf of some salt weed,

---

[3] *pippin* a kind of apple.
[4] *himself* the MS and later editions read "his rump."
[5] *old service* later editions have "his humour's."
[6] *in his turn* later editions have "still more aged."
[7] *Be partner of* the MS and later editions read "Must soon partake."

ON WHICH I DINED THIS DAY
[1] The text is based on the first publication of the poem in *The Private Correspondence of William Cowper, Esq.*, ed. John Johnson (1824).
[2] *waste* "Desolate or uncultivated ground" (Johnson).
[3] *minikin* "Small; diminutive. Used in slight contempt" (Johnson).

Didst outlive tempests, such as wrung and racked
The joints of many a stout and gallant bark,[4]
And whelmed them in the unexplored abyss.   10
Indebted to no magnet and no chart,
Nor under guidance of the polar fire,[5]
Thou wast a voyager on many coasts,
Grazing at large in meadows submarine,
Where flat Batavia just emerging peeps[6]   15
Above the brine, – where Caledonia's rocks[7]
Beat back the surge, – and where Hibernia shoots[8]
Her wondrous causeway far into the main.[9]
– Wherever thou hast fed, thou little thought'st,
And I not more, that I should feed on thee.   20
Peace therefore, and good health, and much good fish,
To him who sent thee! and success, as oft
As it descends into the billowy gulf,
To the same drag that caught thee! – Fare thee well![10]
Thy lot thy brethren of the slimy fin   25
Would envy, could they know that thou wast doomed
To feed a bard, and to be praised in verse.

THE NEGRO'S COMPLAINT (1789)[1]

Forced from home, and all its pleasures,
    Afric's coast I left forlorn;
To increase a stranger's treasures,
    O'er the raging billows borne.
Men from England bought and sold me,   5
    Paid my price in paltry gold;
But, though slave they have enrolled me,
    Minds are never to be sold.

Still in thought as free as ever,
    What are England's rights, I ask,   10
Me from my delights to sever,
    Me to torture, me to task?
Fleecy locks, and black complexion
    Cannot forfeit Nature's claim;
Skins may differ, but affection   15
    Dwells in white and black the same.

---

[4] *bark* boat.
[5] *polar fire* the pole star, used in navigation to determine latitude.
[6] *Batavia* Roman name for the Netherlands.
[7] *Caledonia* Roman name for Scotland.
[8] *Hibernia* a Latin name for Ireland.
[9] *causeway* the Giant's Causeway, cliffs on the northeast coast of Ireland.

[10] *drag* "A net drawn along the bottom of the water" (Johnson).
THE NEGRO'S COMPLAINT
[1] First published in *Stuart's Star* in 1789, this poem was often reprinted with many variations; my text is based on *Poems of William Cowper of the Inner Temple* (1815) but with a few variants substituted from later editions.

Why did all-creating Nature
    Make the plant for which we toil?[2]
Sighs must fan it, tears must water,
    Sweat of ours must dress the soil.   20
Think, ye masters, iron-hearted,
    Lolling at your jovial boards;
Think how many blacks have smarted
    For the sweets your cane affords.

Is there, as ye sometimes tell us,   25
    Is there one who reigns on high?
Has he bid you buy and sell us,
    Speaking from his throne the sky?
Ask him, if your knotted scourges,
    Fetters, blood-extorting screws,[3]   30
Are the means which duty urges
    Agents of his will to use?

Hark! he answers – Wild tornadoes,
    Strewing yonder sea with wrecks;
Wasting towns, plantations, meadows,   35
    Are the voice with which he speaks.
He, foreseeing what vexations
    Afric's sons should undergo,
Fixed their tyrants' habitations
    Where his whirlwinds answer – No.   40

By our blood in Afric wasted,
    Ere our necks received the chain;
By the mis'ries we have tasted,
    Crossing in your barks the main;[4]
By our suff'rings since ye brought us   45
    To the man-degrading mart;
All sustained by patience, taught us
    Only by a broken heart:

Deem our nation brutes no longer
    Till some reason ye shall find   50
Worthier of regard and stronger
    Than the colour of our kind.
Slaves of gold, whose sordid dealings
    Tarnish all your boasted pow'rs,
Prove that you have human feelings,   45
    Ere you proudly question ours!

---

[2] *plant* sugar cane, produced with slave labour in the West Indies.
[3] *Fetters* the edition of 1815 and others have "matches," which I do not understand (short for "matchlock," a gun?); *screw* "An instrument of torture . . . designed to compress the thumbs" (*OED*, citing this passage).
[4] *barks* ships.

On a Spaniel Called Beau Killing a Young Bird[1] (1793)

A Spaniel, Beau, that fares like you,
    Well-fed, and at his ease,
Should wiser be, than to pursue
    Each trifle that he sees.

But you have killed a tiny Bird,   5
    Which flew not till to-day,
Against my orders, whom you heard
    Forbidding you the prey.

Nor did you kill, that you might eat,
    And ease a doggish pain,   10
For him, though chased with furious heat,
    You left where he was slain.

Nor was he of the thievish sort,
    Or one whom blood allures,
But innocent was all his sport,   15
    Whom you have torn for yours.

My Dog! what remedy remains,
    Since, teach you all I can,
I see you, after all my pains,
So much resemble man!   20

Beau's Reply

Sir! when I flew to seize the Bird,
    In spite of your command,
A louder voice than yours I heard,
    And harder to withstand:

You cried – 'Forbear! – but in my breast   5
    A mightier cried – 'Proceed!'
'Twas Nature, Sir, whose strong behest
    Impelled me to the deed.

Yet much as Nature I respect,
    I ventured once to break   10
(As you perhaps may recollect)
    Her precept, for your sake:

And when your Linnet on a day,
    Passing his prison door,
Had fluttered all his strength away,   15
    And panting pressed the floor,

ON A SPANIEL CALLED BEAU KILLING A YOUNG BIRD
[1] The text of this pair of poems is based on the first
printing in William Hayley, *The Life and Posthumous
Writings, William Cowper, Esqr.* 3 vols (1803–4).

Well knowing him a sacred thing,
    Not destined to my tooth,
I only kissed his ruffled wing,
    And licked his feathers smooth.   20

Let my obedience then excuse
    My disobedience now!
Nor some reproof yourself refuse
    From your aggrieved Bow-wow!

If killing Birds be such a crime,   25
    (Which I can hardly see)
What think you, Sir, of killing Time
    With verse addressed to me?

ON THE ICE ISLANDS *Seen floating in the German Ocean*[1] (1799)

What portents, from what distant region, ride,
Unseen till now in ours, th' astonished tide?[2]
In ages past, old Proteus, with his droves[3]
Of sea-calves, sought the mountains and the groves:
But now, descending whence of late they stood,   5
Themselves the mountains seem to rove the flood.
Dire times were they, full-charged with human woes;
And these, scarce less calamitous than those.
What view we now? More wondrous still! Behold!
Like burnished brass they shine, or beaten gold;   10
And all around the pearl's pure splendour show,
And all around the ruby's fiery glow.
Come they from India? where the burning earth,
All-bounteous, gives her richest treasures birth;
And where the costly gems, that beam around   15
The brows of mighty potentates, are found?
No. Never such a countless dazzling store
Had left unseen the Ganges' peopled shore.
Rapacious hands, and ever-watchful eyes,
Should sooner far have marked and seized the prize.   20
Whence sprang they then? Ejected have they come
From Ves'vius', or from Ætna's burning womb?[4]
Thus shine they self-illumed, or but display
The borrowed splendours of a cloudless day?
With borrowed beams they shine. The gales that breathe[5]   25

ON THE ICE ISLANDS
[1] The text is based on the first printing in William Hayley, *The Life and Posthumous Writings, William Cowper, Esqr.* 3 vols (1803–4); Cowper first composed a Latin version of this poem, which he wrote in his last illness, in response to an incident recorded in the newspapers.

[2] *tide* sea.
[3] *Proteus* the shape-shifting, prophetic old man of the sea; a subject of the god Poseidon, he tended his flocks of seals and slept with them on land at midday.
[4] *Ves{u}vius . . . Ætna* volcanoes in Italy.
[5] *gale* "A wind not tempestuous, yet stronger than a breeze" (Johnson).

Now landward, and the current's force beneath,
Have borne them nearer: and the nearer sight,
Advantaged more, contemplates them aright.
Their lofty summits, crested high, they show,
With mingled sleet and long-incumbent snow.   30
The rest is ice. Far hence, where, most severe,
Bleak winter well-nigh saddens all the year,
Their infant growth began. He bade arise
Their uncouth forms, portentous in our eyes.
Oft' as, dissolved by transient suns, the snow   35
Left the tall cliff, to join the flood below,
He caught and curdled, with a freezing blast,
The current, ere it reached the boundless waste.
By slow degrees uprose the wondrous pile,
And long-successive ages rolled the while;   40
Till, ceaseless in its growth, it claimed to stand
Tall as its rival mountains on the land.
Thus stood – and, unremovable by skill
Or force of man, had stood the structure still;
But that, though firmly fixed, supplanted yet   45
By pressure of its own enormous weight,
It left the shelving beach – and, with a sound[6]
That shook the bellowing waves and rocks around,
Self-launched, and swiftly, to the briny wave,
As if instinct with strong desire to lave,   50
Down went the pond'rous mass. So Bards of old,
How Delos swam th' Ægean deep, have told.[7]
But not of ice was Delos; Delos bore
Herb, fruit, and flow'r. She, crowned with laurel, wore,
E'en under wintry skies, a summer-smile;   55
And Delos was Apollo's favourite isle.
But, horrid wand'rers of the deep, to you
He deems Cimmerian darkness only due.[8]
Your hated birth he deigned not to survey,
But, scornful, turned his glorious eyes away.   60
Hence! Seek your home; no longer rashly dare
The darts of Phoebus, and a softer air;[9]
Lest ye regret, too late, your native coast,
In no congenial gulf for ever lost!

---

[6] *shelving* "Sloping; inclining; having declivity" (Johnson).

[7] *Delos* smallest of the Cyclades, it was a floating isle until Zeus chained it to the bottom of the sea to make a secure place for Leto to give birth to Apollo and Artemis.

[8] *Cimmeria* a mythical land of mists and darkness (also a real place near the Caspian sea).

[9] *Phoebus* Apollo, the sun.

THE CASTAWAY[1] (1799)

Obscurest night involved the sky,
 Th' Atlantic billows roared,
When such a destined wretch as I,
 Washed headlong from on board,
Of friends, of hope, of all bereft,   5
His floating home for ever left.

No braver chief could Albion boast[2]
 Than he with whom he went,
Nor ever ship left Albion's coast,
 With warmer wishes sent.   10
He loved them both, but both in vain,
Nor him beheld, nor her again.

Not long beneath the whelming brine,
 Expert to swim, he lay;
Nor soon he felt his strength decline,   15
 Or courage die away;
But waged with death a lasting strife,
Supported by despair of life.

He shouted: nor his friends had failed
 To check the vessel's course,   20
But so the furious blast prevailed,
 That, pitiless perforce,
They left their outcast mate behind,
And scudded still before the wind.

Some succour yet they could afford;   25
 And, such as storms allow,
The cask, the coop, the floated cord,[3]
 Delayed not to bestow.
But he (they knew) nor ship, nor shore,
Whate'er they gave, should visit more.   30

Nor, cruel as it seemed, could he
 Their haste himself condemn,
Aware that flight, in such a sea,
 Alone could rescue them;
Yet bitter felt it still to die   35
Deserted, and his friends so nigh.

He long survives, who lives an hour
 In ocean, self-upheld:
And so long he, with unspent pow'r,
 His destiny repelled;   40

THE CASTAWAY
[1] The text is from the first printing, in Hayley. The
poem, Cowper's last, is based on an account of a sailor
swept overboard, which Hayley says the poet read many

years before in Richard Walter's *A Voyage Round the
World, by George Anson* (1748).
[2] *Albion* England (a Latin name, after its white cliffs).
[3] *coop* barrel.

And ever, as the minutes flew,
Entreated help, or cried – 'Adieu!'

At length, his transient respite past,
   His comrades, who before
Had heard his voice in every blast,   45
   Could catch the sound no more.
For then, by toil subdued, he drank
The stifling wave, and then he sank.

No poet wept him: but the page
   Of narrative sincere,   50
That tells his name, his worth, his age,
   Is wet with Anson's tear.
And tears by bards or heroes shed
Alike immortalize the dead.

I therefore purpose not, or dream,   55
   Descanting on his fate,
To give the melancholy theme
   A more enduring date:
But misery still delights to trace
Its semblance in another's case.   60

No voice divine the storm allayed,
   No light propitious shone;
When, snatched from all effectual aid,
   We perished, each alone:
But I beneath a rougher sea,   65
And whelmed in deeper gulfs than he.

James Macpherson (1736–1796)

The debate about Macpherson continues today. No one now, and relatively few educated people in the eighteenth century, believed for long that Macpherson's poems were, as he claimed, translations of long lost Gaelic epics. At first, Burke was taken in; Hume thought a fragment or two might be genuine; Johnson would have none of it, and the literary community soon followed his sound judgement. But Macpherson's "poems" (most of them really prose poems) were immensely popular and made the author a small fortune. And it should mitigate Johnson's blanket rejection that many of the characters and tales that Macpherson wrote up do exist in Gaelic (Irish and Scottish) folk stories, some in writing (especially in Old Irish). In reviving these traditional tales and embodying them in a kind of feverish prose, Macpherson appealed to the emerging spirit of Romanticism, especially in Germany, where the movement was deeply involved with the rediscovery of folk tales and popular, national cultural life. Macpherson actually sent Johnson a challenge, demanding his retraction (before publication) of his damaging critique in the Journey to the Western Isles of Scotland *(1775). Johnson's response was to arm himself with a large oak stick. Macpherson's dishonesty in itself appalled Johnson, but it seems likely that the nationalistic, Romantic love of folk traditions to which Macpherson appealed, and their popularity added to Johnson's hostility to the work.*

The following fragment comes from Fingal, an Ancient Epic Poem in Six Books, together with Several other Poems composed by Ossian, the Son of Fingal, translated from the Gaelic Language *(1762).*

from Fingal, an Ancient Epic Poem in Six Books, together with Several other Poems composed by Ossian, the Son of Fingal, translated from the Gaelic Language (1762)

FROM BOOK IV[1]

Who comes with her songs from the mountain, like the bow of the showery Lena? It is the maid of the voice of love. The white-armed daughter of Toscar. Often hast thou heard my song, and given the tear of beauty. Dost thou come to the wars of thy people, to hear the actions of Oscar? When shall I cease to mourn by the streams of echoing Cona? My years have passed away in battle, and my age is darkened with sorrow.

Daughter of the hand of snow! I was not so mournful and blind; I was not so dark and forlorn when Everallin loved me. Everallin with the dark-brown hair, the white-bosomed love of Cormac. A thousand heroes sought the maid, she denied her love to a thousand; the sons of the sword were despised: for graceful in her eyes was Ossian.

I went in suit of the maid to Lego's sable surge; twelve of my people were there, the sons of the streamy Morven. We came to Branno friend of strangers: Branno of the sounding mail. – 'From whence', he said, 'are the arms of steel? Not easy to win is the maid that has denied the blue-eyed sons of Erin. But blest be thou, O son of Fingal, happy is the maid that waits thee! Though twelve daughters of beauty were mine, thine were the choice, thou son of fame!' – Then he opened the hall of the maid, the dark-haired Everallin. Joy kindled in our breasts of steel and blessed the maid of Branno.

Above us on the hill appeared the people of stately Cormac. Eight were the heroes of the chief; and the heath flamed with their arms. There Colla, Durra of the wounds, there mighty Toscar, and Tago, there Frestal the victorious stood; Dairo of the happy deeds, and Dala the battle's bulwark in the narrow way. – The sword flamed in the hand of Cormac, and graceful was the look of the hero.

Eight were the heroes of Ossian; Ullin stormy son of war; Mullo of the generous deeds; the noble, the graceful Scelacha; Oglan, and Cerdal the wrathful, and Dumariccan's brows of death. And why should Ogar be the last, so wide renowned on the hills of Ardven?

Ogar met Dala the strong, face to face, on the field of heroes. The battle of the chiefs was like the wind on ocean's foamy waves. The dagger is remembered by Ogar; the weapon which he loved; nine times he drowned it in Dela's side. The stormy battle turned. Three times I broke on Cormac's shield: three times he broke his spear. But, unhappy youth of love! I cut his head away. – Five times I shook it by the lock. The friends of Cormac fled.

---

[1] Fingal being asleep, and the action suspended by night, the poet introduces the story of his courtship of Everallin the daughter of Branno. The episode is necessary to clear up several passages that follow in the poem; at the same time that it naturally brings on the action of the book, which may be supposed to begin about the middle of the third night from the opening of the poem. – This book, as many of Ossian's other compositions, is addressed to the beautiful Malvina the daughter of Toscar. She appears to have been in love with Oscar, and to have affected the company of the father after the death of the son [Macpherson's note].

Whoever would have told me, lovely maid, when then I strove in battle, that blind, forsaken, and forlorn, I now should pass the night, firm ought his mail to have been, and unmatched his arm in battle.

Now on Lena's[2] gloomy health, the voice of music died away. The unconstant blast blew hard, and the high oak shook its leaves around me; of Everallin were my thoughts, when she, in all the light of beauty, and her blue eyes rolling in tears, stood on a cloud before my sight, and spoke with feeble voice.

'O Ossian, rise and save my son; save Oscar, prince of men, near the red oak of Lubar's stream, he fights with Lochlin's sons.' – She sunk into her cloud again. I clothed me with my steel. My spear supported my steps, and my rattling armour rung. I hummed, as I was wont in danger, the songs of heroes of old. Like distant thunder[3] Lochlin heard; they fled; my son pursued.

I called him like a distant stream. 'My son return over Lena. No further pursue the foe, though Ossian is behind thee'. – He came; and lovely in my ear was Oscar's sounding steel. 'Why didst thou stop my hand', he said, 'till death had covered all? For dark and dreadful by the stream they met thy son and Fillan. They watched the terrors of the night. Our swords have conquered some. But as the winds of night pour the ocean over the white sands of Mora, so dark advance the sons of Lochlin over Lena's rustling heath. The ghosts of night shriek afar; I have seen the meteors of death. Let me awake the king of Morven, he that smiles in danger; for he is like the sun of heaven that rises in a storm' . . .

Edward Gibbon (1737–1794)

One of the most frequently quoted passages of eighteenth-century memoirs is the statement that Gibbon assigns to 15 October 1764, while he was touring Rome: "musing amidst the ruins of the Capitol, where the barefooted friars were singing vespers in the temple of Jupiter . . . the idea of writing the decline and fall of the city first started into my mind." The idea may have coalesced for Gibbon at this point, but he had been preparing for his life's work for many years. A more thorough scholar than almost anyone of his time, his reading preparatory to his trip to Italy had itself laid a foundation for his grand idea. In addition to intense periods of study at various times before that, Gibbon had also undergone a period of serious thought about Christianity: he converted to Roman Catholicism in 1753, and, after six months of study (required by his father) under a Calvinist minister at Lausanne, gave it up eighteen months later. This episode is important because Gibbon's Decline and Fall of the Roman Empire *is also the story of the rise of Christianity. One of the "rational" proofs of the validity of the Christian religion presented in many seventeenth- and eighteenth-century handbooks of religion was its miraculous spread, against all odds, in the first*

---

[2] The poet returns to his subject. If one could fix the time of year in which the action of the poem happened, from the scene described here, I should be tempted to place it in autumn. – The trees shed their leaves, and the winds are variable, both which circumstances agree with that season of the year [Macpherson's note].

[3] Ossian gives the reader a high idea of himself. His very song frightens the enemy. This passage resembles one in the eighteenth Iliad, where the voice of Achilles frightens the Trojans from the body of Patroclus [Macpherson's note].

Forth marched the chief, and distant from the crowd
High on the rampart raised his voice aloud . . .
So high his brazen voice the hero reared,
Hosts drop their arms and trembled as they feared.
POPE [*Iliad* 18.255–6, 263–4]

four centuries after the death of Christ. Gibbon's analysis again and again shows that there were *complex political reasons for the popularity of Christianity, and explaining its success does not* *require resort to miracles. Moreover, he was not afraid to point out the excesses of some of the early* *"fanatics," the jealousy and infighting among the various sects, or the philosophical weakness of* *many of the positions they maintained. (In his footnotes especially Gibbon gives free reign to his* *skepticism about unexamined versions of history.) In his lengthy discussions of Julian the Apostate* *and elsewhere, it seemed to many that Gibbon was excessively sympathetic to paganism. Now, his* *willingness so to sympathize, and his ability to look skeptically and realistically at events, without* *failing to appreciate the romantic drapery in which they have been displayed, are among the* *pleasures of reading Gibbon.*

After the publication of volume one of the Decline and Fall *in 1776 Gibbon was embroiled in* *debates with many learned scholars in England and in France, which was a second home to him.* *He was already serving in Parliament and continued to do so, with some interruption, until 1782.* *He then applied to be secretary of the embassy in Paris; the application failed and he went into* *retreat in Lausanne, where he finished his great work in 1787. He went to England several times* *after that, but Lausanne was his headquarters. There he wrote his* Memoirs *near the end of his* *life.*

The small section of The Decline and Fall *presented here is based on the first edition of volume* *II (1781). I also consulted the text and made extensive use of the notes in the landmark editions* *by H. H. Milman (Harper Brothers, 1850) and J. B. Bury (Methuen, 1909–14).*

from *The Decline and Fall of the Roman Empire* (1781)

FROM VOLUME II CHAPTER 23

In the midst of a rocky and barren country, the walls of Jerusalem enclosed the two mountains of Sion and Acra, within an oval figure of about three English miles. Towards the south, the upper town and the fortress of David, were erected on the lofty ascent of Mount Sion: on the north side, the buildings of the lower town covered the spacious summit of Mount Acra; and a part of the hill, distinguished by the name of Moriah, and levelled by human industry, was crowned with the stately temple of the Jewish nation. After the final destruction of the temple by the arms of Titus and Hadrian,[1] a ploughshare was drawn over the consecrated ground, as a sign of perpetual interdiction. Sion was deserted; and the vacant space of the lower city was filled with the public and private edifices of the Ælian colony,[2] which spread themselves over the adjacent hill of Calvary. The holy places were polluted with mountains of idolatry; and, either from design or accident, a chapel was dedicated to Venus, on the spot which had been sanctified by the death and resurrection of Christ. Almost three hundred years after those stupendous events, the profane chapel of Venus was demolished by the order of Constantine; and the removal of the earth and stones revealed the holy sepulchre to the eyes of mankind. A magnificent church was erected on that mystic ground, by the first Christian emperor;[3] and the effects of his pious munificence were

---

FROM VOLUME II CHAPTER 23
[1] *final destruction of the temple . . . Titus and Hadrian* Contrary to the orders of Titus, it was burned at the siege of Jerusalem in 70 CE; the Emperor Hadrian dedicated a temple to Jupiter on the site in 136.

[2] *Ælian colony* after 130 CE Jews were forbidden to enter Jerusalem, and the city became a Roman colony called *Aelia Capitolina.*
[3] *first Christian emperor* Constantine I (Emperor, 306–37).

extended to every spot which had been consecrated by the footsteps of patriarchs, of prophets, and of the Son of God.

The passionate desire of contemplating the original monuments of their redemption attracted to Jerusalem a successive crowd of pilgrims, from the shores of the Atlantic Ocean, and the most distant countries of the East; and their piety was authorised by the example of the empress Helena, who appears to have united the credulity of age with the warm feelings of a recent conversion. Sages and heroes, who have visited the memorable scenes of ancient wisdom or glory, have confessed the inspiration of the genius of the place; and the Christian who knelt before the holy sepulchre, ascribed his lively faith, and his fervent devotion, to the more immediate influence of the Divine spirit. The zeal, perhaps the avarice, of the clergy of Jerusalem, cherished and multiplied these beneficial visits. They fixed, by unquestionable tradition, the scene of each memorable event. They exhibited the instruments which had been used in the passion of Christ; the nails and the lance that had pierced his hands, his feet, and his side; the crown of thorns that was planted on his head; the pillar at which he was scourged; and, above all, they showed the cross on which he suffered, and which was dug out of the earth in the reign of those princes, who inserted the symbol of Christianity in the banners of the Roman legions. Such miracles as seemed necessary to account for its extraordinary preservation, and seasonable discovery, were gradually propagated without opposition. The custody of the *true cross*, which on Easter Sunday was solemnly exposed to the people, was entrusted to the bishop of Jerusalem; and he alone might gratify the curious devotion of the pilgrims, by the gift of small pieces, which they enchased in gold or gems, and carried away in triumph to their respective countries. But as this gainful branch of commerce must soon have been annihilated, it was found convenient to suppose, that the marvellous wood possessed a secret power of vegetation; and that its substance, though continually diminished, still remained entire and unimpaired. It might perhaps have been expected, that the influence of the place and the belief of a perpetual miracle, should have produced some salutary effects on the morals, as well as of the faith, of the people. Yet the most respectable of the ecclesiastical writers have been obliged to confess, not only that the secrets of Jerusalem were filled with the incessant tumult of business and pleasure, but that every species of vice – adultery, theft, idolatry, poisoning, murder – was familiar to the inhabitants of the holy city. The wealth and preeminence of the church of Jerusalem excited the ambition of Arian,[4] as well as orthodox, candidates; and the virtues of Cyril,[5] who, since his death, had been honoured with the title of Saint, were displayed in the exercise, rather than in the acquisition, of his episcopal dignity.

The vain and ambitious mind of Julian might aspire to restore the ancient glory of the temple of Jerusalem.[6] As the Christians were firmly persuaded that a sentence of everlasting destruction had been pronounced against the whole fabric of the Mosaic law, the Imperial sophist would have converted the success of his undertaking into a specious argument against the faith of prophecy, and the truth of revelation. He was displeased with the spiritual worship of the synagogue: but he approved of the institution of Moses, who had not disdained to adopt many of the rites and ceremonies of Egypt. The local and national deity of the Jews was sincerely adored by a polytheist, who desired only to multiply the number of their gods;

---

[4] *Arian* adhering to the heretical beliefs (especially the non-divinity of Jesus) proposed in the fourth century by Arius.

[5] *Cyril* early fifth-century theologian, who argued for the combined divinity and humanity of Jesus and wrote against Julian the Apostate.

[6] *Julian . . . Jerusalem* Julian the Apostate, Emperor of Rome (361–3) returned to traditional Roman paganism and sought to rebuild the temple to embarrass Christians rather than to support Jews.

and such was the appetite of Julian for bloody sacrifice, that his emulation might be excited by the piety of Solomon, who had offered, at the feast of the dedication, twenty-two thousand oxen, and one hundred and twenty thousand sheep.[7] These considerations might influence his designs; but the prospect of an immediate and important advantage would not suffer the impatient monarch to expect the remote and uncertain event of the Persian war. He resolved to erect, without delay, on the commanding eminence of Moriah, a stately temple, which might eclipse the splendour of the church of the resurrection on the adjacent hill of Calvary; to establish an order of priests, whose interested zeal would detect the arts, and resist the ambition, of their Christian rivals; and to invite a numerous colony of Jews, whose stern fanaticism would be always prepared to second, and even to anticipate, the hostile measures of the Pagan government. Among the friends of the emperor (if the names of emperor, and of friend, are not incompatible) the first place was assigned, by Julian himself, to the virtuous and learned Alypius. The humanity of Alypius was tempered by severe justice and manly fortitude; and while he exercised his abilities in the civil administrations of Britain, he imitated, in his poetical compositions, the harmony and softness of the odes of Sappho.[8] This minister, to whom Julian communicated, without reserve, his most careless levities, and his most serious counsels, received an extraordinary commission to restore, in its pristine beauty, the temple of Jerusalem; and the diligence of Alypius required and obtained all the strenuous support of the governor of Palestine. At the call of their great deliverer, the Jews, from all the provinces of the empire, assembled on the holy mountains of their fathers; and their insolent triumph alarmed and exasperated the Christian inhabitants of Jerusalem. The desire of rebuilding the temple has in every age been the ruling passion of the children of Israel. In this propitious moment the men forgot their avarice, and the women their delicacy; spades and pickaxes of silver were provided by the vanity of the rich, and the rubbish was transported in mantles of silk and purple. Every purse was opened in liberal contributions, every hand claimed a share in the pious labour; and the commands of a great monarch were executed by the enthusiasm of a whole people.

Yet, on this occasion, the joint efforts of power and enthusiasm were unsuccessful; and the ground of the Jewish temple, which is now covered by a Mahometan mosque,[9] still continued to exhibit the same edifying spectacle of ruin and desolation. Perhaps the absence and death of the emperor, and the new maxims of a Christian reign, might explain the interruption of an arduous work, which was attempted only in the last six months of the life of Julian. But the Christians entertained a natural and pious expectation, that, in this memorable contest, the honour of religion would be vindicated by some signal miracle. An earthquake, a whirlwind, and a fiery erruption, which overturned and scattered the new foundations of the temple, are attested, with some variations, by contemporary and respectable evidence. This public event is described by Ambrose, bishop of Milan, in an epistle to the emperor Theodosius,[10] which must provoke the severe animadversion of the Jews;[11] by the eloquent Chrysostom, who might appeal to the memory of the elder part of his congregation at Antioch; and by Gregory Nazianzen, who published his account of the miracle before the expiration of the same year. The last of these writers has boldly declared, that this

---

[7]   *twenty-two thousand oxen . . . sheep*   1 Kings 8.63.

[8]   *Sappho*   great Greek lyric poet of the sixth-century BCE, most famous for her love poems.

[9]   *Mahometan mosque*   the Dome of the Rock, built in 661.

[10]   *Theodosius*   Roman Emperor of the East (379–92) and Sole Emperor (392–5), suppressed paganism and Arianism.

[11]   *severe animadversion of the Jews*   [Ambrose] composed this fanatic epistle [CE 388] to justify a bishop, who had been condemned by the civil magistrate for burning a synagogue [Gibbon's note].

præternatural event was not disputed by the infidels; and his assertion, strange as it may seem, is confirmed by the unexceptionable testimony of Ammianus Marcellinus.[12] The philosophic soldier, who loved the virtues, without adopting the prejudices, of his master, has recorded, in a judicious and candid history of his own times, the extraordinary obstacles which interrupted the restoration of the temple of Jerusalem. 'Whilst Alypius assisted by the governor of the province, urged, with vigour and diligence, the execution of the work, horrible balls of fire breaking out near the foundations, with frequent and reiterated attacks, rendered the place, from time to time, inaccessible to the scorched and blasted workmen; and the victorious element continuing in this manner obstinately and resolutely bent, as it were, to drive them to a distance, the undertaking was abandoned'.[13] Such authority should satisfy a believing, and must astonish an incredulous, mind. Yet a philosopher may still require the original evidence of impartial and intelligent spectators. At this important crisis, any singular accident of nature would assume the appearance, and produce the effects of a real prodigy. This glorious deliverance would be speedily improved and magnified by the pious art of the clergy of Jerusalem, and the active credulity of the Christian world; and, at the distance of twenty years, a Roman historian, careless of theological disputes, might adorn his work with the specious and splendid miracle.

The restoration of the Jewish temple was secretly connected with the ruin of the Christian church. Julian still continued to maintain the freedom of religious worship, without distinguishing whether this universal toleration proceeded from his justice or his clemency. He affected to pity the unhappy Christians, who were mistaken in the most important object of their lives; but his pity was degraded by contempt, his contempt was embittered by hatred; and the sentiments of Julian were expressed in a style of sarcastic wit, which inflicts a deep and deadly wound, whenever it issues from the mouth of a sovereign. As he was sensible that the Christians gloried in the name of their Redeemer, he countenanced, and perhaps enjoined, the use of the less honourable appellation of GALILÆANS. He declared, that by the folly of the Galilæans, whom he describes as a sect of fanatics, contemptible to men, and odious to the gods, the empire has been reduced to the brink of destruction; and he insinuates in a public edict, that a frantic patient might sometimes be cured by salutary violence. An ungenerous distinction was admitted into the mind and counsels of Julian, that, according to the difference of their religious sentiments, one part of his subjects deserved his favour and friendship, while the other was entitled only to the common benefits that his justice could not refuse to an obedient people. According to a principle, pregnant with mischief and oppression, the emperor transferred to the pontiff of his own religion the management of liberal allowances from the public revenue, which had been granted to the church by the piety of Constantine and his sons. The proud system of clerical honours and immunities, which had been constructed with so much art and labour, was levelled to the ground; the hopes of testamentary donations were intercepted by the rigour of the laws; and the priests of the Christian sect were confounded with the last and most ignominious class of people. Such of these regulations as appeared necessary to check the ambition and avarice of the ecclesiastics, were soon afterwards imitated by the wisdom of an orthodox prince.[14] The peculiar distinctions which policy has bestowed, or superstition has lavished, on the sacerdotal order, *must* be

---

[12] *Ammianus Marcellinus* (d. 395) major Roman historian, fought under Julian.
[13] *Whilst Alypius . . . abandoned* Ammianus 23.1 . . . [Bishop] Warburton labours to extort a confession of the miracle from the mouths of Julian and Libanius, and to

employ the evidence of a rabbi who lived in the fifteenth century. Such witnesses can only be received by a very favourable judge [Gibbon's note].
[14] *orthodox prince* Jovian (Emperor, 363–4), a Christian.

confined to those priests who profess the religion of the state. But the will of the legislator was not exempt from prejudice and passion; and it was the object of the insidious policy of Julian, to deprive the Christians of all the temporal honours and advantages which rendered them respectable in the eyes of the world.

A just and severe censure has been inflicted on the law which prohibited the Christians from teaching the arts of grammar and rhetoric. The motives alleged by the emperor to justify this partial and oppressive measure, might command, during his lifetime, the silence of slaves and the applause of flatterers. Julian abuses the ambiguous meaning of a word which might be indifferently applied to the language and religion of the GREEKS: he contemptuously observes, that the men who exalt the merit of implicit faith are unfit to claim or to enjoy the advantages of science; and he vainly contends, that if they refuse to adore the gods of Homer and Demosthenes, they ought to content themselves with expounding Luke and Matthew in the church of the Galilæans. In all the cities of the Roman world, the education of the youth was entrusted to masters of grammar and rhetoric, who were elected by the magistrates, maintained at the public expense, and distinguished by many lucrative and honourable privileges. The edict of Julian appears to have included the physicians, and professors of all the liberal arts; and the emperor, who reserved to himself the approbation of the candidates, was authorised by the laws to corrupt, or to punish, the religious constancy of the most learned of all Christians. As soon as the resignation of the more obstinate teachers had established the unrivalled dominion of the Pagan sophists, Julian invited the rising genera-tion to resort with freedom to the public schools, in a just confidence, that their tender minds would receive the impressions of literature and idolatry. If the greatest part of the Christian youth should be deterred by their own scruples, or by those of their own parents, from accepting this dangerous mode of instruction, they must, at the same time, relinquish the benefits of a liberal education. Julian had reason to expect that, in the space of a few years, the church would relapse into its primeval simplicity, and that the theologians, who possessed an adequate share of the learning and eloquence of the age, would be succeed by a generation of blind and ignorant fanatics, incapable of defending the truth of their own principles, or of exposing the various follies of Polytheism.

It was undoubtedly the wish and design of Julian to deprive the Christians of the advantages of wealth, of knowledge, and of power; but the injustice of excluding them from all offices of trust and profit seems to have been the result of his general policy, rather than the immediate consequence of any positive law. Superior merit might deserve and obtain some extraordinary exceptions; but the greater part of the Christian officers were gradually removed from their employments in the state, the army, and the provinces. The hopes of future candidates were extinguished by the declared partiality of a prince, who maliciously reminded them, that it was unlawful for a Christian to use the sword, either of justice, or of war; and who studiously guarded the camp and the tribunals with the ensigns of idolatry. The powers of government were entrusted to the pagans, who professed an ardent zeal for the religion of their ancestors; and as the choice of the emperor was often directed by the rules of divination, the favourites whom he preferred as the most agreeable to the gods, did not always obtain the approbation of mankind. Under the administration of the enemies, the Christians had much to suffer, and more to apprehend. The temper of Julian was adverse to cruelty; and the care of his reputation, which was exposed to the eyes of the universe, restrained the philosophic monarch from violating the laws of justice and toleration, which he himself had so recently established. But the provincial ministers of his authority were placed in a less conspicuous station. In the exercise of arbitrary power, they consulted the wishes, rather than the commands, of their sovereign; and ventured to exercise a secret and vexatious tyranny against the sectaries,[15] on whom they were not permitted to confer the honours of martyrdom. The emperor, who dissembled as long as possible his knowledge of the injustice that was exercised in his name, expressed his real sense of the conduct of his officers, by gentle reproofs and substantial rewards.

The most effectual instrument of oppression, with which they were armed, was the law that obliged the Christians to make full and ample satisfaction for the temples which they had destroyed under the preceding reign. The zeal of the triumphant church had not always expected the sanction of the public authority; and the bishops, who were secure of impunity, had often marched at the head of the congregation, to attack and demolish the fortresses of the prince of darkness. The consecrated lands, which had increased the patrimony of the sovereign or of the clergy, were clearly defined, and easily restored. But on these lands, and on the ruins of Pagan superstition, the Christians had frequently erected their own religious edifices: and as it was necessary to remove the church before the temple could be rebuilt, the justice and piety of the emperor were applauded by one party, while the other deplored and execrated his sacrilegious violence. After the ground was cleared, the restitution of those stately structures which had been levelled with the dust, and of the precious ornaments which had been converted to Christian uses, swelled into a very large account of damages and debt. The authors of the injury had neither the ability nor the inclination to discharge this accumulated demand: and the impartial wisdom of a legislator would have been displayed in balancing the adverse claims and complaints, by an equitable and temperate arbitration. But the whole empire, and particularly the East, was thrown into confusion by the rash edicts of Julian; and the Pagan magistrates, inflamed by zeal and revenge, abused the rigorous privilege of the Roman law, which substitutes, in the place of his inadequate property, the person of the insolvent debtor. Under the preceding reign, Mark, bishop of Arethusa, had laboured in the conversion of his people with arms more effectual than those of persuasion. The magistrates required the full value of a temple which had been destroyed by his intolerant zeal; but as they were satisfied of his poverty, they desired only to bend his inflexible spirit to the promise of the slightest compensation. They apprehended the aged prelate, they inhumanly scourged him, they tore his beard; and his naked body anointed with honey, was suspended, in a net, between heaven and earth, and exposed to the stings of insects and the rays of a Syrian sun. From this lofty station, Mark still persisted to glory in his crime, and to insult the impotent rage of his persecutors. He was at length rescued from their hands, and dismissed to enjoy the honour of his divine triumph. The Arians celebrated the virtue of their pious confessor; the Catholics ambitiously claimed his alliance; and the Pagans, who might be susceptible of shame or remorse, were deterred from the repetition of such unavailing cruelty. Julian spared his life: but if the bishop of Arethusa had saved the infancy of Julian, posterity will condemn the ingratitude, instead of praising the clemency, of the emperor.

At the distance of five miles from Antioch, the Macedonian kings of Syria had consecrated to Apollo one of the most elegant places of devotion in the Pagan world. A magnificent temple rose in honour of the god of light; and his colossal figure almost filled the capacious sanctuary, which was enriched with gold and gems, and adorned by the skill of the Grecian artists. The deity was represented in a bending attitude, with a golden cup in his hand, pouring out a libation on the earth; as if he supplicated the venerable mother to give to his

---

[15] *sectary* "One who divides from public establishment, and joins with those distinguished by some particular whims" (Johnson).

arms the cold and beauteous DAPHNE:[16] for the spot was ennobled by fiction; and the fancy of the Syrian poets had transported the amorous tale from the banks of the Peneus to those of the Orontes.[17] The ancient rites of Greece were imitated by the royal colony of Antioch. A stream of prophecy, which rivalled the truth and reputation of the Delphic oracle, flowed from the *Castalian* fountain of Daphne.[18] In the adjacent fields a stadium was built by a special privilege, which had been purchased from Elis;[19] the Olympic games were celebrated at the expense of the city; and a revenue of thirty thousand pounds sterling was annually applied to the public pleasures. The perpetual resort of pilgrims and spectators insensibly formed, in the neighbourhood of the temple, the stately and populous village of Daphne, which emulated the splendour, without acquiring the title, of a provincial city. The temple and the village were deeply bosomed in a thick grove of laurels and cypresses, which reached as far as a circumference of ten miles, and formed in the most sultry summers a cool and impenetrable shade. A thousand streams of the purest water, issuing from every hill, preserved the verdure of the earth, and the temperature of the air; the senses were gratified with harmonious sounds and aromatic odours; and the peaceful grove was consecrated to health and joy, to luxury and love. The vigorous youth pursued, like Apollo, the object of his desires; and the blushing maid was warned, by the fate of Daphne, to shun the folly of unseasonable coyness. The soldier and the philosopher wisely avoided the temptation of this sensual paradise: where pleasure, assuming the character of religion, imperceptibly dissolved the firmness of manly virtue. But the groves of Daphne continued for many ages to enjoy the veneration of neighbours and strangers; the privileges of the holy ground were enlarged by the munificence of succeeding generations; and every generation added new ornaments to the splendour of the temple.

When Julian, on the day of the annual festival, hastened to adore the Apollo of Daphne, his devotion was raised to the highest pitch of eagerness and impatience. His lively imagination anticipated the grateful pomp of victims, of libations and of incense; a long procession of youths and virgins, clothed in white robes, the symbol of their innocence; and the tumultuous concourse of an innumerable people. But the zeal of Antioch was diverted, since the reign of Christianity, into a different channel. Instead of hecatombs of fat oxen sacrificed by the tribes of a wealthy city to their tutelar deity the emperor complains that he found only a single goose, provided at the expense of a priest, the pale and solitary inhabitant of this decayed temple. The altar was deserted, the oracle had been reduced to silence, and the holy ground was profaned by the introduction of Christian and funeral rites. After Babylas (a bishop of Antioch, who died in prison in the persecution of Decius[20]) had rested near a century in his grave, his body, by the order of Cæsar Gallus,[21] was transported into the midst of the grove of Daphne. A magnificent church was erected over his remains; a portion of the sacred lands was usurped for the maintenance of the clergy, and for the burial of the Christians at Antioch, who were ambitious at lying at the feet of their bishop; and the priests of Apollo retired, with their affrighted and indignant votaries. As soon as another revolution seemed to restore the fortune of Paganism, the church of St. Babylas was demolished, and new buildings were added to the mouldering edifice which had been raised by the piety of Syrian

[16] *Daphne*   daughter of the river god *Peneus*, who escaped the advances of Apollo by being transformed into the laurel tree.

[17] *Orontes*   a river in Syria, near Antioch; the *Peneus* is is on the Peloponnesos in Greece, near Mount Olympus.

[18] *Castalian fountain*   where the nymph Castalia threw herself on Mount Parnassus, near Delphi, site of the oracle of Apollo.

[19] *Elis*   the country around the Peneus river.

[20] *Decius*   Roman emperor in 249–51, instituted persecution of Christians.

[21] *Cæsar Gallus*   ruler of the Eastern provinces from 351–4.

kings. But the first and most serious care of Julian was to deliver his oppressed deity from the odious presence of the dead and living Christians, who had so effectually supressed the voice of fraud or enthusiasm. The scene of infection was purified, according to the forms of ancient rituals; the bodies were decently removed; and the ministers of the church were permitted to convey the remains of St. Babylas to their former habitation within the walls of Antioch. The modest behaviour which might have assuaged the jealousy of a hostile government was neglected, on this occasion, by the zeal of the Christians. The lofty car, that transported the relics of Babylas, was followed, and accompanied, and received, by an innumerable multitude; who chanted, with thundering acclamations, the Psalms of David the most expressive of their contempt for idols and idolaters. The return of the saint was a triumph; and the triumph was an insult on the religion of the emperor, who exerted his pride to dissemble his resentment. During the night which terminated this indiscreet procession, the temple of Daphne was in flames; the statue of Apollo was consumed; and the walls of the edifice were left a naked and awful monument of ruin. The Christians of Antioch asserted, with religious confidence, that the powerful intercession of St. Babylas had pointed the lightning of heaven against the devoted roof: but as Julian was reduced to the alternative of believing either a crime or a miracle, he chose, without hesitation, without evidence, but with some colour of probability, to impute the fire of Daphne to the revenge of the Galilæans. Their offence, had it been sufficiently proved, might have justified the retaliation, which was immediately executed by the order of Julian, of shutting the doors, and confiscating the wealth, of the cathedral of Antioch. To discover the criminals who were guilty of the tumult, of the fire, or of secreting the riches of the church, several of the ecclesiastics were tortured; and a Presbyter,[22] of the name of Theodoret, was beheaded by the sentence of the Count of the East. But this hasty act was blamed by the emperor; who lamented, with real or affected concern, that the imprudent zeal of his ministers would tarnish his reign with the disgrace of persecution.

The zeal of the ministers of Julian was instantly checked by the frown of their sovereign; but when the father of his country declares himself the leader of a faction, the licence of popular fury cannot easily be restrained, nor consistently punished. Julian, in a public composition, applauds the devotion and loyalty of the holy cities of Syria, whose pious inhabitants had destroyed, at the first signal, the sepulchres of the Galilæans; and faintly complains, that they had revenged the injuries of the gods with less moderation than he should have recommended. This imperfect and reluctant confession may appear to confirm the ecclesiastical narratives; that in the cities of Gaza, Ascalon, Cæsarea, Heliopolis, &c., the Pagans abused, without prudence or remorse, the moment of their prosperity. That the unhappy objects of their cruelty were released from torture only by death; and as their mangled bodies were dragged through the streets, they were pierced (such was the universal rage) by the spits of cooks, and the distaffs of enraged women; and that the entrails of Christian priests and virgins, after they had been tasted by those bloody fanatics, were mixed with barley, and contemptuously thrown to the unclean animals of the city. Such scenes of religious madness exhibit the most contemptible and odious picture of human nature; but the massacre of Alexandria attracts still more attention, from the certainty of the fact, the rank of the victims, and the splendour of the capital of Egypt.

George, from his parents or his education, surnamed the Cappadocian[23] was born at Epiphania in Cilicia, in a fuller's shop.[24] From this obscure and servile origin, he raised

---

22 *Presbyter* a priest.
23 *Cappadocian* a native of a highland Roman province of the time in eastern Asia Minor; *Cilicia* is south

of Cappadocia and separated from it by the Taurus mountains.
24 *fuller* "One whose trade is to cleanse cloth" (Johnson).

himself by the talents of a parasite; and the patrons, whom he assiduously flattered, procure for their worthless dependent a lucrative commission, or contract, to supply the army with bacon. His employment was mean; he rendered it infamous. He accumulated wealth by the basest arts of fraud and corruption; but his malversations were so notorious, that George was compelled to escape from the pursuits of justice. After this disgrace, in which he appears to have saved his fortune at the expense of his honour, he embraced, with real or affected zeal, the profession of Arianism. From the love, or the ostentation, of learning, he collected a valuable library of history, rhetoric, philosophy, and theology, and the choice of the prevailing faction promoted George of Cappadocia to the throne of Athanasius.[25] The entrance of a new archbishop was that of a Barbarian conqueror; and each moment of his reign was polluted by cruelty and avarice. The Catholics of Alexandria and Egypt were abandoned to a tyrant, qualified, by nature and education, to exercise the office of persecution; but he oppressed with an impartial hand the various inhabitants of his extensive dioceses. The primate of Egypt assumed the pomp and insolence of his lofty station: but he still betrayed the vices of his base and servile extraction. The merchants of Alexandria were impoverished by the unjust, almost universal, monopoly, which he acquired, of nitre, salt, paper, funerals, &c.: and the spiritual father of a great people condescended to practise the vile and pernicious arts of an informer. The Alexandrians could never forget nor forgive, the tax, which he suggested, on all the houses of the city; under an obsolete claim, that the royal founder had conveyed to his successors, the Ptolemies and the Cæsars, the perpetual property of the soil. The Pagans, who had been flattered with the hopes of freedom and toleration, excited his devout avarice; and the rich temples of Alexandria were either pillaged or insulted by the haughty prince, who exclaimed, in a loud and threatening tone, 'How long will these sepulchres be permitted to stand?' Under the reign of Constantius, he was expelled by the fury, or rather by the justice, of the people; and it was not without a violent struggle, that the civil and military powers of the state could restore his authority, and gratify his revenge. The messenger who proclaimed at Alexandria the accession of Julian, announced the downfall of the archbishop. George, with two of his obsequious ministers, Count Diodorus, and Dracontius, master of the mint, were ignominiously dragged in chains to the public prison. At the end of twenty-four days, the prison was forced open by the rage of a superstitious multitude, impatient of the tedious forms of judicial proceedings. The enemies of gods and men expired under their cruel insults; the lifeless bodies of the archbishop and his associates were carried in triumph through the streets on the back of a camel; and the inactivity of the Athanasian party was esteemed a shining example of evangelical patience. The remains of these guilty wretches were thrown into the sea; and the popular leaders of the tumult declared their resolution to disappoint the devotion of the Christians, and to intercept the future honours of these *martyrs*, who had been punished, like their predecessors, by the enemies of their religion. The fears of the Pagans were just, and their precautions ineffectual. The meritorious death of the archbishop obliterated the memory of his life. The rival of Athanasius was dear and sacred to the Arians, and the seeming conversion of those sectaries introduced his worship into the bosom of the Catholic church. The odious stranger, disguising every circumstance of time and place, assumed the mask of a martyr, a saint, and a Christian hero; and the infamous George of Cappadocia has been transformed[26] into the renowned St. George of England, the patron of arms, of chivalry, and of the garter.

---

[25] *Athanasius* Bishop of Alexandria, replaced and exiled repeatedly for his stand against Arianism.

[26] *transformed* This transformation is not given as absolutely certain, but as *extremely* probable [Gibbon's note].

About the same time that Julian was informed of the tumult of Alexandria, he received intelligence from Edessa, that the proud and wealthy faction of the Arians had insulted the weakness of the Valentinians,[27] and committed such disorders as ought not to be suffered with impunity in a well-regulated state. Without expecting the slow forms of justice, the exasperated prince directed his mandate to the magistrates of Edessa, by which he confiscated the whole property of the church: the money was distributed among the soldiers; the lands were added to the domain; and this act of oppression was aggravated by the most ungenerous irony. 'I show myself', says Julian, 'the true friend of the Galilæans. Their *admirable* law has promised the kingdom of heaven to the poor; and they will advance with more diligence in the paths of virtue and salvation, when they are relieved by my assistance from the load of temporal possessions. Take care', pursued the monarch, in a more serious tone, 'take care how you provoke my patience and humanity. If these disorders continue, I will revenge on the magistrates the crimes of the people; and you will have reason to dread, not only confiscation and exile, but fire and the sword'. The tumults of Alexandria were doubtless of a more bloody and dangerous nature: but a Christian bishop had fallen by the hands of the Pagans; and the public epistle of Julian affords a very lively proof of the partial spirit of his administration. His reproaches to the citizens of Alexandria are mingled with expressions of esteem and tenderness; and he laments, that on this occasion, they should have departed from the gentle and generous manners which attested their Grecian extraction. He gravely censures the offence which they had committed against the laws of justice and humanity; but he recapitulates, with visible complacency, the intolerable provocations which they had so long endured from the impious tyranny of George of Cappadocia. Julian admits this principle, that a wise and vigorous government should chastise the insolence of the people; yet, in consideration of their founder Alexander, and of Serapis their tutelar deity, he grants a free and gracious pardon to the guilty city, for which he again feels the affection of a brother.

After the tumult of Alexandria had subsided, Athanasius, amidst the public acclamations, seated himself on the throne from whence his unworthy competitor had been precipitated: and as the zeal of the archbishop was tempered with discretion, the exercise of his authority tended not to inflame, but to reconcile, the minds of the people. His pastoral labours were not confined to the narrow limits of Egypt. The state of the Christian world was present to his active and capacious mind; and the age, the merit, the reputation of Athanasius, enabled him to assume, in a moment of danger, the office of Ecclesiastical Dictator. Three years were not yet elapsed since the majority of the bishops of the West had ignorantly, or reluctantly, subscribed the Confession of Rimini.[28] They repented, they believed, but they dreaded the unseasonable rigour of their orthodox brethren; and if their pride was stronger than their faith, they might throw themselves into the Arms of the Arians, to escape the indignity of a public penance, which must degrade them to the condition of obscure laymen. At the same time the domestic differences concerning the union and distinction of the divine persons, were agitated with some heat among the Catholic doctors; and the progress of this metaphysical controversy seemed to threaten a public and lasting division of the Greek and Latin churches. By the wisdom of a select synod, to which the name and presence of Athanasius gave the authority of a general council, the bishops, who had unwarily deviated into error, were admitted to the union of the church, on the easy condition of subscribing the Nicene

---

[27] *Valentinians* a Gnostic sect begun in the second century.

[28] *Confession of Rimini* at the Council of Rimini (359), a failed attempt to reconcile orthodoxy and Arianism.

Creed;[29] without any formal acknowledgment of their past fault, or any minute definition of their scholastic opinions. The advice of the primate of Egypt had already prepared the clergy of Gaul and Spain, of Italy and Greece, for the reception of this salutary measure; and, notwithstanding the opposition of some ardent spirits, the fear of the common enemy promoted the peace and harmony of the Christians.

The skill and diligence of the primate of Egypt had improved the season of tranquillity, before it was interrupted by the hostile edicts of the emperor. Julian, who despised the Christians, honoured Athanasius with his sincere and peculiar hatred. For his sake alone, he introduced an arbitrary distinction, repugnant at least to the spirit of his former declarations. He maintained, that the Galilæans, whom he had recalled from exile, were not restored, by that general indulgence, to the possession of their respective churches; and he expressed his astonishment, that a criminal, who had been repeatedly condemned by the judgement of the emperors, should dare to insult the majesty of the laws, and insolently usurp the archepiscopal throne of Alexandria, without expecting the orders of his sovereign. As a punishment for the imaginary offence, he again banished Athanasius from the city; and he was pleased to suppose, that this act of justice would be highly agreeable to his pious subjects. The pressing solicitations of the people soon convinced him, that the majority of Alexandrians were Christians; and that the greatest part of the Christians were firmly attached to the cause of their oppressed primate. But the knowledge of their sentiments, instead of persuading him to recall his decree, provoked him to extend to all Egypt the terms of the exile of Athanasius. The zeal of the multitude rendered Julian still more inexorable: he was alarmed by the danger of leaving at the head of a tumultuous city, a daring and popular leader; and the language of his resentment discovers the opinion which he entertained of the courage and abilities of Athanasius. The execution of the sentence was still delayed, by the caution or negligence of Ecdicius, præfect of Egypt, who was at length awakened from his lethargy by a severe reprimand: 'Though you neglect', says Julian, 'to write me on any other subject, at least it is your duty to inform me of your conduct towards Athanasius, the enemy of the gods. My intentions have been long since communicated to you. I swear by the great Serapis, that unless, on the calends[30] of December, Athanasius has departed from Alexandria, nay, from Egypt, the officers of your government shall pay a fine of one hundred pounds of gold. You know my temper: I am slow to condemn, but I am still slower to forgive'. This epistle was enforced by a short postscript, written with the emperor's own hand: 'The contempt that is shown for all the gods fills me with grief and indignation. There is nothing that I should see, nothing that I should hear, with more pleasure, than the expulsion of Athanasius from all Egypt. The abominable wretch! Under my reign, the baptism of several Grecian ladies of the highest rank has been the effect of his persecutions'. The death of Athanasius was not *expressly* commanded; but the præfect of Egypt understood that it was safer for him to exceed, than to neglect, the orders of an irritated master. The archbishop prudently retired to the monasteries of the Desert; eluded, with his unusual dexterity, the snares of the enemy; and lived to triumph over the ashes of a prince, who, in words of formidable import, had declared his wish that the whole venom of the Galilæan school were contained in the single person of Athanasius.

I have endeavoured faithfully to represent the artful system by which Julian proposed to obtain the effects, without incurring the guilt, or reproach, of persecution. But if the deadly

---

[29]   *Nicene Creed* established at Nicea in 325 CE and   [30]   *calends* the first.
acceptable to all branches of Christianity of the time.

spirit of fanaticism perverted the heart and understanding of a virtuous prince, it must, at the same time, be confessed that the *real* sufferings of the Christians were inflamed and magnified by human passions and religious enthusiasm. The meekness and resignation which had distinguished the primitive disciples of the gospel, was the object of the applause, rather than of the imitation of their successors. The Christians, who had not possessed above forty years the civil and ecclesiastical government of the empire, had contracted the insolent vices of prosperity, and the habit of believing that the saints alone were entitled to reign over the earth. As soon as the enmity of Julian deprived the clergy of the privileges which had been conferred by the favour of Constantine, they complained of the most cruel oppression; and the free toleration of idolators and heretics was a subject of grief and scandal to the orthodox party. The acts of violence, which were no longer countenanced by the magistrates, were still committed by the zeal of the people. At Pessinus, the altar of Cybele[31] was overturned almost in the presence of the emperor; and in the city of Cæsarea in Cappadocia, the temple of Fortune, the sole place of worship which had been left to the Pagans, was destroyed by the rage of a popular tumult. On these occasions, a prince, who felt for the honour of the gods, was not disposed to interrupt the course of justice; and his mind was still more deeply exasperated, when he found that the fanatics, who had deserved and suffered the punishment of incendiaries, were rewarded with the honours of martyrdom. The Christian subjects of Julian were assured of the hostile designs of their sovereign; and, to their jealous apprehension, every circumstance of his government might afford some grounds of discontent and suspicion. In the ordinary administration of the laws, the Christians, who formed so large a part of the people, must frequently be condemned: but their indulgent brethren, without examining the merits of the cause, presumed their innocence, allowed the claims, and imputed the severity of their judge to the partial malice of religious persecution. These present hardships, intolerable as they might appear, were represented as a slight prelude of the impending calamities. The Christians considered Julian as a cruel and crafty tyrant; who suspended the execution of his revenge till he should return victorious from the Persian war. They expected, that as soon as he had triumphed over the foreign enemies of Rome, he would lay aside the irksome mask of dissimulation; that the amphitheatre would stream with the blood of the hermits and bishops; and that the Christians who still persevered in the profession of the faith, would be deprived of the common benefit of nature and society. Every calumny that could wound the reputation of the Apostate, was credulously embraced by the fears and hatred of his adversaries; and their indiscreet clamours provoked the temper of a sovereign, whom it was their duty to respect, and their interest to flatter. They still protested, that prayers and tears were their only weapons against the impious tyrant, whose head they devoted to the justice of offended Heaven. But they insinuated, with sullen resolution, that their submission was no longer the effect of weakness; and that, in the imperfect state of human virtue, the patience, which is founded on principle, may be exhausted by persecution. It is impossible to determine how far the zeal of Julian would have prevailed over his good sense and humanity; but if we seriously reflect on the strength and the spirit of the church, we shall be convinced, that before the emperor could have extinguished the religion of Christ, he must have involved his country in the horrors of a civil war.

---

[31] *Cybele* a fertility goddess.

Thomas Paine (1737–1809)

At the age of thirty-seven Paine met Benjamin Franklin in London. He had been a staymaker and a tax-collector – an excise man, whose job was to search for smuggled goods and assess taxes on tobacco and alcohol. He had tried to raise the rate at which excisemen were paid and lost his job in a climate decidedly unfavorable to job-actions of any kind. Franklin gave him a letter of recommendation and packed him off to Philadelphia. He took work as a contributor and then as editor of the Pennsylvania Magazine or American Museum. *Paine wrote editorials against slavery and the oppression of women before addressing the topic of American independence. Fighting broke out in April 1775, and in October Paine published an article urging a declaration of independence. He expanded his arguments into a pamphlet called* Common Sense, *which came out in January of 1776. By April 120,000 copies were sold, and the work certainly helped ripen the times for the Declaration of Independence, which was signed on 4 July.*

Paine served briefly in the Continental Army before beginning work on his series of Crises; *the first of the eight in the series came out in December 1776 and begins with one of the most famous sentences in journalistic history: "These are the times that try men's souls." The pamphlet sold half a million copies and must be credited with helping to bind the revolutionary nation together.*

After the war Paine was out of work. The State of New York gave him a farm in New Rochelle, but by 1787 he was back in England trying to raise money for a bridge-building scheme. There he read Burke's Reflections on the Revolution in France *and was incensed. He answered in print with* The Rights of Man *(1791), perhaps the most important of the many angry responses to Burke. So well received was the work in France that Paine was elected to a seat in the National Assembly. Unfortunately, the Assembly was finally controlled by the extremists, and Paine, who argued against the execution of Louis, was imprisoned. While in jail he wrote one of the defining statements of his time* The Age of Reason *(1794). However, this work branded him as an atheist and earned him derision; the age was not yet willing to confess the drift of its own assumptions.*

After more than a decade in France, Paine went back to America, where his reputation was just as tarnished as it was in England and France. Paine lived in poverty until 1809 when he died and was buried on his farm in New Rochelle. The great liberal politician and journalist William Cobbett tried unsuccessfully to have Paine's bones moved to England for burial in a more conspicuous site. In the end the bones were lost, and no one knows in which country the physical any more than the literary remains of Paine truly belong. Indeed, he is one of many authors who cannot be seen as belonging exclusively either to America or to Britain, and even France can make some claim to his spirit.

from *COMMON SENSE* (1776)

OF THE ORIGIN AND DESIGN OF GOVERNMENT IN GENERAL, WITH CONCISE REMARKS ON THE ENGLISH CONSTITUTION

Some writers have so confounded society with government, as to leave little or no distinction between them; whereas they are not only different, but have different origins. Society is produced by our wants, and government by our wickedness; the former promotes our happiness *positively* by uniting our affections, the latter *negatively* by restraining our vices. The one encourages intercourse, the other creates distinctions. The first is a patron, the last a punisher.

Society in every state is a blessing, but Government even in its best state is but a necessary evil; in its worst state an intolerable one: for when we suffer, or are exposed to the same miseries *by a Government*, which we might expect in a country *without Government*, our calamity is heightened by reflecting that we furnish the means by which we suffer. Government like dress is the badge of lost innocence; the palaces of kings are built on the ruins of the bowers of paradise. For were the impulses of conscience clear, uniform, and irresistibly obeyed, man would need no other lawgiver; but that not being the case, he finds it necessary to surrender up a part of his property to furnish means for the protection of the rest; and this he is induced to do, by the same prudence which in every other case advises him, out of two evils to choose the least. Wherefore, security being the true design and end of government, it unanswerably follows, that whatever form thereof appears most likely to ensure it to us, with the least expense and greatest benefit, is preferable to all others.

In order to gain a clear and just idea of the design and end of government, let us suppose a small number of persons settled in some sequestered part of the earth, unconnected with the rest; they will then represent the first peopling of any country; or of the world. In this state of natural liberty, society will be their first thought. A thousand motives will excite them thereto, the strength of one man is so unequal to his wants, and his mind so unfitted for perpetual solitude, that he is soon obliged to seek assistance and relief of another, who in his turn requires the same. Four or five united would be able to raise a tolerable dwelling in the midst of a wilderness, but one man might labour out the common period of life without accomplishing any thing; when he had felled his timber he could not remove it, nor erect it after it was removed; hunger in the mean time would urge him from his work, and every different want call him a different way. Disease, nay even misfortune would be death; for though neither might be mortal, yet either would disable him from living, and reduce him to a state in which he might rather be said to perish, than to die.

Thus necessity like a gravitating power would soon form our newly arrived emigrants into society, the reciprocal blessings of which, would supercede, and render the obligations of law and government unnecessary while they remained perfectly just to each other: but as nothing but Heaven is impregnable to vice, it will unavoidably happen that in proportion as they surmount the first difficulties of emigration, which bound them together in common cause, they will begin to relax in their duty and attachment to each other: and this remissness, will point out the necessity of establishing some form of government to supply the defect of moral virtue.

Some convenient tree will afford them a State House, under the branches of which the whole Colony may assemble to deliberate on public matters. It is more than probable that their first laws will have the title only of REGULATIONS and be enforced by no other penalty than public disesteem. In this first parliament every man by natural right will have a seat.

But as the Colony increases, the public concerns will increase likewise, and the distance at which the members may be separated, will render it too inconvenient for all of them to meet on every occasion as at first, when their number was small, their habitations near, and the public concerns few and trifling. This will point out the convenience of their consenting to leave the legislative part to be managed by a select number chosen from the whole body, who are supposed to have the same concerns at stake which those have who appointed them, and who will act in the same manner as the whole body would act were they present. If the colony continues increasing, it will become necessary to augment the number of the representatives, and that the interest of every part of the colony may be attended to, it will be found best to divide the whole into convenient parts, each part sending its proper number: and that the *elected* might never form to themselves an interest separate from the electors, prudence will point out the propriety of having elections often: because as the elected might by that means return and mix again with the general body of the electors in a few months, their fidelity to the public will be secured by the prudent reflection of not making a rod for themselves. And as this frequent interchange will establish a common interest with every part of the community, they will mutually and naturally support each other, and on this (not on the unmeaning name of king) depends the *strength of government; and the happiness of the governed.*

Here then is the origin and rise of government; namely, a mode rendered necessary by the inability of moral virtue to govern the world; here too is the design and end of government, viz. Freedom and security. And however our eyes may be dazzled with snow, or our ears deceived by sound; however prejudice may warp our wills, or interest darken our understanding, the simple voice of nature and of reason will say, ' 'tis right'.

I draw my idea of the form of government from a principle in nature which no art can overturn, viz. That the more simple any thing is, the less liable it is to be disordered, and the easier repaired when disordered; and with this maxim in view I offer a few remarks on the so much boasted constitution of England. That it was noble for the dark and slavish times in which it was erected, is granted. When the world was over-run with tyranny the least remove therefrom was a glorious rescue. But that it is imperfect, subject to convulsions, and incapable of producing what it seems to promise, is easily demonstrated.

Absolute governments (though the disgrace of human nature) have this advantage with them, that they are simple; if the people suffer, they know the head from which their suffering springs; know likewise the remedy; and are not bewildered by a variety of causes and cures. But the constitution of England is so exceedingly complex, that the nation may suffer for years together without being able to discover in which part the fault lies, some will say in one and some in another, and every political physician will advise a different medicine.

I know it is difficult to get over local or long standing prejudices, yet if we will suffer ourselves to examine the component parts of the English constitution, we shall find them to be the base remains of two ancient tyrannies, compounded with some new Republican materials.

First. – The remains of Monarchical tyranny in the person of the King.

Secondly. – The remains of Aristocratical tyranny in the persons of the Peers.

Thirdly. – The new Republican materials, in the persons of the Commons, on whose virtue depends the freedom of England.

The two first by being hereditary are independent of the People; wherefore in a *constitutional sense* they contribute nothing towards the freedom of the State.

To say that the constitution of England is an *union* of three powers reciprocally *checking* each other, is farcical: either the words have no meaning or they are flat contradictions.

To say that the Commons are a check upon the King, presupposes two things.

First. – That the King is not to be trusted without being looked after; or in other words, that a thirst for absolute power is the natural disease of Monarchy.

Secondly. – That the Commons, by being appointed for that purpose, are either wiser or more worthy of confidence than the Crown.

But as the same constitution which gives the Commons a power to check the King by with-holding the supplies, gives afterwards the King a power to check the Commons by empowering him to reject their other bills; it again supposes that the King is wiser than those whom it has already supposed to be wiser than him. A mere absurdity!

There is something exceedingly ridiculous in the composition of Monarchy; it first excludes a man from the means of information, yet empowers him to act in cases where the highest judgement is required. – The state of a king shuts him from the world yet the business of a king requires him to know it thoroughly: wherefore, the different parts by unnaturally opposing and destroying each other, prove the whole character to be absurd and useless.

Some writers have explained the English constitution thus; the King, say they, is one, the people another; the Peers are an house in behalf of the King; the Commons in behalf of the people; but this hath all the distinctions of an house divided against itself;[1] and though the expressions be pleasantly arranged, yet when examined they appear idle and ambiguous: and it will always happen, that the nicest construction that words are capable of, when applied to the description of something which either cannot exist, or is too incomprehensible to be within the compass of description, will be words of sound only, and though they may amuse the ear, they cannot inform the mind: for this explanation includes a previous question, viz. *how came the King by a power which the people are afraid to trust and always obliged to check?* Such a power could not be the gift of a wise people; neither can any power *which needs checking* be from God: yet the provision which the constitution makes, supposes such a power to exist.

But the provision is unequal to the task, the means either cannot or will not accomplish the end, and the whole affair is *Felo de se*:[2] for as the greater weight will always carry up the less, and as all the wheels of a machine are put in motion by one, it only remains to know which power in the constitution has the most weight, for that will govern: and though the others, or a part of them, may clog, or check the rapidity of its motion, yet so long as they cannot stop it, their endeavours will be ineffectual: The first moving power will at last have its way, and what it wants in speed will be supplied by time.

That the crown is this overbearing part in the English constitution needs not be mentioned, and that it derives its whole consequence merely from being the giver of places and pensions is self evident, wherefore, though we have been wise enough to shut and lock a door against absolute Monarchy, we at the same time have been foolish enough to put the Crown in possession of the key.

The prejudice of Englishmen in favour of their own government by King, Lords, and Commons, arises as much or more from national pride than reason. Individuals are undoubtedly safer in England than in some other countries: but the will of the King is as much the law of the land in Britain as in France with this difference, that instead of proceeding directly from his mouth, it is handed to the people under the more formidable shape of an act of parliament. For the fate of Charles the First,[3] hath only made kings more subtle – not more just.

Wherefore laying aside all national pride and prejudice in favour of modes and forms, the plain truth is, that *it is wholly owing to the constitution of the people, and not to the constitution of the government* that the crown is not as oppressive in England as in Turkey.

---

[1] *an house divided against itself* a reference to the saying of Jesus that such a house or such a nation cannot stand (Matthew 12.25).

[2] *Felo de se* legal term for the felony of suicide.

[3] *Charles the First* executed by Parliament, 1649.

An inquiry into the *constitutional errors* in the English form of government, is at this time highly necessary; for as we are never in a proper condition of doing justice to others, while we continue under the influence of some leading partiality, so neither are we capable of doing it to ourselves while we remain fettered by any obstinate prejudice. And as a man who is attached to a prostitute is unfitted to choose or judge of a wife, so any prepossession in favour of a rotten constitution of government will disable us from discerning a good one.

from *The American CRISIS* (1777)

NUMBER I

By the Author of COMMON SENSE

These are the times that try men's souls: The summer soldier and the sunshine patriot will, in this crisis, shrink from the service of his country, but he that stands it NOW, deserves the love and thanks of man and woman. Tyranny, like hell, is not easily conquered; yet we have this consolation with us, that the harder the conflict, the more glorious the triumph. What we obtain too cheap, we esteem too lightly: – 'Tis dearness only that gives every thing its value. Heaven knows how to set a proper price upon its goods; and it would be strange indeed, if so celestial an article as FREEDOM should not be highly rated. Britain, with an army to enforce her tyranny, has declared, that she has a right (*not only to* TAX) but '*to* BIND *us in* ALL CASES WHATSOEVER', and if being *bound in that manner* is not slavery, then is there not such a thing as slavery upon earth. Even the expression is impious, for so unlimited a power can belong only to GOD.

Whether the Independence of the Continent was declared too soon, or delayed too long, I will not now enter into as an argument; my own simple opinion is, that had it been eight months earlier, it would have been much better. We did not make a proper use of last winter, neither could we, while we were in a dependent state. However, the fault, if it were one, was all our own; we have none to blame but ourselves. But no great deal is lost yet; all that Howe[1] has been doing for this month past is rather a ravage than a conquest, which the spirit of the Jersies[2] a year ago would have quickly repulsed, and which time and a little resolution will soon recover.

I have as little superstition in me as any man living, but my secret opinion has ever been, and still is, that GOD almighty will not give up a people to military destruction, or leave them unsupported to perish, who had so earnestly and so repeatedly sought to avoid the calamities of war, by every decent method which wisdom could invent. Neither have I so much of the infidel in me, as to suppose, that HE has relinquished the government of the world, and given us up to the care of devils; and as I do not, I cannot see on what grounds the king of Britain can look up to heaven for help against us: A common murderer, a highwayman, or a housebreaker, has as good a pretence as he.

---

[1] *Howe* Sir William (1729–1814), commander of British forces in America; defeated American forces in and around New York City several times in 1776; beat Washington at Brandywine at the head of the Chesapeake Bay and drove the Continental Congress from its headquarters in Philadelphia in September 1777; resigned his command in 1778.

[2] *the Jersies* recalling Washington's Christmas night attack on the Hessian troops at Trenton in 1776.

from *The Rights of Man*: being an Answer to Mr. Burke's Attack on the French Revolution (1791)

. . . Mr. Burke does not attend to the distinction between *men* and *principles*, and, therefore, he does not see that a revolt may take place against the despotism of the latter, while there lies no charge of despotism against the former.

The natural moderation of Louis XVI contributed nothing to alter the hereditary despotism of the monarchy. All the tyrannies of former reigns, acted under that hereditary despotism, were still liable to be revived in the hands of a successor. It was not the respite of a reign that would satisfy France, enlightened as she was then become. A casual discontinuance of the *practice* of despotism, is not a discontinuance of its *principles*; the former depends on the virtue of the individual who is in immediate possession of the power; the latter, on the virtue and fortitude of the nation. In the case of Charles I and James II of England, the revolt was against the personal despotism of the men; whereas in France, it was against the hereditary despotism of the established government. – But men who can consign over the rights of posterity for ever on the authority of a mouldy parchment, like Mr. Burke, are not qualified to judge of this Revolution. It takes in a field too vast for their views to explore, and proceeds with a mightiness of reason they cannot keep pace with.

But there are many points of view in which this revolution may be considered. When despotism has established itself for ages in a country, as in France, it is not in the person of the King only that it resides. It has the appearance of being so in show, and in nominal authority; but it is not so in practice and in fact. It has its standard every where. Every office and department has its despotism, founded upon custom and usage. Every place has its Bastille, and every Bastille its despot. The original hereditary despotism resident in the person of the King, divides and subdivides itself into a thousand shapes and forms, till at last the whole of it is acted by deputation. This was the case in France; and against this species of despotism, proceeding on through an endless labyrinth of office till the source of it is scarcely perceptible, there is no mode of redress. It strengthens itself by assuming the appearance of duty, and tyrannises under the pretence of obeying.

When a man reflects on the condition which France was in from the nature of her government, he will see other causes for revolt than those which immediately connect themselves with the person or character of Louis XVI. There were, if I may so express it, a thousand despotisms to be reformed in France, which had grown up under the hereditary despotism of the monarchy, and became so rooted as to be in a great measure independent of it. Between the Monarchy, the Parliament, and the Church there was a *rivalship* of despotism; besides the feudal despotism operating locally, and the ministerial despotism operating every where. But Mr. Burke, by considering the King as the only possible object of a revolt, speaks as if France was a village, in which every thing that passed must be known to its commanding officer, and no oppression could be acted but what he could immediately control. Mr. Burke might have been in the Bastille his whole life, as well under Louis XVI as Louis XIV, and neither the one nor the other have known that such a man as Mr. Burke existed. The despotic principles of the government were the same in both reigns, though the dispositions of the men were as remote as tyranny and benevolence.

What Mr. Burke considers as a reproach to the French revolution (that of bringing it forward under a reign more mild than the preceding ones) is one of its highest honours. The revolutions that have taken place in other European countries, have been excited by personal hatred. The rage was against the man, and he became the victim. But, in the instance of

France we see a Revolution generated in the rational contemplation of the rights of man, and distinguishing from the beginning between persons and principles.

But Mr. Burke appears to have no idea of principles, when he is contemplating governments. 'Ten years ago', says he, 'I could have felicitated France on her having a government, without inquiring what the nature of that Government was, or how it was administered'. Is this the language of a rational man? Is it the language of a heart feeling as it ought to feel for the rights and happiness of the human race? On this ground Mr. Burke must compliment every government in the world, while the victims who suffer under them, whether sold into slavery, or tortured out of existence, are wholly forgotten. It is power, and not principles, that Mr. Burke venerates; and under this abominable depravity he is disqualified to judge between them. – Thus much for his opinion as to the occasions of the French Revolution. I now proceed to other considerations.

I know a place in America called Point-no-Point, because as you proceed along the shore, gay and flowery as Mr. Burke's language, it continually recedes and presents itself at a distance ahead; and when you have got as far as you can go, there is no point at all. Just thus it is with Mr. Burke's three hundred and fifty-six pages. It is therefore difficult to reply to him. But as the points he wishes to establish may be inferred from what he abuses, it is in his paradoxes that we must look for his arguments.

As to the tragic paintings by which Mr. Burke has outraged his own imagination, and seeks to work upon that of his readers, they are very well calculated for theatrical representation where facts are manufactured for the sake of show, and accommodated to produce, through the weakness of sympathy, a weeping effect. But Mr. Burke should recollect that he is writing history, and not *Plays*; and that his readers will expect truth, and not the spouting rant of high-toned exclamation.

When we see a man dramatically lamenting in a publication intended to be believed, that 'The age of chivalry is gone!' that 'The glory of Europe is extinguished for ever!' that 'The unbought grace of life' (if anyone knows what it is) 'the cheap defence of nations, the nurse of manly sentiment and heroic enterprise is gone!' and all this because the Quixote age of chivalry nonsense is gone, what opinion can we form of his judgement, or what regard can we pay to his facts? In the rhapsody of his imagination, he has discovered a world of wind mills, and his sorrows are, that there are no Quixotes to attack them. But if the age of aristocracy, like that of chivalry, should fall, and they had originally some connection, Mr. Burke, the trumpeter of the Order, may continue his parody to the end, and finish with exclaiming – 'Othello's occupation's gone!'[1]

Notwithstanding Mr. Burke's horrid paintings, when the French Revolution is compared with that of other countries, the astonishment will be that it is marked with so few sacrifices; but this astonishment will cease when we reflect that it was *principles*, and not persons, that were the meditated objects of destruction. The mind of the nation was acted upon by a higher stimulus than what the consideration of persons could inspire, and sought a higher conquest than could be produced by the downfall of an enemy. Among the few who fell there do not appear to be any that were intentionally singled out. They all of them had their fate in the circumstances of the moment, and were not pursued with that long, cold-blooded, unabated revenge which pursued the unfortunate Scotch in the affair of 1745.[2]

FROM *THE RIGHTS OF MAN*
[1] *Othello's occupation's gone! Othello* 3.3.357: Othello's lament for his loss of honor and purpose when he foolishly believes Desdemona unfaithful.

[2] *the affair of 1745* the last attempt by Jacobites to restore the House of Stuart to power, crushed at Culloden (1746) and severely recriminated thereafter.

Through the whole of Mr. Burke's book I do not observe that the Bastille is mentioned more than once, and that with a kind of implication as if he were sorry it was pulled down, and wished it were built up again. 'We have rebuilt Newgate', says he 'and tenanted the mansion; and we have prisons almost as strong as the Bastille for those who dare to libel the Queens of France'. As to what a madman, like the person called Lord George Gordon,[3] might say, and to whom Newgate is rather a bedlam than a prison, it is unworthy a rational consideration. It was a madman that libelled – and that is sufficient apology; and it afforded an opportunity for confining him, which was the thing that was wished for. But certain it is that Mr. Burke, who does not call himself a madman (whatever other people may do), has libelled, in the most unprovoked manner, and in the grossest style of the most vulgar abuse, the whole representative authority of France; and yet Mr. Burke takes his seat in the British House of Commons! From his violence and his grief, his silence on some points and his excess on others, it is difficult not to believe that Mr. Burke is sorry, extremely sorry, that arbitrary power, the power of the Pope, and the Bastille, are pulled down.

Not one glance of compassion, not one commiserating reflection that I can find through-out his book, has he bestowed on those who lingered out the most wretched of lives, a life without hope, in the most miserable of prisons. It is painful to behold a man employing his talents to corrupt himself. Nature has been kinder to Mr. Burke than he is to her. He is not affected the reality of distress touching upon his heart, but by the showy resemblance of it striking his imagination. He pities the plumage, but forgets the dying bird. Accustomed to kiss the aristocratical hand that hath purloined him from himself, he degenerates into a composition of art, and the genuine soul of nature forsakes him. His hero or heroine must be a tragedy victim expiring in show, and not the real prisoner of misery, sliding into death in the silence of a dungeon . . .

James Boswell (1740–1795)

Scholars specializing in the study of Samuel Johnson have spent a good part of the last two generations trying to reconstruct the "real" Johnson concealed by Boswell's brilliant and captivating biography. Difficult as it has proved to picture Johnson without Boswell, it would be even harder to imagine Boswell without Johnson. It was a part of Boswell's nature to attach himself to great men, to relish describing himself in their company, and to recreate the feeling of being in their presence for future generations. Boswell certainly did not wish to keep himself out of the picture, as more "objective" biographers have attempted to do, and he has been criticized and even ridiculed for this from the beginning. He competed with Hester Thrale for Johnson's intimacy; he resented Goldsmith for attempting "to shine" in company and thus hindering the full blaze of Johnson's talents, which it was always his hope to evoke. Burke evidently did not like to speak in front of Boswell because it was known that he used social occasions as a mine for his literary projects. Reading about his fawning and self-regarding behavior, even in his own books, one is likely to feel that Boswell, as someone in Johnson's circle said bluntly, was "an ass." Yet the appeal of his Life of Johnson *is undeniable. One could argue that he cheapened literature by turning the interest of readers from literature to mere anecdote and that Johnson in particular has*

---

[3] *Lord George Gordon* instigator of the anti-Catholic Gordon riots of 1780 in which many buildings were burned in London and 300 people killed.

suffered because more readers know him through Boswell's account than through his own writing. But this is an argument for academics, and the world of readers must always be grateful to Boswell.

In his notebooks and journals, which are gradually emerging from the immense archive known as the Boswell Papers at Yale University, Boswell often writes more directly about himself. These works provide the richest extant account of life in eighteenth-century Britain. Boswell himself seems to have felt that the unrecorded experience was barely worth having. In this way he is curiously modern: he seems willing to admit that his identity is a sort of fiction or a composition, and he is full of anxiety that can arguably be called existential.

The late director of the Boswell Papers, Frank Brady wrote a fine biography of Boswell, though the pioneering work of Frederick Pottle remains valuable. The Life of Johnson *exists in a magnificent six-volume set, edited by G. B. Hill, and revised by L. F. Powell (Clarendon Press, 1934–64). Although my text comes from the first edition of 1791, I have relied on Hill and Powell in annotating my selection from the* Life. *Under the editorship of Marshall Waingrow and Bruce Redford, the orginal manuscript of the* Life *is also gradually coming out as part of the Boswell Papers.*

from *The Life of Dr. Samuel Johnson, LLD* (1791)

At last, on Monday the 16th of May [1763], when I was sitting in Mr. Davies's[1] back-parlour, after having drunk tea with him and Mrs. Davies, Johnson unexpectedly came into the shop; and Mr. Davies having perceived him through the glass door in the room in which we were sitting, advancing towards us, – he announced his awful approach to me, somewhat in the manner of an actor in the part of Horatio, when he addresses Hamlet on the appearance of his father's ghost, 'Look, my Lord, it comes'. I found that I had a very perfect idea of Johnson's figure, from the portrait of him painted by Sir Joshua Reynolds soon after he had published his *Dictionary*, in the attitude of sitting in his easy chair in deep meditation, which was the first picture his friend did for him, which Sir Joshua has very kindly presented to me, and from which an engraving has been made for this work.[2] Mr. Davies mentioned my name, and respectfully introduced me to him. I was much agitated; and recollecting his prejudice against the Scotch, of which I had heard much, I said to Davies, 'Don't tell him where I come from'. – 'From Scotland', cried Davies roguishly. 'Mr. Johnson', said I 'I do indeed come from Scotland, but I cannot help it'. I am willing to flatter myself that I meant this as light pleasantry to soothe and conciliate him, and not as an humiliating abasement at the expense of my country. But however that might be, this speech was somewhat unlucky; for with that quickness of wit for which he was so remarkable, he seized the expression 'come from Scotland', which I used in the sense of being of that country, and as if I had said that I had come away from it or left it, retorted, 'That, Sir, I find, is what a very great many of your countrymen cannot help'. This stroke stunned me a good deal; and when he had sat down, I felt myself not a little embarrassed, and apprehensive of what might come next. He then addressed himself to Davies: 'What do you think of Garrick?[3] He has refused me an order for

---

FROM *THE LIFE OF DR. SAMUEL JOHNSON*
[1] *Mr. Davies* Thomas (1712?–85), bookseller, actor, and author.
[2] *portrait of him . . . for this work* painted in 1756 and engraved by Heath.

[3] *Garrick* David (1717–79), greatest actor of his age and then co-manager of the Drury Lane Theatre.

the play for Miss Williams,[4] because he knows the house will be full, and that an order would be worth three shillings'. Eager to take any opening to get into conversation with him, I ventured to say, 'O, Sir, I cannot think Mr. Garrick would grudge such a trifle to you'. 'Sir', said he, with a stern look, 'I have known David Garrick longer than you have done; and I know no right you have to talk to me on the subject'. Perhaps I deserved this check; for it was rather presumptuous in me, an entire stranger, to express any doubt of the justice of his animadversion upon his old acquaintance and pupil. I now felt myself much mortified, and began to think that the hope which I had long indulged of obtaining his acquaintance was blasted. And, in truth, had not my ardour been uncommonly strong, and my resolution uncommonly persevering, so rough a reception might have deterred me for ever from making any further attempts. Fortunately, however, I remained upon the field not wholly discomfited; and was soon rewarded by hearing some of his conversation, of which I preserved the following short minute, without marking the questions and observations by which it was produced.

'People' he remarked, 'may be taken in once, who imagine that an author is greater in private life than other men. Uncommon parts require uncommon opportunities for their exertion.

'In barbarous society, superiority of parts is of real consequence. Great strength or great wisdom is of much value to an individual. But in more polished times there are people to do every thing for money, and then there are a number of other superiorities, such as those of birth and fortune, and rank, that dissipate men's attention, and leave no extraordinary share of respect for personal and intellectual superiority. This is wisely ordered by Providence, to preserve some equality among mankind . . .'

Speaking of one[5] who with more than ordinary boldness attacked public measures and the royal family, he said, 'I think he is safe from the law, but he is an abusive scoundrel; and instead of applying to my Lord Chief Justice to punish him, I would send half a dozen footmen and have him well ducked'.

'The notion of liberty amuses the people of England, and helps to keep off the *tædium vitæ*.[6] When a butcher tells you that his heart bleeds for his country, he has, in fact, no uneasy feeling . . .'

I was highly pleased with the extraordinary vigour of his conversation, and regretted that I was drawn away from it by an engagement at another place. I had, for a part of the evening, been left alone with him, and had ventured to make an observation now and then, which he received very civilly; so that I was satisfied that though there was a roughness in his manner, there was no ill-nature in his disposition. Davies followed me to the door, and when I complained to him a little of the hard blows which the great man had given me, he kindly took upon him to console me by saying, 'Don't be uneasy. I can see he likes you very well'.

A few days afterwards I called on Davies, and asked him if he thought I might take the liberty of waiting on Mr. Johnson at his Chambers in the Temple. He said I certainly might, and that Mr. Johnson would take it as a compliment. So upon Tuesday the 24th of May, after having been enlivened by the witty sallies of Messieurs Thornton, Wilkes, Churchill and

---

[4] *Miss Williams* Anna (1706–83), a blind, sometime writer, a close friend and a boarder for many years in Johnson's house.

[5] *one* John Wilkes (1727–97), famous advocate of "Liberty," author in 1763 of the notorious Number 45 of the *North Briton*.

[6] *tædium vitæ* boredom, ennui.

Lloyd,[7] with whom I had passed the morning, I boldly repaired to Johnson. His Chambers were on the first floor of No. 1, Inner Temple-lane, and I entered them with an impression given me by the Reverend Dr. Blair,[8] of Edinburgh, who had been introduced to him not long before, and described his having 'found the Giant in his den'; an expression, which, when I came to be pretty well acquainted with Johnson, I repeated to him, and he was diverted at this picturesque account of himself. Dr. Blair had been presented to him by Dr. James Fordyce.[9] At this time the controversy concerning the pieces published by Mr. James Macpherson,[10] as translations of Ossian, was at its height. Johnson had all along denied their authenticity; and, what was still more provoking to their admirers, maintained that they had no merit. The subject having been introduced by Dr. Fordyce, Dr. Blair, relying on the internal evidence of their antiquity, asked Dr. Johnson whether he thought any man of a modern age could have written such poems? Johnson replied, 'Yes, Sir, many men, many women, and many children'. Johnson, at this time, did not know that Dr. Blair had just published a Dissertation, not only defending their authenticity, but seriously ranking them with the poems of Homer and Virgil; and when he was afterwards informed of this circumstance, he expressed some displeasure at Dr. Fordyce's having suggested the topic, and said, 'I am not sorry that they got thus much for their pains. Sir, it was like leading one to talk of a book, when the author is concealed behind the door'.

He received me very courteously; but, it must be confessed, that his apartment, and furniture, and morning dress, were sufficiently uncouth. His brown suit of clothes looked very rusty; he had on a little old shrivelled unpowdered wig, which was too small for his head; his shirt-neck and knees of his breeches were loose; his black worsted stockings ill drawn up; and he had a pair of unbuckled shoes by way of slippers. But all these slovenly particularities were forgotten the moment that he began to talk. Some gentlemen, whom I do not recollect, were sitting with him; and when they went away, I also rose; but he said to me, 'Nay, don't go'. 'Sir', said I, 'I am afraid that I intrude upon you. It is benevolent to allow me to sit and hear you'. He seemed pleased with this compliment, which I sincerely paid him, and answered, 'Sir, I am obliged to any man who visits me'. I have preserved the following short minute of what passed this day.

'Madness frequently discovers itself merely by unnecessary deviation from the usual modes of the world. My poor friend Smart[11] showed the disturbance of his mind, by falling upon his knees, and saying his prayers in the street, or in any other unusual place. Now although, rationally speaking, it is greater madness not to pray at all, than to pray as Smart did, I am afraid there are so many who do not pray, that their understanding is not called in question'.

Concerning this unfortunate poet, Christopher Smart, who was confined in a mad-house, he had, at another time the following conversation with Dr. Burney. JOHNSON. 'It seems as if his mind had ceased to struggle with the disease; for he grows fat upon it'. BURNEY. 'Perhaps, Sir, that may be from want of exercise'. JOHNSON. 'No, Sir; he has partly as much exercise as he used to have, for he digs in the garden. Indeed, before his confinement, he used for exercise to walk to the alehouse; but he was *carried* back again. I did not think he ought to be shut up. His infirmities were not noxious to society. He insisted on people praying with

[7] *Thornton, Wilkes, Churchill and Lloyd* Bonnell Thornton (1724–68), writer; John Wilkes; Charles Churchill (1731–64), poet and dramatist; Robert Lloyd (1733–64), writer.

[8] *Dr. Blair* Hugh (1718–1800), divine and critic, author of an important work on rhetoric.

[9] *James Fordyce* (1720–96) Presbyterian divine.

[10] *James Macpherson* see the selection from Macpherson, above.

[11] *Smart* Christopher, see the selection from his works above.

him; and I'd as lief pray with Kit Smart as any one else. Another charge was, that he did not love clean linen; and I have no passion for it.

'Mankind have a great aversion to intellectual labour; but even supposing knowledge to be easily attainable, more people would be content to to be ignorant than would take even a little trouble to acquire it.

'The morality of an action depends on the motive from which we act. If I fling half a crown to a beggar with intention to break his head, and he picks it up and buys victuals with it, the physical effect is good; but, with respect to me, the action is very wrong. So, religious exercises, if not performed with an intention to please GOD, avail us nothing. As our Saviour says of those who perform them from other motives, "Verily they have their own reward." ' . . .

Talking of Garrick, he said, 'He is the first man in the world for sprightly conversation'. When I rose a second time he again pressed me to stay, which I did.

He told me, that he generally went abroad at four in the afternoon, and seldom came home till two in the morning. I took the liberty to ask if he did not think it wrong to live thus, and not make more use of his great talents. He owned it was a bad habit. On reviewing, at the distance of many years, my journal of this period, I wonder how, at my first visit, I ventured to talk to him so freely, and that he bore it with so much indulgence.

Before we parted, he was so good as to promise to favour me with his company one evening at my lodgings; and, as I took my leave, shook me cordially by the hand. It is almost needless to add, that I felt no little elation at having now so happily established an acquaintance of which I had been so long ambitious.

My readers will, I trust, excuse me for being thus minutely circumstantial, when it is considered that the acquaintance of Dr. Johnson was to me a most valuable acquisition, and laid the foundation of whatever instruction and entertainment they may receive from my collections concerning the great subject of the work which they are now perusing . . .

A revolution of some importance in my plan of life had just taken place; for instead of procuring a commission in the foot-guards, which was my own inclination, I had, in compliance with my father's wishes, agreed to study the law; and was soon to set out for Utrecht, to hear the lectures of an excellent Civilian[12] in that University, and then to proceed on my travels. Though very desirous of obtaining Dr. Johnson's advice and instructions on the mode of pursuing my studies, I was at this time so occupied, shall I call it? or so dissipated, by the amusements of London, that our next meeting was not till Saturday, June 25, when happening to dine at Clifton's eating-house, in Butcher-row, I was surprised to perceive Johnson come in and take his seat at another table. The mode of dining, or rather being fed, at such houses in London, is well known to many to be particularly unsocial, as there is no Ordinary, or united company, but each person has his own mess, and is under no obligation to hold any intercourse with any one. A liberal and full-minded man, however, who loves to talk, will break through this churlish and unsocial restraint. Johnson and an Irish gentleman got into a dispute concerning the cause of some part of mankind being black. 'Why, Sir', said Johnson, 'it has been accounted for in three ways: either by supposing that they are the posterity of Ham, who was cursed; or that GOD at first created two kinds of men, one black and another white; or that by the heat of the sun the skin is scorched, and so acquires a sooty hue. This matter has been much canvassed among naturalists, but has never

---

[12] *Civilian* "One that possesses the knowledge of the old Roman law, and of general equity" (Johnson); an expert on civil law.

been brought to any certain issue'. What the Irishman said is totally obliterated from my mind; but I remember that he became very warm and intemperate in his expressions; upon which Johnson rose, and quietly walked away. When he had retired, his antagonist took his revenge, as he thought, by saying, 'He has a most ungainly figure, and an affectation of pomposity unworthy of a man of genius'.

Johnson had not observed that I was in the room. I followed him, however, and he agreed to meet me in the evening at the Mitre.[13] I called on him, and we went thither at nine. We had a good supper, and port wine, of which he then sometimes drank a bottle. The orthodox high-church sound of the Mitre, the figure and manner of the celebrated Samuel Johnson, the extraordinary power and precision of his conversation, and the pride arising from finding myself admitted as his companion, produced a variety of sensations, and a pleasing elevation of mind beyond what I had ever before experienced. I find in my journal the following minute of our conversation, which, though it will give but a very faint notion of what passed, is, in some degree, a valuable record; and it will be curious in this view, as showing how habitual to his mind were some opinions which appear in his works . . .

'Sir, I do not think Gray a first-rate poet. He has not a bold imagination, nor much command of words. The obscurity in which he has involved himself will not persuade us that he is sublime. His Elegy in a church-yard has a happy selection of images, but I don't like what are called his great things. His Ode which begins

> Ruin seize thee, ruthless King,
> Confusion on thy banner wait![14]

has been celebrated for its abruptness, and plunging into the subject all at once. But such arts as these have no merit, unless when they are original. We admire them only once; and this abruptness has nothing new in it. We have had it often before. Nay, we have it in the old song of Johnny Armstrong:

> 'Is there ever a man in all Scotland
> From the highest estate to the lowest degree, &c'.

And then, Sir,

> Yes, there is a man in Westmoreland,
> And Johnny Armstrong they do him call.

There, now, you plunge at once into the subject. You have no previous narration to lead you to it. – The two next lines in that Ode are, I think, very good:

> Though fanned by conquest's crimson wing,
> They mock the air with idle state.

Here let it be oberved, that although his opinion of Gray's poetry was widely different from mine, and I believe from that of most men of taste, by whom it is with justice highly admired, there is certainly much absurdity in the clamour which has been raised, as if he had been culpably injurious to the merit of that bard, and had been actuated by envy. Alas! ye

---

[13] *Mitre* a tavern in the Strand.   [14] *Ruin . . . wait* the opening of "The Bard."

little short-sighted critics, could Johnson be envious of the talents of any of his contemporaries? That his opinion on this subject was what in private and in public he uniformly expressed, regardless of what others might think, we may wonder, and perhaps regret; but it is shallow and unjust to charge him with expressing what he did not think.

Finding him in a placid humour, and wishing to avail myself of the opportunity which I fortunately had of consulting a sage, to hear whose wisdom, I conceived in the ardour of youthful imagination, that men filled with a noble enthusiasm for intellectual improvement would gladly have resorted from distant lands; I opened my mind to him ingenuously, and gave him a little sketch of my life, to which he was pleased to listen with great attention.

I acknowledged, that though educated very strictly in the principles of religion, I had for some time been misled into a certain degree of infidelity; but that I was come now to a better way of thinking, and was fully satisfied of the truth of the Christian revelation, though I was not clear as to every point considered to be orthodox. Being at all times a curious examiner of the human mind, and pleased with an undisguised display of what had passed in it, he called to me with warmth, 'Give me your hand; I have taken a liking to you'. He then began to descant upon the force of testimony, and the little we could know of final causes; so that the objections of, why was it so? or why was it not so? ought not to disturb us: adding, that he himself had at one period been guilty of a temporary neglect of religion, but that it was not the result of argument, but mere absence of thought.

After having given credit to reports of his bigotry, I was agreeably surprised when he expressed the following very liberal sentiment, which has the additional value of obviating an objection to our holy religion, founded upon the discordant tenets of Christians themselves: 'For my part, Sir, I think all Christians, whether Papists or Protestants, agree in the essential articles, and that their differences are trivial, and rather political than religious'.

We talked of belief in ghosts. He said, 'Sir, I make a distinction between what a man may experience by the mere strength of his imagination, and what imagination cannot possibly produce. Thus, suppose I should think that I saw a form, and heard a voice cry "Johnson, you are a very wicked fellow, and unless you repent you will certainly be punished"; my own unworthiness is so deeply impressed upon my mind, that I might *imagine* I thus saw and heard, and therefore I should not believe that an external communication had been made to me. But if a form should appear, and a voice should tell me that a particular man had died at a particular place, and a particular hour, a fact which I had no apprehension of, nor any means of knowing, and this fact, with all its circumstances should afterwards be unquestionably proved, I should, in that case be persuaded that I had supernatural intelligence imparted to me' . . .

He proceeded: 'Your going abroad, Sir, and breaking off with idle habits, may be of great importance to you. I would go where there are courts and learned men. There is a good deal of Spain that has not been perambulated. I would have you go thither. A man of inferior talents to yours may furnish us with useful observations upon that country'. His supposing me, at that period of life, capable of writing an account of my travels that would deserve to be read, elated me not a little.

I appeal to every impartial reader whether this faithful detail of his frankness, complacency,[15] and kindness to a young man, a stranger and a Scotchman, does not refute the unjust opinion of the harshness of his general demeanour. His occasional reproofs of folly, impu-

---

[15] *complacency* "Civility; complaisance; softness of manners" (Johnson).

dence, or impiety, and even the sudden sallies of his constitutional irritability of temper, which have been preserved for the poignancy of their wit, have produced that opinion among those who have not considered that such instances, though collected by Mrs. Piozzi into a small volume,[16] and read over in a few hours, were, in fact, scattered through a long series of years; years, in which his time was chiefly spent in instructing and delighting mankind by his writings and conversation, in acts of piety to GOD, and good-will to men.

I complained to him that I had not yet acquired much knowledge, and asked his advice as to my studies. He said, 'Don't talk of study now. I will give you a plan; but it will require some time to consider of it'. 'It is very good in you, Mr. Johnson' I replied, 'to allow me to be with you thus. Had it been foretold to me some years ago that I should pass an evening with the author of The RAMBLER, how should I have exulted!' What I then expressed was sincerely from the heart. He was satisfied that it was, and cordially answered, 'Sir, I am glad we have met. I hope we shall pass many evenings and mornings too, together'. We finished a couple of bottles of port, and sat till between one and two in the morning . . .

He recommended to me to keep a journal of my life, full and unreserved. He said it would be a very good exercise, and would yield me great satisfaction when the particulars were faded from my remembrance. I was uncommonly fortunate in having had a previous coincidence of opinion with him upon this subject, for I had kept such a journal for some time;[17] and it was no small pleasure to me to have this to tell him, and to receive his approbation. He counselled me to keep it private, and said I might surely have a friend who would burn it in case of my death. From this habit I have been enabled to give the world so many anecdotes, which would otherwise have been lost to posterity. I mentioned that I was afraid I put into my journal too many little incidents. JOHNSON. 'There is nothing, Sir, too little for so little a creature as man. It is by studying little things that we attain the great art of having as little misery and as much happiness as possible' . . .

Mr. Levet[18] this day showed me Dr. Johnson's library, which was contained in two garrets over his Chambers, where Lintot,[19] son of the celebrated bookseller of that name, had formerly his printing-house. I found a number of good books, but very dusty and in great confusion. The floor was strewed with manuscript leaves, in Johnson's own handwriting, which I beheld with a degree of veneration, supposing they might contain portions of The Rambler, or of Rasselas. I observed an apparatus for chemical experiments, of which Johnson was all his life very fond. The place seemed to be very favourable for retirement and meditation. Johnson told me, that he went up thither without mentioning it to his servant, when he wanted to study, secure from interruption; for he would not allow his servant to say he was not at home when he really was. 'A servant's strict regard for truth', said he 'must be weakened by such a practice. A philosopher may know that it is merely a form of denial; but few servants are such nice distinguishers. If I accustom a servant to tell a lie for *me*, have I not reason to apprehend that he will tell many lies for *himself*?' I am, however, satisfied that every servant, of any degree of intelligence, understands saying his master is not at home, not at all as the affirmation of a fact, but as customary words, intimating that his master wishes not to be seen; so that there can be no bad effect from it.

[16] *Mrs. Piozzi . . . volume* Hester Lynch Thrale Piozzi (1741–1821) published her *Anecdotes of the Late Samuel Johnson* in 1786; see the selection from her letters below.
[17] *I had kept such a journal for some time* Boswell kept voluminous and "unreserved" journals; he preserved them all, and the work of publishing them and his various notebooks and manuscripts has occupied teams of scholars for three generations.

[18] *Mr. Levet* a physician without university training, who ministered to the poor and lived for many years as a boarder in Johnson's house.
[19] *Lintot* Henry (1709–58), son of Bernard (1675–1736), proprietor of the lucrative copyright for Pope's *Iliad*.

   Mr. Temple, now vicar of St. Gluvias, Cornwall, who had been my intimate friend for many years, had at this time chambers in Farrar's-buildings, at the bottom of Inner Temple-lane, which he kindly lent me upon my quitting my lodgings, he being to return to Trinity Hall, Cambridge. I found them particularly convenient for me, as they were so near Dr. Johnson's.

   On Wednesday, July 20, Dr. Johnson, Mr. Dempster,[20] and my uncle Dr. Boswell, who happened to be now in London, supped with me at these Chambers. JOHNSON. 'Pity is not natural to man. Children are always cruel. Savages are always cruel. Pity is acquired and improved by the cultivation of reason. We may have uneasy sensations from seeing a creature in distress, without pity; for we have not pity unless we wish to relieve them. When I am on my way to dine with a friend, and finding it late, have bid the coachman make haste, if I happen to attend when he whips his horses, I may feel unpleasantly that the animals are put to pain, but I do not wish him to desist. No, Sir, I wish him to drive on'.

   Mr. Alexander Donaldson, bookseller of Edinburgh, had for some time opened a shop in London, and sold his cheap editions of the most popular English books, in defiance of the supposed common-law right of *Literary Property*. Johnson, though he concurred in the opinion which was afterwards sanctioned by a decree from the House of Lords, that there was no such right, was at this time very angry that the booksellers of London, for whom he uniformly professed much regard, should suffer from an invasion of what they had ever considered to be secure: and he was loud and violent against Mr. Donaldson.[21] 'He is a fellow who takes advantage of the law to injure his brethren; for, notwithstanding that the statute[22] secures only fourteen years of exclusive right, it has always been understood by the trade, that he, who buys the copy-right of a book from the author, obtains a perpetual property; and upon that belief, numberless bargains are made to transfer that property after the expiration of the statutory term. Now Donaldson, I say, takes advantage here, of people who have really an equitable title from usage; and if we consider how few of the books, of which they buy the property, succeed so well as to bring profit, we should be of opinion that the term of fourteen years is too short; it should be sixty years'. DEMPSTER. 'Donaldson, Sir, is anxious for the encouragement of literature. He reduces the price of books, so that poor students may buy them'. JOHNSON, (laughing) 'Well, Sir, allowing that to be his motive, he is no better than Robin Hood, who robbed the rich in order to give to the poor'.

   It is remarkable, that when the great question concerning Literary Property came to be ultimately tried before the supreme tribunal of this country,[23] in consequence of the very spirited exertions of Mr. Donaldson, Dr. Johnson was zealous against a perpetuity; but he thought that the term of the exclusive right of authors should be considerably enlarged. He was then for granting a hundred years.[24]

   The conversation now turned upon Mr. David Hume's style. JOHNSON. 'Why, Sir, his style is not English; the structure of his sentences is French. Now the French structure and the English structure may, in the nature of things, be equally good. But if you allow that the English language is established, he is wrong. My name might originally have been

---

[20] *Mr. Dempster* Scottish Member of Parliament and agriculturist.

[21] *Donaldson* several actions were brought against him by London booksellers, but they all failed or were overturned; Boswell acted as his attorney in one suit in 1773.

[22] *statute* "A Bill for the Encouragement of Learning by Vesting the Copies of Printed Books in the Authors, or Purchasers, of such Copies during the Times therein

Mentioned"; a second fourteen-year term was allowed to authors still living after the expiration of the first term; the bill became law in 1710.

[23] *the supreme tribunal of this country* the House of Lords, which determined in 1774 that copyright should be limited.

[24] *a hundred years* Johnson gave his opinion in a letter to William Strahan on 7 March 1774; fifty years is the term he settles on.

Nicholson, as well as Johnson; but were you to call me Nicholson now, you would call me very absurdly'.

Rousseau's treatise on the inequality of mankind[25] was at this time a fashionable topic. It gave rise to an observation by Mr. Dempster, that the advantages of fortune and rank were nothing to a wise man, who ought to value only merit. JOHNSON. 'If man were a savage, living in the woods by himself, this might be true; but in civilised society we all depend on each other, and our happiness is very much owing to the good opinion of mankind. Now, Sir, in civilised society, external advantages make us more respected. A man with a good coat upon his back meets with a better reception than he who has a bad one. Sir, you may analyse this, and say what is there in it? But that will avail you nothing, for it is a part of a general system. Pound St. Paul's Church into atoms, and consider any single atom; it is, to be sure, good for nothing: but, put all these atoms together, and you have St. Paul's Church. So it is with human felicity, which is made up of many ingredients, each of which may be shown to be very insignificant. In civilised society, personal merit will not serve you so much as money will. Sir, you may make the experiment. Go into the street, and give one man a lecture on morality, and another a shilling, and see which will respect you most. If you wish only to support nature, Sir William Petty[26] fixes your allowance at three pounds a year; but as times are much altered, let us call it six pounds. This sum will fill your belly, shelter you from the weather, and even get you a strong lasting coat, supposing it be made of good bull's hide. Now, Sir, all beyond this is artificial, and is desired in order to obtain a greater degree of respect from our fellow-creatures. And, Sir, if six hundred pounds a year procure a man more consequence, and, of course, more happiness than six pounds a year, the same proportion will hold as to six thousand, and so on as far as opulence can be carried. Perhaps he who has a large fortune may not be so happy as he who has a small one; but that must proceed from other causes than from his having the large fortune: for, *cæteris paribus*,[27] he who is rich in a civilised society, must be happier than he who is poor; as riches, if properly used (and it is a man's own fault if they are not) must be productive of the highest advantages. Money, to be sure, of itself is no use; for its only use is to part with it. Rousseau, and all those who deal in paradoxes, are led away by a childish desire of novelty. When I was a boy, I used always to choose the wrong side of a debate, because most ingenious things, that is to say, most new things, could be said upon it. Sir, there is nothing for which you may not muster up more plausible arguments, than those which are urged against wealth and other external advantages. Why, now, there is stealing; why should it be thought a crime? When we consider by what unjust methods property has been often acquired, and that what was unjustly got it must be unjust to keep, where is the harm in one man's taking the property of another from him? Besides, Sir, when we consider the bad use that many people make of their property, and how much better use the thief may make of it, it may be defended as a very allowable practice. Yet, Sir, the experience of mankind has discovered stealing to be so very bad a thing, that they make no scruple to hang a man for it. When I was running about this town a very poor fellow, I was a great arguer for the advantages of poverty; but I was, at the same time, very sorry to be poor. Sir, all the arguments which are brought to represent poverty as no evil, show it to be evidently a great evil. You never find people labouring to convince you that you may live very happily upon a plentiful fortune. – So you hear people talking how miserable a king must be; and yet they all wish to be in his place' . . .

---

[25] *Rousseau's treatise on the inequality of mankind Discours sur l'origine et les fondements de l'inégalité parmi les hommes* (1755).

[26] *Sir William Petty* (1623–87), political economist; he also estimated the mean annual per capita expenditure at £7.

[27] *cæteris paribus*   other things being equal.

At night Mr. Johnson and I supped in a private room at the Turk's Head coffee-house, in the Strand. 'I encourage this house' said he, 'for the mistress is a good civil woman, and has not much business.

'Sir, I love the acquaintance of young people; because, in the first place, I don't like to think myself growing old. In the next place, young acquaintances must last longest, if they do last; and then, Sir, young men have more virtue than old men; they have more generous sentiments in every respect. I love the young dogs of this age: they have more wit and humour and knowledge of life than we had; but then the dogs are not so good scholars. Sir, in my early years I read very hard. It is a sad reflection, but a true one, that I knew almost as much at eighteen as I do now. My judgement, to be sure, was not so good; but, I had all the facts. I remember very well, when I was at Oxford, an old gentleman said to me, "Young man, ply your book diligently now, and acquire a stock of knowledge; for when years come upon you, you will find that poring upon books will be but an irksome task". . .'

He mentioned to me now, for the first time, that he had been distressed by melancholy, and for that reason had been obliged to fly from study and meditation, to the dissipating variety of life. Against melancholy he recommended constant occupation of mind, a great deal of exercise, moderation in eating and drinking, and especially to shun drinking at night. He said melancholy people were apt to fly to intemperance for relief, but that it sunk them much deeper in misery. He observed, that labouring men who work hard, and live sparingly, are seldom or never troubled with low spirits . . .

He maintained, that a boy at school was the happiest of human beings. I supported a different opinion, from which I have never yet varied, that a man is happier; and I enlarged upon the anxiety and sufferings which are endured at school. JOHNSON. 'Ah! Sir, a boy's being flogged is not so severe as a man's having the hiss of the world against him. Men have a solicitude about fame; and the greater share they have of it, the more afraid they are of losing it'. I silently asked myself, 'Is it possible that the great Samuel Johnson really entertains any such apprehension, and is not confident that his exalted fame is established upon a foundation never to be shaken?' . . .

On Tuesday, July 26, I found Mr. Johnson alone. It was a very wet day, and I again complained of the disagreeable effects of such weather. JOHNSON. 'Sir, this is all imagination, which physicians encourage; for man lives in air, as a fish lives in water; so that if the atmosphere press heavy from above, there is an equal resistance from below. To be sure, bad weather is hard upon people who are obliged to be abroad; and men cannot labour so well in the open air in bad weather, as in good: but, Sir, a smith or a tailor, whose work is within doors, will surely do as much in rainy weather as in fair. Some very delicate frames, indeed, may be affected by wet weather, but not common constitutions'.

We talked of the education of children; and I asked him what he thought was best to teach them first. JOHNSON. 'Sir, it is no matter what you teach them first, any more than what leg you shall put into your breeches first. Sir, you may stand disputing which is best to put in first, but in the mean time your breech is bare. Sir, while you are considering which of two things you should teach your child first, another boy has learnt them both'.

On Thursday, July 28, we again supped in private at the Turk's Head coffee-house. JOHNSON. 'Swift has a higher reputation than he deserves. His excellence is strong sense; for his humour, though very well, is not remarkably good. I doubt whether the 'Tale of a Tub' be his; for he never owned it, and it is much above his usual manner.

'Thomson, I think, had as much of the poet about him as most writers. Every thing appeared to him through the medium of his favourite pursuit. He could not have viewed those two candles burning but with a poetical eye' . . .

The conversation then took a philosophical turn. JOHNSON. 'Human experience, which is constantly contradicting theory, is the great test of truth. A system, built upon the discoveries of a great many minds, is always of more strength, than what is produced by the mere workings of any one mind, which, of itself, can do little. There is not so poor a book in the world that would not be a prodigious effort were it wrought out entirely by a single mind, without the aid of prior investigators. The French writers are superficial, because they are not scholars, and so proceed upon the mere power of their own minds; and we see how very little power they have.

'As to the Christian religion, Sir, besides the strong evidence which we have for it, there is a balance in its favour from the number of great men who have been convinced of its truth, after a serious consideration of the question. Grotius[28] was an acute man, a lawyer, a man accustomed to examine evidence, and he was convinced. Grotius was not a recluse, but a man of the world, who certainly had no bias on the side of religion. Sir Isaac Newton set out an infidel, and came to be a very firm believer'.

He this evening again recommended to me to perambulate Spain. I said it would amuse him to get a letter from me dated at Salamancha. JOHNSON. 'I love the University of Salamancha; for when the Spaniards were in doubt as to the lawfulness of their conquering of America, the University of Salamancha gave it as their opinion that it was not lawful'. He spoke this with great emotion . . .

I again begged his advice as to my method of study at Utrecht. 'Come', said he 'let us make a day of it. Let us go down to Greenwich and dine, and talk of it there'. The following Saturday was fixed for this excursion.

As we walked along the Strand to-night, arm in arm, a woman of the town accosted us, in the usual enticing manner. 'No, no, my girl', said Johnson, 'it won't do'. He, however, did not treat her with harshness, and we talked of the wretched life of such women; and agreed, that much more misery than happiness, upon the whole, is produced by illicit commerce between the sexes.[29]

On Saturday, July 30, Dr. Johnson and I took a sculler at the Temple-stairs, and set out for Greenwich.[30] I asked him if he really thought a knowledge of the Greek and Latin languages an essential requisite to a good education. JOHNSON. 'Most certainly, Sir; for those who know them have a very great advantage over those who do not. Nay, Sir, it is wonderful what a difference learning makes upon people even in the common intercourse of life, which does not appear to be much connected with it'. 'And yet', said I, 'people go through the world very well, and carry on the business of life to good advantage, without learning'. JOHNSON. 'Why, Sir, that may be true in cases where learning cannot possibly be any use; for instance, this boy rows as well without learning, as if he could sing the song of Orpheus to the Argonauts, who were the first sailors'. He then called to the boy, 'What would you give, my lad, to know about the Argonauts?' 'Sir', said the boy, 'I would give what I have'. Johnson was much pleased with his answer, and we gave him a double fare. Mr. Johnson then turning to me, 'Sir', said he 'a desire of knowledge is the natural feeling of mankind; and every human being, whose mind is not debauched, will be willing to give all that he has to get knowledge' . . .

---

28 *Grotius* Hugo (1583–1645), legal scholar and author of a fundamental religious handbook, *De veritate religionis*.

29 *illicit commerce between the sexes* Boswell, however, records his very frequent use of such commerce in his journals.

30 *Greenwich* they are crossing the Thames in a small hired boat.

We stayed so long at Greenwich, that our sail up the river, in our return to London, was by no means so pleasant as in the morning; for the night air was so cold that it made me shiver. I was the more sensible of it from having sat up all the night before, recollecting and writing in my journal what I thought worthy of preservation; an exertion, which, during the first part of my acquaintance with Johnson, I frequently made. I remember having sat up four nights in one week, without being much incommoded in the day time.

Johnson, whose robust frame was not in the least affected by the cold, scolded me, as if my shivering had been a paltry effeminacy, saying, 'Why do you shiver?' Sir William Scott, of the Commons, told me, that when he complained of a head-ache in the post-chaise, as they were travelling together to Scotland, Johnson treated him in the same manner: 'At your age, Sir, I had no head-ache'. It is not easy to make allowance for sensations in others, which ourselves have not at the time. We must all have experienced how very differently we are affected by the complaints of our neighbours, when we are well and when we are ill. In full health, we can scarcely believe that they suffer much; so faint is the image of pain upon our imagination: when softened by sickness, we readily sympathise with the sufferings of others . . .

After we had again talked of my setting out for Holland, he said, 'I must see thee out of England: I will accompany you to Harwich'. I could not find words to express what I felt upon this unexpected and very great mark of his affectionate regard . . .

On Friday, August 5, we set out early in the morning in the Harwich stage coach. A fat elderly gentlewoman, and a young Dutchman, seemed the most inclined among us to conversation. At the inn where we dined, the gentlewoman said that she had done her best to educate her children; and particularly, that she had never suffered them to be a moment idle. JOHNSON. 'I wish, madam, you would educate me too; for I have been an idle fellow all my life'. 'I am sure, Sir', said she 'you have not been idle'. JOHNSON. 'Nay, Madam, it is very true; and that gentleman there (pointing to me,) has been idle. He was idle at Edinburgh. His father sent him to Glasgow, where he continued to be idle. He then came to London, where he has been very idle; and now he is going to Utrecht, where he will be as idle as ever'. I asked him privately how he could expose me so. JOHNSON. 'Poh, poh!' said he, 'they knew nothing about you, and will think of it no more'. In the afternoon the gentle-woman talked violently against the Roman Catholics, and of the horrors of the Inquisition. To the utter astonishment of all the passengers but myself, who knew that he could talk upon any side of a question, he defended the Inquisition, and maintained, 'that false doctrine should be checked on its first appearance; that the civil power should unite with the church in punishing those who dared to attack the established religion, and that such only were punished by the Inquisition' . . .

Having stopped a night at Colchester, Johnson talked of that town with veneration, for having stood a siege for Charles the First. The Dutchman alone now remained with us. He spoke English tolerably well; and thinking to recommend himself to us by expatiating on the superiority of the criminal jurisprudence of this country over that of Holland, he inveighed against the barbarity of putting an accused person to the torture, in order to force a confession. But Johnson was as ready for this, as for the Inquisition. 'Why, Sir, you do not, I find, understand the law of your own country. The torture in Holland is considered as a favour to an accused person; for no man is put to the torture there, unless there is as much evidence against him as would amount to a conviction in England. An accused person among you, therefore, has one chance more to escape punishment, than those who are tried among us'.

At supper this night he talked of good eating with uncommon satisfaction. 'Some people' said he, 'have a foolish way of not minding, or pretending not to mind, what they eat. For my part, I mind my belly very studiously, and very carefully; for I look upon it, that he who does not mind his belly will hardly mind anything else'. He now appeared to me *Jean Bull philosophe*,[31] and he was, for the moment, not only serious but vehement. Yet I have heard him, upon other occasions, talk with great contempt of people who were anxious to gratify their palates; and the 206th number of his Rambler is a masterly essay against gulosity. His practice, indeed, I must acknowledge, may be considered as casting the balance of his different opinions upon this subject; for I never knew any man who relished good eating more than he did. When at table, he was totally absorbed in the business of the moment; his looks seemed rivetted to his plate; nor would he, unless when in very high company, say one word, or even pay the least attention to what was said by others, till he had satisfied his appetite, which was so fierce, and indulged with such intenseness, that while in the act of eating, the veins of his forehead swelled, and generally a strong perspiration was visible. To those whose sensations were delicate, this could not but be disgusting; and it was doubtless not very suitable to the character of a philosopher, who should be distinguished by self-command. But it must be owned, that Johnson, though he could be rigidly *abstemious*, was not a *temperate* man either in eating or drinking. He could refrain, but he could not use moderately. He told me, that he had fasted two days without inconvenience, and that he had never been hungry but once. They who beheld with wonder how much he eat[32] upon all occasions when his dinner was to his taste, could not easily conceive what he must have meant by hunger; and not only was he remarkable for the extraordinary quantity which he eat, but he was, or affected to be, a man of very nice discernment in the science of cookery. He used to descant critically on the dishes which had been at table where he had dined or supped, and to recollect very minutely what he had liked. I remember, when he was in Scotland, his praising 'Gordon's palates,' (a dish of palates[33] at the Honourable Alexander Gordon's) with a warmth of expression which might have done honour to more important subjects . . . He about the same time was so much displeased with the performances of a nobleman's French cook, that he exclaimed with vehemence, 'I'd throw such a rascal into the river'; and he then proceeded to alarm a lady at whose house he was to sup, by the following manifesto of his skill: 'I, Madam, who live at a variety of good tables, am a much better judge of cookery, than any person who has a very tolerable cook, but lives much at home; for his palate is gradually adapted to the taste of his cook; whereas, Madam, in trying by a wider range, I can more exquisitely judge'. When invited to dine, even with an intimate friend, he was not pleased if something better than a plain dinner was not prepared for him. I have heard him say on such an occasion, 'This was a good dinner enough, to be sure; but it was not a dinner to *ask* a man to'. On the other hand, he was wont to express, with great glee, his satisfaction when he had been entertained quite to his mind. One day when we had dined with his neighbour and landlord in Bolt-court, Mr. Allen,[34] the printer, whose old housekeeper had studied his taste in every thing, he pronounced this eulogy, 'Sir, we could not have had a better dinner had there been a *Synod of Cooks*'.

While we were left by ourselves, after the Dutchman had gone to bed, Dr. Johnson talked of that studied behaviour which many have recommended and practised. He disapproved of it; and said, 'I never considered whether I should be a grave man, or a merry man, but just let inclination, for the time, have its course' . . .

---

[31]   *Jean Bull philosophe*   John Bull was a caricature of an Englishman invented by John Arbuthnot; Boswell turns the phrase to suggest a caricature of a French *philosophe*, like Voltaire.

[32]   *eat*   an acceptable form of the past tense at this time.

[33]   *palates*   fricasseed ox palates made a fancy dish in the eighteenth century.

[34]   *Allen*   Edmund (d. 1780).

I teased him with fanciful apprehensions of unhappiness. A moth having fluttered round the candle, and burnt itself, he laid hold of this little incident to admonish me; saying, with a sly look, and in a solemn but quiet tone, 'That creature was its own tormentor, and I believe his name was BOSWELL'.

Next day we got to Harwich to dinner; and my passage in the packet-boat to Helvoetsluys being secured, and my baggage put on board, we dined at our inn by ourselves. I happened to say it would be terrible if he should not find a speedy opportunity of returning to London, and be confined to so dull a place. JOHNSON. 'Don't, Sir, accustom yourself to use big words for little matters. It would *not* be *terrible*, though I *were* to be detained some time here'. The practice of using words of disproportionate magnitude, is, no doubt, too frequent every where; but, I think, most remarkable among the French, of which, all who have travelled in France must have been struck with innumerable instances.

We went and looked at the church, and having gone into it and walked up to the altar, Johnson, whose piety was constant and fervent, sent me to my knees, saying, 'Now that you arc going to leave your native country, recommend yourself to the protection of your Creator and Redeemer'.

After we came out of the church, we stood talking for some time together of Bishop Berkeley's[35] ingenious sophistry to prove the non-existence of matter, and that every thing in the universe is merely ideal. I observed, that though we are satisfied his doctrine is not true, it is impossible to refute it. I never shall forget the alacrity with which Johnson answered, striking his foot with mighty force against a large stone, till he rebounded from it, 'I refute it *thus*' . . .

My revered friend walked down with me to the beach, where we embraced and parted with tenderness, and engaged to correspond by letters. I said, 'I hope, Sir, you will not forget me in my absence'. JOHNSON. 'Nay, Sir, it is more likely you should forget me, than that I should forget you'. As the vessel put out to sea, I kept my eyes upon him for a considerable time, while he remained rolling his majestic frame in his usual manner; and at last I perceived him walk back into the town, and he disappeared.

Hester Lynch Thrale Piozzi (1741–1821)

In 1763 Johnson met both Boswell and Hester Thrale for the first time. Although the meeting with Boswell has meant more to literary history, the meeting with Hester Thrale meant more to Johnson personally. She was his closest friend for most of the next twenty years; her house in greater London (Streatham) was often home to Johnson; he had his own room there, with bed made to the full length of his unusually large frame (5 ft 11 in), and even a little gazebo in the garden for writing on pleasant days. Henry Thrale's father had made a small fortune in brewing and his son was enjoying a life on the edges of the upper class. He served in Parliament and he and his beautiful wife knew some of the most interesting people in London. Johnson was in some respects a prize acquisition, but they gave him as much as they got by his friendship. The precise nature of his friendship with Hester will probably never be known. It did involve flirtation of a kind, however, and certainly personal revelations. Johnson evidently told her, as he told her almost everything, something about his vigorous imagination, which occasionally ran to sexual fantasy. There is a

---

long-standing debate in Johnsonian circles about a letter in French that Johnson wrote to Hester Thrale that seems to suggest that he submitted to some sort of sexual bondage in their relationship. (There is a rare echo of that famous letter in the first selection offered here.) This is probably just wishful thinking, and the relationship, in reality, was probably much more decorous. Johnson did depend on this much younger woman in many ways, however, and he submitted to her rules for domestic life in the most elaborately courteous and sometimes suggestive ways.

After the death of Henry Thrale, Johnson's relationship with Hester was diminished. Their relationship flourished in the context of her successful, if not perfect marriage, and fell apart afterward. She married Piozzi, a music teacher and an Italian, both features unforgivable in the spouse of a woman with pretensions to high society. This was virtually the end of her friendship with Johnson, though there was something of a reconciliation. She lived nearly forty years as Mrs Piozzi and was a productive writer much of the time. She had always enjoyed scribbling in the margins of her books, and, partly at Johnson's suggestion, she became an avid diarist. Some of the materials she collected in her Thraliana went to make up her Anecdotes of the Late Samuel Johnson, LLD. My selection from the conclusion is based on the first edition (1786). From Thrale's many letters to Samuel Johnson, I select one that concerns his supposed bondage to her, and another that speaks about the tragic death of one of her children. She lost nine of her twelve and several through a most painful disease of the brain. I reprint the letters from R. W. Chapman's edition of The Letters of Samuel Johnson (Clarendon Press, 1952).

from Anecdotes of the Late Samuel Johnson, LLD during the Last Twenty Years of his Life (1786)

With regard to common occurrences, Mr. Johnson had, when I first knew him, looked on the still-shifting scenes of life till he was weary; for as a mind slow in its own nature, or unenlivened by information, will contentedly read in the same book for twenty times perhaps, the very act of reading it, being more than half the business, and every period[1] being at every reading better understood; while a mind more active or more skilful to comprehend its meaning is made sincerely sick at the second perusal; so a soul like his, acute to discern the truth, vigorous to embrace, and powerful to retain it, soon sees enough of the world's dull prospect, which at first, like that of the sea, pleases by its extent, but soon, like that too, fatigues from its uniformity; a calm and a storm being the only variations that the nature of either will admit.

Of Mr. Johnson's erudition the world has been the judge, and we who produce each a score of his sayings, as proofs of that wit which in him was inexhaustible, resemble travellers who having visited Delhi or Golconda, bring home each a handful of Oriental pearl to evince the riches of the Great Mogul.[2] May the Public condescend to accept my *ill-strung* selection with patience at least, remembering only that they are relics of him who was great on all occasions, and, like a cube in architecture, you beheld him on each side, and his size still appeared undiminished.

FROM ANECDOTES OF THE LATE SAMUEL JOHNSON
[1] *period* sentence.

[2] *the Great Mogul* meaning Akbhar the Great, seventeenth-century ruler of the Mogul empire; at *Golconda*, in the south, was found the largest diamond in India (787 carats).

As his purse was ever open to almsgiving, so was his heart tender to those who wanted relief, and his soul susceptible of gratitude, and of every kind impression: yet though he had refined his sensibility, he had not endangered his quiet, by encouraging in himself a solicitude about trifles, which he treated with the contempt they deserve.

It was well enough known before these sheets were published, that Mr. Johnson had a roughness in his manner which subdued the saucy, and terrified the meek: this was, when I knew him, the prominent part of a character which few durst venture to approach so nearly; and which was for that reason in many respects grossly and frequently mistaken, and it was perhaps peculiar to him, that the lofty consciousness of his own superiority, which animated his looks, and raised his voice in conversation, cast likewise an impenetrable veil over him when he said nothing. His talk therefore had commonly the complexion of arrogance, his silence of superciliousness. He was however seldom inclined to be silent when any moral or literary question was started: and it was on such occasions, that, like the sage in *Rasselas*,[3] he spoke and attention watched his lips; he reasoned, and conviction closed his periods: if poetry was talked of, his quotations were the readiest; and had he not been eminent for more solid and brilliant qualities, mankind would have united to extol his extraordinary memory. His manner of repeating deserves to be described, though at the same time it defeats all power of description; but whoever once heard him repeat an ode of Horace, would be long before they could endure to hear it repeated by another.

His equity in giving the character of living acquaintance ought not undoubtedly to be omitted in his own, whence partiality and prejudice were totally excluded, and truth alone presided in his tongue: a steadiness of conduct the more to be commended, as no man had stronger liking or aversions. His veracity was indeed, from the most trivial to the most solemn occasions, strict, even to severity; he scorned to embellish a story with fictitious circumstances, which (he used to say) took off from its real value. 'A story', says Johnson, 'should be a specimen of life and manners, but if the surrounding circumstances are false, as it is no more a representation of reality, it is no longer worthy our attention'.

For the rest – That beneficence which during his life increased the comforts of so many, may after his death be perhaps ungratefully forgotten; but that piety which dictated the serious papers in the *Rambler*, will be for ever remembered; for ever, I think, revered. That ample repository of religious truth, moral wisdom, and accurate criticism, breathes indeed the genuine emanations of its great Author's mind, expressed too in a style so natural to him, and so much like his common mode of conversing, that I was myself but little astonished when he told me, that he had scarcely read over one of those inimitable essays before they went to the press.

I will add one or two peculiarities more, before I lay down my pen.——Though at an immeasurable distance from content in the contemplation of his own uncouth form and figure, he did not like another man much the less for being a coxcomb. I mentioned two friends who were particularly fond of looking at themselves in a glass – 'They do not surprise me at all by so doing' said Johnson, 'they see, reflected in that glass, men who have risen from almost the lowest situations in life; one to enormous riches, the other to every thing this world can give – rank, fame, and fortune. They see likewise, men who have merited their advancement by the exertion and improvement of those talents which God had given them; and I see not why they should avoid the mirror'.

---

[3] *the sage in Rasselas*   see Johnson, *Rasselas*, chapter 18, above.

The other singularity I promised to record, is this: That though a man of obscure birth himself, his partiality to people of family was visible on every occasion; his zeal for subordination warm even to bigotry; his hatred to innovation, and reverence for the old feudal times, apparent, whenever any possible manner of showing them occurred. I have spoken of his piety, his charity, and his truth, the enlargement of his heart, and the delicacy of his sentiments; and when I search for shadow to my portrait, none can I find but what was formed by pride, differently modified as different occasions showed it; yet never was pride so purified as Johnson's, at once from meanness and from vanity. The mind of this man was indeed expanded beyond the common limits of human nature, and stored with such variety of knowledge, that I used to think it resembled a royal pleasure-ground, where every plant, of every name and nation, flourished in the full perfection of their powers, and where, though lofty woods and falling cataracts first caught the eye, and fixed the earliest attention of beholders, yet neither the trim parterre nor the pleasing shrubbery, nor even the antiquated ever-greens, were denied a place in some fit corner of the happy valley.

from Correspondence with Samuel Johnson (1773–5)

Saturday 29 May '73
from Johnson

Madam

My eye is yet so dark that I could not read your note. I have had a poor darkling week. But the dear Lady[1] is worse. My eye is easier and bears light better, but sees little. I wish you could fetch me on Wednesday. I long to be in my own room. Have you got your key? I hope I shall not add much to your trouble, and will wish at least to give you some little solace or amusement. I long to be under your care.

I am, Madam, your most &c.

Sam: Johnson

Streatham[2].

What care can I promise my dear Mr. Johnson that I have not already taken? what Tenderness that he has not already experienced? yet is it a very gloomy reflection that so much of bad prevails in our best enjoyments, and embitters the purest friendship. You were saying but on Sunday that of all the unhappy you was the happiest, in consequence of my Attention to your Complaint; and to day I have been reproached by you for neglect, and by myself for exciting that generous Confidence which prompts you to repose all Care on me, and tempts you to neglect yourself, and brood in secret upon an Idea hateful in itself, but which your kind partiality to me has unhappily rendered pleasing. If it be possible, shake off these uneasy Weights, heavier to the Mind by far than Fetters to the body. Let not your fancy dwell thus upon Confinement and Severity. I am sorry you are obliged to be so much alone; I foresaw some ill Consequences of your being here while my Mother was dying thus; yet could not resist the temptation of having you near me, but if you find this irksome and dangerous Idea fasten upon your fancy, leave me to struggle with the loss of one Friend, and let me not put to hazard what I esteem beyond Kingdoms, and value beyond the possession of them.

If we go on together your Confinement shall be as strict as possible except when Company comes in, which I shall more willingly endure on your Account.

FROM CORRESPONDENCE WITH SAMUEL JOHNSON
[1] *dear Lady* Hester Thrale's mother.

[2] *Streatham* where the Thrales lived in suburban London.

Dissipation is to you a glorious Medicine, and I believe Mr. Boswell[3] will be at last your best Physician, for the rest you really are well enough now if you will keep so; and not suffer the noblest of human Minds to be tortured with fantastic notions which rob it of all its Quiet. I will detain you no longer, so farewell and be good; and do not quarrel with your Governess for not using the Rod enough. – H:L:T.

8 July 1775
My Dear Sir

This poor unfortunate Child[4] will die at last. The Matter which discharged from his Ear was it seems a temporary Relief, but that was all over when I came down & the Stupor was returned in a most alarming Manner: he has however violent fits of rage – proceeding from Pain I guess – just as Lucy & Miss Anna[5] had – Kipping[6] says the Brain is oppressed of which I have no doubt. What shall I do? What can I do? has the flattery of my Friends made me too proud of my own Brains? & must these poor Children suffer for my Crime? I can neither go on with this Subject nor quit it. – I have heard no more of Mr. Thrale's Intentions about my Estate &c. & you know I am not inquisitive. He spends whole Hours with Scrase[7] engaged in some Business – he does not tell me what. I opened the Ball last Night – tonight I go to the Play: Oh that there was a Play or a Ball for every hour of the four & twenty.

Adieu! my head & my heart are so full I forgot to say how glad I shall be to see you. as I am with the truest Regard

Sir Your most faithful Servant H: L: Thrale

Streatham Saturday 9 July [1775]
Dear Sir

I came home very late last Night and found your sweet Letters all three lying on the Table: I would not have come home at all but Mr. Thrale insisted on it – so I have left this poor Child to die at Brighthelmstone. Doctor Pepys says he will write every Post & Kipping too. What signifies their writing? What signifies anything? the Child will die & I fear in sad Torments too – he is now exactly as Lucy was. The discharge at the Ear stopping on a sudden, they bathed him exactly as you would have bid them youself – by Bromfield's advice indeed but all to no purpose: they are now blistering away about the Ear, Head & Neck, & if he should give them time to do all they intend he will have a Fontanelle cut in his Arm.[8]

Now it is not the Death of this Boy that affects me so; he is very young, & had he lived would probably have been a greater Misfortune to me: but it is the horrible Apprehension of losing the others by the same cruel Disease that haunts my affrighted Imagination & makes me look upon them with an Anxiety scarce to be endured. If Hetty tells me that her Head aches, I am more shocked than if I heard She had broken her Leg.

Poor old Captain Conway is dead. Carter[9] is dolorous still: the Horse is in Weston's Possession at present, nobody would bid above five pounds for him, so Mr. Weston was forced to take him back: as he is now at the Expense of keeping him I will not buy him to ease

3   *Boswell* Johnson and Boswell were about to take their celebrated trip to Scotland.

4   *Child* Ralph, the Thrale's two-year-old.

5   *Lucy & Miss Anna* Lucy died earlier in the year, at the age of four; Anna died at the age of two in 1770.

6   *Kipping* Henry (1726–85), a surgeon and apothecary in Brighton near the Thrale's estate in Brighthelmstone.

7   *Scrase* Charles (1707–92), family lawyer; he was working out the details so that Hester would have the clear, personal disposal of her family's Welsh estate.

8   *Fontanelle* a surgically imposed discharge of fluid from the body; Ralph and several other of the Thrales' children seem to have had some kind of congenital hydrocephalus.

9   *Carter* Charles, Hester Thrale's riding master.

Weston's Pocket & empty my own, but whenever he is going to be parted with I shall step in & save him for Carter . . .

When we came home last Night here to Streatham, the first Man I saw was Perkins;[10] my Spirits were already low, & I feared there was some sad News from London; but it was only a Story about that Crossby who broke[11] in our Debt last Winter, & who has some concerns at Derby – you may remember Avis saying he was struck dumb or stupid or something about it. I warrant you recollect his Expression which I have forgotten. Pray tell me if your Relation Mr. Flint has all his Children alive? there was a sweet little Girl among them very like my poor Lucy – & afflicted with Headaches: do enquire whether She be living or no: I took an Interest in her from the Resemblance, & was not without many Apprehensions for her Life. I have forgotten her name if it was not Lucy – I think it was.

I am ever Sir Your most faithful Servant H L T

Anna Laetitia Aiken Barbauld (1743–1825)

Barbauld learned to read so quickly and mastered French so easily that her father reluctantly agreed to let her go on to Latin and Greek. In the company of her father's pupils and colleagues at a college for dissenters at Warrington, Barbauld grew learned and began writing poetry. She published her first volume in 1773. The next year she married and helped her husband establish a boys school for dissenters. After her husband's death in 1808, she became much more active as a writer and as an editor. One of her projects was an edition of The British Novelists *in fifty volumes. Another was an anthology of passages of English literature for women called* The Female Speaker. *She also edited the letters of Richardson, prepared several books for children's reading, and wrote more poems, including an epistle to the great abolitionist William Wilberforce. "The Mouse's Petition" and "Verses Written in an Alcove" are based on the versions published in* Poems *(1792). "Washing-Day" comes from the* Monthly Magazine, *December 1797.*

from *Poems* (1792)

THE MOUSE'S PETITION[1]

Parcere subjectis, & debellare superbos.
VIRGIL[2]

Oh! hear a pensive prisoner's prayer,
For liberty that sighs;
And never let thine heart be shut
Against the wretch's cries.

For here forlorn and sad I sit,   5
Within the wiry grate;[3]

---

[10] *Perkins* John, chief clerk of the Thrale brewery.
[11] *broke* went bankrupt.
THE MOUSE'S PETITION
[1] *The Mouse's Petition* Found in the trap where he had been confined all night by Dr. [Joseph] Priestly, for the

sake of making experiments with different kinds of air [Barbauld's note].
[2] *Parcere . . . Virgil* "to spare the downtrodden and do battle with the proud" (*Aeneid* 8.653).
[3] *grate* barred walls of a prison.

And tremble at th' approaching morn,
Which brings impending fate.

If e'er thy breast with freedom glowed,
And spurned a tyrant's chain,   10
Let not thy strong oppressive force
A free-born mouse detain.

Oh! do not stain with guiltless blood
Thy hospitable hearth;
Nor triumph that thy wiles betrayed   15
A prize so little worth.

The scattered gleanings of a feast
My frugal meals supply;
But if thine unrelenting heart
That slender boon deny,   20

The cheerful light, the vital air,
Are blessings widely given;
Let nature's commoners enjoy
The common gifts of heaven.

The well-taught philosophic mind   25
To all compassion gives;
Casts round the world an equal eye,
And feels for all that lives.

If mind, as ancient sages taught,
A never dying flame,   30
Still shifts through matter's varying forms,
In every form the same,

Beware, lest in the worm you crush
A brother's soul you find;
And tremble lest thy luckless hand   35
Dislodge a kindred mind.

Or, if this transient gleam of day
Be *all* of life we share,
Let pity plead within thy breast
That little *all* to spare.   40

So may thy hospitable board
With health and peace be crowned;
And every charm of heartfelt ease
Beneath thy roof be found.

So, when destruction lurks unseen,   45
Which men, like mice, may share,
May some kind angel clear thy path,
And break the hidden snare.

VERSES WRITTEN IN AN ALCOVE

Jam Cytherea choros ducit Venus imminente Luna.
HORAT.[1]

Now the moon-beam's trembling lustre
　　Silvers o'er the dewy green,
And in lost and shadowy colours
　　Sweetly paints the chequered fence.

Here between the opening branches　　　　　　　　　5
　　Streams a flood of softened light,
There the thick and twisted foliage
　　Spreads the browner gloom of night.

This is sure the haunt of fairies,
　　In yon cool alcove they play;　　　　　　　　　10
Care can never cross the threshold,
　　Care was only made for day.

Far from hence be noisy clamour,
　　Sick disgust and anxious fear;
Pining grief and wasting anguish　　　　　　　　　15
　　Never keep their vigils here.

Tell no tales of sheeted spectres
　　Rising from the quiet tomb;
Fairer forms this cell shall visit,
　　Brighter visions gild the gloom.　　　　　　　　20

Choral songs and sprightly voices
　　Echo from her cell shall call;
Sweeter, sweeter than the murmur
　　Of the distant water-fall.

Every ruder gust of passion　　　　　　　　　　　25
　　Lulled with music dies away,
Till within the charmèd bosom
　　None but soft affections play:

Soft, as when the evening breezes
　　Gently stir the poplar grove;　　　　　　　　　30
Brighter than the smile of summer,
　　Sweeter than the breath of love.

Thee, th' enchanted Muse shall follow,
　　LISSY! to the rustic cell,
And each careless note repeating　　　　　　　　　35
　　Tune them to her charming shell.[2]

VERSES WRITTEN IN AN ALCOVE
[1] *Jam Cytherea . . . Horat.* "Already Cytherean Venus
leads her chorus beneath the neighbouring Moon"
(Horace, *Odes* 1.4.5).

[2] *shell* a poetic name for the lyre, an instrument originally strung on tortoise shells.

Not the Muse who wreathed with laurel[3]
   Solemn stalks with tragic gait,
And in clear and lofty vision
   Sees the future births of fate;   40

Not the maid who crowned with cypress[4]
   Sweeps along in sceptered pall,
And in sad and solemn accents
   Mourns the crested hero's fall;

But that other smiling sister,[5]   45
   With the blue and laughing eye,
Singing, in a lighter measure,
   Strains of woodland harmony:

All unknown to fame and glory,
   Easy, blithe and debonair,   50
Crowned with flowers, her careless tresses
   Loosely floating on the air.

Then, when next the star of evening
   Softly sheds the silent dew,
Let me in this rustic temple,   55
   LISSY! meet the Muse and you.

from the *Monthly Magazine* (1797)

WASHING-DAY

——— *and their voice,*
Turning again towards childish treble, pipes
And whistles in its sound. —[1]

The Muses are turned gossips; they have lost
Their buskined step, and clear high-sounding phrase,[2]
Language of gods. Come, then, domestic Muse,
In slip-shod measure loosely prattling on
Of farm and orchard, pleasant curds and cream,   5
Or drowning flies, or shoe lost in the mire
By little whimpering boy, with rueful face;
Come, Muse, and sing the dreaded *Washing-Day*.
– Ye who beneath the yoke of wedlock bend,
With bowèd soul, full well ye ken the day   10
Which week, smooth sliding after week, brings on
Too soon; for to that day nor peace belongs

---

[3] *Muse . . . laurel* perhaps Calliope, muse of epic poetry, or one of the three graces.
[4] *maid . . . cypress* perhaps Melpomene, the muse of tragedy.
[5] *smiling sister* perhaps Erato, muse of lyric and love poetry.

WASHING-DAY
[1] *and their voice . . . sound* As You Like It 2.7.161–3, with some changes.
[2] *buskined* shod in the elevated sandals worn in performances of classical Greek tragedy to indicate the great stature of the characters.

Nor comfort; ere the first grey streak of dawn,[3]
The red-armed washers come and chase repose.
Nor pleasant smile, nor quaint device of mirth,   15
E'er visited that day; the very cat,
From the wet kitchen scared, and reeking hearth,
Visits the parlour, and unwonted guest.
The silent breakfast-meal is soon dispatched
Uninterrupted, save by anxious looks   20
Cast at the lowering sky, if sky should lower,
From that last evil, oh preserve us, heavens!
For should the skies pour down, adieu to all
Remains of quiet; then expect to hear
Of sad disasters – dirt and gravel stains   25
Hard to efface, and loaded lines at once
Snapped short – and linen-horse by dog thrown down,
And all the petty miseries of life.
Saints have been calm while stretched upon the rack,
And Montezuma smil'd on burning coals;[4]   30
But never yet did housewife notable
Greet with a smile a rainy washing-day.
– But grant the welkin fair, require not thou
Who call'st thyself perchance the master there,
Or study swept, or nicely dusted coat,[5]   35
Or usual 'tendance; ask not, indiscreet,
Thy stockings mended, though the yawning rents
Gape wide as Erebus, nor hope to find[6]
Some snug recess impervious; should'st thou try
The customed garden walks, thine eye shall rue   40
The budding fragrance of thy tender shrubs,
Myrtle or rose, all crushed beneath the weight
Of coarse checked apron, with impatient hand
Twitched off when showers impend: or crossing lines
Shall mar thy musings, as the wet cold sheet   45
Flaps in thy face abrupt. Woe to the friend
Whose evil stars have urged him forth to claim
On such a day the hospitable rites;
Looks, blank at best, and stinted courtesy,
Shall he receive; vainly he feeds his hopes   50
With dinner of roast chicken, savoury pie,
Or tart or pudding: – pudding he nor tart
That day shall eat; nor, though the husband try,
Mending what can't be helped, to kindle mirth
From cheer deficient, shall his consort's brow   55

---

[3] *nor . . . nor* neither . . . nor.
[4] *Montezuma* in later editions, corrected to Guatimozin, a name for Cuauhtémoc, who became the last emperor of the Aztecs in 1520 on the death of Montezuma II's successor; he stoically resisted the tortures imposed on him by Cortés, the conqueror of his people.
[5] *Or . . . or* either . . . or.
[6] *Erebus* a place of darkness forming a passage from earth to Hades in classical mythology.

Clear up propitious; the unlucky guest
In silence dines, and early slinks away.
    I well remember, when a child, the awe
This day struck into me; for then the maids,
I scarce knew why, looked cross, and drove me from them;   60
Nor soft caress could I obtain, nor hope
Usual indulgencies; jelly or creams,
Relic of costly suppers, and set by
For me their petted one; or buttered toast,
When butter was forbid; or thrilling tale   65
Of ghost, or witch, or murder – so I went
And sheltered me beside the parlour fire,
There my dear grandmother, eldest of forms,
Tended the little ones, and watched from harm,
Anxiously fond, though oft her spectacles   70
With elfin cunning hid, and oft the pins
Drawn from her ravelled stockings, might have soured
One less indulgent –
At intervals my mother's voice was heard,
Urging dispatch; briskly the work went on,   75
All hands employed to wash, to rinse, to wring,
To fold, and starch, and clap, and iron, and plait.
Then would I sit me down, and ponder much
Why washings were. Sometimes through hollow bowl
Of pipe amused we blew, and sent aloft   80
The floating bubbles, little dreaming then
To see, Mongolfier, thy silken ball[7]
Ride buoyant through the clouds – so near approach
The sports of children and the toils of men.
Earth, air, and sky, and ocean, hath its bubbles,[8]   85
And verse is one of them – this most of all.

Olaudah Equiano (1745?–1797)

Sold into slavery and taken from his native Nigerian home at the age of twelve, Equiano became one of the most widely travelled men of his time. After very brief stays in Virginia and the West Indies, he was sold to the owner of a trading ship who named him Gustavus Vassa. The name, which belonged to the sixteenth-century liberator of the Swedes, may have been meant as an ironical comment on Equiano's color, but it came to be somewhat prophetic because Equiano became one of the most powerful eighteenth-century spokesmen for the abolition of slavery. He first went to England in 1757 and was baptised there in 1759. Throughout the Seven Years War (1756–63) he served in the navy and saw action in the Mediterranean and in North America. In 1763 he went to the

---

[7] *Mongolfier* Joseph-Michel (1740–1810) and his brother Jacques-Étienne (1745–1799), inventors of manned balloon flight.

[8] *bubbles* echoes *Macbeth* 1.3.79, where Banquo describes the weird sisters as bubbles from the earth, but also means anything worthless or insubstantial.

West Indies in the possession of a Quaker plantation owner. Partly through this man's protection, he was able to save the money required to buy his freedom (£40), and he became a free man in 1766. He then signed on for voyages to Turkey, the West Indies, and one to the Arctic.

In 1779 Equiano settled in London where he spent most of the rest of his life. He held various posts including Commissary of Provisions for those going to the new free colony in Sierra Leone, established for blacks discharged from the army after the Revolutionary War and former slaves who had sought asylum in England. Equiano published his autobiography in 1789, and it was successful enough to run to eight editions in his lifetime (seven in England and one in America). The book indicts slavery for its cruelty, its inhumanity, its sinfulness, and also its impracticality. Equiano is not only interested in what is fair but also in what will work for the economy of his country and his people. He also anchors his arguments in an intellectual and literary tradition that includes classical aphorisms, the Bible, Hobbes, and Milton. Equiano is very far from rejecting western tradition in his arguments against slavery; in fact, he warmly embraces many liberal elements of that tradition. He styled himself an African in presenting a petition to the Queen "on behalf of his brethren," but England (where he finally married in 1792) was his home.

The text presented here is based on the first American edition (New York, 1791) with some minor corrections from other editions. The whole work is available in Classic Slave Narratives, *edited by Henry Louis Gates, Jr (Penguin, 1987).*

from *The Interesting Narrative of the Life of Olaudah Equiano, or Gustavus Vassa, the African* (1789)

CHAPTER 5

The author's reflections on his situation – Is deceived by a promise of being delivered – His despair at sailing for the West-Indies – Arrives at Montserrat, where he is sold to Mr. King – Various interesting instances of oppression, cruelty, and extortion, which the author saw practised upon the slaves in the West-Indies during his captivity, from the year 1763 to 1766 – Address on it to the Planters.

Thus, at the moment I expected all my toils to end, was I plunged, as I supposed, in a new slavery;[1] in comparison of which all my service hitherto had been perfect freedom; and whose horrors, always present to my mind, now rushed on it with tenfold aggravation. I wept very bitterly for some time; and began to think that I must have done something to displease the Lord, that he thus punished me so severely. This filled me with painful reflections on my past conduct. I recollected that, on the morning of our arrival at Deptford, I had very rashly sworn that as soon as we reached London, I would spend the day in rambling and sport. My conscience smote me for this unguarded expression: I felt that the Lord was able to disappoint me in all things, and immediately considered my present situation as a judgement of Heaven, on account of my presumption in swearing. I therefore, with contrition of heart, acknowledged my transgression to God, and poured out my soul before Him with unfeigned repentance, and with earnest supplications I besought Him not to abandon me in my distress, nor cast me from his mercy for ever. In a little time my grief, spent with its own violence,

---

CHAPTER 5
[1] *at the moment . . . a new slavery* after returning to England from fighting, as a slave, in the Mediterranean theatre of the Seven Years War, Equiano had hoped to disembark and escape in London with the help of his shipmates, but he was sold again and taken off to Portsmouth by a new master.

began to subside; and after the first confusion of my thoughts was over, I reflected with more calmness on my present condition. I considered that trials and disappointments are sometimes for our good; and I thought God might perhaps have permitted this, in order to teach me wisdom and resignation. For he had hitherto shadowed me with the wings of his mercy and by his invisible, but powerful hand, had brought me the way I knew not. These reflections gave me a little comfort, and I arose at last from the deck with dejection and sorrow in my countenance, yet mixed with some faint hope that the *Lord would appear* for my deliverance.

Soon afterwards, as my new master was going on shore, he called me to him, and told me to behave myself well, and do the business of the ship the same as any of the rest of the boys, and that I should fare the better for it; but I made him no answer. I was then asked if I could swim, and I said, 'No'. However, I was made to go under the deck, and was carefully watched. The next tide the ship got under way, and soon arrived at the Mother Bank, Portsmouth; where she waited a few days for some of the West-India convoy. While here I tried every means I could devise amongst the people of the ship to get me a boat from the shore, as there was none suffered to come alongside of the ship; and their own, whenever it was used, was hoisted in again immediately. A sailor on board took a guinea from me, on pretence of getting me a boat; and promised me, time after time, that it was hourly to come off. When he had the watch upon deck I watched also, and looked long enough, but all in vain; I could never see either the boat or my guinea again. And, what I thought was still the worst of all, the fellow gave information, as I afterwards found, all the while to the mates of my intention to go off if possible; but, rogue-like, he never told them he had got a guinea from me to procure my escape. However, after we had sailed, and his trick was made known to the ship's crew, I had some satisfaction in seeing him detested and despised by them all for his behaviour to me.

I was still in hopes that my old shipmates would not forget their promise to come for me to Portsmouth; and, indeed, at last, but not till the day before we sailed, some of them did come there, and sent me off some oranges, and other tokens of their regard. They also sent me word they would come off to me themselves the next day, or the day after: and a lady also who lived in Gosport, wrote to me that she would come and take me out of the ship at the same time. This lady had been once very intimate with my former master. I used to sell and take care of a great deal of property for her, in different ships; and in return she always showed great friendship for me, and used to tell my master she would take me away to live with her. But, unfortunately for me, a disagreement soon afterwards took place between them; and she was succeeded in my master's good graces by another lady, who appeared sole mistress of the Ætna, and mostly lodged on board. I was not so great a favourite with this lady as with the former; she had conceived a pique against me, on some occasion when she was on board, and she did not fail to instigate my master to treat me in the manner he did.[2]

However, the next morning, the 30th of December, the wind being brisk and easterly, the Æolus frigate, which was to escort the convoy, made a signal for sailing. All the ships then got up their anchors; and before any of my friends had an opportunity to come off to my relief, to my inexpressible anguish, our ship had got under way. What tumultuous emotions agitated my soul when the convoy got under sail, and I a prisoner on board, now without

---

[2] *she did not fail to instigate my master to treat me in the manner he did* Thus was I sacrificed to the envy and resentment of this woman, for knowing that the other lady designed to take me into her service; which, had I once got on shore, she would not have been able to prevent. She felt her pride alarmed at the superiority of her rival in being attended by a black servant: it was not less to prevent this, than to be revenged on me, that she caused the captain to treat me thus cruelly [Equiano's note].

hope! I kept my swimming eyes upon the land in a state of unutterable grief; not knowing what to do, and despairing how to help myself. While my mind was in this situation, the fleet sailed on, and in one day's time I lost sight of the wished-for land. In the first expressions of my grief, I reproached my fate, and wished I had never been born. I was ready to curse the tide that bore us; the gale[3] that wafted my prison, and even the ship that conducted us; and, in the despair of the moment, I called on death to relieve me from the horrors I felt and dreaded, that I might be in that place –

> Where slaves are free, and men oppress no more.
> Fool that I was, inured so long to pain,
> To trust to hope, or dream of joy again!
> *   *   *   *   *   *   *
> Now dragged once more beyond the western main,
> To groan beneath some dastard planter's chain;
> Where my poor countrymen in bondage wait
> The long enfranchisément of ling'ring fate:
> Hard ling'ring fate! while, ere the dawn of day,
> Roused by the lash they go their cheerless way;
> And as their souls with shame and anguish burn,
> Salute with groans unwelcome morn's return,
> And, chiding every hour the slow-paced sun,
> Pursue their toils till all his race is run.
> No eye to mark their suff'rings with a tear;
> No friend to comfort, and no hope to cheer:
> Then, like the dull unpitied brutes, repair
> To stalls as wretched, and as coarse a fare;
> Thank heaven one day of mis'ry was o'er,
> Then sink to sleep, and wish to wake no more.[4]

The turbulence of my emotions, however, naturally gave way to calmer thoughts, and I soon perceived what fate had decreed no mortal on earth could prevent. The convoy sailed on without any accident, with a pleasant gale and smooth sea, for six weeks, till February, when one morning the Æolus ran down a brig, one of the convoy, and she instantly went down and was engulfed in the dark recesses of the ocean. The convoy was immediately thrown into great confusion till it was day-light; and the Æolus illuminated with lights to prevent further mischief. On the 13th of February 1763, from the mast-head, we descried our destined island, Montserrat,[5] and soon after I beheld those

> Regions of sorrow, doleful shades, where peace
> And rest can rarely dwell. Hope never comes

---

[3] *gale* "A wind not tempestuous, but stronger than a breeze" (Johnson).

[4] *Where slaves are free . . . wake no more* "The Dying Negro," a poem originally published in 1773. Published anonymously but written by Thomas Day and John Bicknall. Perhaps it may not be deemed impertinent here to add, that this elegant and pathetic little poem, was occasioned by the following incident, as appears from the advertisement prefixed to it: – "A black who, a few days before, had run away from his master, and got himself christened, with intent to marry a white woman, his fellow-servant, being taken and sent on board a ship in the Thames, took an opportunity of shooting himself through the head."

[5] *Montserrat* in the West Indies, near Antigua.

> That comes to all; but torture without end
> Still urges . . .[6]

At the sight of this land of bondage, a fresh horror ran through all my frame, and chilled me to the heart. My former slavery now rose in dreadful review to my mind, and displayed nothing but misery, stripes, and chains; and in the first paroxysm of my grief, I called upon God's thunder, and his avenging power, to direct the stroke of death to me, rather than permit me to become a slave, and to be sold from lord to lord.

In this state of my mind our ship came to an anchor, and soon after discharged her cargo. I now knew what it was to work hard; I was made to help to unload and load the ship. And to comfort me in my distress, at that time two of the sailors robbed me of all my money, and ran away from the ship. I had been so long used to an European climate, that at first I felt the scorching West-India sun very painful, while the dashing surf would toss the boat and the people in it, frequently above high-water-mark. Sometimes our limbs were broken with this, or even attended with instant death, and I was day by day mangled and torn.

About the middle of May, when the ship was got ready to sail for England, I all the time believing that fate's blackest clouds were gathering over my head, and expecting that their bursting would mix me with the dead, Captain Doran sent for me on shore one morning; and I was told by the messenger that my fate was determined. With trembling steps and a fluttering heart I came to the captain, and found with him one Mr. Robert King, a quaker, and the first merchant in the place. The captain then told me my former master had sent me there to be sold; but that he desired him to get me the best master he could, as he told him I was a very deserving boy, which Captain Doran said he found to be true, and if he were to stay in the West-Indies he would be glad to keep me himself; but he could not venture to take me to London, for he was very sure that when I came there, I would leave him. I at that instant burst out a crying, and begged much of him to take me with him to England, but all to no purpose. He told me he had got me the very best master in the whole island, with whom I should be as happy as if I were in England, and for that reason he chose to let him have me, though he could sell me to his own brother-in-law for a great deal more money than what he got from that gentleman. My new master, Mr. King, then made a reply, and said that the reason he had bought me was on account of my good character; and, as I understood something of the rules of arithmetic, when we got there he would put me to school, and fit me for a clerk. This conversation relieved my mind a little, and I left those gentlemen considerably more at ease in myself than when I came to them; and I was very thankful to Captain Doran, and even to my old master, for the character[7] they had given me; a character which I afterwards found of infinite service to me.

I went on board again, and took leave of all my shipmates, and the next day the ship sailed. When she weighed anchor I went to the waterside, and looked at her with a very wishful and aching heart, following her with my eyes until she was totally out of sight. I was so bowed down with grief, that I could not hold up my head for many months; and if my new master had not been kind to me, I believe I should have died under it at last. And indeed I soon found that he fully deserved the good character which Capt. Doran had given me of him; for he possessed a most amiable disposition and temper, and was very charitable and humane. If any of his slaves behaved amiss, he did not beat them or use them ill, but parted with them. This made them afraid of disobliging him; and as he treated his slaves better than any other man

---

6. *Regions of sorrow . . . urges* *Paradise Lost* 1.65–8 imperfectly recalled.

7. *character* "A representation of any man as to his personal qualities" (Johnson).

on the island, so he was better and more faithfully served by them in return. By this kind treatment I did at last endeavour to compose myself; and with fortitude, though moneyless, determined to face whatever fate had decreed for me, Mr. King soon asked me what I could do; and at the same time said he did not mean to treat me as a common slave. I told him I knew something of seamanship, and could shave and dress hair pretty well; I could refine wines, which I had learned on shipboard, where I had often done it; and that I could write, and understood arithmetic tolerably well as far as the Rule of Three.[8] He then asked me if I knew any thing of gauging;[9] and, on my answering that I did not, he said one of his clerks should teach me to gauge.

Mr. King dealt in all manner of merchandize, and kept from one to six clerks. He loaded many vessels in a year, particularly to Philadelphia, where he was born, and was connected with a great mercantile house in that city. He had besides many vessels and doggers,[10] of different sizes, which used to go about the island; and others to collect rum, sugar, and other goods. I understood pulling[11] and managing those boats very well; and this hard work, which was the first that he set me to, in the sugar seasons used to be my constant employment. I have rowed the boat and slaved at the oars, from one hour to sixteen in the twenty-four; during which I had fifteen pence sterling per day to live on, though sometimes only ten pence. However, this was much more than was allowed to other slaves that used to work often with me, and belonged to other gentlemen on the island: these poor souls had never more than ninepence a day, and seldom more than sixpence, from their masters or owners, though they earned them three or four pisterines.[12] For it is a common practice in the West-Indies for men to purchase slaves, though they have not plantations themselves, in order to let them out to planters and merchants, at so much a piece by the day, and they give what they choose, out of this produce of their daily work, to their slaves for subsistence. This allowance is often very scanty.

My master often gave the owners of these slaves two and a half of these pieces per day, and found the poor fellows in victuals[13] himself, because he thought their owners did not feed them well enough, according to the work they did. The slaves used to like this very well; and, as they knew my master to be a man of feeling,[14] they were always glad to work for him in preference to any other gentleman; some of whom, after they had been paid for these poor people's labours, would not give them their allowance out of it. Many times have I seen these unfortunate wretches beaten for asking for their pay; and often severely flogged by their owners, if they did not bring them their daily or weekly money exactly to the time; though the poor creatures were obliged to wait on the gentlemen they had worked for, sometimes more than half the day before they could get their pay, and this generally on Sundays, when they wanted the time for themselves. In particular, I knew a countryman of mine, who once did not bring the weekly money directly that it was earned; and though he brought it the same day to his master, yet he was staked to the ground for his pretended negligence, and was just going to receive a hundred lashes, but for a gentleman who begged him off[15] fifty.

This poor man was very industrious, and by his frugality had saved so much money, by

---

[8]   *Rule of Three*   a method of finding a fourth number when three numbers are known, and the first two are in a proportion equal to that between the third known and the unknown number.

[9]   *gauging*   measuring the contents of barrels and other containers.

[10]   *dogger*   "A small ship with one mast" (Johnson).

[11]   *pulling*   rowing.

[12]   *pisterines*   These pisterines are of the value of a shilling [Equiano's note].

[13]   *found . . . in victuals*   supplied them with food (*OED, find*, sense 19).

[14]   *a man of feeling*   a sensitive person (see the selection from Mackenzie below).

[15]   *begged him off*   successfully pleaded for a reduced sentence.

working on shipboard, that he had got a white man to buy him a boat, unknown to his master. Some time after he had this little estate, the governor wanted a boat to bring his sugar from different parts of the island; and, knowing this to be a negro-man's boat, he seized upon it for himself, and would not pay the owner a farthing. The man on this went to his master, and complained to him of this act of the governor; but the only satisfaction he received was to be damned very heartily by his master, who asked him how he dared any of his negroes to have a boat. If the justly-merited ruin of the governor's fortune could be any gratification to the poor man he had thus robbed, he was not without consolation. Extortion and rapine are poor providers; and some time after this, the governor died in the King's Bench,[16] in England, as I was told, in great poverty. The last war favoured this poor negro-man, and he found some means to escape from his Christian master: he came to England, where I saw him afterwards several times. Such treatment as this often drives these miserable wretches to despair, and they run away from their masters at the hazard of their lives. Many of them, in this place, unable to get their pay when they have earned it, and fearing to be flogged, as usual, if they return home without it, run away where they can for shelter, and a reward is often offered to bring them in dead or alive. My master used sometimes, in these cases, to agree with their owners, and to settle with them himself; and thereby he saved many of them a flogging.

Once, for a few days, I was let out to fit a vessel, and I had no victuals allowed me by either party; at last I told my master of this treatment, and he took me away from it. In many of the estates, on the different islands where I used to be sent for rum or sugar, they would not deliver it to me, or to any other negro; he was therefore obliged to send a white man along with me to those places; and then he used to pay him from six to ten pisterines a day. From being thus employed, during the time I served Mr. King, in going about the different estates on the island, I had all the opportunity I could wish for to see the dreadful usage of the poor men – usage that reconciled me to my situation, and made me bless God for the hands into which I had fallen.

I had the good fortune to please my master in every department in which he employed me; and there was scarcely any part of his business, or household affairs, in which I was not occasionally engaged. I often supplied the place of a clerk, in receiving and delivering cargoes to the ships, in tending stores, and delivering goods; and, besides this, I used to shave and dress my master, when convenient, and take care of his horse; and when it was necessary, which was very often, I worked likewise on board of his different vessels. By these means I became very useful to my master, and saved him, as he used to acknowledge, above a hundred pounds a year. Nor did he scruple to say I was of more advantage to him than any of his clerks; though their usual wages in the West-Indies are from sixty to a hundred pounds current[17] in a year.

I have sometimes heard it asserted that a negro cannot earn his master the first cost; but nothing can be further from the truth. I suppose nine tenths of the mechanics[18] throughout the West-Indies are negro slaves; and I well know the coopers[19] among them earn two dollars a-day; the carpenters the same, and oftentimes more; also the masons, smiths, and fishermen, &c. and I have known many slaves whose masters would not take a thousand pounds current for them. But surely this assertion refutes itself: for, if it be true, why do the planters and merchants pay such a price for slaves? And, above all, why do those, who make this assertion, exclaim the most loudly against the abolition of the slave trade? So much are men blinded,

---

[16]   *King's Bench*   a debtors' prison in London.
[17]   *current*   in currency, cash.
[18]   *mechanic*   "a low workman" (Johnson).
[19]   *cooper*   barrel maker.

and to such inconsistent arguments are they driven by mistaken interest! I grant, indeed, that slaves are sometimes, by half-feeding, half-clothing, over-working, and stripes, reduced so low, that they are turned out as unfit for service, and left to perish in the woods, or to expire on a dunghill.

My master was several times offered by different gentlemen one hundred guineas for me; but he always told them he would not sell me, to my great joy: and I used to double my diligence and care for fear of getting into the hands of these men, who did not allow a valuable slave the common support of life. Many of them used to find fault with my master for feeding his slaves so well as he did; although I often went hungry, and an Englishman might think my fare very indifferent: but he used to tell them he always would do it, because the slaves thereby looked better and did more work.

While I was thus employed by my master, I was often a witness to cruelties of every kind, which were exercised on my unhappy fellow slaves. I used frequently to have different cargoes of new negroes in my care for sale; and it was almost a constant practice with our clerks, and other whites, to commit violent depradations on the chastity of the female slaves; and to these atrocities I was, though with reluctance, obliged to submit at all times, being unable to help them. When we have had some of these slaves on board my master's vessels to carry them to other islands, or to America, I have known our mates commit these acts most shamefully, to the disgrace not of Christians only, but of men. I have even known them gratify their brutal passions with females not ten years old; and these abominations some of them practised to such a scandalous excess, that one of our captains discharged the mate and others on that account. And yet in Montserrat I have seen a negro-man staked to the ground, and cut most shockingly, and then his ears cut off, bit by bit, because he had been connected with a white woman, who was a common prostitute! As if it were no crime in the whites to rob an innocent African girl of her virtue; but most heinous in a black man only to gratify a passion of nature, where the temptation was offered by one of a different colour, though the most abandoned woman of her species.

One Mr. D——, told me he had sold 41,000 negroes, and he once cut off a negro-man's leg for running away. I asked him if the man had died in the operation, how he, as a Christian, could answer, for the horrid act, before God. And he told me, answering was a thing of another world; what he thought and did were policy. I told him that the christian doctrine taught us 'to do unto others as we would that others should do unto us'. He then said that his scheme had the desired effect – it cured that man and some others of running away.

Another negro-man was half-hanged, and then burnt, for attempting to poison a cruel overseer. Thus, by repeated cruelties, are the wretched first urged to despair, and then murdered, because they still retain so much of human nature about them as to wish to put an end to their misery, and to retaliate on their tyrants! These overseers are, indeed, for the most part, persons of the worst character of any denomination of men in the West-Indies. Unfortunately, many humane gentlemen, by not residing on their estates, are obliged to leave the management of them in the hands of these human butchers, who cut and mangle the slaves in a shocking manner, on the most trivial occasions, and altogether treat them, in every respect, like brutes. They pay no regard to the situation of pregnant women, nor the least attention to the lodging of the field negroes. Their huts, which ought to be well covered, and the place where they take their short repose, are often open sheds, built in damp places; so that, when the poor creatures return tired from the toils of the field, they contract many disorders, from being exposed to the damp air in this uncomfortable state, while they are heated, and their pores are open.

The neglect certainly conspires with many others to cause a decrease in the births, as well as in the lives of the grown negroes. I can quote many instances of gentlemen who reside on their own estates in the West-Indies, and then the scene is quite changed; the negroes are treated with lenity and proper care, by which their lives are prolonged, and their masters profited. To the honour of humanity, I know several gentlemen who managed their estates in this manner, and found that benevolence was their true interest. And, among many[20] I could mention in Montserrat, whose slaves looked remarkably well, and never needed any fresh supplies of negroes (and there are many other estates, especially in Barbadoes, which, from such judicious treatment, need no fresh stock of negroes at any time) I have the honour of knowing a most worthy and humane gentleman,[21] who is a native of Barbadoes, and has estates there. This gentleman has written a treatise on the usage of his own slaves. He allows them two hours for refreshment at mid-day, and many other indulgences and comforts, particularly in their lying [in]; and besides this, he raises more provisions on his estate than they can destroy; so that by these attentions he saves the lives of his negroes, and keeps them healthy, and as happy as the condition of slavery can admit. I myself, as shall appear in the sequel, managed an estate, where, by such attentions, the negroes were uncommonly cheerful and healthy, and did more work by half than by the common mode of treatment they usually do. For want, therefore, of such care and attention to the poor negroes, and otherwise oppressed as they are, it is no wonder that the decrease should require 20,000 new negroes annually to fill up the vacant places of the dead.

Even in Barbadoes, notwithstanding those humane exceptions which I have mentioned and others with which I am acquainted that justly make it quoted as a place where slaves meet with the best treatment, and need fewest recruits of any in the West-Indies; yet this island requires 1,000 negroes annually to keep up the original stock, which is only 80,000. So that the whole term of a negro's life may be said to be there, but sixteen years! And yet the climate here is in every respect the same as that from which they are taken, except in being more wholesome. Do the British colonies decrease in this manner? And yet what a prodigious difference is there between an English and West-India climate?

While I was in Montserrat I knew a negro-man, one Emanuel Sankey, who endeavoured to escape from his miserable bondage, by concealing himself on board of a London ship. But fate did not favour the poor oppressed man; for, being discovered when the vessel was under sail, he was delivered up again to his master. This *Christian master* immediately pinned the wretch to the ground, at each wrist and ankle, and then took some sticks of sealing wax, lighted them, and dropped it all over his back. There was another master noted for cruelty: – I believe he had not a slave but had been cut, and pieces fairly taken out of the flesh: and after they had been punished thus, he used to make them get into a long wooden box, or case, he had for that purpose, and shut them up during pleasure. It was just about the height and breadth of a man; and the poor wretches had no room when in the case to move.

It was very common in several of the islands, particularly in St. Kitt's, for the slaves to be branded with the initial letters of their master's name, and a load of heavy iron hooks hung about their necks. Indeed on the most trivial occasions they were loaded with chains, and often instruments of torture were added. The iron muzzle, thumb-screws, &c. are so well known as not to need a description, and were sometimes applied for the slightest faults. I have seen a negro beaten till some of his bones were broken, for only letting a pot boil over. It is not uncommon, after a flogging, to make slaves go on their knees and thank their owners, and

---

[20] *many* Mr. Dubury and many others, in Montserrat [Equiano's note].

[21] *humane gentleman* Sir Philip Gibbes, Bart. Barbadoes [Equiano's note].

pray, or rather say, 'God bless you'. I have often asked many of the men slaves (who used to go several miles to their wives, and late in the night, after having been wearied with a hard day's labour) why they went so far for wives, and did not take them of their own master's negro-women, and particularly those who lived together as household slaves. Their answers have ever been – 'Because when the master or mistress choose to punish the women, they make the husbands flog their own wives, and that we could not bear to do'. Is it surprising such usage should drive the poor creatures to despair, and make them seek a refuge in death, from those evils which render their lives intolerable – while

> With shudd'ring horror pale, and eyes aghast,
> They view their lamentable lot, and find
> No rest?[22]

This they frequently do. A negro-man, on board a vessel of my master's, while I belonged to her, having been put in irons for some trifling misdemeanour, and kept in that state some days, being weary of life, took an opportunity of jumping overboard into the sea; however he was picked up without being drowned. Another, whose life was also a burden to him, resolved to starve himself to death, and refused to eat any victuals; this procured him a severe flogging; and he also on the first occasion that offered, jumped overboard at Charles Town, but was saved.

Nor is there any greater reward shown to the little property than there is to the persons and lives of the negroes. I have already related an instance or two of particular oppression, out of many which I have witnessed; but the following is frequent in all the islands: – The wretched field-slaves, after toiling all the day for an unfeeling owner, who gives them but little victuals, steal sometimes a few moments from rest or refreshment to gather some small portion of grass, according as their time will admit. This they commonly tie up in a parcel; either a bit's worth (sixpence) or half a bit's worth, and bring it to town, or to the market to sell. Nothing is more common than for the white people, on this occasion, to take the grass from them without paying for it; and not only so, but too often also, to my knowledge, our clerks and many others, at the same time have committed acts of violence on the poor, wretched, and helpless females; whom I have seen for hours stand crying to no purpose, and get no redress or pay of any kind. Is not this one common and crying sin enough to bring down God's judgement upon the islands? He tells us the oppressor and the oppressed are both in his hands; and if these are not the poor, the broken-hearted, the blind, the captive, and the bruised,[23] of which our Saviour speaks, who are they?

One of these depredators once, in St. Eustasia, came on board of our vessel, and bought some fowls and pigs of me; and a whole day after his departure with the things, he returned and wanted his money back: – I refused to give it; and, he not seeing my captain on board, began the common pranks with me; and swore he would even break open my chest and take my money. I therefore expected, as my captain was absent, that he would be as good as his word: and he was just proceeding to strike me, when fortunately a British seaman on board, whose heart had not been debauched by a West-India climate, interposed and prevented him. But had the cruel man struck me, I certainly should have defended myself, at the hazard of my life. For what is life to a man thus oppressed? He went away, however, swearing; and threatened that whenever he caught me a-shore he would shoot me, and pay for me afterwards.

---

[22] *With shudd'ring ... No rest Paradise Lost* 2.616–18   [23] *the poor ... bruised* Luke 4.18. imperfectly recalled.

The small account, in which the life of a negro is held in the West-Indies, is so universally known, that it might seem impertinent to quote the following extract, if some people had not been hardy enough of late to assert, that negroes are on the same footing in that respect as Europeans. By the 329th Act, page 125, of the Assembly of Barbadoes, it is enacted. 'That if any negro, or other slave, under punishment by his master, or his order, for running away, or any other crime or misdemeanour towards his said master, unfortunately shall suffer in life or member, no person whatsoever shall be liable to a fine; but if any man out of *wantonness, or only of bloody-mindedness, or cruel intention, wilfully kill a negro, or other slave, of his own, he shall pay into the public treasury £15. sterling*'. And it is the same in most, if not all, of the West-India islands. Is not this one of the many acts of the islands which call loudly for redress? And do not the Assembly, which enacted it, deserve the appellation of savages and brutes rather than of Christians and men? It is an act at once unmerciful, unjust, and unwise; which for cruelty would disgrace an assembly of those who are called barbarians; and for its injustice and insanity would shock the morality and common sense of a Sama[n]ide[24] or Hottentot.[25]

Shocking as this and many other acts of the bloody West-India code at first view appear, how is the iniquity of it heightened when we consider to whom it may be extended! Mr. James Tobin, a zealous labourer in the vineyard of slavery, gives an account[26] of a French planter, of his acquaintance, who showed him many mulattoes working in the fields like beasts of burden; and he told Mr. Tobin these *were all products of his own loins*! And I myself have known similar instances. Pray, reader, are these sons and daughters of the French planter less his children by being begotten on black women? And what must be the virtue of those legislators, and the feelings of those fathers, who estimate the lives of their sons, however begotten, at no more than fifteen pounds; though they should be murdered, as the act says, *out of wantonness and bloody-mindedness*? But is not the slave-trade entirely a war with the heart of man? And surely that which is begun by breaking down the barriers of virtue, involves in its continuance destruction to every principle, and buries all sentiments in ruin!

I have often seen slaves, particularly those who were meagre, in different islands, put into scales and weighed; and then sold from three-pence to six-pence or nine-pence a pound. My master, however, whose humanity was shocked at this mode, used to sell such by the lump. And at or after a sale, even those negroes born in the island it is not uncommon to see taken from their wives, wives from their husbands, and children from their parents, and sent off to other islands, and wherever else their merciless lords choose; and, probably, never more, during life, see each other! Oftentimes my heart has bled at these partings; when the friends of the departed have been at the water-side, and, with sighs and tears, have kept their eyes fixed on the vessel till it went out of sight.

A poor Creole negro I know well, who, after having been thus transported from island to island, at last resided in Montserrat. This man used to tell me many melancholy tales of himself. Generally, after he had done working for his master, he used to employ his few leisure moments to go a fishing. When he had caught any fish, his master would frequently take them from him without paying him; and at other times some other white people would serve him in the same manner. One day he said to me very movingly, 'Sometimes when a white man take away my fish I go to my maser, and he get me my right; and when my maser, by strength, take away my fishes, what me must do? I can't go to any body to be righted;

---

[24] *Sama{n}ide* member of an Islamic Persian dynasty begun in the ninth century.

[25] *Hottentot* one of the native people of southern Africa.

[26] *account* In his *Cursory Remarks* [(Bristol, 1785); Equiano's note].

then', said the poor man, looking up above, 'I must look up to God Mighty in the top for right'. This artless tale moved me much, and I could not help feeling the just cause Moses had in redressing his brother against the Egyptian.[27] I exhorted the man to look up still to the God in the top, since there was no redress below. Though I little thought then that I myself should more than once experience such imposition, and need the same exhortation hereafter, in my own transactions in the islands; and that even this poor man and I should some time after, suffer together in the same manner, as shall be related hereafter.

Nor was such usage as this confined to particular places or individuals; for, in all the different islands in which I have been (and I have visited no less than fifteen) the treatment of the slaves was nearly the same; so nearly, indeed, that the history of an island, or even a plantation, with a few such exceptions as I have mentioned, might serve for a history of the whole. Such a tendency has the slave-trade to debauch men's minds, and harden them to every feeling of humanity! For I will not suppose that the dealers in slaves are born worse than other men. No; it is the fatality of this mistaken avarice, that it corrupts the milk of human kindness and turns it into gall. And, had the pursuits of those men been different, they might have been as generous, as tender-hearted, and just, as they are unfeeling, rapacious and cruel. Surely this traffic cannot be good, which spreads like a pestilence, and taints what it touches! Which violates that first natural right of mankind, equality, and independency; and gives one man a dominion over his fellows which God could never intend! For it raises the owner to a state as far above man as it depresses the slave below it; and, with all the presumption of human pride, sets distinction between them, immeasurable in extent, and endless in duration! Yet how mistaken is the avarice even of the planters. Are slaves more useful by being thus humbled to the condition of brutes, than they would be if suffered to enjoy the privileges of men? The freedom which diffuses health and prosperity throughout Britain answers you – 'No'. When you make men slaves, you deprive them of half their virtue,[28] and you set them, in your own conduct, an example of fraud, rapine, and cruelty, and compel them to live with you in a state of war;[29] and yet you complain that they are not honest or faithful! You stupefy them with stripes, and think it necessary to keep them in a state of ignorance; and yet you assert that they are incapable of learning; that their minds are such a barren soil or moor that culture would be lost on them; and that they came from a climate, where nature, though prodigal of her bounties in a degree unknown to yourselves, has left man alone scant and unfinished, and incapable of enjoying the treasures she has poured out for him! – An assertion at once impious and absurd. Why do you use those instruments of torture? Are they fit to be applied by one rational being to another? And are ye not struck with shame and mortification, to see the partakers of your nature reduced so low? But, above all, are there no dangers attending this mode of treatment? Are you not hourly in dread of an insurrection? Nor would it be surprising: for when

> No peace is given
> To us enslaved, but custody severe;
> And stripes and arbitrary punishment
> Inflicted – What peace can we return?

---

[27] *Moses . . . Egyptian* While still in Egypt, Moses killed an Egyptian for striking his fellow Hebrew (Exodus 2.11–12).

[28] *When you make men slaves, you deprive them of half their virtue* translation of a classical aphorism attributed to Homer (see Johnson's *Dictionary*, s.v. *caitiff*).

[29] *a state of war* a reference to Hobbes's *Leviathan*, see p. 9.

But to our power, hostility and hate,
Untamed reluctance, and revenge, though slow.
Yet ever plotting how the conqueror least
May reap his conquest, and may least rejoice
In doing what we most in suff'ring feel? MILTON.[30]

But by changing your conduct, and treating your slaves as men, every cause of fear would be banished. They would be faithful, honest, intelligent and vigorous; and peace, prosperity, and happiness, would attend you.

Henry Mackenzie (1745–1831)

Unlike many young Scots with literary ambitions, Mackenzie did not emigrate from his native Edinburgh. He visited London on business in 1765, however, and upon his return began his novel The Man of Feeling. *The work shows the influence of Laurence Sterne both in its interest in sentimentality and in its conscious disruption of narrative conventions. The story is framed by an incident in which two friends are out hunting and carrying reading matter, which doubles as wadding for their muskets. They exchange books, and what remains of one of them is the incomplete tale that follows in the rest of novel. The hero of the book is a man named Harley who has a fine sensibility; he is compassionate and sympathetic to his fellow creatures in every way. His "sentimental journey" to the city and back is all the plot we get, but Mackenzie succeeds in establishing a point of view that British readers were ready to adopt, and the book was a hit when it finally appeared in 1771. In fact, it was so popular and struck so responsive a chord that a man named Eccles got carried away and began declaring that he had written the anonymously published book himself.*

Mackenzie lived a long life as an advocate and a prominent member of Edinburgh's literary clubs. He produced several more novels, some dramas, and much journalism. He spanned two literary periods in Scotland: he was a friend of Hume and of Sir Walter Scott. He was also the convener and chairman of a committee established to investigate the legitimacy of Macpherson's Ossian. He came to the sensible conclusion that Macpherson had embellished and reworked fragments of ancient poetry he had heard recited in the Highlands. His claims, then, were not actually false, though they led readers to the false assumption that the sources of his work were intact and palpably existent (presumably in the form of manuscripts).

The following excerpt is based on the first edition.

from *The Man of Feeling* (1771)

CHAPTER 20

He visits Bedlam – The distresses of a daughter

Of those things called Sights, in London, which every stranger is supposed desirous to see, Bedlam is one. To that place, therefore, an acquaintance of Harley's, after having accompa-

---

[30]   *MILTON   Paradise Lost* 2.332–40 (*mutatis*).

nied him to several other shows, proposed a visit. Harley objected to it, 'because', said he, 'I think it an inhuman practice to expose the greatest misery with which our nature is afflicted, to every idle visitant who can afford a trifling perquisite to the keeper; especially as it is a distress which the human must see with the painful reflection, that it is not in their power to alleviate it'. He was overpowered, however, by the solicitations of his friend, and the other persons of the party (amongst whom were several ladies); and they went in a body to Moorfields.[1]

Their conductor led them first to the dismal mansions of those who are in the most horrid state of incurable madness. The clanking of chains, the wildness of their cries, and the imprecations which some of them uttered, formed a scene inexpressibly shocking. Harley and his companions, especially the female part of them, begged their guide to return: he seemed surprised at their uneasiness, and was with difficulty prevailed on to leave that part of the house without showing them some others; who, as he expressed it in the phrase of those that keep wild beasts for a show, were much better worth seeing than any they had passed, being ten times more fierce and unmanageable.

He led them next to that quarter where those reside, who, as they are not dangerous to themselves or others enjoy a certain degree of freedom, according to the state of their distemper.

Harley had fallen behind his companions, looking at a man, who was making pendulums with bits if thread, and little balls of clay. He had delineated a segment of a circle in the wall with chalk, and marked their different vibrations, by intersecting it with cross lines. A decent-looking man came up, and smiling at the maniac, turned to Harley, and told him, that gentleman had once been a very celebrated mathematician. 'He fell a sacrifice', said he, 'to the theory of comets; for, having, with infinite labour, formed a table on the conjectures of Sir Isaac Newton, he was disappointed in the return of one of those luminaries, and was very soon after obliged to be placed here by his friends. If you please to follow me, Sir', continued the stranger, 'I believe I shall be able to give you a more satisfactory account of the unfortunate people you see here, than the man who attends your companions'. Harley bowed, and accepted his offer.

The next person they came up to had scrawled a variety of figures on a piece of slate. Harley had the curiosity to take a nearer view of them. They consisted of different columns, on the top of which were marked South-sea annuities, India-stock, and Three per cent annuities consol.[2] 'This', said Harley's instructor, 'was a gentleman well known in Change-alley.[3] He was once worth fifty thousand pounds, and had actually agreed for the purchase of an estate in the west, in order to realize his money; but he quarrelled with the proprietor about the repairs of the garden-wall, and so returned to town to follow his old trade of stock-jobbing[4] a little longer; when an unlucky fluctuation of stock, in which he was engaged to an immense extent, reduced him at once to poverty and to madness. Poor wretch! he told me t'other day, that against the next payment of differences,[5] he should be some hundreds above a plum'.[6]

'It is a spondee, and I will maintain it', interrupted a voice on his left hand. This assertion was followed by a very rapid recital of some verses from Homer. 'That figure', said the

---

[1]　*Moorfields*　a district in London.
[2]　*South-sea annuities, India-stock, and Three per cent annu-ities consol*　famous investment schemes that failed.
[3]　*Change-alley*　London's financial centre.

[4]　*stock-jobbing*　stock-brokering.
[5]　*difference*　the amount that the price of a stock changes between certain dates.
[6]　*plum*　£100,000.

gentleman, 'whose clothes are so bedaubed with snuff, was a schoolmaster of some reputation: he came hither to be resolved of some doubts he entertained concerning the genuine pronunciation of the Greek vowels. In his highest fits, he makes frequent mention of one Mr. Bentley.[7]

'But delusive ideas, Sir, are the motives of the greatest part of mankind, and a heated imagination the power by which their actions are incited: the world, in the eye of a philosopher, may be said to be a large madhouse'. 'It is true', answered Harley, 'the passions of men are temporary madnesses; and sometimes very fatal in their effects,

From Macedonia's madman to the Swede'.[8]

'It was indeed a very mad thing in Charles, to think of adding so vast a country as Russia to his dominions; that would have been fatal indeed; the balance of the North would then have been lost; but the Sultan and I would never have allowed it'. 'Sir!' said Harley, with no small surprise on his countenance. 'Why, yes', answered the other, 'the Sultan and I; do you know me? I am the Chan of Tartary'.

Harley was a good deal struck by this discovery; he had prudence enough, however, to conceal his amazement, and bowing as low to the monarch as his dignity required, left him immediately, and joined his companions.

He found them in a quarter of the house set apart for the insane of the other sex, several of whom had gathered about the female visitors, and were examining, with rather more accuracy than might have been expected, the particulars of their dress.

Separate from the rest stood one whose appearance had something of superior dignity. Her face, though pale and wasted, was less squalid than those of the others, and showed a dejection of that decent kind, which moves our pity unmixed with horror; upon her, therefore, the eyes of all were immediately turned. The keeper who accompanied them observed it: 'This', said he, 'is a young lady who was born to ride in her coach and six. She was beloved, if the story I have heard is true, by a young gentleman, her equal in birth, though by no means her match in fortune: but love, they say, is blind, and so she fancied him as much as he did her. Her father, it seems, would not hear of their marriage, and threatened to turn her out of doors if ever she saw him again. Upon this the young gentleman took a voyage to the West Indies, in hopes of bettering his fortune, and obtaining his mistress; but he was scarce landed, when he was seized with one of the fevers which are common in those islands, and died in a few days, lamented by every one that knew him. This news soon reached his mistress, who was at the same time pressed by her father to marry a rich miserly fellow, who was old enough to be her grandfather. The death of her lover had no effect on her inhuman parent: he was only the more earnest for her marriage with the man he had provided her; and what between despair at the death of the one, and her aversion to the other, the poor young lady was reduced to the condition you see her in. But God would not prosper such cruelty; her father's affairs soon after went wreck, and he died almost a beggar'.

Though this story was told in very plain language, it had particularly attracted Harley's notice; he had given it the tribute of some tears. The unfortunate young lady had till now seemed entranced in thought, with her eyes fixed on a little garnet ring she wore on her finger; she turned them now upon Harley. 'My Billy is no more!' said she; 'do you weep for my Billy? Blessings on your tears! I would weep too, but my brain is dry; and it burns, it

---

[7]   *Mr. Bentley*   Richard Bentley (1662–1742), important classical scholar; revolutionized Greek prosody through discovery of a lost letter, digamma.

[8]   *From Macedonia's madman to the Swede*   Alexander the Great to Charles XII of Sweden (Pope, *Essay on Man* 4.220).

burns, it burns!' – She drew nearer to Harley. – 'Be comforted, young lady', said he, 'your Billy is in heaven'. – 'Is he, indeed? and shall we meet again? and shall that frightful man' (pointing to the keeper) 'not be there? – Alas! I am grown naughty of late; I have almost forgotten to think of heaven: yet I pray sometimes; when I can, I pray; and sometimes I sing; when I am saddest, I sing: – You shall hear me – hush!

> Light be the earth on Billy's breast,
> And green the sod that wraps his grave'.

There was a plaintive wildness in the air not to be withstood; and, except the keeper's, there was not an unmoistened eye around her.

'Do you weep again?' said she. 'I would not have you weep: you are like my Billy; you are, believe me; just so he looked when he gave me this ring; poor Billy! 'twas the last time ever we met! –

''Twas when the seas were roaring – I love you for resembling my Billy; but I shall never love any man like him'. – She stretched out her hand to Harley; he pressed it between both of his, and bathed it with his tears. – 'Nay, that is Billy's ring', said she, 'you cannot have it indeed; but here is another, look here, which I plaited to-day of some gold-thread from this bit of stuff; will you keep it for my sake? I am a strange girl; but my heart is harmless: my poor heart; it will burst some day; feel how it beats!' She pressed his hand to her bosom, then holding her head in the attitude of listening – 'Hark! one, two, three! be quiet, thou little trembler; my Billy is cold! – but I had forgotten the ring'. – She put it on his finger. – 'Farewell! I must leave you now'. – She would have withdrawn her hand; Harley held it to his lips. – 'I dare not stay longer; my head throbs sadly: farewell!' – She walked with a hurried step to a little apartment at some distance. Harley stood fixed in astonishment and pity; his friend gave money to the keeper. – Harley looked on his ring. – He put a couple of guineas into the man's hand: 'Be kind to that unfortunate'. – He burst into tears and left them.

Hannah More (1745–1833)

Like Henry Mackenzie, Hannah More lived through two distinct literary periods. She was friends with Johnson, Garrick, Burke, Reynolds, and Walpole, but she outlived them all by forty years. Unlike Mackenzie, More did not enjoy the favour in the new regime that she had in the old. She was popular, however, and is said to have earned £30,000 from her writings over her lifetime. She started as a playwright, but soon began writing works with explicit social, moral, and religious purposes. She wrote and campaigned in other ways for the abolition of slavery, for women's rights (especially for women's right to education), and for humane treatment of children and the poor. She was not romantic about her causes in any way. Unlike Romantics, she was horrified by the French Revolution and wrote fifty of her Cheap Repository Tracts *in opposition to the French turmoil and in support of old-fashioned English village politics. More was an old-fashioned Tory with a strong evangelical streak; Johnson recognized her warmly right away, and she was loved by the common readers.*

"Sensibility" was first published in 1782 in More's collection of Bible stories, Sacred Dramas. *"The Slave Trade" was first published independently as* Slavery, a Poem *but took its present title*

in later collections of More. The following texts are based on those in The Works of Hannah
More *(1813).*

from Sensibility (1782)

. . . Sweet Sensibility! thou secret power   231
Who shed'st thy gifts upon the natal hour,
Like fairy favours; art can never seize,
Nor affectation catch thy power to please:
Thy subtle essence still eludes the chains   235
Of definition, and defeats her pains.
Sweet Sensibility! thou keen delight!
Unprompted moral! sudden sense of right!
Perception exquisite! fair virtue's seed!
Thou quick precursor of the liberal deed!   240
Thou hasty conscience! reason's blushing morn!
Instinctive kindness ere reflection's born!
Prompt sense of equity! to thee belongs
The swift redress of unexamined wrongs!
Eager to serve, the cause perhaps untried,   245
But always apt to choose the suff'ring side!
To those who know thee not, no words can paint,
And those who know thee, know all words are faint!
    She does not feel thy pow'r who boasts thy flame
And rounds her every period with thy name;   250
Nor she who vents her disproportioned sighs
With pining Lesbia when her sparrow dies:
Nor she who melts when hapless Shore expires,[1]
While real mis'ry unrelieved retires!
Who thinks feigned sorrows all her tears deserve,   255
And weeps o'er Werter while her children starve.[2]
    As words are but th' external marks to tell
The fair ideas in the mind that dwell;
And only are of things the outward sign,
And not the things themselves they but define;   260
So exclamations, tender tones, fond tears,
And all the graceful drapery feeling wears;
These are her garb, not her, they but express

FROM *SENSIBILITY*
[1] *Shore* Jane Shore a commoner, the mistress of
Edward IV, later accused of sorcery by Richard III, died
in poverty; her rise and fall are the subject of some sad
ballads and a play by Nicholas Rowe (1714).

[2] *Werter* the hero of Goethe's novel *The Sorrows of
Young Werther* (1774).

Her form, her semblance, her appropriate dress;
And these fair marks, reluctant I relate,   265
These lovely symbols may be counterfeit.
There are, who fill with brilliant plaints the page,
If a poor linnet meet the gunner's rage;
There are, who for a dying fawn deplore,
As if friend, parent, country were no more;   270
Who boast quick rapture trembling in their eye,
If from the spider's snare they snatch a fly;
There are, who well-sung plaints each breast inflame,
And break all hearts – but his from whom they came!
He, scorning life's low duties to attend,   275
Writes odes on friendship, while he cheats his friend.
Of jails and punishments he grieves to hear,
And pensions 'prisoned virtue with a tear;
While unpaid bills his creditor presents,
And ruined innocence his crime laments.   280
Not so the tender moralist of Tweed,[3]
His gen'rous Man of Feeling feels indeed.
    O love divine! sole source of charity!
More dear one genuine deed performed for thee,
Than all the periods feeling e'er could turn,[4]   285
Than all thy touching page, perverted Sterne![5]
Not that by deeds alone this love's expressed,
If so the affluent only were the blessed;
One silent wish, one prayer, one soothing word,
The page of mercy shall, well pleased, record;   290
One soul-felt sigh by pow'rless pity given,
Accepted incense! shall ascend to heav'n.

from *The Slave Trade* (1790)

    . . . Whene'er to Afric's shores I turn my eyes,   110
Horrors of deepest, deadliest guilt arise;
I see, by more than fancy's mirror shown,
The burning village and the blazing town:
See the dire victim torn from social life,
The shrieking babe, the agonizing wife;   115
She, wretch forlorn! is dragged by hostile hands,
To distant tyrants sold, in distant lands!
Transmitted miseries, and successive chains,
The sole sad heritage her child obtains!
E'en this last wretched boon their foes deny,   120

---

[3] *the tender moralist of Tweed* Henry Mackenzie, author
of *The Man of Feeling* (see selection above).
[4] *periods* sentences.

[5] *Sterne* Laurence, More is thinking of Sterne's infidelity to his wife.

To weep together, or together die.
By felon hands, by one relentless stroke,
See the fond links of feeling nature broke!
The fibres twisting round a parent's heart,
Torn from their grasp, and bleeding as they part.   125
        Hold, murderers, hold! nor aggravate distress;
Respect the passions you yourselves possess:
E'en you, of ruffian heart and ruthless hand,
Love your own offspring, love your native land:
E'en you, with fond impatient feelings burn,   130
Though free as air, though certain of return.
Then, if to you, who voluntary roam,
So dear the memory of your distant home,
O think how absence the loved scene endears
To him, whose food is groans, whose drink is tears;   135
Think on the wretch, whose aggravated pains,
To exile misery adds, to misery chains.
If warm your heart, to British feelings true,
As dear his land to him, as yours to you;
And liberty, in you a hallowed flame,   140
Burns unextinguished, in his breast the same.
Then leave him holy freedom's cheering smile,
The heav'n-taught fondness for the parent soil;
In every nature, every clime the same;
In all, these feelings equal sway maintain;   145
In all, the love of home and freedom reign:
And Tempe's vale, and parched Angola's sand,[1]
One equal fondness of their sons command.
Th' unconquered savage laughs at pain and toil,
Basking in freedom's beams which gild his native soil.   150
        Does thirst of empire, does desire of fame,
(For these are specious crimes) our rage inflame?
No: sordid lust of gold their fate controls,
The basest appetite of basest souls:
Gold, better gained by what their ripening sky,   155
Their fertile fields, their arts and mines supply.[2]
        What wrongs, what injuries does oppression plead,
To smooth the crime and sanctify the deed?
What strange offence, what aggravated sin?
They stand convicted – of a darker skin!   160
Barbarians, hold! th' opprobrious commerce spare,
Though dark and savage, ignorant and blind,
They claim the common privilege of kind;
Let malice strip them of each other plea,

FROM *THE SLAVE TRADE*
[1] *Tempe's vale* a valley in Thessaly near Mount
Olympus.

[2] *arts* Besides many valuable productions of the soil,
cloths and carpets of exquisite manufacture are brought
from the coast of Guinea [More's note].

They still are men, and men should still be free.   165
Insulted reason loathes th' inverted trade —
Loathes, as she views the human purchase made;
The outraged goddess, with abhorrent eyes,
Sees man the traffic, souls the merchandise!
Man, whom fair commerce taught with judging eye,   170
And liberal hand, to barter or to buy,
Indignant Nature blushes to behold
Degraded man himself trucked, bartered, sold:[3]
Of every native privilege bereft,
Yet cursed with every wounded feeling left.   175
Hard lot! each brutal suff'ring to sustain,
Yet keep the sense acute of human pain.
Plead not, in reason's palpable abuse,
Their sense of feeling callous and obtuse:[4]
From heads to hearts lies nature's plain appeal,   180
Though few can reason, all mankind can feel.
Though wit may boast a livelier dread of shame;
A loftier sense of wrong, refinement claim;
Though polished manners may fresh wants invent,
And nice distinctions nicer souls torment;   185
Though these on finer spirits heavier fall,
Yet natural evils are the same to all.
Though wounds there are which reason's force may heal,
There needs no logic sure to make us feel.
The nerve, howe'er untutored, can sustain   190
A sharp, unutterable sense of pain;
As exquisitely fashioned in a slave,
As where unequal fate a sceptre gave.
Sense is as keen where Gambia's waters glide,[5]
As where proud Tiber rolls his classic tide.   195
Though voice or rhetoric point the feeling line,
They do not whet sensation, but define.
Did ever wretch less feel the galling chain,
When Zeno proved there was no ill in pain?[6]
In vain the sage to smooth its horror tries;   200
Spartans and Helots see with different eyes;[7]
Their miseries philosophic quirks deride,[8]
Slaves groan in pangs disowned by Stoic pride.
   When the fierce sun darts vertical his beams,

---

[3] *trucked* exchanged, bartered.
[4] *feeling* Nothing is more frequent than this cruel and
stupid argument, that they do not feel the miseries inflicted on them as Europeans would do [More's note].
[5] *Gambia* a river in West Africa.

[6] *Zeno* of Citium, Cyprus (335–263 BCE), founder of
Stoicism.
[7] *Helots* an underclass in Sparta, kept in servile positions, yet slightly above true slaves.
[8] *quirk* "Subtlety; nicety; artful distinction"
(Johnson).

And thirst and hunger mix their wild extremes;   205
When the sharp iron wounds his inmost soul,[9]
And his strained eyes in burning anguish roll;
Will the parched negro own, ere he expire,
No pain in hunger, and no heat in fire?
    For him, when agony his frame destroys,   210
What hope of present fame or future joys?
For *that* have heroes shortened nature's date;
For *this* have martyrs gladly met their fate;
But him, forlorn, no hero's pride sustains,
No martyr's blissful visions soothe his pains;   215
Sullen, he mingles with his kindred dust,
For he has learned to dread the Christian's trust;
To him what mercy can that God display,
Whose servants murder, and whose sons betray?
Savage! thy venial errors I deplore,[10]   220
They are *not* Christians who infest thy shore.
    O thou sad spirit, whose preposterous yoke
The great deliverer death, at length, has broke!
Released from misery, and escaped from care,
Go, meet that mercy man denied thee here.   225
In thy dark home, sure refuge of th' oppressed,
The wicked vex not, and the weary rest.
And if some notions, vague and undefined,
Of future terrors have assailed thy mind;
If such thy masters have presumed to teach,   230
As terrors only they are prone to preach;
(For should they paint eternal mercy's reign,
Where were th' oppressor's rod, the captive's chain?)
If, then, thy troubled soul has learned to dread
The dark unknown thy trembling footsteps tread;   235
On Him, who made thee what thou art, depend;
He, who withholds the means, accepts the end.
Thy mental night thy Saviour will not blame,
He died for those who never heard his name.
Not *thine* the reckoning dire of light abused,   240
Knowledge disgraced, and liberty misused;
On *thee* no awful judge incensed shall sit
For parts perverted, and dishonoured wit.
Where ignorance will be found the safest plea,
How many learned and wise shall envy *thee!*   245

---

[9] *iron . . . soul* [an expression taken from Psalm 105.18 meaning to feel the pain of captivity (*OED*, *iron*, 7b)] This is not said figuratively. The writer of these lines has seen a complete set of chains, fitted to every separate limb of these unhappy innocent men; together with instruments for wrenching open the jaws, contrived with such ingenious cruelty as would gratify the tender mercies of an inquisitor [More's note].

[10] *venial* permitted, allowed.

Charlotte Smith (1749–1806)

Married at the age of sixteen, Smith had ten children by the time she was thirty-six. Dogged by debts, her husband fled to Normandy. Smith began writing to earn money and published Elegiac Sonnets and Other Essays *in 1784 at her own expense; the volume made a profit, and she continued to reissue it with corrections and additions for many years under the slightly revised title* Elegiac Sonnets and other Poems. *She followed her husband to Normandy, but soon left him and took her nine surviving children with her to London. After translating some French novels, she wrote one of her own;* Emmeline *(1788) was a great success and launched Smith decisively on her career. She published ten more novels in the next ten years, many of them about heroines who have the virtue of fine sensibility. She knew and influenced Wordsworth, and was befriended by William Hayley, the patron and biographer of Cowper. The texts presented here are based on those printed in* Elegiac Sonnets *(1800).* The Poems of Charlotte Smith *has been edited by Stuart Curran (Oxford University Press, 1993); I am indebted to Curran's work.*

from *Elegiac Sonnets and Other Poems* (1784; revised 1800)

TO HOPE

O Hope! thou soother sweet of human woes!
　　How shall I lure thee to my haunts forlorn?
For me wilt thou renew the withered rose,
　　And clear my painful path of pointed thorn?
Ah, come, sweet nymph! in smiles and softness dressed,　　　　5
　　Like the young Hours that lead the tender Year,[1]
Enchantress! come, and charm my cares to rest: –
　　Alas! the flatterer flies, and will not hear!
A prey to fear, anxiety, and pain,
　　Must I a sad existence still deplore?　　　　　　　　　　10
Lo! – the flowers fade, but all the thorns remain,
　　'For me the vernal garland blooms no more'.[2]
Come then, 'pale Misery's love!' be thou my cure,[3]
And I will bless thee, who, though slow, art sure.

TO FRIENDSHIP

O Thou! whose name too often is profaned;
　　Whose charms celestial few have hearts to feel!
Unknown to Folly – and by Pride disdained!
　　– To thy soft solace may my sorrows steal!

TO HOPE
[1] *Hours*　the Horae, or Seasons, goddesses associated with Venus and the Graces.
[2] *"For . . . more"*　Pope's imitation of the first ode of the fourth book of Horace [l. 32, with slight changes; Smith's note].

[3] *"pale Misery's love!"*　Shakepeare's *King John* [3.4.35, where it means death and does not have the adjective "pale"; Smith's note].

Like the fair moon, thy mild and genuine ray   5
   Through Life's long evening shall unclouded last;
While Pleasure's frail attachments flee away,
   As fades the rainbow from the northern blast!
'Tis thine, O Nymph! with 'balmy hands to bind'[1]
   The wounds inflicted in Misfortune's storm,   10
And blunt severe Affliction's sharpest dart!
   – 'Tis thy pure spirit warms my Anna's mind,
Beams through the pensive softness of her form,
   And holds its altar – on her spotless heart!

THE LAPLANDER

The shivering native who, by Tenglio's side,[1]
   Beholds with fond regret the parting light
Sink far away, beneath the darkening tide,
   And leave him to long months of dreary night,
Yet knows, that springing from the eastern wave   5
   The sun's glad beams shall re-illume his way,
And from the snows secured – within his cave
   He waits in patient hope – returning day.
Not so the sufferer feels, who, o'er the waste
   Of joyless life, is destined to deplore   10
Fond love forgotten, tender friendship past,
   Which, once extinguished, can revive no more!
O'er the blank void he looks with hopeless pain;
For him those beams of heaven shall never shine again.

WRITTEN NEAR A PORT ON A DARK EVENING[1]

Huge vapours brood above the clifted shore,
   Night on the Ocean settles, dark and mute,
Save where is heard the repercussive roar
   Of drowsy billows, on the rugged foot
Of rocks remote; or still more distant tone   5
   Of seamen in the anchored bark that tell
The watch relieved; or one deep voice alone
   Singing the hour, and bidding 'Strike the bell'.
All is black shadow, but the lucid line
   Marked by the light surf on the level sand,   10
Or where afar the ship-lights faintly shine
   Like wandering fairy fire, that oft on land[2]
Mislead the Pilgrim – Such the dubious ray
That wavering Reason lends, in life's long darkling way.

TO FRIENDSHIP
[1] *"balmy hands to bind"* [William] Collins ["Ode to Pity," l. 2; Smith's note].
THE LAPLANDER
[1] *Tenglio* an Arctic river.

WRITTEN NEAR A PORT ON A DARK EVENING
[1] Originally printed in Smith's novel *The Young Philosopher* (1798).
[2] *wandering fairy fire* ignis fatuus or will-o'-the-wisp, gleaming marsh gas.

Mary Scott (*fl.* 1774–1788)

Little is known of the life of Mary Scott, but around 1786 she met her future husband, the dissenting minister John Taylor. She became a convert to Arianism (the belief that God is unitary and Christ was a prophet rather than an aspect of God himself). Like many other dissenters, Scott led a life shaped by religious zeal and an interest in the rights of disenfranchised groups, such as women, slaves, and the poor. She is known principally as the author of The Female Advocate. *This long poem seeks to augment the work of John Duncombe, who celebrated women writers in his* Feminead *(1754), not only by adding names to the list of accomplished women, but also by imagining a future in which women will be freer to fulfill their potential as writers, scholars, and thinkers in all fields of knowledge. It provides a critique of Duncombe's well-meaning effort that offers both historical and conceptual improvements. The text presented here is based on the first edition (1774).*

from The Female Advocate: A Poem Occasioned by Reading Mr. Duncombe's Feminead[1] (1774)

> *Self praised*, and grasping at despotic power,
> *Man* looks on slav'ry as the female dow'r;
> To *nature's* boon ascribes what *force* has giv'n,
> And *usurpation* deems the gift of Heav'n.
>
> Anonymous

Now, big with storms, rough winter issues forth
From the cold bosom of his parent North;
Now, scarce a flow'ret rears its beauteous head
Above the surface of its native bed;
Stripped of its foliage, the late verdant grove,   5
No more invites my devious feet to rove:
How shall I soothe the anguish of a heart,
Yet bleeding from affliction's poignant dart?
A heart that long, alas, hath ceased to glow,
Dead to each hope of happiness below!   10
Propitious come, ye fair Aonian Maids,[2]
And guide a wanderer to your hallowed shades;
O, wrap me in your solitary cells
Where Silence reigns, and Inspiration dwells!
For once this tasteless apathy control,   15
And wake each sprightly passion of my soul.
 But say what theme shall sportive Fancy choose,
Since nature's charms no more delight the Muse?
What theme! and can it then a doubt remain
What theme demands the tributary strain,   20

FROM *THE FEMALE ADVOCATE*
[1] *Mr. Duncombe's Feminead* John Duncombe, *The Feminead, or Female Genius* (1754).

[2] *Aonian Maids* the muses, who lived on Mount Helicon in Aonia, or Boeotia.

Whilst Lordly Man asserts his right divine,
Alone to bow at wisdom's sacred shrine;
With tyrant sway would keep the female mind
In error's cheerless dark abyss confined?
Tell what bright daughters *Britain* once could boast,   25
What daughters now adorn Her happy coast.

. . . .

In thee, illustrious Killigrew, we find[3]
The Poet's and the Painter's Arts combined:
'Twas thine, O all-accomplished maid, to charm   95
Each breast that Virtue, or that Wit could warm:
Though early lost to earth, thy favoured name
In Dryden's verse shall boast immortal fame.
O dire disease! what havoc hast thou made!
What crowds conveyed to death's impervious shade!   100
By thee our fair Orinda too expired,[4]
Loved by the Muses, by the world admired!
(And thou, my Celia, in life's gayest bloom
Felt'st its dread stroke, and met an early tomb:
Listless I touch the long-neglected lyre,   105
Now thy dear name has ceased my songs t'inspire.
No more shall Fancy's glowing page delight,
Or Art's proud trophies charm my aching fight,
Still the keen pangs of parting rend my breast,
And rob my days of peace, my nights of rest!)   105

. . . .

Man, seated high on Learning's awful throne,
Thinks the fair realms of knowledge his alone;
But you, ye fair, his Salic Law disclaim:[5]
Supreme in Science shall the Tyrant reign!   450
When every talent all-indulgent Heav'n
In lavish bounty to your share hath giv'n?
With joy ineffable the Muse surveys
The orient beams of more resplendent days:
As on she raptured looks to future years,   455
What a bright throng to Fancy's view appears!
To them see Genius her best gifts impart,
And Science raise a throne in every heart!

---

[3] *Killigrew* Mrs. *Anne Killigrew*, daughter of *Henry Killigrew* (one of the Prebendaries of *Westminister*) was born a short time before the restoration of King *Charles* II. Her naturally fine genius being improved by a polite education, she made a great proficiency in the kindred-arts of Poetry and Paintings; especially in the latter, in which she probably might have rivalled the greatest masters of her time, had not death arrested her in the bloom of youth and genius. She died of the small-pox, in the twenty-fifth year of her age. Her death was lamented in a long Ode by Mr. *Dryden* [Scott's note; see Dryden's *Ode* and the selection from Killigrew above].

[4] *Orinda* The celebrated Mrs. *Katherine Philips*, who also died of the small pox [Scott's note; see the selection from Philips above].

[5] *Salic Law* one aspect of a Frankish legal code from the sixth century revived by lawyers in the sixteenth century in order to exclude from the thrones of Europe women and men who traced their royal lineage through women.

One turns the moral, one th' historic page;
Another glows with all a Shakespeare's rage!   460
With matchless Newton now one soars on high,
Lost in the boundless wonders of the sky;
Another now, of curious mind, reveals
What treasures in her bowels Earth conceals;
Nature's minuter works attract her eyes;   465
Their laws, their powers, her deep research descries.
From sense abstracted, some, with arduous flight,
Explore the realms of intellectual light;
With unremitting study seek to find,
How mind on matter, matter acts on mind: 470
Alike in nature, arts, and manners read,
In every path of knowledge, see they tread!
Whilst men, convinced of Female Talents, pay
To Female Worth the tributary lay . . .

Frances Burney (later d'Arblay) (1752–1840)

At a very early age Frances Burney moved in exalted literary circles, prized and praised by Samuel Johnson, Hester Thrale, and the rest of the "Streatham" circle. She also knew the world of musicians and composers in which her father constantly moved. Charles Burney was an organist and music-master, who became famous as the author of the most important history of music written in English in his time or before. It was, of course, not his musicianship but rather his humanity that made Burney attractive to Johnson. The two were good friends to start with, and the emergence of his literary, highly good-humoured daughter "Fanny" increased the warmth and affection between them. Frances delighted her friends and the world with her first novel, Evelina, *published when she was only twenty-six.* Cecilia *(1782) was also admired, but then Burney's world began to change: she became estranged from Hester Thrale after her second marriage (1783); Samuel Johnson died (1784); she lost an old family friend whom she called "Daddy Crisp." She was presented to King George III and held an unsatisfactory post in the royal service for a time. She married in 1793 and eventually went to France with her husband to reclaim property he had lost during the Revolution. There were two more novels, the third a mixed success and the fourth a failure. But through it all, from the time she was a teenager in her father's house, through her decade in France and after her return to England during the Napoleonic Wars, Burney kept her diaries and journals. These provide some of the best accounts of what it was like to be in the company of Samuel Johnson and many other luminaries of the period. The view is strikingly different from that found in Boswell's more self-centerd accounts. In addition to writing about her friends and family, her principal interest, Burney also conveys a vivid sense of many of her private and domestic experiences – none more vivid and striking than her account of her mastectomy in 1811 in Paris before the advent of anesthesia.*

    The Journals and Letters *from 1791 on have been produced in twelve volumes by the Clarendon Press (1972–82), and the* Early Journals and Letters *are also coming out from McGill University Press (1988–). Margaret Doody has written a rich critical biography (Rutgers University Press, 1988). My texts are based on those in volume two of the*

McGill production, edited by Lars Troide, and in volume six of the Clarendon Press edition of the Journals, *edited by Joyce Hemlow. I am indebted to these scholars for their commentary as well their texts.*

from *Journals and Letters*

27–8 MARCH 1777

Mrs & Miss Thrale,[1] Miss Owen[2] & Mr. Seward[3] came long before *Lexiphanes*;[4] – Mrs. Thrale is a very pretty woman still, she is extremely lively and chatty, – has no supercilious or pedantic airs, & is really gay and agreeable. Her Daughter is about 12 years old, &, I believe, not all together so amiable as her mother. Miss Owen, who is a Relation, is good humoured & sensible *enough*; she is a sort of *Butt*, & as such, a general favourite: for those sort of characters are prodigiously useful in drawing out the Wit & pleasantry of others: Mr. Seward is a very polite, agreeable young man:

My sister was invited to meet, & play, to them.

The Conversation was supported with a good deal of vivacity – (N.B. my Father being at Home) for about half an Hour, & then Hetty, & *Suzette*, for the first time *in public*, played a Duet, &, in the midst of this performance, Dr. Johnson was announced.

He is, indeed, very ill favoured, – he is tall & stout, but stoops terribly, – he is almost bent double. His mouth is in perpetual motion, as if he was chewing; – he has a strange method of frequently twirling his Fingers, & twisting his Hands; – his Body is in continual agitation, *see sawing* up & down; his Feet are never a moment quiet, – &, in short, his whole person is in perpetual motion:

His Dress, too, considering the Times, & that he had meant to put on his best becomes,[5] being engaged to Dine in a large Company, was as much out of the common Road as his Figure: he had a large Wig, snuff colour coat, & Gold Buttons; but no Ruffles to his Wrist, & Black Worsted Stockings – so, you see, there is another *Worsted Stocking Knave,* besides me, – that's my comfort.

He is shockingly near sighted, & did not, till she held out her Hand to him, even know Mrs. Thrale. He *poked his Nose* over the keys of the Harpsichord, till the Duet was finished, & then, my Father introduced Hetty to him, as an old acquaintance,[6] & he instantly kissed her.

His attention, however, was not to be diverted five minutes from the Books, as we were in the Library; he pored over them, almost brushing the Backs of them, with his Eye lashes, as he read their Titles; at last, having fixed upon one, he began, without further ceremony, to Read, all the time standing at a distance from the Company. We were very much provoked, as we perfectly languished to hear him talk; but, it seems, he is the most silent creature, when not particularly drawn out, in the World.

FROM *JOURNAL AND LETTERS*
[1] *Mrs & Miss Thrale* Hester Lynch Thrale (1741–1821), perhaps Johnson's closest friend until the death of her husband and her subsequent marriage to Gabriel Piozzi, see the selection from her correspondence above, and her daughter Hester Maria (Queeney).
[2] *Miss Owen* Margaret (1743–1816).

[3] *Mr. Seward* William (1747–99), compiler of *Anecdotes of Some Distinguished Persons* (1795–7).
[4] *Lexiphanes* a name taken from a satire by Lucian and applied to Samuel Johnson in a satire by James Callander.
[5] *best becomes* most attractive clothes.
[6] *Hetty* Hester Maria Thrale, Johnson's god-daughter and much more than a mere acquaintance.

My sister then played another Duet, with my Father: but Dr. Johnson was so deep in the Encyclopédie, that, as he is very deaf, I question if he ever knew what was going forward. When this was over, Mrs. Thrale, in a laughing manner, said 'Pray, Dr. Burney, can you tell me what that song was, & whose, which Savoi sung last night at Bach's[7] Concert, & which you did not hear?' My Father confessed himself by no means a good Diviner, not having Time to consult the stars, though in the House of Sir Isaac Newton.[8] However, wishing to draw Dr. Johnson in some Conversation, he told him the Question. The Doctor, seeing his drift, good naturedly put away his Book, & said very drolly 'And pray, Sir – *Who is Bach?* – is he a Piper?' – Many exclamations of surprise, you will believe, followed this Question. 'Why you have Read his name often in the papers', said Mrs. Thrale; & then gave him some account of his Concert, & the number of fine performances she had heard at it.

'Pray', said he, 'Madam, what is the Expense?'

'O', answered she, 'much trouble & solicitation to get a subscriber's Ticket; – or else half a Guinea'.[9]

'Trouble and solicitation', said he, 'I will have nothing to do with; – but I would be willing to give Eighteen Pence'.

Chocolate being then brought, we adjourned to the Dining Room. And here, Dr. Johnson, being taken from the Books, entered freely & most cleverly into conversation: though it is remarkable, that he never speaks at all, but when spoken to; nor does he ever *start*, though he so admirably supports any *subject*.

The whole party was engaged to Dine at Mrs. Montague's:[10] Dr. Johnson said he had received the most flattering note he had ever read, or any body else had ever Read, by way of invitation. 'Well, so have, I, too', cried Mrs. Thrale, 'so if a note from Mrs. Montague is to be boasted of, I beg mine may not be forgot'.

'Your note', cried Dr. Johnson, 'can bear no comparison with *mine*; – I am *at the Head of Philosophers*; she says'.

'And I', cried Mrs. Thrale, '*have all the muses in my Train!*'

'A fair Battle', said my Father; 'come, Compliment for Compliment, & see who will hold out longest'.

'O, I am afraid for Mrs. Thrale!' cried Mr. Seward, 'for I know Mrs. Montague exerts all her forces when she attacks Dr. Johnson'.

'O yes', said Mrs. Thrale, 'she has often, I know, flattered *him* till he has been ready to Faint'.

'Well, Ladies', said my Father, 'You must get him between you to Day, & see which can lay on the paint thickest, Mrs. Thrale or Mrs. Montague'.

'I had rather', cried the Doctor, 'go to Bach's Concert!'

After this, they talked of Mr. Garrick,[11] & his late Exhibition before the King, to whom, & the Queen & Royal Family, he read Lethe,[12] *in character, c'est á dire*,[13] in different Voices, & Theatrically. Mr. Seward gave us an account of a Fable, which Mr. Garrick had written, by way of Prologue, or Introduction, upon the occasion: In this, he says, that a Black Bird, grown old & feeble, droops his Wings, &c, &c, & gives up singing; but, being called upon by the

---

[7] *Bach* Johann Christian (1735–82), the "London Bach," son of the great Johann Sebastian Bach.
[8] The Burneys lived in the house in St Martin's Street where Newton lived and died.
[9] *Guinea* twenty-one shillings, £1.05; half a guinea at this time would be worth about £100 or $160 now.
[10] *Mrs. Montague* Elizabeth (1720–1800), author and socialite.
[11] *Garrick* David (1717–79), greatest actor of his time and one of Johnson's oldest friends.
[12] *Lethe* (1740), a one-act farce by Garrick himself.
[13] *in character, c'est á dire* "in character, that is to say . . ."

Eagle, his Voice recovers its powers, his spirits revive, he sets age at defiance, & sings better than ever. The application is obvious.

'There is not', said Dr. Johnson, 'much of the spirit of *Fabulosity* in this Fable; for the call of an *Eagle* never yet had much tendency to restore the voice of a *Black Bird*! 'Tis true, the Fabulists frequently make the *Wolves* converse with the *Lambs*, – but, when the conversation is over, the *Lambs* are sure to be Eaten! – & so, the *Eagle* may entertain the *Black Bird*, – but the entertainment always ends in a *Feast* for the Eagles!'

'They say', cried Mrs. Thrale, 'that Garrick was extremely hurt by the coolness of the King's applause, & did not find his reception such as he expected'.

'He has been so long accustomed', said Mr. Seward, 'to the Thundering approbation of the Theatre, that a mere *very well*, must necessarily & naturally disappoint him'.

'Sir', said Dr. Johnson, 'he should not, in a Royal apartment, expect the hallooing & clamour of the one shilling gallery. The King, I doubt not, gave him as much applause as was rationally his due: &, indeed, great & uncommon as is the merit of Mr. Garrick, no man will be bold enough to assert that he has not his just proportion both of Fame & Profit: he has long reigned the unequalled favourite of the public, – & therefore, nobody will mourn his hard fate, if the King, & the Royal Family, were not transported into rapture, upon hearing him Read Lethe. Yet, Mr. Garrick will complain to his Friends, & his Friends will lament the King's want of feeling & taste; – then, Mr. Garrick will *excuse* the King! he will say that he might be thinking of something else; – that the affairs of America might occur to him, – or some subject of more importance than Lethe; – but though he will say this himself, he will not forgive his Friends, if they do not contradict him!'

But now, that I have written this *satire*, it is but just both to Mr. Garrick, & Dr. Johnson, to tell you what he said of him afterwards, when he discriminated his character with equal candour & humour.

'Garrick', said he, 'is accused of vanity; – but few men would have borne such unremitting prosperity with greater, if with equal moderation: he is accused, too, of avarice, – but, were he not, he would be accused of just the contrary, for he now Lives rather as a *prince*, than as an Actor: but the frugality he practised when he first appeared in the World, & which, even then, was perhaps beyond his necessity, has marked his character ever since; & now, though his Table, his Equipage, & manner of Living, are all the most expensive, and equal to those of a Nobleman, yet the original stain still blots his name, – though, had he not fixed upon himself the charge of Avarice, he would, long since, have been reproached with *luxury*, & with living beyond his station in magnificence & splendour'.

Another Time, he said of him 'Garrick never enters a Room, but he regards himself as the object of general attention, & from whom the Entertainment of the Company is expected, & true it is, that he seldom disappoints them; for he has infinite humour, a very just proportion of Wit, & more convivial pleasantry than almost any other man. But then, off, as well as *on* the stage, he is always an Actor! for he thinks it so incumbent upon him to be supportive, that his gaiety becomes mechanical, as it is habitual, & [he] can exert his spirits at all Times alike, without consulting his real Disposition to hilarity' . . .

22 MARCH 1812

To Esther Burney[14]

Separated as I have now so long – long been from my dearest Father – BROTHERS – SISTERS – NIECES, & NATIVE FRIENDS, I would spare, at least, their kind hearts any

---

14 *Esther Burney* (1749–1832) Frances's sister.

grief for me but what they must inevitably feel in reflecting upon the sorrow of such an absence to one so tenderly attached to all her first and for-ever so dear & regretted ties – nevertheless, if they should hear that I have been dangerously ill from any hand but my own, they might have doubts of my perfect recovery which my own alone can obviate. And how can I hope they will escape hearing what has reached Seville to the South, and Constantinople to the East? from both I have had messages – yet nothing could urge me to this communication till I heard that M. de Boinville had written it to his Wife, without any precaution, because in ignorance of my plan of silence. Still I must hope it may never travel to my dearest Father – But to You, my beloved Esther, who, living more in the World, will surely hear it ere long, to you I will write the whole history, certain that, from the moment you know any evil has befallen me your kind kind heart will be constantly anxious to learn its extent, & its circumstances, as well as its termination.

About August, in the year 1810, I began to be annoyed by a small pain in my breast, which went on augumenting from week to week, yet, being rather heavy than acute, without causing me any uneasiness with respect to consequences: Alas, 'what was the ignorance?' The most sympathising of Partners, however, was more disturbed: not a start, not a wry face, not a movement that indicated pain was unobserved, & he early conceived apprehensions to which I was a stranger. He pressed me to see some Surgeon; I revolted from the idea, & hoped, by care & warmth, to make all succour unnecessary. Thus passed some months, during which Madame de Maisonneuve, my particularly intimate friend, joined with M. d'Arblay[15] to press me to consent to an examination. I thought their fears groundless, and could not make so great a conquest over my repugnance. I relate this false confidence, now, as a warning to my dear Esther – my Sisters & Nieces, should any similar sensations excite similar alarm. M. d'A. now revealed his uneasiness to another of our kind friends, Mad. de Tracy, who wrote to me a long & eloquent Letter upon the subject, that began to awaken very unpleasant surmises; & a conference with her ensued, in which her urgency & representations, aided by her long experience of disease, & most miserable existence by art, subdued me, and, most painfully & reluctantly, I ceased to object, & M. d'A. summoned a physician – 'M. Bourdois?' Maria will cry; – No, my dear Maria, I would not give your beau frere that trouble; not him, but Dr. Jouart, the physician of Miss Potts. Thinking but slightly of my statement, he gave me some directions that produced no fruit – on the contrary, I grew worse, & M. d'A. now would take no denial to my consulting M. Dubois, who had already attended and cured me in an abscess of which Maria, my dearest Esther, can give you the history. M. Dubois, the most celebrated surgeon of France, was then appointed accoucheur[16] to the Empress, & already lodged in the Tuileries,[17] & in constant attendance: but nothing could slacken the ardour of M. d'A. to obtain the first advice. Fortunately for his kind wishes, M. Dubois had retained a partial regard for me from the time of his former attendance, &, when applied to through a third person, he took the first moment of liberty, granted by a *promenade* taken by the Empress, to come to me. It was now I began to perceive my real danger, M. Dubois gave me a prescription to be pursued for a month, during which time he could not undertake to see me again, & pronounced nothing – but uttered so many charges to me to be tranquil, & to suffer no uneasiness, that I could not but suspect there was room for terrible inquietude. My alarm was increased by the non-appearance of M. d'A. after his departure. They had remained together some time in the Book room, & M. d'A. did not return – till, unable to bear the suspense, I

---

[15] *M. d'Arblay* Alexandre-Jean-Baptiste Piochard d'Arblay (1754–1818), Burney's husband.
[16] *accoucheur* male midwife, obstetrician.
[17] *Tuileries* French royal palace adjacent to the Louvre in Paris.

begged him to come back. He, also, sought then to tranquilize me – but in words only; his looks were shocking! his features, his whole face displayed the bitterest woe. I had not, therefore, much difficulty in telling myself what he endeavoured not to tell me – that a small operation would be necessary to avert evil consequences! – Ah, my dearest Esther, for this I felt no courage – my dread and repugnance, from a thousand reasons *besides* the pain, almost shook all my faculties, &, for some time, I was rather confounded & stupefied than affrighted. – Direful, however, was the effect of this interview; the pains became quicker & more violent, & the hardness of the spot affected increased. I took, but vainly, my prescription, & every symptom grew more serious. At this time, M. de Narbonne spoke to M. d'A. of a Surgeon of great eminence, M. Larrey, who had cured a *polonaise*[18] lady of his acquaintance of a similar malady; & as my horror of an operation was insuperable, M. de N. strongly recommended that I should have recourse to M. Larrey. I thankfully caught at any hope; & another friend of M. d'A. gave the same counsel at the same instant, which other, M. Barbier Neuville, has an influence irresistible over this M. Larrey, to whom he wrote the most earnest injunction that he would use every exertion to rescue me from what I so much dreaded. M. Larrey came, though very unwillingly, & full of scruples concerning M. Dubois; nor would he give me his services till I wrote myself to state my affright at the delay of attendance occasioned by the present high office & royal confinement of M. Dubois, & requesting that I might be made over to M. Larrey. An answer such as might be expected arrived, & I was now put upon a new *regime*, & animated by the fairest hopes. – M. Larrey has proved one of the worthiest, most disinterested, & singularly excellent of men, endowed with real Genius in his profession, though with an ignorance of the World & its usages that induces a *naiveté* that leads those who do not see him thoroughly to think him not alone simple, but weak. They are mistaken; but his attention and thoughts having exclusively turned one way, he is hardly awake any other. His directions seemed all to succeed, for though I had still cruel seizures of terrible pain, the fits were shorter & more rare, & my spirits revived, & I went out almost daily, & quite daily received in my Apartment some friend or intimate acquaintance, contrarily to my usual mode of *sauvagerie*[19] – and what friends I have found! what kind, consoling, zealous friends during all this painful period! In fine,[20] I was much better, & every symptom of alarm abated. My good M. Larrey was enchanted, yet so anxious, that he forced me to see le Docteur Ribe, the first anatomist, he said, in France, from his own fear lest he was under any delusion, from the excess of his desire to save me. I was as rebellious to the first visit of this famous anatomist as Maria will tell you I had been to that of M. Dubois, so odious to me was this sort of process: however, I was obliged to submit: & M. Ribe confirmed our best hopes – – Here, my dearest Esther, I must grow brief, for my theme becomes less pleasant – Sundry circumstances, too long to detail, combined to counter-act all my flattering expectations, & all the skill, & all the cares of my assiduous & excellent Surgeon. The principal of these evils were – the death, broke to me by a newspaper! of the lovely & loved P[rincess] Amelia – the illness of her venerated Father – & the sudden loss of my nearly adored – my Susan's nearly worshipped Mr. Locke[21] – which terrible calamity reached me in *a few lines* from Fanny Waddington, when I knew not of any illness or fear! – Oh my Esther, I must indeed here be brief, for I am not yet strong enough for sorrow. – The good M. Larrey, when he came to me next after the last of these trials, was quite thrown into a consternation, so changed he found

---

18 *polonaise* Polish.
19 *sauvagerie* wildness, incivility.
20 *In fine* in brief,

21 *Locke* William (1732–1810), a close friend of the family.

all for the worse – 'Et qu'est il donc arrive?'[22] he cried, & presently, sadly announced his hope of dissolving the hardness were nearly extinguished. M. Ribe was now again called in – but he only corroborated the terrible judgement: yet they allowed to my pleadings some further essays,[23] & the more easily as the weather was not propitious to any operation. My Exercise, at this time, though always useful & cheering occasioned me great suffering in its conclusion, from mounting up three pair of stairs: my tenderest Partner, therefore, removed me to La Rue de Mirmenil, where I began my Paris residence nearly 10 years ago! – *quite* 10 next Month! Here we are! *au premier*[24] – but alas – to no effect! once only have I yet descended the short flight of steps from which I had entertained new hopes. A Physician was now called in, Dr. Moreau, to hear if he could suggest any new means: but Dr. Larrey had left him no resources untried. A formal consultation now was held, of Larrey, Ribe, & Moreau – &, in fine, I was formally condemned to an operation by all Three. I was as much astonished as disappointed – for the poor breast was no where discoloured, & not much larger than its healthy neighbour. Yet I felt the evil to be deep, so deep, that I often thought if it could not be dissolved, it could only with life be extirpated. I called up, however, all the reason I possessed, or could assume, & told them – that if they saw no other alternative, I would not resist their opinion & experience: – the good Dr. Larrey, who, during his long attendance had conceived for me the warmest friendship, had now tears in his Eyes; from my dread he had expected resistance. He proposed again calling in M. Dubois. No, I told him, if I could not by himself be saved, I had no sort of hope elsewhere, &, if it must be, what I wanted in courage should be supplied by his Confidence. The good man was now dissatisfied with himself, and declared I ought to have the First and most eminent advice his Country could afford; '*Vous êtes si considerée, Madame*', said he, '*ici que le public même sera mecontent si vous n'avez pas tout le secours que nous avons à vous offrir*'.[25] – Yet this modest man is premier chirugien de la Garde Imperiale, & had been lately created a Baron for his eminent services! – M. Dubois, he added, from his super-skill & experience, might yet, perhaps, suggest some cure. This conquered me quickly, ah – Send for him! Send for him! I cried – & Dr. Moreau received the commission to consult with him. – What an interval was this! Yet my poor M. d'A. was more to be pitied than myself, though he knew not the terrible idea I had internally annexed to the trial – but Oh what he suffered! – & with what exquisite tenderness he solaced all I had to bear! My poor Alex[26] I kept as much as possible, and as long, ignorant of my situation. – M. Dubois behaved extremely well, no pique intervened with the interest he had professed in my well-doing, & his conduct was manly & generous. It was difficult still to see him, but he appointed the earliest day in his power for a general & final consultation. I was informed of it only on the Same day, to avoid useless agitation. He met here Drs. Larrey, Ribe, & Moreau. The case, I saw, offered uncommon difficulties, or presented eminent danger, but, the examination over, they desired to consult together. I left them – what an half hour I passed alone! – M. d'A. was at his office. Dr. Larrey then came to summon me. He did not speak, but looked very like my dear Brother James, to whom he has a personal resemblance that has struck M. d'A. as well as myself. I came back, & took my seat, with what calmness I was able. All were silent, & Dr. Larrey, I saw, hid himself nearly behind my Sofa. My heart beat fast: I saw all hope was over. I called upon them to speak. M. Dubois then, after a long & unintelligible harangue, from his own

---

[22]   *Et qu'est il donc arrive?* "And what's happened here?"

[23]   *essays* attempts, efforts.

[24]   *au premier* on the first floor, one flight above the ground floor.

[25]   *Vous êtes ... offrir* "You are so highly regarded, Madame, that here even the public will be displeased if you do not have all the assistance that we can offer you."

[26]   *Alex* her seventeen-year-old son.

disturbance, pronounced my doom. I now saw it was inevitable, and abstained from any further effort. They received my formal consent, & retired to fix a day.

All hope of escaping this evil being now at an end, I could only console or employ my Mind in considering how to render it less dreadful to M. d'A. M. Dubois had pronounced '*il faut s'attendre à souffrir; Je ne veux pas vous trompez — Vous Souffrirez — vous souffrirez beaucoup!*'[27] — M. Ribe had *charged* me to cry! to withhold or restrain myself might have seriously bad consequences, he said. M. Moreau, in echoing this injunction, enquired whether I had cried or screamed at the birth of Alexander — Alas, I told him, it had not been possible to do otherwise; Oh then, he answered, there is no fear! — What terrible inferences were here to be drawn! I desired, therefore, that M. d'A. might be kept in ignorance of the day till the operation should be over. To this they agreed, except M. Larrey, with high approbation: M. Larrey looked dissentient, but was silent. M. Dubois protested he would not undertake to act, after what he had seen of the agitated spirits of M. d'A. if he were present: nor would he suffer me to know the time myself over night; I obtained with difficulty a promise of 4 hours warning, which were essential to me for sundry regulations.

From this time, I assumed the best spirits in my power, *to meet the coming blow;* — & support my too sympathising Partner. They would let me make no preparations, refusing to inform me what would be necessary; I have known, since, that Mad. de Tessé, an admirable old friend of M. d'A., now mine, equally, & one of the first of her sex, in any country, for uncommon abilities, & nearly universal knowledge, had insisted upon sending all that might be necessary, & of keeping me in ignorance. M. d'A. filled a Closet with Charpie,[28] compresses, & bandages — All that to *me* was owned, as wanting, was an arm Chair & some Towels. — Many things, however, joined to the depth of my pains, assured me the business was not without danger. I therefore made my Will — unknown, to this moment, to M. d'A., & entrusted it privately to M. La Tour Maubourg, without even letting my friend his Sister, Mad. de Maisonneuve, share the secret. M. de M. conveyed it for me to Maria's excellent M. Gillet, from whom M. de M. brought me directions. As soon as I am able to go out I shall reveal this clandestine affair to M. d'A. — till then, it might still affect him. Mad. de Maisonneuve desired to be present at the operation; but I would not inflict such pain. M. de Chastel belle sœur to Mad. de Boinville, would also have sustained the shock; but I secured two Guards, one of whom is known to my two dear Charlottes, Ma. Soubiren, portière to l'Hotel Marengo: a very good Creature, who often assumes me by repeating '*ver. vell, Mawm*,' which she tells me she learnt of Charlotte the younger whom she never names but with rapture. The other is a workwoman whom I have often employed. The kindness I received at this period would have made me for-ever love France, had I hitherto been hard enough of heart to hate it — but Mad. d'Henin — the tenderness she showed me surpasses all description. Twice she came to Paris from the Country, to see, watch & sit with me; there is nothing that can be suggested of use or comfort that she omitted. She loves me not only from her kind heart, but also from her love of Mrs. Locke, often, often exclaiming 'Ah! si votre angelique amie étoit ici! —'[29] But I must force myself from these episodes, though my dearest Esther will not think them *de trop*.[30]

After sentence thus passed, I was in hourly expectation of a summons to execution; judge, then, my surprise to be suffered to go on full 3 Weeks in the same state! M. Larrey from time

---

[27] *il faut ... beaucoup* "you must expect pain; I do not wish to deceive you — you will suffer — you will suffer a great deal."

[28] *Charpie* unravelled linen.

[29] *si votre angelique amie étoit ici!* "If only your angelic friend were here".

[30] *de trop* too much, excessive.

to time visited me, but pronounced nothing, & was always melancholy. At length, M. d'A. was told that he waited himself for a Summons! & that, a formal one, & in writing! *I* could not give one. A *consent* was my utmost effort. But poor M. d'A. wrote a desire that the operation, if necessary, might take place without further delay. In my own mind, I had all this time been persuaded there were hopes of a cure: why else, I thought, let me know my doom thus long? But here I must account for this apparently useless, & therefore cruel measure, though I only learnt it myself 2 months afterward. M. Dubois had given his opinion that the evil was too far advanced for any remedy; that the cancer was already internally declared; that I was inevitably destined to that most frightful of deaths, & that an operation would but accelerate my dissolution. Poor M. Larrey was so deeply affected by this sentence, that – as he has lately told me, – he regretted to his Soul ever having known me, & was upon the point of demanding a commission to the furthest end of France in order to force me into other hands. I had said, however, he remembered, once, that I would far rather suffer a quick end without, than a lingering life with this dreadfullest of maladies: he finally, therefore, considered it might be possible to save me by the trial, but that without it my case was desperate, & resolved to make the attempt. Nevertheless, the responsibility was too great to rest upon his own head entirely; & therefore he waited for the formal summons. – In fine, One morning – the last of September, 1811, while I was still in Bed, & M. d'A. was arranging some papers for his office, I received a letter written by M. de Lally to a Journalist, in vindication of the honoured memory of his Father against the assertions of Mad. du Deffand. I read it aloud to My Alexanders, with tears of admiration and sympathy, & then sent it by Alex: to its excellent Author, as I had promised the preceding evening. I then dressed, aided, as usual for many months, by my maid, my right arm being condemned to total inaction; but not yet was the grand business over, when another Letter was delivered to me – another, indeed! – 'twas from M. Larrey, to acquaint me that at 10 o'clock he should be with me, properly accompanied, & to exhort me to rely as much upon his sensibility & his prudence, as upon his dexterity & his experience; he charged to secure the absence of M. d'A: & told me that the young Physician who would deliver me this *annonce*, would prepare for the operation, in which he must lend his aid: & also that it had been the decision of the consultation to allow me but two hours notice. – Judge, my Esther, if I read this unmoved! – yet I had to disguise my sensations & intentions from M. d'A.! – Dr. Aumont, the Messenger & terrible Herald, was in waiting; M. d'A. stood by my bed side; I affected to be long reading the Note, to gain time for forming some plan, & such was my terror of involving M. d'A. in the unavailing wretchedness of witnessing what I must go through, that it conquered every other, & gave me the force to act as if I were directing some third person. The detail would be too *Wordy*, as James[31] says, but *wholesale* is – I called Alex to my Bed side, & sent him to inform M. Barbier Neuville, chef du divison du Bureau de M. d'A. that *the moment was come*, & entreated him to write a summons upon urgent business for M. d'A. & to detain him till all should be over. Speechless & appalled, off went Alex, &, as I have since heard, was forced to sit down & sob in executing his commission. I then, by the Maid, sent word to the young Dr. Aumont that I could not be ready till one o'clock: and finished my breakfast, & not with much appetite, you will believe! forced down a crust of bread, & hurried off, under various pretences, M. d'A. He was scarcely gone, when M. Dubois arrived: I renewed my request for one o'clock: the rest came; all were fain to consent to the delay, for I had an apartment to prepare for my banished Mate. The arrangement, & those for myself, occupied me completely. Two engaged nurses were out of

---

[31] *James* her brother (1750–1821), a rear admiral in the Navy.

the way – I had a bed, Curtains, & heaven knows what to prepare – but business was good for my nerves, I was obliged to quit my room to have it put in order: – Dr. Aumont would not leave the house; he remained in the Salon, folding linen! – He had demanded 4 or 5 old & fine left off under Garments – I glided to our Book Cabinet: sundry necessary works and orders filled up my time entirely till One O'clock, When all was ready – – but Dr. Moreau then arrived, with news that M. Dubois could not attend till three. Dr. Aumont went away & the Coast was clear. This indeed, was a dreadful interval. I had no longer any thing to do – I had only to think – TWO HOURS thus spent seemed never-ending. I would fain have written to my dearest Father – to You, my Esther – to Charlotte James Charles – Amelia Locke – but my arm prohibited me: I strolled to the Salon – I saw it fitted with preparations, & I recoiled – But I soon returned; to what effect disguise from myself what I must so soon know? – yet the sight of the immense quantity of bandages, compresses, sponges, Lint – – Made me a little sick: – I walked backwards & forwards till I quieted all emotion, & became, by degrees, nearly stupid – torpid, without sentiment or consciousness; – & thus I remained till the Clock struck three. A sudden spirit of exertion then returned, – I defied my poor arm, no longer worth sparing, & took my long banished pen to write a few words to M. d'A. – & a few more for Alex, in case of a fatal result. These short billets I could only deposit safely, when the Cabriolets[32] – one – two – three – four – succeeded rapidly to each other in stopping at the door. Dr. Moreau instantly entered my room, to see if I were alive. He gave me a wine cordial, & went to the Salon. I rang for my maid & Nurses, – but before I could speak to them, my room, without previous message, was entered by 7 Men in black, Dr. Larry, M. Dubois, Dr. Moreau, Dr. Aumont, Dr. Ribe, & a pupil of Dr. Larry, & another of M. Dubois. I was now awakened from my stupor – & by sort of indignation – Why so many? & without leave? – But I could not utter a syllable. M. Dubois acted as Commander in Chief. Dr. Larry kept out of sight; M. Dubois ordered a Bed stead into the middle of the room. Astonished, I turned to Dr. Larry, who had promised that an Arm Chair would suffice; but he hung his head, & would not look at me. Two *old mattrasses* M. Dubois then demanded, & an old Sheet. I now began to tremble violently, more with distaste & horror of the preparations even than of the pain. These arranged to his liking, he desired me to mount the Bed stead. I stood suspended, for a moment, whether I should not abruptly escape – I looked at the door, the windows – I felt desperate – but it was only for a moment, my reason then took command, & my fears & feelings struggled vainly against it. I called to my maid – she was crying, & the two Nurses stood, transfixed, at the door. Let those women all go! cried M. Dubois. This order recovered me my Voice – No, I cried, let them stay! *qu'elles restent!* This occasioned a little dispute, that re-animated me – The Maid, however, & one of the nurses ran off – I chid the other to approach, & she obeyed. M. Dubois now tried to issue his commands *en militaire*, but I resisted all that were resistible – I was compelled, however, to submit to taking off my robe de Chambre, which I had meant to retain – Ah, then, how did I think of My Sisters! – not one, at so dreadful an instant, at hand, to protect – adjust – guard me – I regretted that I had refused Madam de Maisonneuve – Madam Chastel – no one upon whom I could rely – my departed Angel! – how did I think of her! – how did I long – long for my Esther – my Charlotte! – My distress was, I suppose, apparent, though not my Wishes, for M. Dubois himself now softened, & spoke soothing. 'Can *You*', I cried, 'feel for an operation that, to *You* must seem so trivial?' – 'Trivial?' he repeated – taking up a bit of paper, which he tore, unconsciously, into a million pieces, *'oui – c'est peu de chose – mais –'*[33] he stammered, & could

---

32 *Cabriolets* carriages.

33 *oui – c'est peu de chose – mais* "Yes, it is a little thing, but . . ."

not go on. No one else attempted to speak, but I was softened myself, when I saw even M. Dubois grow agitated, while Dr. Larrey kept always aloof, yet a glance showed me he was pale as ashes. I knew not, positively, then, the immediate danger, but every thing convinced me danger was hovering about me, & that this experiment could alone save me from its jaws. I mounted, therefore, unbidden, the Bed stead – & M. Dubois placed me upon the Mattress, & spread a cambric handkerchief upon my face. It was transparent, however, & I saw, through it, that the Bed stead was instantly surrounded by the 7 men & my nurse. I refused to be held; but when, Bright through the cambric, I saw the glitter of polished Steel – I closed my Eyes. I would not trust to convulsive fear the sight of the terrible incision. A silence the most profound ensued, which lasted for some minutes, during which, I imagine, they took their orders by signs, & made their examination – Oh what a horrible suspension! – I did not breathe – & M. Dubois tried vainly to find any pulse. This pause, at length, was broken by Dr. Larry, who in a voice of solemn melancholy, said '*Qui me tiendra ce sein?* –'[34]

No one answered; at least not verbally; but this aroused me from my passively submissive state, for I feared they imagined the whole breast infected – feared it too justly, – for, again through the Cambric, I saw the hand of M. Dubois held up, while his fore finger first described a straight line from the top to bottom of the breast, secondly a Cross, & thirdly a circle; intimating that the WHOLE was to be taken off. Excited by this idea, I started up, threw off my veil, &, in answer to the demand '*Qui me tendra ce sein*'? cried '*C'est moi, Monsieur!*' & I held My hand under it, & explained the nature of my sufferings, which all sprang from one point, though they darted into every part. I was heard attentively, but in utter silence, & M. Dubois then re-placed me as before, &, as before, spread my veil over my face. How vain, alas, my representation! immediately again I saw the fatal finger describe the Cross – & the circle – Hopeless, then, desperate, & self-given up, I closed once more my Eyes, relinquishing all watching, all resistance, all interference, & sadly resolute to be wholly resigned.

My dearest Esther, – & all my dears to whom she communicates this doleful ditty, will rejoice to hear that this resolution once taken, was firmly adhered to, in defiance of a terror that surpasses all description, & the most torturing pain. Yet – when the dreadful steel was plunged into the breast – cutting through veins – arteries – flesh – nerves – I needed no injunctions not to restrain my cries. I began a scream that lasted unintermittingly during the whole time of the incision – & I almost marvel that it rings not in my Ears still! so excruciating was the agony. When the wound was made, & the instrument was withdrawn, the pain seemed undiminished, for the air that suddenly rushed into those delicate parts felt like a mass of minute but sharp & forked poniards, that were tearing the edges of the wound – but when again I felt the instrument – describing a curve – cutting against the grain, if I may so say, while the flesh resisted in a manner so forcible to change from the right to the left – then, indeed, I thought I must have expired. I attempted no more to open my Eyes, – they felt as if hermetically shut, & so firmly closed, that the Eyelids seemed indented into the Cheeks. The instrument this second time withdrawn, I concluded the operation over – Oh no! presently the terrible cutting was renewed – & worse than ever, to separate the bottom, the foundation of this dreadful gland from the parts to which it adhered – Again all description would be baffled – yet again all was not over, – Dr. Larrey rested but his own hand, & – Oh Heaven! – I then felt the Knife rackling against the breast bone – scraping it! – This performed, while I yet remained in utterly speechless torture, I heard the Voice of Mr. Larrey,

---

[34]　*Qui me tiendra ce sein?* "Who will take this breast for me?"

– (all others guarded a dead silence) in a tone nearly tragic, desire every one present to pronounce if any thing more remained to be done; The general voice was Yes, – but the finger of Mr. Dubois – which I literally *felt* elevated over the wound, though I saw nothing, & though he touched nothing, so indescribably sensitive was the spot – pointed to some further requisition – & again began the scraping! – and, after this, Dr. Moreau thought he discerned a peccant atom – My dearest Esther, not for days, not for Weeks, but for Months I could not speak of this terrible business without nearly again going through it! I could not *think* of it with impunity! I was sick, I was disordered by a single question – even now, 9 months after it is over, I have a head ache from going on with the account! & this miserable account, which I began 3 Months ago, at least, I dare not revise, nor read, the recollection is still so painful.

To conclude, the evil was so profound, the case so delicate, & the precautions necessary for preventing a return so numerous, that the operation, including the treatment & dressing, lasted 20 minutes! a time, for sufferings so acute, that was hardly supportable – However, I bore it with all the courage I could exert, & never moved, nor stopped them, nor resisted, nor remonstrated, nor spoke – except once or twice, during the dressings, to say '*Ah Messieurs! que je vous plains!* –'[35] for indeed I was sensible to the feeling concern with which they all saw what I endured, though my speech was principally – *very* principally meant for Dr. Larrey. Except this, I uttered not a syllable, save, when they so often re-commenced, calling out '*Avertissez moi, Messieurs! avertissez moi!* –'[36] Twice, I believe, I fainted; at least, I have two total chasms in my memory of this transaction, that impede my tying together what passed. When all was done, & they lifted me up that I might be put to bed, my strength was so totally annihilated, that I was obliged to be carried, & could not even sustain my hands & arms, which hung as if I had been lifeless; while my face, as the Nurse has told me, was utterly colourless. This removal made me open my Eyes – & I then saw my good Dr. Larrey, pale nearly as myself, his face streaked with blood, & its expression depicting grief, apprehension, & almost horror.

When I was in bed, – my poor M. d'Arblay – who ought to write you himself his own history of this Morning – was called to me – & afterwards our Alex. –

[d'Arblay's addition follows]

No! No my dearest & ever more dear friends, I shall not make a fruitless attempt. No language could convey what I felt in the deadly course of these seven hours. Nevertheless, every one *of you, my dearest dearest friends*, can guess must even know it. Alexandre had no less feeling, but showed more fortitude. He, perhaps, will be more able to describe you, nearly at least, the torturing state of my poor heart and soul. Besides, I must own, to you, that these details which were, till just now, quite unknown to me, have almost killed me, & I am only able to thank God that this more than half Angel has had the sublime courage to deny herself the comfort I might have offered her, to spare me, not the sharing of her excruciating pains, that was impossible, but the witnessing so terrific a scene, & perhaps the remorse to have rendered it more tragic. For I don't flatter my self I could have gotten through it – I must confess it.

Thank Heaven! She is now surprisingly well, & in good spirits, & we hope to have many still happy days. May that of peace soon arrive, and enable me to embrace better than with my pen beloved & ever ever more dear friends of the town & country. Amen. Amen!

---

[35] *que je vous plains!* "how I pity you."

[36] *Avertissez moi, Messieurs! avertissez moi!* "Warn me, good sirs! Warn me!."

[Burney proceeds]

God bless my dearest Esther – I fear this is all written confusedly, but I cannot read it – & I can write it no more, therefore I entreat you to let all my dear Brethren male & female take a perusal – and that you will lend it also to my tender & most beloved Mrs. Angerstein, who will pardon, I well know, my sparing myself – which is sparing her, a separate letter upon such a theme. My dearest Father & my dearest Mrs. Locke live so little in the world, that I flatter myself they will never hear of this adventure. I earnestly desire it may never reach them. My kind Miss Cambridge & Miss Baker, also, may easily escape it. I leave all others, & all else, to your own decision.

I ought to have mentioned Sarah[37] when I regretted & sighed for my Sisters, for I am sure she would gladly & affectionately have nursed me had she been at hand: but at that critical moment I only thought of those who had already – & so often – had opportunity as well as Soul to demonstrate their tenderness. – and She who is gone[38] is ever, & on all occasions, still present to me. Adieu, adieu, my beloved Esther –

P.S. I have promised my dearest Esther a Volume – & here it is: I am at this moment quite Well – So are my Alexanders. Read, therefore, this Narrative at your leisure, & without emotion – for all has ended happily. I will send the rest by the very first opportunity: I seize this present with eagerness oh let none – none pass by that may bring me a return! – I have no more yet written.

Enquire means to write to me, my Esther, and All my dears, in pity.

I have not had a Word since the noble packet of M. Wurst!

Thomas Chatterton (1752–1770)

Chatterton's poems have merited a two-volume Clarendon Press edition (1971), and there have been a large number of biographical and critical studies including a novelistic treatment by Peter Ackroyd (1987). Recently, Routledge published a six-volume set entitled Thomas Chatterton, Early Sources and Responses *(1994). What makes all of this remarkable is that Chatterton died at the age of seventeen. His most spectacular literary achievement was the creation of a body of poetry purportedly by a fifteenth-century Bristol poet named Thomas Rowley. Some were taken in by the deception, but, as in the case of Macpherson's Ossian poems, more learned readers soon got it all straightened out. Horace Walpole was one of the most indignant, and his hostility to Chatterton has often been identified as a source of the young poet's despair. It is unclear whether or not Chatterton committed suicide or died of an accidental overdose of the arsenic that he was taking for venereal disease. The romantic myth about "the marvelous boy," as Wordsworth called him was paramount in conceptions of Chatterton's life and works for a long time; he was seen as the type of the Romantic poet, sensitive, spurned by conservative society, and a tragic early suicide. More recently, critics (Claude Rawson, for example) have drawn attention to the ways in which Chatterton's poetry, for all its trumped-up medievalism, adheres to many conventional eighteenth-century poetic standards. "An Excelente Balade of Charitie" has been read romantically as a* cri de coeur *and a suicide note, but it is also a moral fable about charity, the story and theme of which would not be out of place in the works of Isaac Watts or Hanah More or even Samuel Johnson.*

---

[37] *Sarah* Burney's half-sister.

[38] *She who is gone* Burney's mother, Esther, died in 1762.

Because the spelling and punctuation are so important to the medieval deception, I suspend my regular procedure of conservative modernization and present this poem literatim, *just as it appeared the first time it was printed, in* Poems, Supposed to have been Written at Bristol, By Thomas Rowley, and Others, in the Fifteenth Century (*1777*).

from *Poems, Supposed to have been Written at Bristol, By Thomas Rowley, and Others, in the Fifteenth Century* (1777)

AN EXCELENTE BALADE OF CHARITIE:

As wroten bie the gode Prieste Thomas Rowley, 1464[1]

In Virgyne the sweltrie sun gan sheene,
And hotte upon the mees did caste his raie;[2]
The apple rodded from its palie greene,[3]
And the mole peare did bende the leafy spraie;[4]
The peede chelandri sunge the livelong daie;[5]   5
'Twas nowe the pride, the manhode of the yeare,
And eke the ground was dighte in its most defte aumere.[6]

The sun was glemeing in the midde of daie,
Deadde still the aire, and eke the welkin blue,[7]
When from the sea arist in drear arraie[8]   10
A hepe of cloudes of sable sullen hue,
The which full fast unto the woodlande drewe,
Hiltring attenes the sunnis fetive face,[9]
And the blacke tempeste swolne and gatherd up apace.

Beneath an holme, faste by a pathwaie side,[10]   15
Which dide unto Seyncte Godwine's covent lede,[11]
A hapless pilgrim moneynge did abide,[12]
Pore in his viewe, ungentle in his weede,[13]
Longe bretful of the miseries of neede.[14]
Where from the hail-stone coulde the almer flie?[15]   20
He had no housen theere, ne anie covent nie.

AN EXCELENTE BALADE OF CHARITIE
[1] *Rowley* Thomas Rowley, the author, was born at Norton Mal-reward in Somersetshire, educated at the Convent of St. Kenna at Keynesham, and died at Westbury in Gloucestershire [Chatterton's note].
[2] *mees* meads [meadows; Chatterton's note].
[3] *rodded* reddened, ripened [Chatterton's note].
[4] *mole* soft [Chatterton's note].
[5] *chelandri* pied goldfinch [Chatterton's note].
[6] *dighte* dressed, arrayed; *defte* neat, ornamental; *aumere* a loose robe or mantle [Chatterton's notes].
[7] *welkin* the sky, the atmosphere [Chatterton's note].
[8] *arist* arose [Chatterton's note].

[9] *Hiltring* hiding, shrouding; *attenes* at once; *fetive* beautiful [Chatterton's notes].
[10] *holme* holly tree.
[11] *covent* It would have been *charitable*, if the author had not pointed at personal characters in this Ballad of Charity. The Abbot of St. Godwin's at the time of the writing of this was Ralph de Bellomont, a great stickler for the Lancastrian family. Rowley was a Yorkist [Chatterton's note].
[12] *moneynge* moaning.
[13] *ungentle* beggarly [Chatterton's note]; *weede* clothing.
[14] *bretful* filled with [Chatterton's note].
[15] *almer* beggar.

Look in his glommed face, his sprighte there scanne;[16]
Howe woe-be-gone, how withered, forwynd, deade![17]
Haste to thie church-glebe-house, ashrewed manne![18]
Haste to thie kiste, thie onlie dortoure bedde.[19]
Cale as the claie whiche will gre on thie hedde,[20]
Is Charitie and Love aminge highe elves;
Knightis and Barons live for pleasure and themselves.

25

The gatherd storme is rype; the bigge drops falle,
The forswat meadowes smethe, and drenche the raine;[21]
The comyng ghastness doth the cattle pall,[22]
And the full flockes are drivynge ore the plaine;
Dashde from the cloudes, the waters flott againe;[23]
The welkin opes; the yellow levynne flies,[24]
And the hot fierie smothe in the wide lowings dies.[25]

30

35

List! now the thunder's rattling clymmynge sound[26]
Cheves slowlie on, and then embollen clangs,[27]
Shakes the hie spyre, and losst, dispended, drown'd,
Still on the gallard eaer of terroure hanges;[28]
The windes are up; the lofty elmen swanges;
Again the levynne, and the thunder poures,
And the full cloudes are braste attenes in stonen showers.[29]

40

Spurreynge his palfrie oere the watrie plaine,
The Abbote of Seyncte Godwynes convente came;
His chapournette was drented with the reine,[30]
And his pencte gyrdle met with mickle shame;[31]
He aynewarde told his bederoll at the same;[32]
The storme encreasen, and he drew aside,
With the mist almes craver neere to the holme to bide.[33]

45

His cope was all of Lyncolne clothe so fyne,[34]
With a gold button fasten'd neere his chynne;
His autremete was edged with golden twynne,[35]

50

---

[16] *glommed* cloudy, dejected. A person of some note in the literary world is of opinion, that *glum* and *glom* are modern cant words; and from this circumstance doubts the authenticity of Rowley's Manuscripts. *Glum-mong* in the Saxon signifies twilight, a dark or dubious light; and the modern word *gloomy* is derived from the Saxon *glum* [Chatterton's note].
[17] *forwynde* dry, sapless [Chatterton's note].
[18] *church-glebe-house* the grave; *ashrewed* accursed, unfortunate [Chatterton's notes].
[19] *kiste* coffin; *dorture* a sleeping room [Chatterton's notes].
[20] *Cale* cold; *gre* grow.
[21] *forswat* sun-burnt; *smethe* smoke; *drenche* drink [Chatterton's notes].
[22] *pall* a contraction from appall, to fright [Chatterton's note].
[23] *flott* fly [Chatterton's note].

[24] *levynne* lightning [Chatterton's note].
[25] *smothe* steam, or vapours; *lowings* flames [Chatterton's notes].
[26] *clymmynge* noisy [Chatterton's note].
[27] *Cheves* moves; *embollen* swelled, strengthened [Chatterton's note].
[28] *gallard* frighted [Chatterton's note].
[29] *braste* burst [Chatterton's note].
[30] *chapournette* a small round hat, not unlike the shapournette in heraldry, fomerly worn by Ecclesiastics and Lawyers [Chatterton's note].
[31] *pencte* painted [Chatterton's note].
[32] *aynewarde told his bederoll* told his beads backwards [Chatterton's note].
[33] *mist* poor, needy [Chatterton's note].
[34] *cope* a cloak [Chatterton's note].
[35] *autremete* a loose white robe, worn by Priests [Chatterton's note].

And his shoone pyke a loverds mighte have binne;[36]
Full well it shewn he thoughten coste no sinne:
The trammels of his palfrye pleasde his sighte,   55
For the horse-millanare his head with roses dighte.[37]

An almes, sir prieste! the droppynge pilgrim saide,
Oh! let me waite within your covente-dore,
Till the sunne sheneth hie above our heade,
And the loude tempeste of the aire is oer;   60
Helpless and ould am I alas! and poor;
No house, ne friend, ne moneie in my pouche,
All yatte I call my owne is this my silver crouche.[38]

Varlet! replyd the Abbatte, cease your dinne;
This is no season almes and prayers to give,   65
Mie porter never lets a faitour in;[39]
None touch mie ring who not in honour live.
And now the sonne with the blacke cloudes did stryve,
And shettynge on the ground his glairie raie:
The Abbate spurrde his steede, and eftsoones roadde awaie.   70

Once moe the skie was blacke, the thounder rolde;
Faste reyneyng oer the plaine a prieste was seen;
Not dight full proude, ne buttoned up in golde;
His cope and jape were graie, and eke were clene;[40]
A Limitoure he was of order seene;   75
And from the pathwaie side then turned hee,
Where the pore almer laie binethe the holmen tree.

An almes, sir priest! the droppynge pilgrim sayde,
For sweete Seyncte Marie and your order sake.
The Limitour then loosen'd his pouche threade,   80
And did thereoute a groate of silver take;
The mister pilgrim dyd for halline shake.[41]
Here take this silver, it maie eathe thie care;[42]
We are Goddes stewards all, nete of oure owne we bare.[43]

But ah! unhailie pilgrim, lerne of me,[44]   85
Scathe anie give a renttrolle to their Lorde;[45]
Here, take my semecope, thou arte bare, I see;[46]
'Tis thyne; the Seynctes will give me mie rewarde.
He left the pilgrim, and his waie aborde.[47]
Virgynne and hallie Seyncte, who sitte yn gloure,[48]   90
Or give the mittee will, or give the gode man power![49]

---

[36] *loverd* a lord [Chatterton's note].
[37] *horse-millanare* I believe this trade is still in being, though but seldom employed [Chatterton's note].
[38] *yatte* that; *crouche* cross.
[39] *faitour* beggar [Chatterton's note].
[40] *jape* a short surplice, worn by Friars of an inferior class, and secular priests [Chatterton's note].
[41] *halline* joy [Chatterton's note].

[42] *eathe* ease [Chatterton's note].
[43] *nete* nought.
[44] *unhailie* unhappy [Chatterton's note].
[45] *renttrolle* rent-roll, financial statement.
[46] *semecope* a short under-cloak [Chatterton's note].
[47] *aborde* went on.
[48] *gloure* glory [Chatterton's note].
[49] *mittee* mighty, rich; *or . . . or* either . . . or.

George Crabbe (1754–1832)

Like Goldsmith and Smollett, Crabbe devoted himself to literary work after failing to make it in the medical profession. 1780 was the year of decision for Crabbe. He had been an apprentice to a surgeon and apothecary, studied medicine in London, and returned to his native town of Aldeburgh in Suffolk to run his own apothecary shop. His income was inconstant and meagre, however, and his sweetheart declined to marry him in his poverty. So, he went to London with a small stock of the poetry he had been writing. In his second year of professional writing Crabbe attracted the notice and the patronage of Edmund Burke. Burke introduced him to others who helped him greatly, including Samuel Johnson and some noblemen who were interested in poetry and had the where-withal to establish young men in comfortable livings. In 1782 Crabbe wrote The Village, *a poem of over 500 lines that concerns "real life" in a place like Aldeburgh in contrast to fanciful representations of country life in pastoral poetry. The poem appealed to Samuel Johnson, who recommended publication and offered a few changes, including a six-line substitution in the introductory section. Crabbe happily accepted the advice; the poem was published; and Crabbe gained a literary reputation. Meanwhile he had become first a deacon and then an ordained priest; this fitted him for the benefactions of Lord Rutland, whose recently deceased brother Crabbe memorialized in* The Village. *So, all at once, Crabbe was established financially and launched in the literary world. He married his sweetheart, but then a life full of professional and personal vicissitudes was only beginning.*

Crabbe is best known for a series of descriptions of village life and village characters that were published over ten years from 1810 to 1819 as The Borough, Tales, *and* Tales of the Hall. *One of his character portraits has been immortalized in Benjamin Britten's opera* Peter Grimes. *His work removes the golden glow of pastoral poetry from descriptions of common life in the country, and points the way for the movement known as realism that flourished in novels written mainly in the generations after Crabbe's death. He is a link between the highly poetic vision of common life in Gray's* Elegy, *and the more detailed and more comic life-likeness of Dickens or even the depressing depictions of Philip Larkin. Crabbe's poems have been edited by Norma Dalrymple-Champneys in three volumes (Clarendon Press, 1988). The text I present of* The Village *is based on the first edition of 1783 and does not incorporate the many changes Crabbe made when he included the work in his* Poems *(1807).*

from *The Village: A Poem in Two Books* (1783)

BOOK I

The village life, and every care that reigns
O'er youthful peasants and declining swains;
What labour yields, and what, that labour past,
Age, in its hour of languor, finds at last;
What forms the real picture of the poor,   5
Demands a song – The Muse can give no more.
　　Fled are those times, if e'er such times were seen,
When rustic poets praised their native green;
No shepherds now in smooth alternate verse,

Their country's beauty or their nymphs' rehearse;   10
Yet still for these we frame the tender strain,
Still in our lays fond Corydons complain,[1]
And shepherds' boys their amorous pains reveal,
The only pains, alas! they never feel.
 On Mincio's banks, in Caesar's bounteous reign,[2]   15
If TITYRUS found the golden age again,[3]
Must sleepy bards the flattering dreams prolong,
Mechanic echoes of the Mantuan song?
From truth and nature shall we widely stray,
Where VIRGIL, not where fancy leads the way?[4]   20
 Yes, thus the Muses sing of happy swains,
Because the Muses never knew their pains:
They boast their peasants' pipes, but peasants now
Resign their pipes and plod behind the plough;
And few amid the rural tribe have time   25
To number syllables and play with rhyme;
Save honest DUCK, what son of verse could share[5]
The poet's rapture and the peasant's care?
Or the great labours of the field degrade
With the new peril of a poorer trade?   30
 From one chief cause these idle praises spring,
That, themes so easy, few forbear to sing;
They ask no thought, require no deep design,
But swell the song and liquefy the line;
The gentle lover takes the rural strain,   35
A nymph his mistress and himself a swain;
With no sad scenes he clouds his tuneful prayer,
But all, to look like her, is painted fair.
 I grant indeed that fields and flocks have charms,
For him that gazes or for him that farms;   40
But when amid such pleasing scenes I trace
The poor laborious natives of the place,
And see the mid-day sun, with fervid ray,
On their bare heads and dewy temples play;
While some, with feebler hands and fainter hearts,   45
Deplore their fortune, yet sustain their parts,
Then shall I dare these real ills to hide,
In tinsel trapping of poetic pride?
 No, cast by Fortune on a frowning coast,[6]

---

[1] *Corydons*   shepherds, a typical name in pastoral poetry from Virgil and Theocritus onwards.
[2] *On Mincio's . . .*   lines 15–20 stand as they were "corrected" by Samuel Johnson; *Mincio*   a river near Virgil's
home town of Mantua.
[3] *TITYRUS*   Virgil's pastoral poetic name for himself; *golden age*   the imaginary time of peace and simple
nobility represented in pastoral poetry.
[4] *fancy*   imagination.
[5] *DUCK*   Stephen (1705–56), see the selection above.
[6] *frowning coast*   Crabbe uses the terrain of his
native Aldeburgh, Suffolk, as the main source of his
descriptions.

Which can no groves nor happy valleys boast;   50
Where other cares than those the Muse relates,
And other shepherds dwell with other mates;
By such examples taught, I paint the cot,[7]
As truth will paint it, and as bards will not:
Nor you, ye poor, of lettered scorn complain,   55
To you the smoothest song is smooth in vain;
O'ercome by labour and bowed by time,
Feel you the barren flattery of a rhyme?
Can poets soothe you, when you pine for bread,
By winding myrtles round your ruined shed?   60
Can their light tales your weighty griefs o'erpower,
Or glad with airy mirth the toilsome hour?
     Lo! where the heath, with withering brake grown o'er,
Lends the light turf that warms the neighbouring poor;
From thence a length of burning sand appears,   65
Where the thin harvest waves its withered ears;
Rank weeds, that every art and care defy,
Reign o'er the land and rob the blighted rye:
There thistles stretch their prickly arms afar,
And to the ragged infant threaten war;   70
There poppies nodding, mock the hope of toil,
There the blue bugloss paints the sterile soil;[8]
Hardy and high, above the slender sheaf,
The slimy mallow waves her silky leaf;
O'er the young shoot the charlock throws a shade,[9]   75
And the wild tare clings round the sickly blade;[10]
With mingled tints the rocky coasts abound,
And a sad splendour vainly shines around.
     So looks the nymph whom wretched arts adorn,
Betrayed by man, then left for man to scorn;   80
Whose cheek in vain assumes the mimic rose,
While her sad eyes the troubled breast disclose;
Whose outward splendour is but Folly's dress,
Exposing most, when most it gilds distress.
     Here joyless roam a wild amphibious race,   85
With sullen woe displayed in every face;
Who, far from civil arts and social fly,
And scowl at strangers with suspicious eye.
     Here too the lawless vagrant of the main
Draws from his plough the intoxicated swain;   90
Want only claimed the labour of the day,
But vice now steals his nightly rest away.
     Where are the swains, who, daily labour done,

---

[7]   *cot*   cottage.
[8]   *bugloss*   viper's bugloss, blue devil or blue weed, a
bristly plant with blue flowers.

[9]   *charlock*   wild mustard, a plant with stiff bristles on
its stems and leaves.
[10]   *tare*   poisonous ryegrass, a weed often infected with
a poisonous fungus.

With rural games played down the setting sun;
Who struck with matchless force the bounding ball,   95
Or made the ponderous quoit obliquely fall;[11]
While some huge Ajax, terrible and strong,[12]
Engaged some artful stripling of the throng,
And foiled beneath the young Ulysses fell;
When peals of praise the merry mischief tell?   100
Where now are these? Beneath yon cliff they stand,
To show the freighted pinnance where to land;[13]
To load the ready steed with guilty haste,
To fly in terror o'er the pathless waste,
Or when detected in their straggling course,   105
To foil their foes by cunning or by force;
Or yielding part (when equal knaves contest)
To gain a lawless passport for the rest.[14]
     Here wandering long amid these frowning fields,
I sought the simple life that Nature yields;   110
Rapine and Wrong and Fear usurped her place,
And a bold, artful, surly, savage race;
Who, only skilled to take the finny tribe,
The yearly dinner, or septennial bribe,[15]
Wait on the shore, and as the waves run high,   115
On the tossed vessel bend their eager eye;
Which to their coast directs its venturous way,
Theirs, or the ocean's miserable prey.
     As on their neighbouring beach yon swallows stand,
And wait for favourable winds to leave the land;   120
While still for flight the ready wing is spread:
So waited I the favouring hour, and fled;
Fled from these shores where guilt and famine reign,
And cried, Ah! hapless they who still remain;
Who still remain to hear the ocean roar,   125
Whose greedy waves devour the lessening shore;
Till some fierce tide, with more imperious sway,[16]
Sweeps the low hut and all it holds away;
When the sad tenant weeps from door to door,
And begs a poor protection from the poor.   130
     But these are scenes where Nature's niggard hand
Gave a spare portion to the famished land;
Hers is the fault if here mankind complain
Of fruitless toil and labour spent in vain;

---

[11] *quoit* an iron ring used in a game like horseshoes.
[12] *Ajax* Ajax Telamon, the massiest of the Achaeans described in the *Iliad*; he ties in a wrestling match with the smaller wily Ulysses but eventually kills himself when his fellow soldiers decide that Achilles' armor should go to Ulysses rather than him.
[13] *pinnance* ship.

[14] *passport* an authorization to import or export dutiable goods without paying the usual tax.
[15] *yearly dinner* given after annual local elections; *septennial bribe* given to secure votes in the election of Members of Parliament, the period of which was seven years at that time.
[16] *fierce tide* Crabbe recalls a spring-tide in 1779 that destroyed eleven houses in Aldeburgh.

But yet in other scenes more fair in view,   135
Where Plenty smiles – alas! she smiles for few,
And those who taste not, yet behold her store,
Are as the slaves that dig the golden ore,
The wealth around them makes them doubly poor:
Or will you deem them amply paid in health,   140
Labour's fair child, that languishes with Wealth?
Go then! and see them rising with the sun,
Through a long course of daily toil to run;
Like him to make the plenteous harvest grow,
And yet not share the plenty they bestow;   145
See them beneath the dog-star's raging heat,[17]
When the knees tremble and the temples beat;
Behold them leaning on their scythes, look o'er
The labour past, and toils to come explore;
See them alternate suns and showers engage,   150
And hoard up aches and anguish for their age;
Through fens and marshy moors their steps pursue,
When their warm pores imbibe the evening dew;
Then own that labour may as fatal be
To these thy slaves, as luxury to thee.   155

Ann Cromartie Yearsley (1756–1806)

Married to a poor laborer in Bristol, Yearsley was a genuinely poor milk-maid when she was "discovered" by Hannah More. Like Stephen Duck, "the thresher poet" a few generations before, Yearsley, "a milkwoman of Bristol" rose to instant fame. More groomed her work and financed the publication of her Poems on Several Occasions *(1785), to which 1,000 purchasers subscribed. Unfortunately, the kind of regular clerical living into which his patrons thrust Duck was unavailable to Yearsley, and More, with the help of Elizabeth Montagu, cobbled together a financial arrangement that seemed to Yearsley a form of perpetual dependency. She broke with More, got control of the money from the publication and eventually opened a circulating library. This was not a success. She eventually secured another patron and published three more volumes of poetry, but the loss of her first patron and mentor tells on her work, and the opprobrium heaped on her by More's literary and socialite friends restricted her future chances of success.*

Yearsley's work displays a curious combination of the overblown and the conventional melting into a language of Romantic self-expression. She certainly lacks the polish and sophistication of many "transitional" poets, yet there is a fierce personal pride and a vigor in her self-expression that a better sense of poetic tradition might have suppressed. All of Yearsley's poems are being made available through the Brown University Women Writers Project. My text of "On Mrs Montagu" is based on Poems on Several Occasions *(1785), and I take the other two pieces from* Poems on Various Subjects *(1787).*

---

[17]   *dog-star*   the bright star Sirius, which rises with the
sun in late summer and is associated with the heat and
famine of that season.

from *Poems on Several Occasions* (1785)

ON MRS. MONTAGU[1]

Why boast, O arrogant, imperious man,
Perfection so exclusive? are thy powers
Nearer approaching Deity? can'st thou solve
Questions which high Infinity propounds,
Soar nobler flights, or dare immortal deeds,   5
Unknown to woman, if she greatly dares
To use the powers assigned her? Active strength,
The boast of animals, is clearly thine;
By this upheld, thou think'st the lesson rare
That female virtues teach; and poor the height   10
Which female wit obtains. The theme unfolds
Its ample maze, for MONTAGU befriends
The puzzled thought, and, blazing in the eye
Of boldest Opposition, straight presents
The soul's best energies, her keenest powers,   15
Clear, vigorous, enlightened; with firm wing
Swift she o'ertakes *his* Muse, which spread afar
Its brightest glories in the days of yore;
Lo! where she, mounting, spurns the steadfast earth,
And, sailing on the cloud of science, bears[2]   20
The banner of Perfection. –
Ask GALLIA's mimic sons how strong her powers,
Whom, flushed with plunder from her SHAKESPEARE's page,[3]
She swift detects amid their dark retreats;
(Horrid as CACUS in their thievish dens)[4]   25
Regains the trophies, bears in triumph back
The pilfered glories to a wond'ring world.
So STELLA boasts, from her tale I learned;[5]
With pride she told it, I with rapture heard.
  O, MONTAGU! forgive me, if I sing   30
Thy wisdom tempered with the milder ray
Of soft humanity, and kindness bland:
So wide its influence, that the bright beams
Reach the low vale where mists of ignorance lodge,
Strike on the innate spark which lay immersed,   35
Thick clogged, and almost quenched in total night –

ON MRS. MONTAGU
[1] *Mrs Montagu* Elizabeth (1720–1800), writer, socialite, and patron of many women writers; she and Hannah More were Yearsley's patrons.
[2] *science* knowledge.
[3] *her SHAKESPEARE's page* Montagu wrote *An Essay on the Writings and Genius of Shakespeare* (1769), in which she defended the bard from the criticisms of Voltaire and argued his superiority to Gallic (i.e. French) writers.
[4] *CACUS* a fire-breathing monster who dragged some of Hercules' cattle into his cave; Hercules recovered the cattle and killed the beast.
[5] *STELLA* Hannah More (1745–1833); Yearsley's most important patron, who also helped her improve her writing (see selection above).

On me it fell, and cheered my joyless heart.
    Unwelcome is the first bright dawn of light
To that dark soul; impatient, she rejects,
And fain would push the heavenly stranger back;   40
She loathes the cranny which admits the day;
Confused, afraid of the intruding guest;
Disturbed, unwilling to receive the beam,
Which to herself the native darkness shows.
    The effort rude to quench the cheering flame   45
Was mine, and e'en on STELLA could I gaze
With sullen envy, and admiring pride,
Till, doubly roused by MONTAGU, the pair
Conspire to clear my dull, imprisoned sense,
And chase the mists which dimmed my visual beam.   50
    Oft as I trod my native wilds alone,
Strong gusts of thought would rise, but rise to die;
The portals of the swelling soul ne'er oped
By liberal converse, rude ideas strove
Awhile for vent, but found it not, and died.   55
Thus rust the Mind's best powers. Yon starry orbs,
Majestic ocean, flowery vales, gay groves,
Eye-wasting lawns, and Heaven-attempting hills,
Which bound th' horizons, and which curb the view;
All those, with beauteous imagery, awaked   60
My ravished soul to ecstasy untaught,
To all the transport the rapt sense can bear;
But all expired, for want of powers to speak;
All perished in the mind as soon as born,
Erased more quick than ciphers on the shore,   65
O'er which the cruel waves, unheedful, roll.
    Such timid rapture as young EDWIN seized,[6]
When his lone footsteps on the Sage obtrude,
Whose noble precept charmed his wondering
Such rapture filled Lactilla's vacant soul,[7]   70
When the bright Moralist, in softness dressed,[8]
Opes all the glories of the mental world,
Deigns to direct the infant thought, to prune
The budding sentiment, uprear the stalk
Of feeble fancy, bid idea live,   75
Woo the abstracted spirit from its cares,
And gently guide her to the scenes of peace.
Mine was that balm, and mine the grateful heart,
Which breathes its thanks in rough, but timid strains.

---

[6] *young EDWIN*   see *The Minstrel* [(1771–4) by James
Beattie; Yearsley's note].

[7] *Lactilla* Yearsley's poetical name for herself based
on the Latin word for milk because she was a milk-maid.
[8] *bright Moralist* More.

from *Poems on Various Subjects* (1787)

To
INDIFFERENCE

INDIFFERENCE come! thy torpid juices shed
On my keen sense: plunge deep my wounded heart,
In thickest apathy, till it congeal,
Or mix with thee incorp'rate. Come, thou foe
To sharp sensation, in thy cold embrace   5
A death-like slumber shall a respite give
To my long restless soul, tossed on extreme,
From bliss to pointed woe. Oh, gentle Pow'r,
Dear substitute of Patience! thou canst ease
The Soldier's toil, the gloomy Captive's chain,   10
The Lover's anguish, and the Miser's fear.
    Proud Beauty will not own thee! *her* loud boast
Is VIRTUE – while thy chilling breath alone
Blows o'er her soul, bidding her passions sleep.
    Mistaken *Cause*, the frozen Fair denies   15
Thy saving influence. VIRTUE never lives,
But in thy bosom, struggling with its wound:
There she supports the conflict, *there* augments
The pang of *hopeless Love*, the senseless stab
Of gaudy Ign'rance, and more deeply drives   20
The poisoned dart, hurled by the long-loved friend;
Then pants with painful Victory. Bear me hence,
Thou antidote to pain! thy real worth
Mortals can never know. What's the vain boast
Of Sensibility but to be wretched?   25
In *her* best transports lives a latent sting,
Which wounds as they expire. On her high heights
Our souls can never sit; the point so nice,
We quick fly off – secure, but in descent.
    To SENSIBILITY, what is not bliss   30
Is woe. No placid medium's ever held
Beneath her torrid line, when straining high
The fibres of the soul. Of Pain, or Joy,
She gives too large a share; but thou, more kind,
Wrapp'st up the heart from both, and bidd'st it rest   35
In ever-wished-for ease. By all the pow'rs
Which move within the mind for different ends,
I'd rather lose myself with *thee*, and share
Thine happy indolence, for one short hour,
Than live of Sensibility the tool   40
For endless ages. Oh! her points have pierced
My soul, till, like a sponge, it drinks up woe.
    Then leave me, Sensibility! be gone,

Thou chequered angel! Seek the soul refined:
I hate thee! and thy long progressive brood
Of joys and mis'ries. Soft Indifference, come! 45
In this low cottage thou shalt be my guest,
Till Death shuts out the hour: here down I'll sink
With thee upon my couch of homely rush,
Which fading forms of Friendship, Love, or Hope, 50
Must ne'er approach. Ah! – quickly hide, thou pow'r,
Those dear intruding images! Oh, seal
The lids of mental sight, lest I abjure
My freezing supplication.– All is still.
    IDEA, smothered, leaves my mind a waste, 55
Where SENSIBILITY must lose her prey.

TO THOSE WHO ACCUSE THE AUTHOR OF INGRATITUDE[1]

You, who through optics dim, so falsely view
This wondrous maze of things, and rend a part
From the well-ordered whole, to fit your sense
Low, grovelling, and confined; say from what source
Spring your all-wise opinions? Can you dare 5
Pronounce from proof, who ne'er pursued event
To its minutest cause? Yet further soar,
In swift gradation, to the verge of space;
Where, wrapped in worlds, Time's origin exists:
There breathe your question; there the cause explore, 10
Why dark afflictions, borne upon the wing
Of Love invisible, light on the wretch
Inured and patient in the pangs of woe?
    Or Wisdom infinite with Pride arraign;
Rebuke the Deity, and madly ask, 15
Why Man's sad hour of anguish ever ends?
    What are your boasts, ye incapacious souls,
Who would confine, within your narrow orbs,
Th' extensive All? Can sense, like yours, discern
An object, wand'ring from her destined course, 20
Quitting the purer path, where spirit roves,
To sip Mortality's soul-clogging dews,
And feast on Craft's poor dregs? What though she owned
An office, would have borne her to the stars
While list'ning Angels had the plaudit hailed, 25
And blessed her force of soul, unequal proved
Her strongest pow'rs, to top fair Virtue's height,

TO THOSE WHO ACCUSE THE AUTHOR
[1] *Ingratitude* written after Yearsley broke with More
who had invested some £350 in her; Yearsley was widely
and angrily denounced.

Or, on the act, to fix the stamp of *Merit*.
    What's noosed opinion but a creeping curse,
That leads the Idiot through yon beaten track, 30
When keener spirits ask it? Which of you
Dare, on the wing of Candour, stretch afar
To seize the bright sublimity of Truth?
    A wish to share the false, though public din,
In which the popular, not virtuous, live; 35
A fear of being singular, which claims
A fortitude of mind you ne'er could boast;
A love of base detraction, when the charm
Sits on a flowing tongue, and willing moves
Upon its darling topic. These are yours. 40
But were the steadfast adamantine pow'rs
Of Principle unmoved? Fantastic group!
Spread wide your arms and turn yon flaming Sun
From his most fair direction; dash the stars
With Earth's poor pebbles, and ask the World's great Sire, 45
Why, in Creation's system, HE dare fix
More orbs than your weak sense shall e'er discern?
Then scan the feelings of Lactilla's soul.

William Blake (1757–1827)

Blake is one the figures in British literary history who tends to reveal the inadequacy of academic categories. He was more an artist than a poet, but he blended the two in ways that make it impossible to separate his contributions to the two fields; he was startlingly original and yet an immense amount of his work consists in the designs and engravings he produced to illustrate works by others; his political views were radical and he celebrated the French Revolution, but he was devout, inspired, and anti-rationalistic in religion; his work is obscure and apparently dependent on his own personal system of thought, and yet one of the greatest critics of the twentieth century, Northrop Frye, spent the better part of a lifetime showing how profoundly conventional Blake is. Given these larger paradoxes in understanding Blake, it is not surprising that it is difficult to locate him in one or another of the intellectual currents that were crossing each other at the end of the eighteenth century. He is certainly an important Romantic poet, but his Romanticism harks back to Milton and certain kinds of Protestant radicalism that flourished during the interregnum. As E. P. Thompson has shown, Blake was a Muggletonian, a follower of a man who proclaimed himself a prophet in 1651 and preached a radical form of Arianism: he believed God to be completely unitary, even in body, and he obviously believed in a great multiplicity of prophets. Blake himself had visions and regarded his prophetic leanings almost casually, although he could be vociferous in his criticism of those whom he accused of stifling prophecy or the holy imagination. He led a life of continuous, imaginative productivity; the large amount of work that survives is only a fraction of what Blake produced.

    Blake's poetry has been edited by G. E. Bentley in two volumes, one for the engraved and etched writings and one for those in conventional typography (Clarendon Press, 1978). In addition there are numerous wonderful reprints of his engraved works. Songs of Innocence *was his first entirely homemade book. He drew the poems and their surrounding illustrations on copper plates, from which he printed his colored pages; his wife assisted him in printing, tinting and binding the books. A few years later the two produced the companion book* Songs of Experience. *Blake's notion is that these are parallel aspects of life that must be passed through on the way to revelation. But, like so much of Blake's work, the* Songs *have an appeal that goes beyond their place in Blake's or anyone else's explanatory system. The texts here are based on editions made in the first year of printing, though I have been a little freer than usual in adding useful punctuation. The poems should be appreciated in their pictorial context in one or more of the numerous facsimiles that have been produced.*

from *Songs of Innocence* (1789)

INTRODUCTION

Piping down the valleys wild
Piping songs of pleasant glee
On a cloud I saw a child.
And he laughing said to me.

'Pipe a song about a Lamb!'   5
So I piped with merry cheer,
'Piper pipe that song again' –
So I piped, he wept to hear.

'Drop thy pipe thy happy pipe;
Sing thy songs of happy cheer',   10
So I sung the same again
While he wept with joy to hear.

'Piper sit thee down and write
In a book, that all may read' –
So he vanished from my sight,   15
And I plucked a hollow reed.

And I made a rural pen,
And I stained the water clear,
And I wrote my happy songs,
Every child may joy to hear.   20

THE LAMB

Little Lamb who made thee?
    Dost thou know who made thee,
Gave thee life & bid thee feed,
By the stream & o'er the mead;
Gave thee clothing of delight,   5
Softest clothing woolly bright;
Gave thee such a tender voice,
Making all the vales rejoice?
    Little Lamb, who made thee?
    Dost thou know who made thee?   10

Little Lamb I'll tell thee
Little Lamb I'll tell thee;
He is called by thy name,[1]
For he calls himself a Lamb:
He is meek & he is mild,   15
He became a little child:
I a child & thou a lamb,
We are called by his name.
    Little Lamb, God bless thee,
    Little Lamb, God bless thee.   20

THE LITTLE BLACK BOY

My mother bore me in the southern wild,
And I am black, but O! my soul is white,
White as an angel is the English child:
But I am black as if bereaved of light.

My mother taught me underneath a tree   5
And sitting down before the heat of day,
She took me on her lap and kissed me,
And pointing to the east, began to say,

'Look on the rising sun: there God does live
And gives his light, and gives his heat away.   10
And flowers and trees and beasts and men receive
Comfort in morning joy in the noon day.

'And we are put on earth a little space,
That we may learn to bear the beams of love.
And these black bodies and this sun-burnt face   15
Is but a cloud, and like a shady grove.

For when our souls have learned the heat to bear,
The cloud will vanish, we shall hear his voice,
Saying: "Come out from the grove my love & care,
And round my golden tent like lambs rejoice" '.   20

Thus did my mother say and kissed me.
And thus I say to little English boy.
When I from black and he from white cloud free,
And round the tent of God like lambs we joy:

I'll shade him from the heat till he can bear,   25
To lean in joy upon our father's knee.
And then I'll stand and stroke his silver hair,
And be like him and he will then love me.

THE CHIMNEY SWEEPER

When my mother died I was very young,
And my father sold me while yet my tongue,

---

[1] *He* Christ, called the Lamb of God (John 1.29).

Could scarcely cry 'weep weep weep weep'.
So your chimneys I sweep & in soot I sleep.

There's little Tom Dacre, who cried when his head   5
That curled like a lamb's back, was shaved, so I said,
'Hush Tom never mind it, for when your head's bare,
You know that the soot cannot spoil your white hair'.

And so he was quiet, & that very night,
As Tom was a sleeping, he had such a sight,   10
That thousands of sweepers Dick, Joe, Ned & Jack
Were all of them locked up in coffins of black,

And by came an Angel who had a bright key,
And he opened the coffins & set them all free.
Then down a green plain leaping laughing they run   15
And wash in a river, and shine in the Sun.

Then naked and white, all their bags left behind,
They rise upon clouds, and sport in the wind.
And the Angel told Tom, if he'd be a good boy,
He'd have God for his father & never want joy.   20

And so Tom awoke and we rose in the dark,
And got with our bags & our brushes to work.
Though the morning was cold, Tom was happy & warm;
So if all do their duty, they need not fear harm.

HOLY THURSDAY

Twas on a Holy Thursday their innocent faces clean
The children walking two & two in red & blue & green;
Grey headed beadles walked before with wands as white as snow[2]
Till into the high dome of Paul's they like Thames' waters flow.[3]

O what a multitude they seemed these flowers of London town;   5
Seated in companies they sit with radiance all their own;
The hum of multitudes was there but multitudes of lambs,
Thousands of little boys & girls raising their innocent hands.

Now like a mighty wind they raise to heaven the voice of song
Or like harmonious thunderings the seats of heaven among;   10
Beneath them sit the aged men, wise guardians of the poor;
Then cherish pity; lest you drive an angel from your door.

INFANT JOY

'I have no name
I am but two days old'. –
What shall I call thee?
'I happy am
Joy is my name', –   5
Sweet joy befall thee!

---

[2] *beadles* ceremonial church officers.   [3] *Paul's* St Paul's Cathedral, London.

Pretty joy!
Sweet joy but two days old.
Sweet joy I call thee:
Thou dost smile. 10
I sing the while
Sweet joy befall thee.

from *Songs of Experience* (1794)

INTRODUCTION

Hear the voice of the Bard!
Who Present, Past, and Future, sees
Whose ears have heard,
The Holy Word,
That walked among the ancient trees. 5

Calling the lapsèd Soul
And weeping in the evening dew:
That might control
The starry pole:[1]
And fallen fallen light renew! 10

O Earth, O Earth return!
Arise from out the dewy grass;
Night is worn,
And the morn
Rises from the slumberous mass. 15

Turn away no more:
Why wilt thou turn away?
The starry floor
The wat'ry shore
Is giv'n thee till the break of day. 20

HOLY THURSDAY

Is this a holy thing to see,
In a rich and fruitful land,
Babes reduced to misery,
Fed with cold and usurous hand?

Is that trembling cry a song? 5
Can it be a song of joy?
And so many children poor?
It is a land of poverty!

And their sun does never shine.
And their fields are bleak & bare, 10
And their ways are filled with thorns
It is eternal winter there.

INTRODUCTION
[1] *pole* sky.

For where-e'er the sun does shine,
And where-e'er the rain does fall:
Babe can never hunger there, 15
Nor poverty the mind appal.

THE CHIMNEY SWEEPER

A little black thing among the snow:
Crying weep! weep! in notes of woe!
Where are thy father & mother? say?
They are both gone up to the church to pray.

Because I was happy upon the heath, 5
And smiled among the winter's snow:
They clothed me in the clothes of death,
And taught me to sing the notes of woe.

And because I am happy, & dance & sing,
They think they have done me no injury: 10
And are gone to praise God & his Priest & King,
Who make up a heaven of our misery.

THE TYGER

Tyger Tyger, burning bright,
In the forests of the night;
What immortal hand or eye,
Could frame thy fearful symmetry?

In what distant deeps or skies, 5
Burnt the fire of thine eyes?
On what wings dare he aspire?
What the hand dare seize the fire?

And what shoulder, & what art,
Could twist the sinews of thy heart? 10
And when thy heart began to beat,
What dread hand? & what dread feet?

What the hammer? what the chain?
In what furnace was thy brain?
What the anvil? what dread grasp, 15
Dare its deadly terrors clasp?

When the stars threw down their spears
And watered heaven with their tears:
Did he smile his work to see?
Did he who made the Lamb make thee? 20

Tyger Tyger burning bright
In the forests of the night:
What immortal hand or eye,
Dare frame thy fearful symmetry?

AH! SUN-FLOWER

Ah, Sun-flower! weary of time,
Who countest the steps of the Sun:
Seeking after that sweet golden clime,
Where the traveller's journey is done.

Where the Youth pined away with desire,   5
And the pale Virgin shrouded in snow:
Arise from their graves and aspire,
Where my Sun-flower wishes to go.

Robert Burns (1759–1796)

There were certainly earlier poets who wrote successfully in the Scottish dialect of English. Allan Ramsay in the early eighteenth century was important, and there had been a real flowering in the sixteenth century with Henryson, Gavin Douglas, and Dunbar all writing at the same time. Robert Fergusson's (1750–74) poems in vernacular Scots were a key influence. But despite his meager education and his struggles with poverty, whisky, and women, Burns surpassed them all. He hit the perfect medium between repetition and revision of the traditional songs and stories of his native land. He had a reputation for poetry and wild living as a youth and in his early days as a farmer in Ayrshire. Having had an illegitimate child with one woman, he attempted to marry another, Jean Armour, who was also pregnant by him. Her parents blocked him, and Burns was set to go to Jamaica for a fresh start. To fund the expedition, he published Poems, Chiefly in the Scottish Dialect *in 1786. The work was such a success that Burns decided to stay home. He was lionized in Edinburgh, and there were several subsequent, expanded editions of his* Poems. *He also wrote poetry in standard, southern English, but this effort did not amount to much. Most of his best work had been written by 1787, but after that he spent a good deal of time traveling around Scotland collecting and somewhat creatively transcribing folk songs and tales for a large publishing project called* The Scots Musical Museum *(1787–1803).*

To pay the bills, Burns, like Thomas Paine, worked as an excise man, gauging the volume of barrels of liquor and assessing a tax. This ran somewhat counter to his naturally rebellious tendencies; he publicly suppressed his enthusiasm for the French Revolution, but he could not control the opportunities to drink attendant upon his duties. Burns died in poverty at the age of thirty-seven from rheumatic fever.

The Poems and Songs of Robert Burns, *edited by James Kinsley, three volumes (Clarendon Press, 1968) included a glossary of Scottish words to which my notes to the following poems are deeply indebted. I take my texts from the edition of 1787, which came to hand; they vary only slightly from the first edition of 1786, which is preferable as a copytext.*

from *Poems, Chiefly in the Scottish Dialect* (1786)

EPISTLE TO DAVIE, A BROTHER POET[1]

January——

1

While winds frae off *Ben-Lomond* blaw,[2]
And bar the doors wi' driving snaw,
   And hing us owre the ingle,[3]
I set me down, to pass the time,
And spin a verse or twa o' rhyme,   5
   In hamely, *westlin* jingle.[4]
While frosty winds blaw in the drift,
   Ben to the chimla lug,[5]
I grudge a wee the Great-folk's gift,
   That live sae bien an' snug:[6]   10
    I tent less, and want less[7]
      Their roomy fire-side;
    But hanker, and canker,[8]
      To see their cursed pride.

2

It's hardly in a body's pow'r,   15
To keep, at times, frae being sour,
   To see how things are shared;
How best o' chiels are whyles in want,[9]
While Coofs on countless thousands rant,[10]
   And ken na how to wair't:[11]   20
But *Davie*, lad, ne'er fash your head,[12]
   Though we hae little gear,
We're fit to win our daily bread,
   As lang's we're hale and fier:[13]
    'Mair spier na, nor fear na',[14]   25
      Auld age ne'er mind a feg;
    The last o't, the warst o't,
      Is only but to beg.

EPISTLE TO DAVIE
[1] *Davie* David Sillar (1760–1830), author of *Poems* (1789).
[2] *Ben-Lomond* a mountain over 3,000 feet high in the central highlands of Scotland.
[3] *hing* make us hang; *ingle* fire in the hearth.
[4] *westlin* West lands.
[5] *Ben* within; *chimla lug* chimney-corner.
[6] *bien* comfortable.
[7] *tent* care; mind.
[8] *hanker, and canker* mope and become peevish.
[9] *chiels* lads; *whyles* sometimes.
[10] *Coofs* louts, fools; *rant* make merry.
[11] *ken* know; *wair* spend.
[12] *fash* trouble.
[13] *fier* hearty.
[14] "*Mair spier na, nor fear na*" [Allan] Ramsay [Burns's note]; *spier* ask for, require.

3

To lie in kilns and barns at e'en,[15]
When banes are crazed, and bluid is thin,   30
    Is, doubtless, great distress!
Yet then content could make us blest;
Ev'n then, sometimes we'd snatch a taste
    Of truest happiness.
The honest heart that's free frae a'   35
    Intended fraud or guile,
However Fortune kick the ba',
    Has ay some cause to smile:
    And mind still, you'll find still,
      A comfort this nae sma';   40
    Nae mair then, we'll care then,
      Nae farther we can fa'.

4

What though, like Commoners of air,[16]
We wander out, we know not where,
    But either house or hal'?[17]   45
Yet Nature's charms, the hills and woods,
The sweeping vales, and foaming floods,
    Are free alike to all.
In days when Daisies deck the ground,
    And Blackbirds whistle clear,   50
With honest joy our hearts will bound,
    To see the coming year:
    On braes when we please, then,[18]
      We'll sit and sowth a tune;[19]
    Syne *rhyme* till't, we'll time till't,[20]   55
      And sing't when we hae done.

5

It's no in titles nor in rank;
It's no in wealth like Lon'on Bank,
    To purchase peace and rest;
It's no in makin muckle, *mair*:[21]   60
It's no in books, it's no in lear,[22]
    To make us truly blest:
If Happiness hae not her seat
    And centre in the breast,

---

[15] *kilns* places for drying grain.
[16] *Commoner* "One who has a joint right in the common ground" (Johnson, 1773).
[17] *But* without; *hal'* home.
[18] *braes* hillsides.

[19] *sowth* attempt to carry a tune with a low whistle.
[20] *Syne* then; *till 't* to it.
[21] *muckle* much, a great amount.
[22] *lear* learning.

We may be wise, or rich, or great,   65
    But never can be blest:
Nae treasure nor pleasures
    Could make us happy lang;
The *heart* ay's the part ay
    That makes us right or wrang.   70

6

Think ye, that sic as you and I,
Wha drudge and drive through wet and dry,
    Wi' never-ceasing toil;
Think ye, are we less blest than they,
Wha scarcely tent us in their way,   75
    As hardly worth their while?
Alas! how aft, in haughty mood,
    GOD's creatures they oppress!
Or else, neglecting a' that's guid,
    They riot in excess!   80
        Baith careless and fearless
            Of either Heaven or Hell;
        Esteeming, and deeming
            It's a' an idle tale!

7

Then let us cheerfu' acquiesce,   85
Nor make our scanty Pleasures less,
    By pining at our state:
And, ev'n should Misfortunes come,
I here wha sit has met wi' some,
    An's thankfu' for them yet.   90
They gie the wit of Age to Youth;
    They let us ken oursel;
They make us see the naked truth,
    The *real* guid and ill.
        Though losses and crosses   95
            Be lessons right severe,
        There's wit there, ye'll get there,
            Ye'll find nae other where.

8

But tent me, *Davie*, Ace o' Hearts!
(To say aught less wad wrang the cartes,[23]   100
    And flatt'ry I detest)
This life has joys for you and I,
And joys that riches ne'er could buy,

[23] *cartes* cards.

And joys the very best.
There's a' the *Pleasures o' the Heart*,   105
    The Lover an' the Frien';
Ye hae your *Meg,* your dearest part,
    And I my darling *Jean!*
    It warms me, it charms me,
        To mention but her *name*:   110
    It heats me, it beets me,[24]
        And sets me a' on flame!

9

O all you Pow'rs who rule above!
O *Thou*, whose very self art *love!*
    Thou know'st my words sincere!   115
The life-blood streaming through my heart,
Or my more dear Immortal part,
    Is not more fondly dear!
When heart-corroding care and grief
    Deprive my soul of rest,   120
Her dear idea brings relief,
    And solace to my breast.
    Thou *Being*, All-seeing,
        O hear my fervent prayer!
    Still take her, and make her   125
        Thy most peculiar care!

10

All hail! ye tender feelings dear!
The smile of love, the friendly tear,
    The sympathetic glow!
Long since, this world's thorny ways   130
Had numbered out my weary days,
    Had it not been for you!
Fate still has blest me with a friend,
    In every care and ill;
And oft a more endearing band,   135
    A tie more tender still.
    It lightens, it brightens,
        The tenebrific scene,[25]
    To meet with, and greet with
        My *Davie*, or my *Jean!*   140

11

O, how that *name* inspires my style!
The words come skelpin, rank and file,[26]

---

[24] *beets* kindles.
[25] *tenebrific* dark and gloomy.

[26] *skelpin* beating, striking.

Amaist before I ken!
The ready measure rins as fine,
As Phœbus and the famous Nine[27]   145
    Were glowrin owre my pen.[28]
My spaviet *Pegasus* will limp,[29]
    Till ance he's fairly het;[30]
And then he'll hilch, and stilt, and jimp,[31]
    And rin an unco fit:[32]   150
    But least then the beast then[33]
        Should rue this hasty ride,
    I'll light now, and dight now[34]
        His swaety, wizen'd hide.

TO A MOUSE,
ON TURNING HER UP IN HER NEST, WITH THE PLOUGH, NOVEMBER 1785

Wee, sleekit, cowrin, tim'rous beastie,[1]
O, what a panic's in thy breastie!
Thou need na start awa sae hasty,
    Wi' bickering brattle![2]
I wad be laith to rin an' chase thee,
    Wi' murd'ring *pattle!*[3]

I'm truly sorry Man's dominion
Has broken Nature's social union,
An' justifies that ill opinion,
    Which makes thee startle,   10
At me, thy poor, earth-born companion,
    An' *fellow-mortal!*

I doubt na, whyles, but thou may thieve;[4]
What then? poor beastie, thou maun live![5]
A *daimen-icker* in a *thrave*[6]   15
    'S a sma' request;
I'll get a blessin wi' the lave,[7]
    An' never miss't!

---

[27] *Phœbus and the famous Nine* Apollo, god of poetry and the muses.
[28] *glowrin* looking intently.
[29] *spaviet* spavined, stricken with an inflammation of the hock; *Pegasus* the winged horse inhabiting Mount Helicon, sacred to the muses; a symbol of the literary imagination.
[30] *het* heated up.
[31] *hilch, and stilt, and jimp* lurch, and prance, and jump.
[32] *unco* strange.
[33] *least* lest.

[34] *dight* rub down.
TO A MOUSE
[1] *sleekit* sleek, glossy.
[2] *bickering* hurrying; *brattle* the sound of scampering feet.
[3] *pattle* a tool like a spade for removing earth from the plow.
[4] *whyles* sometimes.
[5] *maun* must.
[6] *daimen-icker in a thrave* an occasional ear of corn in two stooks of corn.
[7] *lave* the remainder.

Thy wee-bit *housie*, too, in ruin
It's silly wa's the win's are strewin![8]
An' naething, now, to big a new ane,[9]
    O' foggage green![10]
An' bleak December's winds ensuin,
    Baith snell an' keen![11]   20

Thou saw the fields laid bare an' waste,   25
An' weary Winter comin fast,
An' cozie here, beneath the blast,
    Thou thought to dwell,
Till crash! the cruel *coulter* past[12]
    Out through thy cell.   30

That wee-bit heap o' leaves an' stibble,
Has cost thee monie a weary nibble!
Now thou's turned out, for a' thy trouble,
    But house or hald,[13]
To thole the Winter's sleety dribble,[14]   35
    An cranreuch cauld![15]

But, Mousie, thou art no thy lane,[16]
In proving *foresight* may be vain:
The best-laid schemes o' *Mice* an' *Men*
    Gang aft a-gley,[17]   40
An' lea'e us nought but grief an' pain,
    For promised joy!

Still thou art blest, compared wi' *me!*
The present only toucheth thee:
But, Och! I backward cast my e'e   45
    On prospects drear!
An' forward, though I canna *see*,
    I *guess* an' *fear!*

ADDRESS TO THE DEIL

O Prince! O Chief of many thronèd Pow'rs,
That led th' embattled Seraphim to war——
           MILTON[1]

O Thou! whatever title suit thee,
Auld Hornie, Satan, Nick, or Clootie,[2]
Wha in yon cavern grim an' sootie,

---

[8] *silly wa's* weak walls.
[9] *big* build.
[10] *foggage* rank grass.
[11] *snell* bitter.
[12] *coulter* the vertical cutting blade of the plow.
[13] *But* without; *hald* home.
[14] *thole* endure.

[15] *cranreuch* hoar-frost.
[16] *thy lane* on your own.
[17] *a-gley* astray.
ADDRESS TO THE DEIL
[1] *Milton* *Paradise Lost* 1.128–9.
[2] *Clootie* cloven-hooved.

Closed under hatches,
Spairges about the brunstane cootie,[3]
To scaud poor wretches![4]   5

Hear me, auld *Hangie*, for a wee,[5]
An' let poor damned bodies be;
I'm sure sma' pleasures it can gie,
    Ev'n to a *deil*,   10
To skelp an' scaud poor dogs like me,[6]
    An' hear us squeel!

Great is thy pow'r, an' great thy fame;
Far kend an' rioted is thy name;[7]
An' though yon lowin heugh's thy hame,[8]   15
    Thou travels far;
An' faith! thou's neither lag nor lame,
    Nor blate nor scaur.[9]

Whyles, ranging like a roaring lion,[10]
For prey, a' holes an' corners tryin;   20
Whyles, on the strong-winged Tempest flyin,
    Tirlin the kirks;[11]
Whyles, in the human bosom pryin,
    Unseen thou lurks.

I've heard my reverend *Graunie* say,   25
In lanely glens ye like to stray;
Or where auld, ruined castles, grey,
    Nod to the moon,
Ye fright the nightly wand'rer's way,
    Wi' eldritch croon.[12]   30

When twilight did my *Graunie* summon,
To say her pray'rs, douce, honest woman![13]
Aft yont the dyke she's heard you bummin,[14]
    Wi' eerie drone;
Or, rustlin, through the boortries comin,[15]   35
    Wi' heavy groan.

Ae dreary, windy, winter night,[16]
The stars shot down wi' sklentin light,[17]
Wi' you, mysel, I gat a fright,
    Ayont the lough;[18]   40

---

[3] *Spairges* sprinkles; *brunstane cootie* brimstone tub.
[4] *scaud* scald.
[5] *Hangie* hangman.
[6] *skelp* strike.
[7] *kend* renowned;.
[8] *lowin heugh* flaming crag.
[9] *blate* bashful; *scaur* frightened.
[10] *Whyles* sometimes.
[11] *Tirlin* stripping or rattling; *kirks* churches.
[12] *eldritch croon* unearthly moan.
[13] *douce* kindly, prudent.
[14] *yont* beyond; *dyke* low dry-stone wall; *bummin* humming.
[15] *boortries* the elders, a flowering shrub.
[16] *Ae* one.
[17] *sklentin* slanting, oblique.
[18] *Ayont* beyond.

Ye, like a rash-buss, stood in sight,[19]
    Wi' waving sugh.[20]

The cudgel in my nieve did shake,[21]
Each bristled hair stood like a stake,
When wi' an eldritch, stoor quaick, quaick,[22]   45
    Amang the springs,
Awa ye squattered like a drake,
    On whistling wings.

Let *warlocks* grim, an' wither'd *hags*,
Tell how wi' you on ragweed nags,   50
They skim the muirs an' dizzy crages,[23]
    Wi' wicked speed;
And in kirk-yards renew their leagues,
    Ower howkit dead.[24]

Thence, countra wives, wi' toil an' pain,   55
May plunge an' plunge the kirn in vain;[25]
For, O! the yellow treasure's taen
    By witching skill;
An' dawtit, twal-pint *Hawkie*'s gaen[26]
    As yell's the Bill.[27]   60

Thence, mystic knots mak great abuse,
On young Guidmen, fond, keen, an' crouse;[28]
When the best wark-lume i' the house,[29]
    By cantrip wit,[30]
Is instant made no worth a louse,   65
    Just at the bit.[31]

When thowes dissolve the snawy hoord,
An' float the jinglin icy-boord,[32]
Then, *Water-kelpies* haunt the foord,[33]
    By your direction,   70
An' nighted Trav'llers are allured
    To their destruction.

An' aft your moss-traversing *Spunkies*[34]
Decoy the wight that late an' drunk is:
The bleezin, curst, mischievous monkies   75
    Delude his eyes,

[19] *rash-buss*   clump of rushes.
[20] *sugh*   the rushing sound of wind.
[21] *nieve*   fist.
[22] *stoor*   harsh, hoarse.
[23] *muirs*   moors, bogs.
[24] *howkit*   exhumed.
[25] *kirn*   butter churn.
[26] *dawtit*   spoiled; *Hawkie*   pet name for a cow.
[27] *Bill*   bull.

[28] *crouse*   self-confident.
[29] *wark-lume*   tool; penis.
[30] *cantrip*   witching.
[31] *bit*   crisis.
[32] *icy-boord*   sheet of ice.
[33] *kelpies*   demons.
[34] *Spunkies*   will o' the wisp, ignis fatuus, glowing marsh gas.

Till in some miry slough he sunk is,
        Ne'er mair to rise.

When *Masons* mystic *word* an' *grip*,
In storms an' tempests raise you up,   80
Some cock or cat your rage maun stop,
        Or, strange to tell!
The youngest Brother ye wad whip
        Aff straught to h-ll.

Lang syne, in *Eden*'s bonny yard,[35]   85
When youthfu' lovers first were paired,
An' all the Soul of Love they shared,
        The raptured hour,
Sweet on the fragrant, flow'ry swaird,
        In shady bow'r: 90

Then you, ye auld, snick-drawing dog![36]
Ye cam to Paradise incog.[37]
An' played on man a cursed brogue,[38]
        (Black be your fa'!)
An gied the infant warld a shog,[39]   95
        Maist ruin'd a'.[40]

D'ye mind that day, when in a bizz,[41]
Wi' reekit duds, and reestit gizz,[42]
Ye did present your smoutie phiz,[43]
        'Mang better folk,   100
An' sklented on the *man of Uz*[44]
        Your spitefu' joke?

An' how ye gat him i' your thrall,
An' brak him out o' house an' hal',
While scabs an' botches did him gall,   105
        Wi' bitter claw,
An' lowsed his ill-tongued, wicked Scawl,[45]
        Was warst ava?[46]

But a' your doings to rehearse,
Your wily snares an' fechtin fierce,[47]   110
Sin' that day *Michael* did you pierce,[48]
        Down to this time,

---

[35] *Syne* afterward.
[36] *snick-drawing* crafty.
[37] *incog* incognito, in disguise.
[38] *brogue* trick.
[39] *shog* shock.
[40] *Maist* almost.
[41] *bizz* flurry.
[42] *reekit* smoky; *duds* rags; *reestit* smoke-dried;
gizz wig.

[43] *phiz* face.
[44] *man of Uz* Job.
[45] *Scawl* scold, abusive woman.
[46] *ava* of all.
[47] *fechtin* fighting.
[48] *Michael* stabs Satan in the war in Heaven (*Paradise Lost* 6.320–34).

Wad ding a' Lallan tongue, or Erse,[49]
    In prose or rhyme.

    An' now, auld *Cloots*, I ken ye're thinkin,   115
A certain Bardie's rantin, drinkin,
Some luckless hour will send him linkin,[50]
    To your black pit;
But, faith! he'll turn a corner jinkin,[51]
    An' cheat you yet.   120

    But, fare you weel, auld *Nickie-ben!*
O wad ye tak a thought an' men'!
Ye aiblins might – I dinna ken –[52]
    Still hae a *stake* –
I'm wae to think upo' yon den,[53]   125
    Ev'n for your sake!

Mary Wollstonecraft Godwin (1759–1797)

With his drunken habits, his bullying, and his favoritism for his eldest son, Wollstonecraft's father sensitized his eldest daughter to the unequal place of women in British society. After the death of their mother in 1780, Mary took a great deal of responsibility for the support of her two sisters. She rescued the younger of the two from a hasty and apparently brutal marriage, and with a long-time friend the three started a school in Newington Green, site of the dissenters' academy which Defoe had attended and center of a community of progressive thinkers which included Richard Price, the minister whose sympathetic sermon had stimulated Burke to write his Reflections on the Revolution in France. *After a couple of years of teaching, Wollstonecraft published a treatise called* Thoughts on the Education of Daughters, *published by Joseph Johnson in 1787. She then went to work for the London publisher. She wrote reviews, translated books, wrote some books for children, and compiled* The Female Reader, *an anthology for the education of women. She also wrote* A Vindication of the Rights of Men *(1790), the first of many replies to Burke's* Reflections. *She followed that with* A Vindication of the Rights of Woman *(1792), which is one of the most important documents in the history of feminist thought. She tried herself to live a life liberated from the ordinary restrictions placed on women. She was unlucky in love, however, falling first for the married artist Fuseli and then for a man named Imlay whose infidelities drove her to attempt suicide. Later she found intimacy with William Godwin, another progressive thinker, and though neither of them believed in the institution, they married in expectation of their daughter. Wollstonecraft died from complications in the birth of her child Mary, who later became Mary Shelley, the author of* Frankenstein.

The excerpt presented here is based on the first edition. Wollstonecraft later went to France and was horrified by the excesses of the Revolution. Like Thomas Paine, she became a moderate among the French revolutionaries, but she was always decisive in her rejection of the old regime and the

---

[49] *ding* tire out; *Lallan* Lowland Scots; *Erse* Highland Scots, Gaelic.
[50] *linkin* skipping.
[51] *jinkin* dodging.
[52] *aiblins* perhaps.
[53] *wae* sad.

older Romantic view of women that tended to miniaturize them spiritually and intellectually even when it placed them on pedestals of admiration.

from *A Vindication of the Rights of Men, in a Letter to the Right Honourable Edmund Burke; occasioned by his* Reflections on the Revolution in France (1790)

The only security of property that nature authorises and reason sanctions is, the right a man has to enjoy the acquisitions which his talents or industry have acquired; and happy would it be for the world if there was no other road to wealth or honour; if pride, in the shape of parental affection, did not absorb the man. Luxury and effeminacy would not then introduce so much idiotism into the noble families which form one of the pillars of our state. The ground would not lie fallow, nor would their activity of mind spread the contagion of idleness, and its concomitant vices, through the whole mass of society.

Instead of gaming they might nourish a virtuous ambition, and love might take the place of the gallantry which you,[1] with knightly fealty, venerate. Women would then act like mothers, and the fine lady, become a rational woman, might superintend her family and suckle her children, in order to fulfil her part of the social compact. The unnatural vices, produced in the hot-bed of wealth, would then give place to natural affections, instead 'of losing half their evil by losing all their grossness.' – What a sentiment to come from a moral pen!

A surgeon would tell you that by skinning over a wound you spread disease through the whole frame; and, surely, they indirectly aim at destroying all purity of morals, who poison the very source of virtue, by smearing a sentimental varnish over vice to hide its natural deformity. Stealing, whoring, and drunkenness are gross vices, I presume, though they may not obliterate every moral sentiment, and have a vulgar brand that makes them appear with all their native deformity; but overreaching, adultery, and coquetry, are venial offences, though they reduce virtue to an empty name, and make wisdom consist in saving appearances.

'On this scheme of things[2] a king *is* but a man; a queen *is* but a woman; and woman is but an animal, and an animal not of the highest order.' – All true, Sir; if she is not more attentive to the duties of humanity than fashionable ladies and queens are in general. I will still further accede to the opinion you have so justly conceived of the spirit which begins to animate this age. – 'All homage paid to the sex in general, as such, and without distinct views, is to be regarded as *romance* and folly'. Undoubtedly; because such homage vitiates them, prevents their endeavouring to obtain solid personal merit; and, in short, makes those beings vain inconsiderate dolls, who ought to be prudent mothers and useful members of society. 'Regicide and sacrilege are but fictions of superstition corrupting jurisprudence, by destroying its simplicity. The murder of a king, or a queen, or a bishop, are only common homicide'. – Again I agree with you; but perceive, Sir, that by leaving out the word *father*, I think the comparison invidious . . .

FROM *A VINDICATION OF THE RIGHTS OF MEN*
[1]   *you*   Edmund Burke, to whom the essay is addressed, in answer to his *Reflections on the Revolution in France* (see the selection above for Wollstonecraft's citations of Burke's essay).
[2]   *"On this scheme of things . . ."*   As you ironically observe [Wollstonecraft's note].

But it is not very extraordinary that *you* should, for throughout your letter you frequently advert to a sentimental jargon, which has long been current in conversation, and even in books of morals, though it never received the *regal* stamp of reason. A kind of mysterious instinct is *supposed* to reside in the soul, that instantaneouly discerns truth, without the tedious labour of ratiocination. This instinct, for I know not what other name to give it, has been termed *common sense*, and more frequently *sensibility*; and, by a kind of *indefeasible* right, it has been *supposed*, for rights of this kind are not easily proved, to reign paramount over the other faculties of the mind, and to be an authority from which there is no appeal.

This subtle magnetic fluid, that runs around the whole circle of society, is not subject to any known rule, or, to use an obnoxious phrase, in spite of the sneers of mock humility, or the timid fears of well-meaning Christians, who shrink from any freedom of thought, lest they should rouse the old serpent, to the *eternal fitness of things*. It dips, we know not why, granting it to be an infallible instinct, and, though supposed always to the point to truth, its pole-star; the point is always shifting, and seldom stands due north . . .

Where is the dignity, the infallibility of sensibility, in the fair ladies, whom, if the voice of rumour is to be credited, the captive negroes curse in all agony of bodily pain, for the unheard of tortures they invent? It is probable that some of them, after a flagellation, compose their ruffled spirits and exercise their tender feelings by the perusal of the last new novel. – How true these tears are to nature, I leave you to determine. But these ladies may have read your Enquiries concerning the origin of the Sublime and the Beautiful,[3] and, convinced by your arguments, have laboured to be pretty, by counterfeiting weakness.

You may have convinced them that *littleness* and weakness are the very essence of beauty; and that the Supreme Being, in giving women beauty in the most supereminent degree, seemed to command them, by the powerful voice of Nature, not to cultivate the moral virtues that might chance to excite respect, and interfere with the pleasing sensations they were created to inspire. Confining thus truth, fortitude, and humanity, within the rigid pale of manly morals, they might justly argue, that to be loved, woman's high end and great distinction! they should 'learn to lisp, to totter in the walk', and nick-name God's creatures. Never, they might repeat after you, was any man, much less a woman, rendered amiable by the force of those exalted qualities, fortitude, justice, wisdom, and truth; and thus forewarned of the sacrifice they must make to those austere, unnatural virtues, they would be authorised to turn all their attention to their persons, systematically neglecting morals to secure beauty . . .

---

[3] *Enquiries concerning the origin of the Sublime and the Beautiful* see above, p. 1031.

Bibliography

The following list is intended mainly as a guide to the works used or referred to in the introductions and the footnotes. To avoid redundancy, it excludes works that are properly cited in the headnotes. Therefore, references to both early and standard editions of the works included in the anthology should first be sought in the individual introductions. The companion volume to this anthology will include a guide to secondary sources for studying the literature of the period.

Ackroyd, Peter. *Chatterton.* Hamish Hamilton Ltd, 1987.

Aristophanes. *Aristophanes.* Tr. Benjamin Bickley Rogers. Loeb Library. 3 vols. Heinemann, 1924.

Aristotle. *The Poetics.* Tr. W. H. Fyfe. Loeb Library. Heinemann, 1932.

Athenaeus. *The Deipnosophists.* Tr. Charles Burton Gulick. Loeb Library. 6 vols. Heinemann, 1927.

Blackwell Companion to the Enlightenment. Ed. John Yolton *et al.* Blackwell Publishers, 1992.

Bacon, Sir Francis. *The Essayes or Counsels, Civill and Morall.* Ed. Michael Kiernan. Harvard University Press, 1985.

Bate, W. J. *Samuel Johnson.* Houghton Mifflin, 1977.

Brady, Frank. *James Boswell: the Later Years.* McGraw Hill, 1984.

Brown University Women Writers Project. Http://www.wwp.brown.edu.

Burke, Edmund. *Reflections on the Revolution in France.* Ed. Connor Cruise O'Brien. Penguin Books, 1968.

Burnet, Thomas. *The Sacred Theory of the Earth.* London, 1690.

Burton, Robert. *The Anatomy of Melancholy.* Ed. Thomas C. Faulkner, Nicholas K. Kiessling, and Rhonda L. Blair. 2 vols. Clarendon Press, 1989.

Butler, Samuel. *Hudibras.* Ed. John Wilders. Clarendon Press, 1975.

Cervantes, Miguel. *Don Quixote.* Tr. Charles Jarvis. 2nd edn. London, 1749.

Cheyne, George. *Philosophical Principles of Religion: Natural and Revealed.* 2nd edn. London, 1715.

Cicero. *De Senectute, De Amicitia, De Divinatione.* Tr. W. A. Falconer. Loeb Library. Heinemann, 1979.

——. *Letters to his Friends.* Tr. W. Glynn Williams, M. Cary, and M. Henderson. Loeb Library. 4 vols. Harvard University Press, 1927–72.

Clarke, John. *Essay upon Study.* London, 1731.

Cowley, Abraham. *Davideis.* Ed. Gayle Shadduck. Garland, 1987.

Dictionary of British and American Women Writers 1660–1800. Ed. Janet Todd. Rowman and Littlefield, 1987.

Dictionary of National Biography. Ed. Leslie Stephen. 63 vols. London, 1885–1901. Concise edition. 3 vols. Oxford Univ. Press, 1992.

Donne, John. *The, Elegies, and the Songs and Sonnets.* Ed. Helen Gardner. Clarendon Press, 1965.

Dryden, John. *The Works of John Dryden.* Ed. H. T. Swedenberg *et al.* University of California Press, 1956–.

Eighteenth-Century Resources. World Wide Web: http://www.english.upenn.edu/~jlynch/18th/

Eighteenth-Century Short Title Catalogue (ESTC). CD-ROM and on-line through RLIN or Eureka.

The Eighteenth Century. Microfilm reels. Woodbridge Connecticut: Research Publications, 1982–.

Epistolae Obscurorum Virorum (1516). Ed. and tr. F. G. Stokes. Chatto and Windus, 1909.

Eusebius, Bishop of Caesarea. *The Ecclesiastical History.* Tr. Kirsopp Lake. 2 vols. Loeb Library. Harvard University Press, 1926–32.

Fielding, Henry. *The Wesleyan Edition of the Works of Henry Fielding.* Wesleyan University Press, 1972–. 1: *Miscellanies,* ed. Henry Knight Miller, 1972. 2: *The History of Tom Jones,* ed. Martin C. Battestin and Fredson Bowers, 1975. 3: *Joseph Andrews,* ed. Martin C. Battestin, 1972. 4: *The Jacobite's Journal and Related Writings,* ed. W. B. Coley, 1975.

Florus, Lucius Annaeus. *Epitome of Roman History.* Tr. Edward Seymour Forster and John C. Rolfe. Loeb Library. Heinemann, 1929.

Foxe, John. *Actes and Monuments* [*Book of Martyrs*]. London: John Day, 1563.

Foxon, David. *Libertine Literature in England 1660–1745.*

——. *English Verse 1701–1750.* 2 vols. Cambridge University Press, 1975.

Godwin, Mary Wollstonecraft. *The Works of Mary Wollstonecraft.* Ed. Janet Todd and Marilyn Butler. 7 vols. New York University Press, 1989.

Goreau, Angeline. *Reconstructing Aphra.* Dial Press, 1980.

Grant, Michael. *A Guide to the Ancient World: A Dictionary of Classical Place Names.* H. W. Wilson, 1986.

Greer, Germaine, ed. *Kissing the Rod: An Anthology of Seventeenth-Century Women's Verse.* Farrar, Straus & Giroux, 1989.

Grose, Francis. *A Classical Dictionary of the Vulgar Tongue.* London: S. Hooper, 1785.

Hall, Joseph. *Quo Vadis? A Just Censure of Travel.* London, 1617.

Hammond, Gerald. "Richard Lovelace and the Uses of Obscurity." *Proceedings of the British Academy,* 71 (1985), 203–34.

Hart, Kingsley, ed. *The Letters of Dorothy Osborne to Sir William Temple,* 1652–54. London: Folio Society, 1968.

Herodotus. *Herodotus.* Tr. A. D. Godley. Loeb Library. 4 vols. Heinemann, 1921–24.

Hesiod. *Hesiod, the Homeric Hymns, and Homerica.* Tr. Hugh G. Evelyn-White. Loeb Library. Heinemann, 1914.

Hogarth, William. *Analysis of Beauty.* London, 1753.

Homer, *The Iliad.* Tr. A. T. Murray. Loeb Library. 2 vols. Heinemann, 1924–25.

——. *The Odyssey.* Tr. A. T. Murray. Loeb Library. 2 vols. Heinemann, 1919.

Hooker, Richard. *Of the Laws of Ecclesiastical Polity:* Vols 1–3 of *The Folger Library Edition of the Works of Richard Hooker,* ed. W. Speed Hill, Harvard University Press, 1977–93.

Horace. *The Odes and Epodes.* Tr. C. E. Bennett. Loeb Library. Harvard University Press, 1978.

——. *Satires, Epistles, and Ars Poetica.* Tr. H. R. Fairclough. Loeb Library. Harvard University Press, 1978.

Irenaeus. *Against the Heresies.* Tr. Dominic J. Unger. Paulist Press, 1992.

Johnson, Samuel. *A Dictionary of the English Language.* London, 1755; 4th edn, revised, London, 1773

——. *Lives of the English Poets.* Ed. G. B. Hill. 3 vols. Clarendon Press, 1905.

——. *The Yale Edition of the Works of Samuel Johnson.* Yale University Press, 1958–. 1: *Diaries, Prayers and Annals,* ed. E. L. MacAdam, Jr, with Donald and Mary Hyde. 2: *The Idler and The Adventurer,* ed. Walter J. Bate, John M. Bullitt, and L. F. Powell. 3–5: *The Rambler,* ed. Walter J. Bate and Albrecht B. Strauss. 6: *Poems,* ed. E. L. MacAdam, Jr, with George Milne. 7–8: *Johnson on Shakespeare,* ed. Arthur Sherbo with an introduction by Bertrand Bronson. 9: *A Journey to the Western Islands of Scotland,* ed. Mary Lascelles. 10: *Political Writings,* ed. Donald J. Greene. 14: *Sermons,* ed. Jean H. Hagstrum and James Gray. 15: *A Voyage to Abyssinia,* ed. Joel J. Gold. 16: *Rasselas and Other Tales,* ed. Gwin J. Kolb.

Juvenal. *Juvenal and Persius.* Tr. G. G. Ramsay. Loeb Library. Harvard University Press, 1979.

Le Bossu, René. *Traité du Poeme Epique.* Tr. 1695; facs. rpt. University of Florida Press, 1970

Lewis, Charlton Thomas. *A Latin Dictionary for Schools.* 1889; Clarendon Press, 1962.

Liddell, Henry George and Scott, Robert. *A Greek-English Lexicon (LSJ).* Rev. Henry Stuart Jones, *et al.* Clarendon Press, 1968.

Livy. *Ab Urbe Condita.* Tr. B. O. Foster *et al.* Loeb Library. 14 vols. Heinemann, 1919–59.

Lonsdale, Roger, ed. *Eighteenth-Century Women Poets.* Oxford University Press, 1990.

——, ed. *The New Oxford Book of Eighteenth-Century Verse.* Oxford University Press, 1984.

Lucan. *The Civil War.* Tr. J. D. Duff. Loeb Library. Heinemann, 1928.

Lucretius. *De Rerum Natura.* Tr. W. H. D. Rouse. Loeb Library. Heinemann, 1943.

Martial. *Epigrams.* Tr. Walter C. A. Ker. Loeb Library. 2 vols. Heinemann, 1919–20.

Milton, John. *Complete Prose Works.* General ed. Don M. Wolfe. 8 vols. Yale University Press, 1953–.

——. *The Works of John Milton.* Columbia University Press. 18 vols. 1931–38.

Montaigne, Michel. *Essais.* Tr. Donald M. Frame. Stanford University Press, 1976.

Ogilby, John. *The Fables of Aesop Paraphrased in Verse.* London, 1665.

Ovid. *Metamorphoses.* Tr. Frank Justus Miller. Loeb Library. 2 vols. Harvard University Press, 1946.

——. *Heroides and Amores.* Tr. Grant Showerman. Loeb Library. Heinemann, 1925.

Oxford Classical Dictionary. Ed. N. G. L. Hammond and H. H. Scullard. 2nd edn. Clarendon Press, 1970.

Oxford Companion to Classical Literature. Ed. M. C. Howatson. 2nd edn. Oxford Univ. Press, 1989.

Oxford Dictionary of English Proverbs. 3rd edn. Rev. F. P. Wilson. Clarendon Press, 1970.

Oxford English Dictionary (OED). 2nd edn. Ed J. A. Simpson and E. S. C. Weiner. 20 vols. Oxford University Press, 1989. CD-ROM version, 1993.

Oxford Latin Dictionary. Ed. P. G. W. Glare. Clarendon Press, 1982.

Pausanias. *Description of Greece.* Tr. W. H. S. Jones. Loeb Library. 5 vols. Harvard University Press, 1918–35.

Perry, Ruth. *The Celebrated Astell.* Univ. of Chicago Press, 1986.

Petronius Arbiter. *Petronius*. Tr. Michael Heseltine. Rev. E. H. Warmington. Loeb Library. Heinemann, 1969.

Philips, Ambrose. *The Poems of Ambrose Philips*. Ed. M. G. Segar. Basil Blackwell, 1937.

Pliny, the Elder. *Natural History*. Tr. H. Rackham. Loeb Library. 10 vols. Harvard University Press, 1938–63.

Plutarch. *Parallel Lives*. Tr. Bernadotte Perrin. Loeb Library. 11 vols. Heinemann, 1914–26.

Pope, Alexander. *The Twickenham Edition of the Works of Alexander Pope*. General ed. John Butt (Methuen): 1. *Pastoral Poetry and An Essay on Criticism*, ed. E. Audra and Aubrey Williams (1961); 2. *The Rape of the Lock*, ed. Geoffrey Tillotson, 3rd edn (1962); 3.1. *An Essay on Man*, ed. Maynard Mack (1950); 3.2: *Epistles to Several Persons*, ed. F. W. Bateson, 2nd edn (1961); 4. *Imitations of Horace*, ed. John Butt, 2nd edn (1953); 5. *The Dunciad*, ed. James R. Sutherland, 3rd edn (1963); 6. *Minor Poems*, ed. Norman Ault (1954); 7–8. *The Iliad*, ed. Maynard Mack (1967); 9–10. *The Odyssey*, ed. Maynard Mack (1967); *Index*, ed. Maynard Mack (1969).

Plomer, Henry R. *A Dictionary of the Booksellers and Printers who were at Work in England, Scotland, and Ireland 1641–1775*. 3 vols. Oxford: Bibliographical Society, 1968.

Pottle, Fredrick. *James Boswell, the Earlier Years*. McGraw Hill, 1966.

Propertius. *Elegies*. Ed. and Tr. G. P. Goold. Loeb Library. Harvard University Press, 1990.

Rowe, Nicholas. *The Faire Penitent*. Ed. Malcolm Goldstein. University of Nebraska Press, 1969.

Sandys, J. E. *A History of Classical Scholarship*. 3rd edn, 3 vols. Cambridge University Press, 1927.

Shakespeare, William. *The Riverside Shakespeare*. Ed. G. Blackmore Evans. Houghton Mifflin, 1974.

Sophocles. *Sophocles*. Tr. F. Storr. Loeb Library. 2 vols. Harvard University Press, 1912.

Spenser, Edmund. *The Faerie Queene*. Ed. J. C. Smith. 2 vols. Clarendon Press, 1909.

Swift, Jonathan. The *Prose Works of Jonathan Swift*. Ed Herbert Davis. 14 vols. Basil Blackwell, 1939–68.

Theobald, Lewis. *Shakespeare Restored*. London, 1726.

Tillotson, Geoffrey, Fussell, Paul, and Waingrow, Marshall. *Eighteenth-Century English Literature*. Harcourt Brace Jovanovich, 1969.

Vasari, Giorgio. *The Lives of the Artists*. Tr. Julia Conaway and Peter Bondanella. Oxford University Press, 1991.

Virgil. *Virgil*. Tr. H. Rushton Fairclough. Loeb Library. 2 vols. Harvard University Press, 1934–35.

Voltaire, François Marie Arouet de. *Les Oeuvres Complètes de Voltaire*. Oxford: Voltaire Foundation, 1968–.

Westminster Dictionary of the Bible. Ed. John D. Davis. Rev. Henry Snyder Gehman. Philadelphia: Westminster Press, 1944.

Wilkins, John. *The Discovery of a World in the Moon*. London, 1638.

Wing, Donald. *A Short-title Catalogue of Books Printed in England, Scotland, Ireland, Wales, and British America, and of English Books Printed in Other Countries*. 2nd edn. 3 vols. Modern Language Association of America, 1994.

Wotton, William. *Reflections upon Ancient and Modern Learning*. Londonn, 1694.

——. *A Defense of the Reflections upon Ancient and Modern Learning. . . . With Observations upon the Tale of a Tub*. London, 1705.

Young, Edward. *Night Thoughts*. Ed. Stephen Cornford. Cambridge University Press, 1989.

Index of Titles and First Lines

Index to the Introductions and Footnotes